The Great Tradition in English Literature
from
SHAKESPEARE
to
SHAW

Annette T. Rubinstein

MONTHLY REVIEW PRESS
New York

for
Jean Rubinstein
mother, teacher, comrade

Copyright © 1953, 2010 by Monthly Review Press
Cataloging-in-Publication data available from the publisher

ISBN 978-0-85345-096-2 (paper)

Monthly Review Press
146 West 29th Street, Suite 6W
New York, NY 10001
www.monthlyreview.org

FOREWORD TO THE 1980 EDITION

It is with some trepidation that I return to a work completed over a quarter century before in order to write a note heralding a reprint edition. True, the subject matter was such that few new discoveries or developments could have been expected to upset former judgments, but what about the changes and developments in the author? Would I still agree with my former conclusions and approve my choice of the evidence selected to validate them? To a surprising degree, I have found that the answer was "yes."

Happily, a recent European university lecture tour supported this personal affirmative. English departments in Eastern Europe —Hungary, Czechoslovakia, the German Democratic Republic— are still regularly using the volume. A visit to Bonn found that in the Federal Republic the chapter on Dickens had just been assigned as background reading for an intensive *explication de texte* of *Oliver Twist*, and when my trip ended with a week in Cambridge I learned, amazingly, that an advanced tutorial on Milton was grateful for the unusual material from his relatively neglected prose, here correlated with his life and poetry.

My return to New York in January 1980 provided a climax. A letter awaited me from the head of the English Department of the Institute for Foreign Languages in Peking asking my help in "tracking down copies of the *Great Tradition*, the more the better, new or second-hand."

Since the book first appeared in the United States at the height —or depth—of the cold war, when any serious materialist interpretation of history was anathema and the separation between life and literature in academic circles was all but absolute, the four printings (two hardcover and two paperback) have found their readers largely outside university walls. This was not altogether regrettable since every teacher is glad to have students attracted by their interest in the subject rather than by their need for credits. Nevertheless, in today's freer atmosphere, with its general emphasis on an interdisciplinary approach, it is perhaps not unreasonable to hope that this new edition will find a place in college classrooms and libraries, at home as well as overseas.

Annette T. Rubinstein

New York, N.Y.
April, 1980

FOREWORD TO THE 1953 EDITION

The great tradition in English literature is the tradition of those great writers who could, as Shakespeare said, "sense the future in the instant." The future is always stirring beneath the heart of the present and it is therefore those who live closest to the heart of their own time who can most surely sense the pulse of the life-to-be.

The great tradition in English literature is the tradition of the great realists; that is to say, of the writers who know and are concerned with the vital current which moves steadily beneath the innumerable eddies and confusing crosscurrents of life's surface.

This feeling for the essential direction of history, this profound understanding of the significant events and potentialities of one's own age, has little relation to any skill at observing and reproducing its minutiae. Snobbish or sentimental writers like Pope, Thackeray and Trollope, angry and honest ones like Zola or Gissing or Morrison, can often create an impressive facsimile of the life led by the men and women whom they have had occasion to observe. But, as Bacon said in another context, "a crowd is not company; and faces are but a gallery of pictures; and talk but a tinkling cymbal, where there is no love." And it is in the love which makes them sensitively aware of their fellows' needs, in the respect they feel for man's potentialities, that the work of the great realists is rooted. It is this deep assurance of man's strength, this ardent concern for his rights, that has so often enabled them to "look into the seeds of time and say which grain will grow and which will not." It is this which paradoxically makes their work, written out of the most immediate care for contemporary events, most relevant to those of a far distant future.

This seemingly prophetic insight has taken many forms. One was the daring, closely reasoned scientific prevision of a Bacon or a Huxley. Another was the equally daring, less fully conscious, anticipation of a Blake or a Burns. At some periods we find that this central conviction of man's power to shape his own future expresses itself in the common religious mythology of his time, as with Bunyan. At other periods the writer is forced to create his own myths as Dickens does in his metaphorical use of an apparently factual plot. Often the great humanist was also a fiercely indignant revolutionary like Milton or Hazlitt or Shelley; less often he shared the brief serenity of an optimistic postrevolutionary age like Defoe or Fielding or Jane Austen. But always the great writers have, in one way or another, participated in the essential struggles of their own times. The old miners' song has it, "They say in Harlan County, there are no neutrals here," and that is also so in the great world of art.

True, it has long been a dogma in the academies that art and politics are two separate worlds; that the value of a work of art is unaffected by the artist's relation to the social movements of his own time, his concern with human needs, or his hopes of future progress. And in the last three quarters of a century the artist himself has too often concurred in this belief. But his acceptance of his separation from society, whether melancholy or defiant, was always only a special instance of that alienation of man from himself which has characterized the end of the great bourgeois epoch.

The representative art of the great epochs of human culture have always been political and partisan. Aristotle defined man as *the* political animal, and surely the most human of men—the great artist—are not the least political.

The following pages attempt a rapid survey of one of the greatest of such epochs—that of the expanding bourgeois world in its hopeful youth and its troubled but still rich maturity. The twenty-odd major figures here examined are all chosen from those acknowledged, by the most conservative academicians and critics, to be the greatest writers of their own times, and among the greatest of all time. Yet almost invariably scholarly discussions as well as popular biographies and anthologies minimize, distort, or altogether ignore the political concern and activity which lay at the root of the art they praise. And so, inevitably, they misunderstand and misrepresent vital elements in it, no matter how great their admiration.

A full consideration of the life and work of any of these major figures in the history of English literature soon shows us just how clear, conscious and complete the great writer's consistently progressive partisanship in the political and social conflicts of his own time has always been. But it is difficult for the nonacademic reader to find the time and factual material for such a consideration, and the nonpolitical literary student too often himself unquestioningly accepts the retired tradition of the academies.

This book grew out of one student's attempt first to learn in concrete detail, and then to teach in convincing summary, the part played by the great writers in man's continuing fight for freedom.

It begins with a brief synopsis of the social and political background for the great literature of Shakespeare and his contemporaries, and proceeds to a more detailed consideration of perhaps the two most important Elizabethans—Shakespeare himself and Bacon.

Each of the four succeeding sections similarly opens with a rapid sketch of its age, with emphasis upon those aspects of its history most directly related to the literary development of the period, and proceeds to a more specific consideration of its most representative figures.

There has been little attempt to impose any formal uniformity on the material presented. In some instances a rather full biographical account seemed desirable; in others more space has been devoted to a consideration of certain specific works. Nor is the length of any one chapter an indication of the relative importance of the writer to whom it is devoted. Here again the story to be told determined the manner of its telling. For example, the tragic fact that Keats died at twenty-six, after barely six writing years, made it possible to treat his life and work in less than half the space demanded by Hazlitt or Dickens or Shaw.

In many of the discussions my conclusions as to a writer's political and social attitude necessarily run counter to the conventional impression, so I have thought it best to use the impeccable evidence of direct quotation as far as possible. There are, therefore, substantial extracts from personal letters and diaries as well as from more deliberate literary works included in every chapter but the one on Shakespeare, and even in that there is an unusual amount of such quotation from more or less intimate contemporary sources. I believe that anyone judicially considering these great writers' own statements must conclude, whatever his own opinion may be, that they all felt "that those who are above the struggle are also beside the point."

Finally, although the book presents a continuous development, each of the five major sections of which it is composed can really be read as an independent unit. It may, in fact, be advisable for those readers not well acquainted with the earlier periods of English history and literature to begin with the discussion of the more familiar modern world in the third section, and then to turn back to the Elizabethan Age.

To those lovers of literature who already "think continually of those who are truly great," the book's approach may suggest a different interpretation of familiar beauty, and reveal another dimension in the well-known lives of many long beloved masters. To those men and women who are themselves deeply immersed in the political life of our stirring and difficult age it will, I think, introduce new allies and fresh sources of strength. That, at least, is the hope with which I here complete this long and rewarding labor of love.

ANNETTE T. RUBINSTEIN

New York, N. Y.
September, 1953

ACKNOWLEDGMENTS

For arrangements made with various authors and publishing houses whereby certain copyrighted material was permitted to be reprinted, and for the courtesy extended by them, the following acknowledgments are gratefully made:

D. Appleton & Co., *Bernard Shaw: Playboy and Prophet* by Archibald Henderson; Jonathan Cape, *The Aesthetic Adventure* by William Gaunt; Chanticleer Press, Inc., *John Milton* by Rex Warner; Chatto & Windus, Ltd., *Mliton* by E. M. Tillyard; The Citadel Press, *The Hidden Heritage* by John Howard Lawson; William Collins Sons & Co., Ltd., *The Life of William Cobbett* by G. D. H. and M. Cole; Columbia University Press, *John Bunyan, Mechanick Preacher* by W. Y. Tindall; Cresset Press, Ltd., *Jane Austen and Some Contemporaries* by Mona Wilson; Dodd, Mead & Co., *Charles Dickens* by G. K. Chesterton; Gerald Duckworth & Co., Ltd., *Huxley* by E. W. MacBride; Victor Gollancz, Ltd., *Bernard Shaw: Art and Socialism* by E. Strauss; Harcourt, Brace & Co., Inc., *The Poet in the Theatre* by Ronald Peacock, *The Common Reader* by Virginia Woolf; Harper & Brothers, *Color* by Countee Cullen, *The Poems of Emily Dickinson* by Emily Dickinson; Hodder & Stoughton, Ltd., *Men of Letters* by Dixon Scott; Horizon Press, *Modern Greek Poetry* by Rae Dalven; Hutchinson & Co., Ltd., *Introduction to the English Novel* by Arnold Kettle; International Publishers, *The Novel and the People* by Ralph Fox; The Kenyon Review, "Fiction and the 'Matrix of Analogy'" by Mark Schorer; Alfred A. Knopf, Inc., *Shelley* by Neuman Ivy White; John Lane, The Bodley Head, Ltd., *George Bernard Shaw* by G. K. Chesterton; Lawrence & Wishart, Ltd., *Charles Dickens—The Progress of a Radical* by T. A. Jackson, *A People's History of England* by A. L. Morton, *Crisis and Criticism* by Alick West, *A Good Man Fallen Among Fabians* by Alick West; The Macmillan Co., *Shakespeare and the Rival Tradition* by Alfred Harbage, *Collected Poems* by Thomas Hardy, *History of English Literature* by Legouis and Cazamian, *Science and the Modern World* by A. N. Whitehead; Macmillan & Co., Ltd., *Political Characters of Shakespeare* by John Palmer; McGraw-Hill Book Co., Inc., *Shakespeare Without Tears* by Margaret Webster; Methuen & Co., Ltd., *John Bunyan—Maker of Myths* by Jack Lindsay; New Statesman & Nation, "The Economic Determinism of Jane Austen" by Leonard Woolf; The New Yorker, "Charles Dickens" by Martha Keegan; Oxford University Press, *Shelley, Godwin and Their Circle* by H. N. Brailsford, *The Dickens World* by Humphrey House; Philosophical Library, *Charles Dickens* by Jack Lindsay; Princeton University Press, *Prefaces to Shakespeare* by H. Granville-Barker, *Jane Austen, Irony As Defense and Discovery* by Marvin Mudrick, *The Court Wits of the Restoration* by J. H. Wilson; G. P. Putnam's Sons, *Ellen Terry and Bernard Shaw* by Ellen Terry; The Quarterly Review, "Jane Austen" by Reginald Farrer; Routledge & Kegan Paul, Ltd., *Biography of Bacon* by Mary Sturt; Henry Schuman, Inc., *Francis Bacon* by Benjamin Farrington; Scrutiny (Magazine), "Regulated Hatred" by D. C. W. Harding; Secker & Warburg, *William Blake: A Man Without a Mask* by J. Bronowski; Society of Authors (London), *William Morris As I Knew Him* by Bernard Shaw, *The Works of Bernard Shaw* by Bernard Shaw; George W. Stewart, Inc., *The Great Tradition* by F. R. Leavis; University of California Press, *Swift and Defoe* by John Frederick Ross; Viking Press, Inc., *Collected Works* by Dorothy Parker.

Contents

Foreword v
Acknowledgements ix

THE ELIZABETHAN AGE AND THE BOURGEOIS REVOLUTION

The Elizabethan Age 3
William Shakespeare 20
Francis Bacon 80
Puritans and Cavaliers 111
John Milton 121
The Restoration 163
John Bunyan 170

THE AGE OF REASON

The Augustans 206
Jonathan Swift 224
Daniel Defoe 251
Henry Fielding 287
From the Augustans to the Romantics 315
Jane Austen 328

THE GREAT ROMANTICS AND THE DEMOCRATIC REVOLUTION

The French Revolution 375
An Advance Guard 380
    Robert Burns 381
    William Blake 392
The Spirit of 1789 407
    William Wordsworth 407
    Samuel Taylor Coleridge 426
    William Hazlitt 457
Against the Unholy Alliance 492
    Lord Byron 493
    Percy Bysshe Shelley 516
The Last of the Great Romantics 554
    John Keats 554
    Charles Lamb 579

THE VICTORIAN AGE AND THE INDUSTRIAL REVOLUTION

From the Romantics to the Victorians 617
Industrial England and Its Poetry 628
    Robert Browning 653
Her Majesty's Loyal Opposition 674
The Victorian Novelists 689
    Charles Dickens 693
    George Eliot 752
Thomas Huxley and Human Progress 798

THE END OF AN EPOCH

If Winter Comes 834
George Bernard Shaw 875

Bibliography 927
Index 929

The Elizabethan Age and the Bourgeois Revolution

THE ELIZABETHAN AGE

It is difficult for us today to imagine the reality and vigor of England's great Renaissance age, and of that early period of triumphant revolution which ushered in our modern world.

Sixteenth century England, and especially, its capital city London, were in the full enjoyment of a belated Renaissance, a humanist flowering of secular learning like that which had, a little earlier, reached Italy and France. But partly because of certain political events sketched below and the strong feeling of somewhat aggressive patriotism they engendered, partly because of the powerful current of the Reformation which had affected England almost as much as it did the Netherlands (and had inspired such martyred Protestant leaders as John Wyclif, William Tyndale, and Hugh Latimer) England wore its Renaissance with a difference. As the excellent French critic, Emile Legouis, says in his *History of English Literature*:

> While in France the Renaissance was eminently aristocratic, in England it was always regardful of the masses. It preserved and increased the vogue of the ballads. The theatre, the home of the most magnificent product of the period, was accessible to all men, appealed to the humble as well as to the great.

A striking example of this English integration of the new Renaissance emphasis on learning with the older popular cultural traditions is shown by the development of the medieval morality play in the early sixteenth century. (In France, on the contrary, this flourishing medieval folk art died out entirely during the Renaissance, and after 1548 popular performances of the other medieval religious plays, the mystery plays, were forbidden by law.)

One of the first of these new English morality plays was written by John Skelton in 1516. A famous humanist, noted as a Latinist and grammarian, and appointed tutor to the future Henry VIII, Skelton turned his back on the language of the court and university to write poetry in the still unrespected English vernacular. Thomas More's famous *Utopia*, for example, was written in Latin in 1516 and although widely known in his own time, was not translated into English until 1551. But Skelton said:

> Though my rime be ragged,
> Tatter'd and jagged,
> Rudely raine-beaten
> Rusty and moth-eaten;
> If ye take wel therewith,
> It hath in it some pith.

His morality play, *Magnificence*, does not represent the medieval struggle between heaven and hell for the soul of man. It represents a kingly Renaissance hero, Magnificence, who is almost ruined by following the advice of bad counselors but is saved by the help of such good, but equally worldly, ones as Hope, Circumspection and Perseverance.

An even more interesting secular adaptation of the old religious form, printed anonymously three years later, is called *The Four Elements*. It has as its devil, Ignorance, and as its hero, Humanity, son of the "Natura Naturata" who is saved by his guardian, Studious Desire.

In the late forties *The Play of Wyt and Science* was performed. In this a noble father, Reason, wishes to marry his daughter, Science, to the poor and low-born Human Wit, son of Nature. He answers arguments about the disparity of the match:

> Wherefore, syns they both be so meet matches
> To love each other, strawe for the patches
> Of worldly muckel syence [science] hath inowghe [enough]
> For them both to lyve.

In this play, too, one of the villains is Ignorance, born of Idleness.

About the same time another form of literature which deeply affected the developing Elizabethan drama began to appear.

In 1548 Edward Hall published his *Chronicles* which treated the history of the Civil Wars of Lancaster and York (the Wars of the Roses) and the reigns of Henry VII and VIII. Shakespeare's two great series of History Plays, which we will soon consider, drew much of their material from these very popular *Chronicles*.

In 1561 another *Summarie of English Chronicles* was printed and ran into eleven editions in the following half century.

From 1578-1586 Raphael Holinshed's *Chronicles,* to which Shakespeare was also greatly indebted, appeared and were enthusiastically received by a public deeply interested in political affairs and avid for any lessons that might be learned from history.

The history which those who could not read were soon eagerly following on the bare Elizabethan stage was indeed a thrilling one.

The intoxication of freedom from feudal ties, and the excitement of the new horizons and possibilities which were opening up before the rising young bourgeoisie all over England, were already the very breath of the great Elizabethan Age when Elizabeth came to the throne in 1558.

Her grandfather, Henry VII, founder of the Tudor dynasty, had with his victory ended the hundred and fifty year fratricidal "Wars of the Roses" in which the feudal nobility had been largely destroyed. His need for support and his fear of any reviving rival power in the remnants of the old nobility made his Tudor monarchy from the beginning closely ally itself with the growing new power and wealth of the "middle class." His policies naturally fostered this growth and in many respects met the needs and paralleled the thinking of the most advanced sections of the bourgeoisie.

For example, the only way in which the notoriously thrifty Henry VII willingly spent royal funds was in bounties to encourage shipbuilding. And a century before Geoffrey Chaucer had already noted that, of all the pilgrims en route to Canterbury, only the prosperous "new man"—an active bourgeois merchant—was typically concerned about the neglect of England's sea power.

Henry's son, Henry VIII, had, in the course of England's opposition to Spain, then the center of European reaction, been led to defy the medieval power of the Catholic Church. With amazingly general support and virtually no internal opposition he had succeeded in asserting England's independence of that till then almost unchallenged supernational feudal authority.

By his confiscation and immediate piecemeal resale of the vast church estates, Henry VIII had enormously increased the power of the new monied men, now become landowners as well as merchants, had greatly stimulated trade, and had accelerated the formation of a new nobility whose origins were bourgeois and whose class interest promised loyalty to the throne, which then also meant to the principle of national unity.

At Henry VIII's death in 1547 commerce had grown so enormously that, according to some accounts, the population of London was quadrupled within one generation. The noble Council of Regency, appointed to rule in the name of his young son, did not have, among all its sixteen members, a single one whose title dated back even to the beginning of the century!

It is easy for us today to overlook the genuine advance involved in this substitution of a bourgeois for a feudal nobility.

But we must remember that when we speak of the Elizabethan Age as a revolutionary one we do not refer to a revolution of the miserably poor peasants or of the surprisingly large number of even more miserable "sturdy vagabonds"—the future mechanicks—forced off the land by early capitalist farming.

As Barrows Dunham's profound and witty *Giant in Chains* reminds us: "Feudalism fell . . . not by strength of the class which it directly exploited, but by strength of another class with which it merely interfered." This other class was, of course, the small but rapidly increasing bourgeoisie—some skilled craftsmen, some shipbuilders, some professionals, and above all the merchants.

And in many ways the demands made by this class were more progressive than its predominant composition would lead one to expect.

For, as the history of our own American Revolution and that of the French Revolution have amply illustrated, whenever any such middle class begins to struggle for its own emancipation and the freedom to develop itself, it must, at the beginning, state its case so as to seem to include universal emancipation and freedom of development. That it, as a class, invariably recoils in horror from this broad program as soon as the realization becomes a practical possibility, does not affect the statement's initial validity. And so, in the Elizabethan statement of the essential dignity of generic man, (a statement made in varying ways by Renaissance humanism everywhere at the beginning of the bourgeoisie's assumption of power), we find a universality from which three centuries of bourgeois power were to retreat, leaving its actual realization to a later more comprehensive revolution.

The reality of Tudor progress was emphasized when Edward

VI's death in childhood, and the accession of Elizabeth's older half-sister, the Catholic Mary, ushered in a bloody five years' attempt to reverse the movement of history.

The essential futility of this attempt is evident in the fact that there was never, during her entire reign, any concrete proposal to return even an acre of the confiscated land to the church! But a few of the most public spirited and courageous Protestant Church leaders, and over three hundred small farmers and artisans were burnt at the stake for refusing to disown their heresy. One of these, the brilliant Bishop Latimer, himself a small farmer's son, cried out as the fire was lit, to his colleague and companion in death:

> Play the man, Master Ridley; we shall this day by God's grace, light such a candle in England, as I trust shall never be put out.

The unpopularity of these persecutions was capped by Mary's marriage to the feared and hated king of Spain. Only the knowledge of her fatal illness prevented an uprising in 1558.

Elizabeth's accession was therefore welcomed with great relief and enthusiasm by almost all sections of the population. Even the large number of sincere Catholics were in general more afraid of Spanish domination and renewed civil war than they were of the results of a return to the very "Anglo-Catholic" Episcopalianism of Henry VIII. The event proved them correct. Elizabeth herself was, like her father and grandfather, untroubled with any particular religious convictions, and she was even more superbly gifted with the political sense that created the Tudor "absolutism by consent."

The church settlement she effected was planned to antagonize as few people as possible. The definitions of dogma were deliberately left vague, and the words of the Church services were carefully written so as to make several alternative interpretations equally plausible. A. L. Morton, in his *A People's History of England* summarizes her achievement:

> In the Elizabethan settlement Protestantism assumed the form most compatible with the monarchy and with the system of local government created by the Tudors. The parson in the villages became the close ally of the squire and almost as much a part of the State machine as the Justice of the Peace.

Elizabeth was thus in the happy position of a ruler attuned both temperamentally and intellectually to the tastes as well as the needs of her time.

Her keen interest in exploration and travel and her acknowledged partiality for the grizzled old—as well as the daring young—sea dogs was another taste she shared with the citizens of her city.

This is clear from the tremendous number of travel books and stories of heroic exploits and distant explorations carried on by such curious and unconventional Englishmen as Sir Francis Drake or Sir Walter Raleigh. These books seldom had much literary merit, but they were a vital part of the exciting ferment of an age that bred so great a literature. We must not forget Shakespeare's many references to the "still-vext Bermoothes," the "Antipodes and men whose heads beneath their shoulders grow," and the equally plausible "sea coast of Bohemia."

While the English Renaissance was thus fed by many other streams beside the flow of literature from the ancient world, rediscovered by fifteenth century European culture, it was, of course, largely indebted to that source as well.

After the middle of the sixteenth century there was a flood of translations of Greek and Latin classics, and of the fruits of the earlier Italian and French Renaissance. It was in 1578 that George Chapman published the translation of Homer which John Keats has immortalized for us. Anyone taking the trouble to compare Chapman's version with Pope's elegant and irrelevant eighteenth century one will add a new respect for Elizabethan scholarship to his admiration of Elizabethan poetry.

The great burst of lyric poetry by such sonneteers as Sir Philip Sidney, Sir Thomas Wyatt, and the Earl of Surrey, and the richly pictorial narrative poetry of the *Faerie Queene* by that poet's poet, Edmund Spenser, are all well-known evidences of the Elizabethan age's exuberant vitality.

Less interesting to us today, but also extremely important in the development of our modern English, are the ornate and fantastic early prose narratives like John Lyly's *Euphues* and Sidney's *Arcadia*. But such early literary criticism as Sidney's noble *Apologie for Poetrie* in which he maintains the poet's dignity as the first lawgiver of society, and its prophet, are still important for their content as well as their style.

There are other less known theoretical works which are equally valuable for those who wish fully to realize the meaning of humanism and its respect for man—an attitude absolutely fundamental to any real understanding of Shakespeare's greatness. For example, we may glance at *The Laws of Ecclesiastical Polity* by Richard Hooker, which he had been working on for many years and which was published immediately after his death in 1600.

Hooker was the son of a poor man, destined for an apprenticeship, whose extraordinary brilliance attracted his schoolmaster's attention and won him a scholarship to Oxford. Graduated with high honors in the early seventies, he refused preferment and asked for a small country living where he might "behold God's blessings spring out of my mother earth and eat my own bread without oppositions."

There he devoted himself largely to the huge work he left unfinished at his death. Quiet and conservative in tone, it nevertheless shares the major attitude of his tumultuous and progressive age, its faith in active reason, in man's power to affect the world, and in his full responsibility for whatever he may choose to do or leave undone. A characteristic passage reads:

> Man in perfection of nature being made according to the likeness of his Maker resembleth Him also in the manner of working: so that whatsoever we work as men, the same we do wittingly work and freely; neither are we according to the manner of natural agents any way so tied but that it is in our power to leave done the things we do undone.

Another more obscure ecclesiastical writer, Thomas Starkey, also uses religious terminology to express his regard for the divinity of man's reason:

> Thus, if we with ourself reason, and consider the works of man here upon earth, we shall nothing doubt of his excellent dignity, but plainly affirm that he hath in him a sparkle of Divinity, and is surely of a celestial and divine nature, seeing that by memory and wit also he conceiveth the nature of all things. For there is nothing here in this world, neither in heaven above, nor in earth beneath, but he by his reason comprehendeth it. So that I think we may conclude that man by nature, in excellence and dignity, even so excelleth all other creatures here upon earth, as God exceedeth the nature of man.

These quotations are generally characteristic of Renaissance humanism, but the emphasis on society as an indivisible entity, which alone made it possible for men to realize their potentialities, is more specifically characteristic of the English culture of the period. Even in England there were many great men like Shakespeare's brilliant predecessor, Christopher Marlowe (1564-1593), who stressed the new freedom of individual development as opposed to the older sense of community, but the typical sixteenth century English thought is here better represented by such writers as Hooker, Starkey, and of course Shakespeare himself.

Starkey, for example, says:

> . . . we should have a multitude of people convenient to the place, flourishing with all good abundance of exterior things required to the bodily wealth of man, the which living together in civil life, governed by politic order and rule, should conspire together in amity and love, everyone glad to help another to his power, to the intent that the whole might attain to that perfection which is determined to the dignity of man's nature by the goodness of God, the which is the end of all laws and order, for which purpose they be writ and ordained.

And Hooker adds:

> . . . forasmuch as we are not by ourselves sufficient to furnish ourselves with a competent store of things needful for such a life as our nature doth desire, a life fit for the dignity of man; therefore to supply these defects and imperfections which are in us living single and solely by ourselves, we are naturally induced to seek communion and fellowship with others. This was the cause of men's uniting themselves at the first in politic societies, which societies could not be without government, nor government without a distinct kind of Law. Two foundations there are which bear up public societies; the one, a natural inclination whereby all men desire sociable life and fellowship; the other, an order expressly or secretly agreed upon touching the manner of their union in living together.

Yet for all the variety of Elizabethan literature, its great glory and supreme gift to the world was unquestionably its theatre—still the source of the greatest drama the English-speaking stage has ever known.

This theatre had, as we have seen, roots reaching back to the folk productions of the medieval morality plays, which had been presented by guilds in every sizable English town for centuries. But in its Elizabethan reincarnation this theatre was uniquely the product of late sixteenth century London, and so intimately affected by the queen and her court that we must consider a little more closely the position of the last of the Tudors and her relation to the people Shakespeare's theatre served.

Queen Elizabeth herself was an enlightened representative of her age and seemed surprisingly well aware of the contemporary movement of history. Absolute in power but flexible in policy, aware of the real importance of wealth and careless of military glory, personally interested in her country's welfare and indifferent in matters of religion, she deliberately appealed to widespread support among the common people and jealously repressed the rise of any powerful factions in the nobility. She served during the last third of the sixteenth century as a dramatic center and symbol for a rare—and brief—period in which the real interests of the most progressive class in the country were also the dominant ones of the country, and expressed themselves as those of the nation itself.

In 1608, five years after her death, that great thinker and shrewd observer, Francis Bacon, wrote some notes "On The Fortunate Memory of Elizabeth, Queen of England." These were presented to King James, a ruler under whom Bacon received the rewards and recognition Elizabeth never gave him, and a king who made barely a pretense of any respect or affection for his predecessor. He certainly was not to be favorably impressed by any praise bestowed upon her, and Bacon certainly knew it. We may, therefore, fairly accept what Bacon wrote in this brief essay as the honest and considered opinion of a competent judge who had had unusual opportunities for personal observation.

> Elizabeth both in her nature and her fortune was a wonderful person among women, a memorable person among princes. . . .
>
> The government of a woman has been a rare thing at all times; felicity in such government a rarer thing still; felicity and long continuance together the rarest thing of all. Yet this Queen reigned forty-four years, and did not outlive her felicity. . . .
>
> Observe too that this same humour of her people, over eager for war and impatient of peace, did not prevent her from cultivating and maintaining peace during the whole time of her reign. And this her desire of peace, together with the success of it, I count among her greatest praises; as a thing happy for her times, becoming to her sex, and salutary for her conscience. . . .
>
> Upon another account also this peace so cultivated and

maintained by Elizabeth is matter of admiration; namely, that it proceeded not from any inclination of the times to peace, but from her own prudence and good management. For in a kingdom laboring with intestine faction on account of religion, and standing as a shield and stronghold of defence against the then formidable and overbearing ambition of Spain, matter for war was nowise wanting; it was she who by her forces and her counsels combined kept it under; . . .

Nor was she less fortunate in escaping the treacherous attempts of conspirators than in defeating and repelling the forces of the enemy . . . and yet was not her life made thereby more alarmed or anxious; . . . but still secure and confident, and thinking more of the escape than of the danger, she held her wonted course. . . .

With regard to her moderation in religion there may seem to be a difficulty, on account of the severity of the laws made against popish subjects. But on this point I have some things to advance which I myself carefully observed and know to be true.

Her intention undoubtedly was, on the one hand not to force consciences, but on the other not to let the state, under pretence of conscience and religion, be brought in danger. . . . Not even when provoked by the excommunication pronounced against her by Pius Quintus, did she depart almost at all from this clemency, but perservered in the course which was agreeable to her own nature. For being both wise and of a high spirit, she was little moved with the sound of such terrors: knowing she could depend upon the loyalty and love of her own people, and upon the small power the popish party within the realm had to do harm, as long as they were not seconded by a foreign enemy. . . .

As for those lighter points of character,—as that she allowed herself to be wooed and courted, and even to have love made to her; and liked it; and continued it beyond the natural age for such vanities;—if any of the sadder sort of persons be disposed to make a great matter of this, it may be observed that there is something to admire in these very things, which ever way you take them. For if viewed indulgently, they are much like the accounts we find in romances, of the Queen in the blessed islands, and her court and institutions, who allows of amorous admiration but prohibits desire. But if you take them seriously, they challenge admiration of another kind and of a very high order; for certain it is that these dalliances detracted but little from her fame and nothing at all from her majesty, and neither weakened her power nor sensibly hindered her business:—whereas such things are not infrequently allowed to interfere with the public fortune. . . .

But the truth is that the only true commender of this lady is time, which, so long a course as it has run, has produced nothing in this sex like her, for the administration of civil affairs.

We have already noted the almost universal joy with which England greeted the beginning of Elizabeth's reign because it meant the end of religious persecution, of Spanish influence, and of the dangers of civil war.

For many years Elizabeth deliberately allowed Philip of Spain to think there was a chance of a marriage which would again bind England to a Spanish alliance and, in view of Spain's still greatly superior wealth and power, to Spanish domination. She realized that a test of strength with Spain was almost inevitable but hoped to postpone it as long as possible, partly because of her intense dislike of the waste and destruction war entailed, partly because England was daily becoming a more prosperous manufacturing nation, and every year made her better able to meet Spain's challenge.

Finally in 1587 Mary, Queen of Scots, and claimant to the English throne, was executed for complicity in a plot to assassinate Elizabeth. She bequeathed to Philip of Spain her claim, which was based on the grounds that Henry's non-Catholic marriage to Elizabeth's mother had been illegal, and that Elizabeth herself was therefore illegitimate.

Philip had by then long lost his faith in Elizabeth's susceptibility, and saw no reason for delaying an invasion. The awe-inspiring Armada was equipped and an uprising by the remaining Catholic nobility of the North, with whom he had for years been communicating through the Jesuits, was planned to coincide with the landing in London.

The enormous Spanish galleons were still organized essentially as ships for the transport of troops and, if forced to engage in naval battles, followed the time honored method of grappling with the enemy ship and boarding it, with as many men as possible, to fight on deck.

The lively little English ships, on the other hand, were built for maneuverability on the sea, had cannons fitted at every porthole as well as on deck, and literally sailed circles around the floating castles of Spain, pouring a steady fire of cannon balls which were made more terribly effective by the helplessly crowded Spanish decks.

In a very real sense the battle was a test of strength between the modern and the medieval world, and the rout of the latter was neither an accident nor a miracle but a predictable result.

The new national consciousness reached delirious heights of patriotism and self-confidence at the defeat of the imperial Spanish Armada by a fleet of small merchant ships whose captains and owners largely represented the most daring and representative members of the bourgeoisie.

The popularity of the queen, who had actively identified herself with the defense of London and its citizen-defenders, also reached new heights. Neither Elizabeth nor any other English sovereign was ever again to be so wonderful a symbol of national strength and unity.

Nowhere was this victory more resoundingly celebrated than in the London theatres.

Two parts of *Tamburlaine*, the first play by that extraordinary young Christopher Marlowe, appeared in 1587-88, and were rapidly followed by *The Tragical History* of *Doctor Faustus* in 1588 and *The Jew of Malta* in 1589.

In strange and terrible ways these are three variations on the soaring spirit of man, his eager curiosity, his towering pride, and his insatiable appetite for power whether that be won by military might, knowledge, or gold.

It is interesting to remember that Marlowe's spirit still had vitality enough to trouble a Congressional Committee in 1938 which, investigating the Federal Theatre, demanded, in reference to its production of *Doctor Faustus*, whether that author were "another party member."

But although he was the greatest of them, Marlowe, was only one of the impecunious university men whom the newly organized groups of professional London actors had begun to call on for assistance in supplying their growing public with up-to-date material. They paid writers little but provided a never glutted market, and many learned men condescended to write new plays or rewrite old ones for their vast new largely illiterate public.

The first permanent professional company had been organized in London in 1574 under the protection of the Earl of Leicester and two years later the first playhouse was built at Shoreditch just outside of London. A number of others rapidly followed, each technically of the household of some nobleman who gave them his protection and countenance, although their real economic dependence was then, as now, on the box office.

The queen herself frequently ordered command performance of new or markedly popular plays, and the members of her court followed her example.

Many noblemen themselves attended performances at the regular theatres as well, and the comparatively huge audiences presented an amazing cross section of London. Professor Alfred Harbage, in a carefully documented study of *Shakespeare's Audiences* has shown how representative an audience these plays appealed to, ranging from apprentices who paid tu'ppence for admission to gentlemen who had paid several pounds for a seat.

Legouis correctly relates this broad audience to the extraordinary power of the Elizabethan drama, saying:

> Rich as are all the manifestations of the English literature of the Renaissance, its highest glory and the most direct and original expression of the national genius are dramatic. Elsewhere imitation and artifice play a part; aristocratic sentiment or an ephemeral fashion is a check on spontaneity, ruling out whatever is of the people, . . .
>
> The theatre was open to all: the whole town was attracted by it and enthusiastic for it. It was truly national. For many it took the place of the church they neglected: to most, in this time of no newspapers and few and little-read novels, it was the only source of intellectual pleasure. A secular temple, it provided from time to time a communion of patriotism instead of the old communion of faith.
>
> . . . Never has any other audience been so stimulating to writers, who received their immediate reward in tears or laughter, noisy and multitudinous applause.

As we have already partially indicated, London had experienced an enormous influx of an active and alert but largely illiterate citizenry, keenly interested in matters of public concern, newly curious about the background of their so recently discovered "nation," and deeply stirred by England's sudden assumption of leadership in world affairs and London's growing cosmopolitanism. Their horizons were daily pushed further apart by returning travelers with tales of the antipodes, and stimulated by the talk filtering down to them of other travelers who had visited the starry regions and seen, in the mind's eye at least, the vistas of the ancient Roman world. This audience would in itself almost account for the spontaneous generation of an unequaled theatre.

It is a sad commentary on the distance which professional artists have traveled from the people when we find the last poet laureate of England blaming the "wretched beings" for whom Shakespeare was forced to write, for all the "faults" of his plays, and the sacrifice of an infinitely greater art!

But, of course, this theatre was no spontaneous generation. As we have seen, there was already in England a long and well-loved tradition of truly popular drama in the old miracle, mystery and morality plays, introduced by the Church and taken up and elaborated by the guilds in every sizable town of medieval England. This, together with the well-developed taste for pageantry nourished first by the rich ritual of the Catholic Church and then by the numerous "royal progresses" or processions and frequent public masques and entertainments provide a legitimate ancestry and adequately account for the enormous popularity of the Elizabethan theatre.

There is also another more philosophical sense in which the drama was the logical expression of the Renaissance humanism of the Elizabethan Age. For the Elizabethan mind, man was, essentially, the hero of his own most dramatic story. And not a passive hero or a spectator but one who took it upon himself to change the map of the world and the shape of the heavens. Whether he was a king who redefined the channels through which God's rule might be exercised in England, a merchant adventurer who added a new dimension to the earth, or a lord chancellor who "took all knowledge to be his province," the representative Elizabethan man was an active and effective force in the world, which centered about him and his concerns. There was nothing he might not dare and little he could not do. And everything he dared or did affected the body politic itself, changing the lives of many of his fellows and making a difference to the whole universe. Macbeth's desire to be king does not merely lead to the early death of an old man and the subsequent remorse and sleeplessness of a younger one—Macbeth murdered sleep itself. He confounds the universal peace—the frame of things disjoints—both the worlds suffer until, with the help of the legitimate prince, those fighting against him succeed and give to their tables meat, sleep to their nights, free from their homes and banquets bloody knives, pay faithful homage and receive true honors; in other words, set the frame of things right again.

For such men, who were rooted in the real world, whose desires expressed themselves in practical action, and whose intentions had material results, drama was a natural form of expression and would no doubt have been important even if all rather than only some twenty or twenty-five percent of its audience had known how to read. As it was, it was supreme, and gives us in distillation whatever of woe and wonder occupied the mind of Elizabethan London —the heart of Renaissance England.

What this was we shall see in more detail when we turn to Shakespeare himself and the themes which absorbed the interest of his audiences, and his own interest. First, however, we must very briefly summarize the political movements of Elizabeth's last fifteen years, which were, roughly, also the first fifteen years of Shakespeare's writing career.

The jubilation of a united nation at the defeat of the Spanish Armada was not a triumphant fifth act curtain but only a dramatic second act climax.

The removal of an immediate external threat and the bourgeoisie's dawning realization of their great growing strength as a class made them begin to question the secondary role which was all they had, so far, aspired to play in national politics.

Meanwhile although the throne was no longer as seriously threatened by any revival of feudal power this was by no means an impossible fear. (See the discussion of Essex' rebellion on p. 88 ff.) There were also other ways in which the crown had to demand increased assistance from the commons.

Tudor government was by our standards extremely inexpensive, but compared to the altogether decentralized feudal system of medieval England it was very dear. Today England's national budget makes extravagant provision for a household and personal allowance to the sovereign, but in the sixteenth and seventeenth centuries it was the sovereign who had to provide a national budget out of his private estate.

It was therefore necessary for Elizabeth constantly to secure large sums of money. Many of these were provided by grants more or less voluntarily voted by a House of Commons and by wealthy city councils, which generally approved the royal policy and took a patriotic pride in the respect their queen's personal wit and learning and astute diplomacy won for England.

But there was always a deficit which she made up by granting various noblemen "patents" or monopolies of such products as wines, lace, and, too often, more necessary articles. These were paid for either in lump sums of gold, or in services to the throne, and amounted to a form of indirect taxation.

The growing independence of the large commercial interests and the increasing burden of the longer and longer list of monopolies mounted steadily during the last years of her reign and reached a climax in her last parliament, the year before her death.

The following incident is worth describing for the light it throws on the genuine conflict her successor inherited, and on the political tact with which she had kept it from breaking into open opposition between the commons and the crown during her life.

Elizabeth was almost seventy, and had long been increasingly imperious and notoriously quick tempered in her manner to the court favorites and other members of the nobility. When she heard of the unprecedented criticism which greeted the reading of the long list of monopolies at the opening session of the House of Commons, she immediately sent for the terrified Speaker. To his overwhelming relief she was affability itself. She told him she had just learned that "divers patents" she had granted "were grievous" to her subjects and that this had occupied her thoughts "even in the midst of . . . most great and weighty occasions," and that it should be corrected with all convenient speed.

A delegation from the so recently disaffected Commons arrived, knelt before her and said, in the words of the Speaker:

> In all duty and thankfulness, prostrate at your feet, we present our most loyal and thankful hearts, and the last spirit in our nostrils, to be poured out, to be breathed up, for your safety.

She answered:

> Mr. Speaker, we perceive your coming is to present thanks unto us; know I accept them with no less joy than your loves can have desired to offer such a present, and do more esteem it than any treasure or riches, for those we know how to prize,

but loyalty, love and thanks I account them invaluable; and, though God hath raised me high, yet this I account the glory of my crown, that I have reigned with your loves.

Then, after telling the deputation to rise she continued, graciously and effectively, if disingenuously:

When I heard it, I could give no rest unto to my thoughts until I had reformed it, and those varlets, lewd persons, abusers of my bounty, shall know I will not suffer it. And, Mr. Speaker, tell the House from me that I take it exceeding grateful that the knowledge of these things have come unto me from them.

She concluded, with substantially more honesty:

Of myself, I must say this, I never was any greedy scraping grasper, nor a strict fast-holding prince, nor yet a waster; my heart was never set upon any worldly goods, but only for my subjects' good. . . .
And, though you have had and may have many mightier and wiser princes sitting in this seat, yet you never had nor shall have any love you better.

In addition to this tension of class conflict beginning to appear during the last years of Elizabeth's reign, there was the continual threat of war through Spanish aggression, through England's commitments to the Protestant Netherlands in their fight for freedom, or through the pressure of the young lords of the powerful noble families, who still saw in military glory the main road to both prestige and wealth.

Most serious of all was the danger of a civil war which, many felt, would be precipitated by the queen's death since there was no natural heir to the throne.

These fears were kept alive by the innumerable plots for her assassination, the Catholic intrigues in Ireland made effective by the terrible oppression and justified grievances of that unhappy country—England's first colony—and the still fresh horrors of England's hundred and fifty year long war of the Roses, fought over a disputed succession.

It is this background of national growth, commercial expansion and political concern which gives us the key to the predominantly political drama that culminated in Shakespeare's great plays, where all the terrors of real life are faced and outfaced by an essentially sanguine and self-reliant humanity.

WILLIAM SHAKESPEARE

William Shakespeare was born in Stratford, a small but important market town, during the week of April 23, 1564, the third of a family of eight children. His father, John Shakespeare, was a well-to-do merchant and leading citizen in the town who had repeatedly served as a member of the town council and had held almost all the important town offices at one time or another.

Although there is no record of Shakespeare's education, Stratford is known to have possessed an excellent grammar school, taught by university graduates, and there is no reason to doubt that Shakespeare attended it.

In November, 1582, there is a record of a marriage between Shakespeare, then eighteen and a half, and the twenty-six year old daughter of a yeoman, Ann Hathaway. Since their first child, Susanna, was born less than five months later it is likely that the marriage was one of necessity. Their only remaining children, the twins Judith and Hamnet (who died at twelve), were born in February, 1585.

After this there is no further record of Shakespeare until we find him established as a rising young playwright in 1592. The likelihood is that he left Stratford for London and the theatre soon after the birth of the twins, and lived through the exciting years of the Spanish defeat in the capital.

There are legends of his having held horses outside the playhouses, and certainly he must have lived hard and undertaken many odd jobs before he succeeded in winning admission as a player of small parts and, soon, a refurbisher of old plays, to one of the several companies then using the three London houses.

But by 1592, when he was twenty-eight, his success was such that a contemporary, Robert Greene, one of the best known of the university men who somewhat patronizingly bestowed their talents on the theatre, wrote to his colleagues jealously denouncing the "upstart Crow, beautified with our feathers, that with his *Tiger's heart wrapt in a Player's hide*" (this parodies a line in *Henry VI* "O tiger's heart wrapt in a woman's hide") "supposes he is as well able to bombast out a blank verse as the best of you: and being an absolute Johannes fac totum [Jack of all trades] is in his own conceit the only Shake-scene in the country."

On April 18, 1593, there is an official record of the publication of Shakespeare's first known poem, the long narrative *Venus and Adonis*, which was dedicated to his patron, the Earl of Southampton, a friend and follower of Lord Essex. This poem was immediately popular and was reprinted eleven times in the next few years.

In May, 1594, Shakespeare's second nondramatic poem, *The Rape of Lucrece*, was published with a much warmer and more intimate dedication to the same patron.

That year the Lord Chamberlain's Company was formed. Shakespeare was from the beginning an important member of this leading theatrical company, and appears frequently in its business records from then on.

In 1598 a young scholar, Frances Meres, wrote *A Comparative Discourse of our English poets with the Greek, Latin and Italian poets*. In this he spoke warmly of Shakespeare as one by whom "the English tongue is mightily enriched, and gorgeously invested in rare ornaments and splendid habiliments." He continued:

> As Plautus and Seneca are accounted the best for Comedy and Tragedy among the Latins: so Shakespeare among the English is the most excellent in both kinds for the stage. . . . so I say that the Muses would speak with Shakespeare's fine filed phrase if they would speak English.

Meres included in this article a list of the twelve principal plays which Shakespeare, was, so far, known to have written.

He also referred to the manuscript circulation of the sonnets, saying:

> the sweet witty soul of Ovid lives in mellifluous and honey-tongued Shakespeare, witness his *Venus and Adonis*, his Lucrece, his sugared sonnets among his private friends. . . .

In 1601 there developed a fierce rivalry between the "intellectuals" or classicists who wrote largely for the small aristocratic child-actor theatres, discussed at length in Professor Alfred Harbage's excellent *Shakespeare and the Rival Tradition*, and the less learned, more powerful, favorites of the popular audiences.

A topical satire of the time has an actor exclaim:

> Why, here's our fellow Shakespeare puts them all down; aye, and Ben Jonson too. O that Ben Jonson's a pestilent fellow; he brought up Horace giving the poets a pill, but our fellow Shakespeare hath given him a purge that made him bewray his credit.

Nine years later in an echo of this dispute a John Davies contrasted "W. S." with the bitter sneering favorites of the court coteries, saying:

> Some others rail, but rail as they think fit,
> Thou hast no railing but a reigning wit.

In 1612 a younger Jacobean dramatist, John Webster, author of *The White Devil* and *The Duchess of Malfi*, referred dutifully, but less enthusiastically, to Shakespeare's "right happy and copious industry."

In 1616, immediately after Shakespeare's death, an obscure contemporary poet, W. Basse, wrote charmingly, and on the whole prophetically:

> Renowned Spenser, lie a thought more nigh
> To learned Chaucer; and, rare Beaumont, lie
> A little nearer Spenser, to make room
> For Shakespeare in your threefold, fourfold tomb.
> To lodge all four in one bed make a shift,
> For until doomsday hardly will a fifth
> Betwixt this day and that by fate be slain
> For whom your curtains need be drawn again.

It is of course to this conceit that Ben Jonson is referring in the third, fourth and fifth lines of his tribute below. It was contributed to a formal memorial volume published in 1623, barely seven years after Shakespeare's death.

> . . . Soul of the age!
> The applause! delight! the wonder of our stage!
> My Shakespeare rise! I will not lodge thee by

>   Chaucer, or Spenser, or bid Beaumont lie
>   A little further off, to make thee room:
>   Thou art a monument without a tomb,—
>   . . . .
>   And tell how far thou didst our Lyly outshine
>   Or sporting Kyd, or Marlowe's mighty line.
>   And though thou hadst small Latin and less Greek
>   From thence to honor thee, I will not seek
>   For names: but call forth thundering Aeschylus,
>   Euripides, and Sophocles to us, . . .
>   . . . .
>   Triumph, my Britain, thou hast one to show,
>   To whom all scenes of Europe homage owe.
>   He was not for an age, but for all time!

In the face of all these and many other intimate contemporary references to Shakespeare's work, it is almost incomprehensible that so many men should have found the time, money, and energy to waste in writing, printing, buying, and reading books that "prove" Shakespeare's plays were written by the Baron of Verulam (better known as Francis Bacon); by Lord Rutland; by the Count of Derby; by the Earl of Oxford; or by a half dozen other invariably titled gentlemen.

That England's and, perhaps the world's, greatest poetry should have been written by "our fellow Shakespeare," a man with no title at all, who knew "little Latin and less Greek" has evidently presented insuperable difficulties to many. But, as Legouis says:

> Rather than be surprised that Shakespeare, like Moliere, was an actor and yet wrote plays which were masterpieces, we might well ask if it would have been possible for him to write them in any other walk of life.

However, true as this is, it is only part of the truth. Even after we have said that, if any man were to be able to write Shakespeare's plays he must have been a man of the working theatre, the major question still remains. Why should one human being tower so far above successive generations of his most magnificent fellows? How can one artist be unquestioned master in so rich a field of art as that which modern English literature presents to us?

This question, like so many others in the world of art, cannot be answered unless we see the artist as a part of the life by which he was formed, and which he himself helped to form. It is not the potential Shakespeare whom we have to consider as uniquely great —there may have been others, not many but a few, born with the same capacities—but the actual Shakespeare maturing in an age when the old social and economic order had been destroyed and a new world was coming to birth—and when his nation and indeed his city had taken a leading part in that destruction and that great new birth.

When we today think of a progressive artist it is almost impossible for us not, at the same time, to think of him as an "opposition" artist—as one who, with all his greatness, cannot speak in the tones of easy unself-conscious authority which a great writer, serving as the voice of his time and happily representing a comparatively unquestioned tradition, can use. It was Shakespeare's great good fortune—and ours—that brought him to birth at the brief period in which he could at one and the same time express his own deepest convictions and the central feeling of his age, analytically rather than argumentatively, to an audience which largely shared and embodied both. This period did not last out even his own time, but it sufficed for his formative years and the greater part of his writing life.

In these pages we cannot, of course, attempt anything like a real analysis of Shakespeare's thought. But, naming the plays roughly in the probable order of their appearance, we can glance at certain vital aspects of his political and social philosophy which they illustrate. If this running commentary suggests new questions for each reader's own attention as he returns to reconsider the plays it will be amply justified. This discursive chronological approach may also help us form a more concrete idea of the development of Shakespeare's political and social views in the course of his writing life.

That life began, as we have seen, some time in the late eighties. Before 1594 Shakespeare had written the trilogy of *Henry VI* (parts of which he may have preserved substantially unaltered from an older chronicle play in the possession of his company), *Richard III, Titus Andronicus* (almost certainly, and in much greater part, the work of a crude earlier hand), *Love's Labour Lost, The Two Gentlemen of Verona, The Comedy of Errors,* and *The Taming of the Shrew.*

Much of the mature Shakespeare is here already apparent, in subject matter more than in style, although in *Richard III* the language begins to be unmistakably that of Ben Jonson's "beloved master."

Four of the plays (the three parts of *Henry VI* and *Richard III*) deal concretely with then recent English history, stressing ideas of vital and controversial interest to Elizabethan audiences. Among these are, of course, the incomparable horrors of civil war and the necessity of national unity; the qualities and responsibilities of a real sovereign; the bearing of the personal relations and desires of important public figures on political events; the effect of the political climate of an age on private character; the essential irrelevance of religion to matters of state; and the importance of a legitimate and unquestioned succession to the throne.

This is far from an exhaustive list even of the most interesting general questions raised in these four plays, and there is much else of sheer dramatic and poetic excitement in *Richard III*. However even this brief reference should begin to show some of the major concerns which Shakespeare shared with his alert and politically minded audience.

Titus Andronicus, the poorest of Shakespeare's plays—it is only in very small part his play—deals with some of the same Elizabethan political problems, transposed in scene to Rome. It also has at least one passage of particular interest to modern readers, who know how soon and how far the bourgeoisie was to retreat, in racial terms, from any assertion of human equality.

The Roman empress, after an affair with Aaron, a Moor, gives birth to a black child which her two villainous older sons attempt to kill. Its father, almost equally wicked in other matters, defies them with:

> Stay, murderous villains! will you kill your brother?
> Now, by the burning tapers of the sky,
> That shone so brightly when this boy was got,
> He dies upon my scimitar's sharp point
> That touches this my first-born son and heir!
> I tell you, younglings, not Euceladus,
> With all his threat'ning band of Typhoon's brood,
> Nor great Alcides, nor the god of war,
> Shall seize this prey out of his father's hands.
> What, what, ye sanguine, shallow-hearted boys!
> Ye white-limed walls! ye alehouse painted signs!
> Coal-black is better than another hue;
> For all the water in the ocean
> Can never turn the swan's black legs to white,

> Although she lave them hourly in the flood.
> Tell the empress from me, I am of age
> To keep my own,—excuse it how she can.

The comedies are all amusing, as their frequent repetition for over three centuries has amply certified, and even the least known of them, *Two Gentlemen of Verona*, is precious for the many delightful passages between the poor servant, Launce, and the mongrel dog he treasures. We wait from scene to scene for a resumption of Launce's reproachful but forgiving talk of and to his beast, whom he loves far more than both gentlemen together do all their ladies.

In one such long-suffering monologue Launce begins plaintively to review the dog's misdeeds for the dog's own edification. Speaking in the third person that the lesson may be more impressive, he says:

> He thrusts me himself into the company of three or four gentleman—like dogs, under the dukes table: he had not been there (bless the mark!) a pissing while, but all the Chamber smelt him. "Out with the dog," says one; "What cur is that?" says another; "whip him out," says the third; "Hang him up," says the duke. I, having been acquainted with the smell before, knew it was Crab; and goes me to the fellow that whips the dogs: "Friend," quoth I, "you mean to whip the dog?" "Ay, marry, do I," quoth I, " 't was I did the thing you wot of." He makes me no more ado, but whips me out of the chamber. How many masters would do this for his servant? Nay, I'll be sworn, I have sat in the stock for puddings he hath stolen, otherwise he had been executed; I have stood in the pillory for geese he hath kill'd, otherwise he had suffer'd for 't.

Then in a grand climax of pathos Launce turns directly to his unrepentant hound and feelingly demands:

> Thou think'st not of this now! Nay, I remember the trick you served me when I took my leave of Madam Silvia; did not I bid thee still mark me, and do as I do? When didst thou see me heave up my leg, and make water against a gentlewoman's farthingale? didst thou ever see me do such a trick?

This is his last appearance, but only the first of a long series of increasingly important Shakespearian "clowns" whose simplicity is often shrewdly closer to the mark than all their masters' wisdom.

As T. A. Jackson, the provocative Irish literary critic and historian, says:

> the common people in Shakespeare . . . are more richly individual, more specifically "humorsome," and generally more human, than the lords and ladies who provide the decorative as distinct from the comic background to the plays. (In Hamlet, for instance, the grave digger has far more character than Horatio, or Rosencrantz and Guildenstern; while the most contemptible of the personages in the play is the courtly fop Osric.)

Love's Labour Lost, a far more lyrical comedy, has an interesting reversal of the conventional humorous situation in its mockery of three young aristocrats who proudly forswear love to devote themselves to deep studies, and are rapidly brought to their knees by the wit and beauty of three independent ladies. A comparison with Tennyson's insufferably patronizing *The Princess*, with its bland assumption that "man's love is of his life a thing apart; 'tis woman's whole existence," will show how far the position of women —in comedy as well as life—had deteriorated from Elizabeth to Victoria.

The next group of plays, probably written and produced between 1594 and 1597 were *Romeo and Juliet, A Midsummer Night's Dream, Richard II, King John* and *The Merchant of Venice*. Here there is no longer any question of the master's hand, and to ask which of these plays is best is only, as Keats said, to inquire in which mood you prefer the ocean.

Romeo and Juliet is one of Shakespeare's very few serious love plays, and again it is noteworthy that here, as later, we find an expression of his ungrudging, unreserved equalitarian attitude toward women. This attitude, too, was characteristic of the most progressive part of bourgeois thought in its revolutionary period.

The importance and dignity of Shakespeare's heroines, their frequent leadership in wit, courage, determination, honesty and resourcefulness, are all only one aspect of his thought on the question of woman's position in society. But so far as it goes, his attitude is as worthily represented by his picture of the fourteen-year old Juliet as it is later by his more mature heroines.

Again, just because it is clearly and avowedly a love play, *Romeo and Juliet* offers striking evidence of Shakespeare's consistent, often unconscious, interest in contemporary political and economic problems.

The play begins and ends with the theme of civil war—seen in miniature in Verona, this time. The Prologue opens:

> Two households, both alike in dignity,
> In Fair Verona, where we lay our scene,
> From ancient grudge break to new mutiny,
> Where civil blood makes civil hands unclean.

And in the closing scene the Prince declares:

> And I, for winking at your discords too,
> Have lost a brace of kinsmen: all are punisht.

We get an incidental but penetrating comment on the class nature of the law and the relation of the state to poverty at the very moment when Romeo, no political economist but a desperate and rash young lover, has just been (wrongly) informed that his bride is dead. He naturally wants to commit suicide upon her grave, needs poison, and begins to bethink himself where, in a strange city, he can purchase some.

> Romeo: Well, Juliet, I will lie with thee tonight.
> Let's see for means. O mischief, thou art swift
> To enter in the thoughts of desperate men!
> I do remember an apothecary,
> And hereabouts a' dwells, which late I noted
> In tatter'd weeds, with overwhelming brows,
> Culling of simples; meagre were his looks;
> Sharp misery had worn him to the bones;
> . . . . . .
> Noting this penury, to myself I said,
> "An if a man did need a poison now
> Whose sale is present death in Mantua,
> Here lives a caitiff wretch would sell it him."
> . . . . . .
> What, ho! apothecary!
> Apoth: Who calls so loud?
> Romeo: Come hither, man. I see that thou art poor;
> Hold, there is forty ducats: let me have
> A dram of poison; such soon-speeding gear
> As will disperse itself through all the veins,
> That the life-weary taker may fall dead,
> . . . .

Apoth: Such mortal drugs I have; but Mantua's law
Is death to any he that utters them.
Romeo: Art thou so bare and full of wretchedness,
And fear'st to die? famine is in thy cheeks,
Need and oppression starveth in thy eyes,
Contempt and beggary hangs upon thy back,
The world is not thy friend, nor the world's law:
The world affords no law to make thee rich;
Then be not poor, but break it, and take this.
Apoth: My poverty, but not my will, consents.
Romeo: I pay thy poverty and not thy will.

Richard II, the first of Shakespeare's second series of history plays, is in some ways the most interesting of them all. In it Shakespeare goes back three generations before the outbreak of the civil wars to find their deep-rooted cause. He dramatically presents the contrast between a dying feudalism and the vigorous new bourgeois monarchy, and analyzes the concrete meaning of "the divine right" of kings by posing the question whether it is right to give allegiance to an irresponsible, weak, unjust but legitimate king rather than to replace him by a shrewd, politic and efficient one with no real legal claim to the throne.

The question thus schematically put gives no idea of the richness of its concrete representation in the play, or of the profound political understanding and amazing dramatic skill with which the balance is held.

There is little else in literature at once as subtle and as emphatic as the continual unresolved but uncontradictory distinction Shakespeare draws between the necessity of absolute royal power to end feudal conflicts, and the almost ridiculous arbitrariness of its personal use; between the need for adherence to the doctrine of divine right which insures a peaceful legitimate succession, and the preposterousness of a king's own literal belief in his divinity; between the sanctity of the sovereign's position, and the frequent futility of the individual sovereign.

John Palmer, in his indispensable book on *Political Characters of Shakespeare,* neatly summarizes this paradox in speaking of the "sentiment for royalty" which has survived "so many royal persons who left their country for their country's good."

All this is projected in the two brilliantly contrasted portraits of the immature, capricious, heartless witty and poetic Richard and his practical, self-controlled, reserved and forceful cousin Bolingbroke (later Henry IV).

At the very opening of the play, after a scene of glorious medieval pageantry which Richard has engineered almost as a practical joke, he banishes his cousin for ten years. Insincerely and carelessly he reassures his aged uncle, who mourns that for him this means a last farewell to his son: "Why uncle, thou hast many years to live."

Old John of Gaunt—who has loyally refused to avenge his own brother's murder because it was ordered by the king—retorts, both admitting and setting the limits of royal power:

> But not a minute, king, that thou canst give:
> Shorten my days thou canst with sullen sorrow,
> And pluck nights from me, but not lend a morrow;

The power of life and death, too often confused, are here exactly distinguished:

> Thy word is current with [time] for my death,
> But dead, thy kingdom cannot buy my breath.

Richard presently concedes that his cousin may return from exile in six years and Bolingbroke says bitterly, but seriously:

> Four lagging winters and four wanton springs
> End in a word: such is the breath of kings.

Later Richard describes Bolingbroke's departure. Like Hamlet, he can often better understand what should be done than summon the resolution to do it, and in this description he shrewdly summarizes much of the Tudor art of government without in the least drawing a lesson from Bolingbroke's use of it.

> Richard II: He is our cousin, cousin; but 'tis doubt
> When time shall call him home from banishment,
> Whether our kinsman come to see his friends.
> Ourself and Bushy, Bagot here, and Green
> Observ'd his courtship to the common people;
> How he did seem to dive into their hearts
> With humble and familiar courtesy;
> What reverence he did throw away on slaves,
> Wooing poor craftsmen with the craft of smiles
> And patient underbearing of his fortune,
> As 'twere to banish their affects with him.

> Off goes his bonnet to an oyster-wench;
> A brace of draymen bid God speed him well
> And had the tribute of his supple knee,
> With "Thanks, my countrymen, my loving friends";
> As were our England in reversion his,
> And he our subjects' next degree in hope.

In little more than a hundred words Shakespeare here points the difference between the pre-Tudor feudal monarchs, first among their peers, and the new bourgeois monarchy which exalted the king to incomparable heights while paradoxically basing his absolute power on the tacit consent of the lower classes.

Still more sharply old John of Gaunt on his deathbed makes the same point in eight words when, concluding an indignant remonstrance at Richard's feudal use of his kingdom as a personal estate, he cries: "Landlord of England art thou now, not King."

Almost every scene combines the same richness of psychological insight, dramatic excitement and lyric beauty with a steady development of the underlying political theme.

Nowhere until *Hamlet*, for example, does Shakespeare again give us the clear, cold, biting sarcasm of Richard's great abdication scene, with its double irony at the unadmitted truth of the guilt he, in bitter mockery, assumes, and the overshadowing sense that his well-deserved inevitable fall is nevertheless as great a tragedy for England as he hints it will be.

> God save the king! although I be not he;
> And yet, amen; if heaven do think him me.
> . . . . . .
> Now mark me, how I will undo myself:—
> I give this heavy weight from off my head,
> And this unwieldy sceptre from my hand,
> The pride of kingly sway from out my heart;
> With mine own tears I wash away my balm,
> With mine own hands I give away my crown,
> With mine own tongue deny my sacred state,
> With mine own breath release all duty's rites;
> . . . . . .
> God pardon all oaths that are broke to me!
> God keep all vows unbroke that swear to thee!
> . . . . . .
> God save King Henry, unking'd Richard says,
> And send him many years of sunshine days!

The other play of this period at which we must more particularly look has, partly for extraneous reasons, become one of the most controversial of Shakespeare's works.

The inaccurate but frequent use of the term "a Shylock" for an avaricious or heartless person, and the stereotype of a sadistic Jewish money lender are well known to many who have never read or seen *The Merchant of Venice*.

On the other hand, a long list of distinguished and progressive critics, including Heinrich Heine and William Hazlitt, have taken Shylock as the tragic hero of his own terrible story.

For our time the interpretation of this play in terms of the Jew's position is of such absorbing importance as to dwarf any other themes on which it may touch. This is certainly a valid emphasis, but we should note in passing that Shakespeare was also here concerned with the then new and important bourgeois concepts of laws guaranteeing at least commercial equality and protection to foreign traders, and the possible validity of unprecedented and perhaps antisocial contractual relationships. The idea of free enterprise had not yet in theory, and not wholly in practice, replaced the medieval guild concepts of a "just price" and other traditionally determined conditions.

The late Franklin D. Roosevelt wrote to a friend at the time of the early N.R.A. regulations: "I have just been re-reading a curious old play on the law of contracts. Perhaps you know it under the title of *The Merchant of Venice*."

But for us this is essentially a play on anti-semitism. What does it say about that matter?

The plot in its major outlines was an old one. In 1579 a play had been presented which "set forth the greediness of worldly choosers, and the bloody minds of usurers." In other words, the casket-plot and the pound of flesh motif were already combined in one play.

Marlowe's famous *Jew of Malta*, with its terrifying protagonist, had been enormously successful in the year 1589, and doubtless there had been many other now forgotten similar pieces.

Superficially Shakespeare's work seems to fit into the same genre. But at the very outset it poses a question which is inconceivable in terms of Marlowe's protagonist with his natural, uncaused, all-absorbing malevolence toward every Christian great or small.

Shakespeare, almost immediately at Shylock's first entrance, poses the question of why the Jew hates Antonio. And, in a few lines, he answers it by raising the more primary question as to how Antonio—a generous acquaintance, a magnanimous and loyal friend, a dignified and courteous gentleman—can treat another human being with the contempt and indignity he heaps on Shylock.

Shylock, for the first time able to speak to his old enemy, who has now approached him for a large loan, uses the opportunity to appeal to him on the basis of their common humanity—and their economic equality:

> Signior Antonio, many a time and oft
> In the Rialto you have rated me
> About my moneys and my usances
> Still have I borne it with a patient shrug;
> For sufferance is the badge of all our tribe.
> You call me misbeliever, cut-throat dog,
> And spit upon my Jewish gaberdine,
> And all for use of that which is mine own.
> Well then, it now appears, you need my help:
> Go to then; you come to me, and you say,
> "Shylock, we would have moneys," you say so;
> You, that did void your rheum upon my beard
> And foot me as you spurn a stranger cur
> Over your threshold: moneys is your suit.
> What should I say to you? Should I not say,
> "Hath a dog money? Is it possible,
> A cur can lend three thousand ducats?" or
> Shall I bend low, and in a bondman's key,
> With bated breath, and whispering humbleness,
> Say this:—
> "Fair sir, you spit on me on Wednesday last;
> You spurned me such a day; another time
> You called me dog; and for these courtesies
> I'll lend you thus much moneys!

Antonio, of course, coldly denies the existence of any such bond, replying:

> I am as like to call thee so again,
> To spit on thee again, to spurn thee too.
> If thou wilt lend this money, lend it not
> As to thy friends; for when did friendship take
> A breed of barren metal of his friend?
> But lend it rather to thine enemy;
> Who, if he break, thou may'st with better face
> Exact the penalty.

And Shylock promptly determines that Antonio will yet take him seriously as an enemy at least.

The further events of the money or Venice plot, such as Jessica's willing abduction by Antonio's friends, and her abuse of Shylock's trust which has made her the guardian of his coffers, are all contrived to keep Shylock's hatred at fever heat and intensify his desire for revenge.

Although the major part of the love plot is not here our concern, it is important to note Portia's attitude to the Prince of Morocco—an early sketch of "The Noble Moor"—and see what a deliberate contrast her prejudiced color consciousness affords to Desdemona's happy and candid exclamation, "He jealous? I think the sun where he was born sucked all such humours from him." Portia, on the contrary, at first hearing the Prince of Morocco named, declares: "If he have the condition of a saint, and the complexion of a devil, I had rather he should shrive me than wive me."

She remains unmoved when the Prince, clearly the most disinterested and loving of her suitors, pleads:

> Mislike me not for my complexion,
> The shadowed livery of the burnished sun
> To whom I am a neighbour and near bred.
> Bring me the fairest creature northward born,
> Where Phoebus' fire scarce thaws the icicles,
> And let us make incision for your love
> To prove whose blood is reddest, his or mine.
> . . . .
> I would not change this hue,
> Except to steal your thoughts, my gentle queen.

Her attitude here is important, in view of her later attitude to Shylock, because it so clearly marks Shakespeare's astounding insight into the relatedness of all the prejudices which set barriers between human beings and deny the fundamental bond of their common humanity. We better understand Portia's insensitivity in the courtroom scene because we have here heard her: "Draw the curtains; go. Let all of his complexion choose me so."

Shylock's second passionate assertion of human equality is almost as well known as it deserves to be. Asked what good a pound of Antonio's flesh will do him, he replies:

> To bait fish withal; if it will feed nothing else, it will feed my revenge. He hath disgraced me, and hindered me half a mil-

lion, laughed at my losses, mocked at my gains, scorned my
nation, thwarted my bargains, cooled my friends, heated mine
enemies; and what's his reason? I am a Jew. Hath not a Jew
eyes? hath not a Jew hands, organs, dimensions, senses, affections, passions? fed with the same food, hurt with the same
weapons, subject to the same diseases, healed by the same
means, warmed and cooled by the same winter and summer
as a Christian is? If you prick us, do we not bleed? If you
tickle us, do we not laugh? If you poison us, do we not die?
and if you wrong us, shall we not revenge? If we are like you
in the rest, we will resemble you in that. If a Jew wrong a
Christian, what is his humility? revenge. If a Christian wrong
a Jew, what should his sufferance be by Christian example?
why, revenge. The villainy you teach me, I will execute, and
it shall go hard but I will better the instruction.

There is much that might relevantly be noted in almost every succeeding scene but the final climax of the theme and the play are, of course, found in the fourth act courtroom.

In opening his appeal to Shylock's "better nature" the Duke, with some effort, uses his name, but before its conclusion he has reverted to the direct address of "Jew"—and has, incidentally, urged that Shylock not only forget the forfeit but that he also give Antonio 1,500 ducats as a token of his sympathy!

Shylock's reply has long been recognized as a masterpiece of rhetoric but it has a deeper logic than is generally realized. Twice before, first in the powerful appeal to Antonio for recognition as a human being and then, more formally, in his assertion of the Jew's human identity, Shylock has given the reason for the lodged hate and the certain loathing he bears Antonio. Now, when at last he has a chance to act, he refuses to speak again for deaf ears. But the specious logic of his analogy to a man who kills because he cannot abide a gaping pig or a harmless necessary cat is specious only because of the bond of a common humanity which forbids man to treat his fellows as he may creatures of another species; and Shylock is not the one who has first denied this bond or broken the compact. He warned "Thou calledst me dog before thou hadst a cause; but if I am a dog beware my fangs." Antonio, who was as like to call him so again, has no right to refute the reasoning by analogy.

This underlying justice is emphasized in the next long speech, where after a few lines of witty fencing which demolish Bassanio's verbal attack, Shylock reverts to this serious matter—the essential theme of this play as well as *Othello*—the meaning of that basic prejudice which refuses to accept the bond of a fundamental identity between all human beings.

Choosing this time another form of oppression than the one from which his people had, generally, suffered, Shylock declares:

> You have among you many a purchased slave,
> Which, like your asses, and your dogs, and mules,
> You use in abject and in slavish parts
> Because you bought them:—shall I say to you,
> Let them be free; marry them to your heirs?
> Why sweat they under burdens? let their beds
> Be made as soft as yours, and let their palates
> Be seasoned with such viands? You will answer,
> The slaves are ours. So do I answer you:
> The pound of flesh which I demand of him
> Is dearly bought; 'tis mine, and I will have it.
> If you deny me, fie upon your law!
> There is no force in the decrees of Venice.
> I stand for judgment: answer; shall I have it?

It is easy, and meaningless, to point out earnestly that two wrongs do not make a right, as countless generations of Sunday School teachers have done. Shakespeare is not concerned with this kind of moral. He is again developing the deep significance of such a denial of humanity as slavery implies—a denial so blasphemous that the slaveholder forfeited all right to appeal to any man as one human being to another. There may perhaps be justification for killing a man. There can be no justification for enslaving him. It is, as Milton said a little later, "a sort of treason against the dignity of mankind," to think so.

A complete analysis of the play would provide much more material to this purpose, but it would also show a certain deliberate ambiguity in its presentation. A major example is the omission on the stage of Shylock's tragic homecoming. This is reported by unsympathetic witnesses whom each member of the audience is free to believe literally or to interpret as he chooses. Another evasion is, of course, the entire fifth act of moonlight, music and roses which enables us to forget Shylock's tragic exit, if we wish to do so.

It must be remembered that anti-Semitism was not a practical problem in sixteenth century England. While anti-Semitic expressions were very common and the Jew was a stock symbol for many unpleasant characteristics, there had been no significant number of Jews in England since the expulsion in 1290. The very few exceptions were one or two highly placed physicians attached to the court or to foreign, particularly Spanish, ambassadors' retinues. These were generally of Jewish origin, not Jews in religion or self-identification. Shakespeare, like the overwhelming majority of his countrymen, had in all probability never met a Jew.

But it is clear that Shakespeare, when in advance of a considerable part of his audience, felt no necessity to collide head-on with its prejudices, however clearly he might dissect and condemn them. This will become important in our consideration of his last ten years and his three final plays.

The busy years between 1597 and 1601 saw the production of *Henry IV* (Part I), and *Henry IV* (Part II), *Much Ado About Nothing, Merry Wives of Windsor* (at Queens Elizabeth's express request for more Falstaff), *As You Like It, Julius Caesar, Henry V,* and *Troilus and Cressida.*

The three English history plays complete the second series begun by *Richard II* which, in the chronology of its material, immediately precedes the four plays of the first series. (*King John,* written at about the same time as *Richard II,* dealt with a much earlier period and stands apart. Its general concern does not much differ from the rest of the series, but the construction and language relate rather to the earlier plays.)

The full century of English history thus consecutively dramatized is an amazing achievement. Legouis, discussing the history plays on that level alone, says:

> Nothing is more honourable to Elizabethan audiences than that they sought their amusement in the mere spectacle of great national events; . . . The simplicity and the greatness of conception found in the mysteries are repeated. . . . Country instead of faith is his theme. He imparts knowledge of history as those old poets taught religion: . . . all succeeded each other in the plays, painted almost impartially for a public enabled at once to marvel and to learn.

Jackson more analytically formulates the essence of the history plays, and indicates their importance in the body of Shakespeare's work and their relation to the plays of Roman history, the great tragedies, and even several of the comedies. He says:

> That his Chronicle-Histories deal nominally with feudal times is true. But if they be examined as to their dramatic

content it will be seen that never for a moment are they concerned with feudal issues. All of them turn upon themes then current:—upon the new anti-feudal sentiment of nationality (which Shakespeare voices); upon the perils on the one side of an unbridled tyranny, and on the other of an uncontrolled anarchy; above all on the danger to the State and all peace and harmony of a disturbed or usurped succession to the throne. This last, (with an application to the "popular" endorsement as well as the "legal" right of the Tudor dynasty and its legitimate successors) is the theme of the whole chronicle-history sequence which begins with Richard II, and ends with Henry VIII—nine plays in all. It is also directly and indirectly the theme too of Hamlet, Macbeth, Julius Caesar, and King Lear among the tragedies and As You Like It and the Tempest among the comedies. That is to say; it forms an ingredient, more or less primary, in fifteen out of the thirty-odd plays of Shakespeare. And their net political moral may be summed up in the conclusion that of all political calamities, submission to the clash of aristocratic and clerical ambitions, unrestrained by a wisely directed, and humane but unflinching, central rule, is the calamity most to be feared and most to be guarded against.

No words could better sum up the general opinion of the more thoughtful, and more progressive bourgeois in Shakespeare's own day—faced first with the prospect of the imminent death of the childless Elizabeth, and secondly with succession to the throne of the unpopular and alien but legitimate heir James, King of Scots.

One thing no man wanted—outside of the few cliques of court adventurers—and that was something all men feared: a reopening of the civil wars of the late feudal epoch by one or other of the gangs of the new . . . aristocracy. And this was all the more to be dreaded because already there were indications that the religious quarrels of the Reformation epoch might quite easily break out again in a new and more virulent form.

In the same article Jackson gives a detailed analysis of the way in which, in *Henry IV*, Falstaff and his familiars were, symbolically, developed out of the old "Devil" of the medieval mystery plays, and the "Vices" who were his somewhat degenerate successors in the later morality plays.

At the same time, as Jackson shows, Falstaff with his satellites was a perfectly realistic caricature of the groups of "professional soldiers" who were, between wars, "cut-purses, highway robbers, tavern-bullies, whores' protectors and general spongers." These were essentially composed of the large number of feudal retainers suddenly thrown on their own resources by the dissolution of feudal households under the Tudors. Jackson says, in part:

> In Falstaff and his crew the feudal-order, more than moribund,—decadent to putrescence—still cumbers the world-stage and makes its final grotesquely tragi-comic gesture of defiance in the face of its own inevitable extermination.
> The whole farce of the Falstaff scenes in *Henry IV* turns on this grotesque contrast between the feudal status as it was and that into which it has degenerated. The whole of the tragedy underlying the farce and giving it body and force, is the utter incompatibility between this status and relationship and the new bourgeois world which has come into being, throbbing with exuberant life, and finding fresh outlets for expansion every hour.
> [In one sense] Falstaff is startlingly "up-to-date" in a way Shakespeare could not have forseen. For instance: Falstaff leads the plunder raid upon the merchants on Gads-Hill with this slogan:—
> "Strike! Down with them! Cut the villains' throats! Ah! whoreson catterpillars! bacon-fed knaves! *they hate us youth*! Down with them! fleece them!"
>
> That Falstaff is in fact "some fifty years of age, or may be three-score" only makes this use of the term "youth" all the more startlingly "modern." Do we not know this "youth"? And also its *a-moralism*—its affectation of a super-Nietzschean "transvaluation" of Good and Evil?
> Along with this Shakespeare's genius shines out in that by a whole series of touches, we are made to see in Falstaff the other side to the fact that he is—
>
> "That trunk of humours, that bolting hutch of beastliness, that swollen parcel of dropsies, that huge bombard of sack, that stuffed cloak bag of guts, that roasted Manning tree ox with a pudding in his belly, that reverend Vice, that grey iniquity, that father ruffian, that vanity in years."
>
> All this is there: but there is also the memory of what he once was—a courtly page in the household of one of the highest nobles in the Kingdom, the Duke of Norfolk; a gallant soldier whose reputation as such is still so good that he is given a commission at once, as soon as a civil war breaks out; and so on.

Falstaff is also a real and humorous magnetic personality, but his role as tempter of the young prince, and his final rejection by the newly crowned king, cannot be understood in the purely personal terms used by most of the critics who have argued the matter.

As Jackson's interpretation indicates, Falstaff plays a role in *Henry IV* (Part II) which essentially, balances that of the romantic and gallant but equally reactionary Hotspur in Part I.

Hotspur is witty, he is charming, he is sincere and courageous, he has a perfectly well-justified grievance against *Henry IV* (Bolingbroke) whom he and his father did so much to seat on the throne. But he is as incapable of thinking of England as a nation, or of the king as a responsible sovereign with obligations to his people rather than to his friends, as any prehistoric monster would be.

Shakespeare underlines all this when Hotspur is planning the uprising with his two noble allies. Pointing to a map of England he complains of the proposed three-part division of the fruits of victory:

> Methinks my moiety, north from Burton here,
> In quantity equals not one of yours:
> See how this river comes me cranking in,
> And cuts me from the best of all my land
> A huge half-moon, a monstrous cantle out.
> I'll have the current in this place damn'd up;
> And here the smug and silver Trent shall run
> In a new channel, fair and evenly:
> It shall not wind with such a deep indent
> To rob me of so rich a bottom here.

One of his two confederates realizes that Hotspur is perfectly capable of forfeiting the whole uprising by fighting on this point, once he has made it a point of honor, and ends a delightful quarrel scene by saying: "Come, you shall have Trent turn'd."

Hotspur, as quickly and inconsequentially mollified as he was enraged, responds:

> I do not care: I'll give thrice so much land
> To any well-deserving friend;
> But in the way of bargain, mark ye me
> I'll cavil on the ninth part of a hair.

Shakespeare needs do no more to enlist us on the right side in the coming battle.

Similarly, the spirited old rascal, Falstaff, whom we can afford to enjoy as long as his depredations are limited to petty thievery, underlines by his own words the necessity of Henry V's complete rejection of the boon companion of his less responsible days.

On hearing that his Prince Hal is being crowned king, Falstaff exclaims to his band of petty ruffians and respectable gulls:

> Away, Bardolph! saddle my horse.—Master Robert Shallow, choose what office thou wilt; I am fortune's steward. Get on thy boots: we'll ride all night.—O sweet Pistol . . . devise something to do thyself good.—Boot, boot, Master Shallow! I know the young king is sick for me. Let us take any man's horses; the laws of England are at my commandment. Blessed are they that have been my friends; and woe to my lord chief justice!

Henry V has, on the whole, received less than justice from readers who conceive dramatic interest only in terms of psychological conflict. For in this play the interest is, more exclusively than usual, focused on the struggle between two worlds, and only the new one has a central personal representative.

For that reason Laurence Olivier's extraordinarily effective film was, actually, a far better presentation than any stage production. Shakespeare's equation between the decadent feudalism of sixteenth century Spain and fourteenth century France is brilliantly illuminated by the unwieldy armored French knights, lifted on to their horses by cumbersome machinery, who are helpless before the arrows of the lightly clad and agile English bowmen. The whole scene is, in the film, as it was for Shakespeare's time, a perfect translation of the Elizabethan battle between the heavy Spanish galleons and the agile English privateers.

Democratic language is, today, often an unattended platitude so that we must remind ourselves of the almost universal respect for "gentle blood" to understand the impact of Henry's appeal as a citizen king on a still largely feudal world. Almost two hundred years after Shakespeare, a member of the third estate in France declared "All Frenchmen are brothers of one blood," and was faced with a formal demand for an apology from the noblemen of the first estate! There is then a real sense of the new nationalism in Henry's declaration:

> . . . he to-day that sheds his blood with me
> Shall be my brother; be he ne'er so vile,
> This day shall gentle his condition:

Nor is it an accident that the three gunnery captains who play so staunch a part in England's victory are named Fluellen, Gower and MacMorris and so represent the whole of the British Isles.

The two romantic comedies and the satirical farce all show, in different ways, Shakespeare's respect for the wit, good sense, responsibility, and gallantry of women. In all three plays the absence of any masculine condescension is even more sharply marked by the portrayal of significant independent relationships between women. The friendship of men has been a favorite theme for storytellers ever since the days of Damon and Pythias, and, no doubt, long before. But very few writers have ever considered a relation between women of any importance except as it involved jealousy, generosity, or some other emotion on behalf of a husband, a lover, or a son.

Yet even in the most superficial of these three light-hearted comedies, the *Merry Wives of Windsor,* the very title hints the good-humored, matter-of-fact, practical friendship of Mistress Ford and Mistress Page. This alliance, incidentally, enables them to reverse the conventional intrigue of such a farce by exposing and triumphing over both the knight, who would be a seducer, and the suspicious husband he would cuckold.

In *Much Ado About Nothing* Beatrice is unquestionably the strongest as well as the gayest character, and much of the plot turns upon her firm faith in, and deep concern for, her cousin Hero.

The most important of the three plays, *As You Like it,* not only gives us two equally witty, charming and determined young women as heroines, but also shows us a warmth, loyalty and delight in their personal relations with each other which makes Rosalind's and Celia's friendship comparable to that of David and Jonathan. It is also noteworthy that in this play Rosalind dissects the aristocratic affectation of a cynical and misanthropic melancholy embodied in Jacques.

Julius Caesar, perhaps the most perfect of the Roman plays, must detain us a moment longer.

A large number of the political and social themes we have already noted, and of the subtle psychological development we have so far been constrained to ignore, are raised to new levels of intensity here.

For example, the humorous commoners of whom we have, as

yet, mentioned only a humble first example, appear in full force in the opening scene where their rough wit easily gets the best of a slanging match with their superiors.

> Flavius: Hence! home you idle creatures, get you home:
> Is this a holiday? what! know you not,
> Being mechanical, you ought not walk
> Upon a laboring day without the sign
> Of your profession? Speak, what trade art thou?
> 1st Commoner: Why, sir, a carpenter.
> Marullus: Where is thy leather apron and thy rule?
> What dost thou with thy best apparel on?
> You, sir, what trade are you?
> 2nd Commoner: Truly, sir, in respect of a fine workman, I am but, as you would say, a cobbler.
> Marullus: But what trade art thou? answer me directly.
> 2nd Commoner: A trade, sir, that, I hope, I may use with a safe conscience; which is indeed, sir, a mender of bad soles.
> Marullus: What trade, thou knave? thou naughty knave, what trade?
> 2nd Commoner: Nay, I beseech you, sir, be not out with me: yet if you be out, sir, I can mend you.
> Marullus: What mean'st thou by that? mend me, thou saucy fellow!
> 2nd Commoner: Why, sir, cobble you.
> Flavius: Thou art a cobbler, art thou?
> 2nd Commoner: Truly, sir, all that I live by is with the awl: I meddle with no tradesman's matters, nor women's matters, but with awl. I am indeed, sir, a surgeon to old shoes; when they are in great danger, I re-cover them. As proper men as ever trod upon neats-leather have gone upon my handiwork.
> Flavius: But wherefore are not in thy shop to-day? Why dost thou lead men about the streets?
> 2nd Commoner: Truly, sir, to wear out their shoes, to get myself into more work. But indeed, sir, we make holiday, to see Caesar and to rejoice in his triumph.

There is also in this play a rather elaborate set piece of two carefully arranged scenes which illuminate the contrast in character between imperial Caesar and republican Brutus by showing us the sort of wife each one has chosen, and the nature of their marriage. The deliberate parallel construction of these two short scenes is obvious. In each the wife is concerned about her husband, whom she loves and who loves her; in each she urges him to do something which will, she is convinced, be for his own good; in each she kneels to enforce her request; and in each her husband accedes to it.

But within that framework of similarity the differences are equally apparent and far more important. Brutus is truly shocked at his wife's kneeling to him, and his quick "Kneel not, gentle Portia" is not more conscious of the indignity than Portia's immediate "I should not need, if you were gentle Brutus." Caesar, on the other hand, is so unconscious of any impropriety in his wife's suppliant attitude that he not only makes no comment to her, but later casually repeats to Decius, "Calpurnia here, my wife, stays me at home: . . . and on her knee, Hath begged that I will stay at home today."

Brutus responds with immediate emotion to Portia's first really serious reproach. She asks:

> . . . Am I yourself
> But, as it were, in sort or limitation,
> To keep with you at meals, comfort your bed,
> And talk to you sometimes? Dwell I but in the suburbs
> Of your good pleasure? If it be no more,
> Portia is Brutus' harlot, not his wife.

And he exclaims: "You are my true and honorable wife, As dear to me as are the ruddy drops that visit my sad heart."

He not only agrees to do what she asks because she has convinced him he should, rather than as a favor, but offers an ardent apology for having waited to be asked in his: "O ye gods, Render me worthy of this noble wife."

Caesar treats Calpurnia's request as a childish whim—excusable only in a woman—even when he agrees to grant it. Then, ignoring his promise, he unhesitatingly and unapologetically breaks it when Decius' threat that someone may ridicule him as a henpecked husband changes his mind.

Nor is the contrast of the dictator and the republican any less clear in terms of the kind of woman each has chosen to marry. Portia stands on her dignity as an equal, and bases her right to share her husband's responsibilities on the meaning of a real marriage, anticipating Desdemona's protest that, if she is not allowed to go with Othello to his wars "The rites for which I loved him are denied me." We may also remember Desdemona in the scene where, urging Othello to reinstate Cassio as his lieutenant, she responded to his "I will deny thee nothing" with a proud: "Nay, this is not a boon, 'Tis as I should entreat you wear your gloves, Or feed on nourishing dishes, or keep you warm, Or sue to you to do a peculiar profit To your own person."

Portia similarly refuses to ask as a favor the knowledge "Which by the right and virtue of my place I ought to know of."

Calpurnia, on the other hand, begins with the mock-imperious command—meaningless since she has no power to enforce it, and excusable only in the unrealistic tone of a child's imperative "You shan't go!"—"What mean you Caesar? think you to walk forth? You *shall* not stir out of your house today."

She proceeds to coax—and flatter—her husband and at last diplomatically offers him the face-saving "... call it my fear that keeps you in the house and not your own. Let me upon my knee prevail in this."

She accepts unprotestingly Caesar's condescending "And for thy humor, I will stay at home," just as she later does his cavalier retraction "How foolish do your fears seem now, Calpurnia! I am ashamed that I did yield to them. Give me my robe, for I will go."

But this contrast shows only the best aspect of Brutus' character which, taken as a whole, is really the central pivot of the entire play.

In his *Political Characters of Shakespeare*, Palmer opens a masterly analysis of Brutus' inadequacy to the political action he undertakes by considering Brutus' first hundred and seventy line speech in detail:

> ... Here, then, in one brief scene is an epitome of Brutus in six chapters. He is not gamesome and would leave Cassius to attend the festival alone. He had avoided the company of his friends to brood upon conceptions only proper to himself. He is vexed with passions of some difference, and is with himself at war. He shrinks from the dangers into which he may be led if he should look too deeply into his convictions and admit the necessity to act upon them. He, nevertheless, betrays involuntarily the secret that vexes him and is successfully brought to a full and frank confession by the skilful prompting of his future confederate. The instinctive reluctance of the political philosopher is not yet, however, overcome and he would not for this present be any further moved. He promises to consider what Cassius has said and concludes with a merely general assurance that Brutus would rather be a villager than accept the situation.

Palmer later comments similarly on Brutus' soliloquy before Caesar's assassination, emphasizing Shakespeare's political insight and the way in which it has baffled some of his best nonpolitical commentators:

> This soliloquy of Brutus, in which the dramatist exhibits a salient and abiding characteristic of the doctrinaire in politics, has been condemned by many commentators. Coleridge found the speech to be "singular" and frankly confessed that he did not understand it. How could Brutus, he asks, say that he had no cause to spurn at Caesar in his past conduct as a man? Had Caesar not crossed the Rubicon? Had he not entered Rome as a conqueror? Had he not placed his Gauls in the senate? Coleridge is even more disconcerted by the suggestion that Brutus would have had no objection to Caesar provided he remained as good a ruler as he had hitherto shown himself to be. This brilliant critic not only finds the speech "discordant," but accounts for his inability "to see into Shakespeare's motive" by quoting just those historical facts which give to the soliloquy its true significance. Brutus cannot see persons or events as they are. That is the essence of his character. Caesar has done all the things of which Coleridge reminds us. He is already a full-blown tyrant. But Brutus takes no account of these realities. He is obsessed by a pedantic horror of king-ship, by the republican traditions of his family and by the hypothetical evils which may follow upon the violation of a preconceived theory of government.

The wonderful psychological insight of the play, the unforseen but inevitable development of the contradictions in Brutus' character, and the way in which the reader, like Cassius, grows to love him more deeply while learning ever more sharply to condemn the ineptitude of his leadership, are remarkable. The intellectual intensity of the famous quarrel scene with its profound use of both conscious and unconscious personal and political emotions is seldom surpassed even in Shakespeare.

One is left breathless by the impact of such passages as Cassius' few lines describing how Rome had, like Nazi Germany, first to be enslaved herself in order that she might be fit to enslave the world.

> Those that with haste will make a mighty fire
> Begin it with weak straws; what trash is Rome,
> What rubbish and what offal, when it serves
> For the base matter to illuminate
> So vile a thing as Caesar! . . .

In the next five years the London theatres were several times closed by plague and we find only five Shakespearean plays produced: *Hamlet, Prince of Denmark, Twelfth Night, Measure for Measure, All's Well That Ends Well,* and *Othello, the Moor of Venice.*

It is significant that neither of the two most important plays here listed are ordinarily given their full titles. For if we remember, as no Elizabethan ever forgot, that Hamlet was Prince of Denmark and should have become king, we would be in less danger of reducing the dimensions of his world to those of the queen's bedroom. Not that that center and symbol of the court's corruption was unimportant, or that Hamlet's emotional impotence is unrelated to his political failure. But we should see Hamlet's psychological problems, as Shakespeare's audiences did, as part of a larger whole.

Coleridge, one of the earliest and best of Shakespeare's serious critics, has written a brilliant analysis of the former play's hero. But it is not complete until we add the insight gained by a study of Shakespeare's other plays about bad kings and good ones, about the duties and powers of princes and the needs of government. Specifically, we should ponder the elements of Hamlet's dilemma and character which Shakespeare experimented with in Richard II and Brutus if we wish to understand the play as he wrote it—the play of a prince too sensitive to ignore evil and too lacking in faith, in emotional health, effectively to fight it.

A political reading of the play not only restores the throne of Denmark to its central position but, as in *Othello,* also helps us to understand the psychological problems of its hero. We too often forget that the corruption of the court does not date merely from the late king's death and the queen's "o'er hasty marriage."

Polonius was chosen as prime minister by Hamlet's father, not his uncle; Rosencrantz and Guildenstern were chosen as his childhood companions by Hamlet's father, not his uncle; the queen herself was first chosen as wife by Hamlet's father, not his uncle. It was during his father's lifetime that Hamlet, like Prince Hal, chose to escape the duties and responsibilities of his position by studying philosophy in Wittenberg (rather than life at Eastcheap). And it is from his observation of his father's kingdom that Hamlet knows of:

> . . . the law's delay,
> The insolence of office, and the spurns
> That patient merit of the unworthy takes,

It is no wonder that he has so profound a distrust of the possibilities of good action, so coldly intellectual an admiration of the possibilities of goodness in man, combined with so deep a hatred and so concrete a knowledge of evil.

Our first glimpse of Hamlet shows us his verbal brilliance, the bitter effectiveness of his tongue, and above all the extraordinary quickness of his wit.

In reply to his uncle's dignified greeting: "But now, my cousin [nephew] Hamlet, and my son," he replies with ten swift words which express his utter distrust of the man and fury at the marriage, "A little more than kin and less than kind." And his contempt and anger for his mother's short-lived mourning is as swiftly and clearly stated:

> Seems, madam! nay, it is. I know not seems—
> . . . . . .
> For I have that within which passeth show;
> These but the trappings and the suits of woe.

If we have not already sensed it in this first scene, the soliloquy which immediately follows shows us how little personal grief for his father, or any desire for his inheritance, account for Hamlet's bitterness. Hatred of his uncle, a burning jealous horror at his mother's remarriage, and hopeless disgust for a world in which such corruption flourishes and rules, are the only genuine emotions we find.

This is emphasized by the brief conversation with Horatio, who replies to the question, "And what make you from Wittenberg?", "My Lord, I came to see your father's funeral." Hamlet's bitter self-mockery flashes out:

> I pray thee, do not mock me, fellow-student;
> I think it was to see my mother's wedding.

Horatio reluctantly responds, "Indeed, my lord, it follow'd hard upon." And Hamlet, in perhaps the most searing reference any son ever made to his mother's body, replies:

> Thrift, thrift Horatio! the funeral baked meats
> Did coldly furnish forth the marriage table.

Then there is a complete drop in the emotional temperature as Horatio reveals the ghost's visit and Hamlet asks for details of his appearance.

After Hamlet's interview with the ghost and his oath to revenge the triple wrong of murder, usurpation and seduction, Shakespeare makes his "hero's" inability honestly to undertake action ironically explicit. He echoes the ghost's last words:

> —Remember thee!
> Yea, from the table of my memory
> I'll wipe away all trivial fond records,
> All saws of books, all forms, all pressures past,
> That youth and observation copied there;
> And thy commandment all alone shall live
> Within the book and volume of my brain
> Unmixt with baser matter: yes, by heaven!—

But in the very midst of this renunciation of words and self-dedication to action, Hamlet is struck by a phrase, "O villain, villain, smiling damned villain," and cries, "My tables, meet it is I set it down, That one may smile and smile, and be a villain." And after writing it down he concludes with satisfaction, "So, uncle, there you are."

The scene ends with his painful acceptance of an unwelcome but undisputed responsibility:

> The time is out of joint:—O cursed spite,
> That ever I was born to set it right!—

The arrival of the traveling players is, of course, most important for the plot but it is almost as important for the glimpse it gives us of Hamlet's self-knowledge and self-condemnation.

One of the players is carried away by his recitation of the fall of Troy, and Hamlet is stung to self-reproach by the glaring contrast between the actor's emotional responsiveness and his own real impotence of feeling:

> O, what a rogue and peasant slave am I!
> Is it not monstrous that this player here,
> But in a fiction, in a dream of passion,
> Could force his soul so to his own conceit,
> That, from her working, all his visage wann'd;
> Tears in his eyes, distraction in's aspect,
> A broken voice, and his whole function suiting
> With forms to his conceit? and all for nothing!
> For Hecuba!
> What's Hecuba to him, or he to Hecuba,
> That he should weep for her? What would he do,

> Had he the motive and the cue for passion
> That I have? He would drown the stage with tears,
> And cleave the general ear with horrid speech;
> Make mad the guilty, and appal the free,
> Confound the ignorant; and amaze, indeed,
> The very faculties of eyes and ears.
> Yet I,
> A dull and muddy-mettled rascal, peak,
> Like john-a-dreams, unpregnant of my cause,
> And can say nothing;—

After swearing at his uncle and himself for some dozen lines Hamlet cries out with disgust at this purely verbal assault:

> Why, what an ass am I! This is most brave,
> That I, the son of a dear father murder'd,
> Prompted to my revenge by heaven and hell,
> Must, like a whore, unpack my heart with words,
> And fall a-cursing, like a very drab,
> A scullion!
> Fie upon 't! foh!—

But what is to take the place of such ineffective speech? Action? No; not unless writing be an action. For his conclusion is that he will write a play! And then, if in watching it, the king's guilt (which neither Hamlet nor the audience has hitherto at all doubted), if, Hamlet says, the king's guilt appears—then he'll act.

As we know, the king's reaction to the play makes his guilt clear to the dullest, and Shakespeare obligingly provides Hamlet with an opportunity to act immediately thereafter. But since the king is at prayer Hamlet refuses to kill him, lest his soul go to heaven! The irony is underlined when Shakespeare has the king tell us, as he rises, that he had found himself altogether unable to pray. And Hamlet's inadequacy is recalled when in the next act Laertes, who by then also has a father to avenge, is asked, "what would you undertake To show yourself your father's son indeed More than in words?" He promptly answers that, as for his father's murderer, he would "cut his throat i' th' church," and is approved, "No place, indeed, should murder sanctuarize."

But first, of course, we have the famous scene in the queen's bedroom with Polonius hidden behind the arras. Here Hamlet shows no hesitation in driving his rapier through the curtains when he hears a voice, and we begin more fully to realize that what he shrinks from is neither the physical action nor its immediate personal danger, but the responsibility of a premeditated killing of a king—and its political result. This is emphasized by his prompt and unconcerned disposal of the dead body. And, again to anticipate, the same point is made in the fifth act when he tells how he has arranged for the execution of Rosencrantz and Guildenstern, and answers Horatio's rather shocked, "So Guildenstern and Rosencrantz go to't."

> Why, man, they did make love to this employment,
> They are not near my conscience; . . .

The third act ends with a repetition of Hamlet's self-reproach. This time he contrasts himself with the man of action, Fortinbras. In much the same way as he envied the player's power of feeling for Hecuba, he envies the general's power of fighting even "for a fantasy and trick of fame."

This soliliquy begins, very much like the earlier one:

> How all occasions do inform against me,
> And spur my dull revenge!
> . . . . . .
> Now, whether it be
> Bestial oblivion, or some craven scruple
> Of thinking too precisely on th' event,—
> A thought which, quarter'd, hath but one part wisdom
> And ever three parts coward.—I do not know
> Why yet I live to say "This thing's to do;"
> Sith I have cause, and will, and strength, and means
> To do't. Examples, gross as earth, exhort me:
> Witness this army, of such mass and charge,
> Led by a delicate and tender prince;

It continues some lines later in a passage which deliberately echoes, "What would he do Had he the motive and the cue for passion That I have?":

> How stand I, then,
> That have a father kill'd, a mother stain'd,
> Excitements of my reason and my blood,
> And let all sleep?

Finally Hamlet again concludes:

> . . . O, from this time forth,
> My thoughts be bloody, or be nothing worth!

The last of these three parallel speeches comes in the fifth act. And just because it is the fifth act, there is here a significant difference.

Hamlet, as unable really to mourn Ophelia as he has been to weep for his father or fight for his kingdom, watches Laertes' frenzied expressions of grief at her grave. We must not forget that Laertes, like Fortinbras, has been specifically contrasted with Hamlet in several important respects. His whole-hearted desire to avenge his father's death has already been referred to. And in an earlier scene his recitation of his wrongs aroused the populace to cries of "Laertes shall be king, Laertes king!" This is, of course, an explicit demonstration of how much more easily Hamlet, the legitimate Prince of Denmark, who is "loved by the distracted multitude," could have undone the usurpation had he really wished to.

In this scene then, watching Laertes, Hamlet feels even more intensely his essential impotence. But he can no longer find relief in railing at himself for it and swearing to change. Because he can no longer believe in the possibility of such a change, he no longer dares admit to himself the present fact. So when his misery breaks into speech this time it is not in a self-critical soliloquy but in an angry rationalization attacking Laertes. He fantastically accuses Laertes of mourning Ophelia in order to insult Hamlet with "the bravery of his grief." "Dost thou come here to whine? To outface me with leaping in her grave?" And he too leaps into the grave.

Here again we realize that it is neither physical inhibition nor any fear of direct action which deters Hamlet from fulfilling the responsibility he has undertaken. This is further developed, and his practical abilities are stressed when, in the next scene, he tells Horatio of his adventure with the pirate ship, and of his strategy in disposing of Rosencrantz and Guildenstern. And even here, summarizing his wrongs to Horatio and repeating his determination to kill the king, he asks as though there were a real question:

> Does it not, thinks't thee, stand me now upon,—
> He that hath kill'd my king, and whored my mother;
> Popt in between th' election and my hopes;
> Thrown out his angle for my proper life,
> And with such cozenage,—is't not perfect conscience
> To quit him with this arm? and is't not to be damn'd
> To let this canker of our nature come
> In further evil?

Horatio, who was told two acts before, "Observe my uncle—— O Good Horatio, I'll take the Ghost's word for a thousand pound," has just been rebuked for speaking with some concern of the death of Rosencrantz and Guildenstern. He does not even pretend to take Hamlet's question seriously, but simply reminds his friend that time is short. Hamlet replies, "a man's life's no more than to say one," and reflects that he is sorry he attacked Laertes, "But sure, the bravery of his grief did put me Into a towering passion."

The last scene of the play is, of course, that of Hamlet's fencing match with Laertes. His courtesy in presenting his own weapon to his disarmed opponent and his consequent unwitting use of the secretly poisoned rapier, with which Laertes had already pricked him, are well-known to everyone. But not everyone has noted that Hamlet is even then able to kill the king only after Laertes, dying, has cried out:

> . . . : Hamlet, thou art slain;
> No medicine in the world can do thee good,
> In thee there is not half an hour of life.

There is then no longer any need for delay, since the king's death no longer means that the Prince of Denmark must succeed to real responsibility. Hamlet himself is well aware of this. He uses his last breath to say:

> But I do prophesy th' election lights
> On Fortinbras: he has my dying voice;

For Hamlet death is the escape from responsibility for the world— or, at least, for Denmark—an escape which he was too honest to take deliberately, but is weak enough to welcome. Yet, with all his rationalizations and evasions, he has never denied his obligations or doubted that Fortinbras' was the better part.

It may be no wonder that this prince of wits and of rationalizations should have been eagerly adopted as an alter ego and a justification by generations of disinherited intellectuals, who plead his failure as prima facie evidence of the impossibility of the task he undertook, and so excuse themselves for not undertaking any part in the real world. But we must not forget that Hamlet did undertake such action, however reluctantly. And neither he nor Shakespeare ever doubted that, when the times were out of joint, man was, at whatever inconvenience, born to set them right.

A simple statement of the full title of *Othello, the Moor of Venice*, with its emphatic singular article and immediate emphasis on the hero's origin, centers attention on the still vital social problem of an interracial marriage.

The history of this play, like that of Hamlet, affords a singular illustration of the misinterpretation forced on over a hundred years of criticism by the bourgeois critics' unwillingness or inability to understand Shakespeare's progressive political viewpoint and concrete social interests.

From the beginning of the nineteenth century until its reinstatement by the magnificent production of Paul Robeson and Margaret Webster, *Othello* was one of the most completely misunderstood and, therefore, one of the least popular of Shakespeare's great tragedies. A bourgeois world, unable to countenance the reality of the intermarriage about which the play centers, replaced the Moor, as Margaret Webster says, by a series of "cultured gentlemen, reluctantly and faintly disguising from us their familiar features under a layer of becoming coffee-colored grease paint, rather as if they had recently returned from Palm Beach." But when the central problem of the play had been, thus rudely, thrust out of doors, even the same bourgeois audiences felt a lack of emotional reality in the terms of a conflict which made Othello pitiable, no doubt, but only as a dupe, the victim of an unreasonable, causeless jealousy which robbed him of all tragic stature, and which left the center of the stage to be filled by an Iago whose malignancy had, at the same time, lost the best part of its motivation. Margaret Webster, in her *Shakespeare Without Tears*, concludes:

> For the question of Othello's race is of paramount importance to the play. There has been much controversy as to Shakespeare's intention. It is improbable that he troubled himself greatly with ethnological exactness. The Moor, to an Elizabethan, was a blackamoor, an African, an Ethiopian. Shakespeare's other Moor, Aaron, in *Titus Andronicus*, is specifically black; he has thick lips and a fleece of woolly hair. The Prince of Morocco in *The Merchant of Venice* bears "the shadowed livery of the burnished sun" and even Portia recoils from his "complexion" which he himself is at great pains to excuse.
>
> Othello is repeatedly described, both by himself and others, as black; not pale beige, but black; and for a century and a half after the play's first presentation, he was so represented

on the stage. But after this the close consideration of nice minds began to discern something not quite ladylike about Desdemona's marrying a black man with thick lips. They cannot have been more horrified than Brabantio, her father, who thought that only witchcraft could have caused "nature so preposterously to err," or more convinced of the disastrous outcome of such a match than Iago, who looked upon it as nothing but a "frail vow between an erring Barbarian and a super-subtle Venetian," and declared, with his invincible cynicism, that "when she is sated with his body, she will find the error of her choice: She must have change; she must!"

It is very apparent, and vital to the play, that Othello himself was very conscious of these same considerations and quiveringly aware of what the judgment of the world would be upon his marriage. It is one of the most potent factors in his acceptance of the possibility of Desdemona's infidelity. And she herself loses much in the quality of her steadfastness and courage if it be supposed that she simply married against her father's wishes a man who chanced to be a little darker than his fellows, instead of daring a marriage which would cause universal condemnation among the ladies of polite society. To scamp this consideration in the play is to deprive Othello of his greatest weakness, Desdemona of her highest strength, Iago of his skill and judgment [and, we may add, of much of his essential motive], Emilia of a powerful factor in her behavior both to her master and her mistress, and Venice itself of an arrogance in toleration which was one of the principal hall marks of its civilization—a civilization which frames, first and last the soaring emotions of the play.

Once we realize, however, as Shakespeare did, that Othello is a black man in a white society which then, as now, assumed its racial superiority, we not only have a sufficient cause for an unconscious germ of self-doubt in the strongest hero, but have a clue to help us trace its entirely logical development from the aloofness and reserve overcome only by the surprise attack of Desdemona's love—and in no other circumstances can we imagine a man as warm as Othello waiting until "some nine moons wasted" to find love, nor one as self-confident waiting until "she bade me, if I had a friend that loved her, I should but teach him how to tell my story, and that would woo her," to speak of it.

One of the most discerning of Shakespearian critics, Granville-Barker, says in his famous preface to *Othello*:

> This [Othello's prompt quelling of the midnight brawl in Cyprus and his unforgettable "What, in a town of war—the

people's hearts brimful of fear—to manage private and domestic quarrel—'Tis monstrous . . . Cassio, I love thee, But never more be officer of mine.] is the last capital touch given to the picture of a still unscathed Othello. In retrospect we may recognize the danger that lay in a too inflexible perfection of poise; once upset, hard to regain.

It is the picture of a quite exceptional man; in high repute and conscious of his worth, yet not self-conscious; of a dignity which simplicity does not jeopardize; generous in praise of those who serve him; commanding respect without fear; frank and unsuspicious and ready to reciprocate affection. *Yet he has been a man apart, alone.* He is not young, has fought and adventured the world over, striking root nowhere. *And he is black.* The Venetians, truly, not only value his soldiership but Brabantio, as Othello says "loved me, oft invited me. . . ." They seemed to be treating him in everything as one of themselves. But to have him marry Desdemona! That would be quite another question. Neither he nor she was of the eloping kind; evidently no other way looked open to them . . . yet that the daughter of a Venetian Senator should "to incur a general mock, Run from her guardage to the sooty bosom" even of the renowned Othello . . . and should we, under the spell of his nobility be inclined to forget it—since Desdemona could!—reminder will not be lacking. For Iago's defiling eye sees only this, reads only foulness and perversity into such enfranchisement.

Only in the light of this central fact can we reconcile the course of the play with the proud self-assurance and firm dignity of Othello, as he reveals himself in his early scenes, ignoring all Iago's provocation to bluster or revenge with a quiet:

> . . . My demerits
> May speak unbonneted to as proud a fortune
> As this that I have reached: for know, Iago,
> But that I love the gentle Desdemona,
> I would not my unhoused free condition
> Put into circumscription and confine
> For the sea's worth. . . .
> . . . Not I: I must be found:
> My parts, my title and my perfect soul
> Shall manifest me rightly.

And again:

> . . . Keep up your bright swords
> For the dew will rust them. . . .

> ... Hold your hands,
> Both you of my inclining, and the rest:
> Were it my cue to fight, I should have known it
> Without a prompter. ...

Discussing the character changes Shakespeare made in adapting the story from which he took Othello's plot, Granville-Barker says:

> Again, while Desdemona in the story says to her husband "... you Moors are of so hot a nature that every little trifle moves you to anger and revenge," Shakespeare gives us an Othello calm beneath Brabantio's threats and abuse, in the matter of Cassio's brawl of iron self-control, and against that he sets the gadfly Iago, impatient from the first to be stinging.

The transparent complications of the handkerchief plot (which Shakespeare took almost unchanged from the contemporary story of "the unfaithfulness of husbands and wives" by Cinthio) have too long been used to overshadow the fact that in his insinuations to Othello Iago harps persistently on the two related strings of the unnaturalness of such a marriage as Desdemona's and of Othello's essential ignorance of what "our" women—Venetian women—think and feel.

> I know our country disposition well:
> In Venice they do let heaven see the pranks
> They dare not show their husbands;
>
> . . . . . .
> Ay, there's the point: as, to be bold with you,
> Not to affect many proposed matches
> Of her own clime, complexion and degree,
> Where to, we see, in all things nature tends;
> Fah! one may smell in such, a will most rank,
> Foul disproportion, thoughts unnatural—.

It is here that Othello is vulnerable. His suppressed consciousness of difference—his unadmitted doubts—are appallingly evidenced in such seemingly unrelated references to color as now begin to emerge in fragmentary images and exclamations.

> ... Her name, that was as fresh
> As Dian's visage, is now begrimed and black
> As mine own face. ...
> Arise, black vengeance, from thy hollow cell!

The most explicit of them, indeed, follows immediately upon Iago's first hint, before the handkerchief has been lost or found or mentioned. Iago has barely breathed his pretended suspicions when Othello breaks out:

> Nor from mine own weak merits will I draw
> The smallest fear or doubt of her revolt;
> *For she had eyes*, and chose me. . . . [Italics added.]

and after Iago has concluded:

> . . . I do not in position
> Distinctly speak of her; though I may fear
> Her will, recoiling to her better judgment,
> May fall to match you with her country forms
> And happily repent. . . .

Othello, upon his exit, cries in pain:

> . . . If I do prove her haggard,
> Though that her jesses were my dear heart-strings,
> I'd whistle her off and let her down the wind,
> To prey at fortune. Haply, *for I am black* [italics added]
> And have not those soft parts of conversation
> That chamberers have, or for I'm declined
> Into the vale of years,—yet that's not much—
> She's gone. I am abused; and my relief
> Must be to loathe her. O curse of marriage,
> That we can call these delicate creatures ours
> And not their appetites! I had rather be a toad,
> And live upon the vapour of a dungeon,
> Than keep a corner in the thing I love
> For others' uses.

We see more clearly in every line that for Othello Desdemona's supposed treachery means much more than the most terrible personal loss; it strikes at the very root of his manhood:

> . . . O, now for ever
> Farewell the tranquil mind! farewell content!
> Farewell the plumed troop and the big wars
> That make ambition virtue! O, farewell!
> Farewell the neighing steed and the shrill trump,
> The spirit-stirring drum, the ear-piercing fife,
> The royal banner, and all quality,
> Pride, pomp, and circumstance of glorious war
> Farewell! Othello's occupation's gone.

Finally after the scene in which Othello believes he has heard Cassio pile contempt on contempt—scorning as his strumpet Othello's wife—he bursts forth with what is, indeed, the deepest meaning of the betrayal, "Do you triumph, *Roman*? do you triumph?" After this we can not wonder at the death of Desdemona. Far more than his personal dignity depends upon it. His racial dignity, his very claim to human equality demand revenge. The same understanding of the play's central theme helps us understand how deeply caused Iago's seemingly whimsical malignity to Othello is. Iago's class position as an adventurer without background—a hired professional soldier at an aristocratic court—is in at least one respect, insofar as Othello is concerned, comparable to that of an overseer in the south who can advance as his major claim to respect his bond of color equality with his employers and who is therefore driven to a more apparent, more virulent, and more frequently expressed statement of hatred and contempt for—of difference from—the Negro than they themselves show.

Roderigo, a butt, and therefore to some extent also an inferior struggling for status among his betters, is the only other character in the play who refers disparagingly to Othello's physical characteristics in such remarks as "What a full fortune does the thick lips owe" and "To the gross clasps of a lascivious Moor" but he is then, of course, commenting directly on the marriage of his inamorata. Iago, however, refers bitterly and continually to the racial difference:

> And I—God bless the mark—his Moorship's Ancient.
>
> Even now, now, very now, an old black ram is tupping your white ewe.
>
> You'll have your daughter covered with a Barbary horse;
> You'll have your nephews neigh to you;
> You'll have coursers for cousins and gennets for germans.
>
> The devil will make a grandsire of you.
>
> Her eye must be fed and what delight shall she have to look on the devil? . . . her delicate tenderness will find itself abused, begin to heave the gorge, disrelish and abhor the Moor; very nature will instruct her in it and compel her to some second choice.
>
> Blessed fig's end! the wine she drinks is made of grapes.
> If she had been blessed, she would never have loved the Moor.
>
> . . . and here without are a brace of Cyprus gallants who would fain have a measure to the health of black Othello.

A contemporary psychologist has suggested that we may, in a sense, consider Iago as the concentrated embodiment of all the spite, jealousy and ill will which would, in a literally realistic play on this theme, be focused upon the couple, and which might, in a less deliberate or dramatic manner, accomplish the same intentional destruction. This is, I think, a valid insight well worth our consideration. It calls up a picture very like the contemporary one Countee Cullen has given us in:

> Locked arm in arm they cross the road,
> The black boy and the white:—
> The golden splendor of the day,
> The sable pride of night.
> From lowered blinds the black folk stare
> And here the white folk talk—
> Indignant that the two should dare
> In unison to walk.
> Oblivious to word and look
> They pass, and see no wonder
> That lightning, brilliant as a sword,
> Should blaze the path of thunder!

We must not forget that the most friendly comment on the Moor made by Venetian society is the Duke, his patron's, casually contemptuous:

> If virtue no delighted beauty lack
> Your son-in-law is far more fair than black.

There is a further but not unrelated cause for Iago's directed enmity. Iago, by his own statement, has reached a certain degree of success only through using an active intelligence in flattery, trickery and fraud. He maintains his self-respect by asserting the half-truth that his superiors, if born with his nothing and left to their own resources, would have had to resort to similar measures with, in all probability, far less success. His entire philosophy is thus built on the postulate that the world is divided into cheats and their dupes and that the first class is, at least, superior to the second. Othello, then, by his very existence, challenges Iago's entire universe. "He has a daily beauty in his life that makes me ugly." Othello, beginning with far less than Iago's nothing—without the white skin which entitles Iago to speak of "*our* country disposition —*our* women"—has won a superlative degree of success, never condescending to flattery, trickery or fraud. Since Iago cannot think him a cheat, he must prove him a dupe if he is to keep from self-contempt. And, in fact, he repeatedly expresses this realization in such lines as:

> The Moor is of a free and open nature
> That thinks men honest who but seem to be so
> And will as tenderly be led by the nose
> As asses are.

and:

> Make the Moor thank me, love me, and reward me
> For making him egregiously an ass.

In achieving this purpose, as we have seen above, Iago is not only spurred on by his own resentment and bitterness but is also able to use the insight that hatred gives him into the failures and inadequacies of (interracial) human relationships in his—and our—society to attack the one vulnerable spot and destroy all.

This does not mean that he is conscious of all the strands in the intricately woven fabric of his hate, or could explicitly state the social implications he senses. The central point is underlined in the final scene of the play when *Othello* desperately cries out:

> Will you, I pray, demand that demi-devil
> Why he hath thus ensnared my soul and body?

The answer to that cannot be given on a personal level. It would demand a fully aware social consciousness impossible to Iago. And so there is no answer made. As Granville-Barker says:

> Does Iago even know the answer? "I hate the Moor," rabidly, senselessly, profitlessly; a search through the ruins of his tricks and lies would add nothing real to that. And in the light of the consequences—for him also—such an answer must seem almost less tragic than absurd. . . . "I hate the Moor"—there has been no more to the whole elaborately wicked business than that.

Finally, lest one mistake the matter and distort the argument of the play to conclude that such distrust, misunderstanding and eventual tragedy are the necessary or even natural consequences of an "unnatural" marriage, Shakespeare emphasizes the conclusion that it is intolerance, malice and distrust and not the simple human relationship which is unnatural. This is developed through the complete unconsciousness of Cassio, Cyprus in general, and, of course, the central figure of Desdemona herself. Perhaps of more weight than all her beautiful and passionate love speeches or her utter inability to imagine the cause of Othello's distemper, is the single jesting, altogether unemotional, reference to her husband's color and nativity which Desdemona makes. In response to a question of Emilia's "Is he not jealous?" she replies "Who! he? I think the sun where he was born drew all such humors from him."

This line alone, taken in context, is itself almost a sufficient indication of Shakespeare's complete unquestioning assumption of the irrelevance of the "color line." His almost invariable association of Negro skin pigmentation with the sun, evident in many other plays, in such lines as the Prince of Morocco's, "Mistake me not for my complexion—the shadowed livery of the burnished sun —to whom I am a neighbour and near bred," raises an interesting question. In discussing the common use of "dark" or "black" to connote evil, and its relation to color prejudice in the United States, a contemporary Negro novelist, Lloyd Brown, asks whether the evil or ominous connotations of black or darkness are not "a natural result of the conditions of life, the significance of the sun as the source of light, warmth and growth." If this is so, obviously the effect of Shakespeare's habit of explicitly relating dark skin pigmentation to the sun is, emotionally, to cancel such associations. The sun was, for Elizabethans, even a more potent affirmative symbol than it is for us, since it was a common metaphor for beneficent royalty, and for the principle of order or divinity in the universe.

Before leaving this play we should, perhaps, glance at one other aspect of Shakespeare's social attitude which it, in common with many others, illustrates. That is his remarkable understanding of the nature of a good relationship between men and women, an understanding which completely jumps the period of dawning protest that could create a Nora or a Hedda Gabler, and reaches into the heart of an altogether democratic, or socialist, society.

There are an extraordinary number of instances in which Shakespeare subtly uses a man's attitude toward women to give us a measure of the man himself. Perhaps the most elaborate and deliberate are the carefully contrasted parallel scenes between republican Brutus and his wife, and imperial Caesar and his. These two scenes were described in the discussion of *Julius Caesar* above, where we also cited Portia's statement, often quoted as the simplest and clearest explicit definition the plays afford of the meaning of a real marriage. A close second is certainly Desdemona's claim—indorsed by Othello—that marriage is a serious contract between two free agents, made because of a shared sense of values and community of interests, and gaining its validity from their respect for each other's essential nature and rights. It has, unfortunately, been obscured by the deplorable stage tradition of an ingénue Desdemona, but the briefest glance at the actual lines must dispel this convention.

With unconscious irony her father describes her as a maid "So opposite to marriage that she shunned the wealthy curled darlings of our nation." Not realizing he has answered his own question, he wonders how she could then have fallen in love with a *man* like Othello.

Othello (with some apparent naiveté) reports that on hearing the story of his heroic exploits, Desdemona, with no apparent diffidence:

> . . . wished she had not heard it, yet she wish'd
> That heaven had made her such a man; she thank'd me,
> And bade me, if I had a friend that lov'd her,
> I should but each him how to tell my story,
> And that would woo her.

Finally, Desdemona herself, just married, called in the middle of the night before a formal conclave of Duke and Senate, bitterly attacked by her father, speaks out not only about her love but about the essential meaning of her marriage:

> That I did love the Moor to live with him,
> My downright violence and storm of fortunes
> May trumpet to the world; my heart's subdued
> Even to the very quality of my lord;
> I saw Othello's visage in his mind,
> And to his honour and his valiant parts
> Did I my soul and fortune consecrate.

> So that, dear lords, *if I be left behind*
> *A moth of peace,* and he go to the war,
> *The rites for which I love him are denied me,*
> And I a heavy interim shall support
> By his dear absence. Let me go with him. [Italics added.]

Here we see the swiftly drawn portrait of a woman of energy, power and judgment, as well as emotion, who fell in love, not accidentally, with the man she would have wished to have been. To her marriage means, essentially, an active share in the responsibilities and accomplishments of her husband's life.

Nor is Othello less whole-hearted in his acceptance of this relationship. His immediate response is:

> Let her have your voices.
> Vouch with me, heaven, I therefore beg it not
> To please the palate of my appetite . . .
> But to be free and bounteous to her mind.

And his later spontaneous greeting at a moment of joyfully surprised reunion, "O, happy warrior," accepts Desdemona on her own terms of equality and partnership. Even when racked by agony, his parenthetical descriptive comments show the same equalitarian attitude.

> . . . 'Tis not to make me jealous
> To say my wife is fair, feeds well, loves company
> Is free of speech, sings, plays and dances well.
>
> A fine woman! A fair woman! A sweet woman!
> . . . O! the world hath not a sweeter creature;
> She might lie by an emperor's side and command him tasks
> . . . So delicate with her needle! An admirable musician!
> O, she will sing the savageness out of a bear.
> Of so high and plenteous wit and invention.

All these show how freely and ungrudgingly a man who is secure in his own manhood and strength can acknowledge the independent qualities of a woman—even of a wife!

The next five years saw the production of the last of Shakespeare's great tragedies, *Lear* and *Macbeth,* and the last two Roman plays, *Antony and Cleopatra,* and *Coriolanus,* as well as *Timon of Athens.*

In addition to its magnificent love story, *Antony and Cleopatra* unravels the logical conclusion of the triumvirate's unprincipled triumph in *Julius Caesar*. Again, as in the series of English history plays, we see in this later play a rich development of the subtle indications of character sometimes barely hinted in the earlier one. But we also find here, as in the far more bitter *Timon of Athens* (which may or may not be altogether Shakespeare's) a new note of cynicism. The infatuated Antony has, as one of his devoted followers, Scarus, says, lost "the greater cantle of the world . . . with very ignorance; . . . kist away kingdoms and provinces." His truest friend and adherent, Enobarbus, bitterly describes the general's ignominious desertion of his men in flight:

> Mine eyes did sicken at the sight, and could not
> Endure a further view.

And Scarus concludes:

> I never saw an action of such shame;
> Experience, manhood, honour, ne'er before
> Did violate so itself.

Important protagonists in other plays have been equally ignoble but always before there has been some character who asserted in his very being a kind of integrity. Here Octavius' cold-blooded lust for power is such that it goes far to reconcile us to Antony's warmer egotism. And as for the third of the triumvirate, Lepidus, he is carried off drunk from a meeting with his two peers and Enobarbus comments acidly, pointing to his bearer "There's a strong fellow, . . . 'A bears the third part of the world, man; see'st not?" There was no such sarcasm when Henry V was referred to as "England."

Finally even Enobarbus is driven to desert Antony, declaring "The loyalty well held to fools does make our faith mere folly." When he kills himself in remorse there is no one left alive who still knows the meaning of honor. Four years of James I, and the growing conflict between his interests and those of the nation have evidently had a large part in shaping this play.

Coriolanus too shows this influence but in a more hopeful way.
Shakespeare does not quite envisage any alternative to monarchy—and, in fact, few in the early seventeenth century ever did—

but he is looking for an assertion of national values in new places. One of the early scenes in *Coriolanus* makes this quite clear:

> First. Cit: Before we proceed any further, hear me speak.
> All: Speak, speak.
> First Cit: You are all resolved rather to die than to famish?
> All: Resolved, resolved.
> First Cit: First, you know Caius Marcius is chief enemy to the people.
> All: We know't, we know't.
> First Cit: Let us kill him, and we'll have corn at our own price. Is't a verdict?
> All: No more talking on't; let it be done: away, away!
> Sec. Cit: One word, good citizens.
> First Cit: We are accounted poor citizens, the patricians good. What authority surfeits on would relieve us: if they would yield us but the superfluity, while it were wholesome, we might guess they relieved us humanely: but they think we are too dear: the leanness that afflicts us, the object of our misery, is as an inventory to particularize their abundance; our sufferance is a gain to them. Let us revenge this with our pikes, ere we become rakes; for the gods know I speak this in hunger for bread, not in thirst for revenge.
> Sec. Cit: Would you proceed especially against Caius Marcius?
> First Cit: Against him first: he's a very dog to the commonalty.
> Sec. Cit: Consider you what services he has done for his country?
> First Cit: Very well; and could be content to give him a good report for't, but that he pays himself with being proud.
> Sec. Cit: Nay, but speak not maliciously.
> First Cit: I say unto you, what he hath done famously, he did it to that end: though soft-conscienced men can be content to say it was for his country, he did it to please his mother, and to be partly proud; which he is, even to the altitude of his virtue.
> Sec. Cit: What he cannot help in his nature, you account a vice in him. You must in no way say he is covetous.
> First Cit: If I must not, I need not be barren of accusations; he hath faults, with surplus, to tire in repetition. (Shouts within.) What shouts are these? the other side o' the city is risen; why stay we prating here? to the Capitol!
> All: Come, come.
> First Cit: Soft! who comes here? (Enter Menenius Agrippa)
> Sec. Cit: Worthy Menenius Agrippa; one that hath always loved the people.
> First Cit: He's honest enough; would all the rest were so!

Menenius: What work's, my countrymen, in hand? where go
    you with bats and clubs? The matter? speak, I pray you.
First Cit: Our business is not unknown to the senate; they
    have had inkling this fortnight what we intend to do,
    which now we'll show 'em in deeds. They say poor suitors
    have strong breaths; they shall know we have strong arms
    too.
Menenius: Why, masters, my good friends, mine honest neigh-
    bours, Will you undo yourselves?
First Cit: We cannot, sir, we are undone already.
Menenius: I tell you, friends, most charitable care
Have the patricians of you. For your wants,
Your suffering in this dearth, you may as well
Strike at the heaven with your staves as lift them
Against the Roman state, whose course will on
The way it takes, cracking ten thousand curbs
Of more strong link asunder than can ever
Appear in your impediment. For the dearth,
The gods, not the patricians, make it, and
Your knees to them, not arms, must help. Alack!
You are transported by calamity
Thither where more attends you; and you slander
The helms o' the state, who care for you like fathers,
When you curse them as enemies.
First Cit: Care for us! True, indeed! They ne'er cared for us
    yet:— suffer us to famish, and their store-houses crammed
    with grain; make edicts for usury, to support usurers;
    repeal daily any wholesome act established against the
    rich, and provide more piercing statutes daily to chain up
    and restrain the poor. If the wars eat us not up, they will;
    and there's all the love they bear us.

The whole character of Coriolanus' aristocratic leadership also emphasizes Shakespeare's realization that "noble" leadership was no longer, in any sense, leadership in the interests of the people. And here "noble" does not mean feudal as contrasted with truly kingly. There is here a conscious exposition of the class interests of the aristocracy represented both by the good-natured Menenius and by the insufferable Coriolanus and his more insufferable mother. The class interest of the common people is also represented not only by the rank and file citizens quoted above but also by their chosen leaders.

Palmer summarizes this vital aspect of the play saying:

> For better or worse, these tribunes are Shakespeare's coun-
> terfeit presentment of two labor leaders. They are the natural

products of the class war in the commonwealth. They use their wits to defend the interests of the popular party and to remove from power a declared enemy of the people. They have neither the wish, training nor ability to disguise the quality or intention of their activities. In working for their . . . [class] they do not claim to be working disinterestedly for the nation. In resorting to the lawful and customary tricks of the political trade they neglect the noble postures and impressive mimicries adopted by persons with a longer experience of public life and of the deportment which public life requires. . . . But, essentially, the tribunes are right and they are giving proof of precisely that "realism" and precisely that suspicion of their political rulers which are characteristic of popular leaders in all times and places. Tribunes of the people have notoriously little respect for professions of altruism and of stainless regard for the public welfare uttered by their social superiors. . . . These tribunes are not concerned with the *motives* of Marcius [Coriolanus] in the particular case, but with the dangers inherent in his character. They are diagnosing not the man but the situation, and in their reading of the situation they are, as the event will show, entirely right. They regard themselves as watchdogs of the people, and Shakespeare, in this opening scene, is at some pains to show that they are well-qualified for their office and that they intend to be alert and vigorous in its exercise.

Later Coriolanus, angered by the opposition of the citizens to his election, defies the laws of Rome and is banished. He immediately offers his services to his country's foremost enemy and returns leading an army pledged to the total destruction of Rome.

The frightened patricians blame the commoners—"O! you have made good work! . . . you and your apron-men." But it is noteworthy that not one of them thinks of blaming Coriolanus for his treachery. As Palmer says:

> That Marcius should be bringing up an army to burn Rome is, in fact, regarded by his friends as the perfectly natural gesture of an angry nobleman. . . . [All the patricians seem] equally unaware of the enormity of the situation.

It might have occasioned little more surprise at King James' court, where almost every important figure, including some members of the royal family itself, were in receipt of a pension from the King of Spain.

Palmer concludes this analysis, "[The patricians merely think] it hard lines that the nobility should have to suffer for the sins of the Roman people . . . Only the tribunes plead for Rome, urging the senators to forget their feud and think of the common peril."

But while Shakespeare could envisage such tribunes in ancient Rome, they were still inconceivable in England. The two English plays, *King Lear* and *Macbeth,* which were, in all likelihood, written shortly after King James' accession, present for the last time Shakespeare's characteristic affirmation of national unity and royal responsibility as realistic possibilities.

Again in our consideration of Lear we are too apt to remember the father and forget the king. Mistaking two daughters' fulsome flatteries for sincere love, and the third's somewhat ungracious reserve for indifference, seem very trivial errors to precipitate the terrible action of the play. They are hardly the "tragic flaw" traditionally required to make the protagonist of such a play in some sort the logical cause of its catastrophe.

But we should remember old Gaunt's dying accusation "Landlord of England art thou now, not king" and Hotspur quarreling about his share in the prospective division of England, when we see Lear irresponsibly dividing up his kingdom.

Exposed to the pitiless storm, Lear does not express remorse for having misjudged his children, but compunction at having ignored the needs of his subjects:

> Poor naked wretches, wheresoe'er you are,
> That bide the pelting of this pitiless storm,
> How shall your houseless heads and unfed sides,
> Your loopt and window'd raggedness, defend you
> From seasons such as these? O, I have ta'en
> Too little care of this! Take physic, pomp;
> Expose thyself to feel what wretches feel,
> That thou mayst shake the superflux to them,
> And show the heavens more just.

Again, in his last madness his mind runs more on his kingdom's public corruption than on his private griefs:

> Thou rascal beadle, hold thy bloody hand!
> Why dost thou lash that whore? Strip thine own back;
> That hotly lusts to use her in that kind
> For which thou whipst her. The usurer hangs the cozener.
> Through tatter'd clothes small vices do appear;
> Robes and furr'd gowns hide all. Plate sin with gold,
> And the strong lance of justice hurtless breaks;
> Arm it in rags, a pigmy's straw doth pierce it.

When we turn to *Macbeth* we find one of the supreme illustrations of Shakespeare's assumption that man is essentially a political animal and that his proper sphere of being is action—action which invariably affects large numbers of his fellows.

At the opening of the play the great general, Macbeth, is a national hero who has won "Golden opinions from all sorts of people." Shakespeare's genuine respect for reputation here, as in *Othello* and many other plays, underlines his almost lifelong membership in a society whose major aims he could approve and whose progressive forces were, or seemed about to become, its dominant ones. When we approach the romantic writers two centuries later we realize how impossible this attitude is in a period of divisive protest at a dominant reaction. Then social reputation is bound to seem the hallmark of stupidity, dishonesty, or self-aggrandizement.

But Macbeth's overwhelming ambition does not permit him to wear these opinions "in their newest gloss." By his ambition he is driven to violate all the most fundamental ties of his society, murdering his guest, his kinsman, and his king.

I say driven because Macbeth is no naive murderer or political innocent. He knows that the real object of his desire—a dignified, respected, and assured sovereignty—is unattainable by such means.

Lady Macbeth is unimaginatively certain that the deed in which she helps him is one "Which shall to all our nights and days to come Give solely sovereign sway and masterdom." But Macbeth knows perfectly well that there is no need to await an after-life, which he's willing to chance, for judgment. No:

>   . . . in these cases
>   We still have judgment here; that we but teach
>   Bloody instructions, which, being taught, return
>   To plague the' inventor. . . .

And, as soon as he has murdered the peace and security of the land he knows that:

>   . . . from this instant,
>   There's nothing serious in mortality:
>   All is but toys: renown and grace is dead;
>   The wine of life is drawn, and the mere lees
>   Is left this vault to brag of.

The logic of his position as a usurper who has violated his nation's most fundamental laws, and the constant justified fear that one or another of his peers has already learnt his "bloody instructions," drive Macbeth into more and more terrible deeds until he cries out:

> . . . : I am in blood
> Stept in so far, that, should I wade no more,
> Returning were as tedious as go o'er.

There is not one of his lords but in his house the tyrant keeps "a servant fee'd. The utmost horrors of life under fascism seem succinctly described by a political refugee from Scotland who exclaims:

> Alas! poor country;
> Almost afraid to know itself. It cannot
> Be call'd our mother, but our grave; where nothing
> But who knows nothing, is once seen to smile;
> Where sighs and groans and shrieks that rend the air
> Are made, not mark'd; where violent sorrow seems
> A modern ecstasy; the dead man's knell
> Is there scarce ask'd for who; and good men's lives
> Expire before the flowers in their caps,
> Dying or ere they sicken.

And the simple aims of a war of national liberation have seldom been as well summarized as they are in a plea to the legitimate Prince for his return:

> . . . your eye in Scotland
> Would create soldiers, make our women fight,
> To doff their dire distresses.
> . . . .
> That, by the help of these—with Him above
> To ratify the work—we may again
> Give to our tables meat, sleep to our nights;
> Free from our feasts and banquets bloody knives;
> Do faithful homage, and receive free honours;

A preceding scene gives, in a lighter tone, one of Shakespeare's most explicit statements as to the comparative importance of personal and political virtue in a public man.

In pursuance of a minor stratagem Malcolm, the legitimate heir to the throne, is bent on vilifying himself to test whether or not Macduff's anxiety to have him return to Scotland is based on a sincere wish that he assume the throne.

He begins to protest his unworthiness by accusing himself of voluptuousness and lust, "my desire all continent impediments would o'erbear that did oppose my will." Macduff calmly replies:

> Boundless intemperance in nature is a tyranny. . . .
> But fear not yet to take upon you what is yours;
> . . . .
> We have willing dames enough; there cannot be
> That vulture in you, to devour so many
> As will to greatness dedicate themselves,
> Finding it so inclined. . . .

Malcolm then continues to the more serious self-accusation of avarice which Macduff less confidently counters, "This avarice sticks deeper, grows with more pernicious root Than summer-seeming lust, . . . yet do not fear. . . ." Finally Malcolm concludes, "Nay, had I power, I should Uproar the universal peace, confound All unity on earth. . . . If such a one be fit to govern, speak." Macduff replies, "Fit to govern! No, not to live."

Both the arrangement of this series and the degree of response are amply definitive of the order of importance which Shakespeare attributed to lust, avarice and violence or tyranny. If we compare the number of sermons or even novels written about each of the three in the course of the last three centuries we understand more fully how far artists since Shakespeare have been forced to retreat to a standard of impotent personal morality far less socially conscious or progressive than was his.

As soon as the invading forces, led by the legitimate ruler, land:

> Both more and less have given him the revolt
> And none serve with him but constrained things,
> Whose hearts are absent too.

For Macbeth personally the attack is almost an anticlimax. He has already realized:

> . . . that which should accompany old age,
> As honour, love, obedience, troops of friends,
> I must not look to have; but in their stead,
> Curses not loud but deep, mouth-honour, breath,
> Which the poor heart would fain deny, and dare not. . . .

But tyranny dare not abdicate and the end of the play is a political, not a personal, one. Macbeth is killed in battle, where his own soldiers have joined the enemy ranks, and the true king has the last word:

> . . . What's more to do,
> Which would be planted newly with the time,—
> As calling home our exiled friends abroad,
> That fled the snares of watchful tyranny;
> Producing forth the cruel ministers
> Of this dead butcher and his fiend-like queen,—
> . . . ;—this, and what needful else
> That calls upon us, by the grace of Grace
> We will perform in measure, time and place.

Except for one dubious and at most only partially Shakespearian play, *Pericles*, which was not included in the first collected edition of his dramatic work in 1623, we have nothing new from Shakespeare's pen for almost four years.

Such an unprecedented silence from so prolific a writer, still only in his middle forties, technically at the height of his powers, with a continued practical interest in an active theatre, certainly demands an explanation. And the changing political climate about him clearly offers one.

By the time James I had been a few years on the throne it was apparent that the struggle for power in England would never again lie between the king and the nobility. The real challenge to the increasingly burdensome absolutism of the crown now came entirely from the bourgeoisie, represented by the House of Commons. The throne's most active and influential allies were the powerful bishops, seated in the House of Lords, as well as the important noblemen who held leading positions at court.

The center of this struggle was London, and the theatre was directly and forcibly affected by it in several ways.

Since the new aristocratic domestic policy of the Stuarts involved similar foreign alliances with Spain and other Catholic powers abroad it was essentially antinational and anti-Protestant as well as antipopular.

There was no longer any unanimity on matters of politics between the court and the people and the preponderant political emphasis of the Elizabethan theatre became most repugnant to the court. There were some new, and many newly enforced, censorship regulations to discourage the popular theatre, and there was also an unorganized but general withdrawal of court patronage from it.

We have already mentioned the small private theatres which charged far higher admissions, used expensive artificial lighting, and generally gave evening rather than afternoon performances. They catered to the fashionable hangers-on and devotees of the court, often law students or university men, as well as to the aristocracy, and jeered at the "greasy doublets" and "stinking breath" of the popular theatre's following. As early as *Hamlet* Shakespeare had referred to the companies of child actors, often with trained choir-boy voices, which presented the plays of the private theatres.

Their productions were naturally well adapted to the use of elaborate and elegant masques, often allegorical in nature, fantastic fairy tale material, and a realistic stylized satire. It is possible to imagine talented and precocious children presenting Ben Jonson's *Volpone*. It is not possible to imagine them presenting *Macbeth*.

Since these audiences were all attuned to the court and prided themselves on their knowledge of what went on behind the scenes, there were many veiled references to political events on the level of personal intrigue, but there was, of course, little or no serious consideration of fundamental political questions.

The defection of the aristocratic part of the great audiences might, in itself, have meant little to the dramatists who wrote for the popular theatre. But another more important and seemingly inconsistent antitheatre movement also began to gather momentum in this Jacobean period. That was the growing antagonism of the substantial middle class who had formed so large a part of late sixteenth century audiences.

As the struggle between the king, supported at home by bishops and lords and backed abroad by Rome and Spain, and the bourgeoisie, developed, the strong Protestant feeling which had inspired such early leaders as Wyclif and Tyndale revived. There was a well-known tradition of religious struggle already established in Europe and it was easy for the predominantly Protestant bourgeoisie to fall into this pattern. Attacking the Anglican Church was the most effective and, as yet, the most direct possible way of attacking, at his most vulnerable point, its head, the king.

But Protestantism had been traditionally opposed to the theatre ever since its adherents had criticized the medieval mystery plays as superstitious and mystical. Moreover, most sober hard-working thrifty Protestants were also constitutionally opposed to the theatre as a time-wasting, money-wasting indulgence which too often led to other even more reprehensible ones, like drinking parties and assignations.

All these motivations led to some withdrawal of patronage which was probably more important in terms of quality than quantity, but which was none the less keenly felt by serious dramatists.

Such dramatists, of whom Shakespeare was the preeminent example, were even more fundamentally affected by the apparently hopeless tenor of political events.

All the sixteenth century hardships and injustices, of which Shakespeare was well aware, could be accepted if they were part of a genuinely progressive national movement. But now it seemed as though the whole antifeudal struggle had created only a new, narrow tyranny of church and king, with public funds lavished on such "catterpillars of the commonwealth" as the homosexual favorites James created, like Robert Carr whom he made Viscount Rochester, and George Villiers, whom he named Duke of Buckingham. Here were "Bushy, Bagot, Greene"—the hated royal parasites Shakespeare had seen as so largely instrumental in Richard II's destruction—come to life again in a new and virulent form.

The positive aspect of the revolutionary civil war which was to break out in some thirty short years was not yet apparent. But all the negative conditions of increased dissension and oppression at home, dishonorable and reactionary alliances abroad, and the new ugliness of early seventeenth century imperialism in the Americas and the West Indies were only too evident.

A sadly bitter comment by two serving men in *Coriolanus* sharply points to the situation in Jacobean England. One says that peace "makes men hate one another." And his fellow replies, "Reason; because they then less need one another."

Shakespeare, as we have seen, was not even in his youth a poet of protest. His greatest plays are all plays of powerful clear-eyed affirmation. Later critics, who cannot conceive of an artist as an integrated part of his society, have made much of the obvious necessity a great dramatist feels adequately to present many opposed viewpoints and interests. They have distorted the plain evidence of each play's overall dramatic development to argue that Shakespeare believed all—or none—of the opinions expressed in its course. But, as Professor Harbage concludes his well-documented *Shakespeare and the Rival Tradition:*

> Shakespeare did not acquiesce in discrepancy. That we are forced to *prove* what we instinctively *know* (and what was once taken for granted) is the strange fruit of the art-for-art theorizing that has muddied critical thinking since the mid-nineteenth century. This movement has drawn all its strength from skepticism. As one loses faith in the power of his own age to discriminate between right and wrong, one loses faith in such power in any former age. The evidence of an artist's belief that he shared in this power in his age may be charitably ignored in view of the distinction of his technique. . . . If the symbols used—the characters, actions, the speeches—persist in obtruding ethical ideas, let these symbols be paired in such a way as to cancel each other out, or let them be attributed, like the bawdy jokes, to the demands of the groundlings.

Harbage continues more specifically to define Shakespeare's ethical outlook:

> He wrote for a theatre of a nation, not a theatre of the world, and for a society that was far from classless; yet he faced in the direction of what was in his day (and is in ours) the future, and in his conception of the community there is a breadth of sympathy unequalled among the writers for the theatre of the urban clique.

He concludes with some asperity and a tart but well-justified ad hominem aimed at one of Shakespeare's most fashionable contemporary misinterpreters:

> The statement that perhaps it was part of Shakespeare's "special eminence to have expressed an inferior philosophy in the greatest poetry" (T. S. Eliot) displays at least the virtue of a moment of candor. Provided one recognizes what Shakespeare's philosophy is, he has a right to express his own value judgment on it. More debatable is the right to assume that poetry can be better than its content. It can, of course, be worse.

But it was no longer possible for a great artist to affirm the values presented by the still dominant royal power of Shakespeare's last years. The best of the younger writers like John Ford, Philip Massinger, and John Webster wrote such bitter, impassioned and hopeless studies of corruption and despair as *'Tis Pity She's a Whore*, *A New Way to Pay Old Debts*, and *The Duchess of Malfi*. But as Shakespeare himself had said, he was:

> . . . too old to fawn upon a nurse,
> Too far in years to be a pupil now.

So while he continued active in the business of the theatre, for more than half of his last ten years we find him accepting a "speechless death," which robbed his pen "from breathing native breath."

Then we have the two coldly brilliant, cynical, most un-Shakespearian fairy tales of *Cymbeline* and *The Winter's Tale*, in which he showed the youngsters how easily he could have been master of the rival tradition as well, had he thought such mastery worth the winning. There is also the formal, only partly Shakespearian, *Henry VIII*, and finally, in the same year, the controversial *The Tempest*.

The strongest material in this play, important out of all proportion to the space it occupies, is that dealing with Caliban.

Recent scholarly research has presented more and more minute details to indicate how closely linked Prospero's island—and its "native"—were with the colonial explorations and conquests of the early seventeenth century.

The exciting and troubling news of these early imperialist adventures, and of the rebirth of slavery with which they were accompanied, are reflected in many other contemporary English writers. Francis Bacon, for example, who strongly favored colonies, begins his essay on the subject by recommending that they be "planted" on "pure," that is uninhabited grounds, as otherwise they may fairly be called extirpations of the native inhabitants rather than plantations.

The most casual reference to Shakespeare's introduction of Caliban shows how clearly colonization is the background of Shakespeare's thought as well.

Prospero, the civilized man who has taken over the island, says to his daughter:

> We'll visit Caliban, my slave, who never
> Yields us kind answer.

She objects:

> 'Tis a villain, sir,
> I do not love to look on.

To which he makes the simple and unanswerable reply:

> But, as 'tis,
> We cannot miss him: he does make our fire,
> Fetch in our wood, and serves in offices
> That profit us.

The rationale of "the white man's burden" was evidently not yet required. When Caliban, thus prepared for, enters he complains with evident justice:

> This island's mine, by Sycorax my mother,
> Which thou tak'st from me: when thou camest first
> Thou strok'st me, and made much of me, wouldst give me
> Water with berries in't, and teach me how
> To name the bigger light, and how the less,
> That burn by day and night: and then I loved thee,
> And showed thee all the qualities o' th' isle,
> The fresh springs, brine-pits, barren place and fertile.
> Cursed be I that did so! All the charms
> Of Sycorax, toads, beetles, bats, light on you!
> For I am all the subjects that you have,
> Which first was mine own king: and here you sty me
> In this hard rock, whiles you do keep from me
> The rest o' th' island.
> . . . .
> You taught me language, and my profit on't
> Is, I know how to curse: the red plague rid you
> For learning me your language.

To this striking evaluation of the benefits of civilization Prospero can only respond:

> Hag-seed, hence
> . . . .
> Fetch us in fuel, and be quick thou'rt best
> To answer other business: Shrug'st thou, malice?
> If thou neglect'st, or dost unwillingly
> What I command, I'll rack thee with old cramps,
> Fill all thy bones with aches, make thee roar
> That beasts shall tremble at thy din.

Nevertheless, no matter how strongly justice as well as generosity may range themselves on Caliban's side, he does not win his freedom. Furthermore we are clearly told that, if he did, he would people the isle with Calibans and bind himself to the first drunken sot he met, who would hold him in a more capricious and less fruitful servitude. Nor is there any promise, or hope, that he has a prospect of development toward freedom, or any chance of something better than a fairly well-behaved and less harsh slavery.

The same pessimism, amply warranted by those facts of the time apparent to Shakespeare, permeates every other theme developed in the play.

For example, let us glance at the relations of the evil brother and false friends—a subject treated with unmatched emotional depth and rich indignation in so many of the earlier plays. Here we have again three most unnatural villains—murderers and traitors in intention and attempt if not in act—but instead of a real horror or a real forgiveness we have here a cynically unmoved acceptance:

> You, brother mine, that entertained ambition,
> Expelled remorse, and nature—who, with Sebastian,
> Would here have killed your king—I do forgive thee,
> Unnatural though thou art
> . . . .
> But you, my brace of lords, were I so minded,
> I here could pluck his highness' frown upon you,
> And justify you traitors: at this time
> I will tell no tales.
> . . . .
> For you—most wicked sir—whom to call brother
> Would even infect my mouth, I do forgive
> Thy rankest faults—all of them; and require
> My dukedom of thee, which, perforce, I know,
> Thou must restore.

The cold contempt of this forgiveness is emphasized by Miranda's naive exclamation on seeing this band of traitors: "How many goodly creatures are there here! How beauteous mankind is! O brave new world, That has such people in 't!" And Prospero's condescending " 'tis new to thee."

The world of Shakespeare's youthful hopes and mature accomplishment seemed to have:

> . . . melted into air, thin air:
> And, like the baseless fabric of this vision
> The cloud-capp'd towers, the gorgeous palaces,
> The solemn temples, the great Globe itself
> Yea, all which it inherit, shall dissolve,

Nothing was left to do but break his staff and, "deeper than did ever plummet sound," to drown his book.

At the end of 1611 he retired to Stratford, which he had during the past twenty years only occasionally visited when the theatres were closed by plague, and died there on April 23, 1616.

There are some other trivial facts of his life, including the long series of detailed bequests in his will, available to the curious, but the vital facts for an understanding of his work are all to be found in the broad current of the political and social events of his time. It was the great time of the revolutionary bourgeoisie and to it we owe the greatest realistic literature of hope and affirmation which the bourgeois world has ever known.

FRANCIS BACON

Francis Bacon was born a commoner and died Baron of Verulam and Viscount of St. Albans (1561-1626). Educated to the law which occupied him for over forty years, he became the first "philosopher of industrial science." He sincerely professed himself to have "as vast contemplative ends, as I have moderate civil ends; for I have taken all knowledge to be my province," and picked his way through the intricacies of court politics to achieve the position of Lord Chancellor of England. He was one of the most competent and honest of judges but was correctly, if not quite fairly, impeached for bribery. He devoted the better part of his adult life to the zealous service of an undignified, corrupt and reactionary king but was after his death honored almost as a prophet by Goethe, Voltaire and Milton himself. He was the first great English prose writer, but translated all his important work into Latin so that it should not be wasted, writing:

> These modern languages will at one time or another play the bankrowt with books, and since I have lost much time with this age, I would be glad if God would give me leave to recover it with posterity.

For a farcical conclusion to this series of paradoxes, the one phenomenon he could not really understand was passion, and the one thing he could not write was poetry, but many who would never otherwise have heard his name, have heard vague rumors that he wrote all of Shakespeare's plays!

Bacon's first biographer, Dr. William Rawley, knew him intimately ten or fifteen years, was his chaplain while he was Lord Chancellor, and remained with him as literary secretary during the last five years of his life. In his memoirs written some thirty years later he tells us:

> His father was that famous counsellor to Queen Elizabeth, the second prop of the kingdom in his time, knight, lord-keeper of the great seal of England; a lord of known prudence, sufficiency, moderation and integrity. His mother was Anne, one of the daughters of Sir Anthony Cook; unto whom the erudition of King Edward the Sixth had been committed; a choice lady, and eminent for piety, virtue and learning; being exquisitely skilled, for a woman, in the Greek and Latin tongues.

These facts are, of course, a matter of record, together with many more details about both parents. His mother was ardently religious, an enthusiastic adherent of the extremely "protestant" wing of the Church of England, and actually translated and published several volumes of Calvinist controversy. Although she did her best to impress her views upon both Francis and his older brother neither of them seems to have been much affected.

Francis was persuaded to write a paper on *Controversies in the Church* and was later, for political reasons, much involved in helping to achieve the unification of the Established Church, but his mother could hardly have been much pleased by the mild tone of his early pronouncement:

> God grant that we may contend with other churches, as the vine with the olive, which beareth best fruit; and not as the brier with the thistle, which of us is most unprofitable.

She would have been even more displeased by such a fuller revelation of his mind on the subject as that expressed in a note to a Catholic friend some twenty years later:

> I myself am like the miller of Huntingdon, that was wont to pray for peace amongst the willows; for while the winds

blow, the wind-mills wrought, and the water-mill was less customed. So I see that controversies of religion must hinder the advancement of sciences.

His father was more successful in sharing his ideas with his brilliant youngest son. Mary Sturt, the best of Bacon's recent biographers, tells us that during Henry VIII's reign Nicholas Bacon

> presented a plan for the foundation of a great college to train statesmen. The students were to learn good Latin and French, public policy, domestic management and foreign negotiation. They were to make historical collections of systems of government, and they were to travel in the suites of the King's ministers. . . . The academy that he projected was to train his successors from the upper but not probably the noble classes. . . .

And Benjamin Farrington, in what is probably the best book on Bacon, *Francis Bacon, Philosopher of Industrial Science*, says

> Over the fireplace in the dining hall Nicholas, the improving landlord, had a painting executed showing the goddess Ceres introducing the sowing of grain. This concern of the father with the great invention on which civilization rests sank into the son's mind. The first revolution in man's earthly destiny brought about by the invention of agriculture became the symbol for him of the second revolution brought about by the application of science to industry. . . . In his father's hall the legend beneath the picture of Ceres was *Moniti Meliora* (Instruction brings Progress). The boy whose eyes had rested during dinner on the picture of Ceres became the man who justified his new philosophy of works by appeal to the agricultural revolution.

At the age of fourteen the precocious youngster entered Cambridge and within two years he had learned enough of the essentially medieval philosophy which still formed the staple of academic education to be convinced that he wanted no more. Rawley tells us,

> Whilst he was commorant in the university, about sixteen years of age, (as his lordship hath been pleased to impart unto myself), he first fell into the dislike of the philosophy of Aristotle; not for the worthlessness of the author, to whom he would ever ascribe all high attributes, but for the unfruitfulness of the way; being a philosophy (as his lordship used to

say) strong for disputations and contentions but barren of the production of works for the benefit of the life of man; in which mind he continued to his dying day.

We soon find Bacon's letters and unpublished writings as well as his more formal philosophical works sprinkled with such remarks as: "Will you tell any man's mind before you have conferred with him? So doth Aristotle in raising his axioms upon Nature's mind." And, "Plato corrupted natural philosophy by his theology as thoroughly as Aristotle by his logic."

There are also, of course, many fuller explanations of his "dislike of the philosophy" of the past, like those implied in the selections from the *Novum Organum* and in such passages of his unpublished works as this from the *Cogitata et Visa* which begins, ' 'Franciscus Baconus si cogitarit"—"Francis Bacon thought thus,"—and continues, speaking of himself in the third person throughout:

> In the mechanical arts and their history, especially when compared with philosophy, he (Francis Bacon) observed the following happy omens. The mechanical arts grow toward perfection every day, as if endowed with the spirit of life. Philosophy is like a statue. It draws crowds of admirers, but it cannot move. With their first authors the mechanical arts are crude, clumsy and cumbersome, but they go on to acquire new strength and capacities. Philosophy is most vigorous with its earliest author and exhibits a subsequent decline. The best explanation of these opposite fortunes is that in the mechanical arts the talents of many individuals combine to produce a single result, but in philosophy one individual talent destroys many. The many surrender themselves to the leadership of one, devote themselves to the slavish office of forming a bodyguard in his honour and become incapable of adding anything new. For when philosophy is severed from its roots in experience, whence it first sprouted and grew, it becomes a dead thing.

This criticism of the essential insignificance of the various "schools" of metaphysics, which devote themselves to obscuring with commentary the at least poetically meaningful insights of their founders, is a commonplace of philosophic criticism today. Bacon's sharp contrast of these barren philosophies with the fruitful development of the mechanical arts or, as• we call them, sciences, is also become a truism, although his parallel warnings against pragmatism and crude utilitarianism, at which we must glance later, are not yet either generally accepted or understood. But this opposition to metaphysics was a startling and almost unintelligible attitude for most of his contemporaries in sixteenth century England, and almost two centuries later the radical encyclopedists of France felt they were just beginning to develop his new way of thought.

After leaving Cambridge in disgust the seventeen-year-old spent two years studying and observing men and manners in France. He was recalled by his father's death which, coming rapidly as the result of a sudden chill, had prevented the completion of a special estate that had been planned for the youngster and left him only the very slight provision of a younger son.

Since a profession was now necessary, Bacon entered the Inns of Court in London as a law student, in chambers soon shared by his brother Anthony. His health was not at any time very good but he seems, nevertheless, to have accomplished an extraordinary amount, combining his official studies with much scientific reading and writing, some sustained but unsuccessful attempts at achieving a political position through the influence of his uncle, Lord Burghley, Lord Treasurer of England; and an amazingly ambitious and consistent plan of laying out huge gardens in the unused common ground belonging to Grays Inns. This last work survives not only in his many essays on landscape gardening, but in the actual appearance of the gardens still extant there.

A little pamphlet on the *State of Christendom*, in which he embodied the observations he had made during his stay in France, did not succeed in impressing Elizabeth sufficiently to give him a post in her service, but it helps us to understand his deep desire for a stable, united nation—attainable in England at the time only under the rule of a strong monarch. He says of France:

> The division in this country for matters of religion and state, through discontent of the nobility to see strangers advanced to the greatest charges of the realm, the offices of justice sold, the treasury wasted, the people polled, the country destroyed, hath bred great trouble and like to see more.

When he was twenty-four he was elected to the House of Commons despite the steady though unavowed opposition of his powerful uncle, who had a clever and ambitious son just a few months younger than Francis to provide for. His pen was occasionally employed by the queen in such honorable but unremunerated projects as a paper on *Controversies in the Church* in 1589, and in responding to a sharp Catholic attack on the English Church by a pamphlet called *Observations on a Libel* in 1594. Two years later he was appointed a member of the "Queen's Learned Counsel"—another dignified but unsalaried position.

Rawley summarizes Bacon's uncompensated services to the queen during the ten years with the discreet reflection that: "Nevertheless, though she cheered him much with the bounty of her countenance, yet she never cheered him with the bounty of her hand; . . ."

Ben Jonson, describing his conduct as a lawyer during this period tells us:

> There happened in my time one noble speaker who was full of gravity in his speaking. His language where he could spare or pass by a jest, was nobly censorious. No man ever spoke more neatly, more pressly, more weightily, or suffered less emptiness, less idleness in what he uttered. No member of his speech but consisted of his own graces. His hearers could not cough or look aside from him without loss. He commanded where he spoke, and had his judges angry and pleased at his devotion. No man had their affections more in his power. The fear of every man that heard him was lest he should make an end.

By 1594 when the post of Attorney-General fell vacant Francis and his brother Anthony—returned from a ten-year sojourn on the continent—were advisers to Lord Essex, the queen's favorite, who headed one of the three important factions in court. (The other two were those of their uncle, Lord Burghley and of Sir Walter Raleigh.) Lord Essex made a determined effort to get this appointment, or that of the lesser post of Solicitor General, for Bacon, but was unsuccessful. The cause may have been personal intrigue, but it is probable that the queen was still angry at the part which Bacon, as a member of the House of Commons, had played in the Long Parliament of 1593.

Certain new taxes had been suggested to raise additional revenue for the crown, and he had strongly opposed them, stating:

> The gentlemen must sell their plate, and the farmers their brass pots, ere this will be paid; and for us, we are here to search the wounds of the realm, and not to skim them over.

The dangers are these. First, we shall breed discontent and endanger her Majesty's safety, which must consist more in the love of the people than their wealth. Secondly, this being granted in this sort, other princes hereafter will look for the like; so that we shall put an evil precedent on ourselves and our posterity; and in histories it is to be observed, of all nations the English are not to be subject, base, or taxable.

Furthermore, he had been the only member of the House quick enough to see through a seemingly unobjectionable proposal that the House of Commons meet in a joint session wtih the House of Lords to discuss the matter. He had pointed out the great danger to the Commons' jealousy guarded prerogative of alone introducing financial proposals, and his motion had been almost unanimously carried. The queen might forgive such conduct since she was quite aware of Bacon's genuine devotion to the principles of sovereignty and his practical value to her counsels, but she was was unlikely to forget and much less likely to reward it.

Bacon was, however, sincerely anxious to do all he could for the power and prestige of the crown and, thus, as he saw it, for the stability, peace and prosperity of England. He had also serious hopes of inducing a learned and brilliant ruler to subsidize an ambitious program of scientific research—the first of its kind ever projected—on a scale that would then have been impossible for any other patron.

In 1592 he had had the opportunity to present this project in a speech, *Mr. Bacon in Praise of Learning*, which formed part of a masque presented by Lord Essex for the queen's birthday. It reads, in part:

> Are we the richer by one poor invention by reason of all the learning that hath been these many hundred years? The industry of artificers maketh some small improvement of things invented; and chance sometimes in experimenting maketh us to stumble upon somewhat which is new; but all the disputation of the learned never brought to light one effect of nature before unknown.
>
> All the philosophy of nature which is now received is either the philosophy of the Grecians or that other of the Alchemists. That of the Grecians hath the foundation in words, in ostentation, in confutation, in sects, in schools, in disputations. That of the Alchemists hath the foundation in imposture, in auricular tradion, and obscurity. The one never faileth to multiply words, and the other ever faileth to multiply gold.

He goes on to ask for royal support in substituting for these two false sciences true science which, he says, consists in:

> . . . the happy match between the mind of man and the nature of things. And what the posterity and issue of so honorable a match may be; it is not hard to consider. Printing, a gross invention; artillery, a thing that lay not far out of the way; the compass, a thing partly known before; what a change have these three made in the world in these times; the one in the state of learning, the other in the state of war; the third in the state of treasure, commodities and navigation. And those, I say, were but stumbled upon and lighted upon by chance. Therefore, no doubt the sovereignty of man lieth hid in knowledge; wherein many things are reserved, which kings with their treasure cannot buy, nor with their force command; their spials and intelligence can give no news of them, their seamen and discoverers cannot sail where they grow. Now we govern nature in opinions, but we are thrall unto her in necessity; but if we would be led by her in invention, we should command her in action.

Two years later Bacon wrote a similar masque to be presented as part of the Gray's Inn Christmas revels. Here a philosopher addresses to the king of a mythical kingdom concrete proposals similar to those Bacon had intimated to Queen Elizabeth, and was later, still hopefully, to present to King James. His protagonist says:

> I will wish unto your Highness the exercise of the best and purest part of the mind, and the most innocent and meriting conquest, being the conquest of the works of nature. And to this purpose I will commend to your Highness four principal works and monuments of yourself. First, the collecting of a most perfect and general library, wherein whatever the wit of man hath heretofore committed to books of worth, be they ancient or modern, printed or manuscript, European or of the other parts, of one or other language, may be made contributory to your wisdom.
> Next, a spacious, wonderful garden, wherein whatsoever plant the sun of divers climates, out of the earth of divers moulds, either wild or by the culture of man brought forth, may be with that care that appertaineth to the good prospering there of set and cherished. This garden to be built about with rooms to stable in all rare beasts and to cage in all rare birds; with two lakes adjoining, the one of fresh water, the other of salt, for like variety of fishes. And so you may have in small compass a model of universal nature made private.
> The third, a goodly huge cabinet, wherein whatsoever the

hand of man by exquisite art or engine hath made rare in stuff, form, or motion, whatsoever singularity change and the shuffle of things hath produced, whatsoever Nature hath wrought in things that want life and may be kept; shall be sorted and included.

The fourth such a still-house [laboratory] so furnished with mills, instruments, furnaces and vessels, as may be a place fit for a philosopher's stone.

About this time Lord Essex, who had failed in securing Bacon a political appointment, generously gave him an estate worth (in our money today) over $10,000. It must be remembered that regular remuneration for such work as both Francis and his brother were doing for Essex, in assembling news from foreign agents all over the continent, collating it, and advising policy on the results was not then paid for except through such preferments or gifts.

Anthony, a semi-invalid, was devoting his full time and a considerable part of his own small fortune to this work and it formed an essential part of the Earl of Essex' power and usefulness as a member of the queen's privy council.

Bacon's letter of thanks indicates that he was already troubled by a possible clash between the Earl's ambitions and the sovereignty of the queen. He writes:

> My Lord, I see I must be your homager, and hold land of your gift, but do you know the manner of doing homage in law? Always it is with a saving of his faith to the King and his other Lords, and therefore, my Lord, I can be no more yours than I was, and it must be with the ancient savings; and if I grow to be a rich man, you will give me leave to give it back to some of your unrewarded followers.

Four years later when, in 1599, Essex was setting off as Lord Deputy on the Irish campaign that did, indeed, prove to be the beginning of the romantic attempt at a palace revolution for which he was finally executed, Bacon again included in his letter of good wishes a more explicit warning:

> Therefore I will only add this wish—that your Lordship in this whole action, looking forward, would set down this position, that merit is worthier than fame, and looking back hither, would remember this text, that obedience is better than sacrifice.

In the meantime, in 1597, he had published his first famous series of ten short essays, dedicated to his brother. This small book included the essay "On Studies." The name "essay" was then unknown in England and was of course borrowed from Montaigne's recent description of his book of short prose pieces as attempts, *essais,* to express himself.

When Essex returned from Ireland in defiance of the queen's explicit commands, Bacon exerted himself to effect a reconciliation. The queen seemed not unwilling to envisage such a future result but insisted on a sort of special trial where the Queen's Learned Counsel (including Bacon) were to present the charges against Essex which he would admit, begging for pardon. The indeterminate and mild sentence, "that he should be suspended from the execution of his offices and continue in his own house until it should please Her Majesty to release both this and all the rest," was declared by the president of the privy council, as had, in fact, been arranged in advance, and it seemed possible that with patience Elizabeth's favorite might, in time, regain his offices as well as his freedom from this nominal arrest.

Patience, however, was not among his many gifts and Essex had not enough sense of history to realize that, popular as he undoubtedly was, the time when any part of England could be aroused to support a feudal adventure was long past. He attempted an absurdly ill-prepared and tragically improbable uprising, walking into the city with several hundred followers and calling upon the citizens of London to join him. It seems likely that he intended, as he later intimated, "only" to kill Lord Burghley and Sir Walter Raleigh and force his way to the Queen's presence to secure her promise of reinstatement in public office and, perhaps, in the long coveted position of prince consort.

In any event the scheme was so obviously fantastic that it seemed a sufficiently explicit confession and humble submission would win the royal pardon—as it did, after a comparatively short imprisonment, for his collaborator, the Earl of Southampton. There was no question of his guilt of treason, or of the sentence which would be pronounced; but there seemed to be almost as little question of its remission to nominal imprisonment and banishment from court.

Bacon was explicitly commanded to take part as one of the queen's counsel in the trial and did so. Although there has been considerable criticism of his "disloyalty" and "ingratitude" in accepting the position neither his contemporary biographers nor the best later ones—including the nineteenth century editor of the most complete and authoritative edition of his *Works, Life, and Letters,* James Spedding—feel that such attacks are at all justified.

Bacon was sincerely and correctly opposed to any revival of the feudal power of the nobility which had torn England apart during the Wars of the Roses and he had, as we have seen, warned Essex of the dangers of his attitude several times during the past six years. Essex' guilt was undisputed and the verdict was clear in advance. All intimacy between the two had terminated considerably before Essex' departure for Ireland; the few letters from 1596-1599 are friendly but increasingly formal and largely occupied with more specific advice and warning of the nature of those already quoted. It is true that Bacon would have been ruined and, perhaps, suspected of approval if not complicity had he refused to act, but there is no doubt that his deepest convictions and profound patriotism, as well as his interest, lay on the side of the queen. As Thomas Huxley, another scientific man of letters, a man of unquestioned integrity and disinterestedness, and a great admirer of Bacon's, said three centuries later: "A man ought to be ready to endure persecution for what he does hold; but it is hard to be persecuted for what you don't hold."

Essex' proud refusal to beg the queen for forgiveness, his dramatic execution, and the accession of King James who had always favored him and with whom, as probable successor to the throne, Essex had been illegally corresponding, combined to increase popular sympathy for him, and a corresponding criticism of his prosecutors. In 1604, the year after Elizabeth's death, Bacon felt himself compelled to write on the matter:

> My defence needeth to be but simple and brief: namely, that whatsoever I did concerning that action and proceeding, was done in my duty and service to the Queen and State; in which I would not show myself false-hearted nor faint-hearted for any man's sake living. For every honest man, that hath his heart well planted, will forsake his King rather than forsake God, and forsake his friend rather than forsake his King, and yet will forsake any earthly commodity, yea and his own life in some cases, rather than forsake his friend.

It is so difficult for us today to enter into the emotions of the Elizabethan for whom loyalty to the sovereign was, realistically, the only possible basis of peace and progress, that we can hardly understand the weight of such a statement unless we make a real effort at translating it into the concrete political terms of our own time. Such an effort is, of course, precisely the one we have already found necessary for a real understanding of Shakespeare's history plays and, to a lesser extent, of many of his other tragedies, and is all the more worth emphasizing on that account. Perhaps it will be easier to make it on Bacon's behalf if we keep in mind his notes "On The Fortunate Memory of Elizabeth, Queen of England" (see p. 11 ff.).

When James I succeeded to the throne in 1603, Bacon was already forty-three and although well-known as a lawyer, literary figure and statesman, had still never received a position or substantial income from the political activities which had engrossed so much of his time. His cousin, Robert Cecil, who had succeeded to the position held by Lord Burghley, was even more unfriendly to him than his uncle had been, and there seemed little likelihood of any real political advancement.

Nevertheless, James I had and treasured a reputation as a learned man and patron of philosophy, and Bacon hoped that he could induce him to undertake the project for a combined botanical and zoological garden, museum of arts and industries, and research laboratories, which he had outlined for Elizabeth ten years before. He made an early opportunity of attending court to see the new king—who knighted him together with some three hundred other commoners as a cheap reward for past service to the crown—and was evidently somewhat disappointed. He wrote privately to a friend, "I told your Lordship once before that (methought) his Majesty rather asked counsel of the time past than of the time to come. But it is early yet to ground any settled opinion."

Giving up, for the time, any hope of an official career Bacon evidently made a virtue of necessity, turning to the prospect of devoting his life to the scientific studies with which he was always profoundly if not exclusively concerned. In an unpublished fragment of biography written at this time (like most of his work, in Latin, and here translated by Spedding) he says, in part:

> Believing that I was born for the service of mankind, and regarding the care of the commonwealth as a kind of common property which like the air and the water belongs to everybody, I set myself to consider in what way mankind might

best be served, and what service I was myself by nature best fitted to perform.

Now among all the benefits that could be conferred upon mankind, I found none so great as the discovery of new arts, endowments, and commodities for the bettering of man's life. For I saw that among the rude people in the primitive times the authors of rude inventions and discoveries were consecrated and numbered among the Gods. And it was plain that the good effects wrought by founders of cities, lawgivers, fathers of the people, extirpaters of tyrants, and heroes of that class, extend but over narrow spaces and last but for short times; whereas the work of the Inventor, though a thing of less pomp and show, is felt everywhere and lasts for ever.

But above all, if a man could succeed, not in striking out some particular invention, however useful, but in kindling a light in nature—a light which should in its very rising touch and illuminate all the border-regions that confine upon the circle of our present knowledge; and so spreading further and further should presently disclose and bring into sight all that is most hidden and secret in the world,—that man (I thought) would be the benefactor indeed of the human race,—the propagator of man's empire over the universe, the champion of liberty, the conqueror and subduer of necessities.

For myself, I found that I was fitted for nothing so well as for the study of Truth; as having a mind nimble and versatile enough to catch the resemblance of things (which is the chief point), and at the same time steady enough to fix and distinguish their subtler differences; as being gifted by nature with desire to seek, patience to doubt, fondness to meditate, slowness to assert, readiness to reconsider, carefulness to dispose and set in order; and as being a man that neither affects what is new nor admires what is old, and that hates every kind of imposture. So I thought my nature had a kind of familiarity and relationship with Truth.

Nevertheless, because my birth and education had seasoned me in business of state; and because opinions (so young as I was) would sometimes stagger me; and because I thought that a man's own country has some special claims upon him more than the rest of the world; and because I hoped that, if I rose to any place of honour in the state, I should have a larger command of industry and ability to help me in my work;—for these reasons I both applied myself to acquire the arts of civil life, and commended my service, so far as in modesty and honesty I might, to the favour of such friends as had any influence.

When I found however that my zeal was mistaken for ambition, and my life had already reached the turning-point, and my breaking health reminded me how ill I could afford to be slow, and I reflected moreover that in leaving undone that

good I could do by myself alone, and applying myself to that
which could not be done without the help and consent of
others, I was by no means discharging the duty that lay upon
me,—I put all those thoughts aside, and (in pursuance of my
old determination) betook myself wholly to this work.

It is altogether characteristic of Bacon's consistent reserve that
neither in this solitary fragment of autobiography nor in any of his
letters then or later does he mention the recent death of the brother
who had been so close to him or his courtship of, and subsequent
marriage to, the young Alice Barnham, "an alderman's daughter, an
handsome maiden, to my liking."

However, he had been mistaken in his assumption that the new
regime meant the end of a public career and he was no doubt
pleased as well as surprised to find that King James immediately
gave him a small pension, some slight official position, and an
enormous amount of responsibility in the complicated negotiations
which, largely because of Bacon's work, brought about the immediate, peaceful and complete legal unification of England and
Scotland.

An unfinished essay, *The True Greatness of Britain*, written at
that time, describes the unified nation he wished to see under that
new—or, rather, renewed—title, as a nation not of great nobles and
peasants but one:

> whose wealth resteth in the hands of merchants, burghers,
> craftsmen, free holders, farmers in the country, and the like;
> whereof we have a most evident and present example before
> our eyes, in our neighbours of the Low Countries, who could
> never have endured and continued so inestimable and insupportable charges [of the war with Spain], either by their
> natural frugality or by their mechanical industry, were it not
> also that their wealth was dispersed in many hands, and not
> ingrossed in few, and those hands were not so much of the
> nobility, but most generally of inferior condition.

The king's apparent friendliness revived Bacon's hopes for royal
support of science, and, in 1605, he published *The Advancement of
Learning*, dedicated to the king.

Bacon's practical purposes are immediately apparent in the
preface to the first book which skillfully mingles compliments to
the royal intellect, with appeals to the authority of Plato and the
Bible, that might influence one who "rather asked counsel of

the time past than of the time to come." After developing at some length the value and beauty of true knowledge in the first book, he begins the second with another dedicatory preface which, while somewhat coldly paying its respects to Queen Elizabeth, contrasts her state as a virgin with that of James, already sure of those who would succeed him and, therefore, doubly concerned with improving the world in which they were to succeed.

This second introduction then proceeds with some anxious particularity to explain to the king just what it is that Bacon would like to have him do.

> But to your Majesty, whom God hath already blessed with so much royal issue, worthy to continue and represent you for ever, and whose youthful and fruitful bed doth yet promise many the like renovations, it is proper and agreeable to be conversant not only in the transitory parts of good government, but in those acts also which are in their nature permanent and perpetual. Amongst the which (if affection do not transport me) there is not any more worthy than the further endowment of the world with sound and fruitful knowledge; for why should a few received authors stand up like Hercules' columns, beyond which there should be no sailing or discovering, since we have so bright and benign a star as your majesty to conduct and prosper us?
>
> Let this ground therefore be laid, that all works are overcome by amplitude of reward, by soundness of direction, and by the conjunction of labours. The first multiplieth endeavor, the second preventeth error, and the third, supplieth the frailty of man. . . .

The work achieved no direct results but James was not displeased by it and continued to employ Bacon in his dealings with Parliament, appointing him Solicitor-General in 1607.

The king's relations with the House of Commons were difficult ones and Bacon's part in them was somewhat ambiguous.

The transition from feudalism to absolute monarchy which had been completed by Henry VIII and stabilized by Elizabeth had, naturally, entailed an enormous growth in the central government with a corresponding increase of expense to which the normal royal revenues, derived from the estate held by the family of the sovereign as by any other great family of nobles, was altogether inadequate.

Henry VIII had solved this problem, along with many others,

by his confiscation of church lands. Elizabeth had met it by comparative economy—on a grand scale—by making various nobles bear the expense for the lavish ceremonial which characterized her court, by requesting frequent grants through special taxes or levies which the commons were generally willing to raise since the class they represented still depended on the queen and often benefited by her policy, and by the use of "patents" or monopolies bestowed on nobles important to the court. This last means was one increasingly resorted to and increasingly resented during the latter half of Elizabeth's reign and, sensitive to public opinion and realistically aware of the shifting relationship of class forces, she had promised her last parliament in 1601 a virtual discontinuance of the practise.

In that same parliament Bacon had drawn a distinction between legitimate and illegitimate patents and monopolies, or between what we would now call patents and what we would call monopolies, defining the former to exist: "when any man by his own charge, or by his own wit or invention doth bring any new trade into the realm, or any engine tending to the furtherance of a new trade that never was used before and that for the good of the realm."

But James I, perpetually in need of money both for the necessarily increasing expenses of government and for the aggrandizement of the favorites he slobbered over and bestowed dukedoms upon, was certainly not far-sighted enough voluntarily to give up this power—or any other.

From the beginning to the end his relation with his parliaments were a pattern of farcical futility.

They would be called into being to grant the king a sum of money. They would refuse unless he in turn granted them the redress of a long list of grievances, including repeal of special patents. After long and undignified bargaining some sort of tentative agreement would be reached. The Commons would refuse to hand over the money until they had received the promised redress. The king, equally suspicious, or perhaps meditating a double-cross, would refuse any action until he had received the money. The long vacation might then intervene, and after consultation with their constituents, the Commons would return to drive a harder bargain or the king would in a temper dissolve Parliament with nothing gained and all was to do again.

After such a dissolution in 1611, Bacon wrote the king one of many letters urging a complete change in tactics in his summoning the new parliament. He said, in part:

> My third proposition is that this Parliament may be a little reduced to the more ancient form which was to voice the Parliament to be for some other business of estate and not merely for money; but that to come in upon the bye, whatsoever the truth be. I mean it not in point of dissimulation but in point of majesty and honour; that the people may have somewhat else to talk of and not wholly of the King's estate, and that Parliament-men may not be wholly possessed of these thoughts. What shall be the causes of estate given forth ad populam, whether the opening and increase of trade, or whether the plantation of Ireland, or the reduction and recompiling of the laws, it may be left to further consideration. But I am settled in this, that somewhat be published beside the money matter, and that in this form there is much advantage.

This attempt to restore the royal prestige and unify the king and Commons was far from hypocrisy on Bacon's part, and his tactful understatement of the political role to be played by a genuine parliament was intended to conciliate James into giving the idea a trial.

For although the Elizabethan myth of national unity, which had already outlived its brief truth, was rapidly becoming too threadbare to deceive the most credulous, and the king's pro-Spanish policy and his wife's avowed conversion to Catholicism were destroying his credit with all but the most reactionary, yet Bacon still strove persistently to turn the king's policy into the path of true national interests, and, when he failed in a specific instance, continued, nevertheless, to support the measures actually undertaken by the crown. That is to say, of course, measures for the relief of pressing financial needs or assertion of the royal prerogative in internal affairs. Bacon never in any way furthered or even countenanced the undeclared attempts at rapprochement with Spain or the Vatican, and was practically the only man of his standing at Court never even offered a pension by the King of Spain.

The best explanation of Bacon's role in the reign of James is given by John Howard Lawson's discussion of seventeenth century England in *The Hidden Heritage*. He says, in part:

... Bacon was devoted to the principle of monarchial absolutism, but he differed from many of the crown's advisers in the quality of his intelligence as well as in his class interests. These were the factors which made Bacon invaluable to the government.

Since he did not suffer from the aristocratic astigmatism which afflicted most of the court circle, Bacon could see the problem of power as a national question rather than as a matter of arbitrary class domination. He wanted the king to assert his absolute authority, but he saw the royal will as a means of overcoming class antagonism and forcing the propertied classes to work together for their mutual advantage. . . . He had disapproved of the vulgar bargaining over the *Great Contract* because it exacerbated class differences and exposed the king's selfish aims. As an intellectual structure, Bacon's idea was impressive: James was to reassert his national leadership, balancing the interests of various propertied groups with such open-handed majesty that no one would dare to question his motives or oppose the subsidies which were necessary to maintain the state apparatus. . . .

But the grandeur of Bacon's plan—which doomed it to failure—lay in its abandonment of petty compromises, its large and unwarranted assumption that a unified national policy could be accepted and consistently followed.

One could formulate a policy for the advancement of industry, foreign commerce, territorial expansion and colonial aggrandizement. But such a policy demanded the elimination of monopolistic practices and feudal privileges; . . . it required the strengthening of England's economic and political influence in Europe, which could only be accomplished through opposition to the Hapsburgs and the papacy and an alliance with the Protestant forces on the continent.

All these things constituted the program of the bourgeoisie —which contravened the class interests of the crown and the court. Bacon's reconciliation of classes was an abstraction; it meant that absolutism would take over the program of the bourgeoisie and make it its own.

Nevertheless, for a time James did attempt to put some of Bacon's suggestions into effect, and in 1613 Bacon was made Attorney-General.

In the same year he published a second series of essays and their titles and content show how constantly and profoundly he was thinking of the major political problems of the time. For example, in "Of Plantations" (a name commonly used for colonies), he says first: "I like a plantation in a pure soil; that is, where people are not displanted to the end to plant in others. For else it is rather an extirpation than a plantation."

And again, later:

> Let there be freedom from custom [export duties], till the plantation be full of strength; and not only freedom from custom, but freedom to carry their commodities where they may make their best of them, except there be some special cause of caution.

In another essay "Of Nobility" we find Bacon first saying, as we might expect anyone in his time, place, and position to do:

> A *Monarchy*, where there is no *Nobility* at all, is ever a pure and absolute *Tyranny*; As that of the Turkes. For *Nobility* attempers *Soveraignty*, and draws the Eyes of the People, somewhat aside from the *Line Royall*.

But he then rather surprisingly continues:

> But for *Democracies*, they need it not; And they are commonly, more quiet and lesse subject to Sedition, then where there are Stirps of *Nobles*. For Mens Eyes are upon the Businesse, and not upon the Persons; Or if upon the Persons, it is for the Businesse sake, as fittest, and not for Flags and Pedegree. Wee see the *Switzers* last well, notwithstanding their Diversitie of Religion, and of Cantons. For Utility is their Bond, and not Respects. The united Provinces of the Low Countries, in their Government, excell; For where there is an Equality, the Consultations are more indifferent, and the Payments and Tributes more cheerfull.

"Of Seditions and Troubles" begins:

> The *Matter* of *Seditions* is of two kindes; *Much Poverty*, and *Much Discontentment*. . . . And if this *Poverty*, and Broken Estate, in the better Sort, be joyned with a Want and Necessity, in the meane People, the danger is imminent, and great. For the Rebellions of the Belly are the worst.

The essay continues in shrewd detail:

> The *Causes* and *Motives* of *Seditions* are; *Innovation* in *Religion; Taxes; Alteration of Lawes and Customes; Breaking of Priviledges; General Oppression; Advancement of unworthy*

> *persons; Strangers; Dearths; Disbanded Souldiers; Factions growne desperate;* And whatsoever in offending People, knotteth them, in a Common Cause.

Finally Bacon advises:

> The first *Remedy* or prevention, is to remove by all meanes possible, that *materiall Cause of Sedition,* whereof we spake; which is *Want* and *Poverty* in the *Estate.* To which purpose serveth the Opening, and well Ballancing of Trade; The Cherishing of Manufactures; the Banishing of Idlenesse; the Repressing of waste and Excesse by Sumptuary Lawes; the Improvement and Husbanding of the Soyle; the Regulating of Prices of things vendible; the Moderating of Taxes and Tributes; And the like. Generally, it is to be foreseene, that the Population of a Kingdome, (especially if it be not mowen downe by warrs) does not exceed, the Stock of the Kingdome, which should maintaine them. Neither is the Population, to be reckoned onely by number; For a smaller Number, that spend more, and earne lesse, doe weare out an Estate, sooner then a greater Number, that live lower, and gather more. Therefore the Multiplying of Nobilitie, and other Degrees of Qualitie, in an over proportion, to the Common People, doth speedily bring a State to Necessitie: And so doth likewise an overgrowne Clergie; For they bring nothing to the Stocke; . . .

In another essay, "Of the true Greatnesse of Kingdomes and Estates," there is an extremely interesting discussion of man power and morale, beginning:

> For *Solon* said well to *Croesus* (when in Ostentation he shewd him his Gold) *Sir, if any Other come, that hath better Iron then you, he will be Master of all this Gold.* Therefore let any Prince or State, thinke soberly of his Forces, except his *Militia* of Natives, be of good and Valiant Soldiers. . . . As for Mercenary Forces, (which is the Helpe in this Case) all Examples shew; That, whatsoever Estate or Prince doth rest upon them; *Hee may spread his Feathers for a time, but he will mew* them soone after.

The same essay continues to discuss means of holding as well as winning power, contrasting the Spartans who refused equal rights to aliens with the Romans, and drawing the appropriate moral.

> Never any State was, in this Point, so open to receive *Strangers,* into their Body, as were the *Romans.* Therefore it sorted

with them accordingly; For they grew to the greatest *Monarchy*. Their manner was, to grant Naturalization, (which they called *Jus Civitatis*) and to grant it in the highest Degree; That is, Not onely *Jus Commercij, Jus Connubij, Jus Haereditatis;* But also, *Jus Suffragij,* and *Jus Honorum*. And this, not to Singular Persons alone, but likewise to whole Families; yea to Cities, and sometimes to Nations. Adde to this, their Custome of *Plantation* of *Colonies;* whereby the Roman Plant was removed into the Soile, of other Nations. And putting both Constitutions together, you will say, that it was not the *Romans* that spred upon the *World;* But it was the *World* that spred upon the *Romans;* And that was the sure way of Greatnesse.

In addition to these and the many other specifically political topics, there are many illustrations drawn from the field of politics in the more general consideration of such subjects as, "Of Friendship," "Of Envy," "Of Counsell," and the like. A good example of these is the essay, "Of Wisdome for a Mans selfe," which begins:

An *Ant* is a *wise Creature* for it Selfe; But it is a shrewd Thing, in an Orchard, or Garden. And certainly, Men that are great *Lovers* of *Themselves,* waste the Publique. Divide with reason betweene *Selfe-love* and *Society*: And be so true to thy *Selfe,* as thou be not false to Others; Specially to thy King, and Country. . . . And certainly, it is the Nature of Extreme *Selfe-Lovers*; As they will set an House on Fire, and it were but to roast their Egges; . . .

There are also a few essays dealing explicitly with economic questions. Of these perhaps the most interesting to us is the one "of Usurie." Usury, it must be remembered, was still in early seventeenth century usage as it had been in Shakespeare's time, the correct name for any interest-bearing loan. The medieval prohibition of all interest charges had not yet been formally rescinded, although it was a regulation more honored in the breach than the observance.

Bacon, after summarizing the traditional religious arguments against charging interest, begins:

I say this onely, that *Usury* is a *Concessum propter Duritiem Cordis*: For since there must be Borrowing and Lending, and Men are so hard of Heart, as they will not lend freely, *Usury* must be permitted. . . . But few have spoken of *Usury* use-

fully. It is good to set before us, the *Incommodities*, and *Commodities* of *Usury*; . . .
It appeares by the Ballance, of *Commodities*, and *Discommodities* of *Usury*, Two Things are to be Reconciled. The one, that the *Tooth of Usurie* be grinded, that it bite not too much: The other, that there bee left open a Meanes, to invite Moneyed Men, to lend to the Merchants, for the Continuing and Quickning of Trade. This cannot be done, except you introduce two severall *Sorts* of *Usury*; A *Lesse*, and a *Greater*. For if you reduce *Usury* to one Low Rate, it will ease the common Borrower, but the Merchant will be to seeke for Money. And it is to be noted, that the Trade of Merchandize, being the most Lucrative, may beare *Usury* at a good Rate; other Contracts not so.

To serve both Intentions, the way would be briefly thus. That there be *Two Rates of Usury*, the one Free, and Generall for All; The other under *Licence* only, to *Certaine Persons*, and in *Certaine Places of Merchandizing*. First therefore, let *Usury, in generall, be reduced to Five in the Hundred*; And let that Rate be proclaimed to be Free and Current; And let the State shut it selfe out, to take any Penalty for the same. . . .

Finally, after further description of possible safeguards and means of lowering all interest rates, Bacon concludes with characteristic moderation and realism:

> If it be Objected, that this doth, in a Sort, Authorize *Usury*, which before was, in some places, but Permissive: The Answer is; That it is better, to Mitigate *Usury* by *Declaration*, than to suffer it to Rage by *Connivence*.

Finally in 1616 Bacon succeeded to the office his father had held for twenty years, Lord Keeper of the Great Seal of England, and in 1617 he was, largely through the good offices of the king's then favorite, the Duke of Buckingham, appointed Lord Chancellor.

His predecessor had been ill for some time and there was even without such a delay, an enormous backlog of unheard cases in the ordinary course of events, so that Bacon inherited a court calendar almost two years in arrears. Yet three months after his appointment he was able to write triumphantly, to the Earl of Buckingham:

> This day I have made even with the business of the kingdom for common justice. Not one case unheard. The lawyers

drawn dry of all the motions they were wont to make. Not one petition unanswered, and this I think could not be said in our age before. This I speak not out of ostentation, but out of gladness, that I have done my duty. I know men think I cannot continue, if I should thus oppress myself with business. But that account is made. The duties of life are more than life. And if I die now I shall die before the world is weary of me, which in our times is somewhat rare.

Honors now crowded upon him. In 1618 he was named Baron Verulam and two years later Viscount St. Albans. He spent much time laying out extraordinary gardens about his father's old country house of Gorhamsbury and leased and completely redecorated and furnished York House in London where he had been born.

Nevertheless, he made time to draw up a detailed plan for his master work—*The Great Instauration*—and to complete the second of its six projected parts—*The Novum Organum*.

The work as Bacon envisaged it, was to consist of six independent but related parts. The first was to be called *The Division of the Sciences* and to contain a description of the various fields of natural knowledge with the kinds of activity or inquiry appropriate to each one. The second was *The Novum Organum* (completed in two books) or *Directions Concerning the Interpretation of Nature*. The third was to be what we should today call an Encyclopedia of Natural History and Scientific Experiments. Bacon called it *The Phenomena of the Universe,* or a *Natural and Experimental History for the Foundation of Philosophy*. The fourth section was to be called *The Ladder of the Intellect*. Bacon intended it to be an exposition of the way in which the scientific methods discussed in Part II should be applied to the essential facts or raw materials of science which would be recorded, when collected, in Part III. The fifth was to be *The Forerunners* or *Anticipations of the New Philosophy*. This would have been an illustrative account of various discoveries which had already been made more or less accidentally, and of the way in which man's life had been enriched by them. The last section was to be a summary of *The New Philosophy* or *Active Science*. In describing this sixth part Bacon says:

> The sixth part of my work (to which the rest is subservient and ministrant) discloses and sets forth that philosophy which by the legitimate, chaste, severe course of inquiry which I have explained and provided is at length developed

and established. The completion, however, of this last part is a thing both above my strength and beyond my hopes. What I have been able to do is to give it, as I hope, not a contemptible start. The fortune of the human race will give the issue; such an issue, it may be, as in the present condition of things and men's minds cannot easily be conceived or imagined. For what is at stake is not merely a mental satisfaction but the very reality of men's well being, and all his power of action. Man is the helper and interpreter of Nature. He can act and understand in so far as by working upon her or observing her he has come to perceive her order. Beyond this he has neither knowledge or power. For there is no strength that can break the causal chain: Nature cannot be conquered but by obeying her. Accordingly these twin goals, human science and human power, come in the end to one. To be ignorant of causes is to be frustrated in action.

The Great Instauration in this fragmentary form was published in 1620 and dedicated to King James in an introductory letter which indicated Bacon's feeling that the work could not be completed by one man, and his persistent hope that the king, with his comparatively unlimited resources, might be induced to undertake it.

After the dedication to the king there is a preface addressed to the reader. Bacon begins:

> It seems to me that men do not rightly understand either their store or their strength but overrate the one and under rate the other. Hence it follows that either from an extravagant estimate of the value of the arts which they possess, they seek no further; or else from too mean an estimate of their own powers they spend their strength in small matters and never put it fairly to the trial in those which go to the main. These are as the pillars of fate set in the path of knowledge; for men have neither desire nor hope to encourage them to penetrate further.

Near the conclusion he says:

> Lastly, I would address one general admonition to all, that they consider what are the true ends of knowledge, and that they seek it not either for the pleasure of the mind, or for contention, or for superiority to others, or for profit, or fame, or power, or for any of these inferior things; but for the benefit and use of life; and that they perfect and govern it in charity. For it was from lust of power that the angels fell, from lust of

knowledge that man fell; but of charity there can be no excess, neither did angel or man ever come in danger by it.

The requests I have to make are these. Of myself I say nothing; but in behalf of the business which is in hand I entreat men to believe that *it is not an opinion to be held, but a work to be done*; and to be well assured that I am laboring to lay the foundation, not of any sect, or doctrine, but of human utility and power. Next I ask them to deal fairly by their own interests; and laying aside all emulations and prejudices in favour of this or that opinion, to join in consultation for the common good; and being now fixed and guarded by the securities and helps which I offer from the errors and impediments of the way, to come forward themselves and take part in that which remains to be done. Moreover, to be of good hope, nor to imagine that this Instauration of mine is a thing infinite and beyond the power of man, when it is in fact the true end and termination of error; and seeing also that it is by no means forgetful of the conditions of mortality and humanity, for it does not suppose that the work can be altogether completed within one generation, but provides for its being taken up by another; . . .

Suddenly in 1621, with no real warning, a cataclysm engulfed Bacon—or, at least, the Lord Chancellor.

Parliament convened in a mood of sullen anger at the king and his favorites. The immediate complaint was certain particularly oppressive patents granted to two creatures of Buckingham's and used by them with outrageous presumption, brazen dishonesty, and callous cruelty. The patents had, of course, been granted by the king who could not as yet be openly attacked, but had been legally certified by the Lord Chancellor and two other justices. There was an abortive attempt to take action against the three judges on those grounds, but the two patent holders were cheerfully sacrificed by the crown, and the matter seemed at an end. However, although the specific intrigues involved are still in dispute, it seems clear James learned that a more serious sacrifice was required—either his chief minister or his bedfellow, if not both.

Under the circumstances his choice was a foregone conclusion. Two plaintiffs who had appeared in suits before the Lord Chancellor testified that they had given him bribes which he had accepted—although both had lost their cases and in both instances Bacon's decision had been sustained on appeal.

Everyone available who had been a party to the more than

8,000 actions before Bacon was summoned, and some 28 were found who declared that they had sent him gifts, in most cases after the conclusion of their actions. It is significant that after the most searching investigation the courts failed then or later to reverse a single one of the decisions involved.

Bacon first prepared to make a vigorous defense, but after some communication with the king wrote a general admission of guilt, confessing that he had, as was then customary, taken gifts after the termination of suits and that in at least four cases he had not checked to find out whether the process had actually been terminated. He protested, what seems to have been true, that in no case was his judgment influenced by such gratuities, but submitted himself to the sentence of parliament.

Before the sentence had yet been considered he airily wrote the king:

> But because he that hath taken bribes is apt to give bribes, I will go farther and present your Majesty with a bribe. For if your Majesty give me peace and leisure and God give me life, I will present your Majesty with a good history of England and better digest of your laws.

The sentence, when rendered, read that he should be incapable of any office, place or employment in the State or Commonwealth; never be allowed to sit in Parliament or to come within the verge of the court, which at that time meant London; be imprisoned in the Tower during the King's pleasure; and be fined £40,000. The king's pleasure proved to be less than a week and the fine was transformed into a benefit since Bacon was then, as always, heavily in debt, and the (unpressed) crown lien on his income taking legal priority, prevented any other creditor from putting in a claim until it had been satisfied.

The banishment from London which meant, in this case, from libraries and research facilities, was not so easily overcome since Buckingham wanted the lease of York House and Bacon was unwilling to cede it. After six months exile and some threats of pressing the fine, Bacon gave in, received a limited pardon from the king, and found himself virtually free of penalties although in dishonorable retirement.

The dishonor seems even then to have been a matter of opinion since so censorious a contemporary critic of morals as Ben Jonson

—an acquaintance but by no means a close friend of Bacon's—wrote only a few years later:

> My conceit of his person was never increased toward him by his place or honours, but I have and do reverence him for the greatness that was only proper to himself: in that he seemed to me ever by his works one of the greatest men and most worthy of admiration that had been in many ages: in his adversity I ever prayed that God would give "him strength, for greatness he could not want." Neither could I condole in a word or syllable for him, knowing that no accident could do harm to virtue, but help to make it manifest.

With his usual amazing resilience Bacon spent the next four months writing an excellent history of Henry VII which he presented to the king in partial fulfillment of his promise, and settled down to complete as much as possible of the scientific writings outlined in *The Great Instauration.*

A comment to Rawley, who served as literary secretary for the remainder of Bacon's life, is as good an example of the judicial temperament as literature can afford. He said, after criticizing the custom by which judges were largely paid out of the fees of litigants, that he hoped his case would show the errors which persistence in such a custom could lead to, and concluded, "I was the justest judge that was in England this fifty years. But it was the justest censure of Parliament that was this two hundred years."

In 1622 he published two scientific treatises on *The Winds,* and *Life and Death* (medicine) and in 1623 his *De Augmentis Scientarium,* a greatly enlarged and improved Latin version of *The Advancement of Learning.*

In 1625 he published a revised edition of his Essays with a number of new ones including two cheerful analyses, "Of Judicature," and "Of Vicissitude of Things." Another very interesting new essay, "Of Greatness of Kingdoms and Estates," summarizes a viewpoint which Bacon had expressed at greater length in his survey of the rise of the Tudor absolutism in *The History of King Henry VII.* Its conclusions about small freeholders read remarkably like Thomas Jefferson's. Bacon says:

> Let states that aim at greatness, take heed how their nobility and gentlemen do multiply too fast. For that maketh the common subject grow to be a peasant and base swain, driven out of heart, and in effect but the gentleman's laborer.

Even as you may see in coppice woods; if you leave your staddles too thick, you shall never have clean underwood, but shrubs and bushes. So in countries, if the gentlemen be too many, the commons will be base; . . . This which I speak of hath been no where better seen than by comparing of England and France: whereof England, though far less in territory and population, hath been nevertheless an over-match; in regard the middle people of England make good soldiers which the peasants of France do not. And herein the devices of king Henry the Seventh (whereof I have spoken largely in the history of his life) was profound and admirable; in making farms and houses of husbandry of a standard; that is, maintained with such a proportion of land unto them, as may breed a subject to live in convenient plenty and no servile condition; and to keep the plough in the hands of the owners, and not mere hirelings.

That same March, on King James' death, Bacon gaily and irreverently wrote to the new king, Charles I, that he hoped, as the Father had been his Creator, the Son would be his Redeemer, and in June he was summoned, as a Peer of the Realm, to the House of Lords, although he was too ill that month to attend.

It is apparent that his temperament as well as his ideas justified him in having said: "And it seemeth to me, that most of the doctrines of the philosophers are more fearful and cautionary than the nature of things requireth."

At the beginning of April, 1626, seeing that the ground was still covered with snow, it occurred to him that that would be a good time to try whether flesh could not be preserved by cold as well as salt. He got out of his carriage, bought a fowl from a cottager, had it killed and cleaned, and then himself stuffed it with snow. A letter he dictated from bed a few days later tells of the conclusion of more than the experiment.

To the Earl of Arundel and Surrey.
My Very Good Lord:
I was like to have had the fortune of Caius Plinius the elder, who lost his life by trying an experiment or two touching the conservation and induration of bodies. As for the experiment itself, it succeeded excellently well; but in the journey between London and Highgate I was taken with such a fit of casting, as I knew not whether it were the stone, or some surfeit, or a cold, or indeed a touch of them all three. But when I came to your Lordship's house, I was not able to go back, and therefore was forced to take up my lodging here,

> where your housekeeper is very careful and diligent about me; which I assure myself your lordship will not only pardon towards him, but think the better of him for it. For indeed your Lordship's house was happy to me; and I kiss your noble hands for the welcome which I am sure you give me to it. . . .

Bronchitis rapidly developed and on April 9, 1626, he died and, as his will directed, was buried very quietly near his mother's grave. His wife, with whom he seems to have lived peacefully and pleasantly, although she apparently played no large share in his life, had probably left him shortly before his death. A codicil written that year canceled all bequests to her "for reasons she will understand," and she married a gentleman of her household a few months later. She was then of course still only in her middle thirties.

Today there is little need to urge recognition of scientific achievements. On the contrary, our respect for science is now so unquestioning that we can hardly appreciate Bacon's pioneer work in demanding it. But it is unquestionably true, as Goethe said, that: "The impact of Bacon's genius directed the mind of his age towards reality. This extraordinary man performed the inestimable service of calling attention to the whole field of natural science!"

But there is even more need now than there was four centuries ago to emphasize the other aspect of Bacon's thought which has, with the end of the bourgeois revolution, been forgotten by some of his most devout followers. Lord Macaulay, for example, the Whig historian who thought of himself as the statesman of industrialism, claimed the heritage of Bacon's philosophy for the Victorians, saying:

> To make men perfect was no part of Bacon's plan. His humble aim was to make imperfect men comfortable. . . . In Plato's opinion man was made for philosophy; in Bacon's opinion philosophy was made for man; it was a means to an end; and that end was to increase the pleasures and to mitigate the pains of millions who are not and cannot be philosophers. . . .
> To sum up the whole, we should say that the aim of the Platonic philosophy was to exalt man into a god. The aim of the Baconian philosophy was to provide man with what he requires while he continues to be man. The aim of the Platonic philosophy was to raise us far above vulgar wants. The aim of the Baconian philosophy was to supply our vulgar wants. The former aim was noble; but the latter was attainable.

Bacon himself would have indignantly refuted this interpretation. He says over and over again such things as:

> If there be any one on whose ear my frequent praise of practical activities has a harsh and unpleasing sound because he is wholly devoted to contemplative philosophy, let me assure him that he is the enemy of his own desires. In natural philosophy practical results are not only means to improve human well-being. They are also the guarantee of truth. There is a true rule in religion, that a man must show his faith by his works. The same rule holds good in philosophy. Science too must be known by its works. It is by the witness of works rather than by logic or even observation that truth is revealed and established. *It follows from this that the improvement of man's lot and the improvement of man's mind are one and the same thing.*

He asserts and reasserts that it is not merely inconvenient but morally wrong to despair of human powers or to suppose that man does not have the ability radically to alter nature.

> This philosophy, if it be carefully examined, will be found to advance certain points of view which are deliberately designed to cripple enterprise. Such points of view are the opinion that the heat of the sun is a different thing from the heat of fire; or that men can only juxtapose things while nature alone can make them act upon one another. The effect and intention of these arguments is to convince men that nothing really great, nothing by which nature can be commanded and subdued, is to be expected from human art and labour. Such teachings, if they be justly appraised, will be found to be nothing less than a wicked effort to curtail human power over nature, and to produce a deliberate and artificial despair. This despair in its turn confounds the promptings of hope, cuts the springs and sinews of industry, and makes men unwilling to put anything to the hazard of trial.

He promises that a true scientific history of inventions and their possibilities "will not only be of immediate benefit . . . but will give a more true and real illumination concerning the investigations of the causes of things and axioms of art than has hitherto shone upon mankind."

The true goal of science according to Bacon is not merely "to make imperfect men comfortable," although that may be a useful by-product, as Huxley explains in his essay, "On the Advisableness of Improving Natural Knowledge" (1866). "The true and lawful goal of science," Bacon says, "is the endowing of human life with new discoveries and powers.... For the world is not to be narrowed down till it will go into the understanding, which has been the practice hitherto, but the understanding must be stretched and expanded to take in the image of the world as it is discovered."

No, it is not the Whig Macaulay but rather a great radical contemporary of his who was the true heir to Bacon's philosophy. Bacon would have demolished Macaulay's smug dichotomy between the noble and unattainable objective of raising us above vulgar wants, and the ignoble and attainable one of supplying our vulgar wants. But he would have saluted as a logical next step Engels' conclusion that:

> ... the final, essential distinction between man and other animals ... the animal merely *uses* external nature, and brings about changes in it simply by his presence; man by his changes makes it serve his ends, *masters* it ... all our mastery of it consists in the fact that we have the advantage over all other creatures of being able to know and correctly apply its laws.
> ... by long and often cruel experience and by collecting and analyzing the historical material, we are gradually learning to get a clear view of the indirect, more remote, social effects of our productive activity, and so the possibility is afforded us of controlling and regulating these effects as well.

Almost four centuries ago Bacon could envision such a possibility for the future. In attempting to communicate this vision to his contemporaries he not only became the first "philosopher of industrial science," but also the first English writer of a flexible, varied, precise and colloquial prose.

An impersonal essayist, judicial and detached in tone, he has nevertheless established direct contact with readers' minds in over fifteen generations. For his thought is never an abstraction but always a concrete living thing. The few close-packed sentences of each essay expand and change visibly before our eyes whenever we read them with the attention they demand. And their inspired common sense still stands as one of the most enduring monuments to the practical genius of modern man, which can change the world by understanding it.

PURITANS AND CAVALIERS

If the defeat of the Spanish Armada in 1588 marks the culmination of the century-old alliance between the throne and the bourgeoisie in England, it no less truly marks the beginning of the end of that alliance. Up to that point the middle class may be said to have struggled for mere existence as a class; from that point on its at first unrealized fight was, not for life, but for power.

The alliance disintegrated all the more suddenly because both parties simultaneously felt ready for a test of strength. The still powerful but rapidly declining remnants of the feudal nobility were no longer a real threat to the throne and, with the accession of James I in 1602, the king turned to consolidate relations with them which would, he hoped, enable him successfully and completely to dominate the increasingly defiant House of Commons. While James I's tactlessness, corrupt favorites, personal arrogance, deep ignorance of English history, and unconcealed suspicion of English institutions, undoubtedly accelerated the deterioration of relations between the throne and parliament, and aggravated the new unpopularity of the sovereign, the seeds of the violent struggle which culminated in civil war were inherent in the situation itself, and it would probably have been impossible for the most politic monarch to have avoided it.

The growing divergence between the court and the Commons was soon reflected in the theatre. As early as 1594, Shakespeare comments on the new artificial theatrical fashions which were growing up in response to the demand of the more "precious" aristocratic audience. This drama, presented in far more expensive and exclusive "private theatres," relied heavily on masques, dances, music, and elaborately learned witticisms or flowery conceits, and shrank more and more from themes of serious concern or emotional impact, turning to an unreal fairytale world distinguished only by its verbal skill and pageantry. For such plays the clear cultivated voices of young children and their immature unemotional grace was well fitted—and the popularity of "child actors" (at which Shakespeare makes Hamlet exclaim) was a fad indicative of the real decadence of the drama.

Furthermore, the opposition to the king and court was expressed very largely in religious terms. It must not be forgotten that the king of England was head of church as well as of state, and that there was already a well-established form and tradition of religious struggle while there were not yet set ideological terms for a political struggle. The growing strength and anger of the bourgeoisie was therefore expressed as a renewed Puritan opposition to the Church of England. The Puritans had never been friendly to the theatre on moral and economic grounds, and its official position of existence by favor of, and under protection from, the court, or of individual great noblemen, gave a further edge to their displeasure.

Thus, less than a quarter of a century after it had reached unprecedented heights of almost universal popularity and significance, we find the drama as a great art form virtually disappearing. We must turn for the most important literature of the early seventeenth century to the lyrical poets of the court and to the great pamphleteers of the revolution—the greatest of whom, Milton, was also the single important epic poet whom English literature has, so far, produced.

The cavalier poets, Sir John Suckling, Richard Lovelace, Robert Herrick, whose very names seem set to music and fit burdens for old songs, inherited much of the grace, charm, verbal felicity and lyrical beauty which were the ornament of Elizabethan drama. Sometimes less fresh and spontaneous, often lightly cynical, always less convincing in their emotion, they limit their themes to the confines of an aristocratic court where lovemaking is the business of peace, and courage is shown by a gentleman's defending his king's honor in a war much as he would defend his lady's in a duel.

Oddly enough we find here that a concentration upon lovemaking does not help to create great love poetry—as we shall see with Wordsworth in the nineteenth century, it is impossible to write movingly even about daffodils if one thinks only of daffodils. So if we place some of the most delightful lines of the cavaliers side by side with those of their Elizabethan prototypes we may find that the best flowers of a court are not really as beautiful as those whose roots go deeper into the lives of their time.

Let us, for example, very briefly consider a comparison—and contrast—between the best known lyric by perhaps the most skillful cavalier poet, Robert Herrick (1591-1674), and an Elizabethan song on the same subject from *Twelfth Night*.

The first and last stanzas of Herrick's graceful exhortation "To the Virgins, To Make Much of Time," read:

> Gather ye rosebuds while ye may,
>   Old Time is still a-flying:
> And this same flower that smiles to-day,
>   Tomorrow will be dying.
>
> Then be not coy, but use your time,
>   And while ye may, go marry:
> For, having lost but once your prime
>   You may forever tarry.

Shakespeare seems, more warmly and personally, to urge much the same request in:

> O, Mistress mine, where are you roaming?
> O, stay and hear; your true love's coming,
>   That can sing both high and low.
> Trip no further, pretty sweeting,
> Journeys end in lovers meeting,
>   Every wise man's son doth know.
>
> What is love? 'tis not hereafter;
> Present mirth hath present laughter;
>   What's to come is still unsure.
> In delay there lies no plenty;
> Then come kiss me, sweet and twenty,
>   Youth's a stuff will not endure.

Yet when we come to examine the two poems at all closely we find that the greater emotional power, the sustained contemporary impact of the Elizabethan, is not due simply to a more musical note or more brilliant images. The whole tone of freedom and equality in which the young woman (her virginity is evidently for Shakespeare an irrelevant if not impertinent inquiry) is urged to fulfill herself by making love, as she laughs, at pleasure, with a young man whose voice is exerted to delight her, is sharply contrasted with the virgin whose function it is to please and whose beauty and virginity are perishable commodities to be sold while the market holds. We can be well assured that the latter's husband-to-be will offer nothing so insubstantial as a talent for part-singing, but will rather prove his worth by the tender of a well-filled rent roll.

It is no great step from this to the gay contempt shown by Sir John Suckling (1609-1642):

> Out upon it, I have loved
> Three whole days together!
> And am like to love three more
> If it prove fair weather.

or the pious platitude of Richard Lovelace (1618-1658) in his oft quoted:

> I could not love thee, dear, so much,
> Loved I not honor more.

The religious or "metaphysical" poets of the King and Church of England party have perhaps less to say to us today. Herbert, Crashaw, Vaughan and even the later Donne were turning to God rather to escape the struggle than to strengthen themselves in it, and the frequently contorted and mystical allegory, the involved conceits and the disguised platitudes of their verse are in sharp contrast with the heroic and powerful lines of Milton or the deeply felt, straightforward, and concrete allegory of a simpler nonconformist whom we shall meet a little later—John Bunyan. Even Milton's friend and sometime comrade, Andrew Marvell, lives for us rather in the single famous plea to his coy mistress than in his serious poetry, and for most modern readers it is the originality and, often, the bitterness of Donne's love poetry, with its frequent undertone of the cynicism of "Go and Catch a Falling Star," rather than any more devout emotion which carries conviction.

We may perhaps represent the course of English literature in the seventeenth century by some such image as that of a great and powerful current carrying with it all the rich hopes, accomplishments and aspirations of the Elizabethan age, which split on the rock of the growing national disunity and flowed for a while in two streams. One, the shallow pretty rivulet we have just glanced at; the other a narrow, deep and swift moving current which kept and even intensified some of the earlier emotional power, but had, at least temporarily, lost the tumultuous variety, the playfulness, the breadth and ease which were the particular glory of the parent river.

We have no time to pause with the many vital preachers and pamphleteers whose vocabulary is, sometimes, unfortunately, as foreign to us as their thought is, in many cases, contemporary. Certainly the democratic Levelers and their great spokesman, Lilburne, must be given some individual mention, however brief.

John Lilburne was the leader of the most progressive group which had any substantial following—a group essentially composed of independent farmers and small merchants including some shipowners and well-to-do craftsmen. They stood for individual liberty, absolute legal equality, abolition of all vested interests and most taxes, and complete free trade. Lilburne was jailed under Charles I for writing against the royal prerogative and his fight for a "trial by his peers" and not by the House of Lords or a picked "blue ribbon" jury is an important part of the history of the struggle for constitutional government in England.

When the Civil War actually began, Lilburne served devotedly in the parliamentary army and became a leading figure there. However, with victory, and especially after the decisive defeat of Charles I in 1646-47, the big bourgeoisie who dominated parliament began moving steadily to the right to consolidate their gains and prevent the revolution from going any further. Lilburne, as spokesman for the petty bourgeoisie who had, as yet, secured almost none of the fruits of victory, attacked parliament in a series of sharply worded pamphlets for which he was again jailed and threatened with execution.

This is an excerpt from *England's New Chaines for Old* published in defiance of the press censorship in 1649:

> . . . They have already lost the affections of all People, and are onely supported by their present strength; but when once those good men that hold them up, shall perceive how instrumentall they are made, contrary to their intentions, in advancing a few lofty and imperious mens designes; and how easy it is for them to convert their abilities and power to better, and more common, ends exprest in their former engagements, and with the complaints of the agrieved people, and their owne understandings can furnish them with all, they will then lament that they have so long been out of the way, and set themselves with the utmost courage and resolution to free their distressed country from the fears and captivity it now groans under. They may talk of freedom, but what freedom indeed is there, so long as they stop the Presse, which is indeed and hath been so accounted in all free nations, the most essentiall part thereof? . . .
>
> And as for the prosperity of the Nation; what one thing hath been done that tendeth to it? . . .

> Nay, what sence of the heavy burdens of the people have they manifested of late, hath it not been by their procurement that the Judges their creatures have a thousand pound a yeer allow'd to every one of them above the ordinary fees? which were ever esteemed a heavy oppression in themselves; is there any abridgement of the charge, or length of time, in triall of causes? are the touch'd with the general burthen of Tithes, that canker of industry and tillage? or with that of Exize, which out of the bowells of labourers and other poor people enriches the usurers, and other catterpillars of the Commonwealth; or what have they done to free Trade from the intolerable burden of Customs? except the setting fresh hungry flyes, upon the old sores of the People? . . .

Far to the left even of this stand of the Levelers were the small and much persecuted group of Diggers, a curious early group of "premature communists" who felt, as their name implies, that man should live by the fruits of his own (primarily agrarian) labor and that no land should lie fallow and useless because of legal technicalities of ownership while there lived those able and willing to enrich it and with their labor.

Their courageous and vigorous leader, Gerrard Winstanley, wrote in 1647 a criticism of the fairly radical "Agreement of the People" proposed, after much discussion in Cromwell's New Model Army, as a minimum statement of the army's demands. This "agreement" provided for extreme toleration in religious terms and included much of the early political thinking of the Independents and more of even the Levelers, but completely ignored questions of economic oppression vital to the very poorest rural and city workers. Winstanley said:

> A thing called An Agreement of the People . . . is too low and shallow to free us at all. . . . What stock . . . is provided for the *poor, fatherless, widows,* and *impoverished people*? and what advancement of encouragement for the labouring and industrious, as to take off their burthens, is there?

Although Winstanley supported to the full the middle-class struggle against Charles I and the "tything priests" of the established church, his consistent identification of kings, bishops and "rich men" and his persistent agitation on behalf of the poor agricultural workers was no more welcome to his middle-class allies than to the enemy.

In 1649 he issued the Diggers' Proclamation stating that: "the earth was not made purposely for you to be Lords of it, and we to be your Slaves, Servants and Beggars; but it was to be a common livelihood to all, without respect of persons."

And so as soon as the military victories of Cromwell's armies had culminated in Charles' execution, parliament turned to putting down at least the most extreme of the dissidents in the Commonwealth camp.

Winstanley responded in his last pamphlet; an appeal to Cromwell called *The Law of Freedom* published in November, 1650:

> No man can be rich but he must be rich either by his own labours or by the labours of other men helping him. If a man have no help from his neighbours he shall never gather an estate of hundreds and thousands a year. If other men help him to work then are those riches his neighbours' as well as his own. But all rich men live at ease, feeding and clothing themselves by the labours of other men, not by their own, which is their shame and not their nobility; for it is more blessed to give than to receive. But rich men receive all they have from the labourer's hand, and when they give they give away other men's labours, not their own.

This was so utopian in terms of the practical possibilities of the period that it seems to have been completely ignored, and Winstanley soon after disappears from view, leaving us for remembrance the moving motto he prefixed to his work:

> When these clay bodies are in grave, and children stand in place,
> This shows we stood for truth and peace and freedom in our days.

There was a much greater Puritan poet and pamphleteer, John Milton, England's single epic poet and one of her greatest political prose writers. His life was so intimately related to every stage of the revolution, the short-lived commonwealth and the restoration, that it is impossible to consider his work without, in effect, considering a summary history of England in the crucial years between 1640 and 1670.

We have already summarily examined the roots of the struggle which was basically carried on between bourgeois power fighting its way toward free trade and the rapid development of manufacture, and the royal prerogative using monopolies and other special privileges to maintain absolutism in a commercial society as, in fact, the French throne was to succeed in doing for over a century.

But as soon as this struggle approached an actual rupture, the bourgeoisie's public proclamation of its wrongs and demand for its rights stimulated similar demands on the part of the lower middle class and the poor. These cries for redress of grievances were all the more urgent because the miseries of both peasant and apprentice had been intensified by the rapid consolidation of bourgeois power, the enclosures of "modern" landlords, and the ruthless drive for more efficient large-scale methods of manufacture.

Furthermore, as soon as Civil War actually broke out, it became apparent, as Cromwell said, that you could not fight gentlemen trained in arms and confident of their cause, with hired or pressed starvelings or soft-living prosperous burghers.

The New Model Army which he recruited and organized was so far ahead of its time that it is one of the strangest phenomena in all history.

Composed largely of solid yeomen with a good sprinkling of devoted nonconformist skilled craftsmen, it included every shade of political opinion from the extreme democracy of the Anabaptists, through the large and important section of Levelers, merging into the left-of-center Independents, with whom Milton and Cromwell were most often identified, to the conservative Presbyterians—on the whole, a less conservative, more devoted group than their fellow religionists at home and in parliament. A contemporary writer, Joshua Sprigge, says of this New Model Army:

> The Army was, what by example and justice, kept in good order both respectively to itself and the country; there were many of them differing in opinion, yet not in action nor business: they all agreed to preserve the kingdom; they prospered in their diversity more than in uniformity.

The means by which this unity were achieved and the actual life and organization of the army were as extraordinary as the practical result.

In a time when literacy was still uncommon, the army constituted itself a school for all its members. Political as well as religious discussions of the most searching kind were regularly carried on in military units deliberately kept small for this—ordinarily—most unmilitary purpose. Each regiment had two enlisted men as well as its officers to represent it at the general army councils. The verbatim records kept of these meetings must be read to be believed.

In April, 1647, for example, when the parliamentary victories largely removed fear of any resurgence of royalist strength, there were proposals from parliament that the army be disbanded. Mess after mess refused, saying, in the words of one such resolution, that the army had to continue itself so that: "the poor commons may have a shelter and defence to secure them from oppression and violence." In June the army declared that it was determined: "to promote such an establishment of common and equal right and freedom to the whole, as all might equally partake of but those that do, by denying the same to others or otherwise, render themselves incapable of."

Jack Lindsay, the English literary historian, says in discussing this period of English history:

> The New Model Army that broke the King was an organization of tremendous historical significance. In it there was demonstrated for the first time that unity was possible as a popular construction on a grand scale, not only apart from feudal-religious or monarchial ideas, but in entire opposition to those ideas. Cromwell as the creator of this popular unity was the first great modern revolutionary leader.

He goes on to give us a rapid summary of the events of the next decade, which we will shortly follow in more detail through Milton's eyes:

> The Commonwealth had unshakeably consolidated the bourgeois position. At the same time . . . it aroused democratic hopes among the wider masses—hopes which the bourgeois solution could not satisfy. Cromwell was the leader of the more active sections of bourgeois and petty-bourgeois; he could not, of course, see the struggle in historical perspective; but he had a strong sense of the issues involved. Whenever he came up against one of the nodal points of class in the clashing forces of his day, he blazed out into mysticism. That was the only way he could overcome his sense of the contradictions involved.
>
> . . . Emotionally there was much of him on the side of the Levellers. But he could not merely say to himself that he

rejected the Lilburnean programme as premature; to overcome the strong attraction he felt for it he had to hide in religious outbursts. The leadership of God that he intuited in those outbursts was the pressure of class-forces demanding so-far-and-no-further.

His dilemma was roughly this. He saw that if the Lilburnean plan was carried out while England was at such a low state of productivity, with organization so broken and localized, with literacy still confined to so few, the result would be, not to induce progress but to inhibit it. . . .

Both the Levellers and their opponents knew, and stated, that the achievment of political democracy would mean also an attempt to create economic equality. Such equality, in pre-industrial days, can only mean a sharing-out of the land. That is, a reversion to the ideal of medievalist self-sufficiency. And that would mean a crash of the political edifice, leading to full-blown feudalism. . . .

The difficulty that faced him was to find a way of establishing a collaboration between big and petty bourgeois, as he had established it during the Civil War. And the way was not evident; it was non-existent. What beat him was the deepening conflict between the small and the big land owners, the journeymen and their trade-masters, the small traders and the big companies. Everywhere the same division was showing up. The journeymen were making the last fight to control the masters within the guild organization; they were crushed. A more determined fight in the common council of London won a temporary democratic victory. But there was no means of welding all these forces in a national unity.

All this, however, was still in the undisclosed if imminent future when Milton, the great poet of the Commonwealth, was born a subject of James I in 1608, in circumstances which were peculiarly fortunate for English and, in fact, world literature.

John Milton's family background and education gave him knowledge of classical literature, drama, art, and especially, music, equaled by that of no other Puritan writer.

To this rich endowment and his own extraordinary gifts of sensitivity and expression, he added an understanding and power only to be learned through direct involvement in the sharpest, most important political struggles when their great demand meets, as it did in Milton, a great and willing response.

He himself believed that one rarely, in history, finds great deeds without finding great poets ready fittingly to sing them. Certainly it is then, fitting, that we should be able to survey one of the most heroic periods of English history through the work of the truly heroic poet whom many English critics consider second only to Shakespeare.

JOHN MILTON

Milton's father, disinherited by his father, a well-to-do Catholic yeoman of Oxfordshire, for too soon embracing Protestantism, migrated to London and apprenticed himself to a successful scrivener. The scrivener's profession or business was one which included many of the functions now performed by notaries, law writers, legal stationers or printers, debt collectors and, often, realty loan brokers. John Milton Sr. was evidently both competent and fortunate. Five years before the poet's birth in 1608 he had set up his own business and by 1621 he was employing four apprentices. Four years later he was elected steward of the Scrivener's Company and in 1634 was offered the presidency or mastership, which he declined.

His avocation, and perhaps the reason for that declination and for his comparatively early retirement during Milton's youth, was music. He was an accomplished organist and a composer of real talent, received wide recognition in Protestant circles—a number of hymns are still sung to tunes of his setting—and won a medal from a Polish prince of musical tastes.

He very early recognized his older son's exceptional abilities and encouraged them by providing an excellent day school education, additional private tutoring in Italian, French, music and other similar subjects, a leisurely college education and, more exceptionally, some five years of well-financed leisure for further self-directed study after graduation, climaxed by almost two years expensive travel in France, Switzerland and Italy.

Milton's school days were happy ones. He delighted in study; was fortunate in a courageous, independent and scholarly teacher; enjoyed the companionship of his younger sister and brother; and blossomed in the atmosphere of a sociable home full of music, charity, and respect for learning.

He read and admired Bacon and felt completely at one with his rationalist approach to the world and his emphasis on knowledge as a guide to power—on the necessary unity between fruitful thought and informed action.

For this reason his introduction to the still scholastic and essentially medieval curriculum at Cambridge was not a happy one, and while he rapidly attained a fair competence in the formal Latin disputations which occupied most of the students' hours, he never became reconciled to the waste of time and energy involved. His competence is attested by the fact that he was frequently chosen to deliver the "prolusion" or oration presented at set intervals before the faculty and student body of his own Christ's College and, occasionally, before the combined audience of several colleges.

An excerpt from one of these, translated from its original Latin, will show how strongly rebellious both thought and expression had already become in Milton's late teens.

After defining the true aim of knowledge in Baconian terms as "the enlarging of the bounds of human empire, to the effecting of all things possible," Milton proceeded to a detailed condemnation of the actual subjects and methods of study at the college and concluded his oration "Against the Scholastic Philosophy," by saying:

> Besides all this, it not infrequently happens that those who have entirely devoted and dedicated themselves to this blight of disputation lamentably display their ignorance and absurd childishness when faced with a new situation outside their usual idiotic occupation. Finally, the supreme result of all this earnest labour is to make you a more finished fool and cleverer contriver of conceits, and to endow you with a more expert ignorance; and no wonder, since all these problems at which you have been working in such torment and anxiety have no existence in reality at all, but like unreal ghosts and phantoms without substance obsess minds already disordered and empty of all true wisdom. . . .
>
> But how much better were it, gentlemen, and how much more consonant with your own dignity, now to let your eyes wander as it were over all the lands depicted on the map, . . . then to spy out the customs of mankind and those states which are well ordered; next to seek out and explore the nature of all living creatures, and after that to turn your attention to the secret virtues of stones and herbs. And do not shrink from taking your flight into the skies . . . ; yes, even follow close

upon the sun in all his journeys, and ask account of time itself and demand the reckoning of its eternal passage. . . .

So at length, gentlemen, when universal learning has once completed its cycle, the spirit of man, no longer confined within this dark prison house, will reach out far and wide, until it fills the whole world and the space far beyond with the expansion of its divine greatness. Then at last most of the chances of the world will be so quickly perceived that to him who holds this stronghold of wisdom hardly anything can happen in his life which is unforeseen or fortuitous. He will indeed seem to be one whose rule and dominion the stars obey, to whose command earth and sea hearken, and whom winds and tempests serve; to whom, lastly, Mother Nature herself has surrendered, as if indeed some god had abdicated the throne of the world and entrusted its rights, laws, and administration to him as governor.

Milton's early difficulties at college were not altogether with his teachers, nor were they all occasioned by such intellectual differences.

The medieval traditions of casual wenching and drinking were evidently also present, if not encouraged, and in one of his lighter holiday orations Milton, with the somewhat naive directness he was never to lose, characteristically mingled personal comment with his public address, referring for the first time to his college nickname of "The Lady of Christ's" and, not for the last time, to the chastity he thought more sinfully lost by man than by woman.

> Some people have lately nicknamed me the Lady. But why do I seem to them too little of a man? I suppose because I have never had the strength to drink off a bottle like a prize fighter; or because my hand has never grown horny with holding a plough-share; or because I was not a farm-hand at seven, and so never took a midday nap in the sun—last perhaps I never showed my virility in the way these brothellers do. But I wish they could leave playing the ass as easily as I the woman.

His graduation took place in 1629, a year also marked by his first serious English poem, "On the Morning of Christ's Nativity," with its lovely unpuritanical hymn beginning:

> It was the winter wild
> While the Heaven-born child
>   All meanly wrapped in the rude manger lies;
> Nature in awe to him

> Has doffed her gaudy trim,
>   With her great Master so to sympathize;
> It was no season then for her
> To wanton with the sun, her lusty paramour.

Milton, as was then customary, continued a less consistent residence at Cambridge, interspersed with visits to London until he received his Master's degree in July 1632. He then retired to his father's country estate at Horton for almost six years of truly intensive independent study of ancient and modern history, mathematics, music, and the art of poetry.

During his last years at Cambridge he had written the amazing "apprentice works"—"L'Allegro" and "Il Penseroso," whose ease and lightness make them today perhaps the most generally read of his poems, and at Horton he wrote his deservedly famous sonnet "On Shakespeare."

Although his father had expected him to enter the Established Church, then the normal course for a young man intending to devote his life to serious literary pursuits, Milton could no longer accept the corrupt practises and superstitious beliefs he felt characterized the Church of England. As he said some years later:

> The Church, to whose service, by the intentions of my parents and friends, I was destined of a child, and in mine own resolutions: till coming to some maturity of years, and perceiving what tyranny had invaded the Church, that he who would take orders must subscribe slave and take an oath withal, which unless he took with a conscience that would retch he must either straight perjure or split his faith; I thought it better to prefer a blameless silence before the sacred office of speaking bought, and begun with servitude and forswearing.

A "Latin Epistle in Verse," written at about this time, expresses his appreciation for his father's forbearance in not urging him to enter the ministry against his conscience, or to attempt some such alternative profession as the law, which his brother Christopher was indeed to undertake, against his inclination. He says gratefully:

> You did not, Father, bid me go where a broad way lies open, where the opportunities for gain are easier, and the golden hope of amassing riches shines steadily. Nor do you force me to the civil code, and the ill-guarded principle of national justice, and thus condemn my ears to senseless clamor.

Later in the epistle he tactfully reminds his father that no one so devoted to the art of music can condemn his son's devotion to the sister art of poetry.

A letter written at the same period to an older man, perhaps a friend of his father's or a former tutor, who had evidently more earnestly raised with him the question of the choice of a profession, gives us a valuable revelation of Milton's more serious thoughts on the matter. He says in part:

> Sir,—Besides that in sundry respects I must acknowledge me to profit by you whenever we meet, you are often to me and were yesterday especially as a good watchman to admonish that the hours of the night pass on (for so I call my life, as yet obscure and unserviceable to mankind) and that the day with me is at hand wherein Christ commands us to labour while there is yet light.

He goes on to say that he is not given to overindulgence in useless learning:

> whereby a man cuts himself off from all action and becomes the most helpless, pusillanimous, and unweaponed creature in the world, the most unfit and unable to do that which all mortals must aspire to, either to be useful to his friends or to offend his enemies.

He then concludes:

> Yet, that you may see I am something suspicious of myself, and do take note of a certain belatedness in me, I am the bolder to send you some of my nightward thoughts sometime since.

The "nightward thoughts" inclosed are a copy of his charming sonnet, "On His Having Arrived at the Age of 23,"—which begins with one of the loveliest of sonnet openings:

> How soon hath Time, the subtle thief of youth,
> Stolen on his wing my three-and-twentieth year!
> My hasting days fly on with full career,
> But my late spring no bud or blossom shew'th.

Since Milton had at this time already completed the extraordinarily beautiful ode, "On the Morning of Christ's Nativity," as well as "L'Allegro" and "Il Penseroso," the fourth line might be considered an indication of extreme modesty, which is one of the virtues for which Milton has rarely been criticized, or an extreme stretch of poetic license. More probably, however, it means to state the simple truth, assuming what was in Milton's mind already long axiomatic, that real poetry is always an important public action. Just a few years later he was to write explicitly,

> These abilities [to write poetry] . . . are of power, beside the office of a pulpit, to imbreed and cherish in a great people the seeds of virtue and public civility, to allay the perturbations of the mind, and set the affections in right tune; . . .

and again:

> True poets are the object of my reverence and love and the constant sources of my delight.
> I know that the most of them from the earliest times have been the strenuous enemies of despotism, but these pedlars and milliners of verse who can bear?

Two years later at the request of an older friend, Henry Lawes, already probably the leading English musician of his time, Milton wrote the masque, *Comus*, to be set to music and performed at an important court celebration. It ends with the famous peroration:

> Mortals that would follow me,
> Love Virtue, she alone is free; . . .

This is consistent with Milton's lifelong emphasis on freedom from his invocation in "L'Allegro," to "The mountain nymph, sweet Liberty," to the end of his great tragedy, *Samson Agonistes*, completed over forty years later, but it must have fallen somewhat strangely on courtly ears. *Comus* was, however, well received, and Lawes won Milton's reluctant consent to an at first anonymous publication of it.

In 1637 a young minister, Edward King, who had been a classmate of Milton's at college and had shared—with a difference—his ambition to write poetry, was drowned at sea. The college decided on a memorial volume and Milton was solicited to contribute. His reply was "Lycidas" which has since shared honors with Shelley's "Adonais" as one of the two most famous English elegies.

Milton was far less personally affected by King's death than

Shelley was by that of Keats, and even more directly than the later poet, he turns his thoughts to a general consideration of the life of a young artist whose fate might well be his own. Since King had been about to enter seriously upon his life's work, Milton imagines his own case if an accidental death were now to come as anticlimax to his long and arduous preparation, and asks wistfully:

> Alas! what boots it with uncessant care
> To tend the homely slighted shepherd's trade,
> And strictly meditate the thankless muse?
> Were it not better done as others use,
> To sport with Amaryllis in the shade,
> Or with the tangles of Neaera's hair?
> Fame is the spur that the clear spirit doth raise
> (That last infirmity of noble mind)
> To scorn delight, and live laborious days;
> But the fair guerdon when we hope to find,
> And think to burst out into sudden blaze,
> Comes the blind fury with the abhorred shears,
> And slits the thin-spun life. . . .

Later, assuming that King like Milton himself, if he had continued with his clerical career, would have been a good and conscientious shepherd to his flock, Milton takes the occasion to attack the corrupt, ignorant, and worldly bishops by having St. Peter join in the mourning for his young minister, and say:

> How well could I have spared for thee, young swain,
> Enow of such as for their bellies' sake
> Creep and intrude and climb into the fold!
> Of other care they little reckoning make
> Than how to scramble at the shearers' feast,
> And shove away the worthy bidden guest.
> Blind mouths! that scarce themselves know how to hold
> A sheep-hook, or have learned aught else the least
> That to the faithful herdsman's art belongs!
> What recks it them? What need they? they are sped;
> And when they list, their lean and flashy songs
> Grate on their scrannel pipes of wretched straw;
> The hungry sheep look up and are not fed,
> But swoln with wind and the rank mist they draw,
> Rot inwardly, and foul contagion spread;
> Besides what the grim wolf with privy paw
> Daily devours apace, and nothing said;
> But that two-handed engine at the door
> Stands ready to smite once, and smite no more.

After these last ominous and prophetic two lines, Milton turns to the gentler lamentations of the wild flowers and the welcome no doubt prepared for Lycidas in heaven, and concludes, speaking of himself as singer of the song:

> At last he rose, and twitched his mantle blue:
> Tomorrow to fresh woods, and pastures new.

His plans, probably crystallized by his mother's death and his brother Christopher's marriage, which brought the young couple to live at Horton, had been completed for two year's of foreign travel.

He met and charmed all the leading intellectuals and artists in the major Italian cities and was, in 1639, planning to extend his journey but, as he later said:

> When I was preparing to pass over into Sicily and Greece, the melancholy intelligence which I received of the civil commotions in England made me alter my purpose; for I thought it base to be travelling for amusement abroad, while my fellow-citizens were fighting for their liberty at home. . . .

His return coincided with an interval of uneasy truce between the first overt actions of the civil war—two campaigns known as "The Bishops' Wars."

Although the actual conflict was between the absolute power claimed by the sovereign for his prerogative, and the rights of parliament, the despotism of the Established Church was recognized, on both sides, as the real bulwark of the monarchy. A few years later the famous *Eikon Basilike,* published by the royalists after Charles I's execution as his work, says:

> I find it impossible for a Prince to preserve the State in quiet, unless he hath such an influence upon Church-men; and they such a dependance on Him, as may best restrain the seditions exorbitancies of Ministers tongues, . . .

One of the more moderate divines of the Church of England declared that it was: "natural and consonant that kings should defend the rights of the church, and the church advance the honour of kings."

And in 1641, just after Milton's return, Edmund Waller, speaking in Parliament on the absolute necessity of maintaining the established church, declared:

> I look upon episcopacy as a counterscarp, or outwork, which, if it be taken by this assault of the people, and withal, this mystery once revealed, "That we must deny them nothing when they ask it thus in troops," we may, in the next place have as hard a task to defend our property, as we have lately had to recover it from the [royal] Prerogative. If, by multiplying hands and petitions, they prevail for an equality in things ecclesiastical, the next demand perhaps may be Lex Agraria, equality in things temporal.

The church was thus not only the major defense of tyranny but was also by far the largest single collector of taxes and compulsory fees from all, including the very poor, and a notoriously greedy unimproving landlord of tremendous estates.

The defeat of the king in the first Bishops' War, undertaken to impose the Episcopalian prayer book on Presbyterian Scotland, was therefore the occasion for vigorous attacks on the Established Church in England as well. When the Long Parliament met at the end of 1640, after the brief and inglorious "Second Bishops' War," 1,500 London citizens attended to present a petition signed by over 15,000, urging that the Episcopal Church government "with all its dependencies, roots and branches, may be abolished."

Milton who had, on his return, taken a modest house in London and begun quietly to teach his sister's sons and several other promising private pupils, was stirred to action by the controversy and wrote three powerful pamphlets—*Of Reformation in England, The Reason of Church Government Urged Against Prelaty*, and a series of polemic tracts in defense of a nonconformist publication called *Smectymnus*.

In the *Reason of Church Government* he describes his early life and intimates, as he more explicitly said on a similar occasion later, that his readers may well imagine:

> With what small willingness I endure to interrupt the pursuit of no less hopes than these, and leave a calm and pleasing solitariness fed with cheerful and confident thoughts, to embark in a troubled sea of noise and hoarse disputes, put from beholding the bright countenance of truth in the quiet and still air of delightful studies.

The "troubled sea" was, in truth, fraught with more dangers than Milton here implies. Three leading nonconformist ministers and many laymen of lesser note had only recently had their ears cut off; many more had been publicly whipped through the streets or set in the stocks; and several were indefinitely imprisoned in the tower "at the king's pleasure."

In this pamphlet Milton began, as so often in later ones, with a personal statement personifying religious freedom and dramatizing "her" demands on him.

> I forseee what stories I should hear within myself all my life after, of discourage and reproach: . . . when time was, thou couldst not find a syllable of all that thou hadst read, or studied, to utter in her behalf. Yet ease and leisure was given thee for thy retired thoughts out of the sweat of other men . . . but thou wert dumb as a beast; from henceforward be that which thine own brutish silence hath made thee.

He continued with a half apology for the prose form his present work necessarily had to take:

> Lastly, I should not choose this manner of writing, wherein, knowing myself inferior to myself, led by the genial power of nature to another task, I have the use, as I may account it, but of my left hand. . . . But were it the meanest under-service, if God by his secretary conscience enjoin it, it were sad for me if I should draw back; . . .

He urged the necessity of thorough reform and argued in a variety of ways against the idea of gradualism, concluding that section:

> Speedy and vehement were the reformations of all the good Kings of Judah, though the people had been muzzled in idolatry never so long before.
> And thus I have it as a declared truth, that neither the fear of sects, no, nor rebellion, can be a fit plea to stay reformation, but rather to push it forward with all possible diligence and speed.

Later he speaks with secular joy of "our time of parliament, the very jubilee and resurrection of the state."

In the controversial tracts of 1642 he again begins on a personal note but one of profound general relevance, saying:

> And because I observe that feare and dull disposition, lukewarenesse and sloth are not seldomer wont to cloak themselves under the affected name of moderation, then true and lively zeale is customably dispareg'd with the terme of indiscretion, bitternesse, and choler, I could not to my thinking honor a good cause more from the heart, than by defending it earnestly, as oft as I could judge it to behoove me, not withstanding any false name that could be invented to wrong, or undervalue an honest meaning.

A chief defense advanced even by those moderately critical of the bishops was that at least an established church prevented all kinds of sects, errors, and schisms which would otherwise disrupt the kingdom. Milton made a direct attack upon this argument, often evaded by the nonconformists themselves, and said vehemently:

> If to bring a numb and chill stupidity of soul, an unactive blindness of mind, upon the people by their leaden doctrine or no doctrine at all is to keep away schism, they keep away schism indeed; . . . With as good a plea might the dead-palsy boast to a man. It is I that free you from stitches and pains, and the troublesome feeling of cold and heat, of wounds and strokes; if I were gone, all these would molest you. The winter might as well vaunt itself against the spring, I destroy all noisome and rank weeds, I keep down all pestilent vapours; yes, and all wholesome herbs, and all fresh dews, by your violent and hide-bound frost; but when the gentle west winds shall open the fruitful bosom of the earth, thus overguded by your imprisonment, then the flowers put forth and spring, and then the sun shall scatter the mists, and the manuring hand of the tiller shall root up all that burdens the soil without thanks to your bondage.

His appeal was addressed especially to the waverers and middle-of-the-roaders on his own side, whom he exhorted:

> Let us not make these things [sects and errors] an incumbrance or an excuse of any delay in reforming, which God sends us as an incitement to proceed with more honour and alacrity: for if there were no opposition, where were the trial

of an unfeigned goodness and magnananity? Virtue that wavers is not virtue, but vice revolted from itself, and after a while returning. The actions of just and pious men do not darken in their middle course; but Solomon tells us, they are as the shining light, that shineth more and more unto the perfect day.

Finally, after an impassioned description of the heroic work of Wyclif and other early pioneers and martyrs for religious freedom, he concludes lyrically:

> O if we freeze at noon after their early thaw, let us fear lest the sun forever hide himself, and turn his orient steps from our ungrateful Horizon, justly condemned to be eternally benighted. Which dreadful judgment, O thou the everbegotten Light and perfect Image of thy Father, intercede, may never come upon us. . . .

(When we remember his approaching blindness this and the many other radiant images of light which star Milton's pages have a special poignance for us, no matter what the context is.)

In this tract, bitter and controversial as is its public tone, we find, as in all of Milton, many delightful private passages such as the one in which he refers to his prose, explaining to God that after the final victory has been won:

> . . . he that now for haste snatches up a plain ungarnished present as a thank-offering to thee, which could not be deferred in regard of thy so many late deliverances wrought for us, one upon another, may then perhaps take up a harp and sing an elaborate Song to generations. . . .

The "elaborate song," a great epic Milton was already meditating, was to be postponed through many full and troubled years, but in 1642 he evidently thought that Parliament had both the will and the power to settle affairs with little further trouble. In fact, in the course of the same controversy he elsewhere remarks:

> And indeed if we consider the general concourse of suppliants, the free and ready admittance, the willing and speedy redress in what is possible it will seem not much otherwise than as if some divine compassion from heaven were descended to take into hearing and commiseration the long and remediless affliction of this kingdom.

Years later, when in pain and blindness he had begun more correctly to measure the cost of the struggle both to himself and the nation, he would still speak with satisfaction of his entry into political conflict:

> I saw that a way was opening for the establishment of real liberty; that the foundation was laying for the deliverance of man from the yoke of slavery and superstition; that the principles of religion, which were the first objects of our care, would exert a salutary influence on the manners and constitution of the republic; and as I had from my youth studied the distinctions between religious and civil rights, I perceived that if I ever wished to be of use, I ought not to be wanting to my country, to the Church and to so many of my fellow Christians, in a crisis of so much danger.

However, in 1642 public affairs seemed well on the way to a successful conclusion and Milton turned to think of private ones. He was then almost thirty-five, warmly responsive to all physical beauty, and romantically in love, not, unfortunately, with any particular lady, but with the idea of the joyous companionship of a happy marriage.

Whether there had been some previous tentative arrangement between his father and hers, or whether it was simply a matter of the time, the place and the girl, he rode into the country to collect a family debt of £500 from an extravagant royalist, a landed squire, near Oxford, and returned a month later without the money but with a bride of seventeen, Mary Powell.

The marriage was from the first an unhappy one. The Powell family was strongly royalist, indifferent in matters of religion or learning, and Mary who was altogether unable to share her husband's interests, may well also have been frightened by his intensity. She sadly missed the continual social life and careless easygoing hospitality of her father's home, and less than a month after the wedding she asked permission to pay her family a visit. Once home, she refused to return.

John Aubrey, Milton's contemporary biographer, gives great weight to her royalist beliefs, explaining the divorce by saying: "Two opinions agree not well on one boulster."

It is certainly true that her return home coincided with the early royalist military victories and that she later claimed her mother urged her, on those grounds, not to return to her antiroyalist husband.

Milton, who held a happy marriage one of the great joys of life, who was both sensitive and passionate, and whose morality and pride were equally revolted by the very idea of illicit or casual lovemaking, characteristically integrated his personal beliefs and public actions. He scandalized both his religious and irreligious compatriots by the publication in the next two years of four closely reasoned hard-hitting pamphlets in favor of what is still today an advanced idea, that incompatibility was sufficient cause, and should be made legal reason, for divorce!

While he is concerned almost entirely with the husband's problem and thinks of the need for such relief as almost invariably masculine, he does say explicitly:

> Not but that particular exceptions may have place, if she exceed her husband in prudence and dexterity, and he contentedly yield; for then a superior and more natural law comes in, that the wiser should govern the less wise, whether male or female.

Furthermore, his whole idea of a good marriage, eloquently urged in each of the pamphlets, indicates his high respect for woman as an intellectual companion and comrade, rather than as merely a housekeeper, childbearer and bedmate.

For example, he says in *The Doctrine and Discipline of Divorce*:

> As no man apprehends so well what vice is as he who is truly virtuous, no man knows Hell like him who converses most in Heaven; so there is none that can estimate the evil and affliction of a natural hatred in matrimony unless he have a soul gentle enough and spacious enough to contemplate what is true love. . . . This pure and more inbred desire of joining to itself in conjugal fellowship a fit conversing soul (which desire is properly called love) is stronger than death. . . .

Again in the last of the four pamphlets, *Tetrachordon*:

> . . . there is a peculiar comfort in the married state besides the genial bed, which no other society affords. . . . We cannot therefore always be contemplative, or pragmaticall abroad, but have need of some delightful intermissions, wherein the enlarg'd soul may leave off a while her severe schooling; and like a glad youth in wandring vacancy, may keep her

hollidaies to joy and harmless pastime: which as she cannot well doe without company, so in no company so well as where the different sexe in most resembling unlikeness, and most unlike resemblance cannot but please best and be pleas'd in the aptitude of that variety.

As his custom is, he meets squarely the crucial question of a man's responsibility for making so serious an error, and answers it, with no fear of ridicule, showing concretely his own concern with the situation and the reasons for his tragic mistake:

> The soberest and best governed men are least practised in these affairs; and who knows not that the bashful muteness of a virgin may ofttimes hide all the unliveliness and natural sloth which is really unfit for conversation? Nor is there that freedom of access granted or presumed, as may suffice to a perfect discerning till too late; and where any indisposition is suspected, what more usual than the persuasion of friends, that acquaintance, as it increases, will amend all? And lastly it is not strange though many, who have spent their youth chastely, are in some things not so quick-sighted, while they haste too eagerly to light the nuptial torch; nor is it, therefore, that for a modest error a man should forfeit so great a happiness, and no charitable means to release him, since they who have lived most loosely, by reason of their bold accustoming, prove most successful in their matches, because their wild affections unsettling at will, have been as so many divorces to teach them experience. Whenas the sober man honouring the appearance of modesty, and hoping well of every social virtue under the veil, may easily chance to meet, if not with a body impenetrable, yet often with a mind to all other due conversation inaccessible, and to all the more estimable and superior purposes of matrimony useless and almost lifeless; and what a solace, what a fit help such a consort would be through the whole life of a man, is less pain to conjecture than to have experience.

Far from seeking to disguise his personal need for relief, he generalizes from the pain which did not create, but which made him conscious of, a wrong, saying:

> Indeed man's disposition though prone to search after vain curiosities, yet when points of difficulty are to be discusst, appertaining to the removal of unreasonable wrong and burden from the perplext life of our brother, it is incredible how cold, how dull, and fane from all fellow feeling we are, without the spur of self-concernment.

Although the basis of his argument is an appeal to reason and human kindliness the fashion of the time led him to quote scriptural authority after arguing each point. Thus, for example, referring to Adam's biblically asserted need of congenial companionship, he concludes:

> . . . ; the desire and longing to put off an unkindly solitariness by uniting another body, but not without a fit soul to his, in the cheerful society of wedlock? Which if it were so needful before the fall, when man was much more perfect in himself, how much more is it needful now against all the sorrows and casualties of this life, to have an intimate and speaking help, a ready and reviving associate in marriage? Whereof who misses, by chancing on a mute and spiritless mate, remains more alone than before, and in a burning less to be contained than that which is fleshly, and more to be considered; as being more deeply rooted even in the faultless innocence of nature.

The Protestant Churches did all admit the possibility of divorce for adultery and Milton reasonably protests that:

> The very cause that renders the pollution of the marriage-bed so heavy a calamity is that in its consequences it interrupts peace and affection; much more, therefore, must the perpetual interruption of peace and affection by mutual differences and unkindness be a sufficient reason for granting liberty of divorce.

Similarly, beginning with the Catholic admission of annulment for an unconsummated marriage, he argues:

> that indisposition, unfitness, or contrariety of mind, arising from a cause in nature unchangeable, hindering and ever likely to hinder the main benefits of conjugal society, which are solace and peace, is a greater reason of divorce than natural frigidity, especially if there be no children, and that there be mutual consent.

It is easy to ridicule the naivete and simplicity of Milton's public protest against a private grief, but while he made no pretense about the intensely personal nature of the trouble which had first turned his attention to the problem, that does not gainsay the justice of his position. One of his best nineteenth century critics, a later Sir Walter Raleigh, has summarized the matter with unusual insight.

> . . . ; he was a citizen first and a poet and an unhappy man afterwards. He directed his energies to proving, not that he should be exempted from the operations of the law, but that the law itself should be changed. . . . Thus even in this most personal matter he pleads, not for himself, but for the commonweal. He cannot conceive of happiness as of a private possession, to be secretly enjoyed; it stands rooted, like justice, in the wise and equal ordinances of the State; and the only freedom that he values is freedom under the law.

Of course parliament did not pass the law Milton indignantly demanded, and in 1645, after the decisive defeat of the royalist army, Mary's family decided that a Puritan son-in-law could be an important asset. They arranged matters so that Mary, surprising him at a relative's home, successfully begged for a reconciliation.

Her family as well as his own father, who had been living with the royalist son, Christopher, soon took refuge with Milton. While Mary bore him four children in the next seven years—she died soon after the birth of the last in 1652—there was evidently no joy in the marriage.

A letter to an Italian friend written soon after his own loved father's death in 1647 gives us a sad picture of his domestic life:

> It is often a matter of sorrowful reflection to me that those with whom I have been linked by chance or the law, by propinquity or some connection of no real meaning, are continually at hand to infest my home, to stun me with their noise and wear out my temper, whilst those who are endeared to me by the closest sympathy of tastes and pursuits are almost all denied me either by death or by an insuperable distance of place.

During the stirring early years of the parliamentary victories Milton had not, of course, confined his interests or activities to the discussions on divorce.

He had increased the number of promising students he accepted for instruction and had, in 1644, printed a short account of his system *Of Education*. In this he said: "I call therefore a complete and generous education that which fits a man to perform justly, skilfully and magnanimously all the offices both private and publick of Peace and War."

He felt that pupils should study: "the beginning, end, and reasons of Political Societies; that they may not in a dangerous fit of the Common-wealth be such poor, shaken, uncertain Reeds, of such a tottering Conscience, as many of our great Counsellors have lately shewn themselves, but stedfast pillars of the State."

He emphasized his belief that pupils should be: "stirr'd up with high hopes of living to be brave men, and worthy Patriots, dear to God, and famous to all ages."

While he describes what seems to us an extraordinarily demanding program wherein "they may have easily learnt at any odd hour the Italian Tongue," Milton relaxes into the conclusion:

> In those vernal seasons of the year when the air is calm and pleasant, it were an injury and sullenness against nature not to go out and see her riches, and partake in her rejoicing with heaven and earth . . . to ride out in companies with prudent and staid guides, to all the quarters of the land; learning and observing all places of strength, all commodities of building and of soil, for towns and tillage, harbors and ports for trade. Sometimes taking sea as far as to our navy, to learn there also what they can in the practical knowledge of sailing and of sea-fight.

On the whole, however, his system at best requires Miltons both as instructors and as students, and may be fairly enough characterized by his own summary:

> Only I believe that this is not a Bow for every man to shoot in that counts himself a Teacher; but will require sinews almost equal to those which Homer gave Ulysses; yet I am withall persuaded that it may prove much more easie in the assay, then it now seems at distance, and much more illustrious; . . .

In the same year, 1644, Milton wrote in protest against a parliamentary decree reinstating complete censorship of the press, his best known prose work, *Areopagitica*.

Aereopagitica—A Speech for the Liberty of Unlicensed Printing was dedicated "To the Parliament of England" with a freely translated motto from Euripides:

> This is true Liberty, when freeborn men
> Having to advise the public, may speak free,
> Which he who can, and will, deserves high praise,
> Who neither can nor will, may hold his peace;
> What can be juster in a state than this?

It summarizes Milton's belief in political action, struggle, and fearless inquiry, and his contempt for those who fear error or change more than they love truth.

It is starred with such memorable images as: "Truth is compared in Scripture to a streaming fountain; if her waters flow not in a perpetual progression, they sicken into a muddy pool of conformity." There are also powerful plain statements of direct experience like: "Where there is much desire to learn, there of necessity will be much arguing, much writing, many opinions; for opinion in good men is but knowledge in the making." And there is much biting contempt for bigotry: "Yet when the new light which we beg for shines in upon us, there be who envy and oppose, if it come not first in at their casements."

This magnificent plea for the freedom of the press includes the justly famous statement in which Milton forever rebukes all ivory tower artists and sheltered intellectuals:

> I cannot praise a fugitive and cloistered virtue unexercised and unbreathed, that never sallies out and seeks her adversary, but slinks out of the race, where that immortal garland is to be run for, not without dust and heat. Assuredly we bring not innocence into the world, we bring impurity much rather; that which purifies us is trial, and trial is by what is contrary. That virtue which is but a youngling in the contemplation of evil, and knows not the utmost that vice promises to her followers, and rejects it, is but a blank virtue, not a pure, her whiteness is but an excremental whiteness.

Throughout we feel the same deep personal concern in this pamphlet as in his arguments on divorce. As one of the best historians of English literature—The Frenchman, Taine—said a hundred years ago: "he spoke as a man who is wounded and oppressed, for whom a public prohibition is a personal outrage, who is himself fettered by the fetters of the nation."

On the three hundredth anniversary of Milton's birth, December 9, 1908, an interesting note appeared in the London *Daily News*. It said, referring to the abortive 1905 revolution in Russia:

> At the first sign of the stirring of a new life in Russia, translations of Areopagitica made their appearance, and hawkers sold them for a few kopeks to defy the censor in Nijni Novgorod. When a press was devised at Simla it was on the eternal reasonings of Aeropagitica that Mr. Gokhale based his opinions.

In 1788, the year before the French Revolution, Mirabeau published an article "*Sur la liberte de la presse, imité de l'Anglais de Milton.*" The entire edition was immediately exhausted, as were subsequent editions in 1789 and 1792.

In 1646, two years after *Aeropagitica*, Milton was deeply angered and concerned by the attempt of the conservative Presbyterian majority in Parliament to impose an Established Church of their own on the nation. Using his right hand this time, he wrote a sonnet "On the New Forcers of Conscience under the Long Parliament":

> Because you have thrown off your Prelate Lord,
> And with stiff Vowes renounc'd his Liturgie
> To seize the widowed whore Pluralitie
> From them whose sin ye envi'd, not abhor'd,
> Dare ye for this adjure the Civil Sword
> To force our Consciences that Christ set free?
> . . . .
> When they shall read this clearly in your charge
> New Presbyter is but Old Priest writ Large.

That year, 1646, he also began work on his *History of Britain* which would, he thought, be a practical contribution to statecraft:

> For if it be a high point of wisdom in every private man, much more is it in a Nation to know itself; rather than puft up with vulgar flatteries, and encomiums, for want of self knowledge, to enterprise rashly and come off miserably in great undertakings.

Although he watched the course of public events and the consistent left pressure of Cromwell's New Model on parliament with keen interest during the next two years, the only public statement we find is another sonnet, addressed to one of the great army leaders, Lord Fairfax. This shows Milton's growing awareness of the essentially self-seeking and corrupt policies of the upper middle-class bloc in Parliament, who became less willing to make concessions to their poorer allies as they saw military victory more fully within their grasp:

> Fairfax, whose name in arms through Europe rings,
>   Filling each mouth with envy or with praise,
>   And all her jealous monarchs with amaze,
>   And rumors loud that daunt remotest kings,
> Thy firm unshaken virtue ever brings
>   Victory home, though new rebellions raise
>   Their Hydra heads, and the false North displays
>   Her broken league to imp their serpent wings.
> O yet a nobler task awaits thy hand
>   (For what can war but endless war still breed?)
>   Till truth and right from violence be freed,
> And public faith cleared from the shameful brand
>   Of public fraud. In vain doth Valor bleed,
>   While Avarice and Rapine share the land.

In January, 1649, it had become clear that no firm peace could be made with Charles I, since it was impossible to rely upon his promises and there was ample evidence that he was attempting to secure the intervention of foreign armies to restore his sovereignty. The left and center sections of the parliamentary forces, dominated largely by Cromwell and his New Model Army, therefore determined to execute the king. The right wing were terrified at the audacity of, as Cromwell said, "cutting off his head with the crown on it," and attempted even at the last moment to achieve a compromise.

Even among those really convinced of the necessity of the execution there were many in Parliament who shrank from the direct personal responsibility of so unprecedented a regicide, one, moreover, which would surely be terribly avenged should any turn of fortune restore monarchy to England.

Milton, however, felt no such hesitation and immediately after the sentence had been pronounced began work on *The Tenure of Kings and Magistrates,* a powerful and effective justification of the impending event which was published only a few days after the execution. The argument he presents anticipated in extraordinary detail the basic reasoning of our own Declaration of Independence, and Jefferson may well have used it in some sort as a partial source of that manifesto.

The entire work expresses the most profound admiration of man's dignity and shows almost a solemn joy in the English people's daring so radically to assert it. It begins:

> It being manifest, that the power of kings and magistrates is nothing else but what is only derivative, transferred, and committed to them in trust from the people to the common good of them all, in whom the power yet remains fundamentally, and cannot be taken from them, without a violation of their natural birthright . . . it follows from necessary causes that the titles of sovereign lord, natural lord, and the like are either arrogancies or flatteries.
> . . . unless the people must be thought to be created all for him, he not for them, and they all in one body inferior to him single; which were a kind of treason against the dignity of mankind to affirm.

and that section concludes:

> . . . it follows, lastly, that since the king or magistrate holds his authority of the people both originally and naturally for their good, in the first place, and not his own, then may the people, as oft as they shall judge it for the best, either choose him or reject him, retain him or depose him, though no tyrant, merely by the liberty and right of freeborn men to be governed as seems to them best. . . .

There is, later, some discussion of those afraid to realize their own strength and righteousness:

> . . . who coming in the course of these affairs to have their share in great actions above the form of law or custom, at least to give their voice and approbation, begin to swerve and almost shiver at the majesty and grandeur of some noble deed, as if they were newly entered into a great sin.

A more bitter attack on the feigned kindliness of the upper bourgeoisie, the Presbyterians, concludes:

> If we consider, who and what they are, on a sudden grown so pitiful, we may conclude their pity can be no true and christian commiseration, but either levity and shallowness of mind, or else a carnal admiring of that worldly pomp and

greatness, from whence they see him fallen; or rather, lastly, a dissembled and seditious pity, feigned of industry to get new discord.

The voluntary publication of this work allied Milton more closely than anyone else outside the sixty members of Parliament supposed to act as judges—actually only some forty served—with the full responsibilities of the revolution. Its effectiveness led the Council of State—a smaller and more militant body than Parliament, with more substantial New Model Army representation—to offer Milton the position of Latin Secretary or Secretary for Foreign Tongues. This position he accepted in the spring of 1650, and, on the minutes of the Council, we find the many duties of correspondence, research and pamphleteering which he was assigned.

It is pleasant to record that the only one he did not fulfill was that of writing an answer to Lilburne's *New Chains for Old*, which sharply attacked many of the parliamentary abuses, of which Milton himself was critical. He was enough of a practical politician to realize, or at least accept, a compromise necessitated by the broad coalition of forces which had effected the revolution, but he never neglected an opportunity to press to the left, and he evidently found himself unable or unwilling personally to defend actions he personally condemned.

However, he soon had more serious business on hand.

Immediately after Charles' execution, the royalists had widely published an effectively sentimental religious little book with a frontispiece which pictured the king kneeling in prayer shortly before his death.

This book, which was falsely supposed to have been written by the king himself, purported to give an account of his meditations during the last months of his life. It had a tremendous popular appeal and was widely circulated. Milton was directed to write an answer to *Eikon Basilike*—the King's Book—which he did in *Eikonoklastes*—the King Breaker.

While the conventional form he followed, confuting paragraph by paragraph, makes this less representative than most of Milton's prose, we find every now and then such deeply characteristic thoughts flash out as:

> Truth is but justice in our knowledge and justice is but truth in our practice. . . . Truth is properly no more than contemplation; and her utmost efficiency is but teaching; but

> justice in her very essence is all strength and activity . . . and hath a sword put into her hand, to use against all violence and oppression on the earth. . . . She is the strength, the kingdom, the power, and the majesty of all ages.

The completion of this task led to a far more important one. A famous Latin scholar, Salmasius, had been hired by Charles II's friends abroad to write a book in Latin, entitled *Defensio Regia pro Carolo I*. This *Defense of the King* was a strong and comprehensive attack containing in its most damaging form the whole case against the commonwealth. It was widely circulated on the continent, where English was still considered a somewhat barbarous language, and English envoys sent word home from every court in Europe deploring its effect on England's prestige abroad. Milton was assigned to answer it.

He began his task with great enthusiasm but was soon compelled to heed the increasing deterioration of his always weak eyesight. Physicians warned him that the sight of one eye was already hopelessly destroyed and that only a complete respite from all such close application could save even partial sight in the other. His decision may be given in his own words:

> My resolution was unshaken, though the alternative was either the loss of my sight or the desertion of my duty.
> I considered that many had purchased a less good by a greater evil, the meed of glory by the loss of life; but that I might procure great good by little suffering, that though I am blind I might still discharge the most honourable duties, the performance of which, as it is something more durable than a glory, ought to be an object of superior admiration and esteem. I resolved therefore to make the short interval of sight which was left me to enjoy, as beneficial as possible to the public interest.

His completed work proudly entitled *A Defense of the English People by John Milton, Englishman* was published with enormous acclaim in 1651.

There was a great deal of personal invective against Salmasius' character and scholarship, which the controversial conventions of the time demanded, and which no more than matched the similar attacks Salmasius had already made on Milton. But the heart of the argument merits the dignity of the title.

Milton summarizes the people's case in many such succinct passages as:

> A most potent king, after he had trampled upon the laws of the nation, and given a shock to its religion, and begun to rule at his own will and pleasure, was at last subdued in the field by his own subjects, who had undergone a long slavery under him; . . . afterwards he was cast into prison, and when he gave no ground, either by words or actions, to hope better things of him, was finally by the supreme council of the kingdom condemned to die, and beheaded before the very gates of the royal palace. . . . For what king's majesty sitting upon an exalted throne, ever shone so brightly, as that of the people of England then did, when, shaking off the old superstition, which had prevailed a long time, they gave judgment upon the king himself, or rather upon an enemy who had been their king. . . . By his [God's] manifest impulse being set on work to recover our almost lost liberty, following him as our guide, and adoring the impresses of his divine power manifested upon all occasions, we went on in no obscure but an illustrious passage, pointed out and made plain by God himself.

In terms which recall Shelley's reminder, "the sacred Milton was, let it ever be remembered, a republican and a bold inquirer into morals and religion." Milton celebrates the worth of his countrymen:

> . . . that with so great a resolution, as we hardly find the like recorded in any history, having struggled with, and overcome, not only their enemies in the field, but the superstitious persuasions of the common people, have purchased to themselves in general amongst all posterity the name of deliverers: the body of the people having undertook and performed an enterprise which in other nations is thought to proceed only from a magnanimity that is peculiar to heroes.

Finally Milton restates the argument developed in *The Tenure of Kings and Magistrates*:

> So that wise and prudent men are to consider and to see what is profitable and fit for the people in general, for it is very certain that the same form of government is not equally convenient for all nations, nor for the same nation at all times; but sometimes one, sometimes another, may be more proper,

according as the industry and valour of the people may increase or decay. But if you deprive the people of this liberty of setting up what government they like best among themselves, you take that from them in which the life of all civil liberty consists.

The *Defense* was published in 1651 and by the beginning of 1652 Milton had become totally blind.

The death of his infant son and of his wife that spring seem to have occasioned no interruption in the performance of his duties, assigned or self-assigned, for in addition to his official work we find a sonnet written that May, with an impassioned appeal to Cromwell to prevent the renewed (and, soon, partially successful) attempt of the strong right-wing Presbyterian group to set up their own compulsory established church. It is interesting to note that from the tenth and eleventh lines of this sonnet the late President Franklin D. Roosevelt borrowed the text for one of his most profound and prophetic speeches.

> To *Oliver Cromwell*
> Cromwell our Chief of Men, that through a Croud,
>   Not of War only, but distractions rude;
>   Guided by Faith, and Matchless Fortitude:
>   To Peace and Truth, thy Glorious way hast Plough'd
> And on the neck of crowned Fortune proud
>   Hast rear'd God's Trophies, and his Work pursu'd,
>   While *Darwent* Streams with Blood of *Scots* imbru'd;
>   And *Dunbarfield* resound thy Praises loud,
> And *Worcester's* Laureat Wreath; yet much remains
>   To Conquer still; Peace hath her Victories
>   No less than those of War; new Foes arise
> Threatning to bind our Souls in secular Chains,
>   Help us to save Free Conscience from the paw
>   Of Hireling Wolves, whose Gospel is their Maw.

The conservative parliamentarians were, of course, neither unaware of, nor indifferent to, Milton's attitude, and they showed their hostility in many petty ways hoping, perhaps, to force a resignation which Cromwell would not permit them to demand.

Milton's request for the appointment of Andrew Marvell as assistant secretary to perform those duties his total blindness rendered impossible was refused, and he was grudgingly granted the help of another official not actually under his direction and, probably, unsympathetic to him. He was forced to surrender his official residence to a younger government employee of superior status and may, perhaps, have known of a semipublic apology made to a foreign ambassador for intrusting the translation of some important document to a "blind old man."

These slights must have been particularly painful to a man of the rather touchy personal pride and, indeed, vanity we often see in Milton. Nevertheless, he continued at his post, and at his self-appointed task of helping to keep Cromwell and his Council aware of the support and demands from the left.

In 1653 Cromwell was finally forced to take the drastic step of dissolving parliament, and assumed the title of Lord Protector.

This was, in effect, a virtual dictatorship but as Milton was perhaps even then writing of parliament in his still uncompleted and unpublished *History of Britain*:

> The votes and ordinances which men look'd should have contain'd the repealing of bad laws and the immediate constitution of better, resounded with nothing else but new impositions, taxes, excises, yearly, monthly, weekly, not to reckon the offices, gifts and preferments bestow'd and shar'd among themselves.

A year later we find in his *Second Defense of the People of England* a similar description addressed to Cromwell himself:

> But when you saw that the business was artfully procrastinated, that everyone was more intent on his own selfish interest than the public good, that the people complained of the disappointments which they had experienced, and the fallacious promises by which they had been gulled, that they were the dupes of a few overbearing individuals, you put an end to their domination. . . . In this state of desolation you, O Cromwell! alone remained to conduct the government and to save the country.

There is evident also in that work something of an apology for the necessity under which Milton finds himself, of accepting, temporarily, even a progressive sort of dictatorship:

> The circumstances of the country, which has been so convulsed by the storms of faction, which are yet hardly still, do not permit us to adopt a more perfect or desirable form of government.

The bulk of the *Defensio Secundo*, although it is ostensibly written in reply to an attack on Milton himself and on the argument of the first defense, is an amazingly outspoken warning to Cromwell on the dangers of dictatorship, and an appeal to him for the continued preservation of England's liberty.

After opening with a brief autobiographical sketch in defense against the personal slanders contained in this second royalist attack, Milton continues with extraordinary nobility:

> A grateful recollection of the divine goodness is the first of human obligations; and extraordinary favors demand more solemn and devout acknowledgments: with such acknowledgments I feel it my duty to begin this work. First, because I was born at a time when the virtue of my fellow citizens . . . in greatness of soul and vigour of enterprise . . . has succeeded in delivering the commonwealth from the most grievous tyranny. . . . And next because . . . I . . . was particularly selected . . . openly to vindicate the rights of the English nation, and consequently of liberty itself. Lastly, because in a matter of such moment, and which excited such ardent expectations, I did not disappoint the hopes nor the opinions of my fellow citizens; . . . For who is there, who does not identify the honour of his country with his own? And what can conduce more to the beauty or glory of one's country than the recovery, not only of its civil but its religious liberty? And what nation or state ever obtained both by more successful or more valorous exertion.

He described the acclaim with which the victory of English freedom and his own account of it had been greeted throughout Europe:

> I seem to survey as from a towering height, the far extended tracts of sea and land, and innumerable crowds of spectators, betraying in their looks the liveliest interest, and sensations the most congenial with my own. Here I behold the stout and manly prowess of the Germans disdaining servitude; there the generous and lively impetuosity of the French; on this side the calm and stately valour of the Spaniard; on that, the composed and wary magnanimity of the Italian. Of all the lovers of liberty and virtue, the magnanimous and the wise, in whatsoever quarter they may be found, some secretly favour, others openly approve; some greet me with congratulations and applause; others, who had long been proof against conviction, at last yield themselves captive to the force of truth. Surrounded by congregated multitudes, I now imagine

that, from the columns of Hercules to the Indian Ocean, I behold the nations of the earth recovering that liberty which they so long had lost. . . .

Then he turned to thank—and advise—Cromwell directly:

For you our country owes its liberties, nor can you sustain a character more momentous and more august than that of the author, the guardian and the preserver of our liberties, and hence you have not only eclipsed the achievements of all our kings, but even those which have been fabled of our heroes.

Often reflect what a dear pledge the beloved land of your nativity has entrusted to your care, and that liberty which she once expected only from the chosen flower of her talents and her virtues, she now expects from you only, and by you only hopes to obtain.

You cannot be truly free unless we are free too, for such is the nature of things that he who entrenches on the liberty of others is the first to lose his own and become a slave.

This exhortation he concluded:

Revere also the opinions and the hopes which foreign nations entertain concerning us, who promise to themselves so many advantages from that liberty which we have so bravely acquired, from the establishment of that new government which has begun to shed its splendour on the world, and which, if it be suffered to vanish like a dream, would involve us in the deepest abyss of shame; and lastly, revere yourself; and, after having endured so many sufferings and encountered so many perils for the sake of liberty, do not suffer it, now it is obtained, either to be violated by yourself, or in any one instance impaired by others.

In another section, addressed more generally to the leaders of the English people, he said:

War had made many great whom peace makes small. If after being released from the toils of war, you neglect the arts of peace, if your peace and your liberty be a state of warfare; if war be your only virtue, the summit of your praise, you will, believe me, soon find peace adverse to your interests. Your peace will be only a more distressing war; and that which you imagined liberty will prove the worst of slavery. . . .

If you think that it is a more grand, a more beautiful, or a more wise policy, to invent subtle expedients for increasing the revenue, to multiply our naval and military force, to rival in craft the ambassadors of foreign states, to form skillful treaties and allegiances, than to administer unpolluted justice to the people, to redress the injured, and to succour the distressed, and speedily to restore to everyone his own, you are involved in a cloud of error.

And he added advice which foreshadows Jefferson's "Educate and inform the whole mass of the people. They are the only sure reliance for the preservation of our liberty." His conclusion was an urgent request for the promotion of "education . . . the only genuine source of political and individual liberty, the only true safeguard of states. . . ."

In 1655 Milton was, voluntarily or involuntarily, relieved of most of the duties of his Secretaryship and granted a reduced salary for life—in actuality most likely a pension.

The sonnet "To Mr. Cyriak Skinner Upon His Blindness" (1655) gives a beautifully simple statement of Milton's feelings, his regretful love for the objects of sight, his harmless vanity which clings to the idea that he is at least not disfigured, and his serious consoling pride in the consciousness that his great sacrifice has accomplished its object, and is known to have done so!

> To Mr. *Cyriac Skinner.* Upon his Blindness
> Cyriac this Three years day, these Eyes though clear
>   To outward view of blemish or of Spot,
>   Bereft of Sight, their Seeing have forgot:
>   Nor to their idle Orbs doth day appear,
> Or Sun, or Moon, or Star, throughout the Year;
>   Or Man, or Woman; yet I argue not
>   Against Heaven's Hand, or Will, nor bate one jot
> Of Heart or Hope; but still bear up, and steer
> Right onward. What supports me, dost thou ask?
>   The Conscience, Friend, to have lost them over ply'd
>   In Liberties Defence, my noble task;
> Of which all *Europe* rings from side to side.
>   This thought might lead me through this World's vain mask
>   Content, though blind, had I no other Guide.

This is at least as moving as the better known sonnet written three years before:

> When I consider how my light is spent
> Ere half my days in this dark world and wide
> And that one talent which is death to hide
> Lodged with me useless. . . .

and is far more characteristic. Passive standing and waiting was never, for Milton, a congenial pose.

That year probably saw the beginning of his epic poem, *Paradise Lost,* to whose composition Milton had looked forward some twenty years before, when he wrote:

> I was confirmed in this opinion, that he who would not be frustrated of his hope to write well of hereafter in laudable things, ought himself to be a true poem; that is, a composition and pattern of the best and honorablest things; not presuming to sing high praises of heroic men, or famous cities, unless he have in himself the experience and the practice of all that which is praiseworthy.

He had set up equally demanding conditions for the prose historian, saying:

> One who would be a worthy historian of worthy deeds must possess as noble a spirit and as much practical experience as the hero of the action himself, in order that he may be able to comprehend and measure even the greatest of these actions on equal terms.

But he had already proved himself able to fulfill those, for as he wrote in the *Second Defense*:

> I have delivered my testimony, I would almost say have erected a monument that will not readily be destroyed, to the reality of those singular and mighty achievments which were above all praise.

Nor was this all merely self-praise. Milton's high regard for himself was largely the counterpart of his deep respect for mankind. Saurat, one of his most important contemporary critics, says: "His high opinion of himself is also a high opinion of man! It is also a high opinion of life as it might be lived on earth."

And in one of Milton's first published works we find:

> But he that holds himself in reverence and due esteem, both for the dignity of God's image upon him, and for the price of his redemption, which he thinks is visibly marked upon his forehead, accounts himself a fit person to do the noblest and godliest deeds. . . .

Nor does this faith in man's potentialities waver through all the bitter disappointments and disillusionments of his life.

It is pleasant here to remember that the virtual end of his public career found him enjoying a brief interlude of the kind of happiness he had never known.

In the end of 1656 he married the twenty-eight year old Katherine Woodcock. They seem to have been well suited and deeply devoted to each other and when, in February 1658, she and her infant daughter both died, Milton wrote for the wife he had never seen his only real love poem, the sonnet beginning:

> Methought I saw my late espoused saint.

That September there was another loss whose consequences to England, and perhaps even to Milton himself, were more far-reaching and catastrophic.

As we have seen, the bourgeoisie, having clearly won its struggle for power against the throne, had now little to fear from the monarchy and was, on the other hand, extremely afraid of any increase in strength for the lower classes whom they themselves had had to mobilize, as later in the French Revolution and ours, to help win their own victory. Even during Cromwell's lifetime there were many Presbyterian royalists who wished to reinstate the king, Charles II, now that he had, presumably, learned to know his place. It would then, they felt, no longer be necessary to keep the radical New Model Army in existence, or to fear the anger of the lower classes.

Cromwell's death in the fall of 1658 left the opposition to this bourgeois royalism leaderless; several generals of the New Model Army attempted to use their commands to bolster their personal seizures of power, and the left elements of the coalition both in the army and the nation had long been increasingly disorganized and officially voiceless with, as yet, no really solid class power to back up their demands.

Under the circumstances the weak attempt of Cromwell's peace-loving son to step into his father's shoes was foredoomed to failure, and the resurrection of the remnants of the old Rump Parliament, dissolved by Cromwell in 1653, was obviously also at best a temporary expedient.

Milton, who had been somewhat isolated in his blindness, semi-retirement, and growing disquiet at Cromwell's increasing concessions to the Presbyterians, had evidently no suspicion of the treacherous counter-revolution for which negotiations were already under way. With renewed hopefulness, in February 1659, he addressed *A Treatise of Civil Power in Ecclesiastical Causes* to the old Republican army leaders, urging the end of the established church which Cromwell had given state tax support, though no coercive powers. In May, the reestablishment of the Rump Parliament was greeted by another advisory pamphlet whose message is explicit in the title, *Considerations Touching the likliest means to remove Hirelings from the Church.*

By the end of that year it was, however, apparent that the coalition of former Presbyterians and Royalists was to be established on Parliament's terms, and that the complete Restoration of monarchy was only a matter of months.

At this point Milton stood, as his hero, blind Samson was later to do, sole champion of the liberty of his country.

Almost alone he raised his voice boldly against the imminent reinstatement of the monarchy. He spoke out first in a published letter to General Monk—who had, ironically, just completed negotiations with Charles II. Then he published an enlarged letter or appeal addressed to the new parliament, which had just been called into being to vote approval for the Restoration.

Finally, only a few weeks before Charles II actually landed in England, when practically every republican of note was fleeing the country or frantically attempting to obliterate the record of his past rebellion, Milton published a powerful pamphlet of remonstrance addressed to the last court of appeal—the English people themselves. This was a clarion call for continued resistance to tyranny and devotion to freedom.

The Readie and Easie Way to establish a free Commonwealth describes the sacrifices already made for freedom and decries the shame:

> . . . if by our ingrateful backsliding we make these fruitless;
> . . . making vain and viler than dirt the blood of so many thousand faithful and valiant Englishmen, who left us in this liberty, bought with their lives;

Again he reverts to this theme and passionately demands:

> Are the lives of so many good and faithful men, that died for the freedom of their country, to be so slighted, as to be forgotten in a stupid reconcilement without justice done them.

With no false self-consciousness he cites his own heroic example in speaking out for "that which is not call'd amiss The good Old Cause," and concludes with a desperate appeal:

> That a Nation should be so valorous and courageous to win their Liberty in the Field, and when they have won it, should be so heartless and unwise in the Councils, as not to know how to use it, value it, what to do with it, or with themselves; but . . . basely and besottedly to run their Necks again into the yoke which they have broken, and prostrate all the fruits of their Victory for naught at the feet of the vanquished . . . will be an ignominy if it befal us, that never yet befel any Nation possess'd of their Liberty; worthy indeed themselves, whatsoever they be, to be forever slaves; but that part of the Nation which consents not with them, as I perswade me, of a great number, far worthier than by their means to be brought into the same Bondage. . . .
> What I have spoken, is the Language of that which is not call'd amiss "The good Old Cause": if it seem strange to any, it will not seem more strange, I hope, than convincing to Backsliders. Thus much I should perhaps have said, though I were sure I should have spoken only to Trees and Stones; and had none to cry to, but with the Prophet, "O Earth, Earth, Earth!" to tell the very Soil itself, what her perverse Inhabitants are deaf to. Nay, though what I have spoke, should happ'n . . . to be the last words of an expiring Liberty. But I trust I shall have spoken Persuasion to abundance of sensible and ingenuous men; to some perhaps whom God may raise of these Stones to become Children of reviving Liberty; . . .

God made no sign, and on May 29, 1660, Charles II entered London to receive the homage of his faithful subjects.

Milton spent some months in hiding and was then, briefly, placed under arrest. His £2,000 in government funds—a major part of his estate—was confiscated and various other fines and special charges were imposed which, with the accidental destruction of his house by fire some years later, reduced his income to less than £100 a year. This made it impossible for him to command the secretarial assistance with which he had been composing *Paradise Lost* and completing his *History of Britain*, but considering his voluntary and avowed association with the execution of Charles I, the course the government followed was certainly a lenient one.

Charles II himself was a reasonable and unrevengeful man with a sound instinct against making famous martyrs. For reasons we must examine more closely in our discussion of the restoration in the next section, his course was one of great moderation. The few actual "regicides" left in England, who were barbarously tortured and killed, fell a victim to the animosity of their erstwhile colleagues in parliament—the conservative Presbyterians—who evidently could not rest until they had succeeded in physically destroying all the real republican leaders.

Milton's position was by no means secure. For some time he feared legal penalties, and for a much longer time received threats of assassination which must have been particularly distressing to a blind man. Although it was impossible for him to take any political action, he made no secret of his unchanged opinions. Taine summarizes his situation:

> Milton himself had been constrained to hide; his books had been burned by the hand of the hangman; even after the general act of indemnity he was imprisoned; when set at liberty, he lived in the expectation of being assassinated, for private fanaticism might seize the weapon relinquished by public revenge. Other smaller misfortunes came to aggravate by their stings the great wounds which afflicted him. Confiscation, a bankruptcy, finally the great fire of London, had robbed him of three fourths of his fortune; his daughters neither esteemed nor respected him; he sold his books, knowing that his family could not profit by them after his death; and amid so many private and public miseries he continued calm. Instead of repudiating what he had done, he gloried in it.

The rest of Milton's story is a great one, but soon told. Until 1663 his household consisted of his three daughters, the two elder of whom, then in their late teens, had been brought up largely by Mary Powell's royalist mother. She had expressed bitter animosity to Milton almost from the day of her daughter's marriage, and this had been intensified by his divorce pamphlets and the humiliation she felt when forced to urge her daughter to plead a reconciliation. Although Mrs. Powell and her whole family had been materially indebted to Milton during the years of the commonwealth, she persisted in claiming and, no doubt believing, that he could, somehow, have prevented the fines imposed upon her husband's estate as the penalty of his royalist political activities.

The two daughters were naturally affected by their grandmother's hostility to their father, and must have deeply resented it when the curtailment of his income forced their return to his austere and unhappy home.

His blindness combined with poverty forced him to depend on them not only for some degree of physical care but also for an enforced and uninterested assistance with his writing. There is some contemporary evidence for the story that they read aloud to him in languages they could only pronounce, but none for the idea that it was his wish rather than theirs that kept them in ignorance of all but the minimum accomplishment.

One of the young men who volunteered to read to him daily for some time wrote later:

> He, on the other hand, perceiving with what earnest desire I pursued learning, gave me not only all the encouragement, but all the help, he could. For, having a curious ear, he understood by my tone, when I understood what I read and when I did not, and accordingly would stop me, examine me, and open the most difficult passages to me.

The youngest daughter Deborah, born in 1650 or 1651, had evidently remained at home during Milton's brief second marriage and still spoke with warm affection of her father many years after his death.

We may feel deep sympathy for the unhappy young girls who conspired with the servant to sell their blind father's books, to buy small comforts he could not, or, they thought, would not, afford. But we must spare at least as much for the unhappy patriot living among his enemies, and for the poet who dictated his great epic, ten or twenty lines at a time, to "whatever hand came next"—many of them, as the manuscript shows, almost illiterate hands!

The older of the two nephews he had educated came as often as he could to correct punctuation and spelling, and Milton continued doggedly with his determined effort to "justify the ways of God to man." This objective is stated in the opening lines of *Paradise Lost*:

> Of Mans First Disobedience, and the Fruit
> Of that Forbidden Tree, whose mortal tast
> Brought Death into the World, and all our woe,
> With loss of *Eden*, till one greater Man
> Restore us, and regain the blissful Seat,
> Sing Heav'nly Muse. . . .

> . . . .
> . . . What in me is dark
> Illumin, what is low raise and support;
> That to the highth of this great Argument
> I may assert Eternal Providence,
> And justifie the wayes of God to men.

There were still several close friends who visited him at frequent intervals and one of those, his doctor, did much to remedy his domestic discomfort by introducing a young woman of twenty-four, probably a distant relative of his own, whom Milton married in 1663.

Her education and previous station were humble, and to us the disparity of age seems very great, but the marriage was evidently a happy one. The two elder daughters left home to learn the then very fashionable trade of gold lace making, and we have evidence from Milton's contemporary biographer, Aubrey, his nephew Edward Phillips, and others, that his home life soon settled into a comfortable routine. Two or three hours a day were devoted to singing; time was spent sitting out of doors whenever sun was available; and, of course, study and dictation continued daily under no matter what difficulties.

There are very few letters and almost no other directly autobiographical notes from these last fourteen years, but so personal a poet as Milton has left many revealing glimpses of himself throughout his tremendous epics—*Paradise Lost* and *Paradise Regained*—and his last great work, the triumphant tragedy of *Samson Agonistes* is in a sense pure autobiography throughout.

This is not the place to attempt the difficult and lengthy task of analyzing the still controversial *Paradise Lost*. E. M. W. Tillyard, probably the greatest living Milton scholar, and, more briefly, the novelist Rex Warner, in his excellent short biography of Milton, have written the most interesting recent interpretations of this great and, for modern readers, sometimes forbidding, poem.

Tillyard says in a general discussion of the biblical mythology which so puzzles many contemporary readers, but which obviously had a deep emotional connotation for Milton:

> Largely because of the power he felt in his own mind, Milton believed in the almost boundless possibilities of Man; in the Bible he found this expressed in the statement that God

made Man in his own image. But he sees also, has had it forced upon him by his experience, that actually there is a perverseness in men that brings them to failure without there being any absolute need of their failing. The Fall is a myth at once recounting the perverse nature of men and attaching to them the responsibility. This perverseness is common to all men: through Adam all have fallen. But there is still that in the human mind which can live down this perverseness and lead on to these possibilities: a few take advantage of this possible good. This idea is expressed in Scripture by the possibility of regeneration in Christ.

Rex Warner summarizes his interpretation of the poem by saying:

> Like Lycidas, the poem closes in perfection, but as one looks back over its great events one cannot help feeling that the loss of Heaven for Satan and of Paradise for Adam and Eve symbolise something even greater and wider than what they are intended to do in the successful scheme of the justification of God's ways. Revolt is in the nature of things and so is the violence and enchantment of sexual feeling. Both may lead to disaster, as Milton well knew, yet both are so strong elements in his own character that they command, even against his better judgment, his respect. True, that Satan, whose pride turns to malignity, is lost beyond redemption; yet the original pride was splendid. True, that Adam was more moved by feeling than by the strict injunctions of authority; yet his unhesitating acceptance of death rather than to desert his love has its own nobility. There is a sense in which here, as in all Milton's work, it is man rather than God who is justified. The loss of Paradise gives scope certainly for a greater exercise of God's love, but also for a fuller dignity in man. Such qualities as fortitude and endurance were scarcely required in a life devoted to gardening and love-making. Now they are required in a world "to good malignant, to bad men benigne." Also and even more are necessary those original sins in which Milton so profoundly believed and which can now take on the form of virtue—revolt against unjust authority, and the shared love which can both delight and console.

There are a few passages among the many in the epic carrying special biographical interest which we may stop to note. For example, the beautiful invocation at the opening of the third book, probably still written in the comparative contentment of his semi-retirement, 1655-1658, gives us a restrained but moving statement of what blindness meant to Milton even then, successful, respected and secure in a state he had helped build.

> Thus with the year
> Seasons return, but not to me returns
> Day, or the sweet approach of Ev'n or Morn,
> Or sight of vernal bloom, or Summers Rose,
> Or flocks, or herds, or human face divine;
> But cloud instead, and ever-during dark
> Surrounds me, from the chearful wayes of men
> Cut off, and for the Book of knowledg fair
> Presented with a Universal blanc
> Of Natures works to me expung'd and ras'd,
> And wisdom at one entrance quite shut out.
> So much the rather thou Celestial light
> Shine inward, and the mind through all her powers
> Irradiate, there plant eyes, all mist from thence
> Purge and disperse, that I may see and tell
> Of things invisible to mortal sight.

No one at all familiar with Milton's work can ever be unmindful of the constant loving references to the sun, the stars, and light itself, from his very earliest college poems until the end of his life.

In Book VII, written during his doubly dark days of exile, we find another more bitter reference to the now threatening dark:

> . . . though fall'n on evil dayes,
> On evil dayes though fall'n, and evil tongues;
> In darkness, and with dangers compast round,
> And solitude; yet not alone, while thou
> Visit'st my slumbers nightly, or when Morn
> Purples the East.

The growing dissensions of the commonwealth council were obviously judged with unsparing rigor by their Latin Secretary, who, in Book II, commented on the well-ordered plans of Satan's legions:

> O shame to men! Devil with Devil damn'd
> Firm concord holds, men onely disagree
> Of Creatures rational, though under hope
> Of heavenly Grace; and God proclaiming peace,
> Yet live in hatred, enmitie, and strife
> Among themselves, and levie cruel warre,

> Wasting the Earth, each other to destroy:
> As if (which might induce us to accord)
> Man had not hellish foes anow besides,
> That day and night for his destruction waite.

Yet although Blake, and Shelley after him, felt that as a true poet Milton was "of the devil's party without knowing it," Satan is by no means his hero. The later poets found themselves in a world they never made where the only attitude to be sustained with integrity was that of rebellion. For Milton this was not yet true. He had done as much as any man to make his world; it had been unmade by what he felt to be an accidental not an inevitable failure; and he identified freedom with the just law and order of an improved commonwealth, and not with the violence of a counter-revolutionary rebellion.

His identification with the one great angel, Abdiel, who refuses to fall with Satan but remains firm in his loyalty and faith makes it very clear that Milton was still emotionally far closer to feeling like an honored artist of the republic than an outlaw.

God, welcoming Abdiel, is evidently speaking to the still republican Milton when he says:

> Servant of God, well hast thou fought
> The better fight, who single hast maintained
> Against revolted multitudes the Cause
> Of Truth, in word mightier than they in Armes;
> And for the testimonie of Truth has born
> Universal reproach, far worse to beare
> Than violence; for this was all thy care
> To stand approv'd in sight of God.

Before completing *Paradise Regained,* in 1671, Milton published the *History of Britain* on which he had been working so many years before. It is interesting to note that in this first edition he omitted the strong criticisms of the Long Parliament which we have noted above. He had not come to doubt its justice—the passage was preserved for insertion in later editions—but he saw no reason to give the worse hated monarchy a stick with which to belabor its defeated opponents.

The work is of interest not only for its historical material but also for many shrewd psychological and sociological observations like:

> It is a fond conceit in many great ones, and pernicious in the end, to cease from no violence till they have attain'd the utmost of their ambitions and desires; then to think God appeas'd by their seeking to bribe him with a share however large of their ill-gott'n spoils, and then lastly to grow zealous of doing right, when they have no longer need to do wrong.

Milton's continued defiance of tyranny, and irrepressible tendency to advise men for their own good, are evidenced by a sentence he added, just before publication in 1670, to his discussion of the ease with which Romans, Danes and Normans had all, in former times, conquered England because of its internal divisions and injustice. He concludes with a stern warning:

> If these were the Causes of such misery and thraldom to those our ancestors, with what better close can be concluded, then here in fit season to remember this Age in the midst of her security, to fear from like Vices without amendment the Revolutions of like Calamities.

Paradise Regained, written in 1671, devotes its four books to a description of Christ's temptations in the desert. There is evidently much that is part of Milton's autobiography in Christ's description of his childhood studies and youthful ambitions, and there may well be a topical reference in its opening lines:

> I who e're while the happy Garden sung,
> By one man's disobedience lost, now sing
> Recover'd Paradise to all mankind,
> By one man's firm obedience fully tri'd
> Through all temptation, and the Tempter foil'd
> In all his wiles, defeated and repuls't,
> And Eden rais'd in the vast Wilderness.

But the great creation of Milton's old age was a far different poem—the only true "Greek Tragedy" in English, written about a hero of the Old Testament—*Samson Agonistes*. This must be read as a whole and is far easier for the average reader than any of Milton's other major work.

Samson who had first been betrayed by his cowardly countrymen when he stood as their champion fighting for the freedom of Israel, and who had then been more irremediably betrayed by his own besotted love for Delilah which enabled her to deliver him, weak and helpless, to the Philistines, is, of course, Milton from beginning to end. His miserable blind servitude among his enemies, his agonized longing for sight and freedom, everything except the last terrible triumph of his death is Milton. And the triumph itself is so imaginatively realized we are forced to share Milton's fierce longing that he too could bring destruction down upon the enemy at the negligible cost of his own unhappy life. We also share his tremendous sense of release in the imaginary accomplishment and must hope Milton himself was far-sighted enough to realize that with less than his two bare hands—with no weapon but his poetic imagination—he had created an engine which would help avenge his defeat long after his death. He would have rejoiced to know, for example, that in 1788, the year before the French Revolution, there were twenty-one editions of his great epic published in France!

He lived only three years longer and died peacefully in 1674, leaving all his small property to the wife who had cherished and comforted his old age.

Since in this brief account of Milton's work and life we have been forced almost altogether to ignore the many gentler qualities which so enriched them, we should perhaps include in this story of the patriot poet Rex Warner's reminder:

> Yet, if his great work is, as he wished it to be, "doctrinal to a nation," it is also in itself delightful. . . . One's enjoyment will almost certainly be marred if one thinks of him too exclusively as the blind and defeated patriot, the unflagging scholar, the austere educationist, the anti-clerical, the prophet of a creed of freedom. One should think too of the brilliant young man who astonished Italy with his wit and learning, of the poet who of all others, with the possible exception of Shakespeare, has written most beautifully of flowers and of everything that strikes the sense in an English landscape, of the vigorous believer in the possible goodness of life, who, so far from denying or belittling pleasure, made angels lovers and included in the wholesome delights of Paradise a "sweet reluctant amorous delay."

Although we may be sure Milton would have approved our thinking of "the brilliant young man" with a taste for all the delicate joys of life, he would have been both puzzled and indignant at any hint of a dichotemy that somehow set these qualities in opposition to those of the scholar-patriot fighting for freedom.

Milton did not write beautifully of flowers and friendship *in spite of*, or even in addition to, his militant struggles and heroic self-devotion. He wrote movingly of life *because* he loved it enough to fight for it; he fought for freedom because anything less betrayed the possibilities of human beauty and happiness.

Milton was a whole man, integrated in both his art and his life, and political in the highest sense in both. It is no wonder that every great progressive English poet since his day has claimed his inspiration.

THE RESTORATION

Although the House of Stuarts were installed on the throne in 1660 it was clear to Charles II as well as to his erstwhile opponents that essentially he ruled by the grace of Parliament and not by the divine right of kings.

All the points which had been at issue between his father and the bourgeoisie were explicitly or tacitly ceded by him, and while the Church of England was restored we have seen that the leading Presbyterians themselves (who now found it easy to reconcile their consciences to a friendly Episcopalianism) had already realized the need of an established church to support their state power. They were far more concerned about the dangerous agitation of unlicensed preachers and the subversive activities of nonconformist congregations than they were about the precise ritual of church service—or even about the appointment of bishops by a king, once he himself was, in a sense, their own appointee.

The reality of the situation was so apparent that the French ambassador wrote in a private report to Louis XIV "They think, because there is now a king, that this is a monarchy, but it isn't one." Charles himself, when his less astute brother urged him to punish their father's enemies, reclaim the estates lost by the royalists and, in general, "act like a king," replied succinctly, "I have no wish to start again on my travels."

He made the best of a hard bargain by getting as much money as he could to spend on his titled mistresses and illegitimate children, and assuaged his pride by flaunting an aristocratic debauchery and noble bastards in the face of outraged bourgeois morality.

His court was composed largely of those who had spent idle and dissolute years in exile with him, and of others who had similar reasons for spite against the solid bourgeoisie, and who gratified that spite as well as their tastes in doing all they could to mock and destroy the remnants of Puritanism represented by its personal morality.

The extravagance, intrigue and licentiousness of the court were truly indescribable. J. H. Wilson, a by no means unfriendly or censorious commentator, writes in his book on *The Court Wits of the Restoration Period* that, although contrasted with the general aristocrat and courtier of the time who "with almost complete immunity committed assault, theft, rape, or even murder," the wits were comparatively moral, yet:

> They all wore swords and occasionally used them. They all kept mistresses—ladies of fashion, actresses, miscellaneous willing wenches. Occasionally they drank too much, scoured the town, broke windows, and fought with the watch. They lived in a Godless world [perhaps even more important, in a functionless one as well] and sought their pleasure where it was to be found, certain of being able to "jump the life to come." Nor were they fearful of "judgement here"; their master, the King, was indulgent to their follies and sure to remit their fines. . . . Francis Math, Lord Guilford, a sober lawyer was seriously advised to "keep a whore" because he was ill looked upon at Court for want of doing so!

There are innumerable less authenticated incidents of the same nature as the one which legal records tell us caused Sir Charles Sedley, a leading court figure, to be fined and sentenced to a week's imprisonment. He had appeared naked on a balcony with two noble companions after a drinking bout at Covent Gardens, insulting passers-by with obscene language, and throwing wine bottles at the crowd which then gathered. The records do not verify what popular contemporary anecdote adds, that one of the noble companions, Lord Dickhurst, a member of Parliament, concluded the episode by saying loudly, "Come now, let us go make laws for the nation."

Nor were the ladies of the Court behind the gentlemen. Pepys casually comments in his diary: "Lady Shrewsbury . . . is at this time and hath for a great while been, a whore to the Duke of Buckingham," and there are a tiresome number of far less delicate comments on similar matters in the squibs, epigrams and lampoons with which the court was delighted. The "hero" of Congreve's play, *Way of the World*, wishing to please a lady, gets "a friend to put her into a lampoon and compliment her with the imputation of an affair with a young fellow."

It is not without reason that Wycherly (except for Dryden, perhaps the only other Restoration dramatist of any importance) intimates in his *Plain Dealer* that his heroine's impudence which could "put a court out of countenance" would "debauch a stews."

As we should expect, the only literature which came out of this background, beside a large number of more or less pungent lampoons or epigrams, and a few highly praised formal odes, was that of the licentious comedy of the Restoration theatre—a theatre set up as a part of the Court, officially ruled over by Charles' "Master of Revels," and having no further purpose than any other form of aristocratic dissipation. A gentleman of fashion in the theatre was privileged to cry aloud "Damnme, Jack, 'tis a confounded Play, let's to a Whore and spend our time better," and the playwrights, many of whom were themselves gentlemen of fashion, strove to use their wit and impudence as far as possible (and impudence alone beyond that point) so to amuse the Court audience and its hangers-on as to avoid such an unfavorable comparison.

The two most considerable achievements of the theatre were the plays of Congreve and Wycherly and, partly for their real wit and partly as a mirror of the age, it may be worth one's time to read Wycherly's *The Country Wife* and *The Plain Dealer*, and Congreve's later and more restrained *Love for Love*, *Double Dealer*, or *Way of the World*. Perhaps also the more typical plays of Etheridge, *She Would if She Could* or *The Man of Mode*, would serve to round out the picture for readers especially interested in drama.

If the froth of the aristocracy could provide no better soil for literature, the dominant bulk of the solid bourgeoisie were still less to the purpose. They maintained the pretence of a religion whose real emotion had been spent, continued to use the terms of a hypocritical and meaningless morality, and accepted for their own purposes the rule of a king of whom one of his own favorites unrebuked wrote:

> Restless he rolls about from Whore to Whore,
> A Merry Monarch, Scandalous and Poor.

A better known epigram was posted outside the bedroom door of one of the ladies of the court when Charles II was favoring her with his company:

> Here lies a pretty, witty King,
> Whose word no man relies on,
> Who never said a foolish thing
> Nor ever did a wise one.

For this the Earl of Rochester was publicly thanked by the king, who said that his words were his own but his acts those of his ministers!

The sons and grandsons of Milton's "slaughtered saints" could inded offer no inspiration to art.

It is, therefore, not surprising that the single great work of the period is that of a poor nonconformist tinker and unlicensed minister, three times jailed because he refused to stop preaching the truth as he saw it, and equally opposed to the dissolute extravagance of the Court and the worldly prudence of the bourgeoisie.

Although Bunyan was, in literary terms, by far the greatest of the seventeenth century "mechanick preachers" he was, of course, not a unique phenomenon but part of a deeply rooted and flourishing tradition whose essence his own personal genius enabled him to crystallize in the imperishable form of *Pilgrim's Progress*.

Jack Lindsay, in his excellent biographical study, *John Bunyan —Maker of Myths*, describes in general terms the development of this tradition.

> In England the first great bourgeois wave was at every point vivified by the Protestant idiom; and this unity proceeded up to the Civil War. After that war the inner rifts in the bourgeoisie, the increasing pressure of a dispossessed proletariat, destroyed the vital coherence of the Protestant movement; only with the lower classes did Protestantism remain a living force, compacting their resistance and submission till the day when they could begin to organize for a juster society. . . .
>
> We have seen how in 1649 there occurred the first grand division in the Protestant movement in England. The bourgeois, having won to power, renounced everything in Protestantism that savored of insurgency. . . .

Cromwell and Lilburne on the side of political action, Milton and Bunyan on the side of literary expression, were the four great figures embodying at highest tension the drama and meaning of the seventeenth century revolution. Bunyan gave voice to all the popular feelings of derelict despair, the general stupefaction and suspension that followed the failure of Lilburne, even among those who had not consciously identified themselves with the Lilburnean cause. He, more than any other man, transmuted the cloudy frustration into an ideological weapon of hope which served the masses well in the difficult century and a half awaiting them.

In these comments Lindsay evidently sees, as we have done, that the Restoration was only the logical conclusion to the reactionary course which the major part of the bourgeoisie had followed since the very moment of the king's decisive defeat. To understand the radical religious groups which Bunyan represented we must look back, briefly, to their formation under the commonwealth, precipitated by the revolutionary activities of the early forties, stimulated by the unredressed and, sometimes, increased grievances of the next decade, and protected by Cromwell's sympathetic policy of toleration until his death.

The preaching laymen who led the various groups of working-class dissenters were almost all essentially agitators speaking and, indeed, thinking, in the religious idiom of their time but directing their attacks against social abuses and the oppressors of the poor.

In *John Bunyan, Mechanick Preacher*, W. Y. Tindale, speaking of Bunyan's contemporaries and immediate predecessors, says: "In pulpit or market place they directed and inflamed the passions of the discontented, revealed the corruption of church, society and state, and extended to the vulgar the hope of justice or of baptism." He continues:

> But those saints whose troubles were social and economic as well as religious generally found their way to the company of the radicals, Quakers, Baptists, Fifth Monarchists or Ranters who promised a new society. Though for example the Baptists and even the Quakers secured the loyalty of some polite and eminent men, they claimed the adherence of innumerable laborers, small farmers, shop keepers, and artisans. It is improper, therefore, to ignore the social character of the radical sects or to treat purely as a religious and political revolt that which was also social and economic. The rise of the radical sects . . . gave expression and the hope of relief to men of

all classes, but especially to those whose difficulties were social or economic. The sorrow of the lower orders, which finds expression today in the secular creed of Marxism, embraced in the 17th century the comforts of radical Christianity, whose banners had sanctified the insurrections of the peasants and the revolts of the masses under John of Leyden at Munster.

This study which combines the too infrequently united virtues of scholarship and wit, proceeds to illustrate by an enormous number of lively quotations the fact that both the Presbyterian and Episcopalian attacks on these sects, and the retorts of their far from masochistic adherents, clearly recognized the class basis of the opposition. A judge trying itinerant preachers as vagabonds would declare, "this fellow would have Ministers to be . . . Taylors, Pedlars, and Tinkers, such Fellows as he is." And a lay preacher—who died in jail—would protest indignantly that Christ was a carpenter and Peter a Fisherman "But you cry out that we send . . . Weavers, Smiths, Cappers, Soldiers."

A Presbyterian minister in 1651, one of many harassed by the increasing swarm of articulate workingmen, preached angrily in his church: "Superiors must govern; Inferiors Obey, and be governed; Ministers must study and Preach; People must hear and obey. . . . Baking and Preaching, Nailing and Preaching, Patching and Preaching . . . will not hold." And a gifted cobbler retorted at an open air meeting: "If a Man have the Spirit of God, though he be a Pedler, Tinker, Chimney-sweeper, or Cobbler, he may by the helpe of God's Spirit give a more publique interpretation, than they all."

Attacks on the Ranters in the fifties spoke, truly or falsely, of their sexual orgies, but concluded with a more heartfelt if less picturesque indignation: "They taught that it was quite contrary to the end of the Creation, to Appropriate any thing to any Man or Woman; but that there ought to be a Community of all things."

And a Ranter, later forced to recant by a year's imprisonment in Newgate, justified this accusation by declaring: "Howl, howl, ye nobles, howl honourable, howl ye rich men . . . bow downe, bow downe . . . before those poore, nasty, lousie, ragged wretches . . . you have feared sword-levelling and man-levelling but now you will be levelled by me, the Lord, the real Leveller."

The Leveler leader, Lilburne, ended his life a Quaker, and Quaker preachers by the hundreds during the last years of the Commonwealth took as their texts economic equality and the specific oppression of rack-rent landlords in such sermons as:

Against all those who lay heavie burthens upon the poor by deceipt and oppression, and against all who live in pride and idleness, and fulnesse of bread, by whom the creation is devoured, and many made poor by your meanes, and you who are rich, who live at ease, and in pleasure, you live upon the labours of the poor, and lay heavy burthens upon them grievous to be born. . . .

Was the creature made for that end, to set your hearts upon them: to heape together, out of the reach of the poore and needy; and he who can get the greatest share, should become the greatest man; and all that have little, shall bow downe and worship him. . . .

Woe, woe, woe, to the oppressors of the Earth, who grind the faces of the poor, who rack and stretch out their Rents, till the poor with all the sweat of their brows and hard labour can scarce get Bread to eat, and Raiment to put on. . . .

It is not surprising that the Quaker preacher, in the words of one such who also died in jail, was considered: "a sower of Sedition, a subverter of the Laws, or turner of the World up-side down, a pestilent fellow."

A contemporary wit summarized the matter—as the universities saw it—:

> A Preachers work is not to gelde a Sowe,
> Unseemly 'tis a Judge should milk a Cowe:
> A Cobler to a Pulpit should not mount,
> Nor can an Asse cast up a true account.
> . . . .
> Let tradesmen use their trades, let all men be
> Employ'd in what is fitting their degree.

And an eighteenth century satirist reviewed the troublesome period:

> When tinkers bawl'd aloud to settle
> Church discipline, for patching kettle;
> No sow-gelder did blow his horn
> To geld a cat, but cry'd Reform.

The Fifth Monarchy Men shared with Bunyan's Baptist brethren the seditious belief in the millennium—that is, in Christ's coming, at least in spirit, to rule on earth for a thousand years *before* the end of the world; and unlike the Baptists, they felt that his way should be prepared by the propaganda of the sword as well as that of the word.

In 1661 the general confusion seemed to indicate a favorable opportunity for ending his unaccountable delay and smoothing his path by removing the wicked. A small group of enthusiasts in London went armed to St. Paul's, asked those there whom they were for and, on the reply "King Charles," shot one in the name of "King Jesus."

This hopeless riot was all too easily and bloodily suppressed, but although Bunyan and his colleagues honestly expressed their condemnation of such procedure it was as indicative of the basic social unrest and rebellion they represented as were the actions of the anti-Czarist nihilists, who used a different idiom but the same weapons, two centuries later.

Although even Cromwell had been forced to suppress the proponents of such direct action on a similar occasion years before, Lindsay is undoubtedly correct when he says:

> But meanwhile, in 1660, what the bourgeoisie wanted above all things was to have a sympathetically oppressive state which would allow them to make the fullest use of the Civil War gains and to crush the democratic manifestations which Cromwell tolerated and in so many ways encouraged.

He, more specifically, concludes, "Among the many reasons, the bourgeoisie wanted the King back so that they might put such men as John Bunyan in prison."

Paradoxically enough, then, we must look for the major literature of the Restoration in the work of those for whose suppression it was invoked, just as almost the only surviving literature of our own slave-holding South is still to be found in the magnificent songs of those on whose oppression it was built.

JOHN BUNYAN

John Bunyan was born at the end of November 1628, the son and the grandson of a tinker with, apparently, no specific knowledge of his more remote ancestry. His family has now, however, been traced back for over four hundred years, and it is clear that in the fifteenth and sixteenth century they were among the small independent farmers or yeomen who lost their land in the first enclosures and were forced lower in the world with each successive generation.

Both Bunyan's father and grandfather were named Thomas and there is a record of a Thomas Bunyan innkeeper in the same small village in 1547. However slight Bunyan's knowledge of his forebears he must certainly have known that they had once had, as their birthright, some portion of England's green and pleasant land.

His later repeated use in sermons of this symbol of the land as a precious birthright of which he and his people had been fraudulently deprived is, of course, based on the general practise of the time. Such admonitions as this from his *Heavenly Footman* are ostensibly directed only to the salvation of the soul and are part of the ordinary nonconformist pulpit usage:

> What is before you is worth striving for. As the men of Dan said to their brethren after they had seen the goodness of the land of Canaan, "Arise, for we have seen the land, and behold it is very good. Be not slothful to go and possess the land." . . .

But that usage was, in turn, based on the fact that the congregations were composed of innumerable poor rural laborers and village artisans, as well as of many city apprentices and "mechanicks" (working men) who had also been similarly dispossessed in the transition to a capitalist society.

As early as 1645 Lilburne had used what was evidently already a familiar term, in the title of his pamphlet: "England's Birth-right justified against all arbitrary usurpation, whether regal or parliamentary, or under what rigor soever."

Gerrard Winstanley, when arrested for his attempt to start a colony on the basis of a primitive agricultural communism, had declared:

> And is this not slavery, say the people, that though there be land enough in England to maintain ten times as many people as are in it, yet some must beg of their brethren, or work in hard drudgery for day wages for them, or starve, or steal, and so be hanged out of the way as men not fit to live on the earth?
> Before they are suffered to plant the waste land for a liv-

lihood, they must pay rent to their brethren for it. Well, this is the burden the Creation groans under; and the subjects (so-called) have not their Birthright Freedom granted them from their brethren who hold it from them by club law, but not by righteousness.

In the next century, as we shall see below Swift also used the same term in a similar appeal for the plundered and dispossessed of Ireland. And at the end of the nineteenth century Ruskin was still able to demand:

> Trade Unions of England—Trade Armies of Christendom, what's the roll call of you, and what part or lot have you, hitherto, in this Holy Christian Land of your Fathers?
> Is not that heritage to be claimed, and the Birth Right of it no less than the Death Right?

Of his immediate family background and education Bunyan says in his autobiographical *Grace Abounding*:

> For my Descent then, it was, as is well known by many, of a low and inconsiderable generation; my father's house being of that rank that is meanest, and most despised of all the families in the Land. . . .
> But yet, notwithstanding the meanness and inconsiderableness of my Parents, it pleased God to put it into their hearts, to put me to School, to learn both to read and write; the which I also attained, according to the rate of other poor men's children; though to my shame, I confess, I did soon lose that little I learnt, even almost utterly, and that long before the Lord did work his gracious work of Conversion upon my Soul.

Many of his generous biographers have claimed that Bunyan here modestly exaggerated his lack of social standing, but a less generous contemporary minister in 1659 attacked him as a "Wandering preaching Tinker . . . the meanest of all the vulgar in the Country," so that his description seems to have been reasonably accurate.

There seems to have been some early friction between Bunyan, who was an extremely robust, energetic, and self-willed youngster, and his father, and we learn that he was considered a reckless, vaguely rebellious youth, a ringleader in his companions' more dangerous exploits, given especially to extraordinarily foul and blasphemous language.

In 1642 both his mother and his only sister suddenly took ill and died, and when, barely two months later, his father remarried, Bunyan, not yet sixteen, joined the Parliamentary Army.

The fact that his half-brother, born the next year, was named Charles, leads us to suspect that the friction with his father may have been related, whether as cause or effect, to political as well as other differences.

After reenlisting twice Bunyan was, in 1647, honorably discharged and returned home, a nineteen-year old with a wife of whom we know little except his own statement:

> Presently after this, I changed my condition into a married state; and my mercy was, to light upon a wife, whose father was counted godly: This woman and I, though we came together as poor as poor might be, (not having so much household-stuff as a dish or spoon betwixt us both) yet this she had for her part, *The Plain Man's Path-way to Heaven*, and *The Practice of Piety*, which her father had left her, when he died. In these two books I would sometimes read with her, wherein I also found some things that were somewhat pleasing to me; (but all this while I met with no conviction). She also would be often telling of me, *what a godly man her father was, and how he would reprove and correct vice, both in his house, and amongst his neighbours: what a strict and holy life he lived in his day, both in word and deed.*

Although he was reconciled to his father, who helped him get the tools necessary to set up as a tinker on his own, neither his work nor his happy marriage enabled Bunyan to accept emotionally the world in which he found himself. We feel in his many accounts of his search for God during the next few years a search for the sense of vital purpose, fellowship and direction which he had briefly enjoyed in the army of "the good old cause."

He later wrote in his spiritual autobiography, *Grace Abounding*:

> Wherefore these books, with this relation, though they did not reach my heart, to awaken it about my sad and sinful state, yet they did beget within me some desires to Religion: So that, because I knew no better, I fell in very eagerly with the Religion of the times; to wit, to go to Church twice a day, and that too with the foremost; and there should very devoutly, both say and sing as others did, yet retaining my wicked life: But withal, I was so over-run with the spirit of Superstition, that I adored, and that with great devotion, even all things (both the High-place Priest, Clerk, Vestments, Service, and

what else) belonging to the Church; counting all things holy, that were therein contained; and especially, the Priest and Clerk most happy, and without doubt, greatly blessed, because they were the Servants, as I then thought, of God; and were principal in the holy Temple, to do his work therein.

This conceit grew so strong, in little time, upon my spirit, that had I but seen a Priest (though never so sordid and debauched in his life) I should find my spirit fall under him, reverence him, and knit unto him; yea, I thought, for the love I did bear unto them (supposing they were the Ministers of God) I could have lain down at their feet, and have been trampled upon by them; their Name, their Garb, and Work did so intoxicate and bewitch me.

After I had been thus for some considerable time, another thought came in my mind; and that was, Whether *wê* were of the *Israelites,* or no? For finding in the Scriptures, that they were once the peculiar people of God, thought I, If I were once of this race, my Soul must needs be happy. Now again I found within me a great longing to be resolved about this Question, but could not tell how I should: At last, I asked my father of it; who told me, *No, we were not.* Wherefore then I fell in my spirit, as to the hopes of that, and so remained.

Seeking for a more purposeful and dedicated way of life, and no doubt strongly influenced by memories of the army in which nonconformist, lay preachers of all kinds abounded and spoke as the spirit moved them, Bunyan began a two-and-a-half year internal struggle "for grace."

This army was probably the only one in the world where a near-riot was ever started—as it was in Bunyan's regiment—by a sermon preached on Infant Baptism, An official of the town in which it was stationed explained to a gentleman who protested against such unlicensed preaching by soldiers: "Sir, I assure you, if they have not leave to preach they will not fight; and if they fight not, we must all fly the land and be gone."

Bunyan may have heard, and certainly knew prototypes of, the Colonel who declared at an army council: "The poorest he that is in England hath a life to live as the greatest he. . . . Everyman that is to live under a Government ought first by his own consent to put himself under that government."

It is not surprising that in the years immediately after his return to the narrow, remote village life, he felt, as he tells us, utterly lost, cast away, in short, "damned." Looking for the guilt which had called down this judgment, he found it in such irrelevancies as playing one-a-cat with other young men of the village, dancing, and even bell-ringing for the church.

This last seemingly harmless indulgence was one he found it particularly difficult to give up, and we might well account his agonies about that generally approved amusement as a purely personal idiosyncrasy if it were not for such passages as this; which we find in the journals of his contemporary, the great Quaker leader, George Fox, and others:

> The black earthly spirit of the priests wounded my life; and when I heard the bell toll to call people together to the steeple-house, it struck at my life; for it was just a market-bell, to gather people together that the priest might set forth his wares to sale. Oh! the vast sums of money that are gotten by the trade they make of selling the Scriptures; and by their preaching, from the highest bishop to the lowest priest. . . .

In July 1650, his wife gave birth to a blind baby whom Bunyan had christened Mary and whom, as we shall see, he loved with extraordinary tenderness. Shortly thereafter he experienced, in his own terms, an even more significant birth, or, rather, rebirth. He tells us:

> But upon a day, the good Providence of God did cast me to *Bedford*, to work on my Calling; and in one of the streets of that Town, I came where there were three or four poor women sitting at a door, in the Sun, talking about the things of God; and being now willing to hear them discourse, I drew near to hear what they said, for I was now a brisk Talker also myself, in the matters of Religion: But I may say, *I heard, but I understood not*; for they were far above, out of my reach: . . .
>
> And me-thought they spake, as if joy did make them speak; they spake with such pleasantness of Scripture-language, and with such appearance of Grace in all they said, that they were to me, as if they had found a new world, as if they were *people that dwelt alone, and were not to be reckoned amongst their Neighbours*. Numb. 23.9. . . .
>
> Therefore I should often make it my business to be going again and again into the company of these poor people, for I could not stay away; and the more I went amongst them, the more I did question my condition; and, as I still do remember, presently I found two things within me, at which I did sometimes marvel. . . .

His mental struggles continued for another year or two, but sometime in 1653 he found himself—and was found—fit to join the fellowship of the small Baptist church, and after the birth of his second daughter, Elizabeth, in 1654, he moved his family into Bedford to live as fully as possible with the group of which he had become part.

Such small nonconformist groups formed actual communities rather than mere church congregations, as any study of the minute books in which they recorded the work of their meetings shows us. The relation of their members to each other and the completely democratic community of which they formed a part resembled the life of such utopian nineteenth century colonies as Alcott's Brook Farm and Owen's New Harmony, rather than that of any purely religious group we know. They were, however, composed almost entirely of working people rather than intellectuals, were far more practically rooted in the economic life of their place and time, and carried on a militant and realistic though losing propaganda fight against its values.

Lindsay in his analysis of *Pilgrim's Progress* speaks of Bunyan's relation to this "fellowship," as he himself repeatedly called it, when he says:

> The Celestial City is the dream of all England, all the world, united in Fellowship. Meanwhile there was, for Bunyan, the little congregation of Bedford who were doing their best in a world of distorting pressures.
>
> They [the Independent churches] were, so to speak, constructions *outside society* of what the people felt that society lacked and must continue to lack while operated on a class basis.

It was in this atmosphere of democratic activity that Bunyan wrote his third book—*A Few Sighs from Hell.* It is lurid with hell-terror—and that is the expression of the sense of dissatisfaction and instability, of ceaseless crisis, resulting from the fact that the democratization was based on an outside—society formulation, not on a concrete social order. But it is also a healthy warning to the wealthy classes, the cause of the instability. It is built on the parable of Lazarus and Dives, the poor man who goes to heaven and the heart-less rich man who goes to hell. For if the upper classes were watching with fear masked as scorn the irruption of mechanics into places reserved for their betters, the lower classes were retorting distrust for distrust.

The next few years for Bunyan were strenuous but happy ones. He rapidly became an extremely active and much respected member of the group, discovered a gift for preaching which was recognized and admired by his brethren, and even developed a certain facility with his pen in the course of a number of satisfactorily violent controversies with more educated ministers who were "angry with the Tinker, because he strives to mend Souls as well as Kettles and Pans."

These attacks on lay preachers represented much more than personal jealousy. As Lindsay says:

> The insistence of the masses on their right to think and preach their own religion was an essential part of the revolutionary movement. For such a claim undermined the whole ideology of absolutism. Nothing astonished and outraged the reactionaries so much as the spectacle of a working-man in the pulpit. . . . [A contemporary Restoration historian] never loses a chance to mention the appearance of a weaver, tapster, pedlar, mason, or such as a preacher.

And Bunyan loses no opportunity to vaunt his class consciousness in attacking the learned ministers' addiction to classical quotations and aristocratic manners whereas Christ, he insists, "was born in a stable, laid in a manger, earned his bread with his labour, being by trade a carpenter."

A landed proprietor who, as Parliamentary Chaplain in 1640, had then joined the fight against the bishops, sadly remarked: "We intended not to dig down the banks, or pull up the hedge and lay all waste and common when we desired the prelate's tyranny might cease," and later added, more bitterly, "If any would raise an army to extirpate knowledge and religion the Tinkers and Sowgarters and crate carryers and beggars and bargemen and all the rabble that cannot reade . . . will be the forwardest to come to such a militia."

In 1659, after the birth of two sons, Bunyan's wife died and he, left with four young children, remarried a year later. His choice was again a happy one. Elizabeth, although then only a girl in her teens, soon proved herself a woman of extraordinary spirit and devotion and played a part not less heroic than Bunyan's own in the difficult years upon which they were entering.

In May, 1660, Charles II had been restored to the throne, having first made a general promise of political amnesty and religious toleration. He was willing enough to keep both promises as long as they cost him nothing, but the Presbyterians who were, as we have seen, unable to feel safe until they had secured the death of the few remaining revolutionary leaders, were also most anxious to use the reestablished church as a means for silencing the criticism of the poor, and buttressing the position of the wealthy.

To Charles' mild reminder that he had promised "no forcing of tender consciences," Parliament replied brusquely that "a schismatical conscience was not a tender conscience," and went to work with a will.

Bunyan had the honor not only of being one of the first sufferers under the new law forbidding unlicensed preaching, but of suffering from it before it was actually passed!

His preaching from 1658-1660 had aroused increasing attention from the authorities in his neighborhood and one of the sermons which was published under the title of *The Rich Man and Lazarus* survives to show us why. It is easy to imagine the attitude a magistrate who was also a large landlord would take to such passages as this one, preached in the year of Cromwell's death:

> Oh, what red lines will there be against all those rich ungodly landlords that so keep under their poor tenants that they dare not go out to hear the word for fear that their rent should be raised or they turned out of their houses. Think on this, you drunken rich, and scornful landlords; think on this, you mad brained blasphemous husbands, that are against the godly and chaste conversation of your wives; also you that hold your servants so hard to it that you will not spare them time to hear the Word, unless it will be where and when your lusts will let you . . . the rich man cries to "scrubbed beggarly Lazarus": "What shall I dishonor my fair sumptuous and gay house with such a creephedge as he?" The Lazaruses are not allowed to warn them of the wrath to come, because they are not gentlemen, because they cannot with Pontius Pilate speak Hebrew, Greek and Latin. Nay, they must not, shall not, speak to them, and all because of this.

Before Parliament had actually passed any law against unlicensed preachers, although they had already ordered the compulsory use of the established Common Prayer Book in all regular church services, and were obviously intending to forbid any irregular ones, the neighborhood magistrate had issued a warrant for the arrest of "One Bunyan of Bedford, tinker."

On November 12, 1660, when he arrived at a friend's farmhouse where he had promised to preach, Bunyan's host warned him of the warrant, and urged him to dismiss the meeting being, as Bunyan said, "more afraid of me, than of himself, for he knew better than I what spirit they [the magistrates] were of, living by them."

Bunyan goes on to say:

> After I walked into the close, where I somewhat seriously considering the matter, this came into my mind: That I had shewed myself hearty and couragious in my preaching, and had, blessed be Grace, made it my business to encourage others; therefore thought I, if I should now run, and make an escape, it will be of a very ill savour in the country. For what will my weak and newly converted brethren think of it? But that I was not so strong in deed, as I was in word. Also I feared that if I should run now there was a warrant out for me, I might by so doing make them afraid to stand, when great words only should be spoken to them. Besides I thought, that seeing God of his mercy should chuse me to go upon the forlorn hope in this country; that is, to be the first, that should be opposed, for the Gospel; if I should fly, it might be a discouragement to the whole body that might follow after. And further, I thought the world thereby would take occasion at my cowardliness, to have blasphemed the Gospel, and to have had some ground to suspect worse of me and my profession, than I deserved. These things, with others considered by me, I came in again to the house, with a full resolution to keep the meeting, and not to go away, though I could have been gone about an hour before the officer apprehended me; but I would not; for I was resolved to see the utmost of what they could say or do unto me: For blessed be the Lord, I knew of no evil that I had said or done. And so, as aforesaid, I begun the meeting: But being prevented by the constable's coming in with his warrant to take me, I could not proceed: But before I went away, I spake some few words of counsel and encouragement to the people, declaring to them, that they see we was prevented of our opportunity to speak and hear the word of God, and was like to suffer for the same: desiring them that they should not be discouraged. . . .

Arrested, he was brought before the magistrate who had, perhaps, some qualms at the legality of his action since he arranged for a number of people, including a lawyer and a clergyman, to argue with Bunyan in an attempt to secure his promise that if released he would not again attempt to preach.

Bunyan naturally refused to make such a promise, and entered on several interesting debates, of which he wrote a detailed account in his *Relation of Imprisonment*.

Although, as he correctly indicates, he won the debates, he lost the argument, being remanded to jail for seven weeks until the next quarter session meeting of the county court.

At the trial he continued the argument with the members of the bench who finally declared that by arguing, he had confessed his guilt, and sentenced him to three months imprisonment; after this, if there were another similar offense, he would be banished and, if again found in the realm, hanged.

The illegality of his trial was compounded when at the end of three months, on his refusal to promise that he would, if released, refrain from preaching, he was simply kept in jail with no opportunity to commit a second offense, until such time as he might change his mind!

Although he knew nothing of his legal rights and had no way to enforce them, he directed a number of energetic attempts, carried out with extraordinary courage and spirit by his young wife, to secure a hearing. His own relation gives us a remarkably objective account of her final attempt.

> Now at that assizes, because I would not leave any possible means unattempted that might be lawful; I did, by my wife, present a petition to the Judges three times, that I might be heard, and that they would impartially take my case into consideration.
>
> The first time my wife went, she presented it to Judge *Hales*, who very mildly received it at her hand, telling her that he would do her and me the best good he could; but he feared, he said, he could do none. The next day again, least they should, through the multitude of business forget me, we did throw another petition into the coach to Judge *Twisdon*; who, when he had seen it, snapt her up, and angrily told her that I was a convicted person, and could not be released, unless I would promise to preach no more, etc.
>
> Well, after this, she yet again presented another to Judge *Hales* as he sate on the bench, who, as it seemed, was willing to give her audience. Only Justice *Chester* being present, stept up and said, that I was convicted in the court, and that I was a hot spirited fellow (or words to that purpose) whereat

he waved it, and did not meddle therewith. But yet, my wife being encouraged by the High Sheriff, did venture once more into their presence (as the poor widow did to the unjust Judge) to try what she could do with them for my liberty, before they went forth of the town. The place where she went to them, was to the *Swan Chamber*, where the two Judges, and many Justices and Gentry of the country, was in company together. She then coming into the chamber with a bashed face, and a trembling heart, began her errand to them in this manner.

Woman. My Lord, (directing herself to Judge *Hales*) I make bold to come once again to your Lordship to know what may be done with my husband.

Judge Hales. To whom he said, Woman, I told thee before I could do thee no good; because they have taken that for a conviction which thy husband spoke at the sessions: And unless there be something done to undo that, I can do thee no good.

Woman. My Lord, said she, he is kept unlawfully in prison, they clap'd him up before there were any proclamation against the meetings; the indictment also is false: Besides, they never asked him whether he was guilty or no; neither did he confess the indictment.

One of the Justices. Then one of the Justices that stood by, whom she knew not, said, My Lord, he was lawfully convicted.

Wom. It is false, said she; for when they said to him, do you confess the indictment? He said only this, that he had been at several meetings, both where there was preaching the word, and prayer, and that they had God's presence among them.

Judge Twisdon. Whereat Judge *Twisdon* answered very angrily, saying, what you think we can do what we list; your husband is a breaker of the peace, and is convicted by the law, etc. Whereupon Judges *Hales* called for the Statute Book.

Wom. But said she, my Lord, he was not lawfully convicted.

Chester. Then Justice *Chester* said, my Lord, he was lawfully convicted.

Wom. It is false, said she; it was but a word of discourse that they took for a conviction (as you heard before.)

Chester. But it is recorded, woman, it is recorded, said Justice *Chester*. As if it must be of necessity true because it was recorded. With which words he often endeavoured to stop her mouth, having no other argument to convince her, but it is recorded, it is recorded.

Wom. My Lord, said she, I was a-while since at *London*, to see if I could get my husband's liberty, and there I spoke with my Lord Barkwood, one of the house of Lords, to whom

I delivered a petition, who took it of me and presented to some of the rest of the house of Lords, for my husband's releasement; who, when they had seen it, they said, that they could not release him, but had committed his releasement to the Judges, at the next assizes. This he told me; and now I come to you to see if any thing may be done in this business, and you give neither releasement nor relief. To which they gave her no answer, but made as if they heard her not.

Chest. Only Justice *Chester* was often up with this, He is convicted, and it is recorded.

Woman. If it be, it is false, said she.

Chest. My Lord, said Justice *Chester*, he is a pestilent fellow, there is not such a fellow in the country again.

Twis. What, will your husband leave preaching? If he will do so, then send for him.

Wom. My Lord, said she, he dares not leave preaching, as long as he can speak.

Twis. See here, what should we talk any more about such a fellow? Must he do what he lists? He is a breaker of the peace.

Wom. She told him again, that he desired to live peaceably, and to follow his calling, that his family might be maintained; and moreover said, my Lord, I have four small children, that cannot help themselves, of which one is blind, and have nothing to live upon, but the charity of good people.

Hales. Hast thou four children? said Judge Hales; thou art but a young woman to have four children.

Wom. My Lord, said she, I am but mother-in-law to them, having not been married to him yet full two years. Indeed I was with child when my husband was first apprehended: But being young and unaccustomed to such things, said she, I being smayed at the news, fell into labour, and so continued for eight days, and then was delivered, but my child died.

Hales. Whereat, he looking very soberly on the matter said, Alas poor woman!

Twis. But Judge *Twisdon* told her, that she made poverty her cloak; and said, moreover, that he understood, I was maintained better by running up and down a preaching, than by following my calling.

Hales. What is his calling? said Judge *Hales*.

Answer. Then some of the company that stood by, said, A Tinker, my Lord.

Wom. Yes, said she, and because he is a Tinker, and a poor man; therefore he is despised, and cannot have justice.

Hales. Then Judges *Hales* answered, very mildly, saying, I tell thee, woman, seeing it is so, that they have taken what thy husband spake, for a conviction; thou must either apply thyself to the King, or sue out his pardon, or get a writ of error.

Chest. But when Justice *Chester* heard him give her this

counsel; and especially (as she supposed) because he spoke of a writ of error, he chaffed, and seemed to be very much offended; saying, my Lord, he will preach and do what he lists.

Wom. He preacheth nothing but the word of God, said she.

Twis. He preach the word of God! said *Twisdon* (and withal, she thought he would have struck her) he runneth up and down, and doth harm.

Wom. No, my Lord, said she, it's not so, God hath owned him, and done much good by him.

Twis. God! said he, his doctrine is the doctrine of the Devil.

Wom. My Lord, said she, when the righteous judge shall appear, it will be known, that his doctrine is not the doctrine of the Devil.

Twis. My Lord, said he, to Judge *Hales,* do not mind her, but send her away.

Hales. Then said Judge *Hales,* I am sorry, woman, that I can do thee no good; thou must do one of these three things aforesaid, namely: either to apply thyself to the King, or sue out his pardon, or get a writ of error; but a writ of error will be cheapest.

Wom. At which *Chester* again seemed to be in a chaffe, and put off his hat, and as she thought, scratched his head for anger: But when I saw, said she, that there was no prevailing to have my husband sent for, though I often desired them that they would send for him, that he might speak for himself, telling them, that he could give them better satisfaction than I could, in what they demanded of him; with several other things, which now I forget; only this I remember, that though I was somewhat timerous at my first entrance into the chamber, yet before I went out, I could not but break forth into tears, not so much because they were so hard-hearted against me, and my husband, but to think what a sad account such poor creatures will have to give at the coming of the Lord, when they shall there answer for all things whatsoever they have done in the body, whether it be good, or whether it be bad.

So, when I departed from them, the book of Statute was brought, but what they said of it, I know nothing at all, neither did I hear any more from them.

On these grounds Bunyan was kept in jail for the next six years, knowing that he could at any time secure freedom by giving up his stand for free speech. He said that the parting from his wife and children:

> hath often been to me in this place, as the pulling the Flesh from my Bones; and that not only because I am somewhat

too too fond of these great Mercies, but also because I should have often brought to my mind the many hardships, miseries and wants that my poor Family was like to meet with, should I be taken from them, *especially my poor blind Child*, who lay nearer my heart then all I had besides; O the thoughts of the hardship I thought my blind one might go under, would break my heart to pieces.

Poor Child! thought I, what sorrow art thou like to have for thy Portion in this World? Thou must be beaten, must beg, suffer hunger, cold, nakedness, and a thousand Calamities, though I cannot now endure the Wind should blow upon thee: But yet recalling my self, thought I, I must venture you all with God, though it goeth to the quick to leave you; O, I saw in this condition, I was as a man who was pulling down his House upon the head of his Wife and Children; yet thought I, I must do it, I must do it: . . .

His ignorance of the law and, indeed, the authorities' indifference to it, also made him fear at first that if wearied by his obduracy they might release him by way of the scaffold. He describes these not unreasonable fears:

I will tell you of a pretty business; I was once above all the rest, in a very sad and low Condition for many Weeks, at which time also I being a young Prisoner, and not acquainted with the Laws, had this lay much upon my Spirit, That my Imprisonment might end at the Gallows for ought that I could tell; now therefore Satan laid hard at me to beat me out of heart, by suggesting thus unto me; But how if when you come indeed to die you should be in this Condition; that is, as not to savour the things of God, nor to have any evidence upon your Soul for a better state hereafter? (for indeed at that time all the things of God were hid from my Soul.)

Wherefore when I at first began to think of this, it was a great trouble to me: for I thought with my self, that in the Condition I now was in, I was not fit to die, neither indeed did think I could if I should be called to it: Besides, I thought with my self, if I should make a scrambling shift to clamber up the Ladder, yet I should either with quaking or other symptoms of fainting, give occasion to the Enemy to reproach the Way of God and his People, for their Timorousness. This therefore lay with great trouble upon me, for methought I was ashamed to die with a pale Face, and tottering Knees, for such a Cause as this.

Wherefore I pray'd to God that he would comfort me, and give me strength to do and suffer what he should call me to; yet no comfort appear'd, but all continued hid: I was also at this time so really possessed with the thought of death, that oft I was as if I was on the Ladder with the Rope about my Neck; only this was some Encouragement to me, I thought I might now have an opportunity to speak my last words to a Multitude which I thought would come to see me die; and thought I, if it must be, if God will but convert one Soul by my very last words, I shall not count my Life thrown away, nor lost.

But however short life might be, it was necessary to sustain it, and Bunyan soon found a way to contribute to the support of his family by learning to make shoe laces. Although the physical condition of the jail was bad, the routine was, according to our notions, an informal one. Often as many as thirty-five or forty dissenters were housed there, as well as more ordinary felons and, in private rooms above, a number of debtors. Bunyan immediately resumed his unlicensed preaching and soon hit on a way of earning money for his family by writing and publishing his sermons, or the more elaborate religious pamphlets which grew out of them.

In 1661 his first such publication, a book of verse called *Prison Meditations*, appeared. Bunyan is a real poet only in prose, but his words were always direct and forceful and often arresting by the very boldness and simplicity of their images. For example:

> The Truth and I, were both here cast
> Together, and we do
> Lie arm in arm, and so hold fast
> Each other; this is true.

In 1662 the second, *Praying in the Spirit*, and in 1663 the third, *Christian Behaviour*, both sermons in prose, contained many such charming and unself-conscious illustrations as:

> True Christians are like the several flowers in a garden, that have upon each of them the dew of heaven, which, being shaken with the wind, they let fall their dew at each others roots, whereby they are jointly nourished, and become nourishers of each other.

This plague of militant religious tracts by Bunyan and many like him led the Restoration's chief licenser, Roger L'Estrange, to urge in 1663 that all censors carefully examine and if possible destroy the works of these "great masters of the Popular Stile" which "strike home to the capacity and Humour of the Multitude."

In 1664 Bunyan published two books, *One Thing Needful*, and

The Blessing and the Curse, and in 1665 the better known *Holy City* and *The Resurrection of the Dead.*

In 1666 we have the now classic, spiritual autobiography, quoted above, *Grace Abounding,* which concludes in its first edition: "I was had home to prison again, where I have now lain above five years and a quarter, waiting to see what God will suffer these men to do with me."

In 1666 the disorganization of the prisons due to the great plague forced the discharge of many prisoners whose sentences had not yet expired, and also released Bunyan who was not really under sentence at all.

However, he immediately accepted an invitation to address his brethren, and six months later was again arrested and, this time legally, returned to jail.

The sixth edition of *Grace Abounding,* has a slightly altered conclusion which states that he has "lain now complete twelve years waiting to see what God will suffer these men to do with me."

Either physical illness or discouragement kept Bunyan from much writing during the next six years, and he published only *A Confession of Faith* and *A Defense of the Doctrine of Justification by Faith* during that entire period.

In 1672 Charles II issued a Declaration of Indulgence since, as he truly said, "the sad experience of twelve years—showed . . . very little fruit . . . of the forceable courses." A further reason was that, as he did not say, he had just concluded a secret treaty with Louis XIV binding himself to announce his conversion to Catholicism as soon as practicable, and was therefore anxious to undermine the monopoly of the Church of England.

Bunyan was, immediately upon his release, chosen pastor of his fellowship which had maintained itself, often in hiding, and had met with surprising regularity in secret, during the years of persecution.

When, that May 1672, lay preachers were admitted to license, Bunyan applied for such a license not only for himself and the large barn his congregation had managed to purchase, but for twenty-four other lay preachers and thirty other similar buildings which it was, thenceforward, evidently a part of his duty to supervise.

During the next three years he and Elizabeth had two children. His older sons by his first wife were now assisting him as "braziers" and he continues to sign himself so, although he probably spent little time personally at the forge. In addition to preaching and church organization, he published three more religious works, one of them an attempt to eliminate nonessentials and reconcile the different Baptist sects by proving *Differences in Judgment about Water Baptism No Bar to Communion.*

In 1675 the temporary revocation of licenses and a renewed attempt to silence the nonconformists again led Bunyan to jail, and there he began a parable for the religious instruction of simple folk—a book called *The Pilgrim's Progress.*

This begins conventionally enough as a dream in which the narrator tells us he "saw a man clothed with rags, standing in a certain place, with his face from his own house, a book in his hand, and a great burden upon his back. I looked, and saw him open the book and read therein; and, as he read, he wept, and trembled; and not being able longer to contain, he brake out with a lamentable cry, saying 'What shall I do?' "

The man is, of course, the Pilgrim; his book is the Bible; and the burden on his back is the weight of worldly cares and concerns. (Not, in the ordinary sense of the word, sins. Thrift and ambition are as likely to find a place therein as profligacy or dissipation.)

The formal pattern of the allegory that is to follow is already clearly implied. Aroused to the evils of the world in which he lives, Christian attempts to convince his wife, children and neighbors of the dangers which threaten them, and to enlist their companionship in his search for salvation.

> O my dear wife, said he, and you the children of my bowels, I, your dear friend, am in myself undone by reason of a burden that lieth hard upon me; moreover, I am for certain informed that this our city will be burned with fire from heaven, in which fearful overthrow both myself, with thee my wife, and you my sweet babes, shall miserably come to ruin, except (the which yet I see not) some way of escape can be found, whereby we may be delivered. At this his relations were sore amazed; not for that they believed that what he had said to them was true, but because they thought that some frenzy distemper had got into his head; therefore, it drawing towards night, and they hoping that sleep might settle his brains, with all haste they got him to bed. But the night was as troublesome to him as the day; wherefore, instead of sleeping, he spent it in sighs and tears. So, when the morning was come, they would know how he did. He told them, Worse and worse: he also set to talking to them again: but they began to be hardened. They also thought to drive away his distemper by

harsh and surly carriages to him; sometimes they would deride, sometimes they would chide, and sometimes they would quite neglect him.

Finally he decides to start out alone but at the last minute a friend, Pliable, is so impressed by the strength of his conviction that he offers to go with him. They soon stumble and fall into the slough of Despond, at which Pliable is discouraged and turns back. Christian bravely struggles on but is persuaded to turn off from the right path by Mr. Worldly Wiseman who assures him that a Mr. Legality nearby can show him a much easier way to get rid of his burden. By the help of Mr. Evangelist he eventually gets back to the main road, and is overtaken by a neighbor, Faithful, who had set out later but had made better progress. The two continue together through many adventures, including the great struggle with Apollyon, ruler of this world, who claims them as his subjects and refuses to accept their allegiance to God.

After many other experiences they try to pass through Vanity Fair where both are arrested as foreign agitators. Brought to trial before a lord of the fair, Judge Hate-Good, Faithful is condemned and tortured to death. Christian, however, escapes and continues on his way, assisted by a new friend, Hopeful, who has been converted by Faithful's martyrdom. Although the book should be read as a whole, this chapter alone gives an excellent idea of the amazing contemporary quality it still holds for us today.

They hold to the high road despite many difficulties and dangers but finally, their feet being weary and the road growing hourly more hard and rocky, they are tempted to take a by-path through a pleasant meadow which seems to follow the same general route. It soon diverges, however, and they are warned barely in time by the fate of Mr. Vain-Confidence who, rushing ahead, falls into a deep pit and is dashed to pieces.

Unable to win back to the right road before nightfall, they are captured by Giant Despair and thrown into the dungeon of Doubting Castle. Here they are almost driven to suicide, but again escape and go on their way, posting a warning to help other pilgrims avoid their mistakes. At last they reach the Celestial City, which they enter to enjoy eternal life in the fellowship of the blessed.

Only a small part of the book's real value lies in this familiar framework, although it is extraordinary how much the very fabric of our daily speech has been affected by the language and incidents of Bunyan's classic pilgrimage. But the great literary interest of *Pilgrim's Progress,* the most important forerunner of the English novel, lies in its rich variety of concrete situations, living characters, and vital experiences. The profound psychological insight with which many of the minor characters as well as the hero himself are realized is truly extraordinary. This is all the more amazing when one considers the rapidity of the narrative and the specific allegory it maintains throughout.

For while its central symbol of life as a pilgrimage and man as a pilgrim gives the story much of its emotional power and universality, it also creates certain special problems, and a fundamental contradiction which Bunyan triumphantly ignores, and thus overcomes, without solving it. Superficially the book accepts the idea that this world is merely an ante-chamber through which the soul must pass on the way to everlasting bliss or damnation. Actually it brings us just the opposite message. As Lindsay says:

> The impression conveyed by the allegory is the exact opposite of what it literally professes. The phantasms of good and evil become the real world; and in encountering them the Pilgrim lives through the life that Bunyan had known in definite place and time. The pattern of his experience, the fall and the resolute rising-up, the loss and the finding, the resistance and the overcoming, the despair and the joy, the dark moaning valleys and the singing in the places of the flowers—it is the pattern of Bunyan's strenuous life. There are comrades and enemies, stout-hearts and cravens, men who care only for the good of fellowship and men of greed and fear; and they are the men of contemporary England.

Such a chapter as the trial at "Vanity Fair" will give some idea of the contemporary impact of Bunyan's experiences and of the vivid racy narrative style he had developed, but, like a novel, the book must be read as a whole to be fully appreciated.

It was immediately successful, selling three editions in less than a year and over 100,000 copies before Bunyan's death! It has since been translated into more than 120 languages and has certainly been read by more people than any other single book except the Bible.

But although its popular success and circulation among the bakers, weavers, cobblers, tailors, tinkers, shepherds, ploughmen, dairy maids, seamstresses, and servant girls was immediate, its critical reputation and academic acclaim are much more recent.

In the eighteenth century Dean Swift and Dr. Johnson were, significantly, the only men of any note who had a good word to say for it. Swift wrote that he had been more confirmed and entertained by a few pages in the *Pilgrim's Progress* than by a long discussion upon the will and the intellect, and Johnson compared passages in it to Spenser and Dante, and told Boswell it was one of the only three books which readers wished longer.

But Addison cited Bunyan to prove that even the most despicable of writers had their admirers; the sympathetic Cowper at the end of the eighteenth century hinted a personal liking for the Pilgrim he had met in his childhood but concluded:

> I name thee not, lest so despised a name
> Should move a sneer at thy deserved fame

and Burke spoke of "degrading a book to the style of Pilgrim's Progress."

On the other hand Burns and Blake were both intimately acquainted with this "prose epic of puritanism" and Blake often borrows its very phraseology in his attacks on the Law as opposed to the free grace of the spirit, vouchsafed to those who belong to a true fellowship. Fielding betrays his knowledge of it in more than one passage, and Dickens openly revels in its rich physical detail and high-hearted conflict.

The best of the later academic critics have a sensitive perception of one part of its appeal, its psychological truth and ethical realism, while they ignore or distort its more fundamental impact.

For example the nineteenth century French critic, Taine, says:

> Protestantism . . . could not sing the battles and works of God, but the temptations and salvation of the soul. At the time of Christ came the poems of cosmogony; at the time of Milton, the confessions of psychology. At the time of Christ, each imagination produced a hierarchy of supernatural beings, and a history of the world; at the time of Milton, every heart recorded the series of its upliftings, and the history of grace. Learning and reflection led Milton to a metaphysical poem which was not the natural offspring of the age, whilst inspiration and ignorance revealed to Bunyan the psychological narrative which suited the age, and the great man's genius was feebler than the tinker's simplicity.

This analysis, perceptive as it is in incidentals, ignores both the very substantial difference in class position between Milton and

Bunyan and the small but significant lapse of time between the conception and actual beginning of *Paradise Lost* in the middle fifties, and the creation of the *Pilgrim's Progress* a full generation later.

Milton was, as we have seen, a leading member of that class which was actually responsible for the revolution, and despite his personal disappointment there was nothing at all unreasonable in his envisioning the re-creation of heaven and earth with the assurance of one who has played an active and effective part in such an undertaking.

Bunyan, on the contrary, was a dispossessed member of the lower class whose hopes had been aroused and whose energies had been used in the course of a revolution which, as yet, had only increased the hardships and miseries of their lot.

And although there may have been in his case, as of course there was, to a much greater extent in Milton's, some glimpse of the more profound eventual significance of the bourgeois revolution which England was the first nation in the modern world to complete, yet Bunyan came to full maturity only after the seemingly final defeat of those hopes.

The enormous emotional force of his great work in its very opening scene is derived not simply as Taine implies, from his psychological insight or even his ethical concern, but depends largely on his ability to convey the heart sickness of an enthusiast in an altogether conventional society—the burning indignation of a man who hears the words which are the breath of life not merely denied but, even worse, mouthed and ignored by those whose superficial acceptance is a mockery of the truth.

Bernard Shaw has keenly observed what generations of religious teachers have apparently overlooked when he says of *Pilgrim's Progress*:

> Bunyan's perception that righteousness is filthy rags, his scorn for Mr. Legality in the village of Morality, his defiance of the Church as the supplanter of religion, his insistence on courage as the virtue of virtues, his estimate of the career of the conventionally respectable and sensible Worldly Wiseman as no better at bottom than the life and death of Mr. Badman: all this is expressed by Bunyan in the terms of a tinker's theology. . . . Bunyan makes no attempt to present his pilgrims as more sensible or better conducted than Mr. Worldly Wiseman. Mr. W. W.'s worst enemies, as Mr. Embezzler, Mr. Never-go-to-Church-on-Sunday, Mr. Bad Form, Mr. Murderer, Mr. Burglar, Mr. Co-respondent, Mr. Blackmailer, Mr. Cad,

Mr. Drunkard, Mr. Labour Agitator, and so forth, can read the Pilgrim's Progress without finding a word said against them: whereas the respectable people who snub them and put them in prison, such as Mr. W. W. himself and his young friend Civility; Formalist and Hypocrisy; Wildhead, Inconsiderate and Pragmatick (who were clearly young university men of good family and high feeding); that brisk lad Ignorance, Talkative, By-Ends of Fairspeech and his mother-in-law Lady Feigning, and other reputable gentlemen and citizens, catch it very severely. Even Little Faith, though he gets to heaven at last, is given to understand that it served him right to be mobbed by the brothers Faint Heart, Mistrust and Guilt, all three recognized members of respectable society and veritable pillars of the law. The whole allegory is a consistent attack on morality and respectability, without a word that one can remember against vice and crime.

Bunyan was so concerned about the wickedness of the lawmakers and so unconcerned about the wickedness of the lawbreakers because he realized that the laws themselves are grounded in undemocratic power and sanctify oppression, and that by far the greater social evil is the work of those who live on them rather than that of those who die under them.

This is the measure of Bunyan's greatness and the secret of his appeal to generations of less religious fighters for freedom. He knew that the power of the class state was the power of the oppressor, and that there was no essential merit in obeying its laws even when they were called the ten commandments.

Bunyan would have spoken with more indignation and less cynicism but he was in full accord with the anonymous satirist who said, of the enclosures:

> The law locks up the man or woman
> Who steals the goose from off the common;
> But leaves the man or woman loose
> Who steals the common from the goose.

He does say in a hundred different passionate ways what the realistic and dispassionate dissenter Defoe announced a century later:

> Knowledge of things would teach them every hour
> That Law is but a heathen word for Power.

But unlike his gifted contemporary, the Quaker leader, George Fox, who wandered staring and rapt about the countryside, Bunyan was not, at heart, an anarchist or even an individualist.

During the worst of his early mental struggles he never lost his practical sense of the necessities of life, carried on his daily tinker's work and maintained his family. His search for a meaningful and dedicated way of life was also a search for an organized community with which to share it, and nothing is more common in his writing than such an emphasis on earthly companionship as: "Yea, I could be content to live and die with those people that have the grace of God in their souls."

One of the most moving of his vivid allegories is the dream he relates in *Grace Abounding*:

> About this time, the state and happiness of these poor people at *Bedford* was thus, *in a kind of Vision*, presented to me: I saw, as if they were set on the Sunny-side of some high Mountain, there refreshing themselves with the pleasant beams of the Sun, while I was shivering and shrinking in the Cold, afflicted with Frost, Snow and dark Clouds: Methought also, betwixt me and them, I saw a Wall that did compass about this Mountain; now through this Wall my Soul did greatly desire to pass; concluding, that if I could, I would go even into the very midst of them, and there also comfort my self with the heat of their Sun.

This realistic unmystical consciousness of other people is, as we have noted, one of the reasons for the tremendous appeal of *Pilgrim's Progress* which, using the traditional parable form, brings it so much closer to reality that it trembles on the verge of fiction.

After the publication of several further religious pamphlets, Bunyan in 1680, wrote another story *The Life and Death of Mr. Badman*. The title indicates the book's intention but belies its interest. Again we have real characters sketched in with quick incisive strokes, and recognize a far from conventional or superficial observation. The growing degradation of women in the fashionable literature of the period is highlighted by the wealthy widower's refusal to consider remarriage for: "Who would keep a cow of his own that can have a quart of milk for a penny?"

Bunyan's own idea of woman's position, like Milton's, accepts the general religious assumption of her probable inferiority, but also like Milton's, allows for exceptions. For example, Mr. Badman's good wife, when he tries to influence her conduct and undermine her convictions, says:

> I have a husband, but also a God; my God has commanded me, and that upon pain of damnation, to be a continual wor-

shipper of him, and that in the way of my own appointments. I have a husband but also a soul, and my soul ought to be more unto me than all the world besides.

And, far from the hypocritical denial of sex we associate with a later Victorian "puritanism," Bunyan tolerantly remarks of her error in having accepted Mr. Badman's courtship:

> As to his person, there she was fittest to judge, because she was to be the person pleased, but as to his godliness, there the Word was the fittest judge, and they that could best understand it, because God was therein to be pleased.

Another more conscious and complete opposition between the views of Bunyan and his class-conscious brethren, and those of more respectable Protestant ministers was their attitude to worldly success. In what was to become the accepted Protestant view the Lord, far from chastising those whom he loveth, signifies his love by gifts and favors so that temporal success may be taken as an almost infallible sign of eternal election. Respectable Protestantism held that the poor probably deserve damnation in this world because, whether by predestination or thriftlessness, they are bound to it in the next.

Bunyan, on the other hand, felt that while some of the wealthy might be converted, yet on the whole the accumulation of money was ordinarily accomplished: "by hook and by crook, as we say, by swearing lying, cozening, stealing, covetousness, extortion."

In Mr. Badman he arraigns the wickedness of those who take advantage of the poor, overcharging them because they cannot travel to market or buy in large quantities, as well as of those who hoard grain, and so raise its price.

He consistently contradicts such typical pronouncements from contemporary pulpits as: "Grace in a poor man is grace, and 'tis beautiful, but grace in a rich man is more conspicuous, more useful," and "Faith is a successful grace and hath a promise of prospering."

For example, in one of his later printed sermons, *The Greatness of the Soul* (1682), he builds on a text from Mark:

> For following of me is not like following of some other masters. The wind sits always on my face, and the foaming rage of the sea of this world, and the proud and lofty waves

thereof do continually beat upon the sides of the bark or ship that myself, my cause, and followers are in; he therefore that will not run hazards, and that is afraid to venture a drowning, let him not set foot into this vessel.

And in another, *The Jerusalem Sinner Saved*, which appeared in the year of his death, he asks emphatically about Christ:

> Why should he so easily take a denial of the great ones that were the grandeur of the world, and struggle so hard for hedge-creepers and highway men . . . ?

Again, while he necessarily accepted the idea of a frugal hard working life it was never, for him, precisely the ideal which the preachers from above tried to make it. In a posthumous publication *Paul's Departure and Crown*, he says:

> A horse that is loaded with gold and pearls all day may yet have a foul stable and a galled back at night. And woe be to him that increaseth that which is not his, and that ladeth himself with thick clay.

And in his description of *The House of God* in 1688, he says that all must work there but:

> The work is short, the wages last forever,
> The work like us, the wages like the giver.

To return, however, to *Mr. Badman* there is one kind of sinner whom he there vituperates more severely than any other, and that, interestingly enough, is a latter day saint, the government spy or informer.

Five years later in *The Pharisee and the Publican* he remarks:

> . . . the Publican was counted vile and base and reckoned among the worst of men, even as our informers and bumbaliffs are with us at this day.

And here, in 1680, he gives at full length two "true stories" of the deservedly horrible fate which was visited on wretches who surpassed even the villainous Mr. Badmen in the evil he did not dare to do.

In our town there was one W. S. a man of a very wicked life; and he, when there seemed to be countenance given to it, would needs turn informer. Well, so he did, and was as diligent in his business as most of them could be; he would watch of nights, climb trees, and range the woods of days, if possible, to find out the meeters, for then they were forced to meet in the fields. . . . Well, after he had gone on like a bedlam in his course awhile, and had done some mischiefs to the people, he was stricken by the hand of God, and that in this manner: (1) . . . (2) . . . (3) . . . (4) . . . In that posture . . . half a year or thereabouts. . . . But after that he also walked about until God had made a sufficient spectacle of his judgment for his sin, and then on a sudden he was stricken and died miserably; and so there was an end of him and his doings.

I will tell you of another. About four miles from St. Neots there was a gentleman had a man, and he would needs be an informer, and a lusty young man he was. Well, an informer he was and did much distress some people, and had perfected his informations so effectually against some, that there was nothing further to do but for the constables to make distress on the people, that he might have the money or goods, and, as I heard, he hastened them to do it. Now while he was in the heat of his work . . . a dog, some say his own dog, took distaste at something, and bit his master by the leg . . . that wound was his death and that a dreadful one too. . . .

But what need I instance in particular persons, when the judgment of God against this kind of people was made manifest, I think I may say, if not in all, yet in most of the counties in England where such poor creatures were? But I would if it had been the will of God, that neither I nor anybody else could tell you more of these stories; true stories that are neither lie nor romance.

In 1680 occurred a flurry of exciting political events—intrigues stemming from a number of indirectly related causes. Among these were Parliament's attempt to prevent the Catholic James' being named as eventual successor to his brother, the fraudulent discovery of a "Popish Plot" to murder the king and restore the Catholic Church, and Charles II's conclusion of a secret treaty with the king of France, which guaranteed him a sufficient income to make him, personally, independent of Parliament. These all culminated in Charles' largely successful attempts to cancel the charters of such municipal corporations as Bedfordshire, replacing them by others which gave the throne virtual control of the county councils.

Those events shaped Bunyan's next book—a long and ambitious project, published in 1682—which he himself probably considered his major work.

The Holy War, like *Pilgrim's Progress,* begins with a well-established religious "similitude" or allegory. The city of Mansoul, built by Shaddai (a Hebrew name often used to indicate God), is attacked by the Diabolonians, briefly conquered by entrances forced at the city gates—Eye Gate, Ear Gate, and so forth—and rescued by the leadership of Emanuel (a name which the Fifth Monarchy Men and others often used to denote Jesus in his role as ruler of *earth* during the millenium).

In strictly Calvinist or Baptist terms this would be the end of the story but it is only the beginning of Bunyan's Holy War. For here too the embodiment of the myth becomes intrinsically important, and altogether alters its original significance.

Through the growing indifference of the prosperous godly, and through secret Diabolonians or half-Diabolonians left as citizens of the city, a new conquest, engineered from within, is achieved, which follows very closely the story of the internal defeat of the commonwealth. The major events of *The Holy War* deal with the eventual extirpation of these evil forces, the defense against future assaults, and the firm establishment of Emmanuel's kingdom on earth.

We have already mentioned Bunyan's unadvertised belief in some period—presumably the conventional thousand years—of millennial organization on earth. While there are few explicit statements on the matter, there are many such earlier references as those in *Prison Meditations*:

> Just thus it is, we suffer here
>   For him a little pain,
> Who, when he doth again appear,
>   Will with him let us reign.

In *The Holy City,* written in 1665, which somewhat anticipates the general outline of *The Holy War,* Bunyan said:

> For observe it, Christ hath not only obtained the kingdom of heaven for these that are his, when this world is ended, but hath also, as a reward for his sufferings, the whole world given into his hand; wherefore, as all the kings, and princes, and powers of this world have had their time to reign, and have glory in this world in the face of all, so Christ will have his time, at this day, to show who is "the only Potentate and Lord of Lords" 1.Ti:VI 15. At which day he will not only set up his kingdom in the midst of their kingdoms, as he doth now, but will set it up even upon the top of their kingdoms;

at which day there will not be a nation in the world but must bow to Jerusalem or perish.

In that work, too, as we have seen, he stressed the material nature of this ideal social establishment by denying that Christ would personally rule it, his spirit in the elect brethren being taken to represent him, and by even more strongly contradicting the belief that the new order would be of merely momentary or symbolic duration.

The charter granted by Emmanuel to Mansoul further emphasizes this anticipation of a physically based heaven on earth:

> I do give, grant and bestow upon them freely the world, and what is therein for their good, and they shall have that power over them as shall stand with the honour of my Father, my glory, and their comfort, yea I grant them the benefits of life and death and of things present and things to come.

The overwhelming success of *The Pilgrim's Progress* led Bunyan in 1684 to attempt a second part, popular enough in its time but not comparable to the original.

It deals with the pilgrimage of Christian's widow, children and neighbors, inspired by his example, and is chiefly interesting for the portrait of Roundhead warriors whom he must have known in his army service, like Mr. Greatheart, and Mr. Valiant who says after his last fight:

> My sword I give to him that shall succeed me in my pilgrimage, and my courage and skill to him that can get it. My marks and scars I carry with me, to be a witness for me, that I have fought his battles, who now shall be my rewarder.

It is interesting to note that Mr. Valiant's parents were evidently conventional Protestants who knew the duty of success and warned him not only that the way of the pilgrim was "a dangerous way, yea, the most dangerous way in the World," but also that "it was an idle Life, and if I myself were not inclined to Sloath and Laziness, I would never countenance a Pilgrim's condition."

It is also noteworthy that Bunyan here explicitly and prophetically denies the entire individualistic ethic of a competitive society since Mr. Greatheart and Mr. Valiant slow their pace to accommodate not only women and children but also especially weak or timorous brethren, who have been outstripped by former pilgrims and left to make their difficult way unassisted.

When the cavalcade finally arrives at the Delectable Mountains the good Shepherds give them a particularly warm welcome, saying:

> This is a comfortable Company, you are welcome to us, for we care for the *Feeble*, as for the *Strong:* our Prince has an Eye to what is done to the least of these. Therefore Infirmity must not be a block to our Entertainment. So they had them to the Palace Door, and then said unto them, Come in Mr. *Feeble-mind*, come in Mr. *Ready-to-halt*, come in Mr. *Despondency*, and Mrs. *Much-afraid* [his daughter]. *These* Mr. *Great-heart*, said the Shepherds to the Guide, we call in by Name, for that they are most subject to draw back; but as for you, and the rest that are *strong*, we leave you to your wonted Liberty. Then said Mr. *Great-heart*, This day I see that Grace doth shine in your Faces, and that you are my Lords Shepherds indeed; for that you have not *pushed* these Diseased neither with Side nor Shoulder, but have rather strewed their way into the Palace with Flowers, as you should.
>
> So the Feeble and Weak went in, and Mr. *Great-heart*, and the rest did follow. When they were also set down, the Shepherds said to those of the weakest sort, what is it that you would have? For said they, all things must be managed here, to the supporting of the weak, as well as to the warning of the Unruly.

A later nonconformist who was perhaps the most courageous fighter for freedom on the English literary scene more than a century later, adopted as his motto poor Mr. Feeble's resolution:

> Other Brunts I also look for, but this I have resolved on, to wit, to *run* when I can, to *go* when I cannot *run*, and to *creep* when I cannot *go*.

All those who love Hazlitt must treasure the second part of *Pilgrim's Progress*, if for that quotation alone.

The next year, 1685, James II's accession to the throne caused a renewed fear of prison sentences and heavy fines. Bunyan who was now well-known not only in Bedfordshire but also in London, where he frequently preached as the guest of some independent congregation, was advised that it might be well, for his children's sake if not his own, to be cautious. He replied that "their Heavenly

Father will provide what is necessary, and what is more than necessary is hurtful." His faith, however, was of that practical turn which had led Cromwell's army to "trust in God and keep their powder dry," and Bunyan assisted his children's heavenly father to keep them from want by executing a deed of gift, proof against fines, if not imprisonment, to his wife.

Fortunately James II, himself a Catholic, was set on securing general indulgence for Catholicism as a first step to reestablish the Catholic Church in England, and made no effort to enforce religious conformity.

The next year Bunyan wrote his most successful book in verse, *Country Rhimes for Children*, which contained seventy-four "similitudes." Two of the best are:

"The Hypocrite"
The Frog by nature is but damp and cold,
Her mouth is large, her belly much will hold,
She sits somewhat ascending, loves to be
Croaking in gardens, though unpleasantly.

The hypocrite is like unto this Frog,
And like as is the puppy to the dog.
He is of nature cold, his mouth is wide
To prate, and at true goodness to deride.
And though this world is that which he doth love,
He mounts his head as if he lived above,
And though he seeks in Churches for to croak,
He neither seeketh Jesus nor His Yoke.

"The Formalist"
Thou booby, says't thou nothing but Cuckoo?
The robin and the wren can that out do.
They to us play thorough their little throats
Not one, but sundry pretty tuneful notes.
But thou hast fellows, some like thee can do
Little but suck our eggs, and sing cuckoo.

. . . .

Since Cuckoos forward not our early spring
Nor help with notes to bring our harvest in,
And since while here, she only makes a noise
So pleasing unto none as girls and boys,
The Formalist we may compare her to,
For he doth suck our eggs and sing Cuckoo.

In 1687 political events took a peculiar turn. James II, finding the wealthy ministers and members of the Established Church altogether unwilling to consider any approach toward Catholicism, decided to enlist the aid of the heretofore persecuted dissenters in his campaign for a return to Rome and absolute monarchy.

He proclaimed a Declaration of Indulgence which went much further than Charles II's Declaration of 1672, since it not only suspended all penalties for nonconformity but also abolished religious "tests" or oaths for those appointed to political office.

He also made personal overtures to such leading nonconformists as Bunyan, hoping he could enlist their influence in the election of a parliament pledged to confirm these measures and any further ones he might propose.

Although Bunyan had suffered so seriously from the religious penal laws and had every reason to hate the Established Church and welcome its discomfiture, he saw with extraordinary clarity the whole import of these maneuvers, and subordinated his personal interests and even the immediate interests of his fellowship to defeat their more fundamentally reactionary opponent. An anonymous contemporary biographer, writing in 1692, gives us his first-hand account:

> During these things there were Regulations sent in to all Cities and Towns corporate, to new model the Government in the Magistracy, etc. by turning out some, and putting others; against this, Mr. Bunyan expressed his zeal with some wariness, as foreseeing the bad consequence that would attend it, and laboured with his Congregation to prevent their being imposed on in this kind, and when a great man in those days coming to Bedford, upon some such Errand, sent for him, as 'tis supposed to give him a place of publick trust, he would by no means come to him, but sent his Excuse.

While Bunyan's published work contains the required formal asservations of loyalty toward the king, he was very strongly opposed to absolute monarchy and perhaps to all monarchy. There is the signature of a John Bunyan on a petition signed by a number of his coreligionists in Bedfordshire in 1653 asking Cromwell *not* to assume the crown.

In an *Exposition of the First Ten Chapters of Genesis* which was, perhaps deliberately, not published until after his death, he says: "It is the lot of Cain's brood, to be lords and rulers first, while Abel and his generation have their necks under persecution."

Again in reference to Nimrod in the same work we find:

> I am apt to think he was the first that in this new world sought after absolute monarchy . . . through the pride of his countenance he did scorn that others, or any, should be his equal: nay, could not be content till all made obeisance to him. He therefore would needs be the author and master of what religion he pleased; and would also subject the rest of his brethren thereto, by what ways his lusts thought best. Wherefore he began a fresh persecution.

Readers of *Pilgrim's Progress* will remember the attack of Apollyon, who bears a certain family resemblance to the Stuarts, on those who proclaimed their adherence to a heavenly rather than an earthly ruler, and the pilgrim's assertion that he could not be considered a traitor since his true allegiance was prior to any loyalty oaths. In the later unpublished commentary on Genesis, Bunyan more explicitly defends the seeming disingenuousness of holy men in difficult political situations:

> Hence note, that a man is not to be counted an offender, how contrary soever he lieth, either in doctrine or practice, to men, if both [doctrine and practice] have the command of God. . . . This made Jeremiah, though he preached, That the city of Jerusalem should be burnt with fire, the king and people should go into captivity; yet stand upon his own vindication before his enemies, and plead his innocency against them that persecuted him. . . . Daniel also, though he did openly break the king's decree, and refused to stoop to his idolations and devilish demand; yet purged himself of both treason and sedition, and justifies his act as innocent and harmless even in the sight of God.

A colleague of Bunyan's, had even more forthrightly defended his speaking in parables, clear only to the initiated, by demanding: "Must we counterfeit with you? . . . must we either speak in Tropes and Figures? or else in Ropes and Faggots? or imprisonment at least?"

Tindall summarizes this attitude saying:

> That Bunyan cherished a deep and natural hatred of both king and government, like any normal Baptist of the time, is apparent from remarks scattered throughout his tracts, often next to professions of loyalty, which served to hide his real opinions from all but the elect and the inquisitive. . . . His hope of the conversion of some kings did not lessen his belief

in their present wickedness: he saw and detested the injustice of laws, jails, magistrates, and governors, between whom and the saints was a perpetual war. His denial of sedition was a denial of violence, not of propaganda against the government.

This is borne out by another posthumously published work, *Of Anti Christ, and of the Slaying of the Witnesses*, in which Bunyan even more explicitly indicates his belief, already glanced at in our discussion of *The Holy War*, that some kind of millennium will be established *on earth* when, for the last thousand years of the world's history, things will be rightly ordered here as well as in heaven. In this later unpublished work he seems even to intimate a hope that that millennial period of justice may arrive within an ordinary lifetime:

> God will have his primitive Church state set up in the world (even where Antichrist has set up his), wherefore, in order to do this, Antichrist must be pulled down, stick and stone; and then they that live to see it, will behold the new Jerusalem come down from heaven, as a bride adorned for her husband.

In 1688, just a few months before the then still unexpected "bloodless revolution" which forced James II to abdicate, and made William and Mary rulers of a constitutional monarchy, Bunyan died. He had caught a bad chill riding through forty miles of rain to London, and though he preached the sermon he had planned he died ten or twelve days later, at the end of August 1688.

His first biographer, Charles Doe, was a comb maker who had become acquainted with him some three years before his death and who a year later became a bookseller and finally a publisher because, as he tells us:

> In March, 1686, as I was reading Mr. Bunyan's Book "Saved by Grace," I thought certainly this is the best Book that was ever writ, or I read except the Bible, and then I remembered I had received a great deal of comfort in all of his Books. Some time after my assurance, and being under the sense of the peculiar Love of God, it came into my mind as I was upon my Stair-head what work I should do for God, and about the middle of the Stair I reckoned that to sell books was the best I could do, and by that time I came to the bottom I concluded to sell Mr. Bunyan's and so I began to sell Books

and have sold about 3,000 of Mr. Bunyan's, and also have been concerned in printing the following Books: The Works of Mr. John Bunyan in folio, and the "Heavenly Footman" by John Bunyan.

Elizabeth outlived him for only a year and a half, but all his children except the blind daughter, Mary, whose death had preceded his, survived for many years.

The enormous popularity of his books, or, rather, of his major book, we have already discussed, but its long critical depreciation and sudden glorification in the respectable nineteenth century merits a word of explanation. This has been best given by Lindsay, who concludes his analysis of Bunyan's reputation by saying:

> All that was most vital in the English masses was linked up with the dissenting struggle. Bunyan entered deep into the consciousness of the masses. They were all his Pilgrims accepting the toil and the trial because of the warm light of fellowship on the mountains of the future. They were building a house of fellowship, and Bunyan abode with them as the password of the faithful in a world of environing malignants. The glow in their hearts and the courage of their resistance they felt were owed to him more than to any other one man.

However, his acceptance by the upper classes:

> came at the moment when the class-struggle had sharpened to the point where *any* writer with religious professions became respectable; for the proletarian forces were steadily moving away from the religious formulation, being able to let their sense of unity flow into trade-unions and political agitation. Then was the ripe moment for discovering that the Bedford Tinker was a genius.

Bunyan's position in English literature has survived both denigration and sanctification. Unlike such more sophisticated allegories as *Don Quixote* and *Gulliver's Travels*, children, in enjoying the *Pilgrim's Progress*, appreciate the essential theme as well as the story. And adults, engaged in the same progress, find a more profound relevance in its pages as often as they return to it with a richer experience of life.

It is unfortunately true that today, among the growing number of young people who have not read *Pilgrim's Progress* in their childhood, there is often an impression that he is "old-fashioned religious stuff." But it takes hardly more than a paragraph of direct personal acquaintance with Bunyan to make us realize that his enemies are our enemies, his fight our fight, and his emotional fortitude a source of strength we cannot afford to ignore.

The Age of Reason

THE AUGUSTANS

The pleasures of dissipation are perhaps more limited than has sometimes been supposed, and "épater le bourgeoisie" can be an engrossing objective to writers, artists, or even wits, only in default of any vital alternative possibility. The healthy, rapidly expanding economy of late seventeenth century mercantile England had essentially too much to offer for the mores of the restoration to last long, even at court, and there were already many signs of a growing respectability and decorum even during the lifetime of the returned émigrés and their king.

The immorality of the stage had begun to shock many who could by no stretch of the imagination be called puritans, and the justice of their attacks was tacitly acknowledged by such leading playwrights as John Dryden and William Congreve. Dryden had stopped writing anything but translations long before his death in 1700, and Congreve, who lived until 1729, wrote practically nothing during the last twenty-five years of his life.

Although Dryden's name bulks large in many histories of English literature, his work is of little interest to most twentieth century readers.

His long so-called satirical poems—actually not satires but personal attacks of a burlesque or caricature nature on political opponents and literary rivals—and his frigid plays, of which the best known *All for Love* was hailed by his contemporaries and successors of the eighteenth century as a vastly improved and more civilized version of Shakespeare's *Antony and Cleopatra*, are today practically unread and, for most people, unreadable. Nevertheless, his unquestioned leadership of his own age, the great respect of succeeding generations and his genuine, if limited, abilities as a literary critic and as the originator of a clear forceful prose make his name one that even a casual student of English literature should know. His versatility in style, and convictions, are illustrated by his famous elegy for Cromwell's death in 1659, his ode of rejoicing at the restoration of Cromwell's old enemies, the Stuarts, in 1660, his arguments (in verse) for the Church of England during Charles II's reign, and his prompt celebration in the long poem, *The Hind and the Panther*, of his conversion to Catholicism when James II ascended the throne.

Hazlitt analyzed the essential difference between Dryden and his follower, Pope, on the one hand, and the great poets whom we have so far considered, on the other, in his *Lectures on the English Poets* in 1818. He then said, in part:

> Dryden and Pope are the great masters of the artificial style of poetry in our language as . . . Chaucer, Spenser, Shakespeare and Milton were of the natural; and though this artificial style is generally and very justly acknowledged to be inferior to the other, yet those who stand at the head of that class, ought, perhaps, to rank higher than those who occupy an inferior place in a superior class . . . for it should be recollected, that there may be readers (as well as poets) not of the highest class, though very good sort of people, and not altogether to be despised. . . . The capacious soul of Shakespeare had an intuitive and mighty sympathy with whatever could enter into the heart of man in all possible circumstances; Pope had an exact knowledge of all that he himself loved or hated, loathed or wanted. Milton has winged his daring flight from heaven to earth, through Chaos and old Night. Pope's Muse never wandered with safety, but from his library to his grotto, or from his grotto into his library back again. . . . He lived in the smiles of fortune and basked in the favor of the great.

In 1685, as we have seen, Charles' death brought his brother, James, Duke of York, to the throne. James II was an avowed Catholic who had married a Catholic princess, Mary of Modena, and who was obviously intent not only on restoring Catholicism as the state religion but also, by the help of the Pope and the Catholic monarchs of Europe, on restoring absolute power to the throne of England. For three years there was, as has been noted in the discussion of Bunyan's life, an increasing tension and jockeying for power between the crown on one hand, and a combination of the landed gentry (who would have been represented by Parliament had James not illegally dismissed it) and the powerful dignitaries of the Anglican Church, on the other hand. It was widely believed that James' early dissipations had left him incapable of begetting a son, and if he had died without one his daughter, Mary, then the Protestant queen of Holland, would have been heir to the throne. Therefore matters did not come to a head until 1688. Then, as we saw above, his forcing through of an Act of Indulgence and the announced birth of a son (commonly rumored to have been smuggled into the palace in a warming pan) precipitated a crisis. In this several leaders of the Tory party and the church joined with the leading Whigs to invite William of Orange, Mary's husband and the recognized head of the Protestant powers in Europe, to land in England with an armed force and to ascend the throne.

James II fled to France and the revolution of 1688 was painlessly accomplished. English historians are fond of referring to this as the "glorious" or "bloodless" revolution, in contrast with the more violent revolutions suffered by less fortunate and well-deserving lands. The fact is, of course, that this was merely a postscript to, or reaffirmation of, the prolonged and serious struggle led by Cromwell forty years earlier, and that only the blood then spilled made it unnecessary to spill any more later. The substantial transfer of power to the bourgeoisie had already taken place in 1649 and was, as we have seen, not fundamentally disturbed in 1660. Practically, it mattered only to James II himself that he had delusions of grandeur and thought he was king by divine right. After 1688 not even a king could any longer doubt that he ruled by courtesy of his subjects, and that the throne as well as the church was now an asset of the upper bourgeoisie (which, practically speaking, already included the peerage).

The Augustan Age or "The Age of Enlightenment," as eighteenth century literary England was fond of calling itself, began, and ended, some ten or twenty years before the eighteenth century itself, and what we are to say of it is essentially said of the hundred years from 1688 to 1789—that is, from the "Glorious or Bloodless Revolution" (whose blood had been spilled forty years before), to the "French Revolution" (most of whose bloodshed was necessitated by the long subsequent, and still unfinished, struggle against reaction).

The Augustan Age was, as the name implies, very pleased with itself. The name was chosen by neoclassicist admiration for the culture of Rome under the Emperor Augustus, in the belief that

that greatest height of all preceding civilizations had now found a worthy and comparable successor. Alternatively its fortunate citizens referred to their period as "The Age of Reason" or "The Golden Age."

First Addison, and then Pope, were acknowledged arbiters of the polite letters of the age until their respective deaths in 1713 and 1739. Many literary historians still refer to this half century as the Age of Pope, and Pope was, indeed, an extraordinarily good representative of the time, giving us in brief quotable form a real understanding of its values, objectives, limitations and accomplishments.

If the *Tatler* and *Spectator* papers of Addison and Steele are, in bulk, more readable for us than Pope's work, it is perhaps largely because we are today less impatient of uninspired prose than of uninspired poetry, and expect the emotion which the eighteenth century so conspicuously and contentedly lacked more consistently from a versifier than from an essayist.

But we must remember that poetry was still the dominant form of polite literature at the beginning of that century (though it was no longer so by its end) and that prose was, for an educated man, a far more unconventional medium than verse.

However, in everything but the nonessential matter of rhyme and meter, we find complete agreement among the early eighteenth century literary leaders of society. Addison may speak a trifle more gently, Steele a little more warmly, Pope a great deal more sharply, but all use an elegant and well-turned phrase, a graceful classical allusion, a playful acknowledgment of the detailed realistic surface of contemporary upper-class life, and a generalized stingless satire designed to flatter rather than embarrass readers who would usually have a comfortable assurance of its being aimed only at their neighbors. There were, of course, enough and more than enough stinging insults in such verses as Pope's famous attack on Addison (see p. 223) and others, but these are simply sarcastic personal comments and should not be confused with satire which critically portrays general characteristics or foibles.

Pope, who excels at polishing a platitude, has wrapped up for us in an incomparably neat and portable package the general theme of this select chorus:

> All Nature is but Art unknown to thee;
> All chance direction, which thou canst not see;

> All discord, harmony not understood;
> All partial evil, universal good:
> And spite of Pride, in erring Reason's spite,
> One truth is clear, *Whatever is, is right.*

Of course, this comfortable assurance refers only to fundamentals. In detail Pope, as well as Addison, Lord Chesterfield, Steele, and a whole host of lesser figures knew well enough that there was much to be corrected. Indeed, the entire polite literature of the time is deliberately designed to pare off excrescences, tone down extremes, elaborate impeccable standards of taste, and punish with mockery any deviations from propriety and elegance in sentiment or expression.

From the essayists we learn that some ladies were too promiscuous and others too prudish; that some ambitious literary men forgot their old friends when promoted to high places; that there were still aristocrats who thought ignorance fashionable or who were overly contemptuous of new titles; and that there was already a little too much pushing vulgarity on the part of substantial new fortunes whose owners did not wish to wait for a generation or two of landed proprietorship, or for a noble son-in-law, to sweeten the odor of trade and fit them for the company of their betters. But these were all clearly removable blemishes. The faults were on the surface; the core of England was sound.

It is true that Pope is at his rudest in attacking those luckless denizens of "Grub Street" who have the temerity to write for a bare living without having enough of a gentleman's education to supply either correct Latin mottoes or an intimate knowledge of court intrigues; and the courteous Addison (who later succeeded in marrying a Duchess) is almost sharp about those wretched retail tradesmen, like Defoe, who neglect their shop to take an interest in political news and foreign affairs. But even those regrettable types seemed trivial enough to be laughed out of sight—and forgotten.

Fundamentally the world, or at least England, was a good place, needing just that degree of guidance and polish which its witty and elegant writers were so well equipped to give it—not, indeed, to be much changed, which was both unnecessary and impossible—but to shine eternally refulgent with its virtue all apparent and undimmed. And fundamentally, from the viewpoint of their own class, the fashionable writers were correct.

The bourgoisie was an expanding class, expanding in both directions. New fortunes were being made in trade almost daily by "nobodies" rising from below and, as Addison said:

> It is the happiness of a trading nation like ours, that the younger sons, though incapable of any liberal art or profession may be placed in such a way of life, as may perhaps enable them to vie with the best of their family: accordingly, we find several citizens that were launched into the world with narrow fortunes, rising by an honest industry to greater estates than those of their elder brothers.

Its members were not only increasing but, on the whole, becoming individually wealthier, more powerful and better educated. England's world power and prestige were rising steadily; the long inconclusive series of wars on the continent were comfortably removed, in terms of danger or observable bloodshed; and they provided an unprecedented demand for the products of a vastly improved and more efficient form of agriculture, and for the beginnings of a "mass production" of such manufactured goods as uniforms and weapons. The possibility of religious persecution seemed at an end and a universal toleration, generally credited to the new enlightenment of mankind rather than to skepticism or indifference, was one of the distinguishing marks of the happy island. Newton had opened the door into a world of scientific understanding which Pope complacently hailed with: "Nature and Nature's laws lay hid in Night: God said, *Let* Newton *be!* and all was Light." And, in general, the eighteenth century's pleased description of itself as "The Age of Enlightenment" was, from the point of view of articulate upper middle-class England, not too unrealistic.

What then of inarticulate England? What of the nobodies who remained nobodies? What of the small farmers dispossessed because they lacked the capital necessary for the new agricultural methods? What of the thousands forced into jail, beggary, servitude or emigration by the new Acts of Inclosure, those thousands of whom Morton, in his *People's History of England,* says:

> In other parts of England those of the smaller farmers who were tenants were gradually evicted or were ruined by rents four, five and even ten times as high as had been customary. Land farmed on the new methods could be made to pay these increased rents but this was no help to men whose farms and capital were too small to adopt them successfully. Many of the

small freeholders were also forced to sell out by the impossibility of competing with the up-to-date methods of their richer neighbours. The sums received under conditions amounting virtually to a forced sale were usually too small to be employed successfully in any other business even if the farmer had known how to make good use of them. A few, especially in Lancashire and Yorkshire, became successful manufacturers, but the vast majority spent their money quickly and then sank to the position of wage labourers whether on the land or in the new industrial towns.

A third class, the cottagers, found their rights even more ruthlessly violated. Few were able to establish any legal grounds for the customary rights over the village commons and fewer still received any adequate compensation for the loss of these rights. A whole class that had lived by a combination of domestic industry, the keeping of a few beasts or some poultry and regular or occasional work for wages, now found itself thrown back entirely on the last of these resources, since the period of enclosures was also the period in which domestic industry was being destroyed by the competition of the new factories. Lord Ernle fills nearly three pages of his English Farming Past and Present with a list of local and domestic industries which perished at this time.

From about the middle of the Eighteenth Century the improvement in agricultural technique began to make it possible to economise in labour. Wages fell rapidly in relation to prices: in many parts cottages were destroyed or allowed to become ruinous and there was both a decrease in numbers and a decline in the standards of life of the majority throughout the greater part of rural England. In the later part of the century there was not only an increase in the total population but a marked shifting of population from one part of the country to another. No reliable figures are available, but it is at least probable that the increase was smaller and the shifting greater than was at one time supposed.

The revolution in agriculture had three results which went far beyond the limits of agriculture itself. First it increased the productivity of the land and so made possible the feeding of the great industrial population in the new towns.

Second, it created a reserve army of wage earners, now "freed" completely from any connection with the soil, men without ties of place or property.

Third, there was the creation of a vastly increased internal market for manufactured goods. The subsistence farmer, with his domestic industry and his isolation from the outside world, might consume a good deal and yet buy very little. The labourer into whom he had now evolved was usually compelled to consume a great deal less but everything he consumed had to be bought. And it was only on the firm basis of a substantial home market that a great exporting industry could be built up.

It was his awareness of this vast submerged beggared peasantry and ex-peasantry upon whose misery so much of the prosperity of eighteenth century England was erected, and at whose expense the bourgeoisie conducted its remarkably swift and easy consolidation of power, that gave the greatest writer of the early eighteenth century, Jonathan Swift, the emotional force to create works of universal significance out of the polished periods and satirical wit which are the hallmarks of his time.

Before we turn to consider his towering figure, however, let us, if only for the sake of contrast and a proper perspective, look a little more closely at his contemporaries.

In 1709 Richard Steele sensed the possibilities of a growing fashionable public, wealthy, literate and with some pretensions to education, but without the serious university training which would make it possible for them to read the classics, then almost the only belles lettres in an age which found Shakespeare uncouth, Milton uncomfortable, and Bunyan absurd. Steele published the first English literary periodical, *The Tatler,* which is the ancestor of such widely different contemporary magazines as *The Atlantic Monthly, The Saturday Review of Literature,* the *Sunday Times* or *Tribune Book Review,* and *Magazine Sections,* and *The New Yorker.*

The opening number announced Steele's intention to print a paper every Tuesday, Thursday and Saturday:

> Where politic persons, who are so public-spirited as to neglect their own affairs to look into transactions of state . . . may be instructed, after their reading, what to think . . . also to have something which may be of entertainment to the fair sex, in honour of whom (is) invented the title of this paper . . . all accounts of gallantry, pleasure, and entertainment shall be under the article of White's Chocolate-house; poetry, under that of Will's Coffee-house; learning, under the title of the Grecian; foreign and domestic news, you will hear from Saint James's Coffee-house. . . .

Joseph Addison, a more consistent, prolific, and serious writer, if less quick and imaginative, was soon called on for help and for two years the paper appeared, with remarkable regularity, for the edification of an increasing number of ladies and gentlemen. It offered sketches or "short short stories" with emphasis on character and manner rather than on plot, occasional literary and art criticism of a topical nature, and sprightly satirical comment on such extravagant or crude fads and conventions as duelling, drinking bouts, and exaggerated styles of dress or flirtation. When it was ended in 1711, because of some too indiscreet political reflections and gossip, it was soon replaced by the *Spectator,* under Addison's editorship, which opened with a fictitious picture of the anonymous editor and his declaration:

> Thus I live in the world rather as a Spectator of mankind than as one of the species; by which means I have made myself a speculative statesman, soldier, merchant and artisan without ever meddling with any practical part in my life. I am very well versed in the theory of a husband or a father and can discern the errors in the economy, business and diversion of others, better than those who are engaged in them. . . . I never espoused any part with violence, and am resolved to observe an exact neutrality between the Whigs and Tories, unless I shall be forced to declare myself by the hostilities of either side. [Addison himself was an active and leading Whig and was, in fact, four years later promoted to the position of Secretary of State.]
>
> I have often been told by my friends, that it is pity so many useful discoveries which I have made should be in the possession of a silent man. For this reason, therefore, I shall publish a sheet-full of thoughts every morning for the benefit of my contemporaries; and if I can any way contribute to the diversion or improvement of the country in which I live, I shall leave it, when I am summoned out of it, with the secret satisfaction of thinking that I have not lived in vain.

Although Addison considered himself, and was considered, an unusually religious man, the depth of religious feeling of the period may be judged from his comments in any number of papers, particularly in the famous *Sir Roger de Coverley* series:

> I no sooner saw this venerable [clergy] man in the pulpit, but I very much approved of my friend's insisting upon the qualifications of a good aspect and a clear voice; for I was so charmed with the gracefulness of his figure and delivery, as well as the discourses he pronounced, that I think I never passed time more to my satisfaction. A sermon repeated after this manner is like the composition of a poet in the mouth of a graceful actor.
>
> I could heartily wish that more of our country clergy would follow this example, and, instead of wasting their spirits in

laborious compositions of their own, would endeavor after a handsome elocution, and all those other talents that are proper to enforce what has been penned by greater masters. This would not only be more easy to themselves, but more edifying to the people.

And again:

I am always well pleased with a country Sunday; and think, if keeping holy the seventh day were only a human institution, it would be the best method that could have been thought of for the polishing and civilizing of mankind. It is certain the country-people would soon degenerate into a kind of savages and barbarians, were there not such frequent returns of a stated time, in which the whole village meet together with their best faces, and in their cleanliest habits, to converse with one another upon indifferent subjects, *hear their duties explained to them*, [italics added] and join together in adoration of the Supreme Being.

While the general belief of the early eighteenth century man-of-the-world was a genteel deism or rationalism which would not have been unacceptable to Rousseau or Voltaire, his attitude toward religion was not the Frenchmen's bitter enmity toward a church with power to persecute, but rather tolerant support for a church which was a harmless and necessary part of the existing order. As thorough-going a sceptic as David Hume could advise a clergyman friend to preach the ordinary doctrines, because it was paying far too great a compliment to the vulgar to be punctilious about speaking the truth to them; Hume's political attitude appears more explicitly in his regret that the events of the revolution and subsequent Commonwealth period had changed the English "from a tranquil and submissive people" to a "restless, fanatic and rebellious"; Edward Gibbon could, a little later, more frankly point out that to the statesman a creed may be equally useful, whether it is true or false; and Horace Walpole perfectly expressed the dominant attitude of the educated classes in a letter from Paris saying that he would not allow guests of his to talk of the Old Testament as his French philosophe hosts talked before their servants "if a single footman were in the room."

Addison, however, whether from a more timid and conventional temperament, or a more perspicacious sense of social responsibility, himself held mild religious convictions and pointed out in one of his essays that ordinary people: "who are so used to be dazzled with riches, that they pay as much deference to the understanding of a man of an estate, as of a man of learning . . . are very hardly brought to regard any truth, how important so ever it may be, that is preached to them when they know there are several men of five hundred pounds a year who do not believe it."

Before turning to Addison's friend—and rival—Pope, we may pause a moment to remark on the general upper-class attitude toward women which Addison, in a friendlier but equally unmistakable way, expressed.

The position of woman had indeed deteriorated rapidly since the age when Chaucer's Wife of Bath and his Prioress could, in their own different ways, maintain their independence, fulfill their varying economic functions, and even travel, uncriticized, without masculine guardianship. Women in eighteenth century society (that is, essentially, of course, upper middle-class women—not servants, the rapidly disappearing peasant wives, or the newly appearing group of wives of petty tradesmen) had now become essentially sexual objects. The fashionable literature of the time tells us that the enjoyment of her body by rape or seduction, and the enjoyment of her fortune by marriage, were the only contexts in which it was possible for a man to consider a woman; and she herself seemed but infrequently to consider herself in any other light. Her chastity, or at least her reputation for chastity, is of vital importance before marriage, to enable her to make the best possible bargain; afterwards also she must avoid indiscretion lest she be held too cheap; but the whole business of her life is to arouse and glamorize those appetites from which she derives her importance and for whose satisfaction she may, if skillful, be well paid. Defoe's inimitable Moll Flanders says very sensibly:

> How necessary it is for all Women who expect anything in the World to preserve the character of their Virtue, even when perhaps they may have sacrificed the thing itself.

And Richardson's too often imitated Pamela preserves her "virtue" through three volumes of attack and is, at the end of the prolonged and earnest if involuntary "strip-tease," rewarded by marriage to her would-be ravisher—and by a permanent share in his country house and coach and six.

Addison is unfortunately even further removed from the frank insight of Defoe (of whom we must speak in more detail a little later) than he is from the unmitigated sentimentality of Richardson. He says repeatedly

> I consider woman as a beautiful romantic animal, that may be adorned with furs and feathers, pearls and diamonds, ores and silks. One of the fathers, if I am rightly informed, has defined a woman to be "An animal that delights in finery." ... This observation is so very notorious, that when in ordinary discourse we say a man has a fine head, a long head or a good head, we express ourselves metaphorically, and speak in relation to his understanding; whereas when we say of a woman, she has a fine, a long or a good head, we speak only in relation to her commode [head dress].
> The toilet is their great scene of business, and the right adjustment of their hair the principal employment of their lives. The sorting of a suit of ribands is considered a very good morning's work; and if they make an excursion to a mercer's or a toy-shop, so great a fatigue makes them unfit for anything else all the day after. Their more serious occupations are sewing and embroidering and their greatest drudgery the preparation of jellies and sweetmeats.

More seriously, he says in another essay:

> As our English women excel those of all nations in beauty, they should endeavor to outshine them in all other accomplishments proper to the sex, and to distinguish themselves as tender mothers and faithful wives. . . . Female virtues are of a domestic turn. The family is the proper province for *private* women to shine in. . . . After having addressed himself to the several ranks and orders of his countrymen, and shown them how they should behave themselves in the public cause he [Pericles] turns to the female part of his audience, "And as for you" says he, "I shall advise you in very few words: aspire only to those virtues that are peculiar to your sex; follow your natural modesty, and think it your greatest commendation not to be talked of one way or other."

That a very considerable part of Addison's readers were women shows their own acceptance of their degradation. The saving word "private" preserves Addison from presuming to criticize Queen Anne and, perhaps, such bedchamber politicians as the Duchess of Marlborough. But we are already more than halfway from Elizabeth's un-sex-conscious rebuke to Lord Burghley: "Little man, little man, 'must' is not a word to use to princes" to Victoria's comment (on refusing to consider a petition against the fourteen-hour factory workday for children), "This is a political question and on such questions the queen, being a woman, cannot presume to hold an opinion."

Even the gentle Edward Young wrote:

> Ladies supreme among amusements reign
> By nature born to soothe and entertain.
> Their prudence in a share of folly lies;
> Why will they be so weak as to be wise?

And Thomas Rymer, among the other absurd rules he promulgated to restore classical correctness to the drama, decreed:

> In poetry no woman is to kill a man except her quality gives her the advantage above him. Poetical decency will not suffer death to be dealt to each other by such persons whom the laws of duel allow not to enter the lists together.

When we hear Pope we find, as we should expect, a more brutal directness whose personal spite and occasional violence is, however, perhaps less intolerable than Addison's amiable condescension. He makes a summary statement:

> Nothing so true as what you once let fall;
> "Most women have no character at all,"
> Matter too soft a lasting mark to bear
> And best distinguished by black, brown or fair.

After this it is almost anticlimactic to turn to such other authorities as Lord Chesterfield who said, in a letter of advice to his son:

> A man of sense only trifles with them [women], humours and flatters them as he does with a sprightly, forward child; but he neither consults them about, nor trusts them with, serious matters, though he often makes them believe that he does both, which is the thing in the world that they are proud of. . . . No flattery is either too high or too low for them. They will greedily swallow the highest and gratefully accept of the lowest.

However, it is not only, or even chiefly, in his attitude toward women that Pope best represents his age. We find Pope the epitome of his period whether we accept Carlyle's unkind description of

"The withered unbelieving eighteenth Century," or Austin Dobson's homage:

> So I that love the old Augustan days
> Of formal Courtesies and formal Phrase
> That like, along the finished line to feel
> The Ruffles flutter and the flash of steel
> That like my Couplet as compact as clear,
> That like my Satire sparkling tho severe
> Unmixed with Bathos and unmarr'd by Trope,
> I fling my Cap for Polish—and for Pope.

Pope's choice of the mock heroic *Rape of the Lock* and the sententious *Essay on Man* as titles for two of his major works; his sensible superficial psychology; his correct and uninspired comments on the art of poetry and of life; his pose of fashionable cynicism, and his genuine unashamed egotism; these are all clearly apparent from the beginning to the end of his work, and can be adequately indicated by the briefest of quotations from one poem after the other.

In the *Essay On Criticism,* for example, written in 1709 when Pope was just twenty years old, he begins so deftly and prosaicly that it is easy to see why a later critic exclaimed, "No great poet *would* write like Pope—but no other *could*":

> 'Tis hard to say if greater want of skill
> Appear in writing or in judging ill;
> But of the two less dangerous is th' offence
> To tire our patience than mislead our sense:
> Some few in that, but numbers err in this;
> Ten censure wrong for one who writes amiss;
> A fool might once himself alone expose;
> Now one in verse makes many more in prose.
> 'Tis with our judgments as our watches, none
> Go just alike, yet each believes his own.

The poem continues effortlessly through hundreds of lines as well turned and snobbish as the famous:

> A little learning is a dangerous thing;
> Drink deep or taste not the Pierian spring:
> There shallow draughts intoxicate the brain
> And drinking largely sobers us again;

and through innumerable half-truths as correct and misleading as:

> True wit is Nature to advantage dress'd,
> What oft was thought, but ne'er so well express'd;

or as practical and patronizing as:

> True ease in writing comes from Art, not chance,
> As those move easiest who have learned to dance;

and:

> Men must be taught as if you taught them not
> And things unknown proposed as things forgot.

Pope's next major effort, *The Rape of the Lock,* written about two years later is a mock-epic or, as he calls it, "An Heroi-Comical Poem," on the unauthorized theft of a Lady's lock of hair by an enamored young lord, and on the consequent furor. It is tricked out in pseudohomeric style with an elaborate mythology of fairies, elves, and guardian spirits invented for the occasion, and built on much sharply detailed description of dressing table, ball gown, card-playing mothers and dancing daughters. The confusion of values which equates such possible catastrophes as a seduction and a ruined dress is, of course, deliberately used for humor. But Pope's avowedly moral essays come, as we shall see, so close to the same attitude that we cannot help feeling his parody involved less exaggeration than he supposed.

The poem begins with his heroine preparing for the ball, assisted by her maid Betty and by the invisible Sylphs who wait on beauty. The unself-conscious awareness of colonial commerce in the ninth to the sixteenth lines are as characteristic as the self-conscious classicism of the verses as a whole.

> And now, unveil'd, the toilet stands display'd,
> Each silver vase in mystic order laid.
> First, robed in white, the nymph intent adores,
> With head uncover'd, the Cosmetic powers.
> A heav'nly image in the glass appears;
> To that she bends, to that her eyes she rears.
> Th' inferior priestess, at her altar's side,
> Trembling begins the sacred rites of Pride.

> Unnumber'd treasures ope at once, and here
> The various off'rings of the world appear;
> From each she nicely culls with curious toil,
> And decks the Goddess with the glittering spoil.
> This casket India's glowing gems unlocks
> And all Arabia breathes from yonder box.
> The tortoise here and elephant unite,
> Transform'd to combs, the speckled, and the white.
> Here files of pins extend their shining rows,
> Puffs, powders, patches, trifles, billet-doux.
> Now awful beauty puts on all its arms;
> The Fair each moment rises in her charms,
> Repairs her smiles, awakens every grace,
> And calls forth all the wonders of her face;
> Sees by degrees a purer blush arise,
> And keener lightnings quicken in her eyes
> The busy Sylphs surround their darling care,
> These set the head, and those divide the hair,
> Some fold the sleeve, while others plait the gown;
> And Betty's praised for labours not her own.

Belinda's attendant spirits have an uneasy foreboding of catastrophe:

> This day black omens threat the brightest Fair
> That e'er deserv'd a watchful spirit's care;
> Some dire disaster, or by force or slight;
> But what or where, the Fates have wrapt in night.
> Whether the nymph shall break Diana's law,
> Or some frail China Jar receive a flaw;
> Or stain her honour, or her new brocade,
> Forget her prayers, or miss a masquerade,
> Or lose her heart, or necklace, at a ball;

Meanwhile we see the arbiters of social life:

> Hither the Heroes and the Nymphs resort,
> To taste awhile the pleasures of a court;
> In various talk the instructive hours they past,
> Who gave the ball, or paid the visit last;
> One speaks the glory of the British Queen,
> And one describes a charming Indian screen;
> A third interprets motions, looks, and sighs;
> At every word a reputation dies.

Then suddenly, in the midst of the idyllic scene, the Baron flashes a pair of scissors and:

> The meeting points the sacred hair dissever
> From the fair head, for ever, and for ever!
> Then flash'd the living lightning from her eyes,
> And screams of horror rend th' affrighted skies.
> Not louder shrieks to pitying Heav'n are cast,
> When husbands, or when lapdogs breathe their last;
> Or when rich China vessels, fall'n from high
> In glitt'ring dust and painted fragments lie!

This is excellent foolery, although perhaps too long drawn for modern taste, but in Pope's major philosophical work, the *Essay on Man*, written in 1732-33, we find him concluding, in all seriousness, with a somewhat similar catalogue of human values and their comparative importance, or, rather, unimportance:

> Behold the child, by Nature's kindly law,
> Pleas'd with a rattle, tickled with a straw;
> Some livelier plaything gives his youth delight,
> A little louder, but as empty quite:
> Scarfs, garters, gold, amuse his riper stage,
> And beads and prayer-books are the toys of age:
> Pleas'd with this bauble still, as that before,
> Till tired he sleeps and life's poor play is o'er.

Milton would certainly have been all the more outraged by this view of human life because Pope presumes to open his "essay" by deliberately borrowing the line in which his great predecessor announced the epic purpose of *Paradise Lost*—"to justify the ways of God to man!" Pope declares that the poet's true purpose is to:

> Eye Nature's walks, shoot folly as it flies,
> And catch the manners living as they rise;
> Laugh where we must, be candid where we can,
> But vindicate the ways of God to man.

After a number of such quotable and overquoted pseudoprofundities as:

> Hope springs eternal in the human breast:
> Man never is, but always to be, blest.

Pope completes his vindication and summarizes his philosophy in the famous lines:

THE AUGUSTANS

>All Nature is but Art unknown to thee;
>All chance direction which thou canst not see;
>All discord harmony not understood;
>All partial evil, universal good:
>And spite of Pride in erring Reason's spite,
>One truth is clear, *Whatever is, is right.*

Art has perhaps never more explicitly spoken in the service of the status quo, although Pope himself has often approximated this explicitness in such less solemn recommendations as:

>Be not the first by whom the new is tried
>Nor yet the last to lay the old aside.

Finally, in this same work, Pope anticipates the bourgeois political philosophy of "laissez-faire" and the ethics of "enlightened self-interest":

>For forms of government let fools contest;
>Whate'er is best administered is best;
>For Wit's false mirror hold up Nature's light,
>Show'd erring pride, *Whatever is, is right;*
>That Reason, Passion, answer one great aim;
>That true Self-love and Social are the same;
>That Virtue only makes our bliss below,
>And all our knowledge is, *ourselves to know.*

After this it is, perhaps, anticlimactic to quote anything further, but in justice to Pope's happiest vein of satire we must conclude on a more congenial note with his delightful "Epigram Engraved on the Collar of a Dog Which I Gave to His Royal Highness":

>I am his Highness' dog at Kew;
>Pray tell me, Sir, whose dog are you?

And the even sharper sting that describes his friend, and rival, Addison:

>Peace to all such! but were there one whose fires
>True Genius kindles; and fair Fame inspires,
>Bless'd with each talent and each art to please,
>And born to write, converse, and live with ease;
>Should such a man, too fond to rule alone,
>Bear, like the Turk, no brother near the throne;

> View him with scornful, yet with jealous eyes
> And hate for arts that caus'd himself to rise;
> Damn with faint praise, assent with civil leer,
> And without sneering teach the rest to sneer;
> Willing to wound, and yet afraid to strike,
> Just hint a fault, and hesitate dislike;
> Alike reserved to blame or to commend,
> A tim'rous foe, and a suspicious friend;
> Dreading ev'n fools; by flatterers besieged,
> And so obliging that he ne'er obliged;
> Like Cato give his little Senate laws,
> And sit attentive to his own applause:
> While Wits and Templars ev'ry sentence raise,
> And wonder with a foolish face of praise—
> Who but must laugh if such a man there be?
> Who would not weep, if Atticus were he?

What Pope says of Addison is perhaps reasonably true; if Addison had said it of Pope it would certainly have been even truer; and we might with no great loss here leave the Augustans to each other's company if it were not for Jonathan Swift, the giant who was caught among these Lilliputians.

JONATHAN SWIFT

Jonathan Swift, known throughout the world as the author of *Gulliver's Travels,* and to students of literature as the writer of the most savage, bitter and utterly damning satire ever written in English—*A Modest Proposal*—is still loved and honored all over Ireland as one of the first and greatest of the fighters for Irish freedom.

Some forty years after his death Henry Grattan, securing the adoption of the Declaration of Irish Independence in the Irish House of Commons, cried out, "Spirit of Swift! your genius has prevailed. Ireland is now a nation!' and today, more than two hundred years later, the Drapier's Head still gives its name to scores of Irish inns and taverns, commemorating Swift's series of great political pamphlets published under the title of *The Drapier's Letters.*

Although Swift was born in Dublin his parents were both English, connected with several important families but themselves possessed of little or no financial resources. His father had followed three successful lawyer brothers to Ireland a few years before, but died at twenty-five with his fortune still unmade and his son still unborn. Swift himself entered the world on November 30, 1667, some six months after his father's death. His oldest uncle, Godwin Swift, undertook the expense of his upbringing and education, but in so grudging and "charitable" a fashion that, as Swift said, he "never loved his Uncle Godwin, nor the remembrance of his Uncle to the hour of his death." After attending Trinity College with little satisfaction to either himself or the authorities, he later wrote in a characteristically third person fragment of autobiography:

> By the ill treatment of his nearest relations, he was so discouraged and sunk in his spirits that he too much neglected his academic studies, for some parts of which [notably philosophy and theology, then a very important part of the college curriculum] he had no relish by nature, and turned himself to reading history and poetry.

Later he was to declare, to the scandal of his learned colleagues:

> I have been better entertained, and more informed, by a chapter in the "Pilgrim's Progress" than by a long discourse on the will, and the intellect, and simple and complex ideas.

He reiterated in this and other arguments: "Style? Here's a fine pother about nothing; proper words in proper places make a true definition of a style."

Swift was graduated without honors in 1688. Through family connections a place in England was secured for him as secretary to Sir William Temple, formerly an important English statesman and diplomat, and in 1688 still famous, active, and much visited by leading writers and politicians in his retirement at Moor Park.

This was an interesting position for a novice of twenty-one, which afforded him unusual chances of meeting important men; but it was also in many respects a humiliating one, as Swift's later comments in his private journal make clear. He learned much of the behind-scenes of politics, and the pettiness and dishonesty of successful politicians, and he so bitterly resented the patronage and cavalier treatment with which he met (even family chaplains were still treated rather as upper servants or very poor relations), that twice in the ten years he spent with Temple, he broke away to try his fortune elsewhere. He found no real opening, although he took orders on the promise of a church vacancy by King William III, to whom Temple had recommended him, and he remained at Moor Park in growing discontent until he was thirty-two.

During this time he filled some of his long empty hours by teaching the housekeeper's young daughter Stella, who became his intimate friend and was his close companion for the rest of her life. He also made a bid for fame by writing much utterly valueless poetry on the pompous Augustan model, and, finally, his first two real works—a satirical dialogue *The Battle of the Books*, and a sharp travesty on religious disputes, *The Tale of A Tub*. The latter was not published until 1705, when it was issued anonymously. Swift claimed that this parodied only the Roman Catholic and Dissenting Churches and that it was really a defense of the Episcopalian Church, in which he was seeking preferment; but Queen Anne, who later refused him a bishopric as its author, evidently felt it was essentially an attack on the established church as well. Most modern readers would certainly agree with her.

At Temple's death in 1699 Swift, failing to secure any other appointment, accepted the position of chaplain to the Earl of Berkeley who soon gave him a small living, the vicarage of Laracour in Ireland. From 1701 Swift visited much in London political circles and wrote one or two unimportant political pamphlets mildly defending certain personalities of the Whig ministry then in power. However, the alliance was lukewarm on his part and when it became, or remained, disappointingly cold and unappreciative on the part of the ministers, he returned to Ireland. There he spent most of his time in the duties and pleasures of his country vicarage and in the companionship of Stella, whom he had advised to settle in nearby Dublin under the chaperonage of a distant relative.

In 1707 he undertook a visit to London on behalf of the Irish Church, in hopes of persuading the Queen to give up her claim to an annual tax on that Church's income as she had already given up her claim to any part of the income of the Church of England. Here he entered into long drawn out and, finally, fruitless negotiations on his mission, but meanwhile rapidly made friends of Addison, Steele, Pope, Gay, and almost all the other leading writers of the time. Addison, then already very well known, presented a book to him with the inscription, "To Dr. Jonathan Swift, the most agreeable companion, the truest friend, and the greatest genius of the age," and published a number of his papers and verse in the *Tatler* and *Spectator*. Swift also found time to write a serious attack on contemporary morality in public and private life in his *Project for the Advancement of Religion and Reformation of Manners* which was printed in 1709, just before his return to Ireland.

His unhypocritical but non-religious attitude toward his sacred profession, and the sincere practical support he gave the Church that employed him, are well illustrated in his notebook of private meditations, published after his death. Here, under "Thoughts on Religion" he mused:

> The want of belief is a defect that ought to be concealed, when it cannot be overcome. . . . I look upon myself, in the capacity of a clergyman, to be one appointed by Providence for defending a post assigned to me, and for gaining over as many enemies as I can.

In 1710 political events which threatened the fall of the Whig ministry made Swift hurry back to London. There, partly because of his annoyance with the Whig minister's continued refusal to grant the request of the Irish Church for equal treatment, partly because of his personal liking for the incoming Tory prime minister who made extremely courteous—and witty—overtures to him, and partly because of his genuine lifelong hatred of war (the Whig party and its famous general, the Duke of Marlborough, were pressing for a continuance of the now almost thirty-year old "War of the Protestant Succession"), Swift joined the Tory party.

His first service to the party was a powerful antiwar pamphlet, *The Conduct of the Allies,* which, as a nineteenth century historian said, "knocked Marlborough's sword out of his hand." Dr. Johnson was not fond of Swift and felt that too much fuss had been made about this pamphlet, which, according to him, simply put "all the facts plain." Nevertheless, Johnson said almost half a century later:

> Swift must be confessed to have dictated for a time the political opinions of the English nation. In the succeeding reign he delivered Ireland from plunder and oppression; and shewed that wit confederated with truth, had such force as authority was unable to resist.

Several comments in Swift's private journal to Stella, written shortly before the publication of the pamphlet which made him famous, give an interesting glimpse of his own attitude:

October 23, 1711: I was today in the city concerning something with a printer, and am tomorrow all day busy with Mr. Secretary about the same. I won't tell you now, but the ministers reckon it will do an abundance of good, and open the eyes of the nation, who are half bewitched against a Peace. Few of this generation can remember anything but war and taxes, and they think it is as it should be; whereas 'tis certain we are the most undone people in Europe, as I am afraid I shall make appear beyond all contradiction.

On another occasion, a few months before, Swift had written in his confidential notes to Stella that Marlborough: "is as covetous as Hell, and ambitious as the Prince of it; he would fain have been general for life, and has broken all endeavors for Peace, to keep his greatness and money. . . ."

After the publication of the pamphlet and the termination of the war Swift was probably the most powerful and courted private citizen in England, and with memories of the many snubs and humiliations he had earlier received, amused himself by forcing lords and cabinet ministers to dance attendance on him and put up with his shocking disregard for titles and court etiquette.

Again we find his personal attitude frankly set down in the secret, day-by-day journal he faithfully kept to send Stella whenever he was away from her:

February 12, 1711: I dined today with Mr. Sec. St. John: I went to the Court of Requests at noon, and sent Mr. Harley into the House to call the Secretary, to let him know I would not dine with him if he dined late.

February 17: I took some good walks in the Park today, and then went to Mr. Harley. Lord Rivers was got there before me, and I chid him for presuming to come on a day when only Lord-Keeper and the Secretary and I were to be there.

February 25: I dined today with Mr. Sec. St. John, on condition that I might choose my company.

April 4: Don't you remember how I used to be in pain when Sir Wm. Temple would look cold and out of humour for three or four days, and I used to suspect a hundred reasons? I have plucked up my spirits since then, faith; he spoiled a fine-gentleman.

April 5: I have been used barbarously by the late ministry; I am a little piqued in honour to let people see I am not to be despised.

May 19: Mr. Secretary told me the Duke of Buckingham had been talking to him about me, and desired my acquaintance. I answered, it could not be, for he had not made sufficient advances. Then the Duke of Shrewsbury said he thought the Duke was not used to make advances. I said I could not help that; for I always expected advances in proportion to men's quality, and more from a Duke than other men.

October 7: . . . Lady Oglethorpe brought me and the Duchess of Hamilton together today in the drawing-room, and I have given her some encouragement, but not much.

During these few fashionable London years Swift became friendly with an unpretentious though wealthy widow, Mrs. Vanhomrigh, and her daughter, Vanessa. The daughter's youth made him feel that it was safe to play the "guide, philosopher and friend," direct her education and, after her mother's death, advise her on her business problems. Although she declared herself in love with him he evidently took the affair as a conventional flirtation, and wrote a long formal poem, *Cadenus and Vanessa,* full of elaborate mythological compliments to the lady and much more genuine touches of satire about himself, such as:

> 'Tis an old maxim in the schools,
> That flattery's the food of fools;
> Yet now and then your men of wit
> Will condescend to take a bit.

He told her of Stella and wrote Stella all about her, but Vanessa seems to have been genuinely in love with him, and when he returned to Ireland she followed him to an estate she owned there, still passionately urging marriage.

He was furious both at her insistence and at Stella's uneasiness and refused ever to see Vanessa again during her tragically brief life —she died just two years later. According to some accounts he also, at that time, acceded to Stella's request for a secret and platonic marriage.

There was clearly a pathological element in his insuperable aversion to any sexual relations—a theme developed in Gulliver's return from the Land of Houyhnhnms—and there are many amateur psychologists who have erected tomes over these scanty facts. But Swift's vitally important and well-documented public life and its effect on his work have been largely ignored, and to this we must return.

There seemed no position Swift could not get for his friends— and he got many for the Whig writers he had known, with most of whom he remained very friendly—but his irreverent wit and, perhaps, his pride, barred the way to preferment in the Church, while his being in orders closed the door to any official non-clerical appointment out of it. Finally he accepted the Deanery of St. Patrick's, Dublin, although he had strongly protested against exile from England and bitterly opposed the prospect of more or less permanent banishment to a poverty stricken and subject country. His reluctance seems to have been reciprocated by his congregation and on the day of his installation someone posted a long poem on the door of the Cathedral, beginning:

> This Place He got by Wit and Rhyme
> And many ways most odd;
> And might a Bishop be in time
> Did he believe in God.

it ended:

> Look down, St. Patrick, look, we pray
> On thine own Church and Steeple;
> Convert the Dean on this Great Day;
> Or else, God help the people.

Whether it was St. Patrick's doing or not, the Dean, who never ceased to inveigh against having to live in Ireland, nevertheless soon threw himself heart and soul into the struggles of the nation against its English oppressors:

In 1699 Ireland's flourishing wool industry had been killed by an English law forbidding the exportation of woolen goods and when some of the thousands abruptly thrown out of employment turned to the manufacture of linen, similar laws were passed against the exportation of this and, in fact, all other manufactured goods and even cattle! The bitter struggle for land by a population forced to depend entirely on agricultural pursuits intensified the hardships of an incredibly barbaric system of land tenure, with its heavy drain of enormous profits for absentee landlords. Swift wrote bitterly during his first few months as Dean of St. Patrick's:

> I confess myself to be touched with a very sensitive pleasure when I hear of a mortality in any country parish or village, where the wretches are forced to pay for a filthy cabin and two ridges of potatoes treble their worth; brought up to steal or beg for want of work; to whom death would be the best

thing to be wished for on account both of themselves and the public.

When, in 1719, an Act was passed in England robbing the Irish Parliament and Courts of their last shreds of independence and reaffirming all the general restrictions which had been enacted since 1495, Swift was driven into public action. In 1720 he published his powerful pamphlet, *A Proposal for the Universal Use of Irish Manufacture*, which proposed a virtual boycott of English goods, and an economic declaration of independence for Ireland, with the slogan "Burn everything that comes from England except the coal." This attack was so sharp and stinging that the government brought the printer up for trial as "seditious," since the author was, formally, unknown, although most of Dublin knew perfectly well who he was. Despite the judge's explicit charge the jury refused to convict the printer—they were sent out of court nine times to change their verdict and threatened with prosecution themselves if they did not!—and Swift became the hero of Dublin. One of the sentiments often quoted from this pamphlet by Irish "agitators" for the next hundred years was the characteristic comment:

> The Scripture tells us "oppression makes a wise man mad." Therefore, consequently speaking, the reason why some men are not mad, is because they are not wise: However, it were to be wished that oppression would, in time, teach a little wisdom to fools.

Two years later a particularly obvious "job" (the eighteenth century synonym of our "racket") gave Swift the opportunity he had been waiting for.

One of the King's mistresses, who was already drawing an annual pension of £3,000 from the Irish establishment had, for favors received, been given a "patent" to supply copper coins to Ireland. She arranged with a Mr. William Wood of Birmingham to coin £100,800 worth of coins out of £60,000 worth of metal, and to divide the profits by giving her £10,000 and the King £14,000.

This would have worked some genuine hardship in Ireland by its cheapening of the minor currency but, more important, it was a blatant reminder of Ireland's helpless state of subjection and the callous indifference to her welfare or opinion which permeated the attitude of the English government. Swift realized that this was an issue immediate, concrete and dramatic enough to arouse and unite all classes and religions—he said that "even goslings know enough to huddle together when a kite pauses overhead"—and used it as a springboard for his plunge into serious anti-English agitation. Under the title of *The Drapier's Letters* he issued the first of a series of some of the most effective propaganda leaflets ever written. The first letter is addressed "to the tradesmen, shop keepers, farmers and country people in general of the Kingdom of Ireland," and begins:

> What I intend now to say to you, is, next to your duty to God, and the care of your salvation, of the greatest concern to yourselves, and your children; your bread and clothing, and every common necessary of life, entirely depend on it. Therefore I do most earnestly exhort you as men, as Christians, as parents, and as lovers of your country, to read this paper with the utmost attention, or get it read to you by others, which that you may do at the less expense, I have ordered the printer to sell it at the lowest rate. . . .

The response to this first letter was so overwhelming that a compromise was suggested restricting Wood's coinage to £40,000 worth, and restricting its use to no more than five pence in any one transaction. This brought forth a second letter denouncing the "job" anew, and attacking Wood with every species of ridicule and contumely: "It is no loss of honour to submit to the lion, but who, with the figure of a man, can think with patience of being devoured by a rat?" It called on the people to maintain and increase their resistance. A third letter to the same effect was next addressed "to the nobility and gentry of the Kingdom of Ireland." Public enthusiasm mounted so sharply that there seemed danger of a general uprising, and the Lord Lieutenant wrote to Prime Minister Walpole that it was "impossible to stop the torrent" unless Wood's grant were canceled. Walpole removed him from office and sent over a new Lord Lieutenant. A few days before this dignitary's arrival the fourth and perhaps the greatest of the letters appeared addressed "to the whole people of Ireland." A brief quotation from this will show how important a structure Swift had erected upon the simple foundation of popular opposition to the debased English coinage. Remember that the date is 1724 and anticipates Thomas Paine by almost half a century!

For, *in reason*, all government without the consent of the governed, is the very definition of slavery; but, *in fact*, eleven men well armed will certainly subdue one single man in his shirt. . . . A people long used to hardships lose by degrees the very notions of liberty; they look upon themselves as creatures at mercy, and that all impositions laid on them by a stronger hand are, in the phrase of the report, legal and obligatory. Hence proceed that poverty and lowness of spirit, to which a kingdom may be subject, as well as a particular person. And when Esau came fainting from the field at point to die, it is no wonder that he sold his birthright for a mess of pottage.

The new Lord Lieutenant's first official act was to offer a reward of £300 (subsequently increased) for the name of the author —which was an open secret to every Irishman—and to arrest the printer. However, as Swift later said in his own "Verses on the Death of Dr. Swift":

Ne'er a traitor could be found
To sell him for six hundred pound.

The grand jury, every member of which had mysteriously received an "anonymous" leaflet, "Seasonable Advice to the Grand Jury," refused to indict the printer; so did a second grand jury illegally impaneled by the same Lord Chief Justice who had had such troubles trying to get a sentence of guilty for the earlier printer!

Swift's well-founded trust in the people of Dublin is illustrated by the fact that on the day after the announcement of the reward he publicly attended the new Lord-Lieutenant's reception, strode up to him, and said, in a voice which filled the ballroom: "So, my lord, this is a glorious exploit you performed yesterday, in suffering a proclamation against a poor shopkeeper, whose only crime is an honest endeavor to save his country from ruin."

Wood's patent was revoked (he was consoled with £24,000 paid from the English treasury, of which no doubt the Duchess got her fair share) and in all Ireland, as Johnson later said:

The Drapier was a sign; the Drapier was a health; and which way so ever the eye or the ear was turned, some tokens were found of the nation's gratitude to the Drapier.

Swift made this the occasion for one of his rare sermons—he himself said, "I never preached but twice in my life, and they were not sermons but pamphlets"—and announced as his subject, "Doing Good." The sermon reads in part:

> . . . But, besides this love we owe to every man in his particular capacity, under the title of our neighbour, there is yet a duty of a more large extensive nature incumbent on us; which is, our love to our neighbour in his public capacity, as he is a member of that great body the commonwealth, under the same government with ourselves; and this is usually called love of the public, and is a duty to which we are more strictly obliged than even that of loving ourselves; because therein ourselves are also contained, as well as all our neighbours, in one great body. This love of the public, or of the commonwealth, or love of our country, was in ancient times properly known by the name of virtue, because it was the greatest of all virtues and was supposed to contain all virtues in it; . . .
>
> But here I would not be misunderstood: by the love of our country, I do not mean loyalty to our king, for that is a duty of another nature; and a man may be very loyal, in the common sense of the word, without one grain of public good at his heart. Witness this very kingdom we live in [Ireland] I verily believe, that since the beginning of the world, no nation upon earth ever showed (all circumstances considered) such high constant marks of loyalty, in all their actions and behaviours as we have done: and at the same time, no people ever appeared more utterly void of what is called a public spirit. When I say the people, I mean the bulk or mass of the people; for I have nothing to do with those in power. . . .
>
> Perhaps it may be thought by some, that this way of discoursing is not so proper from the pulpit. But surely, when an open attempt is made, and far carried on, to make a great kingdom a poorhouse, to deprive us of all means to exercise hospitality or charity, to turn our cities and churches into ruins, to make the country a desert for wild beasts and robbers, to destroy all arts and sciences, all trades and manufactures, and the very tillage of the ground, only to enrich one obscure ill–designing proprietor and his followers; it is time for the pastor to cry out "that the wolf is getting into his flock," and to warn them to stand together and all to consult the common safety. And God be praised for his infinite goodness in raising such a spirit of union among us, at least in this point, in the midst of all our former divisions; which union, if it continue, will in all probability defeat the pernicious design of this pestilent enemy to the nation!
>
> . . . I am sensible that what I have now said will not go very far, being confined to this assembly: but I hope it may

stir up others of my brethren to exhort their several congregations, after a more effectual manner, to show their love for their country on this important occasion. And this, I am sure, cannot be called meddling in affairs of state.

The years 1720-1725 which were so busy politically also saw the completion of Swift's best known and most ambitious literary work, *Gulliver's Travels*. This had been begun in jest while Swift was meeting Pope, Gay and other wits at the Scriblerus Club in London, and probably the greater part or all of the "Voyage to Lilliput" had been written there. The touches of personal satire on Walpole and other ministers, and the comparative light-heartedness change rapidly as Swift became more and more immersed in Irish affairs, although even in the first two voyages his deep hatred of war and overwhelming contempt for corrupt politicians are apparent. But the final chapters, culminating in the unforgettable attack on social evils interwoven with the descriptions of the Yahoos, are in another tone altogether and echo the fury of notes like this one, written from Ireland:

> There are thousands of poor wretches who think themselves blessed if they can obtain a hut worse than a squire's dog-kennel, and an acre of ground for a potatoe plantation, on condition of being as very slaves as any in America. What can be more deplorable than to behold wretches starving in the midst of plenty?

The hero of Swift's best known work is one Lemuel Gulliver, a plainspoken simple straightforward man with some education both as a navigator and a doctor. Unable to build a medical practise which will adequately support his wife and young children, he reluctantly accepts an offer to go back to sea as a ship's surgeon and sets sail from Bristol on the first of his now famous voyages, May 4, 1699.

After a successful six months trading cruise in the East Indies they are driven out of their way by a storm and shipwrecked in a strange region northwest of Van Dieman's land.

Gulliver, separated from his companions, is cast up on the shore of what he later discovers to be Lilliput. While asleep he is captured and bound by some thousands of the six-inch tall inhabitants.

His adventures among the Lilliputians have been read in emasulated nursery editions by most children, who enjoy without fully understanding the satire involved in such descriptions as that of the Emperor, "taller by almost the Breadth of my Nail, than any of his Court, which alone is enough to strike an Awe into the Beholders."

There are, of course, many far more elaborate passages which, for Swift's contemporaries, unmistakably indicated current figures of state. And we need no such special knowledge to appreciate their more fundamental satirical attack upon political and court intrigues in general. A well-known illustration opens the third chapter.

Other unmistakable references to the religious wars show how well justified Queen Anne was in her suspicion that Swift's earlier ridicule had been meant impartially to embrace all sects.

After many amusing and some hazardous experiences Gulliver succeeds in returning to England where he makes a small fortune by exhibiting and selling a number of the Lilliputian sheep, cows and other livestock which he had taken with him on his departure.

Two months later, on June 20, 1702, he again goes to sea. The ship is almost immediately driven out of its course by a storm and when the wind subsides several members of the crew row to a strange shore to get drinking water. While Gulliver wanders a little way inland the others are terrified by the approach of one of the gigantic inhabitants and escape, leaving Gulliver alone.

He is soon picked up between thumb and forefinger by one of the sixty-foot tall natives, and naturally gives himself up for lost. "For, as human Creatures are observed to be more Savage and cruel in proportion to their Bulk; what could I expect but to be a Morsel in the Mouth of the first among these enormous Barbarians who should happen to seize me?"

However the Brobdingnagans (as he later learns to call them) prove to be superior to mankind in wisdom and humanity as well as stature. The satire of western civilization is here developed more directly by statement of differences rather than by observation of similarities.

For example, when, after many adventures, Gulliver is purchased by the Queen and becomes something of a court pet the King "desired I would give him as exact an account of the Government of England as I possibly could; because, as fond as Princes commonly are of their own Customs (for so he conjectured of other Monarchs by my former Discourses) he should be glad to hear of anything that might deserve imitation." But the result was disconcerting.

In an effort more favorably to impress the king, Gulliver offers to teach him the arts of war, since the Brobdingnagans have never discovered or invented such things as gunpowder.

> The King was struck with horror at the description I had given of those terrible engines, and the proposal I had made. He was amazed how so impotent and grovelling an insect as I (these were his expressions) could entertain such inhuman ideas, and in so familiar a manner as to appear wholly unmoved at all the scenes of blood and desolation, which I had painted as the common effects of those destructive machines, whereof he said some evil genius, enemy to mankind, must have been the first contriver. As for himself, he protested that although few things delighted him so much as new discoveries in art or in nature, yet he would rather lose half his kingdom than be privy to such a secret, which he commanded me, as I valued my life, never to mention any more.
>
> A strange effect of narrow principles and short views! that a prince possessed of every quality which procures veneration, love, and esteem; of strong parts, great wisdom, and profound learning, endued with admirable talents for government, and almost adored by his subjects, should from a nice unnecessary scruple, whereof in Europe we can have no conception, let slip an opportunity put into his hands, that would have made him absolute master of the lives, the liberties, and the fortunes of his people.

Finally by a strange series of accidents Gulliver is carried out to sea, rescued by an English ship, and returns home.

The third voyage, undertaken a few months later, is the least interesting whether as story or as satire.

Captured by pirates and set adrift in a small boat, Gulliver manages to reach an uninhabited island from which he is rescued by the people of a sort of floating island called Laputa. They are a caste of absent-minded astronomers who rule a small continent, over which they can make their floating island move at will, and who care for nothing but mathematics and music. Despite this promising beginning Gulliver meets with no really exciting adventures here and none of the individuals come alive for us as did many of the persons he met in Lilliput and Brobdingnag.

The object of Swift's satire here is apparently the arid rationalism and formal metaphysical discussions of many eighteenth century literati, but he himself is evidently not clear as to the practical possibilities of scientific investigation, and there seems to be little coherence or discrimination in his attacks on a number of disparate experiments and innovations.

The only detail of this third voyage which strikes the imagination is Gulliver's description of the few individuals in each generation who are, in this region, born immortal.

When he first hears of these Struldbruggs, as they are called, he ecstatically envisions the wisdom, benevolence and happiness which such fortunate beings must achieve, but is rapidly disillusioned. His informant tells him:

> They were not only opinionative, peevish, covetous, morose, vain, talkative, but uncapable of friendship, and dead to all natural affection, which never descended below their grandchildren. Envy and impotent desires are their prevailing passions. . . . The least miserable among them appear to be those who turn to dotage, and entirely lose their memories; these meet with more pity and assistance, because they want many bad qualities which abound in others.

After an absence of five and a half years, Gulliver finally returns to England. "I continued at home with my Wife and Children about five Months in a very happy Condition, if I could have learned the lesson of knowing when I was well. I left my poor Wife big with Child; and accepted an advantageous offer made me to be Captain of the Adventure, a stout Merchantman of 350 Tuns."

Forced to replace a number of his crew by strangers at the Barbadoes, Captain Gulliver learns too late that most of the new recruits had been buccaneers. They seize the ship to use as a pirate vessel, and maroon the captain on a strange shore which, as he later finds out, is the land of the Houyhnhnms. These are rational horses, and the name is intended to be an approximation of a horse's neighing.

The story here loses the close attention to realistic detail which characterises the account of the first two travels, but it is still absorbing and the satire becomes far sharper and more biting.

Among the wild animals in this country are the Yahoos, a vile species which Gulliver, to his infinite horror, finally recognizes as genus Homo. The direct physical elements of his description of these hairy, naked and wild Yahoos becomes amazing when we realize that it was written more than a century before there was any tentative suggestion of evolution or any notion of a link between Man and the Ape.

Gulliver is soon taken into the household of a dapple-gray steed, a Houyhnhnm of quality, and shows the same aptitude in learning the language there as he has displayed in the course of his previous travels. "The Curiosity and Impatience of my Master were so great, that he spent many Hours of his Leisure to instruct me. He was convinced (as he afterwards told me) that I must be a Yahoo, but my teachableness, civility and cleanliness astonished him; which were Qualities altogether so opposite to those Animals."

Requested to tell the history of his country Gulliver does so, dwelling upon the many wars, both domestic and foreign.

> What you have told me (said my master) upon the subject of war, does indeed discover most admirably the effects of that reason you pretend to: however, it is happy that the shame is greater than the danger; and that nature hath left you utterly uncapable of doing much mischief.
>
> For your mouths lying flat with your faces, you can hardly bite each other to any purpose, unless by consent. Then as to the claws upon your feet before and behind, they are so short and tender, that one of our Yahoos would drive a dozen of yours before him. And therefore in recounting the numbers of those who have been killed in battle, I cannot but think that you have *said the thing which is not.*
>
> I could not forbear shaking my head and smiling a little at his ignorance. And being no stranger to the art of war, I gave him a description of cannons, culverins, muskets, carabines, pistols, bullets, powder, swords, bayonets, battles, sieges, retreats, attacks, undermines, countermines, bombardments, sea fights; ships sunk with a thousand men, twenty thousand killed on each side; dying groans, limbs flying in the air, smoke, noise, confusion, trampling to death under horses' feet; flight, pursuit, victory; fields strewed with carcasses left for food to dogs, and wolves, and birds of prey; plundering, stripping, ravishing, burning, and destroying. And to set forth the valour of my own dear countrymen, I assured him that I had seen them blow up a hundred enemies at once in a siege, and as many in a ship, and beheld the dead bodies come down in pieces from the clouds, to the great diversion of the spectators.
>
> I was going on to more particulars, when my master commanded me silence. He said whoever understood the nature of Yahoos might easily believe it possible for so vile an animal to be capable of every action I had named, if their strength and cunning equalled their malice. But as my discourse had increased his abhorrence of the whole species, so he found it

gave him a disturbance in his mind, to which he was wholly a stranger before. He thought his ears being used to such abominable words, might by degrees admit them with less detestation. That although he hated the Yahoos of this country, yet he no more blamed them for their odious qualities, than he did a *gnnayh* (a bird of prey) for its cruelty, or a sharp stone for cutting his hoof. But when a creature pretending to reason could be capable of such enormities, he dreaded lest the corruption of that faculty might be worse than brutality itself. He seemed therefore confident, that instead of reason, we were only possessed of some quality fitted to increase our natural vices; as the reflection from a troubled stream returns the image of an ill-shapen body not only larger, but more distorted.

Gulliver then turned to describe his people's civil rather than their military accomplishments.

Whereupon I was at much pains to describe to him the use of money, the materials it was made of, and the value of the metals; that when a Yahoo had got a great store of this precious substance, he was able to purchase whatever he had a mind to; the finest clothing, the noblest houses, great tracts of land, the most costly meats and drinks, and have his choice of the most beautiful females. Therefore since money alone was able to perform all these feats, our Yahoos thought they could never have enough of it to spend or save, as they found themselves inclined from their natural bent either to profusion or avarice. That the rich man enjoyed the fruit of the poor man's labour, and the latter were a thousand to one in proportion to the former. That the bulk of our people were forced to live miserably, by labouring every day for small wages to make a few live plentifully. I enlarged myself much on these and many other particulars to the same purpose; but his Honour was still to seek; for he went upon a supposition that all animals had a title to their share in the productions of the earth, and especially those who presided over the rest. Therefore he desired I would let him know what these costly meats were, and how any of us happened to want them. Whereupon I enumerated as many sorts as came into my head, with the various methods of dressing them, which could not be done without sending vessels by sea to every part of the world, as well for liquors to drink, as for sauces, and innumerable other conveniences. I assured him that this whole globe of earth must be at least three times gone round, before one of our better female Yahoos could get her breakfast or a cup to put it in. He said that must needs be a miserable country which cannot furnish food for its own inhabitants.

Finally Gulliver completely realized the superiority of the Houyhnhnms and happily settled down to live among them and learn from them.

> When I thought of my family, my friends, my countrymen, or human race in general, I considered them as they really were, Yahoos in shape and disposition, perhaps a little more civilized, and qualified with the gift of speech, but making no other use of reason than to improve and multiply those vices whereof their brethren in this country had only the share that nature allotted them. When I happened to behold the reflection of my own form in a lake or fountain, I turned away my face in horror and detestation of myself, and could better endure the sight of a common Yahoo than of my own person.

Unfortunately the Houyhnhnm Supreme Council was unwilling to allow even a superior Yahoo to remain among them permanently, and decreed his banishment. He was overcome with grief but submitted; contrived to make a boat, and sailed to an uninhabited island. A ship's crew of European Yahoos discovered him there, and despite his urgent remonstrance insisted on taking him back to civilization.

The book, *Travels into Several Remote Nations of the World by Lemuel Gulliver,* was first published anonymously in 1726. It was immediately reprinted in a large number of unauthorized editions. In 1727 a new authorized edition included a letter from Lemuel Gulliver to his cousin, Richard Sympson, who had ostensibly first published the work. There was also an explanatory preface by Richard Sympson himself.

The emphasis in Captain Gulliver's letter makes it very clear that by the time Swift had finished writing the book it was its fourth part which expressed his unqualified condemnation of the world in which he lived.

In 1728 Swift wrote *A Short View of the State of Ireland* which deals trenchantly with absentee landlordism and the deliberate murder of Irish manufacture and commerce by the mercantile interests of England. That same year he wrote in a letter to Pope and Bolingbroke:

> I do profess without affectation, that your kind opinion of me as a patriot, since you call it so, is what I do not deserve; because what I do is owing to perfect rage and resent-

ment, and the mortifying sight of slavery, folly, and baseness about me, among which I am forced to live.

And in a note to an Irish friend he demanded:

Does not corruption of men in high places eat into your heart and exhaust your spirits?

In 1730 he published a brief—and savage—satire on an unofficial suggestion that the French king be allowed to recruit soldiers in Ireland to help relieve the growing "overpopulation" and unemployment in that unhappy island.

This suggestion and similar ones for the emigration of young people as indentured servants to Australia, which were put forth by humane church dignitaries and other public spirited citizens were also, in 1730, responsible for Swift's last political pamphlet, *The Modest Proposal,* which remains the most heart-breaking piece of sarcasm that savage indignation has yet given birth to.

A MODEST PROPOSAL: FOR PREVENTING THE CHILDREN OF POOR PEOPLE IN IRELAND FROM BEING A BURTHEN TO THEIR PARENTS OR COUNTRY, AND FOR MAKING THEM BENEFICIAL TO THE PUBLIC.

It is a melancholy object to those who walk through this great town or travel in the country, when they see the streets, the roads, and cabin doors, crowded with beggars of the female sex, followed by three, four, or six children, all in rags and importuning every passenger for an alms. These mothers, instead of being able to work for their honest livelihood, are forced to employ all their time in strolling to beg sustenance for their helpless infants: who as they grow up either turn thieves for want of work, or leave their dear native country to fight for the pretender in Spain, or sell themselves to the Barbadoes.

I think it is agreed by all parties that this prodigious number of children in the arms, or on the backs, or at the heels of their mothers, and frequently of their fathers, is in the present deplorable state of the kingdom a very great additional grievance; and, therefore, whoever could find out a fair, cheap, and easy method of making these children sound, useful members of the commonwealth, would deserve so well of the public as to have his statue set up for a preserver of the nation.

But my intention is very far from being confined to provide only for the children of professed beggars; it is of a much greater extent, and shall take in the whole number of infants at a certain age who are born of parents in effect as little able to support them as those who demand our charity in the streets.

As to my own part, having turned my thoughts for many years upon this important subject, and maturely weighed the several schemes of our projectors, I have always found them grossly mistaken in their computation. It is true, a child just dropped from its dam may be supported by her milk for a solar year, with little other nourishment; at most not above the value of 2s., which the mother may certainly get, or the value in scraps, by her lawful occupation of begging; and it is exactly at one year old that I propose to provide for them in such a manner as instead of being a charge upon their parents or the parish, or wanting food and raiment for the rest of their lives, they shall on the contrary contribute to the feeding, and partly to the clothing, of many thousands.

There is likewise another great advantage in my scheme, that it will prevent those voluntary abortions, and that horrid practice of women murdering their bastard children, alas! too frequent among us! sacrificing the poor innocent babes I doubt more to avoid the expense than the shame, which would move tears and pity in the most savage and inhuman breast.

The number of souls in this kingdom being usually reckoned one million and a half, of these I calculate there may be about 200,000 couple whose wives are breeders; from which number I subtract 30,000 couple who are able to maintain their own children (although I apprehend there cannot be so many, under the present distresses of the kingdom); but this being granted, there will remain 170,000 breeders. I again subtract 50,000 for those women who miscarry, or whose children die by accident or disease within the year. There only remains 120,000 children of poor parents annually born. The question therefore is, how this number shall be reared and provided for? which, as I have already said, under the present situation of affairs, is utterly impossible by all the methods hitherto proposed. For we can neither employ them in handicraft or agriculture; we neither build houses (I mean in the country) nor cultivate land; they can very seldom pick up a livelihood by stealing, till they arrive at six years old, except where they are of towardly parts; although I confess they learn the rudiments much earlier; during which time, they can however be properly looked upon only as probationers; as I have been informed by a principal gentleman in the county of Cavan, who protested to me that he never knew above one or two instances under the age of six, even in a part of the kingdom so renowned for the quickest proficiency in that art.

I am assured by our merchants, that a boy or a girl before twelve years old is no saleable commodity; and even when they come to this age they will not yield above 3l. or 3l.2s.6d. at most on the exchange; which cannot turn to account either to the parents or kingdom, the charge of nutriment and rags having been at least four times that value.

I shall now therefore humbly propose my own thoughts, which I hope will not be liable to the least objection.

I have been assured by a very knowing American of my acquaintance in London, that a young healthy child well nursed is at a year old a most delicious, nourishing, and wholesome food, whether stewed, roasted, baked, or boiled; and I make no doubt that it will equally serve in a fricassee or a ragout. I do therefore humbly offer it to public consideration that of the 120,000 children already computed, 20,000 may be reserved for breed, whereof only one-fourth part to be males; which is more than we allow to sheep, black cattle or swine; and my reason is, that these children are seldom the fruits of marriage, a circumstance not much regarded by our savages, therefore one male will be sufficient to serve four females. That the remaining 100,000 may, at a year old, be offered in sale to the persons of quality and fortune through the kingdom; always advising the mother to let them suck plentifully in the last month, so as to render them plump and fat for a good table.

A child will make two dishes at an entertainment of friends; and when the family dines alone, the fore or hind quarter will make a reasonable dish, and seasoned with a little pepper or salt will be very good boiled on the fourth day, especially in winter.

I have reckoned upon a medium that a child just born will weight 12 pounds, and in a solar year, if tolerably nursed, will increase to 28 pounds.

I grant this food will be somewhat dear, and therefore very proper for landlords, who, as they have already devoured most of the parents, seem to have the best title to the children.

Infant's flesh will be in season throughout the year, but more plentifully in March, and a little before and after: for we are told by a grave author, an eminent French physician, that fish being a prolific diet, there are more children born in Roman Catholic countries about nine months after Lent than at any other season; therefore, reckoning a year after Lent, the markets will be more glutted than usual, because the number of popish infants is at least three to one in this kingdom: and therefore it will have one other collateral advantage, by lessening the number of papists among us.

I have already computed the charge of nursing a beggar's child (in which list I reckon all cottagers, labourers, and four-fifths of the farmers) to be about 2s. per annum, rags included; and I believe no gentleman would repine to give 10s. for the carcass of a good fat child, which, as I have said, will make four dishes of excellent nurtitive meat, when he has only some particular friend or his own family to dine with him. Thus the squire will learn to be a good landlord, and grow popular among the tenants; the mother will have 8s. net profit, and be fit for work till she produces another child.

Those who are more thrifty (as I must confess the times require) may flay the carcass; the skin of which artificially dressed will make admirable gloves for ladies, and summer boots for fine gentlemen.

As to our city of Dublin, shambles may be appointed for this purpose in the most convenient parts of it, and butchers we may be assured will not be wanting; although I rather recommend buying the children alive than dressing them hot from the knife as we do roasting pigs. . . .

. . . Some persons of a desponding spirit are in great concern about that vast number of poor people, who are aged, diseased, or maimed, and I have been desired to employ my thoughts what course may be taken to ease the nation of so grievous an encumbrance. But I am not in the least pain upon that matter, because it is very well known that they are every day dying and rotting by cold and famine, and filth and vermin, as fast as can be reasonably expected. And as to the young labourers, they are now in as hopeful a condition; they cannot get work, and consequently pine away for want of nourishment, to a degree that if at any time they are accidentally hired for common labour, they have not strength to perform it; and thus the country and themselves are happily delivered from the evils to come. I have too long digressed, and therefore shall return to my subject. I think the advantages by the proposal which I have made are obvious and many, as well as of the highest importance.

For first, as I have already observed, it would greatly lessen the number of papists, with whom we are yearly overrun, being the principal breeders of the nation. . . .

. . . Secondly, The poor tenants will have something valuable of their own, which by law may be made liable to distress and help to pay their landlord's rent, their corn and cattle being already seized, and money a thing unknown.

Thirdly, Whereas the maintenance of 100,000 children, from two years old and upward, cannot be computed at less than 10s. a-piece per annum, the nation's stock will be thereby increased £50,000 per annum, beside the profit of a new dish introduced to the tables of all gentlemen of fortune in the kingdom who have any refinement in taste. And the money will circulate among ourselves, the goods being entirely of our own growth and manufacture.

Fourthly, The constant breeders, beside the gain of 8s. sterling per annum by the sale of their children, will be rid of the charge of maintaining them after the first year.

Fifthly, This food would likewise bring great custom to taverns; where the vintners will certainly be so prudent as to procure the best receipts for dressing it to perfection, and consequently have their houses frequented by all the fine gentlemen, who justly value themselves upon their knowledge in good eating: and a skilful cook, who understands how to oblige his guests, will contrive to make it as expensive as they please.

Sixthly, This would be a great inducement to marriage, which all wise nations have either encouraged by rewards or enforced by laws and penalties.

It would increase the care and tenderness of mothers toward their children, when they were sure of a settlement for life to the poor babes, provided in some sort by the public, to their annual profit or expense. We should see an honest emulation among the married women, which of them could bring the fattest child to the market. Men would become as fond of their wives during the time of their pregnancy as they are now of their mares in foal, their cows in calf, their sows when they are ready to farrow; nor offer to beat or kick them (as is too frequent a practice) for fear of a miscarriage. . . .

. . . I can think of not one objection that will possibly be raised against this proposal, unless it should be urged that the number of people will be thereby much lessened in the kingdom. This I freely own, and it was indeed one principal design in offering it to the world. I desire the reader will observe, that I calculate my remedy for this one individual kingdom of Ireland and for no other that ever was, is, or I think ever can be upon earth. Therefore let no man talk to me of other expedients: of taxing our absentees at 5s. a pound: of using neither clothes nor household furniture except what is of our own growth and manufacture: of utterly rejecting the materials and instruments that promote foreign luxury. . . .

. . . Supposing that 1000 families in this city would be constant customers for infants' flesh, beside others who might have it at merry-meetings, particularly at weddings and christenings, I compute that Dublin would take off annually about 20,000 carcasses; and the rest of the kingdom (where probably they will be sold somewhat cheaper) the remaining 80,000. . . .

. . . I profess, in the sincerity of my heart, that I have not the least personal interest in endeavouring to promote this necessary work, having no other motive than the public good of my country, by advancing our trade, providing for infants, relieving the poor, and giving some pleasure to the rich. I have no children by which I can propose to get a single penny; the youngest being nine years old, and my wife past child-bearing.

In 1733 he received a letter from Pope, congratulating him because his seventieth birthday had been celebrated throughout Ireland with bells, bonfires, and toasts of "Long life to the Drapier, Prosperity to poor Ireland, and the liberty of the press!" He wrote in response:

> My popularity that you mention is wholly confined to the common people, who are more constant than those we miscall their betters. I walk the streets, and so do my lower friends, from whom, and from whom alone, I have a thousand hats and blessings upon old scores [the fight for Irish rights] which those we call the gentry have forgot. But I have not the love, or hardly the civility of any one man in power or station. . . . What has sunk my spirits more than even years and sickness is, reflecting on the most execrable corruptions that run through every branch of public management.

Although his popularity in Ireland never waned, the next ten years were spent in growing loneliness (Stella had died in 1728) and a suppressed hopeless fury at the misery all around him which made him feel, as he said in more than one letter, that he was dying in a trap, poisoned with his own venom. In practical terms he did much, devoting the greater part of his income to such immediate social services as innumerable noninterest-bearing loans of £50 to £100 to set small tradesmen and craftsmen up in business; reductions in the rent and improvements on the farm property his church living controlled; and the more conventional charity demanded to preserve from literal starvation some part of the swarming slum population of Dublin. But he was too clear-sighted to think that any or all of these measures were effective even as an amelioration of conditions, and his growing desperation vented itself in increased irritability, varied by indulgence in all kinds of intellectual, and physical, horseplay with forced, almost hysterical, high spirits.

The "Verses On The Death of Dr. Swift" was one of the wittiest and pleasantest of these elaborate practical jokes. They were first circulated anonymously; Swift then wrote letters to the newspapers indignantly attacking the scurrilous unknown who had written them; and a whole involved series of mystifications and counter-accusations was developed before they were finally published as his in 1739.

They read, in part:

> "O! may we all for death prepare!
> What has he left? and who's his heir?"
> "I know no more than what the news is;
> 'Tis all bequeathed to public uses."—
> "To public uses! there's a whim!
> What had the public done for him?"
> Now Grub-Street wits are all employ'd;
> With elegies the town is cloy'd;
> Some paragraph in every paper
> To curse the Dean, or bless the Drapier.
> From Dublin soon to London spread,
> 'Tis told at court, "The Dean is dead."
> And Lady Suffolk, in the spleen,
> Runs laughing up to tell the queen.
> The queen, so gracious, mild and good,
> Cries, "Is he gone? 'Tis time he should!"
> Here shift the scene to represent
> How those I love my death lament.
> Poor Pope would grieve a month, and Gay
> A week, and Arbuthnot a day.
> The rest will give a shrug, and cry,
> "I'm sorry—but we all must die!"
> My female friends, whose tender hearts
> Have better learn'd to act their parts,
> Receive the news in doleful dumps:
> "The Dean is dead: (Pray, what is trumps?)"
> "His time was come; he ran his race;
> We hope he's in a better place."
> . . . . . .
> He never thought an honour done him
> Because a duke was proud to own him,
> Would rather step aside and choose
> To talk with wits in dirty shoes;
> And would you make him truly sour,
> Provoke him with a slave in power.
> The Irish Senate if you named,
> With what impatience he declaim'd!
> Fair Liberty was all his cry,
> For her he stood prepared to die;
> For her he boldly stood alone;
> For her he oft exposed his own.
> Two kingdoms, just as factions led,
> Had set a price upon his head;
> But not a traitor could be found,
> To sell him for six hundred pound.

> . . . .
> He gave the little wealth he had
> To build a house for fools and mad
> And show'd by one satiric touch
> No nation wanted it as much.
> That kingdom he had left his debtor,
> I wish it soon may have a better.

Madness ran much in his mind; in his *Proposal for the Universal Use of Irish Manufacture*, as early as 1720 he had written: "The Scripture tells us oppression maketh a wise man mad," and in his verses on his own death he referred to the project he later carried out of leaving his estate to found a hospital for the incurably insane—the first of its kind. And when in 1736 the House of Commons passed a bill to facilitate evictions, Swift's wild burlesque attack "The Legion Club" has a particular personal horror mixed with the hatred which describes in detail the inmates of parliament as literal madmen.

In his letters we read of frequent attacks of "age, giddiness, deafness, loss of memory, rage and rancour against persons and proceedings," although we find brief flashes of self-possessed wit reported as late as 1740. One characteristic anecdote tells of his returning from a ride during which he had seen a new armory being built and writing:

> Behold a proof of Irish sense;
> Here Irish wit is seen!
> When nothing's left that's worth defence
> They build a magazine.

It was clear his mind was breaking. As Hazlitt was to say when lecturing about Swift three quarters of a century later:

> There is nothing more likely to drive a man mad, than the being unable to get rid of the idea of the distinction between right and wrong, and an obstinate, constitutional preference of the true to the agreeable.

In 1742 Dean Swift, then already seventy-four years old, was declared insane. He died in 1745 and was buried, as he had directed, with the utmost privacy and simplicity. The Latin epitaph which he himself had composed when making his will in 1735, was, as he had arranged, chiseled in letters "deeply cut and strongly gilded" on his monument of black stone. Translated, it reads:

> Here Lies the Body
> of
> Jonathan Swift
> Once Dean of This Cathedral
> Where Savage Indignation
> [Ubi Saeva Indignatio]
> Can No Longer Tear His Heart
> Go, Passerby,
> And do, if you can, as he did
> A Man's Part in Defense of Human Freedom.

Yeats, a later Irish poet and patriot, not fortunate enough to share Swift's instinctive lifelong loyalty to the people and their interests, has transposed the sonorous Latin into a perhaps somewhat too lightly musical English verse:

> Swift has sailed into his rest;
> Savage indignation there
> Cannot lacerate his breast.
> Imitate him if you dare,
> World besotted traveller; he
> Served human liberty.

Great fighter and superb satirist as Swift was, he cannot be said adequately to represent the progressive force of the early eighteenth century. His hatred of tyranny was deep and strong, and his sympathy with the oppressed a burning painful thing, but although these helped him break through the smug complacency of his class, he could carry on the struggle against its callous corruption only in a desperate and hopeless fashion.

The positive achievements which were made possible by the development of scientific agriculture, skilled manufacture and widespread commerce Swift could not appreciate. Both his essentially aristocratic education and the more or less accidental circumstances of a colonial life made it impossible for him to grasp the limited but real significance of material progress in his age, while his human sympathy for suffering and indignation at injustice kept him keenly aware of the misery, ugliness and destruction involved in the ruthless greed with which it was achieved.

But if he never won, he never surrendered and little as he finally anticipated victory, still less did he ever accept defeat. He did not see how the common man could ever regain his birthright, but he never doubted that he should. Nor did he ever blame the victim for the assault as so many liberal intellectuals have absolved their consciences by doing.

Together with his expressions of furious hatred for those who had stripped and bound man, perhaps the most violent in the great tradition of English literature, we find rare touches of gentleness in his regard for "Esau come fainting from the field . . . [to sell] his birthright for a mess of pottage." And so Swift remains one of the very few who have made satire an effective weapon with which to attack the enemy, rather than merely a shield with which to protect their own sensibilities from him.

DANIEL DEFOE

For a true picture of the real accomplishment of this vigorous postrevolutionary commercial age we must turn to a different figure, a son of lower middle-class nonconformists, a grandson of those who had formed the backbone for Cromwell's New Model Army, and the father of perhaps the greatest art form originated by the bourgeoisie—the novel.

Daniel Foe (he added the "de" forty years later) was born in London, oldest son of an energetic and intelligent London chandler, James Foe, in 1659 or 1660. His family survived both the Great Plague of 1665 and the Great Fire of London in 1666 without mishap, and sometime about the boy's tenth birthday his father, who had evidently been thriving, joined the prosperous London Butchers' Company, securing a membership which carried with it the right to a vote as well as to other substantial benefits.

Defoe, as he was later to call himself, fortunate in his education as well as in his family, was sent to one of the best of the dissenting academies, kept by a Mr. Morton who, like many other nonconformists barred from a clerical career by the Restoration, had turned to teaching.

His school omitted the customary instruction in Greek and spent little time on Latin but stressed English composition, mathematics and even the rudiments of science, then and for long after altogether ignored at both Oxford and Cambridge. Defoe later says that Mr. Morton's "chief excellence lay in Mathematicks, and especially the mechanick part of them," and that he also stressed history, geography, which the boy was to find of absorbing interest all the rest of his life, and political science. This very progressive educator emigrated to New England in 1688 and became the first vice-president of Harvard.

Defoe has also left us a characteristic comment—written as part of a memorial tribute in 1696—on the minister to whose congregation his family belonged, stressing the virtues which seemed to him most important:

> If e'er his Duty focred him to contend,
> Calmness was all his temper, Peace his end.
> His native candor and familiar stile,
> Which did so oft his hearers' hours beguile,

His own religion seems to have been, as indeed it always remained, sincere but by no means immoderate, and he tells us in a characteristically frank and reasonable autobiographical comment that when, on the alarm of a possible Catholic restoration which would confiscate all English Bibles, many of the dissenters copied theirs out in a kind of short-hand:

> ... I myself, then but a boy, worked like a horse, till I wrote out the whole Pentateuch, and then was so tired I was willing to run the risk of the rest.

Years later in a book of advice called *The Complete English Tradesman*, Defoe ingenuously says that a man must not be "so intent upon religious duties, as to neglect the proper times and seasons of business. . . . Works of superrogation are not required at any man's hands." In discussing James II's Declaration of Indulgence, which we have already noted in relation to Bunyan, he makes clear the relative importance of religious and political liberty as far as he is concerned:

> Was anything ever more absurd than this conduct of King James and his party in wheedling the Dissenters, giving them liberty of conscience by his own arbitrary dispensing authority, and expecting they should be content with their religious liberty at the price of the constitution?

His father had expected his oldest son to enter the ministry, but as Defoe later said of his desire to write about economics rather than politics: "trade was the whore I really doated upon and designed to have taken up with." When he left school, trade was growing by leaps and bounds. London's imports, for example, increased from £7,000,000 in 1672 to £11,500,000 in 1688 and the establishment of the Penny Post in 1680 was both an indication of, and an enormous assistance to, the increasing tempo of domestic trade. Defoe, who never in the course of an incredibly tempestuous life was to tire of excitement, plunged enthusiastically into the midst of this busy world of affairs.

About 1680 he became a hose factor or commission merchant, dealing between manufacturer and retailer, and also acting as a jobber for wine, tobacco, woolens, and any other merchandise that seemed interesting.

We have few details of these years but know that he did some commercial traveling in Spain, France, Holland and Italy during the eighties and took many business trips, on horseback, throughout large sections of England. He may have begun his study of French and Italian at school but he evidently became fluent in both languages during this time, and has written some interesting notes on the comparative manners, customs and ways of life in the various European countries he visited. Among the observations he made during his English travels is a rather noncommittal comment on what may have been something like the first industrial strike in England:

> As to Spittle-fields, in about 1679 and 80, if I remember right, when the Weavers in Spittle-fields mutineed upon some occasion of setting up Engine-looms, as they called them, in which one Man might do as much Work as 6 or 8, or more. . . .

By 1684 he was well established with a large enough business to enable him to marry an attractive young woman of twenty, daughter of a rather more important commercial family than his own, who brought him a dowry of over £3,000. By 1688 he had been admitted as a member of the powerful group of "Liverymen of the City of London," had claimed his inherited right to membership in the "Butchers' Company," owned a large warehouse, a London home and a country residence, had several children and seemed likely to be able to retire as a wealthy alderman twenty years later.

Yet, as one of the best of his biographers, James Sutherland, has said, Defoe was always "a citizen first and a man of business afterwards." Twice during these prosperous four years Defoe had imperiled not only his business success but life itself, first by joining in the abortive attempt to place the Protestant Duke of Monmouth on the throne in 1686, and later in the successful rebellion which forced James II's abdication and made William of Orange king in England.

The records of six lawsuits in the next few years show that when Defoe's business began to bore him by a too routine success he looked for more adventurous speculations elsewhere. It may also be true, as he himself claimed, that the war with France caused Defoe, as it did many other merchants, disastrous losses in shipping. At any rate, in 1692, Defoe was forced into bankruptcy, failing for the imposing sum of £17,000—the equivalent of at least $150,000 today.

Years later in one of the many chapters of advice to tradesmen which he wrote in both periodical and book form, he used what was no doubt a summary description of this part of his career. He says:

> . . . nothing is more common than the tradesman when once he finds himself grown rich, to have his head full of great designs, and new undertakings. He finds his cash flow in upon him, and perhaps he is fuller of money than his trade calls for; and as he scarce knows how to employ more stock in it than he does, his ears are the sooner open to any project or proposal that offers itself; and I must add, that this is the most critical time with him in all his life; if ever he is in danger of ruin, 'tis just then. . . . I think, I may safely advance without danger of reprehension, there are more people ruined in England by over-trading than for want of trade; and I would, from my own unhappy experience, advise all men in trade to set a due compass to their ambition.

His creditors seem to have retained faith both in his ability and in his essential honesty, and agreed to an arrangement which enabled him to keep out of the debtors prison, accepting his unsecured and legally unenforcable promise to pay in full as soon as he again made money. (He had paid off over £11,000 by 1705 when circumstances which we shall note as of more than passing interest seriously delayed the remainder.)

Two years later he was offered a good position in Cadiz which he refused, being unwilling permanently to leave England, and in 1695 he was appointed accountant for a newly formed glass-tax commission, trustee for a state lottery, and unofficial unpaid advisor on ways and means to several prominent Whig members of the government.

By 1697 he had organized a pantile factory to make bricks—then imported from Holland—and had received a contract to supply them to the large new Greenwich hospital.

It is interesting to note that excavations for a railroad 160 years later on the site of his factory turned up bricks in sufficient quantity to prove that they were exceptionally well made, of a rather novel design, and extremely durable.

But as always, once a business was successful Defoe lost interest in it and, running it with one hand, turned the other to more exciting and generally more dangerous, matters.

In 1698 he published his first real book, *An Essay Upon Projects*. This included suggestions for improved roads; an enlarged banking system; special simplified legal procedures for commercial disputes; bankruptcy laws which would distinguish between honest and fraudulent failures, allowing the former to work out their debts rather than idle in jail; an asylum or hospital for "idiots"—that is, the feeble-minded; higher education for women; fire and shipwreck insurance; and even an Income Tax! Most of these proposals were adopted within the next two or two and a half centuries.

Perhaps the most interesting to us is the one for "An Academy for Women." This begins:

> I have often thought of it as one of the most barbarous customs in the world considering us as a civilized and a Christian country, that we deny the advantages of learning to women. We reproach the sex every day with folly and impertinence, while I am confident, had they the advantages of education equal to us, they would be guilty of less than ourselves.
>
> One would wonder, indeed, how it should happen that women are conversible at all, since they are only beholding to natural parts for all their knowledge. Their youth is spent to teach them to stitch and sew, or make baubles. They are taught to read indeed, and perhaps to write their names, or so; and this is the height of a woman's education. And I would but ask any who slight the sex for their understanding, what is a man (a gentleman, I mean) good for that is taught no more?

Benjamin Franklin says in his autobiography: "I found besides, a work of Defoe's, entitled an 'Essay on Projects' from which, perhaps, I derived impressions that have since influenced some of the principal events of my life."

Advanced as it was, this was nevertheless a fairly safe publication since those who did not like it found no difficulty in ignoring it. But an article Defoe had published some months before made more enemies.

King William, whom he greatly admired, was making serious efforts to stamp out the remnants of Restoration manners, and at his urging several salutary laws had been passed toward the correction of the public brutality, drunkenness, and gross abuse of women which were still prevalent in London.

These were often enforced against poor and unimportant offenders—and there only. On March 31, 1697 Defoe published an open letter entitled *The Poor Man's Plea* which read, in part:

> These are all cobweb laws, in which the small flies are catched, and the great ones break through. My Lord-Mayor has whipt about the poor beggars, and a few scandalous whores have been sent to the House of Correction; some alehousekeepers and vintners have been fined for drawing drink on the Sabbath-day; but all this falls upon us of the mob, the poor plebian, as if all the vice lay among us; for we do not find the rich drunkard carried before my Lord-Mayor, nor a swearing lewd merchant fined, or set in the stocks. The man with a gold ring may swear before the Justice or at the Justice; may reel home through the open streets, and no man take any notice of it; but if a poor man get drunk, or swear an oath, he must to the stocks without remedy.

Dickens, who knew his Defoe well, may have thought of this when, a hundred and fifty years later, he still found it timely to write the brief dialogue:

> "There's something in his appearance quite—dear, dear, what's that word again?"
> "What word?" enquired Mr. Lillyvick.
> "Why—dear me, how stupid I am," replied Miss Petowker, hesitating. "What do you call it, when Lords break off doorknockers and beat policemen, and play at coaches with other people's money, and all that sort of thing?"
> "Aristocratic?" suggested the collector.
> "Ah! aristocratic," replied Miss Petowker; "something very aristocratic about him, isn't there?"

There was certainly something aristocratic about this conduct in the eighteenth century, and there were many of the Tories who bore Defoe serious ill will from that time on.

In 1698 and 1700 he further antagonized them by two pamphlets defending the King's Whig pro-trade policies, and in 1701 when the landed interest's dislike of William had led to openly racist attacks on his Dutch followers, and covert sneers at the King himself as racially inferior, Defoe wrote an extremely successful burlesque called *The True Born Englishman*.

It traces with broad humor and accuracy the successive invasions of Danes, Romans, Normans and later-day French, as well as the many other strains which make the truest born Englishman a mongrel:

> Thus from a mixture of all kinds began
> That heterogenous thing, an Englishman.

Then it points out, in defense of the forced abdication of James II and, therefore, of the legitimacy of William's title:

> And punishing of Kings is no such crime,
> But Englishmen have done it many a time.

The following stanza gives us a good idea of the generally unsubtle but effective humor which no doubt helped make the verses so extraordinarily popular that there were nine authorized, and at least twelve pirated, editions.

> A Turkish horse can show more ancestry
> To prove his well-descended family. . . .
> These are the heroes that despise the Dutch,
> And rail at new-come foreigners so much,
> Great families of yesterday we show,
> And lords whose parents were the Lord knows who.

A more important effect of the poem was that it won for Defoe an unusual degree of intimacy with the King and made him, for the short remainder of William's life, almost an unofficial private cabinet member advising on all matters pertaining to trade, and on many others.

That spring Defoe, inspired by this relation with the man whom, all his life, he most respected and perhaps most truly loved, carried out an extraordinary exploit.

The party situation in England was a complicated and, basically, an unimportant one. Both Lords and Commons were now divided into Whigs and Tories and while the latter were generally considered the landed interest, and the former the commercial interest, there was often no line of demarcation between moderate Whigs and moderate Tories insofar as policies were concerned. The party battles were really just irrelevant jockeying for personal position and power. During the last years of William's reign, for example, the House of Lords had a Whig majority and the Commons a Tory one! As Defoe was to write, after many years of political journalism, in 1712:

> I have seen the bottom of all parties, the bottom of all their pretences, and the bottom of their sincerity, and as the Preacher said, that all was vanity and vexation of spirit, so I say of these: all is a mere show, outside, and abominable hypocrisy, of every party, in every age, under every government; when they are OUT to get IN, when IN, to prevent being OUT; every sect, every party, and almost every person that we have an account of, have, for ought I see, been guilty, more or less, of the general charge, viz. that their interests governs their principle.

But a more fundamental question was raised when, in May 1701, five Gentlemen of Kent came up to London to present a petition to the Tory House of Commons for more energetic defense measures in Kent. They argued that if the French armies were planning to effect a landing in England, as was rumored, Kent would be their natural destination.

The Tory majority was probably justified in thinking this a publicity stunt whereby the Whigs meant to force them to vote more generous war supplies, but they were certainly altogether unjustified in summarily arresting and imprisoning all five delegates for daring to petition their parliament!

On May 14, in an altogether unprecedented action, Defoe "guarded" as he says, "by about sixteen gentlemen of quality," simply marched into the House, presented the Speaker with a petition he had written entitled, *Legion's Memorial to the House of Commons*, and prudently marched out again before the Speaker had a chance to read it. The memorial was as simple and direct as all Defoe's writing and said, after bluntly describing the outrageous conduct of which the Commons had been guilty:

And though there is no stated proceeding to bring you to your duty, yet the great law of reason says, and all nations allow that, whatever power is above law, it is burdensome and tyrannical; and may be reduced by extra-judicial methods. You are not above the People's resentments! . . .

It then went on to demand:

That the thanks of the House may be given to those Gentlemen who so gallantly appeared in the behalf of their country with the Kentish Petition and have been so scandalously used for it.

and concluded:

We do hereby claim and declare that if the House of Commons, in breach of the Laws and Liberties of the people, do betray the trust reposed in them; and act negligently or arbitrarily and illegally; it is the undoubted Right of the People of England to call them to account for the same; and by Convention, Assembly, or Force, may proceed against them, as traitors and betrayers of their country.

Gentlemen, you have your Duty laid before you! which it is hoped you will think of! But if you continue to neglect it, you may expect to be treated according to the resentments of an injured Nation! For Englishmen are no more to be Slaves to Parliament than to a king!

Our name is Legion, and we are Many.

Parliament was so intimidated that the five delegates were freed before the House adjourned! Defoe was guest of honor at a dinner given for the Gentlemen of Kent, and an anonymous pamphlet on *The History of the Kentish Petition*, written by Defoe himself, sold in the thousands.

His pantile factory was running smoothly with a minimum of attention; his debts were largely paid; his wife and seven children comfortable; and he himself was busy, effective and happy. But his political enemies were by now very many.

We have already seen how he had earned the anger of the London judges and, now, of most Tories. But he had also had a light-hearted fling at antagonizing a substantial part of the Whigs, particularly those who were, like himself, nonconformists or dissenters.

According to laws, many of which remained in force for more

than another century, it was impossible for anyone to attend the universities, hold government office, or enjoy various other privileges, unless he conformed to the requirements of the Established Church.

As the dissenters became respectable and prosperous, however, the Whig party to which they belonged, had approved of the Whig king's various Acts of Toleration. The most notable one of these provided for "Occasional Conformity" whereby a dissenter need only partake of the communion of the Established Church once or twice a year, while regularly attending his own chapel, to be eligible.

In 1698 Defoe had won the enmity of most of the more important dissenters by publishing a pamphlet, *An Enquiry into the Occasional Conformity of Dissenters in Cases of Preferment,* in which he strongly condemned the illogical and irreligious practise of occasional conformity.

We do not know whether he was moved, as a pious biographer suggests, by a memory of the one sermon Bunyan is reputed to have given at his school; by his lifelong hatred of muddled thinking; by the personal pride which would never allow him to belie his own background and class, however careless, as we shall see, about the literal truth in many matters; or by a shrewd idea that if this evasion was ended there would be far more effective pressure brought to have the disabilities removed altogether.

There is some evidence that the last idea played a considerable part in his thinking. John F. Ross, in an interesting comparative study called *Swift and Defoe,* summarizes Defoe's explicit advice to his fellow dissenters, embodied in a burlesque political allegory, *The Consolidator,* in 1705:

> His long and satiric account of English strife was directed toward action in 1705. First it was a long demonstration that no Anglican-Tory leadership could be trusted—that it would lead the nation to disaster for the trading class and for Dissenters. But it was more than attack; it concluded with long "constructive proposals" for the Whigs to act upon. Basically his advice was, "Don't mourn; organize"—and the word he tried to drive home was "Unite." He pointed out in some detail how an organized labor boycott and an economic freeze-out would bring the Anglican-Tories to their knees. He suggested that the Dissenters remove their deposits from the Bank of England and set up their own credit system. But his master

stroke for financial pressure was to show how the Dissenters could even get control of the privileged and chartered companies, like the East India; on concerted agreement, great stock holders among the Dissenters would sell out and start rumors that the stock was worthless; the market would fall; having sold some stock high, the sellers would secretly buy up all the stock at a low figure; and finally, they would run up the price of Funds again as high as ever. . . . Eventually the Dissenters would have economic control of England, and no Tory government could fail to come to terms. Defoe often speaks as if he were concerned with gaining religious toleration; but the measures he urged so vigorously are economic and political, and, if carried out, would have resulted in the destruction of the Anglican-Tory squirearchy. Defoe's class would have gained religious toleration, but also political and economic supremacy. Defoe was not moving in the world of religion, or of the moon; but in the practical world of modern business politics.

However, none of this was indicated in the pamphlet which had been greeted with amazed indignation by Defoe's co-religionists on its publication in 1698.

When in 1702 King William, whose health had for some time been failing, died of shock after an accidental fall from horseback that broke his collarbone, the loss to Defoe was enormous. He lost not only a political leader and personal friend but also his only powerful well-wisher.

The Whigs distrusted and perhaps disliked him; the Tories resented and feared him. Still, if he could have confined himself to building his second fortune—he was to make and lose several more in the course of a long life—he might have done well enough without the help of either. But, although he did not exactly share Milton's passion for political liberty, or Bunyan's utter devotion to religious freedom, he was in his own less heroic fashion equally unable to ignore what seemed to him his civic responsibilities, or to remain silent when it seemed a word of advice might set so many weaker minds right.

Thus when, on the accession of the deeply religious Queen Anne, many Tory High Churchmen began to introduce proposals for increased discrimination against dissenters, Defoe felt he had to take a hand.

In December, 1702, he published an anonymous pamphlet, *The Shortest Way with Dissenters*, which purported to be written by a member of the right wing of the Tory High Church party, and which advocated the most extreme measures to destroy the prosperity, security, and perhaps even the lives of all dissenters.

Defoe's object was a simple one. He intended this extreme statement as a reductio ad absurdem which would show all moderate Tories to what end the doctrines of intolerance tended, and would deter even the most violent diehards, who had not intimated, and probably did not feel, any desire for real physical violence.

But the pamphlet totally failed of its object. It passed for genuine, but it aroused a warm response from extreme Tories and created real terror in the Whigs. For example, a High Church clergyman wrote a friend about it:

> I join with the author in all that he says, and have such a value for the book that, next to the Holy Bible and Sacred Comments, I take it for the most valuable piece I have. I pray God put it into Her Majesty's heart to put what is there proposed in execution.

A few excerpts from the pamphlet would show how all too convincing Defoe had made it, as far as anyone who did not share his absolutely unquestioning assumption of the irrelevance of religious disputes to the serious business of life, was concerned.

The waste of religious struggles was for him so axiomatic that it evidently never occurred to him anyone could desire their resumption. For example, in 1694 he had written in a fragment of English history:

> the Papist, the Church of England, and the Dissenter have all had their turns in administration. . . . Whenever any of them endeavoured their own settlement by the ruin of the parties dissenting, the consequence was supplanting themselves.

And in 1719 he wrote in Robinson Crusoe:

> It was remarkable, too, we had but three subjects, and they were of three different religions. My man Friday was a Protestant, his father was a Pagan and a Cannibal, and the Spaniard was a Papist; however, I allow'd Liberty of Conscience throughout my Dominions.

But it is easy to see why dissenters should have been outraged when they learned who had written the pamphlet, and why their enemies should first have been taken in, and then have been furious because of their own gullibility.

The immediate result of his exploit was that in January, 1703, the Tories procured a warrant for his arrest on general grounds of seditious writing and disturbing the peace, and although the pamphlet had probably been instrumental in turning the twelve moderate Tory votes which defeated the antitoleration bill, the Whigs eyed Defoe with undiminished suspicion and refrained from coming to his defense.

He was more afraid of a lengthy and indefinite jail sentence—"during her majesty's pleasure"—than of death, and went into hiding, attempting by letter to make a bargain with her majesty whereby he would secure a pardon in return for raising "a troop of horse" (a cavalry regiment) at his own expense, and leading them to fight in the French wars!

This was refused and while still a fugitive Defoe frankly wrote a friend:

> Gaols, pillories, and suchlike, with which I have been so much threatened, have convinced me I want passive courage, and I shall never for the future think myself injured if I am called a coward.

Finally captured, he was given an unprecedently severe sentence whose object was obviously to destroy him rather than merely to punish him.

It included a very heavy fine of 200 marks, an indefinite jail sentence clearly intended to be of great duration, and the crowning and really dangerous indignity of three days in the pillory in three separate parts of London. Not infrequently an unpopular prisoner, stoned by the mob while helpless, was fortunate if he emerged with no greater permanent injury than the loss of an eye. Even death from wounds so inflicted was not altogether unlikely or unprecedented.

Defoe was, of course, really being punished for *Legion's Memorial* and perhaps as he himself always claimed, for his refusal even in jail to betray the secrets of policy and ministerial discussions with which the late king had entrusted him.

But although Defoe had confessed himself frightened in advance, as always he rose to the occasion.

Through his wife, of whom we wish we had more personal knowledge than is afforded by tantalizing glimpses at this and succeeding crises, he sent confidential messages to friends and succeeded in getting a *Hymn to the Pillory* printed for street distribution on his first appearance there, and the nucleus of a friendly "mob" organized for the same occasion.

His courage and the humor of his verses won the immediate sympathy of many, and on that and his two subsequent appearances, he was pelted with nothing worse than flowers.

Perhaps the best stanza of the hymn reads:

> Tell them it was because he was too bold,
> And told those truths which should not ha' been told,
>   Extol the justice of the land,
> Who punish what they will not understand.
>   Tell them he stands exalted there
>   For speaking what they would not hear. . . .
> Tell them the Men that placed him here
> Are scandals to the times,
>   Are at a loss to find his guilt,
>   And can't commit his crimes.

Returned to jail, Defoe saw his business going to pieces while he was unable to do anything to save it or help his large family. In desperation he appealed to the very moderate Tory, Harley, who was minister of state, for assistance. Harley who, as we have seen, had shown himself well aware of the value of a skillful pen in his successful efforts to enlist Swift's assistance, was quite willing to secure Defoe's. However he carelessly or deliberately delayed the fulfillment of his half promise until the end of the year and finally, in November 1703, secured for Defoe a pardon from the queen.

One of the many urgent letters with which the prisoner bombarded his dilatory patron is particularly interesting in containing a rare—and characteristic—reference to his children.

> Seven children whose education calls on me to furnish their heads if I cannot their purses, and which debt if not paid now can never be compounded hereafter, is to me a moving article and helps very often to make me sad.

When Defoe emerged from jail he was again bankrupt, a man of forty-three, with a wife and seven children to feed and clothe as well as educate. But the inexhaustible vitality that made it impossible for him to be depressed whenever there was any possibility of action, was no less in evidence now than it had been twelve years before.

He immediately set to work and, with capital secretly furnished by Harley, issued on February 19, 1704, the first number of *A Weekly Review of the Affairs of France, Purged from the Errors and Partiality of News-Writers and Petty Statesmen of all Sides.*

A year later it began to appear three times a week, and in that state continued for nine years.

The Review, as it was soon familiarly called, is in itself an extraordinary achievement. Defoe wrote it himself from cover to cover, personally handled all correspondence—one of his innovations was a weekly supplement which combined the functions of an "Advice to the Lovelorn" column, with an "Information Please" quiz program—was publisher, business manager, and editor as well as reporter, and never missed an issue! This is the more amazing in that, during those nine years, he was often employed as a secret government agent in circumstances of considerable difficulty, had to travel to Scotland and other parts of Great Britain, and was engaged in all sorts of odd and profitable business ventures as opportunity on his travels offered.

A letter to Harley from Edinburgh, where he had spent some time helping to achieve a successful conclusion of the difficult negotiations for "An Act of Union Between England and Scotland," tells of his having been stoned by the anti-English crowd and ends:

> I baulked no cases, I appeared in print when others dared not open their mouths, and without boasting I ran as much risk of my life as a grenadier storming a counter-scarp.

In the vast number of essays which he wrote during the nine years of *The Review*—the equivalent in volume of some twenty or twenty-five average novels—he touched upon the most diverse and personal topics, recurring frequently to questions of woman's position, relations between parents and children, matters of art, journalism, science and religion, as well as to the more obvious questions of economics and politics.

For the paper to be effective it was necessary that it hold its readers' interest, build its circulation, and create respect for the editor's knowledge, intelligence and good will. Although the closely guarded secret of Defoe's government position prevented complete independence he was, as a matter of fact, in sympathy with most of Harley's policies and kept silent about, without defending or attacking, those of which he disapproved.

That he lied about his independence in the pages of the review and, no doubt, outside them, there is no question. But there seems to be as little reason to disbelieve his assertions that he was nevertheless expressing his own opinion in all the matters he chose to discuss, most of which were, of course, unaffected by party policies.

Even when writing more or less "to order" on a specific political controversy, Defoe frequently developed the broader implications of his position in a way altogether different from, and often startlingly more advanced than, any involved in the concrete proposals at issue.

For example, when in the spring of 1709 the government moved to secure general support for its proposal of an immediate peace—largely opposed by the Whigs—Defoe suggested a sort of early League of Nations, or United Nations, to guard against any recurrence of the war. He wrote, on April 19, 1709:

> Nothing then can be a sufficient guarantee for the present peace, but the whole Confederacy, the body of powers that have now acted, being formed into a politic frame or constitution, upon which they can again act in case of an invasion upon any of the branches. Call this what you please, and let the difficulties be as great as you can propose; . . . but if a constitution be formed by which the whole Confederacy may resume and act as a body, then the peace will be always under the protection of the same power that has procured it.
>
> . . . it is now in the power of the present Confederacy forever to prevent any more war in Europe. It is in their power to make themselves arbiters of all the differences and disputes that ever can happen in Europe, whether between kingdom and kingdom, or between sovereign and subjects. A congress of this alliance may be made a court of appeals for all the injured and oppressed, whether they are princes or people that are or ever shall be in Europe to the end of the world. Here the petty states and princes shall be protected against the terror of their powerful neighbours; the great shall no more oppress the small, or the mighty devour the weak; this very

Confederacy have at this time, and if they please may preserve to themselves, the power of banishing war out of Europe. They are able from henceforward to crush the strongest, and support the weakest. .¦. . Perhaps this may pass for a wild thought of mine, and I confess it is new and undigested; but I refer it to the consideration of those in whose hands the power of better modelling this thought lies, whether they have not now the only opportunity that ever Providence entrusted with mankind to make sure the peace of all this part of Europe, as long as the world shall last; and if it be neglected, let them answer for it that ought to have improved it.

Two years earlier, in October, 1707, combating the general clamor for territorial acquisition as a part of England's conditions for making peace, Defoe had with amazing prescience declared:

We want not the dominion of more countries than we have; we sufficiently possess a nation when we have an open and free trade to it. We know how to draw wealth from all nations if we can but trade to them; the value and bulk of our own manufactures have found the way to make themselves necessary to all the world, and they force the wealth from the best and richest countries, be they never so remote; our trading to Old Spain has been a full trade to New Spain, and a trade by which England has always drawn as much money from America as Old Spain itself.

He concluded that essay:

And this is the reason why there are fewer English in foreign parts than of any other nation, and fewer soldiers, and harder to be raised than in any other nation. What should they go abroad for, that live so well at home; what should make the soldier fight at 3s. 6d. a week that can work at home and get near that in a day? 'Tis poverty makes nations scatter, and want of bread drives men into the army. But England, happy in herself, seeks no living abroad, nor dominion abroad; give her peace and trade, she is the happiest, and will be the richest, and in time the most populous, nation in the world.

Since English literature is concerned with Defoe chiefly as a novelist, and since he did not write his first novel until he was sixty, it is of special interest to note how many of the ideas, as well as how much of the technique, which fifteen years later made their appearance in *Robinson Crusoe, Moll Flanders,* and *Roxana,* and in his less well-known fiction, were first formulated in the pages of *The Review.*

For example, in response to a reader's question on "What is the worst sort of husband a sober woman can marry?" Defoe described a number of bad husbands, concluding:

> Well, good people, here are four sorts of ill husbands, and take one of them where you will, the best of them is bad enough, and hard is that woman's case, especially if she be a woman of any merit, whose lot it is; but yet I think my first rate is behind still; there is yet a bad husband that is worse than all these, and a woman of sense had better take up with any of these than with him, and that's a *fool husband.* The drunkard, the debauched, the fighting, and the extravagant; these may all have something attendant which in the intervals of their excesses may serve to alleviate and make a little amends to the poor woman, and help her to carry through the afflicting part; but a fool has something always about him that makes him intolerable; he is ever contemptible and uninterruptedly ridiculous—it is like a handsome woman with some deformity about her that makes all the rest be rejected. If he is kind, it is so apish, so below the rate of manhood, so surfeiting, and so disagreeable, that like an ill smell, it makes the face wrinkle at it; if he be forward, he is so unsufferably insolent that there is no bearing it; his passions are all flashes, struck out of him like fire from a flint. If it be anger, 'tis sullen and senseless; if love, 'tis coarse and brutish. He is in good, wavering; in mischief, obstinate; in society, empty; in management, unthinking; in manners, sordid; in error, incorrigible; and in everything ridiculous.
>
> Wherefore upon the whole, my answer is in short, that the worst thing a sober woman can be married to is a FOOL. Of whom whoever has the lot, Lord have mercy, and a cross should be set on the door as of a house infected with the plague.

And in *Roxana, the Fortunate Mistress,* we find the heroine advising us:

> Never marry a fool. . . . No fool, ladies at all, no kind of fool, whether a mad fool or a sober fool, a wise fool or a silly fool; take anything but a fool; nay, *be* anything, be even an old maid, the worst of fortune's curses, rather than take up with a fool.

Similarly, we find in *The Review* that Defoe draws a sharp distinction between the wickedness of cheating to increase wealth, and the naturalness of stealing to satisfy need:

> The world has a very unhappy notion of honesty, which they take up to the prejudice of the unhappy. Such a man is a fair merchant, a punctual dealer, an honest man, and a rich man. Ay, says one, that makes him a rich man; God blesses him because he is an honest man. *It's a mistake*: God's blessing is the effect of no man's merit. God's blessing may have made him a rich man—*but why is he an honest man, a fair dealer, a punctual merchant?* The answer is plain: Because he is a rich man. The man's circumstances are easy, his trade answers, his cash flows, and his stock increases; this man cannot be otherwise than honest, he has no occasion to be a knave. Cheating in such a man ought to be felony, and that without the benefit of clergy. He has no temptation, no wretched necessity of shifting and tricking, which another man flies to, to do deliver himself from ruin. The man is not rich because he is honest, but he is honest because he is rich. . . .
> And pray, gentlemen, do not vouch too fast for your own honesty; you that have not been tried with distress and disasters, ye know not what you are yourselves. Many a man that thinks himself as honest as (his) neighbours, will find himself as great a r(ogu)e as many of them all, when he comes to the push. How many honest gentlemen have we in England of good estates and noble circumstances that would be highwaymen and come to the gallows if they were poor? How many rich, current, punctual, fair merchants now walk the Exchange that would be errant knaves if they come to be bankrupt? Poverty makes thieves, as bare walls makes giddy housewives; distress makes k(nave)s of honest men, and the exigencies of tradesmen when in declining circumstances, of which none can judge, and which none can express but those that have felt them, will make honest men do that which at another time their very souls abhor. I own to speak this with sad experience, and am not ashamed to confess myself a penitent. *And let him that thinketh he standeth take heed lest he fall.*
> . . . "Give me not poverty, lest I steal," says the wise man; that is, if I am poor I shall be a thief. I tell you all, gentlemen, in your poverty the best of you all will rob your neighbour, ay, and say grace to your meat too. Distress removes from the soul all relation, affection, sense of justice, and all the obligations, either moral or religious, that secure one man against another. Not that I say or suggest the distress makes the violence lawful; but I say it is a trial beyond the ordinary power of human nature to withstand; and therefore that excellent petition of the Lord's Prayer, which I believe

is most wanted and the least thought of, ought to be every moment in our thoughts, "Lead us not into temptation."

And Roxana says, "Honesty is out of the question when Starvation is the case." To which Moll Flanders adds, in her own defense, "Vice came in always at the Door of Necessity, not at the Door of Inclination," and, "As Covetousness is the Root of all Evil, so Poverty is the worst of all Snares." Her God is evidently well aware of the facts of life, for she very reasonably addresses him in prayer, "Give me not poverty, lest I steal."

Defoe himself, in his *"Tour through the whole Island of Great Britain* (1724), adds of a vice which he probably disliked more than either dishonesty or unchastity: "People tell us that Slothfulness begets Poverty, and it is true; but I must add too, that Poverty makes slothfulness."

This attitude toward poverty is, of course, diametrically opposite to any we would expect from the proponent of *The Compleat English Tradesman* and we find in other respects also that Defoe's breadth of intelligence as well as his practical humanity lead him to transcend the fast hardening commercial ethics of the rising class he represents.

The ugly bourgeois ideal of ascetism for profit was not yet, perhaps, fully developed in its application to the master, but it was certainly generally applied to the conditions of his workman, and Defoe was almost alone in the unaffected joy with which he hailed the possibilities of an economy of plenty for all.

He says enthusiastically in *The Compleat English Tradesman*:

> The same trade that keeps our people at home, is the cause of the well living of the people here; for as frugality is not the national virtue of England, so the people that get much spend much; and as they work hard, so they live well, eat and drink well, cloath warm, and lodge soft; in a word, the working manufacturing people of England eat the fat, drink the sweet, live better, and fare better, than the working poor of any other nation in Europe; they make better wages of their work, and spend more of the money upon their Backs and Bellies, than in any other country; . . .

This leads him naturally into one of his favorite discussions, with an explicit emphasis on high wages as the basis of all prosperity for the landed as well as the commercial interests:

This expense of the Poor, as it causes a prodigious consumption both of the provisions and of the manufactures of our country at home, so two things are undeniably the consequence of that part.

1. The consumption of provisions encreases the rent and value of the lands, and this raises the Gentleman's estates, and that again encreases the employment of people, and consequently the numbers of them, as well those who are employ'd in the husbandry of land, breeding and feeding of cattle etc. . . .

2. As the people get better wages, so they, I mean the same poorer part of the people, clothe better, and furnish better, and this encreases the consumption of the very manufactures they make; then that consumption encreases the quantity made, and this creates what we call *Inland Trade*, by which innumerable families are employ'd and the increase of the people maintain'd; and by which encrease of trade and people the present growing prosperity of this nation is produced.

This emphasis on the desirability of high real wages is often repeated in *The Review* in such comments as: ". . . nothing can do them any Service, but what raises the Price of their Labour, or sinks the Price of Provisions; . . ."

Defoe issues repeated warnings on the evils of a subsistence economy:

Again, if you lower the Wages of the Poor, you must of Course sink the Rate of Provisions, and that of Course will sink the Value of Lands, and so you wound the Capital at once; for the Poor cannot earn little and spend much, the End of that is, starving and misery . . . there is no possibility of its being otherwise; it has ever been so, and ever will be so, the Nature of the Thing requires it.

While in general one of the earliest proponents of free trade, he even suggested government subsidies and import duties to protect infant industries without lowering wage standards by the use of workhouse labor in their development, as had then been proposed. He says, for example:

All Manufacturers must have a Beginning and in the Infancy of things, the Government must assist; National Benefits should have National Support, and there are several Ways to do that in this Case, . . . by publick Bounties and Allowances to every Pound of Cotton spun and wrought into Calicoe or Muslin, and by laying yet a higher Duty on the Importation of the same Goods from abroad.

He also argued strenuously (against the prevailing opinion) for the free admission of immigrants, feeling that the number of working people added to a nation's real riches, since:

> Every labouring man is an increase to the public wealth, by how much what he gains by his labour amounts to more than he or his family eats or consumes—for every increase is an article in the credit of the general stock—and for this reason, I say, it is an addition to the public wealth to have the price of labour dear; of which hereafter.
> Every labouring man, then, however poor, increases the public wealth.

This argument he pursued at length in many issues of *The Review*.

At a time when the mercantile theory, with its single emphasis on the balance of gold, stressed only foreign markets and seemed to consider goods consumed at home wasted, Defoe declared:

> But if more foreigners came among us, if it were two millions, it could do us no harm, because they would consume our provisions, and we have land enough to produce much more than we do, and they would consume our manufactures, and we have wool enough for any quantity.

He concluded:

> . . . 't is upon the Gain they make either by their Labour, or their Industry in Trade, and upon their inconceivable Numbers that the Home Consumption of our own Produce, and of the Produce of foreign Nations imported here; is so exceeding great, and that our Trade is raised up to such a Prodigy of Magnitude. . . .

And, almost three quarters of a century before Adam Smith, he carelessly struck out the phrase that has made the latter famous when, in 1704, his *Review* declared:

> The Power of Nations is not now measur'd, as it has been, by Powers, Gallantry and Conduct. 'Tis the *Wealth of Nations* that makes them great.

Defoe was also, as we can see from his fiction, especially interested in the question of colonies whose importance he very early foresaw. In the first year of *The Review* he declared that the growth of the colonies should be England's chief concern for:

> . . . were all, or the greatest part of our Foreign Trade to die, and be no more, our own Colonies in Africk and America are capable of so much Improvement, as is sufficient of themselves to Support our Manufactures, Employ our Shipping, enrich our People, and form all the necessary Articles of Trade within ourselves.

And four years later, in 1707, he rebuked the short-sighted policy which did, indeed, lead to catastrophe in 1776:

> I hinted in a former Review, where I entered on this Subject, that the pernicious Jealousie of making the Colonies independent had always stood in the Way of their Prosperity, and in general in the Way of our own. . . .
> . . . To fear to make our Colonies too great, is, as if a Father, in the educating his Child, should fear to make him too wise, or to give him too much Learning, or in feeding him; should be afraid of making him too strong, or too tall, or too beautiful; for the Plantations being our own Children, the Off-spring of the Commonwealth, they cannot, politically speaking, have too much care taken of them, or be too much tender'd by us.

Other comments of a more personal nature scattered through the issues of *The Review* remind us of the forcible direct style of *Robinson Crusoe* and the realistic insight of *Moll Flanders*.

For example, in one of the first issues, rebutting some attacks upon him in an opposing periodical, he begins:

> But if I must act the Pharisee a little, I must begin thus: God, I thank thee, I am not a drunkard, or a swearer, or a whore-master, or a busie-body, or idle, or revengeful, etc., and I challenge all the world to prove the contrary.

Two years later in response to another attack which evidently dwelt on his writing for profit he replied:

> Oh! but 'tis a scandalous employment, to write for bread! . . . What are all employments in the world pursued for, but for bread? What do you sell, run, fetch, carry, stoop, cringe,

build, pull down, turn and return, what is it all but for bread? And what do you sail, travel, fight, nay, without offense, what preach for? Is it not bread? I hope there are other ends joined in the sacred office, or else I should break in upon my charity, but that office would be thinly supplied if bread were not annext to it.

This was of course only half true about Defoe, as about any other unspoiled human being who genuinely enjoys constructive work. For example, while busy enough with his newspaper, employment as a secret government agent to help bring about the final union of England and Scotland, and with several minor business projects he was investigating in Edinburgh, Defoe wrote Harley a long letter on August 7, 1707, which began: "I am never, you know, for searching an evil to be amazed at it, but to apply the remedies." The letter continued to present an amazingly well thought out "project" for "A Pension Office" that was really an embryo plan of social security insurance by which:

all mankind, be he never so mean, so poor, so unable, shall gain for himself a just claim to a comfortable subsistence whensoever age or casualty shall reduce him to a necessity of making use of it.

This plan included provision for free medical aid, sick and disability benefits, the care of widows and orphans, and support for the families of those confined to debtors' prisons! Defoe concluded: "It is a Shame we should suffer real objects of charity to beg; and for those who are not so, it is a shame but they should work."

Years later, in 1728, he wrote in a similar tone a second book of "projects" which he called *Augusta Triumphan* and which included suggestions for a University of London, and a Hospital, or home, for foundlings. About the latter proposal he very reasonably remarked in defense against accusations that his plan would further immorality:

I am as much against bastards being begot, as I am against their being murdered; but when a child is once begot, it cannot be unbegotten . . . and we ought to show our charity toward it as a fellow creature and Christian, without any regard to its legitimacy or otherwise.

Before leaving this important part of Defoe's work we should remark on how frequently his *Review* discussed woman's position and on how advanced his opinions there were, not only in reference to his own century but even the succeeding one.

We shall have briefly to revert to this in glancing at his second novel, *Moll Flanders,* but should note it here as well.

Defoe not only proposed the education of women (see p. 255), but also repeatedly urged the importance of women's participating in the conduct of their husbands' business or, as widows, of their being able to carry the business on independently; he objected vehemently to the fashion of viewing women simply as sexual objects; and he deplored the injustices of the laws automatically transferring a married woman's property to her husband. We will appreciate Defoe's attitude more adequately if we remember that these laws were still substantially unreformed when Dickens wrote *Nicholas Nickleby,* in which Mr. Mantalini's extravagance bankrupts his wife and forces her to safeguard her reorganized business by conducting it in the name of a spinster forewoman.

Defoe went still further in discussing woman's need for, and right to, full emotional satisfaction in marriage. In several letters of advice to readers he says such things as:

> 'Tis true, Affection is not always Grounded upon Merit; but still they [the imaginary editorial board] reckon Love so Essential to the Happiness of a Conjugal State, that however absurdly that Unaccountable Passion may be Grounded, they think a Woman ought to choose a Man She Loves best. . . .
> If She has not Discretion to govern her Affections, by the real Merit of the Person, that's her Misfortune; but 'tis most certain, She will be but Indifferently Happy with the Man, to whose Person she is indifferent before.

Later, in one of his last books startlingly entitled *On Conjugal Lewdness or Matrimonial Whoredom,* and republished under the comparatively discreet title of *Use and Abuse of the Marriage Bed,* Defoe is even more explicit. He says:

> Some are of the opinion, prudential matches, as they call them, are best. They tell us, it is the parents' business to choose wives for their sons, and husbands for their daughters: . . . that property begets affection, and that if all other things

> hit, they may run the risk of the love with less in inconvenience. . . .
>
> But I must enter my protest here: . . . they seem to know little of the misery of those matches who think they are to be toyed into love after consummation. How often are they cloyed with one another's company before the affection comes in? . . .
>
> The man that marries without love must be a knave; the woman that marries without it must be a fool.

In this book he also advocates a reasonably-sized family—his own would have been so considered when twelve, fourteen and even sixteen births and perhaps many miscarriages in addition were no uncommon lot for a woman—and a divorce law which would accept incompatibility as adequate grounds.

This argument he pursued in later journalistic work, writing in *Applebee's Journal,* April 24, 1725:

> If my Wife and I,—by mere agreeing upon Terms,—came together and married,—why may not my wife and I,—by the like mere agreeing upon Terms,—separate again? For if mutual Consent be the Essence of the Contract of Matrimony, why should not the dissolving that mutual Consent dissolve likewise the Marriage, and disengage the Parties from one another again?

On July 11, 1713 *The Review* came to and end, partly because of the purposely exorbitant stamp tax, designed rather for prohibition than revenue, which Defoe had consistently opposed, and partly because of a change in the political situation, which brought the Whigs into power.

Queen Anne's ill health in that year had raised serious questions of the succession since the choice lay between her Catholic Stuart brother living in exile in France, and the unfamiliar and unpopular German House of Hanover, her nearest Protestant relatives, to whom the succession was legally secured.

Defoe had evidently not learned not to joke with strangers, and burlesqued the Jacobite or Stuart view in two satirical pamphlets, *Reasons Against The Protestant Succession,* which he felt would attract the attention of waverers or opponents and might, if read, convert them to uphold it.

The pamphlets did have an excellent sale and may have been the instrument of converting some, but in 1713, when the Whigs returned to power, Defoe again found himself in jail, on complaint of the Whigs this time, for seditious writing. He succeeded in getting a pardon from the queen in November but immediately after her death, in August 1714, was rearrested for a newspaper squib in which he had attacked a Tory lord who favored the Stuart claims.

Evidently the chief Whig minister thought him useful enough to enlist, and extricated him from his difficulties on condition of certain complicated services which he undertook to perform. Three years later, in 1718, he summarized these in a letter to a new Secretary of State, Lord Stanhope.

He speaks there of the editorship of the *Tory News Letter* which he has been carrying on for the past three years, and traces his negotiations with the Whig ministry preliminary to undertaking it:

> Upon this I engaged in it; and that so far, that though the property was not wholly my own, yet the conduct and government of the style and news was so entirely in me that I ventured to assure his Lordship the sting of that mischievous paper should be entirely taken out, though it was granted that the style should continue Tory, as it was, that the Party might be amused, and not set up another, which would have destroyed the design. And this part I therefore take entirely on myself still. . . .
>
> Upon the whole, however this is the consequence, that by this management the *Weekly Journal,* and *Dormer's Letter,* as also the *Mercurius Politicus,* which is in the same nature of management as the Journal, will be always kept (mistakes excepted) to pass as Tory papers, and yet be so disabled and enervated; so as to do no mischief, or give any offence to the government.
>
> I beg leave to observe, Sir, one thing more to his Lordship in my own behalf, and without which, indeed, I may one time or other run the risk of fatal misconstructions. I am, Sir, for this service posted among Papists, Jacobites, and enraged High Tories—a generation who, I profess, my very soul abhors; I am obliged to hear traitorous expressions and outrageous words against His Majesty's person and government and his most faithful servants, and smile at it all as if I approved it; I am obliged to take all scandalous and, indeed, villainess papers that come, and keep them by me as if I would gather materials from them to put them into the news; nay, I often venture to let things pass which are a little shocking, that I may not render myself suspected.

His enthusiasm for verisimilitude seems again to have overcome him, however, and when Mist, the Tory owner of *Mist's Miscellany* was shortly thereafter fined for an extremely antigovernment article it was asserted with apparent truth that Defoe had been personally responsible for its insertion.

This probably ended his employment by the government and in 1719, at sixty, which was then considered a ripe old age, he retired to the comfortable country house he shared with his wife and two unmarried daughters, and wrote *The Life and Strange Surprizing Adventures of Robinson Crusoe, of York, Mariner: Who lived Eight and Twenty years, all alone in an un-inhabited Island on the Coast of America, near the Mouth of the Great River of Oroonoque; Having been cast on Shore by Shipwreck, wherein all the Men perished but himself. With an Account how he was at last strangely deliver'd by Pyrates. Written by Himself.*

The subject of the book was suggested by the then topical recent adventures of the celebrated Alexander Selkirk, marooned for some years on an island very much like Crusoe's. Superficially the story followed the immensely popular tradition of personal travel books, relating real or pretended adventures of their heroes. This form had been well-established in England ever since Othello won a wife by telling her of:

> . . . antres vast and deserts idle,
> Rough quarries, rocks and hills whose heads touch heaven,
> . . . . . .
> And of the Cannibals that each other eat,
> The Anthropophagi and men whose heads
> Do grow beneath their shoulders. . . .

To all appearances, Defoe simply went a step further by inventing the explorer himself as well as the sights he reported.

Robinson Crusoe purported to be a true history of the life and adventures of an adventurous young businessman. Cast away, not on a desert island, but on an island boasting considerable natural resources, a large number of wild but domesticable animals and even a potentially useful native population, Robinson Crusoe uses the tools civilization has given him, both in his education, ingenuity, and skill, and in the more literal form of iron, seed, and so forth, to build a fruitful, prosperous life. This is not, in the old sense, an adventure story. We do not ask at each step, "What happened to him next?" but "What did he do next?" The emphasis is not on wonderful and terrible events but on resourceful and effective activity. The initiative comes from man throughout. Nature is raw material for his shaping, not a god for his worship. Sometimes stubborn and difficult, it is never purposeful or malicious and can therefore be mastered and used by any educated, intelligent, self-reliant, hard working and prudent man who has a reasonable share of good luck—just such a share as the laws of probability (or the goodness of God) is likely to afford him. One can hardly imagine a more perfect representation of primitive capitalist accumulation building the nucleus of its first small fortunes on industry and thrift, as well as appropriation, and the practical Protestant religion it developed as its rationale, than the passages in chapters IX, XI and XII, in which Defoe describes Crusoe's achievement of a store of grain sufficient to safeguard him from all foreseeable vicissitudes of weather and accident. The kernel of almost every other episode, important or unimportant, is in the same way, profoundly correct as well as realistic.

The surface realism enforced by Defoe's pretense of reportage is valuable and interesting, but was already well-developed in such other earlier and contemporary books of an allegorical nature as *Pilgrim's Progress* and *Gulliver's Travels*. *Robinson Crusoe* derives its honorable position as the first English novel from its subject rather than its technique. Defoe was the first fully to accomplish what Lukasch refers to as the novelist's distinctive task—"to deal with the totality of objects," that is, to deal with a person or group of people in their relations not only to each other, but also to the material and social world around them. In other words, even this early and casually written novel uses the concrete historical world not as an unchanged background but as an essential and changing element in the development of character. It uses nature as a necessary factor in the interaction of man's will with the world, an interaction which shapes the personal as well as social course of history. "The world" Defoe uses here is, of course, socially and economically a simple one, restricted to the dimensions of the island; but we always feel that, like an iceberg, it shows only a small fraction of its bulk above the surface. And we soon realize that our pilot is well aware of the whole great mass beneath. In Crusoe himself we find even more clearly represented all the essentials of the energetic, and individualistic, middle-class man when he still had a future before him and could afford to face the reality he had to know in order to master it.

Here in his masterpiece Defoe has unhesitatingly selected as his theme the essential core of all that was still progressive in the role of the bourgeoisie—their leadership in man's great struggle to conquer and use nature.

And while Crusoe, as well as Defoe, perfectly represents this historic achievement of his class, neither of them are simply average members of that class. We have already seen this in Defoe's life. And we must not forget that it is *against* the urging of his middle-class parents that Crusoe sets out on the adventurous voyage which forces him *physically* to come to grips with nature and create his own fruitful estate in the wilderness. Nor must we forget that Crusoe held it one of his greatest hardships when the store of ink with which he recorded his experience was exhausted!

The inexhaustible vitality, the elasticity of spirit, the intelligent curiosity about life, the self-disciplined ability to work for a far off objective, and the capacity to work experimentally and selectively, learning from each experience, were neither exclusively nor universally bourgeois virtues, but they were typically such at the beginning of the eighteenth century. It is that reality which gives its greatness to this truthful myth of the first postrevolutionary capitalist era.

The book became so enormously and immediately popular that a contemporary critic sneered:

> There is not an old woman that can go to the price of it, but buys thy *Life and Adventures*, and leaves it, as a legacy, with the *Pilgrim's Progress, the Practice of Piety*, and *God's Revenge against Murther* to her posterity.

Defoe responded immediately to the tremendous and widespread demand with a second part, relating Crusoe's adventures after his rescue, which was published within a few months. Next year he followed up his success with the (fictional) *Memoirs of a Cavalier*, ostensibly written by the Cavalier himself—until recently it was still listed as a real autobiography in most bibliographies—and *The Life, Adventures and Piracies of the Famous Captain Singleton*.

This latter pretended biography amazed readers a century later by its accurate descriptions of the then newly explored interior of Africa, and led to wildly improbable surmises of Defoe's access to hidden or forgotten records of unknown explorations. Today scholars are agreed that he used no information which could not have been pieced together by a keen geographer who had studied all the maps and other sources available in England, and was able to make shrewd estimates of topographical probabilities. In any case, the achievement is a most impressive one.

In 1722 he followed his previous successes with his second really important novel, *The Fortunes and Misfortunes of the Famous Moll Flanders etc. Who was Born in Newgate, and during a life of contin'ued Variety for Threescore Years, besides her childhood, was Twelve Year a Whore, five times a Wife (whereof once to her own Brother) Twelve year a Thief, Eight Year a Transported Felon in Virginia, at last grew Rich liv'd Honest, and died a Penitent, Written from her own Memorandums.* . . .

Here again Defoe was following a tradition well-established since pre-Elizabethan times. There were frequently cheap broadsides sold in the streets after the execution of notorious criminals, giving the story of their lives. These generally pretended to be based on last minute confessions and were often written in the first person, supposedly in the very words of the late prisoner. They almost invariably concluded with expressions of penitence and exhortations to virtue, offering the speaker's own life as a horrible example of crime and punishment.

Defoe himself wrote a whole series of these in the miscellaneous journalism of his last ten years. And in *Moll Flanders* he again ostensibly went just a step further in creating the heroine as well as the bulk of her adventures. But we have already seen how deeply concerned Defoe was with the position of woman in his society, so it is no surprise to find that his second important novel deals largely with this question.

In the "true history" of *Moll Flanders* we have what is really a companion piece to *Robinson Crusoe*—the story of his feminine counterpart. She is cast away, not on an uninhabited island, but in the midst of London, and struggles with comparable difficulties in order to carve out her portion of security, comfort and wealth from this wilderness. With deep insight Defoe shows us that whereas middle-class man could, at this time, still deal directly with material things, middle-class woman could secure possession of them only indirectly through her dealings with their owner—man— and had to exercise her ingenuity and wits to make as good a bargain with him as she could. That marriage in which she was subjugated nevertheless gave her some legal rights and put certain limits to her exploitation, and all her shrewdness and resourcefulness is bent upon achieving it on the best possible terms. We have already noted Moll Flanders' blunt summary of what a woman owes herself and how she can best secure it. She says succinctly:

> I hold no woman should allow herself to be taken for a Mistress that hath the means to make herself a Wife.

But since there can be nothing constructive in her efforts to sell herself, legally or illegally, to the best advantage, the book lacks the deeper epic significance we find in *Robinson Crusoe*. Moll Flanders has no creative moment to which we can thrill as we do to Crusoe's exultation when he has finally succeeded in baking a misshapen pot and cries out: "No joy at a thing of so mean a nature was ever equal to mine, when I found that I had made an earthen pot that would bear the fire."

Our interest in her exploits is on the lower level of the picaresque story where we sympathize with society's outlaws and enjoy seeing them get back something of their own. But the more comprehensive ethical understanding which would link these isolated raids on society with a struggle to change it was not a part of Defoe's universe. In his contrast between Swift and Defoe referred to above, Ross correctly says:

> . . . in Defoe's time his culture was at a youthful, vigorous stage, with a promising future predicated on material progress and that useful contradiction in terms, business ethics. Thus, though his own life was full of difficulties, and though he had failed in whatever ambitious dreams he had dreamed in 1702, his work throughout expresses the freshness, the vigor, and the unthinking pioneer optimism which properly reflected the status of his class.

And thus, although he was still human enough to see woman as a person and an equal, it was impossible for him to question the basis of her social degradation—the property relationships which were also the basis of the material progress of his class.

Yet with her robust common sense, warmth, and vitality, Moll has stood as comforter and justification, if not champion, to some of her disinherited sisters in many generations during the past two centuries. We find a striking illustration of this in George Borrow's delightful and too little known *Lavengro*, written in 1851.

There an old apple woman on London Bridge offers the young author help if he is, as she mistakenly thinks, running from the police, and he asks in surprise:

"So you think there is no harm in stealing?"
"No harm in the world, dear! Do you think my own child would have been transported for it, if there had been any harm in it? and what's more, would the blessed woman in the book here have written her life as she has done, and given it to the world, if there had been any harm in faking? She, too, was what they call a thief and a cut-purse; ay, and was transported for it, like my dear son; and do you think she would have told the world so, if there had been any harm in the thing? Oh, it is a comfort to me that the blessed woman was transported, and came back—for come back she did, and rich too—for it is an assurance to me that my dear son, who was transported too, will come back like her."
"What was her name?"
"Her name, blessed Mary Flanders."
"Will you let me look at the book?"
"Yes, dear, that I will, if you promise me not to run away with it."

I took the book from her hand; a short, thick volume, at least a century old, bound with greasy black leather. I turned the yellow and dog's-eared pages, reading here and there a sentence. Yes, and no mistake! *His* pen, his style his spirit might be observed in every line of the uncouth— looking old volume—the air, the style, the spirit of the writer of the book which had first taught me to read. I covered my face with my hand and thought of my childhood. . . .

"This is a singular book," said I at last; "but it does not appear to have been written to prove that thieving is no harm, but rather to show the terrible consequences of crime: it contains a deep moral."
"A deep what, dear?"
"A . . . but no matter, I will give you a crown for this volume."
"No, dear, I will not sell the volume for a crown."
"I am poor," said I; "but I will give you two silver crowns for your volume."
"No, dear, I will not sell my volume for two silver crowns; no, nor for the golden one in the king's tower down there; without my book I should mope and pine, and perhaps fling myself into the river; but I am glad you like it, which shows that I was right about you, after all; you are one of our party, and you have a flash about that eye of yours which puts me just in mind of my dear son. No, dear, I won't sell you my book; but if you like, you may have a peep into it whenever

you come this way. I shall be glad to see you; you are one of the right sort, for if you had been a common one, you would have run away with the thing; but you scorn such behaviour, and, as you are so flash of your money, though you say you are poor, you may give me a tanner to buy a little baccy with: I love baccy, dear, more by token that it comes from the plantations to which the blessed woman was sent."

In 1722 Defoe also published the amazing "eye witness account" of *A Journal of the Plague Year*, the less well-known but interesting relation of *Due Preparations for the Plague*, another novel—*The Adventures of Colonel Jack*—and a four-hundred page book on *Religious Courtship*!

In 1724, in addition to undertaking a number of large-scale business ventures in cheese, oysters and honey and a complicated real estate-pottery factory deal, Defoe found time to write the only other one of his books which is today fairly well known, *Roxana, The Fortunate Mistress*, to complete the first volume of his very interesting *Tour Thro the Whole Island of Great Britain*, and to dash off *A New Voyage round the World*.

The next year saw the second volume of the *Tour* and a new very much enlarged edition of the first volume of *The Compleat English Tradesman, in Familiar Letters, Directing him in all the several Parts and Progressions of Trade*.

Despite his several bankruptcies Defoe writes with undiminished enthusiasm about the wonders of trade, not only in this book but in the novels as well. Roxana, for example, is never so romantic as when she discusses its possibilities. In weighing the merits of alternative suitors, she concludes rapturously:

> That an estate is a pond, but that trade is a spring; that if the first is once mortgaged it seldom gets clear, but embarrasses the person forever; but the merchant has his estate continually flowing; and upon this he named me merchants who lived in more real splendour and spent more money than most of the noblemen in England could singly expend, and that they still grew immensely rich.

Defoe's irrepressible seasoned optimism reminds one of the famous Greek epitaph:

> A shipwrecked sailor, buried on this coast,
> Bids you set sail;

> Full many a gallant bark, when ours was lost,
> Weathered the gale.

Some of the chapter heads of the business handbook are startling and almost disarming in their directness. For example, a section entitled: "Of Honesty in Dealing" has a subhead, "Of Telling Unavoidable Trading Lies," and explains: ". . . there are some latitudes which a tradesman is and must be allowed . . . which cannot be allowed in other cases."

With the same simplicity the pirate Captain Singleton's Quaker first mate, who assists him in the most unscrupulous exploits, finally says to him:

> Now that you're rich, have you not had enough of this wicked life, which will certainly lead you to damnation?

And when, after due consideration, the captain agrees that he has, they both retire to prepare for salvation by living peacefully and virtuously on their piratical spoils.

During all this time Defoe was also engaged in such journalistic writing as a whole series of the "lives, trials, last words and executions" of notorious contemporary criminals, as well as some other less sensational pieces.

That year a journalist describing the manners and morals of the lower classes, could write, with a certainty that the general public would understand his reference:

> Down in the kitchen honest Dick and Doll
> Are studying Colonel Jack and Flanders Moll.

And, although men of letters were all properly contemptuous in public, as fashionable an arbiter of polite taste as Pope felt constrained to admit privately:

> The first part of *Robinson Crusoe* is very good. . . . Defoe wrote a vast many things; and none bad, though none excellent, except this. There is something good in all he had written.

A few years later, Dr. Johnson more enthusiastically exclaimed after reading *Robinson Crusoe*:

> Was there ever anything else written by mere man that was wished longer by its readers except *Don Quixote* and *Pilgrim's Progress*?

And it is with those two immortal classics that succeeding generations have ranked Defoe's almost accidental masterpiece ever since.

Almost accidental because, while he might well never have written a novel at all, only a man who both represented and transcended his special class in the particular way Defoe did, could ever have written anything like this first English novel. Its special place in literature is not won by the simple verisimilitude which convinced its contemporary readers that it must be a true story. A story can be true and damnably dull, or even true and interesting enough as it goes along but, finally, insignificant. As Dr. Arnold Kettle, in his *Introduction to the English Novel*, says on this point:

> It is precisely the fact that the human interest story in our newspapers is nearly always presented from a morally neutral standpoint, without significance, that makes it so often rather disgusting. A concern with the texture of life which is not accompanied by an attempt to evaluate the experiences recorded is bound to be in the end irresponsible.

But *Robinson Crusoe* holds our interest in its first nursery presentation and challenges our maturer understanding at each new rereading. It is concerned not merely with the texture of life, but with its innermost core. It represents the essence of any responsible experience because it summarizes man's successful attempt to impose a state of art on the state of nature, and thus create the material prerequisites for all civilization.

1726 saw the *History of the Devil*, 1727 an *Essay on the History and Reality of Apparitions*, including the well-known account of "The Appearance of Mrs. Veal," and the second volume of *The Compleat English Tradesman*.

The next year Defoe published the *Augusta Triumphans* already mentioned as a second book of *Essays on Projects* and a very sound *Plan of the English Commerce*.

His last publication was another fictional autobiography, *The Military Memoirs of Captain George Carleton*, which some bibliographies still list with anonymous factual material of the preceding century.

The last year of the *Life and Adventures of the Incredible Daniel Defoe*, as one of his biographers has aptly put it, was until very recently a mystery.

In the fall of 1729 he wrote a note to his publisher explaining that he had delayed returning some proof sheets because of illness, and then he disappeared.

There remains one long, emotional and somewhat confused letter the following spring in which Defoe speaks of his loneliness, his intense desire to see his newly born grandson if that could be managed with secrecy. He also urges his son-in-law, to whom the letter is addressed, to give Defoe's wife and unmarried daughter any counsel or assistance they may need in claiming their inheritance after his death. The letter makes it clear that Defoe was in hiding from some unnamed enemy, and that although ill and lonely he was determined to keep his whereabouts a closely guarded secret.

Recent research has finally established the fact that there was a large claim against his estate, which had probably been satisfied in one of his bankruptcy proceedings, as he himself said:

> No man has tasted differing fortune more,
> And thirteen times I have been rich and poor—

but which was now fraudulently or mistakenly revived.

According to the law at the time, this particular claim could be pressed only against Defoe in person and not against his heirs after his death. With a characteristic mixture of adventure and prudence, and with his habitual practical unsentimental devotion to his family, Defoe had acted promptly to preserve their inheritance for his wife and children, and succeeded by dying alone and undiscovered in a London lodging in April, 1730.

The cause of death was noted in the burial certificate as "a lethargy"—surely the only one that had ever visited him in all his varied career.

HENRY FIELDING

Although Defoe wrote the first and most widely read English novel, the novel as a form can hardly be said to have come into being for another quarter of a century.

Robinson Crusoe and even *Moll Flanders* are somewhat special in having only one real character; there are serious limitations to the possible development of the first person hero-narrator form; and, perhaps most important of all, both Defoe and his critics took the question of factual accuracy as a fundamental one.

A contemporary article on *The Life and Strange Adventures of Mr. D. De F. — — of London, Hosier, Who had lived above fifty years by himself in the Kingdoms of North and South Britain* represented Defoe as saying to Crusoe, "I have made you out of nothing," and attacked the book as a lie. Defoe first tried to prove it was true and then fell back, in a third part, on interpreting the entire story as a detailed allegory of his own life and business misadventures.

The interpretation is ingenious though unconvincing, but its importance for us is the evidence it gives that not even its creator yet realized a new literary form had come into being.

It is not until a generation later that we find any further experiments with its possibilities. The first conscious novelist, Henry Fielding, born in 1707, was a skilled writer, a dramatist with a good classical education, who saw the real importance of this new development and half-apologetically, half-proudly, and altogether self-consciously, named it a "comic epic in prose."

Fielding began his literary career as a writer for that theatre which Defoe had called "Satan's work-house where all the manufactures of Hell are propagated." He had both a broad knowledge of, and a deep respect for, the classics which Defoe contemned. He was a highly conscious literary pioneer who spent much thought not only on the experiments which resulted in the first complete modern novel, but also on formulating critical aesthetic theories to evaluate them, while Defoe was, as we have seen, simply concerned to convince his readers that his imaginative creations were just long statements of fact. In addition, Fielding was the great-grandson of a Cavalier, the grandson of a church dignitary who served as royal chaplain, and the son of an army officer. His specific taste differed from Defoe's as much as their varying backgrounds would lead one to expect. Yet what they had in common was a far more essential part of that genius which shaped the great eighteenth century English novel than any or all of their specific differences in training, taste and talent.

Fielding was an impecunious member of the younger branch of an aristocratic family, and his education was much more like that of Swift, whom he greatly admired, than like that of Defoe. But he shared Defoe's central intuition that the world's great age lay ahead, Defoe's fundamental faith in the power of men to change their environment, and Defoe's democratic belief in the goodness and vitality of the common man—and woman—whom he, as well as Defoe, respected without idealizing.

To these attitudes Fielding adds a greater breadth of ethical and aesthetic interest than Defoe's, a keener realization of the joys this world can afford man's senses, a more conscious concern with men's and women's personal relations to each other, and perhaps a wider observation of the rich varieties of character and experience on all levels of society.

Dr. Arnold Kettle summarizes Fielding's refinement of Defoe's attitude when he says:

> Even more basic to the impression of assuredness is the nature of Fielding's philosophy, sceptical but optimistic. He takes the world in his stride, always curious, frequently indignant, but never incurably hurt. . . . He is not complacent but he is fundamentally confident—confident that the problems of human society, that is to say *his* society, can and will be solved by humane feeling and right reason.

Fielding's father was an officer with little but his colonel's pay to live on—fair provision for a fashionable bachelor but altogether inadequate for the comfortable support of a wife and family. He improvidently fell in love with the daughter of a substantial country squire and judge, who defied her parents to elope with him. Her father finally forgave her and settled a small estate of £3,000— an income of about £150 a year—on her and her (future) children on condition that her husband "should have nothing to do nor intermeddle therein."

Five years after Fielding's birth his father temporarily retired on half-pay and set up as a gentleman farmer. The venture was not very successful and Mrs. Fielding was indebted to her mother's help in caring for the family which soon included four little girls and a baby boy. When she died, in 1718, Colonel Fielding rejoined his regiment in London, leaving the family to the care of his mother-in-law. A year later he returned with a second wife—a young Italian woman who is said to have been the widow of an innkeeper.

Fielding, already eleven, seems to have led his sisters in open rebellion against their stepmother—the violent anti-Catholicism which was, in later life, almost his only strong prejudice, no doubt dates from this period. The children's maternal grandmother, now a widow of considerable income and great forcefulness, encouraged them; and their easygoing father sent the young boy to Eton, and the girls to a good boarding school in Salisbury. Their grandmother undertook the care of the baby, and rented a home in Salisbury near the girls' school.

Since Colonel Fielding soon had six children by his second wife, he played little part thereafter in Fielding's life, although the two always remained friendly. On his son's graduation he good-naturedly granted him an allowance of £200 a year which, as Fielding later said, "any body might pay that would," since his father was totally unable to do so.

After two years private study at his grandmother's the young man spent a few months in London, getting a play performed for a few nights at the Drury Lane Theatre. He then enrolled at the University of Leyden.

At the end of a year there his remittances from home stopped altogether, and in 1729 he returned to London with, as he said, "no choice but to be a hackney writer or a hackney coachman."

While his first play, *Love in Several Masques*, had made no money, its reception had been encouraging enough to make him look to the theatre for a living. Read today it seems a slight but promising beginning, with a creditable caricature of a greedy squire, Sir Positive Trap, who thought a man should be able to "carry his daughter to market with the same lawful authority as any other of his cattle." There was also much mockery of the fashionable "beau" or "fine gentleman"—that "empty, gaudy nameless thing" possessing "everything of a woman but the sex and nothing of a man besides it." A few lines of dialogue indicate what was, for a twenty-one year old, an unusually easy tone:

> "That's a pretty suit of yours, Sir Apish, perfectly gay, new, and alamode."
> "He, he, he! the ladies tell me I refine upon them. I think I have studied dress long enough to know a little, and I have the good fortune to have every suit liked better than the former."

Fielding was always a very rapid workman and during the next seven years he must have written four or five plays a year, since he had at least twenty-five produced.

These compare favorably with others of the period, and are, for the most part, in the same genre—a sort of free spoken topical comedy of manners leaning heavily on amorous intrigue, and caricaturing such types as the pedantic scholar, the money-grubbing squire, and the hypocritical prude.

Fielding himself also developed a vein of more serious realistic satire, attacking particularly the corrupt magistrates and law enforcement officers who were in league with the most dangerous elements of the teeming London underworld and who assisted its leaders in exploiting the miserable prostitutes, pickpockets and other weaker brethren. For example, in *Rape upon Rape or The Justice Caught in his own Trap*, which was produced as early as June, 1730, we find such a dialogue as the following between Magistrate Squeezum and his clerk who has just returned from an errand to "Mother Bilkum's" bagnio:

> "She says she does not value your worship's protection at a farthing, for that she can bribe two juries a year to acquit her in Hicks' Hall for half the money which she hath paid you within these three months."
> "Very fine! I will show her that I understand something of juries as well as herself. Quill, make a memorandum against Mother Bilkum's trial that we may remember to have the panel No. 3; they are a set of good men and true, and hearken to no evidence but mine."

In the same play the magistrate commends his subordinates' discretion in having called off a raid when they learned that two lords patronized the gambling house they were supposed to surprise. He says: "Quite right. The laws are turnpikes, only made to stop people who walk on foot, and not to interrupt those who drive through them in their coaches."

These satires clearly owe their inspiration rather to Moliere, several of whose plays Fielding translated and adapted, than to Congreve, who was the model for most of the postrestoration playwrights.

In the later comedies Fielding's attacks became even sharper, and are frequently directed at specific public officials, easily recognized by the delighted audience and their less well-pleased government protectors.

In April, 1731 he went much further with a play called *The Welsh Opera or The Grey Mare is the Better Horse* whose very title impudently commented on the well-known political relationship between George II and his wife Queen Caroline. The body of the play still more dangerously represented the powerful prime minister, Robert Walpole, in the person of a thieving butler Robin. It glanced at his support by other dishonest government officials and parliamentary leaders in such lines as these of the cook's, who is rebuking the coachman for threatening to expose an especially shameless piece of pilfering:

> Fie upon't, William, what have we to do with master's losses? He is rich, and can afford it. Don't let us quarrel among ourselves; let us stand by one another; for, let me tell you, if matters were to be too nicely examined into, I am afraid it would go hard with us all. . . .

The church is represented by Parson Puzzletext, who ponders:

> I think it is a difficult matter to determine which deserves to be hanged most; and if Robin the butler hath cheated more than other people, I see no other reason for it, but because he hath had more opportunity to cheat.

We have already seen in our consideration of the earlier part of the century that while there was an enormous amount of political intrigue and maneuvering, there were really no fundamental political questions involved and that the conflicts were essentially between individuals and groups struggling for the personal rewards of office. In his *People's History of England,* Morton says:

> In England the whole quality of Whiggery was summed up in the commanding person of Robert Walpole. Enterprising Norfolk landowner, financial genius with an understanding of the needs of commerce as keen as any City merchant's, colleague and leader of the great Whig peers, shrewd, predatory and wholly unidealistic, he symbolised the interests and character of the unique alliance which governed England.
> The policy of the Whigs was simple enough. First to avoid foreign wars as being harmful to trade. Then to remove taxes, so far as was possible, from the merchants and manufacturers and place them upon goods consumed by the masses and upon the land. But, as the leading Whigs were themselves landowners and it was considered dangerous to rouse the active hostility of the [Tory] squirearchy, the land tax was kept fairly low and agriculture stimulated by protection and bounties. By avoiding war Walpole was, indeed, able to reduce the land tax considerably. All the politically active classes were thus satisfied and the masses, in this period between the age of spontaneous armed rising and that of organized political

agitation, had no effective means of expressing any discontents that may have existed.

On such a basis party politics became less and less a matter of policies and more and more of simple personal acquisitiveness. It came to be normal and respectable for a gentleman "to get his bread by voting in the House of Commons," and the main concern of such ministers as the Duke of Newcastle was "to find pasture enough for the beasts that they must feed."

Naturally, then, Fielding's dramatic satire was directed against the bribery in parliamentary elections, the dishonesty of government officials, the corruption of such other representatives of vested interests as lawyers, fashionable physicians, and church dignitaries, and dealt with personalities and types rather than issues. It was, however, stinging enough to attract the special attention of the government, and his plays might be better remembered even today if he had not later adapted their best material for use in his novels.

Meanwhile, with the same prodigious vitality we have already marveled at in Defoe, Fielding was not only writing play after play, and living the fast-paced London theatrical life he describes in many of them, but was also maintaining and improving his affectionate intimacy with the Greek and Latin writers to whom he so often refers, and studying such moderns as Shakespeare, Moliere and Cervantes. In addition he found time, during a visit to his sisters' home in Salisbury, to fall romantically and passionately in love with the beautiful young woman whom he immortalized, as a girl, in Tom Jones' Sophia and as a wife and mother in Amelia.

In 1734 she eloped with him to London, and writing for the theatre became a much grimmer affair when every failure meant deprivation for an adored wife and, soon, her dearly loved "little things."

Fielding was writing out of bitter knowledge when he said, in *Tom Jones*:

> To see a woman you love in distress and to be unable to relieve her, and at the same time to reflect that you have brought her into this situation is perhaps a curse of which no imagination can present the horrors to those who have not felt it.

Two years later he took a bold step and invested the greater part of his wife's small inheritance, a total of about £1,500, in a theatre of his own called The Little Theatre.

From the beginning this venture was prodigiously successful. His first play, which was received with enormous enthusiasm and had what was then a very long run, was called *Pasquin or A Dramatic Satire on The Times*.

The first half of the play dealt with bribery in parliamentary elections and the second with similar corruption in the learned professions. The prologue to the second part begins:

> Religion, law and physic were designed
> By heaven the greatest blessings on mankind;
> But priests and lawyers and physicians made
> These general goods to each a private trade;
> With each they rob, with each they fill their purses,
> And turn our benefits into our curses.

His next play, a classical burlesque, was almost as much of a success, and in March, 1737, he topped both of them with his production of *The Historical Register for 1736*. This was a direct satire of Walpole, openly enough presented to provoke the government's *Daily Gazette* into a stern leading article on "An Adventurer in Politics."

Fielding replied to this by printing his two satirical plays in a mock-apologetic pamphlet with a defiant preface that concluded, after discussing plans for enlarging his theatre:

> If nature hath given me any talents at ridiculing vice and imposture, I shall not be indolent, nor afraid of exerting them, while the liberty of the press and stage subsists, that is to say, while we have any liberty left among us.

The pamphlet sold very well, but the government had the last word. In May, 1737, it rushed through a Licensing Act which forced Fielding's theatre to close and made it most unlikely that any other theatrical management would risk the presentation of his plays.

With a wife and two children to provide for, forced out of the profession in which he had made a considerable, if precarious, success, Fielding at 31 enrolled himself as a law student in the Honourable Society of the Middle Temple. Here he somehow managed to complete the normal seven-year course of study in three years, while doing an enormous amount of literary hack work to support a hand-to-mouth existence.

During the last part of this period, from November, 1739, to June, 1741, he served as editor of *The Champion*, a periodical modeled on *The Spectator* and published by a syndicate of booksellers.

Again, we would be more likely to remember these articles if Fielding had not later included and surpassed them in the incidental essays we find scattered through the novels.

The most distinctive emphasis in *The Champion* was Fielding's characteristic development of the contradiction between property values and human values. For example, in discussing the disproportion of the law, he says:

> A boy should, in my opinion, be more severely punished for exercising cruelty on a dog or a cat or any other animal, than for stealing a few pence or shillings or any of those lesser crimes which our courts of justice take note of.

The paper also enabled him to continue his attacks on Walpole who is, for instance, personified as Mammon in one issue and made to say:

> For doubting, sure, thou canst have no pretence;
> To shun a bribe must argue want of sense.
> A wise man's conscience always hath a price;
> Those that are dear are called by blockheads nice.
> Nature 'twixt men no other bounds has set
> Than that of sums—the little and the great.

That month Fielding read an extraordinary book, *Pamela*. This had been published in November, 1740 by Samuel Richardson who, in most literary histories, disputes or shares with Defoe and Fielding the honor of originating the English novel.

It is important to note that Richardson did not, any more than Defoe, think of the novel as a development of the well-established long story form of prose fiction, but as an instrument for the education of the young. As a printer-bookseller he had already published several collections of letters addressed to imaginary correspondents, which were intended to teach young people how to write letters to employers, parents, and so forth. These not only set forth the manner of writing but attempted to inculcate proper attitudes and moral principles.

One of these compendiums was entitled:

> Letters Written to and For Particular Friends on the Most Important Occasions; directing not only the requisite style and form to be observed in writing familiar letters, but how to

think and act justly and prudently in the common concerns of human life.

Some of the letters included were described:

> "From a Maid-servant in Town, acquainting her Father and Mother in the Country with a Proposal of Marriage, and asking their Consent."
> "From a Son reduced by his own Extravagance, requesting his Father's advice on his Intention to turn Player."
> "To a young Lady, advising her not to change her Guardians, nor to encourage any Clandestine address."

In this collection there was a certain continuity of personnel and anecdote in one series of five letters, which proved extremely effective. Richardson had thus been inspired to write, in the form of an extremely long series of letters, the story of a maid servant, Pamela, whose master, failing in his three volume attempt to seduce or rape her, finally has recourse to the desperate expedient of marriage.

The only virtue of this extremely cumbersome self-conscious machinery is that it focuses attention, as did Defoe's simpler autobiographical method, on the apparent truth of the narration and the reality of its subject.

The subject is, of course, again, (as always in the great realistic novels), man's attempt to master his environment, to act on it so that he can shape the kind of life he wants. In conscious terms Pamela plays a somewhat passive part, since the initial attraction that moves Squire B—— is rather her good fortune than her planning, but even there "accomplishments," education, dress and manner—all of which have been acquired through hard work as well as natural ability and good luck—are as important as the accident of beauty; and the stubborn resistance of her thoroughly commercial, though not consciously hypocritical, virtue is the means whereby she makes a deservedly profitable marriage.

The inhuman commercial relations to which capitalism reduced men and women were revolting enough, when displayed by so naive and sentimental a petty bourgeois as Richardson, to shock a more generous and discriminating man like Fielding. He dashed off an amusing though rather superficial burlesque, *An Apology for the Life of Mrs. Shamela Andrews,* which appeared that April with some success, and which Richardson never forgave. In this skit he announced his discovery that Squire B——'s real name was Booby and, less plausibly, that Shamela [Pamela] was a conscious hypocrite, already delivered of an illegitimate child, who wrote her mother: "I thought once of making a little fortune by my person. I now intend to make a great one by my virtue."

When Fielding was called to the Bar that year he had to give up his editorship and so had time to begin a far more powerful and amusing satire, which soon turned into a full length novel, *The Adventures of Joseph Andrews, and of his Friend Mr. Abraham Adams.*

This begins with a parody which is, in itself, a powerful denunciation of the double sexual standard in bourgeois society, and the whole degradation of women implied by it. Pamela's brother, Joseph, was the first hero of the book. It was intended to center about his adventures, as a footman, in defending his chastity against determined attacks by his titled mistress and her housekeeper. But the book soon overflowed the narrow channel planned for it and became a positive assertion of Fielding's own human values of warmth, gratitude, love between men and women, and delight in the pleasures of beef, ale, beauty and scholarship.

Joseph's friend and counselor, Parson Adams, is a figure comparable only to the immortal Don Quixote, by whom he was avowedly inspired; and the journey the two undertake across England, accompanied by the sweetheart who is soon introduced to give Joseph a better reason for his virtue, is a homely modern Odyssey.

Hazlitt speaking of the English Comic writers almost a century afterwards says:

> I should be at a loss where to find in any authentic documents of the same period so satisfactory an account of the general state of society, and of the moral, political and religious feeling in the reign of George II, as we meet with in *The Adventure of Joseph Andrews and his Friend Mr. Abraham Adams.*

Kettle, in a detailed analysis of Fielding's first novel, which must be quoted at some length shows that: "In the conflicts of the novel—which are always those of humanity versus hypocrisy and bogus morality—Adams, for all his idealistic impracticability, is always on the right side."

He refers to a conversation between this absent-minded scholar and the typically down-to-earth man of business, the steward Peter Pounce, as an example not only of the vigor of Fielding's dialogue but also of the subtlety of his dialectic saying: "Pounce begins with a typical, apparently common-sense, materialist definition of charity. But by the end of the dialogue his materialism is revealed as an empty idealism ('the distresses of mankind are mostly imaginary'), while the impractical idealist Adams is left asserting the reality of hunger and thirst, cold and nakedness."

His final description of Fielding's accomplishment is perhaps the best summary of the book we have:

> It is this kind of insight which goes beyond a mere hearty sympathy for what is decent and dislike of what is hypocritical that gives *Joseph Andrews* its quality. But neither should we undervalue the sheer common-sense decency and strong (albeit unsubtle) moral concern which is at the basis of Fielding's vision. In the continual conflicts in *Joseph Andrews* around the theme of charity, conflicts in which Adams and Joseph are always in trouble, generally because they have no money, it is interesting that the unkind are invariably the great and fashionable and lustful, the mercenary and servile and hypocritical—while the kind are the humble people—the postilion who gives Joseph his cloak, the common soldier who pays the bill at the inn, the farmer who has seen through the ways of the world. If we stop to analyse the pervading sense, in Fielding's novels, of generous humanity (and it is, when all is said, the dominant quality of his books), we shall find that it springs not from a vague, undifferentiated bonhomie but from a very explicit social awareness and understanding of the people.

A brief excerpt from the scene where Joseph, stripped and beaten by thieves, is discovered bleeding in a ditch by a stage coach full of passengers, will give us some idea of the book's quality.

> The poor wretch, who lay motionless a long time, just began to recover his senses as a stage-coach came by. The postilion hearing a man's groans, stopt his horses, and told the coachman he was certain there was a dead man lying in the ditch, for he heard him groan. "Go on, sirrah," says the coachman, "we are confounded late, and have no time to look after dead men." A lady, who heard what the postilion said, and likewise heard the groan, called eagerly to the coachman to stop and see what was the matter. Upon which he bid the postilion alight, and look into the ditch. He did so, and returned, "That there was a man sitting upright, as naked as ever he was born."—"O, J-sus!" cried the lady; "A naked

man! Dear coachman, drive on and leave him." Upon this the gentlemen got out of the coach; and Joseph begged them to have mercy upon him: for that he had been robbed and almost beaten to death. "Robbed," cries an old gentleman: "Let us make all the haste imaginable, or we shall be robbed too." A young man, who belonged to the law, answered, "He wished they had passed by without taking any notice: but that now they might be proved to have been last in his company; if he should die they might be called to some account for his murder. He therefore thought it advisable to save the poor creature's life for their own sakes, if possible; at least, if he died, to prevent the jury's finding that they fled for it. He was therefore of opinion, to take the man into the coach, and carry him to the next inn." The lady insisted, "That he should not come into the coach. That if they lifted him in, she would herself alight; for she had rather stay in that place to all eternity, than ride with a naked man." The coachman objected, "That he could not suffer him to be taken in, unless somebody would pay a shilling for his carriage the four miles." Which the two gentlemen refused to do. But the lawyer, who was afraid of some mischief happening to himself, if the wretch was left behind in that condition, saying no man could be too cautious in these matters, and that he remembered very extraordinary cases in the books, threatened the coachman, and bid him deny taking him up at his peril; for that, if he died, he should be indicted for his murder; and if he lived, and brought an action against him, he would willingly take a brief in it. These words had a sensible effect on the coachman, who was well acquainted with the person who spoke them; and the old gentleman above mentioned, thinking the naked man would afford him frequent opportunities of showing his wit to the lady, offered to join the company in giving a mug of beer for his fare; till, partly alarmed by the threats of the one, and partly by the promises of the other, and being perhaps a little moved with compassion at the poor creature's condition, who stood bleeding and shivering with the cold, he at length agreed; and Joseph was now advancing to the coach, where seeing the lady who held the sticks of her fan before her eyes, he absolutely refused, miserable as he was, to enter unless he was furnished with sufficient covering to prevent giving the least offence to decency. . . .

Though there were several greatcoats about the coach, it was not easy to get over this difficulty which Joseph had started. The two gentlemen complained they were cold, and could not spare a rag; the man of wit saying, with a laugh, that charity begins at home; and the coachman, who had two greatcoats spread under him, refused to lend either, lest they should be made bloody; the lady's footman desired to be excused for the same reason, which the lady herself, not withstanding her abhorence of a naked man, approved: and it is more than probable poor Joseph, who obstinately adhered to his modest resolution, must have perished unless the postilion (a lad who hath since been transported for robbing a henroost) had voluntarily stript off a greatcoat, his only outer garment, at the same time swearing a great oath (for which he was rebuked by the passengers), "that he would rather ride in his shirt all his life than suffer a fellow-creature to lie in so miserable a condition."

The book was ignored by the critics but achieved an immediate popular success, selling about 6,500 copies within the year. This enabled Fielding to pay off his debts and provide some much needed comforts for his wife, who had been prostrated by an illness which proved fatal to their beloved first child that winter, and who was still seriously ill.

Fielding himself now became subject to the frequent and excruciatingly severe attacks of gout which were to afflict him for the rest of his life, and found it increasingly difficult to build the substantial law practise for which he had hoped.

He again had recourse to his pen and on April 12, 1743, published a book of *Miscellanies* for which he received almost £800 by subscription. The most important piece included in that volume was the bitter satire, usually referred to as one of his novels, *The Life of Jonathan Wild The Great*.

Jonathan Wild was a notorious criminal—the head of a gang of cutthroats, bullies and pimps, exceeding them all in his utter callousness—who had been one of the first in eighteenth century London to organize crime on a business basis. He had been executed in the late twenties and was included in the series of *Lives of Criminals* written by Defoe at the time.

Fielding, in his introduction, refers to Defoe's "True and Genuine Account of the Life and Actions of the late Jonathan Wild; not made up out of Fiction and Fable, but taken from his own Mouth, and collected from Papers of his own Writing." He handsomely acknowledges his great indebtedness to "that excellent historian, who, from authentic papers and records, etc. hath already given so satisfactory an account of the life and actions of this great man." But, in truth, the facts furnished by Defoe serve merely as raw material for a powerful satire in which Fielding makes it very clear that this "great man," a reference which to his contemporaries invariably meant Walpole, is only the prototype of all corrupt political leaders and military bullies, and that it is they rather than the avowed criminals who merit every decent man's hatred and contempt.

Byron makes an interesting reference to this book in his discussion of Fielding's work in 1821:

> I have lately been reading Fielding over again. They talk of Radicalism, Jacobinism, etc. in England (I am told), but they should turn over the pages of Jonathan Wild the Great. The inequality of conditions and the littleness of the great, were never set forth in stronger terms; and his contempt for Conquerors and the like is such, that, had he lived *now*, he would have been denounced in "the Courier" as the grand Mouth-piece and Factionary of the revolutionists. And yet I never recollect to have heard this turn of Fielding's mind noticed, though it is obvious in every page.

The next winter—November, 1744—his passionately loved wife died, leaving him with two small children. A devoted young housekeeper who had cared for her for many years continued to care for the children, and Fielding's favorite sister, Sarah, joined the little household.

A year later Fielding undertook another periodical, *The True Patriot and The History of Our Own Time*, intended to arouse Londoners to the dangers of a new Jacobite attempt at crowning "The Young Pretender," who actually landed in Scotland and attempted a short-lived invasion of England. Among other interesting nonpolitical notes in the paper was Fielding's brief epitaph for Dean Swift:

> A genius who deserves to be ranked among the first whom the world ever saw. He possessed the talents of a Lucian, a Rabelais and a Cervantes, and in his works exceeded them all. He employed his wit to the noblest purposes . . . in the defence of his country against several pernicious schemes of wicked politicians.

In November 1746 he married his housekeeper and although he still and always spoke of his first wife as his only real love, the marriage was a happy one for both himself and his only surviving little daughter as well as for his second wife. In his *Journal of A Voyage to Lisbon*, written during the last year of his life, Fielding said of her:

My wife, besides discharging excellently well her own, and all the tender offices becoming the female character—besides being a faithful friend, an amiable companion, and tender nurse—could likewise supply the wants of a decrepit husband and occasionally perform his part.

But the attacks upon his taste for "low company," assiduously promoted by Richardson, were, in the thinking of the time, given far more support by this marriage than they would have been by the grossest immorality, and those attacks were partly responsible for his decision to give up his unsuccessful efforts for a legal career.

In 1748 Richardson published his only really fine novel—*Clarissa Harlowe*—which, with all its sentimentality, melodrama and religiosity, nevertheless makes Clarissa an extraordinary spokesman of her sex. Although really in love with her betrayer, she refuses his offer to "make her an honest woman" with the cry "The man who has been the villain to me you have been shall never be my husband," and chooses rather to die in disgrace than to become his wife. In this climax, as well as in her earlier resistance to marrying a wealthy boor of her father's choice, Clarissa stands as an amazingly advanced champion of her sex.

As Kettle says:

> The conflict of Clarissa—the individual hearts vs. the conventional standards of the property-owning class—is one of the essential, recurring conflicts of the modern novel, as of all literature of class society. It is the conflict of love (i.e. human dignity, sympathy, independence) vs. money (i.e. property, position, "respectability," prejudice) which lies at the heart of almost all the novels of Fielding, Jane Austen, the Brontes, ... unlike as they are in almost every respect.

Fielding, with characteristic candor and generosity, lavished enthusiastic praise upon the book in the pages of a new satirical newspaper, *The Jacobite's Journal*, which had succeeded *The True Patriot*. Richardson was, however, far from mollified and continued the venomous and partially successful attempt to destroy his rival's personal as well as his literary reputation.

It was largely owing to these efforts that two of Fielding's patrons, who had replaced Walpole in the forties, refused his application for the judgeship which had been half promised him in recognition of his voluntary assistance against the Jacobite invasion. The malicious gossip retailed as current stories of dissipation that, insofar as they were at all true, dated from Fielding's bachelor days in the theatre. His indisputably low marriage, his unconventional liking for unfashionable company, and his championship of the unrespectable in *Joseph Andrews*, all gave color to these slanders. They were, in fact, still believed and repeated by most Victorian biographers a century later.

However, in October 1748, Fielding was named as magistrate or justice of the peace for Westminster and a few months later this appointment was extended to include all of Middlesex.

Such a position was then considered lucrative but contemptible. In Fielding's hands it became a most ill-paid but honorable one.

There was no salary attached to the office and the magistrate was still, as all Judges had been in Bacon's time, paid by fees collected from the litigants themselves. Fielding gives an excellent brief description of the duties and rewards of this office in the introduction to his *Voyage to Lisbon* written six years later:

> . . . I will therefore confess . . . that my private affairs at the beginning of the winter had but a gloomy aspect; for I had not plundered the public or the poor of those sums which men, who are always ready to plunder both as much as they can, have been pleased to suspect me of taking; on the contrary, by composing instead of inflaming the quarrels of porters and beggars (which I blush to say hath not been universally practised), and by refusing to take a shilling from a man who most undoubtedly would not have had another left, I had reduced an income of about five hundred pounds a year of the dirtiest money on earth to little more than three hundred pounds; a considerable proportion of which remained with my clerk; and, indeed, if the whole had done so, as it ought, he would be but ill paid for sitting almost sixteen hours in the twenty-four in the most unwholesome, as well as nauseous, air in the universe, and which hath in his case corrupted a good constitution without contaminating his morals.

But before we consider further his work as a magistrate, which Fielding himself thought his major claim to public gratitude, we must turn to the publication of *The History of Tom Jones, A Foundling* on February 20, 1749.

The publisher's advertisement early in March announces the six volumes at eighteen shillings a set and happily adds: "it being impossible to get sets bound fast enough to answer the demand for them, such gentlemen and ladies as please, may have them sewed in blue paper and boards, at the price of 16s. a set." There were five more editions within the year and while critical opinion was divided, there were a fair number of appreciative reviews.

The book is some three times the length of *Joseph Andrews* and is even more richly filled with incidents, scenes, and characters, of the English countryside and its capital. In addition Fielding deliberately develops in this book his theory of this new form which he called a "comic epic in prose," but which we recognize as the first fully conscious novel—the form which has most completely expressed the values, and most adequately explored the possibilities, of modern life.

In discussing this great bourgeois art form Kettle says:

> For literature to the bourgeois writers of this period was, above all, a means of taking stock of the new society. A medium which could express a realistic and objective curiosity about man and his world, this was what they were after. It was the search for such a medium that that led Fielding to describe Joseph Andrews as a "comic epic poem in prose." Their task was not so much to adapt themselves to a revolutionary situation as to cull and examine what the revolution had produced. They were themselves revolutionaries only in the sense that they participated in the consequences of a revolution, they were more free and therefore more realistic than their predecessors to just the extent and in just those ways that the English bourgeois revolution involved in fact an increase in human freedom.

Although Fielding used in this new way the time honored apparatus of story-telling—a narrative method heightened and quickened by his long dramatic apprenticeship—his skill and apparent ease should not make us forget the significance of Defoe's and Richardson's seemingly unnecessary technical difficulties. For the very existence of their experiments emphasize what Fielding's mastery conceals—the essentially didactic or ethical nature of the novel.

Fielding himself repeatedly stressed the novelty of the form he was creating. Later critics have, however, too often taken an essentially formal approach, and treated the novel simply as a development of the long romances and the picaresque stories of an earlier day, made more important by the material conditions of the eighteenth century.

Doubtless the comparatively cheap development of printing and the increasing literacy of the population made the novel possible; but a necessary cause is not a sufficient cause, and either of these technical conditions might more easily have accounted for the increased writing and reading of short or long stories, such as we find in magazines today. An understanding of the rich and immediate development of the eighteenth century novel must, I think, be sought in a complex of causes all essentially related as conditions of the developing bourgeois life. Increased literacy has already been mentioned but it must be combined with the increased leisure of at least a part of the middle class, that is, the women; a certain economic margin for leisure-time recreation without a tradition of formal social activity; and a Protestant tradition that disapproved both of the luxurious display of, and of the content involved in, most earlier theatrical performances. All these, however, except for the increasing importance of feminine readers and, soon, writers, are still only a part of the necessary conditions for some popular reading matter suited to a not too educated public, and we must look further into the problems and needs of this public to see why their literature took the form it did.

When we do so we are first struck by their enormous lack of any clearly formulated philosophy of life or ethical system, and the fact that there was really no authority which could formulate or promulgate such a philosophy for them. The church was perhaps at its lowest point in terms of living influence or general authority and respect. Ways of life both in city and country, and especially in the movement from one to the other, were changing almost under men's eyes. Aristocratic mores, as adapted by most upper-class writers and exemplars, were clearly not applicable to most people. Even family authority could not be exercised in the old way. How, for example, could a shopkeeper tell his son to behave as his father had done when clearly his whole object in life was to raise his son to a sphere of activity in which the grandfather would have been completely lost, and in which he himself could barely hope to set an exploratory foot.

Even Addison indicated how sharply traditional family ties must be broken when the younger son could rise "by an honest industry to greater estates than those of their elder brothers," and the brief excerpt from Morton's history, already cited, amply indicates how impossible it must have been for any of the minority who did change from small freeholders to successful manufacturers authoritatively to tell their children or themselves what model to imitate for a successful life.

It is precisely this all important question to which the earliest novels directly address themselves. How shall a man act, in such and such concrete circumstances, to achieve success? What kind of life will make him happy and how can he secure it? Fielding and the other great early novelists were not preachers delivering a memorized answer. They were scientists reproducing in their pages enough of the actual relevant conditions of the world to make possible a laboratory experiment whose results they, as well as their readers, were anxious to learn. Certainly they had a prior hypothesis. But they watched with genuine curiosity and anxiety for its confirmation or correction as the experiment developed in the course of the novel. It is this that gives these early novels—and those later Victorian ones which, with less scope, still used the same serious approach—such genuine and breathless interest. Even in the limited world of a lady like Jane Austen we will find, restricted though the range of her subjects is, the realism and truth of an honest scientific approach to an important experiment. And in such later giants as Balzac and Tolstoi we find that though the size of our crucibles is greater, our mixtures more complex, and the explosive force of our ingredients more dangerous, the attitude of combined exploration and didacticism remains the sign of the great realistic novelist. This is not the place to enter upon a further examination of those distinguishing characteristics of the novel—the persistent consciousness of an irreversible time, the reality of novelty and change, the emphasis on personal relationships, the development of psychological analysis, the concrete contemporary nontransferable nature—which make it the predominant art form of modern bourgeois culture, and made it inevitable that it should have developed only when that culture itself was expanding most fruitfully in its first period of unquestioned dominance.

Tom Jones is an excellent example of all these qualities. There is a vast wealth of amazingly varied formulations in it, ranging from the perfectly eighteenth century equation, "The Cause of King George is the cause of liberty and true religion. In other words, it is the cause of common sense," to the more surprising twentieth or twenty-first century challenge:

> "The delicacy of your 'sex,' " said Tom, "cannot conceive the grossness of ours, nor how little one sort of amour has to do with the heart." "I will never marry a man," replied Sophia, very gravely, "who shall not learn refinement enough to be as incapable as I am myself of making such a distinction."

The central conflict in the novel between property rights and personal rights—between respectability and humanity—comes to a climax in Squire Western's attempt to force his daughter to marry the man who is heir of an estate that happens to adjoin the squire's. He attempts to persuade her by promising an exceptionally large dowry for, as Fielding gravely observes: "so extravagant was the affection of that fond parent, that, provided his child would but consent to be miserable with the husband he chose, he cared not at what price he purchased him."

She refuses, and, locked up in her room for days, is unable to eat or sleep:

> Western beheld the deplorable condition of his daughter with no more contrition or remorse than the turnkey of Newgate feels at viewing the agonies of a tender wife when taking her last farewell of her condemned husband; or rather he looked down on her with the same emotions which arise in an honest fair tradesman who sees his debtor dragged to prison for £10, which, though a just debt, the wretch is wickedly unable to pay. Or, to hit the case more nearly, he felt the same compunction with a bawd when some poor innocent, whom she hath ensnared into her hands, falls into fits at the first proposal of what is called seeing company. Indeed this resemblance would be exact, was it not that the bawd hath an interest in what she doth, and the father, though perhaps he may blindly think otherwise, can, in reality, have none in urging his daughter to almost an equal prostitution.

Although the final happy ending is a somewhat contrived one, this does not really matter. As Kettle says:

> What does matter, because the whole movement and texture of the book depend on it, is that Tom and Sophia fight conventional society, embodied in the character of Blifil. They fight with every strategem including, when necessary, fists and swords and pistols. Unlike Clarissa, they are not passive in their struggle, and that is why *Tom Jones* is not a tragedy but a comedy. It is not the conventionally contrived happy ending but the confidence we feel throughout the book that Tom and Sophia can and will grapple with their situation and change it that gains our acceptance of Fielding's comic view of life.

This is perhaps the best, and certainly the best-known, of Fielding's novels. Coleridge, who seldom accorded unreserved praise to any work of fiction, said:

> What a master of composition Fielding was! Upon my word, I think the Oedipus Tyrannus, the Alchemist, and Tom Jones,

the three most perfect plots ever planned. And how charming, how wholesome, Fielding always is! To take him up after Richardson is like emerging from a sick-room, heated by stoves, into an open lawn, on a breezy day in May.

And Bernard Shaw concluded a discussion by proclaiming that:

> Between the Middle Ages and the nineteenth century, when Fielding was by the Licensing Act driven out of the trade of Moliere and Aristophanes into that of Cervantes, the English novel has been one of the glories of literature, whilst the English drama has been its disgrace.

But while there was still one great novel to come, the next few years found Fielding busy with other though, as it proved, not wholly unrelated matters.

He marked his assumption of office with a grave and searching *Charge To The Grand Jury* which was later printed at the particular request of the jurymen. In the beginning of 1751 he published the result of much thought and careful observation, his *Enquiry into the Causes of the late Increases of Robbers, etc. with some Proposals for Remedying this Growing Evil.*

This first relates a plain unvarnished tale:

> What indeed may not the public apprehend, when they are informed as an unquestionable fact, that there are at this time a great gang of rogues, whose number falls little short of a hundred, who are incorporated in one body, have offices and a treasury, and have reduced theft and robbery into a regular system? There are of this society of men who appear in all disguises, and mix in most companies. Nor are they better versed in every art of cheating, thieving, and robbing than they are armed with every method of evading the law, if they should ever be discovered, and an attempt made to bring them to justice. Here, if they fail in rescuing the prisoner, or (which seldom happens) in bribing or deterring the prosecutor, they have for their last resource some rotten members of the law to forge a defence for them, and a great number of false witnesses ready to support it.

Then it goes on to speak of the truly indescribable and bestial conditions of life in the swollen London slums, saying with considerable restraint:

> Among other mischiefs attending this wretched nuisance the great increase of thieves must necessarily be one. The wonder in fact is that we have not a thousand more robbers than we have; indeed, that all these wretches are not thieves

must give us either a very high idea of their honesty, or a very mean one of their capacity and courage.

It concludes with concrete proposals for a new sort of police force, practical suggestions to make impossible, or at least much more difficult, the kind of collusion then existing between the underworld and law enforcement officers, and recommendations for the drastic reform of prison procedures, particularly in regard to the segregation and treatment of first offenders.

At the end of that year Fielding used his experience as a magistrate, as well as his observations of the world of fashion, and his memories of his rapturous first marriage, in a different form in his last novel, *Amelia*.

The first edition of 5,000 copies was exhausted in twelve hours, partly because of the reputation of *Tom Jones* and partly because of a clever "puffing" or advertising stunt by the publisher. But a second uncorrected impression of 3,000 was not yet completely sold at Fielding's death, and the carefully revised edition he had prepared was not published for some years thereafter.

The realistic exposure of slum and prison conditions, the sharp attacks on the whole machinery of the law, and on such accepted institutions as the imprisonment of debtors, and the general exposure of profligacy and corruption in high places, while it forms a comparatively small part of the book, is unforgettable long after one has closed it. In addition, there is little of the rollicking humour of *Tom Jones* and readers led to expect that overlooked other qualities they might otherwise have found almost equally appealing.

At any rate a large part of respectable public opinion, anxious to ignore the unpleasant truth of the book's social criticism, concurred with Richardson's spiteful judgment:

> I could not help telling his sister that I was equally surprised and concerned for his continued lowness. Had your brother, said I, been born in a stable, or been a runner at a sponging-house, we should have thought him a genius, and wished he had had the advantage of a liberal education, and of being admitted into good company; but it is beyond my conception, that a man of family, and who had some learning, and who really is a writer, should descend so excessively low, in all his pieces. Who can care for any of his people?

This criticism was echoed until, a century later, Dickens angrily countered it with:

> I am not aware of any writer in our language having a respect for himself, or held in any respect by his posterity, who has ever descended to the taste of the fastidious classes. . . . On the other hand, if I look for examples and precedents, I find them in the noblest range of English literature. Fielding, Defoe, . . . for wise purposes . . . brought upon the scene the very scum and refuse of the land . . . and yet, if I turn back . . . I find the same reproach levelled against them . . . each in his turn, by the insects of the hour; who raised their little hum, and died, and were forgotten . . . when Fielding described Newgate, the prison immediately ceased to exist.

Disgust at the cold reception of *Amelia*, whom he spoke of as his favorite child, together with increasing ill health and the pressure of his almost unpaid duties, made Fielding publicly declare his determination to write no more. This resolution he evidently meant to apply to fiction rather than journalism, for in January, 1752, he instituted his last periodical venture—*The Covent Garden Journal*.

The paper had a curious history. In 1749 he and his youngest half-brother John, an intelligent and energetic young man who had had the misfortune to be blinded at nineteen, had organized a "Universal Register Office"—perhaps the first general employment office in England!

This had expanded under John's direction to include real estate and insurance, a sort of travel agency, and in fact a general exchange of all sorts of goods and services. It furnished a good part of Fielding's income, and all of John's until in 1751, Fielding secured him an appointment as assistant magistrate.

By 1751 several rival agencies had sprung up and most of the available London newspapers for political or business reasons, accepted their advertisements but not those of the Fieldings. The brothers therefore decided to publish their own journal. Fielding, despite much dissuasion, personally assumed the editorship in order to use the paper as an organ through which to press for judicial reforms.

Despite its commercial inspiration this periodical affords us more insight into his personal views than any of Fielding's earlier journalistic ventures have done. In one of the first issues he defined his attitude to the political scene declaring:

> I disclaim any dealing in politics. By politics, here, I cannot be understood to mean any disquisitions into those matters which respect the true interest of this kingdom abroad, or

which relate to its domestic economy and government. . . .
By politics I mean that great political cause between *Woodall Out* and *Takeall In* Esqs, which hath been so learnedly handled in papers, pamphlets, and magazines, for above thirty years last past.

A number at the beginning of the second month contains an especially interesting discussion of religion as a means of plundering the poor, although we know from other sources that Fielding himself was a convinced if unexcited Christian. However, here he ironically appeals to gentlemen in power for a revival of religion on politic if on no other grounds:

> . . . if we look into the doctrines and tenets of that institution [Christianity] which was accounted divine by our ancestors . . . we shall find it admirably calculated for the preservation of property; . . .
> Now what can more effectually establish this . . . than the positive assertion of one St. Luke, 20th verse, "Blessed are the poor, for theirs is the kingdom of heaven." If the poor or the people (for in this country the _____ and the _____ are synonymous) could be once firmly persuaded that they had a right to the other world, they might surely be well contented to resign their pretensions to this. Nay, the rich might in that case very fairly withhold everything in this world from them: for it would be manifestly unjust that the poor should enjoy both. . . .
> Could anything, therefore, be so weak in our late governors, as to have suffered a set of poor fellows, who were just able to read and write, to inform their brethren, that the place which the rich had allotted to them was a mere Utopia, and an estate, according to the usual sense of the phrase, in [limbo] only? Could the poor become once unanimously persuaded of this, what should hinder them from an attempt in which the superiority of their numbers might give them some hopes of success; and when they have nothing real to risk in either world in the trial?
> . . . I know so many good people who are pleased with . . . the scheme of the late Dean Swift, to force our poor to eat their own children, as what would not only afford provision for our present poor but prevent their increase.
> But with submission, however proper and humane this proposal might be in Ireland, I must observe it would be extremely cruel and severe here. For there the children of the poor being sustained for the most part with milk and potatoes, must be very delicious food; but here, as the children of the poor are little better than a composition of gin, to force their

parents to eat them would in reality be to force them to poison themselves. . . .

In truth, religion here, as in many other instances, will best do the business of the politician.

As to the restoration of the Christian religion, though I must own the expediency of it, could it be accomplished, I think it is a matter of too much difficulty. . . .

Without further preface then I shall propose the restoration of the ancient heathen religion . . . that consisted in the immolation of human sacrifices.

. . . The objection I would obviate is this; that my scheme is rather too barbarous and inhuman.

To this it might be sufficient to answer that it is for the good of the nation in general; that is to say, for the richer part.

But in truth it is for the advantage of the poor themselves; . . . Do we not daily see instances of men in distressed circumstances, that is to say, who cannot keep a coach and six, who fly to death as to a refuge? What must we think then of wretches in a state of hunger and nakedness; without bread to eat, without clothes to cover them, without a hut or hovel to receive them?

. . . In this light, therefore, I shall be understood by my sensible reader, and instead of that censure of cruelty which hath been bestowed upon Dr. Swift by some very ingenious and learned critics for his above-mentioned proposal, it will be attributed to my humane disposition that I have proposed to lessen the severity of that death, which is suffered by so many persons, who in the most lingering manner do daily perish for want in this metropolis.

Other briefer comments indicate the social views we find developed more fully but sometimes less explicitly in his novels. A good example is his temperate and realistic conclusion:

I do not pretend to say, that the mob have no faults; perhaps they have many. I assert no more than this, that they are in all laudable qualities very greatly superior to those who have hitherto, with much injustice, pretended to look down upon them.

In another article a letter from a purported madman suggests the abolition of money as a cure for many social evils, concluding:

I shall add but one particular more; which is, that my scheme would most certainly provide for the poor, and that by an infallible (perhaps the only infallible) method, by removing the rich. Where there are no rich, there will of consequence be found no poor; for Providence hath in a wonderful manner provided for every country a plentiful subsistence for all its inhabitants; and where none abound, none can want.

After Fielding's ill health had, at the end of 1752, forced him to end the journal, he published one more pamphlet, *A Proposal for Making An Effective Provision for the Poor, for Amending their Morals and for Rendering them Useful Members of the Society.* The specific suggestions are of little interest today, but his description of existing conditions with its indignation at the delicacy that cannot bear to know of horrors but can easily endure their hidden existence is as timely now as then:

> If we were to make a progress through the outskirts of this town, and look into the habitations of the poor, we should there behold such pictures of human misery as must move the compassion of every heart that deserves the name of human. What, indeed, must be his composition who could see whole families in want of every necessary of life, oppressed with hunger, cold, nakedness, and filth, and with diseases, the certain consequences of all these—what, I say, must be his composition, who could look into such a scene as this, and be affected only in his nostrils?

The excellent French literary historian, Louis Cazamian, gives a good description of the strength as well as the limitations of Fielding's thinking in this field when he says:

> As a magistrate Fielding knows well the conflicts of the penal codes and the instincts; he recounts them with the exactitude of a well-informed witness and the zeal of a reformer. For he has a generous conception of justice; no doubt, his ideas on the right to punish, on the responsibility of the criminal, on the social regime, do not go beyond the range of vision of his time; but he quickens them through the susceptibility of a noble conscience, he has felt and shown the crudity of certain legal punishments, the scandals of judicial administration. His calm objective world is at times animated by a humane ardour, just as the independence of his thought does not stop at the inequalities his age deemed necessary.

This pamphlet and the growing fame of Fielding's accomplishments in his district caused the Duke of Newcastle to request in August, 1753, that he submit a plan "for putting an immediate end to those murders and robberies which were everyday committed in the streets."

Although seriously ill, Fielding submitted a plan which he personally undertook to put into effect if supplied with £600 for necessary expenses. This would, he guaranteed, serve to "demolish the then reigning gangs, and to put the civil policy in such order, that no such gangs should ever be able for the future to form themselves into bodies, or at least to remain any time formidable to the public."

The successful upshot of the matter is given very succinctly in an autobiographical fragment, included in the introduction to his *Journal of A Voyage to Lisbon*, which was written two years later and published after his death. Here he says, in part:

> But, not to trouble the reader with anecdotes. . . . I assure him I thought my family was very slenderly provided for; and that my health began to decline so fast that I had very little more of life left to accomplish what I had thought of too late. I rejoiced therefore greatly in seeing an opportunity, as I apprehended, of gaining such merit in the eye of the public, that if my life were the sacrifice to it, my friends [in the government] might think they did a popular act in putting my family at least beyond the reach of necessity, which I myself began to despair of doing. And though I disclaim all pretence to that Spartan or Roman patriotism, which loved the public so well that it was always ready to become a voluntary sacrifice to the public good, I do solemnly declare I have that love for my family.
>
> After this confession therefore, that the public was not the principal deity to which my life was offered a sacrifice, and when it is further considered what a poor sacrifice this was, being indeed no other than the giving up what I saw little likelihood of being able to hold much longer, and which, upon the terms I held it, nothing but the weakness of human nature could represent to me as worth holding at all; the world may, I believe, without envy, allow me all the praise to which I have any title.
>
> My aim, in fact, was not praise, which is the last gift they care to bestow; at least, this was not my aim as an end, but rather as a means, of purchasing some moderate provision for my family, which, though it should exceed my merit, must fall infinitely short of my service, if I succeeded in my attempt.

His health was, actually, so completely destroyed in the work of carrying out his reforms that in April 1754, he retired, happily securing John's appointment to his magistracy. On the urgent advice of his physician, he set sail for Lisbon to attempt recovery in a warm climate.

He was accompanied by his wife and oldest daughter. Unable to walk, suffering from a complication of painful disorders including dropsy, and separated from his children, the "little things," he unfeignedly and unashamedly loved, and with whom he normally spent an extraordinary amount of time, he nevertheless still displayed the liveliest interest in all the incidents of the trip, the eccentricities of the ship's captain, and the novelties to be seen en route.

Two months after reaching his destination he died, and the *Journal* which he had written to defray the expenses of his journey was published posthumously in February, 1755, for the benefit of his wife and children.

His brother John, who published it, also succeeded in getting two of Fielding's old plays produced for their benefit, and in securing them a small pension.

He shared his own income with them for the rest of his life and Fielding's two sons, the only ones of the children to survive their uncle, seem to have been well educated. Charles Lamb half a century later describes the older as a fairly well-known judge whom he went to see for his father's sake.

Hazlitt has, perhaps, written Fielding's best epitaph saying:

> It is a very idle piece of morality, to lament over Fielding for his low indulgence of his appetite for character. If he had been found quietly at his tea, he would never have left behind him the name he had done. There is nothing of a tea inspiration in any of his novels. They are assuredly the finest things of the kind in the language; and we are Englishmen enough to consider them the best in any language. They are indubitably the most English of all the works of Englishmen.

FROM THE AUGUSTANS TO THE ROMANTICS

As late as 1814 a man of letters like Sir Walter Scott could explain the anonymity of his first novel by writing apologetically:

> I shall not own Waverly; . . . In truth I am not sure it would be considered quite decorous of me, as a Clerk of Session, to write novels. . . . I do not see how my silence can be considered as imposing on the public. . . . In point of

emolument everybody knows that I sacrifice much money by withholding my name; and what should I gain by it that any human being has a right to consider as an unfair advantage? In fact, only the freedom of writing trifles with less personal responsibility, and perhaps more frequently than I otherwise might do.

But it must not be supposed that during the preceding fifty years the "official literature" had remained unaffected by this rich and powerful new literary form.

Even a leading intellectual figure like the famous critic and literary dictator Samuel Johnson (1709-1784) read and discussed the novels of Richardson, Fielding and others and, more important, showed in his own writing and way of thinking their influence and that of the social forces which had molded them.

The latter part of the eighteenth century is often referred to as the Age of Johnson, as the earlier one is called that of Addison and Pope, and a comparison of Johnson with the two former writers shows clearly how much even the approved upper-class literature of the period had, insensibly, been changed by the pressure of interests and attitudes from below. Johnson himself was the son of a lower middle-class family. Although he had earned a sort of working scholarship to Oxford, he found it intolerable to remain at the University under the stigma of a sizar's (student waiter's) gown. He was one of the first finally successful representatives of the new class of writers, who made a living entirely by selling their wares to the public through the medium of the new capitalist publisher-booksellers rather than by gaining the patronage of a great nobleman.

His quarrel with Lord Chesterfield is one of the best known anecdotes of literary history, and since it not only marked, but also perfectly summarized, the end of the patronage system—and the establishment of the commodity system—in art, it must again be repeated here.

When Johnson determined to undertake his famous Dictionary, his reason was characteristically eighteenth century, in that he felt the language had reached perfection and must be set in that mold before deterioration, the germs of which were already apparent, overcame it. He naturally thought of securing financial assistance from a leading patron of the arts, and on the hint of some friend or follower of Lord Chesterfield, waited upon him for that purpose. His visits were not encouraged and Johnson, well-known for his independence and touchy pride, made no further efforts in that direction but devoted himself, in great poverty, to doing the work alone. With the assistance of several meager advances from the bookseller who was to bring it out he succeeded. During these years of hardship his wife died.

When the work was about ready for the press its fame had already preceded it. Johnson's literary and critical reputation was also well established by that time, and Chesterfield wrote several very graceful "anonymous" articles in anticipation of its publication, letting it be known that he was not averse to receiving—and rewarding—its dedication to him. Johnson, furious at this belated and unnecessary patronage, wrote his famous letter to Lord Chesterfield on February 7, 1755. In effect this announced the emergence of the modern "independent" intellectual and middle-class professional, free to sell his wares in the market place or starve. The polished style and classical allusions, as well as the gracefully implied insult in the ironically courteous conclusion, all make this an excellent example of the aristocratic eighteenth century style, although the content heralds the end of that epoch.

To the Right Honorable the Earl of Chesterfield

My Lord: I have been lately informed by the proprietor of the World, that two papers, in which my Dictionary is recommended to the public, were written by your Lordship. To be so distinguished is an honor which, being very little accustomed to favors from the great, I know not well how to receive, or in what terms to acknowledge.

When, upon some slight encouragement, I first visited your Lordship, I was overpowered, like the rest of mankind, by the enchantment of your address, and could not forbear to wish that I might boast myself Le vainquer du vainqueur de la terre;—that I might obtain that regard for which I saw the world contending; but I found my attendance so little encouraged that neither pride nor modesty would suffer me to continue it. When I had once addressed your Lordship in public, I had exhausted all the art of pleasing which a retired and uncourtly scholar can possess. I had done all that I could; and no man is well pleased to have his all neglected, be it ever so little.

Seven years, my Lord, have now passed since I waited in your outward rooms, or was repulsed from your door; during which time I have been pushing on my work through difficulties, of which it is useless to complain, and have brought it, at last, to the verge of publication without one act of assistance, one word of encouragement, or one smile of favor. Such treatment I did not expect, for I never had a Patron before. The shepherd in Vergil grew at last acquainted with Love, and found him a native of the rocks.

Is not a Patron, my Lord, one who looks with unconcern on a man struggling for life in the water, and when he has reached ground, encumbers him with help? The notice which you have been pleased to take of my labors, had it been early, had been kind; but it has been delayed till I am indifferent, and cannot enjoy it; till I am solitary, and cannot impart it; till I am known, and do not want it. I hope it is no very cynical asperity not to confess obligations where no benefit has been received, or to be unwilling that the Public should consider me as owing that to a Patron, which Providence has enabled me to do for myself.

Having carried on my work thus far with so little obligation to any favorer of learning, I shall not be disappointed though I should conclude it, if less be possible, with less; for I have been long wakened from that dream of hope, in which I once boasted myself with so much exultation,

My Lord,
Your Lordship's most humble,
Most obedient servant,
Sam Johnson

Before turning to the emergence of "sentiment" and the last two eighteenth century figures we must here mention, we should say that Johnson as well as Swift—the only eighteenth century writers, besides the novelists, who powerfully expressed hatred of oppression and understanding sympathy for poverty—were Tories. This may seem as contradictory as Balzac's official devotion to royalism in Republican France, or Tolstoy's theory of asceticism, non-resistance, resignation and religion in revolutionary Russia. Actually an understanding of these contradictions is of the utmost importance to the student of literature for it requires him to make, and aids him in making, the effort of historical imagination necessary for any real appreciation of the art and creative thinking of other ages.

It is always easier to feel what is wrong than to find a remedy, and those writers sensitive enough to react at that early date to the evils of capitalism were often forced, by their opposition to its inhumanity, to take sides with any who seemed to oppose it. In eighteenth century England, this meant with the Tories. In specific terms, for example, the Whigs were for the War of the Protestant

Succession. The rising merchants and early manufacturers who grew rich through early exploitation of India and other colonies abroad, and through the rooting up of the independent peasantry at home, were all Whigs. The deliberate destruction of Irish industry, which so infuriated Swift, and the defense and extension of the slave trade which aroused Johnson, were largely organized by the Whig interests. Of course, the Tories were fundamentally no better, and in the few cases where there was a genuine difference between them and the Whigs, their stand was hopeless as well as reactionary. But barring an impossible and unhistorical mental leap, there was no stand but the Tory stand for those who could not stomach the commercial bourgeoisie, unless they withdrew from political participation entirely, and became preoccupied with sentimental personal problems as the few later eighteenth century poets like Cowper, Collins and Gray tended to do.

The argument on the slave trade between the "Reactionary Tory" Johnson and his "Progressive Whig" biographer, Boswell shows how very misleading party labels can be if we do not take the trouble to examine their concrete historical content and background. Thus, although we would agree with Boswell and not Johnson in their attitude to the American Revolution, we would certainly sympathize with Johnson's toast: "Here's to the next insurrection of the Negroes in the West Indies"; his statement about "the natural right of the Negroes to liberty and independence"; his argument that "An individual may, indeed forfeit his liberty by a crime, but he cannot by that crime forfeit the liberty of his children"; and his wry comment, with which Swift would have entirely agreed, "I do not much wish well to discoveries for I am always afraid they will end in conquest and robbery." In fact, much of his unfriendly attitude toward the colonies is explained by the sarcastic question, "How is it we hear the loudest yelps for liberty among the drivers of the Negroes?"

Boswell expressed a typically sanctimonious Whig rationalization when he begged leave:

> to enter my most solemn protest against his [Johnson's] general doctrine with respect to the slave trade. . . . To abolish a status which in all ages GOD has sanctioned and man has continued would not only be robbery to an innumerable class of our fellow subjects; but it would be an extreme cruelty to the African savages, a large portion of whom it saves from massacre, or intolerable bondage in their own country, and

introduces into a much happier state of life . . . to abolish that trade would be to shut the gates of mercy on mankind.

This alone makes us realize why some of the most humane men of the age were driven to support any opposition to "Whiggism."

Before leaving Johnson we should, perhaps, look at a few more of the many comments in which he shows how it was his rather amazing insight into the reality of bourgeois ethics (as they were more unmistakably to develop after his time) that motivated his opposition to the party which was their leading representative. The growing bourgeois ideal of a "wealthy but usurious miser and a hard working but ascetic slave," which lies at the root of all the nineteenth century cant about "the deserving poor," was characterized by Johnson as "Whiggism." At one time, in response to a protest that it was no use giving alms to beggars since they would spend it on gin or tobacco, Johnson demanded:

> And why should they be denied such sweeteners of their existence? It is surely very savage to refuse them every possible avenue to pleasure, reckoned too coarse for our own acceptance. Life is a pill which none of us can bear to swallow without gilding; yet for the poor we delight in stripping it still barer, and are not ashamed to shew even visible displeasure if ever the bitter taste is taken from their mouths.

He also related to "Whiggism" the growing middle-class cult of sentimentality at which we must glance before leaving the eighteenth century, and went out of his way to shock his bourgeois "liberal" friends with such remarks as:

> These are the distresses of sentiment which a man who is really to be pitied has no leisure to feel. The sight of people who want food and raiment is so common in great cities, that a surly fellow like me has no compassion to spare for wounds given only to vanity or softness . . . you will find these very feeling people are not very ready to do you good. They *pay* you by *feeling*.

Like Swift, he felt a deep though muffled indignation at the infuriating complacency of articulate eighteenth century opinion, and at the fashionable unfelt world-weariness its successful exponents sometimes affected. A remark he made in his *Life of Pope* summarizes and explains much of this attitude:

Swift's resentment was unreasonable, but it was sincere; Pope's was the mere mimickry of his friend, a fictitious part which he began to play before it became him. When he was only twenty-five years old, he related that "a glut of study and retirement had thrown him on the world" and that there was danger lest "a glut of the world should throw him back upon study and retirement." To this Swift answered with great propriety, that Pope had not yet either acted or suffered enough in the world to have become weary of it.

Johnson's own pessimistic stoicism is well-known—his famous comment on the purpose of writing can bear another repetition: "The only end of writing is to enable the readers better to enjoy life or better to endure it." So can his response to a lady's remark on drunkenness: "I wonder what pleasure men can take in making beasts of themselves?" "I wonder, Madam, that you have not penetration enough to see the strong inducement to this excess; for he who makes a *beast* of himself gets rid of the pain of being a man."

Another time when he was approached by a morbidly conscientious young man who, having stolen some packthread and paper from his employer, wanted Johnson's advice on how best to express repentance, he exploded:

> . . . five hours of the four-and-twenty unemployed are enough for a man to go mad in; so I would advise you Sir, to study algebra . . . your head would get less *muddy* and you will leave off tormenting your neighbors about paper and packthread, while we all live together in a world that is bursting with sin and sorrow.

Even the economic analysis of the origin of the family is foreshadowed in such an amazing statement as Johnson's:

> Consider of what importance the chastity of women is. Upon that, all the property in the world depends. We hang a thief for stealing a sheep. But the unchastity of a woman transfers sheep and farm and all from the right owner.

Finally, before closing this brief survey of some of the landmarks of the eighteenth century, we must turn to the timid reemergence of real poetry in the work of Gray and Goldsmith. This refers, of course, to feeling and content; in terms of technical form poetry—metrical rhymed verse—had never gone out of fashion during the eighteenth century, and while less widely read in comparison with the increasing volume of essays, biographies, memoirs and novels, it remained unquestionably the correct thing to write. Even Johnson found it worth his while to achieve a succes d'estime with several long neoclassical poems, and Swift's early and justly forgotten bids for literary fame all took the shape of elaborate rhetorical odes.

Nor would it be true to imply that Swift's astringent wit and Fielding's healthy, sensuous vigor, and Johnson's solid common sense represent all the important facets of the age. Despite its self-chosen title of "The Age of Reason," the eighteenth century had witnessed the rise of a new and most unpleasant phenomenon in the sentimentality consciously expressed as early as 1768 in Sterne's *Sentimental Journey,* less consciously and more unpleasantly in Richardson's *Pamela, Clarissa Harlowe,* and *Richard Grandison* and as we shall see, still more extravagantly developed in the host of minor novelists who imitated these. Cowper's religious melancholia, Collins' more sedate nature poetry, Thomson's "Seasons" and other lesser work, all show traces of this new devotion to sentiment. It is a difficult attitude to define but if we recollect the somewhat cynical description of faith as "a belief in what we know is not true" we may perhaps describe sentimentality as "emotion about what we know does not matter." It is the indulgence of melancholy for its own sake, the luxurious enjoyment of "a good cry" which has persisted from its eighteenth century birth down to the latest "linked sweetness long drawn out" of the agonized soap opera heroine, or woman's magazine serial or (less frequently in this day of film brutality) the vicissitudes of a sad, sweet, motion picture idyll.

As we shall soon note, Jane Austen unmercifully satirizes this tendency of the host of inferior eighteenth century novelists in her juvenilia as well as in her serious novels, and we find its influence strong in the very inferior sentimental drama which monopolized the American as well as the English theatre of the next century.

It is difficult to discuss this attitude briefly or analyze its causes in a reasonable amount of space. Perhaps Leslie Stephens' explanation in his excellent book on *English Literature and Society in the Eighteenth Century* will suffice for our purpose here. He says:

> No distinct democratic sentiment had yet appeared; the aristocratic order was accepted as inevitable or natural; but there was a vague though growing sentiment that the rulers are selfish and corrupt. There is no strong sceptical or anti-religious sentiment; but a spreading conviction that the official pastors are scandalously careless in supplying the wants

of their flocks. . . . The popular books (among this class) of the preceding generation had been the directly religious books (like Pilgrim's Progress) which had been made obsolete by the growth of rationalism. Still the new public wanted something more savoury than its elegant teachers had given; and, if sermons had ceased to be so stimulating as of old, it could find it in secular moralisers. . . .

Richardson was . . . the first writer who definitely turned sentimentalism to account for a new literary genus . . . sentimentalism at the earlier period naturally took the form of religious meditation upon death and judgement. . . .

Sentimentalism, I suppose, means, roughly speaking, indulgence in emotion for its own sake. The sentimentalist does not weep because painful thoughts are forced upon him but because he finds weeping pleasant in itself. He appreciates the luxury of grief. . . . But the general sense that something is not in order in the general state of things, without as yet any definite aim for the vague discontent was shared by the true sentimentalist.

Although it is apparent that no important art could arise from so unreal and essentially dishonest an emotion, it does tinge at least two poems of more than passing importance, which serve as some transition to the extraordinary outburst of poetic genius we find in the romantic poets of the next quarter century. Gray's *Elegy in a Country Churchyard* and Goldsmith's *The Deserted Village* are both directly referred to as sources of inspiration by Burns, and each has some lines of more than historical value, although their chief interest to us is, perhaps, essentially historical.

Thomas Gray (1716-1771), a classmate and friend of the prime minister's son, Horace Walpole, accompanied him on a continental grand tour of several years' duration after they had, together, been graduated from Cambridge. Then, declining all invitations and possible opportunities to a political or literary career, he settled down on a small income to live the life of a semirecluse in rural retirement near the college. He maintained an increasingly desultory correspondence with Walpole and several other worldly patrons of the arts, and did a great deal of work collecting and editing some of the older folk songs and ballads in which he was the first to take a systematic interest. One of the few autobiographical comments we have purports to explain his retirement, and at any rate gives a good thumbnail sketch of the mores of his age:

Too poor for a bribe and too proud t' importune
He had not the method of making a fortune;

Could love and could hate, so was thought somewhat odd,
No very great wit,—he believed in a God.

His single important poem, *Elegy in a Country Churchyard* maintains a fashionable painless melancholy and uses classical allusions and generalized images from nature in the approved manner, but is memorable for a few lines which strike out to the immediacy of death, give us a powerful symbol for the waste of human potentialities and the role of accident in human life, and make a clear if limited assertion of the claims to consideration, respect, and a certain kind of equality that should be granted all human beings.

Beginning with the eighth stanza, which Burns quotes as an introduction to his own "Cotter's Saturday Night," Gray says, in part:

>   Let not Ambition mock their useful toil,
>   Their homely joys, and destiny obscure;
>   Nor Grandeur hear with a disdainful smile,
>   The short and simple annals of the poor.
>   The boast of heraldry, the pomp of pow'r,
>   And all that beauty, all that wealth e'er gave,
>   Awaits alike th' inevitable hour,
>   The paths of glory lead but to the grave.
>   Nor you, ye Proud, impute to These the fault,
>   If Mem'ry o'er their Tomb no Trophies raise,
>   Where thro' the long-drawn aisle and fretted vault
>   The pealing anthem swells the note of praise.
>   Can storied urn or animated bust
>   Back to its mansion call the fleeting breath?
>   Can Honour's voice provoke the silent dust,
>   Or Flatt'ry sooth the dull cold ear of Death?
>   Perhaps in this neglected spot is laid
>   Some heart once pregnant with celestial fire;
>   Hands, that the rod of empire might have sway'd,
>   Or wak'd to extasy the living lyre.
>   But Knowledge to their eyes her ample page
>   Rich with the spoils of time did ne'er unroll;
>   Chill Penury repress'd their noble rage,
>   And froze the genial current of the soul.
>   Full many a gem of purest ray serene,
>   The dark unfathom'd caves of ocean bear:
>   Full many a flower is born to blush unseen,
>   And waste its sweetness on the desert air.
>   Some village-Hampden, that with dauntless breast
>   The little Tyrant of his fields withstood;
>   Some mute inglorious Milton here may rest,
>   Some Cromwell guiltless of his country's blood.

Th' applause of list'ning senates to command,
  The threats of pain and ruin to despise,
To scatter plenty o'er a smiling land,
  And read their hist'ry in a nation's eyes,
Their lot forbad: nor circumscrib'd alone
  Their growing virtues, but their crimes confin'd;
Forbad to wade through slaughter to a throne,
  And shut the gates of mercy on mankind.
The struggling pangs of conscious truth to hide,
  To quench the blushes of ingenuous shame,
Or heap the shrine of Luxury and Pride
  With incense kindled at the Muse's flame.
Far from the madding crowd's ignoble strife,
  Their sober wishes never learn'd to stray;
Along the cool sequester'd vale of life
  They kept the noiseless tenor of their way.
Yet ev'n these bones from insult to protect
  Some frail memorial still erected nigh,
With uncouth rhymes and shapeless sculpture deck'd,
  Implores the passing tribute of a sigh.
Their name, their years, spelt by the unletter'd muse,
  The place of fame and elegy supply:
And many a holy text around she strews,
  That teach the rustic moralist to die.
For who to dumb Forgetfulness a prey
  This pleasing anxious being e'er resign'd,
Left the warm precincts of the chearful day,
  Nor cast one longing ling'ring look behind?
On some fond breast the parting soul relies,
  Some pious drops the closing eye requires;
Ev'n from the tomb the voice of Nature cries,
  Ev'n in our Ashes live their wonted Fires.

In Goldsmith's *The Deserted Village*, to which Burns also refers in his conclusion of "the Cotter's Saturday Night," we find a more sustained attempt to question the certainty that all was for the best, which the eighteenth century so complacently assumed. Oliver Goldsmith (1728-1774) had had a more varied and eventful life than most of his contemporaries. The son of an Irish gentleman, he was sent to Trinity College in hopes of securing a position in the Church, but after graduation he failed to do so; an uncle gave him some funds to enable him to study law but he immediately lost or spent these; he made shift with various odd jobs for a year or two and finally studied medicine, first in Edinburgh and then in Leyden.

For some years he played the flute and acted with a traveling theatrical company on the continent, visiting many cities and debating and speaking before a number of university audiences. On his return to London, where he became a member of Dr. Johnson's circle, he settled down as a professional writer, doing much hack work, editing, and so forth, but also writing a number of distinguished pieces of different kinds, including a collection of charming essays in *The Citizen of the World*, a delightful seminovel or novelette, *The Vicar of Wakefield*, one of the best known of sentimental comedies, *She Stoops to Conquer*, and the long poem, *The Deserted Village*.

In this poem, centering about the fate of the village of Lissoy, in which he had spent considerable time as a child, Goldsmith raises his most serious questions as to the changes which he saw taking place in England. It is not surprising that he should idealize the pleasantness of country life, whose real hardship he had never known. The description of peasant farming as "light labour" and the general gaiety and charm of village life as he pictures it, are sufficient evidence of the inaccuracy of his nostalgic memory. But it is much more surprising and important to note the clearness with which he understands what was happening to the whole rural population of England. The conversion from "corn" to sheep, by the end of the small freeholdings, the new inclosure acts, and, in Ireland and Scotland, the use of the land as a playground for men whose fortunes were made in trade, forced the peasant off the land. He was left to emigrate or to become a part of the uprooted vagabond population whose remnants settled in city slums and formed the first reservoir of cheap factory labor in the new industrial (late eighteenth, early nineteenth century) period. This all finds a place in *The Deserted Village*.

It is also surprising to find so clear a statement—and criticism—of the whole mercantile theory as Goldsmith packs into the couplet:

> Proud swells the tide with loads of freighted ore
> And shouting Folly hails them from her shore.

Evidently even a minor poet was not abashed at arguing the wealth of nations with a political economist in an earlier time than ours! However, to quote a few of the lines which most clearly show Goldsmith's perspicacity:

> Sweet smiling village, loveliest of the lawn,
> Thy sports are fled, and all thy charms withdrawn;
> Amidst thy bowers the tyrant's hand is seen,
> And desolation saddens all thy green:
> One only master grasps thy whole domain,
> And half a tillage stints thy smiling plain.

. . . .
Sunk are thy bowers in shapeless ruin all,
And the long grass o'ertops the mouldering wall;
And, trembling, shrinking from the spoiler's hand,
Far, far away, thy children leave the land.
Ill fares the land, to hastening ills a prey,
Where wealth accumulates, and men decay;
Princes and lords may flourish, or may fade;
A breath can make them, as a breath has made;
But a bold peasantry, their country's pride,
When once destroyed, can never be supplied.
A time there was, ere England's griefs began,
When every rood of ground maintained its man;
For him light labor spread her wholesome store,
Just gave what life required, but gave no more;
His best companions, innocence and health;
And his best riches, ignorance of wealth.
But times are altered; trade's unfeeling train
Usurp the land and dispossess the swain;
Along the lawn, where scattered hamlets rose,
Unwieldy wealth and cumbrous pomp repose,
And every want to opulence allied,
And every pang that folly pays to pride.
. . . .
Ye friends to truth, ye statesmen who survey
The rich man's joys increase, the poor's decay,
'Tis yours to judge how wide the limits stand
Between a splendid and a happy land.
Proud swells the tide with loads of freighted ore,
And shouting Folly hails them from her shore;
Hoards even beyond the miser's wish abound,
And rich men flock from all the world around.
Yet count our gains. This wealth is but a name
That leaves our useful products still the same.
Not so the loss. The man of wealth and pride
Takes up a place that many poor supplied;
Space for his lake, his park's extended bounds,
Space for his horses, equipage, and hounds;
The robe that wraps his limbs in silken sloth
Has robbed the neighboring fields of half their growth;
His seat, where solitary sports are seen,
Indignant spurns the cottage from the green;
Around the world each needful product flies,
For all the luxuries the world supplies;
While thus the land, adorned for pleasures, all
In barren splendor, feebly waits the fall.
. . . . . .
Thus fares the land by luxury betrayed,
In nature's simplest charms at first arrayed,
But verging to decline, its splendors rise,

> Its vistas strike, its palaces surprise;
> While, scourged by famine, from the smiling land
> The mournful peasant leads his humble band;
> And while he sinks, without one arm to save,
> The country blooms—a garden and a grave.
> . . . .
> Kingdoms, by luxury to sickly greatness grown,
> Boast of a florid vigor not their own.
> At every draft more large and large they grow,
> A bloated mass of rank unwieldy woe;
> Till, sapped their strength, and every part unsound,
> Down, down they sink, and spread a ruin round.

Neither Gray nor Goldsmith were truly great poets, and one of the reasons is apparent in the constant quarrel one senses between traditional form and new content. The heroic couplet, excellently contrived to sharpen the swift sting of Pope's satire, and to provide a more specious plausibility for his sententious epigrams, is not at all suited to the mounting tide of indignation or the flow of sympathy which Goldsmith and Gray wish to express. Gray, in fact, loosened the couplet, placing his rhymes at the end of every other line, and thus securing a little more continuity in the four line stanza; he also gave specific directions—since almost universally ignored—forbidding the printer to break his continuity by spaces between the stanzas. Goldsmith, too, in various ways, struggled against the form which, unsuited to his purpose, had become a strait-jacket instead of a support. But neither of them had the real power of poetic imagination which enabled a Walt Whitman to break through a form that had become irrelevant, and establish his own. This was achieved by two greater poets, Burns and Blake, who, although almost contemporary in time, were in spirit no longer transitional figures, but full-fledged pioneer romantics. They must, therefore, be dealt with in the next section. But first comes one more late eighteenth century figure—the last of the great early novelists, and the first of the great women novelists, Jane Austen, born in 1775.

JANE AUSTEN

After Fielding and Richardson had blazed the path two younger contemporaries, a rough Scottish surgeon, Tobias Smollett, and a most irreverent Yorkshire clergyman, Laurence Sterne, experimented further with what is often referred to as the novel of character and incident on the one hand, and the novel of sensibility on the other. These four who are often grouped as "the first English novelists" or "the great eighteenth century novelists" were all men of affairs and their work shows a breadth of worldly knowledge, a concrete practical observation of people of all classes, and an active energetic interest in the business of contemporary life, which are not again fully expressed by any bourgeois English writer but Dickens.

During the second half of the century, although an extraordinary number of novels were written—and an even more extraordinary number of copies were purchased or rented and read—neither the actual literary value of the form nor its place in critical estimation made any significant advance. The two major lines of development were those of the "Gothick Novel"— bloodchilling melange of ruined castles, haunted rooms, insane prisoners, secret murders, hidden wills and spectral figures, and the "novel of sensibility" with heroines who fainted on the slightest provocation, became frenzied or fell into a decline on very little more, and were dissolved in tears or suffused with blushes on no provocation whatsoever. By far the most important proponent of the former group was Mrs. Radcliffe, while Fanny Burney, Dr. Johnson's young protégée, was certainly the most readable of the latter.

Not only these two novelists but the greater part of their lesser colleagues and by far the major portion of their readers were women, an altogether new phenomenon in literary history.

We have already glanced at one of the most important causes for this huge new audience—the increased leisure and widespread but limited literacy of middle-class women.

Furthermore, the ambiguous position of the novel still prevented self-respecting men of letters from seriously turning to it, and left the field open to the competition of the most adventurous and talented of their sisters. These had few other outlets for their ability and, except through marriage, almost no other way of making or supplementing an income.

Actually the novel was not really accepted as literature until some time after the anonymous publication of *Waverly* in 1814. Its enormous success induced Sir Walter Scott, already well-known as a popular poet, to waive his anonymity and stamp subsequent novels with the hallmark of his undoubted gentility.

Writing as late as 1798 or 1799 Jane Austen found reason to exclaim, in *Northanger Abbey*:

> Yes, novels; for I will not adopt that ungenerous and impolitic custom, so common with novel writers, of degrading, by their contemptuous censure, the very performances to the number of which they are themselves adding: joining with their greatest enemies in bestowing the harshest epithets on such works, and scarcely ever permitting them to be read by their own heroine, who, if she accidentally take up a novel, is sure to turn over its insipid pages with disgust. Alas! If the heroine of one novel be not patronised by the heroine of another, from whom can she expect protection and regard? I cannot approve of it. Let us leave it to the Reviewers to abuse such effusions of fancy at their leisure, and over every new novel to talk in threadbare strains of the trash with which the press now groans. Let us not desert one another; we are an injured body. Although our productions have afforded more extensive and unaffected pleasure than those of any other literary corporation in the world, no species of composition has been so decried. From pride, ignorance, or fashion, our foes are almost as many as our readers; and while the abilities of the nine-hundredth abridger of the History of England, or of the man who collects and publishes in a volume some dozen lines of Milton, Pope and Prior, with a paper from the Spectator, and a chapter from Sterne, are eulogised by a thousand pens, there seems almost a general wish of decrying the capacity and undervaluing the labour of the novelist, and of slighting the performances which have only genius, wit and taste to recommend them. "I am no novel reader; I seldom look into novels; do not imagine that I often read novels; it is really very well for a novel." Such is the common cant. "And what are you reading, Miss ―――?" "Oh! it is only a novel!" replies the young lady; while she lays down her book with affected indifference or momentary shame. "It is only Cecilia, or Camilla, or Belinda"; or, in short, only some work in which the greatest powers of the mind are displayed, in which the most thorough knowledge of human nature, the happiest delineation of its varieties, the liveliest effusions of wit and humour, are conveyed to the world in the best chosen language.

Jane Austen's remarks indicate that it remained the fashion to scorn novels as suitable only for women and lesser tradesmen long after it had become the custom to read them in far better society. Nor, in truth, were there many novels after Fielding's worth critical attention until Jane Austen herself at the turn of the century picked up and adapted his realistic form to her creation of what are, today, almost universally considered the first modern English novels.

The departure of the other later eighteenth century novels from their realistic predecessors and the development of the ridiculous Gothic and even more intolerable lachrymose novel of fashion, have, I think, been correctly accounted for in Marvin Mudrick's stimulating recent study of Jane Austen, entitled *Irony as Defense and Discovery*. His analysis of these phenomena concludes:

> The middle-class woman of the late eighteenth century had good reason to accept and magnify these values [of sensibility and passionate love]. Living in a society dedicated to possession and dominance, with no opportunity for political or economic expression, with no influence, indeed, but such as she might gain by her maneuverability in courtship and marriage and by reading or writing novels in which this maneuverability was exploited, she could hardly fail to examine, claim, and apotheosize—even at the expense of all others—the only values which centered in courtship and marriage, and which could therefore make her feel possessive and dominant. It is significant that an impressive proportion of both lachrymose and Gothic novels—books which disregarded the man's world of property and its cardinal virtue, discretion, or treated them as no more than detestable clogs on sex and sensibility—were written by women; that, in fact, the English novel of the last quarter of the eighteenth century was almost monopolized by women, Fanny Burney and Mrs. Radcliffe being only the preeminent examples; and that Jane Austen was the only woman writer to oppose the tide of feminine sensibility in the novels of her time.

This does not, of course, mean that Jane Austen ignored the specifically feminine problems of her period or the values implicit in varying attempts at their solution. These were, in fact, her essential preoccupation and a great part of her extraordinary power comes from the intensely realistic scrutiny to which she subjected them. But her solutions were serious ones, no matter how ironically presented, and she had nothing but laughter for the escapist fantasies with which sentimental contemporaries solaced their more sentimental readers. In his *Introduction to the English Novel*, Dr. Kettle begins a detailed analysis of perhaps her most mature completed work, *Emma*, by saying:

> . . . a good deal of the moral passion of the book, as of her other novels, does undoubtedly arise from Jane Austen's understanding of and feeling about the problems of women in her society. It is this realistic, unromantic and indeed, by ortho-

dox standards, subversive concern with the position of women that give tang and force to her consideration of marriage.

Before we consider more fully the peculiarly happy satire and the small but perfectly truthful world to which she voluntarily confined her novels, let us look briefly at the very similar world in which she was, perhaps less voluntarily, herself confined all her life. Her world always consisted so largely of the family and its connections that we must enumerate its most important members with some particularity.

Jane Austen was born in 1775 in Hampshire, the sixth of eight children in a pleasant country parsonage. Her family was, like the class to which it belonged, still on the way up. Although her father's father had been a surgeon and so barely a gentleman, and his mother—widowed early—had actually had to take carefully selected lodgers in order to manage an education for her five sons, she *had* managed, and George Austen had won sufficient distinction as a scholar to obtain favorable notice and two fairly good church livings.

His wife, daughter of a clergyman, came of a rather better family with some very wealthy relatives. One of these, a Mr. Knight, was childless and adopted the third son, Edward,—the oldest, James, was of course destined to succeed Jane's father and the second, George, "had fits" and was perhaps feeble-minded from infancy. At any rate he never lived at home and is never mentioned by any of the brothers or sisters.

Edward Knight, as the third son was renamed, inherited a very considerable landed estate and a great deal of Jane's time and that of her older sister, Cassandra, was spent in pleasant visits to him and his family.

Since both the sisters rarely left home together, and since they were always extraordinarily close to each other, the innumerable letters they exchanged furnish a running commentary on Jane's daily life and often enable us to compare the raw material with the highly finished product of the novels. There are, however, exasperating gaps in this correspondence since Cassandra, who long outlived Jane, finally destroyed not only all her own letters, but also all those of Jane's which seemed to her indiscreet, unduly revealing or too emphatically emotional.

Jane's two youngest brothers, Francis and Charles, both entered the navy as midshipmen and rose rapidly through the dangerous opportunities offered by the period of the Napoleonic wars, both finally dying admirals long after Jane's own death.

Her favorite brother, Henry, just a few years older than Jane, had first secured a Colonel's commission in the militia, but resigned this on marrying his cousin Eliza, the Comtesse de Feuillade, widowed by her husband's execution as a royalist emigré in post-revolutionary France. Upon his marriage, Henry entered a London banking house. This venture proved successful and highly remunerative for some time but finally failed in the postwar depression of 1816. With seemingly unclouded spirits Henry, then recently widowed, prepared for ordination, secured a church living, and finished a long life as a highly popular clergyman. He is of particular interest to us because he arranged for the publication of all his sister's six completed novels, and wrote the first brief biographical notice of her after her death.

The family was obviously an extremely energetic, intelligent and good-humored one, and Jane's and Cassandra's enviable position in a household of five brothers was further enhanced by Rev. Austen's custom of tutoring two or three carefully selected young men, sons of friends, who often lived with the family as resident pupils.

The impression of lively good spirits at home which we get from all Jane's early letters is supplemented by her detailed accounts of country balls in which she "danced twenty out of twenty sets" although not fewer than seven less fortunate young ladies were obliged, by the scarcity of gentlemen, to remain partnerless!

Her sophisticated cousin, Eliza Feuillade, wrote on one of her visits to England in 1791: "The two sisters are perfect beauties. They are two of the prettiest girls in England." And after another visit the following year: "Cassandra and Jane are both very much grown and greatly improved in manners as in person. They are, I think, equally sensible and both so to a degree seldom met with, but my heart still gives the preference to Jane."

The Austen brothers were keen hunters, and the whole family enjoyed charades, reading aloud, and the sort of informal youthful hospitality for which such a home easily becomes the center. A number of their rhymed charades have been preserved and enough of Jane's juvenilia—she began writing at twelve or fourteen—exist, formally copied out and ceremoniously dedicated to Henry, Eliza, her father, Cassandra, and other members of the circle, to verify our impression of an unusually happy, spirited and congenial group.

They were evidently much pleased with each other, proud of the abilities of sisters as well as brothers, fond of reading, and confident in their anticipation of future successes of various sorts for all members of the group. There was no luxury, but no feeling of anxiety clouded their easy enjoyment of good health, moderate comfort, and active preparation for the church, the navy, estate managership and marriage.

A cousin of Mrs. Austen's, visiting her for the first time after her marriage wrote of her stay with "the wife of the truly respectable Mr. Austen," saying: "With his sons (all promising to make figures in life) Mr. Austen educates a few youths of chosen friends and acquaintances. When among this Liberal Society, the simplicity, hospitality, and taste which commonly prevail in different families among the delightful valleys of Switzerland ever occurs to my memory."

Cassandra, who had just become engaged to a young clergyman, a former student of her father's, was away on a visit during much of 1796 and Jane wrote her:

> You scold me so much in the nice long letter which I have this moment received from you, that I am almost ashamed to tell you how my Irish friend and I behaved. Imagine to yourself everything most profligate and shocking in the way of dancing and sitting down together. I *can* expose myself, however, *only once* more, because he leaves the country soon after next Friday, on which day *we are* to have a dance at Ashe, after all.

The next year Mrs. Austen welcomed James' second wife—his first wife had died some time before in childbirth, and Jane and Cassandra had been caring for his baby daughter. She wrote her new daughter-in-law: "I look forward to you as a real comfort to me in my old age when Cassandra is gone into Shropshire and Jane the Lord knows where."

However, Jane's Irish friend left to be admitted to the Irish bar, and eight years later married an Irish lady. Many years afterwards, when he had become a Chief Justice and Jane was long dead—and famous—he confided to a nephew that as a boy he had been in love with the younger Miss Austen but there is no strong indication that he was, at most, ever more than one of several possible suitors.

A more serious loss was Cassandra's. Her fiancé died of yellow fever in the West Indies, where he had served as military chaplain while waiting for an appointment to a church living at home.

Yet during this trying period and later, despite all personal vicissitudes, both Jane's letters and her novels breathe undiminished the spirit of stability and security that "characterized the post-revolutionary period of the great English eighteenth century novelists."

For although Jane Austen comes at the very end of that period her general circumstances, family situation, and the somewhat circumscribed practical experiences of a lifelong residence in one of the most prosperous and stable country districts of England, enable her to absorb and recreate its atmosphere with no premonition of an imminent end. Dr. Kettle emphasizes the peculiar advantages this gave her art, while explaining why it was impossible for later English novelists to achieve the same seemingly effortless balance.

> This atmosphere of stability and security Jane Austen emphatically shares. The impulse of realism which permeates her novels is an extension, a refinement of that impulse of controlled and objective curiosity which we have noticed as a by-product of the bourgeois revolution and the underlying characteristic of the eighteenth century novel.
>
> But by the time of Jane Austen the eighteenth century world . . . is almost gone. The industrial revolution is under way and a new and immensely powerful class—that of the industrial capitalists—is in the ascendancy. And the world of the nineteenth century is a world infinitely less amicable to art of any kind than the eighteenth century world.
>
> . . . the [nineteenth century] industrial bourgeoisie as a class . . . hated and feared the implications of any artistic effort of realism and integrity. And throughout the century from the days of Shelley's Castlereagh through those of Dickens' Gradgrind . . . honest writers were bound to feel a deep revulsion against the underlying principles and the warped relationships of the society they lived in.
>
> It is for this reason that, after Jane Austen, the great novels of the nineteenth century are all, in their differing ways, novels of revolt. The task of the novelist was the same as it had always been—to achieve realism, . . . to express the truth about life as it faced them. But to do this, to cut through the whole complex structure of inhumanity and false feeling that ate into the consciousness of the capitalist world, it was necessary to become a rebel. . . .

Jane Austen, needless to say, never became a rebel. And in her satire we find a curious combination of the sharpest and most searching social criticism with a fundamental assurance of social well-being and the likelihood of a reasonable personal happiness. The only analogous satire which comes to mind is found in the early postrevolutionary work of such Russian writers as Ilya Ilf, Eugene Petrov, Valentin Kataeyv, and other minor contemporaries.

This is generally broader and more farcical than anything of Jane Austen's, although the Thorpes and General Tilney in *Northanger Abbey* and Mr. Collins and Lady de Bourgh in *Pride and Prejudice* are almost as explicit. But the fundamental resemblance is that of underlying tone, not that of style. The unsparing exposure of serious social shortcomings, saved from bitterness by a fundamental conviction of the health of the social system, and of its consequent ability to reform itself, are both characteristic of Jane Austen, as they are of those Russian satirists who wrote immediately after the stabilization of the Soviet Union.

When Jane Austen at twenty-one completed her first serious novel—*First Impressions* (later rewritten as *Pride and Prejudice*)—her father evidently esteemed it enough to write a London publisher about the possibilities of its appearance. But he received no answer, and there were no further attempts at negotiation for some time.

That same year, however, she began *Sense and Sensibility* (then named *Elinor and Marianne*) and when that was completed wrote *Northanger Abbey* which she finished in 1799.

We still find some very gay letters to Cassandra, although in many of them it is evident that the gaiety is more a matter of attitude than circumstance. For example, after an entertaining account of a small ball in 1799 she adds: "I do not think it worth while to wait for enjoyment until there is some real opportunity for it." And after a dinner, she writes: "I believe Mary found it dull, but I thought it very pleasant. To sit in idleness over a good fire in a well proportioned room is a luxurious sensation. I said two or three amusing things and Mr. Holder made a few infamous puns."

There is a deliberate—almost a determined—amusement about fashions, as when she reports the result of a buying commission to Cassandra from Bath: "besides, I cannot help thinking that it is more natural to have flowers grow out of the head than fruit. What do you think on that subject?"

There are also pointed observations which might, unchanged, have found their place in the novels. At the conclusion of a dramatic account of a storm, which destroyed some fine elm trees but did no further damage we read: "We grieve therefore in some comfort."

A few years later she more sharply hits at the conventional "mourning in comfort" of her neighbors when she reports the news of a naval engagement in 1811: "How horrible it is to have so many people killed!—And what a blessing that one cares for none of them!"

And a thumbnail sketch is given of "a very young man, just entered of Oxford, wears spectacles and has heard that [Fanny Burney's] Evelina was written by Dr. Johnson."

The unliklihood of publication does not seem to have at all affected Jane's interest in writing, or the high spirits and rapidity with which she wrote. But in 1800 her father's decision to retire (he was already over seventy) and move to Bath with his wife and two daughters, leaving the vicarage and church duties to his oldest son, James, was evidently a great and unwelcome shock to Jane. She was then already twenty-five, and for her this removal evidently put a definite period to youth and its promise of some more significant future. As long as circumstances were relatively unchanged in the home in which she had been born it was still possible to feel that the peaceful, busy, domestic routine was just a pleasant preparation for life. Now, suddenly, a much more circumscribed, less happy domesticity was all too likely to be life itself. When the decision was announced to her, on her return from a visit, she fainted for the first and only time of her life and Cassandra later destroyed all the letters she wrote her during the next month.

Jane had mastered herself enough to announce gaily before their departure: "We plan having a steady cook and a young giddy housemaid, with a sedate middle-aged man, who is to undertake the double office of husband to the former and sweetheart to the latter. No children, of course, to be allowed on either side."

But she was never happy at Bath or, later, Southampton, and despite the sale of *Northanger Abbey* to a publisher in 1803, wrote nothing but the first few chapters of an unfinished novel—*The Watsons*—during the next nine years.

Before we look at that period and at this significantly uncompleted novel, as well as at *Lady Susan*, a rather shocking novelette which had probably been written much earlier, but of which Jane

Austen made a final fair copy in 1805, let us turn to consider the work she had completed before the removal which marked the end of her youth.

The juvenilia to which we have earlier referred was all completed by the time Jane Austen was seventeen, and included a long story told in letters—*Love and Freindship*—which tumultuously parodies the extremes of sensibility fashionable in novels at the time.

The heroine, at fifty, writing the story of her life for the benefit of a friend's daughter, begins in simple burlesque: ". . . I was once beautiful. But lovely as I was the Graces of my Person were the least of my Perfections. Of every accomplishment accustomary to my sex, I was Mistress. When in the Convent, my progress had always exceeded my instructions, my acquirements had been wonderfull for my age, and I had shortly surpassed my Masters."

But even that first letter concludes with more penetrating insight into the relations of sentimentality and egotism: "A sensibility too tremblingly alive to every affliction of my Friends, my Acquaintance and particularly to every affliction of my own, was my only fault, if a fault it could be called. Alas! how altered now! Tho' indeed my own Misfortunes do not make less impression on me than they ever did, yet now I never feel for these of another."

After a doubled and foreshortened but hardly exaggerated version of the then conventional story of love at first sight, elopement and disinheritance, the two young husbands are arrested for debt and the wives: "Ah! what could we do but what we did! We sighed and fainted on the sofa." They refuse to visit the prison for, as one of them explains: "I shall not be able to support the sight of my Augustus in so cruel a confinement—my feelings are sufficiently shocked by the *recital* of his Distress, but to behold it will overpower my Sensibility."

The tenderheartedness that protects itself from any knowledge of suffering was evidently Jane Austen's particular abomination and she returns to the attack later with: "Ah! my beloved Laura (cried Sophia) for pity's sake forbear recalling to my remembrance the unhappy situation of my imprisoned Husband. Alas, what would I not give to learn the fate of my Augustus! to know if he is still in Newgate, or if he is yet hung. But never shall I be able so far to Conquer my tender sensibility as to enquire after him."

Finally they are reunited with their husbands only to see them both perish in a carriage accident. "Sophia immediately sunk again into a swoon—My grief was more audible. . . . For two Hours did I rave thus madly. . . . The morning after . . . Sophia complained of a violent pain in her delicate limbs . . . how could I . . . have escaped the same indisposition but by supposing that the bodily Exertions I had undergone in my repeated fits of frenzy had so effectually circulated and warmed my Blood as to make me proof against the chilling Damps of Night, whereas, Sophia lying totally inactive on the ground must have been exposed to all their severity."

Then, marking the need of common sense even in this fantastic world of sensibility Sophia expires with a solemn moral: "Beware of fainting fits. . . . Though at the time they may be refreshing and agreeable yet believe me they will in the end, if too often repeated, and at improper seasons, prove destructive to your Constitution. . . . Run mad as often as you chuse; but do not faint."

There are other stories parodying such "language of the heart" like *Evelyn* whose heroine: ". . . was the darling of her relations— From the clearness of her skin and the Brilliancy of her Eyes, she was fully entitled to all their partial affection. Another circumstance contributed to the general Love they bore her, and that was one of the finest heads of hair in the world."

But there are also some still more interesting fragments which directly satirize the crudely materialistic values of social snobbery rather than its seeming contradiction in sentimental fantasy. For example, in a collection of fictional letters, *From a Young Lady in distressed Circumstances to her friend* the heroine reports her conversation with a patroness en route to a ball:

"Have you got a new Gown on?"
"Yes Ma'am" replied I with as much indifference as I could assume.
"Why could not you have worn your old striped one? It is not my way to find fault with people because they are poor, for I always think that they are more to be despised and pitied than blamed for it, especially if they cannot help it, but at the same time I must say that in my opinion your old striped Gown would have been quite fine enough for its Wearer—for to tell you the truth (I always speak my mind) I am very much afraid that one half the people in the room will not know whether you have a Gown on or not—But I suppose you intend to make your fortune tonight—Well, the sooner the better; and I wish you success."
"Indeed Ma'am I have no such intention—"

> "Who ever heard a young Lady own that she was a Fortune-hunter?"
>
> ". . . I dare not be impertinent, as my Mother is always admonishing me to be humble and patient if I wish to make my way in the world. She insists on my accepting every invitation of Lady Greville, or you may be certain that I would never enter either her House or her Coach with the disagreeable certainty I always have of being abused for my poverty while I am in them."

It is not surprising that Jane Austen's most recent English biographer, the pleasant but somewhat sentimental popular novelist, Margaret Kennedy, should feel constrained to admit, apologetically, that:

> At some period in her life, probably very early, she seems to have formed a strong prejudice against rich people and great land owners. Some startling encounter with boorish complacency or stupid arrogance created a bias from which she never quite freed herself. Time qualified it. In the course of her life she met with people in this class whom she could love, admire and respect, who were her equals in refinement and who possessed, perhaps, a little more of the world's polish. But the early bias remained and is responsible for the pride of Pemberly, the arrogance of Rosings, the cupidity of Norland, the rustic conviviality of Barton, the instability of Mansfield, the tasteless splendour of Sotherton, the snobbery of Kellynch. It is reflected in the avarice of General Tilney; the selfishness of Lord Osborne, and the insipidity of "our cousins Lady Dalrymple and Miss Carteret.

Miss Kennedy would evidently like to think that Jane Austen's satire was imparatially aimed at all classes but her honesty and detailed knowledge of the novels forces her to conclude that:

> . . . vulgarity of the smaller fry is generally used to set off the false standards, the lack of discrimination shown by their betters. Lucy Steele completely imposes upon Barton and on the Ferrar family. General Tilney knows no better than to gossip with John Thorpe. The designing Mrs. Clay very nearly marries Sir Walter Elliot. Snobbery is shown to impair the judgement; and arrogance has no defence against a toady.

In her last novel, *Sandition,* left unfinished at her death, Jane Austen herself, or, rather, her heroine, said:

But she is very, very mean.—I can see no Good in her. . . .
And she makes everybody mean about her.—This poor Sir Edward and his Sister,—how far Nature meant them to be respectable I cannot tell,—but they are obliged to be Mean in their Servility to her.—And I am Mean too, in giving her my attention, with the appearance of coinciding with her.—Thus it is, when Rich People are Sordid.

Perhaps the most surprising note struck in these very early experiments is that represented by the indignant comment in *Catharine* when the heroine says of a young friend who has been sent to India to make a "good match" there:

. . . do you call it lucky, for a Girl of Genius and Feeling, to be sent in quest of a Husband to Bengal, to be married there to a Man of whose Disposition she has no opportunity of judging till her Judgement is of no use to her, who may be a Tyrant, or a Fool or both for what she knows to the Contrary. . . .

Although the only copy extant of *Lady Susan*, a more ambitious novelette in the form of a series of letters, was made in 1805, that too was probably completed at the end of this early period of inspired preliminary exercises. It is a surprisingly sophisticated and uncompromising self-portrait by a young widow, *Lady Susan*. Her complete lack of maternal feeling, her ambitious worldliness, carefully disciplined self-indulgence, frank physical enjoyment of illicit love, and pride in her power to manipulate both men and women, would all make one think that Vanity Fair's immortal Becky Sharp was deeply indebted to her, were it not for the fact that *Lady Susan* saw the light of print only after Thackeray's death.

The first of Jane Austen's finished novels to be completed in its present form was *Northanger Abbey* which, written in 1798, was, with some slight revisions, sold to a publisher in 1803 for £10. More careful consideration made him hesitate to print so devastating a mockery of the "Gothick novels" which furnished most of the bestsellers on his own book list, as well as on those of his rivals. Since he had no knowledge of the author's identity, her brother Henry was able in 1816 to purchase the manuscript back for the same £10, although in the meantime both *Sense and Sensibility* and *Pride and Prejudice* had made their successful appearance. *Northanger Abbey* was, therefore, not published until after Jane Austen's early death in 1817, but its place in the development of her work is here at the beginning.

In addition to its much more subtle and consistent parody of other popular literary forms, the beginning of which we have already noted in her juvenilia, *Northanger Abbey* touches, lightly it is true, on the essential theme of all Jane Austen's novels.

An interesting article by the liberal English economist, Leonard Woolf, "The Economic Determination of Jane Austen," says:

> ... It is remarkable to what extent the plots and characters are determined by questions of money. The whole opening of Sense and Sensibility turns upon the finance of the Dashwood will and the avarice of Mrs. John Dashwood whose income is £10,000. The finances of the Bennett family and the entail in Pride and Prejudice have an equal importance. The axis of the plot in every novel except Emma is money and marriage or rank and marriage.

But for the most part *Northanger Abbey* deals with the qualities and attitudes required of a marriageable miss rather than with the direct problem of marriage. Its heroine, Jane Austen's youngest, falling easily in love at seventeen with the first personable and intelligent young man she meets, and happily married within the year, has no real problems.

It is very rarely that Jane Austen speaks out in her own person, but in this early book she permits herself the liberty several times. We have already noted her comment on novels and novelists, and there are others which generalize about the qualities of a heroine and the relations of the sexes. For example:

> She was heartily ashamed of her ignorance—a misplaced shame. Where people wish to attach, they should always be ignorant. To come with a well-informed mind is to come with an inability of ministering to the vanity of others, which a sensible person would always wish to avoid. A woman, especially, if she have the misfortune of knowing anything, should conceal it as well as she can.
>
> The advantages of natural folly in a beautiful girl have already been set forth by the capital pen of a sister author; and to her treatment of the subject I will only add, in justice to men, that though, to the larger and more trifling part of the sex, imbecility in females is a great enhancement of their personal charms, there is a portion of them too reasonable, and too well-informed themselves, to desire anything more in

woman than ignorance. But Catherine did not know her own advantages—did not know that a good-looking girl with an affectionate heart and a very ignorant mind cannot help attracting a clever young man, unless circumstances are particularly untoward.

A more characteristic comment, with its arch side glance at Richardson's solemn moral pronouncements, describes the unromantic opening of the acquaintance:

> They danced again; and when the assembly closed, parted, on the lady's side at least, with a strong inclination for continuing the acquaintance. Whether she thought of him so much, while she drank her warm wine and water, and prepared herself for bed, as to dream of him when there, cannot be ascertained; for if it be true, as a celebrated writer has maintained, that no young lady can be justified in falling in love before the gentleman's love is declared; it must be very improper that a young lady should dream of a gentleman before the gentleman is first known to have dreamt of her.

The unconventionally realistic though happy conclusion is even less compatible with romantic standards.

After Henry had declared his affection:

> . . . that heart in return was solicited, which, perhaps, they pretty equally knew was already entirely his own; for, though Henry was now sincerely attached to her,—though he felt and delighted in all the excellencies of her character, and truly loved her society,—I must confess that his affection originated in nothing better than gratitude; or, in other words, that a persuasion of her partiality for him had been the only cause of giving her a serious thought. It is a new circumstance in romance, I acknowledge, and dreadfully derogatory of a heroine's dignity; but if it be as new in common life, the credit of a wild imagination will at least be all my own.

Before writing *Northanger Abbey* Jane had completed the first version of *Sense and Sensibility*, but this was very considerably rewritten when it became her earliest published work in 1811.

Here there is no element of burlesque, but only a realistic satire; and while the heroine's attitude is obviously influenced by the current novels of sensibility, the criticism is directed at a way of living rather than at a way of writing.

There is much outspoken contempt for the mercenary values of good society, and the entire work is colored by an informed indignation at the easy assumption of masculine superiority.

Good-natured Sir John, for example, expresses his delight in telling his attractive but relatively impoverished young cousins of a valuable new acquaintance by saying: "Yes, yes, he is very well worth catching, I can tell you, Miss Dashwood; he has a pretty little estate of his own in Somersetshire."

His widowed cousin, Mrs. Dashwood, Jane Austen's most engaging mother, says with gentle dignity: "I do not believe that Mr. Willoughby will be incommoded by the attempts of either of *my* daughters towards what you call *catching him*. It is not an employment to which they have been brought up."

Sir John persists, however: "Aye, aye, I see how it will be, I see how it will be. You will be setting your cap at him now, and never think of poor Brandon."

And when Marianne sharply retorts: "I abhor every commonplace phrase by which wit is intended; and 'setting one's cap at a man,' or 'making a conquest,' are the most odious of all. Their tendency is gross and illiberal; and if their construction could ever be deemed clever, time has long destroyed all its ingenuity." Sir John "did not much understand this reproof; but he laughed as heartily as if he did, . . ."

Of course, some of the most unpleasant of the characters in the book are women, and their acquiescence in the mores of male supremacy is not among the least unpleasant of their characteristics. For example, after addressing her husband several times with no response, Charlotte Palmer turns to Mrs. Dashwood:

"Mr. Palmer does not hear me," said she, laughing, "he never does sometimes. It is so ridiculous!"

This was quite a new idea to Mrs. Dashwood, she had never been used to find wit in the inattention of any one, and could not help looking with surprise at them both.

Neither Mrs. Palmer nor her mother are among the really unpleasant people, but the same point is illustrated in a number of their scenes. For example, when Mr. Palmer publicly replies to a comment of his wife's:

"I did not know I contradicted any body in calling your mother ill-bred."

"Aye, you may abuse me as you please," said the good-natured old lady, "You have taken Charlotte off my hands, and cannot give her back again. So there I have the whip hand of you."

Charlotte laughed heartily to think that her husband could not get rid of her, and exultingly said, she did not care how cross he was to her, as they must live together. It was impossible for anyone to be more thoroughly good-natured or more determined to be happy than Mrs. Palmer. The studied indifference, insolence, and discontent of her husband gave her no pain; and when he scolded or abused her, she was highly diverted.

But the masterpiece of these three early novels, and, for many people, their favorite Jane Austen novel is *Pride and Prejudice*. This was the earliest of the three to be completed, under the title of *First Impressions*, in 1797, but it was the most completely rewritten from its early letter form into its present one just before publication in 1813.

It was, for some time at least, Jane Austen's own favorite and she wrote her sister when it appeared: "I must confess that I think her [the heroine, Elizabeth] as delightful a creature as ever appeared in print; and how I shall be able to tolerate those who do not like *her* at least I do not know."

Whether Jane Austen realized Elizabeth's resemblance to her creator we do not know, but it is certainly a striking and satisfactory self-portrait.

Dr. Mudrick develops an excellent analysis of Elizabeth's character saying: "Her point of reference is always the complex individual, the individual aware and capable of choice. Her own pride is in her freedom to observe, to analyze, to choose; her continual mistake is to forget that, even for her, there is only one area of choice—marriage—and that this choice is subject to all the powerful and numbing pressures of an acquisitive society." He adds: "Irony here rejects chiefly to discover and illuminate; and though its setting is the same stratified, materialistic, and severely regulated society, its new text and discovery . . . is the free individual."

One of Elizabeth's most delightful scenes is her rejection of Mr. Collins' proposal despite his reminder that, in view of her small fortune: "it is by no means certain that another offer of marriage will ever be made." This scene comes to a climax with a statement of one of Jane Austen's own favorite themes: "Do not consider me now as an elegant female . . . but as a rational creature." It reads, in revealing part:

"You are too hasty, sir," she cried. "You forget that I have made no answer. Let me do it without further loss of time. Accept my thanks for the compliment you are paying me. I am very sensible of the honour of your proposals, but it is impossible for me to do otherwise than decline them."

"I am not now to learn," replied Mr. Collins, with a formal wave of the hand, "that it is usual with young ladies to reject the addresses of the man whom they secretly mean to accept, when he first applies for their favour; and that sometimes the refusal is repeated a second or even a third time. I am therefore by no means discouraged by what you have just said, and shall hope to lead you to the altar ere long."

"Upon my word, sir," cried Elizabeth, "your hope is rather an extraordinary one after my declaration. I do assure you that I am not one of those young ladies (if such young ladies there are) who are so daring as to risk their happiness on the chance of being asked a second time. I am perfectly serious in my refusal. You could not make *me* happy, and I am convinced that I am the last woman in the world who would make you so. Nay, were your friend Lady Catherine to know me, I am persuaded she would find me in every respect ill qualified for the situation."

"Were it certain that Lady Catherine would think so," said Mr. Collins very gravely—"but I cannot imagine that her ladyship would at all disapprove of you. And you may be certain that when I have the honour of seeing her again, I shall speak in the highest terms of your modesty, economy, and other amiable qualifications."

"Indeed, Mr. Collins, all praise of me will be unnecessary. You must give me leave to judge for myself, and pay me the compliment of believing what I say. I wish you very happy and very rich, and by refusing your hand, do all in my power to prevent your being otherwise. In making me the offer, you must have satisfied the delicacy of your feelings with regard to my family, and may take possession of Longbourn estate whenever it falls, without any self-reproach. This matter may be considered, therefore, as finally settled." And rising as she thus spoke, she would have quitted the room, had not Mr. Collins thus addressed her:

"When I do myself the honour of speaking to you next on the subject, I shall hope to receive a more favourable answer than you have now given me; though I am far from accusing you of cruelty at present, because I know it to be the established custom of your sex to reject a man on the first application, and perhaps you have even now said as much to encourage my suit as would be consistent with the true delicacy of the female character."

"Really, Mr. Collins," cried Elizabeth with some warmth, "you puzzle me exceedingly. If what I have hitherto said can appear to you in the form of encouragement, I know not how to express my refusal in such a way as may convince you of its being one."

"You must give me leave to flatter myself, my dear cousin, that your refusal of my addresses is merely words of course. My reasons for believing it are briefly these: It does not appear to me that my hand is unworthy your acceptance, or that the establishment I can offer would be any other than highly desirable. My situation in life, my connections with the family of de Bourgh, and my relationship to your own, are circumstances highly in my favour; and you should take it into further consideration, that in spite of your manifold attractions, it is by no means certain that another offer of marriage may ever be made you. Your portion is unhappily so small that it will in all likelihood undo the effects of your loveliness and amiable qualifications. As I must therefore conclude that you are not serious in your rejection of me, I shall choose to attribute it to your wish of increasing my love by suspense, according to the usual practice of elegant females."

"I do assure you, sir, that I have no pretensions whatever to that kind of elegance which consists in tormenting a respectable man. I would rather be paid the compliment of being believed sincere. I thank you again and again for the honour you have done me in your proposals, but to accept them is absolutely impossible. My feelings in every respect forbid it. Can I speak plainer? Do not consider me now as an elegant female, intending to plague you, but as a rational creature, speaking the truth from her heart."

"You are uniformly charming!" cried he, with an air of awkward gallantry; "and I am persuaded that when sanctioned by the express authority of both your excellent parents, my proposals will not fail of being acceptable."

To such perseverance in wilful self-deception Elizabeth would make no reply, and immediately and in silence withdrew; determined, that if he persisted in considering her repeated refusals as flattering encouragement, to apply to her father, whose negative might be uttered in such a manner as must be decisive, and whose behaviour at least could not be mistaken for the affectation and coquetry of an elegant female."

But Elizabeth, who never hesitates in her determination to prefer even single blessedness to Mr. Collins, is inexpressibly shocked when her best friend, Charlotte, accepts his hand as soon as it is offered to her.

Dr. Mudrick explains: "It is not that Elizabeth misjudges Charlotte's capabilities, but that she underestimates the strength of the pressures acting upon her. . . . She recognizes Mr. Collins' total foolishness and Charlotte's intelligence, and would never have dreamed that any pressure could overcome so natural an opposition. Complex and simple, aware and unaware, do not belong together—except that in marriages made by economics they often unite, however obvious the mismatching."

But although the twenty-year old Elizabeth Bennet cannot understand this, Jane Austen does. She sadly tells us that after accepting the proposal, Charlotte's:

> . . . reflections were in general satisfactory. Mr. Collins, to be sure, was neither sensible nor agreeable; his society was irksome, and his attachment to her must be imaginary. But still he would be her husband. Without thinking highly either of men or of matrimony, marriage had always been her object; it was the only honourable provision for well-educated young women of small fortune, and however uncertain of giving happiness, must be their pleasantest preservative from want. This preservative she had now obtained; and at the age of twenty-seven, without having ever been handsome, she felt all the good luck of it.

This understanding does not mean that Jane Austen herself was prepared to accept safety on such terms. As we shall see from subsequent biographical events, from her letters, and from her later novels, she explicitly refused to settle for anything less than real respect and affection—that is, a real personal relationship, in marriage. But she did not do so under any illusions as to the unpleasant alternative possibilities.

An interesting English article by D. W. Harding, "Regulated Hatred: An Aspect of the Work of Jane Austen," may perhaps overstate the case, but it provides a valuable insight into the importance of Mr. Collins in *Pride and Prejudice*:

> Consequently the proposal scene is not only comic fantasy, but it is also, for Elizabeth, a taste of the fantastic nightmare in which economic and social institutions have such power over the values of personal relationships that the comic monster is nearly able to get her. . . . Elizabeth can never quite become reconciled to the idea that her friend is the wife of her comic monster. And that, of course, is precisely the sort of idea that Jane Austen herself could never grow reconciled to. The people she hated were tolerated, accepted, comfortably ensconced in the only human society she knew; . . .
> It is important to notice that Elizabeth makes no break

with her friend on account of her marriage. This was the sort
of friend—"a friend disgracing herself and sunk in her esteem"
—that went to make up the available social world which one
could neither escape materially nor be independent of psychologically.

Mr. Harding indicates, though without analysis, the one-sided
and therefore somewhat misleading nature of his own comments,
on Jane Austen's attitude to her society, and provocatively concludes: "I have tried to underline one or two features of her work
that claim the sort of readers who sometimes miss her—those who
would turn to her not for relief and escape but as a formidable ally
against things and people which were to her, and still are, hateful."

There is a probable but unsubstantiated family story of Jane's
meeting with an exceptionally intelligent and attractive young man
during a summer trip with Cassandra in 1801. According to Cassandra's account as repeated by a niece, he asked her father's permission to call the following winter but the family were soon
shocked to hear of his sudden death.

This may or may not be a true story. Much more important to
our understanding of Jane Austen's character and sense of values
is an authenticated account of an incident in December, 1802.

Jane and Cassandra had been visiting two friends, sisters, at a
large estate near their old home when their friends' younger
brother, the heir of Manydown, proposed to Jane and was accepted.
After a sleepless night Jane faced him in the morning to declare
that she had changed her mind—a broken engagement then had
at least as much opprobrium attached to it as a divorce does in
most circles today—and she and Cassandra, almost hysterical for
the only time in their brother James' knowledge of them, arrived
before breakfast Friday morning at his rectory, insisting that he
immediately arrange for their transportation home to Bath. Since
he felt bound to escort them himself he urged that they wait until
he had preached that Sunday, but they felt it impossible to remain
an unnecessary hour in the vicinity and he was obliged to arrange
for a substitute and leave immediately.

Jane's attempt at twenty-seven to emulate Charlotte's practical
prudence—not, indeed with as contemptible a figure as Mr. Collins
but with a somewhat younger man in whom she evidently found
nothing particular to enjoy or admire—is apparent in this incident,
as is her essential inability to accept life on such terms.

This experience, or, rather, the long consideration of bleak alternatives which had shaped it, is apparent in the novel she attempted to write during 1803-4, and left barely begun. There is a note of bitterness and almost of desperation in *The Watsons* which no doubt betrayed far more of her social consciousness than she wished known, and forced her to discontinue it after what seems to be a most promising and absorbing beginning.

A dialogue between two sisters, one, an almost resigned spinster of twenty-nine and the other a very beautiful young girl of nineteen, opens the book. The latter, like Fanny Price in Jane Austen's next novel, *Mansfield Park*, has been brought up by wealthy relatives by whom she was to have been adopted, but has been forced to return to her father's poor and barely genteel home.

Miss Watson begins:

> . . . You know, we must marry. I could do very well single for my own part; a little company, and a pleasant ball now and then, would be enough for me, if one could be young forever; but my father cannot provide for us, and it is very bad to grow old and be poor and laughed at. I have lost Purvis, it is true; but very few people marry their first loves. I should not refuse a man because he was not Purvis. . . .

Emma replies, and in reading her reference to a "school" we must remember the realistic boarding schools of Charlotte Bronte's *Jane Eyre*, with their teachers' salaries ranging *up* to £20 a year. She rather cavalierly says:

> "Poverty is a great evil; but to a woman of education and feeling it ought not, it cannot be the greatest. I would rather be a teacher at a school (and I can think of nothing worse), than marry a man I did not like."
> "I would rather do anything than be teacher at a school," said her sister. "I have been at school, Emma, and know what a life they lead; *you* never have. I should not like marrying a disagreeable man any more than yourself; but I do not think there *are* many very disagreeable men; I think I could like any good humoured man with a comfortable income. I suppose my aunt brought you up to be rather refined."

When in January 1805 Reverend Austen died, the major part of his income passed to James, and Mrs. Austen had only £150 a year on which to support herself and her two daughters.

Her five sons agreed among themselves to contribute another £300 a year during her lifetime and were, no doubt, prepared to offer their sisters a home after her death. But the parallel, in circumstances of dependence at least, to the Miss Watsons, was clearly a painful one.

An unmarried friend of Cassandra's, Martha Lloyd, who had been caring for an invalid mother, was at this time left alone by her mother's death, and Mrs. Austen and her daughters invited her to join them. The pooled incomes made living arrangements easier, and her presence made it possible for Jane and Cassandra to pay occasional visits together, but the widowed and essentially rootless household must have been a sad contrast with the busy active life of former years. Anne Elliot's suppressed distaste for Bath, her regret for the duties and dignities of a substantial country residence, and her unspoken comments on the busy littlenesses of a resort town, which later run through Jane Austen's last completed novel, *Persuasion*, all seem to echo the experience of these years.

Jane wrote Cassandra about a visit from James in 1807, when their mother's household had temporarily joined forces with brother Frank's wife, and moved to Southampton for his convenience on brief shore leaves: "I am sorry and angry that his [James'] visits should not give one more pleasure, the company of so good and so clever a man ought to be gratifying in itself; but his chat seems all forced, his opinions on many points, too much copied from his wife's, and his time here I think is spent in walking about the house, banging the doors, and ringing the bell for a glass of water."

The next fall, October 1808, Edward's wife died in childbirth leaving him with eleven children—all under fifteen—and he evidently felt a need for closer relations with his sisters, of whom he had always been very fond.

He offered his mother a choice of two comfortable cottages, one on the estate at which he resided and the other on an estate he owned nearer their former home. They chose the latter and Jane's spirits seemed to rise immediately as they prepared for the move to a new country home of their own in the old neighborhood.

She wrote Cassandra about a last ball at Southampton, to which she had taken a guest: "It was the same room in which we danced fifteen years ago!—I thought it all over,—and in spite of the shame of being so much older, felt with thankfulness that I was quite as happy now as then."

Again, more happily than she had written for years, she jested: "I assure you I am as tired of writing long letters as you can be. What a pity that one should still be so fond of receiving them."

And even when Mrs. Knight, widow of the relative who had made Edward his heir, suggested as one of the advantages of the move that the Rector of Chawton was a middle-aged bachelor, Jane answered imperturbably: "I am very much obliged to Mrs. Knight for such a proof of the interest she takes in me, and she may depend upon it that I *will* marry Mr. Papillon, whatever may be his reluctance or my own."

In her recovered spirits she wrote under an assumed name to the publisher who had six years before purchased *Northanger Abbey*, asking whether he meant to fulfill his contract. He replied that the purchase had carried no obligation to publish but that he was willing to return the manuscript for the £10 he had paid. That was then too large a sum for Jane to spare, and there seemed no advantage in pursuing the matter. She was evidently not seriously discouraged by it, however, for as soon as they had settled in Chawton she turned to a revision of *Sense and Sensibility*, which Henry succeeded in placing with a publisher before the end of the year.

A visit to Henry's home in London enabled her to correct the proofs and although she had undertaken to share any loss the publisher might sustain, she had the great satisfaction of receiving £140 as her share of the profits, the first money she had ever earned.

Her authorship was kept a profound secret, even in the family. Only Cassandra and Henry knew of her negotiations in November, 1812 for the publication of her next book, *Pride and Prejudice*.

During her visit to Henry's to correct those proofs the next May she wrote Cassandra: ". . . I have now therefore written myself in to £250—which only makes me long for more."

The following April Henry's wife, Eliza, died after a long illness and Jane spent over three months with him in London, reporting: "Upon the whole, his spirits are very much recovered.—If I may so express myself, his mind is not a mind for affliction. He is too busy, too active, too sanguine."

She seems genuinely distressed that his pride in her work led him to give away the secret of its authorship on a number of occasions, and she steadfastly resisted his invitations to meet such literary figures as Madame de Stael and others who had expressed a desire to know her. About one lady who wished to meet the author of *Sense and Sensibility*, she wrote: "I am rather frightened by hearing that she wishes to be introduced to me. If I *am* a wild beast I cannot help it. It is not my own fault." And she remarked, on Henry's telling an admirer of *Pride and Prejudice* that she had written that book: "I am trying to harden myself. After all what a trifle it is in all its bearings to the really important part of one's existence, even in this world. . . ."

That August, 1814, she completed the first novel of her second series—*Mansfield Park*—which was published during the fall.

In her letter January 29, 1813, announcing the arrival of her copy of *Pride and Prejudice* Jane had written Cassandra: "I want to tell you that I have got my own darling child from London . . ." and announced the work in progress—*Mansfield Park*: "Now I will try and write of something else, and it shall be a complete change of subject—ordination." The book is not exactly about ordination but it is the only one in which a clergyman's vocation is even hinted at in any terms that would not perfectly well apply to the few other gentlemanly professions.

Whether Jane Austen was practically aware of the increased current demand for books with a religious theme—and she very frankly assured Cassandra she was more interested in gaining money, and independence, by her writing than fame—or whether she was influenced by Cassandra's increasing concern with religious matters, the impulse evidently came from no real interest of her own, and makes *Mansfield Park* with all its added maturity and richness, the only one of her books where we feel a certain distortion of characters and values.

G. K. Chesterton delightfully summarized one aspect of her life and work when he said: "Jane Austen may have been protected from the truth, but precious little of the truth was ever protected from Jane Austen." He discussed her essentially irreligious attitude in his centenary analysis of *Emma* (1917), beginning:

> It is true that Jane Austen did not attempt to teach any history or politics, but it is not true that we cannot learn any history or politics from Jane Austen. . . .
> She is perhaps most typical of her time in being supremely irreligious. Her very virtues glitter with the cold sunlight of the great secular epoch between medieval and modern mysticism. . . .

And a less catholic romantic critic, H. W. Garrod, says indignantly in his frankly named "Jane Austen: A Depreciation": "Human beings act from a variety of motives; but the only motive from which no one ever acts in Miss Austen is the motive of religion."

Another centenary article in the *Quarterly Review* of 1917, by Reginald Farrar, deals generally with the "radiant and remorseless Jane," and discusses her realistic feminism:

> It is not for nothing that "rational" is almost her highest word of praise. . . .
> For her whole sex she revolts against "elegant females," and sums up her ideal woman, not as a "good-natured unaffected girl" (a phrase which, with her, connotes a certain quite kindly contempt), but as a "rational creature." The pretences of "Vanity Fair," for instance, to be an historical novel, fade into the thinnest of hot air when one realizes, with a gasp of amazement, that Amelia Sedley is actually meant to be a contemporary of Anne Elliot. And thus one understands what a deep gulf Victorianism dug between us and the past; how infinitely nearer to Jane Austen are the sane sensible young women of our own day than the flopping vaporous fools who were the fashion among the Turkish-minded male novelists of Queen Victoria's fashions.

This centenary statement here anticipates that of a postwar feminist, Mona Wilson, who wrote in 1938 in *Jane Austen and Some of Her Contemporaries*:

> . . . I wanted to express my conviction that her name should be linked with that of the great Vindicator of the Rights of Women, Mary Wollstonecraft, and that the *vis comica* of the one has been as powerful an agency as the *saeva indignatio* of the other.
> Jane Austen and Mary Wollstonecraft were bent on the destruction of the fair sex, of the ". . . milk-white lamb, that bleats for a man's protection," and the evolution of the rational woman.

Reginald Farrar concluded his article by turning to the one novel where the radiant Jane allowed remorse—or some other equally irrelevant sentiment—to blunt her perception.

> . . . Yet alone of all her books Mansfield Park is vitiated throughout by a radical dishonesty. . . . For example, Jane Austen has vividly and sedulously shown how impossible a

home is Mansfield for the young, with the father an august old Olympian bore, the mother one of literature's most finished fools, and the aunt its very Queen of Shrews; then suddenly for edification, she turns to saying that Tom Bertram's illness converted him to a tardy appreciation of domestic bliss. Having said which, she is soon over mastered by truth once more, and lets slip that he couldn't bear his father near him, that his mother bored him, and that consequently those domestic blisses resolved themselves into better service than you'd get in lodgings, and the ministration of the uninspiring Edmund. . . .

All through "Mansfield Park" in fact Jane Austen is torn between the theory of what she ought to see, and the fact of what she does see. . . . And while in talking of what she does see she is here at her finest, in forcing herself to what she ought to see she is here at her worst; to say nothing of the harm done to her assumptions by her insight and to her insight by her assumptions.

But if, in this first new work undertaken by Jane Austen as an acknowledged author, she allowed herself to be intimidated by the responsibilities of publication, she did not compromise on her statement of woman's wrongs—it never quite reached the status of an explicit demand for woman's rights.

Even Fanny, Jane Austen's most "creep-mouse" heroine stands up to her awe-inspiring uncle with a refusal of a most advantageous proposal, and the daring heresy: "I think it ought not to be set down as certain that a man must be acceptable to every woman he may happen to like himself."

And in her next novel, *Emma*, perhaps her most perfect mature accomplishment, Jane Austen has completely turned her back on any standards but her own.

This novel was, unpredictably, dedicated to the Prince Regent at his own request.

There is almost no other pleasant thing recorded of this monarch—whom we shall have occasion to meet more seriously in the next section—and Jane Austen had herself written to Cassandra when, in February, 1813, he scandalously attempted to divorce his wife: "Poor woman, I shall support her as long as I can, because she *is* a Woman, and because I hate her Husband."

But he evidently had the good taste to enjoy *Sense and Sensibility, Pride and Prejudice*, and *Mansfield Park*. When in 1814 his librarian, Mr. Clarke, learned that Henry Austen's sister had written them, he wrote her telling her that His Royal Highness had a complete set of her books in each of his palaces, and that he would be pleased with the dedication of her next work.

Jane Austen sent a suitable acknowledgment and accepted an invitation to visit the famous library at Carleton House.

Mr. Clarke, a clergyman who might well be compared with Jane Austen's Mr. Elton if not with Mr. Collins himself, was evidently much struck with her on this visit and suggested that in her next novel she should choose as a subject his prototype. He urged:

> Do let us have an English clergyman after your fancy—much novelty may be introduced—show, dear Madam, what good would be done if tithes were taken away entirely, and describe him burying his own mother—as I did—because the High Priest of the parish in which she died did not pay her remains the respect he ought to do. . . . Carry your clergyman to sea as the friend of some distinguished character about a court.

Jane Austen hurriedly replied, with as much trepidation as amusement:

> I am quite honoured by your thinking me capable of drawing such a clergyman as you gave me the sketch of in your note of Nov. 16th. But I assure you I am *not*. The comic part of the character I might be equal to, but not the good, the enthusiastic, the literary. Such a man's conversation must at times be on subjects of science and philosophy, of which I know nothing; or at least be occasionally abundant in quotation and allusions which a woman who, like me, knows only her own mother tongue and has read little in that would be totally without the power of giving. A classical education, or, at any rate, a very extensive acquaintance with English literature, ancient and modern, appears to me quite indispensable for the person who would do any justice to your clergyman; and I think I may boast myself to be, with all possible vanity, the most unlearned and uninformed female who ever dared to be an authoress.

He persisted with offers of virtual collaboration and told her he was sending her two "Sermons I wrote and preached on the ocean" which she was free to use. He also had a new project to suggest. He had just been appointed English Secretary to the Prince Regent's son-in-law, Prince Leopold of Saxe Coburg, and felt that Miss Austen might well write a historical romance dealing with the history of Saxe Coburg.

She ended the correspondence by replying:

> You have my best wishes. Your recent appointments are I hope a step to something still better. In my opinion, the service of a court can hardly be too well paid, for immense must be the sacrifice of time and feeling required by it. . . .
> I am fully sensible that an historical romance, founded on the House of Saxe Coburg, might be much more to the purpose of profit or popularity than such pictures of domestic life in country villages as I deal in. But I could no more write a romance than an epic poem. I could not sit seriously down to write a serious romance under any other motive than to save my life; and if it were indispensable for me to keep it up and never relax into laughing at myself or other people, I am sure I should be hung before I had finished the first chapter. No, I must keep to my own style and go on in my own way; and though I may never succeed again in that, I am convinced that I should totally fail in any other.

During this same period we get another rare glimpse of her conscious artistry in the course of a correspondence with her oldest niece. Anna had begun to write a novel and was sending it to Aunt Jane, chapter by chapter, for criticism.

There are many notes which indicate how scrupulous Jane was about facts—the distance of one town from another, for example, the probability of a small resort being talked of sixty miles away, and such social minutia as: "I have also scratched out the introduction between Lord Portnam and his brother and Mr. Griffin. A country surgeon (don't tell Mr. C. Lylord) would not be introduced to men of their rank."

But there are also more self-revealing comments: "You are now collecting your People delightfully, getting them exactly into such a spot as is the delight of my life;—3 or 4 Families in a Country Village is the very thing to work on." And: "You had better not leave England. Let the Portmans go to Ireland, but as you know nothing of the Manners there, you had better not go with them. You will be in danger of giving false representations. Stick to Bath and the Foresters. There you will be quite at home."

Another note reminds us that Jane Austen's superbly unaccented and effective use of words was not as unconscious as it seems. She writes Anna about one installment: "Devereux Forester's being ruined by his Vanity is extremely good; but I wish you would not let him plunge into a 'Vortex of Dissipation'. I do not object to the Thing, but I cannot bear the expression. . . ."

She would, I think, have been rather pleased by the indignant complaint of Mr. Garrod, in his "Depreciation of Jane Austen," that: "When I call her writing truthful and apt, I have said all that should be said in praise of it. . . . Its qualities, indeed, are, I should be inclined to say, rather those of science than of literature. It does just what it is meant to do, no more, no less. It appears of course a more telling language than the language of science; but that is merely because it has been transferred from the analysis of matter to the analysis of manners."

Another chapter, with one of the interpolated stories so common in the novels of the time, elicited a playful comment which reminds us how carefully prearranged all the most detailed effects in Jane Austen's novels are, even though their freshness and spontaneity often give the effect of improvisation. She writes: "St. Julian's history was quite a surprise to me. You had not very long known it yourself I suspect," and continues with more personal amusement about the antecedent plot complication St. Julian's history had evidently revealed: "His having been in love with the Aunt gives Cecilia an additional interest in him. I like the idea, a very proper compliment to an aunt! I rather imagine indeed that nieces are seldom chosen but out of compliment to some aunt or other." She concludes with a comment on Ben Lefroy—her niece's fiancé, and a nephew of the young Irish gentleman with whom she had flirted so outrageously twenty years before: " I daresay Ben was in love with me once, and would never have thought of you if he had not supposed me dead of scarlet fever."

Two further family correspondences of these years give us valuable glimpses of her personal attitude to several of the major ideas presented, with seeming detachment, in her novels.

Her other motherless niece, Fanny, was involved in a series of courtships, and not sure as to her own feelings, encouraged first one suitor, then another, then decided "never" to marry, then feared lest she would be criticized as fickle for drawing back so late, and wrote her Aunt Jane a day-by-day series of requests for comfort and advice.

Many of the replies might well have been written by Elinor Dashwood or Elizabeth Bennet or Anne Elliot after they had stopped being heroines and become Aunts.

For example, the playful warning in response to her niece's fervent vows of celibacy: "single women have a dreadful propensity for being poor,—which is one very strong argument in favour of matrimony."

And the more serious warning when it seemed the pressure of public opinion might force Fanny into maintaining her consistency even at the cost of an unhappy marriage: "The unpleasantness of appearing fickle is certainly great—but if you think you want Punishment for Past Illusions, there it is—and nothing can be compared to the misery of being bound without Love. . . . That you do not deserve."

These letters came to an end in March, 1817, only a few months before Jane Austen's death. They close happily: "You can hardly think what a pleasure it is to me to have such a thorough picture of your heart.—Oh, what a loss it will be when you are married. You are too agreeable in your single state, too agreeable as a niece —I shall hate you when your delicious play of mind is all settled down into conjugal and maternal affections."

The last letter reads, prophetically as it turned out: "Well, I shall say, as I have often said before, Do not be in a hurry; depend upon it, the right Man will come at last; . . . And then, by not beginning Mothering quite so early in life, you will be young in Constitution and spirits, figure and countenance."

This last bit of advice which would seem, even to many twentieth century readers, remarkably freespoken from a maiden lady to a girl barely out of her teens, reminds us of a whole series of such comments in Jane's letters to Cassandra.

Birth control was evidently altogether unknown in eighteenth century England and three of Jane's own sisters-in-law died in childbirth despite their unusual command of medical attention and care.

Writing of one sister-in-law's pregnancy the twenty-three year old Jane had told Cassandra, evidently with no fear of shocking her, that she had visited Mary: "who is still plagued with the rheumatism, which she would be very glad to get rid of, and still more glad to get rid of [give birth to] her child, of whom she is heartily tired. . . . I believe I never told you that Mrs. Caulthard and Ann, late of Manydown, are both dead, and both died in child-bed. We have not regaled Mary with this news."

Again, some years later, commenting on a neighbour's difficult delivery: "Good Mrs. Deedes!—I hope she will get the better of this Marianne, and then I would recommend to her and Mr. D. the simple regimen of separate rooms."

And in the last years of her life, just a few months after her niece Anna's marriage had put a stop to her novel writing, Jane wrote Cassandra: "Anna has not a chance of escape; her husband called here the other day, and said she was *pretty well* but not equal to so long a walk; she *must come in her Donkey Carriage*. Poor animal, she will be worn out before she is thirty. I am very sorry for her. Mrs. Clement too is in that way again. I am quite tired of so many children. —Mrs. Benn has a 15th."

Unlike her other concerns this one was not directly reflected in the novels—unless we can take the very limited sizes of her heroines' families (all but the first one)—presumably attained by the Spartan regime of separate rooms—as evidence on the matter. But it is important for us to see how fearlessly Jane Austen had considered such aspects of "the woman question" in the light of whatever information was then available.

One other family note, not from her pen, may be instructive before we consider *Emma* and *Persuasion*, the work of her last three years.

A niece, long after Jane Austen's death, when she was already famous and her novels had gone into many editions, described the way in which she had to write even after the successful publication of her first two books. (Jane had never again had a private or semi-private sitting room after the first move from Steventon, where she had shared a dressing room with Cassandra.)

The unconscious contrast her niece's vocabulary assumes between woman's real work and any such personal occupation as authorship, which may be indulged only if not taken too seriously, tells us volumes about the special practical and emotional problems of the woman writer.

According to this undoubtedly accurate account Jane: "would sit quietly working [sewing] beside the fire in the library, saying nothing for a good while, and then would suddenly burst out laughing, jump up and run across the room to a table where pens and paper were lying, write something down, and then come back to the fire and go on quietly working as before."

In this way much of *Emma*, like her other masterpieces, was written.

Dr. Kettle chooses this novel as the greatest and most representative of the works she lived to write (she was only forty-two when she died a year after its publication) and says:

> How does Jane Austen succeed in thus combining intensity with precision, emotional involvement with objective judgment? Part of the answer lies, I think, in her almost complete lack of idealism, the delicate and unpretentious materialism of

her outlook. . . . The clarity of her social observations (the Highbury world is scrupulously seen and analysed down to the exact incomes of its inmates) is matched by the precision of her social judgments, and all her judgments are, in the broadest sense, social. Human happiness not abstract principle is her concern. Such precision—it is both her incomparable strength and her ultimate limitation—is unimaginable except in an extraordinarily stable corner of society. . . .

Sufficient has perhaps been said to suggest that what gives *Emma* its power to move us is the realism and depth of feeling behind Jane Austen's attitudes. She examines with a scrupulous yet passionate and critical precision the actual problems of her world. That this world is narrow cannot be denied. How far its narrowness matters is an important question.

The reason that its narrowness finally does not matter is that none of the implications which could be drawn from the examination of this little corner of society are evaded. Just as the smallest possible section of a circular arc will, when properly examined, allow us to locate the center of the circle from which it was taken, determine the radius, and so reconstruct the circle in its original size and position, so this small section of middle-class relations enables Jane Austen to reach many profound conclusions about her whole society none of which are shirked. She pulls no punches. Her heroine is deliberately presented as a spoiled child and a snobbish, conceited, egotistical young woman, whose false upper-class values are only partially excused as the logical and almost inevitable result of her upbringing. She is, however, both intelligent and warmhearted and the theme of the book is the reeducation of Emma who is, finally, able to learn from her own painful experience.

The cardinal sin in Jane Austen's hierarchy—that one should treat other human beings like inanimate objects, simply as means to one's own ends—is committed by Emma before the end of the third chapter, and the falsity of her relation to her new protégée is lightly and indelibly indicated when she muses about the convenience for companionship of "*a* Harriet Smith," now that Miss Taylor, her former governess-companion, has married.

Emma's genuine affection for Miss Taylor has led her to promote this very happy marriage, but her wealthy father, far more stupid and hopelessly self-engrossed, cannot be brought to believe that anything even mildly inconvenient to him can be at all desirable to anyone, and spends a large part of the first chapter pitying "poor Miss Taylor":

> ... from his habits of gentle selfishness, and of being never able to suppose that other people could feel differently from himself, he was very much disposed to think Miss Taylor had done as sad a thing for herself as for them, and would have been a great deal happier if she had spent all the rest of her life at Hartfield.

This "gentle selfishness," shown in relation to all who come in contact with him, finally gives us as profound and exasperated an understanding of the completely impenetrable righteous self-regard of a ruling class as we could get from the most indignant economic expose of a paternalistic employer. Incidentally it makes us the more ready to welcome even long delayed efforts at self-criticism by his daughter.

Nor is Emma, from the very beginning, with all her deliberate self-delusions, lacking in a certain honesty and understanding of objective facts. For example, although Emma at the beginning sees marriage, as Dr. Kettle says, in "terms of class snobbery and property qualifications ... typical of the ruling class," she has a saving humorous realism about her position. She tells Harriet she has now (at twenty-one) determined never to marry:

> I have none of the usual inducements of women to marry. Were I to fall in love, indeed, it would be a different thing; but I never have been in love; it is not my way or my nature; and I do not think I ever shall. And without love, I am sure I should be a fool to change such a situation as mine. Fortune I do not lack; employment I do not lack; consequence I do not lack; I believe few married women are half as much mistress of their husband's house as I am of Hartfield; ...

In response to Harriet's horrified exclamation: "But still, you will be an old maid—and that's dreadful!" she replies:

> Never mind, Harriet, I shall not be a poor old maid; and it is poverty only which makes celibacy contemptible to a generous public! A single woman with a very narrow income must be a ridiculous, disagreeable old maid! the proper sport of boys and girls; but a single woman of good fortune is always respectable, and may be as sensible and pleasant as anybody else!

However, the real meaning of poverty for a lady is stated not by Emma, but by Jane Fairfax. She is a well-educated, beautiful and exceptionally accomplished young woman whose father's early death has left her, with only a few hundred pounds, to support herself. She must, necessarily, seek a position as governess but has decided to postpone the evil day a few months until her twenty-first birthday.

In reply to the officious vulgarity with which a self-appointed patroness offers to help her find a post she says:

> When I am quite determined as to the time, I am not at all afraid of being long unemployed. There are places in town, offices, where inquiry would soon produce something—offices for the sale, not quite of human flesh, but of human intellect."
> "Oh! my dear, human flesh! You quite shock me; if you mean a fling at the slave trade, I assure you Mr. Suckling was always rather a friend to abolition."
> "I did not mean—I was not thinking of the slave trade," replied Jane; "governess-trade, I assure you, was all that I had in view; widely different, certainly, as to the guilt of those who carry it on; but as to the greater misery of the victims, I do not know where it lies. . . ."

And later Emma herself, despite her snobbish jealousy of Jane's accomplishments, replies to some one who, excusing a serious breach of decorum on Jane's part, has urged:

> "And how much may be said, in her situation, for even that error."
> "Much, indeed!" cried Emma feelingly. "If a woman can ever be excused for thinking only of herself, it is in a situation like Jane Fairfax's." Of such, one might almost say, that "the world is not theirs, nor the world's law!"

Again we see how far an honest, intelligent examination of even the smallest most stable corner of a class society will carry us toward a reexamination of its professions and the values it really lives by. As Kettle concludes:

> Against the element of complacency other forces, too, are at work. . . . Among these positive forces are, as we have seen, her highly critical concern over the fate of women in her society, a concern which involves a reconsideration of its basic values. . . .

It is Jane Austen's sensitive vitality, her genuine concern (based on so large an honesty) that captures imagination. . . . And the concern does not stop at what, among the ruling class at Highbury, is pleasant and easily solved.

It gives us glimpses of something Mr. Woodhouse never dreamed of—the world outside the Hartfield world and yet inseparably bound up with it; the world Jane Fairfax saw in her vision of offices and into which Harriet in spite of (no, *because* of) Emma's patronage was so nearly plunged: the world for which Jane Austen had no answer. It is this vital and unsentimental concern which defeats, to such a very large extent, the limitations.

There were, of course, many contemporary criticisms like those of a church dignitary who "thought the Authoress wrong in such times as these, to draw such Clergymen as Mr. Collins and Mr. Elton."

The Prince Regent's secretary sent formal thanks for the presentation of the "dedicated" *Emma*. Jane evidently found them somewhat inadequate for she wrote to her publisher: "You will be pleased to hear that I have received the Prince's thanks for the *handsome* copy I sent him of *Emma*. Whatever he may think of *my* share of the work, yours seems to have been quite right."

Not only clergymen and princes, but evidently ladies as well, were rendered somewhat uneasy by the unsparing realism and utter lack of sentimentality in *Emma*. Lady Shelley, for example, wrote in 1819, when Jane's first novel, *Northanger Abbey*, and her last, *Persuasion*, were posthumously published together: "the same objection may be made to all Jane Austen's novels. . . . Surely works of imagination should raise us above our everyday feelings, and excite in us those élans passagérès of virtue and sensibility which are exquisite and ennobling."

But perhaps one of the most interesting contemporary criticisms was a long article which Sir Walter Scott wrote anonymously for *The Quarterly* in October 1816.

Although well-known for his poetry, Scott was just entering upon his career as a novelist when Jane Austen was concluding hers, and his position as a lawyer and man of business, influential in literary and political circles in both Edinburgh and London, subjected him to influences quite different from any Jane Austen knew. It is no exaggeration to say that he wrote in an England at least a generation further along the road to industrialism than hers, and that the forces which shaped his world had barely impinged on hers.

His work as a novelist should, therefore, be considered in the context of the great romantic writers of the early nineteenth century rather than in this transitional eighteenth century period (see pp. 617-620).

The review of Jane Austen's work which he wrote in 1816, while friendly, and appreciative enough of some of her minor talents, utterly fails to grasp the essential meaning of her novels. It gives us a glimpse of the good-natured Tory who, unable to face the implications of his own position in an increasingly ruthless capitalist world, turned to a glorification of the medieval past and of luxury emotions which neither he nor any of his readers would have dreamed of obeying in their real lives.

He begins with a good if somewhat patronizing summary of Jane Austen's most obvious subjects and abilities:

> But the author of Emma confines herself chiefly to the middling classes of society; her most distinguished characters do not rise greatly above well-bred country gentlemen and ladies; and those which are sketched with most originality and precision, belong to a class rather below that standard. The narrative of all her novels is composed of such common occurrences as may have fallen under the observation of most folks; and her dramatis personae conduct themselves upon the motives and principles which the reader may recognize as ruling their own and that of most of their acquaintances. . . .
> The author's knowledge of the world, and the peculiar tact with which she presents characters that the reader cannot fail to recognize, reminds us something of the merits of the Flemish school of painting. The subjects are not often elegant, and certainly never grand; but they are finished up to nature; and with a precision which delights the reader. . . .

He is, however, troubled by the unromantic tone in which she discusses marriage. Not that he would recommend *acting* imprudently, but he holds a decent reticence about the real considerations involved more becoming, and would rather the hand were quicker than the eye. It is interesting to note how completely and unquestioningly he assumes that the subject who significantly feels love must be a young man—woman is essentially just its object. And it is also instructive to see how imperceptibly his idealistic argument in favor of romantic self-disregarding early love merges into its utilitarian justification by the practical benefits it may confer.

One word, however, we must say in behalf of that once powerful divinity, Cupid, king of gods and men, who in these times of revolution has been assailed, even in his own kingdom of romance, by the authors who formerly were his devoted priests. We are quite aware that there are few instances of first attachment being brought to a happy conclusion, and that it seldom can be so in a state of society so highly advanced as to render early marriages among the better class, acts, generally speaking, of imprudence. But the youth of this realm need not at present be taught the doctrine of selfishness. It is by no means their error to give the world or the good things of the world all for love; and before the authors of moral fiction couple cupid indivisibly with calculating prudence, we would have them reflect, that they may sometimes lend their aid to substitute more mean, more sordid, and more selfish motives of conduct, for the romantic feelings which their predecessors perhaps fanned into too powerful a flame. Who is it, that in his youth has felt a virtuous attachment, however romantic or however unfortunate, but can trace back to its influence much that his character may possess of what is honourable, dignified and disinterested? If he recollects hours wasted in unavailing hope or saddened by doubt and disappointment; he may also dwell on many which have been snatched from folly or libertinism, and dedicated to studies which might render him worthy of the object of his affections, or pave the way perhaps to that distinction necessary to raise him to an equality with her.

It is most instructive to see here how Sir Walter's panegyric on disinterested love assumes that its romantic object is inevitably chosen from a higher—and richer—social circle and that its occasional result, and natural if unconscious purpose, is to enable the romantic lover to enter that charmed sphere.

"In Belmont is a lady richly left *and* she is fair, and fairer than that word, of wondrous virtue." But Shakespeare knew what he was doing, whereas Sir Walter sees the aristocratic Bassanio as a noble and disinterested hero.

Even the habitual indulgence of feelings totally unconnected with ourself and our own immediate interest, softens, graces, and amends the human mind; and after the pain of disappointment is past, those who survive (and by good fortune those are the greater number) are neither less wise nor less worthy members of society for having felt, for a time, the influence of a passion which has been well qualified as the "tenderest, noblest and best."

Jane Austen said noncommittally that the authoress of *Emma* could not complain of her treatment by the anonymous *Quarterly Reviewer* who was evidently a very clever man.

The depression which followed the peace of 1815-16 forced Henry's banking house into bankruptcy, along with many others, but Jane had only £13 on deposit there, the rest of her earnings—less than £1,000—being with patriotic or more likely sisterly pride, invested in Navy Funds.

However for the first time in her life she now became seriously unwell. Her illness, which proved fatal in little more than a year, was never really diagnosed but the detailed description of her "decline" available from family letters seems clearly to indicate a cancerous affection of some internal organ.

She had begun a new novel shortly after *Emma* was completed and later wrote to Fanny: "I have a something ready for publication which may perhaps come out in a twelve months time." The plan for such a delay was deliberate. Henry in his biographical memoir wrote: "Though in composition she was equally rapid and correct, yet an invincible distrust of her own judgment induced her to withhold her works from the public till time and many perusals had satisfied her that the charm of recent composition was dissolved."

And although *Persuasion* was completed by August 1816, it is likely that had she lived, some scenes—notably that of Mrs. Smith's story—would have been largely rewritten and enriched. The end, too, as far as such important minor characters as Mrs. Clay and Mr. Elliot are concerned, was rather "huddled together" and the novel is, of course, much shorter than any of the others except the first, *Northanger Abbey*. On the whole it seems that while her failing energy made no significant change in the development of characters or theme it did prevent completion of the multitude of felicitous touches which overflow the main channel of all her other books.

But there are also important positive changes that add to our regret for the unwritten novels which should have followed this transitional one.

For the first time we have a mature heroine—Anne Elliot is twenty-seven—and a really sympathetic account of a long-standing love affair.

There is far more sensitivity to the beauty of nature and, on the whole, more emotional awareness of many varied physical sensations.

Relative poverty is touched upon in a daringly uncritical manner. Here again, as in her discussion of childbirth, Jane Austen's private correspondence reveals her awareness of things not directly mentionable in a lady's public writing. Her two favorite contemporary authors were Dr. Johnson, whose discussions of poverty we have already had occasion to note, and a now largely forgotten poet, George Crabbe, who wrote, attacking the sentimental pictures of rural plenty in *The Deserted Village* and elsewhere:

> Will you praise the healthy homely fare
> Plenteous and plain, that happy peasants share?
> O trifle not with wants you cannot feel,
> Nor mock the misery of a stinted meal,
> Homely, not wholesome, plain, not plenteous, such
> As you who praise would never deign to touch;
> By such examples taught, I paint the cot
> As Truth will paint it and as Bards will not.

But while *Persuasion* does not, of course, go so far down the social scale, it does touch almost the very lowest income group in the lower middle class.

Only Miss Bates in *Emma* was previously shown as hospitable in poverty, and she is a sympathetic and amusing, rather than an attractive, character. But here a half-pay navy captain—surely no better off than Captain Price of whose uncomfortable household we have so painfully convincing a view in *Mansfield Park*—is the head of an exceptionally harmonious and generous family.

> Mrs. Harville, a degree less polished than her husband, seemed, however, to have the same good feelings; and nothing could be more pleasant than their desire of considering the whole party as friends of their own, because the friends of Captain Wentworth, or more kindly hospitable than their entreaties for their all promising to dine with them; . . . they seemed almost hurt that Captain Wentworth should have brought any such party [five total strangers] to Lyme without considering it as a thing of course that they should dine with them.

JANE AUSTEN

There was so much attachment to Captain Wentworth in all this, and such a bewitching charm in a degree of hospitality so uncommon, so unlike the usual style of give-and-take invitations and dinners of formality and display, that Anne felt her spirits not likely to be benefited by an increasing acquaintance among his brother-officers. "These would have been all my friends" was her thought; and she had to struggle against a great tendency to lowness.

On quitting the Cobb, they all went indoors with their new friends, and found rooms so small as none but those who invite from the heart could think capable of accommodating so many. Anne had a moment's astonishment on the subject herself; but it was soon lost in the pleasanter feelings which sprang from the sight of all the ingenious contrivances and nice arrangements of Captain Harville to turn the actual space to the best possible account, to supply the deficiencies of lodging-house furniture, and defend the windows and doors against the winter storms to be expected. . . .

. . . He drew, he varnished, he carpentered, he glued, he made toys for the children, he fashioned new netting-needles and pins with improvements; and if everything else was done, sat down to his large fishing net at one corner of the room.

Another new departure is a warm study of a deeply united elderly couple—Admiral and Mrs. Crofts. She especially is an unconventional character who has insisted upon living with her husband aboard ship, and rebukes her brother: "But I hate to hear you talking so, like a fine gentleman, and as if women were all fine ladies instead of rational creatures. We none of us expect to be in smooth water all our days."

Our last glimpse of Mrs. Croft is in Bath where the Admiral:

was ordered to walk to keep off the gout, and Mrs. Croft seemed to go shares with him in everything, and to walk for her life to do him good. . . . Anne . . . delighted to see the Admiral's hearty shake of the hand when he encountered an old friend, and observe their eagerness of conversation when occasionally forming into a little knot of the navy, Mrs. Croft looking as intelligent and keen as any of the officers around her.

The plot of *Persuasion* is much the same as that of Jane Austen's other novels. Dr. Marvin Mudrick says, in discussing the question of Jane Austen's "comedy":

Anne and Wentworth neither overlook nor rebel against the material base of their society: if they overlooked it, they would be deluded, which they are not; if they rebelled, they would be outcasts, which they do not wish to be. Their problem—and they are both wholly aware of it—is to determine just how far the claim of feeling can yield, without effacing itself altogether, to the claim of economics; and this central problem of *Persuasion* is not comic.

And Mark Schorer, in an interesting analysis of the language of the novel, makes a very striking point, although he ignores the presence of those characters who share the author's viewpoint, notably those active or wounded naval officers we have seen who, in a sense, work for their living:

> *Persuasion* is a novel of courtship and marriage with a patina of sentimental scruple and moral punctilio and a stylistic base derived from commerce and property, the counting house and the inherited estate. The first is the expression of the characters, the second is the perception of the author . . . the essence of her comedy resides . . . in the discrepancy between social sentiment and social fact, and the social fact is to be discovered not so much in the professions of her characters as in the texture of her style.

This is true, and his article's subsequent detailed analysis of the language is extremely valuable, but as we have seen, the "essence of the comedy" is not altogether the essence of the book, for "the central problem of *Persuasion* is not comic."

The last novel Jane Austen began, which she found herself unable to continue beyond the first few uncorrected chapters, is an even more apparent departure.

Here for the first time she introduces—and apparently as a center to the book—a commercial scheme for making money.

Sanditon is the name of a new health resort or watering place created by speculative landlords to increase the value of their land.

In previous novels all commercial activities have been pursued off stage, usually before the first chapter began—and money was to be inherited or married but not made. The sole exception lay in the odd system of war office rewards for taking prize-ships referred to by the naval passages of *Persuasion*. Mr. Knightley in *Emma* was a working landlord supervising his farms, and his brother was an energetic barrister, but all the clergymen draw their salaries in dignified repose and no one else comes even that close to earning a living.

Yet Mr. Parker, the first and most important character we meet in *Sanditon*, is on a business errand intended to increase the number of guests at his resort, and we are immediately informed:

> . . . the success of Sanditon as a small fashionable Bathing Place was object, for which he seemed to live. A very few years ago, and it had been a quiet Village of no pretensions; but some natural advantages in its position and some accidental circumstances having suggested to himself, and the other principal Land Holder, the probability of its becoming a profitable Speculation, they had engaged in it, and planned and built and praised and puffed and raised it to something of young Renown—and Mr. Parker could now think of very little besides. . . . Sanditon was a second Wife and 4 children to him—hardly less Dear—and certainly more engrossing.—He could talk of it forever.—It had indeed the highest claims; not only those of Birthplace, Property, and Home,—it was his Mine, his Lottery, his Speculation and his Hobby Horse; his Occupation his Hope and his Futurity. . . .

The wealthy Lady Denham, his greedy but niggardly coinvestor, complains that an increase of visitors will mean higher prices for her household necessities and Jane Austen actually ventures into an economic discussion when Mr. Parker replies:

> My dear Madam, They can only raise the price of consumeable Articles, by such an extraordinary Demand for them and such a diffusion of Money among us, as must do us more Good than harm. Our Butchers and Bakers and Traders in general cannot get rich without bringing Prosperity to *us*.—If they do not gain, our rents will be insecure—and in proportion to their profit must be ours eventually in the increased value of our Houses.

There is a return to the high-spirited burlesque of *Northanger Abbey* but this time it is, significantly, aimed not at an overemotional young heroine but at a determinedly profligate young "villain" with whom the heroine is obviously perfectly competent to deal.

> The truth was that Sir Edw: whom circumstances had confined very much to one spot had read more sentimental novels

than had agreed with him. His fancy had been early caught by all the impassioned, and most exceptionable parts of Richardson's; and such Authors as have since appeared to tread in Richardson's steps, so far as Man's determined pursuit of Woman in defiance of every opposition of feeling and convenience is concerned, had since occupied the greater part of his literary hours, and formed his character. . . .

Clara saw through him; and had not the least intention of being seduced—but she bore with him patiently enough to confirm the sort of attachment which her personal charms had raised.—A greater degree of discouragement indeed would not have affected Sir Edw:—, He was armed against the highest pitch of Disdain or Aversion—If she could not be won by affection he must carry her off. He knew his Business.—

This tantalizing fragment strikes out into such completely new territory that it is impossible even to guess its future development. One can only regret its abrupt termination when, on March 18, 1817, Jane Austen found herself too ill to continue.

On March 28 her wealthy and childless uncle died but the £1,000 legacies of which his sisters' children had been assured were, by the terms of his will, not to be paid until his wife's death—an event which actually did not take place until many years after Jane's.

She had evidently been counting heavily upon the independence which might be assured to Cassandra and herself, and wrote one of her brothers a week later:

> I am ashamed to say that the shock of my uncle's will brought on a relapse and I was so ill on Friday and thought myself so likely to be worse, that I could but press for Cassandra's returning with Frank after the funeral last night, which of course she did, and either her return, or my having seen Mr. Curtis or my disorder choosing to go away, have made me better this morning. I live upstairs however for the present and am coddled. I am the only one of the legatees who has been so silly, but a weak body must excuse weak nerves.

The rally was a very temporary one and on May 24 she and Cassandra took lodgings in the nearby cathedral town of Winchester where there was a surgeon of some reputation who had offered to undertake her treatment.

She wrote gaily enough to a nephew: "Mr. Lyford says he will cure me, and if he fails, I shall draw up a memorial and lay it before the Dean and Chapter, and have no doubt of redress from that pious, learned, and disinterested body." But she also made her will, leaving everything to Cassandra except for one £50 legacy to Henry and another to an old housekeeper who had lost that amount in the failure of his bank.

The disease made rapid progress and on July 18, 1817 she died at the age of forty-two.

Northanger Abbey, of which Henry had repurchased the manuscript, and *Persuasion*, were published in one volume in 1818, and her fame grew slowly but steadily from then on.

Half a century later George Eliot and George Henry Lewes agreed that she was the most perfect artist who had yet used the novel form, unequalled by any male writer—and her popularity with a special but very large public has persisted even though most of the more astringent elements of her art have often been ignored. The best of this traditional appreciation is illustrated by Virginia Woolf who calls her: "the most perfect artist among women," and says:

> Think away the surface animation, the likeness to life, and there remains to provide a deeper pleasure, an exquisite discrimination of human values. . . . Her fool is a fool, her snob is a snob, because he departs from the model of sanity and sense which she has in mind, and conveys to us unmistakably even while she makes us laugh. Never did any novelist make more use of an impeccable sense of human values. It is against the disc of an unerring heart, an unfailing good taste, an almost stern morality, that she shows up those deviations from kindness, truth, and sincerity which are among the most delightful things in English literature.

And Cazamian emphasizes her position as the first *modern* novelist, saying:

> all that a Rochefoucauld had shown up in the strong and bitter note of a straight forward denunciation, and which at a later date the pessimistic novel will dissect with such profuseness and intensity of method, is here indicated or suggested so calmly and with so sober a touch that the author's personal reaction is reduced to a minimum. There is nothing more objective than those stories . . . if a subtle suggestion of irony did not hover over every page, revealing a sharpness of vision that could be unmercifully severe.

This insight into her continuing contemporary relevance is completed by Dr. Kettle with his statement that:

> The intensity of Jane Austen's novels is inseparable from their concreteness and this intensity must be stressed because it is so different from the charming and cosy qualities with which the novels are often associated. Reading . . . [Jane Austen] is a delightful experience but it is not a soothing one. On the contrary, our faculties are aroused, we are called upon to participate in life with an awareness, a fineness of feeling and a moral concern more intense than most of us normally bring to our everyday experience. Everything matters. . . . And in none of the issues of conduct arising in the novel[s] is Jane Austen morally neutral. The intensity with which everything matters to us . . . is the product of this lack of complacency, this passionate concern of Jane Austen for human values.

These widely varied evaluations do not supplant, but rather supplement each other. The fact that as perceptive and sympathetic a critic as Virginia Woolf left so much of Jane Austen's depth unplumbed shows how deceptive the sparkling surface of her work is. For Jane Austen was compelled to accomplish an almost unprecedented feat—to become an artist while remaining a lady.

Only by reading between the lines can one follow the unsparing analysis beneath the imperturbable surface. And then one finds an especial piquancy in the rapid and skillful social dissection carried on while the lady's air of courteous attention to the story disclaims all knowledge of her right hand as well as her left. And of course the need for such a pose is in itself Miss Austen's sharpest comment on woman's position in the best of polite society.

The Great Romantics and the Democratic Revolutions

THE FRENCH REVOLUTION

It is almost impossible for those of us who have not read in detail some of the contemporary records of the period to imagine the extraordinary effect of the French Revolution on the life and thought of England in both cultural and political terms.

It served as a catalytic agent to crystallize, bring to the surface, and make articulate all of the suppressed discontent we have sensed seething far beneath the surface of eighteenth century England; it intensified the general humanitarian sympathy of the more sensitive middle-class intellectuals for the economic hardships of the people, and it made possible an immediate critical expression of the disorientation and bewilderment of the young artists and writers. These young poets and essayists were almost the first of their kind to struggle for a living in the open market, producing their wares as a commodity to sell the public, and finding that this new freedom for the artist was, too often, only freedom to starve.

This expression was not, however, merely unhappy or rebellious. The early success of the revolution so short a distance away, and the enormous wave of popular enthusiasm which swept the mechanics of at least such large cities as London and Manchester, convinced the first generation of romantic writers and philosophers that they spoke for the immediate future and would live to see liberty, equality and fraternity enthroned on earth as it was in heaven—or, rather, in England as well as France and America.

It is interesting and significant to note how for the first time, despite the undeniable influence of Rousseau, the golden age of mankind was assumed by one writer after another to be located, not in the dim mythical past or in some far off hidden island, but in the present place and almost present time.

Even after he had lost faith and hope and gained a comfortable income Wordsworth would still say:

> Bliss was it in that dawn to be alive
> But to be young was very Heaven! O times
> In which the meagre, stale, forbidding ways
> Of custom, law, and statute took at once
> The attraction of a country in romance!
>
> . . . .
>
> Why should I not confess that Earth was then
> To me, what an inheritance, new-fallen,
> Seems, when the first time visited, to one
> Who thither comes to find in it his home?
> He walks about and looks upon the spot
> With cordial transport, moulds it and remoulds,
> And is half-pleased with things that are amiss,
> 'T will be such joy to see them disappear.

The more candid Coleridge, ten years after he had transferred his adherence to church and state, would still wistfully recall his early enthusiasm

> Oh, never can I remember those days with either shame or regret. For I was most sincere, most disinterested. My opinions were, indeed, in many and most important points erroneous; but my heart was single.

This early Jacobinism (as radicalism in the late eighteenth and early nineteenth centuries came to be called) was so widespread that we can read the minutes of an annual dinner in 1789, chaired by a peer of England, Earl Stanhope, where the highly respectable Whig reformer, Dr. Price, made an address congratulating the French National Assembly on the revolution. He said, in part:

> The Revolution in that country . . . the prospect it gives to the two first kingdoms in the world of a common participation in the blessings of civil and religious liberty. . . . I have lived to see 30 millions of people spurning at slavery and demanding liberty with an irresistible voice . . . and now methinks I see the ardour for liberty catching and spreading, a general amendment beginning in human affairs; the dominion of kings changed for the dominion of laws, and the dominion of priests giving way to the dominion of reason and conscience.

By 1792 the repercussions of the revolution in France had reached such heights that a Corresponding Society founded to work for Parliamentary Reform had 30,000 members in London alone, and included such men as William Blake, Thomas Holcroft, Thomas Paine and Horne Tooke. Its founder, a Scottish bootmaker named Thomas Hardy, maintained that every citizen should possess arms and know their use and, more realistically, encouraged combinations of working men for better conditions and wages.

The danger, not of revolution but of real economic reform, was apparent in such a case and "the gentlemen always shoot first." Edmund Burke, whose antiwar stand and speech on *Conciliation With the Colonies* in 1775, had made him the outstanding liberal in Parliament, promptly deserted the Whig party and its co-leader, Fox. Burke then wrote his *Reflections on the French Revolution* with a deliberate demagogic incitement to reactionary terrorism, and a characterization, that soon became infamous, of the "swinish multitude." In his picture of the sufferings of French royalty and nobility, as Thomas Paine said, "He pitied the plumage and forgot the dying bird." And in his panic-mongering threats of invasion, he laid the ground for the real reign of terror which seized, not France, but England, for the next fifteen years.

James Mackintosh, a leading contemporary political writer and speaker (who was himself soon after flattered and bribed into joining the government party), said of Burke's pamphlet:

> His eloquence is not at leisure to deplore the fate of beggared artisans and famished peasants, the victims of suspended industry and languishing commerce. The sensibility which seems scared by the homely miseries of the vulgar is attracted only by the splendid sorrows of royalty and agonizes at the slenderest pang that assails the heart of sottishness and prostitution, if they are placed by fortune on a throne.

And the American Joel Barlow, friend of Thomas Paine and Robert Fulton and semiofficial emissary to France at this time wrote of Burke:

> What is the language proper to be used in describing the character of a man who in his situation, at his time of life, and for a pension of only fifteen hundred pounds a year, could sit down deliberately in his closet and call upon the powers of

earth and hell to inflict such a weight of misery upon the human race?

But whatever we think of Burke we must admit he soon earned his fifteen hundred pounds. (As a matter of fact, the government bound itself to pay the pension for three successive lifetimes so that he could sell it, and he actually realized thirty-seven thousand pounds on the deal before his death in 1797.)

Hundreds of working men and other active political agitators were transported for life on charges of "seditious" utterances. The right of habeas corpus was suspended, all "combinations" of mechanics were declared illegal, public meetings of more than forty were for a time forbidden, and Thomas Paine, who had written *The Rights of Man* in answer to Burke's pamphlet, was found guilty of treason by a jury that declared it did not even have to hear the case for the crown before condemning the accused! Fortunately the accused was not the prisoner. Paine himself did not attend the trial for he had been warned by the poet, Blake, of the likelihood of immediate arrest and, instead of returning to his lodgings where the police waited with a warrant, had escaped to France.

Twelve leaders of the London Corresponding Society were tried for treason, but their personal eminence, an unexpectedly honest jury, and the remarkably able defense of the philosopher, William Godwin (better known in literary history as Shelley's father-in-law), secured a sentence of not guilty seven minutes after the conclusion of the case. The government withdrew warrants already issued for the arrest of over a hundred more members, but the prosecution had succeeded in its major objective of destroying the society and intimidating or rendering ineffective its spokesmen.

Brailsford in his well-known book on *Shelley, Godwin and Their Circle* makes an illuminating comment on the comparative immunity of the group of intellectual leaders. Speaking of Godwin's publication of *Political Justice* in 1793, he says

> Godwin was fortunate in evolving a theory which excused him from attempting the more dangerous exploits of civic courage. His ideal was the Stoic virtue, the isolated strength which can stand firm in *passive* protest against oppression and wrong. He stood firm, and Pitt [the prime minister] was content to leave him standing. . . . The prudence which teaches one man to be a Whig will make of another a Utopian.

However, perhaps only Coleridge, of all the important romantic poets, can fairly be accused of Utopianism. The older men were mostly Jacobins first and reactionaries later—the younger died young in the faith for which they had lived; and Hazlitt, the only one of the former who was long to outlive the Congress of Vienna (which insured the victory of counterrevolution in Europe for almost half a century) never wrote anything more Jacobin than his *Spirit of the Age* in 1825.

Incidentally, Hazlitt gives perhaps as complete an explanation as is necessary for the apostacy of so many of the hopeful young radicals of his youth in his famous essay, published in 1817, two years after the Congress of Vienna and the passage of the Corn Laws, on "Toad Eaters and Tyrants." This reads, in part,

> Thus, in the year 1792, Mr. Burke became a pensioner for writing his book against the French Revolution, and Mr. Thomas Paine was outlawed for his Rights of Man. Since that period, the press has been the great enemy of freedom, the whole weight of that immense engine (whether for good or ill) having a fatal bias given to it by the two mainsprings of fear and favor.... We shall not go over the painful list of instances; neither can we forget them. But they all or almost all contrived to sneak over one by one to the side on which "empty praise or solid pudding" was to be got; they could not live without the smiles of the great, nor provide for an increasing establishment without a loss of character; instead of going into some profitable business and exchanging their lyres for ledgers, their pens for ploughs, they chose rather to prostitute their pens to the mock-heroic defence of the most bare-faced of all mummeries, the pretended alliance of kings and people! ... Such is the history and mystery of literary patriotism and prostitution for the last twenty years.

Hazlitt concludes this essay by showing how much more realistic and steeled with class hatred was the radicalism of those romantics whose revolutionary spirits had weathered the storm. He says:

> We formerly gave the Editor of the Times a definition of a true Jacobin as one "who had seen the evening star set over a poor man's cottage, and connected it with the hope of human happiness." ... Since that time our imagination has grown a little less romantic: so we will give him another, which he may chew the cud upon at his leisure. A true Jacobin, then, is one who does not believe in the divine right of kings, or in any

other alias for it. . . . To be a true Jacobin a man must be a good hater. . . . The love of liberty consists in the hatred of tyrants. The true Jacobin hates the enemies of liberty as they hate liberty, with all his strength and with all his might and with all his heart and with all his soul. . . . He never forgets nor forgives any injury done to the people. . . . He makes neither peace nor truce with tyrants. His hatred of wrong ceases only with the wrong. The sense of it, and of the barefaced assumption of the right to inflict it deprives him of his rest. . . . The love of truth is a passion in his mind as the love of power is a passion in the minds of others. Abstract reason, unassisted by passion, is no match for power and prejudice, armed with force and cunning. . . . Hence the defection of modern apostates.

The main body of the romantics to whom Hazlitt refers were the "Lake Poets"—Coleridge, Wordsworth and, by courtesy, Southey; the younger Byron and Shelley; and the "cockney" Lamb, Keats and their friend, Leigh Hunt. But before we turn to them we must consider two isolated figures, Burns and Blake. These, while not well enough known in their own time to have any substantial influence on this romantic revolution in English literature, nevertheless formed its advance guard and gave surpassing expression to some of its most fundamental ideas and attitudes.

AN ADVANCE GUARD

The dispossessed and inarticulate peasantry—the oppressed and miserable city proletariat—found voices of their own in the first two great writers of the romantic revolution which, briefly, formed the second great age of English poetry.

Robert Burns and William Blake, born within two years of each other in the stony Scottish fields and narrow London streets, were utterly dissimilar in individual taste, temperament and genius. But they were identical in their passionate love of freedom, their hatred for tyranny, their deep, lifelong sympathy with the working class of whom they were born and whose lives they shared, and their vehement partisanship in the revolutionary struggles of their own time—first in America, then in France, and always in Scotland and England.

Robert Burns—1759-1796

Burns was born January 25, 1759, in Ayrshire, in a poor clay farm cottage rented by his father. He himself, in an autobiographical passage, describes how, at his birth

> A blast of Janwar' win'
> Blew hansel in on Robin.

It is a matter of record that only a few days later a storm blew down the badly patched gable and mother and child had to take refuge with a neighbour. Although his father was extremely hard working and frugal, as more babies followed Robert into an inhospitable world, he was forced to leave his poor home for a poorer one. When Burns was seven they moved and the next eleven years were one ceaseless losing struggle to make the stony ground yield enough for both rent and porridge.

Burns' brother Gilbert mentions as a recurrent event the letters and visits from the landlord's agent or "factor" which reduced the whole family to tears and Burns himself describes such scenes:

> I've noticed, on our Laird's court-day,
> An' mony a time my heart's been wae,
> Poor tenant bodies, scant o' cash,
> How they maun thole a factor's smash;
> He'll stamp an' threaten, curse and swear,
> He'll apprehend them, pound their gear,
> While they maun stan', in aspect humble,
> And bear it a', an' fear an' tremble.

However, by the time Burns was eighteen several of the sons could assist with the labor of the farm and the family was able to secure a better lease in a more favorable situation.

Although there had been little time for formal schooling—Burns as the eldest was doing a man's work long before he was fourteen—the father valued learning as part of both religion and patriotism. The children had his example and encouragement in reading during their scanty leisure such books as were available of Scottish history and biography, odd plays of Shakespeare, old issues of the Spectator—in short anything that came to hand—as well as the Bible which they had practically memorized. Furthermore, the father had combined with four neighbours to raise a small salary for a young teacher who boarded with one or another of the group and taught all the children for several years. In some ways Burns strayed far from his father's godly path, but he always admired and himself continued the tradition of sturdy independence of spirit, pride in his own useful, arduous life, and affectionate respect for his poor fellow workers which his father felt and taught. He has given us a moving picture of his father in "The Cotter's Saturday Night" and in such songs as:

> My father was a farmer upon the Carrick border, O
> And carefully he reared me in decency and order, O;
> He bade me act a manly part, though I had ne'er a farthing, O,
> For without an honest, manly heart no man was worth regarding, O.

In addition to his unusually wide reading Burns had early been interested by the remnants of the old Scottish songs and ballads still current in the countryside, and was accustomed to sing or whistle them to lighten a long day behind the plow, fitting in missing verse or chorus or composing new words to an old widowed tune.

Burns was almost always falling in—or out—of love during this time and his seemingly whimsical fickleness had a real base in the obvious impossibility of providing any decent maintenance for a wife and family. He proposed to, and was decisively rejected by, the daughter of a neighboring farmer in 1781 and left the farm to seek his fortune in trade in a nearby town. A small business venture he managed to set up failed completely, and he returned, with a heightened distaste for the monotony and hardships of farm life, to find his father dying of consumption and the farm implements, animals, and even family furniture attached for unpaid rent and other debts.

Burns and his brother Gilbert undertook the lease of a barren upland farm a few miles distant. They salvaged some scanty equipment by putting in a formal claim as their father's creditors for arrears of wages, and moved their widowed mother and young brothers and sisters to this new home in March, 1784. By now, Burns had somewhat of a scandalous reputation, not as an idler but as one who played hard in the intervals of working hard, and who drank strong drinks and sang strong songs in taverns of an evening.

Much of this was no doubt justified but far more was due to a small town's shock at his open mockery of its strict Calvinist religion, and still more to his outspoken championship of such "disreputable" causes as American Independence, Negro freedom, and his undisguised contempt for "the unco guid" of every kind and the increasingly reactionary bourgeois values by which they lived. As early as 1781 he had written in mockery of England's part in the war with the colonies:

> I murder hate, by field or flood,
> Though glory's name may screen us;
> In wars at hame I'll spend my blood,
> Life-giving wars of Venus.
> The deities that I adore,
> Are social peace and plenty;
> I'm better pleased to make one more
> Than be the death o' twenty.

More seriously, a little later when a National Thanksgiving was proclaimed for a naval victory, he wrote:

> Ye hypocrites! are these your pranks,
> To murder men, and gie God thanks?
> For shame! gie o'er, proceed no further—
> God won't accept your thanks for murther!

In a letter a few years later praising some verses a friend had written against the slave trade, Burns said:

> The characters and manners of the dealer in the infernal traffic is well done, though a horrid picture . . . The thought that the oppressor's sorrow on seeing the slave pine is like the butcher's regret when his destined lamb dies a natural death is exceedingly fine.

Burns never wavered in these and his other radical opinions. His free-thinking in religion as well as politics merely became more fixed and mature as he became older, as we can see by comparing a letter written in 1788 with one on the same subject written in 1794. The first reads, in part,

> An honest man has nothing to fear.—If we lie down in the grave, the whole man a piece of broken machinery, to moulder with the clods of the valley—be it so; at least there is an end of pain, care, woes and wants: if that part of us called Mind does survive the apparent destruction of the Man—away with old-wife prejudices and tales. . . .

And the second, in 1794:

> All my fears and cares are of this world: if there is another, an honest man has nothing to fear from it.—I hate a man that wishes to be a Deist, but I fear, every fair unprejudiced Enquirer must in some degree be a Sceptic—It is not that there are any very staggering arguments against the Immortality of Man; but that like Electricity, Phlogiston, etc. the subject is so involved in darkness that we want Data to go upon.—One thing frightens me much: that we are to live forever, seems too good news to be true.

Although Burns never changed his early opinions or beliefs he gradually became aware of the futility of an isolated "Bohemian" revolt against bourgeois values and ideas, which could only express itself in personal recklessness or dissipation. He soon realized that bouts of hard drinking and casual lovemaking were worse than useless expressions of his rebellion at the incessant unprofitable labor of a tenant-farmer's life.

Before that, however, he wrote some of the best expressions of this fruitless but sympathetic rebellion of those to whom "the world is not a friend nor the world's law." Most explicit of these was his comic operetta, *The Jolly Beggars*, completed before the publication of his earliest book in 1785, but not published until some years after his death. The concluding song begins:

> See the smoking bowl before us!
>   Mark our jovial, ragged ring!
> Round and round take up the chorus
>   And in raptures let us sing;
>
> *A fig for those by law protected!*
>   *Liberty's a glorious feast!*
> *Courts for cowards were erected,*
>   *Churches built to please the priest!*
>
> What is title? what is treasure!
>   What is reputation's care?
> If we lead a life of pleasure,
>   'Tis no matter, how or where!
>
> With the ready trick and fable
>   Round we wander all the day;
> And at night in barn or stable
>   Hug our doxies on the hay.

When he and his brother first set up for themselves at Mossgiel, he deluded himself into thinking that prudence and industry might insure sufficient success to provide the material for a tolerable life: ordinary comforts; some money for books and, perhaps, occasional short trips; above all, a reasonable amount of leisure for reading and writing.

A letter to a friend written some two years after his father's death tells us something of these illusory hopes, and shows us that Burns soon realized how useless good resolutions without capital were when faced with the innumerable emergencies characteristic of small commodity farming. He wrote:

> I read farming books, I calculated crops, I attended markets, and, in short, in spite of the devil, the world, and the flesh, I should have been a wise man; but the first year, from unfortunately buying bad seed—the second, from a late harvest, we lost half our crops. This overset all my wisdom, and I returned like the dog to his vomit, and the sow that was washed to her wallowing in the mire.

There is obvious and pathetic autobiography in his deservedly popular poem, "To A Mouse On Turning Her Up In Her Nest With The Plough, November, 1785," which ends:

> That wee bit heap o' leaves an' stibble,
> Has cost thee monie a weary nibble!
> Now thou's turned out, for a' thy trouble,
>   But house or hald,
> To thole the winter's sleety dribble,
>   An' cranreuch cauld!
>
> But Mousie, thou art no thy lane,
> In proving foresight may be vain:
> The best-laid schemes o' mice an' men
>   Gang aft agley,
> An' lea'e us nought but grief an' pain,
>   For promis'd joy!
>
> Still thou art blest, compared wi' me!
> The present only toucheth thee:
> But och! I backward cast my e'e,
>   On prospects drear!
> An' forward, tho' I canna see,
>   I guess an' fear!

Despite hardships, worry and failure during the next two years at Mossgiel, Burns managed to turn more consistently and seriously to what had for some time been a barely acknowledged ambition— his desire of expressing in poetry the heroic exploits of:

> A country where civil, and particularly religious liberty, have ever found their first support and their last asylum—; but alas! I am far unequal to the task, both in native genius and in education.

He completed his "reconstruction" of the large number of Scottish folk love songs and ballads which his work has rescued from obscurity and reconstituted a living part of English literature. In addition, he also wrote many of his best known, longer poems, such as "The Cotter's Saturday Night," "The Jolly Beggars," "To A Mouse," "A Mountain Daisy," "The Twa Dogs," and most of his sharpest antireligious satires such as "Holy Willie's Prayer" and "The Holy Fair."

This first full exercise of his creative power did not prevent Burns from feeling deep discouragement with his own failure and the abject poverty and misery he saw on all sides. His brother Gilbert later said that

> Robert used to remark to me that he could not conceive a more mortifying picture of human life than a man seeking work.

And Burns himself said in "Man Was Made to Mourn":

> See yonder poor, o'erlabored wight,
> So abject, mean and vile,
> Who begs a brother of the earth
> To give him leave to toil. . . .

He described a peasant farmer, worn out by unremitting toil before he had reached the prime of life:

> For, ance that five-and-forty speel'd,
> See crazy, weary, joyless eild,
> Wi' wrinkled face,
> Comes hostin' hirplin', owre the field
> Wi' creepin' pace.

Feeling that he was one "So weary with disaster, tugged with fortune" that he had to set his life on any chance "To mend it, or be rid on't," Burns determined on the desperate expedient of emigration to Jamaica. With that in mind, he solicited subscriptions for a memorial publication of his poetry. Six hundred copies were printed in 1786. Their success in the Scottish capital was so immediate and overwhelming that the poet, who had actually engaged steerage passage to the West Indies and had set out to board the ship, returned and went to Edinburgh instead, to find himself temporarily possessed of a huge number of noble patrons, and to become the six months' lion of fashionable society.

A second edition of his poems in April, 1787, sold over 3,000 copies, and a third was immediately demanded. Burns had already begun to resent the patronizing admiration of the genteel; he wrote in a letter March 22, 1787:

> I have the advice of some very judicious friends among the literati here, but with them I sometimes find it necessary to claim the privilege of thinking for myself.

He began, ungratefully many thought, to seek his friends among "not very select society." In the third edition of his poems Burns defiantly included a new ballad on the American War, and on a trip with a member of the not very select society—a radical school teacher—he wrote on the window of an inn in Stirling his famous lines about the House of Hanover:

> An idiot race, to honor lost;
> Who know them best, despise them most.

On being reproved, he quickly added his "self-reproof":

> Dost not know that old Mansfield, who writes like the Bible,
> Says the more 'tis a truth, sir, the more 'tis a libel?

Commenting on the public acknowledgment of King George's insanity, Burns said:

> I am not sure whether he is not a gainer by how much a madman is a more respectable character than a Fool.

Returning home he loaned his brother the better part of the money he had made, married Jean Armour with whom he had had a troubled love affair and who had borne him an illegitimate child

—or, rather, twins—on the eve of his expected emigration, and looked about him for some more stable way of supporting his growing family.

There was a chance of his getting a government post in the excise but Burns' strong opposition to the government and his detestation of the job—apprehending smugglers whose lawbreaking was hardly regarded as reprehensible by most poor Scots—made him refuse the offer with a note:

> The piebald jacket let me patch once more
> On eighteenpence a week, I've lived before.

However, a man who has a wife and children has given hostages to fortune, and in 1788 he accepted the position, putting a good face on the matter in prose letters:

> . . . what will support my family and keep me independent of the world is to me a very important matter; and I had much rather that my Profession borrowed credit from me, than that I borrowed credit from my Profession.

And again:

> The question is not at what door of fortune's palace shall we enter in, but what doors does she open to us?

Yet he complained more honestly, in verse,

> Searching auld wives' barrels,
>   Ochon, the day
> That clarty barm should stain my laurels!
>   But what'll ye say?
> These movin' things ca'd wives an' weans
>   Wad move the very hearts o' stanes.

One of the worst parts of being a "place man," as Burns bitterly called it, was the need of suppressing his republican sentiments, which gathered strength with the early success of the French revolution. True, Burns was very ineffective in his half-hearted efforts at concealment, but he was constantly irritated by the need to make them at all, and often expressed his anger in deliberately dangerous exploits. For example, when on February 2, 1792, several small cannons from a smuggler ship which Burns had captured were sold at auction, he himself bought them and sent them with a letter of greeting to the French convention then meeting in Paris. He also greeted the growing censorship of political views and discussion in England by dedicating to Fox, who opposed these laws, a set of verses beginning:

> Here's freedom to them that wad read,
> Here's freedom to them that would write!
> There's none ever feared that the truth should be heard
> But they whom the truth would indite.

In December of the same year Burns wrote to a friend in England:

> We, in this country, here, have many alarms of the Reform, or rather, the Republican spirit of your part of the kingdom.— Indeed, we are a good deal in commotion ourselves and in our Theatre here. "God Save the King" has met with some groans and hisses while Ca Ira [a then popular street song of the French Revolution] has been repeatedly called for.—For me, I am a Placeman, you know, a very humble one indeed, Heaven knows, but still so much so as to gag me from joining in the cry.—What my private sentiments are, you will find out without an interpreter.

It was certainly easy enough to discover these sentiments when Burns wrote and spoke so freely in private, and in public proposed such scarcely ambiguous toasts as:

> May our success in the present war be equal to the justice of our cause.

We are hardly surprised to learn that he was denounced to the Board of Excise as an enemy of the government, and an agent was sent to investigate him. Although he escaped with a warning from the friendly investigator, he so much resented the whole situation that he wrote bitterly to his patron, the liberal Earl of Mar:

> Does any man tell me, that my feeble efforts can be of no service, and that it does not belong to my humble station to meddle with the concerns of a People?—I tell him, that it is on such individuals as I, that for the hand of support and the eye of intelligence, a Nation has to rest.

These political "indiscretions" of Burns have been as much ignored by most biographers as his amatory and convivial ones have been overemphasized. For example, one of his earliest patrons, the wealthy Mrs. Dunlop, broke off all relations with him in 1794 and of those biographers who mention the episode, almost all accept her account that it was impossible to continue to know anyone who drank so much, loved so widely and sang such coarse songs in such low company. However, just before severing relations with Burns, Mrs. Dunlop, who had four officer sons in the British Army, and two daughters married to French Royalist Emigrés, had received a letter from the poet in which he described Louis XVI as a perjured blockhead and Marie Antoinette as an unprincipled prostitute who met their deserved fate, adding a guarded hope for more scope for revolutionary principles in England!

Mrs. Dunlop was, of course, not alone in her reprobation and Burns' many imprudences, personal as well as political, made life increasingly difficult for him; effectively barring his expected promotion in the Excise. The constant struggle to make ends meet for his five children (his wife had, in 1792, magnanimously adopted her husband's newly born infant, whose mother was a barmaid at the Globe Tavern) and his sharp sense of being in a false position as a "placeman" and recipient of rich men's half-hearted favors, kept Burns from writing much during these last three or four unhappy years. Nevertheless these same years gave birth to some of his most revolutionary poetry, including "A Man's A Man For A' That." The last stanzas of this proletarian anthem ring out prophetically and, in parenthesis, defiantly:

> A prince can mak a belted knight,
>   A marquis, duke, an' a' that!
> But an honest man's aboon his might—
>   Guid faith, he mauna' fa' that!
> For a' that, an' a' that,
>   Their dignities, an' a' that,
> The pith o' sense an' pride o' worth
>   Are higher rank than a' that.
>
> Then let us pray that come it may
>   (As come it will for a' that)
> That Sense and Worth o'er a' the earth
>   Shall bear the gree an' a' that!
> For a' that, an' a' that,
>   It's coming yet for a' that,
> That man to man the world o'er
>   Shall brithers be for a' that.

Then too he wrote the stirring "Bannockburn" which expressed in terms of the already respectable Scottish revolution of 1314 emotions aroused in Burns by the decidedly unsafe one of 1789. As Burns himself said in 1793 in a letter to his friend Thomson, he was inspired to write the poem when, on passing the ancient battle site of Bannockburn, he recollected "that glorious struggle for Freedom, associated with the glowing ideas of some other struggles of the same nature, *not quite so ancient.*"

>Scots, wha hae wi' Wallace bled,
>Scots, wham Bruce has aften led,
>Welcome to your gory bed
>   Or to victorie!
>
>Now's the day, and now's the hour:
>See the front o' battle lour,
>See approach proud Edward's power—
>   Chains and slaverie!
>
>Wha will be a traitor knave?
>Wha can fill a coward's grave?
>Wha sae base as be a slave?—
>   Let him turn, and flee!
>
>Wha for Scotland's King and Law
>Freedom's sword will strongly draw,
>Freeman stand or freeman fa',
>   Let him follow me!
>
>By Oppression's woes and pains,
>By your sons in servile chains,
>We will drain our dearest veins
>   But they shall be free!
>
>Lay the proud usurpers low!
>Tyrants fall in every foe!
>Liberty's in every blow!
>   Let us do, or die!

Toward the end of 1795 Burns became seriously ill of what he referred to as "flying gout"—probably some form of arthritis or rheumatic fever. As a boy of 14 he had done "a man's work" ploughing the heavy fields and had almost succumbed to an attack of the rheumatic fever which, from then on, had affected his heart. He made a partial recovery but caught a severe chill the following spring and suffered a serious relapse. He was confined to bed throughout April, May and June of 1796 and although he was advised to try sea bathing in July, it was obvious to him that he was a dying man. Harassed by debtors and the thought of his family's penniless future (his wife was about to give birth to another child) he was almost beside himself with pain and worry. A letter to his friend Thomson, dated July 12, 1796, gives us some idea of his state of mind:

> After all my boasted independence, curst necessity compels me to implore you for five pounds. A cruel scoundrel of a haberdasher, to whom I owe an account,—taking it into his head that I am dying, has commenced a process, and will infallibly, put me into jail. Do, for God's sake, send that sum, and that by return of post. Forgive me this earnestness, but the horrors of a jail have made me half distracted.

He returned home a week later, lived three or four days in almost constant delirium and died on July 21, at the age of thirty-seven.

Perhaps his best epitaph is the description Hazlitt gave some twenty years later in his lecture on *The English Poets*:

> He had a strong mind and a strong body, the fellow to it. He had a real heart of flesh and blood beating in his bosom—you can almost hear it throb. Someone said, that if you had shaken hands with him, his hand would have burnt yours. The Gods, indeed, "made him poetical"; but nature had a hand in him first. His heart was in the right place. He did not create a soul under the ribs of death by tinkling siren sounds, or by piling up centos of poetic diction; but for the artificial flowers of poetry, he plucked the mountain daisy under his feet; and a field mouse, hurrying from his ruined dwelling could inspire him with the sentiments of terror and pity. Burns was not like Shakespeare in the range of his genius; but there is something of the same magnanimity, directness, and unaffected character about him. He was not a sickly sentimentalist, a namby-pamby poet, a mincing metre ballad-monger, any more than Shakespeare. He would as soon hear "a brazen candlestick tuned on a dry wheel grate on the axle-tree." He was as much of a man—not a twentieth part as much of a poet—as Shakespeare.

William Blake—1757-1827

Blake was born November 28, 1757, in the back room of a dry goods shop owned by his father, a hosier in a small way of business in Soho, London. His parents, who were Swedenborgian Dissenters, were evidently most progressive in their educational attitude, and after the imaginative highstrung little boy, who was their second son, had reacted with overwhelming fury and terror to any attempt at discipline they let him study what he wished at home—largely reading and drawing. At 10 he was sent to the nearby Pars Drawing School where he showed such great aptitude and ability that four years later his father offered to apprentice him to an eminent artist.

However the premium this required would have made substantial inroads upon the small capital set aside for his brothers' start in life and William refused the sacrifice. Instead he asked to be apprenticed to an engraver where for a premium of 50 pounds he could secure seven years training. This training creditably completed, William at 21 began to work at his trade and to court a pretty flirtatious young girl who, at the end of two years' "keeping company" informed him he was only one of several and that she had no intentions, honorable or otherwise.

William evidently made no secret of his broken heart for when he was bemoaning it one day to some humble neighbors the daughter of the family, whom he had just met, said warmly "I pity you." "Do you so?" "I do indeed." "Then I love you," said Blake. And with no further courtship a proposal and acceptance were concluded.

Catherine Boucher could neither read nor write, and Blake's parents objected to the match, but a year's hard work enabled him to save enough for independent housekeeping and the young couple were married August 18, 1782.

He taught her not only to read and write but also to paint and to assist him in his engraving, and the precipitate engagement began a devoted loving companionship of over forty years. To the end Catherine worshiped her husband, called him Mr. Blake, treasured his work, and assisted at, if she did not actually share in, his visions. Her only recorded complaint is the comment to a friend, "I have very little of Mr. Blake's company. He is always in Paradise."

As for Blake, he refers to her in a letter written after some twenty years marriage as "my dear and too careful and ever-joyous woman" and, discussing a projected move to the seashore, says:

> Eartham will be my first temple and altar; my wife is like a flame of many colours of precious jewels whenever she hears it mentioned.

Some ten years later a friend, Tatham, who was a frequent and intimate visitor in their home, says:

> His wife being to him a very patient woman, he fancied that while she looked on him as he worked, her sitting quite still by his side, doing nothing, soothed his impetuous mind; and he has many a time, when a strong desire presented itself to overcome any difficulty in his plates or drawings, in the middle of the night, risen, and requested her to get up with him, and sit by his side, in which she cheerfully acquiesced.

Working in bed a few days before his death Blake had just finished coloring an etching and put it down saying, "There. I can do no more." The implication that this was his last work distressed his wife who turned away but was arrested by Blake's saying, "Stay, keep as you are; you have ever been an angel to me; I will draw you."

It is comforting to have this picture of a happy marriage, for there was little else of happiness or comfort in Blake's long life. His career has perhaps best been summarized in a few sentences by J. Bronowski, author of *Blake: A Man Without a Mask*, who says:

> At 14 Blake had chosen to be an engraver and he held to that choice until he died. . . . Blake was nearly 40 before he was asked to engrave the first large book of his own designs, to Edward Young's Night Thoughts. It was printed in the slump of 1797 and failed. Thereafter Blake seldom had enough even of hack work, and lived when he could, by patronage. A second book of his designs, to Robert Blair's The Grave was printed in 1808, but it had been given to another to engrave thus making Blake 20 pounds instead of 200. Blake held a show of his work through the summer of 1809. It failed. We do not know how he lived for the next 10 years. The slumps had deepened, inflation and unemployment were growing unchecked. . . . John Linnell [a young painter whom he met in 1818] got the Royal Academy to give Blake 25 pounds in 1822. But to keep Blake alive, he had to commission most of his work. Only thus did Blake at last salvage half a dozen years of passable comfort and dignity. He used them to make his best engravings, for the Book of Job, and his finest designs, for Dante's Divine Comedy. Yet when Job was printed, a year before Blake died, it failed.
>
> It is a story to put its age to shame; decent, humdrum, and hopeless. But it is not an uncommon, it is not even a personal story. . . . The disaster was not in his [Blake's] gifts but in the

everyday of his world. The disaster was the world. . . . There is nothing odd in what happened to Blake; for it was happening to many thousand others. The fine London watchmakers were becoming hands in sweatshops. The learned societies of the Spitalfield silk weavers were rioting for bread. The small owners were losing their place and their skilled workers were losing their livelihood. It is a murderous story and it is Blake's story. But it is not the poet's story nor the painter's. It is the story of Blake, the engraver.

This is true. Blake did not fail because he was a poet but because the growth of industrial wealth and power, in its absolute impoverishment of the working class, destroyed the market for the craft he had been trained to and made it impossible for him to earn a decent living through the use of his skill.

Nevertheless, in another sense this *is* the story of the poet as well as that of the engraver. For Blake not only suffered the same fate as the other craftsmen around him. He felt, understood, and expressed that fate in some of the greatest, most powerful poetry the world has ever known.

Over and over again, in a few unforgettable lines Blake gives us the essence of the factory system—the "dark satanic mills" which left men unemployed, killed children, and forced prostitution through the starvation wages it paid their mothers.

He uses the word "chartered" (monopolized) with the force of a curse or a blow and puts his finger unerringly on the deliberate employment of religion to sanctify tyranny and of both to make property power supreme over human rights.

For example, two poems, "London" and "Holy Thursday," published in his *Songs of Experience* in 1794, read unforgettably:

> I wander through each chartered street,
>   Near where the chartered Thames does flow,
> And mark in every face I meet,
>   Marks of weakness, marks of woe.
>
> In every cry of every man,
>   In every infant's cry of fear,
> In every voice, in every ban,
>   The mind-forged manacles I hear:
>
> How the chimney-sweeper's cry
>   Every blackening church appals,
> And the hapless soldier's sigh
>   Runs in blood down palace-walls.

> But most, through midnight streets I hear
> How the youthful harlot's curse
> Blasts the new-born infant's tear,
> And blights with plagues the marriage-hearse.

And:

> Is this a holy thing to see
> In a rich and fruitful land,—
> Babes reduced to misery,
> Fed with cold and usurous hand?
>
> Is that trembling cry a song?
> Can it be a song of joy?
> And so many children poor?
> It is a land of poverty!
>
> And their sun does never shine,
> And their fields are bleak and bare,
> And their ways are filled with thorns,
> It is eternal winter there.
>
> For where'er the sun does shine,
> And where'er the rain does fall,
> Babe can never hunger there,
> Nor poverty the mind appal.

Even before his lovely *Songs of Innocence* (1787-1789) he had already demanded:

> Why should I care for the men of Thames,
> And the cheating waters of charter'd streams
> Or shrink at the little blasts of fear
> That the hireling blows into mine ear?
>
> Tho' born on the cheating banks of Thames—
> Tho' his waters bathed my infant limbs,
> The Ohio shall wash his stains from me;
> I was born a slave, but I go to be free.

And two years later the *Book of Thel* contained such lyrics as:

> There souls of men are bought and sold,
> And milk-fed infancy for gold;
> And youth to slaughterhouses led,
> And beauty for a bit of bread.

. . . .
         The sword sung on the barren heath
         The sickle in the fruitful field:
         The sword he sung a song of death
         But could not make the sickle yield.

Even his "prophetic books," which he rightly considered oratory rather than poetry, and which finally wound up in an incomprehensible welter of myth and ethical symbolism, begin with a celebration of *The French Revolution* in 1791. It was so forthright a book that the radical printer Joseph Johnson, publisher of Mary Wollstonecraft's *Vindication of the Rights of Women* and William Godwin's *Enquiry Concerning Political Justice,* dared to set up only the first volume in type—we have a proof edition marked "One Shilling"—and never offered even that for sale!

It may surprise many who have heard of Blake only as an unworldly mystic or visionary to see how unambiguous, direct and specific his political statements here are. *The French Revolution,* Book I, begins:

   The dead brood over Europe, the cloud and vision descends
      over cheerful France;
   O cloud well appointed! Sick, sick, the Prince on his couch
      wreath'd in dim
   And appalling mist, his strong hand outstretched, from his
      shoulder down the bond
   Runs aching cold into the scepter, too heavy for mortal grasp,
      no more
   To be swayed by visible hand, nor in cruelty bruise the mild
      flourishing mountains.

Later the book continues even more topically:

   The American War began; all its dark hours passed before my
      face
   Across the Atlantic to France; then the French Revolution
      commenced in thick clouds—
   . . . the Commons convene in the Halls of the Nation; like
      spirits of fire in the beautiful
   Porches of the sun. . . .
   . . . The Ancient dawn calls us
   To awake from slumber of five thousand years.

This first of the prophetic books may not all be real poetry, but certainly it all makes very clear Blake's essential concern with the things of this world. After reading it we are hardly surprised to hear from one of his earliest biographers, Gilchrist, something which later ones have largely overlooked in their eagerness to ascertain whether at the age of eight he did or did not say he had seen a tree full of angels on Peckham Rye. Gilchrist says that at the time of the French Revolution Blake was

> an ardent member of the New School, a vehement republican and sympathizer with the Revolution. . . . [For him] the French Revolution was the herald of the Millenium, of a new age of light and reason. He courageously donned the famous symbol of liberty and equality—the bonnet rouge—in open day, and philosophically walked the streets with the same on his head. . . .

It was at the end of this year, 1791, that Blake saved Thomas Paine's life. Paine had been telling Blake and a few other radical friends, who customarily met at the home of the publisher, Johnson, about a speech he had made the night before. Blake asked, "Did you really say all that?' 'and on being assured by Paine that he had, responded, "Then you must not go home, or you are a dead man." Paine took the matter more lightly but Blake persisted until Paine had agreed to spend the night secretly at a friend's home and leave for France next morning. The next day Paine set sail from Dover less than an hour before an officer with a warrant for his arrest on capital charges, which had been issued the day before, arrived there to intercept him after having vainly sought him at his lodging.

Blake's concrete concern with current events is again apparent in the next of his prophetic books, *America*, written two years later, which begins almost matter of factly:

> The Guardian Prince of Albion [England] burns in his nightly tent.
> Sullen fires across the Atlantic glow to America's shore,
> Piercing the souls of warlike men who rise in silent night.
> Washington, Franklin, Paine & Warren, Gates, Hancock & Green
> Meet on the coast glowing with blood from Albion's fiery Prince.

Washington spoke: "Friends of America! look over the Atlantic sea;
A bended bow is lifted in heaven, & a heavy iron chain
Descends, link by link, from Albion's cliffs across the sea, to bind
Brothers & sons of America till our faces pale & yellow,
Heads deprest, voices weak, eyes downcast, hands work-bruised,
Feet bleeding on the sultry sands, & the furrows of the whip
Descend to generations that in future times forget."

It continues with rising intensity, after describing the outbreak of war:

Albion is sick! America faints! enraged the zenith grew
As human blood shooting its veins all round the orbed heaven,
Red rose the clouds from the Atlantic in vast wheels of blood,
And in the red clouds rose a Wonder o'er the Atlantic Sea,
. . . .
The King of England looking westward trembles at the vision.
. . . . . .
The morning comes, the night decays, the watchmen leave their stations;
The grave is burst, the spices shed, the linen wrapped up;
The bones of death, the cov'ring clay, the sinews shrunk and dry'd
Reviving shake, inspiring move, breathing, awakening,
Spring like redeemed captives when their bonds and bars are burst.
Let the slave grinding at the mill run out into the field,
Let him look up into the heavens and laugh in the bright air;
Let the unchained soul, shut up in darkness and in sighing,
Whose face has never seen a smile in thirty weary years,
Rise and look out; his charms are loose, his dungeon doors are open;
And let his wife and children return from the oppressor's scourge.
They look behind at every step and believe it is a dream,
Singing "The Sun has left this blackness and has found a fresher morning.
And the fair Moon rejoices in the clear and cloudless night;
For Empire is no more, and now the Lion and Wolf shall cease."

Even as reaction deepened in England and Blake was forced to conclude his celebration premature, he still in his next prophetic book, *Europe,* made his practical interest and radical attitude manifest. The book is deeply unhappy and, perhaps, discouraged, but neither resigned nor intimidated:

> Every house a den, every man bound; the shadows are filled
> With spectres, & the windows wove over with curses of iron:
> Over the doors "Thou shalt not," & over the chimney "Fear"
> is written:
> With bands of iron around their necks fasten'd into the walls
> The citizens, in leaden gyves the inhabitants of suburbs
> Walk heavy; soft & bent are the bones of villagers.

In 1793 *The Marriage of Heaven and Hell* has the thought-provoking motto:

> He who loves his enemies, hates his friends;
> This is surely not what Jesus intends.

Other prose "Proverbs of Hell" in the same book are equally noteworthy for their profound and original reflection of social relations, for example: "Where man is not, nature is barren."

Partly because of a growing caution rendered necessary by the antiseditious writings decree of 1792 and the many others which rapidly followed it, and partly because of the total lack of an audience, or even the hope of one, which would have kept Blake thinking in terms of direct communication, his symbolism in the prophetic books became increasingly cloudy and involved. Yet the *Song of Los,* written in 1795, goes on to give an even more penetrating insight into the essential and particular nature of the new kind of economic oppression which industrial capitalism had introduced.

The difference between the accidental natural famines of a more primitive economy and the deliberate man-made famines of industrialism is brilliantly summarized in Blake's description of England as

> Heaps of smoking ruins
> In the midst of prosperity and wantonness.

His amazing, prescient understanding of the world in which unemployment is a necessary condition of production and men starve in the midst of plenty is given in such passages as:

>Shall not the King call for Famine from the heath,
>Nor the Priest for Pestilence from the fen,
>To restrain, to dismay, to thin
>The inhabitants of mountain and plain
>In the day of full-feeding prosperity
>And the night of delicious songs?
>
>Shall not the Councellor throw his curb
>Of Poverty on the laborious,
>To fix the price of labour,
>To invent allegoric riches?
>
>And the privy admonishers of men
>Call for fires in the City,
>For heaps of smoking ruins
>In the night of prosperity & wantonness?
>
>To turn man from his path,
>To restrain the child from the womb,
>To cut off the bread from the city,
>That the remnant may learn to obey,
>
>That the pride of the heart may fail,
>That the lust of the eye may be quench'd,
>That the delicate ear in its infancy
>May be dull'd, & the nostrils clos'd up,
>To teach mortal worms the path
>That leads from the gates of the grave.

Three years later, Blake commented more prosaicly and satirically but scarcely more plainly on Malthus' popular *Essay on The Principle of Population* and those who solemnly quoted it in attacking the "extravagance" of destitution and "the undeserving poor." Blake wrote bitterly:

>When a man looks pale
>With labour & abstinence, say he looks healthy & happy;
>And when his children sicken, let them die; there are enough
>Born, even too many, & our Earth will be overrun
>Without these arts.
>Preach temperance; say he is over gorg'd & drowns his wit
>In strong drink, tho you know that bread & water are all
>He can afford.

But by this time a systematic policy of repression and intimidation had left few who still shared Blake's revolutionary ardors, and fewer still who would have had the courage to discuss or even to read them. Blake therefore wrote very little after the turn of the century except for epigrams and fragments confided to private letters or, more often, his journals.

The *Auguries of Innocence* (1801-1803) contain such characteristic and pregnant couplets as:

> The Babe that weeps the Rod beneath
> Writes Revenge in realms of Death
> The Beggar's Rags, fluttering in Air,
> Does to Rags the Heavens tear.
> The Soldier, armed with Sword & Gun,
> Palsied strikes the Summer's Sun.
> The poor Man's Farthing is worth more
> Than all the Gold on Afric's Shore.
> One Mite wrung from the Labourer's hands
> Shall buy & sell the Miser's Lands;
> Or, if protected from on high,
> Does that whole Nation sell & buy.
> . . . . .
> The Questioner, who sits so sly,
> Shall never know how to Reply.
> He who replies to words of Doubt
> Doth put the Light of Knowledge out.
> The Strongest Poison ever known
> Came from Caesar's Laurel Crown.
> Naught can Deform the Human Race
> Like to the Armour's iron brace.
> When Gold and Gems adorn the Plow
> To peaceful Arts shall Envy bow.
> A Riddle, or the Cricket's Cry,
> Is to Doubt a fit Reply.

As late as 1804 we find an occasional lyric, like the famous one below, written as a preface to *Milton*, which shows the same surpassing power and beauty as the greatest of those composed in his youth.

> And did those feet in ancient time
>   Walk upon England's mountain green?
> And was the holy Lamb of God
>   On England's pleasant pastures seen?
>
> And did the Countenance Divine
>   Shine forth upon our clouded hills?
> And was Jerusalem builded here
>   Among those dark Satanic mills?

> Bring me my bow of burning gold!
> Bring me my arrows of desire!
> Bring me my spear: O clouds, unfold!
> Bring me my chariot of fire!
>
> I will not cease from mental fight,
> Nor shall my sword sleep in my hand,
> Till we have built Jerusalem
> In England's green and pleasant land.

However, public indifference, the long introspection of what was really a twenty-year brooding soliloquy, and a growing detachment from the world around him combined to make the later prophetic books, written in a sort of semireligious arbitrary mythology, increasingly obscure in form and "metaphysical" in content.

This has given some basis for the academic misinterpretation of his whole work which traditionally omits his actual subject matter and distorts his intense imaginative vision of social evil into a rootless mystical abstraction. Yet as Bronowski truly says of the last of the prophetic books,

> Years of greater hardship, for him & for England, had turned his hopes to despair. . . . When men change thus, they commonly also become social reactionaries. Wordsworth, Coleridge and Southey had done so; Blake alone did not. Having grown to hate the wars of nations and of parties, he may even have come to see the social war more sharply. Milton and Jerusalem have put aside the symbols of England at war with France. The symbol of the rich making war upon the poor is the plainer in them.

Naturally the traditional picture of a mystic visionary—sometimes even an insane one—makes frequent use of Blake's many unorthodox statements about the reality of spiritual life—statements made the more often because of his anger at the mechanical materialism and smug utilitarianism by which he was surrounded. However, his insistence on the reality of miracles, for example, should be understood in the context of such a comment as the following which he made on Paine's *Age of Reason*. This shows very clearly how far he was from implying any supernatural force in his assertion of man's miraculous power.

> Is it a greater miracle to feed five thousand men with five loaves than to overthrow all the armies of Europe with a small

pamphlet? Look over the events of your own life & if you do not find that you have both done such miracles & lived by such you do not see as I do. True, I cannot do a miracle thru experiment & to domineer over & prove to others my superior power, as neither could Christ. But I can do work such as both astonish & comfort me & mine. How can Paine, the worker of miracles, ever doubt Christ's in the above sense of the word miracle?

And the meaning of his self named prophetic books can only be understood in the light of his own comment:

> Every honest man is a Prophet; he utters his opinion both of private and public matters. Thus: If you go on so, the result is so, for he never says, such a thing shall happen let you do what you will.

In the same way Blake frequently and, one is tempted to think, often maliciously, puzzled and bewildered his more literal minded acquaintance with his accounts of conversations with such great predecessors as Isaiah, Shakespeare, and Milton. Again it would seem that the following detailed account from one of his most puzzled contemporaries speaks for itself—and for him.

Crabb Robinson, a well meaning literary gossip and friend of poets, attracted to Blake a few years before his death in 1827 by the many stories of eccentricity which were fashionably repeated, visited him a half a dozen times and took detailed notes of their conversations for the benefit of posterity. He reports with great bewilderment such "unChristian" and "insane" remarks as "Jesus is the living god. So am I. And so are you." And "I have spent much time with Socrates. I think I am he—no, a sort of brother of his." And, at more length,

> "I have had," he said, "much intercourse with Voltaire; and he said to me 'I blasphemed the Son of Man, and it shall be forgiven me, but my enemies blasphemed the Holy Ghost in me, and it shall not be forgiven to them.'" I ask him [Robinson's notes solemnly report] in what language Voltaire spoke. His answer was ingenius and gave me no encouragement to cross-questioning. "To my sensations it was English. It was like the touch of a musical key; he touched it probably French but to my ear it became English." I also inquired as I had before about the form of the spirits who appeared to him and asked why he did not draw them. "It is not worth while" he said. "Besides there are so many that the labour would be great. And there would be no use in it."

Crabb Robinson was, however, an honest man who reported the truth even when he could not understand it, and he concludes another note on Blake with the puzzled comment, "At the same time that he asserted his own possession of this gift of Vision, he did not boast of it as peculiar to himself; all men might have it if they would."

Although Blake was evidently sometimes prone to answer a fool according to his folly, he often explained in sober earnest his ideas of the essential truth of art. For example, in a letter written in 1799 to a patron who wished an altogether factual illustration to some work, and objected to Blake's imaginative sketches as being "unnatural" and "unreal" Blake wrote:

> . . . I know that this world is a world of imagination and vision. I see everything I paint in this world, but everybody does not see alike. To the eyes of a miser a guinea is far more beautiful than the sun, & a bag worn with the use of money has more beautiful proportions than a vine filled with grapes. The tree which moves some to tears of joy is in the eyes of others only a green thing which stands in the way. Some see Nature all ridicule & deformity, & by these I shall not regulate my proportions; & some scarce see Nature at all. But to the eyes of the man of imagination, Nature is Imagination itself. As a man is, so he sees. As the eye is formed, such are its powers. You certainly mistake when you say that the visions of fancy are not to be found in this world. To me this world is all one continuous vision of fancy or imagination. . . .

In the course of a similar argument ten years later Blake said even more forcefully:

> "What," it will be questioned, "when the sun rises do you not see a round disk of fire something like a guinea?" Oh! no! no! I see an innumerable company of the heavenly host crying —"Holy, holy, holy, is the Lord God Almighty!" I question not my corporeal eye any more than I would question a window concerning a sight. I look through it & not with it.

Even more succinctly and conclusively he says in verse:

> For double the vision my eyes do see,
> And a double vision is always with me
> With my inward eyes, 'tis an old man grey,
> With my outward, a thistle across my way.

After a completely unsuccessful exhibition of his work in his brother James' draper shop in the year 1809, Blake drops out of sight for almost ten years. Even Charles Lamb, one of the very few who had been favorably impressed by the exhibition, refers to him during this time in terms that make it clear he thinks he may have died, and there is no other contemporary comment at all.

When we catch sight of him again in 1818 he and his wife are living and working in one room in conditions of extreme poverty and complete obscurity. Through a fortunate accident—for Blake and for us—a young painter, John Linnell, met him at this time, was deeply impressed with both his art and his philosophy, and introduced him to a small circle of other young artists and intellectuals who admired him, met frequently at his home which they named "The House of the Interpreter," and warmed his last years with companionship, admiration and some degree of material comfort.

They themselves had grown up after the Congress of Vienna, and were uneasily seeking for some oasis in the desert where only Hazlitt's voice still recalled the hopes of the Romantic Revolution. Already imbued with the acceptance of a false dichotomy between the artist and the ordinary man, they sought an answer in a sort of early pre-Raphaelite return to a wistfully imagined freer ancient world, and in various religious enthusiasms, and they discovered Blake with excitement. They were, of course, largely unaware of the reality of social revolution which had been the original subject and inspiration of his prophetic books and which still gave them, in all their metaphysical rambling, some misunderstood but dimly sensed reality, for as Bronowski says: "There is no doubt what makes Blake's mysticism uncommon; alone among such otherworldly thinkers he founded it on a harsh understanding of the actual."

But Blake was too old and worn out to try to enlist converts or to hope again for any immediate changes. Occasionally a flash of his old spirit showed through as when, one day, weary of the mechanical materialism of contemporary science and its disregard for the significance of man, he interrupted a discussion about the structure of the universe by declaring:

> It is false. I walked the other evening to the end of the world and touched the sky with my finger.

His values, however, had never changed and in the last few months of his life in 1827 he wrote in a letter to a friend:

Since the French Revolution Englishmen are inter-measurable by one another; certainly a happy state of agreement in which I for one do not agree. God help you and me from the divinity of yes and no too—the yea, nay, creeping Jesus—from supposing up and down to be the same thing. . . .

Perhaps the best summary criticism of Blake—and his academic biographers and aesthetic critics—is Bronowski's conclusion:

> . . . Blake's thought rested squarely on the world in which he lived. The two revolutions which shook that world were actual in his life, and are actual in his writings. Unless we see them there, we cannot read his writings rightly; and shall find them eccentric, as his life has been found eccentric. Blake's life was not eccentric, whether Thomas Butts did once see him and his wife naked; or whether he did not. We find it eccentric only if we miss its context, which is made by his writings and his times together; the context of a man living in a public, not a private world. If we give our fancy to the privacy of a man who gave his mind to living in public, we shall needs find him eccentric; but the eccentricity is ours. . . . What is true of Blake's psychological is true of his social outlook. Like others, Blake speaks the discontent of his time. Until we know the discontent, we do not begin to read his writings, because we do not speak their language. It is a noble language, and we should be proud that Blake shared it with Paine, with Priestley and with William Howe. . . .

THE SPIRIT OF 1789

William Wordsworth—1770-1850

William Wordsworth, the second of five children, was born in a small town in the North of England in 1770. When he was eight his mother died, and William and his older brother were sent to a little grammar school in the north country village of Hawkshead. Their only sister, Dorothy, was for some years happily placed with a friend of their mother's.

The school, largely attended by farmers' sons, seems also to have been a happy choice. There were friendly teachers, considerable freedom, and an unusual degree of democracy. The resident pupils boarded in two's and three's with poor cottagers in the village, and were allowed to spend much time on the nearby hills, often making all day fishing and climbing expeditions unsupervised and, in Wordsworth's case at least, unaccompanied.

When his father, a busy lawyer and steward or estate manager, died very suddenly five years later, the younger boys were also sent to school and Dorothy, then eleven, was soon after transferred to the home of their grandparents, who seem to have been exceptionally cold and unpleasant people.

Dorothy writes in a letter in 1787: "I was for a whole week kept in expectation of my brothers, who staid at school all the time after the vacation began owing to the ill nature of my uncle who would not send horses for them. . . . This was the beginning of my mortification, for I felt that if they had had another home to go to, they would have been behaved to in a very different manner, and received with more chearful countenances, indeed nobody but myself expressed one wish to see them."

A little later she writes: ". . . Yesterday morning I parted with the kindest and most affectionate of Brothers, I cannot paint to you my distress at their departure. . . ."

This strong affection William, who is generally the center of her references to "brothers" and is often named individually, fully reciprocated. But otherwise he seems to have been—or, this early, have become—a solitary, self-sufficient, rather reserved boy already extraordinarily affected by "mountains, rocks, and trees" and much more absorbed in reading than he was to be in his later years.

He himself has often, in his poetry, reverted to and described his emotional life in those early school years when

> . . . The sounding cataract
> Haunted me like a passion; the tall rock,
> The mountain, and the deep and gloomy wood,
> Their colours and their forms, were then to me
> An appetite; a feeling and a love
> That had no need of a remoter charm
> By thought supplied, or any interest
> Unborrowed from the eye. . . .

At seventeen, reluctant to become a law student, as his older brother Richard had done, or to commit himself definitely to the Church, he agreed to go to Cambridge which, his uncles felt, would prepare him for—and he himself felt would at least delay his entrance upon—either of the professions.

There he did fairly well, with neither effort nor interest, was mildly but not painfully or conspicuously unsocial, and found the pleasant cultivated south of England countryside no substitute for the wild north country he and Dorothy both loved so fiercely. Most of his vacations were spent in Hawkshead, and he and Dorothy managed to see each other briefly only a few times.

In 1790, before his graduation, he spent the summer on a walking tour in France, Switzerland and Italy, drawn abroad by a strong acknowledged desire for travel and new mountains and perhaps an unconscious, certainly unacknowledged, eagerness to see the place where, as he later wrote:

> The dread Bastille,
> With all the chambers in its horrid towers
> Fell to the ground;—by violence overthrown
> Of indignation; and with shouts that drowned
> The crash it made in falling!

However, to all outward seeming, Wordsworth was, until this time, remarkably unaffected by the year-old excitement over the French Revolution. His detachment from people and their hopes or fears was still undisturbed, and his imagination had yet to thrill to anything besides Nature. He has, later, told us that in his heart

> . . . a passion, she, [Nature]
> A rapture often, and immediate love
> Ever at hand; he [man] only a delight
> Occasional, an accidental grace,
> His hour being not yet come.

His full awakening to vital concern with the struggles of mankind for liberation was not to come for another two years, but even in this first brief visit to France he was thrilled into human sympathy. The French people in 1790 confidently expected encouragement and support from their free neighbor state which had made a revolution and beheaded a king over a century before, and greeted every Englishman as an ambassador of freedom. Wordsworth, again in his autobiographical *Prelude,* says:

> How bright a face is worn when joy of one
> Is joy for tens of millions.

and, in a "Sonnet from Calais":

> A homeless sound of joy was in the sky;
> From hour to hour the antiquated Earth

Beat like the heart of Man; songs, garlands, mirth,
Banners and happy faces far and nigh.

On his return to England he completed his college course and was duly graduated but delayed taking orders, first on the grounds of being too young, and then on no grounds except an unadmitted aversion for the career implied. He wrote to a friend at this time: "It is at present my intention to take orders in the approaching spring. . . . Had it been in my power I should certainly have wished to defer the moment."

Meanwhile he lived rather idly and aimlessly in London on an allowance continued with increasing unwillingness by his guardians and suddenly, in the fall of 1792, after a brief meeting with Dorothy, decided to return to France. His avowed purpose was to learn the language perfectly so that he might secure a position as tutor and traveling companion for one of the many wealthy young men who customarily completed their education by taking the "Grand Tour."

In France he settled in Blois and, for the first time in his life, entered into a close and intimate association with a friend, a man of thirty-seven, Michel Beaupuy. Captain Beaupuy was a nobleman by birth, one of five brothers who had all thrown in their lot with the revolution and fought for the republic for which he and two more of them were soon to die.

Wordsworth soon shared his enthusiasm for and, more unusual, his understanding of, the real meaning of the revolution and, as he described at length in *The Prelude*, spent whole days, weeks and months in talking to and learning from his friend.

He also, naturally, made other acquaintances and, perhaps after Captain Beaupuy was ordered away on active duty, entered into a love affair with a young woman of royalist sympathies, Annette de Vallon, some four years older than himself.

His guardians had for some time been threatening to discontinue his allowance entirely and in the fall, just when Annette's pregnancy made more money necessary, they carried out their threat. Wordsworth waited until the child (a daughter, Caroline) was born and in December left for England promising to come back with funds as soon as possible.

He returned, a convinced republican, to an England of the anti-sedition laws, of Burke's apostasy, and of growing repression and real danger to all outspoken progressives. However, Wordsworth's convictions were deeply felt and openly proclaimed and he soon became friendly with the group of young radicals who surrounded William Godwin, still at this time considered an active political leader.

Even Louis XVI's execution, which was the signal for a wave of reactionary terror by the government and a series of public recantations by former liberals, did not make Wordsworth waver. In fact, one of these recantations by the Bishop of Llandoff, was the occasion for the most complete and explicit statement of Wordsworth's political ideas which we have.

The Bishop, formerly a pseudo-liberal, felt that the time had come to purge himself of his now dangerous reputation and ideas, and on January 15, 1793, preached a shocking sermon on "The Wisdom and Goodness of God in Having Made Both Rich and Poor," which was published with an appendix, "Strictures on the French Revolution and The British Constitution."

Wordsworth immediately wrote "A Letter To The Bishop of Llandoff On The Extraordinary Avowal Of His Political Principles Contained In The Appendix To His Late Sermon—By A Republican."

It proved impossible to find a publisher willing to risk prosecution by printing it, and the letter was finally sent to the Bishop in manuscript, of which several copies had been pretty widely circulated among the young radicals in London. This document, interesting in itself, is doubly important because it contains the only full explicit contemporary statement of Wordsworth's political views in his revolutionary period.

Wordsworth, like Thomas Paine, considered himself an adherent of the French moderate republicans, or Girondists, and the friends he had left in Paris were entirely of that party. But even its fall, the execution of many of its leaders, and the wildly exaggerated reports of the consequent "Reign of Terror" which were circulated and almost universally believed in England, failed to shake his faith in the revolution.

He exulted when Prime Minister Pitt's prophecy of an easy victory for the British forces in two or three engagements was disproved:

> I knew that wound external could not take
> Life from the young Republic; that new foes
> Would only follow, in the path of shame,
> Their brethren, and Her triumph be in the end
> Great, universal, irresistible.

He steadfastly answered those who claimed bloody horrors were the natural and inevitable result of radical ideas by saying (as Dickens later showed in his *Tale of Two Cities*) that actually the excesses (which he believed greater than they were) came from

> . . . a terrific reservoir of guilt
> And ignorance filled up from age to age
> That could no longer hold its loathsome charge
> But burst and spread in fury through the land.

As late as November, 1794, after England had been at war with France for almost a year, he wrote to a radical friend, Matthews, asking his help to secure a job on the staff of an antigovernment paper, for "I cannot abet, in the smallest degree, the measures pursued by the present ministry. They are already so deeply advanced in iniquity that, like Macbeth, they cannot retreat."

The failure of this project left Wordsworth in a serious predicament. The small remainder of his inheritance was tied up in a lawsuit which was not, as it turned out, settled for another ten years, and his guardians were naturally unwilling to advance any further sums to finance an idle and rebellious life. His only published work—a small volume of poems called *Evening Walk and Descriptive Sketches*—written before his stay in France, had attracted even less attention than it deserved. As Wordsworth despondently wrote to a friend: "What is to become of me, I know not."

At this juncture he renewed his acquaintance with a former schoolmate, Raisley Calvert, a young man of republican sympathies who was greatly impressed with Wordsworth's ideas and writing. He quixotically offered to share half his income with him. This Wordsworth refused, but he accepted an invitation to act as traveling companion for a few weeks since that would enable him to visit Dorothy who, although at a distance, was still his closest friend and warmest supporter. Her frequent letters and uncritical adoration must have been a great comfort to him in this period of frustration and indecision and he seems to have shared in her deeply felt desire that the two of them set up a home in some small country cottage where William would be free to study and write.

For Dorothy this was a daydream of very long standing and she often wrote of it to friends as well as to William. In one letter in 1793 she says,

> When I think of winter, I hasten to furnish our little parlor.
> I close the shutters; brighten the fire. When our refreshment is

ended, I produce our work, and William brings his book to our table, and contributes at once to our instruction and amusement; and at intervals we lay aside the book, and each hazards our observations upon what has been read, without the fear of censure or ridicule.

The two were therefore ecstatically happy when young Calvert's loan of a farmhouse enabled them to set up housekeeping together for some five weeks, even though it was necessary for them to make their breakfast and supper of milk and bread, and dine chiefly upon potatoes during the entire period. They both hopelessly wished for some turn of fortune which would make it possible for them to live permanently in more or less the same fashion. When, within the year, young Calvert's death brought William a legacy of £900 they hesitated no longer. They settled at Racedom in a large farmhouse, lent to them rent free for two years on condition that they would perform certain slight chores for the absent owner.

Dorothy was perfectly happy. Her passionate communion with nature and her devoted love for her brother could both be indulged uninterruptedly and she had nothing left to wish for.

William was still deeply troubled by the social evils he had left behind. Yet—he *had* left them behind. Mail came only once a week. A large part of his time was devoted to the necessary work of a vegetable garden, firewood, and other chores. More was devoted to rediscovering nature in Dorothy's sensitive and perceptive company, in reading and in writing. There was no luxury, idleness or superfluity to make him feel guilty, and few of their simple farmer neighbors spent less for material comforts than did the Wordsworths.

Finally, there was no real political organization or practical political activity among the young radicals he had left behind in London to make Wordsworth feel he had deserted a post of duty.

It is, therefore, not difficult to understand how he could, for a while, continue to hold unshaken his republican convictions while gradually losing himself in the delights of a renewed love of nature and the first real home he had known since his mother's death seventeen years before. To this idyllic life was soon added the stimulation of a vital intellectual companionship and plans for a far-reaching cultural revolution.

Two "notorious" young radicals, Samuel Taylor Coleridge and Robert Southey, were in 1795 making themselves a nuisance to the authorities by poems and lectures which attempted to stir the population of nearby Bristol against the war with France.

One of these, the twenty-three-year-old Coleridge, was already, and perhaps correctly, considered by young English intellectuals to be the most brilliant and original thinker of the century. His later analyses of Shakespeare were the first and are still the best of psychological Shakesperian analyses, and he was perhaps the only contemporary keen enough to discern the potential powers of Wordsworth in the little book of first poems published two years before. He had said:

> . . . seldom, if ever, was the emergence of an original poetic genius above the literary horizon more evidently announced. In the form, style and manner of the whole poem, and in the structure of the particular lines and periods, there is an harshness and acerbity connected and combined with words and images all a-glow, which might recall those products of the vegetable world, whose gorgeous blossoms rise out of the hard and thorny rind and shell, within which the rich fruit was elaborating. The language was not only peculiar and strong but at times knotty and contorted, as by its own impatient strength; while the novelty and struggling crowd of images, acting in conjunction with the difficulties of the style, demanded always a greater closeness of attention than poetry, (at all events, than descriptive poetry) has a right to claim.

In Bristol, Coleridge had been endangering his own liberty by such revolutionary sermons as the famous one beginning,

> Are we men? free men? rational men? and shall we carry on this wild and priestly war against reason, against freedom, against human nature?

He was, naturally, delighted when he heard that the author of *Descriptive Sketches* and of the letter "By a Republican" was living nearby and hastened to meet him.

Although this first meeting was brief, and the acquaintance was then interrupted for over a year, it was enthusiastically resumed in the spring of 1797. It is probably difficult to overestimate its importance for either of the young men.

Coleridge, whose reputation at that time was far greater, gave Wordsworth the most unstinted and generously expressed admiration. He listened rapturously to a reading of the long poem, "Guilt and Sorrow," written during the past year, and declared that the advance Wordsworth had made was marvelous. There was, he said, no more obscurity, "no work of strained thought or forced diction, no crowd or turbulence of imagery." The verse form was better; man and nature were more thoroughly assimilated; in short, Wordsworth was now even more clearly what he had said a year before, "The best poet of the age."

With extraordinary disinterestedness Coleridge wrote to one of his admirers, Cottle, a publisher and book seller: "I speak with heart felt sincerity and, I think, unblinded judgment, when I tell you that I feel myself a little man by his side." To another young radical, his brother-in-law, Southey, Coleridge wrote: "Wordsworth is a very great man, the only man to whom at all times and in all modes of excellence I feel myself inferior, the only one, I mean, whom I have yet met with."

To two wealthy patrons of the arts, the Wedgwoods, who were thinking of a grant that would enable Coleridge to write untroubled by practical affairs, he wrote: "He [Wordsworth] strides on so far before you that he dwindles in the distance."

Two years later when one of his best and most generous friends and admirers scolded him for belittling himself with this excessive reverence for Wordsworth, Coleridge replied with a description of the thrill he felt at having been the first to appreciate "the new Milton."

Wordsworth naturally responded to this ardent encouragement and the discerning criticism which accompanied it. While he was no match for Coleridge either in critical perception or in self-forgetful enthusiasm, his company and the example of his steady industrious workmanlike habits seem to have had a most beneficial effect on his friend and enabled Coleridge to complete the only long finished pieces he ever wrote.

That year Wordsworth wrote his great *Prelude* in which he says, speaking of the early years of the revolution,

> Bliss was it in that dawn to be alive
> But to be young was very heaven.

For the young poets then felt they

> Were called upon to exercise their skill
> Not in Utopia—subterranean fields—
> Or some secreted island, heaven knows where,
> But in the very world which is the world
> Of all of us—the place where, in the end,
> We find our happiness, or not at all.

From the long discussions of the two young poets emerged a historic manifesto—the famous *Preface To The Lyrical Ballads*—which introduced a volume containing Coleridge's *Ancient Mariner* and many of Wordsworth's best short lyrical and narrative poems.

The *Preface* is too long and well-known to be included here but a few quotations may show both its relation to Wordsworth's democratic beliefs and its revolutionary character in a literary world still accepting the eighteenth century standards of elegance for poetry.

> The principal object, then, proposed in these Poems was to choose incidents and situations from common life; and to relate or describe them, throughout, as far as was possible in a selection of language really used by men, and, at the same time, to throw over them a certain colouring of imagination, whereby ordinary things should be presented to the mind in an unusual aspect. . . . Humble and rustic life was generally chosen, because in that condition the essential passions of the heart find a better soil in which they can attain their maturity, are less under restraint, and speak a plainer and more emphatic language. . . .
>
> The language, too, of these men has been adopted . . . because such men hourly communicate with the best objects (nature and the material necessities of daily life) from which the best parts of language is originally derived; and because . . . being less under the influence of social vanity, they convey their feelings and notions in simple and unelaborated expressions. Accordingly, such a language, arising out of repeated experience and regular feelings, is a more permanent, and a far more philosophical language, than that which is frequently substituted for it by Poets, who think that they are conferring honour upon themselves and their art, in proportion as they separate themselves from the sympathy of men, and indulge in arbitrary and capricious habits of expression, in order to furnish food for fickle tastes, and fickle appetites, of their own creation. . . .
>
> . . . For all good poetry is the spontaneous overflow of powerful feelings; and though this be true, Poems to which any value can be attached were never produced on any variety of subjects but by a man who, being possessed of more than usual organic sensibility, had also thought long and deeply. For our continued influxes of feeling are modified and directed by our thoughts, which are indeed the representatives of all our past feelings. . . .
>
> . . . What is a Poet? To whom does he address himself? . . . He is a man speaking to men; a man, it is true, endowed with more lively sensibility, more enthusiasm and tenderness, who has a greater knowledge of human nature, and a more

comprehensive soul, than are supposed to be common among mankind; a man pleased with his own passions and volitions; and who rejoices more than other men in the spirit of life that is in him; delighting to contemplate similar volitions and passions as manifested in the goings-on of the Universe, and habitually impelled to create them where he does not find them. . . .

. . . Poetry is the image of man and nature. . . . The Poet writes under one restriction only, namely, the necessity of giving immediate pleasure to a human Being possessed of that information which may be expected from him, not as a lawyer, a physician, a mariner, an astronomer, or a natural philosopher, but as a Man. . . .

Nor let this necessity of producing immediate pleasure be considered as a degradation of the Poet's art. It is far otherwise. It is an acknowledgment of the beauty of the universe; further, it is a homage paid to the native and naked dignity of man, to the grand elementary principle of pleasure, by which he knows and feels and lives and moves. . . . In spite of differences of soil and climate, of language and manners, of laws and customs; in spite of things silently gone out of mind, and things violently destroyed; the Poet binds together by passion and knowledge the vast empire of human society, as it is spread over the whole earth and over all time. . . . If the labours of Men of Science should ever create any material revolution, direct or indirect, in our condition, and in the impressions which we habitually receive, the Poet will sleep then no more than at present; he will be ready to follow the steps of the Man of Science, not only in those general indirect effects, but he will be at his side, carrying sensation into the midst of the objects of the science itself. . . .

. . . The Poet thinks and feels in the spirit of human passions. . . . Poets do not write for Poets alone, but for men. . . .

The publication of this volume marks the high point in Wordsworth's life and work, although he was to write some better poems and over a hundred as good, as well as hundreds if not thousands of bad ones, in the next fifty-two years.

One of the most characteristic of these lovely simple lyrics, with their unselfconscious mingling of a democratic social concern and the spontaneous love of natural beauty, is the brief "Lines written in Early Spring, 1798."

> I heard a thousand blended notes,
> While in a grove I sate reclined,
> In that sweet mood when pleasant thoughts
> Bring sad thoughts to the mind.

To her fair works did Nature link
The human soul that through me ran;
And much it grieved my soul to think
What man has made of man.

Through primrose tufts, in that green bower,
The periwinkle trailed its wreaths;
And 'tis my faith that every flower
Enjoys the air it breathes.

The birds around me hopped and played,
Their thoughts I could not measure:—
But the least motion which they made
It seemed a thrill of pleasure.

The budding twigs spread out their fan,
To catch the breezy air;
And I must think, do all I can,
That there was pleasure there.

If this belief from heaven be sent,
If such be Nature's holy plan,
Have I not reason to lament
What man has made of man?

Half a century later Browning said that his poem "The Lost Leader" in which he referred to Wordsworth with such statements as:

Just for a handful of silver he left us,
Just for riband to stick in his coat,

gave an oversimplified picture of the cause of Wordsworth's defection. Yet in the last analysis, and without the deliberate conscious action implied, it seems to give substantially the correct one.

In 1802 Wordsworth secured an increased income due to a successful end of the inheritance lawsuit, brought about by the intercession of Lord Lonsdale. In the same year, after arranging to make a settlement on his illegitimate daughter, Caroline, and get her mother's consent to his marriage, he married a close childhood friend of Dorothy's, Mary Hutchinson, whom he had known and been fond of even before his first trip to France.

From that time on the responsibilities of a growing family and the continued detachment from all political and social problems made it easier for Wordsworth first to ignore and then to contradict his early principles.

Forgetting the insight of his own *Prelude*, he had turned his back completely on the "world of all of us" and sought his happiness in a private communion with truth and nature. When by 1803 this utopia began to prove as unsatisfying as he had himself foretold, Wordsworth rationalized his loss of active joy and purpose in life in the "Ode on Intimations of Immortality." Its point of view is summarized in the opening lines:

> There was a time when meadow, grove and stream
> The earth, and every common sight,
>   To me did seem
>   Apparelled in celestial light,
> The glory and the freshness of a dream.
> It is not now as it hath been of yore;—
>   Turn wheresoe'er I may,
>   By night or day,
> The things which I have seen I see no more.
>   The Rainbow comes and goes
>   And lovely is the Rose,
>   The Moon doth with delight
> Look round her when the heavens are bare,
>   Waters on a starry night
>   Are beautiful and fair;
>   The sunshine is a glorious birth;
>   But yet I know, where'er I go,
> That there hath passed away a glory from the earth.

This is further developed in the fourth stanza:

> Our birth is but a sleep and a forgetting:
> The Soul that rises with us, our life's Star,
>   Hath had elsewhere its setting,
>   And cometh from afar:
>   Not in entire forgetfulness,
>   And not in utter nakedness,
> But trailing clouds of glory do we come
>   From God, who is our home:
> Heaven lies about us in our infancy!
> Shades of the prison-house begin to close
>   Upon the growing Boy,
> But he beholds the light, and whence it flows,
>   He sees it in his joy;
> The Youth, who daily farther from the east
>   Must travel, still is Nature's Priest
>   And by the vision splendid
>   Is on his way attended;
> At length the Man perceives it die away,
> And fade into the light of common day.

It is interesting to note that one of our own poets—the militant Abolitionist James Russell Lowell—began his *Vision of Sir Launfal* with a sharp attack upon this rationalization. He said, speaking from his very different experience:

> *Not only* about our infancy
> Does Heaven with all its splendors lie—

No doubt Wordsworth's retreat was facilitated by Coleridge's public recantation of his republican beliefs and hopes in his *Ode to France* (see p. 447); Napoleon's coronation and the increasingly aggressive wars his army began to wage must also have made it easy for Wordsworth to rationalize his position by claiming that it was the revolutionary movement and not he who changed.

In any event, beginning with ardent support of the anti-Napoleonic war in 1803, he rapidly turned toward the Tory party in other seemingly unrelated matters.

That same year he met a wealthy patron of the arts, a baronet Sir George Beaumont, who bought a piece of land near his own estate which he presented to Wordsworth in hopes that the poet would build there and settle near him. This Wordsworth did not do, but he kept the substantial gift and with his letter of thanks sent Sir George, who was very much a military man, three poor sonnets written in support of the war!

In 1805 another nobleman, Lord Lonsdale, paid a thousand pounds for a home Wordsworth wished to buy but could not afford, and presented it to him. Wordsworth insisted upon returning that part of the purchase money which he himself had been ready to pay—seven or eight hundred pounds—but his gratitude and its influence on his thinking was probably none the less serious for that.

There was evidently a sore personal regret in his mourning for a lost simplicity of heart, embodied in one of the best-known of sonnets in 1805.

> The world is too much with us; late and soon,
> Getting and spending, we lay waste our powers;
> Little we see in Nature that is ours;
> We have given our hearts away, a sordid boon!
> The Sea that bares her bosom to the moon:
> The winds that will be howling at all hours,
> And are up-gathered now, like sleeping flowers;

For this, for everything, we are out of tune;
It moves us not.—Great God! I'd rather be
A Pagan suckled in a creed outworn;
So might I, standing on this pleasant lea,
Have glimpses that would make me less forlorn;
Have sight of Proteus rising from the sea;
Or hear old Triton blow his wreathed horn.

The next year saw several sonnets of similar autobiographical significance. One beginning "Nuns fret not at their convent's narrow room; And hermits are contented with their cells;" continues with profound untruth "In truth the prison unto which we doom Ourselves, no prison is: . . ." There seems to be more wishful thinking than conviction in these lines, and in such similar ones from the "Ode to Duty" as "Me this uncharted freedom tires; I feel the weight of chance desires; . . ." Taken in connection with the many sorrowful invocations to sleep written in both prose and verse during these years, they suggest that perhaps Wordsworth's reconciliation with the status quo was, as yet, less complete than he liked to think it.

He had, before this time, completed much of the best work published as *Poems in Two Volumes* in 1807. And almost all that Wordsworth contributed to the glory of English poetry was included either in these 1807 volumes or in the revised edition of the *Lyrical Ballads* in 1800. The only important exception was work like *The Prelude* which, completed by 1805, was not published until after his death in 1850.

In 1812 Wordsworth, whose income was of course very inadequate for his growing family, asked Lord Lonsdale to secure him a government position which would pay him well without requiring much of his time. In 1813 this request was granted by his appointment to such a sinecure at an annual salary of from four hundred to six hundred pounds.

Shelley, mourning for his beloved "Lost Leader" wrote sadly when he heard that the great poet had accepted a government sinecure:

Poet of Nature, thou hast wept to know
That things depart which never may return:
Childhood and youth, friendship and love's first glow,
Have fled like sweet dreams, leaving thee to mourn.
These common woes I feel. One loss is mine
Which thou too feel'st, yet I alone deplore.

> Thou wert as a lone star, whose light did shine
> On some frail bark in winter's midnight roar:
> Thou hast like to a rock-built refuge stood
> Above the blind and battling multitude:
> In honoured poverty thy voice did weave
> Songs consecrate to truth and liberty,—
> Deserting these, thou leavest me to grieve,
> Thus having been, that thou shouldst cease to be.

Byron, who had no love for Wordsworth at the best of times, was infuriated that he continued to claim Milton as his inspiration while praising George IV, whose policies were essentially indistinguishable from those of George III, which Wordsworth himself had earlier attacked.

Wordsworth had written, in 1802:

> Milton! thou should'st be living at this hour:
> England hath need of thee: she is a fen
> Of stagnant waters! altar, sword, and pen
> Fireside, the heroic wealth of hall and bower,
> Have forfeited their ancient England dower
> Of inward happiness. We are selfish men;
> Oh! raise us up, return to us again;
> And give us manners, virtue, freedom, power.
> Thy soul was like a Star, and dwelt apart:
> Thou hadst a voice whose sound was like the sea:
> Pure as the naked heavens, majestic, free,
> So didst thou travel on life's common way,
> In cheerful godliness; and yet thy heart
> The lowliest duties on herself did lay.

After Wordsworth had sought and achieved a government sinecure and changed his politics to suit, Byron said sharply:

> If fallen in evil days on evil tongues,
>   Milton appeal'd to the Avenger, Time,
> If Time, the Avenger, execrates his wrongs,
>   And makes the word "Miltonic" mean "sublime,"
> *He* deign'd not to belie his soul in songs,
>   Nor turn his very talent to a crime;
> *He* did not loathe the Sire to laud the Son,
>   But closed the tyrant-hater he begun.

On the whole, during these years Wordsworth's muse at first contented herself with ignoring rather than distorting political affairs, and the bulk of the poems written from 1803 to 1815 deal with nature and the incidents of rural life. His appreciation of these was heightened by the sensitive participation of his sister. Many of the most memorable poems were suggested by her comments on country sights. For example, a few days before he wrote the justly famous "Daffodils" in 1807 we find a note in her journal: "When we were in the woods beyond Gowbarrow Park we saw a few daffodils close to the water-side. We fancied that the sea had floated the seeds ashore, and that the little colony had sprung up. But as we went along there were more, and yet more; and at last under the boughs of the trees we saw that there was a long belt of them along the shore—I never saw daffodils so beautiful—they tossed and reeled and danced as if they verily laughed with the wind that blew upon them over the lake." The genesis of lines 3-14 below is clearly apparent.

> I wandered lonely as a cloud
> That floats on high o'er vales and hills,
> When all at once I saw a crowd,
> A host, of golden daffodils;
> Beside the lake, beneath the trees,
> Fluttering and dancing in the breeze.
>
> Continuous as the stars that shine
> And twinkle on the milky way,
> They stretched in never-ending line
> Along the margin of a bay:
> Ten thousand saw I at a glance,
> Tossing their heads in sprightly dance.
>
> The waves beside them danced; but they
> Out-did the sparkling waves in glee:
> A poet could not but be gay,
> In such a jocund company:

But the loss of integrity cannot be localized and even before Wordsworth began to write incredibly bad poems in support of an established church, in celebration of the Congress of Vienna, and so forth, there was a continued if irregular decline, obvious to any appreciative reader.

By 1816 Wordsworth was writing such utter trash as the sonnet on the "Feeling of a French Royalist On the Disinterment of the Remains of The Duke D'Enghien," and by 1836 (with nothing worth note in all the quantity of banal verse between) he was writing the "Protest Against the Ballot" whose poetic force and style are precisely such as the theme demands. It may, perhaps, be worth quoting a few lines of this "poetry"

> Forth rushed from Envy sprung and Self-conceit,
> A Power misnamed the Spirit of Reform,
> And through the astonished Island swept in storm,
> Threatening to lay all orders at her feet
> That crost her way. Now stoops she to entreat
> License to hide at intervals her head
> Where she may work, safe, undisquieted,
> In a close Box, covert for Justice meet.

Nothing remained to complete Wordsworth's "Decline and Fall" but his appointment as Poet Laureate and his two long prose articles against free public education and the extension of the railroad to his beloved Lake Country. Wordsworth evidently felt that anyone traveling at as cheap a rate as the plan envisaged must desecrate the scenery, and he did his unsuccessful best to defeat the project.

After this it is no wonder that a recent biographer trying to maintain Wordsworth's essential consistency, and the democracy of his later years, could solemnly adduce as evidence: "Although himself a graduate of Cambridge he counted many old Oxonians among his best friends!"

Never was Burns' warning more strikingly vindicated:

> Let folly and knavery
> Freedom oppose;
> 'Tis suicide, Genius,
> To mix with her foes!

The Wordsworth who in the *Prelude* remembered England after the first campaign against the slave trade by Wilberforce and Clarkson in 1792,

> The general air still busy with the stir
> Of that first memorable onset made
> Upon the traffickers in Negro blood;
> Effort which, though defeated, had recalled
> To notice old forgotten principles
> And through the nation spread a novel heat
> Of virtuous feeling.

had said of slavery,

That, if France prospered, good men would not long
Pay fruitless worship to humanity,
And this most rotten branch of human shame,
Would fall together with its parent tree.

But this same Wordsworth in 1840 wrote, in a discussion on Colonial Slavery,

There are 3 parties who must be considered in the question of freeing the slaves:—the slave, the slave-owner, and the British people. The slave owner should be prepared to face *some* financial loss, the slave if given his freedom should be willing to make recompense for the Master's sacrifice [!] and the British people should pass no measure which does not provide for an equivalent to the owner.

He went on to say that those who advocated immediate abolition forgot slavery was sometimes beneficial in that it protected the weak from the strong, for there were worse evils than slavery!

The same Wordsworth in 1802, had written to the heroic and unfortunate Touissant L'Ouverture,

There's not a breathing of the common wind
That will forget thee; thou hast great allies;
Thy friends are exultations, agonies,
And love and man's unconquerable mind.

But in 1822, when the equally heroic and unfortunate Henri Christophe's widow was given a refuge, and treated with due respect, by the Abolitionist, Clarkson, Wordsworth wrote the unspeakable parody:

Queen and Negress, chaste and fair,
Christophe now is laid asleep;
Seated in a British chair
State in humbler manner keep;
Shine for Clarkson's pure delight,
Negro Princess, ebon bright.

Easy indeed is the descent to hell.
There is no profit in pursuing further the rest of Wordsworth's life, which has truly been called "the most dismal anti-climax of which the history of literature holds record." It is merely worth noting that even critics and anthologists who do not see the intimate

relation between poetry and politics rarely refer to any poems written after 1806, still more rarely to those completed after 1812, and almost never to the vast body of works written between 1815 and 1850.

Wordsworth's earlier poetry is often cited by those who would convince us of his later ideas, but for this and for the value of the later Wordsworth who became a poet laureate long after he had ceased being a poet, Hazlitt provides the best comment in his article on "The Courier and 'The Wat Tyler,'" March 30, 1817.

> This we do know, and it is worth attending to; that all that Mr. Southey has done best in poetry, he did before he changed his political creed; that *all* that Mr. Coleridge ever did in poetry, as the Ancient Mariner, Christabel, the Three Graves, his Poems and his Tragedy, he had written when, according to his own (present) account he must have been a very ignorant, idle, thoughtless, person; that much the greater part of what Mr. Wordsworth has done best in poetry was done about the same period; and if what these persons have done in poetry, in indulging "the pleasing fervour of a lively imagination", gives no weight to their political opinions at the time they did it, what they have done since in science or philosophy to establish their authority is more than we know. All the authority that they have as poets and men of genius must be thrown into the scale of Revolution and Reform. Their Jacobin principles indeed gave rise to their Jacobin poetry. Since they gave up the first, their poetical powers have flagged and been comparatively or wholly "in a state of suspended animation". . . . Poet-laureates are courtiers by profession; but we say that poets are naturally Jacobins. All the poets of the present day have been so, with a single exception which it would be invidious to mention. If they have not all continued so, this only shows the instability of their own characters, and that their natural generosity and romantic enthusiasm, "their lofty, imaginative, and innocent spirits," have not been proof against the incessant, unwearied importunities of vulgar ambition. The poets, we say then, are with us, while they are worth keeping.

Samuel Taylor Coleridge—1772–1834

Coleridge was the youngest in a family of 13 children. His father, a liberal clergyman in a country village, was already fifty-three when he was born and both father and mother evidently showed particular tenderness for their baby. The brothers naturally resented such partiality and the child was subject to considerable teasing.

This, together with a great mental precocity and a certain degree of physical awkwardness, set him aside from other children and he spent most of his time, from the age of three, roaming alone about the fields and, very soon, reading. By the time he was six he had read *Belisarius, Robinson Crusoe* and *The Arabian Nights* and peopled his long solitary play days with figures from their authors' imagination as well as his own. His father was master of a small school and from six years on he was the child's teacher as well, delighted with his extraordinary scholastic abilities and adding daily private talks on astronomy and the meaning of grammar to his ordinary lessons. He seems to have been a man of real independence of thought which showed itself not only in these interests but in so dangerous a form as a sermon preached in 1776 or 1777 condemning England's war with the colonies. His death meant even more to Coleridge than the personal loss of a loving and interested father-companion. The family naturally had to move out of the vicarage; several of the older boys left to pursue their various careers; and for the youngest a scholarship at Christ's Church Charity School in London—a large foundation especially designed for orphans and the sons of indigent clergymen—was secured.

For the next eight or nine years the child stayed there—holidays and all—although as he says daydreams and night dreams both took him back to the beloved fields of Ottery.

> . . . But O! how oft,
> How oft, at school, with most believing mind,
> . . . .
> With unclosed lids, already had I dreamt
> Of my sweet birth-place, and the old church-tower,
> Whose bells, the poor man's only music, rang
> . . . .
> So gazed I, till the soothing things, I dreamt,
> Lulled me to sleep, and sleep prolonged my dreams!
> And so I brooded all the following morn,
> Awed by the stern preceptor's face, mine eye
> Fixed with mock study on my swimming book:
> Save if the door half opened, and I snatched
> A hasty glance, and still my heart leaped up,
> For still I hoped to see the *stranger's* face,
> Townsman, or aunt, or sister more beloved,
> My play-mate when we both were clothed alike!

His mother's special fondness seems to have ended with his babyhood and the actual ties with home were largely by correspondence with a sister, who died before his school years were completed. Coleridge eagerly attached himself to a brother who came up to London to "walk the hospitals" as a medical student but he also died a year or so later. The youngster then carried on a correspondence with a much older brother, George, who later became Vicar of Ottery in his father's place. It is to him that a dedicatory poem written fifteen years later, begins: "I have lov'd as a brother, as a son rever'd thee. . . ."

The life at school was a hard one not only because of loneliness and a shocked surprise at the smoky darkness and ugliness of London:

> For I was reared
> In the great city pent 'mid cloisters dim,
> And saw nought lovely but the sky and stars

but also because of serious physical hardships.

The dormitories were crowded, with no real sanitary arrangements; caning or whipping was so very common and severe that thirty years later in nightmares Coleridge still woke crying with the pain, and, worst of all, the food was altogether inadequate. Breakfast consisted of a small piece of dry bread and a pint of bad, watered beer; supper of a larger piece of bread with either butter or cheese and water; meat was served only twice a week at dinner and the portions were so small that not only Coleridge but two school mates, Charles Lamb and Leigh Hunt, have all written of the school saying they rarely had enough to eat as often as once a week.

However, Coleridge was not altogether unhappy. He was a good and rapid student; the formidable head schoolmaster, Boyer, evidently beat him the more lest he should be spoiled but promoted him rapidly and taught him with care; and he found early in his second or third school year a gift of popularity which, in all his tumultuous misadventures, he was never to lose.

His strange, original imagination and complete absorption in intellectual interests was evidently combined with an unself-conscious ability to make immediate sympathetic contact with all sorts of people. While his school fellows told outrageous stories of his absent-mindedness and eccentricity, their laughter was clearly affectionate and they treasured him as an oddity as interesting as strange.

On holidays and leave days when most of the students went

home to friends or relatives in London he wandered through the streets, starting out alone, but generally picking up one or more acquaintances before nightfall. He would talk to anyone who would listen and whether his current interest was Plato's philosophy—into which he tumbled head over heels at fifteen—or Virgil or the new English "landscape poetry," he possessed a genius for communicating his ideas and enthusiasm.

However, despite his aptitude for Latin and his comparatively high position in the school, he made at least one serious attempt to escape either his present life or possibly the prospect of a career in the church for which he was destined. To the incredulous rage of his teacher, a shoemaker whom he had been visiting regularly on leave days for some six months came (at Coleridge's urging) to ask that the boy be discharged and apprenticed to him. Mr. Boyer drove the poor man out with imprecations on the impudence of his request, but the fact that Coleridge himself could have wanted to adopt such a disgraceful trade was evidently beyond his imagination and the boy was not punished.

Four or five years later, in 1791 he was graduated as one of an advanced class of half a dozen students chosen to compete for the most valuable Cambridge scholarship. He won it, and thus secured enough money to cover most of his necessary expenses at college.

At the beginning of his last two school years he had happily found a home in London for holidays and visits. A much younger schoolmate whom he helped with his Latin invited him home to meet his mother and three sisters and Coleridge fell in love with the family immediately. The affection was warmly received, he was adopted as part-time son and brother, and joyously spent all his free days with them, gradually developing a more romantic interest in the oldest daughter, Mary Evans.

During these last two years of his school days a wave of enthusiasm for Freedom and the French Revolution had swept the school—in whose tyranny many of the seniors, no doubt, felt they saw another nearer Bastille—and Coleridge had immediately written an ode on "The Destruction of the Bastille." It is fairly abstract, imitative stuff but a few such lines as "And mark yon peasant's raptur'd eyes; Secure he views his harvests rise;" indicate the concrete understanding of political events which was to characterize him at his highest.

His transfer to Cambridge caused no diminution in his political interest. But the new freedom expressed itself in a growing doubt as to the tenets of the Church of England, and even of orthodox

Christianity in general although he never went quite so far in hetrodoxy as the most extreme Unitarians or Deists, and was always genuinely horrified at Atheism. It also expressed itself in the less laudable collegiate ways of wine parties and unpaid bills. The largest of these bills was, characteristically, due to sheer carelessness. An upholsterer and cabinetmaker's salesman calling upon Coleridge to inquire "How would you like your rooms furnished?" received the lordly answer, "Why, just as you please" and took advantage of his carte blanche for almost £100.

At the end of his first year Coleridge's closest friend, Middleton, an earlier Christ's Church graduate who had welcomed him on his arrival, lost his scholarship for his republicanism and had to leave the college. A professor William Frend, whom they both greatly admired, was expelled, after a lengthy trial for his unorthodox opinions and especially for a pamphlet criticizing England's part in the American war. Coleridge attended sessions of the trial, applauding so loudly at certain points of Frend's defense, that he himself was almost called up for disciplinary action. He then spent a moonlight night in the risky escapade of chalking up "Frend Forever" on all the college walls.

Despite all these extracurricular activities, however, he managed to win several awards including one for a Greek Ode in which he chose as topic "The Slave Trade." He received honorable mention for another Latin one on the same subject.

However, after his two most serious friends had left, he evidently went in more seriously for parties as well as politics, and reports of his debts, drinking and democratic ideas—all three equally disturbing—reached his brothers. One of his college intimates wrote, many years later:

> Coleridge was ready at any time to unbend his mind in conversation; and for the sake of this, his room . . . was a constant rendez-vous of conversation—loving friends. . . . What evenings I have spent in those rooms! What little suppers . . . when Aeschylus and Plato and Thucydides were pushed aside, with a pile of lexicons, to discuss the pamphlets of the day. . . . There was no need of having the book before us. Coleridge had read it in the morning and in the evening he would repeat whole pages verbatim.

His brothers would no doubt have been horrified at hearing even such reports as this, and they were doubtless the recipient of many less friendly. At any rate George wrote letters full of rebuke, admonition, and inquiry, and after some correspondence full of evasive denials and promises of reform, Coleridge confessed his difficulties during the summer holidays of 1793. He was given a sum of money which should have been sufficient to pay his most pressing obligations, and left for college full of good intentions.

Unfortunately he used a good part of the money in a week's visit to London, and found an additional number of forgotten creditors dunning him on his return to Cambridge. Desperately he spent all the remainder for a lottery ticket, wrote an ode praying for good fortune, and went up to London for the drawing. Naturally it lost and Coleridge—despite his genuine hatred of the war and his equally genuine fear of horses—enlisted for an eight-year term in a cavalry regiment! He used an alias—the name of Silas Tomkyn Cumberbach (the last part chosen in anticipatory commiseration with his horse!)

Neither the college nor his family knew his whereabouts and he evidently intended to disappear. However, two months later when part of the regiment was being shipped to France (he himself was still too "indocile a rider" to be included) he decided to get help, if he could, without asking for it. He let some of his friends know where he was, under an ostensible pledge of secrecy. As he had hoped, the news got back to his family. His brother wrote to him and after some correspondence he was released, and returned to Cambridge in April.

It is, I think, significant of his profound hatred for slavery that, whereas Coleridge often returned evasive answers and even disingenuous semidenials to his brothers' distressed inquiries about his political ideas, opposition to the slave trade was one subject on which he would not, or could not, equivocate. For example, in answer to a letter of fraternal rebuke and religious argument from George he replied, in a note dated November 6, 1794:

> Slavery is an abomination to my feeling of the head and heart. Did Jesus teach the *abolition* of it (you ask)? No! He taught those principles of which the necessary *effect* was to abolish slavery!

In June Coleridge went off on a walking trip with a radical friend and, while visiting Oxford, made the acquaintance of a very different kind of young republican there, Robert Southey.

Southey was an intelligent, energetic, rather conventional young man who was a radical partly because it was the fashion in advanced intellectual circles, and partly because his father's early death had left him without the prospects he should have had and which, he felt, any well-organized society would have provided for him.

He had been expelled from a well-known London school, Westminister, two years before as the editor of a school paper, *The Flagellant*, which protested against corporal punishment, and was therefore already something of a hero in radical circles when he arrived at Oxford.

He had heard of Coleridge, welcomed him with enthusiasm, and impressed him by explaining his project for emigrating to America and founding a utopian colony of free souls there. With Southey this was an old daydream in new form. At the age of seven, he and a friend had planned to run away to an island and live alone there, and dressed up in the new terms of equality and the rights of man it was a dazzling plaything for Southey and his college friends, two of whom professed themselves ready to accompany him wherever he went. Although all of them were devoted to the idea, probably none of them would even have thought realistically of putting it into practice, but Coleridge, as we have seen, tolerated no such gap between theory and practice, and, a ready convert, he immediately demanded action.

In addition to inventing a name—"pantisocracy"—and a verb "to aspheritise" (meaning to communize or make property general), he spread the gospel on the rest of his six-week walking tour, and interested a serious republican farmer, Thomas Poole, in helping them.

His belief in direct action may have been a little disturbing to the pantisocrats even so early. One of the three, Allen, immediately dropped out to enter the Church—the ordinary end of a college education for gentlemen without property—and Southey himself wrote a somewhat discouraged letter pointing out the difficulties of raising funds and hinting the possibility of himself entering upon a Church career. Coleridge immediately replied, in September, 1794:

> For God's sake, Southey! enter not the Church. Of Allen I say little but I feel anguish at times. . . . A friend of Hicks' after long struggle between principle and interest, as it is

improperly called, accepted a place under government. He took the oaths, shuddered, went home and threw himself in an agony out of a two-pair of stairs window!

On his way back to Cambridge he met the Fricker family of five daughters of whom one was married to a pantisocrat, Lovell, and another engaged to Southey. He undertook to convert a third— although without an exact proposal, since he was genuinely if hopelessly in love with Mary Evans. In fact he had gone on the tour partly to try to get over the news of her probable engagement to an older man. Nevertheless he was enough in love with pantisocracy to talk ardently of it to any sympathetic listener and was not altogether unhappy, though surprised, when Southey told him he was in honor bound to make love to pretty Sarah Fricker, so that she could accompany the expedition as Coleridge's wife.

A letter to Southey on his return shows how much he was in love with pantisocracy and how little with "Miss Fricker," "America! Southey! Miss Fricker! Yes, Southey, you are right. Even Love is the creature of strong motive. I certainly love her. . . ."

It is not surprising that he was overwhelmed with despair when, a month later, he received a letter from Mary Evans so concerned about his latest plan that it seemed to intimate there might still be a chance if he would give up this desperate venture, even though Mary was evidently still being coaxed into a more advantageous marriage. He refused, as in honor bound, but was naturally even more troubled when some suggestions of Southey's about taking servants along to America—or, rather, continuing to use as a servant his aunt's man, Shad, who had been charmed by Coleridge into volunteering to go along presumably as a pantisocrat. His letter is a characteristic combination of realistic insight and wishful fantasy as these excerpts indicate:

> I was vexed too and alarmed by your letter concerning Mr. and Mrs. Roberts, Shad, and little Sally. . . . Southey, this is *not* our plan, nor can I defend it. "Shad's children will be educated as ours, and the education we shall give them will be such as to render them incapable of blushing at the want of it in their parents."—*Perhaps!* With this one word would every Lilliputian reasoner demolish the system. Wherever men *can* be vicious, some *will* be. The leading idea of pantisocracy is to make men *necessarily* virtuous by removing all motives to evil— all possible temptation. "Let them dine with us and be treated with as much equality as they would wish, but perform that

part of labour for which their education has fitted them."
Southey should not have written this sentence. . . . If your remarks on the other side are just, the inference is that the scheme of pantisocracy is impracticable, but I hope and believe that it is not a *necessary* inference. . . . If Mrs. S. and Mrs. F. go with us, they can at least prepare the food of simplicity for us. Let the married women do only what is absolutely convenient and customary for pregnant women or nurses. Let the husbands do all the rest, and what will that all be? Washing with a machine and cleaning the house. One hour's addition to our daily labor, and *pantisocracy* in its most perfect sense is practicable. That the greater part of our female companions should have the task of maternal exertion at the same time is very *improbable*; but, though it were to happen, an infant is almost always sleeping, and during its slumbers the mother may in the same room perform the little offices of ironing clothes or making shirts.

Coleridge wrote a last desperate proposal to Mary Evans (perhaps making it contingent on her joining the pantisocrats) and, receiving a final definite refusal, wrote to Southey in terms which again show his genius for getting into the worst kind of trouble from the very highest motives.

> To lose her! I can rise above that selfish pang. But to marry another, O Southey! bear with my weakness. Love makes all things pure and heavenly like itself—but to marry a woman whom I do *not* love, to degrade her whom I call my wife by making her the instrument of low desire, and on the removal of a desultory appetite to be perhaps not displeased with her absence! Enough! These refinements are the wildering fires that lead me into vice. Mark you, Southey! I *will* do my duty.

Southey evidently argued in reply to the letter about servitude that since the pantisocrats were to use the labor of oxen for their own benefit, why not that of men? Coleridge answered with understandable heat:

> But who shall dare to transfer "from man to brute" to "from man to man?" To be employed in the toil of the field while we are pursuing philosophical studies—can earldoms or emperorships boast so huge an inequality? Is there a human being of so torpid a nature as that placed in our society he would not feel it? A willing slave is the worst of slaves! His soul is a slave. . . . and to the women, what assistance can little Sally, the wife of Shad, give more than any other of

married women? Is she to have no domestic cares of her own? No house? No husband to provide for? No children?

Whether because of his inability to love Sarah or the increasing difficulty of respecting Southey, Coleridge, when he left Cambridge in December 1794—a month before taking his degree—went to London instead of to Bristol where Southey and Sarah expected him. He made no announcement and perhaps no actual decision as to this being a final departure, but feeling unable to declare his acceptance of the thirty-nine articles of the Church of England—then a formal requirement for graduation—he never returned to take his degree and was after a year's extension dropped from the college rolls.

During this troubled fall of 1794 when all government powers were being used to induce a hysterical horror at the "bloodstained" French, Coleridge wrote in "Lines To A Young Lady—On The French Revolution"

> When slumbering Freedom, roused by high Disdain
> With giant Fury burst her triple chain!
> . . . .
> Amid the yelling of the storm-rent skies
> She came, and scatter'd battles from her eyes!
> Then Exultation waked the patriot fire
> And swept with wild hand the compassionate lyre;
> Red from the Tyrant's wound I shook the lance,
> And strode in joy the reeking plains of France!

In London he plunged into companionship with Charles Lamb, William Godwin, Thomas Holcroft and many of the other leading radicals of the city, "scribbled a few guineas worth" for the newspapers when absolutely penniless, unself-consciously "aspheter- tized" his own scanty guineas and, failing these, his friends', and ignored more and more frequent letters from Southey. Horrified at the declaration of the House of Lords that it was necessary to continue the war against France to protect Christianity, he began his first long serious poem *Religious Musings*, which Lamb rather extravagently declared unequalled by any writer except Milton— and in some respects superior to him! Again, we find in the midst of much sincere but fairly conventional expression of indignation at tyranny, some lines which show a deeper understanding of its specific economic implications. For example, the third, fourth and fifth lines below indicate Coleridge's realization that the seemingly superhuman resources of the ruling class overawe the poor only because they do not see that those impressive resources are simply the sum total of what has been stolen from each of them. Similarly such a line as the eleventh illustrates his insight into the human destruction the rulers achieve in obedience to, rather than in defiance of, their law.

> Ah! far removed from all that glads the sense,
> From all that softens or enables Man,
> The wretched Many! Bent beneath their loads
> They gape at pageant Power, nor recognise
> Their cots' transmuted plunder!
> . . . .
> . . . O ye numberless,
> Whom foul oppression's ruffian gluttony
> Drives from Life's plenteous feast!
> . . . .
> O Aged Women! ye who weekly catch
> The morsel tossed by law-forced charity,
> And die so slowly, that none call it murder!

Although still troubled by the attempt to reconcile his agreement with his friends' political views and his inability to accept completely their irreligious materialist outlook, Coleridge was happy in London, and was rapidly becoming known as a brilliant young radical poet. No doubt he would have managed to resolve or forget these philosophic differences in common activity, but Southey, tired of unanswered letters, and indignant for his fiancée's sister, arrived on the scene. He himself later said:

> Coleridge did not come back to Bristol till January of 1795, nor would he, I believe, have come back at all if I had not gone to London to look for him. For having gone there at the beginning of winter, there he remained without writing to Miss F. or to me, until we actually apprehended that his friends had placed him somewhere in confinement.

The results for Coleridge's personal life were catastrophic. Although he comforted himself with such scraps of uncharacteristic stoic philosophy as, "That which we must do, we had better do willingly; it is a noble chemistry which turns necessity into a pleasure," the need of such self-encouragement did not promise well for his approaching marriage.

But the consequences to his political life—and, subsequently his entire creative genius—were not less fateful. Southey probably thought of himself as a desperate radical and had shocked even his friends by theatrically exclaiming, on hearing of Robespierre's death, "I had rather have heard of the death of my own father" (who had, incidentally died when he was eight). Yet he was essentially ambitious, conventional and snobbish, as he was soon to prove, and as his letters on joining the Church, taking servants to the colony, and so forth, had already shown. Southey's pantisocracy was essentially a device, no less effective for being unconscious, to enable him to assume leadership in the only "genteel" college circles where his lack of fortune would not be a serious handicap, and perhaps to enable him to gain the admiration of his fellows without attracting the serious disapproval of the authorities. Many years later, after he had become an uneasy and unhappy pillar of Church and state, Coleridge wrote an unconsciously revealing analysis of the real nature of such idyllic republicanism:

> It was serviceable in securing myself and perhaps some others from the paths of sedition. We were kept free from the stains and impurities which might have remained upon us had we been travelling with the crowd of less imaginative malcontents through the dark lanes and foul by-roads of ordinary fanaticism!

Again he says, naively exposing the ignoble caution which motivates so much nobly impracticable anarchist fervour: "The prudence which teaches one man to be a Whig will make of another a Utopian."

The *young* Coleridge's beliefs were, however, rooted more deeply and for him there was no real difference between belief and action. With his constant search for a strong, wise, fatherly friend he had given willing allegiance to Southey's plan, and then proceeded to make it truly democratic and dangerous. Now his acknowledged fear of a loveless marriage and his unacknowledged doubt of Southey's genuineness had led him back to the mainstream of the radical movement where he was just beginning to find his place when he was again uprooted by the mingled demands of loyalty, "duty," and the need for immediate precipitate action.

He returned to Bristol, which was then the second largest city in England with an exceptionally large number of well-to-do liberals, many strongly anti-Tory in politics, and many of them members of Unitarian congregations.

The immediate problem was to raise funds for their expedition to the banks of the Susquehanna and the two young men plunged into an orgy of poetry, journalism and lecturing. Southey later claimed he had done four times as much as Coleridge by sitting down and writing while Coleridge walked about and thought, but as Coleridge not unreasonably defended himself, it should be the number of ideas and not the number of words that counted in composition.

At any rate, Coleridge's Bristol lectures made an extraordinary sensation, and the two he gave against the war and against the "sedition laws" and the complete suspension of habeas corpus show not only Coleridge's power of feeling and of thought, but also his courage. Many men had been transported for less than presenting such talks publicly in the England of 1795. The attacks on radicals at the time used "Jacobin" precisely as "Communist" is used today and Coleridge's refusal to be frightened by name-calling led him to quote the epithet with some pride, although actually he felt his serious religious and other differences with the Jacobins made that term altogether inapplicable to him. As he says disgustedly in one of the lectures:

> "It may be very well in theory"—and "the effects of Jacobin principles." Aided by the one and alarmed by the other the shuddering bigot flings the door of argument in your face and excludes all parley by gloomy anticipation of the consequences.

Many entries in his notebook of this period also show the force and clarity of his thinking. In April 1795, for instance, he speaks of the desperate poverty which made it possible to recruit without conscription: "People starved into war. Over an enlisting-place in Bristol a quarter of lamb and a piece of beef hung up!"

And of Burke's *Reflections on the French Revolution* which was being hailed as a literary and philosophic masterpiece and a monument to the human mind: "What repugnant feelings did not Burke's book excite in me! I shuddered while I praised it—a web wrought with admirable beauty from a black bag of poison!"

This year also he wrote the powerful and too little known "War Ecologue," *Fire, Famine and Slaughter*. In less than a hundred dramatic lines it conveys the extraordinary weight of desolation and misery for which England's war ministry was responsible. The brief dialogue below gives an idea of its still immature but evident strength.

Famine:	Can you guess what I saw there?
Fire & Slaughter:	Whisper it, sister! in our ear.
Famine:	A baby beat its dying mother:
	I had starved the one and was starving the other!
Fire & Slaughter:	Who bade you do't?
Famine:	The same! the same!
	Letters four do form his name. [Pitt]
	He let me loose, and cried Halloo!
	To him alone the praise is due.
Fire:	Sisters! I from Ireland came!
	Hedge and corn-fields all on flame,
	I triumphed o'er the setting sun!
	And all the while the work was done,
	On as I strode with my huge strides,
	I flung back my head and I held my sides,
	It was so rare a piece of fun
	To see the sweltered cattle run
	With uncouth gallop through the night,
	Scared by the red and noisy light!
	By the light of his own blazing cot
	Was many a naked Rebel shot;
	The house-stream met the flame and hissed,
	While crash! fell in the roof, I wist,
	On some of those old bed-rid nurses,
	That deal in discontent and curses.
Famine & Slaughter:	Who bade you do't?
Fire:	The same! The same!
	Letters four do form his name.
	He let me loose and cried Halloo!
	To him alone the praise is due.

The temperamental and intellectual difference between the two young men were rapidly becoming apparent—a process accelerated by their enforced sharing of one room for sleep and work, by their meager and unequal financial results, and above all by Southey's now conscious but unacknowledged desire to retreat from the plan without loss of face.

He made proposals, which he hoped Coleridge would unconditionally refuse, for substituting, at least temporarily, a farm colony in Wales instead of the expedition to America; for each earning money privately during a period of fourteen years and then rejoining pantisocracy on a sound financial basis; and so forth.

However, Coleridge had staked his all, emotionally as well as practically, on this association and, as he later truly said, he all his life felt a major need to find permanence and security in loving and respecting those whom he could adopt as older brothers or fathers.

> Me from the spot where I first sprang to light
> Too soon transplanted, ere my soul had fixed
> Its first domestic loves; and hence through life
> Chasing chance-started friendships. . . .

He therefore unhappily and reluctantly accepted the idea of the Welsh farm and was only stung into anger—and a rupture—when Southey added the condition (suggested, perhaps, by the promise he had just received of an annuity of 100 or 150 pounds) that the farm be worked in common, but no other income or property be shared!

This condition, and Southey's obvious unwillingness flatly to refuse two good offers made by his friends and relatives—one to take effect if he studied law, and the other if he entered the church—made it impossible for Coleridge to deceive himself any longer.

Sara and Edith Fricker each took her fiancé's part in the violent quarrels which followed, and in a passion of loneliness and gratitude Coleridge married Sara in October 1795, just when the scheme for which he had undertaken the marriage was definitely given up.

He had by now convinced himself, if with some difficulty, that he was in love—in his long letter to Southey, November 13, 1795, reviewing their association, he says:

> Previously to my departure from Jesus College, and during my melancholy detention in London, what convulsive struggles of feeling I underwent, and what sacrifices I made, you know. The liberal proposal from my family affected me no further than as it pained me to wound a revered brother by the positive and immediate refusal which duty compelled me to return. But there was a—I need not be particular; you remember what a fetter I burst, and that it snapt as if it had been a sinew of my heart. However, I returned to Bristol, and my addresses to Sara, which I at first paid from principle, not feeling, from feeling and from principle I renewed; and I met a reward more than proportionate to the greatness of the effort. I love and I am beloved, and I am happy!

For the first two or three months of married life in a small cottage some twelve miles out of Bristol he was genuinely happy. He wrote a few lyrics to Sara, and in a letter to Thomas Poole, to whom he began now to turn for more intimate friendship, he said:

> God bless you; or rather, God be praised for that he *has* blessed you!
> On Sunday morning I was *married* at St. Mary's Redcliff, poor Chatterton's church! The thought gave a tinge of melancholy to the solemn joy which I felt, united to the woman whom I love best of all created beings. We are settled, nay, quite domesticated, at Clevedon, our comfortable cot!
> *Mrs. Coleridge*! I like to write the name. Well, as I was saying, Mrs. Coleridge desires her affectionate regards to you. I talked of you on my wedding night. God bless you! I hope that some ten years hence you will believe and know of my affection towards you what I will not now profess.
> The prospect around is perhaps more *various* than any in the kingdom. Mine eye gluttonizes the sea, the distant islands, the opposite coast! I shall assuredly write rhymes, let the nine muses prevent it if they can. . . .
> . . . My respectful and grateful remembrance to your mother, and believe me, dear Poole, your affectionate and mindful *friend*, shall I so soon dare to say? Believe me, my heart prompts it.

In his notebook he comments on "Men, eager to adulterise my time by absenting me from my wife," and in sending some verses of thanks for a silver thimble presented to his wife by his publisher he stoutly insisted that she had written the major part of them. He began too, to hope for a family and, perhaps thinking personally as well as politically, wrote in his notebook that "no sentiment has been more detrimental to mankind than the belief that the property we have is our own, and that it is to be hoped that the period is not far removed when every poor man will receive a stipend from the Government under which he lives, rising in proportion to the number of his children."

However, as early as December the honeymoon began to pall and Coleridge felt an unadmitted need for more stimulating mental companionship, and an admitted need for a library, which sent him often to Bristol—and to more frequent and lengthy correspondence with Poole. He writes in his notebook at this time "Good temper and habitual ease are the first ingredients of private society; but wit, knowledge, and originality must break their even surface into some inequality of feeling, or conversation is like a journey on an endless flat."

His publisher, Cottle, was willing and anxious to purchase more poems—the first edition of his first collection for which he had received thirty guineas was already exhausted—but Coleridge felt unable to "write poetry to order" and looked around for some other plan of earning money. He also felt guilty at the withdrawal from political activity and wrote in "Reflections on Having Left a Place of Retirement":

> . . . Was it right
> While my unnumber'd brethren toiled and bled,
> That I should dream away the entrusted hours
> On rose-leaf beds, pampering the coward heart,
> With feelings all too delicate for use?

The result was a plan for a political newspaper, *The Watchman,* which was to appear every eighth day. The reason for this peculiar arrangement was, as Coleridge explained twenty years later in his *Biographia Literaria:*

> In order to exempt it from the stamp-tax [levied on all weekly publications], and likewise to contribute as little as possible to the supposed guilt of a war against freedom, it was to be published on every eighth day. . . .

The motto of *The Watchman* read:

> That All may know the truth
> And that the Truth may make us Free!
> In an Enslaved State the Rulers form and supply
> the opinions of the People:
> A People are free in proportion as they form
> their own opinions.
> In the strictest sense of the word Knowledge is Power.
> We actually transfer the Sovereignty to the
> People, when we make them susceptible of it. In the
> present perilous state of our Constitution the Friends of
> Freedom, of Reason, and of Human Nature, must feel it their
> duty by every means in their power to supply or circulate
> Political information.

After a wonderfully successful speaking tour undertaken to interest readers, Coleridge returned with over 1,000 subscriptions and the paper made its first appearance March 6, 1796.

The March 25 issue had a powerful article against the Slave

Trade, and ended by calling for a boycott of sugar and other leading products of slave labor in the West Indies, to expedite the passage of antislavery laws. During this winter Coleridge had also written a number of political verses like the sonnet on the liberal lord, Earl Stanhope, who stood up alone in the House of Lords to protest the continuation of the war. This began:

> Not, Stanhope! with the Patriot's doubtful name
> I mock thy worth—Friend of the Human Race!

There were other excellent short articles such as "We See Things With Different Eyes":

> He who in company with a fine woman digests an excellent dinner at two guineas a head, perceives *that every thing goes well.* "Thank Heaven, the Jacobins are suppressed, the mouth of sedition is shut. We have men and money in abundance: we shall force the French to make peace on our own terms: shall we not, my Love?" While this Sybarite is yawning and stretching himself in voluptuous indolence, let us turn to the man who has but one penny loaf of mixed bread, and a pound of boiled potatoes to satisfy himself, his wife, and three children, and every instant dreads the entry of his landlord demanding the long delayed payment of his rent.—Ah! (he exclaims with a groan of anguish), formerly I could buy my loaf for eight-pence—my wife had the pot upon the fire every day, and we had a joint of roast meat on Sundays.—Now I have scarcely victuals or clothes; and my neighbors are as bad off as myself. We have neither men nor money left and *God knows when we shall have a peace!*
> Come, come, John! (says his wife) you know, you have partly yourself to blame for this: you were for the War like all the rest: you would vote at the vestry because the Church-Wardens asked you. What business had we with the French?— But come, let us eat our potatoes before they are quite cold.—I wish we had a morsel of butter to them!

There was also some valuable poetry. But there was much padding; the paper came out somewhat irregularly; the more religious readers were alienated by a flippant article against the day of fasting and prayer proclaimed in support of the war, irreverently headed with a text from Isaiah "Wherefore my bowels shall sound like an harp"; and the more radical readers were antagonized by frequent criticisms of the materialism and atheism of certain democrats.

During this winter Coleridge, beginning to think about the relationship of form to content, mercilessly criticized the style as well as the matter of Pitt and the other reactionaries and rather wistfully concluded on the "great apostate" Burke:

> It is consoling to the lovers of human nature to reflect that Edmund Burke, the only writer of that faction "whose name would not sully the page of an opponent," learnt the discipline of his genius in a different corps. At the flames which rise from the altar of freedom he kindled that torch with which he since endeavored to set fire to her temple.

In December 1796 he also wrote an *Ode To The Departing Year*, a sort of companion piece for his *Religious Musings* completed two years before. In this he speaks of England's tyranny as, "doomed to fall, enslaved and vile." In another, similar poem on "The Destiny of Nations" he lists the perfidies committed by England and gives in unusually realistic detail the horrors of war for the common people, ending with a powerful stanza:

> But chief by Afric's wrongs
> Strange, horrible and foul!
> By what deep guilt belongs
> To the deaf Synod "full of gifts and his"
> By Wealth's insensate laugh! By Torture's hand
> Avenger, rise!

Early in 1797 his family, with the addition of little David Hartley born in September, moved to a cottage in Stowey, secured by Thomas Poole with whom Coleridge was now—and remained most of his life—on close and friendly terms.

Here, too, he thought of such desperate expedients for making a living as entering the Unitarian Ministry. Hazlitt in one of his essays describes how he first met Coleridge at a "trial sermon" he gave in 1798. However, Coleridge was saved from entering the ministry by the unconditional gift of a £150 annuity from two brothers, friends of Thomas Poole. They were liberal manufacturers whose father had founded the famous Wedgewood Pottery Works.

Then, in June, Wordsworth and his sister visited Coleridge and the immediate results were the intimate friendship already referred to in the life of Wordsworth, and the rich blossoming of both poets' as yet largely potential powers.

Coleridge spoke of the triumverate as "three people with one soul"; Dorothy described him in a letter to her future sister-in-law:

You had a great loss in not seeing Coleridge. He is a wonderful man. His conversation teems with soul, mind, and spirit. Then he is so benevolent, so good tempered and cheerful, and, like William, interests himself so much about every little trifle. At first I thought him very plain, that is, for about three minutes: he is pale and thin, has a wide mouth, thick lips, and not very good teeth, longish loose-growing half-curling rough black hair. But if you hear him speak for five minutes you think no more of them. His eye is large and full, not dark but grey; such an eye as would receive from a heavy soul the dullest expression; but it speaks every emotion of his animated mind; it has more of the "poet's eye in a fine frenzy rolling" than I ever witnessed. He has fine dark eyebrows, and an overhanging forehead.

Coleridge describes Wordsworth as, "a very great man, the only man to whom *at all times* and *in all modes* of excellence I feel myself inferior." Even the reserved, self-centered Wordsworth speaks of Coleridge's thought as "a majestic river, the sound or sight of whose course you caught at intervals; which was then sometimes concealed by forests, sometimes lost in sand; then came flashing out broad and distinct; and even when it took a turn which your eye could not follow, yet you always felt and knew that there was a connection in its parts, and that it was the same river."

Unwilling to be separated from Coleridge again, the Wordsworths took a house nearby and for over a year the inseparable companionship of the three continued. It flowered in the *Lyrical Ballads* which contained a preface talked by Coleridge and written by Wordsworth, as well as Coleridge's *Ancient Mariner* and many of Wordsworth's best short poems.

The close, creative intercourse of the three is well illustrated by a few cross references between the poems of the two young men and Dorothy's journal. Her note on seeing daffodils and one or two other hints which were immortalized in some of Wordsworth's loveliest poems have already been mentioned. But in Coleridge, too, we often find the same magical process. For example, one note in Dorothy's diary reads: "One only leaf upon the top of a tree—the sole remaining leaf—danced round and round like a rag blown by the wind." And in *Christabel* we find:

> There is not wind enough to twirl
> The one red leaf, the last of its clan,
> That dances as often as dance it can,
> Hanging so light, and hanging so high,
> On the topmost twig that looks up at the sky.

Again, Dorothy's journal reads: "When we left home the moon immensely large, the sky scattered over with clouds. These soon closed in, contracting the dimensions of the moon without concealing her." And in *Christabel* again we find:

> The thin gray cloud is spread on high,
> It covers but not hides the sky.
> The moon is behind, and at the full;
> And yet she looks both small and dull.

Nor was this a one-way process. Many of Wordsworth's finest poems carry further an idea written or half written into one of Coleridge's comparatively few finished poems or many magnificent fragments. For example, the famous Lucy poem beginning "Three years she grew in sun and shower" must have been inspired—and directed—by these lines from Coleridge's "Nightingale."

> . . . my dear babe,
> Who, capable of no articulate sound,
> Mars all things with his imitative lisp.
> How he would place his hand beside his ear,
> His little hand, the small forefinger up,
> And bid us listen! And I deem it wise
> To make him Nature's play-mate. He knows well
> The evening star; and once, when he awoke
> In most distressful mood (some inward pain
> Had made up that strange thing, an infant's dream),
> I hurried with him to our orchard-plot,
> And he beheld the moon, and, hushed at once,
> Suspends his sobs and laughs most silently,
> While his fair eyes, that swam with undropped tears,
> Did glitter in the yellow moonbeam! . . .

Truly ideas as well as coins were here magnificently "aspheterized."

The little group attracted many interesting visitors including Hazlitt, the Lambs, and a certain John Thelwall, a radical who had been barely acquitted of a capital charge of High Treason two years before.

He had written to Coleridge about an article in *The Watchman* and a lively correspondence had followed. Now he visited him, looking for a cottage in which to settle since government surveillance made his life in London impossible. He was taken on many walks and picnics and when, in one visit to a particularly remote romantic glen Dorothy had discovered, Coleridge humorously asked him: "Citizen John, is not this an excellent place to talk treason in?" he answered gravely, "Nay, Citizen Samuel, it is rather a place to make one forget there is any necessity for treason."

The result of his visit, when reported by a government spy who had been sent down independently to investigate the poets, was that next year the Wordsworths found it impossible to renew their lease or secure any other house in the vicinity!

Meanwhile Coleridge had been deeply shaken and disillusioned by Southey's defection and the failure of all his early hopes for a practical political career. His most deep-seated conviction at this time was a hatred of war—in which his religious and political beliefs both joined—and he was shocked at Napoleon's seemingly unprovoked invasion of Republican Switzerland. After waiting a few days in hopes of the French people's revolt against Napoleon, he gave them up as well and wrote his famous *France: An Ode*. This begins, as he himself described it, with "An invocation to those objects in Nature the contemplation of which had inspired the Poet with a devotional love of Liberty." The second stanza, quoted below, then continues, as Coleridge said, with "The exultation of the Poet at the commencement of the French Revolution, and his unqualified abhorrence of the Alliance against the Republic."

> When France in wrath her giant-limbs upreared
> And with that oath, which smote air, earth, and sea,
> Stamped her strong foot and said she would be free,
> Bear witness for me, how I hoped and feared!
> With what a joy my lofty gratulation
>   Unawed I sang, amid a slavish band:
> And when to whelm the disenchanted nation,
>   Like fiends embattled by a wizard's wand,
>   The Monarchs marched in evil day,
>   And Britain joined the dire array;
>   Though dear her shores and circling ocean,
> Though many friendships, many youthful loves,
>   Had swol'n the patriot emotion,
> And flung a magic light o'er all her hills and groves;
> Yet still my voice, unaltered, sang defeat
>   To all that braved the tyrant-quelling lance,
> And shame too long delayed and vain retreat!
> For ne'er, O Liberty! with partial aim
> I dimmed thy light or damped thy holy flame;
>   But blessed the paeans of delivered France,
> And hung my head and wept at Britain's name.

The rest of the poem traces his political beliefs with great truth and power and ends with a less forceful attempt to convince himself—as Wordsworth was beginning to do—that true freedom lay in the individual soul and must be sought in communion with nature, not in politics.

A sad letter to his brother, George, tells of this change:

> Shall a nation of drunkards presume to babble against sickness and the headache? . . . I have scrapped my squeaking baby-trumpet of sedition, and the fragments lie scattered in the lumber-room of penitence. I wish to be a good man and a Christian, but I am no Whig, no Reformist, no Republican.

The same letter goes on, significantly enough, to describe taking laudanum, not for sleep, but for a kind of repose which is "a spot of enchantment, a green spot of fountains and trees in the very heart of a waste of sand." However, at this time he was still keeping a notebook with such remarks as, "Property, intended to secure to every man the produce of his toil—as at present instituted, operates directly contrary to this, Nota Bene."
And in reference to the French Revolution he still said:

> . . . Like a mighty giantess,
> Seized in some travail of prodigious birth,
> Her groans were horrible! but O! most fair
> The Twins she bore—Equality and Peace!

During the same period he wrote "Fears in Solitude" which deals with the general expectation of a French invasion. In this poem, while the poet shares the general fear, he writes angrily of those at home who "swell the war-whoop, passionate for war," and a few lines later, of:

> . . . Boys and girls,
> And women that would groan to see a child
> Pull off an insect's leg, all read of war,
> The best amusement for our morning meal!

Finally in September, unable longer to tolerate his own troubled thoughts, he persuaded the Wordsworths to join him in a year of travel and study in Germany, promising his wife—and himself—that he would return with a *Life of Lessing* that should make their fortune.

In Germany they separated, the Wordsworths traveling and Coleridge settling down, first in a private home to learn the language, and then at the University to study metaphysics to which he turned as a substitute for his earlier ideas and interests.

When he returned in July 1799 he visited home briefly, went on a walking tour with the Wordsworths, and then up to London to begin writing for the *Morning Post*. A letter he sent Wordsworth at this time gives a valuable insight into his state of mind. He said:

> I do entreat you to go on with *The Recluse*; and I wish you would write a poem in blank verse, addressed to those who, in consequence of the complete failure of the French Revolution, have thrown up all hopes of the amelioration of mankind and are sinking into "almost epicurean selfishness."

Here he continued to attack the war, although now entirely on grounds of England's welfare. The essays are closely argued and well-written, and won a very warm response from the Whig public among whom the paper chiefly circulated, but one can feel immediately the loss of "enthusiasm" of which Coleridge complained in his letter to Thomas Wedgwood:

> Thank God I have my health perfectly, and I am working, hard; yet the present state of human affairs presses on me for days together, so as to deprive me of all my cheerfulness. It is probable that a man's private and personal connections and interests ought to be uppermost in his daily and hourly thoughts and that the dedication of much hope and fear to subjects which are perhaps disproportionate to our faculties and powers, is a disease. But I have had the disease so long, and my early education was so undomestic, that I know not how to get rid of it; or even to wish to get rid of it. Life were so flat a thing without enthusiasm, that if for a moment it leaves me, I have a sort of stomach sensation attached to all my thoughts, like those which succeed to the pleasurable sensations of a dose of opium.

Excerpts from a typical article in the issue of February 6, 1800, although still opposing the war as a matter of policy, clearly lack the emotion of the poet, which was so much a part of the Bristol Lectures and *The Watchman:*

> To us the turn of the debate on Monday is a matter of hope and exultation. The harangues of the Ministers were absolute confessions of weakness. Long and tedious details of French

aggressions, which, if they had been as fair and accurate as they were false and partial, would still prove nothing. . . . More than one half of Mr. Pitt's speech was consumed in the old re-repeated tale of the origin of the war. This can be nothing more than an appeal to passion. For let us suppose for a moment, that we and not the French were the aggressors, the unprovoked aggressors; that they were innocent and we guilty—yet how would this affect the subject of peace? Is any man so contemptibly ignorant of the rules and first foundations of State morality, as to affirm that because our Ministers had entered into a war knavishly, that therefore the people were bound in honor or honesty to conclude a peace ruinously? . . . What two nations were ever at war, and did not obstinately charge the aggression, each on the other? Has not this been matter of course since the time that the introduction of the Christian Religion has made the governors of mankind afraid to state conquest or glory as their motives? And to adduce that as a political reason against the propriety of concluding a peace, or even of entering on a negotiation! . . .

Mr. Pitt railed most bitterly at the character of Bonaparte, and charged all the treaties that were broken, to him, upon no other ground, for the greater part, than that he was instrumental in making them! But the truth is, Mr. Pitt knows Bonaparte to be sincere, and, therefore, will not negotiate; because the negotiation would lead to a peace, which peace would baffle that idle hope of restoring the French monarchy, which, spite of the document sent to Petersburgh, is and has been the real object of Ministers, both in beginning and continuing the war.

Another article the next month warms into indignation over the apostacy of a former radical, Arthur Young, and shows how unwilling Coleridge is to give himself up for lost. His bitterness at Young's self-seeking is unquestionably sincere. Twenty years later Hazlitt in an article discussing the three famous renegades. Wordsworth, Coleridge and Southey, points out that only Coleridge refused, half unconsciously, to make any real profit out of the desertion into which disappointment, weakness and loneliness rather than veniality had led him. Coleridge himself says much later, speaking of the years between 1795 and 1800:

> . . . for I was at that period of my life so compleatly hag-ridden by the fear of being influenced by selfish motives, that to know a mode of conduct to be the dictate of prudence was a sort of presumptive proof to my feelings that the contrary was the dictate of duty.

His refusal a few months later to continue with the eminently successful newspaper work he was doing is one of many instances that seem to bear out this statement.

Coleridge's review of Young's book, which tried to analyze the basic reasons and suggest feasible remedies for the hardships caused by a current scarcity of wheat, began by focusing attention on its author's change from ardent liberalism to violent reaction.

> The Public are well acquainted with Arthur Young. Formerly agasp for reform, he now raves against all reformation, as dogs contract hydrophobia from excessive thirst. We impeach him not of insincerity; a proneness to charge either church or state prophets with the guilt of conscious imposture we hold an unequivocal symptom of a vulgar and unreflecting mind. Arthur Young sympathized with his country in a sentiment of horror against the excesses of the French Revolution; he was aware that some portion of this horror would attack all who, like himself, had blown the trump of gratulation on the first approach of that revolution; and he hastened to avow his recantation in a work almost lyrically unconnected, and set to a more boisterous music than would have suited any species of the Lyric except the Palinodia.

Coleridge then spoke with suave irony of the material rewards by which such a renegade's new opinions are more dependably secured than his old ones ever were. Since, however, the book Young had just written was supposedly of a scientific and nonpartisan nature, Coleridge respectfully turned to consider it.

> The Minister accepted and rewarded his conversion, and thereby secured its permanence. Opinions that are the tenure by which a man holds the comforts and luxuries of a good fortune, are commonly very sincere opinions; though it were as absurd to attribute any moral worth to such sincerity as to believe that there is any religious merit in the unusual strictness with which the poor of this kingdom observe the present Lent. Self-interest is a chilling principle; but it is of excellent use to ministers in the condensation and phialling of any hot vapour that suits their purposes, and which might otherwise have passed off "tenures commixtus in auras". But though we consider Arthur Young at present little less than a "gentleman in the confidence of the government" to use the courteous phrase of a learned judge, yet still he is a man of undoubted information, and, in his particular and most important province [economics] entitled on all occasions to the most respectful attention. We procured his present pamphlet, therefore, with eagerness. "The

Question of Scarcity plainly stated, and Remedies considered," and this too by Arthur Young, excited in us not only curiosity, but a deep and serious interest. . . .

After a devastating analysis of Young's arguments in which Coleridge showed how, at each point, it was social injustice rather than physical necessity which was to blame for the hardships caused by scarcity, he concluded with an indignant refutation of the idea that famine is "the will of God."

. . . The third and last quotation is on an awful subject; we take it from P. 85—"It is the hand of the Almighty which has afflicted the nation."—As men and Christians, how can we suppress the indignant feelings which this sentence excited in our inmost soul? By the author's own confession immense tracts of land are lying waste; the evil which we are suffering might have been wholly prevented by suspending the use of oats for pleasure horses; the money which our [military] expeditions to Quiberan and Holland cost would have purchased rice enough to have kept the cheek of every cottager's child fat and rosy, and have made the deficiency of our crops an unfelt evil; and yet we are gravely assured, that it is the hand of the Almighty which afflicts us; and among other reasons for infidelity and atheism. The hirelings of ministers, and the supporters of a sanguinary war, under the blasphemous plea of a war for the religion of Jesus;—these are for the religion of Jesus;—these are not infidels, not atheists—only the occasion of infidelity, the causes of atheism.—The hand of the Almighty afflicts us!—Thou Eternal Goodness!—far rather art thou by gently and fatherly premonitions drawing us back from the brink of that abyss, to which an evil spirit has been luring us; and a placeman [government hireling] dares draw off our eyes from our own follies and those of our rulers, and proclaims to a suffering nation, that it is thy hand alone which has afflicted them!

Furthermore, Coleridge showed a political penetration rare at the time, or, in fact, at any time, in analyzing the relation of a dictator like Napoleon to the economic interests of the propertied class, and drew a parallel between Napoleon and Pitt which was still a good deal too penetrating for most Whigs:

The system he [Bonaparte] has pursued is well calculated to gain the esteem of men of property, and of persons in easy circumstances, who, relieved from the perpetual terrors in which they have hitherto lived, must look to him as their protector. The same feeling which has secured Mr. Pitt in power, must secure Bonaparte. . . . Property will maintain both Mr. Pitt and Bonaparte in authority . . . unless some sudden unforseen event should give a shock to public opinion. . . . But outward tranquility may exist without content; and the mass of the French people may be as little pleased with the Consulate, as the Irish nation are with the military and flogging system by which they are held in subjection.

However, he was increasingly ill-at-ease in his work on the newspaper and, despite offers of a very large increase in salary and a long-time contract, he gave it up in the spring, undertaking instead some far worse paid work of German translation.

In the summer he took a house near the Wordsworths in the North County. The two years he spent there were to be the "Indian Summer" of his poetry—despite his age of barely twenty-eight.

The close association with William and Dorothy was renewed, but this time it seems to have been fruitful chiefly for Wordsworth, rather than Coleridge. Except for the magnificent unfinished *Christabel* the only important poem he was yet to write is the significantly named "Ode to Dejection" completed in April, 1802. In this, like Wordsworth in his "Ode on Intimations of Immortality," which it may have inspired and which was written the next year, Coleridge mourned, without understanding, the loss of his powers of joy and imagination. He says here, in part:

> There was a time when, though my path was rough,
>   This joy within me dallied with distress,
> And all misfortunes were but as the stuff
>   Whence Fancy made me dream of happiness;
> For hope grew round me, like the twining vine,
> And fruits, and foliage, not my own, seemed mine
> But now afflictions bow me down to earth;
> Nor care I though they rob me of my mirth;
>   But oh! each visitation
> Suspends what nature gave me at my birth,
>   My shaping spirit of imagination.

The enthusiasm and joy he had found in his early adherence to the ideals of the revolution were never replaced, and more analytic and self-critical, as well as less disciplined, than his friend Wordsworth, he could not content himself with a second best that gradually degenerated into third, fourth, and finally bore no resemblance whatever to poetry. Instead Coleridge gave up poetry once and for all to drown his loss in opium and metaphysics.

He still wrote much excellent literary criticism including the earliest and some of the best psychological analyses of Shakespeare's plays, notably *Hamlet*. He completed some interesting articles on current affairs from time to time; and a great deal of aesthetics. But the nearest he again approached poetry was in the use of a witty, sharply pointed couplet for such epitaphs as:

> Of him that in this gorgeous tomb doth lie
> This sad brief tale is all that truth can give;
> He liv'd like one who never thought to die,
> He died like one who dared not hope to live.
>
> . . . .
>
> An excellent adage commands that we should
> Relate of the dead that alone which is good;
> But of the great lord, who here lies in lead
> We know nothing good but that he is dead.

or perhaps, his own epitaph in the verses of the "Ode to Tranquillity, 1802," in which he abjured politics as:

> A wild and dream-like trade of blood and guile,
> Too foolish for a tear, too wicked for a smile.

True to this attitude he did not even comment on the fall of the Pitt ministry, against which he had not only written so many articles but also, in 1795, his most powerful dramatic poem, *Fire, Famine and Slaughter,* and he greeted the Peace of Amiens in 1802 without enthusiasm.

Less than two years later we find him writing articles in favor of a new war with France, travestying his old ideas by declaring that this war truly carried on the work of the English Revolution and that the restoration of the Bourbons would be a step toward freedom! (True, the struggles of the Spanish people against Napoleon's invasion was his ostensible theme, but he watched unmoved the later invasion of Spain by the Bourbons.)

In 1809, looking back, he gives us, with his curious characteristic candor, the motivation of his change, and tells us of his relief at reconciling some echo of enthusiasm with the respect of his society.

> It was the noble efforts of Spanish patriotism that first restored us, without distinction of party, to our characteristic enthusiasm for liberty; and presenting it in its genuine form, incapable of being confounded with its French counterfeit enabled us once more to utter the names of our Hampdens, Sidneys and Russells without hazard of alarming the quiet citizen, or of offending the zealous loyalist.

It is hard even then to think of Coleridge as consciously hypocritical and yet, fundamentally, it doesn't matter. Ironically enough, he himself has given us one of the best psychological analyses of such another renegade—and has also shown why the question of sincerity is irrelevant. He says, in part, discussing Mackintosh or some other Whig who followed Burke's early defection:

> Did Curio, the quondam patriot, reformer and semi-revolutionist abjure his opinion, and yell the foremost in the hunt of persecution against his old friends and fellow-philosophists, with a cold clear predetermination, formed at one moment . . . ? I neither know nor care. Probably not. A violent motive may revolutionize a man's opinion and professions. But more frequently his honesty dies away imperceptibly from evening into twilight and from twilight into utter darkness. He turns hypocrite so gradually, and by such tiny atoms of motion that by the time he has arrived at a given point, he forgets his own hypocrisy in the imperceptible degrees of his own conversion.

With Coleridge the degrees were similarly imperceptible. As late as 1808 he described the early Abolitionists as men "who fought and conquered the legalized banditti of men-stealers, the numerous and powerful perpetrators and advocates of rapine, murder, and (of blacker guilt than either) slavery."

In 1815 he fought against the Corn laws and in 1818 gave powerful support to an anti-child labor law (Perl's Factory Reform Act). In his *Biographia Literaria*, 1817, he used "slave ship" as an instance of the ultimate in human horror and said,

> I shall never forget the *disgust* with which Mackintosh's "bear witness", *I recant, abjure,* and *abhor* the principles—i.e. of his Vindicia Gallica [a book which Mackintosh had written in defense of the French Revolution] struck his audience.

But in 1811 he had so completely forgotten his own anger at the use of "Jacobin" as an epithet (see p. 438) that he could write sarcastically about a liberal peer, Sir Frances Burdett, a leader of the antiwar party:

> A Jacobin indeed! No, Sir F. B. wants reform only. What that is to be, and how far it is to go, he does not know at present; "but when great numbers of persons are assembled" then it will come out. For who ever witnessed a great assemblage rudely called a mob . . . but must have acknowledged

its consummate fitness for the complex and difficult questions of legislature? . . . A Jacobin indeed! No! he wishes the legislature to grant him and his party their demands, fairly and in a friendly way; only if they do not, and in a reasonable time too, they must expect "a resumption of power by an aggrieved and oppressed people!" It cannot be denied that an excitement of the people to resume the supreme power . . . has been pronounced by all our law sages to be always sedition, and in aggravated cases, treason. . . . But as to his being a Jacobin, it is really too extravagant!

Mem.—Not a single toast was given at the dinner of these patriots, to our army or to the cause of Portugal and Spain!

In 1814 he no longer recalled his indignation at those who blamed God's will for man's tyranny (see p. 452) and attacked a liberal judge, who had sympathized with the misery of the Irish people:

Your Lordship might have learnt from one of our wisest poets and historians, how unphilosophic it is to transfer the whole blame of disquiet or rebellion from a country to its governors.

Never are the people wholly free
From guilt of wounds they suffer in the war.
Never did any public misery
Rise of itself! God's plagues well grounded are
On common stains of our humanity!

Finally, in 1833 he had actually traveled so far from his youthful hatred of slavery that he could write to an acquaintance who had been urging its abolition:

You are always talking of the *rights* of the Negroes. As a rhetorical mode of stimulating the people of England *here*, I do not object; but I utterly condemn your frantic practice of declaiming about their rights to the blacks themselves. They ought to be forcibly reminded of the state in which their brethren in Africa still are, and taught to be thankful for the providence which has placed them within the reach of the means of grace. [!]

But all this is a posthumous story as far as the poet, Coleridge, is concerned. Emotionally he died in 1800 and it is no wonder that the poor shade he became looked back wistfully to those early days.

Time and time again in the last fifteen years of his life we find such comments as: "My feelings . . . and imagination did not remain unkindled in this general conflagration, and I confess I should be more inclined to be ashamed than proud of myself, if they had. I was a sharer in the general vortex, though my little world described the pattern of its revolution in an orbit of its own." and "Oh never can I remember those days with either shame or regret. For I was most sincere, most disinterested. My opinions were, indeed, in many and most important points erroneous; but my heart was single."

Again, it would be well to let Hazlitt have the last word and sum up the contemporary whom above all others he loved, judged and mourned for.

> . . . this was long after, but all the former while, he had nerved his heart and filled his eyes with tears, as he hailed the rising orb of liberty, since quenched in darkness and in blood, and had kindled his affections at the blaze of the French Revolution, and sang for joy, when the towers of the Bastille and the proud places of the insolent and the oppressor fell, and would have floated his bark, freighted with fondest fancies across the Atlantic wave with Southey and others to seek for peace and freedom. . . .
>
> . . . Liberty (the philosopher's and the poet's bride) had fallen a victim meanwhile to the murderous practises of the hag Legitimacy. [The restoration of the Bourbons.] Proscribed by court-hirelings, too romantic for the herd of vulgar politicians, our enthusiast stood at bay, and at last turned on the pivot of a subtle casuistry to the *unclean side* but his discursive reason would not let him trammel himself into a poet-laureate or stamp-distributor; and he stopped ere he had quite passed that well-known, "Bourne from whence no traveller returns"—and so has sunk into torpid, uneasy repose, tantalized by useless resources, haunted by vain imaginings, his lips idly moving, but his heart forever still, or, as the shattered chords vibrate of themselves, making melancholy music to the ear of memory! Such is the fate of genius in an age when in the unequal contest with sovereign wrong, every man is ground to powder who is not either a born slave, or who does not willingly and at once offer up the yearnings of humanity and the dictates of reason as a welcome sacrifice to besotted prejudice and loathsome power.

William Hazlitt—1778-1830

Hazlitt was unlucky in money and unlucky in love; he lived to see his dearest hopes defeated and most of his closest friends turn against him; he was attacked by political enemies—many of them, former friends—with a personal malignity that destroyed his reputation during his life, robbed him of the better part of a well-deserved fame, and did not end with his death. Yet, dying exhausted and poor at fifty-two, of a stomach cancer which had tortured him intermittently for three years, he could truthfully say "Well, I've had a happy life."

"Give me that man that is not fortune's fool and I will wear him at my heart's core—yea in my heart of hearts." In his youth Hazlitt was fond of saying "I started in life with the French Revolution." In middle age he wrote:

> No man would, I think, exchange his existence with any other man, however fortunate. We had as lief *not be*, as *not be ourselves*. There are some persons of that reach of soul that they would like to live two hundred and fifty years hence, to see to what height of empire America will have grown up in that period, or whether the English constitution will last so long. These are points beyond me. But I confess I should like to live to see the downfall of the Bourbons. That is a vital question with me; and I shall like it the better, the sooner it happens!

Less than a month before his death he struggled out of bed to comment on the deposition of Charles X:

> Let him go where he chooses with a handsome pension, but let him not be sent back again at the expense of millions of lives! . . . Even then I should not despair. The Revolution of the Three Days [July 1830] was like a resurrection from the dead, and showed plainly that liberty too has a spirit of life in it, and that the hatred of oppressors is "the unquenchable flame, the worm that dies not!"

Hazlitt was no stoic. He loved beauty passionately, both in nature and in painting; no essayist but Lamb has ever surpassed him in appreciative description of the small daily joys afforded by the keen and sensitive use of taste and touch and sight and sound and smell—and even Lamb must bow to him when these things are to be enjoyed in the open air; perhaps no one but Coleridge ever read books with so much pleasure or to such good purpose; he loved the theatre and with characteristic sentiment the year before his death he said of his beloved corner in Covent Gardens, "I would, if I could, have it surrounded with a balustrade of gold, for it has been to me a palace of delight."

While fiercely shy, hypersensitive, easily embarrassed or angered, and often seemingly erratic in personal relationships, he was generous with his own time, energy and money, and scrupulous with that of others; unwilling, in the face of extreme provocation, to let private quarrels or ill usage affect his critical opinions and, in the very rare instances where he was stung into allowing this, quick in offering a public correction. Lamb, who was his best friend but was also a clear-eyed and critical judge of men, wrote publicly of Hazlitt during a long period of estrangement:

> I wish he would not quarrel with the world at the rate he does; but the reconciliation must be effected by himself, and I despair of living to see that day. But—protesting against much that he has written, and some things which he chooses to do; judging him by his conversation which I enjoyed so long, and relished so deeply, or by his books, in those places where no clouding passion intervenes—I should belie my own conscience, if I said less than that I think W. H. to be, in his natural state, one of the wisest and finest spirits breathing. So far from being ashamed of that intimacy which was betwixt us, it is my boast that I was able for so many years to have preserved it entire; and I think I shall go to my grave without finding, or expecting to find, such another companion.

While it was impossible for his early republican friends, turned place hunters and Tory apologists, to tolerate him—"He hath a daily beauty in his life that makes mine ugly"—he found warm admirers in many of the younger artists and journalists who got to know him in middle age. These afforded him some companionship although unfortunately none were equal in power and intellect to his older friends—Coleridge, Wordsworth, and Lamb—or to Hazlitt himself. The one exception, Keats, was tragically lost to Hazlitt and the world when their relation had just begun to grow from friendly acquaintance to friendship. The much younger Keats has left behind many expressions of his respect and admiration for Hazlitt; and Hazlitt, in addition to an early remark about his respect for Keats' critical judgment of poetry, has shown his admiration and concern not only in his warm tribute to Keats as one of the English poets, but also in comments scattered through many of his other essays (see p. 572 for example).

Hazlitt's father was a dissenting minister—a Unitarian—who, in addition to his unorthodox religion, was also guilty of even more unpopular political opinions. His honesty and love of freedom made him sympathize so outspokenly with the colonists in the American

Revolution that he lost several pulpits and finally, in 1784 at the close of the war, the family left England for America which, as Hazlitt's older sister, then fourteen, wrote in her diary, was to them "a perfect land where no tyrants were to rule, no bigots to hate and persecute their brethren, no intrigues to feed the flame of discord and fill the land with woe."

Their ship brought the first news of the peace treaty to the Colonies!

Unfortunately, they found that religious bigotry was even more active in the new world than in the old. Reverend Hazlitt was offered several good pulpits and even the presidency of Carlisle College on the condition of his accepting Calvinism. Being his son's father he said he "would rather die in a ditch." Finally a congregation in Boston, having heard him preach, invited him to be their minister but, as his daughter's journal tells us, "the persecuting zeal of the orthodox sent one of their chosen brethren after him, and thus put a stop to his settling there."

After two years of other similarly disheartening experiences, he sadly decided upon a return to England and, leaving his family, went back to try to find a pulpit there. He was able to send for them seven months later, but this separation evidently made a deep impression on the nine-year-old whom he always spoke of as "My William."

William had a deep love and respect for his father and was accustomed to his close daily companionship. The two other children were much older—John, at twenty was already earning his living as a portrait painter—and his mother had been unhappily occupied with the birth, illness, and death of a younger brother and three little sisters during William's short life. In America William had accompanied his father on almost all his numerous trips about the countryside and sat on a footstool in the pulpit, hidden by the rostrum itself, while his father preached. When, for some six months, the elder Hazlitt was walking five miles every Sunday to a temporary pulpit, his daughter notes in her journal: "How often have we stood at the window, looking at my father as he went up this road with William in his nankeen dress, marching by his side, like one that could never be tired."

Both father and son already took it for granted that the son, too, would grow up to "speak for the truth"—as, indeed, he did, although in somewhat different fashion—and the one letter we have from William at this period shows him unhappy at the separation, angry at America, and studying his Latin grammar with a fierce concentration. Finally the father found a poorly paid pulpit in an obscure—though beautiful—village named Wem, and the family was reunited.

William's happiness at the reunion, at the long delightful hours of study with a patient learned teacher, at the uninhibited use of all his physical prowess—he was slight but both strong and skillful —in games with the village children, make the next six years a wonderful unchequered stretch of happiness for him, so that in after life everything pleasant reminds him of Wem and country sights or sounds can often bring him the keenest delight in the middle of the most unhappy moods.

In 1790 he went to some of his father's friends in Liverpool for a lengthy visit and in his letters home we catch glimpses of the forthright, serious, moral concern which was always to characterize Hazlitt's view of men and affairs. His hostess took him to dinner at a wealthy gentleman's and he wrote his mother: "He is a very rich man, but—the man who is a well-wisher to slavery, is always a slave himself. The King, who wishes to enslave all mankind, is a slave to ambition. The man who wishes to enslave all mankind for his king, is himself a slave to his king. . . ."

The next year he first broke into print by a letter to a local newspaper about the burning of Dr. Priestley's house in a government inspired riot, and two years later he entered the New College in Hackney (formerly Hackney Theological Institute) which Dr. Priestley had helped to found.

During the interim he had begun to discover modern literature and to lose his religious beliefs. He later wrote at some length about his introduction to *Tom Jones* and to Burke's orations, but the beginning of his freethinking was too painfully associated with his father's bitter disappointment for him to discuss it in any detail. However, he was still—at fifteen—just beginning to question, and unwilling to shock his father with his doubts, so that he entered the college on a grant intended for prospective clergymen.

There he found an atmosphere which nurtured both his already deeply rooted political radicalism and his growing religious scepticism. In founding the school in April 1791, Dr. Priestley had said:

> Another and most important circumstance which calls us to attend to the proper education of our youth, is the new light which is now—bursting out in favor of the civil rights of men, and the great objects and uses of civil government. While so

favorable a mind is abroad, let every young mind expand itself, catch the rising gale, and partake of the glorious enthusiasm— Let the liberal youth be everywhere encouraged to study the nature of government. . . .

This attitude, despite growing reaction, still formed the spirit of the school in 1793 when Hazlitt entered it. Eighteen or twenty of the students invited Thomas Paine to a college supper; the college as a whole was deeply concerned over the transportation of Palmer and Muir on trumped-up charges of sedition; and when Thomas Hardy and Horne Tooke, on trial for similar charges, were acquitted, the young Hazlitt ran wildly through the streets at six in the morning knocking at every house in which he had any acquaintance to call out joyously, "Not Guilty! Not Guilty!"

Finally, in his last year—1795—he had to tell his father he would never be a minister and was withdrawn from the school. The next three years were useful but unhappy ones. The young man divided his time between his home and his brother's studio in London. At home he read—Rousseau, Shakespeare, political economy, philosophy—and struggled with an essay on political rights which wouldn't get written; in London he met Godwin, Holcroft, Fawcett, Horne Tooke and, a little later, Charles Lamb; but in both places he was conscious of his father's unhappiness, his family's disappointment, his own seeming lack of useful employment or purpose, and the embarrassment which his pennilessness and inexperience caused him when in the presence of the young girls to whom as a group he was becoming strongly attracted.

However, this was a fruitful period, although the fruits were to take some time to ripen. In a political essay written many years later he tells the effect Rousseau had upon him:

> It was Rosseau who brought the feeling of irreconcilable enmity to rank and privileges above humanity home to the bosom of every man,— identified it with all the pride of intellect and with the deepest yearnings of the human heart. He was the founder of Jacobinism, which disclaims the division of the species into two classes, the one the property of the other. It was of the disciples of his school, where principle is converted into a passion, that Mr. Burke said, and said truly—"Once a Jacobin, always a Jacobin."

And in the famous account of his meeting with Coleridge in 1798 we have fully described the most important single event in his life.

It is pleasant, too, to get a glimpse of Hazlitt on his 20th birthday, April 10, 1798, soon after this meeting, when he managed to combine almost all of his dearest loves into one of the perfectly happy days he was to remember for the rest of his life:

> It was on the tenth of April 1798, and I sat down to a volume of the New Eloise, at the inn at Llangollen, over a bottle of sherry and a cold chicken. The letter I chose was that in which St. Preux describes his feelings as he first caught a glimpse from the heights of the Jura of the Pays de Vaud, which I had brought with me as a *bonne bouche* to crown the evening with. It was my birthday, and I had for the first time come from a place in the neighbourhood to visit this delightful spot. The road to Llangollen turns off between Chirk and Wrexham; and on passing a certain point, you come all at once upon the valley, which opens like an amphitheatre, broad, barren hills rising in majestic state on either side, with "green upland swells that echo to the bleat of flocks" below, and the river Dee babbling over its stony bed in the midst of them. The valley at this time "glittered green with sunny showers", and a budding ash-tree dipped its tender branches in the chiding stream. How proud, how glad I was to walk along the high road that overlooks the delicious prospect, repeating the lines which I have just quoted from Mr. Coleridge's poems.

However, when one's father has a living worth just £20 a year and one's older brother is barely able to support his own household in modest comfort, twenty is high time to stop preparing and begin earning. At first, simply in desperation since he wouldn't preach and, it seemed, couldn't write, Hazlitt turned back to the childish purpose he had expressed in a letter to his brother ten years before:

> You want to know what I do. I am a busybody, and do many silly things: I drew eyes and noses till about a fortnight ago. I have drawn a little boy since, a man's face, and a little boy's front face, taken from a bust. Next Monday I shall begin to read Ovid's Metamorphoses and Eutropius. I shall like to know all the Latin and Greek I can. I want to learn how to measure the stars. I shall not, I suppose, paint the worse for knowing everything else.

He still had a facility in drawing; John was doing well as a miniature painter and glad to give his brother all the assistance in his power; and his father seems to have found it easier to accept an attempt at painting than the devotion to a kind of philosophical writing which he associated with his son's loss of faith.

Accordingly he went to London to study art as a matter of expedience, but a few months later when he had his first opportunity to see a collection of truly great paintings, including a number of Titians and Raphaels, he wrote:

> I was staggered when I saw the works there collected, and looked at them with wondering and with longing eyes. A mist passed away from my sight; the scales fell off. A new sense came upon me, a new heaven and a new earth stood before me . . . From that time I lived in a world of pictures. Battles, sieges, speeches in Parliament seemed mere idle noise and fury, "signifying nothing", compared with these mighty works that spoke to me in the eternal silence of thought.

However, this was clearly hyperbole for even while deeply engrossed in art we find him, in 1799, discussing Mackintosh's popular lectures during which occurred the now infamous declaration,

> It is my intention to profess publicly and unequivocally that I abhor, abjure, and forever renounce the French Revolution with its sanguinary history, its abominable principles, and forever execrable leaders.

Hazlitt's comment was:

> If all that body of opinion and principles of which the orator read his recantation was unfounded, if there was an end of all those views and hopes that pointed to future improvement, it was not a matter of triumph or exultation to the lecturer or anybody else, to the young or the old, the wise or the foolish; on the contrary, it was a subject of regret, of slow, reluctant, painful admission—"of lamentation loud through rueful air."

Again, he often refers to the misery of life in the London slums. The only women who would, at that time, pose as models were drawn from the underworld of prostitution with which, as we have seen, the decline of the countryside had already so thickly populated London when Blake was beginning to write a quarter of a century before. Hazlitt, touching on some parliamentary eulogy of the heroism and suffering of soldiers, says :

> The 70,000 prostitutes alone in the streets of London . . . probably experience more bitterness of heart every day of their lives than is caused by any campaign however wild.

He was, by 1802, probably earning his very frugal living by his brush, and he has left us a special note of one painting which marked an important achievement in his personal as well as his professional life:

> To give one instance more, and then I will have done with rambling discourse. One of my first attempts was a picture of my father, who was then in a green old age, with strong-marked features, and scarred with the small-pox. I drew it with a broad light crossing the face, looking down, with spectacles on, reading. . . . The sketch promised well; and I set to work to finish it, determined to spare no time nor pains. My father was willing to sit as long as I pleased; for there is a natural desire in the mind of man to sit for one's picture, to be the object of continued attention, to have one's likeness multiplied; and besides his satisfaction in the picture, he had some pride in the artist, though he would have rather I should have written a sermon than painted like Rembrandt or like Raphael. Those winter days, with the gleams of sunshine coming through the chapel windows, and cheered by the notes of the robin red-breast (that "ever in the haunch of winter sings")—as my afternoon's work drew to a close, were among the happiest of my life. When I gave the effect I intended to any part of the picture for which I had prepared my colours, when I imitated the roughness of the skin by a lucky stroke of the pencil, when I hit the clear pearly tone of a vein, when I gave the ruddy complexion of health, the blood circulating under the broad shadows of one side of the face, I thought my fortune was made; or rather it was already more than made, in my fancying that I might one day be able to say with Correggio, "*I also am a painter!*" It was an idle thought, a boy's conceit; but it did not make me less happy at the time. I used regularly to set my work in the chair to look at it through the long evenings; and many a time did I return to take leave of it before I could go to bed at night. I remember sending it with a throbbing heart to the Exhibition, and seeing it hung up there by the side of one of the Honourable Mr. Skeffington.

That year the Peace of Amiens made it possible for him to go to the Louvre and he secured commissions for ten or twelve copies of pictures to be made there, which paid his way. There too he was thrilled not only by the overwhelming beauty he recognized, but also by the fact that the museum guard and others addressed him as "citoyen"! And in commenting on a picture of the twelve apostles he says that Clarkson, the hero of the antislavery movement whom he had met, resembled several of them and should be added as a thirteenth "a true apostle of human redemption." Evidently nothing Hazlitt deeply felt could long remain divorced from politics in his thinking.

The renewal of the war in 1803 affected him deeply, and despite the fact that many cooling republicans, including most of his old friends, took this occasion to join respectable conservative opinion by supporting the "new" war, Hazlitt, from the first, stoutly maintained that there was nothing new about it and that the Peace had been a government strategy to make possible the union of all factions in support of hostilities. This unpopular belief, openly expressed, lost him many opportunities, but he was fairly successful as an itinerant portrait painter and even earned enough for the extravagance of publishing his finally completed philosophical *Essay in Defense of the Natural Disinterestedness of the Human Mind* at his own expense in 1805. This is almost the only thing Hazlitt ever wrote which was not well written. While the utilitarian philosophy he was attacking is no longer general enough to give it current importance, the conclusion may be worth quoting for the insight it gives us into Hazlitt's thought:

> I naturally desire and pursue my own good (in whatever this consists) simply from my having an idea of it sufficiently warm and vivid to excite in me an emotion of interest, or passion; and I love and pursue the good of others, of a relation, of a friend, of a family, a community, or of mankind for just the same reason. . . . The love of others has the same necessary foundation in the human mind as the love of ourselves.

By 1806 he realized that he would never be a truly great painter—perhaps not even a really good one—and decided to give it up.

One of the last paintings he completed, another one of his father in December 1805, was finished the day Napoleon's victory over Czarist Russia became known in England. Hazlitt wrote years later:

> I think, but am not sure, that I finished this portrait (or another afterwards) on the same day that the news of the battle of Austerlitz came; I walked out in the afternoon, and, as I returned, saw the evening star set over a poor man's cottage with other thoughts than I shall ever have again.

Having laid down his pencil he now necessarily turned to his pen to earn a living, and although it had taken him the better part

of eight years to produce the unremunerative essay which was its
first achievement, from then on he seems to have found no difficulty
in earning—with continuous hard work, it is true—an austere but
sufficient living through his writing, and a little later, lecturing.

A political pamphlet *Free Thoughts On Public Affairs or Advice
to a Patriot*, his second published work, is concise, forceful and
altogether readable as is all of Hazlitt's later writing. In discussing
the changed attitude toward the war he wrote with the dry irony
he was to use so effectively throughout his career:

> As it was a new war, they thought they had a fair right to
> have a new opinion about it; and they exercised their freedom
> of election as eagerly in approving the conduct of ministers in
> entering upon the present war, as they had done in condemning
> their continuance of the former one. For myself, I confess I
> have always looked upon the present war as a continuance of
> the last, carried on upon the same principles and for the same
> purposes.

In his distinction between true patriotism and what we would now
call "jingoism," he rises to heights of impassioned declaration:

> To love one's country is to wish well to it; to prefer its in-
> terests to our own; to oppose every measure inconsistent with
> its welfare; and to be ready to sacrifice ease, health, and life
> itself in its defence. But there is a false kind of patriotism, loud
> and noisy, and ever ready to usurp that name from others, as
> an honourable covering either for selfish designs or blind zeal,
> to which I shall make no pretensions. It has been called pa-
> triotism to flatter those in power at the expense of the people;
> to sail with the stream; to make a popular prejudice the stalking
> horse of ambition, to mislead first and then betray; to enrich
> yourself out of the public treasure; to strengthen your influence
> by pursuing such measures as give to the richest members of
> the community an opportunity of becoming richer, and to laugh
> at the waste of blood and the general misery which they occa-
> sion; to defend every act of a party, and to treat all those as
> enemies of their country who do not think the pride of a min-
> ister and the avarice of a few of his creatures of more conse-
> quence than the safety and happiness of a free, brave, industri-
> ous and honest people; to strike at the liberty of other countries,
> and through them at your own; to change the maxims of a
> state, to degrade its spirit, to insult its feelings and tear from
> it its well-earned and proudest distinctions; to soothe the follies
> of the multitude, to lull them in their sleep, to goad them on
> in their madness, and, under the terror of imaginary evils, to

cheat them of their best privileges; to blow the blast of war for a livelihood in journals and pamphlets and by spreading abroad incessantly a spirit of defiance, animosity, suspicion, distrust, and the most galling contempt, to make it impossible that we should ever remain at peace or in safety.

In economics his opposition to the majority opinion was as prompt and forthright as in politics. The Rev. Malthus' "Essay on Population" had already become a new testament whose revelation was accepted by both Whigs and Tories. In the dispassionate terms of the Encyclopedia Britannica this revelation stated that "—the realization of a happy society will always be hindered by the miseries consequent on the tendency of population to increase faster than the means of subsistence.—Population is prevented from increasing beyond those limits [of the means of subsistence] by the positive [and therefore providential] checks of war, famine and pestilence, and by the influence of misery and vice. From this theory Malthus drew the important practical conclusion for the England of his day that the existing poor law system, with its indiscriminate doles and . . . [increased allowances to] large families, was utterly to be condemned as tending to aggravate the very evils which it was supposed to remedy . . . [the poor should] practice 'moral restraint'. By this term Malthus understood the postponement of the age of marriage, accompanied by strict sexual continence."

For Hazlitt, as for Blake, it was an abomination used to justify the most inhuman cruelties, and the cogent, closely reasoned arguments with which he attacks Malthus are burning with the heat of his indignation. The essay is too substantial an achievement to quote piecemeal, but it should be read in full. It is unfortunately not of just historical interest today when "doom books" solemnly proving the inevitable insufficiency of the earth's food supply, or the fatal deterioration of its climate, are again being seriously read by "liberals." The close relation between theory and practical politics for Hazlitt is illustrated in his attack the next year on a Poor Law Bill supported by Malthus and introduced by a wealthy member of Parliament. In a newspaper article February 19, 1807, Hazlitt wrote:

> The "champion" [of the poor] should be the child of poverty. The author of our religion, when he came to save the world, took our nature upon him, and became as one of us; it

is not likely that any one should ever prove the saviour of the poor, who has not common feelings with them. . . .

During these years he had become very intimate with the Lambs and now, in 1807, Mary Lamb introduced him to a friend of hers, Sarah Stoddart, a very unconventional, brusque, matter-of-fact, not quite young woman of thirty-two with considerable intelligence, education, vitality, and worldly experience. Despite the fact that she was at least three years older than Hazlitt and not particularly attractive—or, perhaps, because of these factors—they were married in 1808. Neither of them was at all in love. Sarah had, in a three-year correspondence with Mary Lamb, spoken frankly of her desire to be well married and of a series of unsuccessful attempts in that direction; she liked Hazlitt, found him willing enough to have her small income secured to her personal use, and realized that at thirty-two there was little or no chance of her making a better match. Hazlitt, who was deeply romantic and worshipped feminine beauty, had developed an external attitude of harsh indifference or even aversion to young girls to hide his almost pathological shyness in their presence. While during his period as an art student he had had considerable sexual experience, he was still at twenty-nine without any experience at all in terms of courtship or romance. His sister and Mary Lamb, both ten years older than himself, were the only respectable women in whose presence he was comfortable and uninhibited, and Sarah's friendship with Mary made her a welcome fourth in the pleasant evenings he spent at the Lambs.

Three letters—one from Charles to Wordsworth, one from Mary to Sarah, and one from Hazlitt himself to his fiancée, give us the background and tone of this rather odd relationship.

From Charles Lamb to Wordsworth:

> William Hazlitt is in town. I took him to see a very pretty girl professedly, where there were two young girls—the very head and sum of the Girlery was two young girls—they neither laughed nor sneered nor giggled nor whispered—but they were young girls—and he sat and frowned blacker and blacker, indignant that there should be such a thing as Youth and Beauty, till he tore me away before supper in perfect misery, and owned he could not bear young girls. They drove him mad. So I took him home to my old Nurse, [Mary] where he recover'd perfect tranquility. Independent of this, and as I am not a young girl myself, he is a great acquisition to us. He is, rather imprudently, I think, printing a political pamphlet on his own

account, and will have to pay for the paper, etc. The first duty of an Author, I take it, is never to pay anything.

From Mary Lamb to Sarah Stoddard:

Farewell — Determine as wisely as you can in regard to Hazlitt, and, if your determination is to have him, Heaven send you many happy years together. If I am not mistaken, I have concluded letters on the Corydon Courtship with this same wish. I hope it is not ominous of change; for if I were sure you would not be quite starved to death, nor beaten to a mummy, I should like to see Hazlitt and you come together, if (as Charles observes) it were only for the joke sake.

From Hazlitt to Sarah:

My Dear Love, — Above a week has passed, and I have received no letter—not one of those letters "in which I live, or have no life at all". What is become of you? Are you married, hearing that I was dead (for so it has been reported)? Or are you gone into a nunnery? Or are you fallen in love with some of the amorous heroes of Boccaccio? Which of them is it? Is it with Chynon, who was transformed from a clown into a lover, and learned to spell by the force of beauty? Or with Lorenzo, the lover of Isabella, whom her three brethren hated (as your brother does me), who was a merchant's clerk? Or with Federigo Alberigi, an honest gentleman, who ran through his fortune, and won his mistress by cooking a fair falcon for her dinner, though it was the only means he had left of getting a dinner for himself? This last is the man; and I am the more persuaded of it, because I think I won your good liking myself by giving you an entertainment—of sausages, when I had no money to buy them with. Nay now, never deny it! Did not I ask your consent that very night after, and did you not give it? Well, I should be confoundedly jealous of those fine gallants, if I did not know that a living dog is better than a dead lion: though, now I think of it, Boccaccio does not in general make much of his lovers: it is his women who are so delicious. I almost wish I had lived in those times, and had been a little *more amiable*. Now, if a woman had written the book, it would not have had this effect upon me: the men would have been heroes and angels, and the women nothing at all. Isn't there some truth in that? Talking of departed loves, I met my old flame the other day in the street. I did dream of her *one* night since, and only one: every other night I have had the same dream I have had for these two months past. Now, if you are at all reasonable, this will satisfy you.

Thursday morning. — The book is come. When I saw it I thought that you had sent it back in a huff, tired out by my sauciness and *coldness*, and delays, and were going to keep an account of dimities and sayes, or to salt pork and chronicle small beer as the dutiful wife of some fresh-looking rural swain; so that you cannot think how surprised and pleased I was to find them all done. I liked your note as well or better than the extracts; it is just such a note as such a nice rogue as you ought to write after the *provocation* you had received. I would not give a pin for a girl "whose cheeks never tingle" nor for myself if I could not make them tingle sometimes. Now, though I am always writing to you about "lips and noses" and such sort of stuff, yet as I sit by my fireside (which I do generally eight or ten hours a day), I oftener think of you in a serious, sober light. For indeed, I never love you so well as when I think of sitting down with you to dinner on a boiled scrag-end of mutton, and hot potatoes. You please my fancy more then than when I think of you in—no, you would never forgive me if I were to finish the sentence. Now I think of it, what do you mean to be dressed in when we are married? But it does not much matter! I wish you would let your hair grow; though perhaps nothing will be better than "the same air and look with which at first my heart was took". But now to business, I mean soon to call upon your brother *in form*, namely, as soon as I get quite well, which I hope to do in about another *fortnight*: and then I hope you will come up by the coach as fast as the horses can carry you, for I long mightily to be in your ladyship's presence—to vindicate my character. I think you had better sell the small house, I mean that at 4.10, and I will borrow £100. So that we shall set off merrily in spite of all the prudence of Edinburgh.

Goodbye, little dear!

The marriage turned out as well as, or perhaps a little better than, one might have expected. There were some three or four years of fairly happy companionship, largely at Winterslow. The Lambs spent a pleasant month with them there the next October of which Hazlitt later wrote: "I used to walk out at this time with Mr. and Miss Lamb of an evening, to look at the Claude Lorraine skies, over our heads, melting from azure into purple and gold, and to gather mushrooms, that sprung up at our feet, to throw into our hashed mutton at supper."

A letter from Lamb in 1811 concluded: "Well, my blessings and heaven's be upon him, and make him like his father, with something a better temper and a smoother head of hair, and then all the men and women must love him."

The "him" referred to was a baby born September 26, to whom Hazlitt was passionately devoted.

During the first two years of his marriage Hazlitt edited and completed his friend Holcroft's autobiography—Thomas Holcroft had been one of those barely acquitted of high treason in the trials ten years before—and an improved English Grammar, but neither of these brought any immediate fame or money.

Fame of a sort he received in 1810 when the powerful *Edinburgh Review* made a belated and vicious attack on his "Reply to Malthus," which occasioned a new and even more crushing reply from Hazlitt. However this bought no milk for a baby, and in 1812 the little family came up to London where Hazlitt began lecturing and journalism in good earnest.

His lectures on philosophy were reasonably successful; he secured a position of Parliamentary reporter for the *Morning Chronicle* at four guineas a week; and the family moved into an apartment which Milton had occupied for six or seven years—a fact ignored until Hazlitt put a plaque to commemorate it.

He rapidly became known as a political columnist, although the sharp attacks on important figures which increased the paper's popularity were received with mixed feelings by the wealthy owner-editor, Perry. Hazlitt writes: "Poor Perry, what bitter complaints he used to make that by running amuck against lords and Scotchmen I should not leave him a place to dine out at! The expression of his face at these moments, as if he were shortly to be without a friend in the world was truly pathetic."

At the beginning of 1813 Leigh Hunt and his brother, editors of the *Examiner*, a more "left" liberal paper, were sentenced to two years in jail on a charge of "libelling" the Prince Regent. Perhaps not coincidentally, Perry that year decided that it was unwise to have a political writer whose kindest comment on a Lord's speech was apt to be a description of him as "soaring into mediocrity with adventurous enthusiasm, harrowed by some plain matter-of-fact, writhing with agony under a truism, and launching a common place with the force of a thunder-bolt."

However, Hazlitt continued with the paper for a while as dramatic critic, and began to write for the *Examiner* and *The Times* as well. The defeat of Napoleon had led the Prime Minister to propose that a peace be concluded on terms "consistent with the honor, rights and interests of France." This had been greeted by the powerful *Times* with outcries of "No Peace with Bonaparte" and a series of articles were written demanding war until the unconditional surrender of France and the restoration of the Bourbons were achieved.

Hazlitt naturally attacked the "exclusive patriotism" which demanded a war to the bitter end. When *The Times*' writer Vetus, said he was "at a loss to understand the patriotism which is not exclusive," Hazlitt replied:

> We will tell Vetus what we mean by exclusive patriotism, such as (we say) his is. We mean by it then, not that patriotism which implies a preference of the rights and welfare of our country, but that which professes to annihilate and proscribe the rights of others—not that patriotism which supposes us to be the creatures of circumstance, habit, and affection, but that which divests us of the character of reasonable beings—which fantastically makes our interests or prejudices the sole measure of right and wrong to other nations, and constitutes us sole arbiters of the empire of the world—in short, which, under the affectation of an overweening anxiety for the welfare of our own country, *excludes* even the shadow of a pretension to common sense, justice, and humanity. It is this wretched solecism which Vetus would fain bolster up into a system, with all the logic and rhetoric he is master of.

Unfortunately, political measures are rarely decided by excellence in debate and *The Times*, which may be said to have lost the argument, nevertheless won the point. Hazlitt said bitterly that the real issue decided at Leipzig was "whether the princes of Europe should be put in a situation to dictate laws and a government to France."

The restoration of the Bourbons affected him so deeply that he even quarreled with Lamb for refusing to take the matter to heart.

Hazlitt was especially furious that, with all England's professions of restoring true freedom and her willingness to ride roughshod over the rights and independence of France in other matters, Lord Castlereagh acquiesced, after barely making a formal protest, to France's retention of the slave trade which had been outlawed by England in 1807. In an article September 18, 1814 Hazlitt wrote that the English government evidently believed:

> That to rob and murder on the coast of Africa is among the internal rights of legislation and domestic privilege of every European and Christian state. . . . We can imagine how the scene took place. The question of Africa being considered as an idle question, in which neither courts nor ministers were

concerned, would naturally be left as a sort of carte blanche for all the flourishes of a national politesse, as a kind of no man's ground for a trial of diplomatic skill and complaisance. So Lord Castlereagh, drawing on his gloves, hemmed once or twice, while the French minister carelessly took snuff; he then introduced the subject with a smile, which was answered by a more gracious smile from M. Talleyrand; his Lordship then bowed, as if to bespeak attention, but the Prince of Benevento bowing still lower, prevented what he had to say, and the cries of Africa were lost amidst the nods and smiles and shrugs of these demi-puppets.

The next year, after Napoleon's brief return and his final crushing defeat at Waterloo, Hazlitt, although in considerable demand for dramatic and literary criticism and general topical writing, was unable to get newspaper assignments of a political nature. Nothing daunted, he began his review of a historical play, *Jane Shore:*

> We think the tragedy of "Jane Shore", which is founded on the dreadful calamity of hunger, is hardly proper to be represented in these starving times, and it ought to be prohibited by the Lord Chamberlain, on a principle of decorum.

Another "nonpolitical" article he wrote this year stressing the importance of partisanship on the side of the people appeared in the shape of a series of letters signed "Peter Pick Thank" written in answer to some signed "Fair Play." The last letter concluded:

> Lastly, Sir, I object to the signature of *Fair Play*, which your correspondent has assumed. There is no such character nor no such thing. . . . Whoever supposes himself to be free from all bias and prejudice in questions of this kind is deficient in self-knowledge; as he who supposes that mere abstract reason, without passion or prejudice, can ever be a match for strong passion and inveterate prejudice with all the aids of venal sophistry to boot, must be ignorant of human affairs and human nature. . . . The love of freedom is no match for the love of power, because the one is urged on by passion, while the other is in general the cold dictate of the understanding. With this natural disadvantage on the side of liberty, I know what I have to expect from those persons who pique themselves on an extreme scrupulousness in the cause of the people. I find none of this scrupulousness in the friends of despotism; *they* are in earnest, the others are not.

During the next few years, Hazlitt began to find a few new allies among the younger liberals like Leigh Hunt. They had been temporarily deceived in the cries of "Liberty Triumphant" over the defeat of Napoleon, whom they had known only as an emperor and aggressive war-maker, but were beginning to realize the appalling results of the Congress of Vienna, and England's true role in the Napoleonic wars.

The end of the war had destroyed the fictitious prosperity of the nation, and the end of war orders and the return of discharged soldiers, added to the already crushing taxation of the poor, created conditions of the most desperate poverty and misery throughout the country. Hunger riots were widespread and the government moved to put them down with ferocious violence and brazen illegality.

A protest meeting in Spar-Fields, London, at the beginning of 1817 gave the authorities a pretext for declaring a national emergency and hanging a poor, unemployed sailor, John Cashman, on the obviously perjured evidence of a government spy. He was taken to execution through crowds calling out "Murder, murder," but subsiding into silence as the officials looked for the source of the protest. Hazlitt recklessly wrote:

> Governments . . . certainly "grow milder" as they grow older. Our government the other day, instead of six hundred citizens taken at a venture from the wards of Cripplegate or Faningdon [slum neighborhoods], only suspended John Cashman and the Habeas Corpus.

Even the well-known anti-Corn Law leader, William Cobbett, publisher of the radical *Political Register*, finally thought it wise to leave the country and renew his criticism of the government from America. But Hazlitt continued to live in Milton's house and never wavered in his running fire of attack on government policies.

In 1816 Wordsworth had written his incredible "Thanksgiving Ode, 18 January, 1816, with other Short Pieces, chiefly referring to Public Events" where the content and form are throughout as well matched as this excerpt indicates:

> But Thy most dreaded instrument
> In working out a pure intent,
> Is Man—arrayed for mutual slaughter—
> —Yea, Carnage is Thy Daughter!

Since the public misery was too apparent to be altogether ignored in his "Thanksgiving Ode," he also wrote a prose introduction beginning

> If the author has given way to exultation, unchecked by these distresses, it might be sufficient to protect him from a charge of insensibility, should he state his own belief that these sufferings will be transitory. . . .

At the same time Coleridge wrote a "Lay Sermon" preaching patience, resignation and humility to the poor as a cure for hunger, and in gentler terms reminding the rich of the beauty and virtue of charity.

Hazlitt exploded into a completely scathing and unanswerable article on "Speeches in Parliament on the Distresses of the Country." A brief excerpt reads:

> We have said that the expenses of the war might as well have been sunk in the sea; and so they might, for they have been sunk in unproductive labour, that is, in maintaining large establishments and employing great numbers of men in doing nothing or mischief; for example, in making ships to destroy other ships, guns and gunpowder to blow out men's brains, pikes and swords to run them through the body, drums and fifes to drown the noise of cannon and the whizzing of bullets; —the price of restoring the Pope, the Inquisition, the Bourbons, and the doctrine of Divine Right, is half of our nine hundred millions of debt. That is the amount of the Government bill of costs, presented to John Bull for payment, not of the principal but the interest; that is what he has got by the war; the load of taxes at his back, with which he comes out of his five and twenty years' struggle, like Christian's load of sins,—. The difference between the expense of a war or a peace establishment is just the difference between a state of productive and unproductive labour.—if the Government pay him so much a day for shooting at Frenchmen and Republicans, this is a tax, a loss, a burthen to the country, without anything got by it; for we cannot, after all, eat Frenchmen and Republicans when we have killed them. War in itself is a thriving, sensible traffic only to cannibals!

After reading this it is easy to understand why Southey should have written, in his article on Parliamentary Reform, that the crime of seditious libel—as exemplified in Cobbett's and Hazlitt's writing—should be made punishable by transportation!

It is pleasant to know that in this year Hazlitt's father was still active and courageous enough to take into his home a Miss Emmett, sister of the Irish patriot, Robert Emmett, who had been hanged as a revolutionary. Hazlitt evidently had good reason to honor his father—as he did specifically in so many of his essays, and generally by the course of his life.

Because he was so frequently involved in bitter political quarrels, Hazlitt has often been described as a man of exceptionally morose temper, quick to take personal offense. This is not true. His quarrels were fought on matters of principle and there have been few men more indifferent than he was on any question of merely personal privilege. A well-authenticated story of a dispute he had with Charles Lamb's older brother shows how good-humored Hazlitt was in private life.

The incident took place at a picture exhibition where John Lamb and Hazlitt differed sharply about the comparative value of Holbein's and Vandyke's coloring. John, losing the verbal battle, moved to another plane of argument and knocked Hazlitt down. As he rose and dusted himself off others in the gallery crowded about, urging him to shake hands and forgive. Hazlitt responded cheerfully: "Well, I don't mind if I do. I am a metaphysician and nothing but an idea hurts me."

Evidently he was telling the truth when he said in an essay in 1826:

> I have often been reproached for considering things only in their abstract principles, and with heat and ill-temper, for getting into a passion about what no ways concerned me. If any one wishes to see me quite calm, they may cheat me in a bargain or tread upon my toes; but a truth repelled, a sophism repeated, totally disconcerts me, and I lose all patience.

When Hazlitt "lost all patience" he was apt to do something about it and in 1817 he hit on a brilliant device which he used repeatedly and with never failing effect, to counter the reactionary publications of the "reformed Jacobins."

The device was simply this. Whenever Southey, Wordsworth or Coleridge made a particularly virulent statement or wrote an especially asinine poem or sermon he would print—with or without comment—some appropriate selection from the writing of their radical youth.

These reprints were always, of course, in direct contradiction to the author's later statements; and, what was far worse, they were also invariably more forceful, convincing and much better written. The self-righteous Southey, as poet laureate, was his most obvious target and since Southey's powers had never, at best been great enough to make Hazlitt mourn their loss, he attacked him with a light-hearted wit that was delightful as well as destructive. For example, in 1813 when Southey was given the laureateship, Hazlitt wrote with happy malice:

> Whatever may be the balance of poetical merit, Mr. Scott [later Sir Walter Scott], we are quite sure, has always been a much better courtier than Mr. Southey; and we are of opinion that the honors of a court can nowhere be so gracefully or deservedly bestowed as on its followers. His acceptance of this mark of court favour would not have broken in upon that uniformity of character, which we think no less beautiful and becoming in life than in a poem. But perhaps a passion for new faces extends to the intrigues of politics as well as of love; and a triumph over the scruples of delicacy enhances the value of the conquest in both cases. *To have been* the poet of the people, may not render Mr. Southey less a court favorite; and one of his old Sonnets to Liberty must give a peculiar zest to his new Birthday Odes. His flaming patriotism will easily subside into the gentle glow of a grateful loyalty; and the most extravagant of his plans of reform end in building castles in Spain.

An immediate clamor arose from the whole host of "liberals" to the effect that Southey's appointment was simply a proof of the growing liberalism of the court and should be hailed as such. After two years of this kind of reasoning Hazlitt replied briefly, and devastatingly, on July 7, 1816:

> That his majesty King George III should make a convert of Mr. Southey rather than Mr. Southey of George III is probable for many reasons. The king, by siding with the cause of the people could not, like King William, have gained a crown: Mr. Southey, by deserting it has got a hundred pounds a year. A certain English ambassador, who had a long time resided at the Court of Rome, was on his return introduced at a levee of Queen Caroline. This lady, who was almost as great a prig as Mr. Southey, asked him why in his absence he did not try to make a convert of the Pope to the Protestant religion. He answered, "Madam, the reason was that I had nothing better to offer his Holiness than what he already has in possession." The Pope would no doubt have been of the same way of thinking.

This is the reason why kings from sire to son pursue "their steady way", and are less changeable than canting cosmopolites.

In a comment on an otherwise forgotten "Ode" by Southey, rejoicing in England's growing power in the East, Hazlitt said:

> In the passage above quoted, Mr. Southey founds his hope of the emancipation of the Eastern World from "the Robber and the Trader's ruthless hand" on our growing empire in India. This is a conclusion which nobody would venture upon but himself.

Now, when Southey was calling for new penal laws to prohibit any freedom of the press, Hazlitt reprinted *Wat Tyler*—a play in verse which Southey had written in his college days almost a quarter of a century before, and which not only contained the best verse he had ever written but also an appeal for armed insurrection far more extreme—verbally at least—than any of Hazlitt's realistic political protests.

Southey appealed to the Lord Chancellor for protection under the copyright laws but that worthy gentleman, shocked by the text of the poem and either insufficiently aware of Southey's current beliefs or deeply suspicious of all poets on principle, solemnly affirmed that material so dangerous, immoral, and wicked, could not claim the protection of any law, and that its author had no property rights in it whatsoever!

Southey, to defend his change of heart, attacked Hazlitt as one of those who "had turned their faces toward the East in the morning, to worship the rising sun, and in the evening were looking eastward still, obstinately affirming that still the sun was there. I, on the contrary, altered my position as the world went round."

Hazlitt promptly replied, "The sun indeed, passes from the East to the West, but it rises in the East again: yet Mr. Southey is still looking in the West—for his pension."

In dealing with the other Lake poets, Wordsworth and Coleridge, Hazlitt's attitude was quite different. They had both deliberately spread untrue personal scandals about him, had repeatedly attempted—with frequent success—to prevent his getting jobs he needed, and had gone far enough to demand of Lamb, as a condition of their continued friendship, that he altogether drop Hazlitt's acquaintance! (Lamb cheerfully ignored these ultimatums and in his own inimitable way, continued to be practically the only friend any one of them kept throughout his lifetime). Nevertheless, Hazlitt never forgot or minimized the truly great, early achievements of their genius and, particularly in speaking of Coleridge, whom he had loved and admired so much during their brief personal acquaintance, his grief for the loss of their powers and their potential value to the cause of freedom is often as great as his anger at their later role. For example, in 1818 in his lecture on Wordsworth as one of the English poets he says:

> He [Wordsworth] was the first poet I ever knew. . . . In his descriptions, you then saw the progress of human happiness and liberty in bright and never-ending succession, like the steps of Jacob's ladder, with airy shapes ascending and descending, and with the voice of God at the top of the ladder, and shall I, who heard him then, listen to him now? Not I! That spell is broke; that time is gone forever; that voice is heard no more; but still the recollection comes rushing by with thoughts of long-past years, and rings in my ears with never-dying sound.

And in 1826, speaking on another topic entirely, he is irresistibly compelled to advert to the possibilities of the Coleridge he once knew:

> I am not, in the ordinary acceptation of the term, a good-natured man; that is, many things annoy me, besides what interferes with my own ease and interest. I hate a lie, a piece of injustice wounds me to the quick, though nothing but the report of it reach me. . . . Coleridge used to complain of my irascibility in this respect, and not without reason. Would that he had possessed a little of my tenaciousness and jealousy of temper; and then, with his eloquence to paint the wrong, and acuteness to detect it, his country and the cause of liberty might not have fallen without a struggle!

Naturally, these skirmishes with the soi-disant poets did not constitute the greater, nor even a great, part of Hazlitt's journalistic work. His major attacks were directly political criticism of government officials and others for specific political action. A good example is his series of articles on the spy system. There was, then as now, growing employment of government spies and informers, recruited from the lowest dregs of the populace, paid to invent any evidence they couldn't find for conspiracies that didn't exist, and used to jail and hang many—and intimidate many, many more.

This practice was the target of several columns on "The Spy System." When Lord Castlereagh rose in Parliament to defend the character of a particularly notorious government tool, Hazlitt concluded an account of his speech in the *Morning Chronicle*, June 30, 1817, as follows:

> According to his Lordship's comprehensive and liberal views, the liberty and independence of nations are best supported abroad by the point of the bayonet; and morality, religion, and social order, are best defended at home by spies and informers. . . . Lord Castlereagh recommended the character of his accomplices, as spies and informers, to the respect and gratitude of the country and the House, he lamented the prejudice entertained against this species of patriotic service, as hindering gentlemen from resorting to it as a liberal and honorable profession.

During these years, in addition to his incessant newspaper work, Hazlitt wrote some articles on art, one for the *Encyclopedia Britannica*, and several volumes of personal essays. He also gave his subsequently printed and now famous series of lectures on "Shakespeare's Characters" and "The British Poets." The latter so impressed Keats that he proclaimed Hazlitt the greatest of all literary critics. Since Keats, however, has left no fuller account of the lectures we must quote another young friend of Hazlitt's, a Mr. Talfourd, who gives an amusing summary picture of him as a lecturer:

> Mr. Hazlitt delivered three courses of lectures at the Surrey Institution . . . before audiences with whom he had but "an imperfect sympathy". They consisted chiefly of Dissenters, who agreed with him in his hatred of Lord Castlereagh, but who "loved no plays"; of Quakers, who approved him as the opponent of Slavery and Capital Punishment, but who "heard no music"; of citizens devoted to the main chance, who had a hankering after the "improvement of the mind", but to whom his favourite doctrine of its natural disinterestedness was a riddle; of a few enemies, who came to sneer; and a few friends, who were eager to learn and to admire. The comparative insensibility of the bulk of his audience to his finest passages, sometimes provoked him to awaken their attention by points which broke the train of his discourse, after which he could make himself amends by some abrupt paradox which might set their prejudices on edge, and make them fancy they were shocked. He startled many of them at the onset, by observing that, since Jacob's dream, "the heavens have gone further off, and become astronomical"—a fine extravagance, which the

ladies and gentlemen who had grown astronomical themselves under the preceding lecturer, felt called on to resent as an attack on their severer studies. . . . He once had an edifying advantage over them. He was enumerating the humanities which endeared Dr. Johnson to his mind, and at the close of an agreeable catalogue, mentioned, as last and noble, "his carrying the poor victim of disease and dissipation on his back through Fleet Street"—at which a titter arose from some who were struck by the picture as ludicrous and a murmur from others, who deemed the allusion unfit for ears polite. He paused for an instant, and then added in his sturdiest and most impressive manner, "an act which realized the parable of the Good Samaritan," at which his moral and delicate hearers shrank rebuked into deep silence. He was not eloquent in the true sense of the term; for his thoughts were too weighty to be moved along the shallow stream of feeling which an evening's excitement can arouse. He wrote all his lectures, and read them as they were written; but his deep voice and earnest manner suited his matter well.

But Hazlitt's chief means of subsistence was his pen, and while he was too quick, versatile and interesting a writer ever to lack employment at a time when the demand for competent writers still exceeded the supply, he was often forced to contribute his newspaper articles anonymously, and the rates he could command were such that to make a living he had to keep incessantly at work. The sale of his books, his access to publishers for more substantial work, and the hope of securing a more stable journalistic position or income, were all blocked by the constant attacks of the great majority of government newspapers and conservative progovernment literati. The latter were not in the direct pay of the government but their eagerness to oblige it was nonetheless keen for that.

Finally, there was a particularly virulent, offensive, and dishonest attack made by William Gifford, the editor of the *Quarterly* —the same magazine which later so viciously and, many think, fatally, attacked Keats.

In January, 1819 Hazlitt published, at his own expense, a pamphlet entitled "A Letter to William Gifford Esq., From William Hazlitt, Esq." which reads in part: "You are a little person but a considerable cat's paw; and so far worthy of notice.—you are the government critic, a character nicely differing from that of a government spy—the invisible link that connects literature with the Police."

Keats quoted the better part of it in a letter to his brother in

America, concluding: "The force and innate power with which it yeasts and works itself up—the feeling for the costume of society, is in a style of genius. He hath a demon, as he himself says of Lord Byron."

At this time Hazlitt had been separated from his wife for about two years; they had been drifting apart for some time before but were both too closely attached to their son to give up his company. His reaching school age seems to have set the date for an amicable separation, which took place. In August 16, 1820, Hazlitt moved into new lodgings and fell madly (the word is well-advised) in love with his landlady's daughter, a beautiful girl of nineteen.

She seems to have been willing to accept any number of gifts from, and willing to give in return a reasonable number of kisses to, a lodger who was evidently not the first so to approach her, and whom she thought a safely married man. However, she had no idea of the depth or violence of Hazlitt's feelings or the seriousness of his intentions. When he declared his determination to get a divorce, she was either terrified by the task of refusing him, or possibly, unwilling to do so until she had more fully ascertained his financial position and her alternative prospects. At any rate, he went through with the expensive, difficult and humiliating procedure of a Scottish divorce—an English one was practically impossible, costing about 5,000 pounds and requiring a special act of the House of Lords—only to find that Sarah Walker had no intention of marrying him. He was, for a short time, truly beside himself with rage, grief and disappointment—wrote letters which were the height of indiscretion, topped that height by indiscreetly allowing their thinly veiled publication as fiction—and, in short, provided a field day for all the respectable writers, speakers and good citizens who felt the Lord had delivered their enemy into their hands. Friends meeting him in 1823 declared he had aged twenty years since 1820. Mary Shelley wrote in 1824:

> Hazlitt is abroad; he will be in Italy in the winter; he wrote an article in the *Edin. Rev.* on the volume of poems I published. I do not know whether he meant it to be favourable or not; I do not like it at all; but when I saw him I could not be angry. I was never so shocked in my life, he has become so thin, his hair so scattered, his cheekbones projecting; but for his voice and smile, I should not have known him; his smile brought tears into my eyes, it was like a sunbeam illuminating the most melancholy of ruins, lightning that assured you on a

dark night of the identity of a friend's ruined and deserted abode.

However, it was not for nothing that Hazlitt had declared some dozen years before: "Other brunts I also look for; but this I have resolved on, to run where I can, to go when I cannot run, and to creep when I cannot go."

He gathered himself together and filed a successful libel suit in answer to the most outrageous of the attacks.

Ignoring the triumphant mockery of his enemies and the coldness of all his "friends" but Lamb, Hazlitt went back to work. "Going back to work" meant not only resuming his journalistic assignments, but also writing a series of lovely sketches on *The Principal Picture Galleries in England* and a number of personal essays, of which one, "Whether Genius is Conscious Of Its Powers," reads defiantly:

> If the reader is not already apprised of it, he will please to take notice that I write this at Winterslow. My style there is apt to be redundant and excursive. At other times it may be cramped, dry, abrupt; but here it flows like a river, and overspreads its banks. . . . Here I came fifteen years ago, a willing exile; and as I trod the lengthened greensward by the low wood-side, repeated the old line,
> "My mind to me a kingdom is!"
> I found it so then, before, and since; and shall I faint, now that I have poured out the spirit of that mind to the world, and treated many subjects with truth, with freedom, and power, because I have been followed with one cry of abuse ever since *for not being a government-tool?* . . . Here too I have written *Table-Talks* without number, and as yet without a falling-off, till now that they are nearly done, or I should not make this boast. I could swear (were they not mine) the thoughts in many of them are founded as the rock, free as air, the tone like an Italian picture. What then? Had the style been like polished steel, as firm and as bright, it would have availed me nothing, for I am not a government-tool! I had endeavoured to guide the taste of the English people to the best old English writers; but I had said that English kings did not reign by right divine, and that his present majesty was descended from an elector of Hanover in a right line; and no loyal subject would after this look into Webster or Deckar because I had pointed them out. I had done something (more than any one except Schlegel) to vindicate the *Characters of Shakespeare's Plays* from the stigma of French criticism; but our anti-Jacobin and

anti-Gallican writers soon found out that I had said and written
that Frenchmen, Englishmen, men were not slaves by birthright. This was enough to *damn* the work. Such has been the
head and front of my offending. . . . Mr. Blackwood, I am
yours—Mr. Croker, my service to you—Mr. T. Moore, I am
alive and well—Really, it is wonderful how little the worse I
am for fifteen years' wear and tear!

To a friend who admired these essays some years later he said,
"You can hardly suppose the depression of body and mind under
which some of them were written." But they were written, and at
the same time he began to write the masterly series of contemporary pen portraits soon printed as *The Spirit of the Age.*

In April, 1824, Hazlitt married a young widow whom he had
just met, but who knew all his books and who fell in love with him
on account of his writings. She was exceptionally attractive and
had a small but sufficient income, and Hazlitt was lonely, grateful
and willing. They went to Paris in September where Hazlitt spent
most of his time in the Louvre, and then traveled through France
and Italy for about a year. These years of his second marriage were
among the very few oases of material comfort since his childhood,
so it is pleasant to read his note:

> The day after my arrival, I found a lodging at a farmhouse,
> a mile out of Vevey, so "lapped in luxury", so retired, so rea-
> sonable, and in every respect convenient, that we remained
> here for the rest of the summer, and felt no small regret at
> leaving it. . . . Days, weeks, months, and even years might
> have passed on much in the same manner, with "but the
> season's difference". We breakfasted at the same hour, and the
> tea-kettle was always boiling (an excellent thing in house-
> wifery)—a lounge in the orchard for an hour or two, and
> twice a week we could see the steam-boat creeping like a spider
> over the surface of the lake; a volume of the Scotch novels (to
> be had in every library on the Continent, in English, French,
> German, or Italian, as the reader pleases), or M. Galignani's
> Paris and London *Observer*, amused us till dinner time; then
> tea and a walk till the moon unveiled itself, "apparent queen
> of night," or the brook, swoln with a transient shower, was
> heard more distinctly in the darkness, mingling with the soft,
> rustling breeze; and the next morning the song of the peasants
> broke upon refreshing sleep, as the sun glanced among the
> clustering vine-leaves, or the shadowy hills, as the mists retired
> from their summit, looked in at our windows.

However, we need never fear, with Hazlitt, that he will yield to what Coleridge had so well described as

> Selfishness, disguised in gentle names
> Of peace and quiet and domestic love. . . .

In the same summer, when his books and pamphlets were temporarily impounded at the Italian border by the "restored" legitimate government, he wrote:

> Go on, obliging creatures! Blot the light out of heaven, tarnish the blue sky with the blight and fog of desolation, deface and trample on the green earth; for while one trace of what is fair or lovely, is left in the earth under our feet, or the sky over our heads, or in the mind of man that is within us, it will remain to mock your impotence and deformity, and to reflect back lasting hatred and contempt upon you.

In an essay on *Reason and Imagination* written at this time, and included in "The Plain Speaker" we again see that comfort had not lessened his sensitivity to wrong and suffering. One of his best general discussions begins:

> It is easy to raise an outcry against violent invective, to talk loud against extravagance and enthusiasm, to pick a quarrel with everything but the most calm, candid, and qualified statement of fact; but there are enormities to which no words can do adequate justice. Are we then, in order to form a complete idea of them, to omit every circumstance of aggravation, or to suppress every feeling of impatience that arises out of the details, lest we should be accused of giving way to the influence of prejudice and passion? This would be to falsify the impression altogether, to misconstrue reason, and fly in the face of nature. Suppose, for instance, that in the discussions on the Slave-Trade, a description to the life was given of the horrors of the *Middle Passage* (as it was termed), that you saw the manner in which thousands of wretches, year after year, were stowed together in the hold of a slave-ship without air, without light, without food, without hope, so that what they suffered in reality was brought home to you in imagination; till you felt in sickness of heart as one of them, could it be said that this was a prejudging of the case, that your knowing the extent of the evil disqualified you from pronouncing sentence upon it, and that your disgust and abhorence were the effects of a heated imagination? No. Those evils that inflame the imagina-

tion and make the heart sick, ought not to leave the head cool. This is the very test and measure of the degree of the enormity, that it involuntarily staggers and appalls the mind. If it were a common iniquity, if it were slight and partial, or necessary, it would not have this effect; but it very properly carries away the feelings, and, if you will, overpowers the judgment, because it is a mass of evil so monstrous and unwarranted as not to be endured, even in thought.

. . . Again, suppose an extreme or individual instance is brought forward in any general question, as that of the cargo of sick slaves that were thrown overboard as so much live lumber by the captain of a Guinea vessel in the year 1775 . . . or the practise of suspending contumacious Negroes in cages to have their eyes pecked out and to be devoured alive by birds of prey—Does this form no rule, because the mischief is solitary or excessive? The rule is absolute; for we feel that nothing of the kind could take place, or be tolerated for an instant, in any system that was not rotten at the core. If such things are ever done in any circumstances with impunity, we know what must be done every day under the same sanction. . . . A state of things where a single instance of the kind can possibly happen without exciting general consternation, ought not to exist for half an hour. . . .

. . . So with respect to the atrocities committed in the Slave-Trade; it could not be set up as a doubtful plea in their favour, that the actual and intolerable sufferings inflicted on the individuals were compensated in a commercial and political point of view—in a moral sense they cannot be compensated. . . . The evil is monstrous and palpable . . . a spectacle of deliberate cruelty that shocks everyone that sees and hears of it, is not to be justified by any calculations of cold-blooded self-interest—is not to be permitted in any case. It is prejudged and self-condemned. . . . Thus, for example, no infinite lumps of sugar put into Mr. Bentham's artificial ethical scales would ever weigh against the pounds of human flesh or drops of human blood that are sacrificed to produce them.

The following spring, June 20, 1826, we find a comment on the pleasant harbor in which Hazlitt was, for the time, anchored, in a letter to him from Leigh Hunt:

I know but one thing that would take me to town sooner than the pleasure of passing an evening with your masculine discourse on one side the table and "the calm of pleasant, womankind" which you have on the other. Pray forgive my saying this, and let Mrs. Hazlitt forgive me, but I am more at ease with you in your own house than anywhere else, and have felt so comfortable there both in Florence and in Down Street

[London] that I trust to please you by saying what I do, and think you should be pleased because it is true.

But the relaxation was a brief one. Less than a month later Hunt reports, "Hazlitt is gone to France and is to write Bonaparte." This had, indeed, been the project closest to his heart since Napoleon's death, if not since Waterloo. Hazlitt was no blind worshiper. For example, he unhesitatingly criticized not only many of Napoleon's actions, but also such of his statements as "I am for the white man against the black because I am white; I am for the French because I am French," saying that Napoleon was not there showing true patriotism because "True patriotism warrants no conclusion contrary to liberty or humanity."

However, his long, almost solitary opposition to England's part in the war, and his insight into the fundamentally more reactionary purposes which masked themselves as opposition to a tyrant, but which planned—and temporarily effected—the restoration of a far worse tyranny, made Hazlitt see Napoleon as a symbol of his fight for freedom. He longed above all things, to compose a full, detailed, life story which would challenge the official English one sure to be written (it was in fact published with great éclat by Sir Walter Scott in 1829) to justify and glorify England's role in the war and the restoration.

It had been impossible for him to secure the leisure for such an undertaking until now when, his moderate household expenses assured by his wife's income, the proceeds of his *Notes of a Journey through France and Italy* and of the two volume collected essays, *The Plain Speaker: Opinions on Books, Men and Things*, sufficed for a year's support of his son and for some contributions to his first wife.

He left for France where records and even eye witnesses of much of Napoleon's life were still available and set to work on his *magnum opus*.

Here he and his wife spent thirteen or fourteen months and here, unfortunately, his fifteen-year-old son joined them. The boy had bitterly opposed the remarriage, and was consistently and unpardonably vituperative to his stepmother, even going so far, according to one biographer, as to deny the validity of a Scottish divorce and to attack the legitimacy of her relations with his father.

Hazlitt was unquestionably fond of, and grateful to, his wife but his tenderness and devotion to his son were far deeper and more demonstrative, and whether this revelation of an emotion he had never shown her *was* a revelation or merely an explanation of what had been lacking in their marriage, she did not accompany him back to England. Whether she explicitly gave him the choice between her companionship and that of his son, as some accounts indicate, is not too important. There is no question which he would have chosen, and in some sense evidently did choose.

At any rate, he did return in the fall of 1827 with the *Life of Napoleon* half written. Despite a violent illness, which he thought caused by a chill but which may have been the first symptoms of the gastric ulcer or stomach cancer that was soon to kill him, he fell hard to work on the last two volumes.

It is neither likely nor desirable that the casual reader go through the almost 1,500 pages of detailed narrative, argument, and documentation which, though written as a labor of love, is none the easier to read for that. But Hazlitt's own statement of his reason for the undertaking should perhaps be quoted in part. The preface tells us:

> Of my object in writing the Life here offered to the public, and of the general tone that pervades it, it may be proper that I should render some account in order to prevent mistakes and false applications. It is true, I admired the man; but what chiefly attached me to him, was his being, as he had been long ago designated, "the child and champion of the Revolution." Of this character he could not divest himself, even though he wished it. He was nothing, he could be nothing, but what he owed to himself and his triumphs over those who claimed mankind as their inheritance by a divine right. . . . He kept off that last indignity and wrong offered to a whole people (and through them to the rest of the world) of being handed over like a herd of cattle, to a particular family and chained to the foot of a legitimate throne. . . . He did many things wrong and foolish; but they were individual acts, and recoiled upon the head of the doer. They stood upon the ground of their own merits, and could not urge in their vindication "the right divine of kings to govern wrong"; they were not precedents; they were not exempt from public censure or opinion; they were not softened by prescription, nor screened by prejudice, nor sanctioned by superstition, nor rendered formidable by a principle that imposed them as sacred obligations on all future generations: either they were state-necessities extorted by the circumstances of the time, or violent acts of the will, that carried their own condemnation in their bosom. Whatever fault might be found with them, they did not proceed on the principle that

"millions were made for one" but one for millions; for it was to establish it (this principle) that the Revolution was commenced, and to overturn it that the enemies of liberty waded through seas of blood, and at last succeeded.

Hazlitt had received £300 for the first two volumes, which were published in 1828, but the bankruptcy of his publisher made it necessary for him to spend that and a little over to see the last two volumes through the press in 1829. During this year he was so ill that on one occasion he wrote the publisher: "I have been nearly in the other world. My regret was 'to die and leave the world rough copy!'" However, he not only completed the four-volume work but wrote enough profitable material on the side to pay for his expenses—and the book's—and in the spring of 1829 returned to London to resume his work on several newspapers as book reviewer, dramatic critic, and general factotum.

When, early in 1830, the first "Jewish Disabilities Bill" was presented in Parliament, he wrote a powerful attack on it, praising Napoleon for having removed such discriminatory legislation in France, and saying that just as the persecution of Jews was a sign of barbarism or retrogression in a nation, so the emancipation of Jews was but "a natural step in the progress of civilization."

Racked by frequently recurring attacks of pain, living in the smallest and barest of the many poor rooms he had occupied during the last twenty years, he was still able to write in his last book, *Conversations with Northcote:*

> Taking one thing with another, I have no great cause to complain. If I had been a merchant, a bookseller, or the proprietor of a newspaper, instead of what I am, I might have had more money or possessed a town and country-house, instead of lodging in a first or second floor, as it may happen. But what then? I see how the man of business and fortune passes his time. He is up and in the city by eight, swallows his breakfast in haste, attends a meeting of creditors, must read Lloyd's lists, consult the price of consols, study the markets, look into his accounts, pay his workmen, and superintend his clerks: he has hardly a minute in the day to himself, and perhaps in the four-and-twenty hours does not do a single thing that he would do if he could help it. Surely, this sacrifice of time and inclination requires some compensation, which it meets with. But how am I entitled to make my fortune (which cannot be done without all this anxiety and drudgery) who do hardly any thing at all, and never any thing but what I like to do? I rise

when I please, breakfast *at length,* write what comes into my head, and after taking a mutton-chop and a dish of strong tea, go to the play, and thus my time passes. Mr.—has no time to go to the play. It was but the other day that I had to get up a little earlier than usual to go into the city about some money transaction, which appeared to me a prodigious hardship: if so, it was plain that I must lead a tolerably easy life: nor should I object to passing mine over again.

By the summer of 1830, however, his theatre going, writing and even reading, were done and the end was near. His son, the Lambs, and one or two other younger friends were almost daily visitors when "he lay, ghastly, shrunk, and helpless, on the bed from which he never afterwards rose. His mind seemed to have weathered all the dangers of extreme sickness, and to be safe and strong as ever. But the physical portion had endured sad decay. He could not lift his hand from the coverlet; and his voice was changed and diminished to a hoarse whisper, resembling the faint scream . . . heard from birds."

Most of his last requirements were unobtrusively supplied by the Lambs, but not realizing that the end was quite so close, and not wishing them burdened with expenses they could ill afford, he dictated a characteristic note to the friendliest and most generous of his former editors a few days before he died. "Dear Sir: I am dying; can you send me 10 pounds and so consummate your many kindnesses to me?" The answer, a warm letter containing £50, arrived Saturday, September 18, 1830, a few hours after his death.

A suitably controversial headstone, erected anonymously by one of his friends declared:

Here rests
WILLIAM HAZLITT
Born April 10, 1778. Died 18 September, 1830.

He lived to see his deepest wishes gratified
as he has expressed them in his Essay,
"On the Fear of Death."
Viz.:
"To see the downfall of the Bourbons,
And some prospect of good to mankind":
(Charles X
was driven from France 29th July, 1830).

"To leave some sterling work to the world":
(He lived to complete his *Life of Napoleon*).

His desire
That some friendly hand should consign
him to the grave was accomplished to a
limited but profound extent; on
these conditions he was ready to depart,
and to have inscribed on his tomb,
"Grateful and Contented."
He was
The first (unanswered) Metaphysician of the age.
A despiser of the merely Rich and Great:
A lover of the People, Poor or Oppressed:
A hater of the Pride and Power of the Few,
as opposed to the happiness of the Many;
A man of true moral courage,
Who sacrified Profit and present Fame
To Principle,
And a yearning for the good of Human Nature,
Who was a burning wound to an Aristocracy,
That could not answer him before men,
And who may confront him before their Maker.
He lived and died
The unconquered Champion
of
Truth, Liberty, and Humanity,
"Dubitantes opera legite."
This stone
is raised by one whose heart is
with him, in his grave.

In 1870 this too honest memorial was removed by his respectable son and a discreetly meaningless one substituted:

WILLIAM HAZLITT, PAINTER, CRITIC, ESSAYIST.
BORN AT MAIDSTONE, APRIL 10, 1778.
DIED IN SOHO, SEPTEMBER 18, 1830.

AGAINST THE UNHOLY ALLIANCE

Byron and Shelley, although separated from the Lake poets by less than a generation, came into a totally different world.

Born about the time of the French Revolution—Byron a year before the storming of the Bastille, Shelley three years after it—they grew up in an England already governed by reaction, committed to an eighteen year long aggressive war, deeply suspicious of all criticism or reform, and moving with the utmost ferocity against internal disturbances precipitated by the incredible poverty and violent suffering of the lower classes.

Any kind of revolutionary thought met with almost as much disapproval from Whigs as from Tories. The blood bath with which first the Napoleonic wars and then the Congress of Vienna had deluged Europe was almost exceeded by the slow murder of starvation, and by the swifter death the law of England too often provided for protesting hunger.

When the wave of unemployment which swept England after the declaration of peace was added to this domestic misery, desperate men who began to hold street demonstrations were ruthlessly shot down by the militia. Workers, forbidden to organize or even to meet in groups of more than five, formed small committees of correspondence. Many were transported or executed upon the perjured evidence of paid government provocateurs and informers. A few—a very few—courageous publishers, like the brothers John and Leigh Hunt, risked and incurred repeated jail sentences for maintaining men's right to speak their minds in print.

It was impossible for young men coming of age in such a world to feel the rapturous idyllic mood of that dawn when it had been "bliss to be alive—and to be young was very heaven." It was all too clear that the Bastille, more firmly grounded than the walls of Jericho, was not really to be destroyed by the very loudest of trumpet blasts. In fact, contrary to all the laws of romance, evil seemed to have grown stronger through attack and, having devoured its most intrepid enemies and enlisted the others under its own banner, finally appeared completely invulnerable.

It is not surprising, therefore, that the younger romantic poets were, like Hazlitt, constrained to fight against rather than for; to concern themselves more directly with attacks on specific evils; and to rely for motive power as much or more on a passionate hatred of oppression as on a joyous confidence in freedom.

Although this statement must be somewhat qualified when we come to consider the greater, many-sided genius of Shelley, it stands unquestionably and wholly true in any discussion of Byron. He, as Hazlitt said, "exists not by sympathy, but by antipathy," and he is, generally, ennobled by the force and justice of his antipathies.

George Gordon, Lord Byron—1788–1824

Byron was born in 1788, the son of a profligate, and irresponsible younger son of the younger son of a lord. His father had married, impoverished, and deserted a wealthy Scottish heiress who embittered, enraged, and at times almost demented by loneliness and frustration, lived alone with her son on an infinitesmal income. Suddenly, when he was ten, the death of the baron who had been his father's uncle (preceded, unexpectedly by the death of two closer relatives) made the youngster Lord Byron, heir to a very large, although mistreated and temporarily embarrassed, estate.

The unhappiness of his first years had been aggravated by a clubfoot of which he was extremely conscious and which his mother in their frequent quarrels did not hesitate to use, calling him "you lame brat."

Sent to Harrow, one of the major English schools, as a ward in Chancery, he forced himself to excel in all sports not affected by his handicap—swimming, horseback riding, fencing, fighting and, later, boxing. In a few years he made himself a leader among the boys of his own age as well as among the younger boys whom he frequently protected from such hazing as he had suffered.

He was ambitious, vain, desperately anxious to lead, and subject to ungovernable rages. But he was also passionately attached to all whom he considered friends, or who treated him with real kindness, and exceedingly sensitive to the suffering others underwent through poverty or physical pain.

At seventeen, after having felt himself wildly in love at least twice—once, in early adolescence with a young cousin who died, and again in his last two years at school, with an older, more distant relative who married—he entered Cambridge, spent many times his generous £500 allowance (one of the largest at the college) in living as he thought a lord should live, drinking and gaming, which he disliked, and giving ostentatious entertainments which he liked very much.

He was always acutely conscious of his slight physical handicap, and also of the more serious handicap of his lack of relatives or connections in the fashionable world; of his mother's vulgarity which had already angered and estranged his guardian, Lord Carlisle; and of his own uncertainty as to how he could really win acceptance from his peers.

However, in his last year at Cambridge (he had played truant for an entire year, living alone in London in expensive quarters with two prize fighters and a bull dog!), he unexpectedly made friends with a small group of extremely intelligent, serious, and progressive students. He joined the undergraduate Whig Club founded by one of them, Hobhouse,—later the second Radical elected to the House of Commons—and published a book of very adolescent poetry under the title *Hours of Idleness*.

Neither his political allegiance nor his poetry was wholly due to his new friends, although the security and encouragement of their association no doubt enabled him to begin expressing himself instead of continuing to live up to his childish ideal of a wicked baron.

His mother, who, while perhaps insane, was not unintelligent, and whom he loved as well as hated, was an ardent sympathizer with the French Revolution. In affectionate intervals she had discussed her ideas freely with the bright youngster who was her only intimate. These ideas are indicated by one of her few remaining letters, addressed to a sister-in-law:

> I am very much interested about the French, but I fancy you and I are on different sides, for I am quite a Democrat and I do not think the King, after his treachery and perjury, deserves to be restored. To be sure, there has been horrid things done by the People, but if the other party had been successful, there would have been as great cruelty committed by them.

Byron himself had excelled in history and general current information at Harrow. There he began to read the great examples of Roman and English oratory with especial interest, identifying himself generally with the opposition, whether that of Brutus or Milton. He had even begun to anticipate a parliamentary career for himself.

In 1807 when he was preparing his *Hours of Idleness* for publication, he wrote

> The poet yields to the orator,, but as nothing can be done in the latter capacity till the extirpation of my Minority, the former occupies my present attention, and both ancients and moderns have declared that the two pursuits are so nearly similar as to require in great measure the same Talents, and he who excels in one, would on application succeed in the other.

The poems were almost wholly a series of imitative exercises and were preceded by a very ill-judged preface which laid stress on the author's being only nineteen years old, mentioned his rank a number of times, and implied, as indeed the title indicates, that serious efforts at writing were beneath a nobleman.

The book was attacked with extreme, though perhaps not unjust, severity in the *Edinburgh Review* and Byron, stung to fury, found his own poetic style in a vitriolic satire, *English Bards and Scotch Reviewers*. In this he pilloried all the leading writers who supported, and were supported by, that journal. He worked on this piece during his last term at Cambridge and also during the half-year which elapsed after graduation before, at twenty-one, he could formally take his seat in the House of Lords.

That event, so happily anticipated, proved to be a matter for defiant self-assertion rather than joy. His cousin, Lord Carlisle, to whom his book had been dedicated, had remained cold and distant and had refused to present him personally to the House of Lords. After some months' delay, caused by a confusion in the family records, he entered totally alone that rather overwhelming body, with no member of which he had any personal acquaintance. He limped across the huge chamber to a seat on the almost empty opposition benches, after rudely snubbing Lord Eldon, the Tory Chancellor who came forward to welcome him.

The satire, with lampoons on Lord Carlisle and on the Whig leader, Lord Holland, added, appeared anonymously in March 1809, and created a real sensation. After enjoying the public amazement and shock at a distance, from a three-months' retirement in his ancestral castle, Byron left England on a two-year tour saying, Byronically:

> I leave England without regret—I shall return to it without pleasure. I am like Adam, the first convict sentenced to transportation, but I have no Eve, and have eaten no apple but what was sour as a crab.

He visited not only most of the regulation European sights but also Albania, Turkey, and other more remote spots, and occupied himself, when not sightseeing, in lovemaking and in reading and writing. Many of his letters to his mother express in different ways such ideas as this one:

> I am so convinced of the advantages of looking at mankind instead of reading about them, and the bitter effects of staying at home with all the narrow prejudices of an islander, that I think there should be a law among us, to set our young men abroad for a term, among the few allies our wars have left us.

Repeated urging from his mother and lawyer, and serious though temporary financial embarrassment, brought him back to

England in 1811. Then his mother's sudden death, before he saw her, and the almost immediate accidental death of two of his closest school friends left him more alone than ever.

However he found the sensation caused by his satire was not altogether forgotten. Lord Holland, the leader of the Whig nobility who was one of those attacked, was unexpectedly friendly, and Byron decided to withdraw the book, which had sold four editions, from circulation, and to embark on a parliamentary career in earnest.

He also gave an older literary man, Dallas (who had made his acquaintance by praising his first book), the manuscript of a new book, *Hints from Horace*, of which he thought very highly, to publish, and the first two cantos of *Childe Harold*, of which he thought little, to do as he liked with! His friend's taste was fortunately better than his own, and since he was preoccupied with other affairs the former work was set aside and the latter immediately prepared for publication.

Meanwhile, on a visit to his estate in Nottingham, Byron had been deeply moved by the misery of the Nottingham hand weavers who, thrown out of work by the introduction of a machine loom, were literally starving with no government relief whatsoever.

There had been a series of desperate attempts to prevent the introduction of these new "frames," which threw six of every seven men out of work. The government, outraged and terrified by these attacks on property, had rushed through the House of Commons a bill making it a capital offense for anyone to break, or conspire to break, or assist in breaking, a frame!

Byron approached Lord Holland, who opposed the bill on party principle as an important Tory measure, to let him speak in the House of Lords for the Whig opposition.

His speech was delivered February 27, 1812, and created a well-deserved sensation. It was short and powerful, and showed a certain understanding of the state of the country, as well as a deeply felt sympathy for the condition of the weavers. Although it made some of the more alert Whig Lords feel that the young Lord Byron might be a dangerous addition to a conservative reform party, its immediate effect was to make him an important figure among the younger men—and a good target for the opposition newspapers who began to watch their opportunity for attack.

The bill which had been almost unopposed in its first two readings in the House of Lords was, almost wholly because of Byron's speech, defeated at the third reading and returned to committee where some of its severest clauses were modified. Thus altered it passed as a compromise measure.

The speech, a surprisingly effective one for an inexperienced young man of twenty-four, reads in part:

> These men were willing to dig, but the spade was in other hands; they were not ashamed to beg, but there was none to relieve them. Their own means of subsistence was cut off; all other employments pre-occupied; and their excesses, however to be deplored or condemned, can hardly be the subject of surprise.
>
> You call these men a mob, desperate, dangerous, and ignorant; and seem to think that the only way to quiet the "Belus multoram capitum" [many-headed multitude] is to lop off a few of its superfluous heads. But even a mob can better be reduced to reason by a mixture of conciliation and firmness, than by additional aggravation and redoubled penalties. Are we aware of our obligation to a mob? It is the mob that labour in your fields and serve in your houses—that man your navy and recruit your army—that have enabled you today to defy the world—and that can also defy you when neglect and calamity have brought them to despair. You may call the people a mob, but do not forget that too often a mob speaks the sentiments of the people.
>
> I have traversed the seat of war in the Peninsula; I have been in some of the most oppressed provinces of Turkey; but never, under the most despotic of infidel governments, did I behold such squalid wretchedness as I have seen since my return, in the very heart of a Christian Country. . . .
>
> Setting aside the palpable injustice and certain inefficiency of the bill, are there not capital punishments sufficient on your statutes? Is there not blood enough upon your penal code, that there must be more poured forth to ascend to heaven and testify against you? How will you carry the bill into effect? Can you commit a whole county to their own prisons? Will you erect a gibbet in every field and hang up men like scarecrows? or will you proceed (as you must, to bring this measure into effect) by decimation; place the country under martial law, depopulate and lay waste all around you, and restore Sherwood Forest as an acceptable gift to the Crown in the former condition of a royal chase, and an asylum for outlaws? Are these the remedies for a starving and desperate population? Will the famished wretch who has braved your bayonets be appalled by your gibbets? When death is a relief, and the only relief that you will afford him, will he be dragooned into tranquillity? Will that which could not be effected by your grenadiers be effected by your executioners? If you proceed by the forms of law, where is your evidence? Those who re-

fused to impeach their accomplices, when transportation only was the punishment, will hardly be tempted to witness against them when death is the penalty. . . .

When a proposal is made to emancipate or relieve, you hesitate, you deliberate for years, you temporise and tamper with the minds of men; but a death bill must be passed off hand, without a thought of the consequences.

He also wrote at this time his sharply stinging "Ode to the Framers of the Frame Bill." A few days later the first two cantos of *Childe Harold* appeared and, as Byron himself says, he awoke one morning to find himself famous.

Dallas, the friend responsible for the publication of *Childe Harold*, wrote in his biography of Byron:

> He was now the universal talk of the town; his speech, and his poem had not only raised his fame, to an extraordinary height, but had dispos'd all minds to bestow on him the most favorable reception. . . . Crowds of eminent persons courted an introduction, and some volunteered their cards . . . never was there such a sudden transition from neglect to courtship. Glory darted thick upon him from all sides; from the Prince Regent and his admirable daughter, to the bookseller and his shopman.

And the fashionable leader, the Duchess of Devonshire, wrote in a letter during that spring season of 1812:

> The subject of conversation, of curiosity, of enthusiasm of the moment is not Spain or Portugal, warriors or patriots, but Lord Byron! . . . The poem is on every table and himself courted, flattered and praised whenever he appears. He has a pale, sickly, but handsome countenance, a bad figure, and, in short, he is really the only topic of every conversation—the men jealous of him, the women of each other.

Despite an invitation from the Prince Regent, Byron did not attend his levee for a formal court presentation. While he did, as hinted by the Duchess, accept several of the many invitations to love tendered by noble ladies, he also found time to make the acquaintance of Leigh Hunt, then serving a two-year prison sentence for "seditious" publications, and to pay him and his radical friends a number of visits in jail.

A curious incident occurred in March when, at a public dinner, the Prince Regent, who had promised that on his accession to power he would invite the Whigs to form a ministry, made it clear he had no intention of keeping his word. His daughter, the Princess Charlotte, who was known to be liberal and was the only member of the Royal Family liked or respected by the people, burst into tears. Byron published, anonymously, in the liberal *Morning Chronicle* a few lines of verse important politically rather than poetically.

> Weep, daughter of a royal line,
> A Sire's disgrace, a realm's decay;
> Ah! happy if each tear of thine
> Could wash a father's fault away!
>
> Weep—for thy tears are Virtue's tears—
> Auspicious to these suffering isles;
> And be each drop in future years
> Repaid thee by thy people's smiles.

Two years later, however, when a new book of his, *The Corsair*, was being printed, he insisted, as a condition of its publication, that these verses be included under his name. His publisher and, in fact, all his very moderate Whig friends objected vehemently but he insisted "The 'Lines to a Lady Weeping' must go with 'The Corsair.' I care nothing for consequences on this point."

Upon their republication by a man of his prominence and social position a real storm burst. Byron returned to London to find "all the newspapers in hysterics and the town in an uproar." Although the Prince Regent was publicly living with at least three noble mistresses and innumerable chambermaids, and publicly accusing his wife of infidelity as prelude to a divorce action, the *Morning Post* solemnly intoned:

> Nothing can be more repugnant to every good heart as well as to the normal and religious feelings of a country, which we are proud to say still cherishes every right sentiment, than an attempt to lower a father in the eyes of his child.

The important *Courier* devoted eight editorials to a detailed attack upon Byron's life and works. *The Sun* urged that, if Byron were as a peer not subject to criminal prosecution, he should at least be expelled by the Lords from his seat in their house; even the *Morning Chronicle* in which the verses had originally been published criticized him severely (and hypocritically) for the cowardice of his earlier anonymity; and the *Morning Post* published a series of badly rhymed attacks.

Naturally all this to-do was not the result of the eight lines which had created no such furor when first written two years before. But during those two years Byron had not only become a social light; he had also become known as the one dangerous radical in the House of Lords. His speech for Catholic Emancipation in the House, while supporting a party stand, was far more ardent than the party thought necessary; his well-known sympathy with those who wished to amend the Insolvent Debtors' Act and abolish debtors' prisons was not even formally approved by the Whigs; and when, in June 1, 1813, in his last parliamentary speech, he presented a sharply worded petition for parliamentary and judicial reform from a well-known radical, John Cartwright, there was not a single member of the Lords who stood with him.

His own attitude during this period was also changing rapidly as he realized how ineffective for any real political purposes the Whig aristocrats were or even wished to be. He wrote in a letter:

> All I like is now gone, and all I abhor remains, viz, the Regent, his government, and most of his subjects. What a fool I was to come back! I shall be wiser next time, unless there is a prospect of alteration in the whole system.

And in a set of verses:

> 'Tis said Indifference marks the present time,
> Then hear the reason—though 'tis told in rhyme
> A king who *can't*, a Prince of Wales who *don't*,
> Patriots who *shan't*, and Ministers who *won't*,
> What matters who are *in* or *out*, of place,
> The *Mad*, the *Bad*, the *Useless*, or the *Base*?

His attendance in Parliament became less and less regular, his social dissipations more and more deliberately shocking, and his unconcealed disgust with himself and the purposeless life he was leading grew pronounced. Protests about his outspoken radicalism from his publishers and others received only such answers as: "I care nothing for the consequences on this point. My politics are to me like a young mistress to an old man—the worse they grow, the fonder I become of them."

His reckless desire to shock the public he despaired of changing was, of course, the reason for his inclusion of the verses to the Princess. His radical reputation was the real reason that then and, a little later, in the personal scandal of his marital separation, he found no more allies among Whigs than Tories.

In 1815 he had married a most extraordinarily unsuitable young woman, a solemnly religious virgin who was the cousin of his most notorious mistress, Lady Caroline Lamb, and who explicitly married him to reform him. A year later, shortly after the birth of a daughter, she left him, having, no doubt, found it impossible to accomplish her mission. (It is only fair to say that Byron, in his disappointment with himself and the world, seems to have married in order to be reformed, although during the brief engagement he repeatedly offered to release his fiancée.)

Lady Byron refused to give any reason for leaving her husband, but her family and friends assiduously spread the most scandalous stories which she refused either to confirm or deny. When Byron, as usual, expressed his feelings in poetry, which was read in manuscript by a number of his friends, the Tory paper, *The Champion*, secured a copy of the manuscript and printed his "Fare Thee Well" and "A Sketch" with the note: "We notice it (this strain of his Lordship's harp), because we think it would not be doing justice to the merits of such political tenets, if they were not coupled with their corresponding practice in regard to moral and domestic obligations."

To us neither the verses to his wife, nor the stories of illicit love affairs, even if, as was whispered, one of these had to do with a half sister by his father's first marriage, seem sufficient to shock a public able to accept the mores of Regency London.

The fashionable reaction can only be understood in terms of the political tensions which had raised such a furor when Byron was less vulnerable two years before, and which had, of course, been intensified by his increasing friendship with the Hunts and other radicals whom he himself outdid in such statements as his forthright declaration on hearing the news of Waterloo: "I am damned sorry for it. I didn't know but I might live to see Lord Castlereagh's head on a pole."

No doubt, too, such lines as those in "Napoleon's Farewell," which had been published in *The Examiner*,

> Farewell to thee, France! but when Liberty rallies
> Once more in thy regions, remember me then,—
> The Violet still grows in the depth of thy vallies
> Though withered, thy tears will unfold it again. . . .

played their part in preventing even the most liberal Whig papers from coming to his defense, as he had expected they would. The fact that the Whigs generally vaunted themselves on the comparative purity or at least discretion of their personal affairs, while pointing at the disgrace the Prince Regent's residence, Carleton House, brought to the nation, may also have inhibited a not too ardent desire to champion a difficult and unreliable member of their party. At any rate, the result was that, since they wouldn't defend him, they energetically joined in the attack to keep it from reflecting on their party, and Byron was virtually forced into exile by the most unanimous storm of obloquy fashionable society had ever raised.

He visited Switzerland, where he met Shelley, and, on being shown the prison in which Bonnivard, the famous fighter for freedom, had been killed, he wrote the well-known long narrative poem, "Prisoner of Chillon" and the sonnet "Chillon":

> Eternal Spirit of the chainless Mind!
> Brightest in dungeons, Liberty, thou art,
> For there thy habitation is the heart—
> The heart which love of thee alone can bind;
> And when thy sons to fetters are consigned—
> To fetters, and the damp vault's dayless gloom,
> Their country conquers with their martyrdom,
> And Freedom's fame finds wings on every wind.
> Chillon! thy prison is a holy place,
> And thy sad floor an altar; for 'twas trod,
> Until his very steps have left a trace
> Worn, as if thy cold pavement were a sod,
> By Bonnivard!—May none those marks efface!
> For they appeal from tyranny to God.

From Switzerland he went to Italy, where he remained from the end of 1816 until his departure for Greece in 1823.

The later cantos of *Childe Harold*, written during Byron's first year in Italy, are far more mature than the first two. Although they created no such immediate sensation as the earlier ones they have, deservedly, been far better remembered. Among their best known lines are such as these which speak for Byron's whole generation:

> Yet, Freedom! yet thy banner, torn, but flying,
> Streams like the thunder-storm against the wind;
> Thy trumpet voice, though broken now and dying,
> The loudest still the tempest leaves behind;
> Thy tree hath lost its blossoms, and the rind,

> Chopp'd by the axe, looks rough and little worth,
> But the sap lasts,—and still the seed we find
> Sown deep, even in the bosom of the North;
> So shall a better spring less bitter fruit bring forth.

The Whigs at home were becoming somewhat more radical in their views as government reaction intensified, and when the death of Princess Charlotte in 1817 destroyed their hope for the early accession of power through an alliance with some member of the Royal Family, the left wing of the party formed a Roto Club which looked to less exalted alliances.

Byron, who was elected a member in absentia, wrote to his friend, John Cam Hobhouse, encouraging him to stand as an opposition candidate within the party, and continued, as letters and diary notes show, to take a lively interest in English politics.

Settling for a while in Venice he wrote his "Ode On Venice" which includes such lines as

> Ye men, who pour your blood for kings as water,
> What have they given your children in return?

The "Ode" ends with a paean of praise to America which alone, by the aid of the ocean, is able to maintain its freedom.

As he hints in this poem, Byron seriously considered emigrating to South America. In his correspondence with English friends about the possibility of selling his English estate to buy land in America he wrote that he did not wish to go to the United States because of slavery there. Later, he wrote more fully in his journal:

> Two or three years ago, I thought of going to one of the Americas, English or Spanish. But the accounts sent from England, in consequence of my enquiries, discouraged me . . . there is *no* freedom, even for *Masters*, in the midst of slaves; it makes my blood boil to see the thing. I sometimes wish that I was the Owner of Africa, to do at once what Wilberforce will do in time, viz.—sweep Slavery from her deserts, and look on upon the first dance of their Freedom!
> As to *political* slavery—so general—it is man's own fault; if they *will* be slaves, let them! Yet it is but "a word and a blow". See how England formerly, France, Spain, Portugal, America, Switzerland, freed themselves! There is no one instance of a *long* contest, in which *men* did not triumph over systems. If Tyranny misses her *first* spring, she is cowardly as the tiger; and retires to be hunted.

However, he was still emotionally much involved in English affairs, as we can see by the *Dedication* to his major poem, *Don Juan*, which he began to write in 1819.

Bob Southey! You're a poet—Poet Laureate,
    And representative of all the race;
Although 'tis true that you turned out a Tory at
    Last—yours has lately been a common case;
And now, my Epic Renegade! what are ye at?
    With all the Lakers, in and out of place?
A nest of tuneful persons, to my eye
Like "four and twenty Blackbirds in a pye;

"Which pye being opened they began to sing"
    (This old song and new simile holds good),
"A dainty dish to set before the King,"
    Or Regent, who admires such kind of food;—
And Coleridge, too, has lately taken wing,
    But like a hawk encumbered with his hood—
Explaining metaphysics to the nation—
I wish he would explain his explanation.

    . . . . . .

I would not imitate the petty thought,
    Nor coin my self-love to so base a vice,
For all the glory your conversion brought,
    Since gold alone should not have been its price,
You have your salary; was't for that you wrought?
    And Wordsworth has his place in the Excise,
You're shabby fellows—true—but poets still,
    And duly seated on the immortal hill.

    . . . . . .

Think'st thou, could he [Milton]—the blind old man arise—
Like Samuel from the grave, to freeze once more
The blood of monarchs with his prophecies,
    Or be alive again—again all hoar
With time and trials, and those helpless eyes,
    And heartless daughters—worn—and pale—and poor;
Would *he* adore a sultan? *he* obey
The intellectual eunuch Castlereagh?

Where shall I turn me not to *view* new bonds,
    For I will never *feel* them?—Italy!
Thy late reviving Roman soul desponds
    Beneath the lie this State-thing breathed o'er thee—
Thy clanking chain, and Erin's yet green wounds,
    Have voices—tongues to cry aloud for me.
Europe has slaves, allies, kings, armies still,
    And Southey lives to sing them very ill.

The third canto of *Don Juan*, also written in 1819, shows that Byron was already deeply concerned with the dawning Greek struggle for independence. In the following stanzas he imagines himself speaking in the person of a contemporary Greek poet, urging his compatriots to rise against Turkish domination and fight for the freedom of Greece.

> The isles of Greece, the isles of Greece!
>   Where burning Sappho loved and sung,
> Where grew the arts of war and peace,
>   Where Delos rose, and Phoebus sprung!
> Eternal summer gilds them yet,
> But all, except their sun, is set.
>
> . . . .
>
> The mountains look on Marathon—
>   And Marathon looks on the sea;
> And musing there an hour alone,
>   I dream'd that Greece might still be free:
> For standing on the Persians' grave,
> I could not deem myself a slave.
>
> . . . .
>
> 'Tis something, in the dearth of fame,
>   Though link'd among a fetter'd race,
> To feel at least a patriot's shame,
>   Even as I sing, suffuse my face;
> For what is left the poet here?
> For Greeks a blush—For Greece a tear.
>
> Must *we* but weep o'er days more blest?
>   Must *we* but blush?—Our fathers bled.
> Earth! render back from out thy breast
>   A remnant of our Spartan dead!
> Of the three hundred grant but three,
> To make a new Thermopylae!
>
> What, silent still? and silent all?
>   Ah, no;—the voices of the dead
> Sound like a distant torrent's fall,
>   And answer, "Let one living head,
> But one arise,—we come, we come!"
> 'Tis but the living who are dumb.

In July 1819 when King Ferdinand of Naples was forced to grant a constitution, Byron was ecstatic at the prospect of a League of Cities which would spread the revolutionary activity and after this had failed he wrote in his journal:

Time and Opinion and the vengeance of a roused-up people will at length manure Italy with their carcasses; it may not be for one year, or two, or ten, but it *will* be, and so that it *could* be sooner, I know not what a man ought to do.

He soon became acquainted with a group of revolutionary Italians (whom he later assisted in an abortive uprising against Austria), and in 1819 wrote *The Prophecy of Dante*. Here he makes that great poet in exile, with whom he obviously identifies himself, say: "They made an Exile—not a slave of me." The second canto ends with Dante's exhortation to his countrymen:

> What is there wanting then to set thee free,
> And show thy beauty in its fullest light?
> To make the Alps impassable; and we,
> Her sons, may do this with one deed—unite!

It is no wonder that when Byron moved to Bologna and began to entertain the liberal elements in the town the Director of Police wrote to his superior in Rome for advice saying: "Byron is a man of letters and his literary merit will attract to him the most distinguished men of learning in Bologna. This class of men has no love for the Government."

A little later when Byron was arranging for an Italian translation of *The Prophecy of Dante* the Royal Commissioner in Florence reported on the project, saying:

> The work is certainly not written in the spirit of our Government or any Italian Government. It seems to me intended to rouse still further the animosities of a populace already sufficiently excited. Lord Byron makes Dante his spokesman, and the prophet of democratic independence, as if this were the salvation of Italy.

Byron's move to Florence had been necessitated by that of the young Countess Teresa Guiccioli, a girl of seventeen or eighteen, who had recently become the third wife of a man of sixty. She and Byron had an acknowledged love relationship which lasted for the rest of his life and soon occasioned an official separation between her and her husband.

The Countess' father, Count Gamba, and her brother were well-known Italian patriots and it had been at her request that

Byron had written *The Prophecy of Dante*. He became close friends with her brother who later, after the failure of the Italian uprising, went with Byron to fight for Greek independence and who lost his life in that victorious struggle. Her father, equally involved in revolutionary activity at home, spent his later years in prison and exile, and died there.

Byron's concern with the abortive Italian revolution was neither superficial nor passive. At the beginning of January, 1821, when King Ferdinand abrogated the constitution granted under pressure two years before, Byron wrote:

> The Powers mean to war with the peoples. Let it be so—they will be beaten in the end. The king-times are fast finishing. There will be bloodshed like water, and tears like mist; but the people will conquer in the end. I shall not live to see it, but I foresee it. . . .
> The waves which dash upon the shore are, one by one, broken, but yet the ocean conquers nevertheless.

A few months later, when immediate plans were put in motion, Byron offered the use of his house—and purse—to establish an arms depot for "no other motive than that of sharing the destiny of a brave nation, defending itself against the self-called Holy Alliance."

His practical activities and his fury at the Neapolitans on whose last minute withdrawal from the plan he blamed its failure, are indicated in his diary notes written May 1, 1821.

During the same week Byron wrote a letter to his friend, the Irish poet, Thomas Moore:

> You cannot have been more disappointed than myself, nor so much deceived. I have been so at some personal risk also, which is not yet done away with. However, no time nor circumstances shall alter my tone nor my feelings of indignation against tyranny triumphant. The present business has been as much a work of treachery as of cowardice, though both may have done their part. If ever you and I meet again, I will have a talk with you upon the subject. At present, for obvious reasons, I can write but little, as all letters are opened.
> In *mine* they shall always find *my* sentiments, but nothing that can lead to the oppression of others. You will please to recollect that the Neapolitans are now nowhere more execrated than in Italy, and not blame a whole people for the vices of a province . . . and now let us be literary; a sad falling off, but it is always a consolation. If "Othello's occupation be gone", let us take to the next best; and, if we cannot contribute to

make mankind more free and wise, we may amuse ourselves
and those who like it. . . .
I have no news. As a very pretty woman said to me a few
nights ago, with the tears in her eyes, as she sat at the harpsi-
chord, "Alas! the Italians must now return to making operas."
I fear *that* and macaroni are their forte, and "motley their only
wear". However, there are some high spirits among them still.
Pray write.

When it became apparent that the struggle for freedom in Italy
was, for the time being, lost, Byron's thoughts turned to his first
love—Greece—whose people were beginning a badly organized and
disunited but courageous struggle for the liberation of their nation.
On September 18, 1821, Byron wrote again to Thomas Moore:

It is awful work, this love, and prevents all a man's projects
of good or glory. I wanted to go to Greece, lately (as everything seems up here) with her brother, who is a very fine brave
fellow . . . and wild about liberty. But the tears of a woman
who has left her husband for a man, and the weakness of one's
own heart, are paramount to these projects, and I can hardly
indulge them!

During the ten or twelve months before Shelley's death in July,
1822, the two poets spent a considerable amount of time together,
and in a letter dated August 8, 1821, Shelley wrote to his wife:

Lord Byron is greatly improved in every respect. . . . The
interest which he took in the politics of Italy, and the actions
he performed in consequence of it, are subjects not fit to be
written, but are such as will delight and surprise you.

In 1822 Byron was delighted to hear of the suicide of the tyrannical English minister, Lord Castlereagh, who had been largely
responsible for the bloodthirsty suppression of unemployed demonstrations at Peterloo and elsewhere (see p. 540 ff.). He expressed his
pleasure in two amusing couplets which appeared in two different
newspapers:

So he has cut his throat at last!—He? Who?
The man who cut his country's long ago.

So Castlereagh has cut his throat! The worst
Of this is—that his own was not the first.

That year Byron also paid his ferociously playful compliments to the Duke of Wellington in the superb ninth canto of *Don Juan*, with its profoundly serious and honest conclusions. This unhappy description of England's postwar foreign policy may perhaps trouble some of us whose nation has today inherited England's leadership in European affairs.

> Though Britain owes (and pays you too) so much,
>   Yet Europe doubtless owes you greatly more:
> You have repaired Legitimacy's crutch,
>   A prop not quite so certain as before:
> The Spanish, and the French, as well as Dutch,
>   Have seen, and felt, how strongly you *restore*;
> And Waterloo has made the world your debtor
> (I wish your bards would sing it rather better).
>
> You are "the best of cut-throats:"—do not start;
>   The phrase is Shakespeare's and not misapplied:
> War's a brain-spattering, windpipe-slitting art,
>   Unless her cause by right be sanctified.
> If you have acted once a generous part,
>   The world, not the world's masters, will decide,
> And I shall be delighted to learn who,
> Save you and yours, have gain'd by Waterloo?
>
> . . . .
>
> Call'd "Saviour of the Nations"—not yet saved,
> And "Europe's Liberator"—still enslaved.
>
> . . . .
>
> Alas! could she [England] but fully, truly, know
>   How her great name is now throughout abhorr'd:
> How eager all the earth is for the blow
>   Which shall lay bare her bosom to the sword;
> How all the nations deem her their worst foe,
>   That worse than *worst of foes*, the once adored
> False friend, who held out freedom to mankind,
> And now would chain them to the very mind:—
>
> Would she be proud, or boast herself the free
>   Who is but first of slaves? The nations are
> In prison,—but the gaoler, what is he?
>   No less a victim to the bolt and bar.
> Is the poor privilege to turn the key
>   Upon the captive, freedom? He's as far
> From the enjoyment of the earth and air
> Who watches o'er the chain, as they who wear.

Finally, in the same rich poetic year, Byron wrote a furious satire, *The Age of Bronze*, addressed to the contemporary "Cincinnatti" or "patriotic farmers"—that is, to the landowners who had profited so richly by more than twenty years of war, and were so reluctant to submit to peace.

> See these inglorious Cincinnatti swarm,
> Farmers of war, dictators of the farm;
> *Their* ploughshare was the sword in hireling hands,
> *Their* fields manured by gore of other lands;
> Safe in their barns, these Sabine tillers sent
> Their brethren out to battle—why? for rent!
> Year after year they voted cent per cent,
> Blood, sweat, and tear-wrung millions—why? for rent!
> They roar'd, they dined, they drank, they swore they meant
> To die for England—why then live? for rent!
> The peace has made one general malcontent
> Of these high-market patriots; war was rent!
> Their love of country, millions all misspent,
> How reconcile? by reconciling rent!
> And will they not repay the treasures lent?
> No: down with everything, and up with rent!
> Their good, ill, health, wealth, joy, or discontent,
> Being, end, aim, religion—rent, rent, rent!

However, Byron was increasingly anxious to join the active struggle for freedom. He spent a restive two years, enriched by his association with Shelley, but disappointed by their unsuccessful joint attempt to found a progressive newspaper, *The Liberal*, in cooperation with Leigh Hunt. In 1823 Byron set sail for Greece.

Before following him there for the last year of his life we must look back at his major poetic work—*Don Juan*—which was published in fourteen cantos, and five or six installments, between 1818 and 1823. The first five cantos were written in 1818 and 1819 and the other, more serious ones in 1822 and 1823.

Byron's unfinished *Don Juan* is generally considered his major work, and is often classed as one of the few epic poems in English. If it is an epic it considerably extends the definition of that term, but at any rate it is certainly one of the few important— and, many critics feel, decidedly the best—of the long satirical poems our literature can offer.

Shelley, to whom Byron had then just read one of the unpublished cantos, wrote on April 15, 1821: "It sets him not only above, but far above, all the poets of the day. Every word has the stamp of immortality."

Byron's purpose in writing it was, as he said in a letter to a friend, "To remove the cloke, which the manners and maxims of society throw over their secret sins, and shew them to the world as they really are. You have not been so much in high and noble life as I have been; but if you had fully entered into it, and seen what was going on, you would have felt convinced that it was time to unmask the specious hypocrisy, and shew it in its native colors."

For Byron the term society meant a political as well as a personal body, and the hypocrisy he wished to unmask was tyrannical as well as marital. For example in the 23rd and 24th stanzas of Canto IX he says:

> For me, I deem an absolute autocrat
> *Not* a barbarian, but much worse than that.
>
> And I will war, at least in words (and—should
>   My chance so happen—deeds), with all who war
> With Thought;—and of Thought's foes by far most rude,
>   Tyrants and sycophants have been and are.
>
> I know not who may conquer; if I could
>   Have such a prescience, it should be no bar
> To this, my plain, sworn, downright detestation
> Of every despotism in every nation.

More lightly, in the 13th stanza of Canto VII he ironically refers to the Turkish Sultan—against whom he was soon to war in good earnest—as:

> His Highness, the sublimest of mankind,—
>   So styled according to the usual forms
> Of every monarch, till they are consigned
>   To those sad hungry Jacobins the worms,
> Who on the very loftiest kings have dined. . . .

Later, in Canto VIII he spends some time distinguishing between just and unjust wars, and after saying that those which are not carried on in "defense of freedom, country, or of laws" are sheer murder, and their heroes murderers, he concludes, in the 5th stanza with:

> And such they are—and such they will be found;
>   Not so Leonidas and Washington,
> Whose every battle-field is holy ground,
>   Which breathes of nations saved, not worlds undone.

How sweetly on the ear such echoes sound!
While the mere victors' may appal or stun
The servile and the vain, such names will be
A watchword till the future shall be free.

There are innumerable such comments scattered through the fourteen cantos and while many of them may seem flippant taken out of the context of the story, they give a revealing picture of the things uppermost in Byron's mind as he wrote. For example, in the 29th and 30th stanzas in Canto V after the hero, Don Juan, has been captured and sold into slavery in the East, Byron remarks:

> And then the merchant giving change, and signing
> Receipts in full, began to think of dining.
> I wonder if his appetite was good?
>   Or, if it were, if also his digestion?
> Methinks at meals some odd thoughts might intrude
>   And conscience ask a curious kind of question,
> About the right divine, how far we should
>   Sell human flesh and blood. . . .

There is a similar passage in Canto XII where Byron is attacking the critics who had written with extraordinary virulence about the three cantos last published (IX, X and XI). While the critics were ostensibly indignant at the "immorality" in the narrower sense, they made it clear that their real fury was aroused by Byron's continuing political contumacy. For example, in *The Literary Gazette* of September, 1823, the critic says that the poem which opens with "a miserable tirade against the Duke of Wellington and Waterloo" is "low blackguard filth," "an extraordinary mixture of everything wicked and silly," outraging "common decency and common feeling." Similarly the *British Critic* for that month refers directly to Byron's revolutionary associations with the Carbonari in Italy and his radical "cockney" friends (like Leigh Hunt) in England.

Byron naturally has a good deal to say of the critics, and beginning with deceptive gentleness, proceeds to exasperate them beyond bearing by his seeming unconsciousness of what it was that really most provoked their anger.

In the 20th stanza, launching into a sort of mock apology for any irreverent humor about sacrosanct names and institutions, he blandly begins:

> Good people all, of every degree
> Ye gentle readers and ungentle writers,
> In this twelfth Canto 'tis my wish to be
> As serious as if I had for inditers
> Malthus and Wilberforce;—the last set free
> The Negroes, and is worth a million fighters.
> While Wellington has but ensalved the Whites
> And Malthus does the thing 'gainst which he writes.

Although *Don Juan* in its entirety may be a too long and leisurely paced poem for general reading in this age of prose, it is hard to say what one would wish omitted. The reactions of both friends and enemies at the time showed how effectively it carried out Byron's intention to "teach, if possible, the stones to rise against earth's tyrants!" However, Byron always felt, as we know, that words were only the second best weapon with which to fight. On July 13, 1823, he sailed for Greece leaving *Don Juan* forever unfinished.

During that year a Committee for Greek Independence had been formed in London and Byron had been elected a member in absentia. His name made it much easier to raise funds and when it became known that not only his personal services but also his very substantial fortune was to be devoted to the cause of the Greeks, a surprisingly large loan for the insurgents was negotiated by private subscription in England.

On reaching Greece August 2, he found that he had not only the anticipated difficulties and dangers of battlefields to contend with, but also those of an uncertain and divided leadership, and an extremely disorganized command. Although he refused the title of commander-in-chief, he actually took the lead in the serious work of organization, was largely instrumental in forcing an accord—on a minimum program of immediate action for independence—between the opposing factions, and instituted vitally necessary health services, supply depots, and some general discipline.

The dangerous recurrence of an old malarial affection made his friends urge him to continue his assistance from a safer distance. He wrote in response to one such letter on April 4: "I am not unaware of the precarious state of my health. But it is proper I should remain in Greece, and it were better die doing something than nothing." Again, in another note, he said: "I cannot quit Greece.

There is a stake worth millions such as I am, and while I can stand at all, I must stand by the cause."

While altogether devoted to the cause of the Greeks, Byron was realistic about their current state and very limited immediate objectives. He said to his companion-in-arms, Teresa's brother, Count Gamba:

> At present there is little difference, in many respects, between Greeks and Turks, nor could there be; but the latter must, in the common course of events, decline in power; and the former must as inevitably become better. . . . The English Government deceived itself at first in thinking it possible to maintain the Turkish Empire in its integrity; but it cannot be done—that unwieldy mass is already putrified, and must dissolve.

After several months of almost continuous exertion and exposure Byron became very ill on May 10 or 11, 1824, and a week later—May 19th—he died in delirium, imagining he led the long anticipated attack on Lepanto and shouting: "Forward! forward! follow me!"

His death was the occasion of such mourning in Greece, such rejoicing in the Turkish army, and such a sensation in England, as have rarely attended the end of a private citizen.

Hazlitt had always been a severe judge of the noble poet who, he said, "may affect the principles of equality but resumes his privilege of peerage upon occasion." On hearing of Lord Byron's death he left unchanged the somewhat critical lecture he had just written, but concluded it: "Lord Byron is dead; he also died a martyr to his zeal in the cause of freedom, for the last, best hopes of man. Let that be his excuse and his epitaph."

In his later, more formal essay on Byron as one of the major romantic poets, Hazlitt repeated his earlier criticisms of Byron's aristocratic attitude. But he concluded:

> Greece, Italy, the world have lost their poet-hero; and his death has spread a wider gloom, and been recorded with a deeper awe, than has waited on the obsequies of any of the many great who have died in our remembrance. Even detraction has been silent at his tomb; and the more generous of his enemies have fallen into the ranks of his mourners. But he set like the sun in his glory; and his orb was greatest and bright-

est at the last; for his memory is now consecrated no less by freedom than genius.

Fifty years after Byron's death the Spanish statesman and revolutionary leader, Castelar, wrote: "What does Spain not owe to Byron? From his mouth came our hopes and fears. He has baptized us with his blood. There is no one with whose being some song of his is not woven. His life is like a funeral torch over our graves."

In 1891 the Italian critic, Chiarni, said that Byron above all contributed "to reestablish in the heart of crushed and servile Europe sentiments of dignity and human liberty."

And in 1947 Nicephonis Vrettakos, a Greek poet of the Resistance, wrote in his long poem, *33 Days:*

> And the Lord Byron' student battalion, fighting
> in the center of the city recited verses from
> the "Curse of Athena" and wondered what could
> console the shade of Byron in this world. . . .
> And that night Byron was sighing as he sat high up
> on the Acropolis over the Saronic Gulf facing England.
> And that night Sophocles awakened and Pindar
> and Solon and Plato
> And they wore the helmets of our dead.
> And there appeared squadrons of French soldiers
> who had been killed fighting in front of the Bastille.
> Russian soldiers who had been killed in snow covered
> Petrograd.
> Soldiers who had fallen in the university city of Madrid.
> Women who had leaped over the cliffs of Zalongo.
> And all of them had formed a circle high up on the Acropolis.
> And they paid homage.
> And they presented arms as they looked at the sun and
> saw in its flame the Lord Byron student battalion
> marching past.

Percy Bysshe Shelley—1792–1822

In August, 1892, Bernard Shaw was invited to speak at two centenary celebrations of Shelley's birth—one, an official ceremony sponsored by all the leading literary figures in England who were dedicating a new Shelley library in his native town of Horsham, Sussex, and the other an almost impromptu affair announced by a Mr. Foote, editor of the *Freethinker,* who had then recently served a year in jail for printing "blasphemy."

Shaw accepted the latter invitation but since that meeting was to be held in the evening when working men were free, he first attended a part of the suburban celebration and heard Shelley described, as he himself later reported, as "so fragile, so irresponsible, so ethereally tender, so passionate a creature that the wonder was that he was not a much greater rascal." He left before the end of the ceremonies to reach the meeting at the Hall of Science in London which, as he said, "consisted for the most part of working men who took Shelley quite seriously and were much more conscious of his opinions and his spirit than his dexterity as a versifier."

A few weeks later Shaw wrote an article for the *Albemarle Review* about Shelley. In this he described both meetings and said, of the latter :

> Finally, Mr. Foote recited Men of England, which brought the meeting to an end amid thunders of applause. What would have happened had anyone recited it at Horsham is more than I can guess. Possibly the police would have been sent for. . . . I think no reasonable man can deny the right of those who appreciate the scope and importance of Shelley's views to refuse to allow the present occasion to be monopolized by triflers to whom he was nothing more than a word-jeweller.

In another part of the same article Shaw points out that:

> In Politics Shelley was a Republican, a Leveller, a Radical of the most extreme type. He was even an Anarchist of the old-fashioned Godwinian school, up to the point at which he perceived Anarchism to be impracticable. He publicly ranged himself with demagogues and gaol-birds like Cobbett and Henry Hunt and not only advocated the Plan of Radical Reform which was afterwards embodied in the proposals of the Chartists, but denounced the rent-roll of the landed aristocracy as the true pension list, thereby classing himself as what we now call a Land Nationalizer. He echoed Cobbett's attack on the National Debt and the Funding System in such a manner as to leave no reasonable doubt that if he had been born half a century later he would have been advocating Social-Democracy with a view to its development into the most democratic form of Communism practically attainable and maintainable.
>
> It only remains to point out that Shelley was not a hot-headed nor an unpractical person. All his writings, whether in prose or verse, have a peculiarly deliberate quality. His political pamphlets are unique in their freedom from all appeal to the destructive passions; there is neither anger, sarcasm, nor frivolity in them; and in this respect his poems exactly resemble his

political pamphlets. . . . Hence it cannot for a moment be argued that his opinions and his conduct were merely his wild oats. His seriousness, his anxious carefulness, are just as obvious in the writings which will expose their publishers to the possibility of a prosecution for sedition or blasphemy as in his writings on Catholic Emancipation, the propriety and practical sagacity of which are not now disputed. And he did not go back upon his opinions in the least as he grew older. By the time he had begun The Triumph of Life, he had naturally come to think Queen Mab a boyish piece of work, not that what it affirmed seemed false to him or what it denied true, but because it did not affirm and deny enough. Thus there is no excuse for Shelley on the ground of his youth or rashness. If he was a sinner, he was a hardened sinner and a deliberate one. . . .

A few years later Henry Salt, another English socialist and friend of Shaw's, who had been present at both centenary meetings, published a biography of Shelley, *Poet and Pioneer*, which he began by saying:

> In estimating the life work of such a character as Shelley's, it must surely be an error to set aside as valueless the central underlying convictions, while professing admiration for the poetry which resulted therefrom, as if the proverb "by their fruits ye shall know them" did not hold good in literature as elsewhere. . . .
> The central facts of his life and the leading points of his life-creed are so obvious and unmistakable, that there is positively no room for the apologetic theory of the academicians. He may have been the "fiend-writer" that his early critics represented him; he certainly was not the nincompoop of Matthew Arnold's epigram, the "beautiful and ineffectual angel, beating in the void his luminous wings in vain".

Percy Bysshe Shelley was born, August 4, 1792, heir to a baronetcy and to a landed estate whose current equivalent would be four or five million dollars. His grandfather, the founder of the family fortune, was an eccentric old man, rough and forceful in his manners, fond of arguing with "low company," and of dressing and living in a plebian manner. He was a radical Whig in politics, and according to a letter written by Shelley on January 26, 1812: "He is a complete atheist, and builds all his hopes on annihilation."

Although Shelley's father, Sir Timothy, was a far more conventional and temperamentally conservative country gentleman, he too, in parliament supported the extremely radical Whig lord, the Duke of Norfolk, who had secured a baronetcy for the family, and he seems to have had little personal concern for orthodoxy in religion even in terms of his children's education. Of Shelley's mother we know very little, though her family was an older and more aristocratic one than her husband's. Shelley sent her some of the early antiwar poems he kept from his father and said of her in a letter to a college friend May 15, 1811: "My mother is quite rational; she says 'I think prayer and thanksgiving are of no use. If a man is a good man, atheist or Christian, he will do very well in whatever future state awaits us.' This I call liberality."

A voracious reader, Shelley early displayed an insatiable appetite for tales of magic, Gothic romances of terror, and chemistry—a science then in its infancy. Even in childhood his interests were essentially active and before he was seventeen he had published two very poor romances, *St. Irvyne* and *Zastrozzi,* written the major part of a book of quite worthless sentimental poetry, and performed with occasionally dangerous or humorous results, a large number of chemical experiments. Of the latter, A. N. Whitehead says in his *Science and the Modern World:*

> What the hills were to the youth of Wordsworth, a chemical laboratory was to Shelley. It is unfortunate that Shelley's literary critics have, in this respect, so little of Shelley in their own mentality. They tend to treat as a casual oddity of Shelley's nature what was, in fact, part of the main structure of his mind, permeating his poetry through and through. If Shelley had been born a hundred years later, the twentieth century would have seen a Newton among chemists.

Shelley himself in his first term at Oxford is reported by his best friend, an upperclassman, Thomas Jefferson Hogg, as saying:

> Is not the time of by far the larger proportion of the human species, wholly consumed in severe labour? . . . What is the cause of the remarkable fertility of some lands, and of the hopeless sterility of others? A spadeful of the most productive soil, does not to the eye differ much from the same quantity taken from the most barren. The real difference is probably very slight; by chemical agency the philosopher may work a total change, and may transmute an unfruitful region into a land of exuberant plenty. Water, like the atmospheric air, is compounded of certain gases: in the progress of scientific discovery a simple and sure method of manufacturing the useful fluid, in every situation and in any quantity, may be detected;

the arid deserts of Africa may then be refreshed by a copious supply, and may be transformed at once into rich meadows, and vast fields of maize and rice. . . . What a comfort would it be to the poor at all times, and especially at this season, if we were capable of solving this problem alone, if we could furnish them with a competent supply of heat! These speculations may appear wild, and it may seem improbable that they will ever be realised, to persons who have not extended their views of what is practicable by closely watching science in its course onward; but there are many mysterious powers, many irresistible agents, with the existence and with some of the phenomena of which, all are acquainted. What a mighty instrument would electricity be in the hands of him who knew how to wield it, in what manner to direct its omnipotent energies? . . . The balloon has not yet received the perfection of which it is surely capable; the art of navigating the air is in its first and most helpless infancy; the aerial mariner still swims on bladders, and has not mounted even the rude raft: if we weigh this invention, curious as it is, with some of the subjects I have mentioned, it will seem trifling, no doubt—a mere toy, a feather, in comparison with the splendid anticipations of the philosophical chemist; yet it ought not altogether to be contemned. It promises prodigious facilities for locomotion, and will enable us to traverse vast tracts with ease and rapidity, and to explore unknown countries without difficulty. Why are we still so ignorant of the interior of Africa?—why do we not despatch intrepid aeronauts to cross it in every direction, and to survey the whole peninsula in a few weeks? The shadow of the first balloon, which a vertical sun would project precisely underneath it, as it glided silently over that hitherto unhappy country, would virtually emancipate every slave, and would annihilate slavery forever.

Although these interests doubtless did much to console him he was extremely unhappy and generally unpopular at school. His incompetence at, and lack of interest in, games; his contempt for the empty mechanical routine of most of his studies; and his opposition to fagging and other related aspects of public school life earned him an enormous amount of group hazing. His fierce, often physically violent, response to this bullying won him the nickname of "mad Shelley." This school reputation was so firmly fixed that half a century after Shelley's death, when the popularity based upon an evasion of the real Shelley was already pretty generally accepted, the headmaster of Eton greeted the eulogistic offer of a memorial bust with a plaintive "All the same, I wish he had gone to Harrow!"

Shelley's identification of all tyranny—whether that of school, father, priest or king—also seems to have become consciously fixed at this time for ten years later, in his dedication of *The Revolt of Islam,* he says:

> I do remember well the hour which burst
> My spirit's sleep. A fresh May-day it was,
> When I walked forth upon the glittering grass,
> And wept, I knew not why; until there rose
> From the near school-room voices that, alas!
> Were but one echo from a world of woes—
> The harsh and grating strife of tyrants and of foes.
>   . . . .
> So without shame I spoke:—"I will be wise,
> And just, and free, and mild, if in me lies
> Such power, for I grow weary to behold
> The selfish and the strong still tyrannize
> Without reproach or check." I then controlled
> My tears, my heart grew calm, and I was meek and bold.

In a letter written several years later to the radical philosopher, Godwin, to tell him what effect the reading of his *Political Justice* had had, Shelley also adverts to this period, saying: "till then I had existed in an ideal world—now I found that in this universe of ours was enough to excite the interest of the heart, enough to employ the discussions of reason; I beheld, in short, that I had duties to perform."

It is, of course, not unusual for an adolescent thus to dedicate himself to reforming the world. It is unusual for the man he becomes to carry out that resolve as steadfastly and powerfully as Shelley did.

He was, with mutual relief, graduated from Eton in 1810 and that fall entered Oxford as a freshman. At first Oxford seems to have given him nothing but negative goods—an end to compulsory games, communal living, and time consuming classes. But even a tutor who querulously insisted, to Shelley's outspoken amazement, "You *must* read you know. You *must* read," did not discourage him from doing just that some ten or twelve hours a day. When he made a close friend of an intelligent, argumentative and skeptical upperclassman he was moved to wish that life would go on in the same way at least another seven years. He and his friend Hogg had already attracted some critical attention from the authorities when Shelley was one of the three students bold enough to print their names in a subscription list for the benefit of an Irish journalist, Peter Finnerty, imprisoned for "seditious" writings. Finnerty's case had already become a cause célèbre in liberal London circles and Shelley was evidently one of the leaders in an attempt to set up a similar defense committee in Oxford. At the same time he published a book of poems for Finnerty's benefit, ostensibly edited by a "Fitz Victor," and purporting to be the posthumous fragments of the notorious Margaret Nicholson who had attempted to assassinate the king in 1785, been adjudged insane, and died in an asylum. While the quality of the verse showed little improvement, the poems attacked war, glorified heroes and heroines of the French Revolution and indicated the truth of Shelley's statement to Godwin, quoted above. A few lines will indicate both the unShelleyan quality of the verse, and the Shelleyan ideas it states:

> Monarchs of earth! thine is the baleful deed,
> Thine are the crimes for which thy subjects bleed.
> Ah! when will come the sacred fated time
> When man unsullied by his leaders' crime,
> Despising wealth, ambition, pomp, and pride
> Will stretch him fearless by his foeman's side?

At this time a graduate member of the college, Charles Sharpe, wrote to a friend or patron:

> Talking of books, we have lately had a literary Sun shine forth upon us here, before whom our former luminaries must hide their undiminished heads—a Mr. Shelley, of University College, who lives upon arsenic, aquafortis, half-an-hour's sleep in the night, and is desperately in love with the memory of Margaret Nicholson. He hath published what he terms the Posthumous Poems, printed for the benefit of Mr. Peter Finnerty, which, I am grieved to say, though stuffed full of treason, is extremely dull; but the author is a great genius, and if he be not clapped up in Bedlam or hanged, will certainly prove one of the sweetest swans on the tuneful margin of the Cherwell. . . . Our Apollo next came out with a prose pamphlet in praise of Atheism, which I have not as yet seen, and there appeared a monstrous Romance in one volume, called St. Irvyne or the Rosicrucian. Here is another pearl of price! all the heroes are confirmed robbers and causeless murderers, while the heroines glide *en chemise* through the streets of Geneva, tap at the palazzo doors of their sweethearts, and on being denied admittance leave no cards, but run home to their warm beds, and

kill themselves. If your lordship would like to see this treasure I will send it. Shelley's last exhibition is a poem on the State of Public Affairs. I fear, my dear Lord, you will be quite disgusted with all this stuff.

The pamphlet referred to was undoubtedly the famous *On the Necessity of Atheism* in which Shelley and Hogg had collaborated and which was privately printed. It had remained officially anonymous until Shelley, impatient to have it reach a wider public, entered an Oxford publisher-bookseller's where he was well-known and strewed copies over the counter and in the windows. The pamphlet was, except for the title, a very mild one and although it formed the occasion for Shelley's expulsion—which Hogg gallantly insisted on sharing—the real reason was, no doubt, to be found in the more dangerous political actvities already indicated.

Both young men repaired to London, to be there visited with the reproaches of their respective parents and to treat with them as to the terms of forgiveness. Each father felt that the other's son had misled his, and made it a condition of the return home that there be not only no visiting, but also no correspondence between them for some considerable time. Although the friends indignantly rejected this condition, lack of money soon forced Hogg to accede and he departed, leaving the nineteen-year-old Shelley alone in London.

Among other prohibitions Sir Timothy had forbidden the continuation of a lively and affectionate correspondence hitherto carried on between Shelley and his young sisters. A very pretty sixteen-year-old schoolmate of theirs, Harriett Westbrook, whose family lived in London, obligingly agreed to act as go-between. Her father was a well-to-do, retired coffee house or tavern keeper, and since most of her classmates were of a superior social position she seems to have suffered some snubs from the more snobbish of them. A school girl crush on the romantic, noble, and persecuted young man was the natural result of her errands. Her somewhat exaggerated accounts of the renewed contumely to which her friendship with him exposed her soon won Shelley's quick sympathy for another victim of tyranny and injustice. Their acquaintance was temporarily interrupted by Shelley's return home after an incomplete reconciliation with his father, arrived at largely through the good offices of the Duke of Norfolk. Unfortunately Harriett's much older sister, Eliza, had evidently realized the possibilities of the situation and efficiently manipulated matters so that, as Shelley wrote a friend of his, a middle-aged schoolteacher, some months later:

> The frequency of her [Harriett's] letters became greater during my stay in Wales, I answered them; they became interesting. They contained complaints of the irrational conduct of her relations, and the misery of living where she could *love* no one. Suicide was with her a favorite theme, her total uselessness was urged as its defence. (This I) admitted, Supposing she could *prove* her inutility, (and that she) was powerless. Her letters became more and more g(loomy) at length one assumed a tone of such despair, as induced me to quit Wales precipitately.—I arrived in London. I was shocked at observing the alteration of her looks. Little did I divine its cause; she had become violently attached to me, and feared that I should not return her attachment . . . prejudice made the confession painful. It was impossible to avoid being much affected, I promised to unite my fate with hers. I staid in London several days, during which she recovered her spirits. I had promised at her bidding to come again to London. They endeavoured to compel her to return to a school where malice and pride embittered every hour; she wrote to me. I came to London. I proposed marriage for the reasons which I have given you, and she complied.

The "reasons" to which he referred were doubtless those summarized in a letter to Hogg only a few days before the elopment:

> In my leisure moments for thought, which since I wrote have been few, I have considered the important point [free love] on which you reprobated my hasty decision. The ties of love and honour are doubtless of sufficient strength to bind congenial souls—they are doubtless indissoluble, but by the brutish force of power; they are delicate and satisfactory. Yet the arguments of impracticability, and what is even worse, the disproportionate sacrifice which the female is called upon to make—these arguments, which you have urged in a manner immediately irresistible, I cannot withstand. Not that I suppose it to be likely that *I* shall directly be called upon to evince my attachment to either theory.

The Duke of Norfolk evidently still thought Shelley was a prospective Whig M. P. worth the saving and invited the young couple to a house party at Greystoke from which Shelley wrote, in rather naive surprise: "I am with people who, strange to say, do not think at all."

Later, the Duke's mediation was successful in getting an allowance of £200 for Shelley from his father, Sir Timothy, who, even more outraged by the misalliance than by the atheism, still refused to see Shelley or receive him at home. This supplemented an equal sum promised by Harriett's father.

Southey, a neighbor of the Duke's, also received his protégé kindly and flattered himself that a few words from a poet laureate would set the foolish young man on the right path.

Two letters written in the same month by Southey and by Shelley form an amusing contrast.

Southey writes in the familiar vein of a tired and mellow old radical:

> . . . Do you know Shelley the member for Shoreham?—His eldest son is here under curious circumstances. . . . His father has cast him off,—but cannot cut off £6000 a year, tho' he may deprive him of as much more,—her's allows them £200 a year, and here they are. The D. of Norfolk is trying to bring about a reconciliation. I, liking him as you may suppose the better for all this, am in a fair way of convincing him that he may enjoy £6000 a year when it comes to him, with a safe conscience, that tho' things are not as good as they will be at some future time, he has been mistaken as to the way of making them better, and that the difference between my own opinion and his is—that he is 19 and I am 8 and 30.

But Shelley's letter might have shaken Southey's comfortable conviction that the difference between them was only a matter of twenty years. Shelley said:

> Southey has changed. I shall see him soon, and I shall reproach him for his tergiversation.—He to whom Bigotry, Tyranny, Law, was hateful has become the votary of these idols in a form the most disgusting.—The Church of England, its Hell and all, has become the subject of his paneygyric, the war in Spain, that prodigal waste of human blood to aggrandize the fame of statesmen, his delight. The Constitution of England —with its Wellesley, its Paget; its Prince—are inflated with the prostituted exertions of his pen. I feel a sickening distrust when I see all that I had considered good, great and imitable fall around me into the gulph of error.

It was apparently during this visit to the Duke of Norfolk that Shelley first planned his trip to Ireland to assist, if possible, in the renewed struggle for Irish freedom then being organized by Daniel O'Connell, leader of the Catholic Committee.

The Duke of Norfolk had been a consistent fighter for Catholic emancipation and was a few months later to refuse the Order of the Garter in protest at the Prince Regent's breaking his promises on the matter. He had, in 1807, staunchly supported a candidate for Parliament on the platform of abolition of the slave trade and as early as 1798 had incurred royal displeasure by making a speech comparing Fox with George Washington, and offering a toast to "Our Sovereign's health—the Majesty of the People."

Shelley had long been interested in the radical Whigs' stand for Irish freedom and doubtless there was at Greystoke considerable discussion of current events in Ireland. Shelley asked the duke to lend him £100 for the trip. He wrote on January 20, 1812 to his friend, Elizabeth Hichener: "I hasten to go to Ireland. I am now writing an 'Address' to the poor Irish Catholics. . . . You shall see the pamphlet when it comes out; it will be cheaply printed, and printed in large sheets to be stuck about the walls of Dublin."

Shelley and Harriet reached Dublin February 12, 1812, and by February 24 he had had some 1,500 copies published to sell at five pence each, although actually the bulk of them were given away in a number of street distributions. The address said, in part:

> The ministers have now in Parliament a very great majority. . . . These men of course, are against you, because their employers are. But the sense of the country is not against you.— They feel warmly for you—in some respects they feel with you. The sense of the English and of their governors is opposite.

The pamphlet was not a discreditable first attempt. However, his second address, *Proposals for An Association*, written after some six weeks first-hand experience in Ireland, was far more interesting and concrete.

The high point of his Irish campaign was evidently an impromptu speech made to a very large meeting at the end of February. This was reported in the *Dublin Evening Post*, beginning:

> Mr. Shelley requested a hearing. He was an Englishman, and when he reflected on *the crimes committed by his nation* on Ireland, he could not but blush for his countrymen, did he

not know that arbitrary power never failed to corrupt the heart of man. (Loud applause for several minutes.)

The Patriot also commented favorably, and on March 7 the *Dublin Weekly Messenger* wrote:

> The highly interesting appearance of this young gentleman at the late Aggregate Meeting of the Catholics of Ireland, has naturally excited a spirit of enquiry, as to his objects and views, in coming forward at *such* a meeting; and the publications which he has circulated with such uncommon industry, through the Metropolis, has set curiosity on the wing to ascertain who he is, from whence he comes, and what his pretensions are to the confidence he solicits, and the character he assumes. To those who have read the productions we have alluded to, we need bring forward no evidence of the cultivation of his mind—the benignity of his principles—or the peculiar fascination with which he seems able to recommend them. . . . Mr. Shelley has come to Ireland to demonstrate in his person that there are hearts in his own country not rendered callous by six hundred years of injustice; . . . Mr. Shelley, commiserating the sufferings of our distinguished country man Mr. Finerty, whose exertions in the cause of political freedom he much admired, wrote a very beautiful poem, the profits of which we understand, from undoubted authority, Mr. Shelley remitted to Mr. Finerty; we have heard they amounted to nearly an hundred pounds. This fact speaks a volume in favour of our new friend.

There were, of course, others less enthusiastic than the liberal Irish newspapers and chief among these as far as Shelley was concerned was the author of the *Political Justice* he so much admired. Godwin, now a tired radical, sent hysterical appeals to his too energetic disciple to stop before his efforts precipitated a violent insurrection. On March 4, he wrote:

> In the pamphlet you have just sent me, your views and mine as to the improvement of mankind are decisively at issue. You profess the immediate object of your efforts to be "the organization of a society, whose institution shall serve as a bond to its members." If I may be allowed to understand my book on "Political Justice," its pervading principle is, that association is a most ill-chosen and ill-qualified mode of endeavouring to promote the political happiness of mankind . . . Discussion, reading, inquiry, perpetual communication, these are my favourite methods for the improvement of mankind: but association, organized societies, I firmly condemn; you may as well tell the adder not to sting . . . as tell organized societies of men,

associated to obtain their rights and to extinguish oppression, prompted by a deep aversion to inequality, luxury, enormous taxes and the evils of war, to be innocent, to employ no violence, and calmly to await the progress of truth.

Shelley promptly and rather sharply replied:

I am not forgetful or unheeding of what you said of associations. But "Political Justice" was first published in 1793; nearly twenty years have elapsed since the general diffusion of its doctrines. What has followed? Have men ceased to fight? Have vice and misery vanished from the earth? Have the fireside communications which it recommends taken place? Out of the many who have read that inestimable book, how many have been blinded by prejudice; how many, in short, have taken it up to gratify an ephemeral vanity, and when the hour of its novelty had passed, threw it aside, and yielded with fashion to the arguments of Mr. Malthus?
I have at length proposed a Philanthropic Association, which I conceive not to be contradictory, but strictly compatible with the principle of "Political Justice."

The chances of immediate organizational results were, however, slight and two days later he wrote to his sympathetic schoolteacher friend, Elizabeth Hichener: "I have at least made a stir here, and set some men's minds afloat. I *may* succeed; but I fear I shall not, in the main object of Association." A month later, shortly after leaving Ireland, Shelley wrote realistically, again to Elizabeth: "We left Dublin because I had done all I could do; if its effects were beneficial, they were not greatly so. I am dissatisfied with my success, but not with the attempt."

They returned to an England where a terrified government was creating new capital offenses to suppress the protests of unemployed workers and savagely prosecuting any publisher who dared print a criticism of its policies. The radical editor, Daniel Isaac Eaton, who had ironically adopted Burke's famous reference to "the swinish multitude" by naming his paper *Politics for the People or A Salamangundi for Swine* was, at the end of May, sentenced by Lord Ellenborough to eighteen months in jail with a monthly two hours in the pillory for publishing Paine's *The Age of Reason*.

On May 31 the *Examiner* gave an account of the case and a few days later Shelley began his first really important literary work—the famous *A Letter to Lord Ellenborough*. In the middle of July he wrote his friend Elizabeth: "I have been writing a defense of Eaton. Today I have not coolness enough to go on." Two or three weeks later the twenty-four page pamphlet had been printed.

The real power and more than topical importance of this work is indicated by its subsequent history. In 1879 it was reprinted in New York when Mr. D. M. Bennett, editor of the atheist *Truth Seeker* was sentenced to over a year in jail for blasphemy. In 1883 Mr. George William Foote, editor of the *Freethinker*, given a similar sentence in London, republished it with an introductory statement:

> Now that the Blasphemy Laws, which have slumbered for fifty years, are once more invoked by the agents of political and spiritual oppression, it is well that Shelley's noble appeal should go forth in a cheap form to the English people, who are the final judges of judges, and the unmakers as well as the makers of law.

Less than six months after the pamphlet had first been printed the same judge, Ellenborough, sentenced Leigh Hunt, editor of the liberal *Examiner*, to two years in prison, a fine of £1,000, with an additional £1,500 five-year security (for future good behavior) to be deposited before his release. He had criticized the Prince Regent in his newspaper! Hunt's brother and co-editor, John Hunt, received a similar sentence. Shelley, who had been attempting to raise a fund for the benefit of the families of seventeen poor weavers, hung for participation in unemployed demonstrations in Yorkshire, wrote hurriedly to his publisher Hookham:

> I am boiling with indignation at the horrible injustice and tyranny of the sentence pronounced on Hunt and his brother, and it is on this subject that I write to you. Surely the seal of abjectness and slavery is indelibly stamped upon the character of England.
> Although I do not retract in the slightest degree my wish for a subscription for the widows and children of those poor men hung at York, yet this £1000 which the Hunts are sentenced to pay is an affair of more consequence. Hunt is a brave, a good, and an enlightened man. Surely the public for whom Hunt has done so much will repay in part the great debt of obligation which they owe the champion of their liberties and virtues. . . . Well I am rather poor at present but I have £20 which is not immediately wanted. Pray begin a subscription for the Hunts. . . . If no other way can be devised for this sub-

scription, will you take the trouble on yourself of writing an appropriate advertisement for the paper, inserting by way of stimulant, my subscription. On second thoughts, I enclose the £20.

Shelley was then, and had been for the better part of the past year, in Wales where he had taken an energetic part in an ambitious and largely successful cooperative attempt to reclaim a tremendous tract of ocean front land for agricultural purposes. During this time he had written the major portion of his first important poem—*Queen Mab*—a long allegorical work about the past, present and future state of the world. This later became, as Karl Marx said, the Chartists' Bible. It was reprinted in innumerable cheap editions by radical publishers, and was quoted more often than any other single literary work in English workingclass newspapers and magazines of the Nineteenth Century.

At the beginning of March 1813, Shelley and Harriett, with her sister Eliza, who had for some time been living with them, paid a second brief visit to Dublin. They stayed at the house of the radical journalist, John Lawless, with whom Shelley had the year before made tentative plans for collaborating on a new newspaper and on a true history of the long Irish struggle for independence.

From Dublin he sent *Queen Mab* to his publisher and by the end of March he and Harriett, then six months pregnant, had returned to London.

Here Shelley undertook the private printing of *Queen Mab* himself, since his publisher refused to bring the poem out, fearing an almost certain prosecution. Shelley had written, in a vain attempt to persuade him: "Indeed, a poem is safe: the iron-souled Attorney general would scarcely dare to attack." But Hookham evidently knew better, for when, some seven years later, a pirated edition *was* publicly printed, its publisher was promptly arrested.

The poem which was destined to be of such importance in the English radical movement of the mid-nineteenth century does not yet show Shelley's mature poetic genius. However, it has considerable literary merit and gives at least a fragmentary first statement of almost all his major political ideas.

The form adopted was the sort of fairy-tale dream already popularized by Southey and others. The first two cantos dealt with a vision of the past, the last two dealt with an ideal view of the happy future, while the five central ones were devoted to a slashing attack on the social evils of the current time. The third canto showed the evils of monarchy, the fourth of political tyranny, the fifth of economic exploitation, and the sixth and seventh, of religion.

The third canto begins with the dreamer Ianthe, guided by Queen Mab, visiting a King at his court where, in the fairy's words:

> Those gilded flies
> That, basking in the sunshine of a court,
> Fatten on its corruption; what are they?—
> The drones of the community; they feed
> On the mechanic's labor; the starved hind,
> For them compels the stubborn glebe to yield
> Its unshared harvests; and yon squalid form,
> Leaner than fleshless misery, that wastes
> A sunless life in the unwholesome mine,
> Drags out in labor a protracted death
> To glut their grandeur; many faint with toil
> That few may know the cares and woe of sloth.

In the next canto, which opens with a description of the death and destruction during Napoleon's retreat from Moscow, Ianthe exclaims at how evil human nature must be to cause such desolation. The fairy sternly replies:

> Nature!—no!
> Kings, priests and statesmen blast the human flower
> Even in its tender bud; their influence darts
> Like subtle poison through the bloodless veins
> Of desolate society.

In the fifth canto Shelley moves on to a discussion of economic exploitation and says:

> Hence commerce springs, the venal interchange
> Of all that human art or Nature yield;
> Which wealth should purchase not, but want demand,
> And natural kindness hasten to supply
> From the full fountain of its boundless love,
> Forever stifled, drained and tainted now.
> . . . . . .
> Commerce has set the mark of selfishness,
> The signet of its all-enslaving power,
> Upon a shining ore, and called it gold;

> Before whose image bow the vulgar great,
> The vainly rich, the miserable proud,
> The mob of peasants, nobles, priests and kings,
> And with blind feelings reverence the power
> That grinds them to the dust of misery.
> But in the temple of their hireling hearts
> Gold is a living god and rules in scorn
> All earthly things but virtue.

This canto moves on to an extraordinary analysis of the difference between the wavering, occasional, easily diverted opposition to tyranny of the middle-class man of good will, and the steady unrelenting hatred of tyranny felt by those "who have nothing to lose but their chains."

> The man of ease, who, by his warm fireside,
> To deeds of charitable intercourse
> And bare fulfilment of the common laws
> Of decency and prejudice confines
> The struggling nature of his human heart,
> Is duped by their cold sophistry; . . .
> . . . But the poor man
> Whose life is misery, and fear and care;
> Whom the morn wakens but to fruitless toil;
> . . . he little heeds
> The rhetoric of tyranny; his hate
> Is quenchless as his wrongs; he laughs to scorn
> The vain and bitter mockery of words,
> Feeling the horror of the tyrant's deeds,
> And unrestrained but by the arm of power,
> That knows and dreads his enmity.

However, despite the poor man's deeper understanding, as yet:

> The iron rod of penury still compels
> Her wretched slave to bow the knee to wealth,
> And poison, with unprofitable toil,
> A life too void of solace to confirm
> The very chains that bind him to his doom.

The sixth and seventh cantos deal with the tyranny of religion and persecution of atheists, foreshadowing in the hero, Ahasuerus, opposition to a tyrannical deity, the great theme of Shelley's epic *Prometheus Unbound*. In the last two cantos the fairy queen comforts Ianthe by a glimpse of the happy future when science will have made a paradise of earth and love will have taught men to enjoy its fruits in peace.

Even these last two cantos, however, are remarkably concrete in stating—and explaining—many of the specific evils which will have been eliminated. For example:

> No longer prostitution's venomed bane
> Poisoned the springs of happiness and life.

Nor will the African then be:

> . . . changed with Christians for their gold
> And dragged to distant isles, where to the sound
> Of the flesh-mangling scourge he does the work
> Of all-polluting luxury and wealth.

During this summer of 1813, two other momentous happenings were expected; the birth of Harriett's first child and Shelley's twenty-first birthday.

The first event duly took place and the little girl was named Eliza Ianthe—Eliza after Harriett's sister whom, by now, Shelley openly detested, and Ianthe for the heroine of his own *Queen Mab*.

Shelley's twenty-first birthday naturally also occurred on time, but he and Harriett were disappointed in their expectation that it would have economic as well as biological significance.

Shelley had by that time debts of some £2000 and had evidently expected some more suitable and permanent financial arrangement to be suggested by his father when he came of age. Harriett had even more sanguinely and, perhaps, more ardently, anticipated full recognition of the young couple. She had written to a friend on May 21: "Mr. Shelley's family are very eager to be reconciled to him and I should not in the least wonder if my next letter were not sent from his Paternal roof, as we expect to be there in a week or two."

Shelley had, at the same time, written to the Duke of Norfolk about a reconciliation and, on his advice, to Sir Timothy declaring his "willingness to make any Concessions that may be judged for the Interest of My Family." By this he evidently meant concessions in terms of financial settlements of the entailed estate he was, eventually, to inherit. When Sir Timothy replied, demanding that Shelley "write to the people at Oxford, and declare his return to Christianity" Shelley, then occupied with the proofs of *Queen Mab*, wrote the Duke: "I was prepared to make my father every reasonable concession, but am not so degraded and miserable a slave as publicly to disavow an opinion which I believe to be true."

Matters were then again at a standstill and on August 8 Harriett somewhat mistakenly wrote: "Mr. S is of age, but no longer heir to the immense property of his sires. They are trying to take it away, and will I am afraid succeed, as it appears there is a flaw in the drawing up of the settlement, by which they can deprive him of everything. . . . We are now in a house 30 miles from London, merely for convenience." [Shelley, being 21, was then constantly in danger of arrest for debt.]

"How long we remain is uncertain, as I fear our necessities will oblige us to remove to a greater distance. Our friends the Newtons are trying to do everything in their power to serve us; but our doom is decided. You who know us may well judge of our feelings. To have all our plans set aside in this manner is a miserable thing. Not that I regret the loss, but for the sake of those I intended to benefit."

Despite the Shelleyan conclusion of this letter, Harriett's natural personal disappointment is clear, and no doubt the increased responsibilities which her child's birth brought, supplemented perhaps by her sister's or father's reminders that all Shelley really had to do was write a letter to Oxford, accentuated and accelerated her growing coldness to her husband's troublesome ideas. She refused to nurse their baby, hiring a wet-nurse despite Shelley's horror that they were thus forcing a woman to sell her own child's milk. According to the later reminiscences of a number of their friends, Harriett at this time also developed considerable interest in fashionable clothes, and she no longer participated in the reading aloud which had theretofore played so large a part in their domestic life.

At the same time Shelley was making the acquaintance of a larger circle of congenial people than he had yet known.

The Newtons mentioned in Harriett's letter were a well-to-do, well-educated and popular couple with five lively children who were being brought up on Rousseauan back-to-nature principles which included vegetarianism, modified nudism, and some similar fads, but which also included a liberal attitude, real interest in music and literature, and seemed to be producing excellent results.

Mrs. Newton's sister, Mrs. Boinville, at whose home Shelley spent much more time, was the center of a circle of liberal French emigrés, republican in politics and free thinkers in religion. Her disapproving nephew, a Presbyterian minister, later wrote of her in his memoirs: "Round her slight figure she wore the badge of republicanism—a wide red band—and I have often heard her call herself une enfant de la Revolution. With this she had unfortunately accepted the principles of the false philosophers of the age. . . ."

Thomas Love Peacock, the novelist, who had recently made the acquaintance of Shelley and Harriett, later wrote of the gatherings at these homes: "I was sometimes irreverent enough to laugh at the fervour with which opinions utterly unconducive to any practical result were battled for as matters of the highest importance to the well being of mankind; Harriett Shelley was always ready to laugh with me, and we thereby both lost caste with some of the more hot-headed of the party."

It is perhaps only fair to add here Shelley's comment on Peacock in a note written to his publisher, Hookham, the summer before:

> Mr. Peacock conceives that commerce is prosperity; that the glory of the British Flag, is the happiness of the British people; that George III. so far from having been a warrior and a Tyrant, has been a Patriot. To me it appears otherwise; and I have rigidly accustomed myself, not to be seduced by the loveliest eloquence or the sweetest strains to regard with intellectual toleration (that) which ought not to be tolerated by those who love Liberty, Truth, and Virtue.

Whatever the merits of the case, the lack of sympathy between Shelley and Harriett continued to increase. It was no doubt accelerated by the growing discomfort of a household constantly moving for fear of bailiffs, and divided by an acknowledged antagonism between Shelley and his sister-in-law, Eliza, on whom Harriett more and more depended.

Shelley had admittedly married for chivalry rather than for love, and while during the first two years of their marriage he had, he said, learned to love his wife, it was an affection based on her cheerful adaptable companionship, devotion, and discipleship, rather than on either intellectual respect or any real physical passion.

By the end of 1813 there was a real, if unacknowledged, estrangement between them, and by March 16, 1814, Shelley was writing to Hogg about Eliza, with whom Harriett almost wholly associated herself: "It is a sight which awakens an inexpressible sensation of disgust and horror, to see her caress my poor little Ianthe, in whom I may hereafter find the consolation of sympathy.

I sometimes feel faint with the fatigue of checking the overflowings of my unbounded abhorrence for this miserable wretch. But she is no more than a blind and loathsome worm, that cannot see to sting."

At this time, he paid a month long visit to the Boinvilles to escape "from the dismaying solitude of myself." Mrs. Boinville wrote to Hogg on April 18: "Shelley is again a widower; his beauteous half went to town on Thursday with Miss Westbrook, who is gone to live, I believe, at Southampton."

Early in June Shelley met Godwin's daughter, Mary, whose brilliant, courageous and unfortunate mother, Mary Wollstonecraft, had been the author of the famous *Vindication of the Rights of Women.*

He walked, read and talked with Mary and soon decided, both in terms of her genuine understanding of, and participation in, his ideas, and of the overwhelming desire he felt for her, that it was necessary to end the marriage with Harriett, which he and Harriett had both originally agreed to treat as a free love union if either ever wished to leave the other. However, Mary's youth (she was not yet 17) and his concern for Harriett kept him from a declaration until the end of the month when Mary herself anticipated it.

He was naively hurt and surprised when Godwin, who had repeatedly declared his firm belief in free love, acted like any other outraged father, and forbade him the house. He was even more naively astonished that Harriett refused to honor their premarital agreement, indignantly rejected his proposal that she meet Mary in friendship, and denounced his request that she thenceforth consider him as a beloved and loving brother, rather than a husband.

Finally, finding everyone so unexpectedly unreasonable, he and Mary, accompanied by her stepsister Jane, eloped to France at the end of July.

After an idyllic six weeks, lack of funds forced them to return to London. There they spent a miserable year dodging creditors, Godwin's emissaries, Harriett's champions, and the increasing numbers of warrants issued for Shelley's arrest as a debtor.

Most of Shelley's time and energy was spent attempting to borrow money, at ruinous rates of 300 and 400 percent, on post-obit notes to fall due whenever he should inherit the estate which was then still in the possession of his grandfather.

Shelley wrote and published a pamphlet—ostensibly a *Refutation of Deism,* but actually also a refutation of Christianity, in which the champions of the two beliefs each so successfully attacked the other's "proofs" that it was clear nothing but atheism was left as a tenable hypothesis. He was too distracted to attempt any more creative work, and rather mournfully asked Peacock one day: "Do you think Wordsworth could have written such poetry if he had ever had dealings with money lenders?"

The young couple's gloom was deepened by the birth of a now unwanted son to Harriett in November, and Mary's premature delivery—in February-of a tiny daughter who died in less than a month.

At the end of the year Sir Bysshe's death and the peculiar condition of his will made it necessary for Sir Timothy to effect a financial settlement with Shelley. He was thereafter to receive £1000 a year, of which at least £200 were made over to Harriett.

Shelley turned back to poetry, completing a rather introspective long poem, *Alastor*, by the end of 1815. After a pleasant sojourn with Lord Byron in Switzerland, during which Mary wrote her first novel, *Frankenstein*, they returned to take a house at Marlow where Shelley began his next important work, *The Revolt of Islam*, an idealized account of the French Revolution.

Their peaceful life was shockingly interrupted when, on December 11, 1816, they learned that Harriett, whom Shelley had not seen for over two years, had drowned herself. She had evidently been lonely and miserable at her father's house and had left her children there, under Eliza's care, in November, taking rooms at an inn in the name of Harriett Smith. The landlady said that she seemed "in the family way" and a newspaper account of the coroner's inquest spoke of the death of "a respectable female far advanced in pregnancy."

She left a pathetic letter to her sister, with messages for Shelley urging his tender guardianship of their son Charles, whom he had never seen, and begging that he allow Ianthe to remain under the care of Eliza.

Shelley was never shown or told of this letter and when, after a hasty marriage to Mary, he communicated with Eliza about the children, the Westbrooks brought a suit against him as an unfit guardian.

Shelley wrote to Mary from London, January 11, 1817:

> Their process is the most insidiously malignant that can be conceived. They have filed a bill to say that I published Queen

Mab, that I now avow myself to be an atheist and a republican, with some other imputations of an infamous nature. . . . If I admit myself or if Chancery decides that I ought not to have the children the Westbrook's will make that decision a basis for a criminal information or common libel attack.

The Westbrooks seem, however, to have had no motive beyond securing guardianship of the children, and proceeded to no further action when Lord Eldon, in an almost unprecedented decision, arranged to appoint a guardian permitting Shelley to visit the children only once a month in his presence.

Shelley wrote a bitter poem "To The Lord Chancellor" in which, after listing the public reasons his country had for cursing Lord Eldon, he proceeded to add private reasons for a father's curse:

> By the false cant which on their innocent lips
> Must hang like poison on an opening bloom,
> By the dark creeds which cover with eclipse
> Their path way from the cradle to the tomb—

This was not published until long after Shelley's death.

However, even during the trial Shelley had not been inactive politically. There had been many discussions with Leigh Hunt and his wife, now close friends and frequent visitors to the Shelleys, and in March 1817 the pamphlet *A Proposal for Putting Reform to the Vote Throughout the Kingdom* was completed and published by "The Hermit of Marlow."

It contained an eminently sensible proposal for a convention in London to arrange the financing and detailed plans for a house-to-house canvass of the United Kingdoms, so as to give all house holders a chance to vote on whether or not they wished the reform of Parliament which would come with a greatly enlarged franchise, abolition of the rotten boroughs, and similar changes. The program of reforms tentatively suggested fell far short of Shelley's own ultimate goal, but were probably the maximum on which it would have been possible to get any broad general agreement among liberals of all kinds. As Shelley was to write to Leigh Hunt about a similar matter two years later: "You know my principles incite me to take all the good I can get in politics, for ever aspiring to something more. I am one of those whom nothing will fully satisfy, but who are ready to be partially satisfied in all that is practicable. We shall see."

Disappointed but not discouraged by the lack of response to this attempt, Shelley continued to work on *The Revolt of Islam*, which was completed by the end of September 1817. In the preface to that poem, which is largely based on a study of the events of the French Revolution, Shelley said that liberty would not be won at one blow but only as the result of "resolute perseverance and indefatigable hope, and long-suffering and long-believing courage, and the systemmatic efforts of generations of men of intellect and virtue." He devoted a considerable portion of the poem to a consideration of what was, for him, one of the major social questions— that of woman's position in society. One passage reads:

> Can man be free, if woman be a slave?
> . . . well ye know
> What woman is, for none of woman born
> Can choose but drain the bitter dregs of woe
> Which ever from the oppressed to the oppressor flow.

Immediately after completing *The Revolt of Islam* (first called *Laon and Cynthna*) Shelley reverted to prose to write a *Lament for the Princess Charlotte*. This only popular and liberal member of the royal family, to whom, it will be remembered, Byron had written a poem some six years before (see p. 500), died in childbirth on November 6, 1817, and was sincerely mourned throughout the country. On the same day, however, three laborers were executed for supposed participation in the Derby riots, to which they had been incited by a notorious police provocateur and spy on whose testimony they were convicted.

Shelley wrote a powerful sixteen page pamphlet in which he discussed the degree of mourning due to each of the two events. He concluded with a threnody for the true Queen of England, the murdered Spirit of Liberty. This pamphlet he rushed to Ollier, asking him to publish it "without an hour's delay." It appeared for the first time in 1843!

Shelley and Mary had been living well within their income but were only gradually able to pay off the accumulation of earlier debts. Some financial vexations, Shelley's ill health (mistakenly diagnosed as consumption), and a probably imaginary alarm that there was a plan on foot to deprive him and Mary of the guardianship of their own two babies, William and Clara, determined the Shelleys to go abroad. The importunities of Mary's stepsister, Jane Claire, who had been Byron's mistress and who wished to take her little daughter, Allegra, to visit Byron, the child's father, made them decide on a trip to Italy. They left England in March 1818.

Although moved by the poverty of the Italian peasants, the brutal treatment of prisoners and the unchallenged rule of a superstitious Catholicism, Shelley was naturally less involved with political questions in Italy than he 'had been in England. Despite some irritating difficulties in his task of mediation between Byron and Mary's stepsister, Shelley's health and spirits improved greatly during their first six months in Italy.

He was keenly interested in all news from England, and when Peacock wrote telling him of Wordsworth's and Southey's active canvass for the most reactionary of Tories in a recent election, and of Wordsworth's publication of two addresses, *To the Freeholders of Westmoreland*, Shelley wrote back, on July 25, 1818: "I wish you had sent me some of the overflowing villainy of those apostates. What a beastly and pitiful wretch that Wordsworth! That such a man should be such a poet!"

A pleasant visit and several days' talk with Byron in the early fall was the basis for another long poem, *Julian and Maddolo*, but this interlude was unhappily ended by the sudden illness and death of the baby, Clara.

Although Shelley was deeply depressed both by the child's death and by Mary's inability to let him comfort or even share her grief, he continued to write poetry of increasingly great beauty and intensity. Despite the terrible blow of little William's death in June—when, however, Mary seemed to turn to him in her double bereavement—the year of 1819 is truly remarkable for the extraordinary work Shelley produced. If everything else he had written were lost, that year's work alone would still assure his place among the world's greatest poets. During that period he completed his great epic poem of man's struggle for freedom, *Prometheus Unbound*, and in August 1819 began his famous tragedy, *The Cenci*.

This was temporarily put aside for an even more important work.

On August 16, 1819, the infamous Peterloo Massacre took place. To quote J. R. Green in his *A Short History of the English People*:

> The disaffected workers and their sympathisers of Lancashire and Cheshire planned a great demonstration to be held at St. Peter's field, Manchester. On the appointed day the demonstrators to the number of at least 60,000 marched to the place of meeting bearing the mottoes "Universal Suffrage," "Annual

Parliaments," "Vote by Ballot," "No Corn Laws," and similar watchwords. As soon as the meeting began, the yeomanry, by order of the Manchester magistrates, charged with drawn swords into the crowd with the object of arresting Orator Hunt, the chairman, and his supporters on the platform. In the melee which followed several people were trampled or sabred to death, and some hundreds were injured. Hunt, Bamford, and others were arrested, and Hunt sentenced to imprisonment for two years and six months, Bamford and two others for twelve months.

. . . An interesting by-product of Peterloo was Shelley's "Masque of Anarchy," with its stirring refrains:

> "Rise like lions after slumber
> In unvanquishable number.
> Shake your chains to earth, like dew,
> Which in sleep have fallen on you:
> Ye are many, they are few,"

which the poet, at the time absent in Italy, was moved to write when reports of the meeting and the conflict with the yeomanry reached him.

When at the beginning of September, Shelley received the news, he wrote to Peacock, "The tyrants here, as in the French Revolution, have first shed blood. May their execrable lessons not be learnt with equal docility."

By the end of September Shelley had completed his magnificent *Mask of Anarchy* and sent it to Leigh Hunt, urging its immediate publication. Hunt evidently thought it too dangerous and, despite repeated inquiries and urgings, suppressed the poem, which first appeared in 1832 long after Shelley's death. This great work is far too long to quote in full, but a few of its ninety-one stanzas will give some idea of its force and quality. Shelley uses "Anarchy" to express the essential nature of a free enterprise, competitive society. In the Masque lawyers, priests, kings and bankers crowd to welcome Anarchy as their "Law and God."

> I met Murder on the way—
> He had a mask like Castlereagh;
> Very smooth he looked, yet grim;
> Seven bloodhounds followed him:
>
> All were fat; and well they might
> Be in admirable plight,
> For one by one, and two by two,
> He tossed them human hearts to chew,
> Which from his wide cloak he drew.

Men of England, heirs of glory,
Heroes of unwritten story,
Nurslings of one mighty mother,
Hopes of her, and one another!

Rise, like lions after slumber,
In unvanquishable number,
Shake your chains to earth like dew
Which in sleep had fall'n on you:
Ye are many, they are few.

What is freedom? Ye can tell
That which Slavery is too well,
For its very name has grown
To an echo of your own.

'Tis to work, and have such pay
As just keeps life from day to day
In your limbs as in a cell,
For the tyrants' use to dwell:

So that ye for them are made,
Loom, and plough, and sword, and spade;
With or without your own will, bent
To their defense and nourishment.

This is slavery—savage men,
Or wild beasts within a den,
Would endure not as ye do:
But such ills they never knew.

What art thou, Freedom? O, could slaves
Answer from their living graves
This demand, tyrants would flee
Like a dream's dim imagery.

Thou art not, as imposters say,
A shadow soon to pass away,
A superstition and a name
Echoing from the cave of Fame.

For the labourer thou art bread
And a comely table spread,
From his daily labour come,
In a neat and happy home.

Thou art clothes, and fire, and food
For the trampled multitude:
No—in countries that are free
Such starvation cannot be,
As in England now we see.

When Shelley heard that Richard Carlile, a radical printer, had been convicted of "blasphemous libel" for attacking the government's actions in Manchester, he wrote Leigh Hunt a long letter to be printed in the next issue of the *Examiner*. This too remained unpublished until 1839. It reads, in part:

> My dear Friend,
> The event of Carlile's trial has filled me with an indignation that will not and ought not to be suppressed. . . .
> It is said that Mr. Carlile has been found guilty by a jury. Juries are frequently in cases of libel illegally and partially constituted, and when ever this can be proved the party accused has a title to a new trial. A view of the question so simple that it is in danger of being overlooked from its very obviousness has presented itself to me, by which I think, it will clearly appear that this illegal and partial character belonged to the jury which pronounced a verdict of guilty against Mr. Carlile, and that he is entitled to a new trial.
> It is the privilege of Englishmen to be tried, not only by a jury, but by a jury of his peers. Who are the peers of any man, and what is the legal import of this word? Let us illustrate the letter by the spirit of the law.
> A nobleman has a right to be tried by his peers—a gentleman, a tradesman, a farmer—the like—. The peers of a man are men of the same station, class denomination with himself. The reason on which this provision is founded is that the person called upon to determine the guilt or innocence of the accused might be so alive to a tender sympathy towards him through common interest, habits and opinion as to render it improbable, either that thro' neglect or aversion they would commit injustice towards him, or that they might be incapable of knowing and weighing the merits of the case. . . .
> On these grounds I think Mr. Carlile is entitled to make application for a new trial, and I am at a loss to conceive how the judges of the King's Bench can refuse to comply with his demands, unless a few modern precedents, founded on an oversight now corrected, are to overturn the very foundations of the law of which they have been perversions.

Shelley also wrote and sent posthaste to England, in the vain hope that it would be printed on cheap paper for immediate distribution to the unemployed, his dramatic "Men of England." It is this short poem to which Shaw refers in his account of the 1892 Centenary meeting (see p. 517).

> Men of England, wherefore plough
> For the lords who lay ye low?

Wherefore weave with toil and care
The rich robes your tyrants wear?

Wherefore feed, and clothe, and save,
From the cradle to the grave,
Those ungrateful drones who would
Drain your sweat—nay, drink your blood!

Wherefore, Bees of England, forge
Many a weapon, chain, and scourge,
That these stingless drones may spoil
The forced produce of your toil?

Have ye leisure, comfort, calm,
Shelter, food, love's gentle balm?
Or what is it ye buy so dear
With your pain and with your fear?

The seed ye sow, another reaps;
The wealth ye find, another keeps;
The robes ye weave, another wears;
The arms ye forge, another bears.

Sow seed,—but let no tyrant reap;
Find wealth,—let no impostor heap;
Weave robes,—let not the idle wear;
Forge arms,—in your defence to bear.
[or]
Shrink to your cellars, holes, and cells;
In halls ye deck, another dwells.
Why shake the chains ye wrought? Ye see
The steel ye tempered glance on ye.

With plough and spade, and hoe and loom,
Trace your grave, and build your tomb,
And weave your winding-sheet, till fair
England be your sepulchre.

And a long series of "Similes for 2 Political Characters of 1819" dedicated To Sidmouth and Castlereagh ends:

As a shark and dog-fish wait
    Under an Atlantic isle,
For the Negro-ship, whose freight
Is the theme of their debate,
    Wrinkling their red gills the while—

Are ye, two vultures sick for battle,
    Two scorpions under one wet stone
Two bloodless wolves whose dry throats rattle,
    Two vipers tangled into one.

The same autumn saw the magnificent "Sonnet: England in 1819" and the superb "Ode to The West Wind" as well as a rousing poem dedicated to the Spaniards fighting for their liberty.

We gain a new understanding for the force of poetry when we see how this sonnet crystallizes the history of an epoch in a hundred words and defines the artificial famines of "overproduction" in its seventh line.

> An old, mad, blind, despised, and dying king,—
> Princes, the dregs of their dull race, who flow
> Through public scorn,—mud from a muddy spring,—
> Rulers who neither see, nor feel, nor know,
> But leech-like to their fainting country cling,
> Till they drop, blind in blood, without a blow,—
> A people starved and stabbed in the untilled field,—
> An army, which liberticide and prey
> Makes as a two-edged sword to all who wield,—
> Golden and sanguine laws which tempt and slay;
> Religion Christless, Godless—a book sealed;
> A Senate,—Time's worst statute unrepealed,—
> Are graves, from which a glorious Phantom may
> Burst, to illumine our tempestuous day.

The subtle symbolism of Shelley's great Ode is no less characteristic than is the explicit frankness of *The Masque of Anarchy* or the political sonnets. Like such major works as *Hellas* and *Prometheus Unbound*, the Ode must be read on several levels at once for a full understanding of its power and meaning. The beautiful realistic description of the autumn storm gives us only by degrees its skilful intimations that we are dealing with men as well as leaves "Yellow and black and pale" and that the "Destroyer and preserver" is not only a spring-prophesying wind but also the "Wild Spirit" of revolutionary change, the very essence of human freedom. The full significance of this rich metaphorical expression can be grasped only in careful and complete rereadings, but the course of its argument may be illustrated by the crucial stanzas selected below:

> O wild West Wind, thou breath of Autumn's being,
> Thou, from whose unseen presence the leaves dead
> Are driven, like ghosts from an enchanter fleeing,
>
> Yellow, and black, and pale, and hectic red,
> Pestilence-stricken multitudes: O thou,
> Who chariotest to their dark wintry bed

The winged seeds, where they lie cold and low,
Each like a corpse within its grave, until
Thine azure sister of the spring shall blow

Her clarion o'er the dreaming earth, and fill
(Driving sweet buds like flocks to feed in air)
With living hues and odours plain and hill:

Wild Spirit, which art moving everywhere;
Destroyer and preserver; hear, oh, hear!
. . . .
If I were a dead leaf thou mightest bear;
If I were a swift cloud to fly with thee;
A wave to pant beneath thy power, and share

The impulse of thy strength, only less free
Than thou, O uncontroulable! If even
I were as in my boyhood, and could be

The comrade of thy wanderings over heaven,
As then, when to outstrip thy skiey speed
Scarce seemed a vision; I would ne'er have striven

As thus with thee in prayer in my sore need.
Oh! lift me as a wave, a leaf, a cloud!
I fall upon the thorns of life! I bleed!

A heavy weight of hours has chained and bowed
One too like thee: tameless, and swift, and proud.

Make me thy lyre, even as the forest is:
What if my leaves are falling like its own!
The tumult of thy mighty harmonies

Will take from both a deep, autumnal tone,
Sweet though in sadness. Be thou, spirit fierce,
My spirit! Be thou me, impetuous one!

Drive my dead thoughts over the universe
Like withered leaves to quicken a new birth;
And, by the incantation of this verse,

Scatter, as from an unextinguished hearth
Ashes and sparks, my words among mankind!
Be through my lips to unawakened earth

The trumpet of a prophecy! O, Wind,
If Winter comes, can Spring be far behind?

Two longer and more playful attacks on reaction were also written in a few days. One was the burlesque "Oedipus Tyrannus or Swellfoot the Tyrant" which allegorized the disgraceful public mudslinging and washing of royal linen in the Prince Regent's attempts to bar his wife from the Coronation ceremonies. The more important piece was the satirical "Peter Bell the Third," a parody on Wordsworth's long poem "Peter Bell," which with unkind accuracy showed how a poet—Wordsworth—forfeited his poetic powers and incurred the curse of dullness as he became reactionary. The third section opens with the much quoted lines:

> Hell is a city much like London—
>   A populous and smoky city;
> There are all sorts of people undone,
> And there is little or no fun done;
>   Small justice shown, and still less pity.

It continues with a description of the early attacks on "Peter" (Wordsworth) which however, reflects more accurately the reviews Shelley was then receiving from England than any which Wordsworth had ever suffered. Shelley paraphrases his own reviewers in:

> By that last book of yours WE think
>   You've double damned yourself to scorn;
> We warned you whilst yet on the brink
> You stood. From your black name will shrink
>   The babe that is unborn.

After some wavering:

> Now Peter ran to seed in soul
>   Into a walking paradox;
> For he was neither part nor whole,
> Nor good, nor bad, nor knave nor fool,—
>   Among the woods and rocks.
> . . . .
> As troubled skies stain waters clear,
>   The storm in Peter's heart and mind
> Now made his verses dark and queer;
> They were the ghosts of what they were,
>   Shaking dim grave clothes in the wind.

The apostacy, of course, soon brought Wordsworth its practical reward and Shelley continues:

> Yet the Reviews, who heaped abuse
>   On Peter while he wrote for freedom,

> So soon as in his song they spy
> The folly which soothes tyranny,
>   Praise him, for those who feed 'em.
>
> He was a man, too great to scan;
>   A planet lost in truth's keen rays;
> His virtue, awful and prodigious;
> He was the most sublime, religious,
>   Pure-minded Poet of these days.

The further course of Wordsworth's decline and fall is summarized:

> Then Peter wrote odes to the Devil,
>   In one of which he meekly said:
> "May Carnage and Slaughter,
> Thy niece and thy daughter,
> May Rapine and Famine,
> Thy gorge ever cramming,
>   Glut thee with living and dead!
>
> "May death and damnation,
> And consternation,
> Flit up from hell with pure intent!
>   Slash them at Manchester,
>   Glasgow, Leeds and Chester;
> Drench all with blood from Avon to Trent."

Finally, with poetic justice retribution falls:

> Peter was dull—he was at first
>   Dull—oh, so dull—so very dull!
> Whether he talked, wrote, or rehearsed—
> Still with this dulness was he cursed—
>   Dull—beyond all conception—dull.
>
>   . . . . . .
>
> The earth under his feet—the springs
>   Which lived within it a quick life,
> The air, the winds of many wings
> That fan it with new murmurings,
>   Were dead to their harmonious strife.
>
>   . . . . . .
>
> Seven miles above—below—around—
>   This pest of dulness holds its sway;
> A ghastly life without a sound;
> To Peter's soul the spell is bound—
>   How should it ever pass away?

This poem, also sent to Ollier for immediate publication as a party squib, was suppressed until 1839. The parody is certainly not unfair to the later Wordsworth but is should be read together with Shelley's respectful lament for the great early Wordsworth, written when he had first requested a government sinecure three years before (see pp. 421-2).

In addition to this year's enormous poetic accomplishment, Shelley was carrying on a lively and energetic correspondence with his few English friends. The letters to Leigh Hunt are particularly interesting. On December 23, 1819, Shelley wrote him:

> What a state England is in! But you will never write politics. I don't wonder; but wish that you would write a paper in the Examiner on the actual state of the country, and what, under all the circumstances of the conflicting passions and interests of men, we are to expect,—not what we ought to expect or what if so and so were to happen we might expect—but what, as things are, there is reason to believe will come—and send it to me for my information. Every word a man has to say is valuable to the public now, and thus you will at once gratify your friend, nay instruct, and either exhilarate him, or force him to be resign'd, and awaken the minds of the people.

That fall, September 1, 1820, separated from Mary for a few days when there was news of an abortive revolt in Naples, he wrote her: "At Naples the constitutional party have declared to the Austrian minister that, if the Emperor should make war upon them, their first action would be to put to death all members of the royal family—a necessary and most just measure, where the forces of the combatants as well as the merits of their respective causes, are so unequal. That kings should be everywhere the hostages for liberty were admirable." At the same time he completed his *Ode to Naples* hailing her fight for freedom and, somewhat prematurely, celebrating her victory and that of her twin city, Florence. The failure of the planned uprising is discussed at some length by Lord Byron who had arranged to take part in it (see pp. 508-9).

Although Shelley does not specifically refer to that failure, it clearly sets the mood for his "Lament" and "Autumn—A Dirge" written immediately thereafter in November. These fragments, published posthumously in 1822, again give us his characteristic metaphorical identification of nature, man and society in one deeply felt personal emotion.

> Rough wind, that moanest loud
> Grief too sad for song;

Wild wind, when sullen cloud
Knells all the night long;
Sad storm, whose tears are vain,

Bare woods, whose branches strain,
Deep caves and dreary main,—
Wail, for the world's wrong!

The next spring, April 1821, Shelley was shocked to hear of Keats' death in Rome. Keats had been invited to join the Shelleys when it became necessary for him to seek a warmer climate, but he was unable to complete his journey. Shelley dedicated to him the beautiful elegy *Adonais* in which he praises Keats' poetry, mourns for his death, and damns the critics whose savage attacks were, he felt, largely responsible for it. The poem is far too long to quote here in its entirety, but luckily even the briefest excerpt gives an unmistakable indication of its power and depth of feeling.

I weep for Adonais—he is dead!
O, weep for Adonais! though our tears
Thaw not the frost which binds so dear a head!
And thou, sad Hour, selected from all years
To mourn our loss, rouse thy obscure compeers,
And teach them thine own sorrow; say: With me
Died Adonais; till the Future dares
Forget the Past, his fate and fame shall be
An echo and a light into eternity! . . .

Although Shelley and Keats were friendly they had not been close friends. It was their common political sympathies and the consciousness of a common enemy rather than an intimate personal loss which so moved Shelley.

The same critics had, of course, been attacking him too, but not quite in the same way. There were in many of their diatribes against Shelley the peculiar attitude we have seen manifested toward Lord Byron of "come back to your class and all will be forgiven; you belong with us and not with cockney vulgarians or foreign radicals." For example, *Blackwood's Magazine*, one of the two most influential reviews which had been as savage as, and more contemptuous than, the *Quarterly*, in its attack on Keats, had said in its review of *The Revolt of Islam* in 1819:

Mr. Shelley has displayed his possession of a mind intensely poetical, and of an exuberance of poetic language, perpetually strong and perpetually varied. In spite, moreover, of a certain perversion in all his modes of thinking, which, unless he gets

rid of it, will ever prevent him from being acceptable to any
considerable or respectable body of readers, he has displayed
many glimpses of right understanding and generous feeling,
which must save him from the unmingled condemnation of even
the most rigorous judges. His destiny is in his own hands; if he
acts wisely, it cannot fail to be a glorious one; if he continues
to pervert his talents, by making them the instruments of a base
sophistry, their splendour will contribute to render his disgrace
the more conspicuous. Mr. Shelley, whatever his errors may
have been, is a scholar, a gentleman and a poet; and he must
therefore despise from his soul the only eulogies to which he
has hitherto been accustomed—paragraphs from the Examiner,
and sonnets from Johnny Keats. He has it in his power to
select better companions, and if he does so, he may very
securely promise himself abundance of better praise.

Shelley was so far from taking this bait, or separating his poetry
from his principles, that he wrote to Ollier: "Do you know, I think
the article in Blackwood could not have been written by a favourer
of Government and a religionist. I don't believe any such one could
sincerely like my writings."

As late as 1821, in its review of *The Cenci*, *Blackwood's* persisted in its attempts to woo Shelley away from bad opinions and worse company, but after his flat declaration of war in *Adonais* it, and all the minor reviews which had been more or less following its lead, outdid even the *Quarterly* in heaping savage abuse upon him.

Another reason for the renewed hostility of the critics may well have been the appearance in 1821 of the first public edition of *Queen Mab*, published without Shelley's consent. Carlile had asked his permission to reprint it, but Shelley felt that its immature and inexpert verse form did not do justice to his poetic ability, and that he had more clearly and profoundly developed his ideas in *The Mask of Anarchy* which he still expected to appear. He therefore refused consent but Carlile's foreman went ahead to publish a pirated version, which he ignobly surrendered to the government at the first threat of prosecution. He received a comparatively light four-month prison sentence and by the middle of the next year there were four different pirated editions on the market. Professor Ivey Newman White summarizes the poem's subsequent history:

> From this moment [1821] Shelley's *Queen Mab* became an important weapon in the arsenal of British working-class radicalism. *John Bull's British Journal*, a radical weekly published by William Benbow, gave it a sympathetic review on

March 11. *The London Magazine and Theatrical Inquisitor*, though only mildly radical, and not a working-man's magazine, reviewed it favourably in the March issue and prophesied that the author was meant to fulfil a high destiny. Within twenty years fourteen or more separate editions were issued by piratical radical publishers. The book took an honoured place with Volney's *Ruins of Empire*, Palmer's *Principles of Nature*, Byron's *Cain*, and works of Tom Paine in the radical "libraries" constantly offered for sale.

In October 1822 the Greek War for Independence had begun and Shelley wrote his last major poem, *Hellas*. This was dedicated to Prince Mavrocordato who was soon to enlist Byron in the struggle. This poem was reviewed in a stupid and hostile tone by only one critic, and left unmentioned in all the other journals!

Meanwhile Shelley had also written two major prose works, an essay *In Defense of Poetry* in which he attacks Peacock's view that poetry is only an ornament of life, saying:

> The most unfailing herald, companion, and follower of the awakening of a great people to work a beneficial change in opinion or institution is poetry. At such periods there is an accumulation of the power of communicating and receiving intense and impassioned conceptions respecting man and nature. It is impossible to read the compositions of the most celebrated writers of the present day without being startled by the electric life which hums within their words.

He also wrote his extraordinary essay on *A Philosophic View of Reform*. This too remained unpublished until many years after his death.

In June, 1822, only a few days before that tragic event, he wrote, to his good friend, Horace Smith: "It seems to me that things have now arrived at such a crisis as requires every man plainly to utter his sentiments on the inefficacy of the existing religions, no less than the political systems, for restraining and guiding mankind. Let us see the truth, whatever that may be."

That summer Shelley and Mary, who had just given birth to a son, Percy Florence, were sharing a summer home on the Bay of Spezia with a young couple, Edward and Jane Williams. At the beginning of July Shelley and his friend Edward left home for a short visit to Byron, making the trip in their new sailboat, *The Ariel*. The occasion was an important one. Shelley had, for the past year, been working to bring about a rapprochement between his friend Leigh Hunt and Byron so that the former could come to Italy to edit a new political journal, *The Liberal*, in which all three poets would collaborate.

Tom Moore and other friends of Byron's—to say nothing of all his enemies—were horrified at this radical and plebian association and did their best to dissuade him. There were other difficulties, chiefly financial ones in terms of Leigh Hunt's own embarrassed circumstances and large family. Shelley, whose object was both to help Hunt and to create an effective new radical medium, had patiently surmounted difficulty after difficulty as is indicated in his letter to Leigh Hunt when the plan was first suggested over a year before (August 26, 1821): "I did not ask Lord Byron to assist me in sending a remittance for your journey; because there are men, however excellent, from whom we would never receive an obligation, in the worldly sense of the word; and I am as jealous for my friend as for myself. I, as you know, have it not, but I suppose that I shall at last make up an impudent face, and ask Horace Smith to add to the many obligations he has conferred on me. I know I need only ask. . . . He [Lord Byron] has many generous and exalted qualities, but the canker of aristocracy wants to be cut out, and something, God knows, wants to be cut out of us all. . . ."

Finally at the end of June, Hunt and his family had arrived and Shelley hastened to welcome them and see him settled in his new quarters in Byron's villa.

There was a full day of excited, hopeful talk and on July 8, 1823, a month before Shelley's thirtieth birthday, he and Williams set off in their little sailboat for the return voyage. A storm arose and ten days later Shelley's body, with a volume of Keats' poems still in his pocket, was cast up on shore.

The respectable English journals greeted the news with undiminished hostility and undisguised joy. One of them said: "Shelley, the writer of some infidel poetry, has been drowned; *now* he knows whether there is a God or no." His father refused to see either Mary or Percy Florence. He grudgingly made his daughter-in-law a small allowance, (to be repaid with interest out of the estate he could not prevent Percy Florence from eventually inheriting since Harriett's son, Charles, died in childhood) only on condition she wrote no biography or memoirs of Shelley. Not until 1839 was she even permitted to publish an annotated edition of Shelley's works. Since that date there has been no question as to his fame, although the nature of his work and the character of his life have been almost incredibly distorted by most of his non-political critics and biographers. But between 1823 and 1840 he was almost unknown in England and his reputation rested almost entirely on the understanding love of radicals. Professor Newman Ivy White counted 134 references to, or quotations from, Shelley in the workingclass and radical periodicals during that period and only 44 in the much greater number of literary or conservative journals. Although he is far from sharing most of Shelley's political ideas, Professor White says in the conclusion of his monumental biography:

> The most characteristic and at the same time the most appealing qualities of Shelley's poetry seem to me to be its peculiar intensity; its unique sense of loneliness, and its superb faith in human destiny. The intensity is a large element in its persuasive power, combined with Shelley's music, it makes him one of the most hypnotic of English poets. The sense of loneliness voices the feeling, which no sensitive person can always entirely escape, of the utter isolation of his own personality. These two traits, mainly, were sufficient to make him a great poet in the eyes of generations that could ignore or belittle his faith in human destiny and his courageous self-dedication to the advance of human freedom. It was well for him that he could be exalted on these traits alone. But the last quality is his greatest glory.

And Karl Marx said:

> The real difference between Byron and Shelley is this: those who understand them and love them rejoice that Byron died at thirty-six, because if he had lived he would have become a reactionary bourgeois; they grieve that Shelley died at twenty-nine, because he was essentially a revolutionist and he would always have been one of the advanced guard of socialism.

THE LAST OF THE GREAT ROMANTICS

John Keats— 1795–1821

To class John Keats and Charles Lamb together as the last of the great romantics is an unusual grouping which requires some justification. For ordinarily in any discussion of the great romantic period of English literature Byron, Shelley and Keats are an inseparable trio and Lamb, who was born in 1775—three years after Coleridge and three years before Hazlitt—is almost as invariably paired with one of these two irreconcilables, who were probably his two most valued friends.

But despite the twenty-year difference in age and the fact that one was a poet and the other an essayist, there is a very fundamental and significant relationship between their work which can, I think, be explained in terms of a common background and somewhat equivalent experience.

There are many indications that, had Keats' short life lasted just a few years longer, his work would have developed in the tradition of direct political and social concern which was, as we have seen, characteristic of all the early major romantic writers. But the fruits of his tragically brief career, like those of Lamb's longer life, also show the beginning of "romanticism" in the sense in which a later age was to use that term; that is, a tendency to live in the private world of personal emotions, solitary daydreams and cultivated tastes, and to use the beauties of art, nature and antiquity as a refuge from the world's wrongs or a substitute for its gifts.

It may seem difficult to reconcile the avowedly political and revolutionary orientation of the work of all the great earlier romantics—Wordsworth, Coleridge, Hazlitt, Byron and Shelley—with this later use of the word. In fact, the latter has so far overshadowed the original meaning that unsophisticated readers might be forgiven for thinking that Coleridge's romanticism was to be found in his opium dreams, Wordsworth's in his retirement to the Lake Country, Byron's in his travels and mistresses, and Shelley's in his elopement with Mary Wollstonecraft Godwin.

Dorothy Parker has summarized nine-tenths of the biographical studies devoted to the three younger poets in her witty:

> Byron and Shelley and Keats,
> A trio of lyrical treats;
> Shelley's fair brow was o'er clustered with curls
> And Byron walked out with a number of girls
> And Keats was never descended from earls—
> Which doesn't detract from the lyrical feats
> Of Byron and Shelley
> And Byron and Shelley
> And Byron and Shelley and Keats.

However, as we have already seen, Wordsworth and Coleridge ended rather than began their great period of romantic writing when they retired from the world, Byron never ceased his direct attacks on its injustices, and Shelley throughout wrote far more lines about exploitation than he did about love.

But now, in Keats and Lamb we find two great writers who were radical in their sympathies, friendships and, to some extent, actions; who, to be sure, occasionally indicated or even stated their political attitudes in their creative writing as well as in their personal letters; but who, on the whole, wrote their most important work in nonpolitical terms.

It is true that in one of his first poems, written in 1816, Keats, then twenty-one, said:

> O for ten years, that I may overwhelm
> Myself in poesy; so I may do the deed
> That my own soul has to itself decreed.
> . . . .
> . . . First the realm I'll pass
> Of Flora, and old Pan: sleep in the grass,
> Feed upon apples red, and strawberries,
> And choose each pleasure that my fancy sees;
> Catch the white handed nymphs in shady places,
> To woo sweet kisses from averted faces, ...
> . . . .
> And can I ever bid these joys farewell?
> Yes, I must pass them for a nobler life,
> Where I may find the agonies, the strife
> Of human hearts. . . .

After less than half those ten years had been granted, his final illness put an end to writing. It interrupted him in the middle of a long unfinished poem, *The Fall of Hyperion*, where the poet venturing into a fantastic and perilous dream finds sanctuary near a mysterious altar and asks the attendant Spirit why he alone is thus saved:

> "None can usurp this height," returned the shade
> "But those to whom the miseries of the world
> Are misery, and will not let them rest.
> All else who find a haven in the world;
> Where they may thoughtless sleep away their days,
> If by a chance into this fane they come,
> Rot on the pavement where thou rotted'st half"—
> "Are there not thousands in the world" said I,

"Who love their fellows even to the death;
Who feel the giant agony of the world;
And more, like slaves to poor humanity,
Labour for mortal good? I sure should see
Other men here, but I am here alone.
"Those whom thou speak'st of are no visionaries,"
Rejoined that voice,—"they are no dreamers weak;
They seek no wonder but the human face,
No music but a happy-noted voice—
They come not here, they have no thought to come—
And thou art here, for thou art less than they."

At about the same time, after much study of one of those "other men"—Milton—Keats wrote in a copy of *Paradise Lost* he was presenting to a friend:

> The genius of Milton, more particularly in respect to its span of immensity, calculated him, by a sort of birthright, for such an "argument" as the Paradise Lost: he had an exquisite passion for what is properly, in the sense of ease and pleasure, poetical Luxury; and with that it appears to me he would fain have been content, if he could in so doing, have preserved his self-respect and feel of duty performed, but there was in him as it were the same sort of thing as operates in the great world to the end of a Prophecy's being accomplished; therefore he devoted himself rather to the ardours than the pleasures of Song, solacing himself at intervals with cups of old wine; and those are with some exceptions the finest parts of the poem.

The year before he had written in a letter to a closer friend, Reynolds:

> [In youth] We see nothing but pleasant wonders, and think of delaying there forever in delight. However among the effects this breathing is father of is that tremendous one of sharpening one's vision into the heart and nature of man—of convincing one's nerves that the world is full of Misery and Heartbreak, Pain, Sickness and Oppression—whereby this Chamber of Maiden-Thought, becomes gradually darkened, and at the same time, on all sides of it, many doors are set open—but all dark—all leading to dark passages.

His letters to different correspondents throughout these two or three years abound in such remarks as: "I am ambitious of doing the world some good: if I should be spared, that may be the work of maturer years;" "The glory of dying for a great human purpose";

"I find there is no worthy pursuit but the idea of doing some good to the world." In a comparison between the aristocratic poets of chivalry and the greater genius of a "miserable and mighty Poet of the human Heart," Keats says that the great English poets are so great because "They have in general been trampled aside into the bye paths of life and seen the festerings of Society."

In addition his letters often contain brief comments on current political events, always from the liberal point of view, and occasionally there is a longer report or analysis such as the one he included in a letter to his brother and sister-in-law in Kentucky which reads, in part:

. . . Three great changes have been in progress.—First for the better, next for the worse, and third time for the better once more. The first was the gradual annihilation of the tyranny of the nobles, when Kings found it in their interest to conciliate the common people, elevate them and be just to them. Just when baronial Power ceased and before standing armies were so dangerous, Taxes were few, Kings were lifted by the people over the heads of their nobles, and those people held a rod over Kings. The change for the worse in Europe was again this. The obligation of Kings to the multitude began to be forgotten. Custom had made noblemen the humble servants of Kings. Then Kings turned to the Nobles as the adorners of their power, the slaves of it and from the people as creatures continually endeavoring to check them. Then in every Kingdom there was a long struggle of Kings to destroy all popular privileges. . . . The example of England, and the liberal writers of France and England sowed the seeds of opposition to this Tyranny—and it was swelling in the ground till it burst out in the French revolution. This has had an unlucky termination. It put a stop to the rapid progress of free sentiments in England; and gave our Court hopes of turning back to the despotism of the 16th Century. They have made a handle of this event in every way to undermine our freedom. They spread a horrid superstition against all innovation and improvement. The present struggle in England is to destroy this superstition. . . . You will see I mean the French Revolution but put a temporary stop to this third change, the change for the better.—Now it is in progress again and I think it an effectual one. This is no contest between Whig and Tory—but between right and wrong. . . . I am convinced however that apparently small causes make great alterations. There are little signs whereby we may know how matters are going on. This makes the business about Carlisle the Bookseller of great moment in my mind. He has been selling deistical pamphlets republished from Tom Paine and many other works held in superstitious horror. He even has been selling for some time immense numbers of a work called "The Deist" which comes out in weekly numbers. For this conduct he has had above a dozen indictments issued against him for which he has found Bail to the amount of many Thousand Pounds. After all they are afraid to prosecute; they are afraid of his defence; it would be published in all the papers all over the Empire: they shudder at this: the Trials would light a flame they could not extinguish. Do you not think this of great import? You will hear by the papers of the proceedings at Manchester and Hunt's triumphant entrance into London. It would take me a whole day to give you anything like detail. I will merely mention that it is calculated that 30,000 people were in the streets waiting for him. The whole distance from the Angel Islington to the Crown and Anchor was lined with Multitudes. . . .

It is also true that no long poem by Keats is altogether devoid of some social comment. We have already mentioned *Hyperion* in this respect, and even the very early and immature *Endymion* has such passages as:

> His first touch of the earth went nigh to kill.
> "Alas!" said he, "were I but always borne
> Through dangerous winds, had but my footsteps worn
> A path in hell, for ever would I bless
> Horrors which nourish an uneasiness
> For my own sullen conquering: to him
> Who lives beyond earth's boundary, grief is dim,
> Sorrow is but a shadow: now I see
> The grass; I feel the solid ground—Ah, me!
> . . . .
> . . . O I have been
> Presumptuous against love, against the sky,
> Against all elements, against the tie
> Of mortals each to each, against the blooms
> Of flowers, rush of rivers, and the tombs
> Of heroes gone! Against his proper glory
> Has my own soul conspired: so my story
> Will I to children utter, and repent.
> There never liv'd a mortal man, who bent
> His appetite beyond his natural sphere,
> But starv'd and died."

In addition, there are a number of short poems written on specifically political subjects. These include the very earliest sonnet, "Written on the Day that Mr. Leigh Hunt Left Prison," (February 2, 1815), which begins:

> What though, for showing truth to flatter'd state,
> Kind Hunt was shut in prison, yet has he,
> In his immortal spirit, been as free
> As the sky-searching lark, and as elate.

and the one "To Kosciusko" written a year later:

> Good Kosciusko, thy great name alone
>   Is a full harvest whence to reap high feeling;
>   It comes upon us like the glorious pealing
> Of the wide spheres—an everlasting tone.

Keats also wrote an epigram on May 29—Restoration Day—against the commemoration of Charles II's return, the antireligious sonnet "Written in Disgust of Vulgar Superstition," as well as many others. But none of these short political poems begin to reach the heights of Keats' best, or even of his representative poetry, nor does any one of these early poems give us a flash of the illumination offered by such a single line of Shelley's as "a people *starved* and stabbed in the *untilled* field."

There are occasionally such insights to be found in several of Keats' greater poems; for example, in the Prologue to *Endymion*, where he gives us a brief, pregnant statement of those conditions against which "a thing of beauty" may serve as a talisman:

> Spite of despondence, of the inhuman dearth
> Of noble natures, of the gloomy days,
> Of all the unhealthy and o'er-darkened ways
> Made for our searching; yes, in spite of all
> Some shape of beauty moves away the pall
> From our dark spirits. . . .

Just as brilliant are the close-packed concrete images in "Ode to A Nightingale," such as:

> Thou wast not born for death, immortal bird,
> No *hungry generations* tread thee down

and:

> The weariness, the fever, and the fret
>   Here, where men sit and hear each other groan;
> Where palsy shakes a few, sad, last gray hairs,

Where youth grows pale, and spectre-thin, and dies;
Where but to think is to be full of sorrow
And leaden-eyed despairs,—

There are also the three amazing stanzas in the long narrative poem of "Isabella; or, The Pot of Basil" which—but we must let Bernard Shaw describe them, though perhaps he somewhat overstated the case to shock the memorial committee that had asked him for a contribution to the 1921 Keats Centennial volume. In his contribution Shaw said, in part:

> Keats achieved the very curious feat of writing one poem of which it may be said that if Karl Marx can be imagined as writing a poem instead of a treatise on Capital, he would have written Isabella. The immense indictment of the profiteers and exploiters with which Marx has shaken capitalistic civilization to its foundations, even to its overthrow in Russia, is epitomized in
>
> > With her two brothers this fair lady dwelt
> > Enriched from ancestral merchandise,
> > And for them many a weary hand did swelt
> > In torched mines and noisy factories,
> > And many once proud-quiver'd loins did melt
> > In blood from stinging whip;—with hollow eyes
> > Many all day in dazzling river stood,
> > To take the rich-ored driftings of the flood.
> >
> > For them the Ceylon diver held his breath,
> > And went all naked to the hungry shark;
> > For them his ears gush'd blood; for them in death
> > The seal on the cold ice with piteous bark
> > Lay full of darts; for them alone did seethe
> > A thousand men in troubles wide and dark:
> > Half-ignorant, they turn'd an easy wheel
> > That set sharp racks at work, to pinch and peel.
> >
> > Why were they proud? Because their marble founts
> > Gush'd with more pride than do a wretch's tears?—
> > Why were they proud? Because fair orange-mounts
> > Were of more soft ascent than lazar stairs?—
> > Why were they proud? Because red-lin'd accounts
> > Were richer than the songs of Grecian years?—
> > Why were they proud? again we ask aloud,
> > Why in the name of Glory were they proud?
>
> Everything that the Bolshevik means and feels when he uses the fatal epithet "bourgeois" is expressed forcibly, com-

pletely; and beautifully in those three stanzas, written half a century before the huge tide of middle-class commercial optimism and complacency began to ebb in the wake of the planet Marx. Nothing could well be more literary than the wording: it is positively euphuistic. But it contains all the Factory Commission Reports that Marx read, and that Keats did not read because they were not yet written in his time. And so Keats is among the prophets with Shelley, and, had he lived, would no doubt have come down from Hyperion and Endymion to tin tacks as a very full blooded modern revolutionist. Karl Marx is more euphuistic in calling the profiteers bourgeoisie than Keats with his "these same ledger-men." Ledger-man is at least better English than bourgeois: there would be some hope for it yet if it had not been supplanted by profiteer.

Certainly, then, despite his oft-quoted remark, "I feel assured I should write from the mere yearning and fondness I have for the beautiful even if my night's labours should be burnt every morning and no eye ever shine upon them," Keats never belonged to the school of "Art for art's sake" which has made such strenuous efforts to claim him. Nor was he a romantic in the decadent sense of that word, which opposes romanticism to realism. Yet with all due respect to Shaw's prophecy and his own unequivocal statement of intention, Keats' great poetry helps us to endure and enjoy the world rather than to change it, and in this sense is at least cousin once removed to the work of those later less fortunate poets of whom Ralph Fox said, "'Art for art's sake' is the hopeless answer of the artist to 'art for money's sake'; hopeless because ivory never was a good material for fortification." Perhaps we will better understand why this was so if we look more closely at the facts of his life, and of Lamb's.

Keats' grandfather was the owner of a thriving livery stable in London. His daughter married the head hostler or foreman and inherited the stables and a small annuity, while a larger one was left to his wife, and two thousand pounds were to be divided among his grandchildren.

John Keats was born October 31, 1795, the oldest of four children. His father seems to have been both liberal and ambitious for his sons and to have planned that they attend the university—then an almost unheard of thing for one in his station in life. John was placed at an excellent small school in 1803, where his two younger brothers shortly followed him, when the family fortunes were abruptly altered by his father's fatal fall from a horse in 1804.

A few months later Keats' mother—hurried perhaps, by the impossibility of running the business herself—remarried, and the stepfather's conduct to the younger children was such that their grandmother took them all to live with her. Their mother was also soon forced to leave her husband; her property, except for the annuity, had, according to the married woman's property laws then in force, become his, and a few years later she retreated to her mother's home, already stricken with consumption.

Here Keats, home for the holidays in 1809–10 nursed her through her final illness and attended her funeral on March 20, 1810.

His life at school was, except for the double tragedy of his parents' deaths, a happy one. The three brothers were, as they remained, extremely close and loving friends, and Keats, who early felt himself the head of the small family, was also very devoted to his young sister.

At school, until he was fifteen, he had the reputation of a good, but not extraordinary, student and of an outstanding athlete and fighter. Although short he was very well built, strong, quick and active and school opinion was unanimous in predicting for him an outstanding career in the army or navy.

When he returned to school after his mother's death he seems to have begun a course of omnivorous and rapid reading in which he made his first experiments at versification with attempts to translate the *Aeneid*. He also, at this time, evidently laid the foundation for a closer and more equal friendship with his young teacher, Charles Cowden Clarke, the son of the headmaster, who loaned him copies of the *Examiner*, Leigh Hunt's liberal paper to which the headmaster subscribed. Later, during Hunt's two year imprisonment, the young Clarke never failed in a weekly visit, bearing as a present from his father a basket of fresh eggs, vegetables in season, and so forth.

The next year, at sixteen, Keats left school not, as had once been hoped, for the university, but to be apprenticed to an apothecary-surgeon. The "trade" at that time did not have the present professional standing of a pharmacist, far less that of a physician, and was considerably closer to the status of such a barber-surgeon as Fielding's Patridge. The "surgeon" referred almost entirely to the much abused function of blood letting then so unfortunately in vogue.

It is characteristic of Keats' common sense and feeling of family responsibility that, much as we know he disliked the prospect of being an apothecary, there is no murmur of resentment or of his even greater disappointment at not going on to prepare for the university. Like Burns and Blake—and unlike the other poets we have here considered, whose families ranged from the top aristocracy through the ranks of the professional upper middle class—Keats assumed that the first duty of man was to earn a living. He felt he must, of necessity, undertake to do that as soon as possible in one of the very few "white collar" avenues open to a young man of his position, means and education. Although he never actually practised his trade, having become convinced he could earn a living by writing, he deferred the announcement of his decision until he had received the final qualifying certificate so that he could fall back on it if necessary.

He continued his reading and the experimental writing of verse during his four-year apprenticeship and, shortly after his grandmother's death in December 1814, entered Guy's Hospital for his final year of training.

He did well at the hospital and was friendly with his fellow students but he liked neither the city, the separation from his family, nor the work itself. It was at this time that he wrote the sonnet to solitude which begins:

> O Solitude! if I must with thee dwell
> Let it not be among the jumbled heap
> Of murky buildings. . . .

A fellow student said of him: "He never attached much consequence to his own studies in medicine, and indeed looked upon the medical career as the career by which to live in a workaday world, without being certain that he could keep up the strain of it." Although accounted an unusually good student at the hospital Keats himself later said "My last operation was the opening of a man's temporal artery. I did it with the utmost nicety, but reflecting on what passed through my mind at the time, my dexterity seemed a miracle and I never took up the lancet again."

He rarely commented on the suffering which he saw during his training but at one time, in a letter on another subject, gave as the reason for his lack of religious sentiment "my dying day—and that women have cancer."

Another friend and fellow student describing him later said

that he "enjoyed good health—a fine flow of animal spirits—was fond of company—could amuse himself admirably with the frivolities of life—and had great confidence in himself." According to the same authority he was, however, "sceptical and republican," and "a fault finder with everything established."

He received his certificate shortly before his twenty-first birthday and immediately thereafter announced to his guardian—a merchant, Mr. Abbey, whom his grandmother had known for many years and whom she had appointed guardian of the grandchildren after their mother's death—that he did not intend to practise, being now confident that he could make his living as a poet. Mr. Abbey was, naturally, both indignant and worried, and took pains to tell Keats after the publication of his first book a year later:

> Well, John! I have read your book, and it reminds me of the Quaker's horse, which was hard to catch, and good for nothing when caught. So your book is hard to understand and good for nothing when it is understood.

His confidence in his ability to earn a living by his pen was largely based on the encouragement of a literary circle headed by the then well-known Leigh Hunt, to which young Keats had been introduced by his friend and former teacher, Clarke.

The *Examiner*, Hunt's paper, had published "O Solitude" in May, 1816, just before Keats' graduation; Hunt printed an article on "Young Poets"—Keats, Shelley, and Reynolds—that December; and plans were already made for the publication of Keats' first book of poetry which did appear in March 1817. Clarke says

> The first volume of Keats' muse was launched amid the cheers and fond anticipation of all his circle. Everyone of us expected (and not unreasonably) that it would create a sensation in the literary world; for such a first production (and a considerable portion of it from a minor) has rarely occurred.

There were seven reviews in well-known journals—all fairly friendly—though one or two of them echoed the warning of the *Edinburgh Magazine* that Keats had better disassociate himself from the "vulgarity" and radical ideas of Leigh Hunt and his friends:

> If Mr. Keats does not forthrite cast off the uncleannesses of this school, he will never make his way to the truest strain

of poetry in which, taking him by himself, it appears he might succeed.

These cheerful prospects were offset by the fact that the book did not sell, that his brother George was not happy with his employment in Mr. Abbey's business, that Fanny, who lived in her guardian's house, was rarely permitted to visit her brother since he had deserted the career marked out for him and, worst of all, that Keats' younger brother, Tom, was already showing unmistakable signs of the consumption which had killed his mother. Keats wrote in a letter to a friend at Oxford that November:

> I scarcely remember counting upon any Happiness—I look not for it if it be not in the present hour—nothing startles me beyond the Moment. The setting Sun will always set me to rights—or if a Sparrow come before my window I take part in its existence and pick about the Gravel.

However, he completed an ambitious long poem, *Endymion,* as well as a number of shorter ones, notably "In a Drear Nighted December," and for a few weeks took his friend Reynolds' place as dramatic critic of *The Champion,* another fairly liberal Whig paper.

One of his comments on Edmund Kean in the part of Othello might well be applied to Paul Robeson in that heroic role, "When he says, in Othello, 'Put up your bright swords, for the dew will rust them,' we feel that his throat had commanded where swords were as thick as reeds. From eternal risk, he speaks as though his body were unassailable."

During this winter Keats became better acquainted with Lamb and Hazlitt, attending the latter's lecture after which he said that Hazlitt's "depth of taste" was one of "the three great things to rejoice at in the age." The other two were the romantic poetry introduced by Wordsworth and the heroic school of painting then being promoted by Haydon.

He went down to Devonshire in March to nurse poor Tom, whom he soon knew to be dying although he affected a light tone in writing about it even to his close friend, Reynolds:

> I hope by this you stand on your right foot—If you are not—that's all,—I intend to cut all sick people if they do not make up their minds to cut sickness—a fellow to whom I have a complete aversion, and who strange to say is harboured and countenanced in several houses where I visit—he is sitting now quite

impudent between me and Tom—He insults me at poor Jem Rice's—and you have seated him before now between us at the Theatre—when I thought he look'd with a longing eye at poor Kean. I shall say, once for all, to my friends generally and severally, cut that fellow, or I cut you—.

Just a year before, in a happier tone he had written to Reynolds on the same subject "Banish money—Banish sofas—Banish wine—Banish music; but right Jack Health, honest Jack Health, true Jack Health—Banish Health and banish all the world."

Endymion was at this time being printed and there was considerable discussion between Keats, his friendly publishers, and other friends, about the preface which he had written for it. His tone in speaking of the Public, to whom the preface is addressed is very different from that of his great contemporaries and, with certain natural differences, fore-shadows that of the later romantics to whom we have referred above.

To Keats the public is neither a sometimes recalcitrant congregation to be instructed, as it was for Coleridge and Wordsworth, nor an occasionally obtuse constituency to be aroused, as it was for Shelley and Byron. It is, on the whole, composed of contemptuous—and contemptible—customers between whom and the artist there exists a certain natural hostility and any concessions to whom indicate the servility of the tradesman. A few months later, discussing his brother George's plan of emigration to America, Keats says:

> He is of too independent and liberal a mind to get on in trade in this country—in which a generous man with a scanty resource must be ruined. I would sooner he should till the ground than than bow to a customer—there is no choice with him—he could not bring himself to the latter.

The tone of his letter to Reynolds in April, 1818, about the proposed preface for *Endymion* makes it clear that Keats considered the necessity for selling his own poetic wares with similar aversion:

> Since you all agree that the thing is bad, it must be so— I have not the slightest feel of humility towards the Public— When I am writing for myself for the mere sake of the Moment's enjoyment, perhaps nature has its course with me—but a Preface is written to the Public; a thing I cannot help looking upon as an Enemy, and which I cannot address without feel-

ings of Hostility—If I write a Preface in a supple or subdued style, it will not be in character with me as a public speaker—I would be subdued before my friends, and thank them for subduing me—but among multitudes of Men—I have no feel of stooping, I hate the idea of humility to them—I never wrote one single Line of Poetry with the least shadow of public thought. I could not live without the love of my friends—I would jump down Aetna for any great Public Good—but I hate a Mawkish Popularity.—I cannot be subdued before them—if there is any fault in the preface it is not affectation but an undersong of disrespect to the Public—if I write another preface it must be without a thought of those people—I will think about it.

On his return to Hampstead, the suburb of London in which they were living, Keats found that George was determined to seek his fortune in America with the assistance of his courageous young fiancée, Georgiana Wylie, who, although only sixteen was planning to marry and accompany him.

While Keats encouraged George's resolution to emigrate, the prospect of his departure and of Tom's almost certain death depressed him more than he would admit—as he wrote to a friend:

I have two Brothers one is driven by the "burden of Society" to America the other, with an exquisite love of life, is in a lingering State. My love for my Brothers from the early loss of my parents and even for our earlier Misfortunes has grown into an affection "passing the Love of Women"—. I have a Sister too and may not follow them, either to America or to the Grave—Life must be undergone, and I certainly derive a consolation from the thought of writing one or two more Poems before it ceases.

When George sailed, at the end of June, Tom seemed somewhat recovered. Keats' health and spirits had been so much affected by George's as well as his own financial worries, and by the strain of the constant nursing of Tom that it seemed advisable for him to take the opportunity of a three-months' walking tour through Northern England and Scotland with a close new friend, Charles Brown.

His letters to Tom and the fifteen-year-old Fanny are among the most delightful travel letters ever written, and are interspersed with the jingles—and more serious verse—he dashed off when too "tired after my day's walking" to write prose! An excellent example is this first one. The erasures and changes of wording in both poems clearly show that they were composed directly on the letter paper.

Dumfries, July 2nd 1818
My dear Fanny,
  I intended to have written you from Kirk(c)udbright, the town I shall be in to-morrow—but I will write now because my Knapsack has worn my coat in the Seams, my coat has gone to the Taylors and I have but one coat to my back in these parts. I must tell you I went to Liverpool with George and our new Sister and the Gentleman my fellow traveller through the Summer and Autumn—we had a tolerable journey to Liverpool —which I left the next morning before George was up for Lancaster—Then we set off from Lancaster on foot with our Knapsacks on, and have walked a Little zig zag through the mountains and lakes of Cumberland and Westmoreland—We came from Carlisle yesterday to this place—We are employed in going up Mountains, looking at strange towns, prying into old ruins and eating very hearty breakfasts. Here we are full in the Midst of broad Scotch "How is it a' wi yoursel"—the Girls are walking about bare footed and in the worst cottages the smoke finds its way out of the door.—Mr. Abbey says we are Don Quixotes—tell him we are more generally taken for Pedlars. All I hope is that we may not be taken for excise men. in this whiskey country. We are generally up about 5 walking before breakfast and we complete our 20 miles before dinner.—Yesterday we visited Burn's Tomb and this morning the fine Ruins of Lincluden.—I had done thus far when my coat came back fortified at all points—so as we lose no time we set forth again through Galloway—all very pleasant and pretty with no fatigue when one is used to it—We are in the midst of Meg Merrilies' country of whom I suppose you have heard.

> Old Meg she was a Gipsy,
>   And liv'd upon the Moors
> Her bed it was the brown heath turf
>   And her house was out of doors.
>
> Her apples were swart blackberries
>   Her currants pods o' broom
> Her wine was dew o' the wild white rose
>   Her book a churchyard tomb.
>
> . . . . . .
> No breakfast had she many a day morn
>   No dinner many a noon
> And 'stead of supper she would stare
>   Full hard against the Moon.
>
> . . . . . .
> Old Meg was brave as Margaret Queen
>   And tall as Amazon:
> An old red blanket cloak she wore;
>   A chip hat had she on.

God rest her aged bones somewhere
She died full long agone!

If you like these sort of Ballads I will now and then scribble one for you—if I send any to Tom I'll tell him to send them to you. I have so many interruptions that I cannot manage to fill a Letter in one day—since I scribbled the song we have walked through a beautiful Country to Kirkcudbright—at which place I will write you a song about myself.

There was a naughty Boy	There was a naughty Boy
A naughty boy was he	And a naughty Boy was he
He would not stop at home	He ran away to Scotland
He could not quiet be—	The people for to see—
He took	Then he found
In his Knapsack	That the ground
A Book	Was as hard
Full of vowels	That a yard
And a shirt	Was as long,
With some towels—	That a song
A slight cap	Was as merry,
For night cap—	That a cherry
A hair brush	Was as red—
Comb ditto,	That lead
New Stockings	Was as weighty
For old ones	That fourscore
Would split O!	Was as eighty
This Knapsack	That a door
Tight at's back	Was as wooden
He rivetted close	As in england—
And followed his Nose	So he stood in
To the North	His shoes
To the North	And he wondered
And follow'd his nose	He wondered
To the North.	He stood in his
. . . .	Shoes and he wonder'd.

My dear Fanny, I am ashamed of writing you such stuff, nor would I if it were not for being tired after my day's walking, and ready to tumble into bed so fatigued that when I am asleep you might sew my nose to my great toe and trundle me round the town, like a Hoop, without waking me. Then I get so hungry a Ham goes but a very little way and fowls are like Larks to me—A Batch of Bread I make no more ado with than a sheet of parliament; and I can eat a Bull's head as easily as I used to do Bull's eyes. I take a whole string of Pork Sausages down as easily as a Pen-orth of Lady's fingers. Ah dear I must soon be contented with an acre or two of oaten cake a hogshead of Milk and a Cloaths basket of Eggs morning noon and night when I get among the Highlanders.

                    Your affectionate Brother John—

From Burns' cottage he wrote to Reynolds, after giving up the attempt at an extempore verse there:

> One song of Burns's is of more worth to you than all I could think for a whole year in his native country.—His misery is a dead weight upon the nimbleness of one's quill.—I tried to forget it—to drink Toddy without any Care—to write a merry Sonnet—it won't do—he talked with Bitches—he drank with blackguards, he was miserable—We can see horribly clear in the works of such a Man his whole life, as if we were God's spies.

The same week, evidently continuing an argument with himself, he wrote in a letter to nineteen-year-old Tom:

> I have not sufficient reasoning faculty to settle the doctrine of thrift—as it is consistent with the dignity of human Society—with the happiness of Cottagers—all I can do is by plump contrasts—Were the fingers made to squeeze a guinea or a white hand? Were the Lips made to hold a pen or a Kiss? And yet in Cities Man is shut out from his fellows if he is poor, the cottager must be dirty and very wretched if she be not thrifty.—The present state of society demands this and this convinces me that the world is very young and in a very ignorant state.—We live in a barbarous age.... On our walk in Ireland we had too much opportunity to see the worse than nakedness, the rags, the dirt and misery of the poor common Irish—A Scotch Cottage, though in that sometimes the Smoke has no exit but at the door, is a palace to an Irish one.... We heard on passing into Belfast through a most wretched suburb that most disgusting of all noises ... I mean the sound of the shuttle. What a tremendous difficulty is the improvement of the conditions of such people. I cannot conceive how a mind "with child" of Philanthropy could grasp at possibility—with me it is absolute despair.

By the end of July, the extreme exertion—they often walked over twenty miles a day—frequent exposure to rain, and rough, insufficient food had so far affected Keats' health that he found it necessary to leave his companion and take a ship back to London. The apparent illness was a badly ulcerated throat, but it seems almost certain that this sore throat—from which he was until the day of his death never completely to recover—was only the first overt sign of the consumption whose germs, perhaps caught during his close nursing of Tom, were already multiplying in him.

At the same time Tom had a serious relapse which necessitated a summons to Keats. The letter crossed him on his homeward journey and he returned in the middle of August to resume his post as nurse.

September 1st, the now infamous attack on *Endymion*—or, rather, on Keats—was published in the *Quarterly Review*, to be followed shortly by a similarly vituperative one in Blackwood's. The *Quarterly* made it clear that it was attacking Keats as a member of the "Cockney School," a friend of such radicals as Leigh Hunt, and a starveling apothecary's apprentice who had the impudence to want to mix with gentlemen and write poetry like his betters.

There is absolutely nothing to be said in defense of these reviews. Keats' friends were certainly justified in using the tragic opportunity afforded by his death, after two years of continuius ill health, to pillory the writers of these and many similar personal attacks on political enemies, always presented under the guise of impartial reviews.

But that Keats himself was unduly moved by the reviews is untrue, although Shelley assumed in his magnificent *Adonais* that the reviews had killed his friend and Byron concurred in his well-known:

>Who killed John Keats?
>"I" said the Quarterly
>Savage and tartarly
>" 'T was one of my feats."

Hazlitt too, agreed:

>. . . Mr. Keats was hooted out of the world, and his fine talents and wounded sensibility consigned to an early grave. In short the treatment of this heedless candidate for poetical fame might serve as a warning, and was intended to serve as a warning to all unfledged tyros, how they venture upon any such doubtful experiments, except under the auspices of some lord of the bed chamber or Government Aristarchus, and how they unprudently associate themselves with men of mere popular talent or independence of feeling. . . . Others . . . have fallen a sacrifice to the obloquy attached to the suspicion of doubting, or of being acquainted with any one who is known to doubt, the divinity of kings. Poor Keats paid the forfeit of the léze majéste with his health and life. What, though his Verses were like the breath of spring and many of his thoughts like flowers—would this, with the circle of critics that beset a throne, lessen the crime of their having been praised in the Examiner?

Certainly the prestige of these magazines made it impossible to sell copies of *Endymion*, and the continual concern about meager daily expenses did much to harass and perhaps shorten the brief remainder of Keats' life. Yet not only the strong testimony of Keats' closest daily companions, but his own outspoken comments as well, show that his reviewers can be credited, at most, with the will to murder. Keats wrote to his publisher, thanking him for clipping several long letters which appeared in literary journals to protest the *Quarterly* articles and added:

> Had I been nervous about its being a perfect piece, and with that view asked advice, and trembled over every page, it would not have been written; for it is not in my nature to fumble—I will write independently.—I have written independently *without Judgment*.—I may write independently, and *with Judgment hereafter*. The Genius of Poetry must work out its own salvation in a man; it cannot be matured by law and precept, but by sensation and watchfulness in itself. That which is creative must create itself—in Endymion I leaped headlong into the Sea, and thereby have become better acquainted with the Soundings, the quick sands, and the rocks, than if I had stayed upon the green shore, and piped a silly pipe and took tea and comfortable advice.—I was never afraid of failure; for I would sooner fail than not be among the greatest.

A pair of sonnets on fame, written the next year, give an equally convincing picture of Keats' philosophical attitude toward such ephemeral reputation as the reviewers could affect, although he never pretended indifference to real immortality. The first of the sonnets below is good advice gaily given to himself and his brother bards, while the second is a hauntingly beautiful statement of more universal human applicability. Both together show us something of the rich maturity of thought and expression Keats had already, at twenty-four, achieved.

> Fame, like a wayward girl, will still be coy
>   To those who woo her with too slavish knees,
> But makes surrender to some thoughtless boy;
>   And dotes the more upon a heart at ease;
> She is a Gipsy will not speak to those
>   Who have not learnt to be content without her;
> A Jilt, whose ear was never whisper'd close,
>   Who thinks they scandal her who talk about her;
> A very Gipsy is she, Nilus-born,
>   Sister-in-law to jealous Potiphar;

Ye love-sick Bards! repay her scorn for scorn;
Ye Artists lovelorn! madmen that ye are!
Make your best bow to her and bid adieu,
Then, if she like it, she will follow you.

. . . .

How fever'd is the man who cannot look
Upon his mortal days with temperate blood,
Who vexes all the leaves of his life's book,
And robs his fair name of its maidenhood.
It is as if the rose should pluck herself,
Or the ripe plum finger its misty bloom,
As if a Naiad, like a meddling elf,
Should darken her pure grot with muddy gloom;
But the rose leaves herself upon the briar,
For winds to kiss and grateful bees to feed,
And the ripe plum still wears its dim attire;
The undisturbed lake has crystal space;
Why then should man, teasing the world for grace,
Spoil his salvation for a fierce miscreed?

Keats immediately began work upon another major work, *Hyperion*, but this went slowly because of his continued "sore throat" and poor Tom's illness. Tom died December 1, 1818, having just passed his nineteenth birthday, and Keats, unable to return to his desolate rooms, gratefully accepted his friend Brown's invitation to share his home.

Brown owned a two-family house and a Mrs. Brawne with her three children soon rented the other part of it. Keats had met Fanny, the eighteen year old daughter, shortly before Tom's death, and had, as he later confessed, fallen in love with her at first meeting despite his tragic preoccupation with Tom.

A month after Tom's death, on Christmas Day, he found she returned his love and although illness and poverty made a formal engagement seem impossible, the couple considered themselves secretly engaged thenceforth.

1819 saw many small ups and downs in Keats' health but only a continued decline in his financial position. His own little capital was all gone and his share of Tom's small residue was held by Mr. Abbey until Fanny should come of age. Brown, himself in possession of the tiniest of incomes, was advancing him money for board and for the most necessary daily expenses. There are several letters from Keats telling his sister, Fanny, that he cannot come to see her until well enough to walk the five or six miles since he cannot afford coach hire.

Nevertheless the close companionship with his beloved Fanny Brawne and the release from other active responsibilities made it possible for Keats to accomplish a tremendous part of his greatest work during this year, including "The Eve of St. Agnes", "La Belle Dame Sans Merci," and the two incomparable odes "On a Grecian Urn" and "To A Nightingale."

He also collaborated with Brown on a melodrama in blank verse, *Otho the Great*. (Brown had once received £300 for a play of his produced at Covent Gardens.) This collaboration took place on the Isle of Wight since a large part of Brown's income came from renting his surburban house as a summer home to wealthier Londoners.

Keats' contributions to *Otho* show promise of considerable though undeveloped dramatic power, and there are many other incomplete experimental verses which seem to indicate that his lifelong absorbing love for Shakespeare was based on a more specific affinity than his short life allowed him to demonstrate. An interesting fragment describing his idea of the real poet implies that such a one must also be essentially a dramatic creator. Keats here said, in part:

> Where's the Poet? show him! show him,
> Muses nine! that I may know him.
> 'Tis the man who with a man
> Is an equal, be he King,
> Or poorest of the beggar-clan,
> Or any other wondrous thing
> A man may be 'twixt ape and Plato;
> 'Tis the man who with a bird,
> Wren, or Eagle, finds his way to
> All its instincts; he hath heard
> The Lion's roaring, and can tell
> What his horny throat expresseth,
> And to him the Tiger's yell
> Comes articulate and presseth
> On his ear like mother-tongue.

Meanwhile George's affairs in America were going very poorly and Keats wrote him reaffirming his promise of any possible assistance, since George had a wife and child and he was, ostensibly, responsible for himself alone.

He also wrote Fanny Brawne offering to release her from her promise if the play did not make his fortune, but was enormously relieved that she refused the offer, and decided that if the worst came to the worst he would take to journalism for a living. He somewhat bitterly told an older friend and admirer in September:

> Even if I am swept away like a Spider from a drawing room I am determined to spin—homespun anything for sale. Yea I will traffic. Anything but Mortgage my brain to Blackwood [a leading Tory journal]. I am determined not to lie like a dead lump.... You may say I want tact—that is easily acquired. You may be up to the slang of the cockpit in three battles. It is fortunate I have not before this been tempted to venture on the common [on the streets]. I should a year or two ago have spoken my mind on every subject with the utmost simplicity. ... I hope sincerely I shall be able to put a Mite of help to the Liberal side of the Question before I die.

In January George desperately made a hurried visit from America, and succeeded in getting his own share of Tom's bequest and practically all of Keats'. He evidently had no idea of his brother's great need for money—Keats seems to have made him think the prospects of the play much brighter than they were—and George knew nothing of Keats' passionate desire for an immediate marriage. In George's preoccupation and concern with the young wife and ailing baby he had left behind, he evidently did not note the clearly visible signs of Keats' serious illness.

February 3, 1820, a week after George's departure, Keats spit blood. Recognizing the bright arterial red he said, "That is the colour of death." To a friend, Jem Rice, he wrote:

> How astonishingly does the chance of leaving the world impress a sense of its natural beauties on us. Like poor Falstaff, though I do not babble, I think of green fields.

And to Fanny Brawne:

> "If I should die," said I to myself, "I have left no immortal work behind me—nothing to make my friends proud of my memory—but I have lov'd the principle of beauty in all things, and if I had had time I would have made myself remembered." Thoughts like these came very feebly when I was in health and every pulse beat for you—now you divide with this (may I say it?) "last infirmity of noble minds" all my reflection.

This letter reminds us of his wonderful sonnet, written some time before, which is one of the few English poems that can stand comparison with Shakespeare's great sonnet sequence.

> When I have fears that I may cease to be
>   Before my pen has glean'd my teeming brain,
> Before high-piled books, in charact'ry
>   Hold like rich garners the full-ripen'd grain;
> When I behold, upon the night's starr'd face,
>   Huge cloudy symbols of a high romance,
> And think that I may never live to trace
>   Their shadows, with the magic hand of chance;
> And when I feel, fair creature of an hour,
>   That I shall never look upon thee more,
> Never have relish in the faery power
>   Of unreflecting love;—then on the shore
> Of the wide world I stand alone, and think,
> Till Love and Fame to nothingness do sink.

Toward spring he rallied a little and when Brown's need to rent the house for the summer again left him temporarily homeless, he took rooms near those in which poor Tom had died. A serious attack which occurred while he was visiting the Hunts made those good friends keep him there to nurse him. In July, when he insisted upon paying a call on Fanny Brawne, her mother, to his great gratitude and relief, refused to let him leave the house, and put him to bed there. During this month his last book appeared and was comparatively well received. There were a number of very laudatory reviews, especially in the more or less liberal journals, and even many of those which carried on their feud with the "Cockney School" wrote in the mild tone of the *Monthly Review,* which spoke of Keats' having "the ore of true poetic genius, though mingled with a large proportion of dross" and blamed his faults on his being "a disciple in a school [Hunt's] in which these peculiarities are virtues."

Keats read the reviews but was too ill to care much about their altered tone. He was much too unhappy over this fatal interruption of all the work he had planned, to accept the critical commendation as a sign of any significant accomplishment.

He was also too feeble to resist his friends' urging that he try the effect of a winter in Italy, and although he certainly knew it was too late he may have harbored the lingering hope for a miracle.

Perhaps also he wished to spare Fanny the torture of watching him die as he had watched poor Tom. He forced himself to leave her, asking Mr. Abbey for a loan which that gentleman, consistent to the last, refused; accepted an "advance" from his generous and friendly publisher; and set sail with a young artist friend, Severn, who had hastily borrowed money himself to be able to accompany him as nurse.

A letter from Shelley inviting him to join the Shelleys near Florence reached Keats shortly before he sailed in September, but by the time he reached Rome he was obviously unable to be moved. He concluded his last letter, written to Brown on November 30:

> I am well disappointed in hearing good news from George, for it runs in my head we shall all die young. I have not written to Reynolds yet, which he must think very neglectful; being anxious to send him a good account of my health, I have delayed it from week to week. If I recover, I will do all in my power to correct the mistakes made during sickness; and if I should not, all my faults will be forgiven. Severn is very well, though he leads so dull a life with me. Remember me to all friends, and tell Haslam I should not have left London without taking leave of him, but from being so low in body and mind. Write to George as soon as you receive this, and tell him how I am, as far as you can guess; and also a note to my sister —who walks about my imagination like a ghost—she is so like Tom. I can scarcely bid you good-bye, even in a letter. I always made an awkward bow. God bless you!

After three months of an agonized "posthumous existence," he died on February 23, 1821, not yet twenty-seven years old. He felt that if he had lived he would have "written something not unworthy to be included with the English poets," but that as it was he had accomplished nothing but practise pieces. At his own direction, therefore, his grave bears the epitaph: "Here lies one whose name is writ in water."

The verdict of the world, however, is better given by the late Countee Cullen, a young Negro poet who was one of America's finest lyricists, and who early adopted Keats as his particular divine. He said:

> Not writ in water nor in mist
> Sweet lyric throat your name;

The singing lips that pale death kissed
Have sear'd his own with flame.

Charles Lamb—1775–1834

"The mass of men lead lives of quiet desperation" said Thoreau not many years after Lamb's death, and in saying so he was surely thinking especially of the growing army of the lower middle class— the clerks, bookkeepers, teachers, hack writers and all the white collar workers for whom Elia spoke. F. W. Morley, in his penetrating study of *Lamb Before Elia* (Elia was, of course, the pen name that Lamb adopted in his middle forties and signed to almost all the essays on which his fame today rests), says:

> . . . so in a wider sense Lamb's writings and his life encouraged a divorce between private existence and public. . . . His conversation was mainly deliberately limited to what couldn't matter very much.

And Leigh Hunt, the one of his contemporaries who best knew his rare expressions of political interest and his infrequent though significant political actions, said:

> The consequence of this exceeding wish to make the best of things as they are (we do not speak politically, but philosophically) is, that his writings tend rather to prepare others for doing public good wisely, than to help the progress of the species themselves. . . . He desires no better Arcadia than Fleet Street; or at least pretends as much, for fear of not finding it.

Fifteen years later, writing just after Lamb's death, Hunt concludes:

> He had felt, thought, and suffered so much that he literally had intolerance for nothing, and never seemed to have it, but when he supposed the sympathies of men, who might have known better, to be imperfect. He was a wit and observer of the first order, as far as the world around him was concerned, and society in its existing state; for as to anything theoretical or transcendental, no man ever had less care for it, or less power. . . . His life had experienced great and peculiar sorrows; but he kept up a balance between those and his consolations, by the goodness of his heart, and the ever-willing sociality of his humour; though now and then, as if he would cram into one

moment the spleen of years, he would throw out a startling and morbid subject for reflection, perhaps in no better shape than a pun; for he was a great punster. It was a levity that relieved the gravity of his thoughts, and kept them from falling too heavily earthwards.

Although Lamb generally refused to become emotionally involved in, or even admit any interest in, politics, and although he maintained unbroken his relationship with the later wavering Coleridge and reactionary Wordsworth, whom he had, of course, met in the days of their early republican ardor, he almost invariably throughout his adult life chose his friends and intimate associates from among the increasingly unpopular radical minority. He was an almost daily visitor to Leigh Hunt during the latter's two-year term of political imprisonment, even though Hunt had previously been an acquaintance rather than a friend; and he gratuitously and publicly championed the ostracized Hazlitt during a period of long personal estrangement.

He himself deliberately eschews all reference to these and similar actions in his private letters as well as his essays, but fortunately we find some of them clearly outlined in such accounts as those of the young Thomas De Quincey who, very much of a High Tory Churchman and something of a snob, was nevertheless a man of fine literary taste and eagerly sought the acquaintance of Lamb. He speaks somewhat patronizingly of Lamb's habitual associates, concluding:

> Take, for example, Thelwall at one time; Holcroft, Godwin, Mrs. Wollstonecraft, Dr. Priestley, Hazlitt; all of whom were, more or less, in a backward or inverse sense, tabood—that is, consecrated to public hatred or scorn. With respect to all these persons . . . Lamb threw his heart and his doors wide open.

Again, although De Quincey evidently did not suspect how thoroughly Lamb shared Hazlitt's opinion of England's role in the war, he comments on his behavior at the occasion of England's victory:

> One might have thought that, if he manifested no sympathy in a direct shape with the primary cause of the public emotion, still he would have sympathized, in a secondary way, with the delirious joy which every street, every alley, then manifested, to the ear as well as the eye. But no! . . . How he felt in the following year, when the mighty drama was consummated by

Waterloo, I cannot say, for I was not then in London. I guess, however, that he would have manifested pretty much the same cynical contempt for us children of the time that he did in all former cases.

This tacit disapproval, although apparent enough to astound De Quincey, was evidently not partisan enough to satisfy Hazlitt. Outraged and sickened by England's part in "restoring legitimacy" to every throne of Europe, he quarreled bitterly with Lamb for seeming so indifferent to the matter. But in 1823, when an article by Southey gave him occasion for it, Lamb deliberately aligned himself with Hazlitt and Leigh Hunt in a totally unexpected and explicit open letter to the poet laureate.

Crabb Robinson, a very conservative Whig friend and great admirer of the Lake Poets, who was also a friend of the Lambs, wrote to Dorothy Wordsworth:

> You have seen Elia's letter to Southey. There are a few passages I could wish away, but with the exception of them it is a delightful composition. . . . There is a generosity in this writing almost heroic. . . . He knows that there are not two characters more generally detested in this country than Leigh Hunt and William Hazlitt and that he will never be forgiven for this voluntary tho qualified and discriminating testimony in their favour. My dislike of Hazlitt almost amounts to hatred, yet I shall have inclination to look kindly on him when I recollect that Lamb has *so* written of him. . . .

But it is true that only rarely, and then almost in spite of himself, does Lamb rise to such heights of earnestness, and of no man could Emily Dickinson more aptly have said:

> The heroism we recite
> Would be a daily thing
> Did not ourselves the cubits warp
> For fear to be a king.

That he should have been able in the face of this determined lifelong self-suppression to maintain the integrity of his understanding, the clarity of his observation and the warmth of his sympathies is an extraordinary and wonderful thing. Because he was able to do this he has left us the fifty-odd *Essays of Elia* which include many of the best, and most of the best-loved, personal essays ever written in English.

Why he was able to do this, when the host of personal essayists since his time have not been able to evade the loss of personality consequent on such a denial, a brief survey of his life may help us to understand.

In considering the life of Lamb it is necessary for us to read between the lines—to understand the silences as well as the words. But it is also necessary for us to feel fully and in detail the real force of those objective conditions which enforced his silence.

Emily Dickinson speaks of some who are free only

> To learn the transport by the pain
> As blind men learn the sun;
> To die of thirst suspecting
> That brooks in meadows run—

To realize how his deeply buried, seldom expressed but never forgotten social passion gave power and warmth to Lamb's writing it is not enough for us just to see the brief ardor of his early youth. Many equally ardent young men have bowed voluntarily to an imagined necessity and have settled down happily, or, at least, comfortably, into indifferent middle age. It is therefore necessary for us not only to know of, but also to feel, Lamb's peculiar obligations if we are fully to understand how he could consciously submit to the conditions of a "life of quiet desperation" and yet maintain unblunted the sensibility and integrity which, near the end of it, created Elia.

Lamb's father had been a footman and was still, at the time of Charles' birth, assistant headwaiter for the lawyers dining under the auspices of "The Worshipful Masters of the Bench of the Honorable Society of the Inner Temple." However, his major position was, by that time, that of valet, general factotum and almost confidential clerk to an important member of the body, Samuel Salt. Since the Lambs occupied some rooms in Mr. Salt's double set of chambers in the Temple, Charles Lamb was born there on February 10, 1775. He had a sister Mary, then eleven, and a brother John, twelve or thirteen years old. Four younger brothers and sisters had died in very early infancy.

Although his parents' social position was thus probably lower than any we have yet had occasion to consider, and in economic terms his family was probably worse off than all but Burns', yet as a child Charles Lamb himself shared in many of the substantial benefits of an older, more aristocratic time.

The Temple Chambers and ground were then—and, in fact, continued to be until the air raids of the second World War—a delightfully green and quiet oasis in the midst of noisy, dirty, crowded London, and the sense of spacious leisure they afforded was very real even to a casual visitor as late as 1940.

The little boy growing up there in 1780 had the further advantage that for him, at the heart of the quiet retreat, was Mr. Salt's large, rather old-fashioned library, exceptionally rich in the then unfashionable literature of sixteenth and seventeenth century England.

Lamb describes in one of his essays how his sister had enjoyed her unlimited access to the same library:

> Her education in youth was not much attended to; and she happily missed all that train of female garniture which passeth by the name of accomplishments. She was tumbled early, by accident or design, into a spacious closet of good old English reading, without much selection or prohibition, and browsed at will upon that fair and wholesome pasturage. Had I twenty girls, they should be brought up exactly in this fashion. I know not whether their chance in wedlock might not be diminished by it; but I can answer for it, that it makes (if the worst come to the worst) most incomparable old maids.

Mary, who was his nurse and first teacher, used to have him practise reading while they played among the tombstones in the old Temple Courtyard, and when he was five or six, found herself much puzzled to answer his logical inquiry: "Mary, where are all the naughty people buried?"

In the summer the two children generally paid long visits to their maternal grandmother who was housekeeper for a very wealthy family, seldom in residence at their beautiful country estate. The tremendous old mansion and lovely well-kept grounds were, as far as the children were concerned, practically Grandmother Field's and formed a wonderful playground for luxurious summer holidays.

Through Salt's influence Charles was admitted, at seven, to the school of Christ's Hospital, where Coleridge had already completed three years. The physical rigors of the place bore much more lightly on him for, as he has himself told in "Christ's Hospital Five-and-Thirty Years Ago," he lived so near home that holidays and even half holidays could be spent there, and his old aunt, who formed a part of the family, would come almost daily with dishes from the home kitchen for her favorite.

Lamb was an exceptionally good student, as his life-long facility in Latin often reminds us, and despite his small stature, frail physique, and special privileges, was a general favorite with boys as well as teachers.

However he had a bad stammer which, it was thought, would disqualify him from taking orders as a clergyman. Since preparation for this career was, ostensibly, the only aim of the graduating class, he was not permitted to prepare for a University Scholarship Examination but was, to his great regret, forced to leave school at fifteen.

For the next two years, while Mary contributed to the family income as a dressmaker, Charles served a sort of informal, unpaid apprenticeship as an office boy in the counting house of one of Mr. Salt's friends. In 1791 he began as a clerk—at a nominal salary of half a guinea a week—in the South Sea House where his brother John was already an accountant.

In 1792 a major change took place in the family circumstances, a change that proved almost fatal for Mary and, in the long run, hardly less catastrophic for Charles.

Mr. Salt died. While he left the Lambs a modest legacy—£300 and an annuity of £10 to John Lamb, and 200 more to his wife— the family was forced to move out of the Temple and secure a small apartment in one of the crowded tenements on Little Queen Street.

The older brother, John, evidently took the opportunity to rent pleasanter bachelor quarters and Charles, who was now at work all day and who for the first time had independent pocket money, began to spend his evenings with a few fellow alumni and with the new friends they brought down to London on frequent visits from the universities most of them were attending. There was much exciting literary and political talk in these evenings at the taverns, which were their informal, inexpensive clubs, many practical jokes of an elaborate erudite nature and, on at least one occasion, Lamb with some of the other young men drew the carriage of the antiwar minister, Fox, through the streets of the city.

But at home life was neither stimulating nor relaxing. John Lamb, the father, had become almost completely senile; his wife, while still energetic and, perhaps, rather domineering, suffered from some form of rheumatism or arthritis which soon confined her entirely to a wheel chair; and the old aunt, Hetty, who had never been on really good terms with her sister-in-law, was now seventy-five and devoted her time almost entirely to religious reading and prayers.

Charles' new interests left Mary alone to cope with the unhappy crowded household, for her dressmaking, although extensive enough to require the services of an apprentice, was carried on entirely in the cramped confines of the family apartment.

The brother and sister were still close and would occasionally read or talk together, but the few minutes they could snatch this way did little to alleviate the steady and, it seemed, interminable, lonely drudgery of her life.

In 1794 Coleridge, escaping from the "Thirty-Nine Articles" to which his imminent graduation at Cambridge would have made it necessary for him to subscribe, took up his quarters at a London tavern, "The Salutation and Cat," and he and Charles rapidly developed an ardent, though at first unequal, friendship.

Southey had vainly written him repeated summons to come and do his duty by Miss Fricker (see pp. 435-6). He called for Coleridge in person and firmly removed the still hopeful Pantisocrat to Bristol. Lamb tried to carry on by correspondence the fiery talk of literature and revolution, which had joined with tobacco smoke in filling the little parlor of the tavern.

The first letter of Charles' which has been preserved is one that begins with characteristic generosity and gives us a startling piece of information.

> Dear Coleridge—Make yourself perfectly easy about [Coleridge's debt to] May. I paid his bill when I sent your clothes. I was flush of money, and am so still to all the purposes of a single life; so give yourself no further concern about it. The money would be superfluous to me if I had it.
>
> When Southey becomes as modest as his predecessor, Milton, and publishes his Epics in duodecimo, I will read 'em; a guinea a book is somewhat exorbitant, nor have I the opportunity of borrowing the work. The extracts from it in the *Monthly Review*, and the short passages in your *Watchman*, seem to me much superior to any thing in his partnership account with Lovell. Your poems I shall procure forthwith. There were noble lines in what you inserted in one of your Numbers from *Religious Musings*; but I thought them elaborate. . . . Coleridge, I know not what suffering scenes you have gone through at Bristol. My life has been somewhat diversified of late. The six weeks that finished last year and began this, your

very humble servant spent very agreeably in a madhouse, at Hoxton. I am got somewhat rational now, and don't bite any one. But mad I was; and many a vagary my imagination played with me, enough to make a volume, if all were told. My Sonnets I have extended to the number of nine since I saw you, and will some day communicate to you. I am beginning a poem in blank verse, which, if I finish, I publish. White is on the eve of publishing (he took the hint from *Vortigern*) "Original letters of Falstaff, Shallow," etc.; a copy you shall have when it comes out. They are without exception the best imitations I ever saw. Coleridge, it may convince you of my regards for you when I tell you my head ran on you in my madness, as much almost as on another person, who I am inclined to think was the more immediate cause of my temporary frenzy. . . .
Yours sincerely,
Lamb

Your *Conciones ad Populum* are the most eloquent politics that ever came in my way.

A week or so later another letter comments further on Coleridge's long antiwar poem, *Religious Musings*, and on his article against the slave trade:

. . . I am sorry there should be any difference between you and Southey. "Between you two there should be peace," tho' I must say I have borne him no good will since he spirited you away from among us. . . . Of your *Watchmen*, the Review of Burke was the best prose. I augured great things from the first Number. There is some exquisite poetry interspersed. I have re-read the extract from the *Religious Musings*, and retract whatever invidious there was in my censure of it as elaborate. There are times when one is not in a disposition thoroughly to relish good writing. I have re-read it in a more favourable moment, and hesitate not to pronounce it sublime. . . . I hunger and thirst to read the poem complete. That is a capital line in your sixth Number:

"This dark, frieze-coated, hoarse, teeth-chattering month."

They are exactly such epithets as Burns would have stumbled on, whose poem on the ploughed-up daisy you seem to have had in mind. . . . I congratulate you on the enemies you must have made by your splendid invective against the barterers in human flesh and sinews.

Letter follows letter in quick succession, and already we find a hint of the distaste for his meaningless clerical work which Lamb was to express with increasing intensity for the next thirty years:

I am now in high hopes to be able to visit you, if perfectly convenient on your part, by the end of next month—perhaps the last week or fortnight in July. A change of scene and a change of faces would do me good, even if that scene were not to be Bristol, and those faces Coleridge's and his friends. In the words of Terence, a little altered, *Toedet me hujus quotidiani mundi*, I am heartily sick of the every-day scenes of life. I shall half wish you unmarried (don't show this to Mrs. C.) for one evening only, to have the pleasure of smoking with you and drinking egg-hot in some little smoky room in a pot-house, for I know not yet how I shall like you in a decent room and looking quite happy. My best love and respects to Sara notwithstanding.

Evidently Coleridge wrote inviting both Charles and Mary, whom he had met and liked, for a visit, and Charles' answer on June 16, 1796, gives us a glimpse of what Mary's life had, for four years, been like:

The first moment I can come I will; but my hopes of coming yet a while yet hang on a ticklish thread. The coach I come by is immaterial, as I shall so easily, by your direction, find ye out. My mother is grown so entirely helpless (not having any use of her limbs) that Mary is necessarily confined from ever sleeping out, she being her bed-fellow. She thanks you though, and will accompany me in spirit. . . . The uncertainty in which I yet stand, whether I can come or no, damps my spirits, reduces me a degree below prosaical, and keeps me in a suspense that fluctuates between hope and fear. Hope is a charming, lively, blue-eyed wench, and I am always glad of her company, but could dispense with the visitor she brings with her—her younger sister, Fear,—a white-livered, lily-cheeked, bashful, palpitating, awkward hussy, that hangs, like a green girl, at her sister's apron-strings, and will go with her whithersoever *she* goes.

The very next day he angrily reports his disappointment that he cannot get leave:

Savory did return, but there are two or three more ill and absent, which was the plea for refusing me. I will never commit my peace of mind by depending on such a wretch for a favour in future, so I shall never have heart to ask for holidays again. The man next him in office, Cartwright, furnished him with the objections.

Even his joy at the subsequent news that Coleridge has been offered an excellent newspaper job and will again be living in London does not, however, prevent Lamb from being concerned at the political implications of such a position and he writes in July:

> But are you really coming to town? The hope of it has entirely disarmed my petty disappointment of its nettles; yet I rejoice so much on my own account, that I fear I do not feel enough pure satisfaction on yours. Why, surely, the joint editorship of the (*Morning*) Chronicle must be a very comfortable and secure living for a man. But . . . can you write with sufficient moderation, as 'tis called, when one suppresses the one half of what one feels or could say on a subject, to chime in the better with popular lukewarmness?

That letter is, incidentally, concluded with a characteristic request:

> White's "Letters" are near publication. Could you review 'em, or get 'em reviewed? Are you not connected with the *Critical Review*?

In all the six or seven hundred letters of Lamb's which we have he never requested a material favor for himself, but we find him tireless in asking his more fortunate friends for jobs, recommendations, subscriptions and other practical assistance of the kind he was himself always supplying to less fortunate ones.

Suddenly, however, all this happy furor of poetry and politics is destroyed forever by an event which Lamb thus briefly reports:

> My dearest Friend — White, or some of my friends, or the public papers, by this time may have informed you of the terrible calamities that have fallen on our family. I will only give you the outlines: My poor dear, dearest sister, in a fit of insanity, has been the death of her own mother. I was at hand only time enough to snatch the knife out of her grasp. She is at present in a madhouse, from whence I fear she must be moved to an hospital. God has preserved my senses: I eat, and drink, and sleep, and have my judgment, I believe, very sound. My poor father was slightly wounded, and I am left to take care of him and my aunt. Mr. Norris, of the Bluecoat School, has been very very kind to us, and we have no other friend; but, thank God, I am very calm and composed, and able to do the best that remains to do. Write as religious a letter as possible, but no mention of what is gone and done with.

With me "the former things are passed away," and I have something more to do than to feel.

God Almighty have us all in His keeping!

[P. S.] Mention nothing of poetry. I have destroyed every vestige of past vanities of that kind. Do as you please, but if you publish, publish mine (I give free leave) without name or initial, and never send me a book, I charge you.

Your own judgment will convince you not to take any notice of this yet to your dear wife. You look after your family; I have my reason and strength left to take care of mine. I charge you, don't think of coming to see me. Write. I will not see you if you come. God Almighty love you and all of us!

The *Morning Chronicle* for September 26, 1796, gives the story more fully:

On Friday afternoon the Coroner and a respectable Jury sat on the body of a Lady in the neighborhood of Holborn, who died in consequence of a wound from her daughter the preceding day. It appeared by the evidence adduced, that while the family were preparing for dinner, the young lady seized a case knife laying on the table; and in a menacing manner pursued a little girl, her apprentice, round the room; on the eager calls of her helpless infirm mother to forbear, she renounced her first object, and with loud shrieks approached her parent.

The child by her cries brought up the landlord of the house, but too late—the dreadful scene presented to him the mother lifeless, pierced to the heart, on a chair, her daughter yet wildly standing over her with the fatal knife, and the venerable old man, her father, weeping by her side, himself bleeding at the forehead from the effects of a severe blow he received from one of the forks she had been madly hurling about the room.

For a few days prior to this the family had observed some symptoms of insanity in her, which had so much increased on the Wednesday evening, that her brother early the next morning went in quest of Dr. Pitcarin—had that gentleman been met with, the fatal catastrophe had, in all probability, been prevented.

It seems the young lady had been once before, in her earlier years, deranged, from the harassing fatigues of too much business.—As her carriage towards her mother was ever affectionate in the extreme, it is believed that to the increased attentiveness, which her parents' infirmities called for by day and night, is to be attributed the present insanity of this ill-fated young woman.

It has been stated in some of the Morning Papers, that she has an insane brother also in confinement—this is without foundation.

The Jury of course brought in their Verdict, Lunacy.

A week later Lamb writes again, simply for the relief of communication, since of all people Coleridge was certainly the last to care about such practical details as Charles painstakingly enumerates:

> Reckoning this, we have, Daddy and I, for our two selves and an old maid-servant to look after him, when I am out, which will be necessary, £170 (or £180 rather) a year, out of which we can spare £50 or £60 at least for Mary, while she stays at Islington, where she must and shall stay during her father's life, for his and her comfort. I know John will make speeches about it but she shall not go into an hospital. The good lady of the madhouse, and her daughter, an elegant, sweet-behaved young lady, love her, are taken with her amazingly; and I know from her own mouth she loves them, and longs to be with them as much. Poor thing, they say she was but the other morning saying she knew she must go to Bedlam for life; that one of her brothers would have it so, but the other would wish it not, but be obliged to go with the stream; that she had often as she passed Bedlam thought it likely, "here it may be my fate to end my days," conscious of a certain flightiness in her poor head oftentimes, and mindful of more than one severe illness of that nature before. A legacy of £100, which my father will have at Christmas, and this £20 I mentioned before, with what is in the house, will much more than set us clear. If my father, an old servant-maid, and I, can't live, and live comfortably, on £130 or £120 a-year, we ought to burn by slow fires; and I almost would, that Mary might not go into an hospital. Let me not leave one unfavourable impression on your mind respecting my brother. Since this has happened, he has been very kind and brotherly; but I fear for his mind: he has taken his ease in the world, and is not fit himself to struggle with difficulties, nor has much accustomed himself to throw himself into their way; and I know his language is already, "Charles, you must take care of yourself; you must not abridge yourself of a single pleasure you have been used to," etc. etc., and in that style of talking.

There seemed to be, and was, in truth, no reason at all to fear for John's mind then or ever, but from this time on we find that Lamb, who had taken his own brief period of mental illness lightly enough before, was seriously fearful of a recurrence which would make it impossible for him to carry through the heavy responsibilities he was now assuming.

Commenting on his consistent refusal to become emotionally involved in political, philosophical, or even literary controversies after this time Morley says that the real reason for this renunciation was Lamb's "impulse of defending himself. He had to manage his responsibilities; he had conditions laid upon him, in particular the threat of mental illness, which were peculiar; therefore his course had to be an individual one." For Lamb thenceforth the act of writing was not an attempt to grapple with the world but, as he himself said, "an endeavor to engage my mind in some constant and innocent pursuit."

For the time being, however, the possibility of writing as a retreat from, rather than as an attack upon, the world had not yet occurred to him, and like Hamlet he felt that his new duties made it necessary for him to destroy "all trivial fond records that youth and observation" had created in order to concentrate on fulfilling the responsibility he was forced to accept.

Although more successful than that unhappy prince in his ultimate objective, he too was unable to stop being "a literary man." We find him ingenuously deceiving himself and acceding to Coleridge's friendly request for the joint publication of their early poems as a part of his renunciation!

> The Fragments I now send you, I want printed to get rid of 'em; for, while they stick burr-like to my memory, they tempt me to go on with the idle trade of versifying, which I long (most sincerely I speak it) I long to leave off, for it is unprofitable to my soul; I feel it is; and these questions about words, and debates about alterations, take me off, I am conscious, from the properer business of my life. Take my Sonnets, once for all; and do not propose any reamendments, or mention them again in any shape to me, I charge you. I blush that my mind can consider them as things of any worth. And, pray, admit or reject these fragments as you like or dislike them, without ceremony. Call 'em Sketches, Fragments, or what you will; but do not entitle any of my *things* Love Sonnets, as I told you to call 'em; 'twill only make me look little in my own eyes; for it is a passion of which I retain nothing. . . . I have another sort of dedication in my head for my few things, which I want to know if you approve of, and can insert. I mean to inscribe them to my sister. It will be unexpected, and it will give her pleasure; or do you think it will look whimsical at all? As I have not spoke to her about it I can easily reject the idea. But there is a monotony in the affections, which people living together, or, as we do now, very frequently seeing each other, are apt to give in to; a sort of indifference in the expression of kindness for each other, which demands that we should sometimes call to our aid the trickery of surprise.

His life at this time was a hard and lonely one, as his frequent letters to his only friend, Coleridge, tell us. In December, 1796, he writes sadly:

> That sonnet, Coleridge, brings afresh to my mind the time when you wrote those on Bowles, Priestley, Burke;—'twas two Christmases ago, and in that nice little smoky room at the *Salutation*, which is even now continually presenting itself to my recollection, with all its associated train of pipes, tobacco, egg-hot, welsh-rabbit, metaphysics, and poetry.—Are we *never* to meet again? How differently I am circumstanced now! I have never met with anyone—never shall meet with anyone—who could or can compensate me for the loss of your society. I have no one to talk all these matters about to; I lack friends. I lack books to supply their absence; but these complaints ill become me. . . . I thank you, from my heart I thank you, for your solicitude about my sister. She is quite well, but must not, I fear, come to live with us yet a good while. In the first place, because, at present, it would hurt her, and hurt my father, for them to be together; secondly, from a regard to the world's good report; for, I fear, tongues will be busy whenever that event takes place. Some have hinted, one man has pressed it on me, that she should be in perpetual confinement: what she hath done to deserve, or the necessity of such an hardship, I see not; do you? I am starving at the India House,—near seven o'clock without my dinner; and so it has been, and will be, almost all the week. I get home at night o'erwearied, quite faint, and then to cards with my father, who will not let me enjoy a meal in peace; but I must conform to my situation; and I hope I am, for the most part, not unthankful.
>
> I am got home at last, and, after repeated games at cribbage, have got my father's leave to write awhile; with difficulty got it, for when I expostulated about playing any more, he very aptly replied, "If you won't play with me, you might as well not come home at all." The argument was unanswerable, and I set to afresh.

But Coleridge had, meanwhile, met the Wordsworths and, unpunctual and irregular at best, was evidently somewhat too absorbed in his new friends and work to meet Lamb's real need for help. A letter from Lamb dated April 7, 1797, says reproachfully:

> Your last letter was dated the 10th of February; in it you promised to write again the next day. At least, I did not expect so long, so unfriendlike a silence. There was a time, Col., when a remissness of this sort in a dear friend would have lain very heavy on my mind; but latterly I have been too familiar with

neglect to feel much from the semblance of it. Yet, to suspect one's self overlooked, and in the way to oblivion, is a feeling rather humbling; perhaps, as tending to self-mortification, not unfavourable to the spiritual state. Still, as you meant to confer no benefit on the soul of your friend, you do not stand quite clear from the imputation of unkindliness (a word, by which I mean the diminutive of unkindness). . . . Coleridge, I am not trifling; nor are these matter-of-fact questions only. You are all very dear and precious to me. Do what you will, Coleridge, you may hurt me and vex me by your silence, but you cannot estrange my heart from you all. I cannot scatter friendships like chuck-farthings, nor let them drop from mine hand like hour-glass sand. I have but two or three people in the world to whom I am more than indifferent, and I can't afford to whistle them off to the winds. . . . Now, do answer this. Friendship, and acts of friendship, should be reciprocal, and free as the air. A friend should never be reduced to beg an alms of his fellow; yet I will beg an alms: I entreat you to write, and tell me all about poor Lloyd, and all of you. God love and preserve you all!

Coleridge evidently did answer, and in June a visit to Bristol by the revolutionary Polish patriot, Kosciusko, makes Lamb ask eagerly: "Did you seize the grand opportunity of seeing Kosciusko while he was at Bristol? I never saw a hero; I wonder how they look."

A little later Coleridge generously and impractically invited Mary, who had been discharged under Charles' guardianship in April and was living alone in lodgings, to stay with him and his wife. Lamb, thanking him, says:

> Mary is recovering; but I see no opening yet of a situation for her. Your invitation went to my very heart; but you have a power of exciting interest, of leading all hearts captive, too forcible to admit of madness. I think you would almost make her dance within an inch of the precipice; she must be with duller fancies, and cooler intellects. I know of a young man of this description, who has suited her these twenty years, and may live to do so still, if we are one day restored to each other.

A few months later in December, 1797, Mary was forced to return to the asylum by another attack and from this time on the fear of her relapse, which he had evidently not before expected, is never out of Charles' mind. Actually Mary was ill for a period of at least two or three months, first every other year and then almost every year for the rest of her long life.

This recurrence also marked the end of Lamb's short-lived attempt to find consolation in a religious interpretation of life. Years later, in 1824, Crabb Robinson notes in his invaluable diary: "C.L.'s impressions against religion are unaccountably strong, and yet he is by nature pious."

Lamb *was* naturally pious, but as early as 1798 he had found the proper objects of his piety on earth, and had begun to come to terms with life as he could best live it. In the middle of his own very real troubles he found time to send a list of the comforts he had discovered to a sentimentally gloomy young Quaker friend:

> My dear Robert — One passage in your Letter a little displeas'd me. The rest was nothing but kindness, which Robert's letters are ever brimful of. You say that "this World to you seems drain'd of all its sweets!" At first I had hoped you only meant to insinuate the high price of Sugar! but I am afraid you meant more. O Robert, I don't know what you call sweet. Honey and the honeycomb, roses and violets, are yet in the earth. The sun and moon yet reign in Heaven, and the lesser lights keep up their pretty twinklings. Meats and drinks, sweet sights and sweet smells, a country walk, spring and autumn, follies and repentance, quarrels and reconcilements, have all a sweetness by turns. Good humour and good nature, friends at home that love you, and friends abroad that miss you, you possess all these things, and more innumerable, and these are all sweet things. . . . You may extract honey from everything; do not go a gathering after gall. The Bees are wiser in their generation than the race of sonnet writers and complainers, Bowles's and Charlotte Smiths, and all that tribe, who can see no joys but what are past, and fill people's heads with notions of the unsatisfying nature of Earthly comforts. I assure you I find this world a very pretty place.

The joint book of verse about which Coleridge had earlier written him appeared in 1798 and was promptly criticized by the reactionary, anti-Jacobin review which attacked Lamb in both the July and August issues.

During the summer Charles also had a romance, *Rosamund Gray*, published. There is a certain autobiographical value in its characters and emotions—the plot and setting are simply standard melodrama—but most readers find it a rather thin and superficial work. Shelley, however, was for some reason much impressed by it and said:

What a lovely thing is his *Rosamund Gray*! How much
knowledge of the sweetest and deepest part of our nature in it!
When I think of such a mind as Lamb's, when I see how un-
noticed remain things of such exquisite and complete perfection, what should I hope for myself, if I had not higher objects
in view than fame?

The book sold moderately well despite the complete silence of
all reviewers, and Lamb began working on an equally implausible
tragedy in blank verse, *John Woodvil*. He finally printed this at his
own expense six years later. Although it has some fine lines and he
always remained especially fond of it, most readers will probably
agree with the verdict of the publishers who refused to undertake
its publication.

In 1799 his poor old father's death made life pleasanter and
easier for him. He and Mary could now make their home together
and she was, when well, a most congenial and profoundly intelligent companion. The *Lamb's Tales from Shakespeare*, and other
children's books, those of her letters which remain, and the unanimous opinion of the many well-known writers who were, later, the
Lambs' intimate friends, all show Mary as an unusually thoughtful
and original woman with a fine quiet sense of humor, great warmth
of generosity, and a deeply tolerant understanding of people.

Some of her most revealing letters were written to her friend,
Sarah Stoddart, later Mrs. Hazlitt, and one of these discusses
Sarah's coming marriage. The Lambs had offered their home for the
wedding, but Sarah's wealthy brother wished her to wait a few
weeks until she could be married from his home, and had asked
Mary to withdraw her invitation. She writes Sarah very frankly
about the practical aspect of the matter, concluding with her delightful and much quoted statement of impractical principle:

> . . . Now though we should be willing to run any hazards
> of disobliging him, if there were no other means of your and
> Hazlitt's meeting, yet he seems so friendly to the match, it
> would not be worthwhile to alienate him from you and our-
> selves too, for the slight accommodation which the difference
> of a few weeks would make, provided always, and be it un-
> derstood, that if you and H made up your minds to be mar-
> ried before the time in which you can be at your brother's
> house, our house stands open and most ready at a moment's
> notice to receive you. Only we would not quarrel unnecessarily

with your brother. Let there be a clear necessity shown, and we will quarrel with anybody's brother.

Even more consistently than Charles, Mary avoided any controversial discussion or the effort of abstract theoretical thought, but the one article she wrote for adults—an essay on "Needle Work" in the *British Lady's Magazine*, 1815—shows mature independent thought considerably in advance of her time:

> Is it too bold an attempt to persuade your readers that it would prove an incalculable addition to general happiness and the domestic comfort of both sexes, if needle-work were never practised but for a remuneration in money? As nearly, however, as the desirable thing can be effected, so much more will women be upon an equality with men as far as respects the mere enjoyment of life. As far as that goes, I believe it is every woman's opinion that the condition of men is far superior to their own....
> *Real business* and *real leisure* make up the portions of men's time;—two sources of happiness which we certainly partake of in a very inferior degree....
> "A penny saved is a penny earned," is a maxim not true unless the penny be saved in the same time in which it might have been earned. I, who have known what it is to work for *money earned*, have since had much experience in working for *money saved*, and I consider, from the closest calculation I can make, that a *penny saved* in that way bears about a true proportion to a *farthing earned*. ... But if the females of a family *nominally* supported by the other sex find it necessary to add something to the common stock, why not endeavor to do something by which they may produce money *in its true shape*?

By the end of 1799, Charles had made another close friend, the only one to rival Coleridge and, later, Hazlitt, in his respect and affection. This was a mathematician, Thomas Manning, whose openly expressed atheism prevented his appointment at Cambridge, but whose ability and reputation had secured for him an unofficial position as a sort of mathematical tutor there.

Perhaps this new, more equal, radical friendship made Lamb quick to resent any reminder of his earlier disciple's attitude toward Coleridge. At any rate when in a new book of poetry there was included "This Lime Tree Tower My Prison"—a poem in which Coleridge lovingly but rather patronizingly addresses Lamb as "my gentle-hearted Charles," there was an explosion and Lamb wrote: "For God's sake (I never was more serious) don't make me ridiculous any more by terming me gentle-hearted in print, or do it in better verses."

However, Coleridge was still, as he always remained, his most dearly loved friend and when that spring Mary was again ill it was to Coleridge that he wrote most freely of his misery.

> My dear Coleridge — I don't know why I write, except from the propensity which misery has to tell her griefs. Hetty died on Friday night, about eleven o'clock, after eight days' illness. Mary, in consequence of fatigue and anxiety, is fallen ill again, and I was obliged to remove her yesterday. I am left alone in a house with nothing but Hetty's dead body to keep me company. To-morrow I bury her, and then I shall be quite alone, with nothing but a cat, to remind me that the house has been full of living beings like myself. My heart is quite sunk, and I don't know where to look for relief. Mary will get better again, but her constantly being liable to such relapses is dreadful; nor is it the least of our evils that her case and all our story is so well known around us. We are in a manner *marked*. Excuse my troubling you, but I have nobody by me to speak to me. I slept out last night, not being able to endure the change and the stillness; but I did not sleep well, and I must come back to my own bed. I am going to try and get a friend to come and be with me tomorrow. I am completely shipwrecked. My head is quite bad. I almost wish that Mary were dead. God bless you! Love to Sara and Hartley.

In this spring of 1800 the Lambs, after several moves caused by neighborhood gossip about Mary's attacks, had finally secured chambers in the Temple, where they were to remain for the next sixteen years.

Lamb also, this year, met Godwin, the author of *Political Justice*, and a number of younger, more active, rather disreputable radical journalists through whom he contributed some satrical verses to the antigovernment papers. Most of them were fairly ordinary competent rhymes on the different ministers such as:

> At Eton School brought up with dull boys,
> We shone like *men* among the *school boys*;
> But since we in the world have been
> We are but *schoolboys* among men.

But Lamb was moved to such biting sarcasm at Mackintosh's public apostacy and attack on his former friends that the *Albion*, the paper in which his epigram appeared, was forced to suspend publication. Unrepentantly, he wrote Manning the news, copying the verse in case his friend had missed it:

> Though thou'rt like Judas, an apostate black,
> In the resemblance one thing thou dost lack:
> When he had gotten his ill-purchased pelf,
> He went away, and wisely hang'd himself:
> This thou may'st do at last; yet much I doubt,
> If thou hast any *bowels* to gush out!

After the end of the *Albion,* Lamb did no more directly political writing until 1812, but he continued to supplement his income by writing humorous paragraphs, which he detested, and an occasional article of dramatic or literary criticism, whenever the opportunity offered.

In 1802 while Charles and Mary were on a long-anticipated visit to the Lake poets, the Wordsworths introduced them to the Clarksons. Lamb was an earnest admirer of Clarkson's long fight against the slave trade, and, since he immediately won his regard by his reference to "those beautiful images of God cut in ebony," the meeting began a lifelong friendship.

Lamb's reputation as a wit and man of letters had begun to spread, and we soon see the beginning of the famous weekly Wednesday night "at homes" which were later so vividly reported by Hazlitt, Leigh Hunt, De Quincey, and half a dozen other literary lights of the day.

He also began to find an occasional safety valve in mild intoxication which troubled both him and Mary, although whatever his morning-after state he never failed to report to the office at his usual hour.

That this was not quite the proper hour is indicated by the plaintive reproach of a friendly superior who said one morning: "Lamb, why are you always the last to arrive?" and was taken aback by the reply, "Well, you must admit I'm always the first to leave."

Lamb also made a joke of his repeated attempts to stop drinking and, later, smoking as well, but that they were serious to him his and Mary's letters both testify. In 1806 Mary wrote Sarah Stoddart:

> I know my dismal faces have been almost as great a drawback upon Charles's comfort as his feverish, teasing ways have been

upon mine. Our love for each other has been the torment of our lives hitherto. I am most seriously intending to bend the whole force of my mind to counteract this, and I think I see some prospect of success.

This resolution, unlike Charles' frequent ones against spirits and tobacco, bore immediate fruit. The plan to write an introductory version for children of some of the Shakespearian plays, took shape and became a cooperative project, for Mary rapidly completed most of the comedies and Charles, with some grumbling, worked on the tragedies.

The *Tales* won an immediate success when they were first published in 1808 and they have been continuously reprinted up until now.

Charles, who had always been a devotee of the theatre, at the same time attempted a farce—*Mr. H.*—which was accepted by the management of Drury Lane. Both Charles and Mary were thrilled at the prospect, but after the first—and last—performance Charles grimly broke the news to a number of friends in notes very much like this one addressed to Wordsworth.

> Dear Wordsworth—*Mr. H.* came out last night, and failed. I had many fears; the subject was not substantial enough. John Bull must have solider fare than *letter*. We are pretty stout about it; have had plenty of condoling friends; but, after all, we had rather it should have succeeded. You will see the *prologue* in most of the morning papers. *It* was attempted to be encored. How hard!—a thing I did merely as a task, because it was wanted, and set no great store by; and *Mr. H.*!! The number of friends we had in the house—my brother and I being in public offices, etc.—was astonishing, but they yielded at length to a few hisses.
>
> A hundred hisses! (Damn the word, I write it like kisses—how different!)—a hundred hisses outweigh a thousand claps. The former come more directly from the heart. Well, 'tis withdrawn, and there is an end.
>
> Better luck to us.

His next work was one of much more importance. Except for Shakespeare, whose plays were then still disfigured by all sorts of eighteenth century improvements—like the infamous happy ending to *King Lear—the* Elizabethan dramatists were almost totally unknown at the beginning of the nineteenth century.

Lamb had, ever since his early acquaintance with them in

Salt's library, developed an enthusiastic and discriminating taste for what is undoubtedly the greatest period of English dramatic literature to date. He now revived a project given up at the time of his mother's death when, as he wrote Coleridge, he had burned his book of "excerpts," for a volume of *Specimens of English Dramatic Poets Who Lived About the Time of Shakespeare.* This, with invaluable introductory remarks and critical comments, was published in 1808.

Here, as in most of his other scattered criticism, Lamb is somewhat off guard and it is in these oblique glimpses that we can best catch sight of the fundamental philosophy of life he spent so much time and energy suppressing.

To begin with, his real favorites were, in art, Hogarth the savage social satirist; in poetry, Milton the devoted revolutionary statesman; in drama the deeply passionate and active Elizabethans; and in prose, his intransigent contemporary, the political essayist, Hazlitt.

Writing of the sonnets of Sir Philip Sidney he remarks:

> . . . They savour of the Courtier, it must be allowed, and not of the Commonwealthsman. But Milton was a Courtier when he wrote the Masque at Ludlow Castle, and still more a Courtier when he composed the Arcades. When the national struggle was to begin, he becomingly cast those vanities behind him; and if the order of time had thrown Sir Philip upon the crisis which preceded the Revolution, there is no reason why he should not have acted the same part in that emergency which has glorified the name of a later Sydney. He did not want for plainness or boldness of spirit. His letter on the French match may testify, he could speak his mind plainly to Princes. The times did not call him to the scaffold.

In a letter to Manning in 1801 he comments on Milton's political pamphlets, which he read in their original Latin:

> If you find the Miltons in certain parts dirtied and soiled with a crumb of right Gloucester, blacked in the candle (my usual supper), or peradventure a stray ash of tobacco wafted into the crevices, look to that passage more especially; depend upon it, it contains good matter. I have got your little Milton, which, as it contains "Salamasius," [Milton's opponent—an apologist for Charles I] and I make a rule of never hearing but one side of the question (why should I distract myself?), I shall return to you when I pick up the *Latina opera*. The first De-

fence is the greatest work among them, because it is uniformly great, and such as is befitting the very mouth of a great nation, speaking for itself. But the second Defence, which is but a succession of splendid episodes, slightly tied together, has one passage, which, if you have not read, I conjure you to lose no time, but read it: it is his consolations in his blindness, which had been made a reproach to him. It begins whimsically, with poetical flourishes about Tiresias and other blind worthies (which still are mainly interesting as displaying his singular mind, and in what degree poetry entered into his daily soul, not by fits and impulses, but engrained and innate), but the concluding page, i.e. of *this passage* (not of the *Defensio*), which you will easily find, divested of all brags and flourishes, gives so rational, so true an enumeration of his comforts, so human, that it cannot be read without the deepest interest.

Another letter to Manning, who had meanwhile gone to China, summarizes his literary activities up to the beginning of 1808:

I have done two books since the failure of my farce; they will both be out this Summer. The one is a juvenile book—the *Adventures of Ulysses*, . . . The other is done for Longman, and is *Specimens of English Dramatic Poets contemporary with Shakespeare*. . . . They used to be called "Beauties." You have seen "Beauties of Shakespeare?" so have many people that never saw any beauties *in* Shakespeare. Longman is to print it, and be at all the expense and risk, and I am to share the profits after all deductions; i.e. a year or two hence I must pocket what they please to tell me is due to me. But the book is such as I am glad there should be.

Similarly, the notes in the *Specimens* themselves afford revealing glimpses of their author as well as their subjects. He says of Thomas Middleton, for example, in a phrase reminiscent of Blake's attack on the conformity of Englishmen after the French Revolution:

The insipid levelling morality to which the modern stage is tied down, would not admit of such admirable passions as these scenes are filled with. . . . With us all is hypocritical meekness.

In commenting on William Rowley, he remarks:

The old play-writers are distinguished by an honest boldness of exhibition. . . . A poor man on our stage is always a gentleman, he may be known by a peculiar neatness of apparel, and by wearing black. Our delicacy in fact forbids the dramatizing of distress at all. It is never shown in its essential properties; it appears but as the adjunct of virtue, as something which is to be relieved, from the approbation of which relief the spectators are to derive a certain soothing of self-refined satisfaction.

Again, although he never idolized Wordsworth—as witness the famous evening when Wordsworth remarked pontifically that he did not see much difficulty in writing like Shakespeare if he had a mind to try, and Lamb retorted "Clearly then, nothing is wanting but the mind"—yet he fully appreciated the real greatness of Wordsworth's best work and, in a review of the *Excursion* wrote:

> The causes which have prevented the poetry of Mr. Wordsworth from attaining its full share of popularity are to be found in the boldness and originality of his genius. The times are past when a poet could securely follow the direction of his own mind into whatever tracts it might lead. A writer who would be popular must timidly coast the shore of prescribed sentiment and sympathy. . . . He must not think or feel too deeply.

For Burns, Lamb always had a deep love and respect. He mentions in one of his early letters to Coleridge, "Burns, the god of my idolatry," and, in a later review of some other poet uses him for purposes of comparison saying, "a predominant feature of independence impresses every page of our glorious Burns."

In this admiration Coleridge, Wordsworth and a few other discriminating readers had already joined Lamb, but he was still practically alone in his knowledge of, and respect for, Blake. Blake, although still alive, had not written for over twenty years and was lost in a deep obscurity when Lamb in 1824 wrote in answer to some question from a friend:

> . . . Blake is a real name, I assure you, and a most extraordinary man if he is still living. . . . His pictures—one in particular, the Canterbury Pilgrims—have great merit, but hard, dry, yet with a grace. He has written a catalogue of them with a most spirited criticism on Chaucer, but mystical and full of Vision. His poems have been sold hitherto only in manuscript. I never read them; but a friend at my desire procured the "Sweep Song." There is one to a tiger which I have heard recited beginning—

"Tiger, Tiger, burning bright
Thro the deserts of the night,"

which is glorious, but, alas! I have not the book: for the man is flown, whither I know not—to Hades or a Mad House. But I must look on him as one of the most extraordinary persons of the age.

Shortly after the publication of the *Specimens* the Tory *Quarterly Review*, in its issue of February, 1812, criticized the book referring, with its customary good taste, to "the blasphemies of a poor maniac."

During this year Lamb was again contributing anonymous political verses and such articles as the one on Guy Faux and parliamentary reform to the Whig *London Magazine* and Leigh Hunt's much more radical *Examiner*.

When, in 1813, Hunt was convicted of "libel" and imprisoned for two years, both Charles and Mary, despite their frequent ill health and Charles' very limited leisure, were his most faithful visitors. Hunt gratefully wrote:

> But what return can I make to the Lambs who came to comfort me in all weathers, hail or sunshine, in day-light or in darkness, even in the dreadful frost and snow of the beginning of 1814? I am always afraid of talking about them, lest my tropical temperament should seem to render me too florid.

After Hunt's release he was, for a time, an intimate of their Wednesday evenings and other occasions, and successfully urged Lamb to collect and publish his "Works" in two volumes—one of prose and one of poetry. Although Lamb was then already forty-two years old these volumes contain none of the work upon which his reputation as the foremost English essayist is based!

His writing days, however, seemed almost over. He had written very little except letters in the past three or four years, and in those he adverted with more and more loathing to his office slavery and with ever increasing pain to Mary's recurrent illness.

However, Lamb had been steadily rising in position, or, at least, salary, and a reorganization in 1817 almost doubled his wages, which then became £450.

That year he and Mary gave up their beloved chambers in the Temple and moved to a more comfortable modern apartment very near the Covent Garden theatre. Many of the actors and managers were already friends of theirs and now often joined the Wednesday evenings after their performances were completed.

Lamb may already, at this time, have fallen in love with Fanny Kelly of whose genius and "divine plain face" he had written so many lyric reviews. In 1819 he sent her the first and only proposal of his life and, on the same day, received a regretful refusal. Miss Kelly tactfully claimed an "early attachment" as her reason, and they remained friends all the rest of his life, but his letter had made it clear that he had no thought of any possible separation from Mary and Miss Kelly later confessed her real feelings to her sister, "I could not give my assent to a proposal which would bring me into that atmosphere of sad mental uncertainty which surrounds his domestic life."

Finally in 1820 Lamb wrote, for a magazine, the first of the famous *Essays of Elia*. He borrowed his pen name from the pseudonym of an old clerk with whom he had worked in the South Sea House more than a quarter of a century before.

The same year, on a visit to Cambridge, the Lambs met an attractive "nut brown maid"—a motherless girl of eleven whom they invited to visit them for the Christmas Holidays. Three years later, on the death of her Italian father, they informally adopted her.

That year, too, Charles again wrote some of his infrequent political satires for Thelwall's *Champion*. Both he and Mary took the side of the Whig Queen Caroline, against the scandalous accusations of her husband, the Tory Prince Regent, although Mary, with rather devastating frankness, said, "I should not think the better of her if I were sure she was what is called innocent."

The gentle wistfulness and lively humor of the essays Charles was now writing give us no hint of the weight with which the bitterly hated office routine and Mary's longer, more frequent illnesses were pressing on him. Only in the letters does he ever express his feelings. In 1822 he wrote to Wordsworth:

> My theory is to enjoy life, but my practice is against it. I grow ominously tired of official confinement. Thirty years have I served the Philistines, and my neck is not subdued to the yoke. You don't know how wearisome it is to breathe the air of four pent walls without relief, day after day, all the golden hours of the day between ten and four, without ease or interposition. . . . Oh for a few years between the grave and the desk!—they are the same, save that at the latter you are the outside machine. . . .

"You don't know how wearisome it is to breathe the air of four pent walls without relief, day after day, all the golden hours between ten and four. . . ." Since Lamb's time we have become so accustomed to this white collar servitude that we may even feel some surprise at the moderation of the hourly sentence at which he bitterly complains.

And in truth even among the writers we have already considered, Bacon spent far more time on exhausting matters of state, Bunyan almost as much, during many years, in the physical labors of his forge, Defoe on the demands of business and Fielding in the duties of his magistracy.

Nor would it be fair to say that the difference lay in their ability to choose their vocations. Many of their nonwriting careers were as accidentally determined by birth or circumstances as was Lamb's bookkeeping.

True, the element of routine presents a more consistent contrast. "—day after day . . . without ease or interposition," from the age of fifteen to—as it happened—that of fifty. Yet when Lamb exclaimed in another letter about the same time, "O! that I had been a shoemaker or a baker or a man of large independent fortune," it is unlikely that he thought the work of the two first named, at any rate, more varied than his own. But they did work that made sense. Shoes must be made and bread be baked. Whether working, as the phrase goes, for himself or for another, the shoemaker and the baker were still working to gratify clearly seen human wants and, in the conditions of 1825, were still carrying through a complete and meaningful process in direct contact with the people whose needs they satisfied.

What happened to such craftsmen as industrialization further divided their labor we shall see in considering the work of Ruskin and Morris in the next two sections, and have no doubt already seen in Charlie Chaplin's *Modern Times*, as well as in the life around us.

But the large army of bookkeepers, correspondents and clerks of all sorts called into being by the growing needs of late eighteenth century English commerce were already completely divorced from the reality of physical manufacture at one end of the process they performed, and from the reality of human needs at the other. Their function was the utterly lifeless one of recording bodiless transactions for the profit of an invisible employer. One of Chesterton's essays explodes into the statement that galley slaves have sometimes been known to sing in melancholy chorus—but banktellers, never! The vigorous overstatement should not be allowed to hide from us an essential truth in his observation on the devitalized and isolated conditions of much white collar employment.

What was the alternative? Was there one for Lamb, if not for his less talented fellow prisoners? We have seen Dr. Johnson celebrate with some gusto the end of the earlier patronage system, and our consideration of Lamb's contemporaries has shown that men like Coleridge and Hazlitt could, even under adverse conditions, manage somehow to live by their pens.

But Lamb with his more imperative family responsibilities was far too clearsighted to view the necessities of a hand-to-mouth existence, the need of daily "selling" and "reselling" oneself to a new purchaser, whether editor or publisher, as any improvement over a single lifelong sale to the bondage of a long-term sentence.

When he was nearing fifty a new friend of the same age, the Quaker poet, Bernard Barton, who disliked his own job in a bank almost as much as Lamb did his very similar one in the East India Company, told Lamb that he had decided to throw it up and write for a living. Lamb, fearing for·his friend's future, wrote in hot haste to undo the mischief committed by his too freespoken ministering to discontent:

> "Throw yourself on the world without any rational plan of support, beyond what the chance employ of booksellers would afford you!!!"

Throw yourself rather, my dear sir, from the steep Tarpeian rock, slap-dash headlong upon iron spikes. If you had but five consolatory minutes between the desk and the bed, make much of them, and live a century in them, rather than turn slave to the booksellers. They are Turks and Tartars when they have poor authors at their beck. Hitherto you have been at arm's length from them. Come not within their grasp. I have known many authors for bread, some repining, others envying the blessed security of a counting-house, all agreeing they would rather have been tailors, weavers,—what not, rather than the things they were. I have known some starved, some to go mad, one dear friend literally dying in a workhouse. You know not what a rapacious, dishonest set these booksellers are. Ask even Southey, who (a single case almost) has made a fortune by book drudgery, what he has found them. Oh, you know not (may you never know!) the miseries of subsisting by authorship. 'Tis a pretty appendage to a situation like yours or mine; but a slavery, worse than all slavery, to be a bookseller's dependant, to drudge your brains for pots of ale and breasts of mutton, to change your free thoughts and voluntary numbers for ungracious task-work. Those fellows hate *us*. The reason I take to be, that contrary to other trades, in which the master gets all the credit (a jeweller or silversmith for instance), and the journeyman, who really does the fine work, is in the background,— in *our* work the world gives all the credit to us, whom *they* consider as *their* journeymen, and therefore do they hate us, and cheat us, and oppress us, and would wring the blood of us out, to put another sixpence in their mechanic pouches! I contend that a bookseller has a *relative honesty* towards authors, not like his honesty to the rest of the world. B., who first engaged me as "Elia," has not paid me up yet (nor any of us without repeated mortifying appeals), yet how the knave fawned when I was of service to him! Yet I dare say the fellow is punctual in settling his milk-score, etc.

Keep to your bank, and the bank will keep you. Trust not to the public; you may hang, starve, drown yourself, for anything that worthy *personage* cares. I bless every star that Providence, not seeing good to make me independent, has seen it next good to settle me upon the stable foundation of Leadenhall. Sit down, good B.B., in the banking-office. What! is there not from six to eleven p.m. six days in the week, and is there not all Sunday? Fie, what a superfluity of man's time, if you could think so!—enough for relaxation, mirth, converse, poetry, good thoughts, quiet thoughts. Oh the corroding; torturing, tormenting thoughts, that disturb the brain of the unlucky wight who must draw upon it for daily sustenance! Henceforth I retract all my fond complaints of mercantile employment; look upon them as lovers' quarrels. I was but half in earnest. Welcome dead timber of a desk, that makes me live. A little grumbling is a wholesome medicine for the spleen; but in my inner heart do I approve and embrace this our close but unharassing way of life. I am quite serious. If you can send me Fox, I will not keep it *six weeks*, and will return it, with warm thanks to yourself and friend, without blot or dog's ear. You will much oblige me by this kindness.

However by the beginning of 1825 he had become "so weary of disaster, tugged with fortune" that he "would set his life on any chance to mend it or be rid of it." In plain prose, as he wrote to Bernard Barton:

Dear B. B.—I have had no impulse to write, or attend to any single object but myself for weeks past—my single self, I— by myself—I. I am sick of hope deferred. The grand wheel is in agitation, that is to turn up my Fortune; but round it rolls, and will turn up nothing. I have a glimpse of freedom, of becoming a Gentleman at large; but I am put off from day to day. I have offered my resignation, and it is neither accepted nor rejected. Eight weeks am I kept in this fearful suspense. Guess what an absorbing stake I feel it. I am not conscious of the existence of friends present or absent. The East India Directors alone can be that thing to me or not. I have just learned that nothing will be decided this week. Why the next? Why any week? It has fretted me into an itch of the fingers; I rub 'em against paper, and write to you, rather than not allay this scorbuta.

The day he learned that he would be retired on a pension of two-thirds his annual salary—then £600—was probably the happiest one of his life. He dropped a note in Crabb Robinson's letter box on his way home: "I have left the d—d Indian House for Ever! Give me great joy!"; he wrote Barton, [B.B.,] "I would not serve another seven years for seven hundred thousand pounds!"; and to Miss Hutchinson, "I would not go back to my prison for seven years longer for £10,000 a year; seven years after one is fifty is no trifle to give up. Still I am a young *pensioner*, and have served but thirty-three years; very few, I assure you, retire before forty." To another friend he wrote that Mary woke every morning "with a sense that some great good has befallen us," and in "The Superannuated Man" he, for once, published a full account of his feelings.

Although he had determined to "scribble occasionally" to make up some of his lost income—private care for Mary during her extended illnesses had absorbed a very large part of it each year since 1817—he spent a great deal of time and energy in first establishing and then contributing to a journal edited by William Hone, who had earlier been imprisoned for his radical activities.

The next year Hone dedicated his *Everyday Book* to Lamb, saying: ". . . your afterwards daring to publish me your 'friend!' with your 'proper name' annexed, I shall never forget."

Lamb used some of his leisure to prepare another series of the Elizabethan dramatists, and wrote some further essays, later collected as *Last Essays of Elia*, but Mary's frequent illnesses depressed him more and more, and when they moved to the country to find out whether quiet and solitude could avert the attacks, he sorely missed his beloved London and the stimulus of its social life.

Mary was ill again in 1830, a year further darkened by Hazlitt's death, and Lamb again wrote to Barton:

I am in an interregnum of thought and feeling. What a beautiful Autumn morning this is, if it was but with me as in times past when the candle of the Lord shined round me! I cannot even muster enthusiasm to admire the French heroism. In better times I hope we may some day meet, and discuss an old poem or two.

Finally by 1833 Mary's illnesses had become so frequent and were followed by such prolonged periods of deep depression that Lamb gave up their lodgings and moved with her into the small private hospital where she had of late been cared for. He describes the move to Wordsworth, whose own beloved sister had recently succumbed to a premature senility:

Dear Wordsworth—Your letter, save in what respects your dear sister's health, cheered me in my new solitude. Mary is ill again. Her illnesses encroach yearly. The last was three months, followed by two of depression most dreadful. I look back upon her earlier attacks with longing: nice little durations of six weeks or so, followed by complete restoration,—shocking as they were to me then. In short, half her life she is dead to me, and the other half is made anxious with fears and lookings forward to the next shock. With such prospects, it seemed to me necessary that she should no longer live with me, and be fluttered with continued removals; so I am come to live with her, at a Mr. Walden's and his wife, who take in patients, and have arranged to lodge and board us only. They have had the care of her before. I see little of her: alas! I too often hear her. *Sunt lachrymoe rerum!* and you and I must bear it.

To lay a little more load on it, a circumstance has happened, *cujus pars magna fui,* and which, at another crisis, I should have more rejoiced in. I am about to lose my old and only walk-companion, whose mirthful spirits were the "youth of our house," Emma Isola. I have her here now for a little while, but she is too nervous, properly to be under such a roof, so she will make short visits,—be no more an inmate. With my perfect approval, and more than concurrence, she is to be wedded to Moxon, at the end of August—so "perish the roses and the flowers"—how is it?

Now to the brighter side. I am emancipated from the Westwoods, and I am with attentive people, and younger. I am three or four miles nearer the great city; coaches half-price less, and going always, of which I will avail myself. I have few friends left there, one or two though, most beloved. But London streets and faces cheer me inexpressibly, though not one known of the latter were remaining.

Thank you for your cordial reception of "Elia." *Inter nos,* the *Ariadne* is not a darling with me, several incongruous things are in it, but in the composition it served me as illustrative.

I want you in the "Popular Fallacies" to like the "Home that is no home," [see below], and "Rising with the lark."

I am feeble, but cheerful in this my genial hot weather. Walked sixteen miles yesterday. I can't read much in summer time.

With my kindest love to all, and prayers for dear Dorothy, I remain most affectionately yours,

C. Lamb

The essay in *Popular Fallacies* to which he calls Wordsworth's attention here—"That Home Is Home Though It Is Never So Homely"—is one of his few outspoken expressions of opinion on the organization of society. In it Lamb tears away the veil of sentiment with which good-natured people soften the realities they do not mean to attack, and angrily describes the plain unvarnished truth. He says, briefly and forcefully:

> Homes there are, we are sure, that are no homes; the home of the very poor man, and another which we shall speak of presently. Crowded places of cheap entertainment, and the benches of ale-houses, if they could speak, might bear mournful testimony to the first. To them the very poor man resorts for an image of the home which he cannot find at home. For a starved grate, and a scanty firing, that is not enough to keep alive the natural heat in the fingers of so many shivering children with their mother, he finds in the depths of winter always a blazing hearth, and a hob to warm his pittance of beer by. Instead of the clamors of a wife, made gaunt by famishing, he meets with a cheerful attendance beyond the merits of the trifle which he can afford to spend. He has companions which his home denies him, for the very poor man has no visitors. He can look into the goings on of the world, and speak a little to politics. At home there are no politics stirring but the domestic. All interests, real or imaginary, all topics that should expand the mind of man, and connect him to a sympathy with general existence, are crushed in the absorbing consideration of food to be obtained for the family. Beyond the price of bread, news is senseless and impertinent. At home there is no larder. . . . Oh, 'tis a fine thing to talk of the humble meal shared together! But what if there be no bread in the cupboard? The innocent prattle of his children takes out the sting of a man's poverty. But the children of the very poor do not prattle. It is none of the least frightful features in that condition, that there is no childishness in its dwellings.

Poor people, said a sensible old nurse to us once, do not bring up their children; they drag them up. . . .
The children of the very poor have no young times. It makes the very heart to bleed to overhear the casual street-talk between a poor woman and her little girl, a woman of the better sort of poor, in a condition rather above the squalid beings which we have been contemplating. It is not of toys, of nursery books, of summer holidays (fitting that age); of the promised sight, or play; of praised sufficiency at school. It is of mangling and clear-starching, of the price of coals, or of potatoes. The questions of the child, that should be the very outpourings of curiosity in idleness, are marked with forecast and melancholy providence. It has come to be a woman before it was a child. It has learned to go to market; it chaffers, it haggles, it envies, it murmurs; it is knowing, acute, sharpened; it never prattles. Had we not reason to say that the home of the very poor is no home?

He was still able, on occasion, to amuse himself and others, making much out of any pleasant trifle that arose. There are many letters like the playful note to Emma's fiancé, who became his last publisher and one of his first biographers.

For God's sake give Emma no more watches; *one* has turned her head. She is arrogant and insulting. She said something very unpleasant to our old clock in the passage, as if he did not keep time, and yet he had made her no appointment. She takes it out every instant to look at the moment-hand. She lugs us out into the fields, because there the bird-boys ask you, "Pray, sir, can you tell us what's o'clock?" and she answers them punctually. She loses all her time looking to see "what the time is." I overheard her whispering, "Just so many hours, minutes, etc., to Tuesday; I think St. George's goes too slow." This little present of Time—why,—'tis Eternity to her!

What can make her so fond of a gingerbread watch? She has spoiled some of the movements. Between ourselves, she has kissed away "half-past twelve," which I suppose to be the canonical hour in Hanover Square.

Well, if "love me, love my watch" answers, she will keep time to you.

It goes right by the Horse Guards.

Dearest M.—Never mind opposite nonsense. She does not love you for the watch, but the watch for you. I will be at the wedding, and keep the 30th July, as long as my poor months last me, as a festival, gloriously.

Yours ever,

Elia.

We have not heard from Cambridge. I will write the moment we do. Edmonton, 24th July, twenty minutes past three by Emma's watch.

After Emma had left he was still lonelier, and writing for company to a young friend of hers who had spent some time with them he gave almost his only detailed description of Mary's distracted state.

She recovered once more and they had one more almost happy season together. A letter to Manning, who had finally returned from China, tells us something of this.

> You made me feel so funny, so happy-like; it was as if I was reading one of your old letters taken out at hazard any time between the last twenty years, 'twas so the same. The unity of place, a garden! The old Dramatis Personae, a landlady and Daughter. The puns the same in mould. Will nothing change you? 'Tis but a short week since honest Ryle and I were lamenting the gone-by days of Manning and Whist. How savourily did he remember them! Might some great year but bring them back again! This was my exclaim, and R. did not ask for an explanation. I have had a scurvy nine years of it, and am now in the sorry fifth act. Twenty weeks nigh has she been now violent, with but a few sound months before, and these in such dejection that her fever might seem a relief to it. I tried to bring her to town in the winter once or twice, but it failed. Tuthill led me to expect that this illness would lengthen with her years, and it has cruelly—with that new feature of despondency after. I am with her alone now in a proper house. She is, I hope, recovering. We play Picquet, and it is like the old times awhile, then goes off. I struggle to town rarely, and then to see London, with little other motive—for what is left there hardly? The streets and shops entertaining ever, else I feel as in a desert, and get me home to my cave. Save that once a month I pass a day, a gleam in my life, with Cary at the Museum (He is the flower of clergymen) and breakfast next morning with Robinson. I look to this as a treat. It sustains me. C. is a dear fellow, with but two vices, which in any less good than himself would be crimes past redemption. He has no relish for Parson Adams— hints that he might not be a very great Greek scholar after all (does Fielding hint that he was a porson?)—and prefers "Ye shepherds so cheerful and gay," and "My banks they are furnished with bees," to "The School-mistress." I have not seen Wright's, but the faithfulness of C., Mary and I can attest. For last year, in a good interval, I giving some lessons to Emma, now Mrs. Moxon, in the *sense* part of her Italian (I knew no words), Mary pertinaciously

undertook, being 69, to read the *Inferno* all thro' with the help of his Translation, and we got thro' it with Dictionaries and Grammars, of course to our satisfaction. Her perseverance was gigantic, almost painful. Her head was over her task, like a sucking bee, morn to night. We were beginning the *Purgatory*, but got on less rapidly, our great authority for grammar, Emma, being fled, but should have proceeded but for this misfortune. Do not come to town without apprising me. We must all three meet somehow and "drink a cup."

[P. S.] Mary strives and struggles to be content when she *is* well. Last year when we talked of being dull (we had just lost our seven-years-nearly inmate), and Cary's invitation came, she said, "Did not I say something or other would turn up?" In her first walk *out* of the house, she would read every Auction advertisement along the road, and when I would stop her she said, "These are *my* Play-bills." She felt glad to get into the world again, but then follows lowness. She is getting about tho', I very much hope. She is rising, and will claim her morning Picquet. I go to put this in the Post first. I walk 9 or 10 miles a day, always up the road, dear London-wards. Fields, flowers, birds, and green lanes, I have no heart for. The bare road is cheerful, and almost as good as a street. I saunter to the Red Lion duly, as you used to the Peacock.

An American journalist who asked Crabb Robinson to invite the Lambs to breakfast with him just a few months before Charles' death in December, 1834, printed an account of his playful behaviour and a verbatim report of his conversation then. In response to a question about American writers Charles answered:

I don't know much of American authors. Mary, there, devours Cooper's novels with a ravenous appetite, with which I have no sympathy. The only American book I have ever read twice was the "Journal of Edward (John) Woolmer," a quaker preacher and tailor, whose character is one of the finest I ever met with. He tells a story or two about Negro slaves that brought the tears into my eyes. I can read no prose now, though Hazlitt sometimes, to be sure—but then Hazlitt is worth all modern prose-writers put together.

That fall Lamb was much shaken by Coleridge's death. They had seen comparatively little of each other during the last few years but their ties were too old and strong to be loosened by that, and on his death bed Coleridge wrote in the margin of the poem whose "gentle hearted" had caused such a tumult over thirty years before, "Charles and Mary Lamb—dear to my heart, yea, as it were, my heart. S.T.C. Aet 63, 1834, 1797–1834=37 years." Four months later Charles fell and scratched his face. It seemed a trivial matter but erysipelas developed and five days later, December 14, 1834, he died.

Mary survived him for eighteen years, well cared for by his friends under the arrangements he had made for her in his will.

Although the well loved Elia was only a character of Lamb's deliberate creation he was, of course, also a real part of Lamb, and his essays, sensitively read, tell us much of their real author. Occasionally in the later ones, particularly in his favorite "Home is home, be it never so homely" (quoted above), Lamb allows himself a bitterness more direct and powerful than Elia admitted. But the general confusion of Elia with Lamb, and the vaguely sympathetic knowledge of his story which includes only its unhappiness and not its heroism, have created the picture of a sentimental, helpless, unworldly figure which has exasperated many of Lamb's most perceptive admirers. One of these, Augustus Birrel exploded to fine effect in his "Obiter Dicta":

> One grows sick of the expression, "poor Charles Lamb," "gentle Charles Lamb," as if he were one of those grown-up children . . . who are perpetually begging and borrowing through the round of every man's acquaintance. Charles Lamb earned his own living, paid his own way, was the helper, not the helped; a man who was beholden to no one, who always came with gifts in his hand, a shrewd man capable of advice, strong in council. Poor Lamb, indeed! Poor Coleridge, robbed of his will; poor Wordsworth, devoured by his own ego; poor Southey writing his tomes and deeming himself a classic: . . . call these men poor, if you feel it decent to do so, but not Lamb, who was rich in all that makes life valuable and memory sweet.

Lamb would, I think, have been pleased with this explosion but it takes us only a part of the way into an understanding of his work—or, rather, as he said, of his play. His real works, he would insist wryly, were bound into the more than twenty large ledgers he had filled and left on the shelves of the East India House.

And they were meaningless works. The whole alienation of man from himself which is so fundamental a characteristic of this era of advanced capitalism is expressed in what Lamb describes as the waste of two-thirds of his lifetime. This waste is most devastatingly complete when not only the fruits but also the very tools and objects of a man's labor have no relationship to his real life. Even such hard and meagerly rewarded physical labor as that of Burns, in an agricultural economy where there is clearly some objective necessity and some material benefit from the application of one's energy, is not as profound a denial of humanity as making the fantastic routine of buying and selling—or its paper representation—the prescribed work of a man's life.

It was this which Ruskin, Morris, Emerson and Thoreau in their different ways inveighed against. It was this, vaguely sensed, which lay at the root of one of Wordsworth's most powerful sonnets:

> The world is too much with us; late and soon
>   Getting and spending we lay waste our powers
>   We have given our lives away, a sordid boon.

But all these as well as the multitude of lesser artists who sensed and expressed this attitude were able somehow to escape the yoke. The means were various. An inherited income; academic retirement; a return to nature; rigorous self-denial and a Spartan simplicity of life; even drugs and death might serve. Lamb alone of the wonderfully articulate ones—the many "mute inglorious" fellow sufferers were and are, of course, legion—by the circumstances of his life and his heroic acceptance of its special responsibilities could not avoid this common lot. And because he entered so fully into these "lives of quiet desperation," he, more than any other writer, is able to supply something of the available consolations. The loving particularity with which he dwells on all the small physical and greater intellectual indulgences, all the "cheap" but fine pleasures which lie, for the city dweller, within the means of a narrow purse and a hard won unacademic culture, has made him as helpful and personal a friend to whole generations of readers as he was to scores of hard pressed contemporaries. Very rarely does he speak out as clearly against the deepening emptiness and irrelevance of life for the ordinary man as in "The Superannuated Man"; just as seldom does he attack the callous sentimentality of bourgeois ethics as directly as in "Homé is Home Though It Be Never So Homely"; but the same warm wholehearted concern that here informs his hatred elsewhere inspires the love with which he offers the best gifts he can find to alleviate a life he dared not think of changing, as in the delightful essay on "Old China" and others. Only the fact that there was a peculiar and real personal prohibition of such thought made it possible for so strong and honest a personality to go thus far and no further. The genuine inescapability of his limits made it unnecessary for him to rationalize his failure to act in, or even systemmatically think about, the broader social scene and created no need for a false political philosophy which would justify his inaction. His personal tragedy made him rather a water boy than a standard bearer in the common man's fight for life, but he never forgot or allowed others to forget which side he was on.

The Victorian Age and the Industrial Revolution

FROM THE ROMANTICS TO THE VICTORIANS

The fifteen or twenty years which elapsed between the death of the younger romantics and the birth of Dickens' Sam Weller were extraordinary not only for the almost complete lack of any new writers of importance, but also because there was practically nothing of significance produced by the few older ones who had survived their age.

The two outstanding exceptions were the inspired journalism of William Cobbett (1762–1835) and the thirty-odd "historical romances" of Sir Walter Scott (1771–1832).

Among the creative writers of the romantic age whom we considered in the last section, Scott was distinguished as the only consistent conservative as well as the only novelist. Many of the poets and essayists were, as we have seen, radicals first and reactionaries later; some were fighting progressives to the very end; but Sir Walter Scott was unique among contemporary men of genius as an unwavering Tory, and was almost unique among important Tory contemporaries as a decent, generous and fair-minded human being.

His paradoxical position was made possible by the fact that he happened to be born in Edinburgh rather than London, and to the day of his death his strong patriotic sentiment remained Scottish rather than English.

There were two ways in which his national interest helped inhibit certain of the prejudices fostered by his class interest and political position. Negatively his life in Edinburgh to a great extent enabled him to remain ignorant of the new alignments and relationships created by the industrial revolution. He sensed its encroachment as a threat, but was not forced to face it as a concrete fact, and the suspicion and fear other more embittered Tories directed at the whole working class, he limited to the almost unknown Glasgow weavers and the wholly unknown English north country colliers. Affirmatively, Sir Walter's Scottish nationalism laid the ground for much of the great popularity and all the enduring value of his novels.

Since the history of an independent Scotland had, legally, ended in 1707 and was, practically, altogether concluded a generation or two before Scott's birth, his patriotism naturally made him seek out and treasure all those distinctive traditions and cultural manifestations which dated from the older days of national independence. His search for living traces of these ancient glories necessarily led him to the solitary shepherds, lonely peasant farmers, and isolated rural villagers in whose speech, life, and clan memories Scotland's earlier history still played a real part. Sir Walter's genuine interest in the past was no doubt greatly intensified by his unconscious desire to avoid any concrete awareness of the social problems and conditions of his own time, but it did enable him to transcend, to some extent, his own class consciousness through respect for, and emotional identification with, those workers who were the only living exemplars of his national tradition.

In *Chronicles of the Canongate*, for example, a kindly well-educated young man is inquiring about conditions of child labor employment in a mill which had been erected in a here-to-fore rural district. From the replies he receives we would get no idea at all of the specific horrors of the time, but in conclusion:

> "For health," said Christie looking gloomily at me, "ye maun ken little o' the world, sir, if ye dinna ken that the health of the poor man's body, as weel as his youth and his strength, are all at the command of the rich man's purse. There never was a trade so unhealthy yet but men would fight to get wark at it for twa pennies a day above the common wage.

In *The Antiquary* written in 1816, some ten years before the first of the *Chronicles*, Saunders Mucklebait, mending the "auld black bitch of a boat" that drowned his son the day before, feels himself reproached by the gentlefolk for his lack of sentiment:

> What would you have me do unless I wanted to see four children starve because ane is drowned? It's weel wi' you

gentles, that can sit in the house wi' handkerchers to your een when ye lose a friend; but the likes o' us maun to our wark again if our hearts were beating as hard as my hammer. . . . Yet what needs ane to be angry at her that has neither soul nor sense?—though I am no that muckle better myself. She's but a rickle o' aul rotten deals nailed thegither, and warped wi' the wind and the sea—and I am a dour carle battered by winds and foul weather at sea and land till I am maist as senseless as hersell. She maun be mended though again' the morning tide —that's a thing of necessity.

Of course Sir Walter pictured himself as a reincarnation, not of the Scottish peasant, but rather of his "laird," and as soon as his enormous literary earnings made it possible, he reenacted the part of a semifeudal lord on his newly created Abbotsford estate. But his conception of the role centered about the democracy of blood kinship and reciprocal responsibilities between a chief and his clan, and he was able to make up all deficits in his pastoral economy through the sale of his work. Thus there never arose any real clash of interests to mar the patriarchal idyll he, for a little time and space, erected in fact as well as fiction.

Long before the days of Abbotsford, however, when Scott was still a far from affluent young lawyer, he had begun to collect and edit the old ballads and folk songs of the Scottish people. True, the most casual comparison with Burns' almost contemporary use of the same material shows how often Scott weakened and sentimentalized this folk literature. Yet he preserved much of value which would otherwise have been lost, and learned much of poetry in doing so.

Echoes of this authentic music sound in his best original verse which, like the "Coronach" of *The Lady of the Lake*, and the little snatches of song that star the pages of his Scottish novels, are unself-conscious lyrics put into the mouths of humble rural characters. And similarly, almost every single memorable personality and scene in all that enormous volume of prose romances which constitute the great bulk of his work, owe their power to the faithfully observed and brilliantly reproduced speech of some old Scottish beggar or cottage woman or farm servant.

For Scott was all his life an energetic and active observer with a prodigious memory, an excellent ear for music and dialogue, a genial unforced friendliness for all sorts of men, and an especial interest in the more distinctive Scottish characteristics which, as we have seen, meant in practice the rural working class. It is actually the realism with which he rendered a background already become picturesque that made his best novels—those placed in eighteenth century Scotland—valuable despite his implausible romanticism and impartially glamorized feudal lords, marauding crusaders, and Stuart pretenders.

For Scott's romanticism did not, of course, at all resemble that of the great romantics who were his contemporaries. When, in the first ten years of the century, he had written as a romantic poet, his poetry was romantic only in the later decadent sense of the word. That is, it enabled its readers, as well as its author, to escape from the troublesome present to a remote, idealized and undemanding past, or from the everyday life of street and farm to the distantly viewed beauties of untamed nature. This was almost diametrically opposed to the spirit of the great romantics who, as we have seen, asserted the value and vitality of human emotions in the contemporary scene and hoped-for future.

When Scott found himself unable to compete with the more passionate and exotic appeal of Byron's early *Childe Harolde* he turned, at first anonymously, to write novels in the same escapist spirit. But there he found more scope for his extraordinary gift of storytelling, his good practical sense of drama, his appreciation of the often grim folk humor, and his ability to sketch the likeness plausibly, if superficially, of hundreds of widely varied and characteristic Scottish figures. Above all, in the novels Scott was able to concentrate on those minor figures, peasants, villagers and servants, not genteel or romantic enough for him to use as heroes or heroines. Like Jeanie in *The Heart of Midlothian* (probably Scott's best novel) they become genteel and colorless before the end of the book when they do wander into such a central position, but when they are left to themselves they constitute the real value of his work and won for him the admiration of such novelists as George Eliot and Dickens, Balzac and Tolstoy.

It is not in these writers, however, that we will find his influence so much as in the curious strain of anti-industrial, humanitarian medievalism which as we shall see largely diverted the nineteenth century protest of Carlyle, Ruskin and the pre-Raphaelites.

Before we turn to consider Cobbett, the only really important progressive writer of this interim period, we must briefly summarize the events in England out of which his work grew.

The passage of the Corn Laws in 1815, setting up a high import tariff on wheat and raising the price of that bread which formed over three quarters of the working man's diet, had intensified the misery and hunger of the people and had led to demonstrations of discontent all over the country. The government's policy of open terrorism came to a climax after the Peterloo Massacre near Manchester, which broke up the largest of these demonstrations. To silence the protests which poured into London from every part of England, as well as from such figures as Byron and Shelley in Italy, Parliament passed the repressive "Six Acts" which included the total suspension of the Habeas Corpus, new gag laws for the press, and more severe penalties for trade union "conspiracies." These measures and the consistent use of Britain's largest professional army effectually stifled all open protest and drove underground any opposition to the government's reign of terror.

When these tactics had accomplished the virtual destruction of all articulate radicalism, and the imprisonment or exile of most militants, there was some relaxation of the government's policy. These factors, together with the gradual revival of industry between 1820 and 1826, occasioned considerable change in the temper of the growing urban population, and large London crowds cheered Lord Castlereagh's funeral cortege in 1822, evidently feeling that his suicide meant the end of an unlamented age.

A. L. Morton provides an admirable summary description of the dominant government attitude, characteristic of moderate Tories as well as Whigs, in the next decade:

> With the new situation new tactics had become necessary. The "Six Acts" had staved off one revolutionary crisis, but the more far-seeing members of the ruling class began to understand that such methods were unlikely to be always effective in the future. They were not unwilling to coerce (as the events of 1830 and, later, of the Chartist period were to show) but they preferred to avoid the necessity of coercion where other methods would serve. The result was a whole series of "liberal" measures, both before and after the Reform Bill, which had as their object the unobtrusive strengthening of the State apparatus, and which, though apparently less repressive than those of the Peterloo era, were in fact much more effective. . . .
>
> For political purposes the police had the advantage of strengthening the power of the State without the danger of serious internal disorder which the use of the yeomanry or of regular troops always involved. At the same time, the decline of Radical agitation after 1820 made it possible to relax the

censorship imposed on the press and to withdraw many of the spies and provacateurs from the Radical and working-class organisations. It was now obviously wise to avoid rather than to provoke disorder. The partial repeal of the Combination Acts in 1824 was similar in effect. So long as Trade Unions were illegal every Union was the ground for a possible conspiracy. Francis Place, to whose astute lobbying the repeal was largely due, had persuaded the Government, and possibly himself, that once legalised, Trade Unions would become unnecessary and would decay and disappear.

Yet these changes actually affected only some part of the city population. Their temporarily lessened militancy left the rural laborers, such village craftsmen as blacksmiths, carpenters and wheelwrights, and many of the small yeoman farmers, to carry on alone a dogged but losing struggle against their constantly deteriorating living standards and decreasing opportunities.

It is, therefore, significant that although not a major figure in English literature, the only writer who made any genuine contribution during this period was William Cobbett, the self-educated radical son of a poor farmer who had himself spent his youth as a hired farm laborer.

His undirected search for some way out of the hopelessness of poorly paid seasonal farm work had led him to enlist in the army. Stationed in Canada from 1783 to 1791, he made extraordinary use of the enforced leisure of a peacetime barrack life to study intensively all the printed matter he could secure.

After narrowly escaping court-martial for an attempt to expose the graft whereby his Quartermaster's Corps appropriated a considerable part of the money intended to feed the entire regiment, Cobbett returned to England as a civilian in 1791. He was determined to use his newly discovered ability of writing in a hard-hitting popular pamphleteer style to expose and overthrow the whole rotten tissue of corruption in high places of which, as he now saw, his particular quartermaster was only a small part.

G.D.H. and M. Cole in the preface to their excellent new edition of Cobbett's major literary work say:

> In some ways his mind was curiously unsophisticated; for some time he was still disposed to believe that, certain things apart, the ruling powers were substantially in accord with his notions of justice, and that, when he found an abuse, he had only to call attention to it loudly enough for it to be remedied.

He regarded abuses as he might stones in his road—as obstacles which needed a kick, possibly two kicks, to remove them, but which were essentially removable. It was only when a long series of kicks, accompanied by the natural language of a full-blooded and indignant man, had failed to make the slightest impression on the obstacles, that it began to dawn upon him that possibly what he had mistaken for casual stones were in reality parts of a monstrous erection which his former friends were actually interested in preserving.

In 1810 Cobbett succeeded in founding *The Political Register* which, through many vicissitudes and several forced interruptions, achieved increasing popularity with workingmen for over a quarter of a century. When, in 1816, a two-penny edition was launched, it became unquestionably the most important radical newspaper in England and remained that until Cobbett's death twenty years later.

In 1817 the passage of the Six Acts forced Cobbett, who had already spent two years in jail for his writing, to fly to the United States for refuge, and on his return in 1819 he rapidly became the most important spokesman and guide of the unorganized, sporadic, but persistent, struggle for life which the rural laborers and ruined yeoman farmers were to carry on with growing desperation during the next ten years.

In 1822 he began to make and report the *Rural Rides* which took him, on horseback, over almost all rural England and through a considerable part of Scotland and Ireland during the next ten years. These essays, published weekly in the *Political Register* and later reprinted in book form, give us an incomparably vivid picture of the cultivated human beauty of the English country side, and of the inhuman misery of the people it should have supported.

They also give us an excellent picture of Cobbett himself—his unself-conscious love of natural sights and sounds, his shrewd practical farmer's wisdom, his warm concern for those who work the land, his taste for a pretty girl or a fine view, his delight in a slashing attack on political enemies, his hatred of the "great Wens" (London, Manchester, or other such cities), and his keen insight into the way in which the country yeomen had been led to destroy their own safeguards by helping to put down the hunger marches of the unemployed weavers.

They show us, too, Cobbett's limitations as a thinker. He understood and hated the war profiteers, the rotten boroughs, the unnecessary expenses of corrupt government bureaus and a useless Established Church, the terrific burden of war debts, the dangerous manipulation of an inflated paper currency, and the financiers who benefited by all. But he never in any way grasped the significance of the new industrialists; although he detested their inhumanity to their workers he thought the factories were of slight—and diminishing—importance.

His hopeless objective was a return to an improved cottage economy and small yeoman farming where the womenfolk would again make most articles of domestic use, assisted by whatever machinery could be employed at home. A reformed Parliament truly representing the people would, he felt, accomplish this by rendering impotent the financial oligarchy, ending government waste, and putting a stop to the high taxes which were ruining the poor farmer and forcing him to starve the rural laborer.

But this incomplete understanding of the total situation did not vitiate the real contribution of the *Political Register* to the people it served. Cobbett was elected to the first "reformed Parliament" in 1832 and although he, like the people he represented, was clearsighted enough to be disillusioned almost immediately, yet he was greeted by wildly enthusiastic crowds throughout his tour of Scotland later that year. The Cole's again summarize his essential achievement, saying:

> He was really an agrarian tribune—the last of line of Gracchus. But living in England of the Industrial Revolution he was foredoomed to disappointment.
> But is disappointment the same as failure? The crowds who welcomed him in 1832 did not think so. They were not welcoming a failure, but a man who had succeeded, all through the time of oppression, in holding the working-classes steadfastly to Reform, and in creating a movement of which the Governments—Whig as well as Tory—were really afraid. In the strictest possible sense of the word, Cobbett, through the dark years, *upheld* the working-class. At a time when those who professed most sympathy with the labourer vied with his open enemies in telling him that he was a poor creature whose whole duty was to restrain his natural impulses and to be obedient and grateful to all set in authority over him, Cobbett, almost alone, told him that he was a man, and that by holding up his head and bearing himself manfully he might gain a man's inheritance. No oppression enraged him so much as the insidious propaganda which hinted that the labourer was not capable of knowing his own mind or of thinking for himself. It is diffi-

cult for the twentieth-century reader, looking back on the Trade Union movement of the 'forties struggling into existence in holes and corners; and upon Social-Democratic leaders haranguing uninterested knots from soap-boxes, to realize what a huge working-class following Cobbett had. At its height, the unstamped Register had a sale of sixty thousand copies, and most of these copies were read, not by a single working-man, but aloud in working-class houses, clubs, and branches throughout the country. If to have inspired sixty thousand groups of people in the battle for Reform, to have kept sixty thousand groups from despair when everything seemed combined to oppress them, is failure, then, and only then, Cobbett may be held to have failed.

In 1830, when general economic depression and an epidemic which killed over two million sheep, had intensified the already unbearable agricultural distress, there was a last outbreak of revolt in the countryside which began with the burning of hay ricks and thrashing machines in Kent and spread throughout the Southern and Eastern Counties.

Troops were called out, the rioters were ruthlessly subdued, nine leaders were hanged, over 450 were transported and over 400 more were given savage prison sentences.

Cobbett himself was put on trial for having, through his writing, aroused the disposition to use force and violence. Such articles as the following enabled the government to assure itself of a conviction.

> My readers will remember how often I have said that it would come to this very thing, burning and destroying; and they will also remember that I have not a few times said also, that it would begin in Sussex or Kent. I knew that English labourers would not lie down and die in any number, with nothing but sour sorrel in their bellies (as two did at Acton in the beginning of the summer); and knew that they would never receive the extreme unction and die of hunger, as the poor Irish did, and be praised for their resignation by Bingham —Baring or Baring—Bingham or whoever else he is.
> I knew that all the palaver in the world, all the wheedling, coaxing, praying; I knew that all the blustering and threatening; I knew that all the imprisoning, whipping, and harnessing to carts and wagons; I knew that all these would fail to persuade the honest, sensible and industrious English labourer, that he had not an *indefensible right to live*. O God! with what indignation did I hear the unfortunate Irish praised because they *died of want*, while their country abounded in the means

of subsistence! There is no man, not of a fiend-like nature, who can view the destruction of property that is now going on in the southern counties without the greatest pain; but I stand to it, that it is the strictly natural course of things, where the labourer, the producer, *will not starve.*

What is his homely reasoning upon the case? "I work twelve hours a day to *produce this food*; I do *all* the real labour, and you, who stand by and look over me, deny me even *subsistence* out of it; no, if you give me none of it, you shall have none yourself, at any rate." And to work he goes, burning and destroying.

But Cobbett conducted his own defense with great abiltiy and courage and when he told how the major government witness had first been threatened with a death sentence for rioting, and had then been promised a pardon for testifying that what he had read in the *Political Register* had incited him to riot, even a hand-picked jury disagreed on its verdict and the accused was discharged.

Undoubtedly the fears aroused by this last flare-up of the countryside induced many of those who had, for over a decade, opposed any parliamentary reform, to join with the more liberal or far-sighted members of parliament in seeing what a very limited degree of conciliation could accomplish. Cobbett characteristically demanded of a proponent of "a moderately reformed parliament" how satisfied he would be with "a moderately chaste wife."

Almost any single account of a "rural ride," printed weekly in the *Political Register* from 1822 until a few years before Cobbett's death in 1835, will give the reader some idea of the rich variety of his comments and observations and the colloquial power of his pen. The typical extract below is taken from one of the earliest such reports, collected and published in the first series of *Rural Rides* in 1826.

Saint Albans
June 24, 1822
   . . . The custom is in this part of Hertfordshire (and, I am told it continues into Bedfordshire) to leave a *border* round the ploughed part of the fields to bear grass and to make hay from, so that, the grass being now made into hay, every corn field has a closely mowed grasswalk about ten feet wide all round it, between the corn and the hedge. This is most beautiful! The hedges are now full of the shepherd's rose, honeysuckles, and all sorts of wild flowers; so that you are upon a grass walk, with this most beautiful of all flower gardens and shrubberies on your one hand; and with the corn

on the other. And thus you go from field to field, (on foot or on horseback) the sort of corn, the sort of underwood and timber, the shape and size of the fields, the height of the hedge-rows, the height of the trees, all continually varying. Talk of *pleasure-grounds* indeed! What, that man ever invented, under the name of pleasure-grounds, can equal these fields in Hertfordshire?—This is a profitable system too; for the ground under hedges bears little corn and it bears very good grass. Something, however, depends on the nature of the soil: for it is not all land that will bear grass, fit for hay, perpetually; and when the land will not do that, these headlands would only be a harbour for weeds and couch-grass, the seeds of which would fill the fields with their mischievous race.—It is curious enough, that these headlands cease soon after you get into Buckinghamshire. At first you see now-and-then a field *without* a grass headland; then it comes to now-and-then a field *with* one; and, at the end of five or six miles, they wholly cease. . . . People do not sow *turnips*, the ground is so dry, and I should think that the Swede-Crop will be very short; for *Swedes* ought to be up at least, by this time. If I had Swedes to sow, I would sow them now, and upon ground very deeply and finely broken. I would sow directly after the plough, not being half an hour behind it, and would roll the ground as hard as possible. I am sure the plants would come up, even without rain. And, the moment the rain came, they would grow famously . . . you . . . see here, as in Kent, Sussex, Surrey and Hampshire, and, indeed, in almost every part of England, that most interesting of all objects, that which is such an honour to England, and that which distinguishes it from all the rest of the world, namely, those *neatly kept and productive little gardens round the labourers' houses*, which are seldom unornamented with more or less of flowers. We have only to look at these to know what sort of people English labourers are; these gardens are the answer to the Malthuses and the Scarletts. Shut your mouths, you Scotch Economists; cease bawling, Mr. Broughan, and you Edinburgh Reviewers, till *you* can show us something, not *like*, but approaching towards a likeness of this! . . . The pay of the labourers varies from eight to twelve shillings a week. Grass mowers get two shillings a day, two quarts of what they call strong beer, and as much small beer as they can drink. . . .

Wycombe is a very fine and clean market town; the people all looking extremely well; the girls somewhat larger featured and larger boned than those in Sussex, and not so fresh-coloured and bright-eyed. More like the girls of America, and that is saying quite as much as any reasonable woman can expect or wish for. The Hills on the Southside of Wycombe form a park and estate, now the property of Smith, who was a banker or stocking-manufacturer at Nottingham, who was made a Lord in the time of Pitt, and who purchased this estate of the Marquis of Landsowne, one of whose titles is Baron Wycombe. Wycombe is one of those famous things called [Rotten] Boroughs, and 34 votes in this Borough send Sir John Dashwood and Sir Thomas Baring to the "collective wisdom." The landlord where I put up *"remembered"* the name of Dashwood, but had *"forgotten"* how the "other" was! There would be no forgettings of this sort, if these thirty-four, together with *their* representatives were called upon to pay the share of the National Debt due from High Wycombe.

INDUSTRIAL ENGLAND AND ITS POETRY

The Victorian Age began, as it ended, a few years before the beginning and the end of the reign of that queen whose name it so dubiously immortalized. For convenience we can mark its outer limits by the passage of the first parliamentary reform bill in 1832 and the outbreak of hostilities against the Boers in 1895.

Morton again gives us an excellent summary of the situation that led up to the passage of this first Reform Bill in 1832—the date which is generally used by historians as the real beginning of the Victorian age.

By 1830 the economic crisis had reached its height. Factories were closing down, unemployment increased rapidly, and the wages of those still employed fell. In the South the movement of revolt already described broke out in the autumn. In the North Trade Unions sprang up like mushrooms and the air was full of wild rumours of workers arming and drilling. The revolution which took place in Paris in July and in Belgium in August helped to increase the tenseness of the atmosphere.

As in 1816, the economic distress led quickly to a demand for Parliamentary Reform. There was this important difference, that while from 1816 to 1820 the demand for Reform had come almost entirely from the working class, it was now a middle class demand as well. Having far closer contact with the masses than the Tories had, the factory owners and shopkeepers realised the dangers of mere repression and set to work to turn the discontent of the people into a weapon for securing their own political supremacy.

The agitation for Reform was therefore more widespread and more dangerous than ever before and though Reform meant quite different things to different classes it was possible for a wire-puller as brilliant as Place to gloss over these differences and even to turn them to good account. When Lovett and the Owenites created their National Union of the Working Classes and Others, . . . with a programme of universal suffrage, a secret ballot, and annual parliaments, Place saw at once the danger and the value of such an organisation. It was dangerous because it meant business, and because it regarded Parliamentary Reform as the first step towards social reform and economic equality. It was useful because it could be turned into a weapon with which to blackmail the Tories into acquiescing in a certain measure of Reform (enough for the needs of the middle classes) as an alternative to Revolution, which Place and the Whigs were never tired of painting in lurid colours while claiming that it was only being averted with the greatest difficulty by their own tact and moderation.

Macaulay, the essayist and historian whose work probably represents "Victorianism" better than that of any other writer, fought for the bill in the House of Commons, threatening that its rejection would mean a violent revolution with "the wreck of laws, the confusion of ranks, the spoilation of property, and the dissolution of the social order"—a series of threats which he repeated with equal success in opposing the extension of the franchise to the working class a quarter of a century later.

The effect of the reform of 1832 was, of course, to place political power in the hands of the wealthy industrialists and their middle-class followers and the workingmen, whose agitation had done so much to secure its passage, found themselves in many ways worse off than before.

The most dramatic and immediate proof that the Whig industrialists were at least as indifferent to the poor man's welfare as the Tory landlords was given by the passage of the inhuman new Poor Law of 1834. The system of "outdoor relief" provided by local authorities was wasteful, often badly administered and certainly far from adequate since the scale of seven and a half gallon loaves established in 1795 as the bare minimum weekly subsistence for a family of four had, by 1831, been reduced to an allowance of five such loaves!

But it helped to keep families together since it was used to supplement subminimum wages for fathers of large families, and it enabled rural laborers to remain in their own cottages during seasons of unemployment. Most important, it was conceived as a means of keeping people alive—if barely so—rather than of starving them to death.

The new law was avowedly conceived as a means of reducing

the poor rate (taxes for relief) by making anything but death—and, not infrequently, death itself—preferable to pauperism.

Families applying for assistance were now denied it unless they entered the workhouse—their poor sticks of furniture and sometimes even their clothes were sold—husband and wife, parents and children, were deliberately separated—food allowances were reduced far below the absolute minimum of the worst of jails—and every hour of the day was systematically filled with painful, monotonous and often useless tasks.

A Methodist minister in Newcastle declared from the pulpit "Sooner than wife and husband and father and son should be sundered and dungeoned and fed on 'skillie'—sooner than wife or daughter should wear the prison dress—sooner than that—Newcastle ought to be, and should be, one blaze of fire with only one way to put it out, and that with the blood of all those who supported this measure."

In many Northern counties the people actually burned the new workhouses and in others their attacks made it impossible to build them for over ten years.

However this struggle, like the other results of the Reform Bill and the concurrent industrialization of England, carries us into the heart of the Victorian Age, the last great period of bourgeois advance, and the work of its greatest writer, Charles Dickens.

The era of middle-class prosperity, smug respectability, intense insularity and material progress which is generally suggested by the term Victorianism actually achieved near perfection during about a third of this period—that is, from the late forties to the early seventies. It was in the heart of this era (1858) that Karl Marx formulated his famous description of England as the most bourgeois of nations which was then attempting to add a bourgeois proletariat to its bourgeois middle class and bourgeois aristocracy.

But, culturally speaking, this mid-Victorian center of the age cast its shadow both before and after, and in terms of literature we may, with certain necessary modifications, treat the period as a whole.

The first thing which astonishes us when we come more closely to examine this age is the seeming paradox that almost all its leading writers—practically everyone with any claim whatsoever to real literary value—were not only severe and outspoken critics of their own time, but were applauded and, on the whole, well paid by that time for their criticism!

This is, of course, true of the famous "prophetic succession" of Carlyle, Ruskin, and, with a difference, William Morris, as well as of the apostle of culture, Matthew Arnold. It is true of the leaders of the tremendously well-publicized Oxford and pre-Raphaelite movements, both consciously movements of opposition to the spirit of their time. It is true not only of such significant novelists as Dickens, George Eliot and the Brontes, but also of the quite popular social problem fiction of writers like Kingsley, today remembered largely for his children's story *The Water Babies*, Mrs. Gaskell represented in most of our libraries solely by her charming vignette, *Cranford*, and Disraeli, now of parliamentary and imperial rather than literary fame.

The actively antireligious agnosticism of a leading scientific writer, Thomas Huxley, president of the Royal Society of Scientists and finally a member of Her Majesty's Privy Council, is almost as amazing in that churchgoing age as the achievement of George Eliot who, living a life of avowed and open "free love," was nevertheless finally visited by bishops and courted by the most respectable of publishers.

Tennyson is now generally and on the whole correctly considered the poet laureate par excellence of a conformist age. Chesterton justly remarked that "Tennyson really did hold a great many of the same views as Queen Victoria, though he was gifted with a more fortunate literary style." Yet even this poet laureate said:

> There lives more faith in honest doubt,
> Believe me, than in half your creeds.

And Thackeray, who unlike Dickens was reputed "able to draw a gentleman," drew his best ones in the satirical portraits of Vanity Fair.

Before we turn to consider more particularly these individual exceptions which almost seem, throughout the Victorian Age, to constitute themselves a rule, let us look at the general tenor of life and thought which they apparently contradict.

Perhaps the first thing that strikes us as we examine the early Victorian ideological landscape is the extraordinary extent and peculiar quality of its dominant religious attitude. This did not, as in the eighteenth century, stop short at gentlemen of fashion. The reaction against the French Revolution and its skeptical philosophers had driven even the aristocracy to see the value of religion as a bulwark against change, and as a means of teaching the lower classes to keep their place.

A clergyman in the late 1830's congratulated himself that, whereas twenty years before not one in over two hundred landed county families with whom he was acquainted had daily prayers for their households, now there was scarce one which did not do so.

Hannah More, the famous children's author who said that the chief purpose of juvenile literature should be to teach children that they were naturally depraved creatures, wrote in 1825:

> It is a singular satisfaction to me that I have lived to see such an increase of genuine religion among the higher classes of society. Mr. Wilberforce and I agree that where we knew one instance of it thirty years ago, there are now a dozen or more.

And poor Lord Melbourne, an eighteenth century survival who was Queen Victoria's first prime minister, was, during a parliamentary debate, moved to voice the shocked protest:

> No one has more respect for the Christian Religion than I have, but really, when it comes to intruding it into private life—

A little later, when reproached by an evangelical bishop for having traveled on a Sunday, he interrupted the rhetorical "You, my lord, a pillar of the Church of England" with a thoughtful "No. Not a pillar, exactly. More like a buttress—I—er—rather support it from outside."

But this wicked and refreshing lord was almost alone in his unregenerate state. Even the far from virtuous heir apparent, Prince Edward, when reproached by Bishop Porteous for his membership in a private (gambling) club which met on Sundays, bowed far enough to respectable public opinion to set its meetings thenceforth on Saturdays.

On the other hand, the lower classes, traditionally the bulwark of religious devotion, seemed in many places distressingly indifferent to their responsibilities.

The *Chambers Edinburgh Journal*, which sold for a penny and a half, and the other cheap working-class newspapers which were so popular in the late thirties and early forties—*The Northern Star, The Voice of the People, The Poor Man's Advocate, The Working*

Man's Friend—were all strongly radical in tone and recommended no books on religious subjects unless the treatment were clearly rationalist or scientific.

Charles Kingsley, writing as a Christian Socialist in his *Politics for the People*, told of visiting a working-class shop where one of the Chartist newspapers was sold and finding that "almost the only books puffed in the advertising columns of the paper were the same French dirt that lay on the counter: Voltaire's Tales, Tom Paine, and by way of a finish The Devil's Pulpit."

A little later in 1852, Florence Nightingale, a self-trained sociologist of real competence, declared after considerable investigation that "The most thinking and conscientious of the artisans have no religion at all."

If we remember Milton, Bunyan, and the other revolutionary nonconformist writers and preachers of the seventeenth century we begin to suspect that there had been a drastic change in the nature of puritanism by the time it became Victorianism, and our suspicions are, of course, quite justified.

Early Protestantism had been in many respects a hard and unlovely philosophy, but it had also been an honest and realistic one. As the religion of a still insurgent undeveloped capitalism its emphasis on self-dedication and the courage of one's convictions, its essentially democratic stress on a direct personal unmediated relationship between each individual and his god, and its requirement of an intense personal effort for salvation, had made toward a heroic if harsh way of life.

Certainly it decried the humanitarian as well as the aesthetic values, and replaced an earlier fellowship of worship where the church was the last refuge of the sinner with a competition for the few places reserved to the elect. In its most rigorous form where, as many Calvinists held, hell was necessary (if for no other reason) because "the bliss of the saved in heaven would lack something of perfection could they not hear the cries of the damned in hell," it was so clear a reflection of competitive capitalism that few of us can contemplate it without a shudder.

But its most extreme asceticism and its denial not only of sensuous pleasures but even of those of the affections had, to begin with, the saving grace of necessity. In that way, and only in that way, could the first all-important accumulations of small scale capitalism be accomplished. With all its ruthlessness and inhumanity those early capitalists had forged of their strange religion a tool for the improvement of the modes of production which would, eventually, make possible a richer more human life.

In the latter part of the eighteenth century John Wesley, the founder of Methodism and perhaps the last of the nonconformist preachers with any claim to greatness, had stated the dilemma of puritanism with an engaging candor. With an ingenuous unhistorical assumption that religion and seventeenth century Protestantism were synonymous, he said:

> I fear, wherever riches have increased, the essence of religion has decreased in the same proportion. Therefore I do not see how it is possible, in the nature of things, for any revival of true religion to continue long. For religion must necessarily produce both industry and frugality, and these cannot but produce riches. But as riches increase, so will pride, anger, and love of the world in all its branches. . . . So, although the form of religion remains, the spirit is swiftly vanishing away.

But when we come to the nineteenth century, we find that such religion had long spent its constructive force. It was no longer a way of self-discipline and asceticism for the leading elements in the bourgeoisie, but rather a way of justifying their own self-indulgence and the enforced asceticism of the working class.

The distinction between the lower middle-class nonconformist chapelgoers and the dominant evangelical trend in the Established Church, which the upper middle class supported, was, by the beginning of the Victorian Era, almost entirely a matter of social habit and preference. Not only the ideas and values but even the language and methods of tract distribution, child training, disapproval of the theatre and, to a great extent, of novels and art in general, were distressingly similar—or perhaps similarly distressing.

The dangerous but useful idea of the early Puritans that God's favor—and, therefore, the recipient's virtue—was to be judged by the worldly success with which He rewarded His worshiper's efforts had had a certain logic when such success meant largely individual influence and leadership rather than luxury and security. But as the Victorians interpreted it, the worldly prosperity itself was the only real meaning of divine election.

Reverend Sydney Smith, an educated and intelligent clergyman, commented with considerable distaste on the growing evangelical trend in 1825, saying:

It was a dangerous practise to test the merit of an individual by counting his strokes of good fortune, or to judge his demerits by the number of his misfortunes. It was dangerous because it implied that the wealthy were virtuous, the poor wicked. It fostered superstition, gave the clergy too much power, and controverted the Christian precept that man receives his retribution, not on earth, but in the life hereafter.

Here Smith has, of course, unwittingly put his finger on one of the major advantages of Evangelicalism.

For the Victorians' religion was no longer used primarily to spur themselves and others on to greater practical efforts, but rather to rationalize their brutal disregard for the hopeless misery of thousands, whom no practical efforts of their own could save from a life and death of desperate poverty.

Partly because this misery, both in the countryside and in the city slums, was greater than so many free men had ever before suffered; partly because of the increasing contrast between this destitution and the more clearly apparent possibilities of material wealth; and partly, no doubt, because it was especially difficult for a growing middle class, many of whose fortunes were only one or two generations old, to assume an inherited difference between those who had and those who had not; it had become very important to blame the poor man for his poverty and to preach the wickedness of relief.

This attitude was not the result, but the cause, of such religious beliefs. Similarly, the irreligion of the age, a similarly motivated and perverted utilitarianism, whose leading spokesman was Herbert Spencer, likewise proclaimed, without blaming God for it, that:

> There is a notion always more or less prevalent and just now vociferously expressed that all social suffering is removable and that it is the duty of somebody or other to remove it. Both these beliefs are false. To separate pain from ill-doing [i.e., misery from lack of capital] is to fight against the constitution of things and will be followed by more pain.

Whatever one may think of the ill-doing, the pain was real enough. The abolition of outdoor relief had forced increased numbers to swell the ranks of factory workers—and slum dwellers—and the conditions of life for these hundreds of thousands were truly indescribable.

The window tax, not repealed until 1851, and more fundamentally the get-rich-quick possibilities of the unregulated building which provided housing in new factory towns and the outlying districts of old cities, created slums. Neighborhoods had grown up in which tenements and hovels crowded back to back on every available inch of space. Nine out of ten rooms were absolutely without daylight.

The shortage of city water supplies, which was met by providing a single faucet for every fifteen or twenty "apartments" in which the water would be turned on for half an hour once, or at most twice, a day, made water as rare and costly a luxury as light.

Breathable air was still more unobtainable since there were literally no sanitary arrangements in such working-class districts except surface cesspools wholly inadequate to handle even the liquid waste for which they had been planned. All solid waste including "human manure" was piled up in the nearest courtyard or alley—on which perhaps forty "homes" opened—to be collected at intervals ranging from once a month to once a year by "dust collectors."

In the first quarter of the century, when cities were smaller, and the transportation of such refuse to farm sections easier, collections were often made weekly and the collector would pay the householder—or landlord—for the privilege. As conditions changed, however, he would either demand payment or wait six months or more until a large enough pile had been accumulated to make his trip worthwhile. Dickens' great novel *Our Mutual Friend* centers about a fortune made by such means.

But even these "living conditions" were not so bad as those in the innumerable cellar dwellings into which thousands upon thousands were crammed, lodging on bare earth floors continually soaked in drippings from the yard above, and often digging holes under the beds into which this matter would finally "flow" to remain until called for.

A government commission in 1845 found that in seven towns there were 67,726 people living in 14,847 such cellars. In one block in Manchester it reported there were 27 cellars discovered where seven or more people shared one bed. The average population density in 20 towns was 5,045 persons to a square mile while in a similar London slum area there were 243,000 to a square mile, and in Liverpool more than that number in an area one half that size! No wonder that a member of the health commission declared:

The annual loss of life from filth and bad ventilation is greater than the loss from death or wounds in any wars in which the country has been engaged in modern times.

To the horrors of these living conditions were, throughout the thirties and early forties, added mass unemployment and literal starvation. In Manchester alone there were over 50,000 unemployed during the summer of 1837. And although the Director of the Liverpool Workhouse certainly succeeded in his "endeavor to make the life of a pauper a life that no man would submit to unless under absolute necessity" there were, nevertheless, over 900,000 on relief as late as 1849—after the beginning of a major trade revival in 1847.

The same year saw a meeting of over 1,000 employed seamstresses in London, of whom only five had earned 6 *shillings* during the preceding week, even though all worked 18 hours a day during a 7-day week.

Terrible and widespread as these conditions were, they would certainly not have received the public attention they did, or aroused the general concern we find reflected in much of the literature of the late thirties and "hungry forties," had it not been for two facts of major importance: first, the constant fear of insurrection aroused by the militant indignation of the workers, and, second, the increasing realization that cholera and the other epidemics frequently spreading beyond the boundaries of the slums recognized no social distinctions.

In 1833 the reformed parliament had thrown an inexpensive sop to liberal sentiment by the abolition of slavery in the West Indies and the passage of some very mild factory legislation forbidding the use of children under nine in all textile mills except silk factories. The immediate result of the legislation was an influx of child labor into silk mills, as well as into the coal mines! The same bill limited the work of children under thirteen to ten hours a day, while those between thirteen and eighteen, and women, were to work no more than a thirteen-hour day.

But the workers, whose long and bitter agitation in the North had forced this minor concession, as well as the reformed parliament itself, were deeply disappointed by the considerably less than half a loaf they had won. When, in 1834, the inhuman New Poor Law (see p. 629 ff.) was passed, they, for a time, gave up what little remaining faith they had in parliamentary action and turned to seek a way out in militant trade unionism.

The "Grand National Consolidated Trades Union," with a membership of over a hundred thousand, centering largely about Manchester and Birmingham, declared in 1834:

> That although the design of the Union is, in the first instance, to raise the wages of the workmen, or prevent any further reductions therein, and to diminish the hours of labour, the great and ultimate object of it must be to establish the paramount rights of Industry and Humanity, by instituting such measures as shall effectually prevent the ignorant, idle and useless parts of Society from having that undue control over the fruits of our toil, which, through the agency of a vicious money system, they at present possess; and that, consequently, the Unionists should lose no opportunity of mutually encouraging and assisting each other in bringing about a DIFFERENT ORDER OF THINGS, in which the really useful and intelligent part of society only shall have the direction of its affairs, and in which a well-directed industry and virtue shall meet their just distinction and reward and vicious idleness its well-merited contempt and destitution.

It is no wonder that Thomas Arnold, famous headmaster of Rugby and father of the more famous Matthew Arnold, wrote to a friend in 1834: "You have heard, I doubt not, of the Trade Union; a fearful engine of mischief, ready to riot and assassinate; and I see no counteracting power."

And it tells us a good deal about the social conscience of the time that he was one of those who proposed, a few years later: "to collect information as to every point in the condition of the poor throughout the kingdom and to call public attention to it by every possible means."

Although a variety of difficulties, internal as well as external, caused the temporary collapse of revolutionary trade unionism, by 1836 the amazing working-class movement known as Chartism had arisen, and for ten years it was to terrify the English bourgeoisie into attempting, by alternate or concurrent policies of charity and intimidation, to effect its dissolution.

The six points demanded in the People's Charter—a monster petition to Parliament—seem now moderate enough democratic reforms, but as Engels declared at the time:

> Chartism is of an essentially social nature, a class movement. The "Six Points" which for the Radical Bourgeoisie are the end of the matter are for the proletariat a mere means to

further ends. "Political power our means, social happiness our end," is now the clearly formulated war-cry of the Chartists.

This war cry was subscribed to by 1,280,000 signatures, but in 1838 a parliament elected by a maximum of 839,000 voters rejected it out of hand.

A series of raids and arrests drove the movement temporarily underground—over 450 leading members had been transported or jailed by 1840—but it continued to organize and by 1842 when most of the leaders began to emerge from jail it had over forty thousand dues paying members in over four hundred local clubs!

A second petition couched in much more revolutionary language was signed by 3,315,000 men—well over half the adult male population of Great Britain in 1842.

When this too was rejected without any hearing or discussion a Trade Union Conference in Manchester almost unanimously passed the resolution:

> That it is our solemn and conscientious conviction that all the evils that afflict society, and which have prostrated the energies of the great body of the producing classes, arise solely from class legislation; and that the only remedy for the present alarming distress and widespread destitution is the immediate and unmutilated adoption and carrying into law the document known as the people's charter.
> That this meeting recommend the people of all trades and callings to forthwith cease work, until the above document becomes the law of the land.

Unfortunately there were not yet organized means to carry out such a general strike policy. Morton, in his *People's History of England,* succinctly describes the immediate outcome.

> Taken by surprise the [Chartist] Association could only recognize the strike, which spread swiftly all over Lancashire, Yorkshire, and the Midlands. London and the South, however, failed to respond. Troops were sent into the strike areas and by September a combination of repression and hunger had forced the strikers back to work. There were over 1,500 arrests, and by the end of the year the movement had once again dwindled to small proportions. A revival of trade between 1843 and 1846 came to the rescue of the authorities.

There was a third attempt in 1847 but this had none of the vitality of the two earlier ones.

The passage of the ten-hour factory bill in that year and the repeal of the Corn Laws the year before had pacified the majority of the employed workers without giving them a real sense of their strength since, ostensibly, the Tory landlords had taken the lead in the fight for factory legislation and the free trade Whig industrialists in the struggle for Corn Law Repeal.

Marx analyzing the situation in 1847 said:

> The English workers have made the English free traders realise that they are not the dupes of their illusions or of their lies; and if, in spite of this, the workers have made common cause with them against the landlords it is for the purpose of destroying the last remnants of feudalism and in order to have only one enemy to deal with. The workers have not miscalculated, for the landlords, in order to revenge themselves upon the manufacturers, have made common cause with the workers to carry the Ten Hour Bill, which the latter have been vainly demanding for thirty years, and which was passed immediately after the repeal of the Corn Laws.

But an enormous part of the Chartist membership and activity had been diverted into the well-financed and comparatively respectable fight for Corn Law Repeal; there was much disillusionment when, in many places, wages were immediately reduced to provide about as little bread at the new price as had been available at the old; and the genuine trade revival now well under way began to provide more stable remunerative occupation for the better educated, skilled operatives who had formed so important a part of the original Chartist movement. The third attempt depended very largely on a small leadership of journalists and speakers (largely arisen from the ranks of the movement itself) and on the still numerous body of the unemployed or casually employed. It rather mechanically repeated the machinery of the twice rejected petition, but this time succeeded in mustering only about one and a half million signatures and, more important, made no realistic plans for any concrete action to be taken when Parliament should again, as, of course, it did, reject the charter.

After this rather ignominious conclusion to the campaign the movement rapidly disintegrated. The revival of trade, which had already begun, continued with only minor and local interruption until late in the seventies, and their prosperity and prospects of advancement isolated the more skilled and better educated part of the working class into a sort of "aristocracy of labor" or, as Marx said, "a bourgeoisified proletariat" largely indifferent to, contemptuous of, or frightened by, their less fortunate brothers.

The bourgeoisie had also been forced, in self-defense, to improve the sanitary conditions of city slums since, as Carlyle sardonically pointed out, a poor seamstress dying of typhus had amply demonstrated her essential sisterhood with her employers by sharing her fate with five of the ladies for whom she had sewed.

It is interesting to note that just as several generations later in the United States Upton Sinclair's *Jungle*, written primarily to expose the working conditions of the foreign-born laborer, succeeded only in arousing the middle class to the need of a Pure Food and Drug Law for their own protection, so the bulk of the social problem novels of the Christian Socialists and others simply convinced the English bourgeoisie of the need for better sanitation and the importance of teaching cleanliness to the poor.

Even when the ardent young Kingsley had become a rather wistful old Tory he retained a passion for washing the poor—there is no accident in his choice of the central metaphor for the *Water Babies*. Such a verse as the following, one of the most widely taught in all the charity Sunday Schools, strikes the same note:

> Though I am but poor and mean
> I will move the rich to love me
> If I'm modest, neat, and clean
> And submit when they reprove me.
>
> The rich man in his castle,
> The poor man at his gate,
> God made them high or lowly
> And ordered their estate.

In 1851, after the opening of the great industrial exhibition by Queen Victoria's hard working consort, Prince Albert, Kingsley could complacently look back on the frightening period just safely concluded. He wrote of the preceding thirty-five years:

> Young lads believed (and not so wrongly) that the masses were their natural enemies and that they might have to fight, any year or any day, for the safety of their property and the honour of their sisters.

Perhaps before we, too, leave this period behind we should pause to consider the almost forgotten and very interesting popular verse which most immediately, directly and simply expressed the anguish of the time.

There were, of course, a number of warm-hearted and generous middle-class sympathizers of whom the best known was poor Thomas Hood. He himself was a poverty-stricken professional journalist whose ill health and heavy family responsibilities had often reduced his uncertain income to the vanishing point. His work generally consisted in light humorous verse or gossipy prose paragraphs for various periodicals, together with many other sorts of literary hack work—editing collections, writing short biographies to order, and so forth.

An occasional pun strikes a note of inspiration—as in the delightful couplet Hood wrote on the appearance of Dickens' *Pickwick Papers* immediately after his *Sketches by Boz*: "Ain't this here Boz a tip-top feller—Some folks write well but he writes Weller." But we now remember him for something very different than the best of his humor.

A poor seamstress had stolen some material worth several shillings and the judge was considering her sentence—which might, legally, have been transportation for over seven years. As a plea for mercy Hood printed his "Song of the Shirt," which not only succeeded in its immediate object but was reprinted in dozens of periodicals, issued as a broadside, and stamped on innumerable handkerchiefs, scarfs, etc. Its particular distinction was that, almost alone among a number of similar poems by different authors, it was actually learned and used by the poor, who were generally completely indifferent to the writings of their betters.

It is not great poetry any more than Thomas Hood was a great poet, but it is his best and its own simple sincerity and sympathy as well as the associations with which it has become enriched make it worth remembering. Perhaps the best stanzas are the often quoted opening one and the literally accurate fifth.

> With fingers weary and worn,
>   With eyelids heavy and red,
> A woman sat, in unwomanly rags,
>   Plying her needle and thread—
> Stitch! stitch! stitch!
>   In poverty, hunger and dirt,
> And still with a voice of dolorous pitch
>   She sang the "Song of the Shirt."

. . . . .
Work—work—work!
    My labour never flags;
And what are its wages? A bed of straw,
    A crust of bread, and rags.
That shatter'd roof, and this naked floor,
    A table, a broken chair,
And a wall so blank, my shadow I thank
    For sometimes falling there. . . .

Another similar poem which, printed in the 1843 Christmas number of *Punch*, tripled the circulation of that issue and played a part in forcing through a bill with some additional antichild-labor provisions in 1844, was Elizabeth Barrett's "The Cry of the Children." Three of its most moving stanzas read:

"For, oh," say the children, "we are weary,
    And we cannot run or leap;
If we cared for any meadows, it were merely
    To drop down in them and sleep.
Our knees tremble sorely in the stooping,
    We fall upon our faces, trying to go;
And, underneath our heavy eyelids drooping
    The reddest flower would look as pale as snow,
For, all day, we drag our burden tiring
    Through the coal-dark, underground;
Or, all day, we drive the wheels of iron
    In the factories, round and round.

For all day the wheels are droning, turning;
    Their wind comes in our faces,
Till our hearts turn, our heads with pulses burning
    And the walls turn in their places.
Turns the sky in the high window, blank and reeling,
    Turns the long light that drops adown the wall,
Turn the black flies that crawl along the ceiling;
    All are turning, all the day—and we with all.
And all day the iron wheels are droning,
    And sometimes we could pray,
"O ye wheels" (breaking out in a mad moaning),
"Stop! be silent for today!"

Aye, be silent! Let them hear each other breathing
    For a moment, mouth to mouth!
Let them touch each other's hands, in a fresh wreathing
    Of their tender human youth!
Let them feel that this cold metallic motion
    Is not all the life God fashions or reveals;

> Let them prove their living souls against the notion
> That they live in you, or under you, O wheels!
> Still, all day, the iron wheels go onward,
> Grinding life down from its mark;
> And the children's souls, which God is calling sunward,
> Spin on blindly in the dark.

Of even more interest, however, are the poems—or, rather songs, for they were generally set to marches and old Methodist hymn tunes—written by the working-class trade unionists, Chartists, and anti-Corn Law agitators of the thirties and forties.

These verses obviously arose out of the immediate situation and often merely adapted or parodied existing songs of a popular religious or patriotic nature. It is significant that, while Victorian poetry as a whole was not profoundly influenced by its great English predecessors these men, when they read, read primarily the great romantic and revolutionary poets of their nation. For example, Samuel Bamford, a self-educated workman exclaims in his autobiographical *Passages in the Life of a Radical:* "Oh! John Milton! John Milton! of all the poetry ever read or heard recited by me, none has spoke out the whole feelings of my heart as have certain passages of thy divine minstrelsy!"

And Thomas Frost, a Chartist leader, testified "the poetry of Coleridge and Shelley was stirring within me and making me a Chartist and more."

One of the most consistent and popular of these people's poets was Ebenezer Elliott, who signed himself C.L.R. (Corn Law Rhymer) and said "I have won my name as 'Rhymer of the Revolution' and am prouder of that distinction than I should be if I were made Poet Laureate of England." His "Jacobin's Prayer," first published in 1831, was reprinted innumerable times. It begins:

> Avenge the plundered poor, O Lord!
> But not with fire, but not with sword—
> Not as at Peterloo they died
> Beneath the hoofs of coward pride;
> Avenge our rags, our chains, our sighs,
> The famine in our children's eyes—.

Another of his very popular songs called "The People's Anthem" reads in part:

When wilt thou save the people?
O God of mercy! when?
Not kings and lords, but nations!
Not thrones and crowns, but men!
Flowers of thy heart, O God, are they!
Let them not pass, like weeds, away!
Their heritage a sunless day!
    God save the people!

Shall crime bring crime for ever,
Strength aiding still the strong?
Is it thy will, O Father!
That man shall toil for wrong?
"No!" say thy mountains; "No!" thy skies;
"Man's clouded sun shall brightly rise,
And songs be heard instead of sighs."
    God save the people!

W. J. Linton, a well-known "agitator" who was active in the distribution of "The Poor Man's Guardian" from 1831 until his death some ten years later, often signed his contributions to that and other similar periodicals "Spartacus." One of his most effective poems, printed over that signature, was "Blade-Time Will Come":

Be patient, O be patient! Put your ear against the earth;
Listen there how noiselessly the germ of the seed has birth;
How noiselessly and gently it upheaves its little way
Till it parts the scarcely-broken ground, and the blade stands
    up in the day!

Be patient, O be patient! the germs of mighty thought
Must have their silent undergrowth, must underground be
    wrought;
But, as sure as ever there's a Power that makes the grass appear,
Our land shall be green with Liberty, the blade-time shall be
    here.

Be patient, O be patient! go and watch the wheat-ears grow,
So imperceptibly that ye can mark nor change nor throe:
Day after day, day after day, till the ear is fully grown;
And then again day after day till the ripened field is brown.

Be patient, O be patient! though yet our hopes are green,
The harvest-field of Freedom shall be crowned with the sunny
    sheen;
Be ripening, be ripening! mature your silent way
Till the whole broad land is tongued with fire on Freedom's
    harvest-day!

A more musical poet was John Bramwich, a stocking weaver and staunch unionist whose songs, set to hymn tunes, were sung at huge meetings throughout the north of England. His "Britannian's Sons," set to the tune of the "New Crucifixion" was sung at his own funeral when he died, worn out by hard work and want, in 1846:

> Britannia's sons, though slaves ye be,
> God, your Creator, made you free;
> He life and thought and being gave,
> But never, never made a slave!
>
> His works are wonderful to see,
> All, all proclaim the Deity;
> He made the earth, and formed the wave,
> But never, never made a slave!
>
> He made the sky with spangles bright,
> The moon to shine by silent night;
> The sun—and spread the vast concave,
> But never, never made a slave!
>
> The verdant earth, on which we tread,
> Was by His hands all carpeted;
> Enough for all He freely gave,
> But never, never made a slave!
>
> All men are equal in His sight,
> The bond, the free, the black, the white:
> He made them all, then freedom gave;
> God made the man—Man made the slave.

Another prolific and popular people's laureate was Ernest Jones, outstanding among the younger Chartist leaders in the late forties. His verses are generally satirical and often, underneath their obvious parody of contemporary material, make oblique reference to, or indirectly quote, some of the great romantic writers. The "Song of the 'Lower Classes'" below is probably influenced by Keats' "Isabella" (p. 561) as well as by Shelley.

> We plow and sow, we're so very very low,
>   That we delve in the dirty clay;
> Till we bless the plain with the golden grain,
>   And the vale with the fragrant hay.
> Our place we know, we're so very very low,
>   'Tis down at the landlord's feet:
> We're not too low the grain to grow,
>   But too low the bread eat.

Down, down we go, we're so very very low,
   To the hell of the deep-sunk mines;
But we gather the proudest gems that glow,
   When the crown of the despot shines;
And whene'er he lacks, upon our backs
   Fresh loads he deigns to lay;
We're far too low to vote the tax,
   But not too low to pay.

We're low, we're low—we're very very low—
   And yet from our fingers glide
The silken flow and the robes that glow
   Round the limbs of the sons of pride;
And what we get, and what we give,
   We know, and we know our share;
We're not too low the cloth to weave,
   But too low the cloth to wear.

We're low, we're low, we're very very low,
   And yet when the trumpets ring,
The thrust of a poor man's arm will go
   Through the heart of the proudest king.
We're low, we're low—mere rabble, we know—
   We're only the rank and file;
We're not too low to kill the foe,
   But too low to share the spoil.

The "Song of the Wage Slave" is clearly indebted, as so much of English working class poetry was, to Shelley's "Men of England" (see pp. 543-4).

   The land it is the landlord's,
      The trader's is the sea,
   The ore the usurer's coffer fills—
      But what remains for me?
   The engine whirls for master's craft;
      The steel shines to defend,
   With labour's arms, what labour raised,
      For labour's foes to spend.

   I pay for all their learning,
      I toil for all their ease;
   They render back, in coin for coin,
      Want, ignorance, disease:
   Toil, toil—and than a cheerless home,
      Where hungry passions cross;
   Eternal gain to them that give
      To me eternal loss!

> The hour of leisured happiness
> The rich alone may see;
> The playful child, the smiling wife—
> But what remains for me?
>
> They render back, those rich men,
> A pauper's niggard fee,
> Mayhap a prison—then a grave,
> And think they're quits with me;
> But not a fond wife's heart that breaks,
> A poor man's child that dies,
> We score not on our hollow cheeks
> And in our sunken eyes;
> We read it there, where'er we meet,
> And as the sum we see,
> Each asks, "The rich have got the earth,
> And what remains for me?"
>
> We bear the wrong in silence,
> We store it in our brain;
> They think us dull, they think us dead,
> But we shall rise again:
> A trumpet through the lands will ring;
> A heaving through the mass;
> A trampling through their palaces
> Until they break like glass:
> We'll cease to weep by cherished graves,
> From lonely homes we'll flee;
> And still, as rolls our million march,
> Its watchword brave shall be—
> The coming hope, the future day,
> When wrong to right shall bow,
> And hearts that have the courage, man,
> To make the future *now*.

Thomas Cooper, often referred to as "the last of the Chartists," who had spoken at Bramwich's funeral, himself created several similar hymns of revolution, including this one written in jail:

> God of the earth, and sea, and sky,
> To Thee Thy mournful children cry;
> Didst Thou the blue that bends o'er all
> Spread for a general funeral pall?
>
> Sadness and gloom pervade the land;
> Death—famine—glare on either hand;
> Didst Thou plant earth upon the wave
> Only to form one general grave?

Finally, to represent the miners or colliers, as they were more frequently called, we must include the well-known "A Grand Time Comin'" by their best known singer, J. P. Robson.

> There's a grand time comin', lads,
> A grand time comin';
> When collier laddies needn't fret,
> For landlords will our rents forget,
> I' the grand time comin'.
> No man shall ax us for his brass,
> But myek our cubbords stranger;
> Then corn shall be as cheap as grass,
>   Wait a wee bit langer!
>
> There's a grand time comin', lads,
> A grand time comin';
> There's a grand time comin', lads,
>   Wait a wee bit langer.
>
> There's a grand time comin', lads,
> A stunnin' time comin':
> A level's sure to come or nowt,
> Smash, then we'll get what lang we've sowt,
> I' the grand time comin'.
> Maisters then will hae to put,
> Nyen need fear thor anger;
> Viewer's sons our traps 'll shut,
>   Wait a wee bit langer.

These men were not great poets. There was no Burns or Blake or Bunyan among them. A literary critic might well question their right to claim the title of poet on any terms. But, as Keats said:

> Who alive can say,
> "Thou art no Poet—mayst not tell thy dreams."
> Since every man whose soul is not a clod
> Hath visions and would speak, if he had loved,
> And been well nurtured in his mother tongue.

From an age which gave us little or no great poetry, although it has left us more than enough of skillful verse, it is worth preserving these fragments of a heartfelt popular poetry with all their serious limitations.

Since there were literally thousands of pages of poetry not only printed but bought, paid for, and, presumably, read, during the Victorian Age it may seem perverse for us to date the at least temporary decline of English poetry, of which our time unhappily affords unmistakable evidence, from that earlier period.

But if we examine afresh even the most admired of the prolific Victorian poets—Tennyson, Arnold, the Rossettis, Swinburne, the Brownings, Edward Fitzgerald—we find that rarely if ever, in their long writing lives, do they reach the profound significance or emotional intensity achieved, in such varied ways, by Shakespeare, Milton, Burns, Blake, Wordsworth, Coleridge, Byron, Shelley and Keats, to name only those of the great poets whose work has been included in these pages.

There probably was never a more skillful musician in verse than Tennyson or, at his best, Swinburne.

No one has ever painted more brilliant word miniatures than Rossetti, who so long preceded the short-lived twentieth century imagist movement.

Few love poems have been so close to so many people as the sonnets of Elizabeth Barrett Browning (see pp. 665-6). There is an almost unmatched fragile lyric beauty in the best of Christina Rossetti.

The sad wit and felicitous phrasing of Fitzgerald's *Rubaiyat* have been quoted by hundreds of thousands who knew little of any poetry—even the poetry they were quoting.

It is difficult to overestimate the virtuosity Robert Browning displayed as a dramatic poet in a period without a drama and a psychologist, before that science had a name (see pp. 661-2).

But not only did such achievements represent (except, perhaps, in Browning's case) only an infinitesmal part of their writer's work; even more important is the fact that the achievements themselves seem somewhat peripheral—somehow lacking in relationship to the central significance, the fundamental meaning, of their author's own experience.

Is is seldom indeed that even one who knows and enjoys the best of Victorian poetry finds himself turning to it for comfort or courage or illumination in a moment of anguish or a period of crisis.

Any real examination of the poetry of the period certainly dispels the impression that it was all "sweetness and light," and yet even the most prolonged and apparently searching debate, as in Tennyson's *In Memoriam*, seems finally to resolve itself into much ado about nothing that really matters—nothing, that is, which would make any difference in the way anyone would actually live his life.

Poetry was no longer a major art intended to change the world. It was an increasingly limited craft which might occasionally touch on the more serious problems that troubled those below the surface, but its essential concern was with the purely personal or "spiritual" difficulties of the author and his peers—such "luxury problems" as shades of religious belief, the conflict between faith and science, and others whose resolution might affect thought but could not affect action. A later poet, since lost at the end of the same road, once pithily summarized such a life of cultured leisure and factitious conflict in the few lines:

> The creepered wall stands up to hide
> The gathering multitude outside
> Whose glances hunger worsens;
> Concealing from their wretchedness
> Our metaphysical distress,
> Our kindness to ten persons.

It is true that most of the Victorian poets, like all the major prose writers of the time, still thought of themselves as inhabiting the rostrum rather than a garret and had, as yet, no notion of retiring from the exclusive groves of the academy to the solitary confinement of an ivory tower.

But their message was increasingly a support, whether direct or diversionary, of the status quo, with a growing emphasis on those higher things which were unaffected by—and could, therefore, not affect—the material circumstances of existence. Even the well-trained poet laureate in the course of his most serious long poem lets us catch a glimpse of the role art was beginning to play when he says:

> But for the unquiet heart and mind
> A use in measured language lies—
> The dull mechanic exercise
> Like some narcotic numbing pain.

Was there ever a more fantastic perversion than that which called on the resources of poetry to deaden feeling and obscure thought? Yet this perversion was, by the end of the era, so generally accepted that not only a conservative like Tennyson, but also an active socialist like William Morris, who later devoted his prose writing and street corner speaking to politics, could consider rhyming as a sort of therapeutic activity and begin his best known series of long narrative poems—*The Earthly Paradise*—with the declaration:

> Of heaven or hell I have no power to sing,
> I cannot ease the burden of your fears,
> Or make quick-coming death a little thing,
> Or bring again the pleasure of past years,
> Nor for my words shall ye forget your tears,
> Or hope again for aught that I can say—
> The idle singer of an empty day.
> . . . .
> The heavy trouble, the bewildering care
> That weighs us down who live and earn our bread,
> These idle verses have no power to bear;
> So let me sing of names remembered,
> Because they, living not, can ne'er be dead,
> Or long time take their memory quite away
> From us poor singers of an empty day.
>
> Dreamer of dreams, born out of my due time,
> Why should I strive to set the crooked straight?
> Let it suffice me that my murmuring rhyme
> Beats with light wing against the ivory gate,
> Telling a tale not too importunate
> To those who in the sleepy region stay,
> Lulled by the singer of an empty day.

Perhaps a partial exception should be made of Robert Browning who realized in an extremely interesting poetic form—or, rather, series of experimental forms—many of the values of the prose writers of his time, as well as most of those developed by the poets who came after him.

He never really comes to grips with the essential questions of his age as do Dickens, George Eliot and Thomas Huxley—he never, as a matter of fact, even recognizes those questions as clearly as do Carlyle, Ruskin or, of course, Morris—yet his genuinely democratic attitude, his lively interest in and fraternal sympathy with all kinds of human beings, his sane un-Victorian feelings for the healthy enjoyment of every sort of sensory, aesthetic, and intellectual experience, and, most unusual, his genuine respect for women as equals in work, play and love, all set him apart from the poets of his time if they do not quite entitle him to the company of his greater predecessors.

It is certainly no accident that he, almost alone in his age, rediscovered Shelley (see p. 669), wrote about Keats, and understood the real meaning of Wordsworth's apostacy (see pp. 658-9).

Robert Browning—1812–1889

Robert Browning's life falls almost absurdly into the pattern of all good fairy tales.

His father and mother were exceptionally wise, kind and loving; and his extraordinary love affair with an adored, adoring and brilliant woman whom he rescued from the clutches of a monster, was truly the center of his life. Even if he and his wife "lived happily ever after" for only fifteen years, yet in the very best of fairy tale traditions she left him a charming, intelligent young son to educate, friends and a devoted sister with whom to live, creative work to complete, a growing though belated fame to enjoy, and even a belief in some sort of reunion after death, to solace his loneliness.

It is no wonder that Browning is preeminently the poet of happy healthy energetic youth, not only in his vital and realistic love lyrics but also in his lively sense of humor, his quick interest in all kinds of people, his warm sympathy for the individual rebel or victim of tyranny, and, above all, in his devouring intellectual curiosity and insatiable appetite for every sort of aesthetic experience.

He has everything except that final power which, as Keats said, belongs to the "miserable and mighty poets of the human heart" to whom "the misery of humanity is misery and will not let them rest," or to those who, as Shakespeare said, can "feel the future in the instant."

Browning's father (also Robert Browning) had inherited some interest in a large plantation in the West Indies belonging to his deceased mother's family, and when he was nineteen his father arranged for him to take up a managerial position there. The young man was so outraged by his first glimpse of slavery that as Browning years later wrote his fiancée, he (Robert Browning Sr.):

> . . . conceived such a hatred of the slave system . . . that he relinquished every prospect—supported himself, while there,

in some other capacity, and came back, while yet a boy, to his father's profound astonishment and rage—one proof of which was, that when he heard that his son was a suitor to *her*, my mother—he benevolently waited on her uncle to assure him that his niece would be thrown away on a man so evidently born to be hanged!—those were his words. My father on his return had the intention of devoting himself to art, for which he had many qualifications and abundant love—but the quarrel with his father,—who had married again and continued to hate him till a few years before his death,—induced him to go at once and consume his life after a fashion he always detested.

The grandfather added a touch of originality to this disinheritance by sending the young man a bill for the full cost of his wasted upbringing, including the expenses incurred at his birth! The disinherited son soon secured a position in the Bank of England. Here he remained seventeen years longer than Lamb's thirty-three before happily retiring, at seventy, to fifteen years of active leisure. Although he never felt any real interest in his commercial career the work was evidently far easier and less painful for him than it had been for Lamb, his hours were short, and promotions were regular and remunerative.

He married, at twenty-nine, a very gently serious young Scotswoman whose German father had given her a small competence as well as an excellent musical education. She was a member of a rather liberal nonconformist sect which he joined, and to which both belonged for the rest of their lives.

When he was thirty-two his only son, our Robert Browning, was born in a very pleasant suburban home in Cambervell and two years later the birth of a daughter, Sarianna, completed the happy family.

Robert Browning was educated almost entirely at home, with brief and unimportant intervals of attendance at private day school. His mother taught him music, arithmetic and gardening and his father, who was not only an amateur of the arts but also a self-taught scholar of real ability, gave him an excellent introduction to the classics and a then far more unusual informed interest in the works of medieval writers, of Italian renaissance poets, scientists and statesmen, and eighteenth century English literature.

Browning in his last book of poetry, published when he was 77, gives us a delightful picture of his education, beginning:

My Father was a scholar, and knew Greek.
When I was five years old, I asked him once,
"What do you read about?" "The siege of Troy."
"What is a siege and what is Troy?" Whereat
He piled up chairs and tables for a town,
Set me atop for Priam, called our cat
—Helen, enticed away from home (he said).
By wicked Paris, who couched somewhere close
Under the footstool, being cowardly,
But whom, since she was worth the pains, poor puss—
Towser and Tray,—our dogs, the Atreidoi,—sought
By taking Troy to get possession of

. . . .
This taught me who was who and what was what:
So far I rightly understood the case
At five years old; a huge delight it proved
And still proves—thanks to the instructor sage,
My Father. . . .
It happened, two or three years afterward,
That—I and playmates playing at Troy's seige
My Father came upon our make-believe
"How would you like to read yourself the tale
Properly told, of which I gave you first
Merely such notion as a boy could bear?
Pope, now, would give you the precise account
Of what, some day, by dint of scholarship,
You'll hear—who knows?—from Homer's very mouth.

. . . .
Time passed, I ripened somewhat; one fine day,
"Quite ready for the Iliad, nothing less?
There's Homer where the big books block the shelf:
Don't skip a word, thumb well the Lexicon!"

To this literary background Browning himself early added a passionate admiration for Byron and although his father much preferred Pope he was so impressed with a series of Byronic juvenilia his son wrote at twelve that he attempted to find a publisher for them.

At fourteen or fifteen Browning picked up in a second-hand bookstore a volume ticketed "Mr. Shelley's Atheistic Poems." This became—and remained—the god of his idolatry and his tolerant mother, despite her sincere religious beliefs, searched far and wide to find someone who could tell her who "Mr. Shelley" was, and triumphantly presented Robert with two more volumes of his work. She also, later, procured for him several collections of poems by a Mr. Keats, an even more completely obscure figure in the late 1820's.

Browning who, at fifteen, had fencing, boxing, riding, dancing, Italian, French and music tutors to occupy his attention was nevertheless so deeply affected by Shelley that he became for about two years a "practising vegetarian and professing atheist," but seemed to give one belief up as easily as the other and to revert to a modified deistic form of his family's unobtrusive faith, as well as to their diet, with no particular pain.

His first poem, a long youthful philosophical monologue *Pauline* was published at his family's expense in 1833, as were his next two volumes.

He was at this time, according to all accounts, an extraordinarily charming, attractive and friendly young man looking, said the famous actor Macready, "more like a youthful poet than any man I ever saw" and, as the daughter of a friend particularized: "He was then slim and dark, and very handsome; and—may I hint it—just a trifle of a dandy, addicted to lemon-coloured kid gloves and such things."

He was also enormously and quite unself-consciously learned, assuming that everyone had as prodigious a memory, as wide a background of varied reading, and as keen a delight in literature, music, and painting as he himself did.

A short visit to St. Petersburg as the nominal secretary of the Russian Consul General who had been much impressed with him at a dinner party; the production of a succes d'éstime in a poetic drama *Strafford*, produced by Macready; the publication of two more long and difficult philosophic poems, *Paracelsus* and *Sordello;* and a thrilling first visit to Italy; filled the next few years with pleasure and promise if no recognized major achievement.

Since it is possible that Browning's absorbing love and the fifteen year expatriate life in Italy which was its result were at least partly responsible for his curious detachment from those social questions that, whatever side they took, agitated most English writers during the next twenty years, we should stop here to see what hints *Strafford* and *Sordello*—written simultaneously—can give us as to Browning's political opinions or interests before he met Elizabeth Barrett. She was herself always very much interested in political questions from a radical point of view.

Strafford was written at Macready's request for a play, but the choice of subject was entirely Browning's and the actor indicated that he thought it was perhaps too political.

The central figure is Charles I's prime minister and the play revolves around the conflict between him and the leader of the parliamentary party, Pym. While Browning shows much sympathy for Strafford and portrays him as motivated entirely by his overwhelming loyalty to his royal master, there is no question as to the justice of Pym's cause or the necessity of Strafford's execution.

Such a summary of the action might lead one to think that the historical conflict had been suggested to Browning by the contemporary struggle for a reformed parliament but a careful study of the play does not indicate any such implicit reference to a parallel. Actually, despite misleading superficial resemblances, there was no such parallel. We have already seen the meaninglessness of the reform in terms of the fundamental conflicts of the nineteenth century. It merely made less ambiguous the relation of the already dominant bourgeoisie to the landed aristocracy, whereas the real struggle had now shifted its ground to the opposition between the proletariat (rural as well as urban) and the bourgeoisie.

There is in *Sordello,* to the writing of which Browning gave much more prolonged and concentrated thought, some indication that his indifference to the parliamentary struggles between Whigs and Tories was a conscious rejection of their essential insignificance. This indifference he later found no difficulty in continuing, but there is also in the early work just a hint of his recognition of some subterranean struggles more fundamental than those rejected, and this insight we do not, later, find Browning develop.

Sordello, the hero, is placed at the end of the thirteenth century when the struggles of the Guelphs and the Ghibellines (which exiled Dante) were convulsing Rome. He attempts to decide whether the Pope's or the Emperor's party will better serve the people and muses:

> Two parties take the world up, and allow
> No third, yet have one principle, subsist
> By the same injustice; whoso shall enlist
> With either ranks with man's inveterate foes.
> So there is one less quarrel to compose
> The Guelf, the Ghibelline may be to curse—
> I have done nothing, but both sides do worse
> than nothing. Nay, to me, forgotten, reft

Of insight, lapped by trees and flowers, was left
The notion of a service—ha? What lured
Me here, what mighty aim was I assured
Must move Taurello? What if there remained
A cause, intact, distinct from these, ordained
For me its true discoverer?

But Sordello dies at the end of the poem, having asserted nothing but his integrity, and Browning explores his discovery no further.

This is, of course, not to say that Browning did not often take a public stand—and sometimes even write a poem—on political questions.

In 1845, when Wordsworth accepted the poet laureateship Browning most powerfully expressed his belief in the progressive nature of art in his famous "Lost Leader." When directly questioned he said that although this poem was not intended as a literal portrait of Wordsworth it had been suggested by his desertion of the progressive principles of his youth, and by his subsequent career. The poem below should be compared with Shelley's more personal sonnet on the same subject addressed to the younger Wordsworth almost half a century before (see pp. 421-2).

Just for a handful of silver he left us,
    Just for a riband to stick in his coat—
Found the one gift of which fortune bereft us,
    Lost all the others she lets us devote;
They, with the gold to give, doled him out silver,
    So much was theirs who so little allowed:
How all our copper had gone for his service!
    Rags—were they purple, his heart had been proud!
We that had loved him so, followed him, honored him,
    Lived in his mild and magnificent eye,
Learned his great language, caught his clear accents,
    Made him our pattern to live and to die!
Shakespeare was of us, Milton was for us,
    Burns, Shelley, were with us,—they watch from their
        graves!
He alone breaks from the van and the freemen,
    He alone sinks to the rear and the slaves!

We shall march prospering,—not thro' his presence;
    Songs may inspirit us,—not from his lyre;
Deeds will be done,—while he boasts his quiescence,
    Still bidding crouch whom the rest bade aspire:
Blot out his name, then, record one lost soul more,

One task more declined, one more footpath untrod,
One more devil's-triumph and sorrow for angels,
One wrong more to man, one more insult to God!
Life's night begins: let him never come back to us!
There would be doubt, hesitation and pain,
Forced praise on our part—the glimmer of twilight,
Never glad confident morning again!
Best fight on well, for we taught him—strike gallantly,
Menace our heart ere we master his own;
Then let him receive the new knowledge and wait us,
Pardoned in heaven, the first by the throne!

The same volume of *Dramatic Romances and Lyrics* contained "The Italian In England," an absorbing long poem in which the speaker, a revolutionary exile, tells of the way he escaped. The major part of his story centers about a young peasant woman. He had intended to bribe or trick her into assisting him.

But when I saw that woman's face,
Its calm simplicity of grace,
Our Italy's own attitude
In which she walked thus far, and stood,
Planting each naked foot so firm,
To crush the snake and spare the worm—
At first sight of her eye, I said,
"I am that man upon whose head
They fix the price, because I hate
The Austrians over us:

In 1846 his Englishman in Italy angrily comments:

Fortuna, in my England at home,
Men meet gravely to-day
And debate, if abolishing Corn Laws
Be righteous and wise—
If 't were proper Scirocco should vanish
In black from the skies!

Throughout his life he was a steady opponent of slavery in the United States and a supporter of Jewish emancipation in England, democracy in France and unification and independence for Italy. In his seventies he answered a question as to his political beliefs by writing "Why I Am a Liberal" for newspaper publication (1885).

"Why?" Because all I haply can and do,
All that I am now, all I hope to be,—

> Whence comes it save from fortune setting free
> Body and soul the purpose to pursue,
> God traced for both? If fetters, not a few,
> Of prejudice, convention, fall from me,
> These shall I bid men—each in his degree
> Also God-guided—bear, and gayly too?
>
> But little do or can the best of us:
> That little is achieved through Liberty.
> Who, then, dares hold, emancipated thus,
> His fellow shall continue bound? Not I,
> Who live, love, labor freely, nor discuss
> A brother's right to freedom. That is "Why."

But he never appears stirred by, or even deeply aware of, any disabilities save legal ones; the economic struggles fundamental to his time seem not really to have reached him; and in the true tradition of middle-class liberalism it is the freedom of the individual from the shackles of priest, king or lord, rather than his right to share with his fellows what was formerly their power, which concerns Browning. Nowhere does he show any awareness of economic problems either in Italy or England, and his attitude is the traditional liberal one which jealously guards the liberty and independence of the individual—his right to freedom of speech and personal action—against any formal legal encroachment, without even noticing the more subtle and pervasive coercion of material necessities. Most of the individual "cases of conscience" he explores are those of cultivated and articulate men not overconcerned with the necessities of material life; and many are explicitly Renaissance figures, as if Browning were half consciously returning to the time for which his individualistic humanism was an adequate and progressive philosophy of life.

The only concrete contemporary social problem with which Browning is deeply concerned is the equality of woman. This is no accident. The problem of woman's position in a bourgeois society is one which can be fruitfully dealt with by an intelligent and sympathetic writer even if his knowledge is largely limited to middle-class relationships. Ibsen's social drama, for example, comes nearest to real understanding and a still valid insight precisely in those plays of his which center in "the woman question."

Nor should we underestimate the importance of Browning's progressive attitude here. Honest thought on this matter was certainly a major Victorian lack, as we shall see in more detail when we come to discuss the work of George Eliot and other important nineteenth century woman writers. Because of his serious independent thought on the question, Browning was able to create a galaxy of living heroines and a series of vivid personal love relationships unequaled in poetry since Shakespeare's time.

Several of these appear in "Pippa Passes," his first successful work (poetically, not financially speaking) which was published in 1841 under the title of *Bells and Pomegranates*. In 1842 an even more impressive group of poems appeared under the same general title as *Dramatic Lyrics*.

Much of Browning's most successful work was done in the form of the Dramatic Monologue which he really originated. One of the best of these is "My Last Duchess," the famous early example given below. Here one can easily visualize the imperious Renaissance figure of the Duke, his great art gallery, and the Count's envoy come to arrange a second marriage. Although the Duke is the only speaker we are led, by his own arrogant condemnation, to sympathize with his former wife's democratic love of life, and his very protestations of indifference show us how much more his dead wife's picture means to him than any other work of art.

>That's my last Duchess painted on the wall,
>Looking as if she were alive. I call
>   That piece a wonder, now: Frà Pandolf's hands
>Worked busily a day, and there she stands.
>Will't please you sit and look at her? I said
>"Frà Pandolf" by design, for never read
>Strangers like you that pictured countenance,
>The depth and passion of its earnest glance,
>But to myself they turned (since none puts by
>The curtain I have drawn for you, but I)
>And seemed as they would ask me, if they durst,
>How such a glance came there; so, not the first
>Are you to turn and ask thus. Sir 'twas not
>Her husband's presence only, called that spot
>Of joy into the Duchess' cheek: perhaps
>Frà Pandolf chanced to say "Her mantle laps
>Over my lady's wrist too much," or "Paint
>Must never hope to reproduce the faint
>Half-flush that dies along her throat:" such stuff
>Was courtesy, she thought, and cause enough
>For calling up that spot of joy. She had
>A heart—how shall I say?—too soon made glad,
>Too easily impressed; she liked whate'er
>She looked on, and her looks went everywhere.

> Sir, 'twas all one! My favor at her breast,
> The drooping of the daylight in the West,
> The bough of cherries some officious fool
> Broke in the orchard for her, the white mule
> She rode with round the terrace—all and each
> Would draw from her alike the approving speech,
> Or blush, at least. She thanked men,—good! but thanked
> Somehow—I know not how—as if she ranked
> My gift of a nine-hundred-years-old name
> With anybody's gift. Who'd stoop to blame
> This sort of trifling? Even had you skill
> In speech—(which I have not)—to make your will
> Quite clear to such an one, and say, "Just this
> Or that in you disgusts me; here you miss,
> Or there exceed the mark"—and if she let
> Herself be lessoned so, nor plainly set
> Her wits to yours, forsooth, and made excuse,
> —E'en then would be some stooping; and I choose
> Never to stoop. Oh sir, she smiled, no doubt,
> Whene'er I passed her; but who passed without
> Much the same smile? This grew; I gave commands;
> Then all smiles stopped together. There she stands
> As if alive. Will't please you rise? We'll meet
> The company below, then. I repeat,
> The Count your master's known munificence
> Is ample warrant that no just pretence
> Of mine for dowry will be disallowed;
> Though his fair daughter's self, as I avowed
> At starting, is my object. Nay, we'll go
> Together down, sir. Notice Neptune, though,
> Taming a sea-horse, thought a rarity,
> Which Claus of Innsbruck cast in bronze for me!

These works were completed before Robert Browning met Elizabeth Barrett. After their marriage Mrs. Browning's active concern with woman's attempt to achieve freedom and equality always had her husband's sincere respect and warmest cooperation. Her attitude is further discussed in the chapter on George Eliot and other Victorian woman writers (see p. 752 ff.).

Browning's early books were rather unkindly and very imperceptively treated by the critics, and a much better known poet, Elizabeth Barrett, who had already, in a private letter to a friend, expressed her great admiration of *Paracelsus*, now wrote an indignant note to the editor of the *Atheneum* declaring "it is easier to find a more faultless writer than a poet of equal genius."

Browning had before read some of her poetry with great enthusiasm and was now interested enough to ask a classmate of his father's who was a distant relative of hers, what Miss Barrett was like. He learned that she was a delightful but very shy woman, no longer quite young, a bed-ridden invalid who received very few friends, a great scholar who read Hebrew as well as Greek and Latin, and a poet since the age of twelve.

Despite much social activity and wide personal popularity Browning was, at the age of thirty, still heart whole and fancy free.

Perhaps partly for this reason the warm, courageous, sympathetic, beauty loving personality which almost all of Elizabeth Barrett's poetry reveals, even when it is weakened by overwriting or some monotony of rhythm, made an extraordinary impression on Browning, and he tried unsuccessfully through his friend, Kenyon, to meet the author. For the time being this was the end of the matter but in 1844, on his return from a second trip to Italy, he found two more volumes which she had just published.

In these were not only a number of poems like *The Cry of the Children* (see pp. 643-4) but also, in a discussion of contemporary poets, the lines:

> Or from Browning some pomegranate which, if cut deep down
>   the middle,
> Shews a heart within blood-tinctured of a veined humanity.

He was, naturally, encouraged to write a note of gratitude telling her how much he liked her poetry and just hinting a wish that he be permitted to meet her.

His letter dated January 10, 1845 begins, "I love your verses with all my heart, dear Miss Barrett, "and three paragraphs later continues, "I do, as I say, love these books with all my heart—and I love you too."

Her reply opens, "Such a letter from such a hand!" and continues: "Sympathy is dear, very dear to me; but the sympathy of a poet, and of such a poet, is the quintessence of sympathy for me." She explains that she is too much of an invalid to receive company— that perhaps, if all goes unusually well with her health there may possibly be some opportunity for a meeting late in spring—and concludes with an invitation to occasional correspondence on literary matters.

Browning's reply is, as we should expect, still warmer and the letters continue with increasing frequency until a letter dated "February" begins "Spring is here! the birds know it. 'I shall see you, I say!"

Finally in May he is permitted to pay his first visit and immediately on returning home startles and alarms Elizabeth by writing a proposal of marriage. There was some cause for her amazement, and perhaps even for alarm.

Elizabeth Barrett was, in 1845, a woman of thirty-nine and had been a semi-invalid since a fall from horseback just after her fifteenth birthday. She had hardly left her room for over ten years and no longer made the passage from bed to sofa unassisted. Browning then thought, as did most people, that she suffered from some incurable spinal affection. Actually, while she did suffer from a comparatively slight affection of one lung, the real cause of her invalidism was a father straight out of the most incredible of bad melodramas. He enjoyed presiding over a prolonged deathbed and would generally visit his favorite daughter at eleven or twelve at night to pray with her for her fortunes in the next world. While Elizabeth furnished the best, she did not by any means provide the only, field for his talents. He refused to allow not only his two healthy younger daughters but also his seven grownup sons to think of marriage and, later, refused ever to speak to the three children who married during his lifetime! He had never resigned himself to the emancipation of the slaves which had reduced him from an extremely wealthy to a very well-to-do absentee owner of a Jamaica plantation, and was determined that if his slaves were no longer absolutely at his disposal, as the Bible said they should be, his children would at least always remain so.

His one domestic virtue was that he always left the house by ten in the morning and almost never returned before six at night.

The brothers and sisters evidently made common cause in evading, since they dared not oppose, his tyranny; and even though Elizabeth loved him and had rarely in her invalid life had occasion to disobey him, we see quite early in her correspondence with Browning that she possessed a surprising impersonal understanding of the situation.

She wrote of her mother, who had died years before, "We lost more in her than she lost in life. . . . One of those women who can never resist; . . ." That Elizabeth herself could resist was not only to be proven in her escape with Browning. Her poetry gives ample evidence of her outspoken expression of views which could not have met with her father's approval and an early note to a friend dated

May 17, 1833, reads, "Of course you know that the late Bill has ruined the West Indians. That is settled. The consternation here is very great. Nevertheless I am glad, and always shall be, that the Negroes are—virtually—free."

However, physical resistance had not been as easy. She accepted her family's ten-year old expectation of an early if not an immediate death; she now often felt unable to use her legs at all, and thought her disability the effect of illness rather than of disuse. The ordinary sick room regime of the time prescribed an airtight overheated atmosphere in which, as she herself noticed, not only cut flowers but even the plants sent by her friends were unable to survive for more than a few days, and had to be constantly replaced.

When Browning first proposed he thought that marriage would mean only sharing a home with the privilege of daily visits to her bedside. But although her ultimatum forced him to burn the letter she returned to him, which is now the only one missing in the published *Letters of Robert Browning and Elizabeth Barrett* that gives us a day-to-day account of the eighteen-month courtship and engagement, he never wavered in his purpose. Soon, however, he had sensibly decided that if she gave up preparing for death to please her father she might well be able to prepare for a happy life with her husband.

Elizabeth Barrett responded with great trepidation but greater courage to his urging that she stand up for a few minutes a day, walk about the room, go out for air in the carriage with her sister, open a door or window, and so forth.

She also responded, less consciously, to his insistence that he loved her and that she would enrich and not blight his life. The wonderful sequence of *Sonnets from the Portugese* completed and published after their marriage give us even more powerfully than the letters her change from fear to doubtful hope and, finally, joyous certainty. Perhaps two of these should be included here; the fourteenth and the forty-third:

> If thou must love me, let it be for naught
> Except for love's sake only. Do not say
> "I love her for her smile . . . her look . . . her way
> Of speaking gently, . . . for a trick of thought
> That falls in well with mine, and certes brought
> A sense of pleasant ease on such a day"—
> For these things in themselves, Beloved, may
> Be changed, or change for thee,—and love, so wrought,

> May be unwrought so. Neither love me for
> Thine own dear pity's wiping my cheeks dry,—
> A creature might forget to weep, who bore
> Thy comfort long, and lose thy love thereby!
> But love me for love's sake, that evermore
> Thou mayst love on, through love's eternity.
>
> . . . .
>
> How do I love thee? Let me count the ways.
> I love thee to the depth and breadth and height
> My soul can reach, when feeling out of sight
> For the ends of Being and ideal Grace.
> I love thee to the level of every day's
> Most quiet need, by sun and candle-light.
> I love thee freely, as men strive for Right,
> I love thee purely, as they turn from Praise.
> I love thee with a passion put to use
> In my old griefs, and with my childhood's faith
> I love thee with a love I seemed to lose
> With my lost saints,—I love thee with the breath,
> Smiles, tears, of all my life!—and, if God choose,
> I shall but love thee better after death.

The course of true love was greatly facilitated by the physicians' unanimous recommendation that she spend the next winter in Italy. This was presented as the only means of staving off almost certain death, and Elizabeth was deeply shocked when her father refused to approve her going since, he said, she should have been thinking only of the next world.

She herself had an annual income of three or four hundred pounds left by an uncle, but the brother and sister who offered to accompany her were altogether dependent on their father and she did not dare allow them to forfeit his support.

Robert Browning, practical and resolute as always, used the occasion to urge that she marry in haste, go to Italy with her husband, and there be cured at leisure. After much hesitation and many delays she finally slipped out of the house one day in late September 1846, and they were secretly married.

A week later they sailed for Italy where, with several visits to France and two to the older Brownings in London, after their son's birth in 1849, they remained for the rest of their happy married life.

A series of delightful intimate letters to her sisters allow us to get still better acquainted with both the newlyweds. For example, just a few months after the elopement she writes:

> Even the pouring of the coffee is a divided labor, and the ordering of the dinner is quite out of my hands. As for me,

when I am so good as to let myself be carried upstairs, and so angelical as to sit still on the sofa and so considerate, moreover, as *not* to put my foot into a puddle, why my duty is considered done to a perfection which is worthy of all adoration.

A year later, after she had, on donkey back, actually made the ascent of a five-mile mountain and performed other feats she writes:

. . . and I have to tell him that he really must not go telling everybody how his wife walked here with him, or walked there with him, as if a wife with two feet were a miracle in nature.

Their happiness was disturbed only by Mr. Barrett's refusal to speak or write to her, or to wish his grandson well, and by their deep concern over Italy's struggle for freedom.

They were generally agreed in their politics but Elizabeth was far more actively interested and emotionally concerned. She complains in 1850 that though Robert was kind enough to go on purpose to the library, which did not admit women, to see the English or French newspapers for her, his report when he returned was unenlightening:

The President's [Louis Napoleon] an ass; he is not worth thinking of. Thiers is a rascal; I make a point of not reading one word said by M. Thiers. Proudhon is a madman; who cares for Proudhon?

But Browning greatly admired her political as well as her love poetry, and encouraged her when, at the end of 1846, she received a request from an abolitionist group in the United States to send them a poem. With his approval she sent one which she described as "too ferocious, perhaps, for the Americans to publish, but they asked for a poem and shall have it."

The poem was certainly an unladylike one, telling of a young Negro woman who, separated from a fellow slave whom she loved and raped by her white master, killed her child and ran to Pilgrims' Point where she was finally flogged to death. *The Runaway Slave at Pilgrims' Point* reads, in part:

I stand on the mark beside the shore
Of the first white pilgrim's bended knee,
Where exile turned to ancestor,
And God was thanked for liberty,
I have run through the night, my skin is as dark,

> I bend my knee down on this mark;
> I look on the sky and the sea.
> . . . .
> O pilgrims! I have gasped and run
> All night long from the whips of one,
> Who, in your names, works sin and woe
> . . . .
> And lift my black face, my black hand,
> Here, in your names, to curse this land
> Ye blessed in freedom's, evermore.

Then, as she is dying, she concludes:

> . . . from these sands
> Up to the mountains lift your hands,
> O slaves, and end what I begun!
>
> Whips, curses: these must answer those!
> For in this union you have set
> Two kinds of men in adverse rows
> Each loathing each, and all forget
> The seven wounds in Christ's body fair,
> While He sees gaping everywhere
> Our countless wounds that pay no debt.

In 1855 Browning published one of his finest books—*Men and Women*—dedicating it as always to Elizabeth Barrett:

> There they are, my fifty men and women
> Naming me the fifty poems finished!
> Take them, Love, the book and me together:
> Where the heart lies, let the head lie also.

This title poem also contains the significant and often quoted lines:

> Dante, who loved well because he hated,
> Hated wickedness that hinders loving.

There are many others in the volume which readers may find of special interest because of their subject matter. Some of these are "Popularity" addressed to the still almost unknown Keats, "Holy Cross Day," a protest at The Papal State's continued persecution of the Jews, "Saul," a vivid psychological retelling of the Old Testament Story, and the powerful dramatic monologue "Andrea del Sarto" in which the artist known as "the faultless painter" summarizes what is, from Browning's viewpoint, his failure. For Browning believes, as Andrea says in a moment of insight:

> Ah, but a man's reach should exceed his grasp
> Or what's a heaven for?

Finally *Men and Women* includes "Memorabilia," Browning's tribute to the then much maligned and little known Shelley.

Four years later when the Brownings received a copy of the *Idylls of the King* they were, despite their personal friendliness to Tennyson, almost the only literary contemporaries to realize how far his very great talent had been injured by his increasing political conservatism. Mrs. Browning wrote a friend in England:

> Perhaps the breathing throbbing life around us in Italy, where a nation is being new-born, may throw King Arthur too far off and flat. But, whatever the cause, the effect was so. The colour, the temperature, the very music left me cold.

In 1860 both Brownings were deeply and sometimes dangerously involved with their Italian friends in planning anti-Austrian activities and then in assisting fugitives. Browning deserted his customary detachment to write:

> I would grasp Metternich until
> I felt his wet red throat distil
> In blood thro' these two hands.

Elizabeth Barrett wrote some of her best work in a series of poems on the Italian political scene published as *Poems Before Congress*. This volume also included *A Curse for a Nation*—a powerful denunciation of slavery in the United States which begins with a prologue:

> I heard an angel speak last night
>   And he said "write!
> Write a Nation's curse for me,
> And send it over the Western Sea."
>
> I faltered, taking up the word:
>   "Not so, my lord!
> If curses must be, choose another
> To send thy curse against my brother.

> For I am bound by gratitude,
>   By love and blood,
> To brothers of mine across the sea,
> Who stretch out kindly hands to me."
>
> . . . .
>
> "Therefore," the voice said, "shalt thou write
>   My curse tonight.
> Because thou hast strength to see and hate
> A foul thing done *within* thy gate."
>
> "Not so," I answered once again.
>   "To curse, choose men.
> For I, a woman, have only known
> How the heart melts and the tears run down."
>
> "Therefore," the voice said, "shalt thou write
>   My curse tonight.
> Some women weep and curse, I say
> (And no one marvels), night and day.
>
> . . . .
>
> So thus I wrote, and mourned indeed,
>   What all may read,
> And this, as was enjoined on me,
> I send it over the Western Sea.
>
> Ye shall watch while kings conspire
> Round the people's smouldering fire,
>   And, warm for your part,
> Shall never dare—O shame!
> To utter the thought into flame
> Which burns in your heart.
>   This is the curse. Write.
>
> Ye shall watch while strong men draw
> The nets of feudal law
>   To strangle the weak;
> And counting the sin for a sin,
> Your soul shall be sadder within
>   Than the word ye shall speak.
>
> . . . .
>
> Go, wherever ill deeds shall be done,
> Go, plant your flag in the sun
>   Beside the ill-doers!
> And recoil from clenching the curse
> Of God's witnessing Universe
>   With a curse of yours.
>   THIS is the curse. Write.

The poem was sharply attacked in the English press and as fiercely defended by Browning. Mrs. Browning took no part in the public controversy but wrote to a friend who had criticized her privately, "Oh, and is it possible that you think a woman has no business with questions like the question of slavery? Then she had better use a pen no more."

Unfortunately her health, always precarious, broke under the strain and a bronchial attack in June, 1861 proved fatal.

Despite Browning's deep and terrible unhappiness he immediately set to work editing her posthumous last poems, and although he could no longer bear the associations of life in Italy he continued to take an active interest in events there. In October, 1862 he could write from Paris to an American friend:

> These last [Civil War] news from the North are admirable and consolatory, and I think, by such poor glimmer of light as comes to me, that the Italian news is far from discouraging.

A year later, he returned to England with his thirteen-year-old son. He had found the heart to begin writing again and in 1868 he published perhaps his major single work—the epic *The Ring and The Book*—with a dedication:

> O lyric love, half angel and half bird
> And all a wonder and a wild desire,
> Boldest of hearts that ever braved the sun,
> Sought sanctuary within the holier blue
> And sang a kindred soul out to his face,—
> Yet human at the red-ripe of the heart—
>
> This is the same voice: can thy soul know change?
> Hail then, and hearken from the realms of help!
> Never may I commence my song, my due
> To God who best taught song by gift of thee,
> Except with bent head and beseeching hand—
> That still, despite the distance and the dark,
> What was, again may be; some interchange
> Of grace, some splendour once thy very thought
> Some benediction anciently thy smile.

The publication of *The Ring and The Book* won Browning a long-delayed critical acclaim and widespread popularity, and although he introduced a later poem with "O British public, ye who like me not," this was no longer accurate.

He now had an eager audience waiting for anything he might write. Despite regular enjoyment of all the concerts, picture exhibitions and literary or artistic London society, he had much lonely time to fill, and he published an enormous amount of good, bad, and indifferent poetry during the last twenty years of his life.

There is surprisingly little difference in freshness or music between the best of the poetry of these later days and the best of the earlier material—and even less in his underlying attitude. The love lyrics are as fresh, the sensuous and aesthetic delight as warm, the wit as sharp, the erudition as lightly carried, and the interest in hearing what every kind of man had to say for himself—or would have had to say, if able—as unflagging. The personal philosophy expressed in his very last poem, the *Epilogue to Asolando*, published on the day of his death in December, 1889 is already clearly apparent in stanzas from the famous *Rabbi Ben Ezra*, first published in 1864.

This longest explicit declaration of faith, opens with the often quoted beginning:

> Grow old along with me!
> The best is yet to be,
> The last of life, for which the first was made:
> Our times are in his hand
> Who saith, "A whole I planned,
> Youth shows but half; trust God: see all, nor be afraid!"

It continues to the energetic:

> Then, welcome each rebuff
> That turns earth's smoothness rough,
> Each sting that bids nor sit nor stand but go!
> Be our joys three-parts pain!
> Strive, and hold cheap the strain;
> Learn, nor account the pang; dare, never grudge the throe!
>
> For thence,—a paradox
> Which comforts while it mocks,—
> Shall life succeed in that it seems to fail:
> What I aspired to be,
> And was not, comforts me:
> A brute I might have been, but would not sink in the scale.

Then, after developing that evolutionary theme, the poem proceeds to another of Browning's favorite ideas:

> Let us not always say,
> "Spite of this flesh to-day
> I strove, made head, gained ground upon the whole!"

> As the bird wings and sings,
> Let us cry, "All good things
> Are ours, nor soul helps flesh more, now, than flesh helps soul!"

In the next three stanzas, Browning shows that without action there can be no real knowledge. His mood is one which all who agree that it is not sufficient to know the world unless we can thereby help to change it must share, even though we may not be able to share his happy expectation of another chance for personal action.

It is significant to note the examples of right and wrong action he selects as typical:

> So, still within this life,
> Though lifted o'er its strife,
> Let me discern, compare, pronounce at last,
> "This rage was right i' the main,
> That acquiescence vain:
> The Future I may face now I have proved the Past."

Finally, we have a clear statement of his courageous—and limited—individualism:

> Now, who shall arbitrate?
> Ten men love what I hate,
> Shun what I follow, slight what I receive;
> Ten, who in ears and eyes
> Match me: we all surmise,
> They this thing, and I that: whom shall my soul believe?

In his seventy-seventh year, shortly before the end of his life, Browning completed *Asolando*. Its epilogue, published on the very day of his death, is a fitting epitaph for this gallant, courageous and high-hearted figure. (Its hopeful vigor makes an instructive contrast with the better known musical resignation of "Crossing the Bar" in which Tennyson, as the Victorian poet laureate, expressed his more typical farewell.)

> At the midnight in the silence of the sleep-time,
>   When you set your fancies free,
> Will they pass to where—by death, fools think, imprisoned—
> Low he lies who once so loved you, whom you loved so,
>   —Pity me?

Oh to love so, be so loved, yet so mistaken!
What had I on earth to do
With the slothful, with the mawkish, the unmanly?
Like the aimless, helpless, hopeless, did I drivel
—Being—who?

One who never turned his back but marched breast forward,
Never doubted clouds would break,
Never dreamed, though right were worsted, wrong would
triumph
Held we fall to rise, are baffled to fight better,
Sleep to wake.

No, at noonday in the bustle of man's work-time
Greet the unseen with a cheer!
Bid him forward, breast and back as either should be,
"Strive and thrive!" cry "Speed,—fight on, fare ever
There as here!"

With all its riches this is not the greatest poetry our English heritage affords. Browning himself, contrasting his own work with that of the supreme masters of his art (among whom he gallantly though mistakenly included Elizabeth Barrett) wrote:

> Can't you imagine a clever sort of angel who plots and plans and tries to build up something; he wants to make you see it as he sees it, shows you one point of view, carries you off to another, hammering into your head the things he wants you to understand; and while all this bother is going on, God Almighty turns you off a little star. That's the difference between us.

Nevertheless Browning's is the greatest poetry the Victorian Age has left us. To find anything more profound and passionate there we must turn from poetry to prose; from the singers to the novelists. These, living closest to the heart of their own time and writing for its most significant audience, were also speaking to and for the future.

HER MAJESTY'S LOYAL OPPOSITION

While the permanent contribution of the Victorian Age was undoubtedly the last major flowering of the bourgeois novel which, especially in Dickens' hands, reached audiences approached by no English literature since Shakespeare, it also possessed a considerable body of prophets whom for lack of a better term we name essayists.

John Henry Newman was a leader of the Oxford Movement toward a more beautiful, dignified and authoritative Church of England—a movement whose general influence ended abruptly when it had taken him and his most logical followers to Rome. Matthew Arnold was the apostle of culture, who made "philistine" an epithet with which to attack her enemies and lukewarm friends. Charles Kingsley was an earnest reformer whose Christian Socialism or, as it was more accurately called, muscular Christianity, led to the establishment of many useful settlement houses and sanitary commissions. Thomas Carlyle was truly a twentieth century Jeremiah whose tremendous denunciations of the callous inhumanity and shameless hypocrisy of his time inspired men as diverse as Kingsley, Ruskin, Browning, Dickens, Huxley, Emerson and Walt Whitman, and whose reactionary solutions for those ills were plausibly claimed as precedent by German Aryans and English Mosleyites. John Ruskin was an art critic whose overwhelming love of beauty was human enough to lead him from contemplating the Stones of Venice to criticizing those of Manchester, and who outraged with social advice chambers of commerce that were waiting to follow his architectural recommendations. William Morris, his great disciple, was perhaps the first English writer really to understand how socialism could free man to be himself. All these must, however briefly, be included in any discussion of Victorian life and literature, although the bulk of Morris' serious writing came after 1880 and will be discussed in the last section with that of his friend and younger contemporary, George Bernard Shaw.

We have already noticed the apparent paradox, that all these severe critics were to a varying but generally extraordinary extent admired, respected, and even rewarded by a very considerable part of the notoriously smug and intolerant public whose ideas and ideals they attacked.

As far as Newman and, in a different way, Arnold are concerned this need hardly puzzle us. Their work grew out of a perfectly genuine and deeply felt need to find some meaning in the increasingly meaningless middle-class life from which they sprang, some living purpose worth their devotion in the deadly dullness of comfort which stretched as far as their eyes could see. Sensitive young men with any truly religious feeling must have been even more shocked than we are at such contemporary sermons as the one of the popular minister, Reverend Baxter, that began: "The man who refuses to take the path which leads to greater profits when that opens before him, is deliberately refusing to obey the will of God."

This need has led many intelligent leisured sons of hardworking successful fathers into many varied and strange paths in every generation of college students since Newman's time. A contemporary account of his *Parochial Sermons*, published in 1834, says:

> It was as if a trumpet had sounded through the land. All read and admired even if they dissented or criticized. The publishers said that the volume put all other sermons out of the market, just as Waverley and Guy Mannering had put all other novels.

But so long as such trumpeters make no effort to change or even explore the substratum that supports them, they are not only harmless but may even be useful.

Charques in his *Literature and Social Revolution*, dealing with the next century, remarks:

> Perhaps there is nobody as willing as the capitalist to admit the importance of an inner reality of things different and finer and altogether apart from the reality under his nose.

And there is no reason to suppose Caesar troubled himself unduly about what things might be rendered to God if he was once satisfied that all which he could fairly call Caesar's had been secured to him.

The testimony of a later generation offered by the last of the Pre-Raphaelite artists, Burne-Jones, gives striking evidence of Newman's significance in this regard. He wrote in 1878:

> When I was fifteen or sixteen he taught me so much that I do mind—things that will never be out of me. In an age of sofas and cushions he taught me to be indifferent to comfort, and in an age of materialism he taught me to venture all on the unseen. . . .

So permanent an effect may occasionally prove embarrassing and unwelcome to an individual father whose heir should put away childish things when he leaves college to become "and Son." But by far the greater number of such heirs do forget sowing spiritual wild oats as easily as they do the more conventional sort, and certainly this contempt for comfort and this disregard of the material world makes a useful cul-de-sac for the restless and rebellious young intellectuals whom the next hundred years of cheaper, more widespread education were to develop in increasing numbers.

Arnold makes clear in *The Function of Criticism at the Present Time* and many subsequent essays that a cultured lion will "roar you as gently an any suckling dove." He says:

> It is of the last importance that English criticism should clearly discern what rule for its course, in order to avail itself of the field now opening to it; and to produce fruit for the future, it ought to take. The rule may be summed up in one word—disinterestedness. And how is criticism to show disinterestedness? By keeping aloof from what is called "the practical view of things;" by resolutely following the law of its own nature, which is to be a free play of the mind on all subjects which it touches. By steadily refusing to lend itself to any of these ulterior, political, practical considerations about ideas, which plenty of people will be sure to attach to them, which perhaps ought to be attached to them, which in this Country at any rate are certain to be attached to them quite sufficiently, but which criticism has really nothing to do with. Its business is, as I have said, simply to know the best that is known and thought in the world, and by in its turn making this known, to create a current of true and fresh ideas. Its business is to do this with inflexible honesty, with due ability; but its business is to do no more, and to leave alone all questions of practical consequences and applications, questions which will never fail to have due prominence given to them.

For the sake of those later devotees of pure truth who, today, follow Arnold in refusing to arrive at any decision which might sully its perfection, we must glance at another essay of his in which he sharply criticized the liberal churchman Bishop Colenso—then under attack from all the more conservative and reactionary elements in the church. The good bishop had become convinced, partly by his study of geology and partly by arguments with some unprejudiced Zulus whom he was trying to convert, that the accounts of Genesis and the bill of lading of Noah's Ark, given in the Bible, were not literally true. He published some of the geological evidences of the earth's extreme antiquity, and a terrific storm broke about his honest head.

His superior excommunicated him; he appealed to the courts; the liberal clergy rallied about him; and Arnold publicly criticized his book—of whose truth he, of course, felt no doubt—as an ill-advised and mischievous publication. Arnold began by saying that any attempt to remove prejudices and enlighten ignorance would, a priori, seem laudable. Why then was this an exception? Because it made its information available not only to the highly instructed few from whom, Arnold thought, it was no secret, but also to the scantily instructed many for whom, he felt, it should have remained one!

> ... the highly instructed few and not the scantily instructed many, will ever be the organ to the human race of knowledge and truth. Knowledge and truth, in the full sense of the words, are not attainable by the great mass of the human race at all. The great mass of the human race have to be softened and humanised through their heart and imagination, before any soil can be found in them where knowledge may strike living roots. Until the softening and humanising process is very far advanced, intellectual demonstrations are uninforming for them; and, if they impede the working of influences which advance this softening and humanising process, they are even noxious; they retard their development, they impair the culture of the world. All the great teachers, divine and human, who have ever appeared, have united in proclaiming this.
>
> Old moral ideas leaven and humanise the multitude: new intellectual ideas filter slowly down to them from the thinking few; and only when they reach them in this manner do they adjust themselves to their practise without convulsing it.

So much for disinterestedness!

In his illuminating recent study of *Critics and Criticism*, Alick West discusses the school represented by Matthew Arnold at one end and by T. S. Eliot at the other. He says, in part:

> Since romanticism, bourgeois thought has been dishonest. ... In particular, criticism refused to face romanticism. Romanticists had stated the social character of literature, the social conditions favorable to it, and the duty of literature to cooperate with all active measures in the creation of those conditions. Then Chartism carried romanticism into action. The men of England fought for the justice and liberty which Shelley had idealised. Bourgeois criticism promptly abjured romanticism.
>
> They did not honestly state what the ideas of romanticism were, and that they would have nothing to do with them for reasons of class. They pronounced in the superior tones of Matthew Arnold, that the romantic poets "did not know

enough." Mr. Eliot, keeping alive at least this tradition, treats Wordsworth like a schoolboy. But of Matthew Arnold he writes: "It is a pleasure certainly after associating with the riff-raff of the early part of the century, to be in the company of a man qui sait se conduire." Riff-raff—that would also be Lord Eldon's word for Shelley.

The romantic poets knew what Matthew Arnold was afraid even to think about—that capitalism is the enemy of poetry. Seeing that "the iron force of adhesion to the old routine" had "wonderfully yielded"; afraid "not that people should obstinately refuse to allow anything but their old routine to pass for reason and the will of God, but either that they should allow some novelty or other to pass for these too easily, or else that they should underrate the importance of them altogether"; Arnold made it his business to change poetry from a revolt against capitalism into its "consolation and stay."

Charles Kingsley (1819–1875) and his friends were less safe but also potentially more useful allies for capitalism since they spoke of, and in extreme cases to, the altogether disinherited of the Victorian age.

Kingsley's *Letters to the Chartists* in *Politics for the People* said many things as radical as:

> We have used the Bible as if it were a mere special constable's handbook—an opium dose for keeping beasts of burden patient while they are being loaded—a mere book to keep the poor in order. . . . We have told you that the Bible preached the rights of property and the duties of labor when (God knows!) for once that it does that, it preaches ten times over the duties of property and the rights of labor.

And over thirty years later, near the end of his life, he was still capable of as searching and original a sermon as the one "Human Soot," preached when he was the honored Canon of Chester Cathedral, for the benefit of the Ragged Schools of Liverpool.

> We know well how, in some manufactures, a certain amount of waste is profitable . . . as in a steam mill every atom of soot is so much wasted fuel; but it pays better not to consume the whole fuel and to let the soot escape. So it is in our present social system; it pays better. Capital is accumulated more rapidly by wasting a certain amount of human life, human health, human intellect, human morals, by producing and throwing away a regular percentage of human soot—of that thinking and acting dirt which lies about, and, alas! breeds and perpetuates

itself in foul alleys and low public-houses, and all and any of the dark places of the earth. But as in the case of the manufactures, the Nemesis comes swift and sure. . . .

But although seemingly so radical in his approach to religion and willing on occasion to frighten his more heartless neighbors into good works, Kingsley and other earnest young parsons like him felt that any real reform must affect primarily the moral fiber of the people, hated extreme poverty even more because of the resultant drunkenness and sexual immorality than because of its disease and misery, feared that most charity led to pauperization, and prided themselves on the extent to which their influence turned the poor from thoughts of violent protest or drastic social change.

The next leader of the loyal opposition is in force of character and intellectual genius perhaps its highest ranking member, and its only working class one. In one way or another every one of his fellow critics owned his inspiration, and even Charles Dickens found him far and away the greatest spirit of the age. Any casual chronological survey of his work makes us feel deeply what a loss he—and the great literature of the progressive tradition—suffered when, in his long solitary search for a way out he too made a wrong turn and plunged with all his extraordinary force into a quagmire of reactionary, semiracist, prefascist idealization of force and feudalism.

Thomas Carlyle (1795–1881), like Burns, was the son of poor Scottish peasants—his father was a village stonemason—and in his brilliant early essay on Burns he has given us a moving picture of their common background:

> The brave, hard-toiling, hard-suffering Father, his brave heroine of a wife; and those children of whom Robert was one. . . . The brave Father, I say always;—a *silent* Hero and Poet; without whom the son had never been a speaking one! . . . And his poor "seven acres of nursery-ground,"—not that, nor the miserable patch of clay-farm, nor anything he tried to get a living by, would prosper with him; he had a sore unequal battle all his days. But he stood to it valiantly; a wise, faithful, unconquerable man; swallowing down how many sore sufferings daily into silence; fighting like an unseen Hero,—nobody publishing newspaper paragraphs about his nobleness; voting pieces of plate to him! However, he was not lost: nothing is lost. Robert is there; the outcome of him,—and indeed of many generations of such as him.

Like Swift and Hazlitt he was a man personally affected by public distress and utterly unable to reduce humanity to statistics. For example, in his first major work, *Sartor Resartus*, he often breaks through the vehement obscurity of the style to declare: "That there should one man die ignorant who had capacity for knowledge, this I call a tragedy, were it to happen more than twenty times a minute as. . . . it does!" And almost twenty years later, when he had long left behind him any consistently progressive or democratic thought he still, almost alone in the chorus of heated parliamentary debates and journalistic wrangling on the Irish Land Question, bore witness to the human meaning of conditions there with the simple statement: "Ireland is a perpetual misery to me; it lies like a nightmare in my thoughts."

But although the passion of his sympathy and indignation far exceeds that of any contemporary save Dickens, it is not that alone which marks him out as the greatest of the might-have-beens in an age which had too many great ones.

His extraordinary insight into the meaning of the social changes which surround him far exceed that of any English contemporary—of any contemporary, in fact, except Marx and Engels.

For example, in his *Signs of the Times*, 1829, he discusses the change in the means of production and its necessary relation to social change in a way quite foreign to any other pre-Marxist thought. He says with a serene optimism all the more surprising in view not only of his own well justified later reputation for furious gloom but also of the state of England and his extreme personal poverty at the time:

> What wonderful accessions have thus been made, and are still making, to the physical power of mankind; how much better fed, clothed, lodged and, in all outward respects, accommodated men now are, *or might be,* by a given quantity of labour, is a grateful reflection which forces itself on every one. What changes, too, this addition of *power* is introducing into the Social System; how wealth has more and more increased, and at the same time gathered itself more and more into masses, strangely altering the old relations and increasing the distance between the rich and the poor will be a question for Political Economists, and a much more complex and important one than any they have yet engaged with. . . .
> Meanwhile, that great outward changes are in progress can be doubtful to no one. The time is sick and out of joint. Many

things have reached their height; and it is a wise adage that tells us, "the darkest hour is nearest the dawn." Wherever we can gather indication of the public thought, whether from printed books as in France or Germany, or from Carbonari rebellions and other political tumults, as in Spain, Portugal, Italy and Greece, the voice it utters is the same. The thinking minds of all nations call for change. There is a deep-lying struggle in the fabric of society; a boundless grinding collision of the New with the Old. The French Revolution as is now visible enough, was not the parent of this mighty movement but its offspring. . . . Political freedom is hitherto the object of these efforts; but they will not stop there. It is towards a higher freedom than mere freedom from oppression by his fellow mortals that man dimly aims. Of this higher freedom which is man's "reasonable service," all his noble institutions, his faithful endeavours and loftiest attainments, are but the body, and more and more approximated emblem.

Three or four years later in *Sartor Resartus* Carlyle wrote still more specifically attacking laissez-faire capitalism, or the system of "free enterprise."

Call ye that a Society where there is no longer any Social Idea extant; not so much as the idea of a Common Home, but only of a common Lodging-House? Where each isolated, regardless of his neighbour, turned against his neighbour, clutches what he can get, and cries "Mine," and calls it Peace because in the cut-purse and cut-throat Scramble no steel knives but only a far cunninger sort can be employed. . . . Thus too does an observant eye discern everywhere that saddest spectacle: The Poor perishing, like neglected, foundered Draught-Cattle of Hunger and Overwork; the Rich, still more wretchedly of Idleness, Satiety and Over-growth.

A few more years and Carlyle had gone so far as to ask himself explicitly what it was that "bursts asunder the bonds of ancient Political Systems, and perplexes all Europe with the fear of change," and to answer himself: "the increase of social resources which the old social methods will no longer sufficiently administer."

After attending one of the large Chartist meetings at the very beginning of the movement Carlyle wrote, with evident satisfaction, in a private letter:

Two thousand most grim looking fellows in bitter earnest! To rule ten million of such by the drill sergeant scheme may be work for Wellington, such as he has not yet tried. Peace be with him! If he want *war* I can promise him plenty of that too; and prettier men have lost their heads in such a cause. . . . For me, I declare I can see nothing but *destruction to the whole concern.*

He was then writing his first—and greatest—major work, *The French Revolution*, which was completed in 1837. Although "the hero as dictator" is already faintly visible here, the spirit and truth of the book are found in the emotional omnipresence of the people, as a weaver's society in Paisley realized when they voted to thank him for writing a book for working men. Meditating its beginning three years before, he had written his brother: "It shall be such a book: quite an epic poem of the Revolution; an apotheosis of Sansculottism! [extreme revolutionary radicalism]." When it was completed he told his wife: "—they have not had for two hundred years any book that came more direct and flamingly from the heart of a living man." And years later he said to his biographer, James Anthony Froude, "I should not have known what to make of this world at all if it had not been for the French Revolution."

This book, completed when Carlyle was forty-two, was in the strictest sense the climax of his life, that is, not only its point of highest interest but also its turning point.

In it we find clearly expressed his fundamental understanding of history, already foreshadowed in the often incoherent philosophy of *Sartor Resartus;* we find emphasized his passionate sympathy for the oppressed and his savage contempt for their oppressors; and we also find intimations of that desperate longing for order and direction, and that fatal underestimation of the common man which, combined, were to lead Carlyle into his final glorification of an authoritarian blood and iron society.

In 1842 Carlyle interrupted his work on a long biography of Cromwell to dash off what he described as a "non-Oxford Tract for the Times:" (*Tracts for the Times* was the title of the famous series of pamphlets which first crystalized and publicized the ideas of Newman and his friends.) Despite Carlyle's description, this essay, *Past and Present*, did resemble the Oxford Movement in its idealization of the feudal past, but its major emphasis was placed on Carlyle's fatal theory of "the hero as master." Still, it contains a realistic, powerful, and just attack on the causes as well as the effects of the people's misery. For example, after scoffing at the theory of "overproduction" in a world where shirt spinners sit idle with bare backs, he vividly describes the insane "Condition of England" when:

> . . . a man willing to work; and unable to find work . . . seeking leave to toil that he might be fed and sheltered! That he might be put on a level with the four-footed workers of the Planet which is his! There is not a horse willing to work but can get food and shelter in requital; a thing this two-footed worker has to seek for, to solicit occasionally in vain.

Then, appears a formulation strangely familiar to those who remember the statement in the *Communist Manifesto:*

> The bourgeoisie has played a most revolutionary role in history. The bourgeoisie, wherever it has got the upper hand, has put an end to all feudal, patriarchal, idyllic relations. It has pitilessly torn asunder the motley feudal ties that bound man to his "natural superiors," and has left no other bond between man and man than naked self-interest, than callous "cash payment."

Carlyle says:

> We have profoundly forgotten everywhere that Cash-payment is not the sole relation of human beings; we think, nothing doubting, that it absolves and liquidates all engagements of man.

There are also many explosions of informed hatred at the whole inhuman system of laissez-faire, which again help us understand Carlyle's reasons for welcoming any conceivable remedy. For example, he says:

> [Laissez-faire means] To have neither superior nor inferior nor equal united man-like to you. Without father, without child, without brother. Man knows no sadder destiny. . . . Encased each as in his transparent ice-palace; our brother visible in his, making signals and gesticulations to us;—visible, but forever unattainable.

But the remedy? His own statements show while he would not have owned the "National Socialists" for sons, yet they had, tragically, some shadow of a right to claim him as father. He appeals to the "captains of industry":

Look around you. Your world-hosts are all in mutiny, in confusion, in destitution; on the eve of fiery wreck and madness! They will not march further for you, on the sixpence a day and supply-and-demand principle: they will not; nor ought they, nor can they. Ye shall reduce them to order, begin reducing them. To order, to just subordination; noble loyalty in return for noble guidance. Their souls are driven nigh mad; let yours be sane and even saner. Not as a bewildered bewildering mob; but as a firm regimented mass, with real captains over them will these men march any more.

Cromwell, published in 1845 and the first of Carlyle's works to find an overwhelming immediate success, is the last that any admirer of his can really take pride or pleasure in. And even here the figure of the dictator and a joy in dictatorship, force, and, almost, cruelty, or at least ruthlessness for its own sake, are disturbingly evident.

The uprisings all over Europe about 1848 seemed to give him some faint echo of his earlier hopes, and in one of his *Latter Day Pamphlets,* published as a complete series in 1850, he says:

> Democracy sure enough, is here: one knows not how long it will keep hidden underground even in Russia;—and here in England, though we object to it absolutely in the form of street barricades and insurrectionary pikes, and decidedly will not open door to it on those terms, the tramp of its million feet is on all streets and thoroughfares, the sound of its bewildered thousandfold voices in all thinkings and modes and activities of men.

But the temporary failure of the revolutionary movement all over Europe and the inglorious end of Chartism in England extinguished this last flicker of hope. In 1852 Carlyle, with unconscious symbolism, retired to a soundproof room built onto the top of his home in London (and no doubt specially designed to keep out the tramp of those million feet, the sound of those thousandfold voices), to spend the next thirteen years writing the hero as emperor, a glorification of the Prussian monarch *Frederick the Great.*

John Ruskin (1819–1900), almost a quarter of a century younger than Carlyle, and as different from him in background, education, temperament and taste as any one man can be from another, nevertheless felt, as did Dickens, that Carlyle was perhaps the only contemporary intellectual who really cared—cared fiercely and desperately—about what he called "the condition of England question," and when Ruskin himself was already at the height of his fame he still referred to himself as a disciple:

> Read your Carlyle with all your heart and with the best of brain you can give; and you will learn from him first, the eternity of good law, and the need of obedience to it; then, concerning your own immediate business, you will learn farther this, that the beginning of all good law, and nearly the end of it, is in these two ordinances,—That every man shall do good work for his bread; and, secondly, that every man shall have good bread for his work.

Nevertheless, in some ways Ruskin went far beyond Carlyle in his understanding of the social problems of his time, as he did in his many practical though unsuccessful attempts to deal with them. Nor should "unsuccessful" be equated with worthless. For not only did William Morris, a founder of the first English socialist party, but many of his followers including, in one sense, at least, Bernard Shaw, truly claim Ruskin as their master. A surprisingly large part of the hopeful young American Socialists of the early twentieth century, who helped build the amazing million copy circulation of *The Appeal To Reason,* had first stumbled on socialist thought in the pages of *Unto This Last, Munera Pulveris,* or *Sesame and Lilies.* Camouflaged by those esoteric names these have remained hidden in the shadow cast by his ponderous tomes of art criticism on library shelves. And when, in 1906, an enterprising journalist polled the first Labour members elected to the English parliament on "Books That Have Changed My Life," over half of them named Ruskin's!

In 1857 Manchester, proud of its booming industry, sought the biggest and best art expert it could find, to speak at its great art exhibit and advise it on the most suitable style of architecture in which to build a town hall that would really express its greatness.

Ruskin accepted the invitation, opened the exhibition, and told the city fathers that although they had had Keats' famous line about a thing of beauty chiseled above the doorway, they had forgotten that "the joy which is indeed a joy forever must be a joy for all."

As for recommending a specific style of architecture, that was impossible until the life of Manchester was beautiful for, as he had already written:

Let a nation be healthy, happy, pure in its enjoyments, brave in its acts, and broad in its affections, and its art will spring round and within it as freely as foam from a fountain; But let the springs of its life be impure and its cause polluted and you will not get the bright spray by treatises on the mathematical structure of bubbles.

After this it was hardly a surprise that two years later he concluded his last chapter of the fifth volume of *Modern Painters* with the announcement to his large and still worshipful public:

Nay, I have many passages of history to examine before I can determine the just limits of the hope in which I may permit myself to continue to labour in any cause of art.

The result of this examination was a series of articles on political economy contributed, until the outraged subscribers stopped them, to Thackeray's *Cornhill Magazine*. When Ruskin was informed, after the third, that only one more could appear, he made it the longest and most intransigent of all, and had the four reprinted a year later under the title of *Unto This Last*.

James Anthony Froude, an admirer of Carlyle's who edited *Fraser's Magazine*, then offered the hospitality of his columns to Ruskin, saying proudly that his subscribers could stomach strong meat. They proved just two issues tougher than Thackeray's public had been, and the six articles were later published by Ruskin under the title of *Munera Pulveris*.

The very heart of Ruskin's social thought is contained in these two works, with their remarkable grasp of such concepts as have, since his time, become familiar to students of economics under the names of "surplus value," "labor theory of value," and so forth.

It is no wonder that *The Manchester Examiner and Times* on October 2, 1860, the year in which the first four of Ruskin's articles on political economy had appeared, editorialized: "he is not worth our powder and shot—yet if we do not crush him his wild words will touch the springs of action in some hearts, and, ere we are aware, a moral flood gate may open and drown us all."

Far from being silenced by the attacks of his enemies or sobered by the warnings of his friends, Ruskin went on saying things like:

Life without industry is guilt and industry without art is brutality.

If you enquire into the vital fact of the matter, this you will find to be the constant structure of European society for the thousand years of the feudal system; it was divided into peasants who lived by digging; priests who lived by begging; and knights who lived by pillaging; and as the luminous public mind becomes fully cognizant of these facts; it will assuredly not suffer things to be altogether arranged that way any more.

This being the nature of labour the "Cost" [value] of anything is the quantity of labour necessary to obtain it; . . .

The extremities of human degradation are not owing to natural causes; but to the habitual preying upon the labor of the poor by the luxury of the rich.

But unfortunately his political understanding was far behind his economic insights. True, he was capable of flashes of inspiration in the field of politics, as when he said "When the privileged classes fall out. . . . the masses do not come into their own, but they come into illuminating information." While stressing the importance of education he constantly warned that "you do not educate a man by telling him what he knew not, but by making him what he was not," and "All education begins in work;. . . . Every youth in the state, from the king's son down, should learn to do something with his hands, so as to let him know what touch meant."

But there with the king's son the secret comes out. It is difficult for us, accustomed to see lip service almost universally paid to political democracy by speakers who would be horrified at any approval of economic democracy, to realize how thoroughly the case was reversed in Ruskin's time. He could steadily and consistently think through the economic obscurantism of his age, but he was utterly unable to conceive of the workers securing their own good, or of any state of society without a king or dictator and body of "good aristocrats" to lead the people. Ruskin meant it as a paradox, but there was an unfortunate element of truth in his frequent assertion:

> I am and my father was before me, a violent Tory of the old school:—Walter Scott's school, that is to say, and Homer's; these two were my masters.

But we must not let his failures obscure the essential greatness of his social thinking, not only as one of the pioneers in realistic economic theory, but also as one of the few really social thinkers in an individualist age, whose strongest opponents, like Carlyle, were usually themselves infected with its disease. For example, if we think of Ibsen's view that "The strongest man is he who can best stand alone," we realize how much more deeply prophetic is Ruskin's idea:

> For the true strength of every human soul is to be dependent on as many noble as it can discern, and to be depended on by as many inferior as it can reach.

It is this human depth of understanding which made Tolstoy say:

> Ruskin was one of the most remarkable men, not only of England and our time, but of all countries and all times. He was one of those rare men who think with their hearts ("les grandes pensees viennent du coeur") and so he thought and said not only what he himself had seen and felt, but what everyone will think and say in future.

THE VICTORIAN NOVELISTS

In the Elizabethan Age the drama was, as we have seen, both the most popular and the most significant literary form. Similarly, in the era of the French Revolution the lyric poetry of the great English romantics, without ever reaching quite as broad an audience did, nevertheless, speak for, as well as to, an advanced section of the working class, in addition to all the many intellectuals revolting against their own middle and upper-class backgrounds. Similarly, in the mid-nineteenth century, the novel became at once the most widely read and the most vital and challenging expression of progressive thought.

The two great figures of the Victorian novel were Charles Dickens and George Eliot, but just below them stand Thackeray and Charlotte and Emily Brontë, as well as a host of lesser contemporaries like Wilkie Collins, Benjamin Disraeli, Mrs. Gaskell, Charles Kingsley, Bulwer Lytton and Anthony Trollope.

We have already briefly mentioned the "social problem novel" whose most illustrious exponents were Disraeli, Kingsley and Mrs.

Gaskell—unless we wish to include Dickens himself. His important though unsuccessful novel—*Hard Times*—certainly falls into this category, and almost all his great early works are closely related to it. But, although he deeply sympathized with Kingsley's efforts and admired and encouraged Mrs. Gaskell's, his own work transcends their limitations in kind as well as degree.

Of the three, Mrs. Gaskell is by far the best observer and finest novelist. Certainly her *Mary Barton* deserves a much larger audience than our time has, so far, afforded it. The mill owner's last minute conversion may be implausible and the significance attributed to it even more misleading, yet essentially the work was so fiercely attacked in its own time not because Mrs. Gaskell's theories were wrong but because her facts and feelings were right.

Nor is the book in any sense a tract or even a documentary disguised as a novel. The characters are alive and deeply rooted in their class and the social struggles of their age; the dialogue is fresh and vivid; there is more than a touch of the easy humor and alertness to distinctive detail which made her still popular *Cranford* almost a minor Jane Austen miracle, and there is a real quality of breathless suspense in Mary's desperate chase after the outward bound "John Cooper."

It is not surprising that Dickens, when in 1850 he assumed the editorship of *Household Words,* should have written to Mrs. Gaskell: ". . . there is no living writer whose aid I would desire to enlist in preference to the authoress of 'Mary Barton' (a book that most profoundly affected and impressed me). . . ."

The novels of Disraeli and Kingsley are perhaps more exclusively of interest only to the literary student or social historian.

Disraeli's *Sybil,* or *The Two Nations,* is memorable chiefly for the insight, hinted at in its title, that the rich and the poor are:

> Two nations; between whom there is no intercourse and no sympathy; who are as ignorant of each other's habits, thoughts and feelings, as if they were dwellers in different zones, or inhabitants of different planets; who are formed by a different breeding, are fed by a different food, are ordered by different manners, and are not governed by the same laws.

There is also a memorable page or two describing conditions in an unemployed weaver's home, and a few more about "Devilsdust," a baby who lived or, rather, refused to die, in one of the typical slum cellars of the hungry forties. But the thesis of salvation through an alliance between workingmen and their natural masters and, even more fundamentally, the author's unquestioning contempt for the poor and his assumption that social reform was largely a matter of tactics whereby the aristocracy could use the working class as a stick with which to beat the bourgeoisie, are more serious defects than the often stilted dialogue and unconvincing glamor of which so many critics have correctly complained. At his best Disraeli's concern never rises above the level of an appeal for the S.P.C.A., and at his worst it falls very far below that.

Kingsley's novels, notably *Alton Locke*, the fictional autobiography of a rank-and-file Chartist leader, and *Yeast*, a work dealing essentially with the rural poor and the "war of the villages" (see pp. 622, 625 ff.) rise as far above Disraeli's work as they fall below that of Mrs. Gaskell.

They share both the strength and weakness we have already, in the last chapter, noted in Kingsley's sermons and theoretical writing. They give an honest and moving picture of conditions and, often of men, with false and mystical suggestions for the reform of both. Perhaps the novels' greatest merit is Kingsley's real respect for the radical working-class figures he consistently introduces. True, he always converts them to faith in both the established Church and the best of the upper class, but he carries out in his fictional portrayal the insight frankly admitted in the letter below, written to a disciple whose clergyman friend was attempting a workingman's cultural club:

> . . . As to the capacities of working men, I am afraid that your excellent friend will find that he has only the refuse of working intellects to form his induction on. The devil has got the best long ago . . . the cream and pith of working intellect is almost exclusively self-educated, and therefore, alas! infidel. If he goes on as he is doing, lecturing on history, poetry, science, and all things which the workmen care for, and can only get from such men as _____ and _____ mixed up with Strausism and infidelity, he will find that he will bring back to his Lord's fold, and to his lecture rooms, slowly, but surely, men whose powers would astonish him, as they have astonished me.

These explicitly "propaganda" novels were widely criticized but even more widely read and discussed throughout the forties and fifties, as were a number of lesser ones, but, of course, they were not the only nor even the most powerful expressions of the deep opposition between progressive art and the alienation of man from his fellows and himself which increasingly characterized nineteenth century capitalist society.

Even the rather snobbish and conventionally minded Thackeray used his great talents to the best effect only in the social satire of *Vanity Fair*. And perhaps the most personal and fragmentary of novelists—the tragic Brontë sisters whose work seems to us far removed from any realistic treatment of social questions—have given us the most passionate denunciation of the inhuman age in which they lived.

Matthew Arnold, with unwitting insight, declared Charlotte Brontë's mind contained "nothing but hunger, rebellion and rage." The *Quarterly Review* had shown similar perspicacity in speaking of *Jane Eyre's* combining "such undoubted power with such horrid taste," and concluding that the spirit of the book was the same as that which had "overthrown authority and violated every code, human and divine, abroad, and fostered Chartism and rebellion at home." Ralph Fox in his *Novel and The People* comments briefly and illuminatingly on the significance of both Charlotte's and Emily's work, as well as that of several of the later Victorian novelists:

> *Wuthering Heights* is certainly the novel become poetry; it is beyond all doubt one of the most extraordinary books which human genius has ever produced; yet it is these things only because it is a cry of despairing agony wrung from Emily by life itself. The life of mid-Victorian England, experienced by a girl of passion and imagination imprisoned in the windswept parsonage on the moors of the West Riding, produced this book. Charlotte expressed the thwarted, lonely lives of these girls in the sublimated love of Rochester and Jane Eyre, in the burning story of Lucy Snowe in *Villette*. Emily could not be satisfied with this. Her love must triumph and in the violent horror-laden atmosphere of the stone farmhouse on the moors it did triumph. Catherine and Heathcliffe are the revenge of love against the nineteenth century. . . .
>
> Indeed, the three greatest books of the age were all such cries of suffering. *Wuthering Heights, Jude the Obscure,* and *The Way of All Flesh*, were the manifestos of English genius that a full human life in a capitalist society was impossible of attainment. The love of woman for man was a waif driven shrieking on to the cold moors; the love of man for his children brought them to that awful end in the Oxford lodging-house, the end the farmer gives to his pigs, while honesty,

intelligence and simplicity bring your nineteenth century hero to prison. . . .

Charlotte Brontë we will again meet when we come to a discussion of "the woman question" in Victorian fiction, and the great work of George Eliot, but first we must attempt to deal with the giant figure of Dickens.

Charles Dickens—1812–1870

Charles Dickens was the second child of a lower middle-class family already, at the time of his birth, fighting a losing battle to maintain their precariously genteel status in the world.

His father, John Dickens, a minor civil servant, was good-natured, sociable and popular but markedly improvident, able to incur and forget debts with unusual ease, and apt more and more frequently to escape from the increasing discomforts of his home to the unimpaired conviviality of the tavern.

As Charles developed into an exceptionally bright and articulate youngster, his easygoing father would often take the six or seven-year-old with him when he escaped from the household, which already seemed overfull of crying babies and their harassed mother, to the more congenial company found out-of-doors.

Until he was nine, Charles and his slightly older sister, Fanny, were taught together at home, sang duets together, and played together in the neighboring fields or on the nearby docks. Charles, who seems already to have been subject to the unexplained attacks of severe pain or cramps from which, despite his generally good health, he suffered all the rest of his life, also spent much time reading alone in his room. He soon became a voracious reader and memorized innumerable stories, as well as the recitations his father frequently called on him to perform.

The family then removed to a somewhat smaller and cheaper house and both Fanny and Charles were entered as day students in a school which stood almost next door. Here they continued until John Dickens' transfer to a London clerkship at the end of 1822 necessitated a farewell to Chatham.

Charles himself stayed behind for a few months to complete the school term, and when he rejoined his family in the spring of 1823 he found that the daily joys and normal expectations of a happy childhood had been forever left behind.

Fanny had won a scholarship to the Royal Academy of Music and was continuing her education there, but the family's straitened circumstances, his father's easy forgetfulness of any unpleasant problem, and his mother's preoccupation with the six younger children who survived—three had already died in infancy—precluded all concern for Charles' education. Nothing was said about plans for further schooling and he rapidly became taken for granted as a helper to the single inadequate young servant, cleaning boots and, soon, carrying articles of furniture to the pawnshop as the family debts became more pressing. Finally, on his twelfth birthday, he began work in a small factory warehouse for six or seven shillings a week. Years later he wrote:

> No words can express the secret agony of my soul as I sunk into this companionship; compared these everyday associates with those of my happier childhood; and felt my early hopes of growing up to be a learned and distinguished man, crushed in my breast. The deep remembrance of the sense I had of being utterly neglected and hopeless; of the shame I felt in my position; of the misery it was to my young heart to believe that, day by day, what I had learned, and thought, and delighted in, and raised my fancy and emulation up by, was passing away from me, never to be brought back any more; cannot be written.
>
> My whole nature was so penetrated with the grief and humiliation of such considerations, that even now, famous and caressed and happy, I often forget in my dreams that I have a dear wife and children; even that I am a man; and wander desolately back to that time of my life.

The entire episode is, of course, described at greater length in the semiautobiographical *David Copperfield* in which Mr. and Mrs. Micawber are somewhat freely modeled on his parents, and the small David rather more exactly on himself.

His father's subsequent stay in a debtor's prison, his own lonely misery in London and, finally, the unexpected rescue when, after his father's release, he was able briefly to attend school again, are also described with substantial truth in his favorite novel.

In 1827 the fifteen-year-old left school for good and secured the position of a lawyer's clerk. This, as he said in 1870, gave him the basis for that subsequently confirmed opinion of the law of England "which one is likely to derive from the impression that it puts all the honest men under the diabolical hooves of all the scoundrels."

It also gave him the originals for the incomparable gallery of legal figures, approached perhaps only in Daumier's cartoons, which play so large a part in the *Pickwick Papers, Bleak House, David Copperfield, Great Expectations,* and many other novels.

John Dickens had forfeited his civil service job in his "insolvent debtor's" proceedings, although he had been granted a small annual pension of about a hundred pounds. He had, with somewhat surprising determination, learned shorthand and was at this time working intermittently as a reporter.

In 1828 Charles more energetically followed his example and after four years of free-lancing secured a fairly good full time position with a newspaper called *The Mirror of Parliament.*

His career as parliamentary reporter and the passionate though unsuccessful first love which filled these early years of his twenties are also vividly traced in *David Copperfield* although Charles did not, of course, win his Maria as David did his Dora. The experience of both has been described by Dickens with gentle mockery:

> Seventeen, eighteen, nineteen, twenty; and then with the waning months came an ever augmenting sense of the dignity of twenty-one. Heaven knows I had nothing to "come into" save the bare birthday and yet I esteemed it as a great possession. . . . I gave a party on the occasion. She was there. It is unnecessary to name Her more particularly; She . . . had pervaded every chink and crevice of my mind for three or four years. I had held volumes of Imaginary Conversations with her mother on the subject of our union, and I had written letters more in number than Horace Walpole's to that discreet matron, soliciting her daughter's hand in marriage. I had never had the remotest intention of sending any of these letters; but to write them, and after a few days tear them up, had been a sublime occupation. Sometimes I had begun "Honoured Madam. I think a lady gifted with those powers of observation which I know you to possess, and endowed with those womanly sympathies with the young and ardent which it were more than heresy to doubt, can scarcely have failed to discover that I love your adorable daughter deeply, devotedly." In less buoyant states of mind I had begun, "Bear with me, Dear Madam, bear with a daring wretch who is about to make a surprising confession to you, wholly unanticipated by yourself, and which he beseeches you to commit to the flames as soon as you have become aware to what towering heights his mad ambition soars." At other times—periods of profound mental depression when She had gone out to balls where I was not—the draft took the affecting form of a paper to be left

on my table after my departure to the confines of the globe. As thus: "For Mrs. Onowenever, these lines when the hand that traces them shall be far away. I could not bear the daily torture of hopelessly loving the dear one whom I will not name. Broiling on the coast of Africa, or congealing on the shores of Greenland, I am far far better there than here." (In this sentiment my cooler judgment perceives that the family of the beloved object would have most completely concurred.) "If I ever emerge from obscurity, and my name is ever heralded by Fame, it will be for her dear sake. If I ever amass Gold, it will be to pour it at her feet. Should I on the other hand become the prey of Ravens—" I doubt if I ever quite made up my mind what was to be done in that affecting case; I tried "then it is better so"; but not feeling convinced that it would be better so, I vacillated between leaving all else blank, which looked expressive and bleak, or winding up with "Farewell!"

Both David and the young Charles again agreed on summarizing their parliamentary experience in Dickens' statement: "Night after night I record predictions that never come to pass, professions that are never fulfilled, explanations that are only meant to mystify."

The single speech which really moved Dickens during his period of parliamentary reporting was O'Connell's passionate denunciation of the Irish Coercion Bill. After sitting through the farce of the compromise Reform Bill (see pp. 628-30), Dickens wrote a crude satirical sketch in which the "Forty Thieves," divided into two robbers' bands of Tories and Whigs, decided to cooperate instead of fight since "There is plunder enough in the cave; so that it is never restored to the original owners and never gets into other hands but ours, why should we quarrel over much!"

Although he was not a political theorist and never even attempted to suggest an alternative to parliamentary government as he knew it, Dickens never thereafter wavered in his understanding of it as an instrument for wielding and disguising the power of the upper classes.

More than twenty years later he planned a series of similar sketches for *Household Words* and on being persuaded to drop them wrote: "I give it up reluctantly, and with it my hope to have made every man in England feel something of the contempt for the House of Commons that I have. We shall never begin to do anything until the sentiment is universal."

In 1855 he wrote:

> I really am serious in thinking—and I have given as painful consideration to this subject as a man with children to live after him can honestly give to it—that representative government is become altogether a failure with us, that the English gentilities and subserviences render the people unfit for it, and that the whole thing has broken down since that great seventeenth century time and has no hope in it.

However, he persevered with his parliamentary reporting, getting some satisfaction from his soon frequent outside assignments to cover by-elections and special contests all over the south and west of England, and setting new records in transcribing and posting back with his notes, often traveling twenty-four hours at a stretch.

His zest in this part of his work is apparent when he writes of some of his experiences in 1834:

> I have had to charge for half-a-dozen break-downs in half-a-dozen times as many miles. I have had to charge for the damage to a great-coat from the drippings of a blazing wax-candle, in writing through the smallest hours of the night in a swift-flying carriage and pair. I have had to charge for all sorts of breakages fifty times in a journey without question, such being the ordinary results of the pace which we went at. I have charged for broken hats, broken luggage, broken chaises, broken harness—everything but a broken head, which is the only thing they would have grumbled to pay for.

By this time he had for over a year been contributing occasional sketches signed "Boz" to several publications and on his twenty-fourth birthday he was thrilled by the appearance of his first book—a collection of these essays under the title *Sketches by Boz*. He was also by that time engaged to Kate Hogarth, the daughter of a colleague, whom he had met a year or so before.

Even in the letters Kate saved from this period, which were printed after Dickens' death, we find none of the passionate romantic excitement of David's—and Charles'—first courtship. And although they are generally humorous and affectionate, there are a surprising number of notes that read, "I hope you will not get low again" or "You are in better spirits than yesterday I hope" or "I hope your cold is better and you have no other complaint bodily or mental."

Charles was at this time still carrying on as a full time journalist and also beginning the soon-to-be famous *Pickwick Papers*, and Kate's apparent inability to understand how the necessities of his work affected their other engagements often evoked rather unloverlike notes such as this:

> If the representations I have so often made you be not sufficient to keep you in good humour . . . why then my dear you must be out of humour, and there is no help for it.

However, he was anxious for an early marriage and the success of *Boz* and the almost simultaneous publication of the first issues of *Pickwick*, soon to skyrocket to unbelievable fame, made it possible for them to be married in April, 1836.

The enormous increase in Pickwick's sales after Sam Weller had entered the sixth number with his inimitable "Number 22 wants his boots? Ask Number 22 vhether he'll have 'em now or vait till he gets 'em," also made it possible for Charles to give up reporting altogether and sign contracts with two separate publishers, for £500 each, for the copyright of two yet to-be-written novels.

Kate was already pregnant when Charles resigned as a reporter in July, and her sixteen-year-old sister Mary came to live with the young couple. Mary soon became Charles' constant companion in excursions Kate could not then make, and their friendship, although altogether platonic, rapidly became so close that Charles was extraordinarily affected when, a year later, Mary suddenly and inexplicably died, apparently of an unsuspected heart ailment. (Her young brother died similarly a few years later.) Florence Dombey, Little Nell, Little Dorrit, and Dickens' many other "little mother" child heroines are evidently based on the deep sense of loss with which Mary's death left him.

However, by the time his first son was born in January, 1837, Charles was already famous, able to move out of lodgings into a twelve-room house, writing two novels at once, fretting at the unauthorized dramatizations and other pirating of his work, and involved in controversy with a publisher whose legal rights were unassailable but whose "unfair" insistence on them would have secured Dickens' services at less than a quarter of their then market value. He had also just met John Forster, who was to be his closest friend for the next ten or fifteen years, to remain his literary and business adviser all his life, and to become his executor and official biographer after his death.

Not only was the external pattern of the next two decades already set; even at this early date certain of Dickens' major themes and social judgments or, rather, insights, had begun to be quite apparent.

For example, in *Pickwick* we find the cockney Sam Weller's unquestioned leadership in good sense, good feeling and general competence; the farcical election contest of the Eatonswill Buffs and Blues; the mockery of army officers and would be socialites; the sharp ridicule of law courts and lawyers on all levels; the vivid description of debtors' prison; the hatred of canting religious hypocrisy; and the keen delight in all the ordinary physical pleasures of life. We also find a stirring of more troubled and troublesome views, such as those hinted at in *The Madman's Story*, where Dickens first describes society's worship of money—and of its possessor whoever he may be.

> I was rich! and when I married the girl, I saw a smile of triumph play upon the faces of her needy relatives, as they thought of their well-planned scheme and their fine prize.

Dickens was, as yet, not really aware of the sharp limits his enormous popularity and worshipful public might set to the things he could directly say, and he was still largely unaware of the most dangerous things he would want to say. Yet there was already a feeling of tension, of suppressed irritability, of unexplored conflict between his natural optimism and zest for life, heightened as it inevitably was by his early popularity and material success, and his uneasy persistent awareness of the scarcely hidden evil and cruelty of that society which was being so generous to him.

For the time being this was relieved in his private life by the extraordinarily wide, but not indiscriminate, acts of private charity which were to continue until his death; by the physically exhausting relaxations of a day's hard riding or rapid walking, in which Forster and two or three other new literary, artistic or theatrical friends often joined him, and by extravagant tirades and "desperate ambrose" vendettas against one or another of the various publishers who were enriching themselves through his labors.

This anger at exploitation was not merely a personal matter of pounds, shillings and pence. Dickens had some years before *Pickwick*, when he was working for *The True Sun*, helped to organize perhaps the first group of reporters to threaten—without so naming it—a strike, and had served as spokesman for the delegation which presented their demands to the publisher, securing the requested salary increase. In 1845 when he himself was, briefly, editor and part proprietor of a newspaper he overruled his partner, the publisher, to effect a substantial raise in the minimum wage rate and general scale of payments, saying of his partner that he "had become possessed of the idea that everyone receiving a salary in return for services is his natural enemy, and should be suspected and mistrusted accordingly." And in 1856, writing to the famous actor Macready, whose daughter's poem he was accepting for publication, Dickens concluded:

> Please to note that I make it a rule to pay for everything that is inserted in "Household Words" holding it to be a part of my trust to make my fellow proprietors understand that they have no right to unrequited labour.

In his writing during the six years between *Boz* and his first American trip (1836-1842), Dickens achieved a temporarily more satisfying resolution of the conflict. In each of these early novels—*Pickwick, Oliver Twist, Nicholas Nickelby, Old Curiosity Shop,* and *Barnaby Rudge*—he attacks one or more specific evils; debtors' prisons, workhouses, Yorkshire schools, legal fraud, capital punishment, envy and self-righteousness disguised as religion and justice. Not only are most of these peripheral social evils which capitalism can afford to outgrow; they almost all have, in these books, as their major victims individual or special groups of children whom a secure capitalist society can afford to protect from certain gross attacks.

There was already implicit a certain deeper criticism of the utilitarian philosophy, the state use of religion, and above all the central position of money in society. But this was still so largely unformulated and unobtrusive that it did not prevent a very general acceptance of the books by the upper as well as the lower class of the reading public. It is, however, noteworthy that the latter were from the very beginning among Dickens' most enthusiastic followers. The cheap serial form of publication which he continued to the end of his life made it possible for even those with a very limited income to purchase each number as it appeared, and in many instances the proprietor of a rooming house, members of various workers' clubs, mutual benefit organizations and other working-class groups would subscribe and read them aloud weekly, biweekly or monthly.

There was among the more discerning or more consciously reactionary critics some disapproval from the very first. For example, Lockhart, editor of the powerful Tory *Quarterly*, grumbled that Pickwick was "all very well—but damned low!" Harriet Martineau, a leading Utilitarian, sharply criticized Dickens' attack on the Poor Law in *Oliver Twist*, referring to his "vigorous erroneousness." The *Quarterly* spoke petulantly in 1839 of Dickens' penchant for the "outcasts of humanity." Gladstone said in disapprobation of *Nicholas Nickelby:* "There is no church in the book and the motives are not those of religion." And Kingsley objected to Dickens' "false ethical theorem" that "The man is not responsible for his faults. They are to be imputed to his circumstances. But he is responsible for, and therefore to be valued solely by, his virtues. They are to be imputed to himself."

It is interesting to compare this disapproving contemporary summary of Dickens' ethical attitude with the statement of the great twentieth century proletarian novelist, Martin Anderson Nexö, who says of his own hero Pelle:

> He was not fond of using great words, but at the bottom of his heart he was convinced that everything had originated in want and misery. Distrust and selfishness came from misusage; they were man's defence against extortion and the extortion came from insecure conditions, from reminders of want or unconscious fear of it. Most crimes could easily be traced back to the distressing conditions, and even where the connection was not perceptible he was sure that it nevertheless existed. It was his experience that every one in reality was good: the evil in them could nearly always be traced back to something definite while the goodness often existed in spite of everything.

And in his own person in the prologue to *Ditte*, speaking of the family Man, Nexö declares:

> In addition to this the family was alike in that most of its members were better than their circumstances. One could recognize the Man family anywhere by their bad qualities being traceable to definite causes, while for the good in them there was no explanation at all; it was inbred.

But on the whole it was not until after the publication of a radically class-conscious Christmas story, *The Chimes*, in 1844, that Dickens' work created any general social uneasiness or resentment in England. For the time being the extraordinary humor, pathos and drama of the individual stories and the more or less specific character of the evils they singled out for attack allowed rich as well as poor to enjoy them without serious misgivings. Dickens himself was also for a time lulled by the practical reforms his work helped to bring about, and the many others in which his growing reputation helped him personally to play an important role. Nor was he himself yet quite aware of the implications of his attitude. The tremendous growth of his understanding only becomes apparent when one compares, for example, his penetrating treatment of the necessary and justified revolution in the oppressed countryside and starved Parisian arrondissements of *The Tale of Two Cities* (1859) with his superficial treatment of the insurrectionary mob in the Gordon riots of *Barnaby Rudge* (1841). Similarly his careless use of anti-Semitic stereotype in *Oliver Twist* (1837–8), although that was based in realistic detail on a current trial of a notorious fence and thief-trainer, should be contrasted with the statement Riah makes in *Our Mutual Friend* (1864–5):

> For it is not, in Christian countries, with the Jews as with other peoples. Men say "this is a bad Greek, but there are good Greeks. This is a bad Turk, but there are good Turks." Not so with the Jews. Men find the bad among us easily enough—among what peoples are the bad not easily found?—but they take the worst of us as samples of the best; they take the lowest of us as presentations of the highest; and they say, "all Jews are alike." If, doing what I was content to do here, because I was grateful for the past and have small need of money now, I had been a Christian, I could have done it, compromising no one but my individual self. But doing it as a Jew, I could not choose but compromise the Jews of all conditions and all countries.

Dickens evidently meant this as a self-critical confession of error. For immediately after the publication of *Oliver Twist* he had replied to a Jewish woman's protest at Fagin with the statement that there were good and bad people in all national and religious groups and that an artist must be free to draw both realistically. He had pointed out the many wicked Christians in the book, some strongly identified with professions of religion, as the Jew was not, and had said that, sorry as he was to have hurt his correspondent's feelings, he could not agree with her opinion that it was worse to draw a bad Jew than a bad Christian.

But by the time Dickens came to write *Our Mutual Friend* over twenty years later he had not only changed his mind but wished publicly to say so. For concluding the statement quoted above, Riah, clearly speaking for his author as well as himself, adds: "I would that all our people remembered it! Though I have little right to say so, seeing that it came home so late to me."

Although in his late twenties it still seemed possible to Dickens that, wrong as many institutions, laws and governments were, an individual wealthy businessman, especially when retired, might play the part of a deus ex machina scattering fairy gold as do Mr. Brownlow, the Cheeryble brothers or Pickwick himself; yet even then this superficial use of the fairy godfather denied his truer vision. Sam Weller helps Mr. Pickwick far more effectively and consistently than Pickwick helps him; no one sees more clearly than Dickens how little Oliver Twist's rescue does for the teeming slums and miserable workhouse children of England; and in 1838 after a visit to the model factory of Manchester whose owners are reputed to be the original of the Cheeryble brothers Dickens wrote:

> I went some weeks ago to Manchester, and saw the *worst* cotton mill. And then I saw the *best*. Ex uno disce omnes. There was no great difference between them. . . . So far as seeing goes, I have seen enough for my purpose, and what I have seen has disgusted and astonished me beyond all measure. I mean to strike the heaviest blow in my power for these unfortunate creatures, but whether I shall do so in *Nickleby* or wait some other opportunity, I have not yet determined.

The reader not yet well acquainted with Dickens should be warned that the emphasis on his fundamental intention here and hereafter in this biographical essay must not be allowed to obscure his incomparable joy in life and the inimitable richness of humorous observations which make almost all his books sheer delight to read.

There is almost no chapter of any book and certainly no complete section from which examples like this one from *Martin Chuzzlewit* could not be multiplied:

> It made Tom melancholy to picture himself walking up the lane and back to Pecksniff's as of old; and being melancholy,

he looked downwards at the basket on his knee, which he had for the moment forgotten.

"She is the kindest and most considerate creature in the world," thought Tom. "Now I know that she particularly told that man of hers not to look at me, on purpose to prevent my throwing him a shilling! I had it ready for him all the time, and he never once looked towards me; whereas that man naturally (for I know him very well) would have done nothing but grin and stare. Upon my word, the kindness of people perfectly melts me."

Here he caught the coachman's eye. The coachman winked. "Remarkable fine woman for her time of life," said the coachman.

"I quite agree with you," returned Tom. "So she is."

"Finer than many a young one, I mean to say," observed the coachman. "Eh?"

"Than many a young one," Tom assented.

"I don't care for 'em myself when they're too young," remarked the coachman.

This was a matter of taste which Tom did not feel himself called upon to discuss.

"You'll seldom find 'em possessing correct opinions about refreshment, for instance, when they're too young, you know," said the coachman. "A woman must have arrived at maturity before her mind's equal to coming provided with a basket like that."

"Perhaps you would like to know what it contains?" said Tom, smiling.

As the coachman only laughed, and as Tom was curious himself, he unpacked it, and put the articles, one by one, upon the footboard—a cold roast fowl, a packet of ham in slices, a crusty loaf, a piece of cheese, a paper of biscuits, half a dozen apples, a knife, some butter, a screw of salt, and a bottle of old sherry. There was a letter besides, which Tom put in his pocket.

The coachman was so earnest in his approval of Mrs. Lupin's provident habits, and congratulated Tom so warmly on his good fortune, that Tom felt it necessary, for the lady's sake, to explain that the basket was a strictly Platonic basket, and had merely been presented to him in the way of friendship. When he had made this statement with perfect gravity—for he felt it incumbent on him to disabuse the mind of this lax rover of any incorrect impressions on the subject—he signified that he would be glad to share the gifts with him, and proposed that they should attack the basket in a spirit of good fellowship at any time in the course of the night which the coachman's experience and knowledge of the road might suggest as being best adapted to the purpose. From this time they chatted so pleasantly together, that although Tom knew infinitely more of unicorns than horses, the coachman informed his friend the guard at the end of the next stage "that rum as the box-seat looked, he was as good a one to go, in point of conversation, as ever he'd wish to sit by."

It is true, as the excellent French critic Cazamian says of Dickens:

> Nowhere do the lightness of spirit and the happy spontaneity of the recital allow the sadness of class struggles to be long forgotten. The opposition of the rich and poor is the sometimes concealed but always present thesis of his moral work.

But the former qualities are also almost always present. And, as Chesterton says in speaking especially of these early novels:

> Nothing that has ever been written about human delights, no Earthly Paradise, no Utopia, has ever come so near the quick nerve of happiness as his description of the rare extravagances of the poor; . . .

Although Dickens learned more from life than from books and rarely in his work referred to any writer but Shakespeare, or, occasionally, the eighteenth century novelists, he had during these eventful first six writing years been deeply impressed by Carlyle's *French Revolution* and *Chartism*. Perhaps those books, as well as his own growing concern with the broader outlines of politico-economic institutions, made him increasingly anxious to visit the United States and see for himself whether that daring republican experiment had really achieved freedom and equality for its people.

In 1840 a general election, in which he declined two invitations to stand for parliament as a Whig, but contributed several strongly anti-Tory songs to the *Whig Examiner*, turned his interest even more powerfully toward political exploration. Finally, in January 1842, he and Kate, leaving their four children with the Macreadys, set sail for the new world.

We cannot understand the depth of Dickens' disillusionment with the United States unless we first realize the height of his expectations. Still only partially aware of the real nature of the inhumanity of nineteenth century England, he thought of the United States as a world in which the relations between men were truly human and where neither class distinctions nor exploitation existed.

His horror at meeting slavery face to face and hearing it defended by men who boasted themselves citizens of "the land of the free" was immeasurable. He himself wrote for publication: "Thus the stars wink upon the bloody stripes and Liberty pulls down her cap upon her eyes, and owns oppression in its vilest aspect for her sister." And in many private letters, a few of which we must quote since they are not otherwise readily accessible, he gave in more concrete and circumstantial detail his experiences in the slave states.

Another thing which profoundly shocked Dickens was the greater pressure for conformity, the tyranny of an illegal but real censorship of opinion by the corrupt press, the lynch spirit it frequently evoked, and the fear even in the North of any open debate on such fundamental questions as slavery.

The meetings of Congress and of the various state legislatures he attended struck him as even more deplorably lacking in sense and dignity than those of Parliament for which, as we know, he already had the most profound contempt. He reports, and apologizes for this indifference in his *American Notes* by saying: "I have born the House of Commons like a man and yielded to no weakness but slumber in the House of Lords." But to most Americans the apology only aggravated the offense.

The perhaps more widespread and certainly more open corruption of governments and their employees; the greater laxity in commercial dealings fostered by the comparatively lax bankruptcy laws; the ease of land swindles, taking advantage especially of the many "green" immigrants; and the open piracy of English novels then protected by no copyright arrangements; were all also important although secondary factors in Dickens' deep disappointment. These criticisms and his disapproval of boarding house life and mannerless familiarity are made sufficiently clear in the pages of *Martin Chuzzlewit*, but his more fundamental condemnation of the United States is made most explicit in the letters written during his four months in America.

On March 20, 1842, he wrote to Macready:

> . . . Still it is of no use. I *am* disappointed. This is not the republic I came to see; this is not the republic of my imagination. I infinitely prefer a liberal monarchy—even with its sickening accompaniment of court circulars—to such a government as this. The more I think of its youth and strength, the poorer and more trifling in a thousand aspects it appears in my eyes. In everything of which it has made a boast—excepting its edu-

cation of the people and its care for poor children—it sinks immeasurably below the level I had placed it upon; and England, even England, bad and faulty as the old land is, and miserable as many of her people are, rises in the comparison. . . .

Freedom of opinion! Where is it? I see a press more mean and paltry and silly and disgraceful than any country I ever knew. . . . I speak of Bancroft, and am advised to be silent on that subject, for he is "a black sheep—a Democrat." I speak of Bryant, and am entreated to be more careful, for the same reason. I speak of international copyright, and am implored not to ruin myself outright. . . .

The sight of slavery in Virginia, the hatred of British feeling upon the subject, and the miserable hints of the impotent indignation of the South have pained me very much; on the last head, of course, I have felt nothing but a mingled pity and amusement; on the other, sheer distress. . . .

The month before, shortly after landing in New York, he had written to Forster:

When we reach Baltimore, we are in the regions of slavery. It exists there in its least shocking and most mitigated form; but there it is. They whisper, here (they dare only whisper, you know, and that below their breaths), that on that place, and all through the South, there is a dull gloomy cloud on which the very word seems written. I shall be able to say, one of these days, that I accepted no public mark of respect in any place where slavery was;—and that's something. . . . I still reserve my opinion of the national character—just whispering that I tremble for a radical coming here, unless he is a radical on principle, by reason and reflection, and from the sense of right. I fear that if he were anything else, he would return home a Tory. . . . I say no more on that head for two months from this time, save that I do fear that the heaviest blow ever dealt at liberty will be dealt by this country, in the failure of its example to the earth. The scenes that are passing in Congress now, all tending to the separation of the States, fill one with such a deep disgust that I dislike the very name of Washington (meaning the place, not the man), and am repelled by the mere thought of approaching it.

On March 17, he wrote from Virginia:

Richmond is a prettily situated town; but, like other towns in slave districts (as the planters themselves admit), has an aspect of decay and gloom which to an unaccustomed eye is *most* distressing. In the black car (for they don't let them sit with the whites), on the railroad as we went there, were a mother and family whom the steamer was conveying away, to sell; retaining the man (the husband and father I mean) on his plantation. The children cried the whole way. Yesterday, on board the boat, a slave owner and two constables were our fellow passengers. They were coming here in search of two Negroes who had run away on the previous day. On the bridge at Richmond there is a notice against fast driving over it, as it is rotten and crazy: penalty—for whites, five dollars; for slaves, fifteen stripes. My heart is lightened as if a great load had been taken from it, when I think that we are turning our backs on this accursed and detested system. I really don't think I could have borne it any longer. It is all very well to say "be silent on the subject." They won't let you be silent. They *will* ask you what you think of it; and *will* expatiate on slavery as if it were one of the greatest blessings of mankind. "It's not," said a hard bad-looking fellow to me the other day, "it's not the interest of a man to use his slaves ill. It's damned nonsense that you hear in England."—I told him quietly that it was not a man's interest to get drunk, or to steal, or to game, or to indulge in any other vice, but he *did* indulge in it for all that. That cruelty, and the abuse of irresponsible power, were two of the bad passions of human nature, with the gratification of which, considerations of interest or of ruin had nothing whatever to do; that bad masters, cruel masters, and masters who disgraced the form they bore, were matters of experience and history, whose existence was as undisputed as that of slaves themselves. He was a little taken aback by this, and asked me if I believed in the bible. Yes, I said, but if any man could prove to me that it sanctioned slavery, I would place no further credence in it. "Well, then," he said, "by God, sir, the n . . . . s must be kept down, and the whites have put down the coloured people wherever they have found them." "That's the whole question," said I. "Yes, and by God," says he, "the British had better not stand out on that point when Lord Ashburton comes over, for I never felt so warlike as I do now,—and that's a fact."

And the next month, April 15, he wrote from St. Louis:

>They won't let me alone about slavery. A certain Judge in St. Louis went so far yesterday, that I fell upon him (to the indescribable horror of the man who brought him) and told him a piece of my mind. I said that I was very averse to speaking on the subject here, and always forbore, if possible; but when he pitied our national ignorance of the truths of slavery, I must remind him that we went upon indisputable records, obtained after many years of careful investigation, and at all sorts of self-sacrifice; and that I believed we were much more competent to judge of its atrocity and horror, than he who had

been brought up in the midst of it. I told him that I could sympathise with men who admitted it to be a dreadful evil, but frankly confessed their inability to devise a means of getting rid of it; but that men who spoke of it as a blessing, as a matter of course, as a state of things to be desired, were out of the pale of reason; and that for them to speak of ignorance or prejudice was an absurdity too ridiculous to be combatted. . . .

It is not six years ago, since a slave in this very same St. Louis, being arrested (I forget for what) and knowing he had no chance of a fair trial be his offence what it might, drew his bowieknife and ripped the constable across the body. A scuffle ensuing, the desperate Negro stabbed two others with the same weapon. The mob who gathered round (among whom were men of mark, wealth, and influence in the place) overpowered him by numbers, carried him away to a piece of open ground beyond the city; and *burned him alive.* This, I say, was done within six years in broad day; in a city with its courts, lawyers, tipstaffs, judges, jails and hangman; and not a hair on the head of one of those men has been hurt to this day. . . .

They say the slaves are fond of their masters. Look at this pretty vignette* (part of the stock-in-trade of a newspaper), and judge how you would feel, when men, looking in your face, told you such tales with the newspaper lying on the table. In all the slave districts, advertisements for runaways are as much matters of course as the announcement of the play for the evening with us.

---

* [RUNAWAY NEGRO IN JAIL was the heading of the advertisement enclosed, which had a woodcut of master and slave in its corner, and announced that Wilford Garner, sheriff and jailér of Chicot County, Arkansas, requested the owner to come and prove his property.]

While formal opposition to slavery was a respectable and even popular view in England, which had abolished it in its colonies ten years before, there were few Englishmen who realized as did Dickens its full horror and the fundamental way in which it affected the entire culture of the United States. Even fewer shared his later realization that the Negro had not received justice when he received merely legal freedom with no special protection or economic provision. Dickens' absolute refusal to countenance the social discrimination which emancipation had not attempted to remove was then shared by almost no one.

During his tour of readings in the United States twenty-six years later (1868) he wrote to his daughter about an incident which had occurred when his business manager, following his directions, refused to accept this prejudice:

> One night at New York, in our second or third row, there were two well-dressed women with a tinge of color—I should say, not even quadroons. But the holder of one ticket who found his seat next to them, demanded of Dolby "What he meant by fixing him next to those two Gord damned cusses of n[....]s?" and insisted on being supplied with another good place. Dolby firmly replied that he was perfectly certain Mr. Dickens would not recognise such an objection on any account, but he could have his money back if he chose. Which, after some squabbling, he had.

It is not surprising that Dickens returned to England in June 1842 convinced that the inhumanity he hated was not to be cured by the simple substitution of a republic for a monarchy, or even by the complete obliteration of legal class distinctions if they were to be replaced by the unbridled power of business.

However, in his *American Notes*, which was written immediately upon his return and published before the end of the year, Dickens praised everything he honestly could, included his admiration of American hospitality, of the unaffected care for strangers, and of the free and easy friendliness of the common man, who did small courtesies as favors for an equal and not for tips from a superior. He also noted and admired at some length the various state laws regulating child labor, free public education, and the size, cleanliness and order of state supported hospitals, prisons, and institutions for the deaf and dumb, the blind, and so forth. He even avoided the copyright question and spoke as little as he could of slavery, government corruption and the tyranny of the commercial press.

The result was a rather dull book—almost the only one Dickens ever succeeded in writing—which was not much liked in England and, for its mild but accurate criticism, was universally execrated throughout the United States.

In *Martin Chuzzlewit*, however, Dickens who could never, in fiction, tell less then he knew of the truth, presented a powerful and radical indictment of the money motive so fundamental in its hypocritical rottenness to the older English civilization and in its shameless raw violence to the younger American one. Only his deep-rooted faith in man's ability to reform himself relieves the somberness of the book. Mark Tapley, while no match for the immortal Weller, plays much the same role as the representative of uncorrupted resourceful humanity to be found only among the poor and is, significantly, both the savior of, and finally the ideal on which, the young gentleman models his new character. Tom Pinch gives an added dimension to the work as an artist and scholar whose unworldly simplicity and indiscriminating faith make him, for a long time, the unconscious accomplice as well as the unsuspecting victim of a greedy and dishonest "pillar of society."

There is small wonder that, despite the popularity in England of the satirical American scenes, the circulation of the book showed a marked decline and Dickens began seriously to worry about holding the more respectable—and wealthy—section of his reading public. The size of his family, to which a fifth child had just been added, the comfortable scale on which they were living, his complete responsibility for his parents' support and his constant contributions not only to his brothers and sisters but also to his wife's family, all made this concern an urgent one, and he began to cast about for some way in which he could avoid so heavy a reliance on his unaided pen.

Yet although his letters at this period frequently express the fear that he may be written out, or that his energy may flag, he was at the very same time not only responding generously and enthusiastically to every appeal for his assistance in drafting or propagandizing for improved social legislation—labor regulations, education, and so forth—and to innumerable requests for help in financing or conducting such institutions as hospitals and free "Ragged schools," but was even seeking out such duties and helping to initiate slum clearance and other similar experiments.

His increasing concern about complete dependence on his popularity as a novelist seems largely to be due to an unadmitted fear of repudiation by the most influential and articulate part of his public. This uneasiness naturally increased as he became more and more aware of his own deep-rooted antagonism to them.

For example, he wrote in a confidential letter dated May, 1843, when he was just beginning *Martin Chuzzlewit*:

> O heaven! if you could have been with me at the hospital dinner last Monday. There were men there—your city aristocracy—who made such speeches, and expressed such sentiments, as any moderately intelligent dustman would have blushed through his cindery bloom to have thought of. Sleek, slobbering, bow-paunched, over-fed, apoplectic, snorting cattle—and

the auditory leaping up in their delight! I never saw such an illustration of the power of purse, or felt so degraded and abased since I have had ears and eyes. The absurdity of the thing was too horrible to laugh at. It was perfectly overwhelming.

And next March when finishing *Martin Chuzzlewit* he wrote prophetically in another letter:

> I believe it is in New Orleans that the man is lying under sentence of death, who, not having the fear of God before his eyes, did not deliver up a captive slave to the torture. The greatest gun in that country has not burst yet—*but it will.*
> Heaven help us too from explosion nearer home! I declare I never go into what is called "society" that I am not aweary of it, despise it, hate it and reject it. The more I see of its extraordinary conceit, and its stupendous ignorance of what is passing out of doors, the more certain I am that it is approaching the period when, being incapable of reforming itself, it will have to submit to be reformed by others off the face of the earth.

Dickens had also begun to write, or rather dictate, during the busy two years since his return from America, an oversimplified *Child's History of England*, important only in that it was written so that Charlie, not yet ten, should begin his education with the right point of view. The "right point of view" and the tone of the book are indicated by such passages as the one about the famous and much maligned peasant revolutionary leader, Wat Tyler:

> Wat was a hard-working man, who had suffered much, and had been foully outraged; and it is probable that he was a man of a much higher nature and a much braver spirit than any of the parasites who exulted then, or have exulted since, over his defeat.

Four months later, in July, 1844, Dickens carried out a much discussed resolution, rented his house, and with Kate, the five children, two nurses, a courier, and his young sister-in-law Georgiana, who had stayed with the children during the American trip and was to remain with them until after his death, he again left England for a two-year sojourn in Italy.

Thackeray comments acidly in a note:

I met on the pier as I was running for the dear life, the great Dickens, with his wife, his children, his Miss Hogarth, all looking abominably coarse and vulgar and happy.

With his family settled in Genoa, Dickens made a number of short trips to other Italian cities, laid the basis for his lifelong affectionate familiarity with Paris, especially its theatre, and paid several flying visits to London. One of these was particularly important to him. His letters to Forster show us how deeply absorbed he was in writing a new Christmas story, *The Chimes*, and how troubled he was by the articulation in that story of his so far unrealized understanding that there was a deep irreconcilable conflict between the rich and the poor in his own society. In several of these letters he asks Forster to invite a select group for a trial reading before he proceeds to publication, and repeats with great urgency that Carlyle—whose *Past and Present* had just appeared—*must* be of the number.

The Chimes would have been startling at any time as perhaps the most class-conscious morality play to be perpetrated in the name of Christmas, but coming at this early period of Dickens' life it is really amazing. Only the year before he had written *The Christmas Carol* in which the happiness of Tiny Tim's whole family are secured by the reform of Bob Cratchit's employer, the miserly Scrooge.

Even there, of course, the story is made moving by Dickens' sense of reality. Humphrey House, in his illuminating discussion of Dickens' use of money in *Dickens' World*, says:

> In fact, one of the reasons why Dickens' benevolent sentiment still has power to bring tears to the eyes, when literary fashion and moral taste incline so heavily against it, is that it has been so well prepared for: he has built up so carefully and realistically scenes of poverty, depression, and unhappiness that the ultimate release—the death, the 5-pound note, the turkey, the job, the smile—brings a break of tension also for the reader. Without such a background Benevolent Sentimentality may justly be sneered at; and we do not weep. The effect is largely got by giving a proper importance to money.

House does not seem to sense the growing uneasiness and final condemnation underlying Dickens' realistic observation of the place of money in his society, nor, of course, the emerging class analysis in which Dickens so clearly shows how those least profoundly affected by the money economy are those who, in ordinary terms, most need money. Yet even this unanalyzed realization of an aspect of Dickens' work so vital and so seldom noted is worth quoting a little more at length:

> This minute attention to the business of life gives Dickens's novels their immense solidity: each is a full world where the characters can fully be themselves, even doing the smallest thing. The prodigious grotesques, like Quilp or Sarah Gamp, maintain their unique life among a caste of more ordinary people because they are so carefully linked to a world of commonplace affairs, the world of moneylending and sickness and birth. The link in nearly every case is money itself. Money is a main theme of nearly every book that Dickens wrote: getting, keeping, spending, owing, bequeathing provide the intricacies of his plots; character after character is constructed round an attitude to money. Social status without it is subordinate. . . . Romance is valued in sterling. Pylades does not show his loyalty to Orestes in the dangers of long journeys and rescues from death, but in surreptitious loans or in sharing the last sixpence. Money is the instrument by which the villain thwarts the hero; and the two are chiefly distinguished by their attitudes towards it; their attitudes to women are secondary. Dickens points a debt at a man's head much as G. P. R. James points a pistol: His heroes are unarmed because they are poor. Money is a weapon of immense power: physical strength, passion, religion, all quail before it; only death shows its weakness.

But the day of the Cheeryble Brothers was over. From now on, in Dickens' books, it is by and large, as he himself says in *The Chimes,* only the poor who help the poor while the rich, with rare personal exceptions try "to put them down."

The Chimes was immediately successful although it never attained the contemporary popularity or, of course, the extraordinarily long-lived fame of the earlier *Christmas Carol.*

Like the *Christmas Carol, The Chimes* begins with a representative of the "deserving poor," a messenger "boy" of sixty who, in addition to cold, hunger and weariness, is oppressed by wondering "whether there is any good at all in us, or whether we are born bad. We seem to be doing dreadful things; we seem to give a deal of trouble; we are always being complained of and guarded against. One way or another, we fill the papers.—I can't make out whether we have any business on the face of the earth or not. Sometimes I think we must have—a little; and sometimes I think we must be intruding."

His young daughter and her sweetheart, who have waited three years for times to get better, suddenly decide not to waste their youth and, having no problems of settlements, trousseaux or furniture to delay them, plan a wedding for the very next day—New Year's Day.

Three gentlemen, a liberal alderman, a conservative enthusiast for the good old days, and a political economist, are all equally shocked at overhearing this anti-Malthusian conspiracy and frighten Trotty into agreeing that such wicked improvidence will result in drunkenness, desertion, and a crowd of shoeless juvenile delinquents.

Convinced that the poor must be wrong to be so miserable, Trotty then returns home and giving up his bed to a still poorer chance-met "vagabond" in search of work, falls uneasily asleep in a chair. He spends the next few hours in a wild nightmare of disembodied visits to various scenes of the future.

In one of these he hears Will Fern, the "vagabond" who has been arrested innumerable times, warn his judges that the time may come when the poor man's Bible will read: "Whither thou goest, I can Not go; where thou lodgest I do Not lodge; thy people are Not my people; Nor thy God my God."

After seeing this and the ruined and wasted lives of his daughter and her sweetheart, Trotty cries out against the weakness in which he had, by doubting them, betrayed his own kind. He ends:

> I know that our inheritance is held in store for us by Time.
> I know there is a sea of Time to rise one day; before which all who wrong us or oppress us will be swept away like leaves. I see it, on the flow, I know that we must trust and hope, and neither doubt ourselves, nor doubt the good in one another.

With this he awakens to find the bells ringing in the New Year. The neighbors rush in to surprise Meg and Richard with a celebration of their wedding eve, and among them even poor Will finds a friend and a job. But despite this seasonable happy ending Dickens concludes: "Had Trotty dreamed?—If it be so, O listener—try to bear in mind the realities from which these shadows come;—."

Both radical and conservative critics reacted quickly to its outspoken partisanship. Jeffrey, the liberal editor of *The Edinburgh Review*, who had befriended the struggling young Carlyle and responded so warmly to Hazlitt's dying appeal, wrote Dickens:

> The aldermen and justices, friends and fathers, etc. and in short, all the tribe of selfishness and cowardice and cant, will hate you in their hearts, and cavil when they can; will accuse you of wicked exaggeration and excitement to discontent; and what they pleasantly call disaffection! But never mind—the good and the brave are with you, and the truth also, and in that sign you will continue.

The more completely radical press exhorted its working-class readers:

> It was written purposely to discontent you with what is daily going on around you. Things so terrible that they should exist but in dreams, are here presented in a dream. . . . For ourselves, we will hope that the challenge may be taken . . . in abatement of the long and dire conspiracy that has been carried on against poverty by the world and the world's law.

And Chesterton, the later warmhearted, albeit sometimes confused, champion of Dickens and his real friends, says of *The Chimes* and its shocked contemporaries:

> He fell furiously on all their ideas; the cheap advice to live cheaply, the base advice to live basely, above all the preposterous primary assumption that the rich are to advise the poor, and not the poor the rich.

Nor were the conservatives less discerning. In a number of the magazines the attack was somewhat oblique. For example, the February 1845 issue of the *London Magazine* pointed out with some asperity that Christianity was the true redresser of the grievances of the poor, and that Dickens necessarily fell short of his goal since he had not got the light of Christian Philanthropy to guide him.

Similarly the May issue of the *North British Review* stated for the guidance of its large body of readers that it could not find the moral tendency of Dickens' books wholesome, since prominence was there given merely to motives of good temper and kindness rather than to those of religion.

More specifically another conservative publication scolded:

There is the same association of beauty and superlative excellence with poverty, and of mental dulness and bodily odiousness (if we may coin the word) with wealth . . . the same spirit of exaggeration in expression.

And still more pertinently we find in yet another paper:

. . . he has gone into the very opposite extreme of ranging party against party and class against class; instead of addressing himself to all men, and for the good of all, he has taken upon himself to separate the good from the bad. . . .

In the autumn of 1845 the family were returning to England. Kate had just had a sixth child and Dickens was struggling with the next Christmas book, *The Cricket On the Hearth*, which was soon attacked by *The Times* and other influential papers as cheap and offensive, and writing to Forster and others of his anxiety to found a new daily newspaper in which he might "strike a blow for the poor."

In contacting and securing backers for the paper Dickens made it apparent that, vague as his specific political objectives were, he felt the need for some sort of coalition between the middle-class Radicals, concerned largely with legislative reforms, and the working-class Chartists, more realistically involved in economic problems.

At the first staff meeting of *The Daily News* in January 1846, Dickens characteristically insisted upon having the compositors, pressmen and other manual workers present. He "expatiated in terms of general brotherhood and invited the sympathy of the men of toil with the men of mind, whose efforts were to be devoted 'in this new channel for the common good.' "

His editorship lasted only until some time in February when he resigned. There had been much friction, particularly about his successful attempt to raise wages substantially over the then prevailing standard, and perhaps he was also discouraged by a realization of the great distance between his social views and that of his reformist colleagues, while he was forced to admit that there was clearly no practical line of general political policy to which he could even try turning the paper. During his short incumbency he had printed a number of interesting personal contributions, notably his "Hymn of the Wiltshire Laborers" inspired by the words of a

Wiltshire working woman. Speaking at an anti-Corn Law meeting she had said, "Don't you all think that we have a great need to cry to our God to put it in the hearts of our generous Queen and her members of Parliament to grant us free bread?"

During the next few months Dickens completed his *Pictures from Italy*—again a somewhat uninspired factual reportage of his travels—and began *Dombey and Son* which appeared in monthly parts, 1846–1848.

The family again went abroad for a prolonged stay in 1846, living first in Switzerland and then in Paris. Dickens wrote:

> Apart from this, you have no conception of the preposterous, insolent little aristocracy of Geneva: the most ridiculous caricature the fancy can suggest of what we know in England. I was talking to two famous gentlemen (very intelligent men) of that place, not long ago, who came over to invite me to a sort of reception there—which I declined. Really their talk about "the people" and "the masses," and the necessity they would shortly be under of shooting a few of them as an example for the rest, . . .

Back in England by the end of 1847, he was beside himself with joy at the news of the French Revolution in February, 1848, and wrote Forster an exuberant letter, which the latter found most disturbing, although he ventured to criticize only its grammar:

> Mon ami, je trouve que j'aime tant la République, qu'il me faut renoncer ma langue et écrire seulement le langage de la République de France—langage des Dieux et des Anges—langage, en un mot, des Francais! . . .
> Vive la gloire de France! Vive la République! Vive le Peuple! Plus de Royauté! Plus de Bourbons! Plus de Guizot! Mort aux traitres! Faisons couler le sang pour la liberté, la justice, la cause populaire!
> Jusqu'a cinq heures et demie ,adieu, mon brave! Recevez de ma consideration distinguée, et croyez-moi, CONCITOYEN! votre tout devoué. CITOYEN CHARLES DICKENS.
>
> [My friend, I find that I love the Republic so much, that it is necessary for me to renounce my tongue and write exclusively in the language of the Republic of France—language of the Gods and of the Angels—language, in a word, of the French! . . .
> Life to the glory of France! Life to the Republic! Life to the People! No more Royalty! No more Bourbons! No more

Guizot! Death to the traitors! Let us make blood run for liberty, justice, and the cause of the people!

Until half past five, adieu, my good fellow! Receive my respectful regards and believe me, fellow citizen, yours devotedly,

Citizen Charles Dickens.]

Dickens took an equally unorthodox view of the hysteria with which the English papers viewed the preparations for the last Chartist petition (see pp. 638-41, 682) and wrote, "Chartist fears and rumours shake us now and then, but I suspect the Government make the most of such things for their purposes."

Another more public statement was occasioned by the publication of Cruikshank's cartoon series, "The Bottle." Dickens who had greatly admired Hogarth's "Rake's Progress" for its realism, found the unrealistic moral emphasis of his talented contemporary much less admirable and wrote:

> When Mr. Cruikshank shows us . . . that side of the metal on which the people in their crimes and faults are stamped he is bound to help us to a glance at that other side on which the government that forms the people, with all its faults and vices is no less plainly impressed.

The illness and death of his sister Fanny and soon thereafter of her young son; Kate's ill health after a miscarriage—they already had seven children; and the sense of growing alienation from the ideas of even his most liberal friends combined to worry Charles during this year, and he sought relief in intensive amateur theatricals and in work on several unusual "social service" projects. Actually these theatricals were conducted on a semiprofessional level and raised literally thousands of pounds for the benefit of various charities. The social service projects were largely financed by a very wealthy philanthropist, Miss Coutts, and included probably the first nonpenitential "home" or rehabilitation center for unmarried mothers, substantial aid to the nondenominational "ragged schools" set up in various slum neighborhoods, and the beginning of a slum clearance housing project which came to fruition in four full blocks of modern flats—the first of their kind—in 1862.

Dickens comments some years later on his interest in one of these projects, writing:

> I sent Miss Coutts (as she was then) a sledge-hammer account of the Ragged Schools, and as I saw her name for two hundred pounds in the Clergy Subscription list, took pains to show her that religious mysteries and difficult creeds wouldn't do for such pupils. I told her, too, that it was of immense importance that they should be *washed*.

This hitherto neglected aspect of Dickens' life has been very well presented by the recent work of Edgar Johnson who, in addition to writing what is to date Dickens' best full length biography, edited a complete volume of Dickens' letters to Lady Burdett-Coutts. These are often most amusing, and indicate how shocked even the charitable of Dickens' acquaintances were by his uncensorious plans for the distressed. He describes one such philanthropist in a note to Lady Burdett-Coutts, concluding:

> I forgot to tell you that she asked me if it were true that the girls at the Shepherd's Bush "had pianos." I shall always regret that I didn't answer yes—each girl a grand, downstairs—and a cottage in her bedroom—besides a small guitar in the washhouse.

When in 1848 Dickens published the completed *Dombey and Son* in book form, it was the first novel he had written since *Martin Chuzzlewit*, completed three years before. It marked a great advance not only in the closely knit and logical plot which from now on replaced the easygoing picaresque romance or series of adventures that essentially constituted the story line of *Pickwick Papers, Oliver Twist, Nicholas Nickleby, The Old Curiosity Shop* and even *Barnaby Rudge*, but also in the keen analytic observation he now brought to bear on the contemporary social scene. It has often been noted that the railroad—a central phenomenon of mid-nineteenth century England—is first used in *Dombey and Son*, and that up to that time Dickens had predated his novels to make rich nostalgic use of the stagecoach world of his childhood.

This is also true in other more fundamental respects. Mr. Dombey is not merely a rich man, benevolent or miserly, or one of the would-be-rich peripheral adventurers who make a dishonest living on the shady outskirts of legitimate business. He is the very center of respectable Victorian prosperity—the capitalist in all his glory. We are directly told:

> The earth was made for Dombey and Son to trade in, and the sun and moon were made to give them light. Rivers and

seas were formed to float their ships; rainbows gave them promise of fair weather; winds blew for or against their enterprises; stars and planets circled in their orbits to preserve inviolate a system of which they were the centre.

All human relations are perverted by this money power. A child exists merely to become "and Son"; a wife as an ornamental object to show the owner's wealth and, if need be, a useful one to produce another son. Even the relative position and different perversions of the remnants of the aristocracy, who exist to be bought as Dombey exists to buy, are clearly traced and vividly projected.

However, the ostensible shift from the broader social view to a study of family relationships, and the fact that the only scene of real squalor upon which the story touches is also one of immorality, seem to have lulled both critics and public into accepting the book at Dickens' own evaluation as simply a study of the pride that goeth before a fall.

Its bitter mockery of a destructive charity school and of a no less inhuman school for gentlemen were taken as isolated exposés rather than parts of an overall theme, and Florence's refuge with the common working people who provide the only warmth and humanity in the book, even for the children of the rich, seemed to fit well enough into the safely generalized moral of humility vs. pride.

Forster breathed a sigh of relief, the public he so well represented shed torrents of tears over the death of Paul Dombey, as they had over that of Little Nell, installed Florence some steps lower in the same pantheon, and felt a delighted shock at the daring but satisfactorily moral treatment of Edith Dombey's elopement. Dickens himself turned away from this temporarily complete statement, and from his deliberately crowded personal life, to a serious consideration of the childhood memories he still found too painful to speak of even with his closest intimates.

David Copperfield, as the barely disguised story of Dickens' own childhood and youth is well-known. The absorbing human interest of the lonely small boy and serious young man; the immortal Micawbers and the literally hundreds of other richly realized figures with which its canvas is crowded; the concentration of tyranny in the form of the Murdstones, Creakle, and other enemies of childhood (here even exploitation is seen only in the use of child labor); all these make it possible to think of this novel almost solely in personal terms. But, as both T. A. Jackson and Jack Lindsay have indicated in their detailed studies of Dickens' work, there is under the personal story an almost diagrammatic simplicity in the view Dickens presents of the classes in his society. Lindsay summarizes their view briefly and accurately when he says:

> Thus, *Copperfield* becomes in many ways the simplest of Charles's novels in its view of society. The gentlemanly party (mainly typified by the Steerforths, though also by some connections of Mrs. Strong) are either sterilely aloof or heartlessly bad. The bourgeoisie are worse because more varied in their evil, which ranges from the villainies of Murdstone or Heap to the lies and cheats of Spenlow or the weakness of Wickfield. The lower middle-class or working-class, from Micawber to the Peggotties, are the repositories of human values.
> The class conflict of the Steerforths and the Peggotties is stated explicitly. Steerforth sees the Peggotties as creatures of another species. "They may be thankful that, like their coarse, rough skins, they are not easily wounded." The seduction of Little Em'ly and her moral murder is Steerforth's carrying out of this proposition, and is Charles's disproof of it. Also, Charles begins in this book his outright campaign against toadyism, the middle-class vice that he grew to hate more and more. The conversation at Mrs. Waterbrook's dinner table is the first full blast in the campaign. And this, it has rightly been pointed out, is a post-1848 symptom, as Charles begins to feel in his bones that the middle-classes all over Europe have somehow funked a great moral and social chance.

While Dickens was writing *David Copperfield*, which appeared in monthly numbers from May 1849 till the fall of 1850, he had undertaken a number of activities to assist the political refugees who flocked to London after the failure of the revolutions of 1848 all over the continent. Of particular interest is an appeal he wrote for the Italian exiles which read, in part:

> They are the good citizens who, when Rome was abandoned by her Monarch and Executives, answered to the general voice, and arose to give her law, tranquility and order; who built upon the ruins of a monstrous system which had fallen of its own rottenness and corruption, one of moderation and truth. . . .
> They are the soldiers who defended that Government against the united arms of bigotry and despotism, and defended it successfully.

This activity and similar exertions in behalf of other such projects or legislative reforms intensified in Dickens the desire for some regular organ of communication with his public. He felt such a project might, at the same time, release him from his recurrent nightmare of a failure of the creative imagination, still forced to carry the too heavy burden of supporting eight (later ten) children and as many more adult dependents. After many proposals and counter-proposals, this dream finally materialized in a weekly magazine devoted to current fiction, poetry, reportage, and editorial essays on contemporary topics of social or general interest.

Dickens was half proprietor and sole editor of *Household Words* until 1859 when, because of a private quarrel with his partners, the publishers, he forced it to close and established a similar periodical, *All the Year 'Round*, which he directed until his death.

The magazine which first appeared in March 1850 took a sharply partisan attitude, almost invariably supporting all Radical proposals for reform and social legislation; opposing religious interference with the pleasures of the poor; pressing for an increase of democracy in all spheres of life; and frequently, as in its reports of specific strike situations, going further than any political party in the fifties was willing to venture.

Since only the long serial novels were ordinarily credited to individual authors, although Dickens later introduced the innovation of signed short stories to help build the reputation of young writers, it is not always possible to know which articles were his. But the entire magazine reflected his policy; he gave extraordinarily detailed direction to those who wrote for or worked under him; and from the casual remarks in his letters, a great many of the specific discussions and reports, including many of the most radical ones, like the report of the Preston strike quoted below, have been definitely assigned to him.

Despite the immediate and continued practical success of this journalistic venture, many of Dickens' respectable friends and admirers deplored his now constant obvious concern with concrete social problems, the closer contact with his huge working-class audience, and the sharper tone of partisanship with which he championed the oppressed.

John Forster, in his long well-documented biography, concludes his description of Dickens' extraordinary success as an editor with an apologetic which accurately summarizes the facts of Dickens' journalistic career and later creative writings while totally misinterpreting the relation between the two and Dickens' own deepening radicalism:

> But periodical writing is not without its drawbacks, and its effect on Dickens, who engaged in it largely from time to time, was observable in the increased impatience of allusion to national institutions and conventional distinctions to be found in his later books. Party divisions he cared for less and less as life moved on; but the decisive, peremptory, dogmatic style, into which a habit of rapid remark on topics of the day will betray the most candid and considerate commentator, displayed its influence, perhaps not always consciously to himself, in the underlying tone of bitterness that runs through the books which followed *Copperfield*. The resentment against remediable wrongs is as praiseworthy in them as in the earlier tales; but the exposure of Chancery abuses, administrative incompetence, politico-economic shortcomings, and social flunkeyism, in *Bleak House, Little Dorrit, Hard Times,* and *Our Mutual Friend*, would not have been made less odious by the cheerier tone that had struck with so much effect at prison abuses, parish wrongs, Yorkshire schools, and hypocritical humbug in *Pickwick, Oliver Twist, Nickleby* and *Chuzzlewit.*

The time, energy, and patience which Dickens devoted to his enthusiastic search for and generous development of young talent is apparent not only from the number of new writers who first appeared in its pages, but also from many grateful contemporary accounts like that of the critic, H. F. Chorley, who wrote immediately after Dickens' death:

> The munificent sacrifices he made of time, money, and sympathy to men of letters, to artists, to obscure persons who had not the shadow of a claim upon him, will never be summed up. There are thousands of persons living who could bear grateful testimony to this boundless generosity of his nature.

More important still is the enormous volume of his editorial correspondence, largely included in the two posthumous volumes edited by his daughter and sister-in-law. In addition to tactful criticism and careful praise, innumerable stimulating suggestions were contained in these letters, which often accompanied rejections as well as acceptances; in some cases Dickens returned as many as five or six manuscripts to the same unknown beginner with continual advice and directions for new attempts on the same or other subjects before he was happily able to accept one! We also find that in his editorial correspondence, Dickens often formulated some of the principles which underlay his own work: For instance, time and again he repeated the concluding remark of the following interesting note—written to his assistant editor, Wills, in October, 1852:

> The fault of ———————'s poem, besides its intrinsic meanness as a composition, is that it goes too glibly with the comfortable ideas (of which we have had too much in England since the Continental commotions) that a man is to sit down and make himself domestic and meek, no matter what is done to him. . . . As it stands, it is at about the tractmark ("Dairyman's Daughter" etc.) of political morality, *and don't think that it is necessary to write down to any part of our audience. I always hold that to be as great a mistake as can be made.*

Again, years later, in a letter which suggested to a young girl the rewriting of her sprightly "Travel Notes" Dickens wrote:

> It is but a word or a touch that expresses this humanity, but without that little embellishment of good nature there is no such thing as humour. In this little Ms everything is too much patronised and condescended to. . . . Again I must say above all things—especially to young people writing: For the love of God don't condescend! Don't assume the attitude of saying "See how clever I am, and what fun everybody else is. . . ." If she considers for a moment within herself, she will know that she derived pleasure from everything she saw, because she saw it with innumerable lights and shades upon it, and bound to humanity by innumerable fine links; she cannot possibly communicate anything of that pleasure to another by showing it from one little limited point only, and that point, observe, the one from which it is impossible to detach the exponent as the patroness of a whole universe of inferior souls.

Shortly after the founding of the magazine Dickens also discovered a young writer, Wilkie Collins, who despite the fifteen year difference in age soon became his closest friend and almost invariable companion. Dickens' family intimacy with, and business reliance upon, Forster, continued and preserved almost intact the outer semblance of the older friendship; but their ideas on life and, therefore, art, were now too far divergent to allow any real continuation of the former relationship.

In March, 1852, Dickens began, for monthly serial publication, the new novel *Bleak House*, which Forster, as we have seen, considered the first of those that show an "underlying tone of bitterness" and which Jackson emphasizes as the beginning of the later novels where "Dickens, consciously and subconsciously, shows himself more and more at odds with bourgeois society and more and more aware of (and exasperated by) the absence of any readily available alternative."

This deepening discontent is the more remarkable for its flat contradiction of the increasingly prevalent smug optimism which characterized English society. As we have already seen, the end of the "hungry forties," aptly symbolized by Prince Albert's Great Industrial Exhibition, ushered in over a generation of the impenetrable and insufferable complacency which their descendants associate more generally with the term "Victorians."

Bleak House is not merely the name of the book and of a house, but is also an apt description of the whole social structure in which the action takes place. The central attack on Chancery, and on all the law and lawyers to which it is so closely related, is no longer a hopeful if urgent appeal for necessary life-saving surgery. It is a hopeless exposure of corruption too deep to be cured by the most drastic means. The physically impossible death by spontaneous combustion of the rag-and-bottle burlesque "Lord Chancellor"— Dickens wasted much energy to "prove" it scientifically possible— was essential to the theme of the book rather than to the drama of the plot. For it enabled Dickens to state in the clearest, most unequivocal terms his realization of the absolute rottenness of mid-Victorian capitalism and his conviction that it would be destroyed by its own inherent evil:

> Help, help, help! come into this for Heaven's sake!
> Plenty will come in, but none can help. The Lord Chancellor of that Court, true to his title in his last act, has died the death of all Lord Chancellors in all Courts, and of all authorities in all places under all names soever, where false pretences are made, and where injustice is done. Call the death by any name Your Highness will, attribute it to whom you will, or say it might have been prevented how you will, it is the same death eternally—inborn, inbred, engendered in the corrupted humours of the vicious body itself, and that only— Spontaneous Corruption, and none other of all the deaths that can be died.

Religion, far from teaching man that he is his brother's keeper, makes Rachel the pitiless destroyer of her sister, Lady Dedlock, and her remorseless persecution is only less odious than the utterly selfish stupid heartless unimaginative cruelty with which the Reverend Chadband helps drive Jo to his miserable death in Tom-All-Alone's.

Philanthropy in the person of the rational Mrs. Jellyby and, worse yet, the religious Mrs. Pardiggle is so utterly false that it stifles in both women all human feeling even for their own children.

The aristocracy are here treated only with good-natured contempt as parasitic survivors, largely ineffective for good or evil, and no doubt doomed to a sufficiently immediate end.

The fog which has swallowed all London at the beginning of the book, a literal phenomenon of the soft coal mid-nineteenth century London has not lifted at the end, and the modified happy ending accorded several of the principal characters is not intended to make us forget or forgive it. The book sold well but the general critical opinion is indicated by Forster's guarded comments and the very qualified praise he gives it in the biography. He says there:

> What in one sense is a merit however may in others be a defect, and this book has suffered by the very completeness with which its Chancery moral is worked out. . . . Dickens has himself described his purpose to have been to dwell on the romantic side of familiar things. But it is the romance of discontent and misery, with a very restless dissatisfied moral, and is too much brought about by agencies disagreeable and sordid. The Guppys, Weevles, Snagsbys, Chadbands, Krooks, and Smallweeds, even the Kenges, Vholeses, and Tulkinghorns, are much too real to be pleasant; . . .

While he was writing *Bleak House,* which was finished in August 1853, Dickens was asked to speak at the annual dinner of a Society of Artists in Birmingham. He willingly accepted the invitation and in his talk developed the idea that the greatest literature was literature for the people and that writing for the people meant writing up, not down. He said that literature "can not be too faithful to the people—cannot too ardently advocate the cause of their advancements, happiness and prosperity." He continued with a discussion of class character concluding with a reference to his own work and the statement:

> Whenever I have tried to hold up to admiration the fortitude, patience, gentleness of the working class, and the reasonableness of their nature, so accessible to persuasion, and their extraordinary goodness towards one another, I have done so because I have first genuinely felt that admiration myself.

In *Bleak House,* at about the same time, he was writing: "What the poor are to the poor is little known except to themselves and God."

After completing the novel, Dickens went for a short vacation trip to Italy. From Turin, where he had hoped to meet several Italian acquaintances, but found them all killed or exiled because of their revolutionary activities, he wrote home a brief account of one interesting conversation with an old Marchese:

> "Dead?" said I.—"In exile."—"O dear me!" said I, "I had looked forward to seeing him again, more than anyone I was acquainted with in the country!" "What would you have!" says the Marchese in a low voice. "He was a remarkable man—full of knowledge, full of spirit, full of generosity. Where should he be but in exile! Where could he be!"

Again in England at the beginning of 1854 he wrote in *Household Words* an account of his visit to Preston where a strike, universally execrated by practically every other periodical in England, was then in progress. He described the strike meeting:

> If the assembly, in respect of quietness and order, were put in comparison with the House of Commons, the Right Honourable the Speaker himself would decide for Preston . . . their astonishing fortitude and perseverance; their high sense of honour among themselves; the extent to which they are impressed with the responsibility that is upon them of setting a example, and keeping their order out of any harm and loss of reputation; the noble readiness in them to help one another. . . .

At the same time he began *Hard Times* which was printed in weekly parts in his own magazine. It more than doubled the circulation among "the lower classes" but aroused extreme concern and perturbation not only to such friends as Forster, but even to his most progressive ones, by its picture of industrial capitalism in action.

In answer to a deeply troubled letter from Mrs. Gaskell, for whose opinion Dickens always had a high respect, and whose own *Mary Barton,* the *Manchester Guardian* had criticized six years before for its "morbid sensibility to the condition of operatives," he wrote in April, 1854:

I have no intention of striking. The monstrous claims of
domination made by a certain class of manufacturers . . . are
within my scheme; but I am not going to strike, so don't be
afraid of me.

However, despite its brilliant parody of utilitarianism, *Hard
Times* is the only novel in which Dickens must be said to have
failed. This is not to say that there is not much of value in the book.
Certainly everyone at all interested in social questions ought to
read it once. But unlike Dickens' other work—or great literature in
general—once is probably enough.

The humor is often journalism, good journalism, rather than
literature. Thus, for example, when Mrs. Sparsit says:

> It is much to be regretted that the united masters allow
> of any such combination. Being united themselves, they ought
> one and all to set their faces against employing any man who
> is united with any other man. . . . These people must be
> conquered, and it's high time it was done, once for all.

it is all too clearly for Dickens' purposes and not her own that she is
set in motion.

The people of the industrial north, men and masters alike (although it matters more with the men than with the masters) were not Dickens' familiars. Here, for the only time, he was writing a book "to order"—even though to his own order—about a situation he had just studied for the occasion, and while the result was valuable, it has neither the power nor the inevitable truth of Dickens' real art. For example, his attempt to create a "third force"—the position of a clear-sighted and even heroic working man who is bound by some sentiment or scruple (in this case an unexplained promise to his sweetheart) not to join a union and who, refusing to betray the union, is then fatally ostracized by both employer and employees—is a serious flaw in the whole fabric of the book and lags far behind Dickens' own personal and public support of trade union organization. It may have been caused by his desire to conciliate Forster and the public he represented, but if the book had been deeply felt as a creation Dickens would have been incapable of such confusion.

Nevertheless, imperfect as it was, *Hard Times* was powerful enough to frighten Macaulay into an angry repudiation of its "Sullen Socialism" and to make the powerful *Blackwood Magazine* comment editorially that the book was dangerous and mischievous as: "a petulant theory of a man in a world of his own making, where he has no fear of being contradicted and is absolutely certain of having everything in his own way." It concluded its review: "We have seldom seen a more lamentable non sequitur than *Hard Times.*"

Ruskin praised it highly and expressed an essential truth about all of Dickens' dealings with social questions when he said:

> Let us not lose the use of Dickens's wit and insight, because he chooses to speak in a circle of stage fire. . . . He is entirely right in his main drift and purpose in every book he has written; and all of them, but especially *Hard Times*, should be studied with close and earnest care by persons interested in social questions. They will find much that is partial, and, because partial, apparently unjust; but if they examine the evidence on the other side, which Dickens seems to overlook, it will appear, after all their trouble, that his view was finally the right one, grossly and sharply told.

However, this book was in essence only an interlude between two major works to which it was related in purpose if not in spirit. Jackson aptly says: "*Hard Times* in fact stands to *Bleak House* and to *Little Dorrit* as a furious raid does to two systemmatic campaigns. Their community of purpose is plain to the most cursory of inspections."

After *Hard Times* Dickens dashed over to Paris for a brief visit most of which was spent in playgoing. From there he sent an interesting note to Forster

> That piece you spoke of is one of the very best melodramas I have ever read. . . . I am very curious indeed to go and see it; and it is an instance to me of the powerful emotions from which art is shut out in England by the conventionalities.

From Boulogne he wrote to Collins about a cobbler's dog whom he had the year before, while the family was summering there, observed daily sitting near his master in the window. This year Dickens writes:

> The cobbler has been ill these many months and unable to work; . . . The little dog sits at the door so unhappy and

anxious to help, that I every day expect to see him beginning a pair of top boots!

This casual personal note illustrates the truth of House's comment, quoted above, that in Dickens' novels, "Romance is valued in sterling. Pylades does not show his loyalty to Orestes in the dangers of long journeys and rescues from death, but in surreptitious loans or in sharing the last sixpence." And the little dog wants to help his master earn a living.

So axiomatic is this understanding for Dickens, that House summarizes its effect on his novels by saying:

> Nearly everybody in Dickens has a job: there is a passionate interest in what people do for a living and how they make do. The shopkeepers and landladies, who contribute so much to the atmosphere of close though honest business, have no monopoly of the working scene. Milliner, washerwoman, engineer, shipwright, glove-cleaner, barber, midwife, wet-nurse, waterman; actors, showmen, detectives, schoolmasters, are traced among the most surprising technical details: the stock-in-trade of Silas Wegg is minutely inventoried; almost every moment of the time of Mortimer Lightwood's office-boy is accounted for; and the time is known when Toodle comes home for tea. The railwayman in "Mugby Junction" is so completely identified with his job that he has no name but Lamps. It is the same with the professions: only the clergy marry, bury and christen rather uneasily against a background of high pews, hassocks, and three-deckers while the pew-opener counts her tips behind the vestry door. The typical rootless, baffled person is one who, like Richard Carstone, cannot settle to a profession and make good.

Work plays an essential part in the characters' approach to life: each sees another first as a business proposition. When Ralph Nickleby has forced his way up Miss La Creevey's staircase she thinks he wants his portrait done in miniature, and he sets out to warn her that she won't get her rent. This professional view of life is most marked and constant in the lawyers: for their profession has a phrase and a fee for all the contingencies of human existence. Every remark of Mr. Jaggers implies a cross-examination: without a word his bitten forefinger implies one. Mr. Guppy's proposal to Esther is all legal jargon, the only language he understands. Wemmick forces the issue home; Walworth sentiments will not do in Little Britain; his whole private life is a piece of fantastic escapism from work, and is therefore thoroughly controlled by it.

The characters not only talk shop, but use shop metaphors when they talk about other things:

"Wery good, wery good," said Mr. Weller. "Always see to the drag ven you go down hill. Is the vay-bill all clear and straight for'erd?"

"The schedule, sir," said Pell, guessing at Mr. Weller's meaning, "The schedule is as plain and satisfactory as pen and ink can make it."

On his return to England, a new friend, Henry Layard, one of the most advanced and uncompromising of the Radical Party, urged Dickens to run for Parliament. He refused but offered even more active assistance as a writer and speaker in behalf of the specific public measures for which the most militant Radicals were fighting.

The outbreak of the Crimean War troubled and depressed him since even progressives, on the whole, supported it in their opposition to the tyranny of the Czar. Dickens, of course, shared this opposition but sensed the opportunistic attitude of the government and the way in which the war was deliberately being used to divert attention from needed reforms at home. He wrote on November 1, 1854:

> I am full of mixed feelings about the war—admiration of our valiant men, burning desires to cut the Emperor of Russia's throat; and something like despair to see how the old cannon-smoke and blood-mists obscure the wrongs and sufferings of the people at home. When I consider the Patriotic Fund on the one hand, and on the other the poverty and wretchedness engendered by Cholera, of which in London alone, an infinitely larger number of English people than are likely to be slain in the whole Russian war have miserably and needlessly died— I feel as if the world had been pushed back five hundred years.

Again two months later, on January 3, 1855, he wrote:

> The absorption of the English mind in the war is, to me, a melancholy thing. . . . I fear I clearly see that for years to come domestic reforms are shaken to the root; every miserable red-tapist flourishes war over the head of every protester against his humbug; . . .

That summer he returned to Paris and seriously considered settling there permanently. He attended an international art exhibition with Wilkie Collins and wrote Forster:

> It is of no use disguising the fact that what we know to be wanting in the men [English painters] is wanting in their works

—character, fire, purpose, and the power of using the vehicle and model as mere means to an end. There is a horrid respectability about most of the best of them—a little, finite, systemmatic routine in them, strangely expressive to me of the state of England itself. . . . There are no end of bad pictures among the French, but Lord! the goodness also!—the fearlessness of them; the bold drawing; the dashing conception; the passion and action in them! The Belgian department is full of merit. It has the best landscape in it, the best portrait of homely life, to be found in the building. Don't think it a part of my despondency about public affairs, and my fear that our national glory is on the decline, when I say that mere form and conventionalities usurp, in English art, as in English government and social relations, the place of living force. . . . I never saw anything so strange. They [the English artists] seem to me to have got a fixed idea that there is no natural manner but the English manner (in itself so exceptional that it is a thing apart, in all countries); and that unless a Frenchman—represented as going to the guillotine, for example—is as calm as Clapham, or as respectable as Richmond Hill, he cannot be right.

The "despondency about public affairs" which was evidently well-known to his friends is succinctly expressed in a letter he wrote to Layard on March 10, 1855, while struggling to begin his next book:

There is nothing in the present time at once so galling and so alarming to me as the alienation of the people from their own public affairs. I have no difficulty in understanding it. They have had so little to do with the game through all these years of Parliamentary Reform, that they have sullenly laid down their cards, and taken to looking on. The players who are left at the table do not see beyond it, conceive that gain and loss and all the interest of the play are in their hands, and will never be wiser till they and the table and the lights and the money are all overturned together. And I believe . . . that it is extremely like the general mind of France before the breaking out of the first Revolution. . . . Finally, round all this is an atmosphere of poverty, hunger, and ignorant desperation of which perhaps not one man in a thousand of those not actually enveloped in it, through the whole extent of the country, has the least idea.

Two months later he indignantly defended Layard's politics to Lady Burdett-Coutts whose opinions, for all her genuine social concern, had not remained entirely unaffected by her position as the wealthiest woman in England.

I differ from you altogether, as to his setting class against class. He finds them already set in opposition. And I think you hardly bear in mind that as there are two classes looking at each other in this question, so there are two sides to the question itself. You assume that the popular class take the initiative. Now as I read the story, the aristocratic class did that years and years ago, and it is *they* who have put *their* class in opposition to the country—not the country which puts itself in opposition to *them*.

Little Dorrit which was at first to be called *Nobody's Fault* was begun in Paris in the fall of 1855 and published in monthly numbers until its completion in 1857.

This novel which Bernard Shaw said, "was a more seditious book than Das Capital" and the one which had made a revolutionary of him, is an extraordinarily rich and powerful work. Jackson, who concludes that "it is near to being the most revolutionary novel that Dickens ever wrote," begins his analysis of the theme:

> The real villain of *Little Dorrit* is neither the scoundrel Blandois, nor the treacherous Flintwich, nor the ineffable Casby, nor the forger Merdle nor the heartless Henry Gowan, nor the self-tormenting Miss Wade, nor is it those rival egoists and social climbers, Mrs. Merdle and Fanny Dorrit; nor the drifting waster, Amy's brother. Nor is it the tragically wilful Mrs. Clennam. Nor all of these put together. Behind all of these human phenomena, using them as its instruments, is a vaster and more impalpable Evil, of whose true being we get indications in the shadow of the Marshalsea walls, in the heartbreaking immobility of the Circumlocution Office, and in the terrifying gloom of Mrs. Clennam's theology. . . .
>
> In *Little Dorrit* while there is a wider and deeper sense of the masses—and a far closer approximation to the proletarian standpoint—there is, in the foreground of the action, little room for optimism. Yet at the same time, too, there is a dawning suggestion of an imminent Doom. In the physical crash of the Clennam mansion—so long the spiritual prison of the young and ardent—so long the stronghold of Wrong inflicted under the guise of Righteousness—one cannot help but sense a prophecy of a like fate awaiting the Circumlocution Office and all that it implies.

Lindsay says:

> Old Dorrit thus becomes a symbol of the Victorian bourgeoisie, living on a lie, afraid above all of having to face up to

origins, afraid of the reality behind the fine words. Old Dorrit, remorselessly impelled towards the moment of self-exposure, is a symbol of his society impelled towards the dreaded reckoning day.

He continues:

> The dynamic of the book comes from the desire to strip away all masks. Old Dorrit is exposed as a jail-bird, Merdle exposed as a swindler, Mrs. Clennam with all her tormented religion exposed as a creature of greed and hate. There is, too, the rowdy exposure of Casby, whose patriarchal exterior is merely a veil for money ruthlessness. The Circumlocution Office itself cannot be exposed, as it stands for the very fabric of the class State; but the exposures of the dominant individuals in the story combine to give the effect of stripping bare the whole basis of lying, hate, fear and exploitation without which there could be no Circumlocution Office, because there would then be nothing to hide.

And, amazingly, the good Catholic, G. K. Chesterton, who knew nothing about Marxism or for that matter capitalism, but knew and loved Dickens, also sensed that there was some evil more profound behind the plot than appeared in it. He credited Dickens with far less understanding than he possessed but since Chesterton himself was at so complete a loss to understand what he did, nevertheless, feel, this is not surprising. He said, in his amusing and provocative book, *Charles Dickens: The Last of the Great Men:*

> The dark house of Arthur Clennam's childhood really depresses us; it is a true glimpse into that quiet street in hell, where live the children of that unique dispensation which theologians call Calvinism and Christians devil-worship. But some stranger crime had really been done there, some more monstrous blasphemy or human sacrifice than the suppression of some silly documents advantageous to the silly Dorrits. Something worse than a common tale of jilting lay behind the masquerade and madness of the awful Miss Havisham. Something worse was whispered by the misshapen Quilp to the sinister Brass in that wild wet summer-house by the river, something worse than the clumsy plot against the clumsy Kit. These dark pictures seem almost as if they were literally visions; things, that is, that Dickens saw but did not understand.

But if Dickens' contemporaries did not fully understand his indictment they were quick to resent it. Thackeray, recognizing perhaps the satire of his own dilettante attitude in the aristocratic Henry Gowan's condescension to his art and its other practitioners, called the book "damned stupid." *The Edinburgh Review,* become less liberal with the passage of time, attacked Dickens for his persistent ridicule "of the institutions of the country, the laws, the administrations, in a word, the government under which we live." *The Saturday Review* of May, 1858 found that all of Dickens' books were "pervaded by that subversive spirit, forming the main basis of his popularity from the outset." And the famous constitutional historian, Walter Bagehot, thought the matter serious enough to devote an article in *The National Review* of October, 1858 to disposing of Dickens' influence, once and for all:

> Nothing can be easier than to make a case, as we may say, against any particular system, by pointing out with emphatic caricature its inevitable miscarriage and by pointing out nothing else. Those who so address us may assume a tone of philanthropy, and for ever exult that they are not so unfeeling as other men are; but the real tendency of their exhortations is to make men dissatisfied with their inevitable condition, and what is worse, to make them fancy that its irremediable evils can be remedied, and indulge in a succession of vague strivings and restless changes. Such, however, is very much the tone with which Mr. Dickens and his followers have in later years made us familiar.

Dickens was now past his middle forties. He had nine children ranging from six to twenty years, of the older of whom he may have been thinking when he noted in his diary: "Copyrights need be hereditary, for genius isn't." He had a wife for whom he felt fondness but neither interest nor respect; a sister-in-law who was by now the acknowledged mistress in a practical sense of his household but for whom, despite her adoration of him, he had only gratitude, admiration and platonic affection. He had a modest estate though a tremendous earning power. He had a host of distinguished friends and admirers who were unable, despite their genuine good will and his sincere efforts at communication, to understand what underlay his increasing restlessness, impatience, and despondency. On April 15, 1857, for example, he wrote in response to a letter from the liberal Earl of Carlisle:

> . . . I have no sympathy with demagogues but am a grievous Radical and think the political signs of the times to be

just about as bad as the spirit of the people will admit of their being. In all other respects I am as healthy, sound and happy as your kindness can wish. So you will set down my political despondency as my only disease.

His closest friend, the bohemian Wilkie Collins, sympathized in a general way with his profound dissatisfaction and helped to ease the tension by aiding and abetting a few casual adventures of a personal nature, but seemed unconcerned with the deeper social forces that underlay Victorian conventionality.

His most radical political associates lagged far behind his penetrating condemnation of the world in which he lived, and they could do nothing to help him formulate constructive demands, or even hopes, for a change. For example, in 1855 he had planned to publish an article on one of the numerous strikes which had followed the Preston affair he himself had so sympathetically reported. Henry Morley, one of the most advanced middle-class friends of labor, had been commissioned to write it. On January 6, 1856, Dickens returned the proofs to his assistant editor with a long determinedly patient letter which reads in part:

> I should like Morley to do a Strike article, and to work into it the greater part of what is here. But I cannot represent myself as holding the opinion that all strikes among this unhappy class of society, who find it so difficult to get a peaceful hearing, are always necessarily wrong, because I don't think so. To open a discussion of the question by saying that the men are "*of course* entirely and painfully in the wrong," surely would be monstrous in any one. . . . Nor can I possibly adopt the representation that these men are wrong because by throwing themselves out of work they throw other people, possibly without their consent. If such a principle had anything in it, there could have been no civil war, no raising by Hampden of a troop of horse, to the detriment of Buckinghamshire agriculture, no self-sacrifice in the political world. And O, good God, when—treats of the suffering of wife and children can he suppose that these mistaken men don't feel it in the depth of their hearts, and don't honestly and honorably, most devoutly and faithfully believe that for those very children, when they shall have children, they are bearing all these miseries now!

It is true that Dickens had one thing more important than all the assets ennumerated above. He had an enormous public including an extraordinary number of lower middle-class and working-class readers—more, probably, than any other English writer has ever yet had at one time—and an even more extraordinary influence with them. But he could find no way of turning this influence to practical account in effecting any real change in his society. He had consciously considered the matter, as we can see from many of his letters, especially those to Layard, the Radical member of Parliament whose understanding most closely approached his own. For example, he had written to him in 1855:

> It seems to me an absolute impossibility to direct the spirit of the people at this pass until it shows itself. If they begin to bestir themselves in the vigorous national manner; if they would appear in political reunion, array themselves peacefully but in vast numbers against a system that they know to be rotten altogether, make themselves heard like the sea all round this island, I for one should be in such a movement heart and soul, and should think it a duty of the plainest kind to go along with it, and try to aid it by all possible means.

Nevertheless, by the time he had completed *Little Dorrit*—and been angered by the critics' attack on it—he felt it was absolutely necessary to take some direct action and, with characteristic energy, he violently broke all precedent in both his personal and his creative life.

This need to destroy whatever part he could of the social ties that bound him may be a less romantic explanation of Dickens' separation from his wife than the conventional one of his sudden overwhelming love for a beautiful young actress. But any careful examination of the circumstances makes it seem infinitely more probable.

Six years earlier, before he had even met the then twelve-year-old Ellen, he had felt compelled to release his young prototype, David Copperfield, from the weight of an unequal marriage although he was forced to use the sentimental device of an obliging and unlikely death to accomplish his purpose. A few years ago an observant contemporary versifier, Martha Keegan, noted accurately, if flippantly, the relation between David's widowed state and Charles' then unforseen separation.

> Copperfield, when first he wed;
> By his fancy was misled.
> David's Dora saved her pride,
> David's Dora up and died.

Charles's Catherine, less discerning,
Had in store a bitter learning—
Like a good Victorian wife,
Thought, her tenure was for life,
Thought, maternal and adoring,
She was licensed to be boring.

Nor was it really necessary for Dickens to destroy the pattern of his domestic life unless he had wished to. For though he soon set up a separate establishment for Ellen which he maintained for the rest of his life—she married some years after his death—this relationship seems to have been at least as much the means as the cause of a violent break with his private past, and of a dangerous test of his ability to defy and yet hold his public. Certainly the discretion with which the affair was thereafter carried on would have more than sufficed to keep up the appearances that preserved innumerable other Victorian marriages, and Kate had even been willing to call on Ellen after she knew of Charles' interest in her. It is impossible not to believe that he seized upon the occasion to help him smash his own small cell in the vast Bastille in which he found himself immured. As he had written from the Parisian Art Exhibition two years before, when debating permanent residence on the Continent, "Mere form and conventionalities usurp in English art, as in English government and social relations, the place of living force and truth."

Dickens had, on his return from France in the fall of 1856, plunged into rehearsals of a new melodrama by Wilkie Collins, *The Frozen Deep*. The amateur theatricals were carried on with an almost frenzied intensity both on stage and off and proved enormously successful. Dickens decided to produce the play for a benefit performance in Manchester and—or, perhaps, in order to—substitute for the ladies of his family three professional actresses in the women's parts. They were the members of a theatrical family whom he had known casually for some time and had perhaps slightly assisted; a widow, Mrs. Ternan, and her two daughters Maria and Ellen Lawless Ternan.

Dickens had four months before applauded the younger daughter, Ellen, then just 18, at her debut in the Haymarket and now, playing opposite her as her fiancée in a comedy curtain-raiser, he fell violently and purposefully in love. Although their relations remained for some time "innocent" he determined on a complete break with Kate, and after considerable misery on all sides succeeded in arranging an apparently amicable separation. Dickens' oldest son, Charlie, was to live with his mother; and her sister Georgiana, was to remain in charge of Dickens' home and of the other children. The young ones, because of Kate's frequent pregnancies and consequent ill health, had apparently been largely in Georgiana's care from infancy.

In Dickens' new novel too he looked for a drastic way out. Jackson says of the former one, *Little Dorrit:* "It would be definitely wrong to say that *Little Dorrit* is revolutionary in the conscious or overt sense. But it would be no less wrong to deny that in the negative or potential sense—in that it shows by the totality of its implications, what things would be if Fate were just—it is near to being the most revolutionary novel that Dickens ever wrote." And as we have seen (p. 734), Jackson also called attention to the physical crash with which at least one of the bastions of injustice fell at the end of that book.

Now, in *The Tale of Two Cities,* Dickens, unable to frame even the image of the revolution he would have liked in the England of 1859, turned back to history to find a temporarily satisfactory revolution in the France of 1789.

There is no question that his deep admiration for Carlyle, the only abstract thinker for whom he ever really cared, was one obvious reason for his choice of revolutions. Another was no doubt his intimate knowledge of France and, especially, Paris. But he must also have sensed the unique importance for his own time of both the democratic spirit it had let loose all over Europe, and of the still unfulfilled promise of its "Liberty, Equality, Fraternity"— a promise whose fulfillment had been so savagely opposed by the English reaction which concretely shaped that society Dickens hated.

On the very first page of *The Tale of Two Cities* Dickens deliberately makes unambiguous his identification of the France which has already had a democratic revolution, with the England which had not.

The second paragraph of the book reads:

> There were a king with a large jaw and a queen with a plain face on the throne of England; there were a king with a large jaw and a queen with a fair face on the throne of France. In both countries it was clearer than crystal to the lords of the

State preserves of loaves and fishes, that things in general were settled for ever.

On the next page, after describing a particularly atrocious execution in France, he speaks of the "Woodman, Fate," and the "Farmer, Death," who had on that day already marked the trees for the guillotine and the farm wagons which were to be used as tumbrils, and concludes:

> But that Woodman and that Farmer, though they work unceasingly, work silently; and no one heard them as they went about with muffled tread: the rather, for as much as to entertain any suspicion that they were awake was to be atheistical and traitorous.

Continually throughout the book he describes the rising tide of revolution with such chapter headings as "Fire Rises," "The Sea Still Rises," and such simple self-comforting allegories as:

> "Well, then," said Defarge, as if a thought were wrung out of his breast, "It is a long time."
> "It is a long time," repeated his wife; "and when is it not a long time? Vengeance and retribution require a long time; it is the rule."
> "It does not take a long time to strike a man with lightening," said Defarge.
> "How long," demanded madame composedly, "does it take to make and store the lightning? Tell me."
> Defarge raised his head thoughtfully, as if there were something in that too.
> "It does not take a long time," said madame, "for an earthquake to swallow a town. Eh, well! Tell me how long it takes to prepare the earthquake?"
> "A long time, I suppose," said Defarge.
> "But when it is ready; it takes place, and grinds to pieces everything before it. In the meantime, it is always preparing, though it is not seen or heard. That is your consolation. Keep it."

Again, in more specific terms, Dickens makes unequivocal statements about the economics as well as the politics of revolution. For example:

> Monseigneur (often a most worthy individual gentleman) was a national blessing, gave a chivalrous tone to things, was

a polite example of luxurious and shining life, and a great deal more to equal purpose; nevertheless, Monseigneur as a class had, somehow or other, brought things to this. Strange that Creation, designed expressly for Monseigneur, should be so soon wrung dry and squeezed out! There must be something short-sighted in the eternal arrangements surely!

He makes his final statement about the revolution in the description of the "Reign of Terror" itself—and it must be remembered that when writing this Dickens took as fact the account of Carlyle and other authorities, which put the number executed in Paris at over 10,000 instead of a bare 1,000, of whom only half were actually political prisoners. Yet he concluded:

> Six tumbrils roll along the streets. Change these back again to what they were, thou powerful enchanter, Time, and they shall be seen to be the carriages of absolute monarchs, the equipages of feudal nobles, the toilets of flaring Jezabels, the churches that are not my father's house but dens of thieves, the huts of millions of starving peasants! No; the great magician who majestically works out the appointed order of the Creator, never reverses his transformations. "If thou be changed into this shape by the will of God," say the seers to the enchanted, in the wise Arabian stories, "then remain so! But, if thou wear this form through mere passing conjuration, then resume thy former aspect!" Changeless and hopeless the tumbrils roll along.

Naturally, in becoming required high school reading, this book has been more deliberately distorted than most of Dickens' of which only the less dangerous early ones are otherwise generally known to the schools.

His vivid description of the dangerous and bloody days of the revolution and his mistaken statistics are stressed, while the underlying theme of the book and his repeated statements of the necessity and essential justice of the revolution are ignored. Much is made of the fact that Darnay is unfairly in danger of being beheaded by the passionate and vengeful Tribunal of the French people and no mention is made of the fact that he is in at least equal danger of being unfairly drawn and quartered by the corrupt and sadistic courts of the English government, yet Dickens himself spends more time on the latter than on the former trial, and devotes a whole chapter to an attack on the paid government spies and perjured witnesses of unrevolutionary England.

Although "Recalled to Life" was originally the title of the book and remained the title of Part I, little attention is given to the fact that Dr. Manette was recalled to life only by the revolution's necessarily violent overthrow of the Bastille.

Dickens' fearful excitement at the frenzy of a mob is emphasized, but his bitter hatred and cold contempt for the French lords, and the English bourgeoisie who sided with them, is altogether ignored.

And, of course, the example of the book's immensely popular contemporary dramatization in a melodrama which reduced the tale of two cities to a frame for the story of Lucie's two suitors, has been conventionally followed ever since.

However, in writing the book Dickens had found one way to say what he had to say, and the tension was at least momentarily relieved.

He had also found or developed another means of securing that closer contact with his huge anonymous audience which became increasingly important to him as his views diverged more widely from those of the articulate and well-known part of it.

He had, ever since the early forties, been in the habit of "trying out" chapters of a work in progress by reading them to groups of friends; actually the desire for an immediate and constant audience reaction was one of the reasons he insisted always on first publishing his novels in periodical form; and since the middle fifties he had given occasional public readings of some of the Christmas Books for the benefit of Children's Hospitals, Mechanics' Institutes, Ragged Schools, and other institutions with which he was particularly in sympathy.

By 1859 he had several times tentatively broached the idea— as a matter of financial desirability—of giving such readings in a more consistent and organized way for his own benefit.

Forster had replied with a horrified negative and had called to his assistance the opinion of almost all Dickens' respectable friends, and Dickens was temporarily deterred, although as soon as *The Tale of Two Cities* was completed in November, 1859 he had turned to a series of readings for charity.

At the same time he began another novel, *Great Expectations*, which appeared in his new magazine, *All The Year 'Round*, throughout 1860 and was completed by the spring of 1861.

The framework of *Great Expectations*, like that of *David Copperfield*, is the first person story of a boy from his early childhood through young manhood with a brief summary statement of the events of his middle age. But within this framework despite the fact that Pip, like David, is essentially the young Charles, we find a very different interpretation of life.

David's life was a variation on the theme of the young Cinderella, or her equally abused brother, who finds a reasonable fairy godmother able and willing to put him in the way of making his fortune. It takes courage and hard work; he finds many ogres in his way and almost loses it through his own vanity or weakness; but eventually he rescues the imprisoned princess, becomes rich and famous and lives happily ever after. We have already noted the ease with which Dickens cleared from David's path the results of those mistakes which so seriously entangled Charles' steps.

But Pip's life is a flat contradiction of the romantic theme. He is no disinherited younger son but a common boy who looks forward to a life of useful work and reasonable comfort with a start provided by his warmhearted blacksmith brother-in-law.

He is dazzled by a mad fairy godmother, captivated by her heartless and snobbish goddaughter, and despises his own people in the new found ambition "to be made a gentleman of." Finally his hopes are disappointed—the actual money he in essence refuses when he could have had it after his disillusionment as to its source; his inamorata makes a mercenary marriage; he is saved from complete wreck only by his blacksmith brother-in-law; and he ends up in a moderately resigned life doing rather less interesting work for a reasonably comfortable but lonelier living. Unfortunately, after the book was completed, Bulwer Lytton persuaded Dickens to add a modified happy ending in which Estelle, happily widowed and reformed by suffering, joins Pip to live with him on his bookkeeper's salary. But as Lindsay says:

> . . . this deformation of the end cannot affect the creative impact of the novel as a whole. Dickens in concise, uncompromising terms sets out the moral that has kept growing ever stronger since the flight of Little Nell with the Old Gambler: The system of capitalist society is based on the denial and distortion of human values. True, human beings are not everywhere broken down into money values, into things of the market; that is because the system cannot swallow everything. But the individual, in so far as he is a member of such a society, is distorted and internally rotted.
>
> Here lies Dickens' greatness, in his capacity to grasp and understand this fact in all its fullness. Only Shakespeare before him had been able to live at this intense heart of the struggle

of values. Dickens maintains an unbroken faith in people with an entire pessimism as to capitalist society.

After *Great Expectations* had been completed Dickens finally broke through the social disapproval and began to give a series of readings as a "paid entertainer." These were tremendously successful and, except for one more great novel, became his major preoccupation for the last nine years of his life. Although he himself always stressed their economic importance, and it is true that they enabled him to provide easily for the three complete households he was now maintaining and to double the sizable estate he left his children, yet this was certainly only a very small part of his motivation. He had for many years been worried about the possibility of exhausting his creative ability and had felt increasingly irksome the thought that he was entirely dependent on the, in a sense uncontrollable, power of his imagination. Furthermore, he was quite aware that he could write truly and successfully only when he was completely absorbed by a theme and was also deeply at one with his public and his combination was clearly becoming more and more impossible. The three years from 1861 to 1864 were, therefore, except for his magazine and a few short stories and sketches, devoted largely to several series of public readings.

Many letters testify to his especial interest in audiences of workingmen and women and his determination always to have a sizeable number of tickets set aside for them at prices they could afford, just as he had always had his books first published in monthly or weekly numbers at prices they could pay.

One such note from his very first series of readings in October, 1859, reads:

> The Norwich people were a noble audience. There, and at Ipswich and Bury, we had the demonstrativeness of the great working towns, and a much finer perception.

During this period Dickens spent an increasing amount of time in "low" company. Kitton, in the memoirs written immediately after his friend's death, says:

> Dickens was an odd fellow regarding the company he sought. I have known him . . . to go down to the Seven Dials, about the worst place in London, and sleep and eat there. He roasted his herring where the rest did and slept with the poor-

est. He loved low society. He never seemed so happy as when seated in a poor coffee house with a crowd of the low classes talking around him.

Forster more apologetically and circumspectly admits, and, to his own satisfaction, explains away, or at least explains, these unfortunate idiosyncrasies in the great man. When we remember that Forster was generally considered extremely liberal, we can better realize the pressure Dickens had, all his life, to withstand.

> To say he was not a gentleman would be as true as to say he was not a writer; but if any one should assert his occasional preference for what was even beneath his level over that which was above it, this would be difficult of disproof . . . the inequalities of rank which he secretly resented took more galling as well as glaring prominence from the contrast of the necessities he had gone through with the fame that had come to him; . . . he was led to appear frequently intolerant (for he very seldom was really so) in opinions and language. . . . The influence from his early life which unconsciously strengthened them in certain social directions has been hinted at, and of his absolute sincerity in the matter there can be no doubt. The mistakes of Dickens were never such as to cast a shade on his integrity. What he said with too much bitterness, in his heart he believed; and had, alas! too much ground for believing. "A country" he wrote . . . with an enormous black cloud of poverty in every town which is spreading and deepening every hour, and not one man in two thousand knowing anything about, or even believing in, its existence; with a nonworking aristocracy, and a silent parliament, and everybody for himself and nobody for the rest; this is the prospect and I think it a very deplorable one.

Finally, in 1864, Dickens gathered his forces to write his last complete and perhaps his very greatest book, *Our Mutual Friend*. Jackson concludes his discussion of this novel by saying:

> A comparison of this last-completed novel with his first brings out sharply the nature of the development he had achieved. In point of plot construction the end novel is as carefully reticulated and planned as the beginning novel is planless and tumbled together. Per contra—the end novel is as deliberately grim, scornful and bitter as the beginning novel is irresponsibly festive, frivolous, and light-hearted.
> There is much more in this than a simple quantitative progression from exuberant youth to sober maturity. There is no note, for instance, of disillusionment as to human nature. On

the contrary, it is the earlier work which in places affects an adolescent cynicism which in the mature work would have jarred inexpressibly. Fundamentally Samuel Pickwick Esq. and Noddy Boffin each finish in an identical position—as each a minor providence in his little world. But contrast the gorgeous absurdity of the Pickwick Club in full session, with the repulsive and vulpine pseudo rationality of the dinner company at the Veneerings and there is revealed in a flash a complete revolution in Dickens' attitude towards bourgeois society.

That Samuel Pickwick belonged as essentially to the bourgeoisie as Noddy Boffin belonged to the proletariat, underscores the moral beyond all cavil. . . .

It was not that the sense of fun had died down in Dickens or that his power of creation had been exhausted. It was the world that had changed for Dickens, and with it his sense of responsibility to, and for, that world.

Lindsay summarizes the book and the three great novels which led up to it:

Dombey, Bleak House, and *Little Dorrit* had been mature works before this, in which he attempted a broadly based picture of the human condition and Victorian society. The first had shown the withering effects of the money-ethic on human values; the second, taking the law as the symbol of the State and all its powers, had uttered a basic rejection of the existing State form; the third had dealt with the lie, the rottenness of guilt and fear, at the social core. In *Our Mutual Friend* Dickens resumes all these judgments in a huge involved novel, in which he carries his forms, artistically and emotionally, to their limit of significant expansion. The fundamental contrast in all his writings, between the vileness of all existing forms of State organization and the indomitable powers of renewal in man, is here carried to breaking point. . . .

The result is one of the greatest works of prose ever written. A work which finally vindicates Dickens' right to stand, as no other English writer can stand, at the side of Shakespeare.

And although this conclusion may seem extravagant it has been shared by critics as diverse as the great French literary historian Cazamian, Chesterton, Gissing, Leacock, Lukasch, Santayana, Shaw, Sitwell, Strindberg, Swinburne, Tolstoy, Zweig, and a surprising number of others. It has seldom been noted that the title of Ibsen's play, which shocked English society and recreated the English theatre, was borrowed from a line in *Our Mutual Friend* in which Bella Rokesmith declares: "I want to be something much worthier than the doll in the *doll's house."*

In 1864, the year which saw the publication of *Our Mutual Friend* begin, a number of periodicals opened a renewed attack on Dickens' lack of correct moral feeling. The *Rambler*, for example, said he was "stone blind to the existence of anything which eye cannot see, and to an hereafter whose woe or joy is dependent on man's conduct here.... Of Christianity as a revelation, of sin as an offence against God, of the law of God as a rule of life, he seems literally unconscious."

During the three years between his completion of *Our Mutual Friend* and his second American tour in 1868, he continued to give readings throughout England, considered a trip to Australia, wrote innumerable articles on topics of the day and spoke at a great many meetings for various progressive institutions and specific reforms. Although he had little faith in parliamentary action, he greeted the general consternation at the idea of universal (manhood) suffrage in 1867 with the statement:

> I have such a very small opinion of what the great genteel have done for us, that I am very philosophical indeed concerning what the great vulgar can do, having a decided opinion that they can't do worse.

Although his health was rapidly deteriorating, his deep dissatisfaction and inability to write creatively drove him to arrange a more and more strenuous program of readings in which he could, without the need for new creative expression, momentarily feel the power to communicate with his public. At the end of 1867 he finally agreed to give a four-week series of readings in the United States.

Despite severe pain and extreme ill health, on his return he undertook a tour in Ireland, and finally suffered a slight unadmitted stroke which forced him home for rest early in 1869.

There he began his last novel, *Edwin Drood*. From the few chapters completed before his death we can see an excellent detective story in the Wilkie Collins tradition with a deeper undertone of evil and social satire. Several comments and characters indicate the probable development of an interest in Asia, and perhaps some attack on the feeling of white supremacy. The spoiled and self-satisfied Edwin Drood sneers at Neville, who has come from the East, "You are no judge of white men," and says he is "going to wake Egypt up a little." However, the book breaks off too soon for us to have any real knowledge of its ultimate direction.

In this year, too, Dickens gave a last talk in Birmingham during which he said:

> I will now discharge my conscience of my political creed, which is contained in two articles, and has no reference to any party or persons. My faith in the people governing is, on the whole, infinitesimal; my faith in the people governed is, on the whole, illimitable.

He also quoted Buckle's history with approval, stressing its thesis that:

> . . . lawgivers are nearly always the obstructors of society instead of its helpers, and . . . in the extremely few cases where their measures have turned out well their success has been owing to the fact that, contrary to their usual custom, they have implicitly obeyed the spirit of their time and have been—as they always should be—the mere servants of the people, to whose wishes they are bound to give a public and legal sanction.

Despite the unequivocal nature of his speech, he was misquoted as having said that he had faith in the people as long as they were governed and did not try to govern themselves! On hearing of this he wrote: "My confession being shortly and elliptically stated, was, with no evil intention I am absolutely sure, in some quarters inversely explained." He went on to say that he had meant to say that he had very little confidence in the people who govern us "with a small p" and very great confidence in the People whom they govern "with a large P." He added that his political opinions had already been not obscurely stated in an "idle book or two."

Forster reports the entire episode accurately and then, with an impenetrable persistence in error, matched only by Jane Austen's ineffable Mr. Collins (see pp. 345-8), concludes:

> It may nevertheless be suspected, with some confidence, that the construction of his real meaning was not far wrong which assumed it as the condition precedent to his illimitable faith, that the people even with the big P, should be governed.

In 1869 Dickens, who had sensed the imminence of the civil war during his first visit to the United States in 1842, seemed to feel across the channel the stirring of the great Paris Commune. In May he wrote:

> I don't know how it may be with you, but it is the fashion here to be absolutely certain that the Emperor of the French is fastened by Providence and the fates on a throne of adamant expressly constructed for him since the foundations of the universe were laid. He knows better, and so do the police of Paris, and both powers must be grimly entertained by the resolute British belief, knowing what they have known, and doing what they have done through the last ten years. What Victor Hugo calls "the drop-curtain, behind which is constructing the great last act of the French Revolution," has been a little shaken at the bottom lately, however. One seems to see the feet of a rather large chorus getting ready.

But he was not to be there for the play. On June 9, 1870, he suffered a second fatal stroke, and died without recovering consciousness.

At his own written request he was privately buried with a minimum of the funeral ceremony he had always hated—but at the insistent request of the nation the private interment took place in Westminister Abbey. Occasional newspaper reports for years after commented on the number of working people and cheap string-tied bunches of flowers to be observed at his grave. Even after the first world war a "Dickens Impersonator" was a common feature of English music halls, and shouted demands for "Mrs. Gamp," "Dick Swiveller" "Sam Weller" and others showed the crowd's familiarity with his repertoire. In 1936, the centennial of his *Pickwick Papers*, *L'Humanite*, the great French communist daily, serialized his *David Copperfield* and in the same year Bastille Day was celebrated in Paris by reprinting extracts from the *The Tale of Two Cities*. Two years later an English survey showed Dickens' work in greater demand than that of any other writer among the prisoners in English jails!

It is no wonder that the growing school of "Art for Art's Sake" and its cult of unintelligibility should condemn Dickens as vulgar. He was vulgar, as one critic has said "in the same way that Shakespeare, Cervantes and Gogol were vulgar, because he and they represent that actual life of which the refined and elegant constitutes but an insignificant and imperceptible particle. He is vulgar in so far as he is expansive, unrestrained in mirth and tears, in so far as there is nothing in him insincere."

Or, as G. K. Chesterton says of the snobbish dichotemy between art and popularity:

> The public does not like bad literature. The public likes a certain kind of literature even when it is bad better than another kind of literature even when it is good. . . . Dickens stands first as a defiant monument of what happens when a great literary genius has a literary taste akin to that of the community. . . . Dickens did not write what the people wanted. Dickens wanted what the people wanted. He talked up to the people.

Chesterton also gives us an illuminating statement of the difference between Dickens and the more naturalistic social novelists who followed him—well-intentioned and earnest as many of the latter unquestionably were. He says:

> If we are to save the oppressed, we must have two apparently antagonistic emotions in us at the same time. We must insist with violence upon his degradation; we must insist with the same violence upon his dignity. . . . There is a school of smug optimists who will deny he is poor. There is a school of scientific pessimists who will deny that he is a man. . . . [Dickens] does not merely pity the lowness of men; he feels an insult to their elevation . . . [the others] feel that the cruelty to the poor is a kind of cruelty to animals. They never feel it is injustice to equals; nay, it is treachery to brothers. . . .

Dickens would certainly have dissented with some violence from Chesterton's opening proposition that "*we* are to save the oppressed." All his correspondence is peppered with such ironical comments as, "Does it not seem a strange thing to consider that I have never yet seen with these eyes of mine, a mechanic in any recognized position on the platform of a Mechanics' Institution?" And in his last series of sketches, *The Uncommercial Traveller*, in 1867 he says flatly, of the working man:

> . . . If his sledge hammers, his spades and pickaxes, his saws and chisels, his paint-pots, and brushes, his forges, furnaces, and engines, the horses that he drove at his work, and the machines that drove him at his work, were all toys in one little paper box, and he the baby who played with them, he could not have been discoursed to, more impertinently and ab-

surdly than I have heard him discoursed to times innumerable.
. . . Whatever is done for the comfort and advancement of the working man must be so far done by himself as that it is maintained by himself.

But Dickens would, I think, otherwise have approved of Chesterton's interpretation, quoted above. And I am sure he would have accepted Chesterton's concluding description of his political position:

> To call Dickens a [conscious] Socialist is a wild exaggeration; but the truth and peculiarity of his position might be expressed thus: that even when everybody thought liberalism meant individualism he was emphatically a liberal and emphatically not an individualist.

George Eliot (Mary Ann Evans Cross) 1819-1880

With the single gigantic exception of Charles Dickens, the significant volume of nineteenth century English novels was, to an amazing extent, the work of women writers like Charlotte and Emily Brontë, Mrs. Gaskell, and George Eliot.

We have already looked briefly at the six perfect books in which Jane Austen so brilliantly crystalized a vital part of late eighteenth century life. Although she was by far the greatest, she was by no means the only, feminine satirist to use her drawing room as an observation post, and to observe with particular care the special difficulties and necessities of women there. Some of these now forgotten early sisters of the pen were: Fanny Burney, Lady Charlotte Bury, Maria Edgeworth, Susan Ferrier, Catherine Gore, Mary Russell Mitford, Lady Sydney Morgan, and Amelia Opie.

The most interesting of Jane Austen's feminine contemporaries was undoubtedly Maria Edgeworth, whose first memorable novel of Irish life, *Castle Rackrent*, published in 1800, is still well worth reading. Its realistic and vivid picture of Irish manners and morals first suggested to Sir Walter Scott his much better known and, generally, much more sentimental use of Scottish society. In his preface to the first edition of *Waverly* (1814) he said he was attempting "in some degree to emulate the admirable Irish portraits of Miss Edgeworth."

Her second novel, *Belinda*, a comedy of manners, was much weakened by the conventional ending and other improvements she added at her father's suggestion. A note to a woman friend, written when she was preparing a new edition nine years after the book's first publication, gives an interesting glimpse of the advice she too often followed in spite of her own better sense:

> So, to return to my own business, *Belinda*, I have taken some, and my father has taken a great deal of pains to improve her. In the first volume the alterations are very slight, and merely verbal. In the second volume "Jackson" is substituted for the husband of Lucy instead of "Juba," many people having been scandalized at the idea of a black man marrying a white woman; my father says that gentlemen have horrors upon this subject, and draw conclusions very unfavorable to a female writer who appeared to recommend such unions; as I do not understand the subject, I trust to his better judgment, and end with—for Juba read Jackson.

These more discreet literary feminists were followed by the violent outspoken protest we find in Charlotte Brontë's novels, especially *Shirley* (1849), and in Elizabeth Barrett Brownings' long narrative poem *Aurora Leigh* (1857).

George Eliot was deeply stirred by both these women. She said of Charlotte Brontë in 1853:

> I am only just returned to a sense of the real world about me, for I have been reading "Villette," a still more wonderful book than "Jane Eyre." There is something almost preternatural in its power. . . . Lewes was describing Currer Bell [Charlotte Brontë's pen name] to me yesterday as a little, plain, provincial, sickly looking old maid. Yet what passion, what fire in her! Quite as much as in George Sand, only the clothing is less voluptuous.

And of Elizabeth Barrett Browning she wrote, in 1857:

> We are reading "Aurora Leigh" for the third time, with more enjoyment than ever. I know no book that gives me a deeper sense of communion with a large as well as beautiful mind.

The essential note struck by both these writers, to which George Eliot so vibrantly responded, was middle-class woman's need for meaningful, valuable, and independent, productive work and the dignity only such work could give her.

Charlotte Brontë had submitted some of her early writings for criticism to Southey, and the poet laureate had replied to her appeal for advice by writing:

> Literature cannot be the business of a woman's life, and it ought not to be. The more she is engaged in her proper duties, the less leisure will she have for it, even as an accomplishment and recreation.

It is no doubt with this in mind that she commented bitterly about the difference between a brother and his sisters, "He is expected to act a part in life; to *do,* while they are only to *be.*" And in a later letter to her publisher after the success of *Jane Eyre,* she wrote:

> Lonely as I am, how should I be if Providence had never given me courage to adopt a career—perseverance to plead through two long weary years with publishers till they admitted me? How should I be with youth past, sisters lost, a resident in a moorland parish where there is not a single educated family? In that case I should have no world at all; the raven weary of surveying the deluge, and without an ark to return to would be my type. As it is, something like a hope and motive sustains me still. I wish all your daughters—I wish every woman in England, had also a hope and a motive. Alas! there are many old maids who have neither.

George Eliot knew, of course, nothing of Miss Brontë's private correspondence but there was no need of that when, in *Shirley,* she found such dialogues as:

> "Caroline," demanded Miss Keeldar, abruptly, "don't you wish you had a profession—a trade?"
> "I wish it fifty times a day. As it is, I often wonder what I came into the world for. I long to have something absorbing and compulsory to fill my head and hands, and to occupy my thoughts."
> "Can labour alone make a human being happy?"
> "No; but it can give varieties of pain and prevent us from breaking our hearts with a single tyrant master-torture. Besides, successful labour has its recompense; a vacant, weary, lonely, hopeless life has none."

In Elizabeth Barrett Browning, George Eliot found the same demand that woman gain an impersonal productive function, with the emphasis somewhat shifted from the value of such work for the worker, to the value of the completed work for society. We have already read Elizabeth Barrett's indignant protest that if a woman were not to meddle with such matters as politics and slavery she had better not write at all. In response to public criticism of her discussion of an even more shocking topic—prostitution —she wrote:

> If a woman ignores these wrongs, then may women as a sex continue to suffer them; there is no help for any of us— let us be decent and die. I have spoken therefore, and in speaking have used plain words—words which look like blots . . . words which, if blurred or softened, would imperil perhaps the force and righteousness of the moral influence.

Again, Thackeray rejected a poem, "Lord Walter's Wife," for the *Cornhill,* saying:

> You see that our Magazine is written not only for men and women but for boys, girls, infants, sucklings almost . . . there are things my squeamish public will not hear on Monday, though on Sundays they listen to them without scruple.

Elizabeth Barrett answered:

> I don't like coarse subjects, or the coarse treatment of any subject. But I am deeply convinced that the corruption of our society requires not shut doors and windows, but light and air; and that it is exactly because pure and prosperous women choose to ignore vice, that miserable women suffer wrong by it everywhere.

And when a more easily satisfied woman friend wrote her with great satisfaction about the universal respect finally accorded Florence Nightingale's work in the hospitals, she replied with some asperity:

> Every man is on his knees before ladies, carrying lint, calling them "angelic she's," whereas if they stir an inch as thinkers or artists from the beaten line (involving more good to general humanity than is involved in lint), the very same men would curse the impudence of the very same women and stop there.

Of course, here too there was no need for George Eliot to read such letters in order to learn what the author of *Aurora Leigh* thought on the "woman question."

As early as 1845 Elizabeth Barrett had made Eve rather than Adam the major protagonist of a poem—*The Drama of Exile*—and had given Eve the vision to see, in the workaday world, an ample recompense for the lost joys of paradise, letting her comfort Adam with:

> I hear a sound of life—of life like ours—
> Of laughter and of wailing,—of grave speech,
> Of little plaintive voices innocent,—
> Of life in separate courses flowing out
> Like our four rivers to one outward main.
> I hear life—life!

A critical poem on the Crystal Palace exhibition in 1851, stressing the evils not placed on exhibit there though they too were "made in England" concluded:

> . . . no light
> Of teaching, liberal nations, for the poor
>   Who sit in darkness when it is not night?
> No cure for wicked children? Christ,—no cure!
>   No help for women sobbing out of sight
> Because men made the laws?

And of course *Aurora Leigh* itself, which George Eliot read three times on its first appearance, was quoted in many of the "Women's Rights" meetings held by the newly-formed Woman Suffrage Association and other similar women's organizations in the seventies and eighties. It is devoted, through all its sometimes wearying ramifications and somewhat improbable plot complications, to a realistic picture of the various stereotypes into which society forced women, crushing those who did not voluntarily stunt their growth to fit men's demands.

Those of us who became women in the 1920's certainly remember the thrill of identification with Millay's indignant sonnet which began:

> Oh, oh! you shall be sorry for that word
> Give back my book and take my kiss instead.
> Was it my enemy or my friend I heard:
> "Such a big book for such a little head?"

I do not know whether Miss Millay had an earlier feminist in mind when writing this, but over half a century before, Aurora Leigh had said:

> I perceive
> The headache is too noble for my sex.
> You think the heartache would sound decenter,
> Since that's the woman's special, proper ache,
> And altogether tolerable, except
> To a woman.

And, in a more frequently quoted passage, Aurora declared a woman must

> . . . get leave to work
> In this world—'tis the best you get at all
> For God in cursing gives us better gifts
> Than men in benediction. . . .
> . . . get work, get work
> Be sure 'tis better than what you work to get.
> . . . .
> The honest earnest man must stand and work.
> The woman also,—otherwise she drops
> At once below the dignity of man
> Accepting serfdom. Free men freely work.

It is hardly surprising that even a comparatively liberal Victorian gentleman like Edward Fitzgerald should have written a friend in 1861:

> Mrs. Browning's death is rather a relief to me, I must say; no more Aurora Leighs, thank God! A woman of real genius, I knew; but what is the upshot of it all? She and her sex had better mind the kitchen and the children—and perhaps the poor.

Nor is it surprising that a fellow woman of genius if not always, by Victorian standards, a lady, should on the contrary have found a "sense of communion with a large as well as beautiful mind" in reading *Aurora Leigh*.

George Eliot, one of the greatest English novelists, had an extraordinarily large mind of her own of which even the ungracious and egotistical Herbert Spencer said: "She had a remarkable capacity for abstract thinking, which so seldom goes along with capacity for concrete observation even in men; ... among women, such a union of the two as existed in her has, I think, never been paralleled."

Although she did not begin to write fiction until she was thirty-eight, she had much earlier managed to put to unconventional use her exceptional intellectual powers.

Her achievement was the more surprising in that neither circumstances, family, nor temperament, were such as would have encouraged literary activity even had she been born a boy.

Her second full length novel, *The Mill on the Floss* (1860), vividly portrays for us her childhood in a substantial conservative farming district with an adored and patronizing older brother, a queer passion for reading, a propensity to dirty her pinafore, tangle her hair, and fall into other less tangible but equally disgraceful errors, and her overwhelming desire to find some way of life strenuous enough to tax all her powers of thought, action and devotion.

This longing to devote oneself to the service of something greater than oneself is a common phenomenon in young people of either sex. A culture which realizes the potential force of such an emotion can cultivate and direct it with terrible effect, whether for good or ill, as we have so recently seen in the heroic youthful guerilla detachments of the Second World War, and in the almost unshakable fanaticism of the Hitler Youth.

But in the individualistic culture of nineteenth century England we find that, while society generally ignores or disapproves a young man's need to identify himself with something more important to him than himself, it encourages and actively inculcates such an attitude on the part of its young women. They are supposed, at best, to find their object in the person of a husband. Failing this good fortune they are expected to substitute parents or other members of the immediate family. At worst, the church and good works for the poor will serve.

Everyone knows Byron's smug dictum, "Man's love is of man's life a thing apart; 'tis woman's whole existence." And even Milton said of the first man and woman, "He for God only; she for God in him."

And, of course, once that to which one owes a selfless loyalty has assumed a human shape it becomes of the utmost importance to please as well as to serve him. So, in the most conventional society, the pressure for conformity bears with a double personal weight upon the woman.

In looking at Jane Austen's life we have found that when she was already a successful author she still left unquestioned the assumption that her literary occupation should be carried on only when it did not interfere with her real function—that of sewing her brothers' shirts. And we have seen that for Mary Lamb even the commercial importance of her professional needlework provided no exemption from the most onerous duties of family attendance. Nor did she, any more than her brothers, feel that these should be shared by them.

Now, despite all the differences of circumstance, we find that this acceptance of "woman's role" is equally important in the development of so seemingly emancipated a figure as George Eliot.

Her early failure in life—her failure, as a girl, to be attractive—is poignantly described in terms of little Maggie Tulliver's heartbreaking disappointments. And it is noteworthy that George Eliot could not bear to touch this autobiographical material until reassured by love, fame, and the practical success of two previous books. Characteristically, Maggie, like all the other heroines in whom we recognize some identification with their creator, is given a gift she herself was never to possess. After an ugly duckling childhood Maggie achieves the swanlike beauty we later see in Dorothea and Romola—but never, alas, in Mary Ann Evans.

However, Mary Ann's too well founded conviction of homeliness was only one of her youthful trials.

Although she greatly admired and deeply loved her father, she had little of his company for he was a very busy practical man who not only conducted his own successful farm and acted as agent for the extremely large Newdigate estate, but also carried on many of the independent tasks of timber valuation, building, and so forth described as Caleb Garth's in *Middlemarch*. He had small time for his difficult younger daughter although her cleverness and quick book learning amused and pleased him—all the more perhaps for the shocked disapproval of his superior sisters-in-law. There is little of him in Maggie's father, but the relation between Mr. Evans and his second wife's snobbish family—he had by his early success earned the right to marry above his station and had, by his vitality and persistence, won the love of his genteel wife though not that of her family—was apparently very much like that which existed between Mr. Tulliver and the Dodsons so immortally pilloried in *The Mill on the Floss*.

But Mary Ann's mother was unwell after her birth and when her brother Isaac (better known to most of us as Tom Tulliver) had already been away at school for several years, she and her older sister Chrissy were also sent to the first of several boarding schools.

Here Mary Ann eagerly and indiscriminately devoured every sort of mental sustenance. She managed a precarious balance between her real need for strenuous and demanding mental exercise and her equally deep craving for social approval and affection by developing a sort of "crush" on her teacher and becoming the "good girl" of the school. In the process she achieved a pedantic and stilted literary style and a painful though sincere tone of evangelical fervor as well as more fortunate accomplishments in languages, arithmetic, music and so forth.

We have often heard how orthodox Hebrew scholars in the restricted world of the small Polish ghettos devoted the full strength of their powerful and hungry minds to fantastic Talmudic commentaries, painfully refining the only material they were permitted to work on. In much the same way Mary Ann became an eager student and critic of the only kind of theoretical material which found its way to a girls' school in early nineteenth century Warwickshire—biblical criticism, evangelical disputes, and morbid ethical self-examinations.

When at fifteen her mother's death called her home and, a year later, her sister's marriage made her the competent, fully responsible keeper of her father's large farm house, she attended to her duties with characteristic intelligence and thoroughness, organizing clothing clubs for the poor and taking a leading part in all neighborhood charities.

She also continued, with a tutor, lessons in Italian, German and music, but as she wrote in one letter after another to her former teacher, Miss Lewis, and to her Methodist aunt, on whom Dinah of *Adam Bede* was later modeled: "My soul seems for weeks together completely benumbed, and when I am aroused from this torpid state the intervals of activity are comparatively short."

In 1841, her brother Isaac's marriage and their father's determination to give up the farm to his son and to take a small house in the neighboring market town of Coventry, made a substantial change in Mary Ann Evans' way of life.

She was still her father's housekeeper and leisure time companion, and almost immediately undertook to organize a clothing club and other volunteer social services which the depression of the early forties made very necessary. But her household occupations were naturally far less demanding with a family of two and no farm yard or dairy to supervise, and while her growing religious doubts had as yet not found expression there is a marked shift of emphasis in the letters from Coventry. The two themes of personal loneliness and social uselessness replace the discussion of "spiritual unease" as we see in such confessions as this of September 1841:

> The prevalence of misery and want in this boasted nation of prosperity and glory is appalling, and really seems to call us away from mental luxury. O to be doing some little towards the regeneration of this groaning, travailing creation. I am supine and stupid—over fed with favors—while the haggard looks and piercing glance of want and conscious hopelessness are to be seen in the streets.

At the same time as Mary Ann Evans' correspondence, even with the deeply religious Miss Lewis, began to stress such this-worldly rather than other-worldly concerns, she found a new intimacy which was to remain for over a decade the most important in her life.

A young couple, Charles and Caroline Bray, had a year before purchased one of Coventry's most luxurious houses—Rosehill—and established a sort of informal intellectual center for all the more or less eccentric theorists of the provinces—and frequent guests from London. Charles himself was the author of a book on *The Philosophy of Necessity*, and while a devotee of phrenology he was also the exponent of many much sounder advanced scientific and social ideas.

His brother-in-law, Charles Hennell, with whom Mary Ann Evans soon developed a warm friendship, was the author of the *Inquiry Concerning the Origin of Christianity* which she had already read and liked. Its purely historical treatment of the life and work of Christ had no doubt helped revive questions her mind was still trying to ignore.

Under the stimulus of these rich new associations and the novel opportunity for speaking her mind freely on philosophical questions and so exploring what she really thought, Mary Ann's imitative faith rapidly dissolved.

Shortly thereafter Mary Ann came to the conclusion that it was dishonest and hypocritical for her to continue her church attendance. She informed her father she would no longer accompany him on Sundays.

She expected no particular excitement or concern at the news since his religion was the matter-of-fact taken for granted kind described in *Silas Marner* where, at Raveloe, everyone belonged to the established church but:

> held that to go to Church every Sunday in the calendar would have shown a greedy desire to stand well with Heaven, and get an undue advantage over their neighbors,—a wish to be better than the "common run," that would have implied a reflection on those who had godfathers and godmothers as well as themselves, and had an equal right to the burying service.

Although religion in his daughter's sense meant little to Mr. Evans, respectability meant everything. He actually prepared to sell his home and move to his married daughter's, while Mary Ann was packed off on a visit to her brother at Griff, to plan on finding lodgings to live in and teaching or translating to live by.

Again we find Mary Ann driven by inner as well as outer compulsions to be a "good girl," and a good daughter.

Her compunction at driving the father she adored into bitter exile in his last years, her love for her own home, and no doubt a deep if unacknowledged fear of the loneliness and difficulties of an unsupported life, begun with the handicap of such serious social disapproval, made her yield willingly to the advice and importunity of all her friends and return to Coventry and to churchgoing in April, 1842.

Life there continued much the same for the next seven years although when, in 1843, her friend Charles Hennell rather suddenly and perhaps disappointingly announced his engagement to Caroline Brabant, daughter of a famous scholar, Mary Ann was persuaded to take over the responsibility of translating David Friedrich Strauss' monumental three volume *Leben Jesu* so as to release the bride who had undertaken but barely begun the task.

The work became a weary trial as Mary Ann's mind, released from concern about her discarded faith, began to seek further afield in literature, mathematics and politics for its sustenance. As soon as it was completed in the spring of 1846, she turned with eagerness to translating Spinoza's *Tractatus Theologico—Politicus* which, she said, was such a rest for her mind!

There was during this period at least one suitor, a slightly younger man, John Sibree, who had left divinity school because of the unsettling doubts raised by his brilliant neighbor. A correspondence with him was welcome, and gives us some glimpses of a more relaxed, humorous, and mature young woman, but it did little to lighten the weight of constant attendance on a sick father, daily hours of tedious translation, and an ever stronger feeling of wasted powers and solitary confinement.

In January 1848 there are in her letters to him interesting comments on several matters of current importance:

> I am glad you detest Mrs. Hannah More's letters. I like neither her letters, nor her books, nor her character. She was the most disagreeable of all monsters, a blue-stocking—a monster that can only exist in a miserably false state of society, in which a woman with but a smattering of learning or philosophy is classed along with singing mice and card-playing pigs. . . . Young Englandism [Disraeli's renovated Toryism] is almost as remote from my sympathies as Jacobitism, as far as its force is concerned, though I love and respect it as an effort on behalf of the people. Disraeli is unquestionably an able man. . . . As to his theory of races, it has not a leg to stand on. . . . Looking at the matter aesthetically, our idea of beauty is never formed on the characteristics of a single race. I confess the types of the pure races, however handsome, always impress me disagreeably; there is an undefined feeling that I am looking not at *man*, but at a specimen of an order under Cuvier's class Bimana. . . .

And a little later in February 1848, at the first news of the French Revolution, we read again to John Sibree:

> Write and tell you that I join you in your happiness about the French Revolution? Very fine, my good friend. If I made you wait for a letter as long as you do me, our little échantillon of a millennium would be over, Satan would be let loose again, and I should have to share your humiliation instead of your triumph.
>
> Nevertheless I absolve you, for the sole merit of thinking rightly (that is, of course, just as I do) about la grande nation and its doings. You and Carlyle (have you seen his article in last week's *Examiner?*) are the only two people who feel just as I would have them—who can glory in what is actually great and beautiful without putting forth any cold reservations and incredulities to save their credit for wisdom. I am all the more delighted with your enthusiasm because I didn't expect it. I feared that you lacked revolutionary ardor. But no—you are just as sans-culottish and rash as I would have you. . . .
>
> I thought we had fallen on such evil days that we were to see no really great movement; that ours was what St. Simon

calls a purely critical epoch, not at all an organic one; but I begin to be glad of my date. . . . I have little patience with people who can find time to pity Louis Philippe and his moustachioed sons. Certainly our decayed monarchs should be pensioned off; we should have a hospital for them, or a sort of zoological garden where these worn out humbugs may be preserved. It is but justice that we should keep them, since we have spoiled them for any honest trade. Let them sit on soft cushions and have their dinner regularly, but, for Heaven's sake, preserve me from sentimentalizing over a pampered old man when the earth has its millions of unfed souls and bodies.

In June she wrote, to Charles Bray this time:

Poor Louis Blanc! The newspapers make me melancholy; but shame upon me that I say "poor"; . . . I worship the man who has written as a climax of his appeal against society, "L'inegalité" des talents *doit aboutir* non à l'inegalité des retributions, mais à l'inegalité des devoirs. [Inequality of talents *ought to lead* not to an inequality of rewards but to an inequality of duties.] You will wonder what has wrought me up into this fury. It is the loathsome fawning, the transparent hypocrisy, the systematic giving as little as possible for as much as possible that one meets with here at every turn. I feel society is training men and women for hell.

A little later the same month she wrote in reply to Charles' enthusiasm about *Jane Eyre* a note that becomes especially interesting in terms of her own great life adventure, then of course still undreamed of:

I have read *Jane Eyre,* and shall be glad to know what you admire in it. All self-sacrifice is good, but one would like it to be in a somewhat nobler cause than that of a diabolical law [the divorce law—or, rather, lack of one] which chains a man, soul and body to a putrefying carcass. However, the book *is* interesting; . . .

A letter to Charles Bray's older sister-in-law, Sara Hennell, with whom Mary Ann Evans had formed what was to remain a lifelong friendship, gives an interesting preview of her ideas about the powers and purposes of the novel. Miss Hennell had evidently criticized her friend's enthusiasm for an immoral woman like the notorious French writer, George Sand, and Mary Ann hastened to reply, despite difficulties:

My life is a perpetual nightmare, and always haunted by something to be done, which I have never the time, or, rather, the energy to do. Opportunity is kind, but only to the industrious; and I, alas! am not one of them. I have sat down in desperation this evening, though dear father is very uneasy, and his moans distract me, just to tell you that you have full absolution for your criticism, which I do not reckon of the impertinent order. I wish you to understand that the writers who have most profoundly influenced me—who have rolled away the waters from their bed, raised new mountains and spread delicious valleys for me—are not in the least oracles to me. . . .

It is thus with George Sand. . . . It is sufficient for me, as a reason·for bowing before her in eternal gratitude to that "great power of God manifested in her," that I cannot read six pages of hers without feeling that it is given to her to delineate human passion and its results, and (I must say, in spite of your judgment) some of the moral instincts and their tendencies, with such truthfulness, such nicety of discrimination, such tragic power, and, withal, such loving, gentle humor, that one might live a century with nothing but one's own dull faculties, and not know so *much* as those six pages will suggest.

On May 31, 1849, when Mary Ann was thirty, her father died. The Brays, who had planned a trip to the continent in June, wisely and kindly insisted on taking her with them and in July, when they began their return trip from Switzerland, she decided to remain in a pleasant pension at Geneva for a few months before making the effort of beginning a new life.

Her father had, as expected, left the farm and the bulk of his property to his son but had invested for Mary Ann £2,000 which assured her an income of £80 to £100 a year—the equivalent of some $2,000 today—and had left her £100 in ready money.

Her letters from Geneva show some concern about finances but also a gradual relief from the low spirits, frequent headaches and general depression which had increasingly characterized her life for the last six or seven years.

In October (1849) she wrote the Brays:

I am beginning to lose respect for the petty acumen that sees difficulties. I love the souls that rush along to their goal with a full stream of sentiment—that have too much of the positive to be harassed by the perpetual negatives—which, after all, are but the disease of the soul, to be expelled by fortifying the principle of vitality.

In February she writes her much older half-sister a letter which includes some penetrating comment on what it means to have a certain standard of living. The significance of this seemingly casual remark is later developed at length in the life of Dr. Lydgate of *Middlemarch* and the choice made by the hero of *Felix Holt, The Radical.*

The same letter includes a brief but vivid account of Mary Ann's intellectual interests during this time. And, more important, it gives us a further illustration of her clinging need for the affection and approval of those around her, a need we must fully understand if we are correctly to estimate the course of her later life.

> Decidedly England is the most comfortable country to be in in winter—at least, for all except those who are rich enough to buy English comforts everywhere. I hate myself for caring about carpets, easy-chairs, and coal fires—one's soul is under a curse, and can reach no truth while one is in bondage to the flesh in this way; but, alas! habit is the purgatory in which we suffer for our past sins. I hear much music. We have a reunion of musical friends every Monday. For the rest, I have refused soireés, which are as stupid and unprofitable at Geneva as in England. . . . I am going now to a séance on Experimental Physics by the celebrated Professor de la Rive.

She finally returned to England in early spring and after a round of rather unsatisfactory family visits settled at Rosehill for the greater part of 1850-1851.

During this period she became better acquainted with John Chapman, the erratic but enterprising publisher who had brought out her *Life of Jesus*. He had just purchased the *Westminster Review* and after a six weeks' stay at his home, or, rather, the boarding house he and his wife kept in London, she agreed to accept the arduous and much underpaid but interesting position of assistant-editor.

Her relations with Chapman, who was married and already carrying on a complicated love affair, were platonic but highly emotional. He seems deliberately to have selected her for the position and to have used all his undoubted personal charm in securing her acceptance because he needed some one of scholarship and literary ability superior to his own but feared to install a man who might rival or outshine him. As it proved, for the next three years Miss Evans did all he had hoped, working twelve and fourteen hours a day in so unobtrusive a manner that his authority was strengthened rather than undermined.

The *Westminster Review*, and Chapman's house to which she moved in the fall of 1851, were a center for the most advanced scientific, philosophical and, to some extent, social thought of London at the time. The contributors were such men as Browning, Carlyle, Froude, Thomas Huxley, George Henry Lewes, John Stuart Mill, and Herbert Spencer, as well as a very few enterprising women like Harriet Martineau.

Miss Evans was soon plunged into all kinds of activity. The spring of 1852 was largely occupied with a battle between Chapman and the ultra-conservative Publishers and Booksellers Association. The question at issue—a removal of trade restrictions on books—was finally referred to a meeting of authors and businessmen for which Miss Evans helped Chapman prepare his brief. She gives a spirited account of the affair in a note to the Bray's, May 5, 1852. It begins:

> The meeting last night went off triumphantly, and I saluted Mr. Chapman with "See the Conquering Hero Comes" on the piano at 12 o'clock; for not until then was the last magnate, except Herbert Spencer, out of the house. I sat at the door for a short time, [there were supposed to be no women in the meeting] but soon got a chair within it, and heard and saw everything.
>
> Dickens in the chair—a position he fills remarkably well, preserving a courteous neutrality of eyebrows, and speaking with clearness and distinction.

Another note in April, 1852, refers to some Americans staying at Chapman's and to an Englishman who was becoming very important to Mary Ann:

> Miss Pugh, an elderly lady, is a great abolitionist, and was one of the Women's Convention that came to England in 1840, and was not allowed to join the Men's Convention. But I suppose we shall soon be able to say, nous avons changé tout cela [we have changed all that].
>
> I went to the opera on Saturday with my "excellent friend, Herbert Spencer," as Lewes calls him. We have agreed that we are not in love with each other, and that there is no reason why we should not have as much of each other's society as we like. He is a good, delightful creature and I always feel better for being with him.

Herbert Spencer too described her as "the most admirable woman, mentally, I ever met," and wrote a friend:

> I am very frequently at Chapman's where she is lodged and the greatness of her intellect, conjoined with her womanly qualities and manner, generally keep me by her side most of the evening.

But he had also written a year before that it was impossible for him, in his financial circumstances, to consider marriage:

> and as for twisting circumstances into better shape, I think it is too much trouble. I think you have heard me say—I don't mean to get on. I don't think getting on is worth the bother. On the whole I am decided not to be a drudge; and as I see no probability of being able to marry without being a drudge, why I have pretty well given up the idea.

Mary Ann Evans was, of course, quite willing to be a drudge for love, and when, after getting his father to call upon her and enjoying her daily companionship, Spencer belatedly decided that further intimacy might seem to compromise him, she was bewildered and deeply hurt.

Again, as in Jane Austen's case—although with a difference—the important point is not whether she was really in love with Spencer or had only persuaded herself that she must be. The essential fact is that Mary Ann Evans, far more completely than Jane Austen, accepted (emotionally, at least) the assumption of her society that the meaning of a woman's life lay primarily in love and marriage and that a woman who could not secure these was a failure—and somehow to blame.

Now Spencer's rejection made her feel not only unloved but also unworthy to be loved and we find a pathetic expression of her bewilderment in a sad little note to an excellent new friend, a Mrs. Taylor:

> Your cordial assurance that you shall be glad to see me sometimes is one of those pleasant things—those life-preservers —which relenting destiny sends me now and then to buoy me up. For you must know that I am not a little desponding now and then, and think that old friends will die off, while I shall be left without the power to make new ones. You know how sad one feels when a great procession has swept by one, and the last notes of its music have died away, leaving one alone

with the fields and sky. I feel so about life sometimes. It is a help to read such a life as Margaret Fuller's. How inexpressibly touching that passage from her journal—"I shall always reign through the intellect, but the life! the life! O my God! shall that never be sweet?" I am thankful, as if for myself, that it was sweet at last.

In July, after the "deliciously calm friendship" was definitely at an end Miss Evans went to the seashore to recover in solitude, writing to Caroline Bray: "I am very well and 'plucky'—a word which I propose to substitute for happy, as more truthful."

However, Spencer had unwittingly done Miss Evans one real service. During one of his last calls he had brought with him a friend, George Henry Lewes. From November 1852 on, mixed with comments on current events, economics, politics, personalities, and literature, are casual but increasingly frequent references to Mr. Lewes.

George Henry Lewes had, when he met Mary Ann Evans, been separated from his wife for over two years, although he was contributing to her personal expenses and furnishing full support for the three sons who were, legally at least, his.

He was two-and-a-half years older than Mary Ann and was very well-known as a dramatic and literary critic, feature writer on scientific subjects, and author of the very good popular *History of Philosophy*.

His father, a theatrical manager and son of a famous comedian, had died in Lewes' youth and he had had a rather checkered education attending school in France as well as England; studying medicine, with a resultant lifelong experimental interest in anatomy; attempting briefly a career in the theatre; and finally making his living as a free-lance writer with two unsuccessful novels and several dramas, as well as numerous adaptations and translation of French plays and much brilliantly successful journalism to his credit.

In 1841, at the age of twenty-three, he had married an exceptionally beautiful nineteen-year-old girl and set up a sort of communal household with several other bohemian young couples, including Leigh Hunt's oldest son, Thornton, and his wife.

Some years later, after the birth of Lewes' son, Charles, his wife fell in love with Thornton, for whom her second child was named. After she had lived with him for some time she returned to her husband who proved that his belief in a single standard was genuine by the ungrudging generosity with which he cooperated in an attempt to rebuild their life together, owning as his the two younger boys whose paternity was extremely doubtful.

However Agnes again left him to return to Hunt, who had separated from his wife, and they had two more children who were acknowledged as Hunt's.

In the 1850's divorce was available only through a special act of Parliament to be achieved at enormous and, for Lewes, utterly prohibitive expense. Furthermore, according to the existing laws, his reconciliation with his wife after her first infidelity was a condoning of the offense which made it impossible for him to appear as the plaintiff. It was, therefore, impossible for him to think of marrying again although he was soon deeply in love with Mary Ann Evans.

She had no knowledge of his circumstances, and aware that he was a hard working and prolific writer who could secure as many assignments as he wished to undertake, she was puzzled as well as concerned by his shabby clothes and meager way of life. Finally she said something about the matter which elicited the explanation that he supported his three young sons and made their mother a regular allowance.

The next two-and-a-half years saw a constantly growing intimacy of daily companionship and mutual dependence, during which Lewes refrained from urging, and Mary Ann Evans from taking, any final step.

Her habitual candor and the complete frankness with which she usually wrote to Sara Hennell and the Brays—and, no doubt, her unconscious desire to mention Lewes' name as often as possible —made it difficult to omit a recital of his doings from her correspondence. The apparent impossibility of any recognized relationship between them made it still more difficult really to discuss his activities. The result is a rather amusing series of non sequiturs in which Miss Evans reports an absurd speech in the House of Lords and concludes that she was prevented from completing her other work, after reading the Parliamentary debate, by "Mr. Lewes, who, of course, sits talking till the second bell rings."

That August her letter to Mrs. Bray, from the seashore, rings a happy contrast to the stoical resignation, reading of Aristotle and being "plucky" the year before. She writes gaily:

> I am on a delightful hill looking over the heads of the houses, and having a vast expanse of sea and sky for my only

view. The bright weather and genial air—so different from what I have had for a year before—make me feel as happy and stupid as a well-conditioned cow. I sit looking at the sea and the sleepy ships with a purely animal bien-être.

On her return to London she moved from Chapman's to more impersonal lodgings where she could receive "visitors" in greater privacy.

In July she prophetically composed a light-hearted "Life of Herbert Spencer" as it would stand a hundred years later in the Biographical Dictionaries of 1954, concluding: "The life of this philosopher, like that of the great Kant, offers little material for the narrator."

And on the 20th of that month she and Lewes left for the continent with, on Miss Evans' part, the briefest of notes to Rosehill,

> Dear Friends—all three—I have only time to say good-bye, and God bless you. P'ste Restante, Weimar, for the next six weeks, and afterwards Berlin. Ever your loving and grateful Marian.

The apparently gratuitous mystification of these letters to her best friends, in which Marian Evans deliberately revealed without explicitly stating her growing intimacy and final elopement with Lewes, is utterly foreign to all we know of the candor and devotion to truth that characterized her all her life. It is, however, easy to understand when we know the essential fact that for this couple marriage was impossible. There was therefore no alternative if he and Marian Evans wished to live together but the illegal union which so troubled her friends and, in a different way, Marian herself.

It is perhaps difficult for us in this day of comparatively easy divorce and, often, casual nonmarital relationships, to realize how shocking the intensely respectable, utterly monogamous, lifelong union, entered into after due deliberation by two mature and independent adults, was to their contemporaries, and how much courage it took for Marian Evans to defy an almost unanimous social disapproval based on a principle with which she herself largely agreed.

Her brother refused to write to, or accept letters from, her until the year of her death; her widowed sister, Chrissie, whom she was assisting financially, continued to accept cheques but interrupted all other correspondence for over five years until she herself was dying of consumption; her friends, the Brays, themselves notoriously "advanced" and, in fact, avowed atheists and free thinkers, did not answer her letters from the continent; and although there was a reconciliation a year later, the former intimacy was never fully resumed.

A letter to Mrs. Bray from Marian Lewes, as she then signed herself, in September, 1855, is of interest both for its statement of her attitude and the implicit revelation it gives of theirs:

> If there is any one action or relation of my life which is, and always has been, profoundly serious, it is my relation to Mr. Lewes. . . . Light and easily broken ties are what I neither desire theoretically nor could live for practically. Women who are satisfied with such ties do *not* act as I have done. That any unworldly unsuperstitious person who is sufficiently acquainted with the realities of life can pronounce my relation to Mr. Lewes immoral, I can only understand by remembering how subtle and complex are the influences that mould opinion. But I *do* remember this; and I indulge in no arrogant or uncharitable thoughts about those who condemn us, even though we might have expected a somewhat different verdict. From the majority of persons, of course, we never looked for anything but condemnation. We are leading no life of self indulgence, except, indeed, that being happy in each other, we find everything easy. We are working hard to provide for others better than we provide for ourselves, and to fulfil every responsibility that lies upon us. Levity and pride would not be a sufficient basis for that. Pardon me if, in vindicating myself from some unjust conclusions, I seem too cold and self-asserting. I should not care to vindicate myself if I did not love you and desire to relieve you of the pain which you say these conclusions have given you. Whatever I may have misinterpreted before, I do not misinterpret your letter this morning, but read in it nothing else than love and kindness towards me, to which my heart fully answers yes. . . .

Of the fourteen months between the farewell note and this letter the Lewes's (as they called themselves) had spent almost nine traveling happily—and industriously—on the continent. During that period George had completed his valuable *Life of Goethe* and Marian had written a number of articles and almost completed a translation of Spinoza's *Ethics*.

On the return to England life became less pleasant. Although Chapman was friendly and had asked her to undertake the responsibility of literary reviewer for the *Westminster* under a cloak of strict anonymity, he dared not be seen with Marian Lewes lest such an association compromise the respectability of his *Review* and publishing house. And this despite the fact that his wife and almost everyone else in their circle knew he had, for many years, been living with his children's governess! Other masculine acquaintances, many of them contributors to the *Review*, either walked around a corner when they saw her so as not to be forced to greet her or, more outrageously, deliberately failed to raise their hats when they spoke so that no one might think they condoned immorality. When, in August 1855, Lewes left her alone in London while he took his three sons, who did not yet know of her, to the seashore for their school holidays, Marian was literally prostrated by these insults.

It is pleasant to note that at least three women friends, whose loyalty she never forgot, wrote to her in terms of immediate cordiality. They were Sara Hennell, Mrs. Taylor, soon a leader of the woman suffrage movement, and Barbara Smith (later Bodichon), a pioneer in the fight for women's education and professional standing.

With Lewes' return things became more cheerful, and during the winter Marian wrote some of her best critical articles, including one on Heine in which she quotes with approval his epigram, "The People have time enough, they are immortal; kings only are mortal." She also wrote an article on Margaret Fuller and Mary Wollstonecraft, one on Carlyle and almost the only appreciative early review of Meredith's novel, *Shaving of Shagpat*. In January 1856 she noted in her journal "Received a charming letter from Barbara Smith, with a petition to Parliament that women may have a right to their earnings."

A friendly note of condolence (on business reverses) to the Brays stresses the importance of anonymity for the continued sale of her writing, with a specific request:

> By the way, when the Spinoza comes out, be so good as not to mention my name in connection with it. I particularly wish not to be known as the translator of the "Ethics," for reasons which it would be "too odious to mention." You don't know what a severely practical person I am become, and what a sharp eye I have to the main chance. I keep the purse, and dole out sovereigns with all the pangs of a miser.

This economy was indeed necessary since the English school which the three Lewes boys were attending had indicated the inadvisability of their returning "under the circumstances" and the Hofwyl school which they were next to attend, was much more expensive.

That spring, too, she began her long critical essay on Riehl's *The Natural History of German Life* in which she explicitly develops much of the aesthetic theory soon to be exemplified in her novels. In that article we find both her mature understanding of the nature and significance of imaginative literature—later to be filled in and confirmed but never essentially altered by her own experience and practice—and her concrete understanding of country life from the viewpoint of the farmer and peasant. This is, of course, more richly illustrated in the agricultural scenes and characters which give her own novels so much of their value, but it is perhaps nowhere more compactly and quotably stated than here.

> The notion that peasants are joyous, that the typical moment to represent a man in a smock-frock is when he is cracking a joke and showing a row of sound teeth, that cottage matrons are usually buxom, and village children necessarily rosy and merry, are prejudices difficult to dislodge from the artistic mind, which looks for its subjects into literature instead of life. . . . But no one who has seen much of actual ploughmen thinks them jocund; no one who is well acquainted with the English peasantry can pronounce them merry. . . . The conventional countryman of the stage, who picks up pocket-books and never looks into them, and who is too simple even to know that honesty has its opposite, represents the still lingering mistake that an unintelligible dialect is a guarantee for ingenuousness, and that slouching shoulders indicate an upright disposition. . . . The selfish instincts are not subdued by the sight of buttercups, nor is integrity in the least established by that classic rural occupation, sheep-washing. To make men moral, something more is requisite than to turn them out to grass. . . . But our social novels profess to represent the people as they are, and the unreality of their representations is a grave evil. The greatest benefit we owe to the artist, whether painter, poet or novelist is the extension of our sympathies. Appeals founded on generalizations and statistics require a sympathy ready-made, a moral sentiment already in activity; but a picture of human life such as a great artist can give, surprises even the trivial and the selfish into that attention to what is apart from themselves, which may be called the raw material of moral sentiment. . . . Art is the nearest thing to life; it is a mode of amplifying experience and extending our contact with our fellow-men beyond the bounds of our personal lot. All the more sacred is the task of the artist

when he undertakes to paint the life of the People. Falsification here is far more pernicious than in the more artificial aspects of life. . . . This perversion is not the less fatal because the misrepresentation which gives rise to it has what the artist considers a moral end. The thing for mankind to know is, not what are the motives and influences which the moralist thinks *ought* to act on the laborer or the artisan, but what are the motives and influences which *do* act on him. . . . However, the unwillingness of the peasant to adopt innovations has a not unreasonable foundation in the fact that for him experiments are practical, not theoretical, and must be made with expense of money instead of brains—a fact that is not, perhaps, sufficiently taken into account by agricultural theorists, who complain of the farmer's obstinacy.

One more article of special interest should be mentioned, which appeared in the *Westminster Review* in September under the title *Silly Novels by Lady Novelists*. In this she contrasted such fashionable effusions with those of serious women writers like Harriet Beecher Stowe, reiterated the fact that the inner truth of woman's life and the special understanding of society which could only be achieved from her special view point would be invaluable to men as well as women if deeply and honestly presented.

This fittingly heralded the major phase of Marian Evans' life work. Her first piece of fiction—a long story, *The Sad Fortunes of the Reverend Amos Barton*—was begun that September and completed in November, 1856, just a few weeks before her thirty-seventh birthday. There is an interesting note in her journal a few months earlier, July 20, 1856:

> I never before longed so much to know the names of things. The desire is part of the tendency that is now constantly growing in me to escape from all vagueness and inaccuracy into the daylight of distinct vivid ideas. . . . I am anxious to begin my fiction writing. . . .

The "names of things" was no doubt a formulation which came to mind because Lewes was then collecting, anatomizing and classifying specimens of crustaceans and other sea animals as the basis of his lively and interesting series of *Seaside Sketches* which appeared in *Blackwood's Magazine* during 1856 and 1857, and was republished as a book in 1858.

But Lewes was responsible for much more than this accidental though illuminating expression of George Eliot's scientific approach to fiction. It is not too much to say that he was altogether responsible for the birth and life of George Eliot. Certainly without his urgent encouragement Marian would never have written a novel. She herself tells the story of this beginning:

> September, 1856, made a new era in my life, for it was then I began to write fiction. It had always been a vague dream of mine that some time or other I might write a novel; and my shadowy conception of what the novel was to be varied, of course, from one epoch of my life to another. But I never went further towards the actual writing of the novel than an introductory chapter describing a Staffordshire village and the life of the neighboring farm-houses; and as the years passed on I lost any hope that I should ever be able to write a novel, just as I desponded about everything else in my future life. . . . My "introductory chapter" . . . happened to be among the papers I had with me in Germany, and one evening at Berlin something led me to read it to George. He was struck with it as a bit of concrete description, and it suggested to him the possibility of my being able to write a novel, . . . He began to say very positively, "You must try and write a story," and when we were at Tenby he urged me to begin at once.

When the story, planned as the first of a series of *Scenes of Clerical Life*, two more of which were subsequently written, was completed, Lewes sent it to G. H. Blackwood, the editor of the famous magazine in which many of his own popular scientific essays had appeared, as the manuscript of a friend.

The editor was enthusiastic and the three stories appeared serially throughout 1857, and were republished as a book in 1858. They are little known today and do not give us any sense of the leisurely masterly handling of a large-size fully peopled canvas which is perhaps George Eliot's greatest gift, but there are in them many of her characteristic succinct thumbnail sketches like the description of virtuous Mrs. Patten in *Amos Barton*:

> quiescence in an easy chair, under the sense of compound interest perpetually accumulating has long seemed an ample function to her.

Another characteristic one is that of the easygoing doctor, Pilgrim, in *Janet's Repentance*, who:

looked with tolerance on all shades of religious opinion that did not include a belief in cures by miracles.

George Eliot, as we may now call her, chose that pen name to preserve her anonymity. It began with Lewes' first name, *George*, and she added *Eliot* as "a good round mouth-filling name" which, she privately explained, meant "To L(ewes) I—owe—it."

On December 31, 1857, George Eliot wrote a final note in her journal for the year:

> *Few women, I fear, have had such reason as I have to think the long, sad years of youth were worth living for the sake of middle age.* Our prospects are very bright too. I am writing my new novel [*Adam Bede*]. G. is full of his "Physiology of Common Life." He has just finished editing Johnson, for which he is to have 100 guineas, and we have both encouragement to think that our books just coming out, ["Sea-side Studies" and "Scenes of Clerical Life"] will be well received. So good-bye dear 1857! May I be able to look back on 1858 with an equal consciousness of advancement in work and in heart.

There was much speculation about who "George Eliot" might be, most people assuming that he was a clergyman. Dickens was the only one who even suspected the possibility of the author's being a woman and just a few weeks after the *Scenes of Clerical Life* had appeared in book form he wrote to "George Eliot," care of the publishers:

> Monday, 17th Jan. 1858
>
> My dear Sir,—
>   I have been so strongly affected by the two first tales in the book you have had the kindness to send me, through Messrs. Blackwood, that I hope you will excuse my writing to you to express my admiration of their extraordinary merit. The exquisite truth and delicacy, both of the humor and the pathos of these stories, I have never seen the like of; and they have impressed me in a manner that I should find it very difficult to describe to you, if I had the impertinence to try.
>   In addressing these few words of thankfulness to the creator of the Sad Fortunes of the Rev. Amos Barton, and the sad love-story of Mr. Gilfil, I am (I presume) bound to adopt the name that it pleases that excellent writer to assume. I can suggest no better one; but I should have been strongly dis-

posed, if I had been left to my own devices, to address the said writer as a woman. I have observed what seemed to me such womanly touches in these moving fictions, that the assurance on the title page is insufficient to satisfy me even now. If they originated with no woman, I believe that no man ever before had the art of making himself mentally so like a woman since the world began.

You will not suppose that I have any vulgar wish to fathom your secret. I mention the point as one of great interest to me —not of mere curiosity. If it should ever suit your convenience and inclination to show me the face of the man, or woman, who has written so charmingly, it will be a very memorable occasion to me. If otherwise, I shall always hold that impalpable personage in loving attachment and respect, and shall yield myself up to all future utterances from the same source, with a perfect confidence in their making me wiser and better.

Your obliged and faithful servant and admirer,
Charles Dickens

A year and a half later, after the publication of *Adam Bede*, Dickens wrote George Eliot, whose identity he had by then learned:

Every high quality that was in the former book, is in that, with a World of Power added thereunto. The conception of Hetty's character is so extraordinarily subtle and true, that I laid the book down fifty times, to shut my eyes and think about it. . . . The whole country life that the story is set in, is so real, so droll and genuine, and yet so select and polished by art, that I cannot praise it enough to you. . . .

. . . if you should ever have the freedom and the inclination to be a fellow labourer with me [in writing for his magazine] it would yield me a pleasure I have never known yet and can never know otherwise, and no channel that even you could command should be so profitable as to yourself.

It is interesting to note two other compliments on *Adam Bede* which George Eliot thought significant enough to copy into her journal. One entry made February 6, 1859, reads:

In this letter Blackwood told me the first ab extra opinion of the book, which happened to be precisely what I most desired. A cabinet maker (brother to Blackwood's managing clerk) had read the sheets, and declared that the writer must have been brought up to the business, or at least had listened to the workmen in their workshop.

Another letter forwarded to her by the publisher she thought important enough to copy in full, although she briefly summarized the praise of such well-known literary figures as Jane Welsh Carlyle, John Murray, Charles Reade and Herbert Spencer.

> Dear Sir,—I got the other day a hasty read of your "Scenes of Clerical Life," and since that a glance at your "Adam Bede," and was delighted more than I can express; but being a poor man, and having enough to do to make ends meet, I am unable to get a read of your inimitable books.
> Forgive, dear sir, my boldness in asking you to give us a cheap edition. You would confer on us a great boon. I can get plenty of trash for a few pence, but I am sick of it. I felt so different when I shut your books, even though it was but a kind of hop-skip-and-jump read.
> I feel so strongly in this matter that I am determined to risk being thought rude and officious, and write to you.
> Many of my working brethren feel as I do, and I express their wish as well as my own. Again asking your forgiveness for intruding myself upon you, I remain, with profoundest respect, yours, etc.,
>
> E. Hall

The third story in *Scenes of Clerical Life* specifically omitted by Dickens' praise, was discussed in a favorable if rather troubled review by Henry James, who began:

> The subject of this tale [Janet's Repentance] might almost be qualified by the French epithet *scabreux*. It would be difficult for what is called *realism* to go further than in the adoption of a heroine stained with the vice of intemperance. The theme is unpleasant; the author chose it at her peril.

It may be a little startling to the young reader who has been taught to think of Henry James as a modern, and of George Eliot as almost prehistoric, to find him so uneasy at her realism. Years later in a discussion of her avowed preference for common subjects and her intimate knowledge of the life she describes, Henry James wrote:

> But even in the absence of any such avowed predilections as these, a brief glance over the principal figures of her different works would assure us that our author's sympathies are with common people. Silas Marner is a linen-weaver, Adam

Bede is a carpenter, Maggie Tulliver is a miller's daughter, Felix Holt is a watchmaker, Dinah Morris works in a factory and Hetty Sorrel is a dairy maid. . . . They [her novels] offer a completeness, a rich density of detail, which could be the fruit only of a long term of conscious contact—such as would make it more difficult for the author to fall into the perversion and suppression of facts, than to set them down literally.

This is true, but it is also true that to a great extent the intimacy with that common life in which George Eliot was most interested ended with the beginning of her "married" life. The way her union with Lewes set her apart from those activities and movements in which she would otherwise have increasingly participated is something very difficult for us in the twentieth century to understand.

While she herself was extremely sensitive to, and involved in, the most advanced theoretical movements of her time, as both her fundamentally dialectical materialist philosophy, and her use of a scientifically psychological approach, show, she was, in terms of large social movements and concrete practical conditions, able to use only the material absorbed in her first thirty years.

True, there are many individuals in her novels who could not have been created except for her contacts during the years of the *Westminster* editorship and her continued association with intellectual leaders which lasted throughout her life with Lewes. One of the few convincing portraits of a musician in all English fiction is Herr Klausner of *Daniel Deronda*, and the part scientific interest can play in personal life has rarely been conveyed as well as through Dr. Lydgate of *Middlemarch*. But the detailed concrete knowledge of a large coherent web of social life ends with the 1850's because of George Eliot's more and more complete seclusion from general society thereafter.

Her imagination could make a brilliant leap to the as yet unarticulated ideology of Zionism in her last book, published a quarter of a century before the establishment of the Zionist movement; and there is still probably no novel which outranks her late masterpiece, *Middlemarch*, as a study of one phase of the woman question.

But even in terms of this question we find the limiting effect of her circumscribed activity.

Soon after the overwhelmingly successful publication of *Adam Bede*, her first full length novel and except for *Middlemarch*, perhaps her greatest, there was a donation of £100 (then the equivalent of at least $2,000) "from the author of *Adam Bede*" for the foundation of Girton as a woman's college, and from time to time a similarly anonymous action or a comment in her letters or journal indicate George Eliot's continued support of such efforts. But the growing interest and broader understanding which active public participation would have developed in her were lacking. Always aware of her anomalous position, fearing lest she bring discredit on a cause she respected or foster the too general identification of "irreligious" and "advanced" with immoral views, she refused to make public statements on any matter whatsoever, even when such friends as Mrs. Taylor later begged her sponsorship.

For example, although she said she would rather have had to her credit the work accomplished by *Uncle Tom's Cabin* than all her own novels, and although she had written Harriet Beecher Stowe, "As healthy human beings we must love and hate—love what is good for mankind and hate what is evil for mankind," she took no public stand on the Civil War. Lewes' name was high on the list of those who backed Huxley's protest against the legal lynching of a Negro senator in Jamaica (see pp. 819-20) but there too George Eliot felt compelled to keep silence.

Lewes himself undertook all dealings with publishers and reviewers, and even removed criticisms from newspapers and magazines before George Eliot read them. He intercepted a letter from Sara Hennell, quoting some adverse reviews, in 1862 and replied to it:

> There is a special reason in her case [why she should see no criticism]. It is that excessive diffidence which prevented her writing at all, for so many years, and would prevent her now, if I were not beside her to encourage her. A thousand eulogies would not give her the slightest confidence, but one objection would increase her doubts . . . it is very desirable she should suffer no more pain in this life than can possibly be avoided.

Although many of the most distinguished men of the time were regular visitors at the Lewes' household, there were until the middle seventies almost no women callers, and until her death George Eliot visited almost nowhere and never invited to her home a woman who had not specifically requested the invitation.

A single disastrous exception must be noted in 1865. By that time the couple had lived in exemplary respectability for over twelve years. As Dickens said

> This irregular pair rehabilitated marriage, the survival of love in the teeth of custom and of sensual delight side by side with fidelity.

George Eliot was famous as the admired author of *Adam Bede, The Mill on the Floss*, and *Silas Marner*; she had been publicly spoken of as the only novelist whose books deserved a place with serious nonfiction work on the shelves of the British Museum; she had been offered £10,000 for the copyright of *Romola*, sight unseen—the largest price ever offered for an as yet unwritten novel.

Lewes, well-known in the world of science and philosophy, had just accepted the editorship of the new *Fortnightly Review* and knowing how much George Eliot was affected by the lack of general social acceptance, he urged the completion of a new luxurious home, The Priory, as an occasion for a housewarming to which they invited his review's distinguished contributors with their wives. Many of these, without their wives, had for several years dropped in almost weekly for informal musical or conversational evenings at the Lewes'.

Of the hundred and fifty guests expected twelve arrived, with no women in the number.

George Eliot attempted to make light of the failure to almost the only intimate woman friend made after her elopement—a Mrs. Congreve. She wrote her:

> Some of the invited were ill and sent regrets, others were not ardent enough to brave the damp evening—in fine, only twelve came. . . . I turn my inward shudders into outward smiles and talk fast with a sense of lead on my tongue. However, Mr. Pigott made a woman's part in the charade so irresistibly comic that I tittered at it at intervals in my sleepless hours.

A few days later, February 21, she noted in her journal, "Ill and very miserable. George has taken my drama" [*The Spanish Gypsy*, later completed as a dramatic poem] "away from me."

All this is not, of course, to say that either as a woman or as an artist she ever regretted her decision.

The manuscript of *Adam Bede*, completed in 1858, bears the

dedication: "To my dear husband, George Henry Lewes, I give the M.S. of a work which would never have been written but for the happiness which his love has conferred on my life."

The Mill on the Floss has the inscription "To my beloved husband, George Henry Lewes, I give this M.S. of my third book, written in the sixth year of our life together, at Holly Lodge, South Field, Wandsworth, and finished 21st March, 1860."

Romola, completed in 1863, is autographed "To the Husband whose perfect love has been the best source of her insight and strength, this manuscript is given by his devoted wife, the writer."

Felix Holt, The Radical, finished in 1866, was inscribed "From George Eliot to her dear Husband, this thirteenth year of their united life, in which the deepening sense of her own imperfectness has the consolation of their deepening love."

Middlemarch was Lewes' favorite among her books, of which he wrote to her friend, Barbara Bodichon:

> So glad you are taken with Dodo [its heroine]. Your letter has been a great comfort to Polly [George Eliot]. I have all along felt that women would owe her peculiar gratitude for that book—such a profound grip of life as it has.

This was, as always, privately dedicated to him by the name which she could not publicly use. "To my dear Husband, George Henry Lewes, in this nineteenth year of our blessed union."

And the manuscript of *Daniel Deronda*, completed in 1876, two years before his death, has with the customary inscription on the title page an appropriate concluding quotation from Shakespeare's twenty-ninth sonnet.

But although personally George Eliot found the world well lost for love, and although she would certainly not have been a novelist at all without it, the world is a serious loss to a novelist. The way in which her otherwise certain touch fumbles whenever she gingerly handles a current matter of specific topical importance, like the secret ballot, manhood suffrage, or even particular demands for women's political rights, shows that for the novelist no conscientious reading and thinking replaces direct observation and experience.

It is not that she is on the wrong side on these issues. It is the excessive shrinking from any disturbance, the extreme reliance on education as a means of change, the idealistic emphasis on motives which falsify the picture when—and only when—she is speaking in her own person of a contemporary proposal of the sixties or seventies.

For not only her basic philosophy, but all her rich and varied concrete observation of life and character, stand against these abstract errors which so shock us in their—fortunately—rare occurrences in her later works.

For example, she gives a profoundly true picture of a working-class leader's character in *Felix Holt, The Radical* where she has him say for himself, when questioned as to his deliberate choice of a workingman's life:

> I would never choose to withdraw myself from the labour and common burthen of the world; but I do choose to withdraw myself from the push and the scramble for money and position. Any man is at liberty to call me a fool, and say that mankind are benefited by the push and scramble in the long-run. . . . As it is, I prefer going shares with the unlucky. . . . It is just because I'm a very ambitious fellow, with very hungry passions, wanting a great deal to satisfy me, that I have chosen to give up what people call worldly good. At least that has been one determining reason. It all depends on what a man gets into his consciousness—what life thrusts into his mind, so that it becomes present to him as remorse is present to the guilty, or a mechanical problem to an inventive genius. There are two things I've got present in that way: one of them is the picture of what I should hate to be. I'm determined never to go about making my face simpering or solemn, and telling professional lies for profit; or to get tangled in affairs where I must wink at dishonesty and pocket the proceeds, and justify that knavery as part of a system that I can't alter. If I once went into that sort of struggle for success, I should want to win—I should defend the wrong that I had once identified myself with.
>
> I should become everything that I now see beforehand to be detestable. And what's more, I should do this, as men are doing it every day, for a ridiculous small prize—perhaps for none at all—perhaps for the sake of two parlours, a rank eligible for the Church wardenship, a discontented wife, and several unhopeful children. . . .
>
> The other thing that's got into mind like a splinter is the life of the miserable—the spawning life of vice and hunger. I'll never be one of the sleek dogs. The old Catholics are right, with their higher rule and their lower. Some are called to subject themselves to a harder discipline, and renounce things voluntarily which are lawful for others. It is the old word—"necessity is laid upon me." . . .
>
> O, I shall go away as soon as I can to some large town

. . . some ugly, wicked, miserable place. I want to be a demagogue of a new sort; an honest one, if possible, who will tell the people they are blind and foolish, and neither flatter them nor fatten on them. I have my heritage—an order I belong to. I have the blood of a line of handicraftsmen in my veins, and I want to stand up for the lot of the handicraftsman as a good lot, in which a man may be better trained to all the best functions of his nature than if he belonged to the grimacing set who have visiting cards and are proud to be thought richer than their neighbours. . . . I have no fellow-feeling with the rich as a class; the habits of their lives are odious to me. Thousands of men have wedded poverty because they expect to go to heaven for it; I don't expect to go to heaven for it, but I wed it because it enables me to do what I most want to do on earth. Whatever the hopes for the world may be—whether great or small—I am a man of this generation; . . . It is held reasonable enough to toil for the fortunes of a family, though it may turn to imbecility in the third generation. I choose a family with more chances in it.

But when a political article was urgently requested by *Blackwood's Magazine* in 1868—immediately after the passage of manhood suffrage—under the title of *Address to Working Men by Felix Holt* we find such statements as Felix Holt would have blushed to make.

George Eliot's artistic practice was, however, here wiser than her theory, and there is neither idealism nor equivocation in the novels themselves or the conclusions to be drawn from them, albeit the specific scenes with which they deal are almost all those of the 1820's and 1830's.

The way in which those conclusions are indicated was expressed by George Eliot herself when she said, in a passage accepted as a guide by one of her most famous admirers, Marcel Proust;

I think aesthetic teaching is the highest of all teaching because it deals with life in its highest complexity. But if it ceases to be purely aesthetic,—if it lapses anywhere from the picture to the diagram,—it becomes the most offensive of all teaching. Avowed Utopias are not offensive, because they are understood to have a scientific and expository character: they do not pretend to work on the emotions; or couldn't do it if they did pretend. . . .

In another discussion of her methods of work she said she wanted "to get breathing individuals, and group them in the needful relations, so that the presentations will lay hold on the emotions as human experience." She referred with approval to an article on *Realism in Art* by Lewes which developed the idea that the true business of art is intensification, not distortion or falsification, of the real; that the common appearances of daily life will furnish all the material the artist ought to ask, and that the true opposite of realism was not idealism, which it included, but rather falsism.

A specific note on her last novel, *Daniel Deronda*, written in answer to an inquiry by Mrs. Stowe, is of interest in explaining her choice of so special a subject as "the Jewish question" in that book—although a large part of the novel is also devoted to her more general concern with "the woman question."

> As to the Jewish element in "Deronda," I expected from first to last, in writing it, that it would create much stronger resistance, and even repulsion, than it has actually met with. But precisely because I felt that the usual attitude of Christians towards Jews is—I hardly know whether to say more impious or more stupid when viewed in the light of their professed principles, I therefore felt urged to treat Jews with such sympathy and understanding as my nature and knowledge could attain to. Moreover, not only towards the Jews, but towards all Oriental peoples with whom we English come in contact, a spirit of arrogance and contemptuous dictatorialness is observable which has become a national disgrace to us. There is nothing I should care more to do, if it were possible, than to rouse the imagination of men and women to a vision of human claims in those races of their fellow-men who most differ from them in customs and beliefs. . . .
>
> To my feeling, this deadness to the history which has prepared half our world for us, this inability to find interest in any form of life that is not clad in the same coat-tails and flounces as our own, lies very close to the worst kind of irreligion. The best that can be said of it is, that it is a sign of the intellectual narrowness—in plain English, the stupidity—which is still the average mark of our culture. . . . I sum up with the writer of the Book of Maccabees—"If I have done well and as befits the subject, it is what I desired; and if I have done ill, it is what I could attain unto."

But while this concern is unquestionably sincere, it does not often appear in George Eliot's work. In fact it is almost certain that the specific interest in the Jews which directed *Daniel Deronda* was rather Lewes' than George Eliot's. In 1849 during a brief venture at a dramatic career he had chosen Shylock to portray, and contemporary comments indicate that his interpretation was the sympathetic and respectful one developed in Heine's analysis of the play. One critic remarked: "There was originality in Lewes' conception of Shylock whom he endeavored to represent as the champion and avenger of an oppressed race." Later, in an article Lewes himself wrote "On Actors and the Art of Acting," he discussed Kean's performance of the role, saying:

> The overpowering remonstrant sarcasm of his address to Antonio, and the sardonic mirth of his proposition about the "Merry bond," were fine preparations for the anguish and rage at the elopement of his daughter, and the gloating anticipations of revenge on the Christian. Anything more impressive than the passionate recrimination and wild justice of argument in his "Hath not a Jew eyes?" has never been seen on our stage.

He also, in an article for the *Fortnightly Review* in 1866, described a workingman's club to which he had belonged in his twenties and spoke of a leading member, Cohn, who was certainly the original of Mordecai—the only significant attempt at a real Jewish figure in *Daniel Deronda*.

The characteristic central themes which appear in almost every book of George Eliot's are first the value of constructive imaginative physical work—illustrated by a skilled carpenter like Adam Bede who says "The best of working is, it gives you a griphold o' things outside your own lot," and, more fully, by a builder and scientific farmer or farm supervisor like Caleb Garth in *Middlemarch*. This theme recurs in almost every novel, but is perhaps best summarized in Caleb's meditations below, if we are careful to use his own rather odd definition of "socially useful labor unrelated to finance" for "business."

> Caleb Garth often shook his head in meditation on the value, the indispensable might of that myriad-headed, myriad-handed labor by which the social body is fed, clothed and housed. It had laid hold of his imagination in boyhood. The echoes of the great hammer where roof or keel were a-making, the signal-shouts of the workmen, the roar of the furnace, the thunder and plash of the engine were a sublime music to him; the felling and lading of timber, and the huge trunk vibrating star-like in the distance along the highway, the crane at work on the wharf, the piled-up produce in warehouses, the precision and variety of muscular effort wherever exact work had

to be turned out—all these sights of his youth had acted on him as poetry without the aid of the poets, had made a philosophy for him without the aid of the philosophers, a religion without the aid of theology. His early ambition had been to have as effective a share as possible in this sublime labor, which was peculiarly dignified by him with the name of "business"; and though he had only been a short time under a surveyor, and had been chiefly his own teacher, he knew more of land, building, and mining than most of the special men in the county.

His classification of human employments was rather crude, and, like the categories of more celebrated men, would not be acceptable in these advanced times. He divided them into "business, politics, preaching, learning and amusement." He had nothing to say against the last four; but he regarded them as a reverential pagan regarded other gods than his own. In the same way, he thought very well of all ranks but he would not himself have liked to be of any rank in which he had not such close contact with "business" as to get often honorably decorated with marks of dust and mortar, the damp of the engine, or the sweet soil of the woods and fields. Though he had never regarded himself as other than an orthodox Christian, and would argue on prevenient grace if the subject were proposed to him, I think his virtual divinities were good practical schemes, accurate work, and the faithful completion of undertakings. But there was no spirit of denial in Caleb, and the world seemed so wondrous to him that he was ready to accept any number of systems, like any number of firmaments, if they did not obviously interfere with the best land-drainage, solid building, correct measuring, and judicious boring for coal. In fact, he had a reverential soul with a strong will, but he had no keenness of imagination for monetary results in the shape of profit and loss: and having ascertained this to his cost; he determined to give up all form of his beloved "business" which required that talent. He gave himself up entirely to the many kinds of work which he could do without handling capital. It is no wonder, then, that the Garths were poor, and "lived in a small way."

An even more constant concern, which appears in virtually every chapter of every book is the relation between actions and character; the importance of practical effects in judging the value of motives; the part played by material factors and personal interest in forming theoretical attitudes; and the fact that a man cannot act freely, in any real sense, unless he understands the real nature and necessities of his situation—in other words, that freedom is the recognition of necessity.

Her very first novel, *Adam Bede*, has an arresting analysis of this in terms of individual psychology and the real meaning of rationalization which concludes:

> Our deeds determine us, as much as we determine our deeds; and until we know what has been or will be the peculiar combination of outward with inward facts, which constitutes a man's critical actions it will be better not to think ourselves wise about his character. There is a terrible coercion in our deeds which may first turn the honest man into a deceiver, and then reconcile him to the change; for this reason —that the second wrong presents itself to him in the guise of the only practicable right. The action which before commission has been seen with that blended common sense and fresh unvarnished feeling which is the healthy eye of the soul, is looked at afterwards with the lens of apologetic ingenuity, through which all things that men call beautiful and ugly are seen to be made up of textures very much alike. Europe adjusts itself to a fait accompli; and so does an individual character,—until the placid adjustment is disturbed by a convulsive retribution.

There is, of course, nothing fatalistic in George Eliot's emphasis on cause and effect here.

In his extraordinarily fine recent study—*An Introduction to the English Novel*—Dr. Arnold Kettle has been at some pains to show that,

> as a matter of fact, the figure of a sarcastic fate does not preside over *Middlemarch*. On the contrary George Eliot is at pains to dissociate herself from any such concept. Throughout the novel with an almost remorseless insistence, each moral crisis, each necessary decision is presented to the participants and to us with the minimum of suggestion of an all-powerful Destiny. It is the very core of George Eliot's morality and of the peculiar moral force of the book that her characters, despite most powerful pressures, and above all the prevailing pressure of the Middlemarch way of life, are not impelled to meet each particular choice in the way they do. Lydgate need not have married Rosamond, though we understand well enough why he did. Neither need Fred Vincy have reformed; it is George Eliot's particular achievement here that she convinces us of a transformation against which all the cards of "Destiny" have been stacked.

And in a later novel, *Romola*, where the same argument is carried a step further, George Eliot begins by stressing the element of repeated choice.

Tito was experiencing that inexorable law of human souls, that we prepare ourselves for sudden deeds by the reiterated choice of good or evil which gradually determines character.

In the same book we find:

The contaminating effect of deeds often lies less in the commission than in the consequent adjustment of our desires, [we have already seen a specific example of this knowledge in Felix Holt's refusal to become a business man]—the enlistment of self-interest on the side of falsity; as, on the other hand, the purifying influence of public confession springs—from the fact that by it the hope in lies is forever swept away, and the soul recovers the noble attitude of simplicity.

In the *Spanish Gypsy* we find another favorite theme of George Eliot's when the hero says:

'T is a vile life that like a garden pool
Lies stagnant in the round of personal loves;
. . . . . .
A miserable, petty, low-roofed life,
That knows the mighty orbits of the skies
Through nought save light or dark in its own cabin.

This unusual combination of an unfailing sense of the social structure and the material world with the keenest possible perception of emotional states and personal relations is emphasized by the English critic, Dr. F. R. Leavis, when he writes:

George Eliot had said in *Felix Holt*, by way of apology for the space she devoted to "social changes" and "public matters": "there is no private life which has not been determined by a wider public life." The aim implicit in this remark is magnificently achieved in *Middlemarch*, and it is achieved by a novelist whose genius manifests itself in a profound analysis of the individual.

And of course the importance of constructive work and of more than personal interests both play a great part in George Eliot's attitude toward woman's struggles for emancipation, as expressed in almost every one of her works.

Her first book, *Silas Marner* (written immediately after the *Scenes of Clerical Life*), is memorable for the outstanding yet representative independence and quiet competence of both the cottager, Dolly Winthrop, and the well-to-do young woman, Nancy Lammeter.

Adam Bede, her first full-length novel and, except for *Middlemarch*, perhaps her best one, not only presents the strength of the Methodist preacher, Dinah, and Caleb Garth's unusual wife and daughter, but also a more typical countrywoman, Mrs. Poyser. A farmer's wife with little formal education, she is not only exceptionally capable in managing house and dairy, but is also far keener than her husband in her understanding of human beings and social relationships.

A brief excerpt from a scene in which their landlord, the squire, is attempting to persuade or intimidate Poyser into an unfavorable exchange of land, illustrates all these qualities as well as George Eliot's superb ear for dialogue on all social levels.

"Well, Poyser," said the Squire, shifting his tactics, and looking as if he thought Mrs. Poyser had suddenly withdrawn from the proceedings and left the room, "you can turn the Hollows into feeding-land. I can easily make another arrangement about supplying my house. And I shall not forget your readiness to accommodate your landlord as well as a neighbour. I know you will be glad to have your lease renewed for three years when the present one expires; otherwise, I daresay Thurle, who is a man of some capital, would be glad to take both the farms, as they could be worked so well together. But I don't want to part with an old tenant like you."

To be thrust out of the discussion in this way would have been enough to complete Mrs. Poyser's exasperation, even without the final threat. Her husband, really alarmed at the possibility of their leaving the old place where he had been bred and born—for he believed the old Squire had small spite enough for anything—was beginning a mild remonstrance explanatory of the inconvenience he should find in having to buy and sell more stock, with—

"Well, sir, I think as it's rether hard" . . . when Mrs. Poyser burst in with the desperate determination to have her say out this once, though it were to rain notices to quit, and the only shelter were the workhouse.

"Then, sir, if I may speak—as, for all I'm a woman, and there's folks as thinks a woman's fool enough to stan' by an' look on while the men sign her soul away, I've a right to speak, for I make one quarter o' the rent, and save another quarter—I say, if Mr. Thurle's so ready to take farms under you, it's a pity but what he should take this, and see if he likes to live in a house wi' all the plagues o' Egypt in't—wi' the cellar full o' water, and frogs and toads hoppin' up the steps by dozens—and the floors rotten and the rats and mice gnawing every bit o' cheese, and runnin' over our heads as we lie i' bed till we expect 'em to eat us up alive—as it's a mercy they hanna eat the children long ago. I should like to see if there's another tenant besides Poyser as 'ud put up wi' never having a bit o' repairs done till a place tumbles down—and not then, on'y wi' begging and praying, and having to pay half—and being strung up wi' the rent as it's much if he gets enough out o' the land to pay, for all he's put his own money into the ground beforehand. Se if you'll get a stranger to lead such a life here as that: a maggot must be born i' the rotten cheese to like it I reckon. You may run away from my words, sir," continued Mrs. Poyser, following the old Squire beyond the door—for after the first moments of stunned surprise he had got up, and waving his hand towards her with a smile, had walked out towards his pony. But it was impossible for him to get away immediately, for John was walking the pony up and down the yard, and was some distance from the cause-way when his master beckoned.

"You may run away from my words, sir, and you may go spinnin' underhand ways o' doing us a mischief, for you've got Old Harry to your friend, though nobody else is, but I tell you for once as we're not dumb creatures to be abused and made money on by them as ha' got the lash i' their hands, for want o' knowin' how t' undo the tackle. An' if I'm the only one as speaks my mind, there's plenty o' the same way o' thinking i' this parish and the next to't, for your name's no better than a brimstone match in everybody's nose—if it isna two-three old folks as you think o' having your soul by giving 'em a bit o' flannel and a drop o' porridge. An' you may be right i' thinking it'll take but little to save your soul, for it'll be the smallest savin' y' iver made wi' all your scrapin'."

There are occasions on which two servant-girls and a waggoner may be a formidable audience, and as the Squire rode away on his black pony, even the gift of short-sightedness did not prevent him from being aware that Molly and Nancy and Tim were grinning not far from him. Perhaps he suspected that sour old John was grinning behind him—which was also the fact. Meanwhile the bull-dog, the black-and-tan terrier, Alick's sheep-dog, and the gander hissing at a safe distance from the pony's heels, carried out the idea of Mrs. Poyser's solo in an impressive quartett.

Mrs. Poyser, however, had no sooner seen the pony move off than she turned round, gave the two hilarious damsels a look which drove them into the back kitchen, and, unspearing her knitting, began to knit again with her usual rapidity, as she re-entered the house.

"Thee'st done it now," said Mr. Poyser, a little alarmed and uneasy, but not without some triumphant amusement at his wife's outbreak.

"Yes, I know I've done it," said Mrs. Poyser; "but I've had my say out, and I shall be th' easier for't all my life. There's no pleasure i' living, if you're to be corked up forever, and only dribble your mind out by the sly, like a leaky barrel. I shan't repent saying what I think, if I live to be as old as th' old Squire; and there's little likelihoods—for it seems as if them as aren't wanted here are th' only folks as aren't wanted i' th' other world."

In *Felix Holt*, Esther Lyon declares defensively "A woman must choose mean things because only mean things are offered her." Daniel Deronda's mother exclaims bitterly:

You may try—but you can never imagine what it is to have a man's form of genius, and yet to suffer the slavery of being a girl. To have a pattern cut out—"this is what you must be; this is what you are wanted for; a woman's heart must be of such a size and no larger, else it must be pressed small, like Chinese feet; her happiness is to be made as cakes are, by a fixed receipt."

Poor Maggie Tulliver is always bruising herself against the rigid senseless barriers of what the well-bred young girl must do, and is finally destroyed in a conflict where her own loving nature leaves her weaponless.

In the poem, Armgart, the heroine says pointedly:

Men did not say, when I had sung last night,
" 'Twas good, nay, wonderful, considering
She is a woman"—and then turn to add,
"Tenor or baritone had sung her songs
Better, of course; she's but a woman spoiled."

And in the heroine of *Middlemarch*, of whom George Eliot says:

It was not in Dorothea's nature, for more than the duration of a paroxysm, to sit in the narrow cell of her calamity, in the besotted misery of a consciousness that only sees another's lot as an accident of its own;

we find a full-length treatment of the problem of the intelligent middle-class woman, more representative than Eliot herself in that she is not an artist or, in fact, a genius of any kind, and so any answer she can find must be one available to the great majority of her sisters.

When we first meet the twenty-year-old Dorothea we see her, like the nineteen-year-old Mary Ann Evans some thirty-three years before, already looking for work meaningful enough to demand her devotion.

> For a long while she had been oppressed by the indefiniteness which hung in her mind, like a thick summer haze, over all her desire to make her life greatly effective. What could she do, what ought she to do?—she, hardly more than a budding woman, but yet with an active conscience and a great mental need, not to be satisfied by a girlish instruction comparable to the nibblings and judgments of a discursive mouse. . . .
> The intensity of her religious disposition, the coercion it exercised over her life, was but one aspect of a nature altogether ardent, theoretic, and intellectually consequent; and with such a nature struggling in the bands of a narrow teaching, hemmed in by a social life which seemed nothing but a labyrinth of petty courses, a walled-in maze of small paths that led no whither, the outcome was sure to strike others as at once exaggeration and inconsistency. The thing which seemed to her best, she wanted to justify by the completest knowledge; and not to live in a pretended admission of rules which were never acted on. . . .

Unlike the young Mary Ann Evans, Dorothea is beautiful, wealthy and has an altogether eligible suitor. But although not averse to marriage she cannot consider it apart from the solution of her real problem.

> She felt sure that she would have accepted the judicious Hooker if she had been born in time to save him from that wretched mistake he made in matrimony; or John Milton when his blindness had come on; or any of the other great men whose odd habits it would have been glorious piety to endure; but an amiable, handsome baronet, who said "Exactly," to her remarks even when she expressed uncertainty,—how could he affect her as a lover? The really delightful marriage must be that where your husband was a sort of father, and could teach you even Hebrew, if you wished.

When an elderly clergyman who was devoting his life to constructing a meaningless concordance of religious myths which, to Dorothea's uninformed vision, was necessarily a work of profound scholarship and social significance, proposed to her, she was therefore overwhelmed with joy. She felt that in the life he offered her:

> She was going to have room for the energies which stirred uneasily under the dimness and pressure of her own ignorance and the petty peremptoriness of the world's habits.
> "I should learn everything then," she said to herself, still walking quickly along the bridle path through the wood. "It would be my duty to study that I might help him the better in his great works. There would be nothing trivial about our lives. Every-day things with us would mean the greatest things. It would be like marrying Pascal. I should learn to see the truth by the same light as great men have seen it by and then I should know what to do, when I got older; I should see how it was possible to lead a grand life here—now—in England. I don't feel sure about doing good in any way now; everything seems like going on a mission to a people whose language I don't know; unless it were building good cottages—there can be no doubt about that.

With this opening, the book broadens out to a wonderfully vivid and subtle study of the complexities and concrete substance of all of *Middlemarch*, including of course, many other women and, particularly interesting among the men, the brilliant young scientist Lydgate. We learn of Lydgate, for example, that:

> In warming himself at French social theories he had brought away no smell of scorching. We may handle even extreme opinions with impunity while our furniture, our dinner-giving, and preference for armorial bearings in our own case link us indissolubly with the established order. And Lydgate's tendency was not to extreme opinions: he would have liked no barefoot doctrines, being particular about his buots; he was no radical about anything but medical reform and the prosecution of discovery.
> Lydgate meant to innovate in his treatment also, and he was wise enough to see that the best security for his practising honestly according to his belief was to get rid of systematic temptations to the contrary.

Virginia Woolf speaks of "the mature *Middlemarch*, the magnificent book which with all its imperfections is one of the few

English novels written for grown-up people." And it is true that George Eliot's power is at its highest there.

However, few readers would be willing to give up *Felix Holt*, despite its overcomplicated coincidental plot, and certainly *Daniel Deronda* is of much more than historical interest, for all that its hero is the most improbable figure ever seriously presented by a great novelist.

This last, completed in 1876, was the last novel George Eliot wrote.

Ill health, the search for a permanent country home, and the foreign travel which had formed so large a part of her life with Lewes, occupied their last two years together and when, on November 7, 1878, Lewes died, it seemed as though her life, too, would end.

She was utterly prostrated by the loss, could hardly bear to see anyone, including his son Charles, of whom she had always been extremely fond, and was aroused to any kind of activity only by her desire to found a perpetual research scholarship in his memory, and to see his last work—*Problems of Physiology*—through the press.

In the arrangements for the scholarship George Eliot was assisted by a middle-aged friend—a retired banker, Mr. J. W. Cross —whose mother and sisters she and Lewes had met some twelve years before, and who had introduced him to the Lewes' in Rome in 1869.

He was at that time just twenty-nine, had long been a great admirer of her books, and rapidly became friendly with the illustrious elderly couple.

George Eliot was particularly fond of Mr. Cross' mother, who was perhaps the first older woman of position to welcome her during her life with Lewes, and the Cross's home was one of the very few she visited.

Mrs. Cross died just before Lewes, and her son, who had been deeply devoted to her, evidently found comfort in the companionship of George Eliot, whom he soon began to relieve of all the business, letter writing, and so forth for which she had so long depended on Lewes.

Eighteen months after her bereavement George Eliot, then sixty-one, was married at St. George's Hanover Square, a very fashionable Episcopalian church, to the forty-year-old John Cross.

Her stepson, Charles, and Cross's sisters were almost the only ones present at the wedding which George Eliot had consented to just three weeks before it took place.

Her loneliness; possibly her fear of a new scandal if his frequent visits and intimate association with her affairs continued; her practical and emotional need for some such care and companionship as he urged her to accept; and perhaps a desire for social acceptance may explain the marriage which so amazed all her friends. Although she had, surprisingly, been the guest of one of Queen Victoria's married daughters and had been taken down to dinner on the arm of a bishop in 1878 she still felt herself at a serious disadvantage and shrank from general society. She wrote to Barbara Bodichon a week before her marriage:

> I am going to do what not very long ago I should have pronounced impossible for me, and therefore I should not wonder at any one else who found my action incomprehensible. By the time you receive this letter I shall (so far as the future can be a matter of assertion) have been married to Mr. J. W. Cross, who you know, is a friend of years, a friend much loved and trusted by Mr. Lewes, and who, now that I am alone, sees his happpiness in the dedication of his life to me. This change in my position will make no change in my care for Mr. Lewes's family, and in the ultimate disposition of my property. Mr. Cross has a sufficient fortune of his own. We are going abroad for a few months, and I shall not return to live at this house. [The Priory where she and Lewes had lived since 1865.] Mr. Cross has taken the lease of a house, No. 4 Cheyne Walk, Chelsea, where we shall spend the winter and early spring making Witley our summer home.

An ironic postscript to this event was a letter from her brother Isaac who broke a thirty-year silence to welcome his rehabilitated sister back to the family. To this George Eliot replied with a surprising cordiality that helps us understand her amazing action:

> . . . it was a great joy to me to have your kind words of sympathy, for our long silence has never broken the affection for you which began when we were little ones. My husband, too, was much pleased to read your letter. I have known his family for eleven years, and they have received me among them very lovingly. The only point to be regretted in our marriage is that I am much older than he; but his affection has

made him choose this lot of caring for me rather than any other of the various lots open to him.

The trip abroad was successful and George Eliot's health seemed much improved. However, shortly after they had settled into their new home, she caught a chill and died on December 19, 1880, after eight months of marriage.

Her "irregular" life and unorthodox beliefs prevented her burial in Westminster Abbey, where she would otherwise have been the first woman writer so honored.

THOMAS HUXLEY AND HUMAN PROGRESS

Some years before Huxley's death, when he was everywhere acknowledged as one of the world's greatest living scientists and an outstanding English man of letters, an editor of *Who's Who* was much perturbed to discover that there was hardly any information available as to his grandfather and none at all beyond that! Huxley, veteran of a twenty-year fight for the theory of evolution, replied to the urgent request for such data: "My own genealogical inquiries have taken me so far back that I confess the later stages do not interest me."

A year or so later, in 1890, he commented tersely upon the then current pseudo-scientific discussion of the contribution made by the Celtic, Anglo-Saxon, and other strains to "English character," and concluded: "The combination of swarthiness with stature above the average and a long skull confer upon me the serene impartiality of a mongrel."

This utter lack of snobbishness, impatience with irrelevancies, and gift for the "apt and acid phrase" were among the essential characteristics which distinguished Huxley all his life and enabled him to accomplish the work of three or four lifetimes in his seventy years.

His consistent refusal to dogmatize, his concern with basic social as well as scientific questions, his profoundly materialistic outlook are all interestingly illustrated in embryo by a page of the diary he kept irregularly during his teens.

The first brief note written in 1840, concludes with a typically scientific—and nonadolescent—note of caution.

> Had a long talk with my mother and father about the right to make Dissenters pay Church rates—and whether there ought to be any Establishment. I maintain that there ought not in both cases—I wonder what will be my opinion ten years hence?

The next summarizes a discussion with his family's minister which must have disturbed the good clergyman far more than it did his young parishioner.

> Had a long argument with Mr. Maz on the nature of the soul and the difference between it and matter. I maintained that it could not be proved that matter is essentially—as to its base—different from soul.

The last note culminates in a quotation copied into his journal as the gist of his precocious fifteen-year-old understanding—an understanding only faintly and tardily perceived by such a major contemporary thinker as Thoreau, for example:

> "One solitary philosopher may be great, virtuous and happy in the midst of poverty, but not a whole nation."

At this time Huxley had had two years desultory and unpleasant "education" in a very poor school where his father was assistant-master, and, upon the failure of the school, he had begun his own intensive self-education at home. At twelve he had devoured a ponderous, difficult, but somewhat unorthodox geological treatise, *Theory of the Earth*, and at fourteen the reading of Carlyle's *Sartor Resartus* had set him upon a rapid and thorough study of German. This language was then almost unknown in England, even to men of science, though little of the vast work of nineteenth century German scholarship was yet available in translation.

Although Huxley differed sharply from Carlyle in fundamental beliefs and attitudes he often reverted to the great effect of this early acquaintance on his own development.

In 1880, when he was fifty-five, he wrote to a friend:

> Few men can have dissented more strongly from his [Carlyle's] way of looking at things than I; but I should not

yield to the most devoted of his followers in gratitude for the bracing influence of his writings when, as a very young man, I was essaying without rudder or compass to strike out a course for myself.

And again in a personal letter ten years later:

> There is nothing of permanent value (putting aside a few human affections) nothing that satisfies quiet reflection—except the sense of having worked according to one's capacity and light, to make things clear and get rid of cant and shams of all sorts. That was the lesson I learned from Carlyle's books when I was a boy, and it has stuck by me all my life.

We may doubt whether such a lesson is, in this sense, to be learned except by one who already knows it, but certainly in the young Carlyle's most vigorous and stirring works the still younger Huxley found an inspiring expression of his own as yet unformulated basic philosophy of honest hard work, devoted social concern, and fearless personal integrity. This gives all the more force to the pathos of a meeting some forty years later, when Huxley, at the height of his achievement and honors, came out of the Royal Society of Scientists to see the aged Carlyle, who had long differed violently with his defense of evolution—and democracy—walking slowly down the other side of the street. Touched by the old man's lonely appearance he crossed over and attempted to speak of his early appreciation, but Carlyle, ignoring the proffered hand, muttered bleakly, "You're Huxley—the man who says we're all monkeys, aren't you?" and walked on in solitary bitterness.

While Huxley was studying German his two much older sisters both married doctors, and, his already keen scientific interest made it natural for him to see this as a providential answer to the problem of establishing a career with no money or family influence to assist him.

At sixteen he went to London as apprentice to his beloved Lizzie's husband, Dr. Scott, and the next year he won a scholarship at the Charing Cross Hospital.

The subsequent experience as an interne visiting the poorest slum homes in London affected him profoundly. His son Leonard, writing his biography, includes the few pages of autobiographical material Huxley was once prevailed upon to publish, and adds, provokingly without quotations:

I found, however, among his papers, an entirely different sketch of his early life, half-a-dozen sheets describing the time he spent in the East End, with an almost Carlylean sense of the horrible disproportions of life.

There is included, even in the official material, a brief description of Huxley's hospital experience which reads, in part:

> I saw strange things there—among the rest, people who came to me for medical aid, and who were really suffering nothing but slow starvation. . . . I have not forgotten . . . a visit to a sick girl in a wretched garret where two or three other women . . . were busy shirt-making. After the examination even my small medical knowledge sufficed to show that my patient was merely in want of some better food than the bread and bad tea upon which these people were living. I said so as gently as I could and the sister turned upon me with a kind of choking passion. Pulling out of her pocket a few pence and half pence, and holding them out, "That is all I get for six and thirty hours' work and you talk about giving her proper food."

However, despite his strong human concern, Huxley's primary interest was research rather than treatment. His room was known to fellow students as "The Sign of the Head and Microscope" because that image was so regularly to be seen outlined on his window shade at the most unseasonable hours of the night. At the age of eighteen he made, in the now disregarded description of doctoral requirements, a tiny but genuine "original contribution to human knowledge" with the discovery of a cell layer in the root sheath of hair, still known as *Huxley's Layer*.

His graduation at twenty found him a year too young to be admitted to practise and in urgent need of a job, so he applied for and received an appointment as assistant-surgeon to *H.M.S. The Rattlesnake*, outfitted for a three-year voyage of chart making and scientific observation about the Great Barrier Reef off Australia.

From Rio de Janeiro, where for the first time he saw slavery in action, he wrote to his mother an indignant description of the Negro slaves, concluding,

> I have a much greater respect for them than for their beastly Portuguese masters. . . .

Later, after some time spent observing the Polynesian settlements in the South Seas, he concluded, as he wrote in an article on *Science at Sea*, that

> "the blessings of civilization" mean for the darker race, labour, care, drunkenness, disease, and ultimate subjection and extinction.

However most of his time was spent in observing and dissecting jellyfish, about whom he made several fundamental discoveries which were discussed in two papers printed in the journal of the Royal Society of Scientists during his absence. On his return he found they had been acknowledged as important contributions to the morphology of invertebrates, and on that basis, and that of the value of the additional material he brought back with him, he was, in 1851, one of the youngest men ever to be elected a Fellow of the Royal Society.

The next year he received the society's medal, and won the respect of almost all the scientific leaders of England—especially that of his contemporaries—the physicist, Tyndale, the botanist, Hooker, and the rather older Darwin. These all became his lifelong friends.

Despite this recognition and the further honor of an invitation to lecture at the Royal Institution, Huxley was still an assistant-surgeon of the Royal Navy on leave—and on half-pay! There were at the time perhaps a dozen positions for scientists in all England and unless death or resignation vacated one, such success as his, Huxley said, procured a young man dinner invitations to the most distinguished homes in London, but did not provide him with the necessary cab fare to reach them. It is, therefore, not surprising that an extraordinary proportion of English scientists up through the nineteenth century were men of independent income.

Huxley was epecially worried because during his trip he had become engaged to a young Englishwoman in Sydney, Australia, and had confidently promised to send for her as soon as he should have secured a position on his return.

To his sister Lizzie, who had emigrated to Tennessee, and who was his chief confidante after his mother's death, he wrote in 1850:

> I hate the incessant struggle and toil to cut one another's throat among us men. . . . The worst of it is I have no am-

bition, except as means to an end, and that end is the possession of a sufficient income to marry upon. . . . A worker I must always be—it is my nature—but if I had £400 a year. . . .

Again a few months later he told her:

The necessity for these little strategems utterly disgusts me. I would so willingly reverence and trust any man of high standing and ability. . . . I do so long to be able to trust men implicitly.

The next year he wrote with increasing discouragement:

The world is no better than an arena of gladiators, and I, a stray savage, have been turned into it to fight my way with my rude club among the steel-clad fighters.

His applications for the very few science-teaching vacancies in Scotland, Canada and even Australia were turned down in favor of candidates with greater local influence. The governor's nephew, for example, secured the one in Toronto. Huxley became more and more torn between his desire for an immediate marriage and his reluctance to forsake research and enter upon the medical practise which would make that possible.

He wrote his fiancée in 1852, after five years of waiting:

Sometimes I am half mad with the notion of burying all my powers [as a doctor in Sydney] in a mere struggle for a livelihood. Sometimes I am equally wild at thinking of the long weary while that has passed since we met. . . .

Feeling that the delay must be even more maddening for her he asked her to make the decision. She evidently made the right one and his next letter expressed his great gratitude for her:

noble and self-sacrificing letter, which has given me more comfort than anything for a long while. . . . The spectre of a wasted life has passed before me—a vision of that servant who hid his talent in a napkin and buried it.

A short time before he had written to a common friend of theirs in Sydney speaking of the almost certain poverty involved in his choice of a scientific career and his disillusionment with some of the great figures of the scientific world seen close to. His letter concluded however,

> But it is equally clear to me that for a man of my temperament, at any rate, the sole secret of getting through this life with anything like contentment is to have full scope for the development of one's faculties. Science alone seems to me to afford this scope—Law, Divinity, Physic and Politics being in a state of chaotic vibration between utter humbug and utter skepticism.

A year later when marriage still seemed as far off as ever he again thanked his fiancée for her encouragement, saying:

> and depend, however painful our present separation may be, the spectacle of a man who had given up the cherished purpose of his life, the Esau who had sold his birthright for a mess of pottage and with it his self-respect, would before long years were over our heads be infinitely more painful.

In 1854, when they had waited, as he said, as long as Jacob served for Rachel, he suddenly received a lectureship at the Government School of Mines, another in Comparative Anatomy at St. Thomas Hospital, and a grant from the Royal Society for the publication of his monograph on *The Oceanic Hydrozoa*.

In that year, too, his fiancée's father unexpectedly returned to London, bringing with him his daughter, just as Huxley was about to send for her. The meeting was not a happy one. Henrietta had caught some tropical fever, had been repeatedly bled and dosed according to the still too common medical practice of the time, and when Huxley introduced her as his patient, not his fiancée, to a specialist friend, he was bluntly informed that she had not six months to live!

A second opinion was slightly more encouraging in terms of a possible eventual cure, but Huxley insisted that he would marry her first and cure her afterwards. He carried out his program so successfully that after almost half a century of marriage she outlived him by almost twenty years!

In the rather curious formulation of Huxley's most recent historian:

> His married life, apart from the unavoidable ups and downs occasioned by illness, was uniformly happy, and so affords no material whatever to the biographer.

He himself would have accepted the statement of fact, but not the conclusion, nor do the variety, length and frequency of his letters to and about his wife at all bear out the latter.

In 1867, after thirteen years of marriage he writes, congratulating his friend, the great German biologist Haeckel, on his engagement, and concludes:

> The one thing for men, who like you and I stand pretty much alone, and have a good deal of fighting to do in the external world, is to have light and warmth and confidence within the four walls of home. May all these good things await you.

Another delightful letter the next year to his wife not only indicates his invariable habit of showing her all his work before publication, but also indicates that he was practically, as well as theoretically, in favor of self-criticism.

His scientific career abounds in evidences of his scrupulous readiness to correct his conclusions—published or unpublished—in the light of new knowledge, and his general discussions often repeat the idea that:

> The most considerable difference I note among men is not in their readiness to fall into error, but in their readiness to acknowledge these inevitable lapses.

But there were—and are—many men able to admit error to a colleague who do their best to preserve the legend of domestic omniscience.

Huxley, on the contrary, writes his wife:

> I met Grove who edits Macmillan at the soiree. He pulled the proof of my lecture out of his pocket and said, "Look here, there is one paragraph in your lecture I can make neither top nor tail of. I can't understand what it means." I looked to wher his finger pointed, and behold it was the paragraph you objected to when I read you the lecture on the sea shore! I told him, and said I should confess, however set up it might make you.

And when they were both sixty-four and he had gone off on a trip with his youngest son, just graduated from medical school, he wrote home:

Catch me going out of reach of letters again. I have been horribly anxious. Nobody—children or any one else—can be to me what you are. Ulysses preferred his old woman to immortality, and this absence has led me to see that he was as wise in that as other things. . . .

During the first five years of his married life, Huxley laid the foundation of his reputation as a great teacher, did a large amount of experimental work of direct interest to scientists, and established the tremendously important and successful "Lectures to Workingmen" which remained a vital part of the famous scientific institute on Jermyn Street long after his death.

There had been some small beginning of such lectures—notably by the brilliant physicist Michael Faraday who was himself the son of a blacksmith—but the scale on which Huxley organized the series in terms of size, consistency, and significance of subjects treated, was altogether unprecedented. So, too, was his avowed belief that on the whole the working class was the class that could be most successfully enlisted in the fight for a thorough going application of science which would revolutionize society and man's life on earth.

Many years later he declared, defending Haeckel's association with the German revolutionaries, "Science *ought* to be in league with the radicals." And in February, 1855, when first inaugurating his lectures for working men, he wrote to a friend:

> I enclose a prospectus of some People's Lectures (Popular lectures I hold to be an abomination unto the Lord) I am about to give here. . . .
> I am sick of the dilettante middle class, and mean to try what I can do with these hard-handed fellows who live among facts. . . .

Again three months later we find in a letter discussing a promised visit to the seashore, and the proposal that he lecture there:

> . . . in point of earnestness and attention my audience was all I could wish. I am now giving a course of the same kind to working men exclusively. . . . The theatre holds 600; and is crammed full.
> I believe in the fustian, and can talk better to it than to any amount of gauze and Saxony; and to a fustian audience (but to that only) I would willingly give some when I come to Tenby.

These lectures, like everything else in Huxley's public life, were profoundly affected by the publication of Darwin's epochmaking *Origin of Species* in November, 1859.

Darwin later said he had determined that, to his mind, the book would be successful if it convinced three English scientists—Lyell, the geologist, Hooker, the botanist, and Huxley, the zoologist. And eleven days before publication he wrote "If I can convert Huxley I shall be content."

Huxley read the book immediately, and ten days after its publication wrote Darwin of his whole-hearted "conversion." He fully realized the terrific furor that would follow, despite Darwin's caution in omitting from his text all the materials he had gathered on man's relation to the apes—actually *Origin of Species* contains only one sentence on page 488, referring to man, and this reads discreetly, "Light will be thrown on the origin of man and his history.'

In a lecture a year or two later, Huxley explicitly accepted his responsibility as the first to begin throwing light on that matter when he said:

> Before concluding these lectures there is one point to which I must advert—though, as Mr. Darwin has said nothing about man in his book; it concerns myself rather than him;—for I have strongly maintained on sundry occasions that if Mr. Darwin's views are sound they apply as much to man as to the lower mammals, seeing that it is perfectly demonstrable that the structural differences which separate man from the apes are not greater than those which separate some apes from others.

He concluded his letter of congratulation on the publication of the book with a warning—and a promise.

> I trust you will not allow yourself to be in any way disgusted or annoyed by the considerable abuse and misrepresentation which, unless I greatly mistake, is in store for you.
>
> Depend upon it, you have earned the gratitude of all thoughtful men. And as to the curs which will bark and yelp, you must recollect that some of your friends, at any rate, are endowed with an amount of combativeness which (though you have often and justly rebuked it) may stand you in good stead.
>
> I am sharpening up my claws and beak in readiness.

Events proved the promise as well justified as the warning and for the next twenty years Huxley was known as "Darwin's bulldog"

—always ready and anxious to fly at anyone who attacked his friend or, rather, his friend's teaching.

He immediately set about developing the theory of evolution in its most controversial and, in many respects, most vital aspect by announcing as his next series of Lectures to Working Men, *The Relation of Man to the Rest of the Animal Kingdom.*

Darwin himself was a little uneasy at this development and warned against such a presentation to such an audience, but Huxley declared: "I will stop at no point so long as clear reasoning will carry me further."

He made it clear (as he later wrote to another friend on a similar occasion):

> I quite appreciate your view of the matter, though it is diametrically opposed to my own conviction that the more rapidly truth is spread among mankind the better it will be for them.

In March, 1861 he wrote triumphantly to his wife:

> My working men stick by me wonderfully, the house being fuller than ever last night. By next Friday evening they will all be convinced they are monkeys. . . . Lyell came and was rather astonished at the magnitude and attentiveness of the audience.

Frederic Harrison, who had come to observe the beginning of the series, wrote a report worth quoting at some length.

> The intimate alliance foretold by Comte between philosophers and the Proletariat has undoubtedly commenced. Last night I was at Professor Huxley's lecture at the Jermyn Street Institution. They are, you know, courses for working men exclusively. . . . The 600 tickets were taken up in 1½ hours after the first distribution commenced. I never saw an audience more intent, intelligent, and sympathetic. They were literally thirsting for knowledge. . . .
> Last night's lecture I thought a type of a popular exposition, central, broad, clear, positive, suggestive and elementary. It at once took me into the radical ideas of biology and handled them from a social and practical point of view. . . .
> The proposition to which his six lectures are devoted is this, "Biology shows less structural difference between man and the higher apes than between the higher and lower apes; and far less than between the highest apes and lower animals."

This is the provocatio ad populum with a vengeance. . . .
It will take many sermons to undo last night's words!

Naturally the established church, then in complete control of both the universities and most of the important schools in England, did not ignore this challenge, and the famous debate in which Bishop Wilberforce attempted to annihilate Huxley by a seemingly courteous inquiry as to whether he claimed descent from the ape through his grandmother or his grandfather, was only the opening gun.

Although Huxley himself later said in response to questions about these early debates that "there is no literary fare so unappetizing as cold controversy," this is certainly not true of his own polemics. For one thing his quick hard-hitting wit was always used to project the essential truth of an idea, often even broader in scope than its application to the immediate situation required.

An example is his response to one of the many similar gibes the bishop's inquiry had heralded. He retorted that there was far more hope for man if one thought he had reached his present state in an ascent from the ape than in a descent from the angels! In his lecture in Edinburgh the next year—1862—he more fully stated this:

> Nay more, thoughtful men, escaped from the blinding influences of traditional prejudice, will find in the lowly stock whence man has sprung, the best evidence of the splendour of his capacities; and will discern in his long progress through the Past a reasonable ground of faith in his attainment of a nobler Future.

The lecture was well received but the *Edinburgh Review* cited Huxley's discussion *On Species and Races and their Origin* as an abuse of science like those which had led to the French Revolution seventy years before.

Nor was that editor alone in sensing the political nature of Huxley's thought and its similarity to the political upsurge of the romantic writers at the end of the eighteenth century.

A more sympathetic contemporary, John Morley (editor of the *Fortnightly Review* after George Henry Lewes), wrote of another radical departure by Huxley a decade later:

> No article that has appeared in any periodical for a generation back excited so profound a sensation as Huxley's memor-

able paper "On the Physical Bases of Life." The stir was like the stir that in a political epoch was made by Swift's *Conduct of the Allies.*

Professor Houston Peterson, one of Huxley's more interesting twentieth century biographers, wrote in 1932:

> For Huxley, Hooker and a few others *The Origin of Species* inspired the kind of enthusiasm that "Liberty, Equality and Fraternity" had inspired seventy years earlier.
>
> "Bliss was it in that dawn to be alive
> But to be young was very heaven."

And Blake's best biographer and critic, Bronowski, declared in a BBC broadcast in 1949:

> Huxley felt himself to be the spokesman of . . . the unbelievers in the Mechanics' Institute. . . .
> . . . the anticlerical tradition of English workingmen since the days of Tom Paine. . . . Methodism in Victorian England had become what Wesley himself had feared, the religion of success. The men in the Mechanics' Institutes turned from it to unbelief.

In an earlier BBC broadcast in 1945 Huxley's grandson, the well-known biologist, Julian Huxley, summarized the meaning of the great struggle in which his distinguished grandfather was the leading protagonist:

> But it [the controversy over evolution] was in some way the most decisive event in the history of 19th century thought. It was as decisive as the 17th century controversy over the ideas of Galileo and Newton, and in some ways more revolutionary, since it was directly concerned with men and human affairs instead of with matter and the stars in their courses. The theory of evolution through natural selection revolutionized biology by providing that central, unifying concept which it had previously lacked. It revolutionized general thought by dethroning man from the position of Lord of Creation assigned to him by orthodox theology, and even more by substituting a dynamic for a static concept of existence by making us discard all absolute ideas, such as perfection or fixity, and forcing us to think of nature and human affairs in terms of change and progress. And the controversy had a special significance at the time as symbolizing the conflict between authority and free

inquiry, between the claims of revelation and those of scientific truth.

Finally Huxley's latest official biographer, Macbride, discussing, in 1934, the unabashed materialism summarized in Huxley's article *On the Physical Basis of Life* half a century before, concluded with an apology its author was fortunately unable to hear:

> His definition of the agnostic position was a lasting contribution to clarity and honesty of thought, but his philosophy of materialism was radically unsound, and, propagated by his influence and authority, had done enormous damage; it has led to results which would have horrified Huxley could he have forseen them [?]; for example, it has certainly been one of the contributing causes to the establishment of Bolshevism in Russia.

But while Huxley's controversies with the church and traditional prejudices still make delightful reading, we must shortly turn to his more prophetic ones with the pseudoscientific "social Darwinists" and businessmen, remembering his rejoinder, when asked to reenter upon an argument he had already won: "No; life is too short to spend it in slaying again the twice slain."

Yet the reorganization of mystical obscurantism as a prop for reaction in this second half of the 20th century gives a timeliness he had not foreseen to such statements as that in a letter to his wife in 1873:

> . . . We are in the midst of a gigantic movement greater than that which preceded and produced the Reformation . . . nor is any reconcilement possible between free thought and traditional authority. One or other will have to succumb after a struggle of unknown duration, which will have as its side issues vast political and social troubles. I have no more doubt that free thought will win in the long run than I have that I sit here writing to you, or that this free thought will organise itself into a coherent system, embracing human life and the world as one harmonious whole. But this organization will be the work of generations of men, and those who further it most will be those who teach men to rest in no lie, and to rest in no verbal delusions. I may be able to help a little in that direction —perhaps I may have helped already.

When we remember the unrepealed antievolution law Tennessee passed in the 1920's there is especial irony in learning from a Nashville paper of 1876 that when, on his visit to the United States in that year, Huxley went to Tennessee to meet his sister "the best people of Nashville—the professional men, the solid business men, and the beauty and fashion of the city . . ." cheered him at the end of the lecture he gave there. This concluded:

> . . . I need not say that this [evolutionary] view of the past history of the globe is a very different one from that which is commonly taken. It is so widely different that it is impossible to effect any kind of community, any kind of parallel, far less any reconciliation between these two. One of these must be true. The other is not.

It was on this American visit that he opened his inaugural address, dedicating the then just-founded John Hopkins with the warning:

> A great warrior is said to have made a desert and called it peace. Administrators of education funds have sometimes made a palace and called it a university.

And it was then, too, that he all unknowingly received his most flattering tribute from an outraged Presbyterian clergyman in New York who commented on the prayerless ceremony, writing to a colleague in Baltimore:

> It was bad enough to invite Huxley. It were better to have asked God to be present. It would have been absurd to ask them both.

The pressing John Hopkins invitation which had brought Huxley to the United States was based not only on his general eminence as a scientist but on his specific work for public education in England and his almost singlehanded, successful fight to introduce science into the curriculum of English schools and universities.

He had succeeded in adding laboratory work to the lecture instruction he gave in his own institution, and had labored tirelessly to have others follow this example.

Even in medical training there was at the time little practical experimentation and Huxley insisted day in and day out that sound medical treatment could only be based on "the sort of familiar, finger-end knowledge which a watchmaker has of a watch."

He had with even more vehemence and persistence supported

the (in England) then novel idea that there had to be a completely free school system open to all. Actually, his formulation which included every level of higher education is still not altogether accepted even in the United States.

For he insisted:

> I conceive it to be our duty to make a ladder from the gutter to the university along which every child in the three kingdoms should have the chance of climbing as far as he was fit to go.

And in opposing all kinds of caste education he added that he sometimes thought what was needed even more than the means to help capacity rise was "machinery by which to facilitate the descent of incapacity from the highest strata to the lower."

The university of a scientifically reorganized society, he declared, "will be a place for men to get knowledge; not for boys and adolescents to get degrees."

All too often, he said students "work to pass, not to know; and outraged Science takes her revenge. They do pass, and they don't know."

When in 1870 a new law was passed authorizing the use of public funds for free schools, and organizing new school boards to define and apply these conditions under which they were to be established, Huxley was persuaded, despite the pressure of his other work, that he should in consistency offer his services. He stood for election, half hoping that he would be defeated; made no campaign whatsoever; and was returned with the highest number of votes in London.

The only thing which infuriated him more than the attempt of the clergymen on the board to turn the new schools to sectarian religious purposes was the attitude that poor children should be trained to become docile unquestioning "hands." He opposed narrow vocational education saying:

> . . . the preparatory education of the handicraftsman ought to have nothing of what is ordinarily understood by "technical" about it. . . . The education which precedes that of the workshop should be entirely devoted to the strengthening of the body, the elevation of the moral faculties, and the cultivation of the intelligence; and, especially, to the imbuing the mind with a broad and clear view of the laws of that natural world

with the components of which the handicraftsman will have to deal.

And, the earlier the period of life at which the handicraftsman has to enter into actual practise of his craft, the more important is it that he should devote the precious hours of preliminary education to things of the mind, which have no direct and immediate bearing on his branch of industry, though they lie at the foundation of all realities.

He wrote angrily:

> The politician tells us, "You must educate the masses because they are going to be masters." The clergy join in the cry for education, for they affirm that the people are drifting away from church and chapel into broadest infidelity. The manufacturers and the capitalist swell the chorus lustily. They declare that ignorance makes bad workmen; that England will soon be unable to turn out cotton goods or steam engines, cheaper than other people; and then, Ichabod! Ichabod! the glory will be departed from us. And a few voices are lifted up in favour of the doctrine that the masses should be educated because they are men and women with unlimited capacities of being, doing, and suffering, and that it is as true now as ever it was, that the people perish for lack of knowledge.

However he proved himself as adroit and practical in the committee room as he was in the laboratory, and accomplished seemingly superhuman feats of reconciliation between the avowed and militant free thinkers and the clergymen of various denominations who composed the board. Although he made no secret of his conviction that: "The principle of strict secularity in State education is sound, and must eventually prevail," he shocked some of his best friends by agreeing to a nonsectarian teaching of the Bible (by laymen) when he realized that he could not otherwise get a vote carried for the actual opening of the new schools. Almost a quarter of a century later he still found it necessary to explain this action and wrote, in response to a serious inquiry:

> The persons who agreed to the compromise, did exactly what all sincere men who agree to compromise, do. For the sake of the enormous advantage of giving the rudiments of a decent education to several generations of the people, they accepted what was practically an armistice in respect of certain matters about which the contending parties were absolutely irreconcilable.

It may have been somewhat easier for him to agree to the compromise because of his firm personal conviction that victory would be on the side of the free thinkers. He said privately:

> I am not afraid of the priests in the long-run. Scientific method is the white ant which will slowly but surely destroy their fortifications. And the importance of scientific method in modern practical life—always growing and increasing—is the guarantee for the gradual emancipation of the ignorant upper and lower classes, the former of whom especially are the strength of the priests.

A further important element in the compromise was the adoption, in large part, of the progressive curriculum he advised which included physical education, art for all—he made an especially determined fight against its omission for girls—and science.

Here, too, he opened fire on the whole commercial concept of "applied science," wishing that the term had never been invented or could be destroyed. "The great end of life," he said, "is not knowledge but action." And "All science is meaningless unless applied to life, while it is altogether impossible to set limits to the seemingly farfetched investigations which will one day prove themselves vital."

> Science is nothing but trained and organized common sense, differing from the latter only as a veteran may differ from a raw recruit; and its methods differ from those of common sense only so far as the guardsman's cut and thrust differ from the manner in which a savage wields his club.
>
> I myself entirely agree . . . "that the scope of all speculation is the performance of some action or thing to be done," and I have not any very great respect for, or interest in, mere knowing as such. I judge of the value of human pursuits by their bearing upon human interests; in other words, by their utility; but I should like that we should quite clearly understand what it is that we mean by this word "utility." In an Englishman's mouth it generally means that by which we get pudding or praise or both. . . . I think that knowledge of every kind is useful in proportion as it tends to give people right ideas, which are essential to the foundation of right practice, and to remove wrong ideas, which are the no less essential foundations and fertile mothers of every description of error in practice.

Some fourteen months after his election to the school board ill health forced him to resign, but his active interest in the work of the free schools and in general education on the lower levels did not end.

It was necessary rapidly to train an enormous number of elementary teachers in the rudiments of scientific instruction. He energetically undertook the personal supervision of a huge elementary retraining program, and recruited many of his distinguished colleagues to assist him. He succeeded in persuading Hooker to act as an examiner in the London school by urging that "The English nation will not take science from above, so it must get it from below."

On the university level Huxley was largely responsible for the development of those institutions which soon after his death merged to form London University. The scientific curriculum they emphasized was, in turn, a great part of the pressure that finally compelled Cambridge and even Oxford to include science as a part of their course of study.

His attitude to higher education was in other respects also far in advance of that of most of his contemporaries. For example, he said:

> The educational abomination of desolation of the present day is the stimulation of young people to work at high pressure by incessant competitive examination. Some wise man has said of early risers in general that they are conceited all the forenoon and stupid all the afternoon. . . . I have no compassion for sloth but youth has more need for intellectual rest than age; and the cheerfulness, the tenacity of purpose, the power of work, which make many a successful man what he is, must often be placed to the credit, not of his hours of industry but to that of his hours of idleness in boyhood.

He not only fought for the introduction of English literature—then taught, where it was taught at all, in Latin or as a matter of philology—but urged the universities to add music as well as art to their curriculum, in such statements as this, which may seem strange to our narrower view of the scientist:

> But the man who is all morality and intellect, although he may be good and great, is, after all, only half a man. There is beauty in the moral world and in the intellectual world; but there is also a beauty which is neither moral nor intellectual—the beauty of the world of Art. . . . But in the mass of mankind the aesthetic faculty, like the reasoning power and the moral sense, needs to be roused, directed, and cultivated; and

I know not why the development of that side of his nature, through which man has access to a perennial spring of ennobling pleasure, should be omitted from any comprehensive scheme of University education. . . . I should like to see Professors of the Fine Arts in every university; and instruction in some branch of their work made a part of the Arts curriculum.

Before leaving this survey of Huxley's educational views we must include an indication of his attitude to the then highly controversial question of woman's education.

Queen Victoria, terrified by the demand for higher education of women had, in 1860, written:

> The Queen is most anxious to enlist everyone who can speak or write to join in checking this mad wicked folly of Women's Rights, with all its attendant horrors, on which her poor feeble sex is bent, forgetting every sense of womanly feeling and propriety.

In the same year Huxley wrote to his friend Lyell:

> I am far from wishing to place any obstacle in the way of the intellectual advancement and development of women. On the contrary, I don't see how we are to make any permanent advancement while one-half of the race is sunk, as nine-tenth of women are, in mere ignorant parsonese superstitutions; and to show you that my ideas are practical I have fully made up my mind, if I can carry out my own plans, to give my daughters the same training in physical science as their brother will get, so long as he is a boy. They, at any rate, shall not be got up as man-traps for the matrimonial market.

Ten or twelve years later, when the demand for women's rights included the right to medical training, the queen expressed herself in even more unbridled fashion. In 1874 Huxley wrote in a semi-public statement:

> We have heard a great deal lately about the physical disabilities of women. Some of these alleged impediments, no doubt, are really inherent in their organization, but nine-tenths of them are artificial—the products of their modes of life. I believe that nothing would tend so effectually to get rid of these creations of idleness, weariness, and that "over stimulation of the emotions" which, in plainer spoken days, used to be called wantonness, than a fair share of healthy work, di-

rected toward a definite object, combined with an equally fair share of healthy play, during the years of adolescence; and those who are best acquainted with the acquirements of an average medical practitioner will find it hardest to believe that the attempt to reach that standard is like to prove exhausting to an ordinarily intelligent and well-educated young woman.

We have already seen how closely his domestic practise followed his professional theory so we are not surprised to find such a note as this to conclude the question: "My second daughter has taken to art, and will make a painter if she be wise enough not to marry for some years."

The last specific current controversy with which we must deal before ascertaining Huxley's views on the general philosophical, ethical, and aesthetic questions on which he wrote so much, is his attitude toward slavery in the United States, and the oppression of the native population in the British colonies.

His much loved oldest sister had, as we have noted, emigrated to the United States at the end of the forties, and had settled in the South. In 1864 her sixteen-year-old son was a volunteer in the Confederate army, and she wrote her brother a heartbroken letter desperately trying to convince him that despite whatever Yankee propaganda and sentimental glorification of the Negro he might have heard, the South was right.

His answer, in which he attempts to meet her feelings by waiving every nonessential point on which she insists, is nevertheless crystal clear in the stubborn honesty of conviction of its conclusion. He begins:

> I have read all that you tell me about the south with much interest and with the warmest sympathy, so far as the fate of the south affects you. . . . I have not the smallest sentimental sympathy with the Negro; don't believe in him at all, in short. I have no love for the Yankees and I delight in the energy and self-sacrifice of your people; but for all that, I cannot doubt that whether you beat the Yankees or not, you are struggling to uphold a system which must, sooner or later, break down. . . . But it is clear to me that slavery means, for the white man, bad political economy; bad social morality; bad internal political organization, and bad influence upon free labour and freedom all over the world. For the sake of the white man, therefore, for your children and grandchildren directly, and for mine, indirectly, I wish to see this system ended. Would that the south had had the wisdom to initiate that end without this miserable war!

All this must jar upon you sadly, and I grieve that it does so; but I could not pretend to be other than I am, even to please you. . . .

Of course, many English liberals joined Huxley in his stand on the American Civil War. But two years later, in the terrific furor created by the Eyre case in Jamaica, even Dickens followed Carlyle, Kingsley and Tennyson into an indefensible position on the wrong side.

There had been an insurrection on the island and Governor Eyre had summarily arrested, court-martialed and executed one of the Negro members of the legislature, a Mr. Gordon who had been outspoken in his demand for Negro rights.

Huxley, with John Stuart Mill, took the lead in organizing a committee to demand the recall and trial of Governor Eyre. Darwin stood, or at least agreed, with them as we see from a note to him dated November 11, 1866:

> I am glad to hear from Spencer that you are on the right (that is *my*) side in the Jamaica business. But it is wonderful how people who commonly act together are divided about it.

At the end of the month he responded to taunts in the *Pall Mall Gazette*, which jeered that his preoccuption with monkeys prevented his understanding the value of white men's lives, by writing that paper a powerful open letter which read, in part:

> Unless the Royal Commissioners have greatly erred, therefore, the killing of Mr. Gordon can only be defended on the ground that he was a bad and troublesome man; in short, that although he might not be guilty, it served him right.
> I entertain so deeply-rooted an objection to this method of killing people—the act itself appears to me to be so frightful a precedent, that I desire to see it stigmatised by the highest authority as a crime. And I have joined the Committee which proposes to indict Mr. Eyre, in the hope that I may hear a court of justice declare that the only defence which can be set up (if the Royal Commissioners are right) is no defence, and that the killing of Mr. Gordon was the greatest offence known to the law—murder.

He wrote even more fully in response to a personal appeal by Kingsley, who was a close friend of Governor Eyre's, and who deprecated Huxley's "vindictiveness" in pressing the case:

I desire to see Mr. Eyre indicted and a verdict of guilty in a criminal court obtained, because I have, from its commencement, carefully watched the Gordon case; and because a new study of all the evidence which has now been collected has confirmed my first conviction that Gordon's execution was as bad a specimen as we have had since Jeffries' time of political murder. . . .

Ex-Governor Eyre seized the man, put him in the hands of the preposterous subalterns, who pretended to try him—saw the evidence and approved of the sentence. He is as much responsible for Gordon's death as if he had shot him through the head with his own hand. I dare say he did all this with the best of motives, and in a heroic vein. But if English law will not declare that heroes have no more right to kill people in this fashion than other folk, I shall take an early opportunity of migrating to Texas [!] or some other quiet place where there is less hero-worship and more respect for justice. . . .

In point of fact, men take sides on this question, not so much by looking at the mere facts of the case, but rather as their deepest political convictions lead them. . . .

The hero-worshippers who believe that the world is to be governed by its great men, who are to lead the little ones, justly if they can; but if not, unjustly drive or kick them the right way, will sympathize with Mr. Eyre.

The other sect (to which I belong) who look upon hero-worship as no better than any other idolatry, and upon the attitude of mind of the hero-worshipper as essentially immoral; who think it is better for a man to go wrong in freedom than to go right in chains; who look upon the observance of inflexible justice between man and man as of far greater importance than even the preservation of the social order, will believe that Mr. Eyre has committed one of the greatest crimes of which a person in authority can be guilty, and will strain every nerve to obtain a declaration that their belief is in accordance with the law of England.

The same democratic distaste for the "great man theory of history" which was so characteristic of the age shows itself in a more peaceful form in Huxley's answer to a journalist's questionnaire in 1894.

The paper had circularized leaders in all fields of thought for an opinion as to whether the nineteenth century would be known to history as the age of Comte, Darwin, Renan, Edison, Pasteur or Gladstone. Huxley answered, refusing to indicate any one man, even Darwin:

I conceive that the leading characteristic of the 19th century has been the rapid growth of the scientific spirit, the consequent application of scientific methods of investigation to all the problems with which the human mind is occupied; and the correlative rejection of traditional beliefs which have proved their incompetence to bear such investigation.

He concluded, characteristically,

Science reckons many prophets, but there is not even a promise of a Messiah.

As we have seen, in addition to an enormous teaching load, a great deal of general scientific writing, a decreasing but still large amount of laboratory research, and the cares and pleasures of a growing family, Huxley devoted the sixties largely to the fight for popular scientific acceptance of evolution and the seventies to his work for the improvement of education.

The need for additional income—he had seven children, five of whom survived him—induced him to accept a post as Inspector of Fisheries in 1881. There he did some valuable work but too often wasted precious time and energy as one letter grumblingly indicates: "All this week I shall be hearing one Jackass contradict another Jackass about questions which are of no importance. I would almost as soon be in the House of Commons."

In 1885 physical exhaustion and dyspepsia, which had much earlier threatened a breakdown averted only by a long vacation (made possible by the generosity of Darwin and other friends ten years before), forced Huxley to resign his active posts. He retired on a comparatively generous pension of £1,200 (later £1,500), the equivalent of his combined teaching and government salaries.

This decade saw the development of a new, more difficult polemic against Spencer and the other pseudoscientific priests of a new superstition—the rationalization of a cutthroat competitive society which borrowed the language of evolution to deny its significance. This philosophy is often misleadingly referred to as "Social Darwinism."

We have seen in our survey at the beginning of the Victorian Age how the ruthless exploitation of poverty was equally justified by the distortions of evangelical religion and the smug "scientific" proponents of English political economy. Truly, "The Victorian followed his conscience as the driver follows his horse," whether he sanctified his cause by invoking God or free trade.

Spencer, the archbishop of the scientific dispensation, was untroubled by the "necessary" misery of a competitive system. He said:

> The poverty of the incapable, the distresses that come upon the imprudent, the starvation of the idle, and those shoulderings aside of the weak by the strong, which leave so many "in shallows and in miseries," are the decree of a large far-seeing benevolence . . . the process *must* be undergone, and the sufferings *must* be endured. No power on earth, no cunningly devised laws of statesmen, no world-rectifying schemes of the humane, no communist panaceas, no reforms that men ever did or ever will broach, can diminish them one jot.

Although he justified his ethics by a reference to the "struggle for existence," "survival of the fittest," and other phrases borrowed from advanced scientific thought, Spencer carefully set boundaries to the exercise of such thought in exploring the universe, reinstating a chillier, more remote God as his sacrosanct "Unknowable."

Huxley, despite personal friendship and a common anticlerical cause, was not slow to attack both Spencer's metaphysics and his ethics as thoroughly irrational, wickedly inhuman, and essentially dishonest. Objecting to the metaphysics first, he said he did "not very much like to speak of anything as 'unknowable' and 'regretted' that Spencer 'made the mistake of wasting a capital upon it.'"

He then more sharply and frequently attacked the fundamental confusion of an "ethics" which claimed its justification in the struggle for survival, declaring time and time again:

> There are two very different questions which people fail to discriminate. One is whether the principle of evolution accounts for morality, the other whether the principle of evolution in general can be adopted as an ethical principle.
> The first, of course, I advocate; and have constantly insisted upon. The second I deny, and reject all so-called evolutional ethics based upon it. . . .

In his famous essay *Evolution and Ethics*, published in 1893, Huxley systematically formulated his views on this subject saying, in part:

There is another fallacy which appears to me to pervade the so-called "ethics of evolution." It is the notion that because, on the whole, animals and plants have advanced in perfection of organization by means of the struggle for existence and the consequent "survival of the fittest"; therefore men in society, men as ethical beings, must look to the same process to help them towards perfection. I suspect that this fallacy has arisen out of the unfortunate ambiguity of the phrase "survival of the fittest." "Fittest" has a connotation of "best"; and about "best" there hangs a moral flavour. In cosmic nature, however, what is "fittest" depends upon the conditions. . . .

. . . But the influence of the cosmic process on the evolution of society is the greater the more rudimentary its civilization. Social progress means a checking of the cosmic process at every step and the substitution for it of another, which may be called the ethical process; the end of which is not the survival of those who may happen to be fittest in respect of the whole of those conditions which obtain, but of those who are ethically best.

As I have already urged, the practice of that which is ethically best—what we call goodness or virtue—involves a course of conduct which in all respects, is opposed to that which leads to success in the cosmic struggle for existence. In place of ruthless self-assertion it demands self-restraint; in place of thrusting aside, or treading down, all competitors, it requires that the individual shall not merely respect, but shall help his fellows; its influence is directed, not so much to the survival of the fittest, as to the fitting of as many as possible to survive. It repudiates the gladiatorial theory of existence. It demands that each man who enters into the enjoyment of the advantages of a polity shall be mindful of his debt to those who have laboriously constructed it; and shall take heed that no act of his weakens the fabric in which he has been permitted to live. Laws and moral precepts are directed to the end of curbing the cosmic process and reminding the individual of his duty to the community, to the protection and influence of which he owes, if not existence itself, at least the life of something better than a brutal savage.

It is from neglect of these plain considerations that the fanatical individualism of our time attempts to apply the analogy of cosmic nature to society. . . . Let us understand, once for all, that the ethical progress of society depends, not on imitating the cosmic process, still less in running away from it, but in combating it. It may seem an audacious proposal thus to pit the microcosm against the macrocosm and to set man to subdue nature to his higher ends; but I venture to think that the great intellectual difference between the ancient times with which we have been occupied and our day, lies in the

> solid foundation we have acquired for the hope that such an enterprise may meet with a certain measure of success.
>
> ... As civilization has advanced, so has the extent of this interference increased; until the organized and highly developed sciences and arts of the present day have endowed man with a command over the course of non-human nature greater than that once attributed to the magicians. The most impressive, I might say startling, of these changes have been brought about in the course of the last two centuries; while a right comprehension of the process of life and of the means of influencing its manifestations is only just dawning upon us. ...
>
> ... Ethical nature may count upon having to reckon with a tenacious and powerful enemy as long as the world lasts. But, on the other hand, I see no limit to the extent to which intelligence and will, guided by sound principles of investigation, and organized in common effort, may modify the conditions of existence, for a period longer than that now covered by history. And much may be done to change the nature of man himself. The intelligence which has converted the brother of the wolf into a faithful guardian of the flock ought to be able to do something towards curbing the instincts of savagery in civilized men.

He especially resented the irresponsible use of the term "unfit" by the eugenicists and remarked pointedly in the course of one such discussion "I sometimes wonder whether people who talk so freely about extirpating the unfit ever dispassionately consider their own history."

Even more directly opposed to the fatalistic acceptance of other people's misery which characterized the thought of "scientific" businessmen, was Huxley's repeated emphasis on the true objectives of science.

His many personal and impersonal discussions of this subject all begin with the assumption that it is not the scientist's business merely to understand the world; he must also be able to change it. And the direction indicated for such change is equally unambiguous.

In direct contradiction to Spencer's statement of the inevitable necessity of poverty Huxley said:

> ... if there is no hope of a large improvement of the conditions of the greater part of the human family; if it is true that the increase of knowledge, the winning of a greater dominion over Nature which is its consequence, and the wealth which follows upon that dominion, are to make no

difference in the extent and intensity of want, with its concomitant physical and moral degradation, among the masses of the people, I should hail the advent of some kindly comet, which would sweep the whole affair away, as a desirable concomitant . . . the natural order of things—the order, that is to say, as unmodified by human effort—does not tend to bring about what we understand as welfare.

One of the great questions presented to modern man he declared was:

to what extent modern progress in natural knowledge, and more especially the general outcome of that progress in the doctrine of evolution, is competent to help us in the great work of helping one another.

And challenged for a personal definition of morality to replace the slavish acceptance of the "natural" struggle for existence as a norm, he wrote simply and clearly:

Moral duty consists in the observance of those rules of conduct which contribute to the welfare of society, and by implication, of the individuals who compose it.
The end of society is peace and mutual protection, so that the individual may reach the fullest and highest life attainable by man. The rules of conduct by which' this end is to be attained are discoverable—like the other so-called laws of Nature—by observation and experiment, and only in that way.

This emphasis on morality as a social and not an individual concept—so unusual in an age that gave birth to the aphorism "business is business" and generally equated "immoral conduct" with lack of chastity—appears even more forcefully in the prolegoma to his famous Oxford lecture in 1892:

That man as a "political animal" is susceptible of a vast amount of improvement, by education, by instruction, and by the application of his intelligence to the adaptation of the conditions of life to his higher needs, I entertain not the slightest doubt. . . .
That which lies before the human race is a constant struggle to maintain and improve, in opposition to the State of Nature, the State of Art of an organised polity; in which, and by which, man may develop a worthy civilisation, capable of maintaining itself and constantly improving itself. . . .

And, in opposition to Matthew Arnold's comfortably passive definition of culture as a knowledge of "the best that has been taught and said in the world," he emphasized the importance of activity and active work in as yet unexplored fields, declaring:

> The modern knows that the only source of real knowledge lies in the application of scientific methods of inquiry to the ascertainment of the facts of existence; that the ascertainable is infinitely greater than the ascertained, and that the chief business of the teacher is not so much to make scholars as to train pioneers.

He was not tempted to any approval of the best people by their approval of him. On the contrary he ungratefully pointed out that "the ignorance of the so-called educated classes in this country is stupendous, and in the hands of people like Gladstone it is a political force." Later he remarked that "every society has its scum at the top and its dregs on the bottom."

He spoke of his growing conviction:

> . . . that the organization of society upon a new and purely scientific basis is not only practicable, but is the only political object much worth fighting for.

When, at the Royal Society dinner in 1892, a V.I.P. publicly regretted that Huxley had never placed his abilities at the service of the House of Commons, he responded with an anecdote of his youth when he had declined an offer of training in the law because "so far as I understand myself, my faculties are so entirely confined to the discovery of truth, that I have no sort of power of obscuring it."

He referred to himself as "a plebian who stands by his order" and when from the highest quarters, it was intimated that a title would be offered him if he were prepared to accept it he commented with something less than courtesy,

> The sole order of merit which, in my judgment, becomes a philosopher, is the rank which he holds in the estimation of his fellow-workers, who are the only competent judges in such matters. Newton and Cuvier lowered themselves when the one accepted an idle knighthood, and the other became a baron of the empire. The great men who went to their graves as Michael Faraday and George Grote seem to me to have

understood the dignity of knowledge better when they declined all such meretricious trappings.

He sometimes attempted to don the robe of a peaceful elder statesman, advising a former student: "Seriously, I wish you would let an old man, who has had his share of fighting, remind you that battles, like hypotheses, are not to be multiplied beyond necessity . . . ," and continued his advice, "Now you do *not* 'suffer fools gladly'; on the contrary you 'gladly make fools suffer.' I do not say you are wrong—but that is where the danger of the explosion lies. . . ."

Yet as he enthusiastically entered on new controversies with Gladstone and the Salvation Army, instead of confining himself to the editing of his collected works (which he described as "the coordination of my eruptions when I was an active volcano"), he was forced, somewhat disingenuously, to apologize:

> The deuce of it is, that however much the weary want to be at rest the wicked won't cease from troubling. Hence the occasional skirmishes and alarms which may lead my friends to misdoubt my absolute detachment from sublunary affairs.

More frankly, he admitted at another time that: "of the few innocent pleasures left to men past middle life—the jamming of common-sense down the throats of fools is perhaps the keenest." His amusements were not, however, either as scarce or all as stormy as this would seem to imply. Few men have combined such happy and unruffled personal relationships with such vigorous public warfare.

A few quotations from family letters will serve to show that Huxley was one of the very few who manage to do all their fighting where they get mad.

A charming note to his older son and biographer, Leonard, father of both Aldous and Julian Huxley, written in the year of Huxley's "retirement"—1885—reads in part:

> . . . If you had taken to physical science it would have been delightful to me for us to have worked together, and I am half inclined to take to history that I may earn that pleasure. . . . Joking apart, I believe that history might be, and ought to be, taught in a new fashion so as to make the meaning of it as a process of evolution intelligible to the young.

A letter to one of his daughters in 1892, after a visit she paid her parents in the home Huxley and his wife had built at Eastburn, begins, "The love you children show us, warms our old age better than the sun." After some discussion of the art of being a parent he concludes:

> . . . Depend upon it, that confounded "just man who needed no repentance" was a very poor sort of a father. But perhaps his daughters were "just women" of the same type; and the family circle as warm as the interior of an ice pail.

A letter to an old friend discusses a more recently acquired dignity than that of fatherhood:

> I forget whether you have had any experience of the "Art d'etre Grandpere" or not—but I can assure you, from 14 such experiences, that it is easy and pleasant of acquirement, and that the objects of it are veritable "articles deluxe," involving much amusement and no sort of responsibility on the part of the possessor.

Several notes refer to Julian, Leonard's younger son, who was, at four, already evidently singled out as a youngster of special interest by his observant grandfather.

> He is a most delightful imp, and the way in which he used to defy me on occasion, when he was here, was quite refreshing. The strength of his conviction that people who interfere with his freedom are certainly foolish, probably wicked, is quite Gladstonian.

Half a century later Julian returned the compliment of an appraisal in his article on "T. H. Huxley—A New Judgment" where he says, summarizing the character and achievements of his redoubtable grandfather:

> As a scientist he was outstanding, though he was not in the very restricted class of men like Newton, Faraday or Darwin, who have made fundamental discoveries or revolutionized scientific thinking. He was outstanding in education, both in reforming teaching methods in his own subject and in securing to science in general its place in the curriculum, while yet emphatic as to the place to be assigned to other subjects such as literature and the arts. He played perhaps the greatest role of any single man in the intellectual struggle which

followed the publication of Darwin's *Origin of Species*. For not only was he more responsible than any one else in gaining acceptance of Darwinism, but he followed out the implications of evolution in almost every field—from anthropology to ethics, from philosophy to theology. He stood, and still stands, as the highest embodiment of scientific integrity, of passionate devotion to truth and equally passionate hatred of shams and humbug. . . . He retained an immense variety of interests; his character was outstanding; he made himself a secure place among English prose-writers; he had a genius for friendship and for social life. . . .

Huxley's perhaps even more generally known grandson, Aldous, far less akin to him in taste, temperament, training or beliefs, has nevertheless also a special claim of kinship with his famous grandfather as a man of letters. When in 1932 Aldous was invited to speak in the series of Annual Huxley Memorial Lectures for the Institute he devoted most of his tribute to fairly technical matters of literary style. But after quoting his grandfather's dictum that "Veracity is the heart of morality," he added, "It was also the heart of his literary style."

This is undeniable as any or all of the above quotations may be taken to illustrate. But Huxley was also a very conscious writer. Sometimes he even explicitly commented upon the course he himself pursued. In one discussion of the matter he said:

For my part, I venture to doubt the wisdom of attempting to mould one's style by any other process than that of striving after the clear and forcible expression of definite conceptions; in which process the Glassian precept, "first catch your definite conceptions" is probably the most difficult to obey. But still I mark among distinguished contemporary speakers and writers of English, saturated with antiquity, not a few to whom, it seems to me, the study of Hobbes might have taught dignity; of Swift, concision and clearness; of Goldsmith and Defoe, simplicity.

Another discussion more specifically directed to young scientific writers concluded:

Be clear though you may be convicted of error. If you are clearly wrong, you will run up against a fact some time and get set right. If you shuffle with your subject and study chiefly to use language which will give a loophole of escape either way, there is no hope for you.

And he repeated the same favorite idea as an introduction to a talk on certain educational problems, beginning:

> A great lawyer-statesman and philosopher of a former age— I mean Francis Bacon—said that truth came out of error much more rapidly than out of confusion. There is a wonderful truth in that saying. Next to being right in this world, the best of all things is to be clearly and definitely wrong, because you will come out somewhere. If you go buzzing about between right and wrong, vibrating and fluctuating, you come out nowhere; but if you are absolutely and thoroughly and persistently wrong, you must, some of these days, have the extreme good fortune of knocking your head against a fact and that sets you all straight again.

Since what is true of all good writers—that the style is the man—is especially true of writers like Huxley, this bit of advice highlights an important facet of his thought—his realization that the refusal to act or believe is in itself an action, and that such responsibility weighs no less heavily than affirmative action.

True, he often spoke of "the sanctity of doubt," having even answered Kingsley's condolences and invocation to belief in immortality as a comfort on the death of his baby son with:

> But the longer I live, the more obvious it is to me that the most sacred act of a man's life is to say and to feel, "I believe such and such to be true." All the greatest rewards and all the heaviest penalties of existence cling about that act. The universe is one and the same throughout; and if the condition of my success in unravelling some little difficulty of anatomy or physiology is that I shall rigorously refuse to put faith in that which does not rest on sufficient evidence, I cannot believe that the great mysteries of existence will be laid open to me on other terms. . . .

But he never confused such necessary scientific caution with the deliberate use of intellectual uncertainty to rationalize inaction. He speaks of the "active doubt" of a real scientist, saying:

> It is doubt which so loves truth that it neither dares rest in doubting, nor extinguish itself by unjust belief.

He rates those who use the lack of absolute certainty to evade the responsibilities of decision in such passages as:

To quarrel with the uncertainty that besets us in intellectual affairs would be about as reasonable as to object to live one's life with due thought for the morrow, because no man can be sure he will be alive an hour hence.

His emphasis on clarity and a straightforward, unaffected prose led Huxley to the conclusion that "It is an excellent rule always to erase anything that strikes one as particularly smart when writing it."

He followed this rule so consistently that a lady in one of his later audiences asked in some perplexity, "Why do they call him a great lecturer? He just makes things perfectly plain, that's all."

However, as Aldous said in his lecture *On Huxley as a Man of Letters*,

> Huxley realized very well the importance of being an artist. Of the Germans he writes: "As men of research in positive science they are magnificently laborious and accurate. But most of them have no notion of style, and seem to compose their books with a pitchfork."

Huxley himself told his wife, after attending a 25th anniversary dinner of the popular scientific magazine, *Nature*, which he had really founded, that in his speech he, "scolded the young fellows pretty sharply for their slovenly writing."

Several years earlier, in 1891, he wrote more complacently than apologetically to the French translator of some of his works:

> . . . I am quite conscious that the condensed and idiomatic English into which I always try to put my thoughts must present many difficulties to a translator.
> The fact is that I have a great love and respect for my native tongue, and take great pains to use it properly.

Nor did all his love and respect for Darwin restrain him from the irreverent private comment: "Exposition is not Darwin's forte and his English is sometimes wonderful."

He had enough faith in Darwin's judgment, however, even in literary matters, to be particularly delighted when, in congratulating him on the publication of his first real book, *Evidences as to Man's Place in Nature*, Darwin wrote:

> I never fail to admire the clearness and condensed vigour of your style, as one calls it, but really of your thought. . . .

Bacon himself could not have charged a few paragraphs with more condensed and cutting sense than you have done.

His special feeling for the importance of language may, perhaps, be related to the insight which led him to expect that future research might—as it has—indicate speech as a major factor in the development of man as a human being. He answered a question as to the probable explanation of the enormous gap between man and his ancestors:

> What is it that constitutes and makes man what he is? What is it but his power of language—that language giving him the means of recording his experience—making every generation somewhat wiser than its predecessor . . . which enables men to be men—looking before and after and, in some dim sense, understanding the working of this wondrous universe—and which distinguishes man from the whole of the brute world. I say that this functional difference is vast, unfathomable, and truly infinite in its consequences; and I say at the same time, that it may depend upon structural differences which shall be absolutely inappreciable to us with our present means of investigation.

But of course language, fond as he was of it, represented to Huxley rather a tool to use than an object of art to contemplate.

And it is not surprising that in his own evaluation of his career he, with all due modesty, comes closer to Julian's than Aldous' estimate.

In 1887, thanking the Royal Society for its presentation to him of their most coveted scientific honor—the Darwin award instituted on Darwin's death in 1885—Huxley said of himself:

> As for me, in part from force of circumstances and in part from a conviction I could be of most use in that way, I have played the part of something between maid-of-all-work and gladiator-general for Science, and deserve no such prominence as your kindness has assigned to me.

And in a more complete formal evaluation of his full and energetic life he finally wrote:

> To promote the increase of natural knowledge and to forward the application of scientific methods of investigation to all the processes of life to the best of my ability, in the conviction which has grown with my growth and strengthened

with my strength, that there is no alleviation for the sufferings of mankind except veracity of thought and of action, and the resolute facing of the world as it is when the garment of make-believe by which pious hands have hidden its ugliest features is stripped off.

It is with this intent that I have subordinated any reasonable, or unreasonable, ambition for scientific fame which I may have permitted myself to entertain, to other ends; to the popularisation of science; to the development and organisation of scientific education; to the endless series of battles and skirmishes over evolution; and to untiring opposition to that ecclesiastical spirit, that clericalism, which in England, as everywhere else, and to whatever denomination it may belong, is the deadly enemy of science.

In striving for the attainment of these objects I have been but one among many, and I shall be well content to be remembered, or even not remembered, as such.

We may fittingly appropriate for this brilliant essayist, who was one of the very few Victorians to remain a complete man and fulfill himself happily in both his work and his life, the epitaph he himself pronounced on a great teacher:

He had intellect to comprehend his highest duty distinctly, and force of character to do it; which of us dare ask for a higher summary of his life than that?

The End of an Epoch

IF WINTER COMES

The twenty-five years after the Crystal Palace Exhibition of 1851 were, for England, years of almost unexampled prosperity and uninterrupted material gain.

Her practical monopoly of the world industrial markets provided ever larger fortunes for a still increasing number of middle-class merchants and manufacturers. It also enabled the bourgeoisie to provide a comparatively high living standard for a small but important part of the working class—the skilled workers who composed the "aristocracy of labor," and who had formed so large a part of the leadership of the early Chartist movement.

This enormous margin of profit also allowed for certain necessary reforms in city sanitation, factory working conditions, and a general ten-hour day. Every one of these concessions, largely forced by the growing strength of the craft unions, was acclaimed by the bourgeoisie as an instance of its own progressive democratic concern and when, in 1867, a surprise move by Disraeli's "Radical Tories" established universal manhood suffrage, it was clear that the millennium had arrived.

Twenty-five years before, at the time of the deeply class conscious Chartist demonstrations, the Whig, Macaulay, had cried in genuine terror:

> I am opposed to universal suffrage. I believe universal suffrage would be fatal to all purposes for which government exists, and that it is utterly incompatible with the very existence of civilization. I conceive that civilisation rests on the security of property. While property is insecure, it is not in the power of the finest soil, or of the moral and intellectual constitution of any country, to prevent the country sinking into barbarism, while, on the other hand, so long as property is

secure it is not possible to prevent a country advancing in prosperity. [Therefore the extension of the franchise to the working class] which would, to a moral certainty, be induced to commit great and systematic inroads against the security of property [would be fatal].

But by the end of the sixties the class struggle was, for Liberals and Conservatives alike, a thing of the past. Poverty still existed but there had been no general unemployment for over twenty years and the unalleviated misery of the casual or unskilled laborer was hardly a matter of concern even to his more fortunate fellows. The powerful London Trade Union Council, for example, had publicly declared the tens of thousands of dock workers, match girls, and other casuals in that city "unorganizable" and of no interest to sober, steady, ambitious workmen.

To most upper-class Englishmen the extension of the franchise in 1867 merely meant that almost everyone could now help decide whether it was the turn of the respectable Mr. Gladstone or of the picturesque Mr. Disraeli to serve as prime minister. The loser would, of course, act as head of the loyal opposition to Her Majesty's government until it was again his chance to lead it.

We have seen Dickens' earlier description of this parliamentary farce. He himself had, not very hopefully, welcomed the slight possibilities of a change suggested by manhood suffrage but after seeing it in action for some twenty years, his admirer, William Morris, was to declare that Parliament still was:

> On the one side a kind of watch committee, sitting to see that the interests of the upper classes took no hurt; and on the other a sort of blind to delude people into supposing that they had some share in the management of their own affairs.

England, which had been terrified by the continental revolutions of 1848 was, by 1870, so complacently sure of her virtuous immunity that the Paris Commune barely stirred a ripple of interest. But another result of the Franco-Prussian War was destined to cause her more serious disturbance.

German industry, under the iron direction of Bismarck, forged ahead so rapidly in the postwar years that it soon appeared as an active, and often as a successful, competitor in markets England had long taken completely for granted.

The United States too had recovered from the Civil War and

was beginning to launch an unprecedented program of industrial expansion.

Both Germany and the United States were, naturally, building improved modern factories which made the smaller older English ones seem antiquated in comparison. Yet it was, in most cases, economically impossible for English industrialists to scrap their investments in their now inefficient pioneer plants and rebuild to meet the new international competition.

The immediate response to these unfavorable conditions were, first, wage cuts; then an elimination of the margin which had made certain paternalistic practises possible for individual employers; and, finally, widespread unemployment. It is significant that the term "the unemployed" was not generally used until the early eighties and appears in a dictionary for the first time as a noun in 1886.

By the late seventies a nation-wide depression had set in which was to last for the next ten years, and which provides much of the background for the emergence of the self-named "fin de siècle" literature and art of the eighties and nineties.

Before we turn to consider this and other literary developments of the period, however, we must complete our rapid survey of their economic foundation.

English capitalism was to enjoy one more period of prosperity after the collapse of its industrial monopoly, but on a very different basis.

1884-86 saw the real beginning (in the Sudan) of her bloody conquest of Africa, and from that time on the wealth of the nation was more and more largely derived from superprofits on colonial investments.

This meant, of course, the end of any constructive role for the now increasingly functionless bourgeoisie, and a long interruption of all serious productive development for the nation. In 1874, for example, over half the workers in England were employed in textiles and heavy industry. Less than twenty years later, on the other hand, over half were employed in the service and retail consumer fields, with a large proportion altogether dependent on luxury trade.

The public climax of this decline and fall of bourgeois English economy may be seen in the openly imperialistic adventure of the Boer war. This ushered in the "era of wars and revolutions" which so ingloriously concluded an epoch gloriously begun by the repulse of the invading Spanish Armada some three hundred years before.

Let us, therefore, think for a moment of the great Elizabethan renaissance as we turn to the literature of this period, which can no longer be called Victorian even though Victoria was yet to celebrate her Diamond Jubilee.

Of course, even from the depths of national prosperity and domestic tranquility there had been some voices raised in protest at the life created by industrial capitalism. We have already seen how the best of the Victorians were almost unanimous in their criticism of Victorian culture, although their diagnoses of its ills were somewhat beside the mark and their suggested remedies were therefore generally impossible or irrelevant. But the major energies of the powerful middle class, from which they almost all came, and to which they all finally belonged, were then still devoted to the progressive task of expanding man's powers of production. The writers were still, therefore, despite their deep dissatisfaction, somewhat able to identify themselves with their society, and to work in and for it.

Even Dickens felt, almost to the end of his life, that there was hope for a reformed world in an appeal to the basic common sense, good will, and emotional strength of the average Englishman, and Huxley never lost faith in the possibility of building a better world through a truly liberal scientific education for the nation. Whether as novelists or essayists the great Victorians all maintained a steady stream of propagandist writing intended to win their countrymen to their own more or less progressive views.

Even in the world of the fine arts we find that the original Pre-Raphaelite Brotherhood, defended by Ruskin at the turn of the century, had made their social belief in cooperation rather than competition as explicit and important a cornerstone of their movement as the aesthetic principle of a return to a prerenaissance, preindustrial technique.

The four Pre-Raphaelite artists who organized the revolt against the standards of the Royal Academy in the middle of the century—Holman Hunt, John Everett Millais, Dante Gabriel Rossetti, and Thomas Woolner—were in no sense proclaiming the doctrine of antisocial individualism or the slogan of "art for art's sake" which characterized the later aesthetic movement that closed the century.

The Pre-Raphaelites would have been deeply shocked at the

formulation with which one of the later aesthetic leaders in the eighties traced a descent from Pre-Raphaelitism, saying:

> Under different names the irregular recurrence of an aesthetic movement—that is to say, the aspiration of a select few to a higher culture than that of the many—has been a peculiar feature in the social history of the modern world.

It was not the higher sophistication of an elect, but the lost simplicity in which all men could appreciate the beauties of nature and a natural art, that the Pre-Raphaelites sought. Whistler, an outstanding forerunner of the later aesthetic movement, would not allow an ordinary house painter to mix the colors to be used on a wall of his rooms. Ruskin, honored by the Pre-Raphaelites, felt that real architecture would be possible only when every stonemason should again feel free to carve gargoyles according to his own fancy, as in the medieval cathedrals.

But easel painting was obviously an instrument even less adapted to the fundamental regeneration of the many than to the higher education of the few. Like the contemporary critics at whom we have already glanced in "Her Majesty's Loyal Opposition" the Pre-Raphaelites were themselves too completely a part of the class whose values they opposed to create any real movement or any truly major works of art. Yet almost a generation later their banner still served as a rallying point for such different expressions of antibourgeois feeling as Swinburne's *Poems and Ballads* (1866) and the painting of the young Edward Burne-Jones and William Morris who were both, for a while, personal disciples of Rossetti's.

Even such very alien figures as the last two important nineteenth century novelists—George Meredith and Thomas Hardy—gravitated toward the Pre-Raphaelites as the best cultural symbol of anti-Victorianism in the third quarter of the century.

In both novelists we see the beginning of the development which was to transform so highly social a literary form as the novel into a private rather than a public medium during the final decline of bourgeois culture.

George Meredith (1828-1909) for some years in the sixties shared a house with Rossetti and Swinburne. His first novel had, on its publication in 1856, been enthusiastically hailed by George Eliot as the appearance of a powerful new talent. But neither it nor any of his subsequent books were actually addressed to the general reader and when, twenty years later, he had become the idol of a slowly increasing number of "Meredithians" a considerable part of their approval was based on his being above the heads of the many.

He himself sublimated his uneasiness at Victorian civilization in terms of the "comic spirit" which sees through all societies and serves as a corrective to their values—for the elect, at least. Despite his bitter private disappointment at the lack of public recognition, he was able to say with some sincerity near the end of his career, "Thank God, I have never written a word to please the public"— or, of course, to correct it.

The intellectual snobbishness apparent in his writing appeared more grossly in his life, where he concealed his father's ownership of the successful and prosperous tailoring establishment founded by his grandfather, under a vague claim to illegitimate aristocratic parentage. Here in this seemingly trivial and personal manifestation, as in the later aesthetic movement, we find that where the artist, alienated by the increasing degeneracy of the bourgeoisie, has no knowledge of, or imaginative sympathy with, the working class, his hunger for an emotional home often leads him to idealize the more distant and now harmless aristocracy who were, in the "good old times," he thinks, cultivated patrons of art. This is another fundamental difference between the later aestheticism and that preached by Ruskin, who attacked nothing more fiercely than the individual patronage system of the Renaissance, correctly finding in that period the beginning of the inhuman antisocial competitive system he hated.

Not many years later a great novelist, Maxim Gorky, was to say:

> It seems to me that the unhappiness of intellectuals is due to their loneliness, their aloofness from life. Comparatively few of them live among the masses of the people; mostly they exist between the common people and the capitalists as between the hammer and the anvil, in perpetual danger of being shattered.
> Where lies the way out of this tragic position?
> Bring the people over to your side, attract them by spiritual interests, give the people a chance to understand you and to become as spiritually rich as yourselves. Then you will no longer be lonely; then you will be strong and only then can culture triumph and true humanity be victorious. Life will then be joyous and easy and even the stones will smile.

And a contemporary and countryman of Meredith's, William Morris, was as we shall see, already able to act on this possibility in the last twenty years of the century.

But although Meredith was still utterly confused as to the artist's possible allies he was already clear about his enemies. In his creative work he riddled Victorian pomposity and respectability with laughter, challenged the conventional categories of personal relationships, and championed the "new woman" whose feminist claims became the storm center of the eighties. And in his serious consideration of her position he was forced to a more fundamental analysis of many social phenomena. In one of his best novels, *Diana of the Crossways* (1884), we find, for example, such insight as:

> Whenever I am distracted by existing circumstances, I lay my finger on the material conditions and I touch the secret. Individually, it *may* be moral within; collectively it is material —gross wrongs, gross hungers.

Thomas Hardy (1840-1928) was in many ways a much greater writer. His stoical pessimism and deep rooted love of the bleak Wessex countryside seem even more opposed than Meredith's sophisticated wit to Swinburne's romantic pseudoclassical hedonism. Nevertheless in the face of a common enemy he too briefly joined forces with the "King of the aesthetic poets." He greeted the appearance of *Poems and Ballads* in 1866, writing:

> It was as though a garland of red roses
> Had fallen about the hood of some smug nun
> When irresponsibly dropped as from the sun
> In fulfth of numbers freaked with musical closes
> Upon Victoria's formal middle time
> His leaves of rhythm and rhyme.

Hardy's novels were also at first approved by a very limited circle, but this was because of his bitter realistic criticism and deeply felt pessimism rather than because of any difficulty they presented to the ordinary reader. The censors' angry complaint was that they were all too intelligible in their attack on the comfortable Victorian view of life.

One of the best of the conservative critics, Andrew Lang, significantly coupled Hardy with outstanding foreign iconoclasts in his disapproval. He wrote of the latter:

... the famed foreigner, Dostoievsky, and M. Zola, and M. Maupassant often seem to be in the mood when man delights them not, nor woman either. A piercing consciousness of the misery in the world fills their pages, and to read them is about as gay as to read the daily papers.

And of Hardy (in the early eighties) Lang said that he did not intend "to speak again about any work of Mr. Hardy's."

We have referred to Hardy as a social critic and a realist. In a sense, both terms are misleading. He was far too hopeless to see any use in criticizing society, and no melodrama ever depended more on wildly improbable coincidences to bring about a happy ending than Hardy ordinarily did to arrange a catastrophic one.

But essentially Hardy, like the American writer, Herman Melville, had simply displaced his realistic understanding of society so that it appeared as a seemingly fantastic misunderstanding of nature.

It is not true that natural laws intentionally operate so as to destroy the ordinary man's most modest hopes of happiness or freedom. It is not true that all decent human feeling logically involves its possessor in a nightmare of dead end roads and uncharted quicksands. But this was increasingly true of the viciously competitive society and narrowing economic opportunities which made Hardy miserable in London and led him to leave it forever as soon as he could afford to. He himself was freer and happier after his return to the lonely countryside of his birth, but the effects of predatory capitalism were even more universally apparent in the hopeless struggle of small farmers, shepherds, and rural laborers to compete for subsistence with the unseen power of industrialism.

It is his half-conscious understanding of this losing struggle for life that gives Hardy's grim Wessex novels, like Melville's *Moby Dick*, the power to communicate a deeply felt reality beneath the surface melodrama. Nor can Hardy's "fatalism," bitter as that is, be completely understood unless we remember his belief that, "Whatever may be the inherent good or evil of life, it is certain that men make it much worse than it need be."

His condemnation of the world in which he lived was not weakened by the accident of personal success. When, in 1896, he had achieved fame and a moderate fortune, he announced his determination to write no more novels, and for the last thirty years of his long life he did not!

On his deathbed he asked his wife to read him the eighty-first stanza of the *Rubaiyat* which, he felt, most adequately expressed his gloomy reconciliation with the world:

> Oh Thou, who man of baser earth didst make
> And ev'n with paradise devise the snake:
>   For all the sin where with the face of man
> Is blackened—man's forgiveness give—and take.

Although Hardy remained to the end far more democratic than Melville this substitution of "the universe" for "society" served him, too, as a release from the heartbreaking task of attempting to remake his world—a truly hopeless task as long as the artist, in isolation from his own class, had not yet learned to look below for allies.

The growing clarity, as well as the continuing passivity, of his attitude is well illustrated by a poem Hardy wrote after the Boer war, "The Man He Killed," which concludes:

> I shot him dead because—
> Because he was my foe,
> Just so—my foe of course he was;
> That's clear enough; although
>
> He thought he'd 'list, perhaps,
> Off-hand like—just as I—
> Was out of work—had sold his traps—
> No other reason why.
>
> Yes; quaint and curious war is!
> You shoot a fellow down
> You'd treat if met where any bar is,
> Or help to half-a-crown.

This return from prose to poetry by an established novelist dramatized the general movement of the period. For novel writing is essentially a philosophic occupation which cannot be practised without a strong conviction of the significance as well as the existence of an objective world. The novel's power depends on the strength of its writer's convictions, and his ability to assert the validity of his values. As Ralph Fox said:

> No novelist has ever been able to create without possessing that ability for generalization about his characters which is the result of a philosophical attitude toward life.

And Virginia Woolf declared of the post-Victorian novelists a few years later:

> The most sincere of them will only tell us what it is that happens to himself. They cannot make a world because they are not free of [that is, free to enter into, as one is free of one's home or is given the freedom of a city] other human beings. They cannot tell stories because they do not believe the stories are true. To believe that your impressions hold good for others is to be released from the cramp and confinement of personality. It is to be free as Scott was free, to explore with a vigor that holds us spellbound, the whole world of adventure and romance. It is also the first step in that mysterious process in which Jane Austen was so great an adept. The little grain of experience once selected, believed in, and set outside herself, could be put precisely in its place, and she was then free to make of it, by a process which never yields its secret to the analyst, into that complete statement which is literature.

But the writers who most dramatically expressed the last twenty years of the century, the self-styled "decadents of the Aubrey Beardsley period," the followers of James Whistler and Oscar Wilde and their thesis of "art for art's sake," neither were nor wished to be "released from the cramp and confinement of personality."

On the contrary, for them the only certainty left in a disintegrating world seemed to be the individual ego of the artist himself. They shared Ruskin's and Morris' horrified recoil from the ugliness of Victorian England as well as their sense of the deep moral degradation expressed by aesthetic standards based on the laws of conspicuous consumption or its cheap machine-made imitation. But they did not consider it even remotely possible to remake the world, and they found something ludicrous as well as futile in any attempt to convert it.

This attitude of melancholy withdrawal from an alien world was far more widespread than the special reaction of any one group of artists. We have already seen something of it in Meredith's aloof humor, and another expression in Hardy's compassionate tragedy. Perhaps its fullest and certainly its most valuable poetic expression can be found in the austere lyrics of the classicist, A. E. Housman (1859-1936).

His work begins with the mild irony of a poem on Queen Victoria's golden jubilee in 1887:

> Oh, God will save her, fear you not!
> Be you the men you've been,
> Get you the sons your fathers got
> And God will save the queen.

It concludes, with the repetition of a recurrent note, in *Last Poems* (1922):

> Could man be drunk forever
> With liquor, love, or fights,
> Lief should I rouse at morning
> And lief lie down of nights.
>
> But men at whiles are sober
> And think by fits and starts
> And if they think, they fasten
> Their hands upon their hearts.

In the thirty-five years between, the two slender carefully selected volumes of poetry rang the changes on a few dignified and melancholy themes.

The beauty of nature, and its indifference to humanity; the brevity of youth and friendship; the good will of the ordinary simple man and its utter ineffectiveness to change the course of events; all are repeated with an oddly detached grave compassion.

For example, "The Carpenter's Son" (1896) says, unemphatically:

> Oh, at home had I but stayed
> 'Prenticed to my father's trade,
> Had I stuck to plane and adze
> I had not been lost, my lads.
>
> Then I might have built perhaps
> Gallows-trees for other chaps,
> Never dangled on my own
> Had I but left ill alone.
>
> . . . .
>
> Here hang I, and right and left
> Two poor fellows hang for theft:
> All the same's the luck we prove,
> Though the midmost hangs for love.
>
> Comrades all, that stand and gaze,
> Walk henceforth in other ways;

See my neck and save your own;
Comrades all, leave ill alone.

Make some day a decent end,
Shrewder fellows than your friend.
Fare you well, for ill fare I:
Live, lads, and I will die.

The irony of the second stanza above is made unwontedly explicit in an occasional verse like:

Little is the luck I've had
And oh, 'tis comfort small
To know that many a better lad
Has had no luck at all.

There are also a large number of sorrowful war poems, more disturbed but also even more hopeless than Hardy's "The Man He Killed." However, perhaps the most important poems for our purpose are those few in which Housman, from time to time, developed his idea of the function of poetry and the place of the artist.

The most complete of these has already provided titles for several novels by later literary decadents, and offers as explicit a statement of the "pure artist's" apology as one can find.

The laws of God, the laws of man,
He may keep that will and can;
Not I: let God and man decree
Laws for themselves and not for me;
And if my ways are not as theirs
Let them mind their own affairs.
Their deeds I judge and much condemn,
Yet when did I make laws for them?
Please yourselves, say I, and they
Need only look the other way.
But no, they will not; they must still
Wrest their neighbour to their will,
And make me dance as they desire
With jail and gallows and hell-fire.
And how am I to face the odds
Of man's bedevilment and God's?
I, a stranger and afraid
In a world I never made.
They will be master, right or wrong;
Though both are foolish, both are strong.

> And since, my soul, we cannot fly
> To Saturn nor to Mercury,
> Keep we must, if keep we can,
> These foreign laws of God and man.

But this dignified stoical withdrawal from the world—made possible, in Housman's case, by a classics professorship at London and Cambridge—was possible, even as a personal solution, for very few late nineteenth century writers. For most of them neither such economic independence nor the emotional detachment it facilitated were feasible.

Far more typical than Housman's circumstances were those of the poor young insurance clerk, Aubrey Beardsley, who was finally able to throw up his job and make some sort of living as an illustrator, but who died of neglected tuberculosis at twenty-six; or those of the penniless ghost writer and translator, John Davidson, who drowned himself at fifty-two, worn out by the struggle to support a family and still save time and energy for his creative writing; or those of the impoverished journalist, Ernest Dowson, who died of drugs and consumption at thirty-three; or those of the unsuccessful candidate for the priesthood, three times failed medical student, and discharged shoemaker's apprentice, Francis Thompson, who, already a hopeless drug addict, was literally rescued from the gutter by an appreciative Catholic editor and enabled to complete some extraordinary poetry before his death at forty-eight.

This lyric, "In No Strange Land," found among his papers after his death, gives a good idea of the quality of his longer work.

> O world invisible, we view thee,
> O world intangible, we touch thee,
> O world unknowable, we know thee,
> Inapprehensible, we clutch thee!
>
> Does the fish soar to find the ocean,
> The eagle plunge to find the air—
> That we ask of the stars in motion
> If they have rumor of thee there?
>
> Not where the wheeling systems darken,
> And our benumbed conceiving soars!—
> The drift of pinions, would we hearken,
> Beats at our own clay-shuttered doors.
>
> The angels keep their ancient places;
> Turn but a stone, and start a wing!

'Tis ye, 'tis your estranged faces
That miss the many-splendored thing.

But when so sad thou canst not sadder,
Cry; and upon thy so sore loss
Shall shine the traffic of Jacob's ladder
Pitched betwixt Heaven and Charing Cross.

Yea, in the night, my Soul, my daughter,
Cry, clinging Heaven by the hems;
And lo, Christ walking on the water
Not of Gennesaret, but Thames.

Even those who made a moderate success in the world of journalism or scholarship, and the few whose small inherited incomes assured them of a less precarious, if inadequate, livelihood, felt that they were daily forced to sell themselves into a hated servitude to keep alive, and masked their fear of the public's power only by contempt for its ignorance and insensitivity.

Loathing their bourgeois masters they thought that these were "the people." Far from identifying themselves with other differently oppressed workers, they assumed that the lower classes, of whom they were but distantly aware, were as much worse than the middle class as that was worse than the legendary aristocracy. Noble patrons had once, they wistfully thought, supplied the artist with a cultured audience and an elegant life.

Arthur Symons, one of the most successful critics of the group, and editor of their best magazine, wrote a valuable description of "decadence," from the viewpoint of the "decadents" themselves. This totally ignores the economic and social conditions that created the movement but gives us some sense of its essentially homeless and functionless quality, as well as of the superior sophistication and sensitivity with which it supported its rejection of bourgeois values and its claim to belong to a higher, more aristocratic civilization than that of the hated bourgeoisie.

He says, in part:

> The most representative literature of the day—the writing which appeals to, which has done so much to form, the younger generation—is certainly not classic, nor has it any relation with the old antithesis of the classic, the Romantic. After a fashion it is no doubt a decadence; it has all the qualities that mark the end of great periods, the qualities that we find in the Greek, the Latin, decadence: an intense self-consciousness, a restless curiosity in research, an oversubtiliz-

ing refinement upon refinement, a spiritual and moral perversity. . . .

. . . For its very disease of form, this literature is certainly typical of a civilization grown over-luxurious, over-inquiring, too languid for the relief of action, too uncertain for any emphasis in opinion or conduct.

The philosophy of the very varied group which finally enrolled under this banner had received its earliest important English expression in the work of the scholarly aesthete, Walter Pater (1839-1894), a student of Ruskin's and a teacher of Wilde's.

His cultivated hedonism was developed at some length in *Marius, the Epicurean* which served as bible for the comparatively small number that achieved decadence by way of the universities, and the much larger number of those who admired it in their salad days there.

The essence of Pater's message (which he tempered in later editions, alarmed by the thoroughgoing acceptance of his less academic disciples) seemed to be that the sole duty of the aesthete was to develop his aesthetic sensibilities, enjoy all possible varieties of artistic and sensuous experience, and "burn always with a hard gemlike flame." Pater's own life was spent in the cloistered precincts of Oxford and his experiences were intellectual ones, enriched by a cultivated eye and ear. But the young men who contributed to the *Yellow Book* and spent their brief maturity in the London of the starving eighties and "gay nineties" had neither the material security, the timid or austere temperament, nor the stable world in which Pater had grown up, to make his kind of prudent aestheticism possible for them. It is only by an unkind irony of fate that his dictum appears to have borne so much more fruit than does most professorial advice.

Actually the more important influence which did, to some extent, channelize the spontaneous development of this English aesthetic movement was that of its French prototype, from which the famous slogan of "art for art's sake" was borrowed.

William Gaunt, in his excellent book on *The Aesthetic Adventure*, describes the earlier French trend in terms which also help us to understand its belated English appearance.

. . . in France, Bohemia was, like the middle class itself, a by-product of the Revolution [of 1830] and its radical displacement of the social order.

Cloud-cuckoo-land was the result of the operation of economic laws. Painters, writers, musicians, no longer had a niche in society, because no class existed which felt any need for their productions or identified itself with their interests. Thus the Bohemian was a sort of anarchist. He must contrive to live without wage or settled income and therefore was unpractical and imprudent from necessity. The bourgeois was his enemy not simply because he was, as the great Daumier was representing him in lithographs for La Charivari, a creature of greed and craft, of physical and mental ugliness, but still more because the bourgeois had an objection to the arts, and to artists, as performing no useful function he could understand. Such an attitude constituted, for the artist, a release from social obligations.

And Ralph Fox epigrammatically summarizes the whole tradition from Gautier and Baudelaire to Whistler, Beardsley, and Wilde, when he says:

"Art for Art's sake" is only the hopeless answer of the artist to the slogan "Art for money's sake":—hopeless because ivory never was a good material for fortifications.

The completely philistine contempt for art of the late-Victorian bourgeois is strikingly illustrated in an etiquette book of the middle seventies, which gives several exemplary conversations for the benefit of ladies and gentlemen meeting at such social affairs as picnics, balls, and musicales.

At one of the last-named the model young man is advised to begin: "I suppose one ought not to talk while the music is going on, but I should like to tell you a story I heard the other day." The well-bred young woman naturally responds: "Oh please do, I should so like to hear it."

It is no wonder that the most serious young artists should have begun to equate popularity with insensitive mediocrity, and should have concurred in Degas' assertion that:

Painting was private life. You practised it for two or three living friends and some who were dead!
The others knew nothing about it and never would know anything and consequently you did not care what they thought.

However the desire to communicate with their fellows dies hard in human beings and the central figures of the English aesthetic movement, at first defined as a group only by the vicious attacks of *Punch* and the good-natured mockery of Gilbert and Sullivan's *Patience*, finally more or less defined themselves by cooperating to issue the first number of the short-lived but famous *Yellow Book* in April, 1894.

Aubrey Beardsley served as its art editor for the first four issues and its contributors included such writers as Max Beerbohm, John Davidson, Ernest Dowson, Richard le Gallienne, Lionel Johnson, George Moore, Arthur Symons and Francis Thompson.

After the fourth issue the sensational trial and imprisonment of Oscar Wilde set off a storm of "antidecadent" feeling and Aubrey Beardsley, as Wilde's friend, was asked to withdraw.

He and many of the more talented men then organized *The Savoy* under Arthur Symons' editorship. To this much better magazine not only several Fabians, including Bernard Shaw, but also W. B. Yeats and other leaders of the "Irish Renaissance" contributed during its short eight months' existence.

A large number of the inner circle of the aesthetes, including Beardsley and Wilde, died before they were forty, and many of them, like these two and Ernest Dowson, sought refuge from "a world they never made" in a deathbed conversion to Catholicism. Their literary immortality rests on a handful of memorable lyrics, some provocative art criticism, a few witty or wistful essays, and Wilde's two or three most brilliant plays, especially *The Importance of Being Earnest*.

But their significance is far greater than this meagre accomplishment would indicate. For the suicidal "fin de siècle" aesthetic which their brief appearance crystallized has survived to reappear in the many literary perversions from surrealism to existentialism through which the increasing degeneracy of twentieth century bourgeois culture has expressed itself. And, more important, it has served as a basis for the curious utterly unhistorical theory of "pure art" with which reactionary critics today seek to outlaw all progressive contemporary literature.

Since this is so we should pause for a moment, before turning to the emergence of the new social literature which revitalized the English drama, to consider this aspect of the work of the nineteenth century decadents who were, after all, not yet as far gone in decay as their twentieth century successors.

It is true that not all propaganda is art—although undeniably the most effective, enduring and truthful propaganda is. But it is not at all true that no art is propaganda. It would, in fact, be difficult to find any great work of literature which was not propaganda, whether it proved to be as direct as Shelley's "Men of England" or as subtle as his "Ode to the West Wind."

This is so apparent that it has taken over half a century of the desperate antihumanism of a dying culture before its spokesmen became brazen enough to deny the fact of art's historical function, whatever ideals they personally set for its future. And so it may be with some surprise that many modern formalists would note the genuine social concern still fitfully apparent in the work of the best of their own rebellious and consciously antisocial founding fathers.

We have already spoken of Swinburne, considered an early forerunner of the aesthetic movement, but we have not mentioned his deep admiration for Walt Whitman and his love for the exiled Italian revolutionary, Mazzini. His acquaintance with Mazzini and sympathy for his aims inspired Swinburne's *Songs Before Sunrise* (1871). The volume begins:

> Watchman, what of the night?
> Storm and thunder and rain,
> Lights that waver and wane,
> Leaving the watchfires unlit.
> Only the bale fires are bright,
> And the flash of the lamps now and then
> From a palace where spoilers sit,
> Trampling the children of men.

Arthur O'Shaughnessy, a young disciple of Swinburne's and Baudelaire's, who died in the early days of the aesthetic movement, is now best remembered for his "Music Makers" (1880) with its decidedly social claim that the poet is the builder of civilizations and:

> . . . overthrows them with prophesying
> To the old of the new world's worth;
> For each age is a dream that is dying,
> Or one that is coming to birth.

Finally Oscar Wilde himself (1854-1900), the admitted spokesman of the movement whose destruction precipitated its collapse, was in both theory and practise far closer to William Morris, for example, than we can conceive of, say, T. S. Eliot's being to Bernard Shaw.

During his lecture tour in the United States in 1882 Wilde formulated the theory which traces the pedigree of the aesthetic movement back to a (retreating) romanticism, and notes the relation of the early romantics to the French Revolution. His talk began:

> I trace the first tendencies of the modern Renaissance to the French Revolution, and the desire for perfection which lay at the base of that revolution found in a young English poet its most complete and flawless realisation. . . . Byron was a rebel and Shelley a dreamer; but in the calmness and clearness of his vision, his self-control, his unerring sense of beauty, and his recognition of a separate realm for the imagination, Keats was the pure and serene artist, the fore-runner of the Pre-Raphaelite school, and so of the great romantic movement of which I am to speak.

He concluded with his movement's better known credo of art's "purity":

> . . . But all things are not fit subjects for poetry. Into the sacred house of Beauty the true artist will admit nothing about which men argue. If he writes on these subjects, he does so, as Milton expresses it, with his left hand.
> . . . In its primary aspect a painting has no more spiritual message than an exquisite fragment of Venetian glass.

However, presumably using his left hand he himself, at the height of his career in 1895, wrote an extremely interesting essay, *The Soul of Man under Socialism*. The deliberate snobbishness of many passages is startling even when one realizes how completely "The People" means, for Wilde, "The Bourgeoisie." But his essential understanding of the relation between society and art, between socialized production and free human development, is still more amazing.

Before turning to the fuller exploration of this thesis in the works of William Morris and Bernard Shaw let us do Wilde the justice of glancing at some of his early insights:

> But their [philanthropists'] remedies do not cure the disease; they merely prolong it. Indeed, their remedies are part of the disease.

... The proper aim is to try and reconstruct society on such a basis that poverty will be impossible.
... We are often told that the poor are grateful for charity. Some of them are, no doubt, but the best amongst the poor are never grateful. ... Charity they feel to be a ridiculously inadequate mode of partial restitution; ... to recommend thrift to the poor is both grotesque and insulting. It is like advising a man who is starving to eat less. ...
... Most personalities have been obliged to be rebels. Half their strength has been wasted in friction. Byron's personality, for instance, was terribly wasted in its battle with the stupidity, and hypocrisy and Philistinism of the English. ... Shelley escaped better. ... Still, even in Shelley, the note of rebellion is sometimes too strong. ... When private property is abolished there will be no necessity for crime, no demand for it, and it will cease to exist. ... [For] though a crime may not be against property it may spring from the misery and rage and depression produced by our wrong system of property-holding, and so, when that system is abolished, will disappear. ... Jealousy, which is an extraordinary source of [non-property] crime in modern life, is an emotion closely bound up with the conception of property, ...
... Up to the present, man has been, to a certain extent, the slave of machinery, ... This, however, is, of course, the result of our property system and our system of competition. ... Were that machine the property of all, every one would benefit by it. It would be an immense advantage to the community. ... The fact is, that civilisation requires slaves. ... Human slavery is wrong, insecure and demoralising. On mechanical slavery on the slavery of the machine, the future of the world depends. ... There will be great storages of force for every city, and for every house if required, and this force man will convert into heat, light, or according to his needs. Is this Utopian? A map of the world that does not include Utopia is not worth even glancing at, for it leaves out the one country at which Humanity is always landing.
... It is often said that force is no argument. That, however, entirely depends on what one wants to prove. Many of the most important problems of the last few centuries, such as the continuance of a personal government in England, or of feudalism in France, have been solved entirely by means of physical force. ... Behind the barricades there may be much that is noble and heroic. But what is there behind the leading article but prejudice, stupidity, cant and twaddle? ...
It will, of course, be said that such a scheme as is set forth here is quite unpractical and goes against human nature. ... A practical scheme is ... a scheme that could be carried out under existing conditions. But it is exactly the existing conditions that one objects to; and any scheme that could accept

these conditions is wrong and foolish. The conditions will be done away with, and human nature will change. . . . The error of Louis XIV was that he thought human nature would always be the same. The result of his error was the French Revolution.

Finally, we may conclude Wilde's story with a reminiscence of Shaw's which tells us much about both men. Shaw wrote in his *16 Self Sketches* (1949):

> What first established a friendly feeling in me [to Oscar Wilde] was, unexpectedly enough, the affair of the Chicago anarchists [the victims of the Haymarket frame-up in Chicago, 1886], . . . I tried to get some literary men in London, all heroic rebels and sceptics on paper, to sign a memorial asking for the reprieve of these unfortunate men. The only signature I got was Oscar's. It was a completely disinterested act on his part; and it secured my distinguished consideration for him for the rest of his life.

After Wilde had been sentenced to two years penal servitude in a burst of savage indignation which owed at least as much of its venom to his social criticism as to his homosexuality, Shaw was the only English writer who dared attempt a petition for his release.

When this failed he frequently referred, in his subsequent columns of dramatic criticism, to the witty playwright whose name was otherwise altogether unmentionable in England and whose closest friends denied ever having known him.

But this tells us more of Shaw than of Wilde, who died miserably in France a few years after his release, and whose place in the public eye had, by then, been fittingly taken by almost the only avowed poet of modern imperialism—Rudyard Kipling.

Before we turn to our final consideration of late nineteenth century English literature in the work of the Fabian Socialist, Bernard Shaw, we must look briefly at the accomplishments of his early friend, the Communist, William Morris (1834-1896).

G. K. Chesterton, whose wildly sweeping generalizations about English literature seem so very often to hit the bullseye, said "By Morris' time and ever since, England has been divided into three classes: Knaves, Fools, and Revolutionists." And no one has ever called William Morris either a knave or a fool. True, many pious biographers have attempted to evade Chesterton's ugly alternative by treating Morris as a utopian dreamer, although for the last thirteen years of his life he persistently declared himself a Marxist and a revolutionary, summarizing his stand in a speech in Glasgow on his fifty-fourth birthday:

> I call myself a revolutionary Socialist because I aim at a complete revolution in social conditions. I do not aim at reforming the present system, but at abolishing it. . . . But, mark you again, what I aim at is Socialism or Communism, not Anarchism.

On other occasions he more explicitly defined socialism as a transitional stage between the revolutionary capture of state power by the working class and the almost complete disappearance of the state after the establishment of pure communism.

It is therefore somewhat surprising that most American readers, at least, associate Morris, somewhat vaguely, with the revival of a rather medieval form of long narrative poetry, the creation of the "Morris chair," and the formation of a nostalgic sort of arts and crafts movement.

Few have read much of his poetry and even fewer have seen his extraordinary series of lectures on socialism—only a selection is included in his collected works under the title *Signs of Change*—or his discussions of art and society, published as *Hopes and Fears for Art*. Almost no one in the present generation on this side of the Atlantic has read the charming pastoral *News from Nowhere*—a deliberately one-sided "utopia" presented in conscious correction of Bellamy's useful but unimaginative and mechanical socialist romance, *Looking Backward*—or the limited but often stirring *Chants for Socialists*, or the truly great and powerful *Dream of John Ball*.

After college Morris, who then had a large inherited income, spent several years in an apprenticeship to architecture which he, like Ruskin, considered the master art, but for which he found he had no personal talent. Under Rossetti's influence Morris and his closest friend, Edward Burne-Jones, began to study painting. Burne-Jones succeeded and became the last of the important Pre-Raphaelite painters, but Morris soon decided that his vocation, while certainly for visual art, was not really for painting. He had developed a great interest in illuminated manuscripts; some of his own exceptionally beautiful ones rival in their borders and decoration if not in their lettering the best work of medieval craftsmen. He had also begun to experiment with weaving and embroidery, winning from Rossetti the disgusted comment, "Top's taken to worsteds."

When Morris was married it was not difficult for him to find an imaginative architect friend to design an unconventional, strikingly plain and beautiful house, large enough for the sort of perpetual informal house party his hospitality created during the next five years. But the fantastic ugliness of mid-Victorian furniture and furnishings is almost impossible to imagine without such detailed knowledge as one can get, for example, by poring over a descriptive catalogue of the objets d'art at the great Crystal Palace Exhibition.

To surround "the most beautiful woman in the world" with even the best of such objects—to fill the large, simple, gracious rooms of the already beloved Red House with them—was for Morris obviously unthinkable. Luckily the solution was to him equally obvious. He had enormous energy, enough money, and a group of very talented but only partially employed artistic friends. And so, as his excellent first official biographer, J. W. Mackail, said in 1899, "the monastery of his Oxford dreams rose into being as a workshop and the Brotherhood became a firm registered under the Companies Act."

Morris, Marshall, Faulkner and Company, later Morris and Company, undertook all kinds of decoration, from murals and stained glass windows to wallpapers, draperies, dishes and the smallest objects of applied art.

From the beginning the firm paid high wages, refused to compromise on quality—finally setting up their own dye works, for example, to use the expensive indigo and vegetable dyes that industry had replaced with cheaper, less fast, chemical products—and charged commensurate prices. They lost money for some time but that Morris was prepared for and, fortunately, when five years later the copper shares he had inherited dropped in value, the company's reputation was firmly established and it was possible for Morris to continue to make a comfortable living by making things he would have enjoyed creating "for nothing."

A number of delightful bills exist from those early years, including one for a "cartoon" of a stained glass window by Burne-Jones headed, "Norse heroes on the sea, making for other people's property." The detailed story of Morris' technical experiments—from baking tiles to dying embroidery thread to carpet-weaving—is a fascinating one, given in some detail in Mackail's long biography. But although the extraordinary combination of antiquarian literary research, international visits, and explorations in the north textile country for old workmen who had, as boys, been apprenticed to hand industries, is of much more than technical interest in revealing Morris' power of imaginatively recreating history to form a living tradition, we cannot take time to discuss it here.

One aspect of his work shop experience is, however, essential for us since it prevented him from paralleling the errors of intellectual snobbery which were characteristic of the scientific Fabians like Bernard Shaw as well as the aesthetic socialists like Ruskin.

Most middle-class reformers, no matter how sincere their good will, knew workmen—if at all—only through speech, and naturally found them largely inferior according to their own highly specialized training. Morris knew them in terms of their work and never wavered in his conviction of the more than middle-class competence of the skilled workman. For example, speaking of the ordinary medieval workman he said:

> We who have studied the remains of his handicraft have been, without any further research, long instinctively sure that he was no priest-ridden down-trodden savage, but a thoughtful and vigorous man, and in some sense at least free.

His general manager, describing their association of almost twenty years, after Morris' death said in part:

> It is worth while to note that there was no sort of selection of these boys [trained to weave tapestries] or of any others who were brought up by us to one or other branches of Mr. Morris' business. John Smith, who is now the dyer at Merton, was taken into the dye-shop because it was just being set up at the time he was getting too old to remain errand boy. Others were put to the [tapestry] loom because at the time we were starting this we were asked to do something for them. . . . The same rule applied to all the others and it justified Mr. Morris's contention that the modern system, which he called that of Devil take the hindmost, is frightfully wasteful of human intelligence.

The year before his marriage Morris had published a book of narrative poems, including *The Defence of Guenevere*, of which Swinburne said: "In all the noble roll of our poets there has been no second teller of tales comparable to the first till the advent of this one." A second volume, *The Life and Death of Jason*, still written in highly decorative medieval imagery, received much more general acclaim in 1867, and in 1870 he completed *The Earthly Paradise*.

The significantly named "An Apology: Prologue to the Earthly Paradise" is perhaps the best known of Morris' poems. The poetry formally restates the conclusion of a letter written twelve years before. "I can't enter into politico-social subjects, for on the whole I see that things are in a muddle, and I have no power or vocation to set them right," he had said then, and now he said: "Dreamer of dreams, born out of my due time, Why should I strive to set the crooked straight."

But the last stanza concludes with two lines that hint an unresolved conflict, perhaps already an unadmitted determination, in the poet's mind:

> So with this Earthly Paradise it is,
> If ye will read aright, and pardon me,
> Who strive to build a shadowy isle of bliss
> Midmost the beatings of the steely sea,
> Where tossed about all hearts of men must be;
> Whose ravening monsters mighty men shall slay,
> Not the poor singer of an empty day.

However, the immediate result of this dissatisfaction took Morris to what most of us would consider a still more remote world in the serious study of Icelandic literature. He began that in 1869 and continued it almost to the end of his life.

A talk he gave some years later on the Icelandic Chieftains gives us a better idea of what he found in the epics of the north—and to some extent recreated in his own later sagas. He said in this informal lecture:

> As to the manners of these early settlers, they were naturally exceedingly simple, yet not lacking in dignity: contrary to the absurd feeling of the feudal or hierarchical period manual labour was far from being considered a disgrace: the mythical heroes have often nearly as much fame given them for their skill as weapon smiths as for their fighting qualities. . . . The greatest men lent a hand in ordinary field or house work, pretty much as they do in the Homeric poems; one chief is working in his hayfield at a crisis in his fortune; another is mending a gate, a third is sowing his corn, his Cloak and

sword laid by in a corner of the field; another is a great house builder; another a ship-builder; one chief says to his brother one eventful morning:

"There's the calf to be killed and the viking to be fought. . . . Which of us shall kill the calf, and which shall fight the viking?"

In 1876 he published his epic saga of *Sigurd the Volsung* which he himself always considered his finest and most important literary work.

The note of concern for the ploughmen and the fishermen, the "lowly people," is unmistakable and his hero is a much more seriously conceived champion of the poor than such folk heroes as Robin Hood, for example. There are many lines which illustrate this very simply, like these:

The sheaf shall be for the plougher, and the loaf for him that sowed,
Through every furrowed acre where the Son of Sigmund rode.

The next year, 1877, Morris was stirred into public action in two ways. The first was his organization of the Society for the Protection of Ancient Buildings which he and his friends irreverently called the Antiscrape. This did much valuable work and was important to Morris for many years, but need hardly concern us here except as an instance of his consistent impulse to do something in association with other people about any concern which he felt deeply at heart. The second was his precipitate entry on political life to stem a tide of propaganda intended to involve England in a Balkan War between the indistinguishable despotisms of Turkey and Czarist Russia.

The "Manifesto to Working Men of England," his first completely political composition, is well worth the respectful attention of much more seasoned political writers. It reads in part:

[Those who would lead you to war are] Greedy gamblers on the Stock Exchange, idle officers of the army and navy (poor fellows!), worn-out mockers of the clubs, desperate purveyors of exciting war-news for the comfortable breakfast-tables of those who have nothing to lose by war; and lastly, in the place of honor, the Tory Rump that we fools, weary of peace, reason, and justice, chose at the last election to represent us. Shame and double shame, if we march under such leadership as this in an unjust war against a people who are not our enemies, against Europe, against freedom, against nature, against the hope of the world. . . .

Working men of England, one word of warning yet: I doubt if you know the bitterness of hatred against freedom and progress that lies at the hearts of a certain part of the richer classes in this country: their newspapers veil it in a kind of decent language; but do but hear them talk among themselves, as I have often, and I know not whether scorn or anger would prevail in you at their folly and insolence. These men cannot speak of your order, of its aims, of its leaders, without a sneer or an insult: these men, if they had the power (may England perish rather!) would thwart your just aspirations, would silence you, would deliver you bound hand and foot forever to irresponsible capital. Fellow-citizens, look to it, and if you have any wrongs to be redressed, if you cherish your most worthy hope of raising your whole order peacefully and solidly, if you thirst for leisure and knowledge, if you long to lessen those inequalities which have been our stumbling-block since the beginning of the world, then cast aside sloth and cry out against an unjust war and urge the middle classes to do no less.

Morris' conclusion, when the government fear of working-class resentment in the forthcoming general elections had been an important factor in their giving up the hope of war, was "More and more I feel how right the flattest democracy is."

Next month he wrote:

Thanks for sending me Arnold's lecture, with the main part of which I heartily agree: the only thing is that if he has any idea of a remedy he doesn't mention it. I think myself that no rose-water will cure us: . . . in short, nothing can be done until all rich men are made poor by common consent. I suppose he dimly senses this, but is afraid to say it, being, although naturally a courageous man, somewhat infected with the great vice of that cultivated class he was praising so much —cowardice, to wit.

And in a lecture on "Art and Socialism" which must have been something of a shock to the liberal middle-class group that had urged his attendance as a speaker, he said:

Can the middle classes regenerate themselves? At first glance one would say that body of people so powerful, who have built up the great edifice of modern Commerce, whose science, invention and energy have subdued the forces of nature . . . could do anything they please. And yet I doubt it: their own creation, the Commerce they are so proud of, has become their master; and we . . . are compelled to admit not that Commerce was made for man, but that man was made for Commerce.

On all sides we are forced to admit it. There are in the English middle class today . . . men of the highest aspirations. . . . But both the leaders and the led are incapable of saving so much as half-a-dozen commons from the grasp of inexorable Commerce: they are as helpless in spite of their culture and their genius as if they were so many over-worked shoe-makers. . . . Things grow worse year by year, day by day. Let us eat and drink, for to-morrow we die, choked by filth? . . .

How can we of the middle classes, we the capitalists and our hangers-on, help? . . . By renouncing our class, and on all occasions when antagonism rises up between the classes, casting in our lot with the victims; those who are condemned at the best to lack of education, refinement, leisure, pleasure and renown; and at the worst, to a life lower than that of the most brutal of savages. There is no other way.

He was delighted by hearing vague rumors of the gradual awakening of a number of "malcontents," which was, a year later to lead to the formation of the [Social] Democratic Federation organized by a Marxist of sorts, H. M. Hyndman.

Morris wrote verse with extraordinary facility but he had not yet learned to use it directly in the service of his new social interests. In response to a question ostensibly about a new poem by Swinburne, but actually referring also to his own long interrupted writing, he replied:

As to the poem, ["Tristram of Lyonnesse"] I have made two or three attempts to read it, but have failed, . . . in these days the issue between art, that is the godlike part of man, and mere bestiality, is so momentous, and the surroundings of life are so stern and unplayful, that nothing can take serious hold of people, or should do so, but that which is rooted deepest in reality and is quite at first hand; there is no room for anything which is not forced out of a man of deep feeling because of its innate strength and vision.

Although Morris was still to write a considerable amount of poetry, some of it very different from his previous work, the significant literary accomplishment of his last fifteen years was chiefly prose.

In addition to several works which will be considered very briefly below, there were almost forty major essays, each originally presented as a carefully prepared lecture. A selection of these were published in 1882 as *Hopes and Fears for Art*, and a later volume in 1888 as *Signs of Change*. The final edition of his collected works also included eight interesting *Lectures on Socialism*, of unusual literary merit.

January 13, 1883, the day on which he was elected an Honorary Fellow of his college at Oxford, Morris publicly joined the [Social] Democratic Federation. This aroused a storm of horrified protest. To his closest friend, Mrs. Burne-Jones, who wrote urging that he put his faith in education which alone could make the rich altruistic and the poor prosperous, he replied:

> Think of many not uneducated people that you know, and you will I am sure see that education will not cure people of the grossest social selfishness and tyranny unless Socialistic principles form part of it. Meantime I am sure it is right, whatever the apparent consequences may be, to stir up the lower classes (damn the word) to demand a higher standard of life for themselves, not merely for themselves or for the sake of the material comfort it will bring, but for the good of the whole world and the regeneration of the conscience of man; and this stirring up is part of the necessary education which must in good truth go before the reconstruction of society: but I repeat that without laying before people this reconstruction, our education will but breed tyrants and cowards, big, little and least, down to the smallest who can screw out money from standing by to see another man working for him.
>
> The one thing I want you to be clear about is that *I cannot help* acting in the matter, and associating myself with anybody which has the root of the matter; and you know, and it may ease your kind heart respecting me, that those who are in the thick of it, and trying to do something, are not likely to feel so much of the hope deferred which hangs about the cause as onlookers do.

There were other criticisms, more difficult to meet, aimed at the character of the S. D. F. chairman, Hyndman. Many of the most serious socialists or communists—the names were until 1917 largely interchangeable—including Marx and Engels themselves, were seriously distrustful of his leadership, and Morris seems from the first to have shared some of their doubts.

He realized the necessary weakness of middle-class leadership for a movement which, as he had said, was based on the "antagonism of classes" as the "natural and necessary instrument of its [capitalism's] destruction." One of his letters which oddly echoes George Eliot's Felix Holt, shows how much concrete thought he had already given to the practical aspect of the question during his first year's membership in the S. D. F.:

> Some of the more ardent disciples look upon Hyndman as too opportunist, and there is truth in that; he is sanguine of speedy change happening somehow, and is inclined to intrigue and the making of a party [faction]: . . . What we want is real leaders themselves working men, and content to be so till classes are abolished. But you see where a man has gifts for that kind of thing he finds himself tending to rise out of his class before he has begun to think of class politics as a matter of principle, and too often he is just simply "got at" by the governing classes, not formally, but by circumstances I mean. Education is the word doubtless; but then in comes the commercial system and defends itself against that in a terrible unconscious way with the struggle for bread, and lack of leisure and squalid housing. . . .

But even the most serious misgivings could not prevent his whole-hearted allegiance to what was, at the time, the only possible organization through which a "practical Socialist" could work. As he himself said a little later in a very similar situation:

> Even this don't shake me; means we must use the best we can get; but one thing I won't do, wait forever till perfect means are made for very imperfect me to work with.

There was another organization that had been set up at about the same time as the Social Democratic Federation, which Morris could far more easily have joined. Its most famous member, Bernard Shaw, said of the early English Socialist movement: "Morris was our one acknowledged great man." His memorial essay, "William Morris As I Knew Him," shows throughout, the tone of sincere admiration and almost humble tenderness which Shaw uses only when speaking of this much older friend, whom he first met in 1883 or 1884.

His explanation of Morris' refusal to join the Fabian Society, in which Shaw was then just becoming active, gives us so good a picture of both men and some of their essential differences that a considerable part of it must be quoted:

It may be asked why Morris, as a practical man, did not join the Fabians. . . .

The answer is that he would have been more out of place in our drawing rooms than in any gang of manual laborers or craftsmen . . . and the discussions would have ended in his dashing out of the room in a rage, and damning us all for a parcel of half baked shortsighted suburban snobs, as ugly in our ideas as in our lives. He could be patient with the strivings of ignorance and poverty toward the light if the striver had the reality that comes from hard work on tough materials with dirty hands, and weekly struggles with exploitation and oppression; but the sophistication of middle class minds hurt him physically. . . .

We must have got on fairly well together; for I presently found myself not only lecturing at the little meeting hall into which he had converted his Hammersmith coach house, but appearing with him at the neighboring street corners on Sunday mornings conducting what most of the passers-by took to be prayer meetings. He and I complemented one another admirably; for I had a positive taste for abstract economics, and used my knowledge so effectively against the capitalist enemy that Morris said in the course of one of his addresses "In economics Shaw is my master." The shock this gave me, which I still remember vividly, shows how far I placed him above myself. I was positively scandalized. . . .

Morris's writings about Socialism, which the most uppish of his friends regarded as a deplorable waste of the time and genius of a great artist, really called up all his mental reserves for the first time. His verse, though it cannot have been so effortless as it seemed, had not taken him to his limit. . . .

In short, Morris was a readymade poet and decorative draughtsman; but no man is a readymade street corner agitator if his subject is one which requires strenuous thought and makes him feel so deeply that he must preach it as a gospel in spite of all inaptitudes, timidities, repugnances.

. . . It is true that there was no lack of practised and even powerful speakers in the movement, spouting Marxism, Fabianism, and all the other brands; but not one of them could propagate his vision of the life to come on a happy earth, and his values that went so much deeper into eternity than the surplus value of Marx.

. . .; he would never have written *Sigurd* if it had cost him half the hard brain work Socialism extorted from him. But that was how the idle singer of an empty day became a prophet and a saint.

The major events of the next few years belong to the story of Shaw as well as that of Morris and their climax was, in fact, to be a more serious turning point in the thought of the playwright, although its influence on the poet was far clearer at the time.

As Shaw intimated, Morris had immediately plunged into the work of street speaking and organization, careless of the cost to him in time, energy, and health, or of the practical effect upon his business. He himself said:

> . . . every man who has a cause at heart is bound to act as if it depended on him alone, however well he may know his own unworthiness; and thus is action brought forth from mere opinion.

In addition to some forty lectures involving trips to Birmingham, Bradford, Edinburgh, Glasgow, Leeds, Manchester, Newcastle and Sheffield during a year, he spoke outdoors twice each Sunday in London, whenever the weather permitted, and at innumerable evening meetings there. He also did an enormous amount of the necessary drudgery of fund raising, besides contributing substantially himself, and made optimistic attempts to recruit members for the society among his own rather startled circle of acquaintances.

Although Morris may have been unrealistic in some of his attempts at recruiting, he cannot be accused of having given his chosen candidates an overoptimistic view of the responsibilities their consent would entail. In one talk to a liberal middle-class audience he concluded an appeal to them to join the S. D. F. by saying:

> You will run the risk of losing position, reputation, money, friends even. Nor can I assure you that you will forever escape scotfree from the attacks of open tyranny. It is true that at present capitalist society only looks on Socialism in England with dry grins. But remember that the body of people who have for instance ruined India, starved and gagged Ireland, and tortured Egypt, have capacities in them, some ominous signs of which they have lately shown, for openly playing the tyrants' game nearer home.

He confessed himself unable to debate the intricacies of the surplus value theory with the Fabians or other non-Marxist and ultradoctrinaire Marxist Socialists, declaring bluntly:

> It is enough political economy for me to know that the idle class is rich and the working class is poor, and that the

rich are rich because they rob the poor. That I know because I see it with my own eyes. I need read no books to convince me of it. And it does not matter a rap, it seems to me, whether the robbery is accomplished by what is termed surplus value, or by means of serfage or open brigandage. The whole system is monstrous and intolerable, and what we Socialists have got to do is to work together for its complete overthrow, and for the establishment in its stead of a system of cooperation where there shall be no masters or slaves, but where everyone will live and work jollily together as neighbours and comrades for the equal good of all.

The spring of 1884 saw "No Master," the first of his songs, collected next year as *Chants for Socialists*, of which one stanza reads:

> And we—shall we, too, crouch and quail,
> Ashamed, afraid of strife,
> And lest our lives untimely fail,
> Embrace the Death in Life?
> Nay, cry aloud, and have no fear,
> We few against the world:
> Awake! Arise! The hope we bear
> Against the curse is hurled.

Another of the Chants, written a few months later, is the better known "March of the Workers," which concludes:

> On we march then, we the workers, and the rumor that ye hear
> Is the blended sound of battle and deliv'rance drawing near;
> For the hope of every creature is the banner that we bear,
> And the world is marching on.
>
> Hark the rolling of the thunder!
> Lo the sun! and lo there under
> Riseth wrath, and hope, and wonder,
> And the host comes marching on.

At the same time Morris began as a serial a more formal long narrative poem, *Pilgrims of Hope*, which was interesting but very uneven in quality, and was finally left incomplete. In this there was an incongruous but oddly charming mingling of his most esoteric private joys, in illuminated manuscripts, for example, and the general theme of man's struggle toward a better life. The stanza below gives an idea of the unaffected simplicity with which Morris spoke of his special interests to his broader audience, winning a remarkable response:

> The singers have sung and the builders have builded
> The painters have fashioned their tales of delight;
> For what and for whom hath the world's book been gilded
> When all is for these but the blackness of night?

In 1887 the practical day-to-day work of street meetings and other forms of agitation culminated in the "Bloody Sunday" at Trafalgar Square which was, as we shall soon see, crucial for Bernard Shaw and the whole Fabian Society.

In 1885 Morris' Socialist League had withdrawn from the Social Democratic Federation. Nevertheless, largely through his influence, the S. D. F. and even sometimes the Fabian Society acted together with the Socialist League in a number of special demonstrations during the middle eighties. One of these took place on Monday, February 8, 1886.

A surprisingly great open air meeting called by a "Radical Tory" land league in Dodds Field was "captured" by a number of Socialist speakers and after vaguely incendiary calls for "immediate revolution" by Hyndman a more or less spontaneous march to Hyde Park, to demand unemployment relief, was undertaken by many thousands of those present, themselves almost all unemployed.

Angered by the deliberate mockery of some gentlemen standing at the windows of a fashionable club en route, members of the demonstration threw stones, and the shattering of the glass seemed a signal for a general riot such as London had not known since the Lord Gordon "No Popery" riots in 1780.

There was no physical harm done to anyone, although many ladies and gentlemen were forced out of carriages and boisterously insulted. But shop windows in all the fashionable districts were broken and there was considerable looting—not for the most part by the demonstrators but by the enormous number of petty thieves, beggars and, perhaps, police spies with which London swarmed in those years of depression.

The immediate result was most revealing. The Mansion House Fund for unemployment relief shot up from a slowly gathered £30,000 to over £70,000 in less than a week, and half the wealthy houses in London were shut up while their owners took a long vacation in the country—or even a sea voyage.

Morris wrote in the Socialist League Newspaper—*Commonweal* —on February 8, 1886:

> Such abject cowardice has perhaps seldom been so frankly shown as was shown by the middling bourgeoisie on those two days. Whatever were they afraid of? Of nothing? No; they were afraid of their own position, so suddenly revealed to them as by a flash of lightning; their position as a class dominating a class injured by them, and more numerous than they.

Burne-Jones wrote him a horrified and pathetic plea to "cease and desist" when his editorial appeared, and Morris answered good-naturedly:

> If you had only suffered as I have from the apathy of the English lower classes . . . you would rejoice at their awakening, however ugly the forms it took. As to my capacity for leadership in this turmoil, believe me I feel as humble as could be wished: yet after all it is my life, and the work of it, and I must do my best.

In another letter about the same time he wrote, "We have been overtaken unprepared by a revolutionary incident, but that incident was practically aimless." And a fuller account of the incident some six weeks later concluded:

> For the rest, contemptible as the riot was, as a riot, it no doubt has had a great effect, both here and on the continent: in fact the surprise of people that the British workman will not stand everything is extreme. . . . I fancy there will be another attempt on our meetings this summer and I rather expect to learn one more new craft—oakum—picking to wit, [in jail] though I assure you I don't want to—far from it.

The prospect of a jail sentence was far from imaginary. During the hard winter of 1885-86 there had been a police drive to suppress open air meetings and Sunday after Sunday speakers had been arrested and given stiff sentences on the charge of "obstructing traffic." Bernard Shaw tells how he narrowly escaped arrest on two such occasions and Morris writes in a Socialist diary he kept for a few months, which he described in a note to his daughter as "the Socialist movement from inside," or "Jonah's view of the whale":

> I may note here for the benefit of well-to-do West-enders that the police are incredibly rough and brutal to the poor people in the East end; and that they treated Allman [arrested for open air speaking] very ill.

The riot naturally did nothing to relax police severity and until the early spring of 1887 there were an increasing number of such small skirmishes ending in individual arrests.

War again seemed to threaten and an article in the 1887 New Year's issue of the *Commonweal* states Morris' uncompromising attitude on the matter:

> Meanwhile if war really becomes imminent our duties as Socialists are clear enough, and do not differ from those we have to act on ordinarily. To further the spread of international feeling between the workers by all means possible, to point out to our own workmen that foreign competition and rivalry, or commercial war, culminating at last in open war, are necessities of the plundering classes; and that the race and commercial quarrels of these classes only concern us so far as we can use them as opportunities for fostering discontent and revolution; and that the interests of the workmen are the same in all countries and they can never be really enemies of each other.

Finally on Sunday, November 13, 1887 all the socialist organizations, together with a number of others, planned a huge "free speech" demonstration in Trafalgar Square. The London Times the next day reported:

> Mr. William Morris . . . then proceeded to say that wherever free speech was attempted to be put down, it was their bounden duty to resist the attempt by every means in their power . . . mounted and on foot [the police] charged in among the people, striking indiscriminately . . . and causing complete disorder in the ranks.

Morris himself wrote:

> Our comrades fought valiantly, but they had not learned how to stand and turn their columns into a line, or to march on to the front—there was no rallying point . . . and all that

the people composing our strong column could do was to struggle into the square as helpless units.

In a private letter he also said: "In fact, this affair, as far as it has gone, has been an ominous flash from the smouldering volcano of class war which underlies modern sham-society."

Three hundred people were arrested during "Bloody Sunday" and at least three died as an immediate result of the injuries inflicted by the police. One of these, Alfred Linnell, was a socialist workingman and Morris was asked to speak at his funeral on December 18, 1887. He said:

> Our friend who lies here has had a hard life; and he has met with a hard death; but if society had been differently constituted, his life might have been a delightful, beautiful and happy one. It is our business to begin to organize for the purpose of seeing that such things shall not happen.

The mourners then sang a moving song which Morris had written for the occasion. The second and third stanzas, which are probably the best known, read:

> We asked them for a life of toilsome earning,
> They bade us bide their leisure for our bread,
> We craved to speak to tell our woeful learning,
> We come back speechless, bringing back our dead.
> Not one, not one, nor thousands must they slay,
> But one and all if they would dusk the day.
>
> They will not learn; they have no ears to hearken
> They turn their faces from the eyes of fate;
> Their gay-lit halls shut out the skies that darken
> —But lo! This dead man, knocking at the gate.
> Not one, not one, nor thousands must they slay,
> But one and all if they would dusk the day.

The struggles in which he had participated during the past few years were translated by Morris into artistic form in what may well be his most enduring literary creation—published as a serial in *Commonweal* from November 1886 to January 1887—*A Dream of John Ball*.

This great peasant revolt of 1381, two of whose best known leaders were the rebel, Wat Tyler, and a village priest, John Ball, provided a perfect subject for Morris. It allowed him to integrate his extraordinary knowledge of the middle ages, his love of the medieval English countryside, architecture and craftsmanship, his profoundly imaginative understanding of the science of history, and his own brief but deeply felt experience of active class warfare.

But Morris' story is far more than merely an excellent historical recreation. By a simple and subtly handled device he succeeds in giving the reader a sort of double concern and double vision whereby the struggles of 1381 illuminate, and are illuminated with, the development of the next five centuries. The foreknowledge of his own fate is, essentially, shared by John Ball so that instead of a dramatic irony the reader feels a deeper respect for, and identification with, him. And his uninformed but penetrating questions and comments as to what will come after, help the nineteenth century figure, who is his visitor, to a deeper comprehension of his own greater factual knowledge. The impact of this short book can only be felt by reading it as a whole.

The creative literary impulse revived in this work carried Morris through a series of nine more prose romances, one of which was his well-known "utopia," *News from Nowhere*, that appeared as a serial in the *Commonweal* from January to November, 1890. The other romances, from *The House of the Wolfungs* in 1888 to *The Sundering Flood* in 1898, were recreations of Norse tales and myths somewhat like those used in the earlier poetry of *Sigurd the Volsung*.

During this period he continued an active, original, and extraordinarily fruitful approach to the "lesser arts" which he felt were still potentially closer to the people than the sophisticated poetry and easel painting of the time.

In one of his lectures on art he said:

> As things go, it is impossible for any one who is not highly educated to understand the higher kind of pictures. The aspect of this as regards people in general is to my mind much more important than that which has to do with the unlucky artist: but he also has some claim upon our consideration; and I am sure that this lack of the general sympathy of simple people weighs very heavily on him, and makes his work feverish and dreamy, or crabbed and perverse.

And in his ostensibly technical discussions of various "popular arts" he often opened up extraordinary vistas by a few casual remarks. For example he was almost the only one to realize, before the pioneer work of the great sociologist Dr. W. E. B. DuBois in the next century, the decisive effect of African culture on other better known traditions, remarking that Egyptian art was not essentially Oriental but rather Negroid in its initial impulse.

With the publication of *The House of The Wolfungs* in 1888 he developed a new interest in typography that soon led to the foundation of the famous Kelmscott Press and the creation of printed books which recreated in a new industrial form much of the beauty of the best illuminated manuscripts.

This absorbing interest did not, however, detract from his Socialist activities which received fresh encouragement from the unprecedented organization of unskilled and semiskilled workers in the Great Dock Strike of 1888.

He was delighted beyond measure by the strikers' socially conscious manifesto and felt about this strike, as he wrote to *The Daily Chronicle* in reference to the general miners' strike of 1893 some years later, that:

> . . . this change for the better can only be realized by the efforts of the workers themselves. "By us, and not for us," must be their motto. That they are now finding this out for themselves and acting on it makes this year a memorable one indeed, small as is the actual gain they are claiming. So I not only "admit" but joyfully insist on the fact "that the miners are laying the foundation of something better." The struggle against the terrible power of the profit-grinder is now practically proclaimed by them as a matter of principle, and no longer a mere chance-hap business dispute, and though the importance of this is acknowledged here and there, I think it is even yet under rated. For my part I look upon the swift progress towards equality now as certain. . . .

This serene optimism colors the gently pastoral *News from Nowhere* which Morris wrote in 1890, but it was directly occasioned by his irritation at Bellamy's *Looking Backward.*

In reviewing that book when it first appeared in England Morris said with exasperation that Mr. Bellamy appeared to be:

> . . . perfectly satisfied with modern civilization, if only the injustice, misery and waste could be got rid of—which half-

change seems possible to him. . . . Bellamy has his mind fixed on the mere machinery of life.

Another discussion of "The Simple Life Under Socialism" evidently carries on Morris' quarrel with Bellamy between the lines, although he does not choose explicitly to attack a socialist in a non-socialist forum. He says:

> What is simplicity? Do you think by chance that I mean a row of yellow-brick, blue-slated houses, or a phalangstere like an improved Peabody lodging-house; and the dinner-bell ringing one into a row of white basins of broth with a piece of bread cut nice and square by each, with boiler-made tea and ill-cooked rice pudding to follow? No. That's the philanthropist's idea, not mine.

Finally he decided to write his own "Looking Backward" as a corrective to the American one, calling it *News from Nowhere.*

Under the circumstances it is easy to understand why he here, more than anywhere else, overstresses the pastoral quality of the future, the conscious desire for work, the emphasis on beauty and the comparative disuse of machinery, which will be found there.

The tale is none the less a charming one, with much more concrete characterization of places and people than we find in most utopias, and many such characteristic touches as the old man's musing: ". . . even now, when all is won, and has been for a long time, my heart is sickened with thinking of all the waste of life that has gone on for so many years." This sounds very much like Morris' own statement: ". . . it is not revenge we want for poor people but happiness; indeed, what revenge can be taken for all the thousands of years of suffering of the poor?" So too does the old man's devastatingly simple refutation of Fabianism which he declared to be impossible because: "it involves the making of a machinery by those who didn't know what they wanted the machines to do."

This concreteness is no more than we should expect of the far from "Unsocial Socialist" who had, unlike many intellectual revolutionaries, repeatedly declared:

> I don't want to get out from among my fellow men, for with all their faults—which are not theirs but only our own— I like them and want to live and work among them. My

Utopia must be pitched square in the midst of them or nowhere.

Despite the deliberately idyllic picture of the future there is also a highly realistic picture, in the seventeenth chapter, of "How The Change Came," which is startling in its prevision of the advent of fascism.

That spring Morris had his first serious attack of illness and although he rallied and continued to work in many fields for the next five years, he never really recovered his full strength.

In 1891 he wrote a lovely set of verses which his daughter May worked into the embroidered hangings of the beautiful oaken bed at Kelmscott, where he was forced to spend an increasing number of hours during the next few years.

> The wind's on the wold
> And the night is a-cold,
> And Thames runs chill
> 'Twixt mead and hill.
> But kind and dear
> Is the old house here
> And my heart is warm
> 'Midst winter's harm.
> Rest then and rest,
> And think of the best
> 'Twixt summer and spring,
> When all birds sing
> In the town of the tree,
> And ye lie in me
>
> And scarce dare move,
> Lest earth and its love
> Should fade away
> Ere the full of the day.
> I am old and have seen
> Many things that have been;
> Both grief and peace
> And wane and increase.
> No tale I tell
> Of ill or well,
> But this I say,
> Night treadeth on day,
> And for worst and best
> Right good is rest.

In 1893 he completed a systemmatic work in collaboration with Belfort Bax—*Socialism: Its Growth and Outcome*—and he remained active as a speaker for the Hammersmith Socialists and a contributor to Socialist periodicals until the very end.

That year also Morris was unofficially but definitely asked whether he would be willing to accept the poet laureateship, left vacant by Tennyson's death the year before. Of course he refused, but the incident reminds us that Bernard Shaw was by no means alone in his opinion that Morris was "the greatest living master of the English language both in prose and verse."

His last article in *Justice* appeared on May 1, 1896 and that October he died.

The obituary article in *Justice* appropriately quoted two lines from one of his own poems:

> There amidst the world new builded shall our earthly deeds abide,
> Though our names be all forgotten, and the tale of how we died.

(GEORGE) BERNARD SHAW

In 1905, near the midpoint of his long life, (1856-1950) Bernard Shaw wrote to a young man, Archibald Henderson, who later became his official biographer:

> I knew that you thought you were dealing simply with a "new dramatist," whereas to myself, all the fuss about Candida was only a remote ripple from the splashes I made in the days of my warfare long ago. I do not think what you propose is important as *my* biography; but a thorough biography of any man who is up to the chin in the life of his own time as I have been is worth writing as a historical document; and therefore if you still care to face it I am willing to give you what help I can.

This is profoundly true of Shaw himself, not only in the essential sense in which he meant it, but also in the way in which the accidental circumstances of his early years conspired to make him the most typical as well as the greatest of the antibourgeois critical intelligentsia, who were themselves the best representatives of bourgeois culture in its last period.

Like Shakespeare, Shaw was by his personal and class position exposed to the full force of the powerful social currents stirring in his time. Less fortunate than Shakespeare, his genius was formed in a storm apparently raised by the death throes of an old world rather than the birth of a new one.

Shaw's exceptional powers of perception enabled him to catch the still feeble cry of the not yet delivered future and, in some fashion, to respond to it. But it proved impossible for him altogether to transcend the limitations of his age and class, and in his response there is always something tortuous and self-defeating that permits us only a glimpse of what his great genius, freed, might really have created.

In spite of his enormous accomplishment, artistic achievement, public success and personal happiness, Shaw himself often echoed Frank Harris' assertion that he was, somehow, a defeated man.

Like Swift, Shaw was born a Protestant in Ireland and, like Swift, he never felt himself to be in a complete sense either an Englishman or an Irishman, far less an English or an Irish patriot.

Shaw's family was a part of what G. K. Chesterton has aptly called not a settlement nor a colony, but essentially an Anglo-Irish garrison formed by the descendants of transplanted English Protestants. Their dislike and scorn for the Roman Catholic "natives" by whom they were surrounded was matched and kept in check by their fear and resentment of the English government by which they were ruled.

Shaw himself has vividly described the formal Protestantism whose only positive quality was its genteel exclusiveness, and he has told of his own childish conviction that neither Roman Catholics nor shopkeepers could ever hope to meet a gentlemanlike God.

In *16 Self Sketches* Shaw tells how he was first brought to question this snobbish assumption by his mother's interest in music and his discovery that some of the best voices in Dublin belonged to petty tradesmen and were raised in the choirs of the Roman Catholic churches. Characteristically he concludes "Days of My Youth" (1898):

> If religion is that which binds men to one another, and irreligion that which sunders, then must I confess that I found the religion of my country in its musical genius, and its irreligion in its churches and drawing rooms.

The peculiar rootlessness of the society into which Shaw was born was reinforced by the still more peculiarly unintegrated family of which he found himself a very lonely part.

His mother had been rigidly brought up by a deformed and wealthy aunt to erase, through an aristocratic marriage, the stain of the pawnbroker grandfather who had founded the family fortune. She loathed her upbringing and escaped its tyranny by accepting the first proposal she received. This happened to be made by an amiable, middle-aged, poor relative of the wealthy baronet, Sir Robert Shaw. George Carr Shaw was a theoretical teetotaler with a small civil service pension of £60 a year, and a miserable secret dipsomania.

Shaw says: "I can only imagine the hell into which my mother descended when she found out what shabby genteel poverty with a drunken husband is like." A few lapses at the ceremonial dinners to which the young couple were invited estranged them from the husband's family as effectively as the marriage itself had estranged them from the wife's. Shaw and his two older sisters would, he said, have been far less astonished by an earthquake than by the spectacle of their parents receiving visitors or going out to dinner.

He tells how, as a child, he went for a walk one day with his father who playfully pretended to throw him into the canal—and nearly did. Returning home he ran to share with his mother his incredible suspicion that "Papa is drunk." Her bitter reply, "When is he anything else?" was so sudden and violent a destruction of his universe that, he felt, it was only a slight exaggeration to say "I have never since believed in anything or anybody."

Withdrawing from a disappointing world of personal relationships, Shaw's mother found the meaning of life in an absorbing passion for music. Under the direction of a famous orchestral conductor, Vandaleur Lee, with an original method of voice training, she cultivated her really beautiful voice and engaged in its serious though amateur use.

When Lee's brother died the Shaws arranged to share his large house with him. His contempt for doctors, insistence upon open windows, and preference for brown bread and other "health" foods remained a permanent influence in Shaw's life as did, in its own way, his father's whiskey and wistful teetotalism.

After a series of four ineffective gentlemanly schools which did not even teach the Latin that was their sole subject of specialization, Shaw at fifteen entered upon the dignities of a junior clerkship in a land agent's office. This position was secured for him by the recommendation of one of his father's more successful brothers.

Unemotional as are all Shaw's references to his childhood, the extreme coldness and inhuman isolation of that home are apparent in his specific memories of the few occasions on which his mother took him for a walk or gave him supper, spreading the butter thicker on his toast than the servant ever did. He remarked at one time: "We as children had to find our way in a household where there was neither hate nor love, fear nor reverence, but always personality."

And at another, he said: "The fact that nobody cared for me particularly gave me a frightful self-sufficiency."

His mother and sisters left for London soon after his fifteenth birthday and Shaw remained in Dublin with his father for another five years. Mrs. Shaw later confirmed her son's statement that she had never had a picture of him, or received a letter from him, or written one to him, in her life.

Shaw achieved rapid promotion through the defection of the cashier. He was first called upon to fill the position as an emergency stop gap, and did so well that he was then formally inducted into it with a considerable increase in salary. But he was never at all interested in the job and, when it threatened to become permanent in 1876 he suddenly threw it up to follow his mother to London.

The five years of his office life were memorable to him chiefly for the many hours spent with the excellent picture collection in the Dublin National Gallery, to which Shaw eventually left a large part of his fortune. He devoted most of the rest of his leisure to a painful unassisted mastery of the piano. Left by his mother's and sisters' departure in a house suddenly emptied of music Shaw found it a simple necessity that he learn to make music for himself; and did so with characteristic persistence and originality.

In London he quartered himself upon his mother, who was teaching singing for a living, and doggedly set to work to educate himself in libraries, galleries and free concerts, and to become a writer.

In the four years from 1879 to 1883 Shaw wrote five long novels and sent them to as many publishers as he could find stamps to reach. Some fifty years later he said: "When my manuscripts were returned, my mother was not in the least interested. I don't think she ever read a single one of them. She accepted me as a burdensome good-for-nothing, just what she would expect from a son of her husband."

The last of these novels, *An Unsocial Socialist*, was, as the name implies, written after Shaw had discovered, first in socialist meetings and then in a reading of Karl Marx, another medium of adult education. In 1946, presenting the manuscripts of his novels to Dublin, Shaw wrote:

The title of this [last] novel finished me with the publishers. One of them even refused to read it. I had read the first volume of Karl Marx's *Capital,* and made my hero a Marxian Socialist. This was beyond endurance. A clerk for a hero (my first) was not a recommendation; but at least he accepted the world as it was and wore a white linen collar in its social eddies. I was perhaps to be encouraged. But my second, a working electrical engineer crashing through the castes and mastering them: that was distasteful and incorrect. I was going wrong. Then a British Beethoven, careless of his clothes, ungovernable, incomprehensible, poor, living in mean lodgings at an unfashionable address· this was absurd. The next, a prizefighter, wooing and marrying a priggishly refined lady of property was a bit of romance without a child dying in it, but with a fight or two.

But a Socialist! A Red, an enemy of civilization, a universal thief, atheist, adulterer, anarchist and apostle of Satan he disbelieved in!! and presented as a rich young gentleman, eccentric but not socially unpresentable!!! Too bad.

And all the time I did not know that I was being ostracized on social and political grounds instead of, as I thought, declined on my literary demerits, which, as is now clear, were never in question.

The Unsocial Socialist was the first of Shaw's novels to be printed. Published as an unpaid-for serial in a Socialist magazine, *To-Day,* it attracted the attention of William Morris, whose interest surprised and delighted the unknown young author.

The path by which Shaw reached Socialism was, with some differences, a fairly common one for a poor young intellectual in the London of the early eighties. One of his few friends had introduced him to a "debating society called the Zetetical: a junior copy of the once well known Dialectical Society founded to discuss John Stuart Mill's Essay on Liberty when that was new. . . . The tone was strongly individualistic, atheistic, Malthusian, Ingersollian, Darwinian, and Herbert Spencerian."

Feeling compelled to speak, Shaw says he:

> . . . suffered agonies that no one suspected. During the speech of the debater I resolved to follow, my heart used to beat as painfully as a recruit's going under fire for the first time. . . .
>
> I persevered doggedly. I haunted all the meetings in London where debates followed lectures. I spoke in the streets, in the parks, at demonstrations, anywhere and everywhere pos-

sible. In short, I infested public meetings like an officer afflicted with cowardice, who takes every opportunity of going under fire to learn his business.

In the course of this heroic self-discipline Shaw happened on a meeting in the Nonconformist Memorial Hall where Henry George was scheduled to speak. After this lecture:

> It flashed on me then for the first time that "the conflict between Religion and Science," . . . the overthrow of the Bible, the higher education of women, Mill on Liberty, and all the rest of the storm that raged around Darwin, Tyndall, Huxley, Spencer and the rest, on which I had brought myself up intellectually, was a mere middle-class business. . . . The importance of the economic basis dawned on me.

Although Henry George never understood the limitations of his Land Nationalization and Single Tax program as applied to an industrial society, and later attacked those who were actually developing his own fundamental principle, many of the late nineteenth century socialists owed their first interest in economic change to him. William Morris spoke for most of them when he said: "People read between the lines of his book, not his economical errors, but his deep love of truth and his never-ceasing desire to benefit his fellow-men."

A young English critic, Dixon Scott, who died in the first world war at the opening of a promising career, left us an interesting thumbnail sketch of the intellectual ferment in which Henry George's message germinated for so many beside Shaw. Scott was himself a part of the later aesthetic reaction in a generation educated by open Imperialism, and his report of writers still hopeful enough to be socially conscious is all the more vivid for his own wondering disapproval. His essay on Shaw was, as we shall have later occasion to note, remarkable in its concrete analysis of the origin and nature of Shaw's extraordinarily effective dramatic style. Yet in the same essay we also find the peculiar twentieth century interpretation of art as something historically divorced from social movements—a heresy which was, as we have seen, not shared even by the late nineteenth century "art for art's sake" aesthetes.

It was no doubt in reaction against this attitude that Shaw commented, on reading the article: "It was very much as if I had told him the house was on fire, and he had said, 'How admirably monosyllabic!'" For otherwise Shaw was not averse to intelligent technical discussion of his artistry. He was delighted with the perception of a director who advised his cast to treat Shaw's long speeches as arias, not conversations, and he never tired of quoting Einstein's remark that his words were like Mozart's notes, since "every one of them meant something and was exactly in its proper place."

Scott said, in "The Innocence of Bernard Shaw":

> Remember the hour; it was the eve of the eighties, when the arts joined the isms. And Carlyle begot Ruskin, and Ruskin begot Morris, and Morris begot Cunninghame-Graham, and the Carpenters and the Cranes and the Salts; instead of velvet jackets and slap-dash joviality, young artists took to *saeva indignatio* and sandals . . . the arts went over with a rush to their traditional enemy. They joined the majority. They made friends with the mob. Sculptors, painters, and poets, for the first time in English history, deserted the aristocrats and lined up with the proletariat. . . . In place of priding themselves on their immunity from the vulgar hobby known as politics, they began to boom and bleat like a lot of leading articles. . . . They became infidels, atheists, anarchists, cosmogenists, vegetarians, anti-vivisectionists, anti-vaccinationists.

Shaw did, of course, accept many of these peripheral "isms." Several of them, with the unpopular addition of teetotalism, he had already adopted through the influence of childhood memories, and at the opening session of the Shelley Society he had frightened two ladies into withdrawing by declaring himself to be "like Shelley, a Socialist, Atheist, and Vegetarian."

But after reading George's *Progress and Poverty* Shaw began to attend the newly founded Social Democratic Federation, organized by H. M. Hyndman, which Morris was at this time (1883) about to join.

Attempting to defend Henry George's thesis there, he was told that he had no right to discuss such matters unless he had read the first volume of Marx's *Capital*. There had, as yet, been no English translation made, but the Reading Room of the British Museum, where Shaw spent much of his first nine years in London, and to which he finally left a considerable portion of his estate, had a copy of the French translation.

This he promptly read and, as he said in various ways on so

many occasions during the next seventy years: "From that hour I became a man with some business in the world." "I was a coward until Marx made a Communist of me and gave me a faith: Marx made a man of me."

However, at the very outset we find a fatal flaw in his understanding of Marx—a flaw which accounts for so much in his subsequent career, and is itself so easily accounted for in terms of his whole background. Shaw himself summarizes the matter when he tells us of:

> . . . the enormous advantage the founders of the Fabian Society had in their homogeneity of class and age. There were no illiterate working-men among them; there were no born-poor men; there was not five years' difference between the eldest and the youngest.

As we have already seen in his comment on William Morris (see p. 864) as well as in the one above, the vital element of Marxism which the young intellectual could not accept was the importance and potential leadership of the uneducated, uncultured working class. Shaw's own special isolation in both personal and class terms, his long and arduous self-education which he jealously —and no doubt correctly—vaunted as superior to that of most university graduates, and his extraordinary brilliance and verbal facility, all made it almost impossible for him to accept or even conceive of working-class leadership.

This was, of course, true of the intelligentsia as a whole, and particularly of their characteristic political expression in the Fabians. But Shaw was not a typical Fabian. He was much more persistent than the average Fabian in his attempt to spread the gospel; he was indefatigable in his twelve years of committee work and street meetings; he was ready to welcome the Russian revolution in 1917 and eager to understand and applaud its great achievements throughout the late twenties and thirties; he was even able to foresee the "cold war" and the betrayal of the democracies by their reactionary governments in the postwar (World War II) world, saying in 1942:

> The defeat of Germany and her relapse into the Fascism of the British-American type will throw her into the arms of the victorious Allies in a new world-war to suppress Communism.

Yet throughout both his work and life we find the painful, often conscious inner conflict between his sincere desire for the new world, which could be built only by a complete emancipation from bourgeois institutions and mentality, and his inability to break out of the snobbish intellectual isolation of that mentality and its institutions.

Even in the pre-Marxist novels of 1879-1883 we find something of this conflict underlying the strongest scenes.

Alick West in his excellent study of Shaw, entitled *Bernard Shaw: A Good Man Fallen Among Fabians*, summarizes the general theme of the novels in their relation to Shaw's background and early development. He says:

> The exclusion of his family from the respectable society of Dublin, his own solitariness within the family, and his loneliness in London were the immediate experience of life from which Shaw made his novels. . . .
> Yet in the very fact that Shaw wrote the novels, and in the care with which he wrote them, lay a contradiction of this detachment of the hero from his fellows. . . .
> . . . His work expresses not only personal resentments, but also a human vitality which is in conflict with the heroes' negative aloofness.
> . . . It continues in its objectivity the tradition of the classical period of the English novel. . . .
> The conflict is that of the living energy of human beings thwarted by and fighting against stupidity, snobbishness, hypocrisy and tyranny, against the vices of English middle-class respectability.

To a great extent the conflict in the novels was centered, as Shaw described the debates in the Zetetical Society, on issues already clearly decided in London, though not in the Dublin of Shaw's youth. But in several ways, notably in his treatment of the artist, we find a new note introduced. For example, in *Love Among The Artists* (1881), we find a recognition of the strength the artist can draw, not from his self-sufficient aloofness or superior culture, but from his contact with the common people. Madge Brailsford has run away from home to become an actress. She is read out of all good society but she is compensated by beginning to feel "a certain respect for the silently listening, earnest audiences that crowded the house."

Shaw comments:

The ostracism which is so terrible to women whose sole aim is to know and be known by people of admitted social standing cannot reach the woman who is busily working with a company bound together by a common co-operative occupation, and who obtains at least some word or sign of welcome from the people every night.

Although the author's sympathy in this novel swings back to his lonely hero, a more conventionally misunderstood musician living in his "holy garret," yet as West says, linking Shaw's attitude up with the aesthetic revolt which had already led Morris to socialism:

> The artist of contemporary aestheticism as represented by Pater, is a contemplative, who feels little call to right society's wrongs; the artist in Shaw's novels is a fighter. . . .
> It is in the closeness of the artist to the common people that Shaw already at this time reveals a certain kinship with William Morris.

Another novel completed the year before, *The Irrational Knot*, presents a hero, Conolly, a self-educated workingman who has won to success as an engineer. In a development somewhat paralleling that of Jack London's *Martin Eden*, Conolly's thirst for culture leads him to marry a lady. He finds that her culture is that of "the class that does not work," an unreal culture of "made-up faces, trashy pictures, drawling and lounging and strutting and tailoring, drawing-room singing and drawing-room dancing."

Conolly does not, like Martin Eden, physically commit suicide. But despite his undiminished self-sufficiency and Shaw's apparent belief that he has achieved a happy ending, his hero's triumph over his own youthful ideas seems the sort of Pyrrhic victory which suicide snatches from death. Conolly finally says:

> I once thought, like you, that freedom was the one condition to be gained at all cost and hazard. My favorite psalm was that nonsense of John Hay's
> "For always in thine eyes, O Liberty,
> Shines that high light whereby the world is saved;
> And though thou slay us, we will trust in thee."
> And she does slay us. Now I am for the fullest attainable life. That involves the least endurable liberty.

It is significant that four years later Shaw, who had by then discovered Socialism, himself quoted Hay's lines at the head of his first Fabian Tract (Tract No. 2).

West concludes his discussion of *The Irrational Knot* with an analysis which also illuminates much of its author's essential conflict.

> His [Conolly's] rationalism is a defence of his own integrity against emotion that would cloud his sense of values. It is also a weapon of attack that disintegrates the group opposing him by dissipating the collective emotion that helps to unite it: . . .
> On the other hand, rationalism is used to justify the hero's remaining within that class of whose ideology the very conception of the hero as isolated from his environment is an expression. . . . Rationalism gives Conolly the excuse for forgetting that he has been false to the working class, and for posing as the one wise man who has understood that to be free is to obey the main rules of the game—as made by the bourgeois class.

In Shaw's last novel, *An Unsocial Socialist*, the fundamental weakness of his socialism is painfully clear. The very title underlines his failure as soon as we realize that it is intended as sympathetic description rather than satire. As always thereafter, Shaw's picture of the exploitation upon which his society was built is crystal clear. But as always there is no hint of any potential power in the exploited to overthrow their masters or save themselves. In fact, it is only the superior, educated, wealthy individual—the hero, Trefusis—who is really aware of the workers' predicament or able to envisage and desire a remedy. Here we see, in embryo, the logical self-deception which was to proclaim the superman the only savior capable of achieving a better collective society, and even, for a time, to make Shaw find his embodiment in Mussolini.

An article in *The Christian Socialist* for April, 1885 reads almost like a parody of socialism from above, but there seems no doubt that in that prefascist age Shaw meant it seriously.

> Now if Socialism be not made respectable and formidable by the support of *our* class—if it be left entirely to the poor, then the proprietors [capitalists] will attempt to suppress it by such measures as they have already taken in Austria and Ireland. Dynamite will follow. Terror will follow dynamite. Cruelty will follow terror. More dynamite will follow cruelty. Both sides will thus drive one another from atrocity to atrocity. . . . If, on the other hand, the middle class will educate themselves to understand this question, they will be able to

fortify whatever is just in Socialism and to crush whatever is dangerous in it. No English government dare enact a Coercion Law or declare a Minor State of Siege against the Radical [left wing Liberal] party.

But Shaw was never quite as unreal or unsocial a revolutionary as his novel's millionaire hero. In 1884 he had already begun to apply for membership in the Social Democratic Federation. Hesitating about the final step "because I wanted to work with men of my own mental training" he came across the newly organized Fabian Society's first tract, *Why Are The Many Poor?*

The very name of the society convinced him "that there was a good title which immediately suggested an educated body." He attended the next meeting, and was elected a member on September 5, 1884.

Shaw says, in his *16 Self Sketches:*

> I at once applied for membership of the Democratic Federation, but withdrew my application on discovering the newly founded Fabian Society, in which I recognized a more appropriate *milieu* as a body of educated middle-class intelligentsia: my own class in fact. Hyndman's congregation of manual-working pseudo-Marxists could for me be only hindrances.

At this time the Fabians considered themselves Marxists and did, in actuality, accept a very unrealistic mechanical materialism. They spoke glibly of the "fact" that just as gunpowder had meant the death of feudalism, so the capitalist system could not long survive the invention of dynamite; they felt that the truth of scientific socialism had only to be clearly presented to the exploited workers in order to precipitate an immediate revolution under Fabian leadership; and they agreed in setting the probable date of the revolution "no later than 1889"—the centenary anniversary of Bastille Day!

The shock of "Bloody Sunday" in Trafalgar Square (p. 867 ff.) November, 1887 marked a turning point for the Fabians to whose executive board Shaw had been elected in January, 1885. The events leading up to that demonstration, and the unprovoked police attack which killed at least three men, have already been briefly described in the discussion of William Morris.

It is noteworthy that the Fabians had until this time participated with other Socialist groups in the struggle for freedom of speech at street meetings which had begun in 1885 and led up to the Trafalgar Square Demonstration. Shaw, commenting on the change in his organization's attitude, said in Fabian Tract No. 41:

> In 1885, a conflict with the Government arose over the right of free speech at Dodd Street. . . . But nobody dreamt of giving the Fabian delegate to the Vigilance Committee [composed of representatives of the S. D. F., of Morris' Socialist League, and other organizations] the strict injunctions which bind the delegates of 1892 to use all their influence to avert a conflict with the police. He was simply to throw himself into the struggle on the side of the Socialists, and take the consequences.

The consequences on November 17, 1887 proved so much more serious than the Fabians had ever supposed possible that the event precipitated a reevaluation of their entire policy. They were, moreover, discouraged by the fact that they had been putting "Socialism . . . clearly before the working classes" for almost three years and had not yet seen any signs that those classes were ready "to concentrate the power of their immense numbers in one irresistible organization." Under the circumstances the rout which led Morris to a realistic analysis of the need for organization and training, led the Fabians to seek a safer road to socialism, one which would make it unnecessary for them to depend on unworthy working-class allies.

Shaw's first Fabian Tract in 1884 had begun with the statement: "That, under existing circumstances, wealth cannot be enjoyed without dishonour, or foregone without misery." And it had concluded: "We had rather face a Civil War than such another century of suffering as the present one has been."

At the meeting held immediately after "Bloody Sunday" Mrs. Besant, a member of the executive, proposed a return to Trafalgar Square next Sunday. Her moving speech was greeted with enthusiastic cheers. Shaw arose to discuss the motion, and drew so vivid a picture of the slaughter which would ensue should the Fabians provoke the government to use their machine guns, firing 250 rounds a minute, that there was, finally, only one vote for the motion. Even its seconder abstained! One critic has convincingly suggested that in a sense all Shaw's subsequent work resolved itself into the effort to achieve socialism without facing the necessity of reversing the defeat in Trafalgar Square.

In 1888 Shaw presented another report to the Fabian Society—

The Transition to Social Democracy—which outlined their new policy of "permeation" and "gradualism."

The "success" of this policy in its creation of England's "socialist" Labour Party and the postwar (World War I) cabinet of Ramsay Macdonald is a matter of history. The fine English film, *Fame Is the Spur*, gives an excellent picture of that ambiguous achievement. But we should not overlook the unsolved conflict which made Shaw conclude his report:

> . . . if we feel relieved that the change is to be slow enough to avert personal risk to ourselves; if we feel anything less than acute disappointment and bitter humiliation at the discovery that there is yet between us and the promised land a wilderness in which many must perish miserably of want and despair: then I submit to you that our institutions have corrupted us to the most dastardly degree of selfishness.

Incidentally here, as so often in his moments of deepest emotion, he was developing an idea suggested by William Morris. Morris had, in a speech at Oxford five years earlier, concluded:

> It may be that it will not be hard to keep the working classes down for awhile—possibly for a long while. The hope that this may be so I will say plainly is a dastard's hope.

It was not only in a rhetorical peroration that Shaw showed his reluctance to give up the hope of what Morris called "educating for revolution." The partial expression of this hope in Shaw's dramatic work we will examine shortly. But he also continued, somewhat inconsistently, to carry on the strenuous thankless task of day-to-day propaganda which had been gratefully abandoned by almost all the other Fabians. As he himself describes it:

> This went on for about twelve years [until his marriage in 1898] during which I sermonized on Socialism at least three times a fortnight average. I preached whenever and wherever I was asked. It was first come first served with me: when I got an application for a lecture I gave the applicant the first date I had vacant, whether it was for a street corner, a public-house parlor, a market place, the economic section of the British Association, the City Temple, a cellar or a drawing room. My audiences varied from tens to thousands. I expected opposition but got hardly any. Twice, in difficulties raised by attempts of the police to stop Socialist street meetings (they

always failed in the end because the religious sects, equally active in the open air, helped the Socialists to resist them), I was within an ace of going to prison. The first time was in Dodd Street in dockland, where the police capitulated on the morning of the day when I volunteered to defy them. The second time, many years later at the World's End in Chelsea, a member of a rival Socialist Society disputed the martyr's palm with me, and, on a division, defeated me by two votes, to my secret relief. My longest oration lasted four hours in the open air on a Sunday morning to crowds at Trafford Bridge in Manchester. One of my best speeches was delivered in Hyde Park in torrents of rain to six policemen sent to watch me, plus only the secretary of the Society that had asked me to speak, who held an umbrella over me. I made up my mind to interest those policemen, though as they were on duty to listen to me, their usual practice, after being convinced that I was harmless, was to pay no further attention. I entertained them for more than an hour. I can still see their waterproof capes shining in the rain when I shut my eyes.

Shaw's discovery of Marx had had other less predictable consequences besides those outlined above. A well-known dramatic critic, William Archer, had been intrigued to notice a red-haired young man in the Reading Room intently studying a French copy of *Das Kapital* and a complete musical score of Wagner's *Tristan und Isolde*. Both works were then almost utterly unknown in England and Archer, who was the first to translate Ibsen's plays, was interested in making the acquaintance of a fellow explorer.

He soon learned Shaw's circumstances, appreciated his literary ability, and realized the overwhelming shyness which had prevented his making any attempt to secure journalistic work.

Archer himself was much in demand for book reviews and special articles in addition to his regular column of criticism. He began to hand these assignments over to his protégé and in 1885 Shaw finally earned £112, or just about enough to cover his modest expenses for the year.

In 1886 Archer was asked to take on the job of art critic for *The World*, on which he was already dramatic critic. Instead of accepting he secured Shaw's appointment.

In 1888 another friend succeeded in having Shaw appointed as music critic to a new paper, *The Star*. Under the pseudonym of Corno di Bassetto, Shaw wrote an extraordinary weekly column for over two years. He indicated the theory—and practise—that made his work valuable in a statement several years later when, over the signature G.B.S., he had begun a similar weekly column of music criticism in *The World*.

> It is my special merit that I have always seen plainly that in this Philistine country a musical critic, if he is to do any good, must put off the learned commentator and become a propagandist, versed in all the arts that attract a crowd, and wholly regardless of personal dignity. I have propagated my ideas on other subjects at street corners to the music of the big drum; and I should not hesitate to propagate Wagnerism there with a harmonium if I were sufficiently master of that instrument. . . .

As he had fought for the new men in music, he had also supported them in art, writing with real understanding of the much abused impressionists:

> . . . being the outcome of heightened attention and quickened consciousness on the part of its disciples, it was evidently destined to improve pictures greatly by substituting a natural, observant real style for a conventional, taken-for-granted ideal one.

He praised Madox Brown "because he had vitality enough to find intense enjoyment in the world as it really is, unbeautified, unidealized, untitivated in any way for artistic consumption."

Of still greater importance than his enthusiasm for either Wagnerism or Impressionism was his "discovery" of Ibsen in 1889. To this was due a whole series of major literary and dramatic events from *The Quintessence of Ibsenism* in 1890 to Shaw's first play in 1892 and, in all probability, much of his career in the theatre thereafter.

One of the many Socialist lectures he gave during this period must, however, be quoted in part at least, before we turn to the drama. During 1888, in a talk entitled "The Impossibilities of Anarchy," which was published a few years later, Shaw made a statement about the nature of the capitalist state. We should keep this clearly expressed understanding of his in mind as a touchstone while we examine the series of powerful but ambiguous plays which lead up to *Major Barbara* in 1905.

> I fully admit and vehemently urge that the State at present is simply a huge machine for robbing and slave-driving the poor by brute force. . . . the primary function of the

policeman . . . is to see that you do not lie down to sleep
in this country without paying an idler for the privilege; that
you do not taste bread until you have paid the idler's toll in
the price of it; that you do not resist the starving blackleg
[scab] who is dragging you down to his level for the idler's
profit by offering to do your work for a starvation wage.
Attempt any of these things, and you will be haled off and
tortured in the name of law and order, honesty, social
equilibrium, safety of property and person, public duty,
Christianity, morality, and what not, as a vagrant, a thief, and
a sinner. . . . And his [the soldier's] primary function is to
come to the rescue of the policeman when the latter is overpowered. Members of Parliament . . . parsons quoting scripture for the benefit of the squire; lawyers selling their services
to the highest bidder at the bar, and maintaining the supremacy of the money class on the bench; juries of employers
masquerading as the peers of proletarians in the dock; University professors elaborating the process known as the education of a gentleman; artists striving to tickle the fancy or
flatter the vanity of the aristocrat or plutocrat; workmen doing
their work as badly and slowly as they dare so as to make the
most of their job; employers starving and overworking their
hands and adulterating their goods as much as they dare;
these are the actual living materials of those imposing abstrac-
tions known as the State, the Church, the Law, the Constitution, Education, the Fine Arts, and Industry. Every institution
. . . is corrupted by the fact that the men in it either belong
to the propertied class themselves or must sell themselves to it
in order to live. All the purchasing power that is left to buy
men's souls with after their bodies are fed is in the hands of the
rich; and everywhere, from the Parliament which wields the
irresistible coercive forces of the bludgeon, bayonet, machine
gun, dynamite shell, prison and scaffold, down to the pettiest
centre of shabby-genteel social pretension, the rich pay the
piper and call the tune. . . . With this hint I leave the matter,
in the full conviction that the State, in spite of the Anarchists,
will continue to be used against the people by the classes until
it is used by the people against the classes with equal ability
and equal resolution.

Another passage from a symposium on "The Socialist Ideal,"
in which Morris discussed art, Henry Salt literature, and Shaw
politics, is important to our understanding of Shaw's later dramatic
work. In this discussion, published in *The New Review*, 1891,
Shaw said:

Confront me with a respectable audience, and my sense
of humour gets the better of me; the truths they ignore assume

flippant and fantastic disguises in spite of me: the deportment of the truth teller sinks to the occasion and I become egotistical and shameless.

. . . The change will not be made by them but by men with whom they dare not walk arm-in-arm down Piccadilly. . . .

The well-to-do thrust the poor down into the cellar and make them rats—to nibble with their million teeth at the foundation pillars of society. And they are making fair progress, I assure you.

By that time Shaw had joined and perhaps rather eclipsed Archer as a champion of Ibsenism, and after a number of lectures on *The Doll's House, Ghosts,* and other plays of Ibsen's he had in 1890, written *The Quintessence of Ibsenism.*

Most of his lectures were presented to Socialist groups, and since Ibsen had always declared himself outside of politics, an enterprising reporter sought to secure his repudiation of the socialist viewpoint in an interview for a conservative paper.

On August 28, 1890, a letter of Ibsen's appeared in *The Daily Chronicle* correcting the distorted report of his attitude. This letter read, in part:

. . . I was surprised that I, who had made it my chief life-task to depict human characters and destinies, should, without conscious or direct intention, have arrived in several matters at the same conclusions the social-democratic moral philosophers had arrived at by scientific processes.

What led me to express this surprise (and, I may here add, satisfaction) was a statement made by the correspondent to the effect that one or more lectures had lately been given in London, dealing, according to him chiefly with *A Doll's House.*

From his earliest years art had, for Shaw, provided the meaning and warmth which is supplied for most men by religion and intimate personal relations. In Ibsen he found the high seriousness and technical mastery he demanded from art, together with a direct progressive attack on the evils of contemporary life. Although he had not yet really thought of play writing as his own medium, he already had a feeling of the wasted possibilities of the theatre. It should, he felt, take itself seriously "as a factory of thought, a prompter of conscience, an elucidation of social conduct, an armoury against despair and dullness, a temple of the ascent of Man."

Yet the English drama, never a great social art form since the early seventeenth century was, at the end of the nineteenth century, almost completely meaningless.

Famous actor-managers played fragmentary and distorted versions of those Shakespearean plays whose heroes offered them a "vehicle" for personal display, and the rest of the dramatic fare was a cheap mixture of translated French farce or skillfully meretricious intrigue, and sentimental English melodrama.

When a small band of enthusiasts initiated The Independent Theatre with *Ghosts*, while two other noncommercial groups presented *Rosmersholm* at the Vaudeville Theatre and *Hedda Gabler* in a private experiment, there was a hysterical outcry from the pulpits, the universities and the newspapers.

Shaw summarized the current dramatic criticism, supplemented in many papers by leading articles and editorials attacking Ibsen. *The Daily Telegraph* for March 1891, he reported, compared *Ghosts* "to an open drain, a loathsome sore unbandaged, a dirty act done publicly, or a lazar house with all its doors and windows open." Ibsen's work was described as, "Bestial, cynical, disgusting, poisonous, sickly, delirious, indecent, loathsome, fetid, literary carrion, crapulous stuff, clinical confessions." One writer concluded, "It is difficult to expose in words the gross and almost putrid indecorum of this play." Another urged that "proceedings should be taken against the theatre . . . under the Act for the suppression of disorderly houses."

After this sensational opening the public-spirited producer Grein, wished to present a contemporary English masterpiece, feeling certain that there were many which had been summarily rejected by commercial managers. Shaw recalled two acts of a play he had written in 1885—originally intending a collaboration with Archer who had volunteered to supply the plot while his friend wrote the dialogue.

Archer's patience had been sorely tried when Shaw declared that he had written a whole act and not yet come to the plot, which he had, moreover, forgotten. However, Archer was prevailed on to repeat the plot, but altogether refused cooperation when, a few days later, Shaw appeared to say he had completed only the second act but had used up all the plot and needed some more to go on with.

This play Shaw hastily finished, drawing heavily on his experiences collecting rents in a Dublin land office agency—experiences which, he said, he had altogether forgotten until Henry George's talk brought them into focus. The result was *Widowers' Houses*. Shaw described its first presentation in his *16 Self Sketches:*

> Two performances were all he [Grein] could afford. The first provoked a sensational mixture of applause and hooting, which I countered successfully in a speech before the curtain. A unanimously favorable reception of the second was followed by a press discussion of the play which lasted a fortnight. I was denounced as a pamphleteer void of dramatic faculty; but all the stage effects I had planned came off perfectly; and this was what convinced me that I was a born master of the theatre.

The play is dramatically effective; its dialogue already shows considerable use of the special and inimitable Shavian style he was rapidly perfecting; and the material is more explicitly and wholly social in nature than that of almost any other play. And yet the impact of the work, powerful as it is, is somehow less powerful than it should be. Here, as so often in the later plays, the whole is something less than the sum of its parts.

Shaw's own analysis in the preface gives us the clue to this puzzling lack. He says, very truly, that:

> The notion that the people in *Widowers' houses* are abnormally vicious or odious could only prevail in a community in which Sartorius is absolutely typical in his unconscious villainy.

Then he continues to explain:

> Now the didactic object of my play is to bring conviction of sin—to make the Pharisee who repudiates Sartorius . . . recognize that Sartorius is his own photograph.

And no one can doubt that this objective is largely achieved. But its very statement reveals its inadequacy. Shaw's drama, like his Fabianism, is impregnable in its exposure of the existing evil. But when the audience is convicted of sin, what then? Again Shaw's drama, like his Fabianism, permits no real answer, Alick West summarizes the matter when he says:

But, like Trefusis in *Unsocial Socialist* he [Shaw] is more concerned to bring conviction of sin than to inspire to a new life; for he shows no escape from sin. The whole manner of posing the dramatic issue . . . confronts Trench not with the real choice of fighting or not fighting capitalism, but with an unreal choice of participating or not participating in exploitation. . . .

It does not stir the collective energy of the audience; it makes them shrink from contact with one another. Therefore it is wrong to call it a great play; but only by comparison with great plays can it be judged.

A far from socially conscious critic, Ronald Peacock, verifies from his own point of view this conclusion about the audience's reaction. He says in an interesting study of Shaw in *The Poet in The Theatre*:

As they [Shaw's plays] draw to a close they do not give the feeling of a building being completed; the forces which propel them are indeed bent all the other way, towards demolition. These works do not, after their emergence in time, solidify, as the great dramas do, into a shape for the memory; they leave us without the retrospective vision of form achieved.

And Shaw himself concurred when, in his preface to the published play (1892), he remarked:

I offer it as my own criticism of the author of *Widowers' Houses* that the disillusion which makes all great dramatic poets tragic has here made him only derisive; and derision is by common consent a baser atmosphere than that of tragedy.

In his very early and exceptionally valuable *George Bernard Shaw*, G. K. Chesterton is also clearly referring to *Widowers' Houses* when he says:

I hear many people complain that Bernard Shaw deliberately mystifies them. I cannot imagine what they mean; it seems to me that he deliberately insults them. . . .
The prosperous English Philistine complains that Mr. Shaw is making a fool of him. Whereas Mr. Shaw is not in the least making a fool of him; Mr. Shaw is with laborious lucidity calling him a fool. G. B. S. calls a landlord a thief; and the landlord, instead of denying or resenting it, says, "Ah, that

fellow hides his meaning so cleverly that one can never make out what he means, it is all so fine spun and fantastical."

And E. Strauss drives this point home in *Bernard Shaw: Art and Socialism*. He says there, after quoting Chesterton's statement:

> As the same landlord is very sharp-witted when he suspects a serious attack on his material interests, the bluntness of his perception in this case may be accepted as weighty evidence against the dangers of Shaw's attacks for his intended victims.

The Philanderer, a rather forced and uncertain comedy, produced in 1893, is almost the only one of Shaw's plays to depend for its humor on topical material. The opposition of "Ibsenites" and "anti-Ibsenites" and the rather heavy play on "unwomanly women" and "unmanly men" dates it too obviously for permanence, and it was the one play of his own that Shaw came thoroughly to dislike.

The same year also saw a major work in Shaw's only other really socialist play—*Mrs. Warren's Profession*.

Her profession was large-scale organized prostitution, and the play was banned by the censor, allegedly for its presentation of sex but actually for its presentation of business. Chesterton says, referring to the eighteenth century origin of the bill under which the censor acted (see p. 294):

> Fielding was a free writer; but they did not resent his sexual freedom; the Censor would not have objected if he had torn away the most intimate curtains of decency or rent the last rag from private life. What the Censor disliked was his rending the curtain from public life.

And the same motivation accounted for the late nineteenth century application of the censorship bill to Shaw.

Mrs. Warren's Profession is in its conception one of the most powerful and shocking plays that has ever enriched the English theatre. It is also, in its development, one of the worst examples of an author's deliberate distortion of his own creations.

In this play for almost the first time in two and a half centuries a dramatic writer broke the tacit conspiracy of silence about the world outside the middle class. Ibsen had already presented searching studies of the unmentionable horrors within that life, but the lower limit of his world was really marked by the petty bourgeoisie. He is therefore completely successful only when dealing with problems like those of *The Doll's House* or *Ghosts* which can, to some extent, be truthfully developed within the limits of a single class. With all its power such a play as *The Enemy of The People* too often talks nonsense as soon as its hero touches on politics or economics.

Although he always held that Ibsen was the greater dramatist of the two, Shaw was fully aware that he had, in this respect, gone a step further than the writer he admired. He said of Ibsen's audiences:

> In the theatre of Ibsen we are not flattered spectators killing an idle hour with an ingenious and amusing entertainment: we are "guilty creatures sitting at a play."

But when *Widowers' Houses* was published, together with *Mrs. Warren's Profession*, in a volume called *Unpleasant Plays*, he said of his own audiences:

> For the first time on any stage, as far as I know, the audience saw the citizen with his share in the guilt of our industrial system brought home to him as "guilty creatures sitting at a play."

Yet even Hamlet, with whom Shaw frequently and illuminatingly identified himself, had a plan for the next step after his play should have "unkennelled all occulted guilt." Shaw had none beside the barren exclamation "So uncle, there you are!" And, like Hamlet, he was driven to strange shifts to conceal the fact.

That becomes most painfully apparent in *Mrs. Warren's Profession*. Alick West concludes his lengthy and closely reasoned analysis of Shaw's deliberate anticlimax in that play by saying:

> The play is divided against itself. Its potential greatness, its moments of actual greatness, come from its theme of the conflict between the bourgeois ideology of individualistic, rationalist self-sufficiency and the individual's realization of his part in society. But the theme is blurred because Shaw's Fabianism blurs the character of capitalism. . . . By uniting worker and capitalist in one and the same person [Mrs. Warren] he obliterates the fundamental cleavage in class society. He opposes his heroine neither as capitalist to the working class nor as worker to the capitalist class. He opposes her as pure virgin to the impurity of capitalism in general. He thus

reverts to the bourgeois ideology of individual on the one hand and society on the other from which he was trying to free himself.

The desire for such freedom is an underlying impulse of the play; and in that great scene when Vivie is transformed by the realization that her very life comes from a woman of the people, the freedom is momentarily achieved.

The next three plays, *Arms and The Man*, *Candida*, and *You Never Can Tell*—later published with the first three as *Plays Pleasant and Unpleasant*—mark a significant retreat.

The first of these, under all its excellently planned and executed foolery, gives us a bitter parody of Shaw's own genuine idealism, deliberately confused with an imitative sentimentality, and therefore easily defeated by a Philistine opportunism. This opportunism also parodies Shaw's own genuine realism—and flatters the audience into thinking they share it. The insolent serving girl, Louka, rebuffs her would-be husband when he offers to buy a caress with a part of a tip won by his servility, saying, "Yes; sell your manhood for 30 levas, and buy me for 10! Keep your money." Yet she too is made ridiculous in a pseudoromantic conversation with the discredited idealist Sergius, whom Shaw had originally planned as a "comic Hamlet."

Although he himself had skillfully contrived it so, Shaw was bitterly disappointed when an enthusiastic first night audience failed to sense his own statement of values, hidden between the lines, and cheered the play as a satirical farce. He wrote a fellow playright:

> . . . the clever people feel the discrepancy between the real and theatrical feeling only as a Gilbertian satire on the latter, and, appreciating the wit well enough, are eager to show their cleverness by proclaiming me as a monstrously clever sparkler in the cynical line. . . . I had the curious experience of witnessing an apparently insane success, . . . and of going before the curtain to enormous applause, the only person in the theatre who knew that the whole affair was a ghastly failure.

The next play, *Candida*, produced the same year (1894) was his first really popular—and commercial—success. Shaw himself referred to the heroine as the prototype of "the virgin mother" but his clear-sighted friend, Beatrice Webb, declared that she was nothing but a "sentimental prostitute." Most women would, I think, tend to agree with Mrs. Webb.

Here the clergymen, whose Socialism his wife effectively dismisses as ridiculous and unreal, is given lines which might well have been taken directly from one of Shaw's own autobiographical sketches:

> Reverend Morell: "The Hoxton Freedom Group want me to address them on Sunday morning. . . . Just like Anarchists not to know that they can't have a parson on Sundays! . . . Say I can come on Mondays and Thursdays only. . . . Have I any lecture on for next Monday?"
> Proserpine: "Tower Hamlets Radical Club."
> Rev. Morell: "Well, Thursday then?"
> Proserpine: "English Land Restoration League."
> Rev. Morell: "What next."
> Proserpine: "Guild of St. Matthew on Monday. Independent Labor Party, Greenwich Branch, on Thursday. Monday, Social-Democratic Federation, Mile End Branch. Thursday, first Confirmation Class. Oh, I'd better tell them you can't come. They're only half a dozen ignorant and conceited costermongers without five shillings between them."
> Rev. Morell: ". . . Come, Miss Proserpine: can't you find a date for the costers? What about the 25th? That was vacant the day before yesterday."
> Proserpine: "Engaged. The Fabian Society."
> Rev. Morell: "Bother the Fabian Society!"

Incidentally, this passage contains almost the only reference to the Fabian Society in all of Shaw's half a hundred plays.

You Never Can Tell, keyed throughout to the tone of high farce, presents an even more explicit self-betrayal and ends on a note of despair masked by hysteria.

Mrs. Clendening, an "advanced woman" of the late sixties, has anticipated Ibsen's Nora by leaving her proprietary husband, and England, some twenty years before the opening curtain. More foresighted than Nora, she took her children with her and her daughter Gloria has been educated as an agnostic, rationalist and feminist.

Returning to England, Gloria is prepared to suffer social ostracism and obloquy in order to carry on her mother's work. Mrs. Clendening, meeting a former colleague, announces their joint determination for martyrdom and is shocked to find, first, that all her old opinions are now perfectly safe and respectable and, second, that Gloria's generation has actually taken to Socialism and that Gloria herself is likely to be plunged head over heels in it before the month is out.

But at the first skillfully contrived approach of a lover Gloria succumbs to the "Life Force," and bitterly reproaches her mother for having taught her "Nothing—nothing!" about the *only* important thing in life. When her suitor admits he has, before meeting her, made love to others she rushes at him "with her fist clenched." As West says:

> The end of the play is horrible. Gloria, who had looked most eagerly and passionately into the future and within a month was to have been up to her ears in the socialism of which she will now never hear, is swept off into the fancy-dress dance, not by Valentine, but by her symbolic husband, the masterful money-making, bullying Bohun, . . . Despite the freshness of its comedy, . . . the play seems a senseless, intolerable farce, in which all the promise of life comes to nothing.

And Chesterton, writing from a very different view point in 1909, nevertheless concurred:

> In Gloria's collapse before her bullying lover there is something at once cold and unclean; it calls up all the modern supermen with their cruel and fishy eyes.

It is interesting to note in passing that the program of the play, at its first presentation in 1896, featured a cover picture by Aubrey Beardsley and that in the same year Shaw contributed an essay "On Going to Church" to the famous *Yellow Book* of which Beardsley was art editor. The same first production had a short play by W. B. Yeats, *The Land of Heart's Desire,* used as a curtain raiser. The bohemian rebellion of the "decadents," the nostalgic nationalism of the Irish theatre, and the social realism of the new "problem plays" have been so completely separated in most literary histories that it is well to remind ourselves they all felt themselves, as indeed they were, related expressions of discontent with late nineteenth century industrial civilization.

The Devil's Disciple, produced in 1897, was immediately popular, especially in the United States. The American Revolution provided the background for its action which skillfully combines all the excitement of melodrama with a light satire of melodrama.

The same year saw a long Socialist article on "The Illusions of Socialism" contributed to an anthology, *Forecasts of the Coming Century* or *Hand and Brain*. It also saw a significant statement in Shaw's letter to Ellen Terry:

> In this world you must know *all* the points of view, and take One, and stick to it. In taking your side, don't trouble about its being the right side—north is no righter or wronger than south—but be sure that it is really *yours*, and then back it for all you are worth.

Another letter five months later in May, 1897, gives us an even more significant comment on *Mrs. Warren's Profession:*

> It's much my best play; but it makes my blood run cold: I can hardly bear the most appalling bits of it. Ah, when I wrote that, I *had* some nerve.

When Shaw had joined the Fabian Society over ten years before he had also induced a young acquaintance, an economist Sidney Webb, to desert the zetetical debating society and join with him. Sidney Webb remained all his life Shaw's closest friend and when he married the very wealthy and progressive Beatrice Potter, who was herself a leading Fabian, she too soon became an intimate friend of Shaw's.

In 1893 or 1894 Shaw had, through the Webbs, met an Irishwoman, Charlotte Payne-Townshend, whom Beatrice had interested in working with the Fabians.

Staying with the Webbs during the summer of 1896 he wrote Ellen Terry:

> This time we have been joined by an Irish millionairess who has had cleverness and character enough to decline the station of life—"great catch for somebody"—to which it pleased God to call her, and whom we have incorporated into our Fabian family with great success. I am going to refresh my heart by falling in love with her. I love falling in love—but, mind, only with her, not with the million; so someone else must marry her if she can stand him after me.

Evidently she couldn't. When Shaw developed a serious necrosis of the bone after a badly treated foot injury she took the then unconventional step of visiting him at his home in May, 1898.

Finding him in a room covered with dust, littered with old papers and unarranged books, and decorated with the cold fried eggs he had forgotten to eat for lunch, she insisted on his coming to her house where he could be properly cared for. (He was living with his mother and sister whom she had imagined devotedly nursing him, but neither of them had stepped into his room for over a week.)

Shaw protested that since she was living alone her reputation would be hopelessly compromised by a bachelor protégé, and the upshot was a marriage to his "green-eyed millionairess" on June 1, 1898. He asked her to arrange a trust fund for his mother which would make her independent, should anything happen to him, but his own income was already considerable and within a few years had become even larger than his wife's.

The complete though temporary breakdown of his health before his foot injury was altogether healed, and the general change of habits and living routine caused by his marriage made this a definite end of the first period of Shaw's maturity.

Thereafter there were no street meetings, no real contact with the working class, and few socialist lectures outside of the highly intellectual Fabian circle. His return to health was accompanied by a growing professional concentration on the theatre, and an increased emphasis on vegetarianism and other such superficial means of marking the difference between himself and the other members of the wealthy bourgeois society to which he now belonged.

Shaw's vegetarianism was never altogether a matter of sentimental principle or a simple humanitarian response. It was essentially a gesture of nonparticipation like that Trent had attempted to make in *Widowers' Houses*.

Just as Trent could cheerfully give up the prospect of wealth to avoid sharing the guilt of the bourgeoisie, but could not imagine giving up his own moderate income for that purpose, so Shaw could cheerfully give up those things society left optional. He did without meat because he could not do without money and, like Kingsley, transferred most of his emotional horror from the basic ugliness of human exploitation to other more symbolic ugliness.

He himself says: "Some day, I hope, we shall live on air, and get rid of all the sanitary preoccupations which are so unpleasantly aggravated by meat-eating." And Chesterton aptly remarks:

"That fixed fancy sticks to the mind; that Bernard Shaw is a vegetarian more because he dislikes dead bodies than because he likes live ones."

Shaw continued to work hard as a County Councilman until he failed of reelection in 1904 and the book he wrote then—*The Commonsense of Municipal Trading*—he always considered, or at least referred to, as one of his most important works. But it is clear he got little inspiration out of his conscientious devotion to what Morris contemptuously called "gas and water socialism."

In 1904 Shaw wrote to his biographer, Henderson:

> My latest book, *The Common Sense of Municipal Trading*, is in its way one of the best and most important I have ever written. I beg you, if you write about my "extraordinary career," to make it clear to all young aspirants, that its extraordinariness lies in its ordinariness—that, like a greengrocer and unlike a minor poet, I have lived instead of dreaming and feeding myself with artistic confectionery.

More important for us in his nondramatic work between 1895 and 1905 was his dramatic criticism.

In 1894 Frank Harris who had then just bought the *Saturday Review* had appointed Shaw as its dramatic critic, and in 1907 a two-volume selection of his critiques was published by the American, James Huneker. Later Shaw himself published a three-volume selection under the title *Our Theatres in the Nineties*.

As we should expect, this is a brilliant and provocative analysis of much beside technical dramaturgy. Shaw wrote a contemporary colleague in 1895:

> The best-established truth in the world is that no man produces a work of art of the very first order except under the pressure of a strong conviction and definite meaning as to the constitution of the world.

Nor does this primary concern for the "message," the propaganda value of the plays he was reviewing, at all lessen Shaw's urgent concern with their essential literary and dramatic value. On the contrary he, like Gorky, realized that the reason one had to be so uncompromising in one's judgment of art was precisely because what it said was of such fundamental importance to life. As he remarked in a discussion of his own critical work:

> People have pointed out evidence of personal feeling in my notices as if they were accusing me of a misdemeanour, not knowing that a criticism written without personal feeling is not worth reading. It is the capacity for making good or bad art a personal matter that makes a man a critic.

Over forty years later he reaffirmed this, saying:

> The few born critics cannot help themselves: they know what good work is, crave for it, are tortured by the lack of it, will fight tooth and nail for it, and would do so even if the managers were their fathers and the prima donnas their sweethearts.

And in the preface to his *Dramatic Opinions and Essays*, when these were published together in 1907, he explained more fully:

> I must warn the reader that what he is about to study is not a series of judgments aiming at impartiality, but a siege laid to the theatre of the nineteenth century by an author who had to cut his own way into it at the point of the pen and throw some of its defenders into the moat.
>
> Pray do not conclude from this that the things hereinafter written were not true, or not the deepest and best things I know how to say. Only they must be construed in the light of the fact that all through I was accusing my opponents of failure because they were not doing what I wanted, whereas they were often succeeding very brilliantly in doing what they themselves wanted . . . ; and I brought everybody—authors, actors, managers—to the one test: were they coming my way or staying in the old grooves.

What exactly it was that he wanted his contemporaries to do we can gather not only from his own plays—and Ibsen's—but from such perfectly serious if emphatic statements as:

> The theatre is as important as the Church was in the Middle Ages, and much more important than the Church in London now. [It can be] a factory of thought, a prompter of conscience, an elucidator of conduct, an armoury against despair and dullness, and a temple of the Ascent of Man.

Since the particular kinds of realistic drama the social theatre of the nineties emphasized have often been referred to as "problem plays," it is worth noting Shaw's own definition of this form, contributed to a symposium on "The Problem Play" in 1895. He said there:

> The material of the dramatist is always some conflict of human feeling with circumstances: so that, since institutions are circumstances, every social question furnishes material for drama. But every drama does not involve a social question, because human feeling may be in conflict with circumstances which are not institutions, which raise no question at all, which are part of human destiny.

Whatever the inadequacies we may find in the final account of his life's work—and Shaw himself after the first world war said repeatedly, although not consistently, that despite his great accomplishments he had failed completely to effect any part of the social change which was his sole real objective—we must never forget his achievement in the regeneration of the English theatre. Chesterton summarized this:

> He has brought back into English drama all the streams of fact or tendency which are commonly called undramatic. They were there in Shakespeare's time; but they have scarcely been there since until Shaw. . . . In this great sense Shaw has brought philosophy back into drama—philosophy in the sense of a certain freedom of the mind. This is not a freedom to think what one likes (which is absurd, for one can only think what one thinks); it is a freedom to think about what one likes, which is quite a different thing and the spring of all thought. Shakespeare (in a weak moment, I think) said that all the world is a stage. But Shakespeare acted on the much finer principle that a stage is all the world. . . . A variety of solutions in philosophy is as silly as it is in arithmetic, but one may be justly proud of a variety of materials for a solution.

One other important critical work dates from this period, *The Sanity of Art*.

A German journalist, Max Nordau, had written an idiotic and irritating book on the degeneracy of genius—a thesis revived in more scholarly and sophisticated form by much reactionary literary criticism today. An anarchist, Benjamin Tucker, who then financed and edited the American magazine *Liberty*, was so outraged by this attack on art that he wrote Shaw offering to pay the highest rate ever received by any Englishman—"even Mr. Gladstone"—for a newspaper article, if Shaw would write a reply. Shaw refused to accept any payment for this useful and congenial task, but utterly demolished Nordau as well as his contention in a long open letter addressed to Tucker, and reprinted in pamphlet form as *The Sanity of Art.*

The controversial material is still interesting, but of even greater significance is Shaw's statement about propaganda, which he refers to as "journalism," and art. This reads:

> Journalism [propaganda] can claim to be the highest form of literature; for all the highest literature is journalism. . . . The writer who aims at producing the platitudes which are "not for an age, but for all time" has his reward in being unreadable in all ages; whilst Plato and Aristophanes trying to knock some sense into the Athens of their day, Shakespeare peopling that same Athens with Elizabethan mechanics and Warwickshire hunts, Ibsen photographing the local doctors and vestrymen of a Norwegian parish, Carpaccio painting the life of St. Ursula exactly as if she were a lady living in the next street to him, are still alive and at home everywhere among the dust and ashes of many thousands of academic, punctilious, most archaeologicaly correct men of letters and art who spend their lives haughtily avoiding the journalist's vulgar obsession with the ephemeral.
>
> . . . nothing that is not journalism will live as long as literature, or be of any use whilst it does live.

A similar note is sounded in his review of Tolstoy's *What is Art* in 1898. He quotes Tolstoy's definition of art: "an activity by means of which one man, having experienced a feeling, intentionally transmits it to others." Then he comments: "This is the simple truth: the moment it is uttered, whoever is really conversant with art recognizes in it the voice of the master."

But that year saw the third of his major critical essays, *The Perfect Wagnerite,* which substitutes a mystical idealist interpretation of history in terms of an age of faith (the past), an age of reason (the present), and an age of will (the future) for the Fabians' earlier historical materialism, of which Shaw now began to speak so patronizingly. He said, for instance, in Fabian Tract No. 41:

> We had a convenient stock of imposing generalizations about the evolution from slavery to serfdom and from serfdom to free labor. . . . We gave lightning sketches of the development of

the medieval craftsman into the manufacturer and finally into the factory hand. . . .

Caesar and Cleopatra, produced in 1898, also makes clear Shaw's lack of the real sense of history, which was Morris' great gift. It emphasizes, too, his inability to think of intelligence or power in any but highly self-conscious and articulate forms.

Not only is the great man here taken to be the cause of historical events; he is also a highly critical figure with progressive twentieth century intellectual standards, while the conservative first century British islander (who still dyes himself blue before going into battle) is interpreted as simply a stupid figure with conventional nineteenth century standards.

Furthermore the real secret of greatness lies, according to Shaw, in the great man's essentially passionless nonhumanity. Only once, in *St. Joan,* was Shaw able to grasp the conception of the "hero" as a man so deeply rooted in the progressive humanity of his own time that (sometimes without himself realizing it) he can become an effective factor in helping humanity to move forward. And even in that play the epilogue deliberately controverts this deeper understanding and takes us back to the idealist hero whose kingdom is not really of this world.

The same idea, that true wisdom is inconsistent with passionate desire or justified anger, underlies the effective melodrama of *Captain Brassbound's Conversion* produced in 1899. Here Captain Brassbound is the son of a native woman of Morocco. His English uncle (a lord chief justice) has cheated her of the estate she should have inherited from her husband, and ever since her death her son has vowed revenge. Fate delivers his uncle into his hand, but a charming and implausible relative, Lady Waynefleet, persuades him that revenge is vulgar. The captain finally agrees, saying: "My uncle is no worse a man than myself—better, most likely; for he has a better head and a higher place." The apparent change from melodramatic sentiment to realistic common sense reads well and acts well, but one cannot help agreeing with Chesterton:

> Of course, it was very natural in an aristocrat like Lady Cicely Waynefleet to wish to let sleeping dogs lie, especially . . . under dogs. Of course it was natural for her to wish everything to be smooth and sweet-tempered. But I have the obstinate question in the corner of my brain, whether if a few

Captain Brassbounds did revenge themselves on judges, the quality of our judges might not materially improve.

There is, too, an ominous note struck when Lady Cicely replies comfortingly to the Captain's angry "Damn you! you have belittled my whole life to me," with: "Oh no. I am sure you have done lots of kind things and brave things, if you could only recollect them. With Gordon [in the Sudan] for instance? Nobody can belittle that." Shaw then, without a trace of satire, describes the way in which the captain gratefully kisses her hand while her eyes fill with tears!

Yet even this hardly prepares us for the imperialistic pamphlet *Fabianism and the Empire* in 1900 in which Shaw justified and supported the Boer war.

Here we have a willfully unrealistic view of the disinterestedness of imperialism which can be compared only with Walter Lippman's fatuous exposition of the disinterestedness of big business, written in 1929, as an uneasy apologetic for his own betrayal of his youthful socialism.

Shaw says, in part:

. . . democracy in the popular sense of government by the masses, is clearly contrary to common sense. . . . The result is that our ccnstitution, whatever it may be nominally, is in fact a plutocracy. . . . The primary conditions of Imperial stability are not the same throughout the Empire. The democratic institutions that mean freedom in Australasia and Canada would mean slavery in India and the Soudan. . . .

. . . Great Power, consciously or unconsciously, must govern in the interests of civilization as a whole; and it is not to those interests that such mighty forces as gold-fields, and the formidable armaments that can be built upon them, should be wielded irresponsibly by small communities of frontiersman. Theoretically they should be internationalized, not British-Imperialized; but until the Federation of the World becomes an accomplished fact we must accept the most responsible Imperial Federation available as a substitute for it.

Naturally socialists of all kinds, including many Fabians, were outraged by this stand, and Shaw wrote a long personal letter to Hyndman on April 28, 1900, attempting to justify it. Here we find a germ of much that emerges in one of his most powerful and troubling plays, *Major Barbara*, a few years later.

Now I am a pure natural-history student, and feel no more indignation against a Rockefeller or a Rhodes than I do against a dog following a fox. I know the capitalist—a poor devil who follows the slot of money without the faintest consciousness of himself either as a beast of prey or as a captain of industry. Ask him to give you an idea of himself; and he will stutter out something about the Golden Rule and our Lord Jesus Christ with perfect sincerity. He preys on the proletariat as a cat preys on mice, through his instinct for gain. Even though you would restrain him from such predaciousness, that is no reason why you should not take him up and stroke him and pet him if he is a nice animal (which he sometimes is), instead of allowing your instinct for righteousness to transform you into a talented terrier and worrying him. It is out of that sort of worrying that the whole evil comes. You will resist moral evil. So, please observe, will Rockefeller. But, you will say, Rockefeller is robbing the poor all the time. So are you. So am I. Society leaves us no personal alternative at all. But in no ways calls us for sacrifices to expiate the evil. If Rockefeller *deserves* hanging (an expression which belongs to your moral system), so does every man who would do the same as Rockefeller if he got the chance, say 99 per cent. of his indignant fellow men. You cannot hang everybody, including yourself; and yet moralism leads to that or nothing.

This goes a step further in Shaw's seemingly complete surrender of the fight for socialism. We have seen how he had, almost at the outset of his career, given up any hope that the poor would move toward it under pressure of their material necessities. In fact, he later actually said that the Fabian propaganda in the eighties was so ineffective, popularly, because working people were preoccupied with their increasing material problems and socialist agitation was "overlooked in the excitements of the unemployed agitation."

Yet he had then said that Marx had been "a revelation" and "the turning point in my career" because "he rent the veil. He opened my eyes to the facts of history and civilization, gave me an entirely fresh conception of the universe, provided me with a purpose and mission in life." And Marx had done all this, he concluded, although "His abstract economics, I discovered later, were wrong." (Shaw thought that Jevons' theory of marginal utility provided a better formulation for prosocialist argument than Marx' surplus value.) How had Marx done all that, then? Simply by appealing so powerfully to "a generous passion" in the rebellious intellectual sons of the middle class—their "passion of hatred" for all the "accursed middle-class institutions that have starved, thwarted, misled and corrupted us from our cradles."

In 1900, however, he was informing Hyndman that this passion of social indignation was an outworn fallacy and a hindrance to progress! But though this rationalization was to take even more significant form in *Major Barbara* it was by no means Shaw's final stand. In 1935, for example, he declared:

> William Morris is described by Wells as a poet and decorator. That is not the significance of William Morris to us; there are plenty of poets and decorators about. Morris's significant specialty was his freely expressed opinion that idle capitalists are "damned thieves." And the word "damned" was more than mere decoration. One misses that note in Clissold; [Wells' "progressive" capitalist hero] yet it is the key-note of Socialism.

From 1901 to 1903 while Shaw was occupied with *Man and Superman*, a number of his earlier plays were revived. Although by no means indifferent to success he was unhappily aware that it was only a small and unvalued part of himself which he had expressed in them. He said, comparing the reception of the *Pleasant Plays* and *Three Plays for Puritans* with the earlier rejection of *Mrs. Warren's Profession*:

> No author who has ever known the exultation of sending the Press into an hysterical tumult of protest, of moral panic, of involuntary and frantic confession of sin, of a horror of conscience in which the power of distinguishing between the work of art on the stage and the real life of the spectator is confused and overwhelmed, will ever care for the stereotyped compliments which every successful farce or melodrama elicits from the newspapers.

In many respects, indeed, his comedies from 1894 on had actually travestied his ideas. Strauss, discussing this strange phenomenon of a man who mocked in his central work the cause he was still devoting himself to, says:

> And the skilful technique of the author not only exposes the weakness of the Socialist parson, [Morell in *Candida*, 1894] but also undermines the beliefs behind the individual character.

An even more startling development was Shaw's apparently irresistible urge to endow the most contemptible blackguards which his powerful imagination and his keen observation could produce, with at least a smattering of Socialist phraseology which was, of course, debased by mere contact with such characters. . . . This applies to . . . Drinkwater (*Captain Brassbound's Conversion* 1899), to the Social Democrats and Anarchists among the brigands in *Man and Superman*, (1903) to Gunner (*Misalliance* 1910) and, above all, to Snobby Price (*Major Barbara* 1905).

. . . The mere fact that allusions to Socialism are in all these cases very far-fetched and, from an artistic point of view, utterly misplaced, shows the author's special intention in introducing them.

. . . The simplest explanation of this curious fact is to be found in Bernard Shaw's resentment against a movement which has deeply disappointed him.

In *Man and Superman* Shaw explicitly turned from considering concrete social problems, even ambiguously, to the beginning of his preoccupation with a "Life Force." This mystical force was exemplified for him in almost all women's desire for procreation, and in a very few men's desire for artistic or intellectual achievment.

In his hero's "Revolutionist's Handbook," included as an appendix when the play was published, Shaw was already very specifically contradicting his earlier assumption of the "responsible" nature of imperialism. He says:

> We have demanded the decapitation of the Chinese Boxer princes as any Tartar would have done; and our military and naval expeditions to kill, burn, and destroy tribes and villages for knocking an Englishman on the head [in protection of their own property] are so common a part of our Imperial routine that the last dozen of them has not called forth as much pity as can be counted on by any lady criminal. . . . The world will not bear thinking of to those who know what it is. . . .

But after discussing the futility of offering Fabianism as a remedy, the handbook says hopelessly:

> Are we then to repudiate Fabian methods, and return to those of the barricades, or adopt those of the dynamitard and the assassin? On the contrary, we are to recognize that both are fundamentally futile.

What then is the answer? Eugenics!

> The only fundamental and possible Socialism is the socialization of the selective breeding of Man: in other terms of human evolution.

This play, too, betrays the intellectual arrogance which assumes a permanent division between the manual worker and the thinker. In the long scene in heaven, supposed to take place in the interlude between two acts and seldom presented except as a separate playlet, the Life Force says:

> I want to know myself and my destination, and choose my path; so I have made a special brain—to grasp this knowledge for me as the husbandman's hand grasps the plough for me.

One can imagine what Morris, for whom the central function of socialism was the destruction of this inhuman division, would have said!

John Bull's Other Island in 1904 was written for, but rejected by, Yeats' Irish National Theatre. It is, as Chesterton says, Shaw's "only play with a geography." In this play, which is essentially a tragedy all the more tragic for its author's complete acceptance of defeat, Father Keegan sees with absolute clarity the inhumanity underlying Broadbent's practical geniality. Nevertheless he concludes:

> Well, perhaps I had better vote for an efficient devil who knows his own mind and his own business than for a foolish patriot who has no mind and no business.

This is an even more complete surrender than the lonely withdrawal in which Keegan echoes Shaw's long outgrown preface to his first novel, *Immaturity* (1879):

> Whether it be that I was born mad or a little too sane, my kingdom was not of this world: I was at home only in the realms of my imagination, and at my ease only with the mighty dead.

The next year, 1905, brought one of the most powerful and distressing of Shaw's plays. Before its appearance Max Beer, a German socialist, had in a way anticipated the path Shaw's thinking was for many years to follow—although never consistently or willingly. Beer had written:

> Having no objective guide, no leading principle to go by, Shaw necessarily arrives at hero-worship—at the hankering after a Superman to guide mankind. I have noticed the same mental development in several continental critics. . . . They began with Social Democracy, passed through the Ibsen period, worshipped *The Enemy of the People*, finally becoming adherents of Nietzsche in theory and of Bismarck or some other social imperialist in practice. . . . The Revisionists or Fabians, say: "Socialism is, before all, an administrative problem; it is not a class struggle, but a clever management of public affairs! It is the Superman in local government."

And in *Major Barbara* Shaw distorted his most searching and most deeply felt analysis of contemporary capitalist society into an attempt to recommend a sort of idealized fascism.

The dramatic construction of the play is a magnificent one; the characterization is perhaps the finest Shaw ever achieved; and the humor is on his own most meaningful level. The modern stage has rarely if ever trembled to lines more devastating than Barbara's, when she learns that the Salvation Army, through which she was working for the salvation of the poor, was for sale like every other capitalist institution and had, long ago, been bought by the rich. Her cry when she finds her army an instrument in the hands of the big armament manufacturers and whiskey distilleries is:

> Undershaft and Bodger: their hands stretch everywhere: when we feed a starving fellow-creature, it is with their bread, because there is no other bread; when we tend the sick, it is in the hospitals they endow, if we turn from the churches they build, we must kneel on the stones of the street they pave. As long as that lasts, there is no getting away from them.

But how does she conclude that terrible denunciation? Her last sentence is, incredibly, "Turning our backs on Bodger and Undershaft is turning our backs on life." And her solution is—marriage to the man who will inherit the armaments factory!

Even Ruskin had asked, "If capital is necessary, are capitalists so?" And Morris' John Ball had demanded, "What else shall ye lack when ye lack masters?"

West concludes a long and illuminating analysis of *Major Barbara* with:

... and the curtain comes down on a great play gone wrong.

For it is a great play in the scope of its conception. It boldly takes as its theme what it is Shaw's merit to have made the theme of contemporary English drama—men and women as members of capitalist society. There is in it the vision, movingly and powerfully expressed, that capitalism degrades human relations into money relations. Beneath its wild anarchism there is a frantic desire to destroy capitalism. But Shaw's Fabianism made him choose the wrong hero, the capitalist himself.

While the period which we are considering actually ends at this point, it is necessary for us very briefly to refer to Shaw's most important later work, and to summarize even more briefly the most significant developments in his thinking during his last half century of life.

In 1906 the Shaws bought the New Rectory, Ayot St. Lawrence, which they renamed Shaw's Corner. At first used only for long week-ends and holidays, it finally became their permanent home. Shaw had cared little for travel but his wife enjoyed it, and after *St. Joan* was completed in 1923 they spent some part of almost every year abroad, until just before the second world war.

However the major part of their time after the first world war was passed in tranquil and hard working domesticity at Ayot St. Lawrence.

Mrs. Shaw died in September, 1943 and Shaw acknowledged the thousands of sympathetic messages he received with a card:

> Mr. Bernard Shaw has received such a prodigious mass of letters on occasion of his wife's death that, although he has read and values them all, any attempt to acknowledge them individually is beyond his powers. He therefore begs his friends and hers to be content with this omnibus reply, and to assure them that a very happy ending to a long life has left him awaiting his own in perfect serenity.

Misalliance (1909-1910) is funny, but it is also sad. The millionaire is a weaker but still dynamic and sympathetic version of Undershaft, and his crude energy and magnetism are supplemented by the mellow aristocratic wisdom of a retired colonial governor, who says "Yes, Democracy reads well. But it doesn't act well, like some people's plays."

There is an absurdly sentimental, cowardly, and ignorant

pseudosocialist who attempts a revenge assassination of his dead mother's generous millionaire lover, but bungles that like everything else, and is saved from the police by the kindness of the millionaire's wife. Yet one cannot help realizing how much it must have hurt Shaw to hear a bourgeois audience laughing with relief at such lines as these, skillfully made ridiculous by the situation.

> I enter and enter, and add and add, and take money and give change, and fill cheques and stamp receipts; and not a penny of that money is my own; not one of those transactions has the smallest interest for me or anyone else in the world but him; and even he couldn't stand it if he had to do it all himself. And I'm envied, aye, envied for the variety and liveliness of my job by the poor devil of a bookkeeper that has to copy all my entries over again.

And what a deep feeling of guilt he must have suffered to express his condemnation through the same ineffective and ignorant little clerk in the hysterical outburst below, ended by Mrs. Tarleton's comfortable "Oh, did you ever hear such silly nonsense."

> Girl students in Russia go to the gallows; let themselves be cut in pieces with the knout or driven through the frozen snows of Siberia sooner than stand looking on tamely at the world being made a hell for the toiling millions. If you were not all skunks and cowards you'd be suffering with them instead of battening here on the plunder of the poor.

In *Androcles and The Lion* (1911-1912) we find Shaw returning both to the character and the problem of Barbara Undershaft. (The same character later forms a large part of his most famous heroine, Joan of Arc.)

But Lavinia in *Androcles and The Lion* refuses to believe that, "Turning our backs on Undershaft and Bodger [or its Roman equivalent] "is turning our backs on life." She refuses to sacrifice even a pinch of incense to the imperial power, declaring:

> When men who believe neither in my gods nor in their own . . . drag me to the foot of an iron statue that has become the symbol of the terror and darkness through which they walk, of their cruelty and greed, of their hatred of God and their oppression of man . . . I cannot do it.

Yet as Strauss points out in his discussion of the play, this refusal to accept the world as it is, is here made on an idealistic level "carefully pruned of every practical application to social problems." He also makes the interesting comment that Ferrovius too offers a solution of sorts when he, in effect, repeats Barbara's decision: "The Christian God is not yet, . . . meanwhile I must serve the gods that are, not the God that will be."

Heartbreak House, the most unShavian of Shaw's plays, was begun in 1913 and completed by 1916, although it was not produced until 1921.

It is, clearly, much influenced by Chekhov by whose plays Shaw was deeply impressed at his first acquaintance with them in those prewar years. When he saw the *Cherry Orchard,* while writing *Heartbreak House,* he said, "I feel as if I want to tear up all my plays and begin over again."

Here for the first time since the early *Unpleasant Plays* (and perhaps *Candida*) the capitalist is presented as a despicable figure rather than a superman. And the whole mood is one of despair, with a cultured, witty, charming group of people whose best hope is for a dramatic and sudden death. Yet the central figure, the erratic and half drunk old inventor Captain Shotover, speaks out more clearly than any Shavian protagonist since Mrs. Warren herself.

When Elie repeats some of Undershaft's ideas about the sin of poverty, to justify herself for seeking a mercenary marriage, Captain Shotover declares:

> I can't argue; I'm too old: my mind is made up and finished . . . old-fashioned or new-fashioned, if you sell yourself, you deal your soul a blow that all the books and pictures and concerts and scenery in the world won't heal!
> . . . You are looking for a rich husband. At your age I looked for hardship, danger, horror and death that I might feel the life in me more intensely. I did not let the fear of death govern my life; and my reward was, I had my life. You are going to let the fear of poverty govern your life; and your reward will be that you will eat, but you will not live.

Again, in a conversation with his handsome, courageous and useless son-in-law, Shotover sounds a more profound truth than Shaw has ever before permitted a character to state.

> Shotover: Are we to be kept forever in the mud by these hogs to whom the universe is nothing but a machine for greasing their bristles and filling their snouts? . . . We must

win powers of life and death over them both. I refuse to
die until I have invented the means.
Hector: Who are we that we should judge them?
Shotover: What are they that they should judge us? Yet they
do, unhesitatingly. There is enmity between our seed and
their seed. They know it and act on it strangling our
souls. They believe in themselves. When we believe in
ourselves, we shall kill them. . . .
Hector: They are too stupid to use their power.
Shotover: Do not deceive yourself: they do use it. We kill the
better half of ourselves every day to propitiate them. The
knowledge that these people are there to render all our
aspirations barren prevents us having the aspirations.

The play was probably too sharply critical of Britain's rulers to
find a producer during the war, and Shaw himself had so seriously
offended respectable public opinion with his article *Commonsense
About the War,* published at the end of 1914, that he would probably not have been able to secure a theatre in any event.

The pamphlet sold 75,000 copies in two months. Yet it was not
exactly an antiwar stand that Shaw took. He himself, in 1923, accurately stated his purpose in writing the article:

> I was fiercely determined, like Ramsay Macdonald, that the
> diplomatists and militarists who brought about the war should
> not get credit for having saved the world from the peril which
> they had in fact created. They were pretending—or allowing
> greenhorns and journalists to pretend for them—that the war
> was a war to end war, an act of pure defense against an unprovoked attack by Germany, a crusade against tyranny, oppression, imperialism and foreign domination led by a peaceful,
> unambitious, unaggressive, idyllic England: and in that faith
> many young men enlisted, fought and died.

But again, as in *Widowers' Houses,* his purpose was merely to
convince the audience of sin, not to arouse them to resist it. The
conclusion Shaw came to, and acted on in writing propaganda and
recruiting material for the government during the next four years,
was that one should not deceive oneself with belief in any ethical
difference, but that one should nevertheless fight for "one's own"
side. He said:

> I felt as if I were witnessing an engagement between two
> pirate fleets, with, however, the very important qualification
> that as I and my family and friends were on board British

ships, I did not intend the British section to be defeated if I could help it.

Chesterton had evidently been prophetic in his remark, in 1909, on *Caesar and Cleopatra*:

> Before the temple of Mars, Tolstoy stands and thunders, "There shall be no wars"; Bernard Shaw merely murmurs, "Wars if you must; but for God's sake, not war songs."

Shaw himself told the story of a speech he made in support of a Labour Party candidate some years after the war when a soldier in the audience said to him: " 'If I had known all that in 1914, they would never have got khaki on *my back*.' My reply was: 'That is precisely why I did not tell you in 1914.' "

Yet although Shaw had altogether discounted the possibility, and would perhaps hardly have welcomed its realization in England, he *had* said: "No doubt the heroic remedy . . . is that both armies should shoot their officers and go home to gather in their harvests in the villages and make revolutions in the towns."

When in 1917 the Russians did just that there was a storm of vituperation and abuse in which most English socialists joined. At a stormy meeting of the Fabian Society Bernard Shaw sat in unwonted silence, and then arose abruptly to terminate the discussion with the flat statement, "We are socialists. The Russian side is our side."

That same year he wrote to the United States:

> Dear Frank Harris,—
> Good news from Russia, eh? Not quite what any of the belligerents intended, any more than Bismarck intended to make France a republic in 1870; but the Lord fulfils Himself in many ways. It is probably not the last surprise He has up His sleeve for us.
> Yours ever,
> G. Bernard Shaw
>
> I say that Life Force is God, but the Englishman objects to this. He says that Life Force is a foreigner, while God is an Englishman. That is where we disagree.

Yet in 1919 he had forgotten the illiterate Russian soldiers who "voted with their feet" and said in his *Peace Conference Hints*:

The people can no more govern than they can write plays or use the infinitesimal calculus. Even government by the consent of the governed is impossible as long as people are so uneducated politically that they will not consent to be governed at all, and must therefore be governed, under one pretence or another, by main force. But government for the people is possible, and is the goal of democracy.

Nevertheless he watched the establishment of socialism in the Soviet Union with the keenest sympathy and interest, and largely because of the new realistic hope he found in it he finally wrote his most affirmative play, *St. Joan*, in 1923.

Back to Methusalah, produced two years earlier, is one of the very few Shavian plays which are neither readable nor actable. He wrote it in the conviction with which the war had left him:

> The circumstances of this catastrophe confirmed a doubt which had steadily grown in my mind during my forty years of public work as a Socialist: namely, whether the human animal, as he exists at present, is capable of solving the social problems raised by his own aggregation, or, as he calls it, his civilization.

The play substitutes extreme longevity for the breeding of supermen as the sole hope of civilization! There is a certain extraneous interest in its probable inception from a casual remark of William Morris: "Surely if people lived five hundred years instead of three score and ten they would find some better way of living than in such a sordid loathsome place [as London], but now it seems to be nobody's business to try to better things—isn't mine, you see, in spite of all my grumbling."

But *St. Joan* is another matter entirely. Here in many scenes we get a real feeling of the movement of history and of the hero's essentially representative quality. Here we find—until the whole tenor of the play is flatly contradicted by the epilogue—a powerful identification of the truly great individual, real progress, and the common people.

Joan's defiance of the reactionary court and church rings out with the accent of the great antifeudal struggles:

> Remember the day your knights and captains refused to follow me to attack the English at Orleans! You locked the gates to keep me in; and it was the townsfolk and the common

people that followed me, and forced the gate, and shewed you the way to fight in earnest.
And her last words before the nobles she led and the king she crowned sell her to her enemies are:

> I will go out now to the common people, and let the love in their eyes comfort me for the hate in yours. You will all be glad to see me burnt; but if I go through the fire I shall go through it to their hearts for ever and ever. And so, God be with me!

In 1926 at a seventieth birthday dinner Shaw said:

> Karl Marx made a man of me. Socialism made a man of me. Otherwise I should be like so many of my literary colleagues who have just as much literary ability as I have. Socialism made a man of Mr. Wells and he has done something. But look at the rest of the literary people and you will understand why I am inordinately proud of being a Socialist.

That this statement was, for all the inadequacies of Shaw's Socialism, literally true, is evidenced in any careful consideration of the bulk of his plays. Not only the subject matter, and the essential tension often underlying the most trivial plots, but the very language itself shows in every line the effect of Shaw's political life.

Dixon Scott, who was himself inclined to regard such participation unworthy of, and hampering to, an artist, nevertheless made an extraordinarily brilliant and valuable analysis of its result in the style of Shaw's plays.

Scott's article on "The Innocence of Bernard Shaw" was reprinted in a memorial volume, *Men of Letters*, after the author's death in the first World War. It says, in part:

> It [Shaw's style] was an instrument built expressly for cut-and-thrust platform work; and every irrelevant qualification or charm was ruthlessly threshed out of its texture. . . . Conditioned absolutely by the special nature of the campaign he had in view—submitting to every qualification without shuffling, and taking advantage of every license without shame—it is the very finest example in the whole range of English letters of prose written to be uttered with physical forcibleness on the rapid levels of man-to-man speech, and yet retaining, unsuspected, all those subtle powers of balance, of rhythm and

picturesqueness, whose aid must be employed before all defences can be carried and which steal triumphantly into the citadel of the mind of the hearer through insidious emotional doorways whilst the colloquialisms keep the common sense engaged. . . .
Lightened of all adjectives, nimble with nouns, turning categories into keyboards, he is wont to ripple us a run and, avoiding vowels in order to get the snap of consonants, it rattles past at a rate that makes the best of Swift seem slow, and pelts the brain with stinging drops like driving hail. . . . And just as an athlete is more beautiful than an aesthete, so it grows more sensuous the more austere it becomes, positively practising a bodily seductiveness by seeming wholly to rely on an appeal to cold-blooded intelligence.

Finally, in 1931, Shaw accepted an invitation to visit the Soviet Union. At a reception in his honor on his arrival in Moscow he said:

If the experiment which Lenin started succeeds, it will be the opening of a new world era. If the experiment fails, then I shall have to take leave of you when I die with something of melancholy; but if the future is the future as Lenin saw it, then we may smile and look forward to the future without fear. . . .
I look round and see all these faces with a new look on them, a look you cannot see yet in the capitalist West, but which I hope to see everywhere some day.

And at the farewell dinner he declared: "I am leaving the land of hope, and returning to the lands of despair."
To the leading questions of a reporter who met him in Warsaw, eager for some word of condemnation to print, Shaw replied uncompromisingly:

It is torture to get back to Capitalism. When you have seen Bolshevism on the spot, there can be no doubt that Capitalism is doomed.

Four years later, commenting on H. G. Wells' report of his interview with Stalin in 1935 Shaw remarked:

. . . I have long been laughed at in Russia as "a good man fallen among Fabians"; but the two old hyperfabian Fabians, Webb and Shaw, have stuck to their guns . . . whilst the sentimental Socialists have been bolting in all directions from Stalin, screaming, like St. Peter, "I know not the man."

He criticized Wells' underestimation of the Soviet accomplishment, saying:

> First, the Russian statesmen have discovered that in a really free country—that is to say, a country which really belongs to its people . . . the response to this freedom is so far greater than could have been conceived without practical demonstration, that Russia has been able to effect social transformations in ten years that under our system would take a hundred, if indeed the mere proposal of them had not involved immediate seclusion in a mental hospital for their advocates. It is this revelation of reserves of organizing and administrative ability in the masses which has impressed Stalin so deeply with the indispensability of "the people" as a political force.

Urged to visit the United States he responded in what then seemed wild hyperbole: "Americans do not know that I should not be allowed to land if I told the truth about my political and religious convictions."

But despite these and many similarly unconventional insights Shaw continued to shock his admirers with new tangents as startling as his early support of the Boer war had been. The great Soviet critic, Lunacharsky, said in 1931:

> Bernard Shaw has rendered great services to the nascent new world. Yet, if the fighters for the new world should consist only of people like Bernard Shaw, this new world would never be born.
> Therefore, our attitude towards Bernard Shaw is this. We have before us a brilliant man, but "he is not a warrior in either camp; only a chance guest." When Bernard Shaw is a guest in the bourgeois camp, we see on his face an impression of humour mingled with scorn, and when he pays a visit to the camp of the fighters "for the cause of liberty," we see on his face an expression of sympathy that is mingled with humour, because it seems to him that these fighters are rather ponderous, dogmatically credulous people.
> We realise that Bernard Shaw is our ally. Yet, we know quite well that he may sometimes execute some amazing zigzag (he has done so occasionally, indulging in witticism at our expense) and do so in a manner calculated to evoke a satisfied grunt from the bourgeoisie.

We find some of the most amazing of these zigzags in his complete misunderstanding of fascism, his continued underestimation of the possibilities of democracy, and his persistently unrealistic idealist interpretation of history. This reliance on the magical power of words could lead him to say, with genuine disappointment:

> For 48 years I have been addressing speeches to the Fabian Society and to other assemblies in this country. So far as I can make out, those speeches have not produced any effect whatsoever.
> I have solved practically all the pressing questions of our time, but . . . they keep on being propounded as insoluble just as if I had never existed.
> I have produced no permanent impression because nobody has ever believed me.

In more sanguine moods Shaw would, with equal lack of realism, assert:

> I haven't done too badly. When you consider who we were who set out to reverse the basis of society: a few refugees working in the British Museum, a few spouters, a few saints, and one or two cracked writers and artists who spoiled their limited chances of ever making a livelihood, and now capitalism is reeling and rocking. I know too much about boxing to take for granted that capitalism is going to be counted out. What seems a deadly blow often makes no impression. It's had to take some hard knocks; *The Fabian Essays,* my *Intelligent Woman's Guide,* and soon my new book, *A Gentle Swing to the Left.*

But at 81 he was still a pioneer. The Federal Theatre, America's short-lived but magnificent experiment with a truly national theatre based on the people themselves, at first found it difficult to get permission for the production of plays by leading dramatists. Many of these evidently feared it would compromise their reputations to have their plays produced by a relief project. Others were willing to release their plays only upon specific guarantees of well-known professional casts. One of the best known dramatists in the United States withdrew his consent when he learned that a play of his was being presented by the Harlem unit.

Finally the directors of the project determined on a bold stroke.

They wrote directly to the most famous living dramatist and asked his permission to use all his plays—including the latest as yet unproduced one—and to present them, where possible, with interracial casts. Shaw promptly replied in a letter (hitherto unpublished) which was evidently one of those his secretary complained of his typing himself (see reproduction of letter following).

22nd May 1937

I cannot let you have On The Rocks until Mr. Milton Shubert has given it a send off by his New York production, or until his failure to produce next autumn makes an end of his contract with me.

Now as to the rest of the repertory, will you kindly, to start with, put clean out of your head all the silly legends that the American newspapers keep repeating about me, and regard me, if you possibly can, as a fellow creature?

I know quite well what you are up against in this undertaking. It is useless to hope that you can find "groups with a high degree of skill in acting and direction" everywhere. You may not be able to find them anywhere. The plays will be murdered more or less barbarically all the time. That happens on Broadway too; and you must take what you can get in the way of casting and direction just as if you were a fashionable manager. So far from avoiding Negro casts you will be very lucky if you can get them; for Negroes act with a delicacy and sweetness that make white actors look like a gang of roughnecks in comparison.

You must leave the Theatre Guild out of account, and deal directly with me. The Guild people are my very good friends; but their object in life is to prevent anyone except themselves doing my plays; and their interference is quite unnecessary. I want them to perform my plays and not to complicate my business affairs.

They tell me that your theatre, being a federal institution, is unable to move without miles of red tape being consumed, and that money can be extracted from it only after signing nine receipts. They also seem to think that every production will be a separate transaction involving a special licence and weekly payments and acknowledgments. That will never do for me. As long as you stick to your fifty cent maximum for admission, and send me the accounts and payments quarterly, or half yearly if you prefer it, so that I shall have to sign only four or two receipts a year, and forget all about you in the meantime, you can play anything of mine you like unless you hear from me to the contrary as in the case of On The Rocks, which will soon be at your disposal like the rest.

Can you arrange things in this fashion for me?

Any author of serious plays who does not follow my example does not know what is good for him. I am not making a public spirited sacrifice: I am jumping at an unprecedentedly good offer.

Faithfully,
G. Bernard Shaw

Federal Theatre Projects
701—8th Avenue
New York City
U.S. America.

From Bernard Shaw.

22nd May 1937

I cannot let you have *On the Rocks* ~~Too True To Be Good~~ until Mr Milton Shubert has given it a send off by his New York production, or until his failure to produce next autumn makes an end of his contract with me.

Now as to the rest of the repertory, will you kindly, to start with, put clean out of your head all the silly legends that the American newspapers keep repeating about me, and regard me, if you possibly can, as a fellow creature?

I know quite well what you are up against in this undertaking. It is useless to hope that you can find "groups with a high degree of skill in acting and direction" everywhere. You may not be able to find them anywhere. The plays will be murdered more or less barbarically all the time. That happens on Broadway too; and you must take what you can get in the way of casting and direction just as if you were a fashionable manager. So far from avoiding Negro casts you will be very lucky if you can get them; for Negroes act with a delicacy and sweetness that make white actors look like a gang of roughnecks in comparison.

You must leave the Theatre Child out of account, and deal directly with me. The Guild people are my very good friends; but their object in life is to prevent anyone except themselves doing my plays; and their interference is quite unnecessary. I want them to perform my plays and not to complicate my business affairs.

They tell me that your theatre, being a federal institution, is unable to move without miles of red tape being consumed, and that money can be extracted from it only after signing nine receipts. They also seem to think that every production will be a separate transaction involving a special licence and weekly payments and acknowledgments. That will never do for me. As long as you stick to your fifty cent maximum for admission, and send me the accounts and payments quarterly, or half yearly if you prefer it, so that I shall have to sign only four or two receipts a year, and forget all about you in the meantime, you can play anything of mine you like unless you hear from me to the contrary as in the case of *On the Rocks* ~~Too True~~, which will be soon be at your disposal like the rest.

Can you arrange things in this fashion for me?

Any author of serious plays who does not follow my example does not know what is good for him. I am not making a public spirited sacrifice: I am jumping at an unprecedentedly good offer.

Faithfully,
G. Bernard Shaw

Federal Theatre Projects
701- 8th Avenue
New York City
U.S.America.

The letter was triplicated innumerable times and until the destruction of the Federal Theatre in 1939 it served as probably the most informal contract ever honored by the United States Treasury. Over ten thousand performances of Shaw's plays were presented during those two years, and other dramatists were delighted to follow his example in responding to requests for the use of their work by the Federal Theatre.

To summarize a life of ninety-four years which remained alert and creative almost to the very end is an impossible task. Bernard Shaw himself did as good a job as anyone when he said to a friend and late biographer, Stephen Winsten:

> You talked of the age into which I was born as a great age. I regard it as the most villainous page of recorded history, redeemed only by men like Morris, and Tolstoy, Ibsen, and Gorki, Zola and Dickens. And the twentieth century is no better. We need minds larger than those of villagers. I have been described as a man laughing in a wilderness. That is correct enough, if you accept me as preparing the way for better things.

BIBLIOGRAPHY

A complete bibliography of the books read during the preparation of this work would include several thousand titles and would therefore be of little or no value to the reader. Even a selected bibliography of those books actually used, rather than eliminated after a first reading, would comprise a list of several hundred, and would require at least brief comments to render intelligible the widely varied reasons for the inclusion of many of the titles.

It has therefore seemed best to name here only a very few works of exceptional interest. Most of the biographical and critical studies listed below are notable for their own literary value, and the originality of their authors' viewpoints as well as for the significant material they include. Naturally they do not agree in toto either with each other or with the foregoing pages, but they do, on the whole, agree about the relation of literature to society and the progressive, humanist character of all great art.

Although the long, documented "official" biographies available for almost all the major figures of English literature are, of course, indispensable for anyone wishing to make a real study of a specific writer, they are generally too bulky and detailed, and often too discreet for general interest, and have almost all been omitted below, although often quoted in the text, as have many other valuable studies of too special an interest to be included here.

Arnot, Robert Page, *William Morris: A Vindication*, (pamphlet published by the author), London, 1934.
Bronowski, Jacob, *William Blake 1757-1827: A man without a mask*, London, Secker and Warburg, 1944.
Cameron, Kenneth Neill, *The Young Shelley: genesis of a radical*, New York, Macmillan, 1950.
Cauldwell, Christopher, *Studies in a Dying Culture*, New York, Dodd, 1938.
Cazamian, Louis, *A History of English Literature*, London, Macmillan, 1935.
Charques, R. D., *Contemporary Literature & Social Revolution*, London, Martin Secker, 1933.
Chesterton, G. K., *Robert Browning*, London, Macmillan, 1903.
Charles Dickens: a critical study, New York, Dodd, 1906.
George Bernard Shaw, London, Lane, 1909.

Farrington, Benjamin, *Francis Bacon: Philosopher of Industrial Science*, New York, Henry Schuman, 1949.
Fox, Ralph, *The Novel and the People*, New York, International Publishers, 1937.
Gilchrist, Alexander, *Life of Blake*, London, 1863.
Granville-Barker, Harley, *Prefaces to Shakespeare*, Princeton, Princeton University Press, 1946.
Grennan, Margaret, *William Morris: Medievalist and Revolutionary*, New York, King's Crown Press, 1945.
Harbage, Alfred, *As They Liked It*, New York, Macmillan, 1947.
Harrison, G. B., *Introducing Shakespeare*, London, Penguin, 1939.
Howe, P. P., *The Life of William Hazlitt*, London, Penguin, 1922.
Jackson, T. A., *Charles Dickens: the progress of a radical*, London, Lawrence & Wishart, 1937.
Johnson, Edgar, *Charles Dickens: his tragedy and triumph*, New York, Simon & Schuster, 1953.
Kettle, Arnold, *An Introduction to the English Novel*, London, Hutchinson & Co., 1951.
Legouis, Emile, *A History of English Literature*, London, Macmillan, 1935.
Lindsay, Jack, *John Bunyan, Maker of Myths*, London, Methuen, 1937.
Charles Dickens: a biographical and critical study, New York, Philosophical Library, 1950.
Lukacs, George, *Studies in European Realism*, London, Hillway, 1950.
Mirsky, Dmitri, *The Intelligentsia of Great Britain* (1885-1935), New York, Covici, 1935.
Morley, F. V., *Lamb Before Elia*, London, Cape, 1932.
Morton, A. L., *A People's History of England*, London, Lawrence & Wishart, 1948.
Mudrick, Marvin, *Jane Austen: irony as defense and discovery*, Princeton, Princeton University Press, 1953.
Palmer, John, *Political Characters of Shakespeare*, London, Macmillan, 1945.
Payne, William Lytton, *Mr. Review; Daniel Defoe as author of the Review*, New York, King's Crown Press, 1947.
Rattray, R. F., *Bernard Shaw: A Chronicle*, New York, Roy Publishers, 1951.
Strauss, E., *Bernard Shaw: Art and Socialism*, London, Gollancz, 1942.
Sturt, Mary, *Francis Bacon: a biography*, New York, Morrow, 1932.
Tillyard, E. M., *Milton*, London, Chatto, 1951.
Warner, Rex, *John Milton*, New York, Chanticleer Press, 1950.
Watson, Francis, *Daniel Defoe*, London, Longmans, 1952.
Webster, Margaret, *Shakespeare Without Tears*, London, McGraw, 1942.
West, Alick, *George Bernard Shaw: "A good man fallen among Fabians,"* New York, International Publishers, 1950.
Crisis and Criticism, London, Lawrence & Wishart, 1937.
White, Newman Ivy, *Portrait of Shelley*, New York, Knopf, 1945.

INDEX

Academy for Women, An (Defoe), 255-56
Adam Bede (Eliot), 760, 777-80, 782, 791
Addison, Joseph, 190, 209, 210, 211, 213-18, 223-24, 226, 305, 316
Adonais (Shelley), 126, 550, 551, 572
Advancement of Learning, The (Bacon), 93, 106
Adventures of Colonel Jack, The (Defoe), 284
Adventure of Ulysses, The (Lamb), 601
Aesthetic Adventure (Gaunt), 848
Against the Scholastic Philosophy (Milton), 122-23
Age of Bronze, The (Byron), 510, 511
Age of Reason, The (Paine), 403, 528
Alastor (Shelley), 537
Albemarle Review, 517
All for Love (Dryden), 206
All the Year 'Round (Dickens), 723, 743
All's Well That Ends Well (Shakespeare), 47
Alton Locke (Kingsley), 691
Amelia (Fielding), 293, 309-10
America (Blake), 398
American Notes (Dickens), 706, 710
American Revolution, 6, 319, 383, 900
Ancient Mariner, The (Coleridge), 416, 426, 445
Androcles and the Lion (Shaw), 915
Anne, Queen, 217, 226, 236, 261, 276
Antiquary, The (Scott), 618
Antony and Cleopatra (Shakespeare), 64-65, 206
Apologie for Poetrie (Sidney), 8
Apology for the Life of Mrs. Shamela Andrews, An (Fielding), 296-97
An Apology: Prologue to the Earthly Paradise (Morris), 858
Appeal to Reason, The, 686
Appearance of Mrs. Veal, The (Defoe), 286
Applebee's Journal, 276

Arcadia (Sidney), 8
Archer, William, 892, 893
Areopagetica—A Speech for Liberty of Unlicensed Printing (Milton), 138, 140
Armgart (Eliot), 793
Aristotle, 82, 83, 770
Armada, Spanish, 13, 14, 17, 111, 837
Arms and the Man (Shaw), 898
Arnold, Matthew, 631, 638, 650, 675, 677-79, 692, 826, 860
Art & Socialism (Morris), 860
Aurora Leigh (Browning, E. B.), 753, 755, 757
Austen, Jane, 302, 306, 322, 328-74, 690, 749, 752, 759, 768, 843
Asolando (Browning, R.), 673
As You Like It (Shakespeare), 37, 38, 42
Aubrey, John, 133, 157
Auguries of Innocence (Blake), 402
Augusta Triumphan (Defoe), 274, 286
Augustans, The, 206-24

Back to Methusalah (Shaw), 919
Bacon, Anthony, 84, 85, 88
Bacon, Francis, 11, 23, 77, 80-111, 122, 303, 605, 830, 832
Balzac, Honore de, 306, 318, 620
Bamford, Samuel, 541, 644
Bannockburn (Burns), 391
Baptists, 118, 167, 169
Barkwood, Lord, 181-82
Barnaby Rudge (Dickens), 702, 720, 760
Barrett, Elizabeth, See Browning, Elizabeth Barrett
Barton, Bernard, 606, 607, 608
Basse, W., 22
Battle of the Books, The (Swift), 226
Bax, Belfort, 874
Baudelaire, Pierre Charles, 849, 851
Beardsley, Aubrey, 843, 846, 849, 850, 900
Beaumont, Francis, 22, 23

Beer, Max, 912, 913
Belinda (Edgeworth), 752, 753
Bellamy, Edward, 855, 872, 873
Bells and Pomegranates (Browning, R.), 661
Belle Dame Sans Merci, La (Keats), 575
Bible, The, 93, 187, 189, 203, 215, 252, 262, 814
Biographia Literaria (Coleridge), 442, 455
Birrel, Augustus, 614
Blackwood's Magazine, 485, 550, 551, 730, 775, 776, 777, 778, 785
Blanc, Louis, 764
Blade-Time Will Come (Linton), 645
Blake, William, 160, 190, 328, 337, 378, 380, 392-407, 464, 468, 564, 601, 602, 649, 650
Bleak House (Dickens), 695, 724, 726, 727, 730, 747
"Bloody Sunday," 867, 870, 886, 887
Bodichon, Barbara Smith, 773, 783, 797
Boer War, 836, 842, 922
Book of Thel (Blake), 396
Borrow, George, 282-84
Boswell, James, 190, 319-20
Bramwich, John, 646, 648
Brawne, Fanny, 575, 576, 577, 578
Bray, Charles and Caroline, 761, 764, 765, 769, 770, 771, 772, 773
British Critic, The, 513
British Lady's Magazine, The, 596
British Poets, The (Hazlitt), 481
Britannia's Son (Bramwich), 646
Bronowski, J., 394, 395, 403, 406, 407, 810
Bronte, Charlotte, 302, 350, 631, 689, 692, 693, 752, 753-55
Bronte, Emily, 302, 631, 689, 752
Brook Farm, 176
Brown, Charles, 568, 574, 575, 577, 578
Browning, Elizabeth Barrett, 643, 650, 663-68, 669-71, 674, 753-57
Browning, Robert, 418, 650, 652, 653-74, 675, 767
Buckingham, Duke of (George Villiers), 75, 101, 104, 105, 165
Bunyan, John, 114, 166, 167, 169, 170-205, 207, 213, 252, 261, 605, 633, 649
Burdett-Coutts, Lady, 719, 720, 733

Burghley, Lord, 84, 85, 89, 91, 217
Burke, Edmund, 190, 377, 378, 379, 444, 455, 461, 528
Burney, Fanny, 329, 331, 337, 752
Burne-Jones, Edward and Mrs., 672, 855, 856, 862, 868
Burns, Gilbert, 381, 382
Burns, Robert, 190, 323, 324, 325, 328, 380, 381-92, 424, 564, 569, 571, 582, 586, 602, 619, 649, 650, 680
Byron, George Gordon, Lord, 301, 380, 422, 483, 492-516, 537, 539, 549, 550, 552, 554, 555-56, 567, 620, 621, 650, 655, 852, 867

Cadenus and Vanessa (Swift), 229
Caesar and Cleopatra (Shaw), 907, 918
Cain (Byron), 552
Candida (Shaw), 898, 910, 916
Canterbury Tales (Chaucer), 5, 602
Capital (*Das Kapital*), 734, 879, 881, 889
Captain Brassbound's Conversion (Shaw), 907, 911
Captain Singleton (Defoe), 280-81, 285
Carlile, Richard, 543, 551, 558
Carlyle, Thomas, 218, 219, 620, 631, 652, 680-85, 705, 713, 740, 742, 763, 767, 773, 779, 799, 800, 801, 819
Caroline, Queen, 291, 478, 604
Carpenters Son, The (Housman), 844
Castle Rackrent (Edgeworth), 752
Castelar y Ripoll, Emilio, 516
Castlereagh, Lord, 335, 473, 481, 502, 505, 509, 621
Catherine (Austen), 341
Cazamian, Louis, 313, 373, 705, 747
Cenci, The (Shelley), 540-51
Cervantes, Miguel de, 293, 301, 308, 750
Chambers Edinburgh Journal, 632
Champion, The, 294, 295, 502, 604
Chants for Socialists (Morris), 855, 865
Chapman, John, 766, 767, 768, 771, 772
Characters of Shakespeare's Plays (Hazlitt), 484
Charge to the Grand Jury (Fielding), 308

INDEX   931

Charles I, 107, 115, 116, 117, 128, 141, 143, 154, 657
Charles II, 144, 152, 153, 154, 163-64, 165, 166, 170 177, 178, 186, 196, 201, 207, 560
Charles Dickens: The Last of the Great Men (Chesterton), 735
Charlotte, Princess, 500, 504
Charques, R. D., 676
Chartism, 638, 678, 685
Chartism (Carlyle), 705, 706
Chaucer, Geoffrey, 5, 22, 23, 207, 216, 602
Chekhov, Anton, 916
Chesterfield, Lord, 210, 218, 316-18
Chesterton, G. K., 353, 605, 631, 705, 716, 735, 747, 750, 752, 854, 876, 895, 896, 900, 902, 905, 912, 918
Childe Harold (Byron), 497, 499, 503, 620
Child's History of England (Dickens), 712
Chillon (Byron), 503
Chimes, The (Dickens), 702, 713, 714, 716
Christabel (Coleridge), 426, 445, 446, 453
Christian Behaviour (Bunyan), 185
Christian Socialist, The, 885
Christmas Carol (Dickens), 713, 714
Christ's Hospital (Lamb), 583
Chronicles of the Canongate (Scott), 618
Chronicles (Hall), 5
Chronicles (Holinshed), 5
Citizen of the World, The (Goldsmith), 326
Civil War (U. S.), 671, 781, 835
Civil War (English), 115, 118, 120, 128, 129, *See also* Cromwell
Clarissa Harlowe (Richardson), 302, 322
Clarke, Charles Cowden, 563
Clarke, Rev. M., 355, 356
Clarkson, Thomas, 424, 425, 465, 598
Cobbett, William, 475, 476, 517, 617, 620, 620-28, 622, 623, 625, 626, 627
Cole, G. D. H. and M., 622, 624
Colenso, Bishop, 677
Coleridge, Samuel Taylor, 46, 47, 307, 308, 376, 379, 380, 403, 413, 414, 415, 416, 420, 426-57, 458, 459, 462, 463, 476-79, 480, 486, 505, 555-56, 567, 580, 583, 585, 586, 587, 588, 590, 591, 592, 593, 596, 597, 600, 602, 606, 613, 614, 644, 650
Collins, Wilkie, 689, 725, 730, 732, 737, 739, 748
Collins, William, 319, 322
Colonel Jack, The Adventures of (Defoe), 284, 285
Comedy of Errors, The (Shakespeare), 24
Commonsense About the War (Shaw), 917
Commonsense of Municipal Trading, The (Shaw), 903
Commonweal, 868, 869, 871
Communist Manifesto (Marx and Engels), 684
Comparative Discourse of our English Poets with the Greek, Latin and Italian Poets, A (Meres), 21
Compleat English Tradesman, The (Defoe), 252, 270-71, 284, 285, 286
Comus (Milton), 126
Conciliation with the Colonies (Burke), 377
Conciones ad Populum (Coleridge), 586
Conduct of the Allies (Swift), 227, 810
Confession of Faith, A (Bunyan), 186
Congreve, William, 165, 206, 291
Consolidator, The (Defoe), 260
Controversies in the Church (Bacon), 81, 85
Covent Garden Journal, The (Fielding), 310
Conversations with Northcote (Hazlitt), 490
Cooper, Thomas, 648, 649
Coriolanus (Shakespeare), 64, 65-69, 75
Corn Law Rhymer, *See* Elliott, Ebenezer
Cornhill Magazine, 687, 755
Corsair, The (Byron), 500
Cotter's Saturday Night, The (Burns), 324, 325, 382, 386
Cottle, Joseph, 415, 442
Country Rhimes for Children (Bunyan), 200
Country Wife, The (Wycherly), 165

Court Wits of the Restoration Period, The (Wilson), 164
Covent Garden Journal, The, 310-13
Courier and Wat Tyler, The (Hazlitt), 426
Courier, The, 500
Cowper, William, 190, 319, 322
Crabbe, George, 368
Cranford (Gaskell), 631, 690
Crashaw, Richard, 114
Cricket on the Hearth, The (Dickens), 717
Crisis and Criticism (West), 678, 679
Cromwell, Oliver, 116, 117, 118, 119, 140, 141, 146, 147, 148, 149, 153, 167, 170, 178, 200, 201, 207, 208, 251
Cromwell (Carlyle), 683, 684
Cromwell, our Chief of Men (Milton), 146
Cross, John W., 796, 797
Cross, Mary Ann Evans, See Eliot, George
Cruikshank, George, 719
Cry of the Children, The (Browning, E. B.), 643, 663
Crystal Palace Exhibition, 834, 856
Curse for a Nation, A (Browning, E. B.), 669, 670
Cuvier, George Leopold, Baron, 763, 826
Cymbeline (Shakespeare), 77

Daffodils (Wordsworth), 423
Daily Chronicle, The, 892
Daily Gazette, The, 294
Daily News (London), The, 140, 717
Daily Telegraph, The, 893
Daniel Deronda (Eliot), 780, 783, 786, 787, 796
Dante, Alighieri, 190, 507-08, 613, 657, 668
Darwin, Charles, 802, 807, 820, 828, 829, 831, 879, 880
Daumier, Honoré, 695, 849
David Copperfield (Dickens), 694, 695, 721, 722, 743, 750
Davidson, John, 846, 850
Declaration of Independence, 141, 142
Dedication to Don Juan (Byron), 505
Defense of Guenevere, The (Morris), 857
Defense of the English People by John Milton, Englishman, A, 144, 145, 146
Defense of the King (Defensio Regia pro-Carolo I) (Salmasius), 144
Defoe, Daniel, 192, 210, 216, 217, 251-87, 288, 289, 293, 295, 296, 300, 304, 310, 605, 829
Deist, The, 559
De Quincey, Thomas, 580, 581, 598
Descriptive Sketches (Wordsworth), 412, 414
Deserted Village, The (Goldsmith), 323, 325, 326-28, 368
De Stael, Madame, 352
Destiny of Nations, The (Coleridge), 444
Destruction of the Bastille, The (Coleridge), 429
de Vallon, Annette and Caroline, 410, 418
Devil's Disciple, The (Shaw), 900
Diana of the Crossways (Meredith), 840
Dickens, Charles, 190, 256, 275, 309, 310, 329, 335, 412, 616, 620, 630, 631, 636, 642, 652, 674, 675, 680, 681, 685, 689, 690, 693-752, 767, 777, 778, 819, 925
Dickens' World (House), 713-14, 731-32
Dickinson, Emily, 581, 582
Dictionary (Johnson), 316-18
Diggers, 116, 117
Disraeli, Benjamin, 631, 689, 690, 691, 763, 834, 835
Ditte (Nexo), 701
Division of the Sciences, The (Bacon), 102
Dobson, Austin, 219
Doctrine & Discipline of Divorce, The (Milton), 134
Doe, Charles, 203-04
Doing Good (Swift), 234-35
Doll's House, The (Ibsen), 747, 892, 897
Dombey and Son (Dickens), 718, 720, 747
Donne, John, 114
Don Juan (Byron), 505, 506, 510, 511-514
Don Quixote (Cervantes), 204, 285, 297
Double Dealer, The (Congreve), 165
Dowson, Ernest, 846, 850

INDEX

Drake, Sir Francis, 8
Drama of Exile, The (Browning, E. B.), 756
Dramatic Lyrics (Browning, R.), 661
Dramatic Opinions and Essays (Shaw), 904
Dramatic Romances and Lyrics (Browning, R.), 659
Drapier's Letters, The (Swift), 224, 232, 233, 247
Dream of John Ball, A (Morris), 855, 870
Dryden, John, 165, 206, 207
Dublin Evening Post, 526
Dublin Weekly Messenger, 527
Du Bois, W. E. B., 872
Duchess of Malfi, The (Webster), 22, 77
Due Preparations for the Plague (Defoe), 284

Earthly Paradise, The (Morris), 652, 658
Eaton, Daniel Isaac, 528, 529
Economic Determination of Jane Austen, The (Woolf, Leonard), 342-43
Edgeworth, Maria, 752-53
Edinburgh Review, The, 472, 483, 495, 565, 716, 736, 809
Edward, VI, King, 6-7, 81
Eikon Basilike (Charles I), 128, 143
Eikonoklastis (Milton), 143, 144
Eldon, Lord, 476, 538
Elegy in a Country Churchyard (Gray), 323, 324
Elia, See Lamb, Charles
Eliot, George, 373, 429, 433, 434, 620, 631, 652, 661, 662, 689, 693, 752-98, 838
Eliot, T. S., 76, 678, 679, 852, 863
Ellenborough, Lord, 528, 529
Elliott, Ebenezer, 644, 645
Elizabeth, Queen, 5, 7, 11, 12, 13, 14, 17, 18, 19, 27, 37, 38, 81, 84, 85, 86, 87, 89, 90, 91, 94, 95, 217
Emerson, Ralph Waldo, 615, 618
Emma (Austen), 331, 342, 353, 355, 360-65, 367, 368, 370, 611, 612
Encyclopedia Britannica, 468, 481
Endymion (Keats), 559, 560, 566, 572, 573
Enemy of the People, An (Ibsen), 897, 913

Engels, Friedrich, 110, 638, 639, 681, 862
England's New Chaines for Old (Lilburne), 114
English Bards and Scotch Reviewers (Byron), 496
English Literature and Society in the Eighteenth Century (Stephens), 322-23
Englishman in Italy, The (Browning), 659
Enquiry Concerning Political Justice (Godwin), 397
Enquiry Into the Causes of the Late Increase of Robbers (Fielding), 308-09
Enquiry into the Occasional Conformity of Dissenters (Defoe), 260
Epilogue to Asolando (Browning, R.), 672, 673-74
Essay in Defense of the Natural Disinterestedness of the Human Mind (Hazlitt), 466
Essays of Elia (Lamb), 581, 604, 608, 609
Essay on Criticism (Pope), 219-20
Essay on Liberty (Mill, J. S.), 899
Essay on Man (Pope), 219, 222
Essay on Population (Malthus), 401, 468
Essay on the History and Reality of Apparitions (Defoe), 286
Essay Upon Projects, An (Defoe), 255, 256, 286
Essex, Lord, 17, 21, 85, 86, 88, 89, 90
Etheridge (also Etherege), Sir George, 165
Euphues, Lyly, 8
Europe (Blake), 400
Euripides, 23, 138, 139
Eve of St. Agnes, The (Keats), 575
Evelina (Burning), 337
Evelyn (Austen), 339
Evening Walk and Descriptive Sketches (Wordsworth), 412
Everyday Book (Hone), 608
Evidences as to Man's Place in Nature (Huxley), 831
Evolution and Ethics (Huxley), 822, 831
Examiner, The, 472, 502, 528, 529, 543, 551, 563, 565, 572, 603
Examiner, The, 763

Excursion, The (Wordsworth), 602
Eyre, Governor, 819, 820

Fabians, 857, 863, 865, 867, 882, 884, 886, 887, 894, 899, 901, 906, 908, 909, 911, 918, 921, 923
Faerie Queene (Spenser), 8
Fall of Hyperion, The (Keats), 556
Faraday, Michael, 806, 826, 828
Fare Thee Well (Byron), 502
Fairfax Whose Name in Arms Thru Europe Rings (Milton), 141
Farrar, Reginald, 354, 355
Farrington, Benjamin, 82-83
Fears in Solitude (Coleridge), 448
Feelings of a French Royalist (Wordsworth), 423
Felix Holt, The Radical (Eliot), 766, 783, 784, 790, 793, 796
Ferrier, Susan, 752
Feuillade, Eliza, Comtesse de, 333, 352
Few Sighs from Hell, A (Bunyan), 176
Fielding, Henry, 190, 287-315, 316, 322, 328, 330, 562, 605, 896
Fifth Monarchy Men, 167-69, 197
Finnerty, Peter, 522, 527
Fire, Famine and Slaughter (Coleridge), 438, 439, 454
Fitz Victor (Shelley), 522
Fitzgerald, Edward, 650, 757
Foe, Daniel, *See* Defoe, Daniel
Forecasts of the Coming Century or Hand and Brain (Shaw), 901
Ford, John, 76
Forerunners or Anticipations of the New Philosophy, The (Bacon), 102
Formalist, The (Bunyan), 200
Forster, John, 698, 707, 713, 717, 718, 721, 723, 726, 727, 729, 732, 746, 749
Fortnightly Review, 782, 787, 809
Fox, Charles, 377, 389, 526
Fox, George, 175, 192
Fox, Ralph, 562, 584, 692, 842, 849
France: An Ode (Coleridge), 447
Francis Bacon, Philosopher of Industrial Science (Farrington), 82
Frankenstein (Shelley, Mary), 537
Franklin, Benjamin, 256, 398
Fraser's Magazine, 687
Frederick the Great (Carlyle), 685
Freethinker, The, 516-29

Free Thoughts on Public Affairs or Advice to a Patriot (Hazlitt), 467
French Revolutions, 6, 375-80, 409-12, 448, 451, 458, 464, 492, 495, 539, 541, 558, 609, 631, 683, 689, 718-19, 742, 750, 854
French Revolution, The (Blake), 397, 398
French Revolution, The (Carlyle), 683, 705
Frend, William, 430
From a Young Lady in Distressed Circumstances to Her Friend (Austen), 339-40
Frost, Thomas, 644
Froude, James Anthony, 683, 687, 767
The Frozen Deep (Wilkie Collins), 739
Fuller, Margaret, 769, 773
Function of Criticism, The (Arnold), 677

Garrod, H. W., 354, 358
Gaskell, Elizabeth C., Mrs., 631, 689, 690, 691, 728, 752
Gaunt, John of, 30, 31, 69
Gaunt, William, 848-49
Gay, John, 226, 235, 248
George II, 291, 297, 306
George, III, 387, 422, 478, 535
George IV, 355, 364, 422, 472, 499, 500, 501, 502, 505, 526, 546, 604
George, Henry, 880, 881, 894
Ghosts (Ibsen), 892, 893, 897
Gibbon, Edward, 215
Gifford, William, 482
Gilbert and Sullivan, 850, 898
Gilchrist, Alexander, 398
Gissing, George, 747
Gladstone, William, 701, 820, 826, 827, 828, 835, 905, 906
Godwin, William, 378, 397, 411, 435, 462, 517, 521, 527-36, 580, 597
Goethe, Johan Wolfgang, 80, 108
Goldsmith, Oliver, 321, 323, 325-28, 829
Gorky, Maxim, 839, 903, 925
Grace Abounding (Bunyan), 172, 173, 186, 193
Grand Time Comin', A (Robson), 649
Granville-Barker, Harley, 55, 56, 57, 61

INDEX 935

Grattan, Henry, 224
Gray, Thomas, 319, 321, 323-25, 328
Great Expectations (Dickens), 695, 743, 745
Great Instauration, The (Bacon), 102, 103, 104, 106
Greatness of the Soul, The (Bunyan), 194-95
Green, J. R., 540, 541
Greene, Robert, 20-21
Guilt and Sorrow (Wordsworth), 414
Gulliver's Travels (Swift), 204, 224, 229, 235-41, 279
Guy Mannering (Scott), 676

Haeckel, Ernest Heinrich, 805, 806
Hall, Edward, 5
Hamlet (Shakespeare), 27, 30, 31, 38, 47-53, 54, 74, 112, 454
Hancock, John, 398
Hanover, House of, 276, 387, 484
Hard Times (Dickens), 690, 724, 728, 729, 730
Harding, D. W., 348-49
Hardy, Thomas, 377, 462
Hardy, Thomas, 838, 840, 841, 842, 843, 845
Harley, Robert, 228, 264, 265, 266, 274
Harris, Frank, 876, 903, 918
Harrison, Frederic, 808-09
Hazlitt, William, 32, 199, 207, 249, 297, 315, 379, 380, 392, 426, 444, 446, 450, 457-92, 493, 515, 555, 572, 580, 581, 595, 596, 598, 606, 608, 613, 681, 716
Heart of Midlothian, The (Scott), 620
Heartbreak House (Shaw), 916
Hedda Gabler (Ibsen), 62, 893
Heine, Heinrich, 32, 787
Hellas (Shelley), 552
Henderson, Archibald, 875, 903
Hennell, Sara, 764, 770, 773, 781
Henry IV, 29, 30, 31
Henry IV (Shakespeare), 37, 38-41
Henry V (Shakespeare), 30, 37, 41-42, 47, 65, 69
Henry VI (Shakespeare), 21, 24, 25
Henry VII, 5, 106, 107
Henry VIII, 4, 5, 6, 7, 13, 82, 94
Henry VIII (Shakespeare), 38, 77, 106
Herbert, George, 114

Hermit of Marlow, The (Shelley), 538
Herrick, Robert, 112, 113
Hichener, Elizabeth, 524, 526, 528
Hidden Heritage, The (Lawson), 96, 97
Hints from Horace (Byron), 497
Historical Register for 1736, The (Fielding), 294
History of Britain (Milton), 140, 147, 154, 160, 161
History of King Henry VII, The (Bacon), 106, 107
History of the Kentish Petition, The (Defoe), 259
History of Philosophy (Lewes), 769
Hobhouse, John Cam, 494, 495, 504
Hogarth, William, 600, 719
Hogg, Thomas Jefferson, 519, 520, 523, 535, 536
Holcroft, Thomas, 377, 435, 462, 472, 580
Holinshed, Raphael, 5
Holland, Lord, 496, 497
Holy City, The (Bunyan), 186, 197-98
Holy Fair, The (Burns), 386
Holy Thursday (Blake), 395
Holy War, The (Bunyan), 197, 203
Holy Willie's Prayer (Burns), 386
Home Is Home Be It Never So Homely (Lamb), 610-13, 614, 615
Hone, William, 608
Hooker, Richard, 8, 9, 10
Hooker, Sir Joseph Dalton, 802, 807, 810, 816
Hooker, Thomas, 794
Hopes and Fears for Art (Morris), 855, 862
Housman, A. E., 843-46
Hours of Idleness (Byron), 495
House, Humphrey, 713, 731
House of God, The (Bunyan), 195
Household Words (Dickens), 690, 696, 709, 723, 728
How the Change Came (Morris), 874
Human Soot (Kingsley), 679-80
Hume, David, 215
Hunt, Henry, 517, 541, 559
Hunt, John, 493, 529
Hunt, Leigh, 380, 428, 472, 475, 487, 488, 493, 499, 502, 511, 513, 529, 538, 541, 549, 552, 553, 572, 577, 579, 580, 581, 598, 603, 769

Hunt, Thornton, 769, 770
Hutchinson, Mary, 418, 608
Huxley, Aldous, 827, 829, 831, 832
Huxley, Julian, 810, 827, 828, 832
Huxley, Leonard, 800, 827, 828
Huxley, Thomas, 90, 110, 651, 652, 675, 767, 781, 798-833, 880
Howe, William, 407
Hymn of the Wiltshire Laborers (Dickens), 717
Hymn to the Pillory (Defoe), 264
Hyndman, H. M., 862, 867, 881, 886, 908, 910
Hyperion (Keats), 559, 574

Ibsen, Henrik, 747, 889, 890, 892, 896, 897, 899, 904, 906, 925
Idyls of the King (Tennyson), 669
Ilf, Ilya, 336
Illusions of Socialism, The (Shaw), 901
Immaturity (Shaw), 912
Importance of Being Ernest, The (Wilde), 850
Il Penseroso (Milton), 124, 126
Impossibilities of Anarchy, The (Shaw), 890
Impressionism, 890
In Defense of Poetry (Shelley), 552
In Memoriam (Tennyson), 650
Independents, The, 116, 118
Innocence of Bernard Shaw, The (Scott, D.), 881, 920
In No Strange Land (Thompson), 846
Intelligent Woman's Guide to Socialism, The (Shaw), 923
Introduction to the English Novel, An (Kettle), See Kettle, Arnold
Irony as Defense and Discovery (Mudrick), 331
Irrational Knot, The (Shaw), 884, 885
Isabella or, The Pot of Basil (Keats), 561, 646
Isola, Emma (Moxon), 609, 611-12
Italian in England, The (Browning, R.), 659

Jacobin, 376, 426, 438, 455, 462, 477, 512, 594
Jacobin's Prayer, The (Elliott), 644
Jackson, T. A., 27, 37, 39, 40, 721, 726, 734, 740, 746

Jacobite's Journal, The, 302
James, Henry, 779
James I, 11, 38, 65, 69, 73, 75, 87, 90, 91, 93, 94, 95, 96, 97, 103, 104, 105, 107, 111, 120
James II, 196, 199, 200-01, 202, 203, 207, 208, 252, 254, 257
James, Duke of York, See James II
James, Kings of Scots, See James I
Jane Austen, A Depreciation (Garrod), 354, 358
Jane Austen and Some of Her Contemporaries (Wilson), 354
Jane Eyre (Bronte, C.), 350, 692, 753, 754, 764
Janet's Repentance (Eliot), 776
Jefferson, Thomas, 106, 142, 150
Jeffrey, Francis, 716, 820
Jew of Malta, The (Marlowe), 14, 32
John Bull's British Journal, 551
John Bull's Other Island (Shaw), 912
John Bunyan Maker of Myths (Lindsay), 166-67
John Bunyan, Mechanick Preacher (Tindale), 167-68
John Woodvil (Lamb), 595
Johnson, Edgar, 720
Johnson, Joseph, 397, 398
Johnson, Dr. Samuel, 190, 227, 233, 285, 311, 316-22, 326, 329, 337, 368, 482, 606, 777
Jonathan Wild, the Great (Fielding), 300-01
Jolly Beggars, The (Burns), 384, 386
Jones, Ernest, 646
Jonson, Ben, 22, 25, 74, 85, 105, 106
Joseph Andrews, 297-300
Journal of a Voyage to Lisbon (Fielding, 301, 303, 314, 315
Journal of the Plague Year, A (Defoe), 284
Jude the Obscure (Hardy), 692
Julius Caesar (Shakespeare), 37, 38, 42-46, 47, 63, 65
Justice, 874

Kataeyv, Valentin, 336
Kean, Edmund, 566, 567, 787
Keats, John, 8, 27, 127, 380, 459, 481, 482, 550, 551, 553, 554, 555-79, 646, 649, 650, 653, 655, 668, 686, 852
Keats, Fanny, 568, 569-70, 574, 578
Keegan, Martha, 738

Kelly, Fanny, 604
Kennedy, Margaret, 340
Kettle, Arnold, 286, 289, 297-98, 302, 304, 307, 331-32, 335, 360, 361, 362, 363, 364, 374, 789
King, Edward, 126, 127
King John (Shakespeare), 27, 37
King Lear (Shakespeare), 38, 64, 69-70, 599
Kingsley, Charles, 631, 633, 641, 675, 679, 680, 689, 690, 691, 701, 819, 830, 902
Kipling, Rudyard, 854
Kosciusko, Thaddeus, 560, 593
Kyd, Thomas, 23

Lady of the Lake, The (Scott), 619
Lady Susan (Austen), 337, 341
L'Allegro (Milton), 124, 126
Lamb Before Elia (Morley), 579
Lamb, Charles, 315, 380, 406, 428, 435, 446, 459, 462, 469, 471, 473, 477, 479, 484, 491, 554-56, 562, 579-616, 654
Lamb, Mary, 469-70, 471, 583, 584, 587, 590, 593, 595, 596, 597, 598, 599, 603, 604, 605, 609, 612, 613-14, 759
Lament for the Princess Charlotte (Shelley), 539
Land of Heart's Desire, The (Yeats), 900
Lang, Andrew, 840, 841
Laon and Cynthna (Shelley), 539
Last Essays of Elia (Lamb), 608
Last Poems (Housman), 844
Latimer, Bishop Hugh, 3, 7
Latin Epistle in Verse (Milton), 124
Latter Day Pamphlets (Carlyle), 685
Lavengro (Borrow), 282-84
Law of Freedom, The (Winstanley), 117
Laws of Ecclesiastical Polity, The (Hooker), 8
Laws of God, The, Laws of Man, The (Housman), 845-46
Layard, Henry, 732, 733, 738
League of Nations, 266-67
Lectures on Socialism (Morris), 862
Lectures to Working-men (Huxley), 806, 808
Lectures on the English Poets (Hazlitt), 207, 392

Legion's Memorial to the House of Commons (Defoe), 258-59, 263
Legouis, Emile, 3, 15, 23, 37
Letter to the Bishop of Llandoff, A (Wordsworth), 411
Letter to Lord Ellenborough, A (Shelley), 528
Letter to William Gifford, A (Hazlitt), 482
Letters to the Chartists (Kingsley), 679
Letters of Robert Browning and Elizabeth Barrett Browning, 665
Levelers, 115, 116, 118, 120, 168
Lewes, George Henry, 373, 753, 767, 769, 771, 772, 773, 775, 781, 782, 783, 787, 796, 797, 809
L'Humanite, 750
Liberal, The, 511, 553
Life Adventures and Piracies of the Famous Captain Singleton, The (Defoe), 280-81, 285
Life and Adventures of the Incredible Daniel Defoe, The (Defoe), 286
Life and Death of Jason, The (Morris), 858
Life and Death of Mr. Badman, The (Bunyan), 193-94, 195
Life of Jonathan Wild the Great, The (Fielding), 300
Life of Napoleon (Hazlitt), 489
Life of Pope (Johnson), 320
Lilburne, John, 115, 116, 120, 143, 167, 168, 171
Lindsay, Jack, 119, 166, 167, 170, 176, 177, 189, 204, 721, 722, 734, 744, 747
Lines to a Lady Weeping (Byron), 500
Lines written in Early Spring (Wordsworth), 417
Linnell, Alfred, 870
Linnell, John, 394, 406
Linton, W. J., 645
Literary Gazette, The, 513
Little Dorrit (Dickens), 724, 730, 734, 738, 740, 747
Lives of Criminals (Defoe), 300
London (Blake), 395
London, Jack, 884
London Magazine, 716
London Magazine and Theatrical Inquisitor, The, 552

London Times, The, 869
London Trade Union Council, 835
Lonsdale, Lord, 418, 420, 421
Looking Backward (Bellamy), 855, 872, 873
Lord Walter's Wife (Browning, R.), 755
Lost Leader, The (Browning, R.), 418, 421, 658
Louis XIV, 163, 186, 854
Louis XVI, 390, 411
L'Ouverture, Touissant, 425
Love Among the Artists (Shaw), 883
Love for Love (Congreve), 165
Love in Several Masques (Fielding), 290
Love and Freindship (Sic) (Austen), 338-39
Lovelace, Richard, 112, 114
Love's Labour Lost (Shakespeare), 24, 27
Lowell, James Russell, 420
Lukasch (Lukacs), George, 279, 747
Lycidas (Milton), 126-28, 158
Lyell, Sir Charles, 807, 808, 817
Lylord, C., 357, 372
Lyly, John, 8, 23
Lyrical Ballads (Coleridge and Wordsworth), 421, 445
Lytton, Bulwer, 689, 744

Macaulay, Wm. Babington (Lord), 108, 110, 629, 834
Macbeth (Shakespeare), 16, 38, 64, 69, 70-74
MacBride, E. W., 811
Macdonald, Ramsay, 888, 917
Mackail, J. W., 856
Mackintosh, James, 377, 455, 464, 597
Macready, William Charles, 656, 705, 706
Madman's Story, The (Dickens), 699
Magnificence (Skelton), 4
Major Barbara (Shaw), 890, 891, 911, 913
Malthus, Rev. T. R., 401, 468, 514, 528
Malthusian, 715, 879
Man He Killed, The (Housman), 842, 845
Man Was Made to Mourn (Burns), 386
Man and Superman (Shaw), 910, 911

Manchester Guardian, The, 728
Manchester Examiner & Times, The, 687
Manifesto to Workingmen of England (Morris), 859
Manning, Thomas, 596, 598, 600, 601, 612
Man's a Man for A' That, A (Burns), 390
Mansfield Park (Austen), 350, 353-55, 368
March of the Workers (Morris), 866
Marlborough, Duke and Duchess, 217, 227, 228
Marlowe, Christopher, 10, 14, 23, 32
Marriage of Heaven and Hell, The (Blake), 400
Martin Chuzzlewit (Dickens), 703, 710, 711, 712, 720, 724
Martineau, Harriet, 701, 767
Marvell, Andrew, 114, 146
Marx, Karl, 554, 561, 562, 630, 640, 681, 862, 863, 878, 881, 882, 889, 909, 920
Marxism, 168, 681, 855, 865, 882, 883, 886
Mary Barton (Gaskell), 690, 728
Mary, Queen of Scots, 13
Mary, Queen (Tudor), 7, 13
Mask of Anarchy (also *Masque*) (Shelley), 541-43, 545
Massinger, Philip, 76
Mavrocordato, Prince, 552
Mazzini, Guiseppe, 851
Measure for Measure (Shakespeare), 47
Mechanics Institutes, 743, 751
Melville, Herman, 841, 842
Memoirs of a Cavalier (Defoe), 280
Men of England (Shelley), 517, 543-44, 647, 851
Men & Women (Browning, R.), 668
Merchant of Venice, The (Shakespeare), 27, 32-36, 54, 55
Meredith, George, 773, 838, 839, 840, 893
Meres, Frances, 21
Merry Wives of Windsor, The (Shakespeare), 37, 42
Middlemarch (Eliot), 759, 766, 780, 783, 787, 789, 790, 791, 793, 795
Middleton, Thomas, 430, 601
Midsummer Night's Dream, A (Shakespeare), 27

INDEX 939

Mill, John Stuart, 767, 819, 879
The Mill on the Floss (Eliot), 758, 759, 782, 783
Military Memoirs of Capt. Geo. Carleton, The (Defoe), 286
Milton, John, 80, 112, 114, 117, 118, 119, 120, 121-63, 166, 167, 190, 191, 193, 207, 213, 222, 233, 261, 402, 403, 404, 415, 422, 435, 472, 475, 495, 505, 557, 585, 600, 633, 644, 650, 758, 794, 852
Milton (Wordsworth), 422
Misalliance (Shaw), 911, 914
Miscellanies (Fielding), 300
Mirror of Parliament, The, 695
Mist's Miscellany, 278
Mitford, Mary Russell, 752
Moby Dick (Melville), 841
Modern Painters (Ruskin), 686
Modest Proposal, A (Swift), 224, 242-46
Moliere, Jean Baptiste Poquelin, 23, 291, 293, 308
Moll Flanders (Defoe), 216, 268, 270, 273, 275, 281-84, 285, 287
Moore, George, 850
Moore, Thomas, 485, 508, 509, 553
Monk, General, 153
Montaigne, Michel Eyquem, Seigneur de, 89
Monthly Review, The, 577, 585
More, Mrs. Hannah, 632, 763
More, Thomas, 4
Morley, F. W., 579, 591
Morley, John, 809
Morley, Henry, 737
Morning Chronicle, The, 472, 481, 500, 588
Morning Post, The, 449, 500
Morris, William, 605, 615, 631, 651, 652, 675, 686, 835, 838, 840, 843, 851, 852, 854-75, 879, 880, 881, 882, 884, 887, 888, 891, 903, 907, 910, 913, 919, 925
Morton, A. L., 7, 211-13, 292-93, 305, 621, 628, 639
Mr. H. (Lamb), 599
Mrs. Warren's Profession (Shaw), 896, 897, 910
Much Ado About Nothing (Shakespeare), 37, 42
Mudrick, Marvin, 331, 345-48, 369, 370
Munera Pulveris (Ruskin), 686, 687

Music Makers (O'Shaughnessy), 851
My Last Duchess (Browning, R.), 661, 662

Napoleon Bonaparte, 420, 447, 450, 452, 454, 466, 472, 474, 488, 490, 531
Napoleon's Farewell (Byron), 502
Natural and Experimental History for the Foundations of Philosophy (Bacon), 102
Nature, 831
Needle Work (Lamb, Mary), 596
Negro-ship (Shelley), 544
New Chains for Old (Lilburne), 143
New Forcers of Conscience, On the (Milton), 140
New Review, The, 891
Newman, John Henry, 675, 676
News from Nowhere (Morris), 855, 871, 872, 873
Newton, Isaac Sir, 211, 519, 810, 826, 828
New Model Army, 116, 118, 119, 141, 143, 152, 251, (See also Cromwell)
New Philosophy or Active Science, The (Bacon), 102, 103
New Voyage Round the World, A (Defoe), 284
New Way to Pay Old Debts, A (Massinger), 77
Nexo, Martin Anderson, 701
Nicholas Nickleby (Dickens), 275, 700, 701, 720, 724
Nietzche, Friedrich Wilhelm, 39, 913
Nightingale, The (Coleridge), 446
Nightingale, Florence, 633, 755
No Master (Morris), 866
Nordau, Max, 905, 906
Norfolk, Duke of, 39, 519, 523, 524, 526, 533
North British Review, The, 716
Northanger Abbey (Austen), 330, 336, 337, 341-43, 352, 364, 367, 371, 373
Northern Star, The, 632
Notes on a Journey through France and Italy (Hazlitt), 488
Novan Organum, The (Bacon), 83, 102
Novel and the People, The (Fox), 692, 693

940 INDEX

Obiter Dicta (Birrel), 614
Observations on a Libel (Bacon), 85
Oceanic Hydrozoa, The (Huxley), 804
O'Connell, Daniel, 526, 696
Ode on Intimations of Immortality (Wordsworth), 419, 453
Ode To A Grecian Urn (Keats), 575
Ode to a Nightingale (Keats), 560
Ode to Dejection (Coleridge), 453
Ode to Duty (Wordsworth), 421
Ode to France (Coleridge), 420
Ode to Naples (Shelley), 549
Ode To The Departing Year (Coleridge), 444
Ode to the Framers of the Frame Bill (Byron), 499
Ode to the West Wind (Shelley), 545-46, 851
Ode to Tranquility (Coleridge), 454
Oedipus Tyrranus or Swellfoot the Tyrant (Shelley), 546
Of Anti-Christ, and of the Slaying of the Witnesses (Bunyan), 203
Old Curiosity Shop, The (Dickens), 700, 720
Old China (Lamb), 615
Oliver Twist (Dickens), 700, 701, 702, 720, 724
O, Mistress Mine (Shakespeare), 113
On Actors and the Art of Acting (Lewes), 787
On Going to Church (Shaw), 900
On the Necessity of Atheism (Shelley and Hogg), 523
On the Physical Bases of Life (Huxley), 810
On the Rocks (Shaw), 924
Otho the Great (Keats), 575
Our Mutual Friend (Dickens), 636, 702, 703, 724, 746, 747, 748
Of Counsell (Bacon), 100
Of Education (Milton), 137
Of Envy (Bacon), 100
Of Friendship (Bacon), 100
Of Greatness of Kingdoms & Estates (Bacon), 20, 99, 106
Of Judicature (Bacon), 106
Of Nobility (Bacon), 98
Of Plantations (Bacon), 97, 98
Of Sedition and Troubles (Bacon), 98, 99
Of Usurie (Bacon), 100-01

Of Vicissitude of Things (Bacon), 106
Of Wisdome for a Mans Selfe (Bacon), 100
On Conjugal Lewdness or Matrimonial Whoredom (Defoe), 275-76
On His Having Arrived at the Age of 23 (Milton), 125, 163
On Shakespeare (Milton), 124
On Studies (Bacon), 89
On the Advisableness of Improving Natural Knowledge (Huxley), 110
On the Fortunate Memory of Elizabeth, Queen of England (Bacon), 11, 91
On the Morning of Christ's Nativity (Milton), 123-24, 125
One Thing Needful (Bunyan), 185
O'Shaughnessy, Arthur, 851
Othello (Shakespeare), 34, 36, 44, 45, 47, 54, 64, 70, 278
Our Theatres in the Nineties (Shaw), 903
Owen, Robert, 176

Paine, Thomas, 232, 377, 378, 379, 398, 400, 407, 411, 462, 528, 552, 558, 633, 810
Palmer, John, 29, 45, 46, 67, 68, 69
Pall Mall Gazette, 819
Pamela (Richardson), 216, 295, 296, 322
Paracelsus (Browning, R.), 656, 662
Paradise Lost (Milton), 151, 154, 156-61, 191, 222, 555
Paradise Regained (Milton), 157, 160, 161
Paris Commune, 750, 835
Parochial Sermons (Newman), 676
Pasquin or A Dramatic Satire on the Times (Fielding), 294
Passages in the Life of a Radical (Bamford), 644
Past & Present (Carlyle), 683, 713
Pater, Walter, 848, 884
Patriot, The (Browning, R.), 527
Pauline (Browning, R.), 656
Peace Conference Hints (Shaw), 918
Peacock, Ronald, 895
Peacock, Thomas Love, 535, 537, 541, 549, 552
Peoples Anthem, The (Elliott), 644, 645
People's History of England, A (Mor-

INDEX 941

ton), 7, 211, 212, 213, 292, 293, 621, 639
Pepys, Samuel, 164
The Perfect Wagnerite (Shaw), 906
Pericles (Shakespeare), 73
Persuasion (Austen), 351, 360, 364, 367-70, 373
Peter Bell the Third (Shelley), 547
Peterloo Massacre, 509, 540-41, 621
Petrov, Eugene, 336
Pharisee and the Publican, The (Bunyan), 195
Phenomena of the Universe, The (Bacon), 102
Philanderer, The (Shaw), 896
Philosophic View of Reform, A (Shelley), 552
Pickwick Papers, The (Dickens), 642, 695, 698, 699, 700, 720, 724, 750
Pictures from Italy (Dickens), 718
Pilgrims of Hope (Morris), 866
Pilgrim's Progress (Bunyan), 166, 176, 187-93, 197, 198-99, 202, 204, 225, 279, 280, 285, 323
Pippa Passes (Browning, R.), 661
Pitt, William, 378, 411, 450, 452, 454
Place, Francis, 622, 628, 629
Plain Dealer, The (Wycherly), 165
Plain Speaker, The (Hazlitt), 486, 488
Plan of the English Commerce (Defoe), 286
Plato, 83, 93, 108, 429, 906
Play of Wyt and Science, The, 4
Plays Pleasant and Unpleasant (Shaw), 898, 910
Poems and Ballads (Swinburne), 838, 840
Poems Before Congress (Browning, E. B.), 669
Poems in Two Volumes (Wordsworth), 421
Poet and Pioneer (Salt), 518
Poet in the Theatre, The (Peacock), 895
Political Characters in Shakespeare (Palmer), 29, 45, 46
Political Justice (Godwin), 378, 521, 527, 597
Political Register (Cobbett), 475, 623, 624, 626
Politics for the People (Kingsley), 528, 633, 679
Poole, Thomas, 432, 440, 441, 444

Poor Man's Advocate, The, 632
Poor Man's Guardian, The, 645
Poor Man's Plea, The (Defoe), 256
Pope, Alexander, 8, 207, 209, 210, 211, 216, 218-24, 226, 235, 241, 247, 248, 285, 316, 320, 321, 328, 330, 655
Popular Fallacies (Lamb), 610
Powell, Mary (Milton), 133, 137, 155
Preface to the Lyrical Ballads (Wordsworth), 416
Prelude, The (Wordsworth), 410, 415, 418, 421, 424
Pre-Raphaelite Brotherhood, 837-40
Presbyterians, 118, 140, 146, 155, 168
Pride and Prejudice (Austen), 336, 341, 342, 345-49, 352, 353, 355
Priestley, Dr. Joseph 407, 461, 580, 592
Prince Regent, See George IV
Princess, The (Tennyson), 27
Prison Meditations (Bunyan), 185, 197
Prisoner of Chillon (Byron), 503
Problems of Physiology (Lewes), 796
Progress and Poverty (George), 881
Project for the Advancement of Religion (Swift), 227
Prometheus Unbound (Shelley), 532, 540, 545
Prophecy of Dante, The (Byron), 507, 508
Proposals for An Association (Shelley), 526
Proposal for Making an Effective Provision for the Poor, A (Fielding), 313
Proposal for Putting Reform to the Vote Throughout the Kingdom, A (Shelley), 538
Proposal for the Universal Use of Irish Manufacture, A (Swift), 231, 249
Protest Against the Ballot, A (Wordsworth), 423
Proust, Marcel, 785
Proverbs of Hell (Blake), 400
Punch, 643, 850

Quakers, 167-69
Quarterly Review, 354, 364, 367, 482, 550, 551, 572, 573, 603, 692, 701

Queen Mab (Shelley), 518, 530-33, 537, 538, 551
Quintessence of Ibsenism, The (Shaw), 890, 892

Rabbi Ben Ezra (Browning, R.), 672
Radcliffe, Mrs. Ann, 329, 331
Ragged Schools, 719, 720, 743
Rake's Progress (Hogarth), 719
Rambler, The (Johnson), 748
Ranters, 167-68
Rape of the Lock, The (Pope), 219, 220-22
Rape of Lucrece, The (Shakespeare), 21
Rape upon Rape or The Justice Caught In His Own Trap (Fielding), 291
Rawley, Dr. William, 81, 82, 85, 106
Reade, Charles, 779
Readie and Easie Way to establish a free Commonwealth, The (Milton), 153
Realism in Art (Lewes), 786
Reason and Imagination (Hazlitt), 486, 487
Reason of Church Government Urged Against Prelaty, The (Milton), 129, 132
Reasons Against the Protestant Succession (Defoe), 276
Recluse, The (Wordsworth), 449
Reflections on Having Left a Place of Retirement (Coleridge), 442
Reflections on the French Revolution (Burke), 377, 438
Reformation, 3, 811
Reformation in England, Of (Milton), 129-32
Refutation of Deism (Shelley), 536
Regulated Hatred: An Aspect of the Work of Jane Austen (Harding), 348-49
Relation of Man to the Rest of the Animal Kingdom, The (Huxley), 808
Relation of Imprisonment (Bunyan), 180
Religious Courtship (Defoe), 284
Religious Musings (Coleridge), 435, 444, 585, 586
Renaissance, 3, 6, 8, 9, 15,·16, 17
Reply to Malthus (Hazlitt), 472

Resurrection of the Dead, The (Bunyan), 186
Review, The (Defoe), 265-69, 271, 272, 273, 275, 276
Revolt of Islam, The (Shelley), 521, 537, 539, 550
Revolutionist's Handbook, The (Shaw), 911
Reynolds, J. H., 557, 565, 566, 571, 578
Rich Man and Lazarus, The (Bunyan), 178
Richard II (Shakespeare), 27, 29-31, 37, 38, 47, 75
Richard III (Shakespeare), 24, 25
Richardson, Samuel, 216, 217, 295, 302, 304, 308, 309, 316, 322, 323, 328, 343, 372
Rights of Man, The (Paine), 378, 379
Ring and the Book, The (Browning, R.), 671
Robeson, Paul, 54, 566
Robinson Crusoe (Defoe), 262, 268, 373, 278-80, 281, 282, 285, 286, 287
Robinson, Henry Crabb, 404, 405, 427, 581, 594, 608, 613
Robson, J. P., 649
Romeo and Juliet (Shakespeare), 27-29
Romola (Eliot), 782, 783, 789
Roosevelt, Franklin D., 32, 146
Rosamund Gray (Lamb), 594, 595
Rosmersholm (Ibsen), 893
Ross, John F., 260-61, 282
Rossetti, Christina and Dante Gabriel, 650, 837, 838, 856
Rousseau, Jean Jacques, 215, 375, 462, 463
Rowley, William, 601
Roxana, The Fortunate Mistress (Defoe), 268, 270, 284
Rubaiyat, The (Fitzgerald), 650, 842
Runaway Slave at Pilgrims Point, The (Browning, E. B.), 667, 668
Rural Rides (Cobbett), 623, 626
Ruskin, John, 172, 605, 615, 620, 631, 652, 675, 685, 686, 687, 688, 689, 730, 837, 838, 843, 851, 855, 913
Rymer, Thomas, 218

Sad Fortunes of the Reverend Amos Barton, The (Eliot), 775, 776

INDEX 943

Saint Joan (Shaw), 907, 914, 919
Salamagundi for Swine, A, 528
Salt, Henry, 518, 891
Salt, Samuel, 582, 584, 600
Samson Agonistes (Milton), 126, 157, 161-62
Sand, George, 713, 764, 765
Sandition (Austen), 340, 370, 371
Sanity of Art, The (Shaw), 905, 906
Sartor Resartus (Carlyle), 681, 682, 799
Saturday Review (London), 736, 903
Saurat, Dennis, 151
Saved by Grace (Bunyan), 203
Savoy, The, 850
Schorer, Mark, 370
Scenes of Clerical Life (Eliot), 776, 777, 779, 790
Science at Sea (Huxley), 802
Scott, Dixon, 880, 920
Scott, Sir Walter, 315, 329, 364, 366, 367, 465, 478, 488, 617-20, 688, 752, 881
Scriblerus Club, 235
Science and the Modern World (Whitehead), 519
Seaside Sketches (Lewes), 775, 777
Seasonable Advice to the Grand Jury (Swift), 233
Seasons, The (Thomson), 322
Second Defense of the People of England (Defensio Secundo) (Milton), 147-50, 151, 601
Sense and Sensibility (Austen), 336, 341, 342, 343-45, 352, 353, 355
Sentimental Journey (Sterne), 322
Sesame and Lillies (Carlyle), 686
Shakespeare, William, 5, 8, 9, 10, 11, 16, 17, 20-80, 81, 91, 100, 111, 112, 113, 121, 124, 206, 207, 213, 293, 366, 381, 392, 404, 414, 454, 462, 481, 575, 595, 599, 600, 601, 603, 650, 653, 661, 674, 705, 744, 750, 783, 875, 893, 905
Shakespeare's Characters (Hazlitt), 481
Shakespeare and the Rival Tradition (Harbage), 22, 76
Shakespeare's Audiences (Harbage), 15
Shakespeare Without Tears (Webster), 54, 55
Shaving of Shagpat, The (Meredith), 773

Shaw, Charlotte Payne-Townshend, 878, 901, 914
Shaw, George Bernard, 191, 192, 308, 516, 517, 518, 675, 686, 734, 747, 850, 852, 854, 857, 863, 864, 867, 868, 874, 875-926
Shaw, George Carr and Mrs. George Carr, 877-78
She Stoops to Conquer (Goldsmith), 326
Shelley, Mary (Wollstonecroft Godwin), 483, 536, 537, 539, 549, 552, 553
Shelley, Percy Bysshe, 126, 127, 145, 160, 335, 378, 380, 421, 492, 503, 509, 511, 516-54, 555, 556, 560, 565, 567, 572, 578, 595, 621, 644, 646, 647, 650, 653, 655, 669, 679, 851, 852, 881
Shelley, Godwin and Their Circle (Brailsford), 378
Shelley, Sir Timothy, 518, 523, 525, 533, 537
Shirley (Bronte, C.), 753, 754
Short History of the English People, A (Green), 540
Short View of the State of Ireland, A (Swift), 241
Shortest Way with Dissenters, The (Defoe), 261-62
Signs of Change (Morris), 855, 862
Simple Life Under Socialism, The (Morris), 873
Sir Richard Grandison (Richardson), 322
16 Self Sketches (Shaw), 854, 876, 886
Sketch, A (Byron), 502
Sketches by Boz (Dickens), 642, 697, 698, 700
Sidney, Sir Philip, 8, 600
Signs of the Times (Carlyle), 681, 682
Sigurd the Volsung (Morris), 859, 864, 871
Silas Marner (Eliot), 762, 782, 790
Silly Novels by Lady Novelists (Eliot), 775
Similes for 2 Political Characters of 1819 (Shelley), 544
Sinclair, Upton, 641
Sir Roger de Coverley (Addison), 214-15
Skelton, John, 4-5

Smectymnus (Milton), 129-32
Smith, Horace, 552, 553
Smith, Rev. Sydney, 634, 635
Smollett, Tobias, 328-29
Social Darwinism, 821-25
Social Democratic Federation (S. D. F.), 861, 862, 863, 865, 867, 886
Socialism Its Growth and Outcome (Bax and Morris), 874
Socialist League, 867, 868
Song of the "Lower Classes", The (Jones), 646
Song of the Shirt, The (Hood), 642, 643
Song of the Wage Slave (Jones), 647
Songs Before Sunrise (Swinburne), 851
Songs of Experience (Blake), 395
Songs of Innocence (Blake), 396
Songs of Los (Blake), 400
Sonnet: England in 1819 (Shelley), 545
Sonnets from the Portugese (Browning, E. B.), 665, 666
Sordello (Browning, R.), 656, 657, 658
Soul of Man Under Socialism, The (Wilde), 852
Southampton, Earl of, 21, 89
Southey, Robert, 380, 403, 413, 415, 426, 431, 447, 450, 457, 476, 477, 478, 479, 505, 525, 530, 540, 581, 585, 586, 754
Soviet Union, 918, 921-22
Spanish Gypsy, The (Eliot), 782, 790
Spartacus, *See* Linton, W. J.
Specimens of the English Dramatic Poets (Lamb), 600, 601, 603
Spectator, 209, 214-16, 227, 295, 330
Speeches in Parliament on the Distresses of the Country (Hazlitt), 476
Spedding, James, 90, 91
Spencer, Herbert, 635, 757, 767, 768, 771, 819, 822, 824, 879
Spenser, Edmund, 8, 22, 23, 190, 207, 880
Spinoza, Baruch, 762, 773
Spirit of the Age (Hazlitt), 379
St. Irvyne (Shelley), 519
Star, The, 889
Starkey, Thomas, 9, 10
State of Christendom, The (Bacon), 84

Steele, Richard, 209, 210, 213, 226
Stephens, Leslie, 322-23
Sterne, Laurence, 322, 328-30
Stoddart, Sarah (Hazlitt), 469, 470, 595, 598, 599
Stowe, Harriet Beecher, 775, 786
Strafford (Browning, R.), 656, 657
Strauss, David Friedrick, 762, 896, 910, 915
Stuarts, The, 163, 202, 207, 276, 277
Sturt, Mary, 82
Suckling, Sir John, 112, 114
Summarie of English Chronicles, 5
Sun, The, 500
Superannuated Man, The (Lamb), 608, 615
Sutherland, James, 253-54
Swift and Defoe (Ross), 260
Swift, Jonathan, 172, 190, 213, 224-51, 264, 282, 288, 301, 311, 312, 318, 319, 320, 321, 322, 681, 810, 829, 876
Swinburne, Algernon C., 650, 747, 838, 840, 851, 857
Sybil, or The Two Nations (Disraeli), 690
Symons, Arthur, 847, 850

Taine, Hippolyte, 139, 155, 190, 191
Tale of a Tub, The (Swift), 226
Tale of Two Cities, The (Dickens), 412, 702, 740, 742, 743, 750
Tales from Shakespeare (Lamb), 595, 599
Talfourd, Sir Thomas, 481-82
Tamburlaine (Marlowe), 14
Taming of the Shrew, The (Shakespeare), 24
Tatler, 209, 213-14, 227
Taylor, Mrs. Peter, 768, 773, 781
Tempest, The (Shakespeare), 38, 77-80
Temple, Sir Williams, 225, 226, 228
Tennyson, Alfred Lord, 27, 631, 650, 651, 669, 673, 758, 819, 874
Tenure of Kings and Magistrates, The (Milton), 141-43, 145
Ternan, Ellen Lawless, 738-40
Terry, Ellen, 901-02
Tetrachordon (Milton), 134
Thackeray, William Makepiece, 341, 631, 687, 689, 692, 712, 735, 755
Thanksgiving Ode (Wordsworth), 475, 476

INDEX 945

Thelwall, John, 446, 580, 604
33 Days (Vrettakos), 516
This Lime Tree Bower My Prison (Coleridge), 596, 613
Thomson, James, 322, 392
Thoreau, Henry David, 579, 619, 799
Thoughts on Religion (Swift), 227
Thompson, Frances, 846, 850
Three Play for Puritans (Shaw), 910
Tillyard, E. M. W., 157-58
Times, The (London), 472-73, 717
Timon of Athens (Shakespeare), 64, 65
Tindale, W. Y., 167-68, 202, 203
'Tis Pity She's a Whore (Ford), 77
Titus Andronicus (Shakespeare), 24, 25, 54
To A Mouse (Burns), 385, 386
To A Mountain Daisy (Burns), 386
To A Nightingale (Keats), 575
To Mr. Cyriak Skinner Upon His Blindness (Milton), 150
To Oliver Cromwell (Milton), 146
To The Lord Chancellor (Shelley), 538
To The Virgins, To Make Much of Time (Herrick), 113
Toad Eaters and Tyrants (Hazlitt), 379
To-Day, 879
Tolstoy, Leo, 306, 318, 620, 747, 906, 918, 925
Tom Jones (Fielding), 293, 303-08, 309, 461
Tooke, Horne, 377, 462
Tory News Letter, 277
Tour Through the Whole Island of Great Britain (Defoe), 270, 284
Tragical History of Doctor Faustus, The (Marlowe), 14-15
Transition to Social Democracy, The (Shaw), 888
Troilus and Cressida (Shakespeare), 37
Trollope, Anthony, 689
True and Genuine Account of the Life and Actions of the Late Jonathan Wild (Defoe), 300
True Born Englishman, The (Defoe), 257
True Greatness of Britain, The (Bacon), 93
True Patriot and the History of Our Own Time, The (Fielding), 301, 302
True Sun, The, 699
Truth Seeker, 529
Tucker, Benjamin, 905
Tudor Monarchy, 5, 6, 7, 11, 17
Twelfth Night (Shakespeare), 47, 113
Two Dogs, The (Burns), 386
Two Gentlemen of Verona, The (Shakespeare), 24, 26
Tyler, Wat, 712, 870
Wat Tyler (Southey), 479
Tyndale, William, 3, 74
Tyndall, John, 802, 880

Uncle Tom's Cabin (Stowe), 781
Uncommercial Traveler, The (Dickens), 751
Unpleasant Plays, 897, 916
Unsocial Socialist, The (Shaw), 878, 879, 885, 895
Unto This Last (Ruskin), 686, 687
Use and Abuse of the Marriage Bed (Defoe), 275-76
Utopia (More), 4

Vanity Fair (Bunyan), 188, 189, 341, 354
Vanity Fair (Thackeray), 692
Vaughan, Henry, 114
Venus and Adonis (Shakespeare), 21
Verses on the Death of Dr. Swift (Swift), 233, 247-49
Vicar of Wakefield, The (Goldsmith), 326
Victoria, Queen, 27, 217-18, 354, 641, 797, 817, 837, 843
Victorian, 108, 303, 306, 354, 628, 629, 630, 633, 634, 640, 644, 650, 652, 674, 679, 689, 726, 737, 739, 757, 821, 837, 839, 840, 843, 849, 856
Villiers, George, See Duke of Buckingham
Villette (Bronte, C.), 753
Vindication of the Rights of Women, A (Wollstonecraft), 397, 536
Vision of Sir Launfal, The (Lowell), 420
Voice of the People, The, 632
Volpone (Jonson), 74
Voltaire, Francois Marie Arouet de, 80, 215, 633
Vrettakos, Nicephonis, 516

Wagner, Richard, 889, 890
Waller, Edmund, 128-29
Walpole, Robert, 232, 235, 292, 294, 295, 300, 302
Warner, Rex, 157, 158, 162
Wars of the Roses, 5, 90
Washington, George, 398, 399, 512, 526
Watchman, The, 442, 446, 449, 585, 586
Water Babies, The (Kingsley), 631, 641
Watsons, The (Austen), 337, 350
Waverly, Scott, 315, 329, 676, 752
Way of All Flesh, The (Butler), 692
Way of the World, The (Congreve), 165
We See Things With Different Eyes (Coleridge), 443
Wealth of Nations, The (Smith), 272, 326
Webb, Beatrice and Sidney, 898, 899, 901, 921
Wells, H. G., 920, 921, 922
Webster, John, 22, 76
Webster, Margaret, 54-55
Wedgwood, Thomas, 415, 449
Wellington, Duke of, 510, 513, 514, 682
Wesley, John, 634, 810
Welsh Opera or the Grey Mare is the Better Horse, The (Fielding), 291
West, Alick, 678, 679, 883, 884, 885, 894, 897, 900
Westbrook, Eliza, 524, 530, 533, 535, 536, 537, 538
Westbrook, Harriet, 523, 530, 533, 535, 536, 537
Westminster Review, 766, 767, 772, 773, 775, 780
What is Art? (Tolstoy), 906
Whether Genius is Conscious of its Power (Hazlitt), 404, 485
Whig Examiner, The, 705
Whistler, James, 838, 843, 849
White, Ivy Newman, 551, 554
Whitehead, A. N., 519
Whitman, Walt, 328, 675, 851
Why I Am A Liberal (Browning, R.), 659
Widowers' Houses (Shaw), 894, 895, 897, 902, 917

Wilberforce, William, 424, 514, 632
Wilde, Oscar, 843, 848, 849, 850, 851, 852
William and Mary (Of Orange), 203, 208, 226, 254, 256, 257, 261
William Morris As I Knew Him (Shaw), 863
Williams, Edward and Jane, 552, 553
Wilson, J. H., 164-65
Wilson, Mona, 354-55
Wisdom and Goodness of God, The (Llandoff), 411
Winstanley, Gerrard, 116, 117, 171
Winter's Tale, The (Shakespeare), 77
Wollstonecraft, Mary, 354, 397, 536, 580, 773
Wood, William, 231, 232, 233
Woolf, Leonard, 342-43
Woolf, Virginia, 373, 374, 795, 842
Wordsworth, Dorothy, 407-10, 412-13, 444-46, 453, 581, 592, 610
Wordsworth, William, 112, 376, 380, 403, 407-26, 444, 445, 446, 447, 448, 449, 450, 453, 459, 469, 475, 477, 479, 480, 505, 519, 537, 540, 547, 548, 556, 567, 580, 592, 598, 599, 602, 604, 609, 610, 614, 615, 650, 653, 658, 679
Work, Life and Letters (of Bacon), (Spedding), 90
Working Man's Friend, The, 632, 633
Works (Lamb), 603
World, The, 889, 890
Wuthering Heights (Bronte, E.), 692
Wyatt, Sir Thomas, 8
Wycherly, William, 165
Wyclif, John, 3, 74, 132

Yeast (Kingsley), 691
Yeats, William Butler, 250, 850, 900, 912
Yellow Book, The, 848, 850, 900
You Never Can Tell (Shaw), 898, 899
Young, Arthur, 450-52
Young, Edward, 218

Zastrozzi (Shelley), 519
Zola, Emile, 925

www.ingramcontent.com/pod-product-compliance
Lightning Source LLC
Chambersburg PA
CBHW032334300426
44109CB00041B/725

9780853450962